American Casebook Series
Hornbook Series and Basic Legal Texts
Nutshell Series

of

WEST PUBLISHING COMPANY
P.O. Box 64526
St. Paul, Minnesota 55164–0526

ACCOUNTING

Faris' Accounting and Law in a Nutshell, 377 pages, 1984 (Text)

Fiflis, Kripke and Foster's Teaching Materials on Accounting for Business Lawyers, 3rd Ed., 838 pages, 1984 (Casebook)

Siegel and Siegel's Accounting and Financial Disclosure: A Guide to Basic Concepts, 259 pages, 1983 (Text)

ADMINISTRATIVE LAW

Davis' Cases, Text and Problems on Administrative Law, 6th Ed., 683 pages, 1977 (Casebook)

Davis' Basic Text on Administrative Law, 3rd Ed., 617 pages, 1972 (Text)

Gellhorn and Boyer's Administrative Law and Process in a Nutshell, 2nd Ed., 445 pages, 1981 (Text)

Mashaw and Merrill's Cases and Materials on Administrative Law–The American Public Law System, 2nd Ed., 976 pages, 1985 (Casebook)

Robinson, Gellhorn and Bruff's The Administrative Process, 3rd Ed., 978 pages, 1986 (Casebook)

ADMIRALTY

Healy and Sharpe's Cases and Materials on Admiralty, 2nd Ed., 876 pages, 1986 (Casebook)

Maraist's Admiralty in a Nutshell, 390 pages, 1983 (Text)

Sohn and Gustafson's Law of the Sea in a Nutshell, 264 pages, 1984 (Text)

AGENCY—PARTNERSHIP

Fessler's Alternatives to Incorporation for Persons in Quest of Profit, 2nd Ed., 326 pages, 1986 (Casebook)

AGENCY—PARTNERSHIP—Cont'd

Henn's Cases and Materials on Agency, Partnership and Other Unincorporated Business Enterprises, 2nd Ed., 733 pages, 1985 (Casebook)

Reuschlein and Gregory's Hornbook on the Law of Agency and Partnership, 625 pages, 1979, with 1981 pocket part (Text)

Seavey, Reuschlein and Hall's Cases on Agency and Partnership, 599 pages, 1962 (Casebook)

Selected Corporation and Partnership Statutes and Forms, 555 pages, 1985

Steffen and Kerr's Cases and Materials on Agency-Partnership, 4th Ed., 859 pages, 1980 (Casebook)

Steffen's Agency-Partnership in a Nutshell, 364 pages, 1977 (Text)

AGRICULTURAL LAW

Meyer, Pedersen, Thorson and Davidson's Agricultural Law: Cases and Materials, 931 pages, 1985 (Casebook)

ALTERNATIVE DISPUTE RESOLUTION

Kanowitz' Cases and Materials on Alternative Dispute Resolution, 1024 pages, 1986 (Casebook)

AMERICAN INDIAN LAW

Canby's American Indian Law in a Nutshell, 288 pages, 1981 (Text)

Getches and Wilkinson's Cases on Federal Indian Law, 2nd Ed., approximately 870 pages, 1986 (Casebook)

ANTITRUST LAW

Gellhorn's Antitrust Law and Economics in a Nutshell, 3rd Ed., about 425 pages, 1987 (Text)

List current as of July, 1986

T7202—1g

I

LAW SCHOOL PUBLICATIONS—Continued

ANTITRUST LAW—Cont'd

Gifford and Raskind's Cases and Materials on Antitrust, 694 pages, 1983 with 1985 Supplement (Casebook)

Hovenkamp's Hornbook on Economics and Federal Antitrust Law, Student Ed., 414 pages, 1985 (Text)

Oppenheim, Weston and McCarthy's Cases and Comments on Federal Antitrust Laws, 4th Ed., 1168 pages, 1981 with 1985 Supplement (Casebook)

Posner and Easterbrook's Cases and Economic Notes on Antitrust, 2nd Ed., 1077 pages, 1981, with 1984-85 Supplement (Casebook)

Sullivan's Hornbook of the Law of Antitrust, 886 pages, 1977 (Text)

See also Regulated Industries, Trade Regulation

ART LAW

DuBoff's Art Law in a Nutshell, 335 pages, 1984 (Text)

BANKING LAW

Lovett's Banking and Financial Institutions in a Nutshell, 409 pages, 1984 (Text)

Symons and White's Teaching Materials on Banking Law, 2nd Ed., 993 pages, 1984 (Casebook)

BUSINESS PLANNING

Painter's Problems and Materials in Business Planning, 2nd Ed., 1008 pages, 1984 (Casebook)

Selected Securities and Business Planning Statutes, Rules and Forms, 470 pages, 1985

CIVIL PROCEDURE

Casad's Res Judicata in a Nutshell, 310 pages, 1976 (text)

Cound, Friedenthal, Miller and Sexton's Cases and Materials on Civil Procedure, 4th Ed., 1202 pages, 1985 with 1985 Supplement (Casebook)

Ehrenzweig, Louisell and Hazard's Jurisdiction in a Nutshell, 4th Ed., 232 pages, 1980 (Text)

Federal Rules of Civil-Appellate Procedure—West Law School Edition, about 550 pages, 1986

Friedenthal, Kane and Miller's Hornbook on Civil Procedure, 876 pages, 1985 (Text)

Kane's Civil Procedure in a Nutshell, 2nd Ed., 306 pages, 1986 (Text)

Koffler and Reppy's Hornbook on Common Law Pleading, 663 pages, 1969 (Text)

Marcus and Sherman's Complex Litigation—Cases and Materials on Advanced Civil Procedure, 846 pages, 1985 (Casebook)

Park's Computer-Aided Exercises on Civil Procedure, 2nd Ed., 167 pages, 1983 (Coursebook)

CIVIL PROCEDURE—Cont'd

Siegel's Hornbook on New York Practice, 1011 pages, 1978 with 1985 Pocket Part (Text)

See also Federal Jurisdiction and Procedure

CIVIL RIGHTS

Abernathy's Cases and Materials on Civil Rights, 660 pages, 1980 (Casebook)

Cohen's Cases on the Law of Deprivation of Liberty: A Study in Social Control, 755 pages, 1980 (Casebook)

Lockhart, Kamisar, Choper and Shiffrin's Cases on Constitutional Rights and Liberties, 6th Ed., about 1300 pages, 1986 with 1986 Supplement (Casebook)—reprint from Lockhart, et al. Cases on Constitutional Law, 6th Ed., 1986

Vieira's Civil Rights in a Nutshell, 279 pages, 1978 (Text)

COMMERCIAL LAW

Bailey's Secured Transactions in a Nutshell, 2nd Ed., 391 pages, 1981 (Text)

Epstein and Martin's Basic Uniform Commercial Code Teaching Materials, 2nd Ed., 667 pages, 1983 (Casebook)

Henson's Hornbook on Secured Transactions Under the U.C.C., 2nd Ed., 504 pages, 1979 with 1979 P.P. (Text)

Murray's Commercial Law, Problems and Materials, 366 pages, 1975 (Coursebook)

Nordstrom and Clovis' Problems and Materials on Commercial Paper, 458 pages, 1972 (Casebook)

Nordstrom, Murray and Clovis' Problems and Materials on Sales, 515 pages, 1982 (Casebook)

Nordstrom, Murray and Clovis' Problems and Materials on Secured Transactions, about 500 pages, 1987 (Casebook)

Selected Commercial Statutes, 1389 pages, 1985

Speidel, Summers and White's Teaching Materials on Commercial and Consumer Law, 3rd Ed., 1490 pages, 1981 (Casebook)

Stockton's Sales in a Nutshell, 2nd Ed., 370 pages, 1981 (Text)

Stone's Uniform Commercial Code in a Nutshell, 2nd Ed., 516 pages, 1984 (Text)

Uniform Commercial Code, Official Text with Comments, 994 pages, 1978

UCC Article 9, Reprint from 1962 Code, 128 pages, 1976

UCC Article 9, 1972 Amendments, 304 pages, 1978

Weber and Speidel's Commercial Paper in a Nutshell, 3rd Ed., 404 pages, 1982 (Text)

White and Summers' Hornbook on the Uniform Commercial Code, 2nd Ed., 1250 pages, 1980 (Text)

COMMUNITY PROPERTY

Mennell's Community Property in a Nutshell, 447 pages, 1982 (Text)

Verrall and Bird's Cases and Materials on California Community Property, 4th Ed., 549 pages, 1983 (Casebook)

COMPARATIVE LAW

Barton, Gibbs, Li and Merryman's Law in Radically Different Cultures, 960 pages, 1983 (Casebook)

Glendon, Gordon and Osakive's Comparative Legal Traditions: Text, Materials and Cases on the Civil Law, Common Law, and Socialist Law Traditions, 1091 pages, 1985 (Casebook)

Glendon, Gordon, and Osakwe's Comparative Legal Traditions in a Nutshell, 402 pages, 1982 (Text)

Langbein's Comparative Criminal Procedure: Germany, 172 pages, 1977 (Casebook)

COMPUTERS AND LAW

Maggs and Sprowl's Computer Applications in the Law, about 300 pages, 1986 (Text)

Mason's An Introduction to the Use of Computers in Law, 223 pages, 1984 (Text)

CONFLICT OF LAWS

Cramton, Currie and Kay's Cases-Comments-Questions on Conflict of Laws, 3rd Ed., 1026 pages, 1981 (Casebook)

Scoles and Hay's Hornbook on Conflict of Laws, Student Ed., 1085 pages, 1982 with 1986 P.P. (Text)

Scoles and Weintraub's Cases and Materials on Conflict of Laws, 2nd Ed., 966 pages, 1972, with 1978 Supplement (Casebook)

Siegel's Conflicts in a Nutshell, 469 pages, 1982 (Text)

CONSTITUTIONAL LAW

Barron and Dienes' Constitutional Law in a Nutshell, about 400 pages, 1986 (Text)

Engdahl's Constitutional Power in a Nutshell: Federal and State, 411 pages, 1974 (Text)

Lockhart, Kamisar, Choper and Shiffrin's Cases-Comments-Questions on Constitutional Law, 6th Ed., 1601 pages, 1986 with 1986 Supplement (Casebook)

Lockhart, Kamisar, Choper and Shiffrin's Cases-Comments-Questions on the American Constitution, 6th Ed., about 1200 pages, 1986 with 1986 Supplement (Casebook)—abridgment of Lockhart, et al. Cases on Constitutional Law, 6th Ed., 1986

Manning's The Law of Church-State Relations in a Nutshell, 305 pages, 1981 (Text)

Miller's Presidential Power in a Nutshell, 328 pages, 1977 (Text)

CONSTITUTIONAL LAW—Cont'd

Nowak, Rotunda and Young's Hornbook on Constitutional Law, 3rd Ed., Student Ed., approximately 1100 pages, 1986 (Text)

Rotunda's Modern Constitutional Law: Cases and Notes, 2nd Ed., 1004 pages, 1985, with 1986 Supplement (Casebook)

Williams' Constitutional Analysis in a Nutshell, 388 pages, 1979 (Text)

See also Civil Rights

CONSUMER LAW

Epstein and Nickles' Consumer Law in a Nutshell, 2nd Ed., 418 pages, 1981 (Text)

McCall's Consumer Protection, Cases, Notes and Materials, 594 pages, 1977, with 1977 Statutory Supplement (Casebook)

Selected Commercial Statutes, 1389 pages, 1985

Spanogle and Rohner's Cases and Materials on Consumer Law, 693 pages, 1979, with 1982 Supplement (Casebook)

See also Commercial Law

CONTRACTS

Calamari & Perillo's Cases and Problems on Contracts, 1061 pages, 1978 (Casebook)

Calamari and Perillo's Hornbook on Contracts, 2nd Ed., 878 pages, 1977 (Text)

Corbin's Text on Contracts, One Volume Student Edition, 1224 pages, 1952 (Text)

Fessler and Loiseaux's Cases and Materials on Contracts, 837 pages, 1982 (Casebook)

Friedman's Contract Remedies in a Nutshell, 323 pages, 1981 (Text)

Fuller and Eisenberg's Cases on Basic Contract Law, 4th Ed., 1203 pages, 1981 (Casebook)

Hamilton, Rau and Weintraub's Cases and Materials on Contracts, 830 pages, 1984 (Casebook)

Jackson and Bollinger's Cases on Contract Law in Modern Society, 2nd Ed., 1329 pages, 1980 (Casebook)

Keyes' Government Contracts in a Nutshell, 423 pages, 1979 (Text)

Schaber and Rohwer's Contracts in a Nutshell, 2nd Ed., 425 pages, 1984 (Text)

COPYRIGHT

See Patent and Copyright Law

CORPORATIONS

Hamilton's Cases on Corporations—Including Partnerships and Limited Partnerships, 3rd Ed., 1213 pages, 1986 with 1986 Statutory Supplement (Casebook)

Hamilton's Law of Corporations in a Nutshell, 379 pages, 1980 (Text)

Henn's Teaching Materials on Corporations, 2nd Ed., about 1200 pages, 1986 (Casebook)

LAW SCHOOL PUBLICATIONS—Continued

CORPORATIONS—Cont'd

Henn and Alexander's Hornbook on Corporations, 3rd Ed., Student Ed., 1371 pages, 1983 with 1986 P.P. (Text)

Jennings and Buxbaum's Cases and Materials on Corporations, 5th Ed., 1180 pages, 1979 (Casebook)

Selected Corporation and Partnership Statutes, Regulations and Forms, 555 pages, 1985

Solomon, Stevenson and Schwartz' Materials and Problems on Corporations: Law and Policy, 1172 pages, 1982 with 1986 Supplement (Casebook)

CORPORATE FINANCE

Hamilton's Cases and Materials on Corporate Finance, 895 pages, 1984 with 1986 Supplement (Casebook)

CORRECTIONS

Krantz's Cases and Materials on the Law of Corrections and Prisoners' Rights, 3rd Ed., 855 pages, 1986 (Casebook)

Krantz's Law of Corrections and Prisoners' Rights in a Nutshell, 2nd Ed., 386 pages, 1983 (Text)

Popper's Post-Conviction Remedies in a Nutshell, 360 pages, 1978 (Text)

Robbins' Cases and Materials on Post Conviction Remedies, 506 pages, 1982 (Casebook)

CREDITOR'S RIGHTS

Bankruptcy Code, Rules and Forms, Law School and C.L.E. Ed., about 800 pages, 1986

Epstein's Debtor-Creditor Law in a Nutshell, 3rd Ed., 383 pages, 1986 (Text)

Epstein and Landers' Debtors and Creditors: Cases and Materials, 2nd Ed., 689 pages, 1982 (Casebook)

LoPucki's Player's Manual for the Debtor-Creditor Game, 123 pages, 1985 (Coursebook)

Riesenfeld's Cases and Materials on Creditors' Remedies and Debtors' Protection, 4th Ed., about 800 pages, 1987 (Casebook)

White's Bankruptcy and Creditor's Rights: Cases and Materials, 812 pages, 1985 (Casebook)

CRIMINAL LAW AND CRIMINAL PROCEDURE

Abrams', Federal Criminal Law and its Enforcement, 882 pages, 1986 (Casebook)

Carlson's Adjudication of Criminal Justice, Problems and References, about 124 pages, 1986 (Casebook)

Dix and Sharlot's Cases and Materials on Criminal Law, 2nd Ed., 771 pages, 1979 (Casebook)

CRIMINAL LAW AND CRIMINAL PROCEDURE—Cont'd

Federal Rules of Criminal Procedure—West Law School Edition, about 465 pages, 1986

Grano's Problems in Criminal Procedure, 2nd Ed., 176 pages, 1981 (Problem book)

Israel and LaFave's Criminal Procedure in a Nutshell, 3rd Ed., 438 pages, 1980 (Text)

Johnson's Cases, Materials and Text on Criminal Law, 3rd Ed., 783 pages, 1985 (Casebook)

Kamisar, LaFave and Israel's Cases, Comments and Questions on Modern Criminal Procedure, 6th Ed., about 1600 pages, 1986 with 1986 Supplement (Casebook)

Kamisar, LaFave and Israel's Cases, Comments and Questions on Basic Criminal Procedure, 6th Ed., about 800 pages, 1986 with 1986 Supplement (Casebook)—reprint from Kamisar, et al. Modern Criminal Procedure, 6th ed., 1986

LaFave's Modern Criminal Law: Cases, Comments and Questions, 789 pages, 1978 (Casebook)

LaFave and Israel's Hornbook on Criminal Procedure, Student Ed., 1142 pages, 1985 with 1985 P.P. (Text)

LaFave and Scott's Hornbook on Criminal Law, 2nd Ed., Student Ed., about 800 pages, 1986 (Text)

Langbein's Comparative Criminal Procedure: Germany, 172 pages, 1977 (Casebook)

Loewy's Criminal Law in a Nutshell, 302 pages, 1975 (Text)

Saltzburg's American Criminal Procedure, Cases and Commentary, 2nd Ed., 1193 pages, 1985 with 1986 Supplement (Casebook)

Uviller's The Processes of Criminal Justice: Investigation and Adjudication, 2nd Ed., 1384 pages, 1979 with 1979 Statutory Supplement and 1986 Update (Casebook)

Uviller's The Processes of Criminal Justice: Adjudication, 2nd Ed., 730 pages, 1979. Soft-cover reprint from Uviller's The Processes of Criminal Justice: Investigation and Adjudication, 2nd Ed. (Casebook)

Uviller's The Processes of Criminal Justice: Investigation, 2nd Ed., 655 pages, 1979. Soft-cover reprint from Uviller's The Processes of Criminal Justice: Investigation and Adjudication, 2nd Ed. (Casebook)

Vorenberg's Cases on Criminal Law and Procedure, 2nd Ed., 1088 pages, 1981 with 1985 Supplement (Casebook)

See also Corrections, Juvenile Justice

DECEDENTS ESTATES

See Trusts and Estates

LAW SCHOOL PUBLICATIONS—Continued

DOMESTIC RELATIONS

Clark's Cases and Problems on Domestic Relations, 3rd Ed., 1153 pages, 1980 (Casebook)

Clark's Hornbook on Domestic Relations, 754 pages, 1968 (Text)

Krause's Cases and Materials on Family Law, 2nd Ed., 1221 pages, 1983 with 1986 Supplement (Casebook)

Krause's Family Law in a Nutshell, 2nd Ed., 444 pages, 1986 (Text)

Krauskopf's Cases on Property Division at Marriage Dissolution, 250 pages, 1984 (Casebook)

ECONOMICS, LAW AND

Goetz' Cases and Materials on Law and Economics, 547 pages, 1984 (Casebook)

See also Antitrust, Regulated Industries

EDUCATION LAW

Alexander and Alexander's The Law of Schools, Students and Teachers in a Nutshell, 409 pages, 1984 (Text)

Morris' The Constitution and American Education, 2nd Ed., 992 pages, 1980 (Casebook)

EMPLOYMENT DISCRIMINATION

Jones, Murphy and Belton's Cases on Discrimination in Employment, about 930 pages, 1986 (Casebook)

Player's Cases and Materials on Employment Discrimination Law, 2nd Ed., 782 pages, 1984 (Casebook)

Player's Federal Law of Employment Discrimination in a Nutshell, 2nd Ed., 402 pages, 1981 (Text)

See also Women and the Law

ENERGY AND NATURAL RESOURCES LAW

Laitos' Cases and Materials on Natural Resources Law, 938 pages, 1985 (Casebook)

Rodgers' Cases and Materials on Energy and Natural Resources Law, 2nd Ed., 877 pages, 1983 (Casebook)

Selected Environmental Law Statutes, about 850 pages, 1986

Tomain's Energy Law in a Nutshell, 338 pages, 1981 (Text)

See also Environmental Law, Oil and Gas, Water Law

ENVIRONMENTAL LAW

Bonine and McGarity's Cases and Materials on the Law of Environment and Pollution, 1076 pages, 1984 (Casebook)

Findley and Farber's Cases and Materials on Environmental Law, 2nd Ed., 813 pages, 1985 (Casebook)

Findley and Farber's Environmental Law in a Nutshell, 343 pages, 1983 (Text)

ENVIRONMENTAL LAW—Cont'd

Rodgers' Hornbook on Environmental Law, 956 pages, 1977 with 1984 pocket part (Text)

Selected Environmental Law Statutes, about 950 pages, 1986

See also Energy Law, Natural Resources Law, Water Law

EQUITY

See Remedies

ESTATES

See Trusts and Estates

ESTATE PLANNING

Kurtz' Cases, Materials and Problems on Family Estate Planning, 853 pages, 1983 (Casebook)

Lynn's Introduction to Estate Planning, in a Nutshell, 3rd Ed., 370 pages, 1983 (Text)

See also Taxation

EVIDENCE

Broun and Meisenholder's Problems in Evidence, 2nd Ed., 304 pages, 1981 (Problem book)

Cleary and Strong's Cases, Materials and Problems on Evidence, 3rd Ed., 1143 pages, 1981 (Casebook)

Federal Rules of Evidence for United States Courts and Magistrates, 337 pages, 1984

Graham's Federal Rules of Evidence in a Nutshell, 429 pages, 1981 (Text)

Kimball's Programmed Materials on Problems in Evidence, 380 pages, 1978 (Problem book)

Lempert and Saltzburg's A Modern Approach to Evidence: Text, Problems, Transcripts and Cases, 2nd Ed., 1232 pages, 1983 (Casebook)

Lilly's Introduction to the Law of Evidence, 490 pages, 1978 (Text)

McCormick, Elliott and Sutton's Cases and Materials on Evidence, 5th Ed., 1212 pages, 1981 (Casebook)

McCormick's Hornbook on Evidence, 3rd Ed., Student Ed., 1156 pages, 1984 (Text)

Rothstein's Evidence, State and Federal Rules in a Nutshell, 2nd Ed., 514 pages, 1981 (Text)

Saltzburg's Evidence Supplement: Rules, Statutes, Commentary, 245 pages, 1980 (Casebook Supplement)

FEDERAL JURISDICTION AND PROCEDURE

Currie's Cases and Materials on Federal Courts, 3rd Ed., 1042 pages, 1982 with 1985 Supplement (Casebook)

Currie's Federal Jurisdiction in a Nutshell, 2nd Ed., 258 pages, 1981 (Text)

LAW SCHOOL PUBLICATIONS—Continued

LAND USE

Callies and Freilich's Cases and Materials on Land Use, 1233 pages, 1986 (Casebook)

Hagman's Cases on Public Planning and Control of Urban and Land Development, 2nd Ed., 1301 pages, 1980 (Casebook)

Hagman and Juergensmeyer's Hornbook on Urban Planning and Land Development Control Law, 2nd Ed., Student Edition, approximately 580 pages, 1986 (Text)

Wright and Gitelman's Cases and Materials on Land Use, 3rd Ed., 1300 pages, 1982 (Casebook)

Wright and Wright's Land Use in a Nutshell, 2nd Ed., 356 pages, 1985 (Text)

LEGAL HISTORY

Presser and Zainaldin's Cases on Law and American History, 855 pages, 1980 (Casebook)

See also Legal Method and Legal System

LEGAL METHOD AND LEGAL SYSTEM

Aldisert's Readings, Materials and Cases in the Judicial Process, 948 pages, 1976 (Casebook)

Berch and Berch's Introduction to Legal Method and Process, 550 pages, 1985 (Casebook)

Bodenheimer, Oakley and Love's Readings and Cases on an Introduction to the Anglo-American Legal System, 161 pages, 1980 (Casebook)

Davies and Lawry's Institutions and Methods of the Law—Introductory Teaching Materials, 547 pages, 1982 (Casebook)

Dvorkin, Himmelstein and Lesnick's Becoming a Lawyer: A Humanistic Perspective on Legal Education and Professionalism, 211 pages, 1981 (Text)

Greenberg's Judicial Process and Social Change, 666 pages, 1977 (Casebook)

Kelso and Kelso's Studying Law: An Introduction, 587 pages, 1984 (Coursebook)

Kempin's Historical Introduction to Anglo-American Law in a Nutshell, 2nd Ed., 280 pages, 1973 (Text)

Kimball's Historical Introduction to the Legal System, 610 pages, 1966 (Casebook)

Murphy's Cases and Materials on Introduction to Law—Legal Process and Procedure, 772 pages, 1977 (Casebook)

Reynolds' Judicial Process in a Nutshell, 292 pages, 1980 (Text)

See also Legal Research and Writing

LEGAL PROFESSION

Aronson, Devine and Fisch's Problems, Cases and Materials on Professional Responsibility, 745 pages, 1985 (Casebook)

Aronson and Weckstein's Professional Responsibility in a Nutshell, 399 pages, 1980 (Text)

LEGAL PROFESSION—Cont'd

Mellinkoff's The Conscience of a Lawyer, 304 pages, 1973 (Text)

Mellinkoff's Lawyers and the System of Justice, 983 pages, 1976 (Casebook)

Pirsig and Kirwin's Cases and Materials on Professional Responsibility, 4th Ed., 603 pages, 1984 (Casebook)

Schwartz and Wydick's Problems in Legal Ethics, 285 pages, 1983 (Casebook)

Selected Statutes, Rules and Standards on the Legal Profession, 276 pages, Revised 1984

Smith's Preventing Legal Malpractice, 142 pages, 1981 (Text)

Wolfram's Hornbook on Modern Legal Ethics, Student Edition, 1120 pages, 1986 (Text)

LEGAL RESEARCH AND WRITING

Cohen's Legal Research in a Nutshell, 4th Ed., 450 pages, 1985 (Text)

Cohen and Berring's How to Find the Law, 8th Ed., 790 pages, 1983. Problem book by Foster, Johnson and Kelly available (Casebook)

Cohen and Berring's Finding the Law, 8th Ed., Abridged Ed., 556 pages, 1984 (Casebook)

Dickerson's Materials on Legal Drafting, 425 pages, 1981 (Casebook)

Felsenfeld and Siegel's Writing Contracts in Plain English, 290 pages, 1981 (Text)

Gopen's Writing From a Legal Perspective, 225 pages, 1981 (Text)

Mellinkoff's Legal Writing—Sense and Nonsense, 242 pages, 1982 (Text)

Rombauer's Legal Problem Solving—Analysis, Research and Writing, 4th Ed., 424 pages, 1983 (Coursebook)

Squires and Rombauer's Legal Writing in a Nutshell, 294 pages, 1982 (Text)

Statsky's Legal Research, Writing and Analysis, 2nd Ed., 167 pages, 1982 (Coursebook)

Statsky and Wernet's Case Analysis and Fundamentals of Legal Writing, 2nd Ed., 441 pages, 1984 (Text)

Teply's Programmed Materials on Legal Research and Citation, 2nd Ed., 358 pages, 1986. Student Library Exercises available (Coursebook)

Weihofen's Legal Writing Style, 2nd Ed., 332 pages, 1980 (Text)

LEGISLATION

Davies' Legislative Law and Process in a Nutshell, 2nd Ed., 346 pages, 1986 (Text)

Nutting and Dickerson's Cases and Materials on Legislation, 5th Ed., 744 pages, 1978 (Casebook)

LAW SCHOOL PUBLICATIONS—Continued

LEGISLATION—Cont'd

Statsky's Legislative Analysis: How to Use Statutes and Regulations, 2nd Ed., 217 pages, 1984 (Text)

LOCAL GOVERNMENT

McCarthy's Local Government Law in a Nutshell, 2nd Ed., 404 pages, 1983 (Text)

Reynolds' Hornbook on Local Government Law, 860 pages, 1982 (Text)

Valente's Cases and Materials on Local Government Law, 2nd Ed., 980 pages, 1980 with 1982 Supplement (Casebook)

MASS COMMUNICATION LAW

Gillmor and Barron's Cases and Comment on Mass Communication Law, 4th Ed., 1076 pages, 1984 (Casebook)

Ginsburg's Regulation of Broadcasting: Law and Policy Towards Radio, Television and Cable Communications, 741 pages, 1979, with 1983 Supplement (Casebook)

Zuckman and Gayne's Mass Communications Law in a Nutshell, 2nd Ed., 473 pages, 1983 (Text)

MEDICINE, LAW AND

King's The Law of Medical Malpractice in a Nutshell, 2nd Ed., 342 pages, 1986 (Text)

Shapiro and Spece's Problems, Cases and Materials on Bioethics and Law, 892 pages, 1981 (Casebook)

Sharpe, Fiscina and Head's Cases on Law and Medicine, 882 pages, 1978 (Casebook)

MILITARY LAW

Shanor and Terrell's Military Law in a Nutshell, 378 pages, 1980 (Text)

MORTGAGES

See Real Estate Transactions

NATURAL RESOURCES LAW

See Energy and Natural Resources Law

NEGOTIATION

Edwards and White's Problems, Readings and Materials on the Lawyer as a Negotiator, 484 pages, 1977 (Casebook)

Williams' Legal Negotiation and Settlement, 207 pages, 1983 (Coursebook)

OFFICE PRACTICE

Hegland's Trial and Practice Skills in a Nutshell, 346 pages, 1978 (Text)

Strong and Clark's Law Office Management, 424 pages, 1974 (Casebook)

See also Computers and Law, Interviewing and Counseling, Negotiation

OIL AND GAS

Hemingway's Hornbook on Oil and Gas, 2nd Ed., Student Ed., 543 pages, 1983 with 1986 P.P. (Text)

OIL AND GAS—Cont'd

Kuntz, Lowe, Anderson and Smith's Cases and Materials on Oil and Gas Law, 857 pages, 1986 (Casebook)

Lowe's Oil and Gas Law in a Nutshell, 443 pages, 1983 (Text)

See also Energy and Natural Resources Law

PARTNERSHIP

See Agency—Partnership

PATENT AND COPYRIGHT LAW

Choate and Francis' Cases and Materials on Patent Law, 2nd Ed., 1110 pages, 1981 (Casebook)

Miller and Davis' Intellectual Property—Patents, Trademarks and Copyright in a Nutshell, 428 pages, 1983 (Text)

Nimmer's Cases on Copyright and Other Aspects of Entertainment Litigation, 3rd Ed., 1025 pages, 1985 (Casebook)

PRODUCTS LIABILITY

Noel and Phillips' Cases on Products Liability, 2nd Ed., 821 pages, 1982 (Casebook)

Noel and Phillips' Products Liability in a Nutshell, 2nd Ed., 341 pages, 1981 (Text)

PROPERTY

Bernhardt's Real Property in a Nutshell, 2nd Ed., 448 pages, 1981 (Text)

Boyer's Survey of the Law of Property, 766 pages, 1981 (Text)

Browder, Cunningham and Smith's Cases on Basic Property Law, 4th Ed., 1431 pages, 1984 (Casebook)

Bruce, Ely and Bostick's Cases and Materials on Modern Property Law, 1004 pages, 1984 (Casebook)

Burke's Personal Property in a Nutshell, 322 pages, 1983 (Text)

Cunningham, Stoebuck and Whitman's Hornbook on the Law of Property, Student Ed., 916 pages, 1984 (Text)

Donahue, Kauper and Martin's Cases on Property, 2nd Ed., 1362 pages, 1983 (Casebook)

Hill's Landlord and Tenant Law in a Nutshell, 2nd Ed., 311 pages, 1986 (Text)

Moynihan's Introduction to Real Property, 254 pages, 1962 (Text)

Uniform Land Transactions Act, Uniform Simplification of Land Transfers Act, Uniform Condominium Act, 1977 Official Text with Comments, 462 pages, 1978

See also Real Estate Transactions, Land Use

PSYCHIATRY, LAW AND

Reisner's Law and the Mental Health System, Civil and Criminal Aspects, 696 pages, 1985 (Casebooks)

LAW SCHOOL PUBLICATIONS—Continued

REAL ESTATE TRANSACTIONS

Bruce's Real Estate Finance in a Nutshell, 2nd Ed., 262 pages, 1985 (Text)

Maxwell, Riesenfeld, Hetland and Warren's Cases on California Security Transactions in Land, 3rd Ed., 728 pages, 1984 (Casebook)

Nelson and Whitman's Cases on Real Estate Transfer, Finance and Development, 2nd Ed., 1114 pages, 1981, with 1986 Supplement (Casebook)

Nelson and Whitman's Hornbook on Real Estate Finance Law, 2nd Ed., Student Ed., 941 pages, 1985 (Text)

Osborne's Cases and Materials on Secured Transactions, 559 pages, 1967 (Casebook)

REGULATED INDUSTRIES

Gellhorn and Pierce's Regulated Industries in a Nutshell, 394 pages, 1982 (Text)

Morgan, Harrison and Verkuil's Cases and Materials on Economic Regulation of Business, 2nd Ed., 666 pages, 1985 (Casebook)

See also Mass Communication Law, Banking Law

REMEDIES

Dobbs' Hornbook on Remedies, 1067 pages, 1973 (Text)

Dobbs' Problems in Remedies, 137 pages, 1974 (Problem book)

Dobbyn's Injunctions in a Nutshell, 264 pages, 1974 (Text)

Friedman's Contract Remedies in a Nutshell, 323 pages, 1981 (Text)

Leavell, Love and Nelson's Cases and Materials on Equitable Remedies and Restitution, 4th Ed., 1111 pages, 1986 (Casebook)

McCormick's Hornbook on Damages, 811 pages, 1935 (Text)

O'Connell's Remedies in a Nutshell, 2nd Ed., 320 pages, 1985 (Text)

York, Bauman and Rendleman's Cases and Materials on Remedies, 4th Ed., 1029 pages, 1985 (Casebook)

REVIEW MATERIALS

Ballantine's Problems

Black Letter Series

Smith's Review Series

West's Review Covering Multistate Subjects

SECURITIES REGULATION

Hazen's Hornbook on The Law of Securities Regulation, Student Ed., 739 pages, 1985 (Text)

Ratner's Securities Regulation: Materials for a Basic Course, 3rd Ed., 1000 pages, 1986 (Casebook)

Ratner's Securities Regulation in a Nutshell, 2nd Ed., 322 pages, 1982 (Text)

SECURITIES REGULATION—Cont'd

Selected Securities and Business Planning Statutes, Rules and Forms, 470 pages, 1985

SOCIAL LEGISLATION

Hood and Hardy's Workers' Compensation and Employee Protection Laws in a Nutshell, 274 pages, 1984 (Text)

LaFrance's Welfare Law: Structure and Entitlement in a Nutshell, 455 pages, 1979 (Text)

Malone, Plant and Little's Cases on Workers' Compensation and Employment Rights, 2nd Ed., 951 pages, 1980 (Casebook)

SPORTS LAW

Schubert, Smith and Trentadue's Sports Law, 395 pages, 1986 (Text)

TAXATION

Dodge's Cases and Materials on Federal Income Taxation, 820 pages, 1985 (Casebook)

Dodge's Federal Taxation of Estates, Trusts and Gifts: Principles and Planning, 771 pages, 1981 with 1982 Supplement (Casebook)

Garbis and Struntz' Cases and Materials on Tax Procedure and Tax Fraud, 829 pages, 1982 with 1984 Supplement (Casebook)

Gelfand and Salsich's State and Local Taxation and Finance in a Nutshell, 309 pages, 1986 (Text)

Gunn's Cases and Materials on Federal Income Taxation of Individuals, 785 pages, 1981 with 1985 Supplement (Casebook)

Hellerstein and Hellerstein's Cases on State and Local Taxation, 4th Ed., 1041 pages, 1978 with 1982 Supplement (Casebook)

Kahn and Gann's Corporate Taxation and Taxation of Partnerships and Partners, 2nd Ed., 1204 pages, 1985 (Casebook)

Kragen and McNulty's Cases and Materials on Federal Income Taxation: Individuals, Corporations, Partnerships, 4th Ed., 1287 pages, 1985 (Casebook)

McNulty's Federal Estate and Gift Taxation in a Nutshell, 3rd Ed., 509 pages, 1983 (Text)

McNulty's Federal Income Taxation of Individuals in a Nutshell, 3rd Ed., 487 pages, 1983 (Text)

Posin's Hornbook on Federal Income Taxation of Individuals, Student Ed., 491 pages, 1983 with 1985 pocket part (Text)

Selected Federal Taxation Statutes and Regulations, about 1400 pages, 1986

Solomon and Hesch's Cases on Federal Income Taxation of Individuals, about 800 pages, 1987 (Casebook)

LAW SCHOOL PUBLICATIONS—Continued

TAXATION—Cont'd

Sobeloff and Weidenbruch's Federal Income Taxation of Corporations and Stockholders in a Nutshell, 362 pages, 1981 (Text)

TORTS

Christie's Cases and Materials on the Law of Torts, 1264 pages, 1983 (Casebook)

Dobbs' Torts and Compensation—Personal Accountability and Social Responsibility for Injury, 955 pages, 1985 (Casebook)

Green, Pedrick, Rahl, Thode, Hawkins, Smith and Treece's Cases and Materials on Torts, 2nd Ed., 1360 pages, 1977 (Casebook)

Green, Pedrick, Rahl, Thode, Hawkins, Smith, and Treece's Advanced Torts: Injuries to Business, Political and Family Interests, 2nd Ed., 544 pages, 1977 (Casebook)—reprint from Green, et al. Cases and Materials on Torts, 2nd Ed., 1977

Keeton, Keeton, Sargentich and Steiner's Cases and Materials on Torts, and Accident Law, 1360 pages, 1983 (Casebook)

Kionka's Torts in a Nutshell: Injuries to Persons and Property, 434 pages, 1977 (Text)

Malone's Torts in a Nutshell: Injuries to Family, Social and Trade Relations, 358 pages, 1979 (Text)

Prosser and Keeton's Hornbook on Torts, 5th Ed., Student Ed., 1286 pages, 1984 (Text)

Shapo's Cases on Tort and Compensation Law, 1244 pages, 1976 (Casebook)

See also Products Liability

TRADE REGULATION

McManis' Unfair Trade Practices in a Nutshell, 444 pages, 1982 (Text)

Oppenheim, Weston, Maggs and Schechter's Cases and Materials on Unfair Trade Practices and Consumer Protection, 4th Ed., 1038 pages, 1983 with 1986 Supplement (Casebook)

See also Antitrust, Regulated Industries

TRIAL AND APPELLATE ADVOCACY

Appellate Advocacy, Handbook of, 2nd Ed., 182 pages, 1986 (Text)

Bergman's Trial Advocacy in a Nutshell, 402 pages, 1979 (Text)

Binder and Bergman's Fact Investigation: From Hypothesis to Proof, 354 pages, 1984 (Coursebook)

Goldberg's The First Trial (Where Do I Sit?, What Do I Say?) in a Nutshell, 396 pages, 1982 (Text)

Haydock, Herr and Stempel's, Fundamentals of Pre-Trial Litigation, 768 pages, 1985 (Casebook)

Hegland's Trial and Practice Skills in a Nutshell, 346 pages, 1978 (Text)

Hornstein's Appellate Advocacy in a Nutshell, 325 pages, 1984 (Text)

TRIAL AND APPELLATE ADVOCACY—Cont'd

Jeans' Handbook on Trial Advocacy, Student Ed., 473 pages, 1975 (Text)

Martineau's Cases and Materials on Appellate Practice and Procedure, about 550 pages, 1987 (Casebook)

McElhaney's Effective Litigation, 457 pages, 1974 (Casebook)

Nolan's Cases and Materials on Trial Practice, 518 pages, 1981 (Casebook)

Parnell and Shellhaas' Cases, Exercises and Problems for Trial Advocacy, 171 pages, 1982 (Coursebook)

Sonsteng, Haydock and Boyd's The Trialbook: A Total System for Preparation and Presentation of a Case, Student Ed., 404 pages, 1984 (Coursebook)

TRUSTS AND ESTATES

Atkinson's Hornbook on Wills, 2nd Ed., 975 pages, 1953 (Text)

Averill's Uniform Probate Code in a Nutshell, 425 pages, 1978 (Text)

Bogert's Hornbook on Trusts, 5th Ed., 726 pages, 1973 (Text)

Clark, Lusky and Murphy's Cases and Materials on Gratuitous Transfers, 3rd Ed., 970 pages, 1985 (Casebook)

Gulliver's Cases and Materials on Future Interests, 624 pages, 1959 (Casebook)

Gulliver's Introduction to the Law of Future Interests, 87 pages, 1959 (Casebook)—reprint from Gulliver's Cases and Materials on Future Interests, 1959

McGovern's Cases and Materials on Wills, Trusts and Future Interests: An Introduction to Estate Planning, 750 pages, 1983 (Casebook)

Mennell's Cases and Materials on California Decedent's Estates, 566 pages, 1973 (Casebook)

Mennell's Wills and Trusts in a Nutshell, 392 pages, 1979 (Text)

Powell's The Law of Future Interests in California, 91 pages, 1980 (Text)

Simes' Hornbook on Future Interests, 2nd Ed., 355 pages, 1966 (Text)

Turano and Radigan's Hornbook on New York Estate Administration, approximately 575 pages, 1986 (Text)

Uniform Probate Code, 5th Ed., Official Text With Comments, 384 pages, 1977

Waggoner's Future Interests in a Nutshell, 361 pages, 1981 (Text)

Waterbury's Materials on Trusts and Estates, 1039 pages, 1986 (Casebook)

WATER LAW

Getches' Water Law in a Nutshell, 439 pages, 1984 (Text)

LAW SCHOOL PUBLICATIONS—Continued

WATER LAW—Cont'd

Sax and Abram's Cases and Materials on Legal Control of Water Resources in the United States, 941 pages, 1986 (Casebook)

Trelease and Gould's Cases and Materials on Water Law, 4th Ed., 816 pages, 1986 (Casebook)

See also Energy and Natural Resources Law, Environmental Law

WILLS

See Trusts and Estates

WOMEN AND THE LAW

Kay's Text, Cases and Materials on Sex-Based Discrimination, 2nd Ed., 1045 pages, 1981, with 1986 Supplement (Casebook)

Thomas' Sex Discrimination in a Nutshell, 399 pages, 1982 (Text)

See also Employment Discrimination

WORKERS' COMPENSATION

See Social Legislation

CASES AND MATERIALS ON
LABOR LAW
COLLECTIVE BARGAINING IN A FREE SOCIETY
Third Edition

By

Walter E. Oberer
Professor of Law
University of Utah

Kurt L. Hanslowe
Late Professor of Law and of
Industrial and Labor Relations
Cornell University

Jerry R. Andersen
Late Professor of Law
University of Utah

Timothy J. Heinsz
Professor of Law
University of Missouri—Columbia

AMERICAN CASEBOOK SERIES

WEST PUBLISHING CO.
ST. PAUL, MINN., 1986

Library of Congress Cataloging in Publication Data

Oberer, Walter E.
  Labor law, collective bargaining in a free society.

  (American casebook series)
  Rev. ed. of: Cases and materials on labor law.
1979.
  Includes index.
  1. Collective labor agreements—United States—
Cases. 2. Labor laws and legislation—United States—
Cases. I. Oberer, Walter E. Cases and materials
on labor law. II. Heinsz,
Timothy J. III. Series.

KF3408.A402 1986   344.73'0189   86–13245
                        347.304189

ISBN 0–314–25183–9

Labor Law, 3rd Ed. (O., H., A. & H.) ACB

To
Ann and Nan
Freya, Jill, and Megan
David, Nicholas, and Theodora
Ida and Leopoldine

Second Edition Addendum
Mary Lou
Michael, Alyssa, and David
Monty

Third Edition Addendum
Susan
Jennifer, Megan and Mary

And to the memory of our fathers
Walter
Ernst
Silas
Vernon

*

Preface to Third Edition

Since the publication of the Second Edition in 1979, two of its co-editors, Kurt Hanslowe and Jerry Andersen, have died untimely deaths. The deaths of good people are always untimely, but these were two of nature's noblemen, young beyond years, wise beyond time, good comrades beyond the telling. We, the present editors, one a colleague on the past editions, the other a former student of both of his and Kurt's and a kindred spirit with Jerry, have striven to maintain the central thrust of this casebook.

The course in labor law is arguably the best vehicle in the law school curriculum for analyzing and coming to understand the meaning of a free society—the "what" and the "how" and the "why." The potential of the course therefore reaches far beyond the production of labor lawyers. This has been the philosophical basis, the spinal cord, the *rationale* of the organization and the selection of the cases and materials in the casebook from the time of its First Edition.

This Third Edition retains the basic organizational approach utilized in the prior editions to impart to students the development of labor relations and the law, i.e., the meaning of "Collective Bargaining in a Free Society." The emphasis remains the teaching of the "why" of labor law, as well as the "what." The authors have continued to consider case selection the most important aspect of this (or any other) casebook. In this regard, past users will find that most "old friends" remain as teaching vehicles. At the same time we have included the recent decisions and statutes which demand attention. In so doing, we have culled and weeded the older materials to the extent warranted by the new.

The new materials include the following subject areas: the erosion of the employment-at-will doctrine, the impact of bankruptcy on collective bargaining, the legality of affirmative action programs, and the expansion of labor-managment relations in the federal sector. In addition, the Third Edition focuses upon the continuing change and ferment in the case law in the more traditional areas of secondary boycotts, "hot cargo" agreements, "individual" concerted activity, permanent replacements, discharge for union activities, the duty to bargain in good faith, the deferral doctrine, the duty of fair representation, the union's power to compel its members to engage in concerted activities, union security agreements, campaign misrepresentation, and developments in public sector labor relations, particularly with regard to the ever-present strike issue.

We have also striven to honor two other cardinal principles of the prior editions:

(1) The principle of *interest*; this is *not* Cases and Materials on Embalming.

(2) The principle of *self-containment*; with rare exception, the users of this casebook should be able to prepare for class without involuntary research beyond its covers and those of its Statutory Supplement.

The current authors harbor the thought that both Kurt and Jerry would have approved of the changes made in this Third Edition and of their continued association with it. We also acknowledge, with gratitude, the contributions made by Donald T. Weckstein, of the University of San Diego School of Law, a revered friend and colleague.

We cannot close without a further expression of gratitude to two University of Missouri law students, Michael Pritchett and Ronald Smith, who performed yeoman service as research assistants and to Norma Castleman for her ever-diligent word processing support.

WALTER E. OBERER
TIMOTHY J. HEINSZ

September, 1986

Preface to Second Edition

The second edition of this casebook is very much like the first—only pruned and updated. The pruning, performed with surgical concern, permits a second edition reflective of all of consequence that has occurred between 1972 and 1979 yet unswollen in size. The materials are still mainstream—as clearly and teachably presented as we are able. There is little meandering, some impishness.

The major structural changes, other than the pruning and updating, are these: The old Chapter 9 (last), "The Individual and the Union: 'I Versus We'—A Study in Irony," is now Chapter 8. The old Chapter 8, "The Conflict Between Free Collective Bargaining and the Public Interest," is now Chapter 9, retitled "The Conflict Between Free Collective Bargaining and Other Public Interests." The first section of the new Chapter 9, "Employment Discrimination" (dealt with in the first edition in Chapter 7), reflects the most serious decision in restructuring. When the first edition was published, employment discrimination litigation had not yet peaked. Griggs v. Duke Power Co. alone had reached the Supreme Court. The authoritative high points of the pertinent law could then be reasonably canvassed in a half-dozen cases. That, to say the least, is no longer the situation. The veritable gush of litigation since then, much of it welling up to the Supreme Court, has required rethinking of the manner of treatment of employment discrimination in this casebook on "Labor Law"; the discrimination area has bourgeoned into a law school course in itself. Our decision has been neither to jettison completely nor to freight fully, but rather to present a highly select handful of cases bearing most heavily upon the *overlap* between traditional collective bargaining law and the newer employment discrimination developments. The remainder of those developments are left to separate treatment in the emerging casebooks devoted to the regulation of employment (and other) discrimination.

Two new features in the second edition, rendering its use a bit more convenient, perhaps bear mentioning. They are a Detailed Table of Contents, which includes not only principal cases but also major cases *noted*, and a plaintiff-defendant *and* defendant-plaintiff Table of Cases.

For the rest, we leave the reader to the Preface to the first edition, still largely viable for all of the age now on its whimsy. We add only the assurance that the original authors, aided and abetted by a third, have duly debated all marginal questions (those that do not really matter and therefore carry no decisional onus) and have resolved them, to a one, in a manner inconsistently consistent. We commend this criterion to all editorial teams as a lubricant to peace and publication.

Our second and last "add only" is to recognize a trio of University of Utah law students who aided staunchly in one or another research effort:

Richard Wasserman, Vilate Stewart, Dennis Farley; *and* a virtuoso of the office keyboard, true-blue, Tina Allred.

WALTER E. OBERER
KURT L. HANSLOWE
JERRY R. ANDERSEN

December, 1978

Preface to First Edition

The Blueprint

This casebook has a plot. The strand upon which the "cases and materials" of Part I are strung is the evolution of labor relations and the law in the United States. The student is led through the "why" of the developments, as well as the "what"—not by the hand, via textual exegesis, but by problems, in the form, principally, of cases. When he gets onto the "story-line," the plan is that he will begin to anticipate the parts as yet unread, even unwritten.

This is Part I, institutional and historical in its approach, as well as analytical. With completion of its 199 pages, the student will have had a small course in the law of labor relations, from 1806 through April, 1972, from the common law through the Sherman and Clayton Acts, through the Railway Labor Act, Norris-LaGuardia, Wagner, Taft-Hartley, Landrum-Griffin, the Civil Rights Act of 1964, Executive Order 10988 and its *public* employment progeny. He will have identified the forces and interests in competition in what is called "labor relations," the evolving conflicts between and among these forces and interests, the law's evolving efforts to control and direct the waging of the struggle. He will also have learned the "Greek" of labor law: "strikes"; "picketing"—"peaceful," "organizational," "recognitional"; "boycotts"—"primary," "secondary," "consumption," "labor"; "exclusivity"; "bargaining unit"; "duty to bargain"; "unfair labor practice"; "union security"; "duty of fair representation"; etc.

Teaching Part I (in xerox form) has been fun for the authors because it permits dealing *at large* with the major problems in the labor law arena—i. e., in a manner little circumscribed by the intricacies of current statutory law (although these intricacies are not ignored, and much of the law of Part I is the law today). Relationships between the large-group conflicts of labor relations and other large-group conflicts—e. g., those of race relations and of the campus—may be explored, a kind of venture the materials in Part I encourage.

Forearmed with this "overview," the more traditional journey of Part II is taken by its travelers in stride. The labyrinths of the current law, statutory and gloss, are there explored in detail, but the problems encountered appear as old friends, seen simply anew. The forest is not lost in the trees.

The materials in Part II are arranged functionally, in a kind of chronology. Organization and representation problems are considered first, then bargaining weapons, the structure of bargaining and its reciprocal duties, the administration of the agreement, including problems of race and sex discrimination. At this point, a step backward is taken, for perspective. The public interest is brought into focus. Resurgent antitrust implications are considered, as well as the contradictions inherent in the attempted union of free collective bargaining, full employment, stable prices. Emergency labor disputes are dealt with next, in a manner anticipating the section which follows, collective bargaining in public employment. The cases and materials comprising the public employment section have been selected with an eye to the *differences* between the public and private sectors in respects relevant to the process of bilateralism imported into public employment from private.

Part II and the book end on a note of irony—"I Versus We," materials dealing with the need of the worker for protection from the institution which he created for his own economic and social advancement.

A closing thought with regard to Parts I and II. A pedagogue pressed for time may, without mortal injury to his students, deny to himself and them the pleasures of Part I, launching directly into "The Principle of Exclusivity" with which Part II begins. One of the authors has tried this approach on an experimental basis and found that it works well. All kinds of permutations in between are, of course, available.

Potential users of this casebook may benefit from an understanding of some further, more specific principles guiding the authors in the selection and presentation of the materials it contains:

(1) [Not remembered clearly enough, after four years, for restatement, except that it was profound.]

(2) The principle of *leanness*. We have tried throughout to stick to mainstreams and major tributaries. Lacy refinements have been eschewed. We have sought to construct a teaching vehicle, not a hornbook.

(3) The principle of *interest*. Like pack-rats, we were attracted to bright, shiny objects. We reminded ourselves periodically that we were not constructing Cases and Materials on Embalming. (Caution: There is an occasional needle imbedded in this haystack.)

(4) The principle of *continuity*. We wanted the materials to "flow," and positioned them to facilitate this process. The "story-line" (not always the same story) presented in the interstitial "Notes" was calculated to the same end. The reader might not know where he was at a particular point, but we wanted him to know how he got there.

(5) The principle of *nonoverediting*. We did not want to drive pedagogues and students to the official reports by reason of ambiguities *edited into* a case. Remaining ambiguities, to the extent they exist, will likely be found, upon inspection, to be *birth* defects. As a corollary to this principle of clarity, we have on occasion clarified pristine ambiguity by reporting in brackets or footnotes additional information from other sources. Similarly, we have striven to state cases textually with a clarity rendering resort to the original report unnecessary.

(6) The principle of *self-containment*. With what we hope is rare exception, the users of this book should be able to prepare for class without involuntary research beyond its covers and those of its Statutory Supplement.

(7) The principle of *broader application.* Of all of the courses in the curriculum, Labor Law is perhaps the best vehicle for communicating an understanding of what a free society is, and how, and why. This may well be Labor Law's major contribution to the curriculum, since most of the students taking the course will probably not practice in the area. In our selection of materials and in our textual passages we have sought to maximize this dimension of the course, without, however, slighting the interests of prospective labor lawyers.

Footnotes and Omissions

The omission of footnotes in the cases and materials reported has not been indicated other than as implied by adherence to the original numbering system in the footnotes retained. Footnotes prepared by the authors are lettered. Omissions of citations, as well as of other textual material, are indicated by asterisks.

Responsibility for Errors

The preparation of this casebook has taken four years. It might well have taken eight had not the authors somewhere in the third year hit upon the following pacification: One of them, in the interests of expedition, at that point agreed to assume responsibility for any errors which might, despite all, smuggle their way into the casebook and by dint of clever concealment escape detection through seventeen rereadings. The author who assumed this responsibility, and thereby enabled this imperfect book to see the light of present publication, in lieu of a *perfect* book four years later, is too modest to take credit for his courage.

Acknowledgements

We are deeply obliged to many people for their help in putting this casebook together. One of these, Professor George Schatzki of the University of Texas School of Law, gave invaluable assistance in the preparation of Chapters 6 and 7 and Section A of Chapter 8, particularly with regard to the selection and organization of materials.

Several Cornell law students provided stalwart service: checking citations and secondary authorities, proofreading, indexing. Individually, their support was considerable; collectively, it was indispensable. They are: Jeffrey N. Cole, James A. DeMent, John J. Gallagher, Paul G. Hughes, James G. Szymanski, Jay W. Waks, Christopher C. Wheeler.

No book gets published without the dedication of a corps of loyalists of the typewriter and other office arts. This one is an exemplar of that truth. Ruth J. Shaw, Jylanda M. Diles, and Ann B. Pendleton are, in a special way, co-authors of this book. Sherry A. Hurley, Rosemary Tinker, and Cynthia M. Whiteman also contributed staunchly.

We thank these women, these former students, Professor Schatzki, deeply.

We must also express our gratitude to the Cornell Law School and those responsible for its administration for the generous provision of the facilities and materials with which casebooks are made. The thousands of pages of xeroxing turned out over the years made it possible to put the book, in pre-publication form, through the experiment of the classroom. We also thank the guinea pigs.

WALTER E. OBERER
KURT L. HANSLOWE

Cornell University
June, 1972

Acknowledgments and Permissions

The authors gratefully acknowledge receiving the following permissions to reprint copyrighted materials:

Clark, The Fiduciary Duties of Union Officials Under Section 501 of the LMRDA, 52 Minn.L.Rev. 440–44 (1967). Reprinted by permission of the Minnesota Law Review and the author, R. Theodore Clark, Jr.

Cox, Internal Affairs of Labor Unions Under the Labor Reform Act of 1959, 58 Mich.L.Rev. 819, 824–27 (1960). Reprinted by permission of the Michigan Law Review.

Dulles, Labor in America 355–360. From Labor in America by Foster Rhea Dulles. Copyright 1949, 1955, 1960, © 1966 by Foster Rhea Dulles. Reprinted by permission of the publisher, Thomas Y. Crowell Company, Inc.

Frankfurter and Greene, The Labor Injunction 86–88, 123–126, 200–205. Copyright © 1930 by Macmillan Publishing Co., Inc., renewed 1958 by Felix Frankfurter and Nathan Greene. Reprinted by permission of Macmillan Publishing Co., Inc.

Green, The Case for the Sit-Down Strike, The New Republic, March 24, 1937, 199–200. Reprinted by permission of The New Republic.

Gregory, The Collective Bargaining Agreement: Its Nature and Scope, 1949 Wash.U.L.Q. 3, 11. Reprinted by permission of the Washington University Law Quarterly.

Hanslowe and Oberer, Determining the Scope of Negotiations Under Public Employment Relations Statutes (PERB and the Scope of Negotiations Under the Taylor Law), 24 Indus. & Lab.Rel.Rev. 432 (1971). Reprinted by permission of the Industrial and Labor Relations Review.

Kennedy, Robert F., The Enemy Within 126–128. Copyright © 1960 by Robert F. Kennedy. Reprinted by permission of Harper & Row, Publishers, Inc.

Madden, Origin and Early Years of the National Labor Relations Act, 18 Hastings L.J. 571 (1967). Copyright © 1967, Hastings College of Law. Reprinted by permission of the Hastings Law Journal.

McGuiness, How to Take A Case Before the National Labor Relations Board 34–38. Copyright 1976 by the BNA, Inc. Washington, D.C. Reprinted by permission of The Bureau of National Affairs, Inc.

McKelvey, Fact Finding in Public Employment Disputes: Promise or Illusion, 22 Indus. & Lab.Rel.Rev. 528, 543 (1969). Reprinted by permission of the Industrial and Labor Relations Review.

From *The Developing Labor Law*, 2nd edition, by Charles Morris. Copyright © 1971, 1983 American Bar Association. Reprinted by permission.

Negroes Enjoined from Boycotting Mississippi Stores, New York Times, July 6, 1968, p. 22, Col. 1 (City ed.). © 1968 by The New York Times Company. Reprinted by permission of The New York Times.

Nelles, A Strike and Its Legal Consequences—An Examination of the Receivership Precedent for the Labor Injunction. Reprinted by permission of the Yale Law Journal Company and Fred B. Rothman & Co. from The Yale Law Journal, Vol. 40, pp. 507–10, 515–27, 529–30 (1931).

Nelles, The First American Labor Case. Reprinted by permission of the Yale Law Journal Company and Fred B. Rothman & Company from The Yale Law Journal, Vol. 41, pp. 165, 166–70, 172–80, 184–87, 190–93 (1931).

Oberer, The Scienter Factor in Sections 8(a)(1) and (3) of the Labor Act: Of Balancing, Hostile Motive, Dogs and Tails, 52 Cornell L.Q. 491, 493–94, 505–06 (1967). Copyright © 1967 by Cornell University. Reprinted by permission of the Cornell Law Review and Fred B. Rothman & Co.

Oberer, Sections 8(a)(1) and (3) of the Labor Act in the Wake of the Lockout Decisions: Of Balancing, Hostile Motive, Dogs and Tails. Reprinted by permission from Proceedings of the 19th Annual Winter Meeting, copyright © 1967 by the Industrial Relations Research Association, Madison, Wis. 53706.

Summers, A Summary Evaluation of the Taft-Hartley Act, 11 Indus. & Lab. Rel.Rev. 405, 409–10 (1958). Reprinted by permission of the Industrial and Labor Relations Review.

Summary of Contents

*

Table of Contents *

* Brackets around case names indicate that the cases are treated in Notes following principal cases or within a principal case.

PART II. A LONG ANALYSIS OF PROBLEMS GLOSSED OVER IN THE SHORT HISTORY

*

Table of Cases

The principal cases are in bold type. Cases cited or discussed in the text are roman type. References are to Pages. Cases cited in principal cases and within other quoted materials are not included.

CASES AND MATERIALS ON
LABOR LAW
COLLECTIVE BARGAINING IN A FREE SOCIETY
Third Edition

*

Part I

A SHORT HISTORY OF COLLECTIVE BARGAINING AND THE LAW IN THE UNITED STATES: THE SEARCH FOR BALANCE

Chapter 1

LABOR AS A COMMODITY: THE RISE AND DECLINE OF THE DOUBLE STANDARD

A. THE COMMON LAW

Like everything else in life (other places too, presumably), a casebook on labor law must have a beginning. Among the many possibilities is one of appealing simplicity. Indeed, there is more to be said for the Philadelphia Cordwainers' Case of 1806 as a point of departure than that it is "America's first labor case." Adequately analyzed and despite its age, that case provides the wherewithal for an understanding of the basic economic, political, and social forces at work and in conflict in what is now called "labor relations." The Federalists and Jeffersonians of that period have their counterparts today, not only in the United States but in other countries as well. They represent, to paraphrase a letter from Jefferson to Lafayette, forces "of nature." [a] The interplay between these forces and the changes in the environment in which they meet and contest determine the posture of the law with regard to labor relations ("labor policy") at any given time and place.

THE PHILADELPHIA CORDWAINERS' CASE

(COMMONWEALTH v. PULLIS)

Mayor's Court of Philadelphia, 1806.

[The case is reported in Volume 3 of John R. Commons' famous Documentary History of American Industrial Society (1910), at page 59. The title page of the case reads:

"THE TRIAL OF THE BOOT & SHOEMAKERS OF PHILADELPHIA, ON AN INDICTMENT FOR A COMBINATION AND CONSPIRACY TO RAISE THEIR WAGES. * * *

"TO THOMAS M'KEAN, Governor, and THE GENERAL ASSEMBLY OF PENNSYLVANIA,

a. See footnote 17, infra p. 4.

2

"Is dedicated the report of the most interesting law case, which has occurred in this state since our revolution * * * with the hope of attracting their particular attention, at the next meeting of the Legislature.

" 'It is better that the law be known and certain, than that it be right.' With respect, I am, fellow citizens, your most obedient,

"THOMAS LLOYD

[Shorthand Reporter]."

The stenographic report of the case runs almost 200 pages in the Commons book. The essence of the case and of the environment in which it arose has been captured in the following article by Walter Nelles.]

NELLES, THE FIRST AMERICAN LABOR CASE
41 Yale Law Journal 165, 166–70, 172–80, 184–87, 190–93 (1931).

I

The first case * * * arose from a cordwainers' strike at Philadelphia in the fall of 1805.

The on-coming of the Industrial Revolution seems in this country to have been first felt in the foot-wear industry. Before the end of the eighteenth century master cordwainers at Philadelphia and other eastern cities had passed from manufacture only for people who "bespoke" boots or shoes for their own wear to comparative quantity production of stocks for their retail stores. Thenceforth counter-organizations of masters and journeymen were in intermittent conflict.

The journeymen's standard of living was not luxurious. As a matter of course, as in all manual employments, the workday was from sun-rise to sun-set, and was often protracted by candlelight. A slow workman testified that he could not earn ten dollars a week at the piece work rates paid in 1805 if he should work all the twenty-four hours of the day. One first-rate workman, making only the finest shoes at the highest rate, averaged six or seven dollars a week; another averaged nine or ten.

Since journeymen worked at their own speed in their own houses with their own tools, their only direct object of pressure was to maintain or advance piece-work wages. Their success was at first considerable. They maintained the closed shop; "scabbed" [7] masters and workmen, though they might hobble along for a time, had ultimately to make their peace with the society [of journeymen]. The society seems to have been sensitive to the limit within which masters could advance wages, and sale prices, without curtailing production and, consequently, employment. Governing its wage demands by this limit, and so controlling the labor supply that submissive masters could not be hurt by open-shop competition, it won consistently until 1805.

But with the passing of the industry beyond the stage of manufacture for a local market, the society's strategic position was impaired. During the

---

7. The word "scab" was already in common use, carrying its full modern connotation. A spectator at the cordwainers' trial was fined five dollars for his contempt in exclaiming in court, "A scab is a shelter for lice."

Napoleonic wars, ✻ ✻ ✻ it became possible for Philadelphia manufacturers to sell boots in the South in competition with boots made in England. The journeymen were not farsighted enough to perceive the menace of this trade. They helped it grow by accepting—initially doubtless by way of special favor to masters in what seemed exceptional cases—a twenty-five cent reduction of the regular piece-work rate when boots were made for export. That both masters and journeymen should become increasingly dependent upon the export trade was inevitable. In 1805, aware too late that it was regular instead of occasional, the society conjoined demands for a higher regular rate for boots and for discontinuance of the rebate of wages for export or "order" work.[9]

[The masters resisted these demands.]

The journeymen "turned out." They were weakened not only by their impotence to affect the price of competitive English boots but also by internal disharmony; the vote to turn out was sixty to fifty. The best workmen, being employed exclusively upon fine footwear for the local market, saw no benefit to themselves. They turned out only to avoid being "scabbed." And it seems likely, though there was no such testimony, that the growth of the export trade had made room for inferior workmen who feared that to win the demands might kill the export trade and throw them out of employment. Both classes of unwilling strikers stood out, however, for several weeks. But after the arrest of eight leaders on a charge of criminal conspiracy they went back to work at the old rates, and the strike ended in total failure.

II

The trial of the eight for the supposed common law crime of "conspiracy to raise their wages" was in the following spring. The legal controversy, both out of court and in, was part of the major political controversy of the time—then still usually expressed as between "aristocracy" and "republicanism" (which meant Jeffersonian democracy).

✻   ✻   ✻

The essence of Jeffersonianism was humane concern for "the security of each and the welfare of all," and conviction that those ends were, for the time being, best served by a maximum of individual freedom and a minimum of law and government. Jeffersonian freedom was not a sterile dogma; it meant freedom to obtain as well as to pursue a fair degree of happiness. It was obviously not possible for the journeymen cordwainers to obtain such happiness as better wages could confer if the only effective way to raise their wages was closed to them. It was natural, therefore, that Jeffersonian feeling should rally to their defense. ✻ ✻ ✻ After 1800, with Republicanism both nationally and, except in New England, locally in the saddle, most ambitious self-seekers whose commitment to Federalism had not been such as to hold them loyal through shame were ready enough to profess Republicanism in the abstract.[17] ✻ ✻ ✻ Only the bench and bar remained both strongly and openly Federalist.

9. ✻ ✻ ✻ The demand was for the same wages that prevailed at New York and Baltimore. ✻ ✻ ✻

17. In 1823, when all politicians were calling themselves Republicans, Jefferson wrote to La Fayette: "You are not to believe that

The *Cordwainers' Case* fell neatly into place in the line of Federalist common law holdings over which Jeffersonianism had been boiling for years. Jefferson himself felt that his "revolution" would not be complete until it had republicanized the law as judicially declared. With him, and those who followed him rather from conviction than interest, the object of the impeachment [of judges] campaign was not to man the courts with Republican politicians—though of course its success would have had that result—but to take the Federalist judges *out* of politics, in which they had been immersed to their ears. One of the Republican cries was for repudiation of the English common law. "English common law" meant, concretely, a series of decisions and charges in political cases in which Federalist judges had invoked it, with much violence to what had been Federalist constructions of the Constitution in the campaign to placate opposition to its adoption. The English common law as to crimes against governmental authority was, it was held, "the common law of the United States;" though the Federal government possessed no powers not delegated to it by the Constitution, and the Constitution entrusted implied powers to Congress only, the Federal courts, without warrant from Congress, had "inherent" power to punish as violative of the common law of the United States conduct prejudicial to the policies of the Federalist administration. * * * Common law doctrines of seditious libel, long disputed in England and there repudiated in 1791 by Fox's Libel Act, were held compatible with the nature of American government and not repugnant to the First Amendment; freedom of the press consisted only in freedom from censorship prior to publication. Republican publications reviling Federalist officials and policies were punishable as seditious libels under the common law of the United States even without the Sedition Act of 1798. * * *

The prosecution and conviction of the cordwainers * * * added still another count to the majority Republican indictment of the common law. The British authorities * * * were said by the court to establish that a "conspiracy of workmen to raise their wages" was criminal at common law. * * *

The case was tried in the Mayor's Court of Philadelphia. * * * The prosecution was conducted by two of the ablest members of the brilliant Philadelphia bar of that period: Joseph Hopkinson and Jared Ingersoll. * * *.

Caesar A. Rodney had been imported from Delaware * * * to Philadelphia to defend the journeymen cordwainers * * *.

III

The practice of arguing law as well as fact to juries in criminal cases was still universal at the time of the cordwainers' trial. There was no controversy as to the facts. The question of law involved was novel in the United States. It would have been rash, therefore, for the court to undertake to prevent counsel from appealing to the jury on grounds of public policy as well as by citation of English authorities. And since the issues of public policy with respect to organized labor have not changed greatly in a century

these two parties are amalgamated, that the   * * * For in truth, the parties of Whig and lion and the lamb are lying down together.   Tory, are those of nature." * * *

and a quarter, the most interesting of the arguments of counsel are those which touched them.

The major premise of the prosecution's case was that unlimited expansion of manufactures is beneficial to the community. It is therefore proper, said Hopkinson, "to support this manufacture. Will you permit men to destroy it who have no permanent stake in the city; men who can pack up their all in a knapsack, or carry them in their pockets to New York or Baltimore?" The journeymen's confederacy, said Ingersoll, will destroy the industry, to the ruin, not of the masters, who could stand the shock, but of the journeymen themselves.

Another of the prosecution's scarecrows may have seemed to the jury more perturbing: if the masters pay higher wages, "you must pay higher for the articles." From this was drawn the inference, perhaps plausible if the export trade had not yet become important to the masters, that the masters "have no interest to serve in the prosecution * * *. They, in truth, are protecting the community."

Rodney, for the defendants, speciously denied that higher wages meant higher prices: "If you banish from this place (as it is morally certain you will) a great number of the best workmen, by a verdict of guilty, can you reasonably expect, that labour will be cheaper? Will it not rise in value, in exact proportion to the scarcity of hands, and the demand for boots and shoes, like every other article in the market?" It followed, he argued, that it was not the journeymen's society but the prosecution that endangered the export trade and the prosperity which "must be the sincere wish of us all." * * *

That the prosecution was subversive of American freedom was the main contention of the defence. Even if it were conceded (as of course it was not) that at English common law the cordwainers' society would be a criminal conspiracy, that common law was not American common law. In support of this, counsel argued, relying upon * * * Blackstone, that if a doctrine of labor conspiracy had been used in this country during the colonial period— which it had not—it could not survive as law in one of the United States, even under a constitution or statute which continued "the common law" in general terms. For it would be in derogation of the natural and unalienable rights of man, and inconsistent with democracy.

The anomalies of freedom were, however, as striking then as now. To associate for betterment is an exercise of freedom. And the associates may claim freedom of collective action. * * * But efficient [collective action] may involve a variety of coercions of unwilling individuals—to join, or to conform with its regulations, or to concede its demands.

So Ingersoll had also freedom points, with which * * * he could play more effectively than Rodney upon the feelings of both judges and jury.

"The defendants formed a society, the object of which was * * * What? That they should not be obliged to work for wages which they did not think a reasonable compensation? No: * * * they may legally and properly associate for that purpose. * * *" The object of the society was not freedom, but compulsion:

"We charge a combination, by means of rewards and punishments, threats, insults, starvings and beatings, to compel the employers to accede to terms, they the journeymen present and dictate."

In repeated instances the society had substituted compulsion for freedom of contract in fixing wages. A turn-out in 1798 had forced wages above the contract rate; and when, in 1799, the masters combined to restore the contract rate, another turn-out kept them up. The evidence—which had not been confined to the events of 1805, but had ranged back into the eighteenth century—was full of concrete hardships suffered by individuals. Ingersoll adroitly, without heightening or cumulation of details, refreshed the jury's sense of the moving quality of this evidence as it had come from the lips of the witnesses. Job Harrison had joined the society in 1794 for fear of being scabbed: "if I did not join the body, no man would set upon the seat where I worked, * * * nor board or lodge in the same house, nor would they work at all for the same employer." Most of the turn-outs were for wages on boots; he, making only fine shoes, had nothing to gain. During the turn-out of 1799, having "a sick wife and a large young family," he scabbed secretly for Mr. Bedford until, having been detected by the "tramping committee" and roused to indignation by the strikers' rejection of the tearful plea of one Dobbin for leave to support his children, he resolved to scab openly. Mr. Bedford promised to protect him, and kept him on after the strike had been won. Mr. Bedford's shop was therefore scabbed; his force, which before the strike had been twenty, was for a year and a half reduced to four or five journeymen, of whom only two were competent. While his shop was scabbed his shop window was broken with potatoes which had pieces of broken shoemakers' tacks in them—"at least the one had which they aimed at my person, and was near hitting me in the face." Harrison having finally been readmitted to the society on payment of a fine, Mr. Bedford could get workmen again. He went South and secured many customers; but soon after his return, business becoming a little brisk, his new force compelled him to raise their wages and demand higher prices of his Southern customers—with the result that he lost trade to the amount of $4,000 a year. Mr. Blair testified: "At the turn-out in 1798, I had six men working for me; who were willing to continue notwithstanding the turn-out. These men were kept up in a garret, but sometimes after dark, they would venture out to Mrs. Finch's, next door but one, to get a drink of beer; one Sunday evening * * * I found them hid away in the cellar; they had been beaten, and the girl was crying, and had been beaten also. I was very angry, and determined next day to buy a cowskin, and whip the first that came near the house. Their clerk, Nelson, was the first, and I fell foul and beat him; he sued me for it, and my men sued them afterwards; we dropped the whole and squared the yards. * * * I afterwards had to pay fines for my men, to get them into the body again." A journeyman testified: "The name of a scab is very dangerous; men of this description have been hurt when out at nights. I myself have been threatened for working at wages with which I was satisfied. I was afraid of going near any of the body: I have seen them twisting and making wry faces at me, and heard two men call out scab, as I passed by. I was obliged to join, for fear of personal injury. * * *" There was no evidence, however, of any violence within five years of the

1805 turn-out, or that any of the defendants had ever done more than take part in strikes and live up to the no-association-with-scabs rule of the society.

IV

An open-minded judge might have felt bound to caution a jury which was judge of the law applicable to undisputed facts in this political case of first impression against the superficiality of counsel on both sides as well as against their "appeals to passion." The fairest of practical judges might well, however, have shrunk from undertaking himself to marshal fully and fairly all the arguments and inferences that might properly have been weighed. Even after one hundred and twenty-five years this difficult job cannot be undertaken without diffidence. And though it is here attempted as of 1806, with an eye mainly to facts then evident and inferences then reasonable, what is said must inevitably reflect consideration of later experience.

Whether the journeymen cordwainers were guilty of crime depended, not upon the English authorities * * *, but upon whether a Jeffersonian or a Tory judgment of tendency with respect to the prosperity and happiness of people, standing in thought as *the* people, should prevail.

To American commercial Toryism (except that of New England ship-owners) the beneficence of rapid development of manufactures was not open to question. Hamilton would have thought *per se* excellent the increased wealth that would result. Wealth tends inevitably, to be sure, to become concentrated in the most capable hands. But such happiness as poverty and incapacity may hope for depends upon the wealth of the rich. The richer the rich, the more employment they provide, and the greater their power to be generous should they be so disposed. Manufactures would, moreover, increase the aggregate wealth, power and importance, however distributed among individuals, not only of the city, but also of the nation. We should escape dependence upon Europe for necessities; and find ourselves better equipped for aggression and defence in wars which no observer of the Napoleonic world could feel as escapable. Private wealth is national power. It is better to live in a strong nation than in a weak one. Since journeymen's societies were clearly obstructive of rapid increase in manufacturing wealth, they were obstructive of both public and private security and prosperity.

A more humane Tory than Hamilton could in 1806 have reinforced this contention. At the trial no one either dared or wished to challenge the beneficence of manufactures. It could not have been denied that the proceeds of increased manufactures would be widely distributed among persons then living at Philadelphia. The jury was composed of one merchant, three inn-keepers, three grocers, a bottler, a watch-maker, a tailor, a hatter, and a tobacconist. If, for non-inclusion of persons dependent upon wages, it was not fairly representative of the economic interests of all the people of Philadelphia, it represented a probable majority. All such as those jurors, having a head-start upon the competitors who would be sure to arise, stood to fatten their pocket-books through increase in the total amount of money to be spent in Philadelphia. Export manufacture would clearly bring to town much money; there would be more employers with more money to spend before there would be fewer, with still more; and however low the wages of manufacturing labor, their aggregate would be enormous. Manufacturing wage-earners then present in Philadelphia would obviously suffer loss, but opportunities to re-coup were many and hopeful. If their wages became unsatisfactory, it was true that a good many could pack their all in a knap-sack and better themselves at New York or Baltimore, or by going West, or by changing occupation. * * * As for the immigrants who pushed natives and earlier comers sometimes up and sometimes down, doubtless they lived meanly. But even they could sometimes rise; and at worst they lived better than in famished Ireland. An observer who conclud-ed that manufacturing laborers had little need of defensive-aggressive orga-nization in 1806, and that their closed shops impaired the freedom and happiness of the majority, was not obviously biased or uninformed.

A weighty other side to the case could however, be seen or felt even in 1806. Economic factors are not the sole factors in human welfare, and wealth is neither an equivalent of happiness nor its necessary condition. Our Twentieth Century preoccupation with economics tends to make think-ing lop-sided. The pendulum has swung from extravagant denial of the heresy of economic determination to counter-extravagance of affirmation.

The Eighteenth Century produced men who, like Jefferson and Madison, saw things in better proportion. Candid though they were in recognition of economic motives and values, they did not deem it soft-headed to perceive that economic gains may be human losses, even to their gainers.

It was obvious to Jefferson that somewhat autonomous work (whether or not stimulated by gain or need) in which main attention is upon excellence of product—whether tobacco leaves, a civilization, poetry, or tables and chairs—develops more satisfactory human animals than work whose doing fails to shut from view a gain or need which prompts it. The effects upon human quality of the pursuit of gain dissociated from creation were evident * * *. Wealth, moreover, makes poverty. Even European economists were not yet definitely committed to the theory that the Iron Law of Wages is a law of Nature and therefore both immutable and excellent;[55] Jefferson might have said that the actual reduction of English manufacturing labor to bare life, without liberty or happiness, was not natural but artificial. Since their human products are so undesirable, we could properly, according to the man to whom *laissez faire* individualism is ascribed as a dogmatic faith, outlaw manufactures. If we subordinate our other pursuits to agriculture, he said, we are more likely to be happy than if we mimic an Amsterdam, a Hamburg, or a city of London. * * *

Freedom, like interstate commerce, is a practical conception, and its practical boundaries are even more shifting and elusive. Freedom in gener-al is in perpetual conflict with freedom in particular. None have ever enjoyed freedom either absolutely or equally. Anyone's freedom is inevita-bly either more or less than anyone else's. A man's possession or lack of freedom is not measured by his legal rights, which can only affect his power to become more free. How much freedom he actually enjoys is a question not of law but of fact, and the answer is different in every instance. A free

---

55. The Iron Law—that wages cannot "naturally" exceed the minimum essential to subsistence—was intimated in the Eighteenth Century by Quesnay and Turgot, but got its main impetus from Ricardo in 1817. * * *

society is a society in which fairly substantial freedom is fairly generally enjoyed—of course in various and unequal degrees.

* * * [F]reedom is in proportion to autonomy, which is in proportion to power * * *. A "free society" which permits inequalities of power *ipso facto* permits inequalities of freedom.

To reduce citizens of unequal capacities to equality of power is of course impossible. And a free society has good reason for not going nearly so far towards compulsion of equality as might be possible. That good reason is not, however, its concern for freedom, which is qualitatively neutral. It is concern for the qualities of its freemen. The freest society conceivable might be a society of morons. Concern for general enjoyment of substantial freedoms conflicts with and yields somewhat to concern for human excellence. The freest of free societies, if it were likewise intelligent, though its regulations would often be of leveling tendency, would check leveling short of the point at which it would defeat that full and ardent competitive cultivation and use of superior faculties which is a supreme excellence of living.

In Jeffersonian America the danger of too much leveling was supposed to be met by the policy of letting people alone to do their utmost for themselves within the limits of the tolerable. That policy meant that life would be a rough-and-tumble in which much coercion and loss would have to go without legal remedy and be written off as due to the "inevitable friction of society." But while disparities were moderate, fairly substantial freedom somewhat general, and opportunities abundant, it stimulated most people to better their qualities and to enrich their lives. Whether it would also result in the conservation of as satisfactory a diffusion of substantial freedom as there was to start with depended upon * * * what it should be construed as requiring in concrete instances such as the *Cordwainers' Case.*

No rule, maxim or principle of law or policy will necessarily and always result in conservation or increase of freedom. The question of what legal regulations or omissions to regulate will serve those ends is always practical. * * * To say that because men's abstract rights are equal they are equally free is indeed a crude and violent *non sequitur.* "Consider," said Anatole France, "the majestic equality of the law, which visits the same punishment upon rich and poor for begging in the streets, for sleeping under bridges, and for stealing bread." Equality of property rights results in freedoms somewhat, though very roughly, in proportion to property owned, and in lacks of freedom somewhat in proportion to property lacked. In the conditions of Jefferson's time equality of property rights could be felt on the whole as practically serviceable to freedom generally. But even then it was seen * * * that the tendency of accumulations of wealth to impair freedoms would call ultimately for correction "by the equalizing tendency of our laws." Since freedom depends on power, and legal rights are elements of power, when disparities of power widen, the inferior may need superior rights or privileges and immunities in order to enjoy such freedoms as it is desirable and practicable that they should have.

The *Cordwainers' Case* involved no claim for the defendants of unequal rights or special privileges or immunities in a strict sense of those words.[65] * * * The stress of the prosecution was upon the coercions incident to the activities and objects of the association, * * * without distinction between whether they were effected by acts then recognized as unlawful (beating of strike-breakers) or by acts which were not (refusal of association). * * *

V

A safe and sensible position for a court in 1806 might have been this: The question is of American public policy and cannot be deemed controlled by English authorities. Society is divided with respect to it; there is no such approach to unanimity as might justify a court in feeling that it had a mandate from society to decide it, and no such indifference as to make a decision either way preferable to none at all. Such a question of policy is more appropriate for legislative than for judicial consideration; and so long as the legislature has not spoken, society may be presumed to will that the subject shall remain unregulated by law.

A different position, however, was taken by Recorder [Moses] Levy [who presided at the trial]. In his charge to the jury such sensitiveness as he showed to considerations which have been here adduced was not catholic.

It was proper, he said, to consider whether the journeymen's combination was injurious to the public welfare. It interferes with the "natural" regulation of wages and prices by supply and demand. If journeymen may combine to exact "artificial" wages "dependent upon the will of the few who are interested," it follows that the masters may combine to exact artificial prices for boots. "If they could stand out three or four weeks in winter, they might raise the price of boots to thirty, forty, or fifty dollars a pair, at least for some time. * * * In every point of view this measure is pregnant with public mischief and private injury—tends to demoralize the workmen— destroy the trade of the city, and leaves the pockets of the whole community to the discretion of the concerned." No merchant can do business if, after he has contracted to deliver articles, his journeymen may arbitrarily jump their wages. Consider, moreover, the effects upon the journeymen themselves. "The botch, incapable of doing justice to his work," is put on a level with the best workman. Indigent workmen, with families to maintain, "however sharp and pressing their necessities, were obliged to stand the turn-out, or never afterwards be employed." They were not free to use their own good sense and return to work. Does not this tend to lead "neccessitous men * * * to take other courses for the support of their wives and children? It might lead them to procure it by crimes—by burglary, larceny, or highway

65. It may be necessary to repeat that there was no claim or evidence that anything which an individual might not lawfully have done had been done in the 1805 strike. The defendants might therefore have claimed that they were denied equality of right.

Since there is no wish to palliate the fact that instances of violent and intimidatory coercion such as had occurred in 1798 are naturally incident to collective labor pressures, especially to an initial establishment of a closed shop, the fairness of trying the defendants for the whole past history of their organization is not discussed. No claim of legal immunity for the instigators or perpetrators of violent coercions is involved in the argument that in spite of the likelihood of occasional incidents of lawlessness if the society survived, membership in the society would better not have been held unlawful. Occasional lawlessness is incident to many lawful activities.

robbery! A father cannot stand by and see, without agony, his children suffer."

The laws of the journeymen "leave no individual at liberty to join the society or reject it. * * * They are not the laws of Pennsylvania." Are we to have, "besides our state legislature, a new legislature consisting of journeymen shoemakers"—an *imperium in imperio?* * * *

"An attempt has been made," he continued, "to shew that the spirit of the revolution and the principle of the common law, are opposite in this case. That the common law, if applied in this case, would operate an attack upon the rights of man. The enquiry on that point, was unnecessary and improper. Nothing more was required than to ascertain what the law is." * * *

Though the Recorder had charged, as was then orthodox, that it was for the jury as well as the court "to decide what the rule of law is," and though he had stated that it was proper to consider the public welfare and had undertaken to do so, he exerted himself to foreclose the jury from deciding the law upon grounds of public policy. The rule of law, "whatever may be its spirit or tendency," must control. The common law has introduced and perpetuated "that admirable institution, the freeman's boast, the trial by jury." It is an "invaluable code" which has "ascertained and defined" both civil rights and crimes with consistency and "critical precision." Only those who understand it as a whole are competent judges of it. "As well might a circle of a thousand miles diameter be described by the man, whose eye could only see a single inch, as the common law be characterized by those who have not devoted years to its study." It "regulates with a sound discretion most of our concerns. * * * Its rules are the result of the wisdom of the ages." He then stated its rules for the case:

"If the purpose to be obtained, be an object of individual interest, it may fairly be attempted by an individual. * * * Many are prohibited from combining for the attainment of it.

" * * * a combination of workmen to raise their wages may be considered in a two fold point of view: one is to benefit themselves * * * the other is to injure those who do not join their society. The rule of law condemns both. If the rule be clear, we are bound to conform to it even though we do not comprehend the principle upon which it is founded. * * * It is enough, that it is the will of the majority. It is law because it is their will—if it is law, there may be good reasons for it though we cannot find them out."

He proceeded, however, to adduce as a reason the coercion incident to such a combination. A unanimous court, he said in conclusion, "have given you the rule as they have found it in the book. * * * If you can reconcile it to your consciences, to find the defendants not guilty, you will do so; if not, the alternative that remains, is a verdict of guilty."

In *Aurora* [a Jeffersonian newspaper] for March 31, 1806, [the editor] wrote as follows:

"A man who did not know the purposes for which the law contemplated the appointment of a *recorder* to preside in the mayor's court, would unquestionably have concluded that Mr. Recorder Levy had been paid by the master shoemakers for his discourse in the mayor's court on Friday last—

never did we hear a charge to a jury delivered in a more prejudiced and partial manner—from such courts recorders and juries, good lord deliver us."

It is inferrable that the majority Republican faction of which *Aurora* was the organ may not have been unrepresented on the jury, and that its representatives may have been responsible for a form of verdict reminiscent of a famous case which may still somewhat have lived in Pennsylvania tradition. When William Penn was tried at London for the crime of unlawful assembly, the jury returned as its verdict: "Guilty of holding a meeting in Fenchurch Street." This, the court held, was not a verdict of Guilty. And since the jury would find no other, Penn went free. The sealed verdict signed by the jurors in the *Cordwainers' Case* was as follows:

"We find the defendants guilty of a combination to raise their wages."

Whatever may have been the intention of the jurors, or some of them, this was entered as a verdict of Guilty.

Counsel for the prosecuting masters had assured the jury that they were concerned only to establish a principle, and were not desirous that the defendants be punished. The court, doubtless anxious to avoid further exasperation of popular feeling, kept their implied promise. The defendants were each fined eight dollars. ✱ ✱ ✱

VI

The *Cordwainers' Case* is important mainly for affording distinct view of a conflict of values, interests, and ideas which has survived changes of conditions—exhibiting that conflict in an air which, since time has laid some of its dust, is clearer than the air of the present. ✱ ✱ ✱

Note

1. Why was the Philadelphia Cordwainers' Case characterized by the court reporter as the "most interesting law case" in Pennsylvania since the Revolution?

2. Are the basic conflicts involved in the case peculiar to the conditions prevailing in Philadelphia in 1806? Or are they present today in countries with economies which are (1) developing, (2) mature, (3) aged—e.g., India, the United States, Great Britain?

Suppose that you were suddenly made (elected, crowned, couped) president, emperor, potentate of a new, undeveloped nation; suppose, further, that your concerns for your people were entirely benevolent: What would your labor policy be?

3. What, precisely, was the conduct found to be criminal in the Cordwainers' Case?

4. What does Nelles mean when he writes (supra p. 10): "The freest society conceivable might be a society of morons"?

5. How can a free society reconcile the theoretical equality of individual freedom with the actual inequality of individual power? What are the functions and limits of law in dealing with group conflicts of the sort involved in the Cordwainers' Case? Are these problems peculiar to employer-employee relations?

How, for example, should the law deal with the problems presented in the following news item (New York Times, July 6, 1968, p. 22, col. 1 (city ed.))?

"Negroes Enjoined
From Boycotting
Mississippi Stores

"GREENWOOD, Miss., July 5 (UPI)—Judge W.H. Bizzell issued a temporary injunction today forbidding Negroes to continue a boycott against white-owned stores.

"Sixty-one merchants, who said the boycott had amounted to economic strangulation in this small Mississippi Delta city, had sought the injunction.

"The Greenwood Movement, a civil rights group headed by a white Roman Catholic priest, the Rev. Nathaniel Machesky, began the boycott three months ago to seek more jobs for Negroes and improvements in housing and sanitation services.

"Judge Bizzell issued the injunction after hearing testimony of fire-bombing, window smashing and other acts of retaliation against Negroes who patronized the white-owned stores.

"The injunction prohibits movement members from 'picketing or marching or persuading or inducing any other person or persons to picket and march with or without signs' within 300 feet of any of the stores.

"It also prohibited 'lookouts' who had observed the stores and recorded the names of customers and the use of violence in preventing Negroes from shopping in the stores.

"Judge Bizzell said the injunction would remain in effect 'until this court can reasonably feel that the Negroes of Greenwood can realize that they are able to patronize the business district if they wish without fear or intimidation.'

"Boycott leaders have already filed a plea in United States District Court to void any injunctions issued by state courts. The plea is pending."

COMMONWEALTH v. HUNT
Supreme Judicial Court of Massachusetts, 1842.
45 Mass. (4 Metc.) 111, 38 Am.Dec. 346.

This was an indictment against the defendants, (seven in number,) for a conspiracy. The first count alleged that the defendants, together with divers other persons unknown to the grand jurors, "on the first Monday of September 1840, at Boston, being workmen and journeymen in the art and manual occupation of bootmakers, unlawfully, perniciously and deceitfully designing and intending to continue, keep up, form, and unite themselves into an unlawful club, society and combination and make unlawful by-laws, rules and orders among themselves, and thereby govern themselves and other workmen in said art, and unlawfully and unjustly to extort great sums of money by means thereof, did unlawfully assemble and meet together, and, being so assembled, did then and there unjustly and corruptly combine, confederate and agree together, that none of them should thereafter, and that none of them would, work for any master or person whatsoever, in the said art, mystery or occupation, who should employ any workman or journeyman, or other person, in the said art, who was not a member of said club, society or combination, after notice given him to discharge such workman from the employ of such master; to the great damage and oppression, not only of their said masters employing them in said art and occupation, but also of divers other workmen and journeymen in the said art, mystery and occupation; to the evil example of all others in like case offending, and against the peace and dignity of the Commonwealth." * * *

[The indictment contained four additional counts which, without adding anything of consequence to the allegation of the conspiracy in the first count, alleged the execution of the conspiracy, i.e., the refusal by the defendants to work for certain masters because of their employment of journeymen who were not members in good standing of the society, thereby causing loss to such masters and journeymen. The four additional counts contained no allegation of any unlawful purpose or of the use of any unlawful means not already set forth in the first count. With regard to the second count, for example, the court observed: "It is simply an averment of an agreement amongst themselves not to work for a person, who should employ any person not a member of a certain association. It sets forth no illegal or criminal purpose to be accomplished, nor any illegal or criminal means to be adopted for the accomplishment of any purpose. It was an agreement, as to the manner in which they would exercise an acknowledged right to contract with others for their labor. It does not aver a conspiracy or even an intention to raise their wages; and it appears by the bill of exceptions, that the case was not put upon the footing of a conspiracy to raise their wages."]

The defendants were found guilty, at the October term, 1840, of the municipal court, and thereupon several exceptions were alleged by them to the ruling of the judge at the trial. The only exception, which was considered in this court, was this: "The defendants' counsel contended that the indictment did not set forth any agreement to do a criminal act, or to do any lawful act by criminal means; and that the agreements, therein set forth, did not constitute a conspiracy indictable by any law of this Commonwealth; and they moved the court so to instruct the jury: But the judge refused so to do, and instructed the jury that the indictment against the defendants did, in his opinion, describe a confederacy among the defendants to do an unlawful act, and to effect the same by unlawful means * * *.

A printed copy of the constitution of the Boston Journeymen Bootmakers' Society was given in evidence against the defendants, at the trial; and it was agreed that the same might be referred to by the counsel, in the argument, and by the court, in considering the exceptions. * * *

SHAW, C.J. Considerable time has elapsed since the argument of this case. It has been retained long under advisement, partly because we were desirous of examining, with some attention, the great number of cases cited at the argument, and others which have presented themselves in course, and partly because we considered it a question of great importance to the Commonwealth, and one which had been much examined and considered by the learned judge of the municipal court.

* * * Without attempting to review and reconcile all the cases, we are of opinion, that as a general description, though perhaps not a precise and accurate definition, a conspiracy must be a combination of two or more persons, by some concerted action, to accomplish some criminal or unlawful purpose, or to accomplish some purpose, not in itself criminal or unlawful,

by criminal or unlawful means. We use the terms criminal or unlawful, because it is manifest that many acts are unlawful, which are not punishable by indictment or other public prosecution; and yet there is no doubt, we think, that a combination by numbers to do them would be an unlawful conspiracy, and punishable by indictment. ⁕ ⁕ ⁕

Several rules upon the subject seem to be well established, to wit, that the unlawful agreement constitutes the gist of the offence, and therefore that it is not necessary to charge the execution of the unlawful agreement. ⁕ ⁕ ⁕

Another rule is a necessary consequence of the former, which is, that the crime is consummate and complete by the fact of unlawful combination, and, therefore, that if the execution of the unlawful purpose is averred, it is by way of aggravation, and proof of it is not necessary to conviction; and therefore the jury may find the conspiracy, and negative the execution, and it will be a good conviction.

And it follows, as another necessary legal consequence, from the same principle, that the indictment must—by averring the unlawful purpose of the conspiracy, or the unlawful means by which it is contemplated and agreed to accomplish a lawful purpose ⁕ ⁕ ⁕—set out an offence complete in itself ⁕ ⁕ ⁕; and that an illegal combination, imperfectly and insufficiently set out in the indictment, will not be aided by averments of acts done in pursuance of it.

From this view of the law respecting conspiracy, we think it an offence which especially demands the application of that wise and humane rule of the common law, that an indictment shall state, with as much certainty as the nature of the case will admit, the facts which constitute the crime intended to be charged. This is required, to enable the defendant to meet the charge and prepare for his defence, and, in case of acquittal or conviction, to show by the record the identity of the charge, so that he may not be indicted a second time for the same offence. It is also necessary, in order that a person, charged by the grand jury for one offence, may not substantially be convicted, on his trial, of another. ⁕ ⁕ ⁕

From these views of the rules of criminal pleading, it appears to us to follow, as a necessary legal conclusion, that when the criminality of a conspiracy consists in an unlawful agreement of two or more persons to compass or promote some criminal or illegal purpose, that purpose must be fully and clearly stated in the indictment; and if the criminality of the offence, which is intended to be charged, consists in the agreement to compass or promote some purpose, not of itself criminal or unlawful, by the use of fraud, force, falsehood, or other criminal or unlawful means, such intended use of fraud, force, falsehood, or other criminal or unlawful means, must be set out in the indictment. ⁕ ⁕ ⁕

We are here carefully to distinguish between the confederacy set forth in the indictment, and the confederacy or association contained in the constitution of the Boston Journeymen Bootmakers' Society, as stated in the little printed book, which was admitted as evidence on the trial. Because, though it was thus admitted as evidence, it would not warrant a conviction for any thing not stated in the indictment. It was proof, as far as it went to support the averments in the indictment. If it contained any criminal matter not set forth in the indictment, it is of no avail. * * *

[The court here repeats the allegations of the first count as reported in the opening paragraph of the case.]

Now it is to be considered, that the preamble and introductory matter in the indictment—such as unlawfully and deceitfully designing and intending unjustly to extort great sums, &c.—is mere recital, and not traversable, and therefore cannot aid an imperfect averment of the facts constituting the description of the offence. The same may be said of the concluding matter, which follows the averment, as to the great damage and oppression not only of their said masters, employing them in said art and occupation, but also of divers other workmen in the same art, mystery and occupation, to the evil example, &c. If the facts averred constitute the crime, these are properly stated as the legal inferences to be drawn from them. If they do not constitute the charge of such an offence, they cannot be aided by these alleged consequences.

Stripped then of these introductory recitals and alleged injurious consequences, and of the qualifying epithets attached to the facts, the averment is this; that the defendants and others formed themselves into a society, and agreed not to work for any person, who should employ any journeyman or other person, not a member of such society, after notice given him to discharge such workman.

The manifest intent of the association is, to induce all those engaged in the same occupation to become members of it. Such a purpose is not unlawful. It would give them a power which might be exerted for useful and honorable purposes, or for dangerous and pernicious ones. If the latter were the real and actual object, and susceptible of proof, it should have been specially charged. Such an association might be used to afford each other assistance in times of poverty, sickness and distress; or to raise their intellectual, moral and social condition; or to make improvement in their art; or for other proper purposes. Or the association might be designed for purposes of oppression and injustice. But in order to charge all those, who become members of an association, with the guilt of a criminal conspiracy, it must be averred and proved that the actual, if not the avowed object of the association, was criminal. An association may be formed, the declared objects of which are innocent and laudable, and yet they may have secret articles, or an agreement communicated only to the members, by which they are banded together for purposes injurious to the peace of society or the rights of its members. Such would undoubtedly be a criminal conspiracy, on proof of the fact, however meritorious and praiseworthy the declared objects might be. The law is not to be hoodwinked by colorable pretences. It looks at truth and reality, through whatever disguise it may assume. But to make such an association, ostensibly innocent, the subject of prosecution as a criminal conspiracy, the secret agreement, which makes it so, is to be averred and proved as the gist of the offence. But when an association is formed for purposes actually innocent, and afterwards its powers are abused, by those who have the control and management of it, to purposes of oppression and injustice, it will be criminal in those who thus misuse it, or give consent thereto, but not in the other members of the association. In this case, no such secret agreement, varying the objects of the association from those avowed, is set forth in this count of the indictment.

Nor can we perceive that the objects of this association, whatever they may have been, were to be attained by criminal means. The means which they proposed to employ, as averred in this count, and which, as we are now to presume, were established by the proof, were, that they would not work for a person, who, after due notice, should employ a journeyman not a member of their society. Supposing the object of the association to be laudable and lawful, or at least not unlawful, are these means criminal? The case supposes that these persons are not bound by contract, but free to work for whom they please, or not to work, if they so prefer. In this state of things, we cannot perceive, that it is criminal for men to agree together to exercise their own acknowledged rights, in such a manner as best to subserve their own interests. One way to test this is, to consider the effect of such an agreement, where the object of the association is acknowledged on all hands to be a laudable one. Suppose a class of workmen, impressed with the manifold evils of intemperance, should agree with each other not to work in a shop in which ardent spirit was furnished, or not to work in a shop with any one who used it, or not to work for an employer, who should, after notice, employ a journeyman who habitually used it. The consequences might be the same. A workman, who should still persist in the use of ardent spirit, would find it more difficult to get employment; a master employing such an one might, at times experience inconvenience in his work, in losing the services of a skillful but intemperate workman. Still it seems to us, that as the object would be lawful, and the means not unlawful, such an agreement could not be pronounced a criminal conspiracy. * * *

Suppose a baker in a small village had the exclusive custom of his neighborhood, and was making large profits by the sale of his bread. Supposing a number of those neighbors, believing the price of his bread too high, should propose to him to reduce his prices, or if he did not, that they would introduce another baker; and on his refusal, such other baker should, under their encouragement, set up a rival establishment, and sell his bread at lower prices; the effect would be to diminish the profit of the former baker, and to the same extent to impoverish him. And it might be said and proved, that the purpose of the associates was to diminish his profits, and thus impoverish him, though the ultimate and laudable object of the combination was to reduce the cost of bread to themselves and their neighbors. The same thing may be said of all competition in every branch of trade and industry; and yet it is through that competition, that the best interests of trade and industry are promoted. It is scarcely necessary to allude to the familiar instances of opposition lines of conveyance, rival hotels, and the thousand other instances, where each strives to gain custom to himself, by ingenious improvements, by increased industry, and by all the means by which he may lessen the price of commodities, and thereby diminish the profits of others.

We think, therefore, that associations may be entered into, the object of which is to adopt measures that may have a tendency to impoverish another, that is, to diminish his gains and profits, and yet so far from being criminal or unlawful, the object may be highly meritorious and public spirited. The legality of such an association will therefore depend upon the means to be used for its accomplishment. If it is to be carried into effect by fair or honorable and lawful means, it is, to say the least, innocent; if by falsehood or force, it may be stamped with the character of conspiracy. It follows as a necessary consequence, that if criminal and indictable, it is so by reason of the criminal means intended to be employed for its accomplishment; and as a further legal consequence, that as the criminality will depend on the means, those means must be stated in the indictment. If the same rule were to prevail in criminal, which holds in civil proceedings—that a case defectively stated may be aided by a verdict—then a court might presume, after verdict, that the indictment was supported by proof of criminal or unlawful means to effect the object. But it is an established rule in criminal cases, that the indictment must state a complete indictable offence, and cannot be aided by the proof offered at the trial. * * *

* * * Whatever illegal purpose can be found in the constitution of the Bootmakers' Society, it not being clearly set forth in the indictment, cannot be relied upon to support this conviction. * * * [L]ooking solely at the indictment, disregarding the qualifying epithets, recitals and immaterial allegations, and confining ourselves to facts so averred as to be capable of being traversed and put in issue, we cannot perceive that it charges a criminal conspiracy punishable by law. The exceptions must therefore, be sustained, and the judgment arrested.

Note

1. Should the Boston Journeymen Bootmakers' Society have been named, instead, the "Boston Journeymen Bootmakers' Christian Temperance Union"?

The above question may serve to introduce an interpretation of the judicial process peculiarly well exemplified in Commonwealth v. Hunt. This form of analysis, the practitioners of which are called "legal realists," proceeds on the premise that environment is more important than legal doctrine in deciding cases. As explained by one of the pioneers of legal realism (Leon Green, Tort Law Public Law in Disguise, 38 Tex.L.Rev. 1 (Part I), 257 (Part II) (1959–60)), there are three ingredients in the decisional mix: (1) environmental facts, (2) litigated facts (those introduced into evidence), (3) legal doctrine. Their importance to decision-making is in the order stated. The order is, however, inverted in judicial opinions. Doctrine dominates, litigated facts appear in highly abstracted form only, environmental facts are seldom seen at all. The farther removed one is, therefore, from the time and place of a particular decision, the more difficult it is to understand the real rationale. Indeed, the more one studies the opinion of the court, the more misled one may be. A study of the trial record would flesh out the litigated facts but not necessarily communicate much of the environment.

To illustrate, less demand would have been placed upon Chief Justice Shaw's talents as a lawyer and judge in writing the opinion in Commonwealth v. Hunt had the decision been to affirm the convictions, rather than to reverse the trial court. This is typically the situation in great leading cases. Rationalizing, through legal doctrine and facts abstracted from the record, important changes in the law, which changes are impelled if not dictated by changes in the environment, is one of the highest challenges for advocates and judges. The challenge is to make as socially palatable as possible legal changes which, because of their magnitude, must necessarily gore many and alarm more.

To further illustrate, the following paragraph does more to explain the difference in result between the Philadelphia Cordwainers' Case and Commonwealth v. Hunt than the twenty-five pages of opinion and statement of facts in the official report of the latter:

"[N]umerous * * * criminal convictions of workers [between 1806 and 1842] for taking advantage of what they regarded as their ordinary civil privilege to exercise their right to work or not work, under such terms as they saw fit, bred ill-feeling throughout the East. Mobs of laborers held mock trials of judges and hung them in effigy to show their resentment at being treated as common criminals for having done what they believed they had a perfect right to do. Juries were refusing to convict in some of these prosecutions, in spite of clearly proved cases of criminal conspiracy under the prevailing law. Even the press attacked judicial statements that the unions were of foreign origin or were mainly upheld by foreigners." Gregory, Labor and the Law 27 (2d rev. ed. 1961).

2. What *is* the holding in Commonwealth v. Hunt? What benefits might a union lawyer have sought to draw from the case?

Chief Justice Shaw's focusing upon (1) *purpose* (object, end) and (2) *means* in assaying the lawfulness of concerted union activity was a forerunner of the analytical method by which such activity was later to be regulated, whether by courts, statutes, or administrative agencies. The controlling questions are: (1) *What* did they do? (2) *Why* did they do it? The what and the why are then measured against a yardstick of current social acceptability (as perceived by the particular court, legislature, agency). There is nothing unique, of course, in this process; the lawfulness of all human conduct is so measured.

3. Despite Commonwealth v. Hunt, the criminal conspiracy doctrine retained some vitality until about 1890. See, e.g., Commons and Andrews, Principles of Labor Legislation 383 (4th rev.ed. 1967). In the interim, however, experimentation with other remedies took place. These developments are outlined in the materials which follow.

WALKER v. CRONIN

Supreme Judicial Court of Massachusetts, 1871.
107 Mass. 555.

[Plaintiffs sued for damages in tort. Defendant demurred to plaintiffs' declaration. The trial court sustained the demurrer, and plaintiffs appealed.]

WELLS, J. The declaration, in its first count, alleges that the defendant did, "unlawfully and without justifiable cause, molest, obstruct and hinder the plaintiffs from carrying on" their business of manufacture and sale of boots and shoes, "with the unlawful purpose of preventing the plaintiffs from carrying on their said business, and wilfully persuaded and induced a large number of persons who were in the employment of the plaintiffs," and others "who were about to enter into" their employment, "to leave and abandon the employment of the plaintiffs, without their consent and against their will;" whereby the plaintiffs lost the services of said persons, and the profits and advantages they would otherwise have made and received therefrom, and were put to large expenses to procure other suitable workmen, and suffered losses in their said business.

This sets forth sufficiently (1) intentional and wilful acts (2) calculated to cause damage to the plaintiffs in their lawful business, (3) done with the unlawful purpose to cause such damage and loss, without right or justifiable cause on the part of the defendant, (which constitutes malice,) and (4) actual damage and loss resulting.

The general principle is announced in Com.Dig.Action on the Case, A.: "In all cases where a man has a temporal loss or damage by the wrong of another, he may have an action upon the case to be repaired in damages." The intentional causing of such loss to another, without justifiable cause, and with the malicious purpose to inflict it, is of itself a wrong. * * *

In the case of Keeble v. Hickeringill, as contained in a note to Carrington v. Taylor, 11 East, 571, 574, both actions being for damages by reason of frightening wild fowl from the plaintiff's decoy, Chief Justice Holt alludes to actions maintained for scandalous words which are actionable only by reason of being injurious to a man in his profession or trade, and adds: "How much more, when the defendant doth an actual and real damage to another when he is in the very act of receiving profit in his employment. Now there are two sorts of acts for doing damage to a man's employment, for which an action lies; the one is in respect of a man's privilege, the other is in respect of his property." After considering injuries to a man's franchise or privilege, he proceeds: "The other is where a violent or malicious act is done to a man's occupation, profession, or way of getting a livelihood; there an action lies in all cases." From the several reports of this case it is not clear whether the action was maintained on the ground that the wild ducks were frightened out of the plaintiff's decoy, as would appear from 3 Salk. 9, and Holt, 14, 17, 18; or upon the broader one, that they were driven away and prevented from resorting there, as the case is stated in 11 Mod. 74, 130. But the doctrine thus enunciated by Lord Holt covers both aspects of the case; as does his illustration of frightening boys from going to school, whereby loss was occasioned to the master. Of like import is the case of Tarleton v. McGawley, Peake, 205, in which Lord Kenyon held that an action would lie for frightening the natives upon the coast of Africa, and thus preventing them from coming to the plaintiff's vessel to trade, whereby he lost the profits of such trade.

There are indeed many authorities which appear to hold that to constitute an actionable wrong there must be a violation of some definite legal right of the plaintiff. But those are cases, for the most part at least, where the defendants were themselves acting in the lawful exercise of some distinct right, which furnished the defence of a justifiable cause for their acts, except so far as they were in violation of a superior right in another.

Thus every one has an equal right to employ workmen in his business or service; and if, by the exercise of this right in such manner as he may see fit, persons are induced to leave their employment elsewhere, no wrong is done to him whose employment they leave, unless a contract exists by which such other person has a legal right to the further continuance of their services. If such a contract exists, one who knowingly and intentionally procures it to be violated may be held liable for the wrong, although he did it for the purpose of promoting his own business. * * *

Every one has a right to enjoy the fruits and advantages of his own enterprise, industry, skill and credit. He has no right to be protected against competition; but he has a right to be free from malicious and wanton interference, disturbance or annoyance. If disturbance or loss come as a result of competition, or the exercise of like rights by others, it is *damnum absque injuria*, unless some superior right by contract or otherwise is interfered with. But if it come from the merely wanton or malicious acts of others, without the justification of competition or the service of any interest or lawful purpose, it then stands upon a different footing, and falls within the principle of the authorities first referred to. * * *

The difficulty in such cases is to make certain, by proof, that there has been in fact such loss as entitles the party to reparation; but that difficulty is not encountered in the present stage of this case, where all the facts alleged are admitted by the demurrer. The demurrer also admits the absence of any justifiable cause whatever. This decision is made upon the case thus presented, and does not apply to a case of interference by way of friendly advice, honestly given; nor is it in denial of the right of free expression of opinion. We have no occasion now to consider what would constitute justifiable cause.

The second and third counts recite contracts of the plaintiffs with their workmen for the performance of certain work in the manufacture of boots and shoes; and allege that the defendant, well knowing thereof, with the unlawful purpose of hindering and preventing the plaintiffs from carrying on their business, induced said persons to refuse and neglect to perform their contracts, whereby the plaintiffs suffered great damage in their business.

It is a familiar and well established doctrine of the law upon the relation of master and servant, that one who entices away a servant, or induces him to leave his master, may be held liable in damages therefor, provided there exists a valid contract for continued service, known to the defendant. It has sometimes been supposed that this doctrine sprang from the English statute of laborers, and was confined to menial service. But we are satisfied that it is founded upon the legal right derived from the contract, and not merely upon the relation of master and servant; and that it applies to all contracts of employment, if not to contracts of every description. * * *

In Lumley v. Gye, 2 El. & Bl. 216, the plaintiff had engaged Miss Wagner to sing in his opera, and the defendant knowingly induced her to break her contract and refuse to sing. It was objected that the action would not lie, because her contract was merely executory, and she had never actually entered into the service of the plaintiff; and Coleridge, J., dissented, insisting that the only foundation for such an action was the statute of laborers, which did not apply to service of that character; but after full discussion and deliberation it was held that the action would lie for the damages thus caused by the defendant. * * *

Upon careful consideration of the authorities, as well as of the principles involved, we are of opinion that a legal cause of action is sufficiently stated in each of the three counts of the declaration.

Demurrer overruled.

Note

1. What would an employer have to prove to recover damages in tort under Walker v. Cronin? How effective would this remedy be?

2. Is the precedential value of Keeble v. Hickeringill, as applied to the facts of Walker v. Cronin, fatally affected by the circumstance that, as stated by Justice Wells, "it is not clear whether the action was maintained on the ground that the wild ducks were frightened *out of* the plaintiff's decoy, as would appear from 3 Salk. 9, and Holt, 14, 17, 18; or upon the broader one, that they were driven away *and prevented from* resorting there, as the case is stated in 11 Mod. 74, 130"? (Emphasis added.) Or, on the other hand, does this circumstance render the impact of that decision even more compelling since there would then be in *both* cases two sets of objects of the tortious conduct of the actor through which he harms the plaintiff: (1) objects already present, in the one case in the plaintiffs' employ, in the other case in the plaintiff's decoy; (2) objects not yet, but desirous of being, in the employ or decoy, as the case may be? (Excerpted from unpublished notes of one of the authors on the subject "The Common Law Mind at Work (and Play).")

3. In the evolution of employer efforts to cope with concerted labor activities, a fortuitous development occurred in the late 1870's which was to affect profoundly the course of labor relations in the United States for more than half a century. The development took place in the railroad industry, to which, with the opening of the American continent after the Civil War, the focus of "labor law" shifted. (The shift was largely away from shoemakers; the early monuments of American labor law might with fair accuracy be captioned "Cases on Cordwainers.") The following materials reveal the unlikely origin of the "labor injunction" and the manner in which this technique for the control of labor strife swelled to fill a vacuum in the law.

SECOR v. TOLEDO, P. & W. RY.

Circuit Court, Northern District of Illinois, 1877.
21 Fed.Cas. 968, 971.

DRUMMOND, CIRCUIT JUDGE [on rehearing]. The defendants were brought before the court some time since, for being engaged with others at Peoria, on the 26th of July last, in forcibly stopping the trains of the Toledo, Peoria & Warsaw Railway Company, then in the possession of a receiver appointed by the court, and for preventing by intimidation and violence, the employes of the company from performing their duties in the running of the trains. They were found guilty of the offense, and a penalty imposed by the court. [The penalties were imprisonment for four months in the case of one defendant and for two months in the case of the others.]

The order of the court, appointing the receiver and putting him in possession of the railway and its appendages, required him to operate the road * * *. Where property is delivered to a receiver, the authority of the court is directly impressed on it by its order or decree, entered of record, which is considered notice to all persons that it is in custody of the court through its receiver. * * * The receiver holds it under a continuing order, which remains in force till rescinded or modified by the court.

* * * The property being thus in possession of the court, it becomes its duty to protect the receiver in its use by all the means in its power, and if he is deprived of it, to restore it to him by the necessary orders or writs of assistance to the marshal. And if that is unavailing, it can call on the general government to aid in enforcing its lawful process or orders. And among the means at the disposal of the court are summary proceedings against persons who unwarrantably interfere with property in its custody in disobedience of its orders. * * *

The right of a court to punish summarily by fine or imprisonment for contempt of its authority, is undoubtedly a power requiring great caution in its exercise, but it has always been considered, that in some form and with some limitations it ought to exist. The court must have the means without delay to protect itself, its process and the property in its custody by punishing those who wrongfully and forcibly disturb the possession held under its authority. * * *

Under our federal judicial system the power of the court to punish for contempt is limited to the misbehavior of any person in its presence or so near as to obstruct the administration of justice; the misbehavior of its officers in their official acts, and the disobedience or resistance by any person to any lawful writ, process, order, rule, decree or command of the court.

In addition to the order of the court placing the railway in possession of the receiver, there was on the 26th of July a special order of the court requiring the marshal to prevent any interference with it and to assist the receiver in retaining it, and restore it if he were deprived of the possession. * * *

Such has been the embarrassed condition of the railroads in this part of the country within a few years past, that many of them are in the possession of the circuit court of the United States for this circuit, the gross annual earnings of which amount to more than fifteen millions of dollars. This statement shows the magnitude of the interests intrusted to our care. The theory is that our possession is only temporary, but there is generally such a multitude of claims to be adjudged in each case, and so great are the difficulties in arranging conflicting rights among the mortgagees preparatory to a sale and reorganization, that it sometimes happens in spite of the earnest efforts of the court to hasten the sale by foreclosure, that they remain in the custody of the court for some years. The Toledo, Peoria & Warsaw Railway Company has been in the hands of a receiver for more than two years.

It will be seen therefore, that the forcible interruption of the traffic of so many railroads for days, was a very serious matter, and the judges were of opinion, after the fact, that it was not possible to pass by so great an outrage upon the rights of property in our possession, by a reprimand or mere nominal punishment of the guilty persons. If it had been a few cars or engines that had been interfered with, it would have been different, but there was the business of many railroads, for a time struck down by men who bade defiance to the law and to the authority of the court. There seemed to be a necessity to exercise the power vested in the court. If such things could be repeated, then was not only a great wrong done to those whose interests we were obliged to protect, but the government itself had ceased to accomplish one of the chief objects of its creation.

We could take no part in any supposed conflict between capital and labor, if there can be a conflict in a country where the laborer of to-day may be the capitalist of tomorrow. All men are equal before the law. Neither the capitalist nor the laborer has a right to violate it. We personally desire that the laborer in all departments of life should obtain adequate reward for his services. What that should be, it was not for us as a general question to decide. We can only say that we found no sufficient excuse for the wrong done to the property in possession of the court. The men who committed it had no claim whatever to it, and if they had, the result would have been the same. Those who may be said, in one sense, to own the property of the Toledo, Peoria & Warsaw Railway Company, and who will be entitled to its proceeds when sold, are the bondholders under the mortgages, but though many of them may be capitalists, still even they would be guilty of a contempt if they violently took possession of the property while in the custody of the court. It is the act committed that constitutes the offense, whether by capitalists or strikers, the forcible seizure of property not in the possession of an individual or of a corporation, but of the court.

But while these circumstances have influenced us to impose a penalty, we do not desire to continue it, if the purpose has been effected—the maintenance of the authority of the court and the prevention of similar offenses hereafter. And after due consideration we have come to the conclusion, the court still being in session, that we may remit the penalty and discharge the defendants.

The railroads have resumed their ordinary traffic. There seems at present no danger of future trouble. Railroad employes have returned to their duties. It is to be hoped that the lessons of the time have not been lost on the public, nor on employers or employes. The defendants have expressed regret for what has been done, and promise that the offense shall not be repeated. And then it is to be remembered that we consider only the disobedience of the orders of the court and not the general criminal act. And though the wrong done was great, still it is but justice to say that at Peoria, as elsewhere in this circuit, there was no destruction of property as at Pittsburgh; on the contrary, there were in some places earnest efforts made by the strikers to preserve property.

Again, we do not lose sight of the fact that at Peoria, as elsewhere in the circuit, persons who aided in depriving the receiver of control over the property, did not fully realize the nature of the offense as against the court. They must to a great extent be held answerable for all the consequences which followed from their wrongful and violent acts, but it must be admitted that after a time, when they fully comprehended that they were obstructing the orders of the courts and the possible results, they relinquished the control of the trains and allowed the receiver to retake possession. In Peoria this was sooner accomplished than in some other places. So, that in view of these considerations, and with the concurrence of the district attorney and the counsel of the receiver, all the defendants will now be discharged, on each one giving his own recognizance to observe the laws of the United States, and to abstain from all wrongful interference with any property in the possession of a receiver of this court, for one year from this time. * * *

NELLES, A STRIKE AND ITS LEGAL CONSEQUENCES—AN EXAMINATION OF THE RECEIVERSHIP PRECEDENT FOR THE LABOR INJUNCTION

40 Yale Law Journal 507–10, 515–27, 529–30 (1931).

The questions of labor law are indissociable from the question of what Madison called "the most difficult of all political arrangements"—that of so adjusting the conflicting claims of those with and those without property "as to give security to each and to promote the welfare of all." To deal with them on the basis only of what is contained in law books is to miss many factors which have influenced the judgments both of courts and of their critics. * * *

In the case of the American labor injunction the insufficiency of the law's own explanations of itself is singularly evident. The first reported instance of a labor injunction—in England in 1868 [2]—was of minor and deferred importance. The cases examined in this paper—summary punishments of strike sympathizers for contempt of court in obstructing the operation of railways in the hands of receivers—were of greater consequence. * * * The punishments were responsive less to legal principles than to emotions inspired by the great railway strike of 1877. And that strike was responsive to conditions concerning which it will be the first task of this paper to refresh recollection.

I

The economic expansion of the United States after the Civil War was disorderly. It involved enormous waste, both material and human. If "men of vision" built for the future, it was not for the sake of the future. Railways were built to be "milked" by their promoters of subsidies obtained through legislative corruption. Many railroads, to finance which middle western pioneers mortgaged their farms or issued municipal bonds, were not built at all. In boom times nothing but expansion seemed important. Before production exceeded the buying power of old markets, new markets were planted by new railways on the prairies. Alternate links of transportation and industry composed an ever-lengthening endless chain which, primed with immigrants, pumped wealth—enriching life in some respects, impoverishing it in others. The boom was prolonged by abnormal European demand for American food stuffs due to wars and crop shortages. While this accident obscured the hard truth that new farmers along the lines of new railways were producing more wheat, corn, hogs and cattle than normal

---

2. Springhead Spinning Co. v. Riley, L.R. 6 Eq. 551 (1868). * * * The case was not followed in the United States until Sherry v. Perkins, 147 Mass. 212, 17 N.E. 307 (1888). It had meanwhile been but slightly noted—and then with reprobation: Prudential Assurance Co. v. Knott, L.R. 10 ch. 142 (1875); Boston Diatite Co. v. Florence Manufacturing Co., 114 Mass. 69 (1873).

markets could buy, it seemed that the middle west could not be developed too fast for its own good, that no railway building was overbuilding. But peace and comparative plenty returned to Europe, and after the resultant Panic of 1873 people at large paid heavily for the creation and concentration of great wealth. The depression lasted until 1879. Prices fell to unprecedented depths. Farm and railway mortgages were foreclosed. Small independent business men and manufacturers closed their establishments forever and took salaried jobs—if they could get them. The tramp, in thousands, appeared for the first time in America. ∗ ∗ ∗

II

It was during the administration of Hayes that the unregulated private operation of railways, the effects of its anarchy intensified by the depression, produced the strike which a good many contemporary binoculars magnified, for the moment, to the proportions of a social revolution.

During the depression the primary object of every owner of a business was to survive. Present profit, if possible at all, was secondary. The immediate aims were to keep one's apparatus for future profit in working order, and not to part with its ownership or control. The owners of many Middle Western railways, unable to meet fixed charges, had to call on the courts to take care of their properties through receivers; some were, others were not, able to profit by the receivership and reorganization proceedings and find themselves still in the drivers' seats at their conclusion. Of the lines between New York and Chicago, already combined into four great competing systems, only the pilfered Erie had recourse to receivership. But in the struggle to survive even the New York Central and the Pennsylvania cut viciously at one another's throats. In 1876 Mr. James Ford Rhodes bought a ticket from Cleveland to Boston for $6.80. Cattle were carried from Chicago to New York at a dollar a carload.

Losses on competitive through traffic were in part recouped by exorbitant rates from way stations such as Pittsburgh. Railway employees also were naturally required to contribute to the costs of cutthroat competition. Reductions of wages were not negotiated in those days; they were announced. There had been successive reductions since the Panic. Many of the men, moreover, were on part time and subject to onerous boarding house charges at the end of runs which left them far from home. And upon a truce in the rate war effective July 1, 1877, came announcement of a further ten per cent cut in wages.

There was never a strike less organized and more spontaneous than that which followed. The British *Chargé d'affaires* conjectured that but for some panicky firing into an unarmed crowd by frightened militiamen at Baltimore on July 20th, it would have remained local to the Baltimore and Ohio. It spread "more by contagion than by organization." ∗ ∗ ∗ Casual local leaderships there inevitably were, but no policy or direction more definite than could spring from the concurring wills of an indignant mass.

Colonel Thomas A. Scott, president of the Pennsylvania Railroad, wrote about the strike in the *North American Review* soon after it was over. His analysis of causes and motives is interested and inadequate. But his outline of events is succint and sufficient:

"On the 16th of July it became known that the firemen and freight brakemen of the Baltimore and Ohio Railroad were on a strike at Martinsburg, West Virginia, and that no freight trains were allowed to pass that point in either direction. This proved to be the beginning of a movement which spread with great rapidity from New York to Kansas and from Michigan to Texas, which placed an embargo on the entire freight traffic of more than twenty thousand miles of railway, put passenger travel and the movement of the United States mails at the mercy of a mob, subjected great commercial centers like Chicago and St. Louis to the violent disturbance of their business relations, and made the great manufacturing city of Pittsburgh for twenty-four hours such a scene of riot, arson, and bloodshed as can never be erased from the memory of its inhabitants."

The strike mobs were composed of the miscellaneous unemployed; the proportion of striking railway employees is unascertainable but was probably minor. The incidents of riot, arson, and bloodshed, though appalling, were exceptional. The usual mob procedure was to block tracks, yards and stations, and prevent the movement of trains. In general, the strikers "did everything they could to keep up the regular running of all trains carrying the United States mails" in proof that they were fighting the corporations only. Troops, Federal and state (the civil authorities did little or nothing), soon broke up the mobs and "moved the trains." Within a fortnight the strike was over.

III

It is striking, though not at all extraordinary, that there were few, if any, prosecutions in state courts for participation in any of the thousands of crimes incident to that fortnight of disorder. The state of public opinion accounts for this suspension of the criminal law. "The system of corporate life and corporate power" was still in its infancy. The majority of the population was still dependent upon agriculture. The units of commerce and industry were still, for the most part, small. The local mine owner, the small shopkeeper, the contracting carpenter, had the dignity of independence. Their voices dominated public opinion. However crudely the ordinary citizen thought and talked about public affairs, he did think and talk about them, with a proud sense that his opinion was worth something. Democracy was operative.

The ordinary man hated and feared the railroads, not alone for their discriminations, extortions and frauds, but also because they symbolized for him the "Big Business" that was commencing to impinge on many sides. The newspapers were small and still his. Politicians and office holders, though they might secretly be for sale, had assiduously to cultivate the conviction that they also were his. Wage earners, unless they were unassimilated alien immigrants, seemed potential allies of the farmers and small businessmen in the coming struggle for independence.

* * * In many parts of the country it would have been a foolhardy chief of police who interfered with the mobs and a still more foolhardy district attorney who asked a grand jury to indict their members.

Yet sober men in responsible positions could not rest quiescent in the face of anarchy manifest. * * * [W]hen governors applied for soldiers

President Hayes of course proclaimed a constitutional occasion and furnished them. The notion that the Federal government might file bills in equity and obtain injunctions against unlawful interference with railways, as was done in 1894, would, had anyone even thought of it, have seemed preposterous. But it is possible to infer that Attorney General Devens may have instigated—he certainly supported—the extraordinary activities of Federal courts "in their administrative capacity" presently to be described. Many railways in the Seventh Circuit (Illinois, Indiana and Wisconsin) were in the hands of receivers appointed to operate them pending suits to foreclose mortgages. Thomas Drummond was Circuit Judge. Walter Q. Gresham was District Judge in Indiana.

Full details of what Judge Gresham did in Indiana are preserved in his valuable biography. When the strike mob occupied the station at Indianapolis, Gresham held in his court room a mass-meeting of prominent citizens, most of whom had served in the Civil war. He said "that the community was in possession of the mob; that the governor, the mayor, and the sheriff, whose duty it was to act, were supine; life and property were in danger; that society was disintegrating, if it had not dissolved."

He organized a vigilance committee, promising "that he would take no action as Federal judge in an administrative capacity" without the committee's approval. He called for military volunteers, himself enrolling first. * * * Gresham's first thought was to act in subordination to the governmental executive of the state. But first the Governor, and then the Mayor rejected his services. So he instructed the United States marshal, General Spooner, to use the volunteers as a *posse*. There being no ammunition for the *posse*, General Spooner went alone to the station at Indianapolis. Upon his proclamation to the mob that they were in contempt of court, they peaceably permitted receivers' trains to move. Some of the leaders were subsequently arrested for their prior "contempt." Federal troops, furnished at Judge Gresham's request, were put under the command of the marshal. Upon his approach at the head of a detachment, receivers' trains moved at Terre Haute and Vincennes. At the request of the president of the Vandalia, a solvent road with no receiver, Judge Gresham ordered General Spooner to keep troops at Terre Haute "for moral effect." General Spooner somewhat exceeded his orders. "He considered it a duty, in view of President Hayes' proclamation, the Judge's telegrams, his authority as United States Marshal, and his practical experience as a man," to move the Vandalia mail train, escorting it from the Terre Haute station under orders to his men to shoot the first who should attempt to interfere. "The legal lights of Indianapolis including the Judge," said that General Spooner "did right."

At Indianapolis the Judge's "Committee on Safety" hesitated to move trains on roads not in the hands of receivers. Finally, however, the Governor, yielding to importunities, added Gresham's volunteers to the organized militia under General Lew Wallace, and the strike was broken on all roads.

Though no such wealth of detail is accessible as to events in Illinois, it is inferrable that they were similar, except in the degree of directness of judicial participation, to events in Indiana.

IV

In the excitement of the strike the Federal judges in Indiana and Illinois were but incidentally concerned with whether the direction of military forces was compatible with the judicial function in a government built upon the principle of the separation of powers. They conceived themselves as dealing with a situation of revolutionary exigency. They were doing their duty as citizens. Their position as judges made them powerful as citizens. To have stayed their hands, in a lacuna of law incident to an insurrection, upon the ground that judicial power did not extend to empanelling an army or a police force, would have been pusillanimous.

Had they not been judges their activities as military volunteers would have been without significance in legal history. The powers exercised would have disappeared with the emergency that legitimized them. For judges, however, intervention in public affairs except in a judicial capacity is conventionally improper. The propriety of judicial conduct is normally established by judicial opinions. Occasion for judicial opinions arose when an extraordinary assumption of judicial power was superimposed upon the assumption of military power which might better have been justified as natural than as judicial. The mob leaders arrested by the United States marshals were tried without jury and sentenced to imprisonment for contempt of court.

Judge Gresham refused to sit in the contempt cases. Judge Drummond tried and sentenced the men arrested both in Indiana and in Illinois.

The extension in these cases of the power to punish summarily for contempt of court was radical. That power theoretically exists because of its "necessity" in order to prevent obstruction of the administration of justice, and extends no further than that "necessity" requires. It is hard to find a more reasonable theory on which to construe obstruction of a receiver's administration of a railway as obstruction of the administration of justice than this: courts administer justice; courts also administer railways through receivers; therefore the administration of a railway by a court through a receiver is an administration of justice. * * * Operating receiverships had already in this country had a curious effect upon procedural rights in civil cases; a passenger injured by the negligent operation of a receiver's train could sue at law for damages only by leave of the court that appointed the receiver, and permission ordinarily was denied. But never before had a court assimilated to contempt an interference with receivership assets by a thief or a casual turbulent. For nonprivies to the suit in equity to which the receivership is incident, nothing earmarks a business operated by a receiver as under special protection of judicial prerogative. It elbows its way, like other businesses, in a crowded world. It seeks the same end— private profit. It is exposed to the same weather, physical and social. Why should an outsider who, in the course even of his unlawful affairs, touches that business or is touched by it, find himself by the magic of that touch transported to another realm?

Judge Drummond was not forced by counsel who appeared for the defendants in the contempt cases to consider the deeper questions which might have been raised: the nature and limits of judicial power; the nature and objects of receiverships and of the contempt power; the compatibility of the summary punishments with constitutional guarantees of trial by jury and due process of law. Conceding that under the statute passed to *restrict* the power of Federal courts to punish for contempt he could not punish the defendants unless they had *disobeyed or resisted a lawful order of the court,* Judge Drummond held that the defendants' interference with the running of trains amounted to *disobedience* of the orders of the court directing the receivers to operate trains. Though he recognized that disobedience of the orders of the court "is the only offense of which we can take cognizance," he enlarged rather in his opinions upon the enormity of the defendants' offenses against society. His arguments were such as might have been addressed to a jury, under a latitude of deviation from technical issues such as jury lawyers are apt to strive for, or to a legislature in support of the adoption of a novel policy. He referred with feeling to the hardness of the times and conceded that the railway employees might have reason for dissatisfaction. Still, a majority of the people of the country probably have to support their families on less than railway pay. No one has a "right," moreover, to any particular rate of pay. The right of a laborer is simply to contract with his employer for the pay which the employer is willing to give and the laborer is willing to take—which is determined "by the demand and supply of labor." "It is a matter of common bargain and agreement, and unless it can be settled in this way we have to destroy all the relations of life." "The proper way, as it seems to the court, for any class who desire to have the service which they perform compensated at a better rate, is to spread the facts touching that service before the community and thus create a public sentiment in their favor, so that justice may ultimately be done to them by their employers." If receivers' employees have grievances, "the court is always open to hear those grievances, consider them and instruct the receiver to do complete justice to all employers [sic]. * * *" "When it is claimed that the rights of labor consist in not only refusing to labor, but in interfering with the labor of others we, of course, can have no feeling of respect for any such right as that. * * *" Every man * * * has a right to leave the service of his employer * * * but men ought not to combine together and cause at once a strike among all railroad employees * * * because the injury there is public in character. * * * Suppose in seed time the farm hands throughout a large section of this state should come to the conclusion that the farmers did not pay them wages enough, and should combine together and go around to the various farms * * * and prevent in this way the planting of seed? * * * Would that be right? * * * And yet that would be the same thing in principle as these railroad employes have done in this case. * * * Suppose that on any of these trains there was money or property which was to save a man's farm or house from loss or sacrifice. Suppose that there was a traveler who was going to the bedside of a dying wife, husband, son or daughter. * * *" "These railroads are among the principal means of modern civilization by which the business of the country is transacted. Therefore when a man interferes with a property whose object is so important, which affects so materially all the relations of society, he commits as great an offense against the rights of individuals and against the rights of the public as can well be imagined. * * * A public example must be made, and it must be made emphatically. * * * It is * * * indispensably necessary that the court should not tolerate any interference, however slight, with the management of the railroads * * * in its custody. * * * This thing must be stopped, and, so far as this court has the power to do it, it shall be stopped."

This disquisition was unquestionably as sincere as it was fervent. In spite of occasional interjections to the effect that he considered "only the disobedience of the orders of the court and not the general criminal act," it is obvious that Judge Drummond was but slightly concerned to disguise the fact that the policy which determined his punishments was not the policy of the contempt power, but the policy of protecting society, already disturbed by the internecine competition of capital, from the further disturbances of competition between capital and labor.

V

The policy of summary punishment for disorders incident to strikes which Judge Drummond inaugurated is at least debatable. It is also debatable whether courts should have power to establish an innovation so radical. * * *

Judge Drummond's decisions, moreover, begged a question of priority. Which was more important in 1877—that persons guilty of disturbance should be punished; or that pressure should be exerted to abate the cruelties of the economic anarchy of which such disturbance was an inevitable by-product? Judge Drummond spoke for a large constituency in making concern for law and order exclusive. A writer in the *Nation* echoed him: the kindest thing to untaught immigrants would be to show them that "society as here organized, on individual freedom of thought and action, is impregnable." Wages are fixed by supply and demand; "society does not owe any particular rate of wages to anybody." It owes "protection of life and property and personal rights to all its members." We should therefore strengthen the army and militia. And philanthropists should hold their tongues and not treat all things as open to discussion. * * *

Labor pressure gained cohesion and momentum after 1877. To Samuel Gompers, then a young cigar maker in the New York East Side, the strike "was the tocsin which sounded a ringing message of hope to us all." He recognized that the unorganized and tumultuous character of the strike had made it barren of direct benefit to the strikers. But it showed the possibility of a labor power which, with organization and discipline, might affect the "natural" law that fixes wages.

The question for a humane impartial realist in 1877 was as to the extent to which even the interest in law enforcement is subordinate to the interest in a labor pressure sufficient to lead to compromises. Anarchic competition can be conducive towards the general welfare only if under as well as upper dogs can bite. There is sense in Jefferson's somewhat hair-raising dictum as to Shay's Rebellion: "What country can preserve its liberties if their rulers are not warned from time to time that their people preserve the spirit of resistance?" The sense is the same as that of the insistence of Socrates upon his own social value as a gad-fly.

If government, as an impartial umpire of competition, is to exert a degree of control upon anarchic individualism, it must see to it that the fangs of one competitor be not too drastically blunted while those of his rival are strong. In the nineteenth century there was available no governmental mechanism more adequate to this service as between labor and capital than the system of trial by jury. Courts cannot be expected to recognize even the existence of a question as to the extent to which it is desirable that society shall permit itself to be stung by labor gad-flies. The answer, moreover, varies from time to time. Was not society in truth served by the state of public feeling in 1877 which made criminal convictions of mob leaders by juries unthinkable? * * * If law is not to become master instead of servant to society, it is essential that natural feeling should in special instances have power to prevent unnatural rigor of law enforcement. And it is as true in law as in mechanics that a structure which must oppose extraordinary stresses with unyielding rigidity is less durable than a structure which is flexible, or from which pressure can be diverted. The jury's power of exception in cases where the grounds of exception, though strongly felt, elude legal generalization, has served rather to maintain than to impair the integrity of normally satisfactory rules of law. Without it hard cases would make bad law more often than they do. * * * For when law is administered by judges *and* juries, the justice and injustice that result are more truly the justice and injustice *of society* than when law is administered by judges only. When a jury verdict is felt as oppressive, the grievance is against society and its law. But a sense of grievance toward a judicial decision is against the judge or the courts.

Note

1. What order of the court were the defendants held to have contemned in the Secor case? How could they have known that their action constituted contempt of court, exposing them to summary punishment?

2. Why does Judge Drummond find it necessary to state (p. 25): "[I]t is to be remembered that we consider only the disobedience of the orders of the court, and not the general criminal act"?

3. The difficulty of limiting the exercise of the contempt power, as invoked in Secor, to the receivership situation was demonstrated shortly after the strike by President Scott of the Pennsylvania Railroad, who branded such a limitation as arbitrarily discriminatory. As reported by Nelles: "He advocated Congressional legislation extending the summary power to all cases of disturbance of the operation of roads carrying mails or interstate commerce:

> " 'It will hardly be contended [Scott stated] that the railroad companies must become bankrupt in order to make secure the uninterrupted movement of traffic over their lines, or to entitle them to the efficient protection of the United States government. * * * The laws which give the Federal courts the summary process of *injunction* to restrain so comparatively trifling a wrong as infringement of a patent right certainly must have been intended or ought to give the United States authority to prevent a wrongdoing which not only destroys a particular road but also paralyzes the commerce of the country and wastes the national wealth.'

"This, it is believed, was the first suggestion of the possibility of labor injunctions in the United States." 40 Yale L.J. at 533.

VEGELAHN v. GUNTNER

Supreme Judicial Court of Massachusetts, 1896.
167 Mass. 92, 44 N.E. 1077.

Bill in equity, filed December 7, 1894, against fourteen individual defendants and two trades unions, alleging that the plaintiff was engaged in business as a manufacturer of furniture * * * in Boston, and employed a large number of men carrying on his business there, that there were in Boston certain associations named as defendants, which were composed of persons engaged in similar occupations to that of the individual defendants, of whom the defendant Guntner was agent; that on or about October 11, 1894, the plaintiff received a communication from the defendant unions as follows: "Your upholsterers do hereby kindly submit enclosed Price-list for your earnest consideration, the object is to institute a more equal competition this we would asked [sic] to go into effect on and after Oct. 29, 1894, and we kindly request that after said date Nine hours constitute a day's work", that on or about November 21, 1894, without notice and without warning, all of the individual defendants, except Guntner, struck, and left the plaintiff's employment and premises in a body; that since that date the plaintiff had endeavored to carry on his business, and to employ other men to fill the places of the defendants, but the defendants, their agents and servants, had wilfully and maliciously patrolled the streets in front of his premises in groups and squads continuously, and had used indecent language and epithets to those working in his employ in the places made vacant by the defendants, that they had wilfully and maliciously blocked up the doorway and entrance of his premises, and there intercepted, interfered with, and intimidated persons who desired to visit the premises for the purpose of engaging in the employment of the plaintiff, and for the purpose of trading with the plaintiff; that they had wilfully and maliciously intimidated and threatened the persons whom he had employed to take their places with bodily harm if they continued in the plaintiff's employment, and had caused certain new men so employed to leave his employment, that they had notified the insurance companies that the property there insured was in danger, and had attempted to effect a cancellation of the insurance carried by the plaintiff on his stock of goods; that they had followed the delivery team of the plaintiff in divers places and cities, and had been to several customers of the plaintiff and threatened to injure them and their business if they continued to trade with the plaintiff, and generally to injure the plaintiff in his said business, and to prevent his continuing to carry on his business; that the defendants, their agents and servants, had been and were a nuisance and obstruction to persons travelling on the street, and to persons in the employ of the plaintiff, and to persons intending to trade with the plaintiff at his premises; that all acts of the defendants were a part of a scheme to prevent persons from entering the employment of the plaintiff and from continuing in his employment, that the business carried on by the plaintiff was a large one, and the good will was of considerable value, in both of which the plaintiff had already been injured; and that, if the defendants were permitted to continue their acts, both the business and the good will would be further seriously injured and destroyed. * * *

The following decree was entered at a preliminary hearing upon the bill: "This cause came on to be heard upon the plaintiff's motion for a temporary injunction; and after due hearing, at which the several defendants were represented by counsel, it is ordered, adjudged, and decreed that an injunction issue *pendente lite,* to remain in force until the further order of this court, or of some justice thereof, restraining the respondents and each and every of them, their agents and servants, from interfering with the plaintiff's business by patrolling the sidewalk or street in front or in the vicinity of the premises occupied by him, for the purpose of preventing any person or persons who now are or may hereafter be in his employment, or desirous of entering the same, from entering it, or continuing in it; or by obstructing or interfering with such persons, or any others, in entering or leaving the plaintiff's said premises; or by intimidating, by threats or otherwise, any person or persons who now are or may hereafter be in the employment of the plaintiff, or desirous of entering the same, from entering it, or continuing in it; or by any scheme or conspiracy among themselves or with others, organized for the purpose of annoying, hindering, interfering with, or preventing any person or persons who now are or may hereafter be in the employment of the plaintiff, or desirous of entering the same, from entering it, or from continuing therein."

Hearing upon the bill and answers before Holmes, J., who reported the case for the consideration of the full court, as follows:

"The facts admitted or proved are that, following upon a strike of the plaintiff's workmen, the defendants have conspired to prevent the plaintiff from getting workmen, and thereby to prevent him from carrying on his business unless and until he will adopt a schedule of prices which has been exhibited to him, and for the purpose of compelling him to accede to that schedule, but for no other purpose. If he adopts that schedule he will not be interfered with further. The means adopted for preventing the plaintiff from getting workmen are, (1) in the first place, persuasion and social pressure. And these means are sufficient to affect the plaintiff disadvantageously, although it does not appear, if that be material, that they are sufficient to crush him. I ruled that the employment of these means for the said purpose was lawful, and for that reason refused an injunction against the employment of them. If the ruling was wrong, I find that an injunction ought to be granted.

"(2) I find also, that, as a further means for accomplishing the desired end, threats of personal injury or unlawful harm were conveyed to persons seeking employment or employed, although no actual violence was used beyond a technical battery, and although the threats were a good deal disguised, and express words were avoided. It appeared to me that there was danger of similar acts in the future. I ruled that conduct of this kind should be enjoined.

"The defendants established a patrol of two men in front of the plaintiff's factory, as one of the instrumentalities of their plan. The patrol was changed every hour, and continued from half-past six in the morning until half-past five in the afternoon, on one of the busy streets of Boston. The number of men was greater at times, and at times showed some little inclination to stop the plaintiff's door, which was not serious, but seemed to me proper to be enjoined. The patrol proper at times went further than simple advice, not obtruded beyond the point where the other person was willing to listen, and conduct of that sort is covered by (2) above, but its main purpose was in aid of the plan held lawful in (1) above. I was satisfied that there was probability of the patrol being continued if not enjoined. I ruled that the patrol, so far as it confined itself to persuasion and giving notice of the strike, was not unlawful, and limited the injunction accordingly.

"There was some evidence of persuasion to break existing contracts. I ruled that this was unlawful, and should be enjoined.

"I made the final decree appended hereto. If, on the foregoing facts, it ought to be reversed or modified, such decree is to be entered as the full court may think proper; otherwise, the decree is to stand."

The final decree was as follows: "This cause came on to be heard, and was argued by counsel; and thereupon, on consideration thereof, it is ordered, adjudged, and decreed that the defendants, and each and every of them, their agents and servants, be restrained and enjoined from interfering with the plaintiff's business by obstructing or physically interfering with any persons in entering or leaving the plaintiff's premises * * *, or by intimidating, by threats, express or implied, of violence or physical harm to body or property, any person or persons who now are or hereafter may be in the employment of the plaintiff, or desirous of entering the same, from entering or continuing in it, or by in any way hindering, interfering with, or preventing any person or persons who now are in the employment of the plaintiff from continuing therein, so long as they may be bound so to do by lawful contract."

The case was argued at the bar in March, 1896 * * *.

ALLEN, J. The principal question in this case is whether the defendants should be enjoined against maintaining the patrol. * * *

The patrol was * * * used in combination with social pressure, threats of personal injury or unlawful harm, and persuasion to break existing contracts. It was thus one means of intimidation indirectly to the plaintiff, and directly to persons actually employed, or seeking to be employed, by the plaintiff, and of rendering such employment unpleasant or intolerable to such persons. Such an act is an unlawful interference with the rights both of employer and of employed. An employer has a right to engage all persons who are willing to work for him, at such prices as may be mutually agreed upon; and persons employed or seeking employment have a corresponding right to enter into or remain in the employment of any person or corporation willing to employ them. These rights are secured by the Constitution itself. * * * No one can lawfully interfere by force or intimidation to prevent employers or persons employed or wishing to be employed from the exercise of these rights. In Massachusetts, as in some other States, it is even made a criminal offence for one by intimidation or force to prevent or seek to prevent a person from entering into or continuing in the employment of a person or corporation. Pub.Sts. c. 74, § 2. Intimidation is not limited to threats of violence or of physical injury to person or property. It has a broader signification, and there also may be a moral intimidation which is illegal. Patrolling or picketing, under the circumstances stated in the report, has elements of intimidation like those which were found to exist in

Sherry v. Perkins, 147 Mass. 212. It was declared to be unlawful in Regina v. Druitt, 10 Cox C.C. 592; Regina v. Hibbert, 13 Cox C.C. 32; and Regina v. Bauld, 13 Cox C.C. 282. * * * The patrol was an unlawful interference both with the plaintiff and with the workmen, within the principle of many cases, and, when instituted for the purpose of interfering with his business, it became a private nuisance. See * * * Walker v. Cronin, 107 Mass. 555 * * *.

The defendants contend that these acts were justifiable, because they were only seeking to secure better wages for themselves by compelling the plaintiff to accept their schedule of wages. This motive or purpose does not justify maintaining a patrol in front of the plaintiff's premises, as a means of carrying out their conspiracy. A combination among persons merely to regulate their own conduct is within allowable competition, and is lawful, although others may be indirectly affected thereby. But a combination to do injurious acts expressly directed to another, by way of intimidation or constraint, either of himself or of persons employed or seeking to be employed by him, is outside of allowable competition, and is unlawful. Various decided cases fall within the former class, for example: * * * Bowen v. Matheson, 14 Allen, 499; Commonwealth v. Hunt, 4 Met. 111; * * * Mogul Steamship Co. v. McGregor, [1892] A.C. 25 * * *. The present case falls within the latter class.

Nor does the fact that the defendants' acts might subject them to an indictment prevent a court of equity from issuing an injunction. It is true that ordinarily a court of equity will decline to issue an injunction to restrain the commission of a crime; but a continuing injury to property or business may be enjoined, although it may also be punishable as a nuisance or other crime. * * * In re Debs, 158 U.S. 564, 593, 599. * * *

A question is also presented whether the court should enjoin such interference with persons in the employment of the plaintiff who are not bound by contract to remain with him, or with persons who are not under any existing contract, but who are seeking or intending to enter into his employment. A conspiracy to interfere with the plaintiff's business by means of threats and intimidation, and by maintaining a patrol in front of his premises in order to prevent persons from entering his employment, or in order to prevent persons who are in his employment from continuing therein, is unlawful, even though such persons are not bound by contract to enter into or to continue in his employment; and the injunction should not be so limited as to relate only to persons who are bound by existing contracts. Walker v. Cronin, 107 Mass. 555, 565. * * *

In the opinion of a majority of the court the injunction should be in the form originally issued.

So ordered.

FIELD, C.J. The practice of issuing injunctions in cases of this kind is of very recent origin. One of the earliest authorities in the United States for enjoining in equity acts somewhat like those alleged against the defendants in the present case is Sherry v. Perkins, 147 Mass. 212, decided in 1888 [See footnote 2, supra p. 26]. * * *

* * * In the present case, if the establishment of a patrol is using intimidation or force within the meaning of our statutes, it is illegal and criminal; if it does not amount to intimidation or force, but is carried to such a degree as to interfere with the use by the plaintiff of his property, it may be illegal and actionable, but something more is necessary to justify issuing an injunction; if it is in violation of any ordinance of the city regulating the use of streets, there may be a prosecution for that, and the police can enforce the ordinance; but if it is merely a peaceful mode of finding out the persons who intend to go to the plaintiff's premises to apply for work, and of informing them of the actual facts of the case in order to induce them not to enter into the plaintiff's employment, in the absence of any statute relating to the subject I doubt if it is illegal, and I see no ground for issuing an injunction against it.

As no objection is now made by the defendants to the equitable jurisdiction, I am of opinion, on the facts reported, as I understand them, that the decree entered by Mr. Justice Holmes should be affirmed without modification.

HOLMES, J. In a case like the present, it seems to me that, whatever the true result may be, it will be of advantage to sound thinking to have the less popular view of the law stated, and therefore, although when I have been unable to bring my brethren to share my convictions my almost invariable practice is to defer to them in silence, I depart from that practice in this case, notwithstanding my unwillingness to do so in support of an already rendered judgment of my own.

In the first place, a word or two should be said as to the meaning of the report. I assume that my brethren construe it as I meant it to be construed, and that, if they were not prepared to do so, they would give an opportunity to the defendants to have it amended in accordance with what I state my meaning to be. There was no proof of any threat or danger of a patrol exceeding two men, and as of course an injunction is not granted except with reference to what there is reason to expect in its absence, the question on that point is whether a patrol of two men should be enjoined. Again, the defendants are enjoined by the final decree from intimidating by threats, express or implied, of physical harm to body or property, any person who may be desirous of entering into the employment of the plaintiff so far as to prevent him from entering the same. In order to test the correctness of the refusal to go further, it must be assumed that the defendants obey the express prohibition of the decree. If they do not, they fall within the injunction as it now stands, and are liable to summary punishment. The important difference between the preliminary and the final injunction is that the former goes further, and forbids the defendants to interfere with the plaintiff's business "by any scheme * * * organized for the purpose of * * * preventing any person or persons who now are or may hereafter be * * * desirous of entering the [plaintiff's employment] from entering it." I quote only a part, and the part which seems to me most objectionable. This includes refusal of social intercourse, and even organized persuasion or argument, although free from any threat of violence, either express or implied. And this is with reference to persons who have a legal right to contract or not to contract with the plaintiff, as they may see fit. Interference with existing contracts is forbidden by the final decree. I wish to insist a little that the only point of difference which involves a difference of principle between the final decree and the preliminary injunction which it is proposed to restore, is what I have mentioned, in order that it may be seen exactly what we are to discuss. It appears to me that the judgment of the majority turns in part on the assumption that the patrol necessarily carries with it a threat of bodily harm. That assumption I think unwarranted, for the reasons which I have given. Furthermore, it cannot be said, I think, that two men walking together up and down a sidewalk and speaking to those who enter a certain shop do necessarily and always thereby convey a threat of force. I do not think it possible to discriminate, and to say that two workmen, or even two representatives of an organization of workmen, do,— especially when they are, and are known to be, under the injunction of this court not to do so. * * * I may add, that I think the more intelligent workingmen believe as fully as I do that they no more can be permitted to usurp the State's prerogative of force than can their opponents in their controversies. But if I am wrong, then the decree as it stands reaches the patrol, since it applies to all threats of force. With this I pass to the real difference between the interlocutory and the final decree.

I agree, whatever may be the law in the case of a single defendant * * *, that when a plaintiff proves that several persons have combined and conspired to injure his business, and have done acts producing that effect, he shows temporal damage and a cause of action, unless the facts disclose, or the defendants prove, some ground of excuse or justification. And I take it to be settled, and rightly settled, that doing that damage by combined persuasion is actionable, as well as doing it by falsehood or by force. Walker v. Cronin, 107 Mass. 555. * * *

Nevertheless, in numberless instances the law warrants the intentional infliction of temporal damage because it regards it as justified. It is on the question of what shall amount to a justification, and more especially on the nature of the considerations which really determine or ought to determine the answer to that question, that judicial reasoning seems to me often to be inadequate. The true grounds of decision are considerations of policy and of social advantage, and it is vain to suppose that solutions can be attained merely by logic and the general propositions of law which nobody disputes. Propositions as to public policy rarely are unanimously accepted, and still more rarely, if ever, are capable of unanswerable proof. They require a special training to enable any one even to form an intelligent opinion about them. In the early stages of law, at least, they generally are acted on rather as inarticulate instincts than as definite ideas for which a rational defence is ready.

To illustrate what I have said in the last paragraph, it has been the law for centuries that a man may set up a business in a country town too small to support more than one, although he expects and intends thereby to ruin some one already there and succeeds in his intent. In such a case he is not held to act "unlawfully and without justifiable cause," as was alleged in Walker v. Cronin * * *. The reason, of course, is that the doctrine generally has been accepted that free competition is worth more to society than it costs, and that on this ground the infliction of the damage is privileged. Commonwealth v. Hunt, 4 Met. 111, 134. Yet even this proposition nowadays is disputed by a considerable body of persons, including many whose intelligence is not to be denied, little as we may agree with them.

I have chosen this illustration partly with reference to what I have to say next. It shows without the need of further authority that the policy of allowing free competition justifies the intentional inflicting of temporal damage, including the damage of interference with a man's business, by some means, when the damage is done not for its own sake, but as an instrumentality in reaching the end of victory in the battle of trade. In such a case it cannot matter whether the plaintiff is the only rival of the defendant, and so is aimed at specifically, or is one of a class all of whom are hit. The only debatable ground is the nature of the means by which such damage may be inflicted. We all agree that it cannot be done by force or threats of force. We all agree, I presume, that it may be done by persuasion to leave a rival's shop and come to the defendant's. It may be done by the refusal or withdrawal of various pecuniary advantages which, apart from this consequence, are within the defendant's lawful control. It may be done by the withdrawal, or threat to withdraw, such advantages from third persons who have a right to deal or not to deal with the plaintiff, as a means of inducing them not to deal with him either as customers or servants. Commonwealth v. Hunt, 4 Met. 111, 132, 133. Bowen v. Matheson, 14 Allen, 499. * * * Mogul Steamship Co. v. McGregor, [1892] A.C. 25.

I pause here to remark that the word "threats" often is used as if, when it appeared that threats had been made, it appeared that unlawful conduct had begun. But it depends on what you threaten. As a general rule, even if subject to some exceptions, what you may do in a certain event you may threaten to do, that is, give warning of your intention to do in that event, and thus allow the other person the chance of avoiding the consequences. So as to "compulsion," it depends on how you "compel." * * * So as to "annoyance" or "intimidation." * * * In Sherry v. Perkins, 147 Mass. 212, it was found as a fact that the display of banners which was enjoined was part of a scheme to prevent workmen from entering or remaining in the plaintiff's employment, "by threats and intimidation." The context showed that the words as there used meant threats of personal violence, and intimidation by causing fear of it.

I have seen the suggestion made that the conflict between employers and employed is not competition. But I venture to assume that none of my brethren would rely on that suggestion. If the policy on which our law is founded is too narrowly expressed in the term free competition, we may substitute free struggle for life. Certainly the policy is not limited to struggles between persons of the same class competing for the same end. It applies to all conflicts of temporal interests.

So far, I suppose, we are agreed. But there is a notion which latterly has been insisted on a good deal, that a combination of persons to do what any one of them lawfully might do by himself will make the otherwise lawful conduct unlawful. It would be rash to say that some as yet unformulated truth may not be hidden under this proposition. But in the general form in which it has been presented and accepted by many courts, I think it plainly untrue, both on authority and on principle. Commonwealth v. Hunt, 4 Met.

111. * * * There was combination of the most flagrant and dominant kind in Bowen v. Matheson and in the Mogul Steamship Company's case, and combination was essential to the success achieved. But it is not necessary to cite cases; it is plain from the slightest consideration of practical affairs, or the most superficial reading of industrial history, that free competition means combination, and that the organization of the world, now going on so fast, means an ever increasing might and scope of combination. It seems to me futile to set our faces against this tendency. Whether beneficial on the whole, as I think it, or detrimental, it is inevitable, unless the fundamental axioms of society, and even the fundamental conditions of life, are to be changed.

One of the eternal conflicts out of which life is made up is that between the effort of every man to get the most he can for his services, and that of society, disguised under the name of capital, to get his services for the least possible return. Combination on the one side is patent and powerful. Combination on the other is the necessary and desirable counterpart, if the battle is to be carried on in a fair and equal way. * * *

If it be true that workingmen may combine with a view, among other things, to getting as much as they can for their labor, just as capital may combine with a view to getting the greatest possible return, it must be true that when combined they have the same liberty that combined capital has to support their interests by argument, persuasion, and the bestowal or refusal of those advantages which they otherwise lawfully control. I can remember when many people thought that, apart from violence or breach of contract, strikes were wicked, as organized refusals to work. I suppose that intelligent economists and legislators have given up that notion to-day. I feel pretty confident that they equally will abandon the idea that an organized refusal by workmen of social intercourse with a man who shall enter their antagonist's employ is wrong, if it is dissociated from any threat of violence, and is made for the sole object of prevailing if possible in a contest with their employer about the rate of wages. The fact, that the immediate object of the act by which the benefit to themselves is to be gained is to injure their antagonist, does not necessarily make it unlawful, any more than when a great house lowers the price of certain goods for the purpose, and with the effect, of driving a smaller antagonist from the business. Indeed, the question seems to me to have been decided as long ago as 1842 by the good sense of Chief Justice Shaw, in Commonwealth v. Hunt, 4 Met. 111. I repeat at the end, as I said at the beginning, that this is the point of difference in principle, and the only one, between the interlocutory and the final decree. * * *

The general question of the propriety of dealing with this kind of case by injunction I say nothing about, because I understand that the defendants have no objection to the final decree if it goes no further, and that both parties wish a decision upon the matters which I have discussed.

Note

1. Why do both Chief Justice Field and Justice Holmes impliedly question the propriety of the granting of *any* injunction in the case? What is the basis for equitable jurisdiction here?

2. In Commonwealth v. Hunt, the court defined an unlawful conspiracy as "a combination of two or more persons, by some concerted action, to accomplish some * * * unlawful purpose, or to accomplish some purpose, not in itself * * * unlawful, by * * * unlawful means." (Supra pp. 15–16.) Was the concerted activity in Vegelahn unlawful (i.e., enjoinable) because of the purpose for which the defendants acted, the means they used to achieve that purpose, or both? Did the majority treat the strike itself as unlawful?

3. What are the differences between the temporary injunction (approved by the majority) and the amended version issued by Justice Holmes after the hearing on the merits? Which of these two injunctions do you deem most appropriate?

4. How does Vegelahn relate to Walker v. Cronin and Secor v. Toledo, P. & W. Ry.?

5. Two short sentences in Holmes' dissent contain the kernel of what has since been called the "theory of countervailing power": "Combination on the one side [capital] is patent and powerful. Combination on the other [labor] is the necessary and desirable counterpart, if the battle is to be carried on in a fair and equal way." (Supra p. 41.) Briefly stated, the theory is that in a free society the accumulation of power on the part of any one group motivates those adversely affected by the exercise of that power to seek to protect themselves by collectivizing their own power. The theory is developed by John Kenneth Galbraith in American Capitalism: The Concept of Countervailing Power (1952). One way of defining a free society may indeed be: a society the members of which are free to assert their individual interests collectively; the function of the law in such a society is to establish ground rules by which this process can be both continued and contained.

PLANT v. WOODS

Supreme Judicial Court of Massachusetts, 1900.
176 Mass. 492, 57 N.E. 1011.

Bill in equity, filed in the Superior Court, by the officers and members "of the voluntary association known as Union 257, Painters and Decorators of America of Springfield, Massachusetts, which Union is affiliated with a national organization of the same name, with headquarters at Lafayette in the State of Indiana," against the officers and members "of the voluntary association known as Union 257, Painters and Decorators of America, which Union is affiliated with a national organization of the same name, with headquarters at Baltimore in the State of Maryland," to restrain the defendants from any acts or the use of any methods tending to prevent the members of the plaintiff association from securing employment or continuing in their employment. * * *

HAMMOND, J. This case arises out of a contest for supremacy between two labor unions of the same craft, having substantially the same constitution and by-laws. * * * The plaintiff union was composed of workmen who in 1897 withdrew from the defendant union.

There does not appear to be anything illegal in the object of either union as expressed in its constitution and by-laws. The defendant union is also represented by delegates in the Central Labor Union, which is an organization composed of five delegates from each trade union in the city of

Springfield, and had in its constitution a provision for levying a boycott upon a complaint made by any union.

The case is before us upon a report after a final decree in favor of the plaintiffs, based upon the findings stated in the report of the master.

The contest became active early in the fall of 1898. In September of that year, the members of the defendant union declared "all painters not affiliated with the Baltimore headquarters to be non-union men," and voted to "notify the bosses" of that declaration. The manifest object of the defendants was to have all the members of the craft subjected to the rules and discipline of their particular union, in order that they might have better control over the whole business, and to that end they combined and conspired to get the plaintiffs and each of them to join the defendant association, peaceably if possible, but by threat and intimidation if necessary. Accordingly, on October 7, they voted that "if our demands are not complied with, all men working in shops where Lafayette people are employed refuse to go to work." The plaintiffs resisting whatever persuasive measures, if any, were used by the defendants, the latter proceeded to carry out their plan in the manner fully set forth in the master's report. Without rehearsing the circumstances in detail it is sufficient to say here that the general method of operations was substantially as follows.

A duly authorized agent of the defendants would visit a shop where one or more of the plaintiffs were at work and inform the employer of the action of the defendant union with reference to the plaintiffs, and ask him to induce such of the plaintiffs as were in his employ to sign applications for reinstatement in the defendant union. As to the general nature of these interviews the master finds that the defendants have been courteous in manner, have made no threats of personal violence, have referred to the plaintiffs as non-union men, but have not otherwise represented them as men lacking good standing in their craft; that they have not asked that the Lafayette men be discharged, and in some cases have expressly stated that they did not wish to have them discharged, but only that they sign the blanks for reinstatement in the defendant union. The master, however, further finds, from all the circumstances under which those requests were made, that the defendants intended that employers of Lafayette men should fear trouble in their business if they continued to employ such men, and that employers to whom these requests were made were justified in believing that a failure on the part of their employees who were Lafayette men to sign such reinstatement blanks, and a failure on the part of the employers to discharge them for not doing so, would lead to trouble in the business of the employers in the nature of strikes or a boycott, and the employers to whom these requests were made did believe that such results would follow, and did suggest their belief to the defendants, and the defendants did not deny that such results might occur; that the strikes which did occur appear to have been steps taken by the defendants to obtain the discharge of such employees as were Lafayette men who declined to sign application blanks for reinstatement; that these defendants did not in all cases threaten a boycott of the employers' business, but did threaten that the place of business of at least one such employer would be left off from a so-called "fair list" to be published by the Baltimore Union. The master also found that, from all the evidence presented, the object which the Baltimore men and the defendant association sought to accomplish in all the acts which were testified to was to compel the members of the Lafayette Union to join the Baltimore Union, and as a means to this end they caused strikes to be instituted in the shops where strikes would seriously interfere with the business of the shops, and in all other shops they made such representations as would lead the proprietors thereof to expect trouble in their business.

We have, therefore, a case where the defendants have conspired to compel the members of the plaintiff union to join the defendant union, and to carry out their purpose have resolved upon such coercion and intimidation as naturally may be caused by threats of loss of property by strikes and boycotts, to induce the employers either to get the plaintiffs to ask for reinstatement in the defendant union, or that failing, then to discharge them. * * *

It is well to see what is the meaning of this threat to strike, when taken in connection with the intimation that the employer may "expect trouble in his business." It means more than that the strikers will cease to work. That is only the preliminary skirmish. It means that those who have ceased to work will, by strong, persistent, and organized persuasion and social pressure of every description, do all they can to prevent the employer from procuring workmen to take their places. It means much more. It means that, if these peaceful measures fail, the employer may reasonably expect that unlawful physical injury may be done to his property; that attempts in all the ways practised by organized labor will be made to injure him in his business, even to his ruin, if possible; and that, by the use of vile and opprobrious epithets and other annoying conduct, and actual and threatened personal violence, attempts will be made to intimidate those who enter or desire to enter his employ; and that whether or not all this be done by the strikers or only by their sympathizers, or with the open sanction and approval of the former, he will have no help from them in his efforts to protect himself.

However mild the language or suave the manner in which the threat to strike is made under such circumstances as are disclosed in this case, the employer knows that he is in danger of passing through such an ordeal as that above described, and those who make the threat know that as well as he does. Even if the intent of the strikers, so far as respects their own conduct and influence, be to discountenance all actual or threatened injury to person or property or business, except that which is the direct necessary result of the interruption of the work, and even if their connection with the injurious and violent conduct of the turbulent among them or of their sympathizers be not such as to make them liable criminally or even answerable civilly in damages to those who suffer, still with full knowledge of what is to be expected they give the signal, and in so doing must be held to avail themselves of the degree of fear and dread which the knowledge of such consequences will cause in the mind of those—whether their employer or fellow workmen—against whom the strike is directed; and the measure of coercion and intimidation imposed upon those against whom the strike is threatened or directed is not fully realized until all those probable consequences are considered.

Such is the nature of the threat, and such the degree of coercion and intimidation involved in it.

If the defendants can lawfully perform the acts complained of in the city of Springfield, they can pursue the plaintiffs all over the State in the same manner, and compel them to abandon their trade or bow to the behests of their pursuers.

It is to be observed that this is not a case between the employer and employed, or, to use a hackneyed expression, between capital and labor, but between laborers all of the same craft, and each having the same right as any one of the others to pursue his calling. In this, as in every other case of equal rights, the right of each individual is to be exercised with due regard to the similar right of all others, and the right of one be said to end where that of another begins.

The right involved is the right to dispose of one's labor with full freedom. This is a legal right, and it is entitled to legal protection. Sir William Erle in his book on Trade Unions, page 12, has stated this in the following language, which has been several times quoted with approval by judges in England: "Every person has a right under the law, as between him and his fellow subjects, to full freedom in disposing of his own labor or his own capital according to his own will. It follows that every other person is subject to the correlative duty arising therefrom, and is prohibited from any obstruction to the fullest exercise of this right which can be made compatible with the exercise of similar rights by others. Every act causing an obstruction to another in the exercise of the right comprised within this description—done, not in the exercise of the actor's own right, but for the purpose of obstruction—would, if damage should be caused thereby to the party obstructed, be a violation of this prohibition." * * *

In this case the acts complained of were calculated to cause damage to the plaintiffs, and did actually cause such damage; and they were intentionally done for that purpose. Unless, therefore, there was justifiable cause, the acts were malicious and unlawful. Walker v. Cronin * * *.

The defendants contend that they have done nothing unlawful, and, in support of that contention, they say that a person may work for whom he pleases; and, in the absence of any contract to the contrary, may cease to work when he pleases, and for any reason whatever, whether the same be good or bad; that he may give notice of his intention in advance, with or without stating the reason; that what one man may do several men acting in concert may do, and may agree beforehand that they will do, and may give notice of the agreement; and that all this may be lawfully done notwithstanding such concerted action may, by reason of the consequent interruption of the work, result in great loss to the employer and his other employees, and that such a result was intended. In a general sense, and without reference to exceptions arising out of conflicting public and private interests, all this may be true.

     * * *

Still standing for solution is the question, Under what circumstances, including the motive of the actor, is the act complained of lawful, and to what extent?

In cases somewhat akin to the one at bar this court has had occasion to consider the question how far acts, manifestly coercive and intimidating in their nature, which cause damage and injury to the business or property of another, and are done with intent to cause such injury and partly in reliance upon such coercion, are justifiable.

In Bowen v. Matheson, 14 Allen, 499, it was held to be lawful for persons engaged in the business of shipping seamen to combine together into a society for the purpose of competing with other persons engaged in the same business, and it was held lawful for them, in pursuance of that purpose, to take men out of a ship, if men shipped by a non-member were in that ship; to refuse to furnish seamen through a non-member; to notify the public that they had combined against non-members, and had "laid the plaintiff on the shelf"; to notify the plaintiff's customers and friends that the plaintiff could not ship seamen for them; and to interfere in all these ways with the business of the plaintiff as a shipping agent, and compel him to abandon the same.[b] The justification for these acts, so injurious to the business of the plaintiff and so intimidating in their nature, is to be found in the law of competition. No legal right of the plaintiff was infringed upon, and, as stated by Chapman, J., in giving the opinion of the court (p. 503), "if their effect is to destroy the business of shipping-masters who are not members of the association, it is such a result as in the competition of business often follows from a course of proceeding that the law permits." The primary object of the defendants was to build up their own business, and this they might lawfully do to the extent disclosed in that case, even to the injury of their rivals.

Similar decisions have been made in other courts where acts somewhat coercive in their nature and effect have been held justifiable under the law of competition. Mogul Steamship Co. v. McGregor, [1892] A.C. 25.   *   *   *

On the other hand, it was held in Carew v. Rutherford, 106 Mass. 1, that a conspiracy against a mechanic,—who is under the necessity of employing workmen in order to carry on his business,—to obtain a sum of money from him which he is under no legal obligation to pay, by inducing his workmen to leave him, or by deterring others from entering into his employ, or by threatening to do this so that he is induced to pay the money demanded, under a reasonable apprehension that he cannot carry on his business without yielding to the demands, is an illegal, if not a criminal, conspiracy; that the acts done under it are illegal, and that the money thus obtained may be recovered back. Chapman, C.J., speaking for the court, says that there is no doubt that, if the parties under such circumstances succeed in injuring the business of the mechanic, they are liable to pay all the damages done to him.

b. Plaintiff John Bowen was in the business of housing and boarding seamen and of supplying them, for a fee, to masters of ships sailing out of Boston. He ran, in effect, a kind of "hiring hall" for profit. The defendants, proprietors of competing hiring halls, had organized the Seamen's Mutual Benefit Association of Boston for the purpose of establishing minimum wage rates for seamen shipping out of Boston, thereby enhancing defendants' own profits. Plaintiff refused to comply with these minimum rates, as a result of which he was driven out of business: masters of ships who dealt with him were denied the supply of any seamen by the defendants; plaintiff alone was not able to meet the requirements of his customers; ship masters could not, as a consequence, afford to deal with him. Plaintiff sued for damages in tort. He lost.

That case bears a close analogy to the one at bar. The acts there threatened were like those in this case, and the purpose was, in substance, to force the plaintiff to give his work to the defendants, and to extort from him a fine because he had given some of his work to other persons.

Without now indicating to what extent workmen may combine and in pursuance of an agreement may act by means of strikes and boycotts to get the hours of labor reduced or their wages increased, or to procure from their employers any other concession directly and immediately affecting their own interests, or to help themselves in competition with their fellow-workmen, we think this case must be governed by the principles laid down in Carew v. Rutherford, ubi supra. The purpose of these defendants was to force the plaintiffs to join the defendant association, and to that end they injured the plaintiffs in their business, and molested and disturbed them in their efforts to work at their trade. It is true they committed no acts of personal violence, or of physical injury to property, although they threatened to do something which might reasonably be expected to lead to such results. In their threat, however, there was plainly that which was coercive in its effect upon the will. It is not necessary that the liberty of the body should be restrained. Restraint of the mind, provided it would be such as would be likely to force a man against his will to grant the thing demanded, and actually has that effect, is sufficient in cases like this. * * *

It was not the intention of the defendants to give fairly to the employer the option to employ them or the plaintiffs, but to compel the latter against their will to join the association, and to that end to molest and interfere with them in their efforts to procure work by acts and threats well calculated by their coercive and intimidating nature to overcome the will.

The defendants might make such lawful rules as they please for the regulation of their own conduct, but they had no right to force other persons to join them.

The necessity that the plaintiffs should join this association is not so great, nor is its relation to the rights of the defendants, as compared with the right of the plaintiffs to be free from molestation, such as to bring the acts of the defendants under the shelter of the principles of trade competition. Such acts are without justification, and therefore are malicious and unlawful, and the conspiracy thus to force the plaintiffs was unlawful. Such conduct is intolerable, and inconsistent with the spirit of our laws. * * *

There must be, therefore, a decree for the plaintiffs. * * *

Inasmuch as the association of the defendants is not a corporation, an injunction cannot be issued against it as such, but only against its members, their agents and servants. * * *

Decree accordingly.

HOLMES, C.J. * * * If the decision in the present case simply had relied upon Vegelahn v. Guntner, 167 Mass. 92, I should have hesitated to say anything * * *. But much to my satisfaction, if I may say so, the court has seen fit to adopt the mode of approaching the question which I believe to be the correct one, and to open an issue which otherwise I might have thought closed. The difference between my brethren and me now seems to be a difference of degree, and the line of reasoning followed makes it proper for me to explain where the difference lies.

I agree that the conduct of the defendants is actionable unless justified. * * * I agree that the presence or absence of justification may depend upon the object of their conduct, that is, upon the motive with which they acted. Vegelahn v. Guntner, 167 Mass. 92, 105, 106. * * * On the other hand, I infer that a majority of my brethren would admit that a boycott or strike intended to raise wages directly might be lawful, if it did not embrace in its scheme or intent violence, breach of contract, or other conduct unlawful on grounds independent of the mere fact that the action of the defendants was combined. A sensible workingman would not contend that the courts should sanction a combination for the purpose of inflicting or threatening violence or the infraction of admitted rights. To come directly to the point, the issue is narrowed to the question whether, assuming that some purposes would be a justification, the purpose in this case of the threatened boycotts and strikes was such as to justify the threats. That purpose was not directly concerned with wages. It was one degree more remote. The immediate object and motive was to strengthen the defendants' society as a preliminary means to enable it to make a better fight on questions of wages or other matters of clashing interests. I differ from my brethren in thinking that the threats were as lawful for this preliminary purpose as for the final one to which strengthening the union was a means. I think that unity of organization is necessary to make the contest of labor effectual, and that societies of laborers lawfully may employ in their preparation the means which they might use in the final contest.

Although this is not the place for extended economic discussion, and although the law may not always reach ultimate economic conceptions, I think it well to add that I cherish no illusions as to the meaning and effect of strikes. While I think the strike a lawful instrument in the universal struggle of life, I think it pure phantasy to suppose that there is a body of capital of which labor as a whole secures a larger share by that means. The annual product, subject to an infinitesimal deduction for the luxuries of the few, is directed to consumption by the multitude, and is consumed by the multitude, always. Organization and strikes may get a larger share for the members of an organization, but, if they do, they get it at the expense of the less organized and less powerful portion of the laboring mass. They do not create something out of nothing. It is only by divesting our minds of questions of ownership and other machinery of distribution, and by looking solely at the question of consumption,—asking ourselves what is the annual product, who consumes it, and what changes would or could we make,—that we can keep in the world of realities. But, subject to the qualifications which I have expressed, I think it lawful for a body of workmen to try by combination to get more than they now are getting, although they do it at the expense of their fellows, and to that end to strengthen their union by the boycott and the strike.

Note

1. Why does Justice Holmes state at the outset of his dissent: "If the decision in the present case simply had relied upon Vegelahn v. Guntner * * * I should have hesitated to say anything"?

2. The "illegal purpose" doctrine enunciated in Plant v. Woods (and anticipated in Walker v. Cronin and in Holmes' dissent in Vegelahn v. Guntner) is a variation of the "prima facie tort" doctrine, "the classic statement of which is that 'intentionally to do that which is calculated in the ordinary course of events to damage, and which does, in fact, damage another in that person's property or trade, is actionable if done without just cause or excuse.'" Prosser, The Law of Torts 26 (4th ed.1971).

What was the basis of the disagreement between the majority and Holmes in the application of the foregoing doctrine in Plant v. Woods? With whom do you agree?

3. In Vegelahn and in Plant the issuance of the injunction was premised upon the use of illegal means and/or the presence of an illegal purpose. While the question of the legality of the means may be difficult in some situations, a greater difficulty is encountered when the question is one of legality of purpose. Since the illegal purpose (prima facie tort) doctrine is so broadly, and therefore amorphously, stated (what is *just* cause or excuse—i.e., *lawful* purpose?), there is considerable room for the exercise of judicial discretion. Where does a judge, thus set at large, look for guidance? Are questions of social policy of the sort presented in Plant v. Woods properly for the courts or for the legislature? Should legislators, like judges, be required to be lawyers? Does legal training (as opposed to, say, training in economics or history) provide special preparation for answering the type of question posed in Plant v. Woods?

Assuming, *arguendo,* the propriety of judicial, rather than legislative, resolution of questions of the kind involved in Plant v. Woods, what are the implications of resolving them in courts of equity (via the injunction) as opposed to courts of law (via criminal prosecutions or tort actions)? "[W]hen law is administered by judges *and* juries, the justice and injustice that result are more truly the justice and injustice *of society* than when law is administered by judges only." Nelles, A Strike and Its Legal Consequences—An Examination of the Receivership Precedent for the Labor Injunction, 40 Yale Law Journal 507, 530 (1931). (This proposition is elaborated in brief and brilliant fashion by Nelles, supra pp. 32–33.)

4. The courts were not unanimous in either the acceptance or application of the illegal purpose doctrine. In National Protective Association of Steam Fitters v. Cumming, 170 N.Y. 315, 63 N.E. 369 (1902), the New York Court of Appeals, on facts substantially the same as in Plant v. Woods, rejected the illegal purpose doctrine in favor of what has been called the "civil rights" test, which focuses solely upon the legality of the means employed. The court indicated, however, that the decision would have been in favor of the defendant under either test. "They [members of a labor organization] are free to secure the furtherance of their common interests in every way which is not within the prohibition of some statute, or which does not involve the commission of illegal acts. The struggle on the part of individuals to prefer themselves, and to prevent the work which they are fitted to do from being given to others, may be keen, and may have unhappy results in individual cases; but the law is not

concerned with such results, when not caused by illegal means or acts." 170 N.Y. at 335, 63 N.E. at 375 (concurring opinion).

For a discussion of the divergent approaches of the courts of Massachusetts and New York, favoring the more liberal approach of the latter, see Gregory, Labor and the Law 52–82 (2d rev.ed.1961).

5. In Mogul Steamship Co. v. McGregor, [1892] A.C. 25, cited in Plant v. Woods, the defendants were an association of shipowners organized to achieve a monopoly of the carrying trade from China to Europe. To this end they (1) granted a rebate of five per cent to shippers who shipped exclusively with members of the association, and (2) refused to carry any cargo of shippers who dealt with the plaintiffs. The plaintiffs, competing shipowners excluded from the association, sought damages and an injunction. The House of Lords held for the defendants. The prima facie tort test set forth in the quote from Prosser, supra Note 2, is from Lord Bowen's opinion in the court below. 23 Q.B.D. 598, 613 (1889).

Does the court in Plant v. Woods succeed in distinguishing Mogul Steamship and Bowen v. Matheson? For a discussion of this question, see Gregory, Labor and the Law 31–82 (2d rev.ed.1961).

6. What is the logic of the proposition of economics proclaimed by Justice Holmes in the last paragraph of his dissent in Plant v. Woods? Do you agree with him?

COPPAGE v. KANSAS

Supreme Court of the United States, 1915.
236 U.S. 1, 35 S.Ct. 240, 59 L.Ed. 441.

MR. JUSTICE PITNEY delivered the opinion of the court.

In a local court in one of the counties of Kansas, plaintiff in error was found guilty and adjudged to pay a fine, with imprisonment as the alternative, upon an information charging him with a violation of an act of the legislature of that State, approved March 13, 1903, being Chap. 222 of the session laws of that year, found also as §§ 4674 and 4675, Gen.Stat. Kansas 1909. The act reads as follows:

"An Act to provide a penalty for coercing or influencing or making demands upon or requirements of employes, servants, laborers, and persons seeking employment.

"*Be it Enacted, etc.:*

"Section 1. That it shall be unlawful for any individual or member of any firm, or any agent, officer or employé of any company or corporation, to coerce, require, demand or influence any person or persons to enter into any agreement, either written or verbal, not to join or become or remain a member of any labor organization or association, as a condition of such person or persons securing employment, or continuing in the employment of such individual, firm, or corporation.

"Sec. 2. Any individual or member of any firm or any agent, officer or employé of any company or corporation violating the provisions of this act shall be deemed guilty of a misdemeanor, and upon conviction thereof shall be fined in a sum not less than fifty dollars or imprisoned in the county jail not less than thirty days."

The judgment was affirmed by the Supreme Court of the State, two justices dissenting (87 Kansas, 752), and the case is brought here upon the ground that the statute, as construed and applied in this case, is in conflict with that provision of the Fourteenth Amendment of the Constitution of the United States which declares that no State shall deprive any person of liberty or property without due process of law.

The facts, as recited in the opinion of the Supreme Court, are as follows: About July 1, 1911, one Hedges was employed as a switchman by the St. Louis & San Francisco Railway Company, and was a member of a labor organization called the Switchmen's Union of North America. Plaintiff in error was employed by the railway company as superintendent, and as such he requested Hedges to sign an agreement, which he presented to him in writing, at the same time informing him that if he did not sign it he could not remain in the employ of the company. The following is a copy of the paper thus presented:

Fort Scott, Kansas,

_____, 1911.

Mr. T.B. Coppage, Superintendent Frisco Lines, Fort Scott:

We, the undersigned have agreed to abide by your request, that is, to withdraw from the Switchmen's Union, while in the service of the Frisco Company.

(Signed) _____

Hedges refused to sign this, and refused to withdraw from the labor organization. Thereupon plaintiff in error, as such superintendent, discharged him from the service of the company.

At the outset, a few words should be said respecting the construction of the act. It uses the term "coerce," and some stress is laid upon this in the opinion of the Kansas Supreme Court. But, on this record, we have nothing to do with any question of actual or implied coercion or duress, such as might overcome the will of the employé by means unlawful without the act. In the case before us, the state court treated the term "coerce" as applying to the mere insistence by the employer, or its agent, upon its right to prescribe terms upon which alone it would consent to a continuance of the relationship of employer and employé. * * * There is neither finding nor evidence that the contract of employment was other than a general or indefinite hiring, such as is presumed to be terminable at the will of either party. The evidence shows that it would have been to the advantage of Hedges, from a pecuniary point of view and otherwise, to have been permitted to retain his membership in the union, and at the same time to remain in the employ of the railway company. In particular, it shows (although no reference is made to this in the opinion of the court) that as a member of the union he was entitled to benefits in the nature of insurance to the amount of fifteen hundred dollars, which he would have been obliged to forego if he had ceased to be a member. But, aside from this matter of pecuniary interest, there is nothing to show that Hedges was subjected to the least pressure or influence, or that he was not a free agent, in all respects competent, and at liberty to choose what was best from the standpoint of his own interests. Of course, if plaintiff in error, acting as the representative of the railway company, was otherwise within his legal rights in insisting that Hedges should elect whether to remain in the employ of the company or to retain his membership in the union, that insistence is not rendered unlawful by the fact that the choice involved a pecuniary sacrifice to Hedges. * * * And if the right that plaintiff in error exercised is founded upon a constitutional basis it cannot be impaired by merely applying to its exercise the term "coercion." We have to deal, therefore, with a statute that, as construed and applied, makes it a criminal offense punishable with fine or imprisonment for an employer or his agent to merely prescribe, as a condition upon which one may secure certain employment or remain in such employment (the employment being terminable at will), that the employé shall enter into an agreement not to become or remain a member of any labor organization while so employed; the employé being subject to no incapacity or disability, but on the contrary free to exercise a voluntary choice.

In Adair v. United States, 208 U.S. 161, this court had to deal with a question not distinguishable in principle from the one now presented. Congress, in § 10 of an act of June 1, 1898, entitled "An Act concerning carriers engaged in interstate commerce and their employés" (c. 370, 30 Stat. 424, 428), had [made it a misdemeanor, subject to a fine of one hundred to one thousand dollars, to condition railroad employment on nonmembership in a labor union. Adair, an agent of a railroad, was convicted for having discharged an employee because of union membership.] The court held that portion of the Act upon which the conviction rested to be an invasion of the personal liberty as well as of the right of property guaranteed by the Fifth Amendment, which declares that no person shall be deprived of liberty or property without due process of law. * * *

Unless it is to be overruled, this decision is controlling upon the present controversy; for if Congress is prevented from arbitrary interference with the liberty of contract because of the "due process" provision of the Fifth Amendment, it is too clear for argument that the States are prevented from the like interference by virtue of the corresponding clause of the Fourteenth Amendment * * *.

The decision in [Adair] was reached as the result of elaborate argument and full consideration. * * * We are now asked, in effect, to overrule it; and in view of the importance of the issue we have re-examined the question from the standpoint of both reason and authority. As a result, we are constrained to re-affirm the doctrine there applied. Neither the doctrine nor this application of it is novel; we will endeavor to re-state some of the grounds upon which it rests. The principle is fundamental and vital. Included in the right of personal liberty and the right of private property— partaking of the nature of each—is the right to make contracts for the acquisition of property. Chief among such contracts is that of personal employment, by which labor and other services are exchanged for money or other forms of property. If this right be struck down or arbitrarily interfered with, there is a substantial impairment of liberty in the long-established constitutional sense. The right is as essential to the laborer as to the capitalist, to the poor as to the rich; for the vast majority of persons have no other honest way to begin to acquire property, save by working for money.

An interference with this liberty so serious as that now under consideration, and so disturbing of equality of right, must be deemed to be arbitrary, unless it be supportable as a reasonable exercise of the police power of the State. But, notwithstanding the strong general presumption in favor of the validity of state laws, we do not think the statute in question, as construed and applied in this case, can be sustained as a legitimate exercise of that power. * * * We do not mean to say * * * that a State may not properly exert its police power to prevent coercion on the part of employers towards employés, or *vice versa*. But, in this case, the Kansas court of last resort has held that Coppage, the plaintiff in error, is a criminal punishable with fine or imprisonment under this statute simply and merely because while acting as the representative of the Railroad Company and dealing with Hedges, an employee at will and a man of full age and understanding, subject to no restraint or disability, Coppage insisted that Hedges should freely choose whether he would leave the employ of the Company or would agree to refrain from association with the union while so employed. This construction is, for all purposes of our jurisdiction, conclusive evidence that the State of Kansas intends by this legislation to punish conduct such as that of Coppage, although entirely devoid of any element of coercion, compulsion, duress, or undue influence, just as certainly as it intends to punish coercion and the like. * * *

Laying aside, therefore, as immaterial for present purposes, so much of the statute as indicates a purpose to repress coercive practices, what possible relation has the residue of the Act to the public health, safety, morals or general welfare? None is suggested, and we are unable to conceive of any. The Act, as the construction given to it by the state court shows, is intended to deprive employers of a part of their liberty of contract, to the corresponding advantage of the employed and the upbuilding of the labor organizations. But no attempt is made, or could reasonably be made, to sustain the purpose to strengthen these voluntary organizations, any more than other voluntary associations of persons, as a legitimate object for the exercise of the police power. They are not public institutions, charged by law with public or governmental duties, such as would render the maintenance of their membership a matter of direct concern to the general welfare. If they were, a different question would be presented.

As to the interest of the employed, it is said by the Kansas Supreme Court (87 Kansas, p. 759) to be a matter of common knowledge that "employés, as a rule, are not financially able to be as independent in making contracts for the sale of their labor as are employers in making contracts of purchase thereof." No doubt, wherever the right of private property exists, there must and will be inequalities of fortune; and thus it naturally happens that parties negotiating about a contract are not equally unhampered by circumstances. This applies to all contracts, and not merely to that between employer and employé. Indeed a little reflection will show that wherever the right of private property and the right of free contract coexist, each party when contracting is inevitably more or less influenced by the question whether he has much property, or little, or none; for the contract is made to the very end that each may gain something that he needs or desires more urgently than that which he proposes to give in exchange. And, since it is self-evident that, unless all things are held in common, some persons must have more property than others, it is from the nature of things impossible to uphold freedom of contract and the right of private property without at the same time recognizing as legitimate those inequalities of fortune that are the necessary result of the exercise of those rights. But the Fourteenth Amendment, in declaring that a State shall not "deprive any person of life, liberty or property without due process of law," gives to each of these an equal sanction; it recognizes "liberty" and "property" as coexistent human rights, and debars the States from any unwarranted interference with either.

And since a State may not strike them down directly it is clear that it may not do so indirectly, as by declaring in effect that the public good requires the removal of those inequalities that are but the normal and inevitable result of their exercise, and then invoking the police power in order to remove the inequalities, without other object in view.[c] The police power is broad, and not easily defined, but it cannot be given the wide scope that is here asserted for it, without in effect nullifying the constitutional guaranty. * * *

Of course we do not intend to say, nor to intimate, anything inconsistent with the right of individuals to join labor unions, nor do we question the legitimacy of such organizations so long as they conform to the laws of the land as others are required to do. Conceding the full right of the individual to join the union, he has no inherent right to do this and still remain in the employ of one who is unwilling to employ a union man, any more than the same individual has a right to join the union without the consent of that organization. Can it be doubted that a labor organization—a voluntary association of working men—has the inherent and constitutional right to deny membership to any man who will not agree that during such membership he will not accept or retain employment in company with non-union men? Or that a union man has the constitutional right to decline proffered employment unless the employer will agree not to employ any non-union man? * * * And can there be one rule of liberty for the labor organization and its members, and a different and more restrictive rule for employers? We think not; and since the relation of employer and employé is a voluntary relation, as clearly as is that between the members of a labor organization, the employer has the same inherent right to prescribe the terms upon which he will consent to the relationship, and to have them fairly understood and expressed in advance. * * *

The decision in the *Adair Case* is in accord with the almost unbroken current of authorities in the state courts. In many States enactments not distinguishable in principle from the one now in question have been passed, but, except in two instances (one, the decision of an inferior court in Ohio, since repudiated; the other, the decision now under review), we are unable to find that they have been judicially enforced. It is not too much to say that such laws have by common consent been treated as unconstitutional, for while many state courts of last resort have adjudged them void, we have found no decision by such a court sustaining legislation of this character, excepting that which is now under review. * * *

c. For an argument at the opposite end of the spectrum, see Nelles, supra pp. 9–10.

Upon both principle and authority, therefore, we are constrained to hold that the Kansas act of March 13, 1903, * * * is repugnant to the "due process" clause of the Fourteenth Amendment, and therefore void.

Judgment reversed, and the cause remanded for further proceedings not inconsistent with this opinion.

MR. JUSTICE HOLMES, dissenting.

I think the judgment should be affirmed. In present conditions a workman not unnaturally may believe that only by belonging to a union can he secure a contract that shall be fair to him. * * * If that belief, whether right or wrong, may be held by a reasonable man, it seems to me that it may be enforced by law in order to establish the equality of position between the parties in which liberty of contract begins. Whether in the long run it is wise for the workingmen to enact legislation of this sort is not my concern, but I am strongly of opinion that there is nothing in the Constitution of the United States to prevent it, and that Adair v. United States, 208 U.S. 161, and Lochner v. New York, 198 U.S. 45, should be overruled. I have stated my grounds in those cases and think it unnecessary to add others that I think exist. See further Vegelahn v. Guntner, 167 Massachusetts, 92, 104, 108. Plant v. Woods, 176 Massachusetts, 492, 505. I still entertain the opinions expressed by me in Massachusetts.

[The dissenting opinion of Justice Day, with whom Justice Hughes concurred, is omitted.]

Note

1. The so-called "yellow-dog contract," upheld in Coppage v. Kansas, provided the basis for courts to find that efforts by a union to organize employees who had entered such contracts constituted the tort of inducing breach of contract. This tort was encountered, it may be recalled, in another usage in Walker v. Cronin and Vegelahn v. Guntner. In the leading case of Hitchman Coal & Coke Co. v. Mitchell, 245 U.S. 229, 38 S.Ct. 65, 62 L.Ed. 260 (1917), the tort served as a basis for enjoining the efforts of the United Mine Workers to organize employees who had entered such contracts, even though their employment was "at will."

2. What are the implications of the decisions in Coppage and in Adair for the development of a national labor policy founded upon recognition of the right of employees to form and join unions and to engage in collective bargaining?

B. EARLY STATUTES: ANTI–TRUST AND ANTI–ANTI–TRUST (SHERMAN ACT OF 1890, CLAYTON ACT OF 1914, NORRIS–LAGUARDIA ACT OF 1932)

LOEWE v. LAWLOR

Supreme Court of the United States, 1908.
208 U.S. 274, 28 S.Ct. 301, 52 L.Ed. 488.

MR. CHIEF JUSTICE FULLER delivered the opinion of the court.

This was an action brought in the Circuit Court for the District of Connecticut under § 7 of the Anti-Trust Act of July 2, 1890, c. 647, 26 Stat.

209, claiming three-fold damages for injuries inflicted on plaintiffs by a combination or conspiracy declared to be unlawful by the act.

Defendants filed a demurrer to the complaint * * *. The demurrer was sustained * * * on the ground that the combination stated was not within the Sherman Act * * *; and upon plaintiffs declining to amend their complaint the court dismissed it with costs. 148 Fed.Rep. 924; and see 142 Fed.Rep. 216; 130 Fed.Rep. 633.

The case was then carried by writ of error to the Circuit Court of Appeals for the Second Circuit, and that court, desiring the instruction of this court upon a question arising on the writ of error, certified that question to this court. The certificate consisted of a brief statement of facts, and put the question thus: "Upon this state of facts can plaintiffs maintain an action against defendants under section 7 of the Anti-Trust Act of July 2, 1890?" * * *

The question is whether upon the facts * * * averred and admitted by the demurrer this action can be maintained under the Anti-Trust Act. [The facts averred in the complaint are set forth more fully later in the opinion. In essence, the complaint alleged that the defendants, members of a union known as the United Hatters of North America, affiliated with the American Federation of Labor, called a strike against D.E. Loewe & Co., the plaintiffs' partnership, doing business as manufacturer and seller of hats in Danbury, Connecticut. The purpose of the strike was to unionize the plaintiffs' business. In support of the strike, a national consumers' boycott was instituted by the United Hatters and the AFL against the sale of plaintiffs' hats in various states across the country.]

The first, second and seventh sections of [the Sherman Act] are as follows:

1. "Every contract, combination in the form of trust or otherwise, or conspiracy, in restraint of trade or commerce among the several States, or with foreign nations, is hereby declared to be illegal. Every person who shall make any such contract or engage in any such combination or conspiracy, shall be deemed guilty of a misdemeanor, and, on conviction thereof, shall be punished by fine not exceeding five thousand dollars, or by imprisonment not exceeding one year, or by both said punishments, in the discretion of the court.[a]

2. "Every person who shall monopolize, or attempt to monopolize, or combine or conspire with any other person or persons, to monopolize any part of the trade or commerce among the several States, or with foreign nations, shall be deemed guilty of a misdemeanor, and, on conviction thereof, shall be punished by fine not exceeding five thousand dollars, or by imprisonment not exceeding one year, or by both said punishments, in the discretion of the court."[a]

a. The ceiling amount of the fine was changed in 1955 to $50,000. 69 Stat. 282. In 1974 the entire sanction structure was amended so as to make the offense a felony instead of a misdemeanor and to increase the penalties to a "fine not exceeding one million dollars if a corporation, or, if any other person, one hundred thousand dollars or * * * imprisonment not exceeding three years, or * * * both said punishments, in the discretion of the court." 88 Stat. 1708.

7. "Any person who shall be injured in his business or property by any other person or corporation by reason of anything forbidden or declared to be unlawful by this act, may sue therefor in any Circuit Court of the United States in the district in which the defendant resides or is found, without respect to the amount in controversy, and shall recover three fold the damages by him sustained, and the costs of suit, including a reasonable attorney's fee."

In our opinion, the combination described in the declaration is a combination "in restraint of trade or commerce among the several States," in the sense in which those words are used in the act, and the action can be maintained accordingly.

And that conclusion rests on many judgments of this court, to the effect that the act prohibits any combination whatever to secure action which essentially obstructs the free flow of commerce between the States, or restricts, in that regard, the liberty of a trader to engage in business.

* * *

* * * [I]t was said * * * in the *Northern Securities Case,* 193 U.S. 331, that, "the act declares illegal every contract, combination or conspiracy, in whatever form, of whatever nature, and whoever may be the parties to it, which directly or necessarily operates in restraint of trade or commerce among the several States." * * *

The averments here are that there was an existing interstate traffic between plaintiffs and citizens of other States, and that for the direct purpose of destroying such interstate traffic defendants combined not merely to prevent plaintiffs from manufacturing articles then and there intended for transportation beyond the State, but also to prevent the vendees from reselling the hats which they had imported from Connecticut, or from further negotiating with plaintiffs for the purchase and intertransportation of such hats from Connecticut to the various places of destination. So that, although some of the means whereby the interstate traffic was to be destroyed were acts within a State, and some of them were in themselves as a part of their obvious purpose and effect beyond the scope of Federal authority, still * * * the acts must be considered as a whole, and the plan is open to condemnation * * *. If the purposes of the combination were, as alleged, to prevent any interstate transportation at all, the fact that the means operated at one end before physical transportation commenced and at the other end after the physical transportation ended was immaterial.

Nor can the act in question be held inapplicable because defendants were not themselves engaged in interstate commerce. The act made no distinction between classes. It provided that "every" contract, combination or conspiracy in restraint of trade was illegal. The records of Congress show that several efforts were made to exempt, by legislation, organizations of farmers and laborers from the operation of the act and that all these efforts failed, so that the act remained as we have it before us.

In an early case, United States v. Workingmen's Amalgamated Council, 54 Fed.Rep. 994, the United States filed a bill under the Sherman Act in the Circuit Court for the Eastern District of Louisiana, averring the existence of "a gigantic and widespread combination of the members of a multitude of separate organizations for the purpose of restraining the commerce among the several States and with foreign countries," and it was contended that the statute did not refer to combinations of laborers. But the court, granting the injunction, said:

> "I think the Congressional debates show that the statute had its origin in the evils of massed capital; but, when the Congress came to formulating the prohibition, which is the yardstick for measuring the complainant's right to the injunction, it expressed it in these words: 'Every contract or combination in the form of trust, or otherwise in restraint of trade or commerce among the several States or with foreign nations, is hereby declared to be illegal.' The subject had so broadened in the minds of the legislators that the source of the evil was not regarded as material, and the evil in its entirety is dealt with. They made the interdiction include combinations of labor, as well as of capital; in fact, all combinations in restraint of commerce, without reference to the character of the persons who entered into them. It is true this statute has not been much expounded by judges, but, as it seems to me, its meaning, as far as relates to the sort of combinations to which it is to apply, is manifest, and that it includes combinations which are composed of laborers acting in the interest of laborers. ＊ ＊ ＊"

The case was affirmed on appeal by the Circuit Court of Appeals for the Fifth Circuit. 57 Fed.Rep. 85.

Subsequently came the litigation over the Pullman strike and the decisions, In re Debs, 64 Fed.Rep. 724, 745, 755; S.C., 158 U.S. 564. The bill in that case was filed by the United States against the officers of the American Railway Union, which alleged that a labor dispute existed between the Pullman Palace Car Company and its employés; that thereafter the four officers of the railway union combined together and with others to compel an adjustment of such dispute by creating a boycott against the cars of the car company; that to make such boycott effective they had already prevented certain of the railroads running out of Chicago from operating their trains; that they asserted that they could and would tie up, paralyze and break down any and every railroad which did not accede to their demands, and that the purpose and intention of the combination was "to secure unto themselves the entire control of the interstate, industrial and commercial business in which the population of the city of Chicago and of other communities along the lines of road of said railways are engaged with each other, and to restrain any and all other persons from any independent control or management of such interstate, industrial or commercial enterprises, save according to the will and with the consent of the defendants."

The Circuit Court proceeded principally upon the Sherman Anti-Trust law, and granted an injunction. In this court the case was rested upon the broader ground that the Federal Government had full power over interstate commerce and over the transmission of the mails, and in the exercise of those powers could remove everything put upon highways, natural or artificial, to obstruct the passage of interstate commerce, or the carrying of the mails. But in reference to the Anti-Trust Act the court expressly stated (158 U.S. 600):

> "We enter into no examination of the act of July 2, 1890, c. 647, 26 Stat. 209, upon which the Circuit Court relied mainly to sustain its jurisdiction. It must not be understood from this that we dissent from the conclusions of

that court in reference to the scope of the act, but simply that we prefer to rest our judgment on the broader ground which has been discussed in this opinion, believing it of importance that the principles underlying it should be fully stated and affirmed."

And in the opinion, Mr. Justice Brewer, among other things, said (p. 581):

"It is curious to note the fact that in a large proportion of the cases in respect to interstate commerce brought to this court the question presented was of the validity of state legislation in its bearings upon interstate commerce, and the uniform course of decision has been to declare that it is not within the competency of a State to legislate in such a manner as to obstruct interstate commerce. If a State, with its recognized powers of sovereignty, is impotent to obstruct interstate commerce, can it be that any mere voluntary association of individuals within the limits of that State has a power which the State itself does not possess?"

The question answers itself, and in the light of the authorities the only inquiry is as to the sufficiency of the averments of fact. * * * [It is charged in the case at bar] that defendants formed a combination to directly restrain plaintiffs' trade; that the trade to be restrained was interstate; that certain means to attain such restraint were contrived to be used and employed to that end; that those means were so used and employed by defendants, and that thereby they injured plaintiffs' property and business.

* * * [T]he complaint averred that plaintiffs were manufacturers of hats in Danbury, Connecticut, having a factory there, and were then and there engaged in an interstate trade in some twenty States other than the State of Connecticut; that they were practically dependent upon such interstate trade to consume the product of their factory, only a small percentage of their entire output being consumed in the State of Connecticut; that at the time the alleged combination was formed they were in the process of manufacturing a large number of hats for the purpose of fulfilling engagements then actually made with consignees and wholesale dealers in States other than Connecticut, and that if prevented from carrying on the work of manufacturing these hats they would be unable to complete their engagements.

That defendants were members of a vast combination called The United Hatters of North America, comprising about 9,000 members and including a large number of subordinate unions, and that they were combined with some 1,400,000 others into another association known as The American Federation of Labor, of which they were members, whose members resided in all the places in the several States where the wholesale dealers in hats and their customers resided and did business; that defendants were "engaged in a combined scheme and effort to force all manufacturers of fur hats in the United States, including the plaintiffs, against their will and their previous policy of carrying on their business, to organize their workmen in the departments of making and finishing, in each of their factories, into an organization, to be part and parcel of the said combination known as The United Hatters of North America, or as the defendants and their confederates term it, to unionize their shops, with the intent thereby to control the employment of labor in and the operation of said factories, and to subject the same to the direction and control of persons, other than the owners of the same, in a manner extremely onerous and distasteful to such owners, and to carry out such scheme, effort and purpose, by restraining and destroying the interstate trade and commerce of such manufacturers, by means of intimidation of and threats made to such manufacturers and their customers in the several States, of boycotting them, their product and their customers, using therefor all the powerful means at their command, as aforesaid, until such time as, from the damage and loss of business resulting therefrom, the said manufacturers should yield to the said demand to unionize their factories."

That the conspiracy or combination was so far progressed that out of eighty-two manufacturers of this country engaged in the production of fur hats seventy had accepted the terms and acceded to the demand that the shop should be conducted in accordance, so far as conditions of employment were concerned, with the will of the American Federation of Labor; that the local union demanded of plaintiffs that they should unionize their shop under peril of being boycotted by this combination, which demand defendants [plaintiffs?] declined to comply with; that thereupon the American Federation of Labor, acting through its official organ and through its organizers, declared a boycott. * * *

And then followed the averments that the defendants proceeded to carry out their combination to restrain and destroy interstate trade and commerce between plaintiffs and their customers in other States by employing the identical means contrived for that purpose; and that by reason of those acts plaintiffs were damaged in their business and property in some $80,000.

We think a case within the statute was set up and that the demurrer should have been overruled.

Judgment reversed and cause remanded with a direction to proceed accordingly.

Note

1. What motivated the union to seek to organize plaintiffs' employees?

2. Was the strike against the plaintiffs in Danbury, Connecticut, without more, a violation of the Sherman Act? Or was the national boycott essential to the violation?

3. What is a boycott? How does it relate to or differ from a strike? What kind of boycott was involved here?

Refined analysis of the nature and scope of boycotts requires a closer examination of the facts involved than was articulated, for example, by Chief Justice Fuller in Loewe v. Lawlor. Such analysis requires the answering of at least three questions: (1) Who is doing the boycotting? (2) What, specifically, are they doing? (3) To whom are they doing it? Or, more briefly, who is doing what to whom?

The bill of complaint in Loewe v. Lawlor, set out in a footnote of the Court's opinion, provides the following answers to those questions: (1) The "who" were the United Hatters of North America and their allies—the American Federation of Labor, "union men," "friends of organized labor," "those desiring the patronage of organized workers." (2) The "what" was a concerted refusal to patronize D.E. Loewe & Co., any person or concern which itself patronized D.E.

Loewe & Co., and any person or concern which patronized any person or concern which patronized D.E. Loewe & Co. (3) The "whom" were, of course, D.E. Loewe & Co., persons and concerns which patronized D.E. Loewe & Co., and persons and concerns which, in turn, patronized persons or concerns which themselves patronized D.E. Loewe & Co.

Representative of the technique by which the boycott was conducted is the following circular, quoted verbatim in the complaint:

"San Francisco Labor Council,
"Affiliated with the American Federation of Labor,
"Secretary's Office, 927 Market Street,
"Rooms 405, 406, 407 Emma Spreckel's Building,
"Meets every Friday, at 1159 Mission St.

"Telephone South 447.

"Address all communications to 927 Market Street.

"San Francisco, July 3, 1903.

"To whom it may concern:

"At a special meeting of the San Francisco Labor Council held on the above date, the hat jobbing concern known as Triest & Co., 116 Sansome St., San Francisco, was declared unfair for persistently patronizing the unfair hat manufacturing concern of D.E. Loewe & Co., Danbury, Connecticut, where the union hatters have been on strike, for union conditions, since August 20, 1902. Triest & Co. will be retained on the unfair list as long as they handle the product of this unfair hat manufacturing concern. Union men do not usually patronize retail stores who buy from unfair jobbing houses or manufacturers. Under these circumstances, all friends of organized labor, and those desiring the patronage of organized workers, will not buy goods from Triest & Co., 116 Sansome St., San Francisco.

"Yours respectfully,   G.B. BENHAM,
                                                   "*President S.F. Labor Council.*

"T.E. ZANT,
  "*Secretary S.F. Labor Council.*
[L.S.]

"W.C. HENNELLY,

"D.F. KELLY,
  "*Representing United Hatters
of North America.*"

4. Loewe v. Lawlor, known in the trade as the "Danbury Hatters" case, was the first case in which the Supreme Court held the Sherman Antitrust Act of 1890 to apply to organized labor. The decision produced considerable controversy. For the view favoring such application, see, e.g., Mason, Organized Labor and the Law 119–142 (1925); for the opposing view, see, e.g., Berman, Labor and the Sherman Act 3–54 (1930). Whatever conclusion one reaches on this question, it is clear that organized labor was not the focal point of congressional concern in enacting the statute.

5. The Danbury Hatters case was a *cause célèbre* —fourteen years in the courts, twice tried by a jury, four times reviewed, in one form or another, by the Circuit Court of Appeals and three times by the Supreme Court. The final judgment was in excess of $250,000, for which amount the more than a hundred individual defendants, all members of the United Hatters and residing in Connecticut, were held personally liable in Lawlor v. Loewe, 235 U.S. 522, 35 S.Ct. 170, 59 L.Ed. 341 (1915) (Holmes writing for the Court). The case was finally settled in 1917 for over $234,000, of which the AFL, having sought voluntary contributions from union members across the country, furnished $216,000. This settlement forestalled, at the last moment, foreclosure sales of the homes of individual defendants to satisfy judgment liens. "Probably no case, except the Dred Scott decision, ever caused greater agitation in legal and political circles, and few, if any, have exercised greater influence on our industrial institutions. It forbade that the closed shop be forced by interstate boycotts." Merritt, History of the League for Industrial Rights 31 (1925). See generally, Merritt, op. cit. 22–35; Witte, The Government in Labor Disputes 134–136 (1932).

DUPLEX PRINTING PRESS CO. v. DEERING

Supreme Court of the United States, 1921.
254 U.S. 443, 41 S.Ct. 172, 65 L.Ed. 349, 16 A.L.R. 196.

MR. JUSTICE PITNEY delivered the opinion of the court.

This was a suit in equity brought by appellant in the District Court for the Southern District of New York for an injunction to restrain a course of conduct carried on by defendants in that District and vicinity in maintaining a boycott against the products of complainant's factory, in furtherance of a conspiracy to injure and destroy its good will, trade, and business—especially to obstruct and destroy its interstate trade. There was also a prayer for damages, but this has not been pressed and calls for no further mention. Complainant is a Michigan corporation and manufactures printing presses at a factory in Battle Creek, in that State, employing about 200 machinists in the factory in addition to 50 office-employees, traveling salesmen, and expert machinists or road men who supervise the erection of the presses for complainant's customers at their various places of business. The defendants who were brought into court and answered the bill are Emil J. Deering and William Bramley, sued individually and as business agents and representatives of District No. 15 of the International Association of Machinists, and Michael T. Neyland, sued individually and as business agent and representative of Local Lodge No. 328 of the same association. The District Council and the Lodge are unincorporated associations having headquarters in New York City, with numerous members resident in that city and vicinity. There were averments and proof to show that it was impracticable to bring all the members before the court and that the named defendants properly represented them; and those named were called upon to defend for all, pursuant to Equity Rule 38 (226 U.S. 659). * * * The District Court, on final hearing, dismissed the bill, 247 Fed.Rep. 192; the Circuit Court of Appeals affirmed its decree, 252 Fed.Rep. 722; and the present appeal was taken.

The jurisdiction of the federal court was invoked both by reason of diverse citizenship and on the ground that defendants were engaged in a conspiracy to restrain complainant's interstate trade and commerce in printing presses, contrary to the Sherman Anti-Trust Act of July 2, 1890, c.

647, 26 Stat. 209. The suit was begun before but brought to hearing after the passage of the Clayton Act of October 15, 1914, c. 323, 38 Stat. 730. Both parties invoked the provisions of the latter act, and both courts treated them as applicable. Complainant relied also upon the common law; but we shall deal first with the effect of the acts of Congress. * * *

[The facts] may be summarized as follows. Complainant conducts its business on the "open shop" policy, without discrimination against either union or nonunion men. The individual defendants and the local organizations of which they are the representatives are affiliated with the International Association of Machinists, an unincorporated association having a membership of more than 60,000; and are united in a combination, to which the International Association also is a party, having the object of compelling complainant to unionize its factory and enforce the "closed shop," the eight-hour day, and the union scale of wages, by means of interfering with and restraining its interstate trade in the products of the factory. Complainant's principal manufacture is newspaper presses of large size and complicated mechanism, varying in weight from 10,000 to 100,000 pounds, and requiring a considerable force of labor and a considerable expenditure of time—a week or more—to handle, haul and erect them at the point of delivery. These presses are sold throughout the United States and in foreign countries; and, as they are especially designed for the production of daily papers, there is a large market for them in and about the City of New York. They are delivered there in the ordinary course of interstate commerce, the handling, hauling and installation work at destination being done by employees of the purchaser under the supervision of a specially skilled machinist supplied by complainant. The acts complained of and sought to be restrained have nothing to do with the conduct or management of the factory in Michigan, but solely with the installation and operation of the presses by complainant's customers. None of the defendants is or ever was an employee of complainant, and complainant at no time has had relations with either of the organizations that they represent. In August, 1913 (eight months before the filing of the bill), the International Association called a strike at complainant's factory in Battle Creek, as a result of which union machinists to the number of about eleven in the factory and three who supervised the erection of presses in the field left complainant's employ. But the defection of so small a number did not materially interfere with the operation of the factory, and sales and shipments in interstate commerce continued. The acts complained of made up the details of an elaborate programme adopted and carried out by defendants and their organizations in and about the City of New York as part of a country-wide programme adopted by the International Association, for the purpose of enforcing a boycott of complainant's product. The acts embraced the following, with others: warning customers that it would be better for them not to purchase, or having purchased not to install, presses made by complainant, and threatening them with loss should they do so; threatening customers with sympathetic strikes in other trades; notifying a trucking company usually employed by customers to haul the presses not to do so, and threatening it with trouble if it should; inciting employees of the trucking company, and other men employed by customers of complainant, to strike against their respective employers in order to interfere with the hauling and installation of presses, and thus bring pressure to bear upon the customers; notifying repair shops not to do repair work on Duplex presses; coercing union men by threatening them with loss of union cards and with being blacklisted as "scabs" if they assisted in installing the presses; threatening an exposition company with a strike if it permitted complainant's presses to be exhibited; and resorting to a variety of other modes of preventing the sale of presses of complainant's manufacture in or about New York City, and delivery of them in interstate commerce, such as injuring and threatening to injure complainant's customers and prospective customers, and persons concerned in hauling, handling, or installing the presses. In some cases the threats were undisguised, in other cases polite in form but none the less sinister in purpose and effect. All the judges of the Circuit Court of Appeals concurred in the view that defendants' conduct consisted essentially of efforts to render it impossible for complainant to carry on any commerce in printing presses between Michigan and New York; and that defendants had agreed to do and were endeavoring to accomplish the very thing pronounced unlawful by this court in Loewe v. Lawlor, 208 U.S. 274; 235 U.S. 522. The judges also agreed that the interference with interstate commerce was such as ought to be enjoined, unless the Clayton Act of October 15, 1914, forbade such injunction.

That act was passed after the beginning of the suit but more than two years before it was brought to hearing. We are clear that the courts below were right in giving effect to it; the real question being, whether they gave it the proper effect. In so far as the act (a) provided for relief by injunction to private suitors, (b) imposed conditions upon granting such relief under particular circumstances, and (c) otherwise modified the Sherman Act, it was effective from the time of its passage, and applicable to pending suits for injunction. Obviously, this form of relief operates only *in futuro,* and the right to it must be determined as of the time of the hearing. * * *

The Clayton Act, in § 1, includes the Sherman Act in a definition of "anti-trust laws," and, in § 16 (38 Stat. 737), gives to private parties a right to relief by injunction in any court of the United States against threatened loss or damage by a violation of the anti-trust laws, under the conditions and principles regulating the granting of such relief by courts of equity. Evidently this provision was intended to supplement the Sherman Act, under which some of the federal courts had held, as this court afterwards held in Paine Lumber Co. v. Neal, 244 U.S. 459, 471, that a private party could not maintain a suit for injunction.

That complainant's business of manufacturing printing presses and disposing of them in commerce is a property right, entitled to protection against unlawful injury or interference; that unrestrained access to the channels of interstate commerce is necessary for the successful conduct of the business; that a widespread combination exists, to which defendants and the associations represented by them are parties, to hinder and obstruct complainant's interstate trade and commerce by the means that have been indicated; and that as a result of it complainant has sustained substantial damage to its interstate trade, and is threatened with further and irreparable loss and damage in the future; is proved by clear and undisputed evidence. Hence the right to an injunction is clear if the threatened loss is due to a violation of the Sherman Act as amended by the Clayton Act. * * *

The substance of the matters here complained of is an interference with complainant's interstate trade, intended to have coercive effect upon complainant, and produced by what is commonly known as a "secondary boycott," that is, a combination not merely to refrain from dealing with complainant, or to advise or by peaceful means persuade complainant's customers to refrain ("primary boycott"), but to exercise coercive pressure upon such customers, actual or prospective, in order to cause them to withhold or withdraw patronage from complainant through fear of loss or damage to themselves should they deal with it.

As we shall see, the recognized distinction between a primary and a secondary boycott is material to be considered upon the question of the proper construction of the Clayton Act. But, in determining the right to an injunction under that and the Sherman Act, it is of minor consequence whether either kind of boycott is lawful or unlawful at common law or under the statutes of particular States. Those acts, passed in the exercise of the power of Congress to regulate commerce among the States, are of paramount authority, and their prohibitions must be given full effect irrespective of whether the things prohibited are lawful or unlawful at common law or under local statutes. * * *

Upon the question whether the provisions of the Clayton Act forbade the grant of an injunction under the circumstances of the present case, the Circuit Court of Appeals was divided; the majority holding that under § 20, "perhaps in conjunction with section 6," there could be no injunction. These sections are set forth in the margin.[1] Defendants seek to derive from them some authority for their conduct. As to § 6, it seems to us its principal

---

1. "Sec. 6. That the labor of a human being is not a commodity or article of commerce. Nothing contained in the antitrust laws shall be construed to forbid the existence and operation of labor, agricultural, or horticultural organizations, instituted for the purposes of mutual help, and not having capital stock or conducted for profit, or to forbid or restrain individual members of such organizations from lawfully carrying out the legitimate objects thereof; nor shall such organizations, or the members thereof, be held or construed to be illegal combinations or conspiracies in restraint of trade, under the antitrust laws."

"Sec. 20. That no restraining order or injunction shall be granted by any court of the United States, or a judge or the judges thereof, in any case between an employer and employees, or between employers and employees, or between employees, or between persons employed and persons seeking employment, involving, or growing out of, a dispute concerning terms or conditions of employment, unless necessary to prevent irreparable injury to property, or to a property right, of the party making the application, for which injury there is no adequate remedy at law, and such property or property right must be described with

particularity in the application, which must be in writing and sworn to by the applicant or by his agent or attorney.

"And no such restraining order or injunction shall prohibit any person or persons, whether singly or in concert, from terminating any relation of employment, or from ceasing to perform any work or labor, or from recommending, advising, or persuading others by peaceful means so to do; or from attending at any place where any such person or persons may lawfully be, for the purpose of peacefully obtaining or communicating information, or from peacefully persuading any person to work or to abstain from working; or from ceasing to patronize or to employ any party to such dispute, or from recommending, advising, or persuading others by peaceful and lawful means so to do; or from paying or giving to, or withholding from, any person engaged in such dispute, any strike benefits or other moneys or things of value; or from peaceably assembling in a lawful manner, and for lawful purposes; or from doing any act or thing which might lawfully be done in the absence of such dispute by any party thereto; nor shall any of the acts specified in this paragraph be considered or held to be violations of any law of the United States."

importance in this discussion is for what it does *not* authorize, and for the limit it sets to the immunity conferred. The section assumes the normal objects of a labor organization to be legitimate, and declares that nothing in the anti-trust laws shall be construed to forbid the existence and operation of such organizations or to forbid their members from *lawfully* carrying out their *legitimate* objects; and that such an organization shall not be held in itself—merely because of its existence and operation—to be an illegal combination or conspiracy in restraint of trade. But there is nothing in the section to exempt such an organization or its members from accountability where it or they depart from its normal and legitimate objects and engage in an actual combination or conspiracy in restraint of trade. And by no fair or permissible construction can it be taken as authorizing any activity otherwise unlawful, or enabling a normally lawful organization to become a cloak for an illegal combination or conspiracy in restraint of trade as defined by the anti-trust laws.

The principal reliance is upon § 20. This regulates the granting of restraining orders and injunctions by the courts of the United States in a designated class of cases, with respect to (a) the terms and conditions of the relief and the practice to be pursued, and (b) the character of acts that are to be exempted from the restraint; and in the concluding words it declares (c) that none of the acts specified shall be held to be violations of any law of the United States. All its provisions are subject to a general qualification respecting the nature of the controversy and the parties affected. It is to be a "case between an employer and employees, or between employers and employees or between employees, or between persons employed and persons seeking employment, involving, or growing out of, a dispute concerning terms or conditions of employment."

The first paragraph merely puts into statutory form familiar restrictions upon the granting of injunctions already established and of general application in the equity practice of the courts of the United States. It is but declaratory of the law as it stood before. The second paragraph declares that "no *such* restraining order or injunction" shall prohibit certain conduct specified—manifestly still referring to a "case between an employer and employees, * * * involving, or growing out of, a dispute concerning terms or conditions of employment," as designated in the first paragraph. It is very clear that the restriction upon the use of the injunction is in favor only of those concerned as parties to such a dispute as is described. The words defining the permitted conduct include particular qualifications consistent with the general one respecting the nature of the case and dispute intended; and the concluding words, "nor shall any of the acts specified in this paragraph be considered or held to be violations of any law of the United States," are to be read in the light of the context, and mean only that those acts are not to be so held when committed by parties concerned in "a dispute concerning terms or conditions of employment." If the qualifying words are to have any effect, they must operate to confine the restriction upon the granting of injunctions, and also the relaxation of the provisions of the anti-trust and other laws of the United States, to parties standing in proximate relation to a controversy such as is particularly described.

The majority of the Circuit Court of Appeals appear to have entertained the view that the words "employers and employees," as used in § 20, should be treated as referring to "the business class or clan to which the parties litigant respectively belong"; and that, as there had been a dispute at complainant's factory in Michigan concerning the conditions of employment there—a dispute created, it is said, if it did not exist before, by the act of the Machinists' Union in calling a strike at the factory—§ 20 operated to permit members of the Machinists' Union elsewhere—some 60,000 in number—although standing in no relation of employment under complainant, past, present, or prospective, to make that dispute their own and proceed to instigate sympathetic strikes, picketing, and boycotting against employers wholly unconnected with complainant's factory and having relations with complainant only in the way of purchasing its product in the ordinary course of interstate commerce—and this where there was no dispute between such employers and their employees respecting terms or conditions of employment.

We deem this construction altogether inadmissible. Section 20 must be given full effect according to its terms as an expression of the purpose of Congress; but it must be borne in mind that the section imposes an exceptional and extraordinary restriction upon the equity powers of the courts of the United States and upon the general operation of the anti-trust laws, a restriction in the nature of a special privilege or immunity to a particular class, with corresponding detriment to the general public; and it would violate rules of statutory construction having general application and far-reaching importance to enlarge that special privilege by resorting to a loose construction of the section, not to speak of ignoring or slighting the qualifying words that are found in it. Full and fair effect will be given to every word if the exceptional privilege be confined—as the natural meaning of the words confines it—to those who are proximately and substantially concerned as parties to an actual dispute respecting the terms or conditions of their own employment, past, present, or prospective. The extensive construction adopted by the majority of the court below virtually ignores the effect of the qualifying words. Congress had in mind particular industrial controversies, not a general class war. "Terms or conditions of employment" are the only grounds of dispute recognized as adequate to bring into play the exemptions; and it would do violence to the guarded language employed were the exemption extended beyond the parties affected in a proximate and substantial, not merely a sentimental or sympathetic, sense by the cause of dispute. * * *

The qualifying effect of the words descriptive of the nature of the dispute and the parties concerned is further borne out by the phrases defining the conduct that is not to be subjected to injunction or treated as a violation of the laws of the United States, that is to say: (a) "terminating any relation of employment, * * * or persuading others by peaceful and lawful means so to do"; (b) "attending at any place where any such person or persons may lawfully be, for the purpose of peacefully obtaining or communicating information, or from peacefully persuading any person to work or to abstain from working;" (c) "ceasing to patronize or to employ any party to such dispute, or * * * recommending, advising, or persuading others by peaceful and lawful means so to do"; (d) "paying or giving to, or withholding from, any person engaged in such dispute, any strike benefits * * * "; (e) "doing any act or thing which might lawfully be done in the absence of such dispute by any party thereto." The emphasis placed on the words "lawful" and "lawfully," "peaceful" and "peacefully," and the references to the dispute and the parties to it, strongly rebut a legislative intent to confer a general immunity for conduct violative of the anti-trust laws, or otherwise unlawful. The subject of the boycott is dealt with specifically in the "ceasing to patronize" provision, and by the clear force of the language employed the exemption is limited to pressure exerted upon a "party to such dispute" by means of "peaceful and *lawful*" influence upon neutrals. There is nothing here to justify defendants or the organizations they represent in using either threats or persuasion to bring about strikes or a cessation of work on the part of employees of complainant's customers or prospective customers, or of the trucking company employed by the customers, with the object of compelling such customers to withdraw or refrain from commercial relations with complainant, and of thereby constraining complainant to yield the matter in dispute. To instigate a sympathetic strike in aid of a secondary boycott cannot be deemed "peaceful and lawful" persuasion. In essence it is a threat to inflict damage upon the immediate employer, between whom and his employees no dispute exists, in order to bring him against his will into a concerted plan to inflict damage upon another employer who is in dispute with his employees.

The majority of the Circuit Court of Appeals, very properly treating the case as involving a secondary boycott, based the decision upon the view that it was the purpose of § 20 to legalize the secondary boycott "at least in so far as it rests on, or consists of, refusing to work for any one who deals with the principal offender." Characterizing the section as "blindly drawn," and conceding that the meaning attributed to it was broad, the court referred to the legislative history of the enactment as a warrant for the construction adopted. Let us consider this.

By repeated decisions of this court it has come to be well established that the debates in Congress expressive of the views and motives of individual members are not a safe guide, and hence may not be resorted to, in ascertaining the meaning and purpose of the law-making body. * * * But reports of committees of House or Senate stand upon a more solid footing, and may be regarded as an exposition of the legislative intent in a case where otherwise the meaning of a statute is obscure. * * * And this has been extended to include explanatory statements in the nature of a supplemental report made by the committee member in charge of a bill in course of passage. * * *

In the case of the Clayton Act, the printed committee reports are not explicit with respect to the meaning of the "ceasing to patronize" clause of what is now § 20. (See House Rept. No. 627, 63d Cong., 2nd sess., pp. 33–36; Senate Rept. No. 698, 63d Cong., 2nd sess., pp. 29–31; the latter being a reproduction of the former.) But they contain extracts from judicial opinions and a then recent textbook sustaining the "primary boycott," and expressing an adverse view as to the secondary or coercive boycott; and, on the whole, are far from manifesting a purpose to relax the prohibition against restraints of trade in favor of the secondary boycott.

Moreover, the report was supplemented in this regard by the spokesman of the House committee (Mr. Webb) who had the bill in charge when it was under consideration by the House. The question whether the bill legalized the secondary boycott having been raised, it was emphatically and unequivocally answered by him in the negative. The subject—he declared in substance or effect—was under consideration when the bill was framed, and the section as reported was carefully prepared with the settled purpose of excluding the secondary boycott and confining boycotting to the parties to the dispute, allowing parties to cease to patronize and to ask others to cease to patronize a party to the dispute * * *.

The extreme and harmful consequences of the construction adopted in the court below are not to be ignored. The present case furnishes an apt and convincing example. An ordinary controversy in a manufacturing establishment, said to concern the terms or conditions of employment there, has been held a sufficient occasion for imposing a general embargo upon the products of the establishment and a nation-wide blockade of the channels of interstate commerce against them, carried out by inciting sympathetic strikes and a secondary boycott against complainant's customers, to the great and incalculable damage of many innocent people far remote from any connection with or control over the original and actual dispute—people constituting, indeed, the general public upon whom the cost must ultimately fall, and whose vital interest in unobstructed commerce constituted the prime and paramount concern of Congress in enacting the anti-trust laws, of which the section under consideration forms after all a part.

Reaching the conclusion, as we do, that complainant has a clear right to an injunction under the Sherman Act as amended by the Clayton Act, it becomes unnecessary to consider whether a like result would follow under the common law or local statutes; there being no suggestion that relief thereunder could be broader than that to which complainant is entitled under the acts of Congress.

There should be an injunction against defendants and the associations represented by them, and all members of those associations, restraining them, according to the prayer of the bill * * *.

Decree reversed, and the cause remanded to the District Court for further proceedings in conformity with this opinion.

MR. JUSTICE BRANDEIS, dissenting, with whom MR. JUSTICE HOLMES and MR. JUSTICE CLARKE concur.

The Duplex Company, a manufacturer of newspaper printing presses, seeks to enjoin officials of the machinists' and affiliated unions from interfering with its business by inducing their members not to work for plaintiff or its customers in connection with the setting up of presses made by it. Unlike Hitchman Coal & Coke Co. v. Mitchell, 245 U.S. 229, there is here no charge that defendants are inducing employees to break their contracts. Nor is it now urged that defendants threaten acts of violence. But plaintiff insists that the acts complained of violate both the common law of New York and the Sherman Act and that, accordingly, it is entitled to relief by injunction under the state law and under § 16 of the Clayton Act * * *.

The defendants admit interference with plaintiff's business but justify on the following ground: There are in the United States only four manufacturers of such presses; and they are in active competition. Between 1909 and 1913 the machinists' union induced three of them to recognize and deal with the union, to grant the eight-hour day, to establish a minimum wage scale and to comply with other union requirements. The fourth, the Duplex Company, refused to recognize the union; insisted upon conducting its factory on the open shop principle; refused to introduce the eight-hour day and operated for the most part, ten hours a day; refused to establish a minimum wage scale; and disregarded other union standards. Thereupon two of the three manufacturers who had assented to union conditions, notified the union that they should be obliged to terminate their agreements with it unless their competitor, the Duplex Company, also entered into the agreement with the union, which, in giving more favorable terms to labor, imposed correspondingly greater burdens upon the employer. Because the Duplex Company refused to enter into such an agreement and in order to induce it to do so, the machinists' union declared a strike at its factory, and in aid of that strike instructed its members and the members of affiliated unions not to work on the installation of presses which plaintiff had delivered in New York. Defendants insist that by the common law of New York, where the acts complained of were done, and where this suit was brought, and also by § 20 of the Clayton Act, * * * the facts constitute a justification for this interference with plaintiff's business.

First. As to the rights at common law: Defendants' justification is that of self-interest. They have supported the strike at the employer's factory by a strike elsewhere against its product. They have injured the plaintiff, not maliciously, but in self-defense. They contend that the Duplex Company's refusal to deal with the machinists' union and to observe its standards threatened the interest not only of such union members as were its factory employees, but even more of all members of the several affiliated unions employed by plaintiff's competitors and by others whose more advanced standards the plaintiff was, in reality, attacking; and that none of the defendants and no person whom they are endeavoring to induce to refrain from working in connection with the setting up of presses made by plaintiff is an outsider, an interloper. In other words, that the contest between the company and the machinists' union involves vitally the interest of every person whose coöperation is sought. May not all with a common interest join in refusing to expend their labor upon articles whose very production constitutes an attack upon their standard of living and the institution which they are convinced supports it? Applying common-law principles the answer should, in my opinion, be: Yes, if as matter of fact those who so coöperate have a common interest.

The change in the law by which strikes once illegal and even criminal are now recognized as lawful was effected in America largely without the intervention of legislation. This reversal of a common-law rule was not due to the rejection by the courts of one principle and the adoption in its stead of another, but to a better realization of the facts of industrial life. It is conceded that, although the strike of the workmen in plaintiff's factory injured its business, the strike was not an actionable wrong; because the obvious self-interest of the strikers constituted a justification. * * *

Formerly courts held that self-interest could not be so served. Commons, History of Labor in the United States, vol. 2, c. 5. But even after strikes to raise wages or reduce hours were held to be legal because of the self-interest, some courts held that there was not sufficient causal relationship between a strike to unionize a shop and the self-interest of the strikers to justify injuries inflicted. Plant v. Woods, 176 Massachusetts, 492; Lucke v. Clothing Cutters' Assembly, 77 Maryland, 396; Erdman v. Mitchell, 207 Pa.St. 79. But other courts, repeating the same legal formula, found that there was justification, because they viewed the facts differently. National Protective Association v. Cumming, 170 N.Y. 315; Kemp v. Division No. 241, 255 Illinois, 213; Roddy v. United Mine Workers, 41 Oklahoma, 621. When centralization in the control of business brought its corresponding centralization in the organization of workingmen, new facts had to be appraised. A single employer might, as in this case, threaten the standing of the whole organization and the standards of all its members; and when he did so the union, in order to protect itself, would naturally refuse to work on his materials wherever found. When such a situation was first presented to the courts, judges concluded that the intervention of the purchaser of the materials established an insulation through which the direct relationship of the employer and the workingmen did not penetrate; and the strike against the material was considered a strike against the purchaser by unaffected third parties. Burnham v. Dowd, 217 Massachusetts, 351; Purvis v. United Brotherhood, 214 Pa.St. 348; Booth v. Burgess, 72 N.J.Eq. 181. But other courts, with better appreciation of the facts of industry, recognized the unity of interest throughout the union, and that, in refusing to work on materials which threatened it, the union was only refusing to aid in destroying itself. Bossert v. Dhuy, 221 N.Y. 342; Cohn & Roth Electric Co. v. Bricklayers Union, 92 Connecticut, 161; Gill Engraving Co. v. Doerr, 214 Fed.Rep. 111; State v. Van Pelt, 136 N.C. 633; Grant Construction Co. v. St. Paul Building Trades Council, 136 Minnesota, 167; Pierce v. Stablemen's Union, 156 California, 70, 76.

So, in the case at bar, deciding a question of fact upon the evidence introduced and matters of common knowledge, I should say, as the two lower courts apparently have said, that the defendants and those from whom they sought coöperation have a common interest which the plaintiff threatened.[b] This view is in harmony with the views of the Court of Appeals of New York. For in New York, although boycotts like that in Loewe v. Lawlor, 208 U.S. 274, are illegal because they are conducted not against a product but against those who deal in it and are carried out by a combination of persons not united by common interest but only by sympathy, Auburn Draying Co. v. Wardell, 227 N.Y. 1, it is lawful for all members of a union by whomever employed to refuse to handle materials whose production weakens the union. Bossert v. Dhuy, supra; P. Reardon, Inc. v. Caton, 189 App.Div. 501;

b. A close reader may notice that Justice Brandeis' characterization of the facts is somewhat different from that of Justice Pitney. Justice Pitney's emphasis is on the secondary and sympathetic aspect of the defendants' activities and of the conduct they induced and sought to induce. Justice Brandeis, on the other hand, emphasized the unity of interest among all of those whose aid was sought by the defendants. While this difference of view led Justice Brandeis to minimize the involvement of other than Machinists, the fact that Machinists employed by employers other than Duplex were urged to join the boycott was itself sufficiently secondary in nature to prompt Justice Pitney to conclude as he did.

compare Paine Lumber Co. v. Neal, 244 U.S. 459, 471. "The voluntary adoption of a rule not to work on non-union made material and its enforcement * * * differs entirely from a general boycott of a particular dealer or manufacturer with a malicious intent and purpose to destroy the good will or business of such dealer or manufacturer." Bossert v. Dhuy, supra, p. 355. In my opinion, therefore, plaintiff had no cause of action by the common law of New York.

Second. As to the anti-trust laws of the United States: * * *

[The Clayton Act] was the fruit of unceasing agitation, which extended over more than twenty years and was designed to equalize before the law the position of workingmen and employer as industrial combatants. Aside from the use of the injunction, the chief source of dissatisfaction with the existing law lay in the doctrine of malicious combination, and, in many parts of the country, in the judicial declarations of the illegality at common law of picketing and persuading others to leave work. The grounds for objection to the latter are obvious. The objection to the doctrine of malicious combinations requires some explanation. By virtue of that doctrine, damage resulting from conduct such as striking or withholding patronage or persuading others to do either, which without more might be *damnum absque injuria* because the result of trade competition, became actionable when done for a purpose which a judge considered socially or economically harmful and therefore branded as malicious and unlawful. It was objected that, due largely to environment, the social and economic ideas of judges, which thus became translated into law, were prejudicial to a position of equality between workingman and employer; that due to this dependence upon the individual opinion of judges great confusion existed as to what purposes were lawful and what unlawful; and that in any event Congress, not the judges, was the body which should declare what public policy in regard to the industrial struggle demands.

By 1914 the ideas of the advocates of legislation had fairly crystallized upon the manner in which the inequality and uncertainty of the law should be removed. It was to be done by expressly legalizing certain acts regardless of the effects produced by them upon other persons. As to them Congress was to extract the element of *injuria* from the damages thereby inflicted, instead of leaving judges to determine according to their own economic and social views whether the damage inflicted on an employer in an industrial struggle was *damnum absque injuria,* because an incident of trade competition, or a legal injury, because in their opinion, economically and socially objectionable. This idea was presented to the committees which reported the Clayton Act. The resulting law set out certain acts which had previously been held unlawful, whenever courts had disapproved of the ends for which they were performed; it then declared that, when these acts were committed in the course of an industrial dispute, they should not be held to violate any law of the United States. In other words the Clayton Act substituted the opinion of Congress as to the propriety of the purpose for that of different judges; and thereby it declared that the relations between employers of labor and workingmen were competitive relations, that organized competition was not harmful and that it justified injuries necessarily inflicted in its course. Both the majority and the minority report of the

House Committee indicate that such was its purpose. If, therefore, the act applies to the case at bar, the acts here complained of cannot "be considered or held to be violations of any law of the United States," and, hence, do not violate the Sherman Act.

The Duplex Company contends that § 20 of the Clayton Act does not apply to the case at bar, because it is restricted to cases "between an employer and employees, or between employers and employees, or between employees, or between persons employed and persons seeking employment, involving, or growing out of, a dispute concerning terms or conditions of employment"; whereas the case at bar arises between an employer in Michigan and workingmen in New York not in its employ, and does not involve their conditions of employment. But Congress did not restrict the provision to employers and workingmen *in their employ*. By including "employers and employees" and "persons employed and persons seeking employment" it showed that it was not aiming merely at a legal relationship between a specific employer and his employees. Furthermore, the plaintiff's contention proves too much. If the words are to receive a strict technical construction, the statute will have no application to disputes between employers of labor and workingmen, since the very acts to which it applies sever the continuity of the legal relationship. * * * The further contention that this case is not one arising out of a dispute concerning the conditions of work of one of the parties, is, in my opinion, founded upon a misconception of the facts.

Because I have come to the conclusion that both the common law of a State and a statute of the United States declare the right of industrial combatants to push their struggle to the limits of the justification of self-interest, I do not wish to be understood as attaching any constitutional or moral sanction to that right. All rights are derived from the purposes of the society in which they exist; above all rights rises duty to the community. The conditions developed in industry may be such that those engaged in it cannot continue their struggle without danger to the community. But it is not for judges to determine whether such conditions exist, nor is it their function to set the limits of permissible contest and to declare the duties which the new situation demands. This is the function of the legislature which, while limiting individual and group rights of aggression and defense, may substitute processes of justice for the more primitive method of trial by combat.

Note

1. Which of the two interpretations of the Clayton Act in Duplex is the more persuasive?

The heat generated by the controversy over the meaning of the Clayton Act was presaged by Samuel Gompers' hailing of the Act as labor's "Magna Carta." One of the more trenchant commentaries on this controversy is that of Frankfurter and Greene, The Labor Injunction 169 (1930): "With a legislative history like that which surrounds the Clayton Act, talk about the legislative intent as a means of construing legislation is simply repeating an empty formula. * * * Statutory construction in doubtful cases, in the last analysis, is a choice among competing policies as starting points for reasoning." For a relatively recent

discussion analyzing the competing views and setting forth the relevant literature, see Jones, The Enigma of the Clayton Act, 10 Industrial and Labor
Relations Review 201 (1957).

2. Justice Pitney characterizes (supra p. 65) the condemned activities of the
defendants as a "secondary boycott," as distinguished from a "primary boycott."
What is the difference between the two?

Why does Justice Brandeis take a more charitable view of the defendants'
conduct? Do you agree with the distinction he makes between a boycott directed
against a non-union-made product and a boycott directed against those who deal
in the product? By what criteria would he determine what groups of employees
might lawfully refuse to handle the "hot" product?

3. The above distinctions demonstrate a continuing problem in formulating
the law of labor relations. The problem may be posed in this fashion: What is
the arena to be allowed to labor and capital in resolving their conflicts of
interest? Another way of posing the same question is: What weapons should
either side be permitted to use in asserting its cause? A few moments' reflection
will reveal, for example, the crescendoing impact and scope of involvement of:
(1) a strike; (2) picketing; (3) a primary consumption boycott; (4) a secondary
labor or consumption boycott, directed (a) specifically at the product of the
primary employer, (b) generally at the business of one or more otherwise neutral
parties dealing in the product of the primary employer; (5) a sympathetic strike;
(6) a general strike. What factors would you deem properly to be taken into
account in drawing the line between permitted and prohibited weapons of
economic coercion in shaping the law of a free society?

4. The Duplex interpretation of the Clayton Act was reaffirmed by the
Supreme Court in Bedford Cut Stone Co. v. Journeymen Stone Cutters' Association, 274 U.S. 37, 47 S.Ct. 522, 71 L.Ed. 916 (1927). The plaintiff employers in
that case, some twenty-four in number, had previously had an agreement with
the union but had subsequently closed "their shops and quarries against the
members" of the union. The union thereupon declared the stone produced by
the plaintiffs to be "unfair," and the members refused to work on or handle it.
Justice Brandeis, again in dissent, wrote the following: "The Sherman Law was
held in United States v. United States Steel Corporation, 251 U.S. 417, to permit
capitalists to combine in a single corporation 50 per cent of the steel industry of
the United States dominating the trade through its vast resources. The Sherman Law was held in United States v. United Shoe Machinery Co., 247 U.S. 32,
to permit capitalists to combine in another corporation practically the whole
shoe machinery industry of the country, necessarily giving it a position of
dominance over shoe-manufacturing in America. It would indeed, be strange if
Congress had by the same Act willed to deny to members of a small craft of
workingmen [some 5,000 in number] the right to cooperate in simply refraining
from work, when that course was the only means of self-protection against a
combination of militant and powerful employers. I cannot believe that Congress
did so." 274 U.S. at 65, 47 S.Ct. at 531.

CORONADO COAL CO. v. UNITED MINE WORKERS

Supreme Court of the United States, 1925.
268 U.S. 295, 45 S.Ct. 551, 69 L.Ed. 963.

MR. CHIEF JUSTICE TAFT delivered the opinion of the Court.

This is a suit for damages for the effect of an alleged conspiracy of the defendants unlawfully to restrain and prevent plaintiffs' interstate trade in coal in violation of the first and second sections of the Federal Anti-Trust Act. The charge is that the defendants, in 1914, for the purpose of consummating the conspiracy, destroyed valuable mining properties of the plaintiffs. Treble damages and an attorney's fee are asked under the seventh section of the Act. The suit was brought in the District Court for the Western District of Arkansas. The plaintiffs are the Bache-Denman Coal Company and eight other corporations in each of which the first named owns a controlling amount of stock. One of them is the Coronado Company, which gives the case its name. The corporations were correlated in organization and in the physical location of their mines. They had been operated for some years as a unit in the Prairie Creek Valley in Sebastian County, Arkansas. Immediately after the destruction of the property the District Court in a proper proceeding appointed receivers for the mines, and they or their successors are also parties to this suit. The original complaint was filed in September, 1914. It was demurred to, and the demurrer sustained. On error in the Court of Appeals the ruling was reversed. Dowd v. United Mine Workers of America, 235 Fed. 1. The case then came on for trial on the third amended complaint and the answers of the defendants. The trial resulted in a verdict of $200,000 for the plaintiffs, which was trebled by the court, and a counsel fee of $25,000 and interest to the date of the judgment were added. The Court of Appeals reversed the judgment as to interest, but in other respects affirmed it. 258 Fed. 829. On error from this Court under § 241 of the Judicial Code, the judgments of both courts were reversed, and the cause remanded to the District Court for further proceedings. The opinion is reported in 259th United States, 344. The new trial, in October, 1923, resulted in a directed verdict and judgment for the defendants, which was affirmed by the Circuit Court of Appeals. The case is here on error for a second time.

In our previous opinion we held that the International Union, known as the United Mine Workers of America, the union known as United Mine Workers, District No. 21, and the subordinate local unions which were made defendants, were, though unincorporated associations, subject to suit under the Anti-Trust Act, but that there was not sufficient evidence to go to the jury to show participation by the International Union in the conspiracy and the wrongs done. We found evidence tending to show that District No. 21 and other defendants were engaged in the conspiracy and the destruction of the property, but not enough to show an intentional restraint of interstate trade and a violation of the Anti-Trust Act. The plaintiffs contend that they have now supplied the links lacking at the first trial against each of the principal defendants.

The Bache-Denman mines lie near the west line of Arkansas, next to Oklahoma. In all the Arkansas mines, except a small one, union miners were engaged. The towns of the neighborhood—Hartford, Huntington, Midland, Frogtown and others—were peopled by them. District No. 21 was a regional organization of the United Mine Workers which included Arkansas, Texas and Oklahoma. Mr. Bache as manager of the plaintiffs' mines had been operating them for a number of years with union labor and under a District No. 21 contract and scale of wages, which did not expire until July 1, 1914. In March of that year he determined to run his mines thereafter on a non-union or open basis, and notified Pete Stewart, the president of the District No. 21, that he intended to do so. He shut down his mines and prepared to open them on an open shop basis on April 6th. He anticipated trouble. He employed three guards from the Burns Detective Agency and a number of others to aid him. He bought a number of Winchester rifles and ammunition, and surrounded his principal mining plant at Prairie Creek, No. 4, with cables strung on posts. He had notices prepared and sent to his employees who occupied the company's houses that they should vacate unless they remained in his employ. He sent out for non-union men and had gathered some thirty or more for the day fixed for the opening. The people in all that part of the country were urged by the members of the local unions to come to a meeting at the school house, a short distance from the Prairie Creek mine, for a public protest. The meeting appointed a committee to visit the superintendent and insist that the mine remain a union mine. The guards, directed not to use their guns save to defend their own lives, were at the mercy of the union miners, who assaulted them, took their guns away and injured a number of them. The employees deserted the mine, which filled with water upon the stopping of the pumps. One of the crowd went up to the top of the coal tipple and planted a flag on which was the legend, "This is a union man's country."

Mr. Bache obtained from the federal District Court an injunction against the union miners and others taking part in this lawless violence, including among them the President of No. 21, Pete Stewart, and Holt, its Secretary-Treasurer. Bache then prepared to resume mining. The work progressed under the protection of United States deputy marshals. Meanwhile non-union miners and other employees were brought in from out of the State. The United States marshals were after some weeks withdrawn from the property and only private guards were retained. Meanwhile the water had been pumped out and the mining and shipping of coal were about to begin. A large force of union miners of the local unions and of District No. 21, and their sympathizers, armed themselves with rifles and other guns furnished and paid for by the District No. 21 organization, and before day on July 17th began an attack upon the men who Bache had brought together, and proceeded to destroy the property and equipment. It was a battle, in which two of the employees of the mine, after capture, were deliberately murdered, and not only gunfire and bullets but also dynamite and the torch were used to destroy all the property on the premises of the Prairie Creek Mine and of three of the other mines of the plaintiffs.

First. Is there any evidence in the present record tending to show that the International Union of the United Mine Workers participated? * * *

* * * In our previous opinion we held that a trades-union, organized as effectively as this United Mine Workers' organization was, might be held liable, and all its funds raised for the purpose of strikes might be levied upon to pay damages suffered through illegal methods in carrying them on; but certainly it must be clearly shown in order to impose such a liability on an association of 450,000 men that what was done was done by their agents in accordance with their fundamental agreement of association.

As we said in our previous opinion, 259 U.S. 395:

"A corporation is responsible for the wrongs committed by its agents in the course of its business, and this principle is enforced against the contention that torts are *ultra vires* of the corporation. But it must be shown that it is in the business of the corporation. Surely no stricter rule can be enforced against an unincorporated organization like this. * * * It is a mere question of actual agency * * *."

[The Court found the evidence of agency to be insufficient.]

The action of the trial court in its direction of a verdict for the defendant, the International Union, must be affirmed.

Second. The tendency of the evidence to show that District No. 21 through its authorized leaders and agents and certain of its subordinate local unions organized and carried through the two attacks of April 6th and July 17th is so clear that it does not need further discussion. The only issue is whether the outrages, destruction and crimes committed were intentionally directed toward a restraint of interstate commerce. On the first trial we held that the evidence did not show this. The circumstances seemed amply to supply a different and a merely local motive for the conspiracy. The hostility of the head of District No. 21 and that of his men seemed sufficiently aroused by the coming of non-union men into that local community, by Mr. Bache's alleged breach of his contract with District No. 21 in employing non-union men three months before it expired, by his charged evasion of it through a manipulation of his numerous corporations, by his advertised anticipation of trespass and violence in his warning notices, in his enclosing his mining premises with a cable, and in stationing guards with guns to defend them. These preparations in the heart of a territory that had been completely unionized for years were likely to stir a bitterness of spirit in the neighborhood. Bache had himself foreseen such a spirit when he took part in the formulation of a letter to his stockholders for his superintendent to sign, in which it was said: "To do this means a bitter fight, but in my opinion it can be accomplished by proper organization." He testified that he was entering into a matter he knew was perilous and dangerous to his companies. In view of these circumstances, we said in the previous opinion:

"Nothing of this is recited to justify in the slightest the lawlessness and outrages committed, but only to point out that as it was a local strike within the meaning of the International and District constitutions, so it was in fact a local strike, local in its origin and motive, local in its waging, and local in its felonious and murderous ending."

Were we concerned only with the riot of April 6th, we should reach the same conclusion now; but at the second trial plaintiffs were able to present a large amount of new evidence as to the attitude and purpose of the leaders and members of District No. 21, shown especially in the interval between the riot of April 6th and the destruction of the mine property on July 17th following. This is attributed by counsel for the plaintiffs to the fact that the new witnesses had moved away from Sebastian County, Arkansas, and were freed from local restraint and to grievances of former union sympathizers and participants who thought themselves not sufficiently appreciated.

Part of the new evidence was an extract from the convention proceedings of District No. 21 at Fort Smith, Arkansas, in February, 1914, in which the delegates discussed the difficulties presented in their maintenance of the union scale in Arkansas, Oklahoma and Texas because of the keen competition from the non-union fields of Southern Colorado and the non-union fields of the South in Alabama and Tennessee. Stewart, the president, called attention to a new field in Oklahoma which he said would be a great competitor of union coal fields, and that District No. 21 would be forced to call a strike to bring into line certain operators in that section, and in the event that they did so the District would fight such a conflict to the bitter end regardless of cost. They also discussed a proposal to reduce the scale at the union mines at McCurtain, Oklahoma, which Stewart advocated, in order that the McCurtain operators might be put on a proper competitive basis in interstate markets with other operators. Several of the delegates at this convention took part in the riot of April 6th and the battle of July 17th following.

A new witness was one Hanraty, who was for seven years president of District No. 21, then a state mine inspector for three years, and then national organizer from 1912 to 1914, and president of District No. 21 again in 1915, but subsequently separated from the union. He testified that he had been closely associated as president of the District with Stewart as a member of the District executive board. He had been frequently in close conference with most of the leading men who had taken part in the violence at Prairie Creek. He said that he made speeches all through District No. 21 and did not remember a speech in which he did not mention the danger from non-union coal in taking the markets of union coal and forcing a non-union scale, and that it was a constant subject of discussion among the officers and members. * * *

[From this and other testimony] the jury could reasonably infer that the purpose of the union miners in District No. 21 and the local unions engaged in the plan was to destroy the power of the owners and lessees of the Bache-Denman mines to send their output into interstate commerce to compete with that of union mines in Oklahoma, in Kansas, in Louisiana markets and elsewhere. It appeared that 80 per cent. of all the product of the mines in Sebastian County went into other States. * * *

The mere reduction in the supply of an article to be shipped in interstate commerce by the illegal or tortious prevention of its manufacture or production is ordinarily an indirect and remote obstruction to that commerce. But when the intent of those unlawfully preventing the manufacture or production is shown to be to restrain or control the supply entering and moving in interstate commerce or the price of it in interstate markets, their action is a direct violation of the Anti-Trust Act. United Mines Workers v. Coronado Co., 259 U.S. 344, 408, 409 * * *. We think there was substantial evidence at the second trial in this case tending to show that the purpose of the destruction of the mines was to stop the production of non-union coal and prevent its shipment to markets of other States than Arkansas, where it would by competition tend to reduce the price of the commodity and affect injuriously the maintenance of wages for union labor in competing mines, and that the direction by the District Judge to return a verdict for the defendants other than the International Union was erroneous.

We affirm the judgment of the District Court and the Circuit Court of Appeals in favor of the International Union of United Mine Workers of America, and reverse that in favor of District No. 21 and the other local unions and the individual defendants and remand the cause as to them for a new trial.

Affirmed in part and reversed in part.

Note

1. Is the theory of liability in the Coronado case the same as in Loewe v. Lawlor and Duplex? Was a specific finding of intent to restrain interstate commerce required to be made in the latter cases? If not, why not?

2. Both Coronado and Loewe v. Lawlor were actions for treble damages under the Sherman Act. The other two remedies available under that Act, prior to the Clayton Act, were criminal prosecution and injunctive relief in proceedings *initiated by the Attorney General*. The Clayton Act altered the latter in a significant respect. As stated by Justice Pitney (supra p. 64) in Duplex, that Act gave "to *private parties* a right to relief by injunction in any court of the United States against threatened loss or damage by a violation of the anti-trust laws." (Emphasis added.) This opening of the federal courts to suits for injunctions by private parties, even in the absence of diversity jurisdiction, greatly facilitated what came to be called by disillusioned observers "government by injunction." For political reasons related to life-tenure of federal judges and their greater insulation than state courts from local pressures antagonistic to large-scale "foreign" corporate employers, the federal courts became a preferred forum for the seeking of injunctive relief.

While the substantive basis for liability under the antitrust statutes was the same whatever remedy was sought, the injunctive remedy carried with it a potential for abuse not similarly encountered in criminal prosecutions or in actions for treble damages. The materials immediately following are intended to focus upon the abuses peculiar to the labor injunction, particularly as manifested in the federal courts.

GREAT NORTHERN RY. v. BROSSEAU

District Court, North Dakota, 1923.
286 Fed. 414.

AMIDON, DISTRICT JUDGE. This is a suit * * * to restrain [defendants] from threats and acts of violence in connection with the strike of the railway shop crafts which was started on July 1, 1922. A temporary restraining order was issued, and has been continued in force after a full hearing until quite recently, when a preliminary injunction was issued. * * * During the three months the case has been pending, and the different proceedings have been taken, the court has been called upon to investigate the law applicable to such a case, and a few matters that I have learned are of sufficient importance to justify their statement.

Neither the restraining order nor the preliminary injunction prepared by counsel was signed by the court. During the 30 years that courts have been dealing with strikes by means of injunctions, these orders have steadily grown in length, complexity, and the vehemence of their rhetoric. They are full of the rich vocabulary of synonyms which is a part of our English language. They are also replete with superlative words and the superlative phrases of which the legal mind is fond. The result has been that such writs have steadily become more and more complex and prolix. * * * They ought to be so brief and plain that laymen can understand them. They ought to be framed in the fewest possible words. The order should not express the bias or violence of a party to such a controversy or his attorney. I therefore framed the orders in this case with these objects in view. The purpose ought to be to state the specific acts that are forbidden. It also helps to show where the line separating wrong from right conduct lies, to state what acts are not forbidden. So I attempted to do that in the orders that were issued. A copy of the restraining part of the injunction will be found in the margin.[1] The result has been that the strikers have been able to understand the orders, and have shown a keen desire to do so and obey them. * * *

The experience [gained in the hearings in this case has] convinced me that affidavits are an untrustworthy guide for judicial action. That is the case in all legal proceedings, but it is peculiarly true of litigation growing out of a strike, where feelings on both sides are necessarily wrought up, and the desire for victory is likely to obscure nice moral questions and poison the minds of men by prejudice. Many of the affidavits submitted on behalf of plaintiffs have been made by private detectives or guards. As a class they are overzealous, through their desire to prove to the detective bureaus that they are efficient, and to the railway company that they are indispensable. Speaking generally, such detectives are mostly drawn from a class of people in large cities which would cause little credence to be given to their statements in ordinary litigation. * * *

* * * I have required in all important matters the presence of the chief witnesses upon each side at the hearing. * * * A comparison of the picture produced by their testimony with that produced by their affidavits has proven the utter untrustworthiness of affidavits. * * *

The most serious complaint that can be made against injunctions, which have become so prominent a part of the law in dealing with strikes in the United States, is the fact that courts have become accustomed to decide the most important questions of fact, often involving the citizen's liberty, upon this wholly untrustworthy class of proof.

In England, the acts which American courts are accustomed to restrain have been made crimes in the Conspiracy Statute of 1875 and its amendments. There injunctions have completely ceased in the theater of strikes. The acts having been made criminal, any party who is guilty of doing them is promptly arrested, tried, and, if found guilty, punished. * * *

---

1. See note at end of case.

I have had occasion to make a careful study of section 20 of the Clayton Act * * * and section 2 of the English Trades Dispute Act of 1906. The reports of the judicial committee both of the House and the Senate state that the section of our statute referred to was copied from the English section. The form in which they are framed differs, but their legal effect is the same.

* * *

I am convinced that the American statute does not authorize strikers to go upon the property of the company without its consent for the purpose "of attending at any place" where new employés may be, "for the purpose of peacefully obtaining or communicating information, or peacefully persuading such new employés to abstain from working." That is the natural interpretation of the statute, and had been placed upon it before its adoption here. Slesser & Baker, "The Law of Trade Unions," p. 217.

The difference in the civil life habits of England and the United States results in widely different effects from the same statute in the two countries. In Great Britain strikers and the new employés are a part of the common life of the community. They mingle freely with one another. The opportunities for peaceful persuasion are a part of the daily intercourse. There the private armed detective is unknown. Nobody carries arms in England, but members of the army and navy; even policemen carry nothing but their sticks, and soldiers, in the rare cases in which they are called out to repress riots in connection with strikes, use nothing but their hand arms. In such a field the right of peaceful persuasion is natural and easy. It results sometimes in violent words, occasionally in violent acts with fists, and more rarely with bricks. The policemen, however, are quite equal to coping with such a situation. Guilty parties are promptly arrested, tried, and, if found guilty, promptly punished. The writ of injunction in strike cases has been unknown in England during the period when it has attained such universal use with us.

In the United States new workmen are recruited from fields remote from the strike. They are brought into the company's yards in cars. They sleep and eat on the ground, and are surrounded by a cordon of private detectives. This practice in no small degree nullifies the provisions of the Clayton Act * * *. There are no opportunities for peaceful persuasion. The new employés are schooled in the notion that if they leave the stockade they will be in imminent danger. The contrast between the situations in England and America presents an impressive example of how differently the same statute works in countries whose habits of life are different.

In American Steel Foundries Co. v. Tri-State Central Trades Council, 257 U.S. 184, 42 S.Ct. 72, 66 L.Ed. 189, the number of pickets at any single point was limited to one. The court, however, is careful to state that no mathematical formula was intended for the purpose of all cases. Each case must depend to some extent upon the local situation. The danger of intimidation and attack is not confined to aggressions by strikers. The impartial history of strikes teaches that there is as much danger to strikers on the picket line from private detectives and sometimes from new employés, as there is of the same kind of wrong on the part of strikers against new employés. My experience in the present strike clearly confirms that view. The strikers on the picket line are entitled to have enough present to shield

them against the temptation of their adversaries to resort to violent methods. They also need the same protection against trumped-up charges or
unfair evidence relative to any assaults that may occur on either side. At
the beginning of the present strike the pickets had large tents at important
points of ingress to the company's property, and were accustomed to assemble there, especially in the nighttime, in large numbers. I became convinced
from the evidence that such tents, or the assembling of large numbers at or
near the company's property, was a serious intimidation to workmen going
about the yards in the necessary performance of their duties. I therefore
required all such tents to be removed. The place for union men to meet for
conference or in any considerable numbers is at their union hall. I limited
the number of pickets at points of ingress and egress to three, and experience has justified that limitation as fair to both sides.

The Clayton Act, in both sections 17 and 20 * * *, uses the words
"irreparable injury," and declares that such injury is necessary to support
injunctive relief. What is the meaning of these words as used in the statute?
Every strike as its natural consequence causes irreparable injury to the
employer, and if the employment is quasi public, it causes the same kind of
injury to the public. That is the purpose of the strike. * * *. Notwithstanding this injury, Congress in express terms grants to employés the right
to strike and to inflict such injuries. The Clayton Act was passed in 1914.
Congress acted with a full knowledge of the disastrous consequences resulting from strikes, particularly in the case of coal mining and transportation.
* * *

Notwithstanding the legislative history of the statute, and its highly
remedial character, as indicated by its history and the reports of the
committees having it in charge, many lower federal courts have studiously
striven to disregard its plain language, as well as the actual intent of
Congress, as disclosed by the history of the statute. Some have held that all
the strikes cause irreparable injury, and therefore the employer is entitled to
an injunction to prevent such injury. Other courts have gone so far as to
hold that the entire statute was a trick by Congress to so frame the measure
that one part of it would nullify the other. Other courts have said there was
no such thing as peaceful picketing, and hence no such thing as peaceful
persuasion, and therefore the plain language of the statute must be disregarded by the court, and all picketing and all attempts by strikers to exercise
their rights of peaceful persuasion were to be restrained, and injunctions
have been accordingly issued. Other courts, notwithstanding the specific
language of the last clause of section 20 that the doing of the acts which it
permits should not be held to be in conflict with any federal law, have
restrained strikes upon the ground that they have violated the Sherman
Anti-Trust Law and statutes forbidding the obstruction of the United States
mails.

In my judgment, all such action by courts is a gross abuse of judicial
power, and a direct refusal on their part to obey a statute which was
intended to limit their powers. It may be that the statute is economically
and socially unwise, because of the vast injuries which strikes inflict upon
society. Those considerations, however, are for Congress and not for the
courts. * * *

It must result from the foregoing that the irreparable injury referred to in the Clayton Act is something other and different from the irreparable injury to which I have referred above, and which is the natural result of a strike, and the sanction which gives it force. The history of trade disputes shows that these words are intended to embrace direct injuries to new employés, or to the property of the employer, by acts of trespass or violence, and also obstruction of the employer in obtaining new employés by means of threats, abuse, or violence—in a word, conduct which prevents by means of violence or duress the employer from carrying on his business.

These are the only legitimate fields for injunctive relief, and to gather up the natural and inevitable consequences of the strike, and use them as the basis of injunctive relief, is simply to proceed in a mental circle. * * *

[Court's] Note

The restraining part of the injunction order is as follows:

"Ordered and adjudged that the defendants and all persons acting with them be and they are hereby enjoined and restrained as follows:

"1. From using threats or vulgar or abusive epithets or language towards plaintiff's employés, agents or officers, or towards persons about to become such.

"2. From injuring plaintiff's employés, agents or officers, or persons about to become such, or their families, or their property.

"3. From injuring any of plaintiff's property, personal or real, or any property or passengers in plaintiff's care, or being transported upon any of its lines.

"4. From trespassing upon plaintiff's property.

"5. From warning plaintiff's employés, agents or officers, or persons about to become such, or the families of either, that they will suffer or be likely to suffer any of the wrongs or injuries enjoined in this order, if they enter plaintiff's employment or continue therein.

"6. From aiding or advising any person to commit any of said wrongs or injuries.

"7. From going upon or near plaintiff's said properties, or the homes of plaintiff's employés, agents or officers, for the purpose of doing any of said wrongs or injuries:

"8. From having and keeping at or near any point of ingress or egress to or from plaintiff's property more than three pickets, all other defendants and persons acting with them being restrained and enjoined from being present, and from assembling or loitering at or about any of said points or at or near plaintiff's property. If other persons desire to confer with pickets, they must choose occasions when they are not acting as pickets.

"A small tent may be erected at or near any point at which such pickets are stationed to protect them from the weather while they are on duty; but there must not be present at any such tent at any single time any one but the pickets who are there on duty. It is to be used by them and not by others.

"The defendants and those acting with them are enjoined from erecting or maintaining at or near plaintiff's property any other tents than those permitted by this section. If any other tents have been heretofore erected, they must be promptly removed.

"9. From attempting to do any of the acts above forbidden.

"This order does not enjoin or restrain the defendants, or persons acting with them, from using towards plaintiff's employés, or persons about to become such, language of peaceable persuasion or entreaty, for the purpose of inducing them not to enter plaintiff's employment or to cease therefrom; nor does it restrain or enjoin the defendants or persons acting with them from peacefully imparting information to such employés of plaintiff or persons about to become such, for the purpose just specified; but this order is intended to and does enjoin and restrain the defendants and persons acting with them from doing any of the things hereinbefore forbidden in this order under the claim or pretense of using peaceful persuasion or entreaty, or peacefully imparting information. So long as the defendants and those acting with them confine themselves to a peaceful and orderly exercise of their rights specified in this section, the plaintiff, its officers, agents, employés and guards are enjoined from interfering with them, and particularly—

"1. From using towards them threatening or abusive language or epithets.

"2. From inflicting upon them any personal injuries or attempting to do so.

"3. The armed guards of plaintiff are enjoined specifically from drawing or exhibiting firearms or other dangerous weapons, for the purpose of intimidating such pickets, and from using firearms or other dangerous weapons at all except in the presence of imminent peril such as threatens very serious injury to the person of the party using such weapons, or others in the employ of the company, or to resist the imminent and immediate danger of the destruction of personal property or injury to engines or switches, or any other similar property that would imperil the public in using the company's railway, or the employés of plaintiff in the prosecution of its business, and on such occasions from using said firearms or other dangerous weapons when there is any other reasonable means of preventing the aforesaid wrongful acts.

"It is further ordered that a copy of this preliminary injunction shall be mailed to each of the defendants and to all persons known to be acting with them, at his present address, in so far as such address can reasonably be ascertained, and that ten copies of said order be posted in conspicuous public places in the vicinity of the roundhouse, shops, yards and other property of the Great Northern Railway Company, in each of the following places in North Dakota, namely, New Rockford, Devils Lake, Grand Forks, Minot and Williston, and that a copy of this preliminary injunction be also mailed to the principal officers and agents of the plaintiff, and each of the special guards employed by plaintiff, at the points above mentioned; that such mailing and posting be done by the United States marshal for the district of North Dakota.

"That a copy of this preliminary injunction may also be published in a newspaper published in the places above specified, which publication shall be attended to by said Great Northern Railway Company or its representative.

"It is further ordered, that any person who shall tear down, deface, destroy, or in any manner interfere with any of the copies of this preliminary injunction that shall be posted pursuant to this order, shall be held in contempt of this court, and shall be punished accordingly."

Note

The injunction issued by Judge Amidon restrained "the defendants and all persons acting with them" (supra p. 83). Language such as this, found in one form or another in all labor injunctions, raises important questions not specifically dealt with by Judge Amidon: (1) What persons are subject to contempt proceedings for failing to obey the injunction—only the parties named as defendants in the lawsuit, their agents also, others? (2) What kind of notice must the persons thus subject to the decree receive in order to be bound by it— personal service, actual notice, constructive notice? These questions are answered in the excerpt from Frankfurter and Greene which follows this Note.

The breadth of the answer given by the federal courts to the first question is interestingly demonstrated in Taliaferro v. United States, 290 Fed. 906 (4th Cir. 1923), where, under the following circumstances, a barber was held guilty of contempt of injunctions (of which he had actual notice) issued against striking railway unions and certain of their officers and members: "He was not a member of any of the unions named, and as he was a barber operating a shop of his own he had no direct material interest in the controversy. Many of his patrons were, however, out on the strike, and he was a warm sympathizer with it, as it goes without saying he had a perfect right to be. His shop in Clifton Forge was not far from one of the entrances to plaintiff's yards or shops and on a street habitually traversed by those working for it. Subsequent to the issue of the injunctions, a couple of the unionists brought to him a placard and asked him to display it. It had the words 'No Scabs Wanted in Here,' printed in letters sufficiently large to be readable at a distance of from 50 to 100 feet. He hung it up in his window facing the street ＊ ＊ ＊." 290 Fed. at 907.

FRANKFURTER AND GREENE, THE LABOR INJUNCTION
86–88, 123–26, 200–05 (1930).

[This book is recognized as the classic study of the labor injunction and its attendant abuses. The legislative reforms it proposed were enacted by Congress in 1932 as the Norris-LaGuardia Act.]

PERSONS BOUND BY INJUNCTIONS

＊ ＊ ＊ Injunction suits have been entitled by naming as defendants the union and its officers, or, less frequently, persons prominent in activities deemed illegal. But the parties defendant named in the moving papers by no means disclose the sway of injunctive relief in labor disputes ＊ ＊ ＊.

The federal courts have given the labor injunction its farthest reach of application. In the *Debs Case*, the famous "omnibus" injunction was issued against the defendants, "and all persons combining and conspiring with them and all other persons whomsoever".[25] ＊ ＊ ＊ When the phrasing of the Debs injunction was still warm, Mr. Dunbar, a conservative leader of the

25. In re Debs, Petitioner, 158 U.S. 564, 570 (1895).

Bar, protested against it: "If the course there followed can be supported, the principles of equity jurisprudence have received an important extension which may render 'government by injunction' more than a mere epithet." [27] Later decrees have followed and extended the early models, bringing within the area of potential contempt the conduct of all undefined persons who in the future might threaten or encourage or commit violation of the ambiguous schedule of forbidden acts. * * *

The ductile quality of phrase "all persons whomsoever" is now conventionally imparted, in one form or another, to federal labor injunctions. * * *

* * * The whole world is asked to pay heed. To what extent is it bound to do so? Parties to the suit, persons named and served, their agents and employees—of these there is no doubt in all jurisdictions. Injunctions against representatives of a class bind the class. And one who knowingly assists a person named in the injunction to violate it may be held in contempt. But this does not exhaust the range of responsibility. All who have knowledge of a decree must obey it.[162] Actual notice proven in any way is enough. Publicity is the only limit to the injunction's authority. As a consequence, the complainant uses every available device to spread knowledge of the decree. The injunction is printed, sometimes in all the languages prevalent in the community, distributed by deputy marshals, posted in conspicuous places throughout the city or county, published in newspapers of general circulation, and mailed to all possible offenders. * * * Given knowledge of the injunction, the tradesman who exhibited a notice "No Scabs Wanted in Here", and the newspaper publisher who characterized strike-breakers as "dirty scabs", though otherwise completely outside the area of contention, were held to be within the class of persons subject to attachment for contempt.

To the "standing injunction" of the criminal law [172] there is thus added another compendium of restrictions upon the freedom of speech and action of "all persons whomsoever". The imminent threat of irreparable harm to property, the basis of the chancellor's restraint upon the conduct of the person who actually so threatened, does service against all persons, indefinable and undefined, who might subsequently injure or threaten to injure the

---

27. Dunbar, Government by Injunction (1897) 13 L.Q.Rev. 347, 354. For similar criticisms of the early injunction orders, see Allen, Injunction and Organized Labor (1894) 28 Am. L.Rev. 828, where it was said of those injunctions that they are directed against "ten thousand strikers and all the world besides." (at 857.)

"To be obliged to wait until the injunction is violated to determine against whom it was issued ought to be enough to show that it is not an injunction at all, but in the nature of a police proclamation, putting the community in general under peril of contempt if the proclamation be disobeyed." Note in (1894) 8 Harv.L.Rev. at 228.

162. American Steel & Wire Co. v. Wire Drawers', etc., Unions, 90 Fed. 598 (N.D.Ohio, 1898), where the court said (at 604): "And it is

one of the features of an interlocutory injunction that it reaches all who are parties, whether they have been served with process of subpoena or not, whether they have appeared or not, whether they have answered or not; and it binds all who have notice of it, whether they are parties or not. It is old as the practice of injunctions that all having notice of it must obey it. If not parties to the suit, they aid or abet those who are, if the injunction be violated by those who know of it." * * *

172. "The Penal Law is a standing injunction against crime. * * * If the defendants are committing crime, the quick, summary, regular remedy is arrest and prosecution." Wood Mowing & Reaping M. Co. v. Toohey, 114 Misc. 185, 196 (N.Y., 1921).

congeries of interest protected as complainant's "property". A particular controversy between particular parties—which is the limited sphere of judicial power—is made the occasion for a code of conduct governing the whole community.[174]   *   *   *

CONCLUSIONS

*   *   * The history of the labor injunction in action puts some matters beyond question. In large part, dissatisfaction and resentment are caused, first, by the refusal of courts to recognize that breaches of the peace may be redressed through criminal prosecution and civil action for damages, and, second, by the expansion of a simple, judicial device to an enveloping code of prohibited conduct, absorbing, *en masse,* executive and police functions and affecting the livelihood, and even lives, of multitudes. Especially those zealous for the unimpaired prestige of our courts have observed how the administration of law by decrees which through vast and vague phrases surmount law, undermines the esteem of courts upon which our reign of law depends. Not government, but "government by injunction", characterized by the consequences of a criminal prosecution without its safeguards, has been challenged.

The restraining order and the preliminary injunction invoked in labor disputes reveal the most crucial points of legal maladjustment. Temporary injunctive relief without notice, or, if upon notice, relying upon dubious affidavits, serves the important function of staying defendant's conduct regardless of the ultimate justification of such restraint. The preliminary proceedings, in other words, make the issue of final relief a practical nullity. Undoubtedly, the law is here confronted with a very perplexing situation. Where the plaintiff on the surface presents a meritorious case, he should not be exposed to the peril of irreparable damage before the court can make available to him its slower, though much more scrutinizing, processes of fact-finding. This form of relief presents no difficulty when the temporary suspension of defendant's activities results in no very great damage to him, at least no damage that cannot be adequately compensated by money, security for which is provided by plaintiff's bond. In labor cases, however, complicating factors enter. The injunction cannot preserve the so-called *status quo;* the situation does not remain in equilibrium awaiting judgment upon full knowledge. The suspension of activities affects only the strikers; the employer resumes his efforts to defeat the strike, and resumes them free from the interdicted interferences. Moreover, the suspension of strike activities, even temporarily, may defeat the strike for practical purposes and foredoom its resumption, even if the injunction is later lifted. Choice is not between irreparable damage to one side and compensable damage to the other. The law's conundrum is which side should bear the risk of *unavoidable* irreparable damage. Improvident denial of the injunction may be

---

174. Again to quote from Mr. Dunbar: "Courts of equity, like courts of law, are established for the determination of controversies between individuals. The power to issue preliminary injunctions is incidental to the power of determining such controversies. The right to lay down general rules for the government of the community, to declare ex cathedra, in advance of any contentious proceedings in which the question arises, what may and what may not lawfully be done, to impose on the whole community a duty to refrain from doing a certain act, is in its nature a legislative right." Dunbar, Government by Injunction (1897) 13 L.Q.Rev. 347, 362.

irreparable to the complainant; improvident issue of the injunction may be irreparable to the defendant. For this situation the ordinary mechanics of the provisional injunction proceedings are plainly inadequate. Judicial error is too costly to either side of a labor dispute to permit perfunctory determination of the crucial issues; even in the first instance, it must be searching. The necessity of finding the facts quickly from sources vague, embittered and partisan, colored at the start by the passionate intensities of a labor controversy, calls at best for rare judicial qualities. It becomes an impossible assignment when judges rely solely upon the complaint and the affidavits of interested or professional witnesses, untested by the safeguards of common law trials—personal appearance of witnesses, confrontation and cross-examination.

But the treacherous difficulties presented by an application for an injunction are not confined to the ascertainment of fact; the legal doctrines that must be applied are even more illusory and ambiguous. Even where the rules of law in a particular jurisdiction can be stated, as we have tried to state them, with a show of precision and a definiteness of contour, the unknowns and the variables in the equation—intent, motive, malice, justification—make its application in a given case a discipline in clarity and detachment requiring time and anxious thought. With such issues of fact and of law, demanding insight into human behavior and nicety of juristic reasoning, we now confront a single judge to whom they are usually unfamiliar, and we ask him to decide forthwith, allowing him less opportunity for consideration than would be available if the question were one concerning the negotiability of a new form of commercial paper. We ease his difficulty and his conscience by telling him that his decision is only tentative.

Emphasis upon procedural safeguards in the use of the injunction must therefore rank first. Whatever differences there may be as to the particular stages of the procedure at which changes are to be made or as to the character of the changes, there should be no reasonable basis for opposing such correctives, once the unique elements that enter into labor litigation are fully recognized. * * *

But after all, procedural safeguards are not enough. Judges have to apply "the law"—the coercing will of society. As to labor law, the governing rules of conduct are essentially not legislative formulations; largely they are judge-made law. * * * Legislatures must decide whether such rules conform to prevailing conceptions of public policy or, if these demand a change of rules, the desirable extent of such change within constitutional limits. * * *

Judged by authoritative utterances, contemporary society rests upon certain assumptions: that social progress depends upon economic welfare; that our economic system is founded upon the doctrine of free competition, accepting for its gains the cost of its ravages; that large aggregations of capital are not inconsistent with the doctrine of free competition, but are, indeed, inevitable and socially desirable; that the individual workers must combine in order thereby to achieve the possibility of free competition with concentrated capital. The task of law, whether expressed by judicial decision or newly formulated by statute, is to accept or reject concretely the implications of these assumptions.

Recognition of the social utility and, indeed, of the necessity of trade unions implies acceptance of the economic and social pressure that can come from united action. Such acceptance does not solve all difficulties; it leaves open the most troublesome of questions—the questions of how far and when. The possible ramifications that the power of concerted action may take and the various uses to which it may be put raise bristling issues of policy, and, therefore, of law. Thus, the employees of a plant may call a strike to gain some immediate advantage such as higher wages, shorter hours, improved working conditions. Or, they may seek an end of less immediate benefit, such as the right of collective bargaining or complete unionization, in order to strengthen their resources in a future contest for the satisfaction of economic needs. Again, extension of its membership by a trade union may become a condition of retention of gains already won and a requisite of further gains in the betterment of industrial conditions. And so, a union imperilled by the fact that its employer, subject to union restrictions, may be unable to compete with non-union employers in the same or a related industry, may seek one of two ways to protect its standards: it may refuse to spend its labor upon the materials or products from such non-union plants; it may seek to unionize those plants by diverse appeals to the non-union employees or to the public. By picketing and by debate directed to non-union employees and by appeals to the world at large, it may bring new recruits within the orbit of trade unionism; it may accomplish its aim by more drastic measures, through the disciplinary devices of organized labor and through pressure upon the public not to patronize or deal with non-union shops for their products. Finally, a union may conceive the realization of its own aims, in themselves socially desirable, to be dependent upon association with workers in unrelated industries, and hence exert its powers of concerted action in their aid and, in turn, invite their help in its own struggles.

By some such analysis the issues involved in labor controversies must be pierced to their true meaning and cleared of the fog of incriminating terminology. Once we recognize that the right of combination by workers is in itself a corollary to the dogma of free competition, as a means of equalizing the factors that determine bargaining power, the consequences of making the power of union effective will be seen in truer perspective. Undoubtedly, hardships and even cruelties are involved in this phase, as in other aspects, of our competitive system. Wise statesmanship here enters to determine at precisely what points the cost of competition is too great. Primarily this is the task of legislatures. Only within very narrow limits is it the function of courts to apply their own notions of policy. And it is immaterial whether this is done by judges with the frank avowal that they also are organs of policy or under the subtler guise of enforcing constitutional coercions. To count the cost of union weapons is to count the cost of free competition in industrial controversy.   *   *   *

THE NORRIS–LAGUARDIA ACT OF 1932

As we have seen, from the founding of the Republic, American law was a frequent ally of employers in their contests with their employees. The criminal conspiracy doctrine, the illegal purpose (prima facie tort) doctrine, the unlawful means test, the antitrust laws, and, most important, the labor injunction—all of these contributed to what Chief Justice Taft once characterized in private correspondence as the effort "to prevent the Bolsheviki from getting control." [c]

The Great Depression, which followed the financial collapse of 1929, made evident the need for major social reform and provided the climate for reversal of policies long considered sacrosanct. The Norris-LaGuardia Act of 1932 was one of the earliest Congressional responses to this need. In practical effect, it took the federal courts, a favored forum of employers, out of the labor-regulating business. In so doing, it applied a kind of laissez-faire to labor relations. "No court of the United States," Section 1 of the Act declared, "shall have jurisdiction to issue any restraining order or temporary or permanent injunction in a case involving or growing out of a labor dispute, except in conformity with the provisions of this Act. * * *"

The framers of the Norris-LaGuardia Act, having before them the abortive efforts in the Clayton Act to place conditions upon the issuance of labor injunctions by the federal courts, were astute to leave no loopholes for judicial interpretation in this later effort. The starting point for an analysis of the structure of the Act is Section 13, which defines a "labor dispute" in language so sweeping and yet so specific as to preclude any Duplex-type escape from its reach. The next step in the logical progression of the Act is Section 4, which provides that, in any case involving or growing out of a "labor dispute," no order may be issued by a federal court restraining or enjoining any of the union activities meticulously defined in that section. Generally stated, the protected activities set forth in Section 4 encompass all of the pressure tactics which we have encountered in the cases thus far presented, except for conduct involving violence or fraud.

And even where violence or fraud is involved, and therefore the absolution of Section 4 unavailable, an order restraining or enjoining such conduct may be issued only after a hearing and the findings of fact specified in Section 7. The requisite findings must be based upon "the testimony of witnesses in open court (with opportunity for cross-examination)." Two of these findings are that "as to each item of relief granted greater injury will be inflicted upon complainant by the denial of relief than will be inflicted upon defendants by the granting of relief," and that "the public officers charged with the duty to protect complainant's property are unable or unwilling to furnish adequate protection." Moreover, the hearing required by Section 7 must be preceded by "due and personal notice * * * to all known persons against whom relief is sought." The sole exception to the requirement of such notice is contained in a proviso of Section 7, permitting the issuance of a temporary restraining order "effective for no longer than five days"; but even such an order is issuable only upon testimony under

c. Pringle, The Life and Times of William Howard Taft 967 (1939).

oath to the effect that "unless a temporary restraining order shall be issued without notice a substantial and irreparable injury to complainant's property will be unavoidable * * *." Furthermore, no temporary restraining order or temporary injunction may be issued except on condition that the complainant first file an adequate bond to "recompense those enjoined for any loss, expense, or damage caused by the improvident or erroneous issuance of such order or injunction," including court costs and attorney fees.

Section 9 of the Act declares that every restraining order or injunction which is granted, in cases of violence or fraud pursuant to Section 7, "shall include only a prohibition of such specific act or acts as may be expressly complained of in a bill of complaint * * * and as shall be expressly included" in the findings of fact required to be made by the court.

Section 11 guarantees any person charged with contempt of an order issued in accordance with Section 7 the right to trial by jury.

Section 3 declares the "yellow dog" contract to be "contrary to the public policy of the United States" and therefore unenforceable "in any court of the United States."

Section 6 provides that no labor organization or officer or member thereof "shall be held responsible or liable in any court of the United States for the unlawful acts of individual officers, members, or agents, except upon clear proof of actual participation in, or actual authorization of such acts, or of ratification of such acts after actual knowledge thereof."

Section 10 provides for expedited appeals in any case where a court of the United States has issued or denied a temporary injunction in a situation involving a labor dispute, giving such proceedings in the court of appeals "precedence over all other matters except older matters of the same character."

No commentary upon the Norris-LaGuardia Act and its impact would be complete without reference to what was probably the major social shortcoming of the "government by injunction" which preceded it, namely, that the granting of an injunction in a labor dispute dealt not at all with the grievances which caused the dispute, but rather was akin to tying the lid on a boiling kettle of water and stuffing a rag down its spout.

The forces which produced the Norris-LaGuardia Act in the federal jurisdiction also produced its counterparts in several of the states. These enactments, popularly called "little Norris-LaGuardia Acts," parallel the provisions of the federal Act in one degree or another and deny jurisdiction to the state courts, as the federal Act does to the "courts of the United States," to issue injunctions in cases arising out of labor disputes, except under carefully defined conditions.[d]

d. The state anti-injunction statutes, along with other state labor laws, are set forth, state by state, in volumes 4 and 4A of BNA (Bureau of National Affairs) Labor Relations Reporter and in CCH (Commerce Clearing House) Labor Law Reporter, State Laws. Both BNA and CCH are multi-volume loose-leaf services which are kept abreast of changes in the law.

UNITED STATES v. HUTCHESON

Supreme Court of the United States, 1941.
312 U.S. 219, 61 S.Ct. 463, 85 L.Ed. 788.

MR. JUSTICE FRANKFURTER delivered the opinion of the Court.

Whether the use of conventional, peaceful activities by a union in controversy with a rival union over certain jobs is a violation of the Sherman Law * * * is the question. It is sharply presented in this case because it arises in a criminal prosecution. Concededly an injunction either at the suit of the Government or of the employer could not issue.

Summarizing the long indictment, these are the facts. Anheuser-Busch, Inc., operating a large plant in St. Louis, contracted with Borsari Tank Corporation for the erection of an additional facility. The Gaylord Container Corporation, a lessee of adjacent property from Anheuser-Busch, made a similar contract for a new building with the Stocker Company. Anheuser-Busch obtained the materials for its brewing and other operations and sold its finished products largely through interstate shipments. The Gaylord Corporation was equally dependent on interstate commerce for marketing its goods, as were the construction companies for their building materials. Among the employees of Anheuser-Busch were members of the United Brotherhood of Carpenters and Joiners of America and of the International Association of Machinists. The conflicting claims of these two organizations, affiliated with the American Federation of Labor, in regard to the erection and dismantling of machinery had long been a source of controversy between them. Anheuser-Busch had had agreements with both organizations whereby the Machinists were given the disputed jobs and the Carpenters agreed to submit all disputes to arbitration. But in 1939 the president of the Carpenters, their general representative, and two officials of the Carpenters' local organization, the four men under indictment, stood on the claims of the Carpenters for the jobs. Rejection by the employer of the Carpenters' demand and the refusal of the latter to submit to arbitration were followed by a strike of the Carpenters, called by the defendants against Anheuser-Busch and the construction companies, a picketing of Anheuser-Busch and its tenant, and a request through circular letters and the official publication of the Carpenters that union members and their friends refrain from buying Anheuser-Busch beer.[e]

e. Additional facts set forth in the indictment are the following:

"* * * Anheuser-Busch, Inc., had in its employ in its brewery and manufacturing plant in the City of St. Louis * * * approximately two so-called millwrights, approximately sixteen maintenance carpenters, and approximately sixty cabinet-makers, all of whom were members of United Brotherhood of Carpenters and Joiners of America * * * ; and also approximately eighty machinists, all of whom were members of International Association of Machinists * * *." Record, p. 6.

The demand of the defendants upon Anheuser-Busch which produced the instant labor dispute was that Anheuser-Busch "employ millwrights who were members of United Brotherhood of Carpenters and Joiners of America, instead of machinists, to perform * * * the work of erecting, assembling, installing, and setting machinery in the St. Louis brewery and manufacturing plant of Anheuser-Busch, Inc." Id. at 7. In other words, the defendants were demanding that machinists who were members of the IAM be replaced by millwrights who were members of the Carpenters Union.

"Throughout the formation and execution of their * * * combination and conspiracy neither the defendants * * * nor their coconspirators [other officials of the

These activities on behalf of the Carpenters formed the charge of the indictment as a criminal combination and conspiracy in violation of the Sherman Law. Demurrers denying that what was charged constituted a violation of the laws of the United States were sustained, 32 F.Supp. 600, and the case came here under the Criminal Appeals Act. * * *

In order to determine whether an indictment charges an offense against the United States, designation by the pleader of the statute under which he purported to lay the charge is immaterial. He may have conceived the charge under one statute which would not sustain the indictment but it may nevertheless come within the terms of another statute. See Williams v. United States, 168 U.S. 382. On the other hand, an indictment may validly satisfy the statute under which the pleader proceeded, but other statutes not referred to by him may draw the sting of criminality from the allegations. Here we must consider not merely the Sherman Law but the related enactments which entered into the decision of the district court.

* * * The controversies engendered by application [of the Sherman Law] to trade union activities and the efforts to secure legislative relief from its consequences are familiar history. The Clayton Act of 1914 was the result. * * * Section 20 of the Act * * * withdrew from the general interdict of the Sherman Law specifically enumerated practices of labor unions by prohibiting injunctions against them—since the use of the injunction had been the major source of dissatisfaction—and also relieved such practices of all illegal taint by the catch-all provision, "nor shall any of the acts specified in this paragraph be considered or held to be violations of any law of the United States." The Clayton Act gave rise to new litigation and to renewed controversy in and out of Congress regarding the status of trade unions. By the generality of its terms the Sherman Law had necessarily compelled the courts to work out its meaning from case to case. It was widely believed that into the Clayton Act courts read the very beliefs which that Act was designed to remove. Specifically the courts restricted the scope of § 20 to trade union activities directed against an employer by his own employees. Duplex Co. v. Deering, * * *. Such a view it was urged, both by powerful judicial dissents and informed lay opinion, misconceived the area of economic conflict that had best be left to economic forces and the pressure of public opinion and not subjected to the judgment of courts. * * * Agitation again led to legislation and in 1932 Congress wrote the Norris-LaGuardia Act. * * *

Carpenters Union] were employees of Anheuser-Busch, Inc.; and no dispute existed between Anheuser-Busch, Inc. and the millwrights, carpenters, and cabinetmakers in its employ concerning the terms and conditions of their employment * * *." Id. at 8.

"The indictment alleges that defendants picketed or caused to be picketed the premises of Anheuser-Busch, Inc., and the premises of its tenant, Gaylord Container Corporation, the latter adjoining the premises of Anheuser-Busch, Inc.; that defendants refused to allow their members to be employed by Borsari Tank Corporation of America, which was about to construct a tank building for Anheuser-Busch, Inc.; that defendants refused to allow their members to be employed by L.O. Stocker Company, which had a contract to build an office building for Gaylord Container Company; and that defendants distributed circulars and letters and caused notices to be printed throughout the country in 'The Carpenter', the official publication of defendants' union, denouncing Anheuser-Busch, Inc., as unfair to organized labor and calling upon all union members and friends of organized labor to refrain from purchasing and drinking beer brewed by that company." United States v. Hutcheson, 32 F.Supp. 600, 601 (E.D.Mo. 1940).

The Norris-LaGuardia Act removed the fetters upon trade union activities, which according to judicial construction § 20 of the Clayton Act had left untouched, by still further narrowing the circumstances under which the federal courts could grant injunctions in labor disputes. More especially, the Act explicitly formulated the "public policy of the United States" in regard to the industrial conflict, and by its light established that the allowable area of union activity was not to be restricted, as it had been in the *Duplex* case, to an immediate employer-employee relation. Therefore, whether trade union conduct constitutes a violation of the Sherman Law is to be determined only by reading the Sherman Law and § 20 of the Clayton Act and the Norris-LaGuardia Act as a harmonizing text of outlawry of labor conduct.

Were, then, the acts charged against the defendants prohibited, or permitted, by these three interlacing statutes? If the facts laid in the indictment come within the conduct enumerated in § 20 of the Clayton Act they do not constitute a crime within the general terms of the Sherman Law because of the explicit command of that section that such conduct shall not be "considered or held to be violations of any law of the United States." So long as a union acts in its self-interest and does not combine with non-labor groups,[3] the licit and the illicit under § 20 are not to be distinguished by any judgment regarding the wisdom or unwisdom, the rightness or wrongness, the selfishness or unselfishness of the end of which the particular union activities are the means. * * *

It is at once apparent that the acts with which the defendants are charged are the kind of acts protected by § 20 of the Clayton Act. The refusal of the Carpenters to work for Anheuser-Busch or on construction work being done for it and its adjoining tenant, and the peaceful attempt to get members of other unions similarly to refuse to work, are plainly within the free scope accorded to workers by § 20 for "terminating any relation of employment," or "ceasing to perform any work or labor," or "recommending, advising, or persuading others by peaceful means so to do." The picketing of Anheuser-Busch premises with signs to indicate that Anheuser-Busch was unfair to organized labor, a familiar practice in these situations, comes within the language "attending at any place where any such person or persons may lawfully be, for the purpose of peacefully obtaining or communicating information, or from peacefully persuading any person to work or to abstain from working." Finally, the recommendation to union members and their friends not to buy or use the product of Anheuser-Busch is explicitly covered by "ceasing to patronize * * * any party to such dispute, or from recommending, advising, or persuading others by peaceful and lawful means so to do."

Clearly, then, the facts here charged constitute lawful conduct under the Clayton Act unless the defendants cannot invoke that Act because outsiders to the immediate dispute also shared in the conduct. But we need not determine whether the conduct is legal within the restrictions which Duplex Co. v. Deering gave to the immunities of § 20 of the Clayton Act. Congress in the Norris-LaGuardia Act has expressed the public policy of the United

---

3. Cf. United States v. Brims, 272 U.S. 549, involving a conspiracy of mill work manufac- turers, building contractors and union carpenters.

States and defined its conception of a "labor dispute" in terms that no longer leave room for doubt. * * * This was done, as we recently said, in order to "obviate the results of the judicial construction" theretofore given the Clayton Act. New Negro Alliance v. Sanitary Grocery Co., 303 U.S. 552, 562; see Apex Hosiery Co. v. Leader, 310 U.S. 469, 507, n. 26. Such a dispute, § 13(c) provides, "includes any controversy concerning terms or conditions of employment, or concerning the association or representation of persons in negotiating, fixing, maintaining, changing, or seeking to arrange terms or conditions of employment, regardless of whether or not the disputants stand in the proximate relation of employer and employee." And under § 13(b) a person is "participating or interested in a labor dispute" if he "is engaged in the same industry, trade, craft, or occupation, in which such dispute occurs, or has a direct or indirect interest therein, or is a member, officer, or agent of any association composed in whole or in part of employers or employees engaged in such industry, trade, craft, or occupation."

To be sure, Congress expressed this national policy and determined the bounds of a labor dispute in an act explicitly dealing with the further withdrawal of injunctions in labor controversies. But to argue, as it was urged before us, that the *Duplex* case still governs for purposes of a criminal prosecution is to say that that which on the equity side of the court is allowable conduct may in a criminal proceeding become the road to prison. It would be strange indeed that although neither the Government nor Anheuser-Busch could have sought an injunction against the acts here challenged, the elaborate efforts to permit such conduct failed to prevent criminal liability punishable with imprisonment and heavy fines. That is not the way to read the will of Congress, particularly when expressed by a statute which, as we have already indicated, is practically and historically one of a series of enactments touching one of the most sensitive national problems. Such legislation must not be read in a spirit of mutilating narrowness. * * *

The relation of the Norris-LaGuardia Act to the Clayton Act is not that of a tightly drawn amendment to a technically phrased tax provision. The underlying aim of the Norris-LaGuardia Act was to restore the broad purpose which Congress thought it had formulated in the Clayton Act but which was frustrated, so Congress believed, by unduly restrictive judicial construction. This was authoritatively stated by the House Committee on the Judiciary. "The purpose of the bill is to protect the rights of labor in the same manner the Congress intended when it enacted the Clayton Act * * * which act, by reason of its construction and application by the Federal courts, is ineffectual to accomplish the congressional intent." H.Rep. No. 669, 72d Congress, 1st Session, p. 3. The Norris-LaGuardia Act was a disapproval of Duplex Printing Press Co. v. Deering, * * * and Bedford Cut Stone Co. v. Journeymen Stone Cutters' Assn., 274 U.S. 37, as the authoritative interpretation of § 20 of the Clayton Act, for Congress now placed its own meaning upon that section. The Norris-LaGuardia Act reasserted the original purpose of the Clayton Act by infusing into it the immunized trade union activities as redefined by the later Act. In this light § 20 removes all such allowable conduct from the taint of being a "violation of any law of the United States" including the Sherman Law.

There is no profit in discussing those cases under the Clayton Act which were decided before the courts were furnished the light shed by the Norris-LaGuardia Act on the nature of the industrial conflict. And since the facts in the indictment are made lawful by the Clayton Act in so far as "any law of the United States" is concerned, it would be idle to consider the Sherman Law apart from the Clayton Act as interpreted by Congress. * * * It was precisely in order to minimize the difficulties to which the general language of the Sherman Law in its application to workers had given rise, that Congress cut through all the tangled verbalisms and enumerated concretely the types of activities which had become familiar incidents of union procedure.

Affirmed.

MR. JUSTICE MURPHY took no part in the disposition of this case.

MR. JUSTICE STONE, concurring.

As I think it clear that the indictment fails to charge an offense under the Sherman Act, as it has been interpreted and applied by this Court, I find no occasion to consider the impact of the Norris-LaGuardia Act on the definition of participants in a labor dispute in the Clayton Act, as construed by this Court in Duplex Printing Press Co. v. Deering, * * * an application of the Norris-LaGuardia Act which is not free from doubt and which some of my brethren sharply challenge. * * *

[The following is a distillation of Justice Stone's reasoning in reaching the conclusion that no Sherman Act offense had been charged: There were two varieties of boycott alleged. The first was a labor boycott, the second a consumption boycott. As to the first, he concluded that the decision of a year earlier in Apex Hosiery Co. v. Leader, 310 U.S. 469, 60 S.Ct. 982, 84 L.Ed. 1311, 128 A.L.R. 1044 (1940) (opinion by Stone, discussed infra p. 97), rendered the strike by the employees of Anheuser-Busch and the supportive picketing mere "local" activity; the refusal to work for the two construction companies and the picketing of the premises of Anheuser-Busch's tenant, the Gaylord Container Corporation, did not make the activity any less "local." "If," Justice Stone observed, "the counts of the indictment which we are now considering make out an offense, then every local strike aimed at closing a shop whose products or supplies move in interstate commerce is, without more, a violation of the Sherman Act." 312 U.S. at 241, 61 S.Ct. at 470.

[As for the consumption boycott, Justice Stone "thought that, since the strike against Anheuser-Busch was by its employees and there is no intimation that there is any strike against the distributors of the beer, that the strike was a labor dispute between employer and employees within the labor provisions of the Clayton Act as they were construed in Duplex Printing Press Co. v. Deering * * *" In such a situation, he said, "§ 20, * * * makes lawful the action of any person 'ceasing to patronize * * * any party to such dispute' or 'recommending, advising, or persuading others by peaceful [and lawful] means so to do.'" 312 U.S. at 242, 61 S.Ct. at 471. He further asserted that "publication, unaccompanied by violence, of a notice that the employer is unfair to organized labor and requesting the public not to patronize him is an exercise of the right of free speech guaranteed by the First Amendment which cannot be made unlawful by act of Congress." 312 U.S. at 243, 61 S.Ct. at 471.]

MR. JUSTICE ROBERTS, dissenting.

I am of opinion that the judgment should be reversed. * * *

Without detailing the allegations of the indictment, it is sufficient to say that they undeniably charge a secondary boycott, affecting interstate commerce.

This court, and many state tribunals, over a long period of years, have held such a secondary boycott illegal. * * *

By a process of construction never, as I think, heretofore indulged by this court, it is now found that, because Congress forbade the issuing of injunctions to restrain certain conduct, it intended to repeal the provisions of the Sherman Act authorizing actions at law and criminal prosecutions for the commission of torts and crimes defined by the anti-trust laws. * * * I venture to say that no court has ever undertaken so radically to legislate where Congress has refused so to do.

The construction of the act now adopted is the more clearly inadmissible when we remember that the scope of proposed amendments and repeals of the anti-trust laws in respect of labor organizations has been the subject of constant controversy and consideration in Congress. In the light of this history, to attribute to Congress an intent to repeal legislation which has had a definite and well understood scope and effect for decades past, by resurrecting a rejected construction of the Clayton Act and extending a policy strictly limited by the Congress itself in the Norris-LaGuardia Act, seems to me a usurpation by the courts of the function of the Congress not only novel but fraught, as well, with the most serious dangers to our constitutional system of division of powers.

THE CHIEF JUSTICE joins in this opinion.

Note

1. Were the defendants' activities protected by Section 20 of the Clayton Act as interpreted in Duplex?

2. Was Justice Roberts' outrage over the Court's interpretation of the Norris-LaGuardia Act well-founded?

> "[T]he proposed bill ['Proposed Law Governing Labor Injunctions in Federal Courts,' enacted, with minor changes, as the Norris-LaGuardia Act] * * * explicitly applies only to the authority of United States courts 'to issue any restraining order or injunction.' All other remedies in federal courts and all remedies in state courts remain available." Frankfurter and Greene, The Labor Injunction 220, 279 (1930).

For a scathing commentary on Justice Frankfurter's opinion, see Gregory, The New Sherman-Clayton-Norris-LaGuardia Act, 8 U.Chi.L.Rev. 503 (1941).

3. Some critics of the breadth of the exemption from the antitrust laws accorded organized labor in the Hutcheson case have argued for the narrower exemption adopted by the Court a year before in APEX HOSIERY CO. v. LEADER, 310 U.S. 469, 60 S.Ct. 982, 84 L.Ed. 1311, 128 A.L.R. 1044 (1940). See, e.g., Gregory, Labor and the Law 255–279 (2d rev. ed. 1961). In Apex, members of a labor union, intent upon unionizing a hosiery factory in Philadelphia, forcibly took possession of the plant and held it during a protracted "sit-down" strike accompanied by much violence and destruction of property. The employer

sued for treble damages under the Sherman Act, prevailing to the tune of over $700,000 in the trial court. The Supreme Court, Justice Stone writing, held that the defendants had not violated the Sherman Act, despite the fact that they had clearly prevented the production and shipment of a substantial volume of hosiery destined for markets in other states. The basis for the Court's decision was that the Sherman Act reached only conduct which constituted a "restraint upon commercial competition in the [interstate] marketing of goods or services," i.e., simply put, efforts to control market prices. An *interference* with the production or shipment of a commodity in interstate commerce was not a "restraint upon commercial competition" unless its purpose was to control the price of the commodity. (For example, a conspiracy to derail and rob a train laden with goods for interstate markets would not, of itself, constitute a violation of the Sherman Act.)

The only respect in which the defendants in Apex could be said to have sought to restrain "commercial competition in the [interstate] marketing of goods or services" was that they had combined together to establish a monopoly on the supply of labor to a Philadelphia manufacturer of hosiery destined for out-of-state markets. This type of combination, the Court said, had been expressly exempted from the reach of the antitrust laws by Section 6 of the Clayton Act, which declares that "the labor of a human being is not a commodity or article of commerce * * * nor shall [labor] organizations, or the members thereof, be held or construed to be illegal combinations or conspiracies in restraint of trade. * * *" (In other words, the marketing to an employer by his employees of their *labor* is not the marketing of a "commodity or article of commerce"—i.e., is not the "marketing of goods or services." "Labor" in this sense differs from "services" in that *wages* are paid for the former whereas a price is paid for the latter. For example, a plumbing firm which employs a hundred plumbers would be engaged in marketing the "services" of those plumbers to the firm's customers; each of the employee plumbers who actually performed those "services" for the customers would, on the contrary, *not* be engaged in the marketing of "services" to those customers, but rather in the sale of "labor" to the plumbing firm.) The Court further observed in Apex that "an elimination of price competition based on differences in labor standards is the objective of any national labor organization. But this effect on competition has not been considered to be the kind of curtailment of price competition prohibited by the Sherman Act." 310 U.S. at 503–04, 60 S.Ct. at 997–98.

If the Court had said only the above *and* overruled Loewe v. Lawlor, Duplex, Second Coronado, and like cases, the meaning of Apex would have been reasonably clear. Instead, Justice Stone sought to distinguish those cases on the following grounds: Loewe v. Lawlor and Duplex entailed secondary boycotts against goods produced in one state and sold in other states; the boycotts were therefore necessarily directed at, and intended to restrain, the interstate marketing of, in the one case, hats, and, in the other, printing presses. "[T]he restraint itself, in contrast to the interference with shipments caused by a local factory strike * * * was held to offend against the Sherman Act because it * * * was aimed at suppression of competition with union made goods in the interstate market." 310 U.S. at 507, 60 S.Ct. at 999. Coronado, on the other hand, involved a local strike, as in Apex, which strike constituted, at most, an *indirect* restraint on the interstate marketing of coal. In such a case, specific proof of the subjective intent to restrain (suppress competition in) the interstate marketing of coal was held to be necessary; if specific evidence of such an *actual* intent were not required, *every* strike (e.g., for higher wages) against an employer producing goods for interstate commerce would violate the Sherman Act, since it would necessarily suppress competition in the interstate marketing of those goods to the extent that the strike reduced the supply of the goods. In Apex, the specific finding of this necessary intent was lacking; the trial court had permitted the jury to *infer* the intent to restrain (suppress competition in) the interstate marketing of hosiery on the basis that such a restraint was "the natural and probable consequence of [the defendants'] acts." In short, Justice Stone seemed (his opinion is not a model of clarity) to categorize the secondary boycott cases as *direct* restraints upon interstate commerce and local strikes as *indirect* restraints upon interstate commerce; in the first category, specific evidence of an intention to restrain (suppress competition in) such commerce was not necessary, while in the second it was.

The difficulty with Justice Stone's analysis, apart from its inscrutability, is that it is highly artificial. The union actors in *all* of the foregoing cases had precisely the same purpose, namely to eliminate "price competition based on differences in labor standards." And, as we have seen, Justice Stone expressly stated in his opinion that *this* was *not* "the kind of curtailment of price competition prohibited by the Sherman Act"!

The Apex case demonstrates in tortuous fashion the problems inherent in seeking to regulate traditional labor union activities via the Sherman Act. Treating *all* such activities which restrain interstate commerce by interfering with it as unlawful would be simple in theory, but dangerous—indeed impossible—in practice. But drawing the line between those activities which, though interfering with interstate commerce, do not "restrain" it, within the meaning of the Act, and those which do is a task of such complexity and sensitivity as almost to defy accomplishment by means as simplistic as Section 1 of the Sherman Act. Analysis of the Apex opinion may thus demonstrate the reason Justice Frankfurter was able to persuade a majority of the Court to subscribe to his opinion in Hutcheson, however peculiar it was, whereas Justice Stone, riding the old Apex horse, was not. The former view, though perhaps hard to swallow, rested easy on the judicial stomach once it had been downed; the latter promised continuing indigestion.

The Hutcheson decision resulted in a moratorium on the application of the antitrust laws to labor "so long as a union acts in its self-interest and does not combine with non-labor groups," as Justice Frankfurter put it. But this pronouncement harbored the seed of further entanglement of labor in the antitrust toils. An account of this later episode in the antitrust drama must be postponed, however, until a new and leading character has been introduced. That character is the National Labor Relations Act. The post-Hutcheson application of the antitrust laws to organized labor entails the effort to reconcile an old antitrust policy with a new labor relations policy. Since the latter is premised upon collective bargaining, and since in collective bargaining a union necessarily acts both "in its self-interest" *and* in combination "with non-labor groups"—But we mustn't give the plot away! [f]

f. The story is resumed infra, Chapter 9, Section B, p. 994.

Chapter 2

PATERNAL PROTECTION: OF LAW, COLLECTIVE BARGAINING, AND SOCIAL THERAPY

INTRODUCTORY NOTE

Workers waged a long struggle to break through barriers, erected by the law, to achieve what amounted to the right of freedom of competition in a competitive economy. Eventually, a kind of laissez-faire policy evolved, as we have seen, according to organized labor a relatively large freedom to engage in efforts at self-help, albeit necessarily confined within the channels of civilized behavior.

The next step in the evolution of the law in seeking to engineer the resolution of conflicts between capital and labor was the imposition of duties on employers, thus affording affirmative protection to employees in their efforts to organize, gain recognition, and bargain collectively over the terms and conditions of their employment. This development might be called the advent of paternal protection. It was presaged by certain policies established by President Wilson in the handling of labor disputes during World War I. A National War Labor Board and a National War Labor Policies Board were created to deal with labor disputes affecting the war effort. These agencies adopted, among others, the following principles: "Full recognition of the right of both employers and workers to organize in their trade unions and associations respectively and to bargain collectively through their chosen representatives. This right was in no way to be denied, abridged, or interfered with by either side, and all discrimination for legitimate activities with such organizations was forbidden." [a] The Boards went out of existence shortly after the war, and their policies in the regulation of labor relations were not carried over into peace time. The wartime experiment had little immediate influence upon subsequent developments in the handling of labor disputes. It did, however, provide a pattern for future reference. [b]

a. Watkins, Labor Problems and Labor Administration in the United States during the World War, University of Illinois, Studies in the Social Sciences, Vol. VIII, No. 3, p. 165 (1919).

b. See, generally, Witte, The Government in Labor Disputes 246–251 (1932).

The statutory adoption of the principle of paternal protection as a national labor policy first occurred in the railroad industry. There were several reasons for this priority. That industry was the first major national industry to develop in the United States, and labor disputes of a crippling magnitude were first encountered there. The large corporate structures necessary to finance and operate railroads, and the vast aggregation of workers required to construct, maintain, and operate them provided the environment for unionization. That environment included the bureaucracy of management necessary to administer such a large enterprise, the consequent gulf between employer and employee, the relative wealth of the industry and resultant ability to pay, and the boom-and-bust proclivity of the economy which periodically produced panics adversely affecting job security, wage rates, and other work standards. See, e.g., Secor v. Toledo, P. & W.R. Co., supra p. 23 and the Nelles article following it, supra p. 26.

Another reason for the pioneering role of the railroad industry in the development of national labor policy inheres in the Federal Constitution. That industry was the prime candidate for regulation under the Commerce Clause. The most conservative of judges with respect to the scope of congressional power could hardly deny that an interstate railroad was engaged in interstate commerce. If the Commerce Clause had any scope at all in labor matters, it began here.[c]

The materials in Sections A and B below, on the Railway Labor Act of 1926 and the Wagner Act of 1935, are intended to achieve three purposes. The first is to continue the story of the response of the law to the conflicts involved in labor relations—to establish, more specifically, the mood of the next epoch of development. The second purpose is to provide a preliminary overview of the two statutory schemes, an orientation as to their structures. The third purpose is to indicate some of the more important problems which the policy of paternal protection itself engendered. Such is the growth of the law—problems produce solutions which in turn produce new problems.

A. THE RAILWAY LABOR ACT OF 1926

The Railway Labor Act of 1926 had forebears going back as far as the Arbitration Act of 1888,[a] all entailing efforts by Congress to deal with

---

c. But see Adair v. United States, 208 U.S. 161, 28 S.Ct. 277, 52 L.Ed. 436, 13 Ann.Cas. 764 (1908), in which a divided Court held, *inter alia,* that Congress lacked power under the Commerce Clause to prohibit interstate railroads from discriminating against employees because of union membership. The Court asked: "[W]hat possible legal or logical connection is there between an employee's membership in a labor organization and the carrying on of interstate commerce?" Justice McKenna, dissenting, observed caustically: "A provision of law which will prevent, or tend to prevent, the stoppage of every wheel in every car of an entire railroad system, certainly has as direct influence on interstate commerce as the way in which one car may be coupled to another, or the rule of liability for personal injuries to an employee"—the latter two subjects being admittedly within the power of Congress to regulate.

The limitation which the decision in Adair sought to impose on the Commerce Clause with regard to the regulation of labor relations was so incredible in a nation heavily dependent upon rail carriers that it was never again given credence by the Supreme Court. Adair was never even granted a decent burial; it was simply ignored to death. The alternative due process ground for the Adair decision was relied upon in Coppage v. Kansas, supra p. 50, but cryptically put to rest in Texas & N.O.R. Co. v. Brotherhood of Railway & S.S. Clerks, infra p. 110. See Phelps Dodge Corp. v. NLRB, 313 U.S. 177, 61 S.Ct. 845, 85 L.Ed. 1271 (1941).

a. 25 Stat. 501.

recurrent railway labor crises.[b] The Act of 1888 provided for voluntary arbitration and, where necessary, compulsory "investigation," the latter involving what would presently be called "fact finding." The law was ineffective. The only proceeding initiated under it was the product of the Pullman Strike of 1894, which occasioned the appointment of a presidential commission to report on that dispute. The report of that commission is one of the classic documents of American industrial history.[c] The recommendations made by the commission resulted in the passage of the Erdman Act of 1898,[d] which provided for mediation and voluntary arbitration of disputes. (For a discussion of other aspects of the Erdman Act, see Adair v. United States, cited and discussed in Coppage v. Kansas, supra p. 50). The Erdman Act was also ineffective for several years of its existence, largely because the carriers were opposed to intervention. But as the unions became more powerful the situation changed, and from 1906 to 1913 the machinery of the act was resorted to with such success that over sixty railroad disputes were settled without one serious interruption of rail service due to strikes. Problems developed, however, because of the burden which the act cast upon the statutorily designated part-time mediators (until 1911, the Chairman of the Interstate Commerce Commission and the Commissioner of Labor; after 1911, any member of the ICC or of the Commerce Court designated by the President). The Newlands Act of 1913[e] sought to remedy this defect by creating a Board of Mediation and Conciliation consisting of four full-time members. This act worked satisfactorily until 1916, when a nation-wide railroad strike on the issue of the eight-hour day was averted by the hurried passage of the Adamson Act,[f] which in effect granted the employees' demands.

On the eve of America's entrance into World War I, Congress empowered President Wilson to take over the operation of the railroads. He did so in December 1917. For the short period the railroads were under government operation, liberal labor policies were pursued. Upon the return of the railroads to private ownership in April 1920, further problems arose. The Congressional response to these problems was the Transportation Act of 1920.[g] The inadequacies of that Act in turn produced the Railway Labor Act of 1926[h] and the amendment thereof in 1934.[i]

These three acts and the problems with which they dealt are the subject matter of the next two cases. Before submerging in those cases, however, the reader may profit from a cursory commentary upon the structure of the Railway Labor Act, distinguishing it from the Wagner Act of 1935 (National Labor Relations Act). (The structure of the latter Act, as it has evolved, will be examined in detail in the remaining pages of this casebook; the Railway Labor Act, on the other hand, will receive little further attention beyond the Railway Clerks and the Virginian Railway cases.)

b. For a fuller treatment of the developments outlined in this introductory section, see Millis and Montgomery, Organized Labor 730–48 (1945), and Witte, The Government in Labor Disputes 238–44 (1932).

c. U.S. Strike Commission, Report on the Chicago Strike of June–July, 1894 (1895).

d. 30 Stat. 424.

e. 38 Stat. 103.

f. 39 Stat. 721.

g. 41 Stat. 456.

h. 44 Stat. 577.

i. 48 Stat. 1185.

STRUCTURE OF THE RAILWAY LABOR ACT

The Railway Labor Act regulates collective bargaining in the railroad industry and, since 1936, in the airline industry as well (Title II, Sections 201–207). The policies and the procedures of the Act are administered by two bodies: the National Mediation Board and the National Railroad Adjustment Board.

The Mediation Board is "composed of three members appointed by the President, by and with the advice and consent of the Senate, not more than two of whom shall be of the same political party" (Section 4, First). The Mediation Board (as its name connotes) deals with disputes arising in the effort to negotiate collective bargaining agreements (Section 5, First), so-called "major disputes." (The Mediation Board also resolves disputes as to who shall be the collective bargaining representatives of employees (Section 2, Ninth).) In the event of an impasse in collective bargaining, the Board first seeks to mediate a resolution. If unsuccessful in such effort, the Board then seeks to induce the parties to submit their controversy to arbitration, and if the parties so agree, the arbitration award is final and binding (Section 9, Second). If, on the contrary, the parties refuse to submit the bargaining dispute to arbitration and it is not otherwise resolved, the parties are free to resort to the standard economic pressures of collective bargaining, having exhausted the Act's conditions precedent to the use of self-help. (One of these conditions precedent is that such self-help—e.g., a strike—must be delayed until 30 days after notification by the Mediation Board to the parties "in writing that its mediatory efforts have failed" (Section 5, First).) Where, however, the bargaining dispute is deemed by the Mediation Board to "threaten substantially to interrupt interstate commerce to a degree such as to deprive any section of the country of essential transportation service," the Board is required to notify the President, who may then invoke the emergency provisions of the Act: appoint an Emergency Board to investigate and report concerning the dispute, during which procedure a 60-day moratorium on work stoppages or changes in terms or conditions of employment is in effect (Section 10).

The National Railroad Adjustment Board (or in the case of airlines, the National Air Transport Adjustment Board—Section 205) deals, on the contrary, with "minor disputes," i.e., disputes as to the interpretation and application of existing collective bargaining agreements (Section 3). The Adjustment Board is made up of equal numbers of representatives of the carriers and labor organizations involved and functions typically through subsidiary divisions of equal-membership bodies. If any such body deadlocks, the impasse is resolved through the selection by mutual agreement of a neutral person to sit as a "referee," or, failing such agreement, the selection of such referee by the Mediation Board. The awards of these bodies in these "grievances" are final and binding (Section 3, First (m)).

TEXAS & NEW ORLEANS R.R. COMPANY v.
BROTHERHOOD OF RAILWAY &
STEAMSHIP CLERKS

Supreme Court of the United States, 1930.
281 U.S. 548, 50 S.Ct. 427, 74 L.Ed. 1034.

MR. CHIEF JUSTICE HUGHES delivered the opinion of the Court.

This suit was brought in the District Court by the Brotherhood of Railway and Steamship Clerks, Freight Handlers, Express and Station Employees, Southern Pacific Lines in Texas and Louisiana, a voluntary association, and H.W. Harper, General Chairman of its System Board of Adjustment, against the Texas and New Orleans Railroad Company, and certain officers and agents of that Company, to obtain an injunction restraining the defendants from interfering with, influencing or coercing the clerical employees of the Railroad Company in the matter of their organization and designation of representatives for the purposes set forth in the Railway Labor Act of May 20, 1926 * * *.

The substance of the allegations of the bill of complaint was that the Brotherhood, since its organization in September, 1918, had been authorized by a majority of the railway clerks in the employ of the Railroad Company (apart from general office employees) to represent them in all matters relating to their employment; that this representation was recognized by the Railroad Company before and after the application by the Brotherhood in November, 1925, for an increase of the wages of the railway clerks and after the denial of that application by the Railroad Company and the reference of the controversy by the Brotherhood to the United States Board of Mediation; that, while the controversy was pending before that Board, the Railroad Company instigated the formation of a union of its railway clerks (other than general office employees) known as the "Association of Clerical Employees—Southern Pacific Lines"; and that the Railroad Company had endeavored to intimidate members of the Brotherhood and to coerce them to withdraw from it and to make the Association their representative in dealings with the Railroad Company, and thus to prevent the railway clerks from freely designating their representatives by collective action.

The District Court granted a temporary injunction. Thereafter the Railroad Company recognized the Association of Clerical Employees—Southern Pacific Lines as the representative of the clerical employees of the Company. The Railroad Company stated that this course was taken after a committee of the Association had shown authorizations signed by those who were regarded as constituting a majority of the employees of the described class. The subsequent action of the Railroad Company and its officers and agents was in accord with this recognition of the Association and the consequent non-recognition of the Brotherhood. In proceedings to punish for contempt, the District Court decided that the Railroad Company and certain of its officers who were defendants had violated the order of injunction and completely nullified it. The Court directed that, in order to purge themselves of this contempt, the Railroad Company and these officers should completely "disestablish the Association of Clerical Employees," as it was then constituted as the recognized representative of the clerical employees of the Railroad Company, and should reinstate the Brotherhood as such representative, until such time as these employees by a secret ballot taken in accordance with the further direction of the Court, and without the dictation or interference of the Railroad Company and its officers, should choose other representatives. The order also required the restoration to service and to stated privileges of certain employees who had been discharged by the Railroad Company. 24 F.(2d) 426. Punishment was prescribed in case the defendants did not purge themselves of contempt as directed.

On final hearing, the temporary injunction was made permanent. * * * The Circuit Court of Appeals affirmed the decree, holding that the injunction was properly granted and that, in imposing conditions for the purging of the defendants of contempt, the District Court had not gone beyond the appropriate exercise of its authority in providing for the restoration of the *status quo*. 33 F.(2d) 13. This Court granted a writ of certiorari. * * *

The bill of complaint invoked subdivision third of section 2 of the Railway Labor Act of 1926 * * * which provides as follows:

"Third. Representatives, for the purposes of this Act, shall be designated by the respective parties in such manner as may be provided in their corporate organization or unincorporated association, or by other means of collective action, without interference, influence, or coercion exercised by either party over the self-organization or designation of representatives by the other."

The controversy is with respect to the construction, validity and application of this statutory provision. The petitioners, the Railroad Company and its officers, contend that the provision confers merely an abstract right which was not intended to be enforced by legal proceedings; that, in so far as the statute undertakes to prevent either party from influencing the other in the selection of representatives, it is unconstitutional because it seeks to take away an inherent and inalienable right in violation of the First and Fifth Amendments of the Federal Constitution; * * * that in any event the action taken by the Railroad Company and its officers in the recognition of the Association of Clerical Employees, and in other preceedings following upon that recognition, was not contrary to law and that there was no warrant for the interposition of the court either in granting the injunction order or in the proceedings for punishment for the alleged contempt.

* * * Both the District Court and the Circuit Court of Appeals approached the consideration of the evidence as to intimidation and coercion, and resolved such conflicts as the evidence presented, in the light of the demonstration that a strong motive existed on the part of the Railroad Company to oppose the demands of the Brotherhood and to promote another organization of the clerical employees which would be more favorable to the interests and contentions of the Company. Both courts found the explanation of the Company's attitude in the letter addressed by H.M. Lull, executive vice-president of the Railroad Company, to A.D. McDonald, its president, under date of May 24, 1927, shortly before the activities of which complaint was made in this suit. In this letter Mr. Lull referred to the pendency before the United States Board of Mediation of the demand of the Brotherhood for an increase of wages for the clerical employees, and it was stated

that if the matter went to arbitration, and the award was made on the same basis as one which had recently been made with respect to the lines west of El Paso, it would mean an increased pay-roll cost of approximately $340,000 per annum. Mr. Lull said that from the best information obtainable the majority of the clerical and station service employees of the Railroad Company did not belong to the national organization (the Brotherhood), and that "it is our intention, when handling the matter in mediation proceedings, to raise the question of the right of this organization to represent these employees and if arbitration is proposed we shall decline to arbitrate on the basis that the petitioner does not represent the majority of the employees. This will permit us to get away from the interference of this organization, and if successful in this, I am satisfied we can make settlement with our own employees at a cost not to exceed $75,000 per annum."

Motive is a persuasive interpreter of equivocal conduct, and the petitioners are not entitled to complain because their activities were viewed in the light of manifest interest and purpose. The most that can be said in favor of the petitioners on the questions of fact is that the evidence permits conflicting inferences, and this is not enough. The circumstances of the soliciting of authorizations and memberships on behalf of the Association, the fact that employees of the Railroad Company who were active in promoting the development of the Association were permitted to devote their time to that enterprise without deduction from their pay, the charge to the Railroad Company of expenses incurred in recruiting members of the Association, the reports made to the Railroad Company of the progress of these efforts, and the discharge from the service of the Railroad Company of leading representatives of the Brotherhood and the cancellation of their passes, gave support, despite the attempted justification of these proceedings, to the conclusion of the courts below that the Railroad Company and its officers were actually engaged in promoting the organization of the Association in the interest of the Company and in opposition to the Brotherhood, and that these activities constituted an actual interference with the liberty of the clerical employees in the selection of their representatives. In this view, * * * we pass to the important questions of law whether the statute imposed a legal duty upon the Railroad Company, that is, an obligation enforceable by judicial proceedings.

It is unnecessary to review the history of the legislation enacted by Congress in relation to the settlement of railway labor disputes, as earlier efforts culminated in Title III of the Transportation Act, 1920 (c. 91, 41 Stat. 456, 469) the purpose and effect of which have been determined by this Court. In Pennsylvania Railroad Company v. United States Railroad Labor Board, 261 U.S. 72, the question was whether the members of the Railroad Labor Board [j] as constituted under the provisions of the Transportation Act, 1920, had exceeded their powers. The Court held that the Board had jurisdiction to hear and decide a dispute over rules and working conditions upon the application of either side, when the parties had failed to agree and an adjustment board had not been organized. The Board also had jurisdiction to decide who might represent the employees in the conferences contem-

---

j. The Railroad Labor Board was comprised of nine members appointed by the President, three each representing employers, employees, and the public.

plated by the statute and to make reasonable rules for ascertaining the will of the employees in this respect. Interference by injunction with the exercise of the discretion of the Board in the matters committed to it, and with the publication of its opinions, was decided to be unwarranted. The Court thought it evident that Congress considered it to be "of the highest public interest to prevent the interruption of interstate commerce by labor disputes and strikes," and that its plan was "to encourage settlement without strikes, first by conference between the parties; failing that, by reference to adjustment boards of the parties' own choosing," and, if this proved to be ineffective, "by a full hearing before a National Board" organized as the statute provided. But the Court added: "The decisions of the Labor Board are not to be enforced by process. The only sanction of its decision is to be the force of public opinion invoked by the fairness of a full hearing, the intrinsic justice of the conclusion, strengthened by the official prestige of the Board, and the full publication of the violation of such decision by any party to the proceeding." It was said to be the evident thought of Congress "that the economic interest of every member of the Public in the undisturbed flow of interstate commerce and the acute inconvenience to which all must be subjected by an interruption caused by a serious and widespread labor dispute, fastens public attention closely on all the circumstances of the controversy and arouses public criticism of the side thought to be at fault." Id. pp. 79, 80. The Court concluded that the Labor Board was "to act as a Board of Arbitration," but that there was "no constraint" upon the parties "to do what the Board decides they should do except the moral constraint of publication of its decision." Id. p. 84.

* * *

It was with clear appreciation of the infirmity of the existing legislation, and in the endeavor to establish a more practicable plan in order to accomplish the desired result, that Congress enacted the Railway Labor Act of 1926. It was decided to make a fresh start. The situation was thus described in the report of the bill to the Senate by the Committee on Interstate Commerce (69th Cong., 1st sess., Sen. Rep. No. 222): "In view of the fact that the employees absolutely refuse to appear before the labor board and that many of the important railroads are themselves opposed to it, that it has been held by the Supreme Court to have no power to enforce its judgments, that its authority is not recognized or respected by the employees and by a number of important railroads, that the President has suggested that it would be wise to seek a substitute for it, and that the party platforms of both the Republican and Democratic Parties in 1924 clearly indicated dissatisfaction with the provisions of the transportation act relating to labor, the committee concluded that the time had arrived when the labor board should be abolished and the provisions relating to labor in the transportation act, 1920, should be repealed."

The bill was introduced as the result of prolonged conferences between representative committees of railroad presidents and of executives of railroad labor organizations, and embodied an agreement of a large majority of both.[2] The provisions of Title III of the Transportation Act, 1920, and also the Act of July 15, 1913 (c. 6, 38 Stat. 103) which provided for mediation,

2. In the report of the bill by the Committee on Interstate and Foreign Commerce to the House of Representatives, it was said (69th Cong. 1st sess., H.R.Rep. No. 328):

conciliation and arbitration in controversies with railway employees, were repealed.

While adhering in the new statute to the policy of providing for the amicable adjustment of labor disputes, and for voluntary submissions to arbitration as opposed to a system of compulsory arbitration, Congress buttressed this policy by creating certain definite legal obligations. The outstanding feature of the Act of 1926 is the provision for an enforceable award in arbitration proceedings. The arbitration is voluntary, but the award pursuant to the arbitration is conclusive upon the parties as to the merits and facts of the controversy submitted. (Section 9.) The award is to be filed in the clerk's office of the District Court of the United States designated in the agreement to arbitrate, and * * * the court is to enter judgment on the award * * *. Thus it is contemplated that the proceedings for the amicable adjustment of disputes will have an appropriate termination in a binding adjudication, enforceable as such.

Another definite object of the Act of 1926 is to provide, in case of a dispute between a carrier and its employees which has not been adjusted under the provisions of the Act, for the more effectual protection of interstate commerce from interruption to such a degree as to deprive any section of the country of essential transportation service. (Section 10.) In case the Board of Mediation established by the Act, as an independent agency in the executive branch of the Government, finds that such an interruption of interstate commerce is threatened, that Board is to notify the President, who may thereupon in his discretion create an emergency board of investigation to report, within thirty days, with respect to the dispute. The Act then provides that "After the creation of such board and for thirty days after such board has made its report to the President, no change, except by agreement, shall be made by the parties to the controversy in the conditions out of which the dispute arose." (Id.) This prohibition, in order to safeguard the vital interests of the country while an investigation is in progress, manifestly imports a legal obligation. The Brotherhood insists, and we think rightly, that the major purpose of Congress in passing the Railway Labor Act was "to provide a machinery to prevent strikes." Section 10 is described by counsel for the Brotherhood as "a provision limiting the right to strike," and in this view it is insisted that there "is no possible question that Congress intended to make the provisions of Section 10 enforceable to the extent of authorizing any court of competent jurisdiction to restrain either party to the controver-

"The bill was introduced as the product of negotiations and conferences between a representative committee of railroad presidents and a representative committee of railroad labor organization executives, extending over several months, which were concluded with the approval of the bill, respectively, by the Association of Railway Executives and by the executives of 20 railroad labor organizations. As introduced, it represented the agreement of railway managements operating over 80 per cent of the railroad mileage and labor organizations representing an overwhelming majority of the railroad employees."

The committee of the Senate on Interstate Commerce reported to the Senate on this point, as follows (69th Cong., 1st sess., Sen. Rep. No. 222):

"The railroads favoring the bill appeared before the committee through their representatives and advocated it. None of the railroads opposing the bill appeared either in person or by any representative. The bill was agreed to also by all the organizations known as 'standard recognized railway labor organizations,' 20 in number, and these appeared by their representatives before the committee in advocacy of the bill."

sy from changing the existing status during the sixty-day period provided for the emergency board."

* * *

It is thus apparent that Congress, in the legislation of 1926, while elaborating a plan for amicable adjustments and voluntary arbitration of disputes between common carriers and their employees, thought it necessary to impose, and did impose, certain definite obligations enforceable by judicial proceedings. The question before us is whether a legal obligation of this sort is also to be found in the provisions of subdivision third of Section 2 of the Act providing that "Representatives for the purposes of this Act, shall be designated by the respective parties * * * without interference, influence, or coercion exercised by either party over the self-organization or designation of representatives by the other."

It is at once to be observed that Congress was not content with the general declaration of the duty of carriers and employees to make every reasonable effort to enter into and maintain agreements concerning rates of pay, rules and working conditions, and to settle disputes with all expedition in conference between authorized representatives, but added this distinct prohibition against coercive measures. This addition can not be treated as superfluous or insignificant, or as intended to be without effect. * * * While an affirmative declaration of duty contained in a legislative enactment may be of imperfect obligation because not enforceable in terms, a definite statutory prohibition of conduct which would thwart the declared purpose of the legislation cannot be disregarded. The intent of Congress is clear with respect to the sort of conduct that is prohibited. "Interference" with freedom of action and "coercion" refer to well understood concepts of the law. The meaning of the word "influence" in this clause may be gathered from the context. *Noscitur a sociis.* * * * The use of the word is not to be taken as interdicting the normal relations and innocent communications which are a part of all friendly intercourse, albeit between employer and employee. "Influence" in this context plainly means pressure, the use of the authority or power of either party to induce action by the other in derogation of what the statute calls "self-organization." * * *

In reaching a conclusion as to the intent of Congress, the importance of the prohibition in its relation to the plan devised by the Act must have appropriate consideration. Freedom of choice in the selection of representatives on each side of the dispute is the essential foundation of the statutory scheme. All the proceedings looking to amicable adjustments and to agreements for arbitration of disputes, the entire policy of the Act, must depend for success on the uncoerced action of each party through its own representatives to the end that agreements satisfactory to both may be reached and the peace essential to the uninterrupted service of the instrumentalities of interstate commerce may be maintained. There is no impairment of the voluntary character of arrangements for the adjustment of disputes in the imposition of a legal obligation not to interfere with the free choice of those who are to make such adjustments. On the contrary, it is of the essence of a voluntary scheme, if it is to accomplish its purpose, that this liberty should be safeguarded. The definite prohibition which Congress inserted in the Act can not therefore be overridden in the view that Congress intended it to be ignored. As the prohibition was appropriate to the aim of Congress, and is capable of enforcement, the conclusion must be that enforcement was contemplated. * * *

We entertain no doubt of the constitutional authority of Congress to enact the prohibition. The power to regulate commerce is the power to enact "all appropriate legislation" for its "protection and advancement" * * *. Exercising this authority, Congress may facilitate the amicable settlement of disputes which threaten the service of the necessary agencies of interstate transportation. In shaping its legislation to this end, Congress was entitled to take cognizance of actual conditions and to address itself to practicable measures. The legality of collective action on the part of employees in order to safeguard their proper interests is not to be disputed. It has long been recognized that employees are entitled to organize for the purpose of securing the redress of grievances and to promote agreements with employers relating to rates of pay and conditions of work. American Steel Foundries v. Tri-City Central Trades Council, 257 U.S. 184, 209. Congress was not required to ignore this right of the employees but could safeguard it and seek to make their appropriate collective action an instrument of peace rather than of strife. Such collective action would be a mockery if representation were made futile by interferences with freedom of choice. Thus the prohibition by Congress of interference with the selection of representatives for the purpose of negotiation and conference between employers and employees, instead of being an invasion of the constitutional right of either, was based on the recognition of the rights of both. The petitioners invoke the principle declared in Adair v. United States, 208 U.S. 161, and Coppage v. Kansas, 236 U.S. 1, but these decisions are inapplicable. The Railway Labor Act of 1926 does not interfere with the normal exercise of the right of the carrier to select its employees or to discharge them. The statute is not aimed at this right of the employers but at the interference with the right of employees to have representatives of their own choosing. As the carriers subject to the Act have no constitutional right to interfere with the freedom of the employees in making their selections, they cannot complain of the statute on constitutional grounds. * * *

We do not find that the decree below goes beyond the proper enforcement of the provision of the Railway Labor Act.

Decree affirmed.

MR. JUSTICE MCREYNOLDS did not hear the argument and took no part in the decision of this case.

Note

1. What is the significance of the Railway Clerks case in the development of the law of labor relations? Do you agree with Chief Justice Hughes (supra p. 109) that "[f]reedom of choice in the selection of representatives on each side of the dispute is the essential foundation of the statutory scheme"?

What conduct of the railroad was held to be unlawful "interference" with the freedom of the employees to select their representative? In this regard, why should support by the employer of a company union be deemed such "interference" where the employees are *satisfied* with the company union?

2. Does the Court succeed in distinguishing Coppage v. Kansas, supra p. 50, and Adair v. United States, discussed in Coppage, supra p. 52? Were not employees in all three of these cases discharged for union membership?

3. The Railway Labor Act has been several times amended since its adoption in 1926. Major changes were made in 1934. Some of these are treated in the Virginian Railway case which follows. The provisions of the Act set forth in the Statutory Supplement to this book are those presently in effect, reflecting the changes made in the several amendments since 1926. (Citations and dates of these amendments are noted in the Supplement.) The changes effected in the 1934 Act included making the employer conduct involved in the Railway Clerks case a criminal offense. Section 2, Tenth.

4. As appears in the Railway Clerks opinion, the Railway Labor Act of 1926, a seminal statute in the scheme of labor relations in the United States, was the product of a broad consensus among railroads and railway brotherhoods. Indeed, it might be characterized as an industry-wide collective bargaining agreement which was then ratified by congressional action. This genesis of a protected collective bargaining system may provide insight concerning methods for resolving large group conflicts in a free society. It may also provide insight into the sources, functions, and limits of law in dealing with such conflicts. In the latter regard, there is profit in comparing the Railway Labor Act of 1926, a still viable law, with the prior abortive efforts to legislate industrial peace on the railroads.

VIRGINIAN RY. v. SYSTEM FEDERATION NO. 40

Supreme Court of the United States, 1937.
300 U.S. 515, 57 S.Ct. 592, 81 L.Ed. 789.

MR. JUSTICE STONE delivered the opinion of the Court.

This case presents questions as to the constitutional validity of certain provisions of the Railway Labor Act of May 20, 1926, * * * as amended by the Act of June 21, 1934, * * * and as to the nature and extent of the relief which courts are authorized by the Act to give.

Respondents are System Federation No. 40, which will be referred to as the Federation, a labor organization affiliated with the American Federation of Labor and representing shop craft employees of petitioner railway, and certain individuals who are officers and members of the System Federation. They brought the present suit in equity in the District Court for Eastern Virginia, to compel petitioner, an interstate rail carrier, to recognize and treat with respondent Federation, as the duly accredited representative of the mechanical department employees of petitioner * * *.

In 1927 the American Federation of Labor formed a local organization, which, in 1934, demanded recognition by petitioner of its authority to represent the shop craft employees, and invoked the aid of the National Mediation Board, constituted under the Railway Labor Act as amended, to establish its authority. The Board, pursuant to agreement between the petitioner, the Federation, and the Association, and in conformity to the statute, held an election by petitioner's shop craft employees, to choose representatives for the purpose of collective bargaining with petitioner. As the result of the election, the Board certified that the Federation was the duly accredited representative of petitioner's employees in the six shop crafts. * * *

[The trial court] directed petitioner to "treat with" the Federation [instead of a company union] and to "exert every reasonable effort to make and maintain agreements concerning rates of pay, rules and working conditions, and to settle all disputes, whether arising out of the application of such agreements or otherwise, * * *." It restrained petitioner from "entering into any contract, undertaking or agreement of whatsoever kind concerning rules, rates of pay or working conditions affecting its Mechanical Department employees, * * * except * * * with the Federation" * * *. The decree further restrained the petitioner from organizing or fostering any union of its mechanical department employees for the purpose of interfering with the Federation as the accredited representative of such employees. 11 F.Supp. 621.

On appeal the Court of Appeals for the Fourth Circuit approved and adopted the findings of the district court and affirmed its decree. 84 F.(2d) 641. This Court granted certiorari to review the cause as one of public importance.

Petitioner here, as below, makes two main contentions: First, with respect to the relief granted, it maintains that § 2, Ninth, of the Railway Labor Act, which provides that a carrier shall treat with those certified by the Mediation Board to be the representatives of a craft or class, imposes no legally enforcible obligation upon the carrier to negotiate with the representative so certified, and that in any case the statute imposes no obligation to treat or negotiate which can be appropriately enforced by a court of equity. Second, that § 2, Ninth, in so far as it * * * imposes on the carrier any obligation to negotiate with a labor union authorized to represent its employees, and restrains it from making agreements with any other labor organization, * * * is a denial of due process guaranteed by the Fifth Amendment. * * *

First. The Obligation Imposed by the Statute. * * *

[P]etitioner insists that the statute affords no legal sanction for so much of the decree as directs petitioner to "treat with" respondent Federation "and exert every reasonable effort to make and maintain agreements concerning rates of pay, rules and working conditions, and to settle all disputes whether arising out of the application of such agreements or otherwise." It points out that the requirement for reasonable effort to reach an agreement is couched in the very words of § 2, First, which were taken from § 301 of the Transportation Act, and which were held to be without legal sanction in that Act. * * * It is argued that they cannot now be given greater force as reënacted in the Railway Labor Act of 1926, and continued in the 1934 amendment. But these words no longer stand alone and unaided by mandatory provision of the statute as they did when first enacted. The amendment of the Railway Labor Act added new provisions in § 2, Ninth, which makes it the duty of the Mediation Board, when any dispute arises among the carrier's employees, "as to who are the representatives of such employees," to investigate the dispute and to certify, as was done in this case, the name of the organization authorized to represent the employees. It commands that "Upon receipt of such certification the carrier shall treat with the representative so certified as the representative of the craft or class for the purposes of this Act."   *   *   *

Experience had shown, before the amendment of 1934, that when there was no dispute as to the organizations authorized to represent the employees, and when there was willingness of the employer to meet such representative for a discussion of their grievances, amicable adjustment of differences had generally followed and strikes had been avoided. On the other hand, a prolific source of dispute had been the maintenance by the railroads of company unions and the denial by railway management of the authority of representatives chosen by their employees. * * * Section 2, Ninth, of the amended Act, was specifically aimed at this practice. It provided a means for ascertaining who are the authorized representatives of the employees through intervention and certification by the Mediation Board, and commanded the carrier to treat with the representative so certified. * * *

* * * The command to the employer to "treat with" the authorized representative of the employees adds nothing to the 1926 Act, unless it requires some affirmative act on the part of the employer. * * * As we cannot assume that its addition to the statute was purposeless, we must take its meaning to be that which the words suggest, which alone would add something to the statute as it was before amendment, and which alone would tend to effect the purpose of the legislation. The statute does not undertake to compel agreement between the employer and employees, but it does command those preliminary steps without which no agreement can be reached: It at least requires the employer to meet and confer with the authorized representative of its employees, to listen to their complaints, to make reasonable effort to compose differences—in short, to enter into a negotiation for the settlement of labor disputes such as is contemplated by § 2, First. * * *

Propriety of Relief in Equity. Petitioner contends that if the statute is interpreted as requiring the employer to negotiate with the representative of his employees, its obligation is not the appropriate subject of a decree in equity; that negotiation depends on desires and mental attitudes which are beyond judicial control, and that since equity cannot compel the parties to agree, it will not compel them to take the preliminary steps which may result in agreement.

There is no want of capacity in the court to direct complete performance of the entire obligation: both the negative duties not to maintain a company union and not to negotiate with any representative of the employees other than respondent and the affirmative duty to treat with respondent. Full performance of both is commanded by the decree in terms which leave in no uncertainty the requisites of performance. * * * Whether an obligation has been discharged, and whether action taken or omitted is in good faith or reasonable, are everyday subjects of inquiry by courts in framing and enforcing their decrees. * * *

In considering the propriety of the equitable relief granted here, we cannot ignore the judgment of Congress, deliberately expressed in legislation, that where the obstruction of the company union is removed, the meeting of employers and employees at the conference table is a powerful aid to industrial peace. Moreover, the resources of the Railway Labor Act are not exhausted if negotiation fails in the first instance to result in agreement. If disputes concerning changes in rates of pay, rules or working conditions, are "not adjusted by the parties in conference," either party may invoke the mediation services of the Mediation Board, § 5, First, or the parties may agree to seek the benefits of the arbitration provision of § 7. With the coercive influence of the company union ended, and in view of the interest of both parties in avoiding a strike, we cannot assume that negotiation, as required by the decree, will not result in agreement, or lead to successful mediation or arbitration, or that the attempt to secure one or another through the relief which the district court gave is not worth the effort. * * *

The decree is authorized by the statute and was granted in an appropriate exercise of the equity powers of the court.

Second. Constitutionality of § 2 of the Railway Labor Act. (A) Validity Under the Commerce Clause. * * * [The Court held that § 2 of the Railway Labor Act was a valid exercise of congressional power under the Commerce Clause.]

(B) Validity of § 2 of the Railway Labor Act Under the Fifth Amendment. The provisions of the Railway Labor Act applied in this case * * * do not require petitioner to enter into any agreement with its employees * * *. They prohibit only * * * use of the company union * * *, and they impose on petitioner only the affirmative duty of "treating with" the authorized representatives of its employees for the purpose of negotiating a labor dispute.

Even though Congress, in the choice of means to effect a permissible regulation of commerce, must conform to due process, * * * it is evident that where, as here, the means chosen are appropriate to the permissible end, there is little scope for the operation of the due process clause. * * * And the Fifth Amendment, like the Fourteenth, * * * is not a guarantee of untrammeled freedom of action and of contract. In the exercise of its power to regulate commerce, Congress can subject both to restraints not shown to be unreasonable. * * *

Each of the limited duties imposed upon petitioner by the statute and the decree do not differ in their purpose and nature from those imposed under the earlier statute and enforced in the *Railway Clerks* case * * *.

Affirmed.

Note

What is the content of the employer's duty to "treat with" (i.e., to bargain with) the certified representative of the employees? What *should* that content be in a model labor code: To make reasonable efforts to meet and confer? To make reasonable efforts to reach agreement? To make good faith efforts to reach agreement? Something else?

What difference does it make?

B. THE WAGNER ACT OF 1935

The two fundamental propositions of the existing law of collective bargaining in the United States are demonstrated in Railway Clerks and Virginian Railway, the Railway Labor Act cases: (1) that employees have the right to organize and to bargain collectively through a representative of their own choosing; (2) that the employer has the correlative duties (a) not to interfere with the exercise of those rights by employees, and (b) to recognize and bargain with the chosen representative of the employees.

In 1935 Congress enacted the Wagner Act (National Labor Relations Act), which accorded to a large number of employees not covered by the Railway Labor Act the same basic rights, and imposed upon employers the same basic duties, as in the earlier act. While the language and structure of the two acts are different, the scheme of collective bargaining is the same. Unlike its counterpart in the railroad industry, the line of descent of the Wagner Act was short. It was the offspring of the economic collapse which followed the crash of 1929. As part of the "New Deal" effort to cope with the national crisis provoked by that collapse, Congress in 1933 enacted the National Industrial Recovery Act. A primary purpose of this Act was to induce American business to establish "codes of fair competition" for each industry, thereby stabilizing the economy by eliminating destructive competition. Section 7(a) of the Act provided:

> "Every code of fair competition, agreement, and license approved, prescribed, or issued under this title shall contain the following conditions: (1) That employees shall have the right to organize and bargain collectively through representatives of their own choosing, and shall be free from the interference, restraint, or coercion of employers of labor, or their agents, in the designation of such representatives or in self-organization or in other concerted activities for the purpose of collective bargaining or other mutual aid or protection; (2) that no employee and no one seeking employment shall be required as a condition of employment to join any company union or to refrain from joining, organizing, or assisting a labor organization of his own choosing; and (3) that employers shall comply with the maximum hours of labor, minimum rates of pay, and other conditions of employment, approved or prescribed by the President." [a]

The agency entrusted with the administration of the foregoing provision (first called the National Labor Board and later the National Labor Relations Board) functioned until May 27, 1935, when the Supreme Court invalidated the NIRA in Schechter Poultry Corporation v. United States, 295 U.S. 495, 55 S.Ct. 837, 79 L.Ed. 1570. During the agency's short and rather ineffective life, it nonetheless rendered a number of decisions applying the principles of Section 7(a). These principles and decisions anticipated basic features of the Wagner Act. [b]

The Wagner Act, signed into law by President Roosevelt on July 5, 1935, had two primary purposes. Ostensibly, it was designed to resolve labor disputes which would otherwise adversely affect interstate commerce. This

[a]. 48 Stat. 198 (1933).

[b]. For further discussion of the NIRA and Section 7(a), see infra pp. 124–125.

was the constitutional hook upon which congressional jurisdiction was hung. More basically, the Act was intended to deal with the economic crisis of the Great Depression by enhancing the bargaining, and therefore purchasing, power of workers.

The Wagner Act was shortly to produce a constitutional drama before the same Supreme Court which had demonstrated its hostility to the "New Deal" legislation in Schechter and other celebrated cases. The drama was heightened by the highly controversial "Court-packing" plan of the President, the idea of which was to increase the number of justices on the Supreme Court sufficiently to permit the President, by the appointment of "liberals" to these vacancies, to achieve a more sympathetic reading of the Constitution.[c] The drama was further heightened by the advice afforded by many of the country's outstanding lawyers to employers the country over that they could lawfully ignore the Wagner Act because of its patent unconstitutionality. The constitutional issue was joined and resolved in the following case.

NATIONAL LABOR RELATIONS BOARD v. JONES & LAUGHLIN STEEL CORP.

Supreme Court of the United States, 1937.
301 U.S. 1, 57 S.Ct. 615, 81 L.Ed. 893, 108 A.L.R. 1352.

MR. CHIEF JUSTICE HUGHES delivered the opinion of the Court.

In a proceeding under the National Labor Relations Act of 1935 the National Labor Relations Board found that the respondent, Jones & Laughlin Steel Corporation, had violated the Act by engaging in unfair labor practices affecting commerce. The proceeding was instituted by the Beaver Valley Lodge No. 200, affiliated with the Amalgamated Association of Iron, Steel and Tin Workers of America, a labor organization. The unfair labor practices charged were that the corporation was discriminating against members of the union with regard to hire and tenure of employment, and was coercing and intimidating its employees in order to interfere with their self-organization. The discriminatory and coercive action alleged was the discharge of certain employees.

The National Labor Relations Board, sustaining the charge, ordered the corporation to cease and desist from such discrimination and coercion, to offer reinstatement to ten of the employees named, to make good their losses in pay, and to post for thirty days notices that the corporation would not discharge or discriminate against members, or those desiring to become members, of the labor union. As the corporation failed to comply, the Board petitioned the Circuit Court of Appeals to enforce the order. The court denied the petition holding that the order lay beyond the range of federal power. 83 F.(2d) 998. We granted certiorari. * * *

The scheme of the National Labor Relations Act * * * may be briefly stated. The first section sets forth findings with respect to the injury to commerce resulting from the denial by employers of the right of employees to organize and from the refusal of employers to accept the procedure of

---

c. For an account of the "Court-packing" episode, see, e.g., 2 Pusey, Charles Evans Hughes 749–765 (1951).

collective bargaining. There follows a declaration that it is the policy of the United States to eliminate these causes of obstruction to the free flow of commerce. The Act then defines the terms it uses, including the terms "commerce" and "affecting commerce." Section 2. It creates the National Labor Relations Board and prescribes its organization. Sections 3–6. It sets forth the right of employees to self-organization and to bargain collectively through representatives of their own choosing. Section 7. It defines "unfair labor practices." Section 8. It lays down rules as to the representation of employees for the purpose of collective bargaining. Section 9. The Board is empowered to prevent the described unfair labor practices affecting commerce and the Act prescribes the procedure to that end. The Board is authorized to petition designated courts to secure the enforcement of its order. The findings of the Board as to the facts, if supported by evidence, are to be conclusive. * * * Any person aggrieved by a final order of the Board may obtain a review in the designated courts with the same procedure as in the case of an application by the Board for the enforcement of its order. Section 10. The Board has broad powers of investigation. Section 11. Interference with members of the Board or its agents in the performance of their duties is punishable by fine and imprisonment. Section 12. Nothing in the Act is to be construed to interfere with the right to strike. Section 13. * * *

The procedure in the instant case followed the statute. The labor union filed with the Board its verified charge.

The Board thereupon issued its complaint against the respondent, alleging that its action in discharging the employees in question constituted unfair labor practices affecting commerce within the meaning of section 8, subdivisions (1) and (3), and section 2, subdivisions (6) and (7), of the Act. Respondent, appearing specially for the purpose of objecting to the jurisdiction of the Board, filed its answer. Respondent admitted the discharges, but alleged that they were made because of inefficiency or violation of rules or for other good reasons and were not ascribable to union membership or activities. As an affirmative defense respondent challenged the constitutional validity of the statute and its applicability in the instant case. Notice of hearing was given and respondent appeared by counsel. The Board first took up the issue of jurisdiction and evidence was presented by both the Board and the respondent. Respondent then moved to dismiss the complaint for lack of jurisdiction and, on denial of that motion, respondent in accordance with its special appearance withdrew from further participation in the hearing. The Board received evidence upon the merits and at its close made its findings and order.

Contesting the ruling of the Board, the respondent argues (1) that the Act is in reality a regulation of labor relations and not of interstate commerce; (2) that the Act can have no application to the respondent's relations with its production employees because they are not subject to regulation by the federal government; and (3) that the provisions of the Act violate * * * the Fifth and Seventh Amendments of the Constitution of the United States.

The facts as to the nature and scope of the business of the Jones & Laughlin Steel Corporation have been found by the Labor Board, and, so far as they are essential to the determination of this controversy, they are not in dispute. The Labor Board has found: The corporation is organized under the laws of Pennsylvania and has its principal office at Pittsburgh. It is engaged in the business of manufacturing iron and steel in plants situated in Pittsburgh and nearby Aliquippa, Pa. It manufactures and distributes a widely diversified line of steel and pig iron, being the fourth largest producer of steel in the United States. With its subsidiaries—nineteen in number—it is a completely integrated enterprise, owning and operating ore, coal and limestone properties, lake and river transportation facilities and terminal railroads located at its manufacturing plants. * * * Approximately 75 per cent. of its product is shipped out of Pennsylvania.

Summarizing these operations, the Labor Board concluded that the works in Pittsburgh and Aliquippa "might be likened to the heart of a self-contained, highly integrated body. They draw in the raw materials from Michigan, Minnesota, West Virginia, Pennsylvania in part through arteries and by means controlled by the respondent; they transform the materials and then pump them out to all parts of the nation through the vast mechanism which the respondent has elaborated."

* * * Respondent has about 10,000 employees in its Aliquippa plant, which is located in a community of about 30,000 persons. * * *

While respondent criticizes the evidence and the attitude of the Board, which is described as being hostile toward employers and particularly toward those who insisted upon their constitutional rights, respondent did not take advantage of its opportunity to present evidence to refute that which was offered to show discrimination and coercion. In this situation, the record presents no ground for setting aside the order of the Board so far as the facts pertaining to the circumstances and purpose of the discharge of the employees are concerned. Upon that point it is sufficient to say that the evidence supports the findings of the Board that respondent discharged these men "because of their union activity and for the purpose of discouraging membership in the union." We turn to the questions of law which respondent urges in contesting the validity and application of the Act.

* * *

We think it clear that the National Labor Relations Act may be construed so as to operate within the sphere of constitutional authority. The jurisdiction conferred upon the Board, and invoked in this instance, is found in section 10(a), which provides:

"Sec. 10(a). The Board is empowered, as hereinafter provided, to prevent any person from engaging in any unfair labor practice (listed in section 8) affecting commerce."

The critical words of this provision, prescribing the limits of the Board's authority in dealing with the labor practices, are "affecting commerce." The Act specifically defines the "commerce" to which it refers (section 2(6)):

"The term 'commerce' means trade, traffic, commerce, transportation, or communication among the several States * * *."

There can be no question that the commerce thus contemplated by the Act (aside from that within a Territory or the District of Columbia) is interstate and foreign commerce in the constitutional sense. The Act also defines the term "affecting commerce" section 2(7):

"The term 'affecting commerce' means in commerce, or burdening or obstructing commerce or the free flow of commerce, or having led or tending to lead to a labor dispute burdening or obstructing commerce or the free flow of commerce."

* * * Whether or not particular action does affect commerce in such a close and intimate fashion as to be subject to federal control, and hence to lie within the authority conferred upon the Board, is left by the statute to be determined as individual cases arise. We are thus to inquire whether in the instant case the constitutional boundary has been passed.

* * * The unfair labor practices found by the Board are those defined in section 8, subdivisions (1) and (3). These provide:

"Sec. 8. It shall be an unfair labor practice for an employer—

"(1) To interfere with, restrain, or coerce employees in the exercise of the rights guaranteed in section 7. * * *

"(3) By discrimination in regard to hire or tenure of employment or any term or condition of employment to encourage or discourage membership in any labor organization."

Section 8, subdivision (1), refers to section 7, which is as follows:

"Section 7. Employees shall have the right to self-organization, to form, join, or assist labor organizations, to bargain collectively through representatives of their own choosing, and to engage in concerted activities, for the purpose of collective bargaining or other mutual aid or protection."

Thus, in its present application, the statute goes no further than to safeguard the right of employees to self-organization and to select representatives of their own choosing for collective bargaining or other mutual protection without restraint or coercion by their employer.

That is a fundamental right. Employees have as clear a right to organize and select their representatives for lawful purposes as the respondent has to organize its business and select its own officers and agents. Discrimination and coercion to prevent the free exercise of the right of employees to self-organization and representation is a proper subject for condemnation by competent legislative authority. * * *

* * * Respondent says that, whatever may be said of employees engaged in interstate commerce, the industrial relations and activities in the manufacturing department of respondent's enterprise are not subject to federal regulation. The argument rests upon the proposition that manufacturing in itself is not commerce. * * *

[But] the stoppage of [respondent's manufacturing] operations by industrial strife would have a most serious effect upon interstate commerce. In view of respondent's far-flung activities, it is idle to say that the effect would be indirect or remote. It is obvious that it would be immediate and might be catastrophic. * * * When industries organize themselves on a national scale, making their relation to interstate commerce the dominant factor in their activities, how can it be maintained that their industrial labor relations constitute a forbidden field into which Congress may not enter when it is necessary to protect interstate commerce from the paralyzing consequences of industrial war? * * *

Experience has abundantly demonstrated that the recognition of the right of employees to self-organization and to have representatives of their own choosing for the purpose of collective bargaining is often an essential condition of industrial peace. Refusal to confer and negotiate has been one of the most prolific causes of strife. This is such an outstanding fact in the history of labor disturbances that it is a proper subject of judicial notice and requires no citation of instances. The opinion in the case of Virginian Railway Co. v. System Federation No. 40 * * * points to the large measure of success of the labor policy embodied in the Railway Labor Act. But, with respect to the appropriateness of the recognition of self-organization and representation in the promotion of peace, the question is not essentially different in the case of employees in industries of such a character that interstate commerce is put in jeopardy from the case of employees of transportation companies. And of what avail is it to protect the facility of transportation, if interstate commerce is throttled with respect to the commodities to be transported!

       * * *

       * * * Respondent asserts its right [under the Due Process Clause] to conduct its business in an orderly manner without being subjected to arbitrary restraints. What we have said points to the fallacy in the argument. Employees have their correlative right to organize for the purpose of securing the redress of grievances and to promote agreements with employers relating to rates of pay and conditions of work. Texas & N.O. R. Co. v. Railway S.S. Clerks * * *; Virginian Railway Co. v. System Federation No. 40. Restraint for the purpose of preventing an unjust interference with that right cannot be considered arbitrary or capricious. * * *

The Act does not compel agreements between employers and employees. * * * The theory of the Act is that free opportunity for negotiation with accredited representatives of employees is likely to promote industrial peace and may bring about the adjustments and agreements which the Act in itself does not attempt to compel. As we said in Texas & N.O. R. Co. v. Railway & S.S. Clerks, supra, and repeated in Virginian Railway Co. v. System Federation No. 40, the cases of Adair v. United States, 208 U.S. 161, 28 S.Ct. 277, 52 L.Ed. 436, 13 Ann.Cas. 764, and Coppage v. Kansas, 236 U.S. 1, 35 S.Ct. 240, 59 L.Ed. 441, L.R.A. 1915C, 960, are inapplicable to legislation of this character. The Act does not interfere with the normal exercise of the right of the employer to select its employees or to discharge them. The employer may not, under cover of that right, intimidate or coerce its employees with respect to their self-organization and representation, and, on the other hand, the Board is not entitled to make its authority a pretext for interference with the right of discharge when that right is exercised for other reasons than such intimidation and coercion. The true purpose is the subject of investigation with full opportunity to show the facts. It would seem that when employers freely recognize the right of their employees to their own organizations and their unrestricted right of representation there will be much less occasion for controversy in respect to the free and appropriate exercise of the right of selection and discharge.

The Act has been criticized as one-sided in its application; that it subjects the employer to supervision and restraint and leaves untouched the abuses for which employees may be responsible; that it fails to provide a more comprehensive plan,—with better assurances of fairness to both sides and with increased chances of success in bringing about, if not compelling, equitable solutions of industrial disputes affecting interstate commerce. But we are dealing with the power of Congress, not with a particular policy or with the extent to which policy should go. We have frequently said that the legislative authority, exerted within its proper field, need not embrace all the evils within its reach. The Constitution does not forbid "cautious advance, step by step," in dealing with the evils which are exhibited in activities within the range of legislative power. * * *

The procedural provisions of the Act are assailed. But these provisions, as we construe them, do not offend against the constitutional requirements governing the creation and action of administrative bodies. * * * The Act establishes standards to which the Board must conform. There must be complaint, notice and hearing. The Board must receive evidence and make findings. The findings as to the facts are to be conclusive, but only if supported by evidence. The order of the Board is subject to review by the designated court, and only when sustained by the court may the order be enforced. Upon that review all questions of the jurisdiction of the Board and the regularity of its proceedings, all questions of constitutional right or statutory authority are open to examination by the court. We construe the procedural provisions as affording adequate opportunity to secure judicial protection against arbitrary action in accordance with the well-settled rules applicable to administrative agencies set up by Congress to aid in the enforcement of valid legislation. * * *

The order of the Board required the reinstatement of the employees who were found to have been discharged because of their "union activity" and for the purpose of "discouraging membership in the union." That requirement was authorized by the Act. Section 10(c). * * *

Respondent complains that the Board not only ordered reinstatement but directed the payment of wages for the time lost by the discharge, less amounts earned by the employee during that period. This part of the order was also authorized by the act. Section 10(c). It is argued that the requirement is equivalent to a money judgment and hence contravenes the Seventh Amendment with respect to trial by jury. The Seventh Amendment provides that "In suits at common law, where the value in controversy shall exceed twenty dollars; the right of trial by jury shall be preserved." The amendment thus preserves the right which existed under the common law when the amendment was adopted. * * * Thus it has no application to cases where recovery of money damages is an incident to equitable relief even though damages might have been recovered in an action at law. * * *

The instant case is not a suit at common law or in the nature of such a suit. The proceeding is one unknown to the common law. It is a statutory proceeding. * * * The contention under the Seventh Amendment is without merit.

Our conclusion is that the order of the Board was within its competency and that the Act is valid as here applied. The judgment of the Circuit Court of Appeals is reversed and the cause is remanded for further proceedings in conformity with this opinion. It is so ordered.

Reversed and remanded.

[The dissenting opinion of Justice McReynolds, joined in by Justices Van Devanter, Sutherland, and Butler, is omitted. Its basic premise was the following: "It is unreasonable and unprecedented to say that the commerce clause confers upon Congress power to govern relations between employers and employees in * * * local activities." Manufacturing was found to be a "local activity" even where the raw materials used in the process of the manufacturing came from other states and where the products of such manufacturing were regularly sold in other states. If the position of the majority were adopted, the dissent stated, "Almost anything—marriage, birth, death—may in some fashion affect commerce."]

Note

1. The fears expressed by Justice McReynolds in his dissenting opinion were partially realized in NLRB v. Pierce Bros., 206 F.2d 569 (9th Cir.1953), in which a California undertaking establishment was held subject to the National Labor Relations Act on the grounds that it shipped bodies and ashes to points outside California and purchased equipment and supplies from out of the state. The argument that the business was "of a purely local nature not involving commerce" was rejected.

2. The "camel's head" potential of the decision in Jones & Laughlin (and four companion cases [d]) has been fully realized in subsequent decisions. Specific aspects and problems of the NLRB's expansive jurisdiction will be dealt with later. For the present, it suffices to say that Congress has been held to have exercised its power under the Commerce Clause to the hilt in the "affecting commerce" standard [e] and that the full exercise of that power brings within the NLRB's reach every enterprise of consequence in the country.

3. Those introduced to the study of labor law today find themselves confronted by a highly bureaucratized institution, i.e., the NLRB, the dimensions and power of which belie its short life. The following address by its first chairman may provide some humanizing insight into the origins of this bureaucracy and of the law it administers.

d. NLRB v. Fruehauf Trailer Co., 301 U.S. 49, 57 S.Ct. 642, 81 L.Ed. 893; NLRB v. Friedman-Harry Marks Clothing Co., 301 U.S. 58, 57 S.Ct. 645, 81 L.Ed. 893; Associated Press v. NLRB, 301 U.S. 103, 57 S.Ct. 650, 81 L.Ed. 953; Washington, Virginia & Maryland Coach Co. v. NLRB, 301 U.S. 142, 57 S.Ct. 648, 81 L.Ed. 965.

e. E.g., NLRB v. Fainblatt, 306 U.S. 601, 59 S.Ct. 668, 83 L.Ed. 1014 (1939).

MADDEN,* ORIGIN AND EARLY YEARS OF THE
NATIONAL LABOR RELATIONS ACT **

18 Hastings Law Journal 571 (1967).

It is good for the participants in any institution to think about and discuss the history of their institution, even though this folklore is entirely familiar to them. The institution of the law of labor relations has a Founding Father, Senator Robert F. Wagner of New York. Starting as an immigrant boy from Germany, he found in the city and state of New York the opportunity to forge for himself a career which culminated in his service for several terms in the United States Senate. During the critical periods of the Great Depression, he brought into being more important and enduring legislation than any other member of Congress has done in our history. Of this legislation, the statute which, in common speech, bears his name is, of course, the one which is the foundation of the imposing structure of labor law in the United States.

Something of the story of the enactment of the Wagner Act should be recounted here. In June, 1933, shortly after the new administration had taken office, the National Industrial Recovery Act was passed. It provided that the various industries could establish codes providing minimum wages and maximum hours to prevent cut-throat competition. The act contained section 7(a), which provided that every code should contain a provision that employees should have the right to organize and bargain collectively through representatives of their own choosing. Even though section 7(a) created no enforcement machinery, the President, without any statutory authority, appointed a National Labor Board consisting of distinguished representatives of labor and of industry, with Senator Wagner as chairman.

In spite of the low level of some 3,000,000 to which union membership had fallen and the continued high level of unemployment, unions, incited by section 7(a), demanded recognition and collective bargaining but were rebuffed by most employers, including all the big employers. The Senator, in his experience as Chairman of the Labor Board, learned that the refusal of employers to bargain, and their creation of "employee representation plans," better known as company unions, were prolific causes of strikes.

Within a year after the passage of the National Industrial Recovery Act, Senator Wagner drafted a statute, modeled after the Federal Trade Commission Act, creating a quasi-judicial tribunal with defined legal authority and power to have its orders enforced by court decree. In February, 1934, the proposed statute was introduced in the Senate, and extensive hearings were held in the Senate Committee. Mr. Wagner urged that the National Industrial Recovery Act was having little success due to the lack of mass purchasing power which resulted from low wages and high unemployment and that section 7(a) was not being obeyed since it contained no enforcement

* Professor of Law, University of California, Hastings College of the Law. Senior Judge, United States Court of Claims. Sits frequently by assignment of Chief Justice of United States Supreme Court with United States Court of Appeals, Ninth Circuit. [Deceased, 1972.]

** This article was the basis of an address delivered at the Luncheon Meeting of the Section of Labor Law of the American Bar Association at Montreal, Canada on August 9, 1966.

power. Industry's spokesmen were unanimously opposed to the bill, and it became apparent that it could not be enacted at that session. As a compromise, in June, 1934, Congress enacted Resolution 44,[4] which authorized the President to establish a board or boards to investigate situations relating to section 7(a) of the Recovery Act. The only power, other than the power to investigate, given to the board by Resolution 44, was the power to conduct elections by secret ballot in order to determine the employees' choice as to representatives for collective bargaining.

The President promptly appointed a distinguished board of three men, none of whom represented industry or labor. The experience of this board may have been educational but it was also completely frustrating. It functioned until May, 1935, when the United States Supreme Court held the National Industrial Recovery Act unconstitutional. In the meantime, Senator Wagner, recognizing that Resolution 44 was substantially worthless, introduced a bill similar to his 1934 bill. Again, extensive hearings were held and the same opposition developed. Leon Keyserling, the Senator's Administrative Assistant who worked intimately with the Senator on this project, writes:

> "[T]he legislation was opposed by organized industry with a force and fervor and expenditure of funds perhaps unparalleled. It was vehemently opposed by almost all of the press, ranging from the persistent opposition of the *New York Times* to the less responsible tirades of less circumspect journals. It was roundly condemned by so eminent and sincere an editorialist as Mr. Walter Lippman, who said: 'If the bill were passed, it could not be made to work. * * * It is preposterous to put such a burden upon mortal men * * *. The bill should, I believe, be scrapped. * * *'"[6]

Frank R. Kent of the Baltimore Sun called the Senator a "labor addict" for championing the bill. Some left wing labor spokesmen opposed the bill because it would lead to government intervention in unionism.

In the presence of the President, influential senators asked Mr. Wagner to withdraw the bill. Only after the bill's passage by the Senate, and when it seemed certain that the House would pass it, did the President give it his endorsement. No member of the President's cabinet, or of his brain trust, gave Wagner any help in getting the bill passed. And Keyserling points out that even in their memoirs, in which they admitted participation in the great accomplishments of the New Deal Era, none claimed any credit for the Wagner Act. To again quote Keyserling:

> "While it is true that * * * [Wagner's] proposal could not have become law in the political climate of 1928, nor perhaps in the climate of 1938, it is equally true that there would never have been a Wagner Act or anything like it at any time if the Senator had not spent himself in this cause to a degree which almost defies description."[8]

The Senator's hope was that his law would make American working men free, by permitting them to join forces with their fellow workmen instead of standing alone and insignificant; that it would, in time, make

---

4. 48 Stat. 1183 (1934).

6. Keyserling, The Wagner Act: Its Origin and Current Significance, 29 Geo.Wash.L.Rev. 199, 201–02 (1961).

8. Keyserling, supra note 6, at 201.

them and their country affluent, by creating a great mass purchasing power for the products of American industry. He was right on both counts.

The United States Supreme Court, as mentioned above, invalidated the National Industrial Recovery Act in May of 1935. Congress was anxious to do something but doubtful as to what it had power to do. It was aware that if it passed an unconstitutional law the Supreme Court would correct its error. Nevertheless, Senator Wagner's bill was passed by Congress on July 2, 1935, and signed by the President on July 5. The new act was to be administered by a three-man board appointed by the President. Ultimately the appointees were to serve five year terms, but the terms of the initial three appointees were to run for one, three, and five years so that expiration of the terms would be staggered. Although it was July, and Congress in those days was often hopeful of adjourning in July, the President did not hurry to appoint the members of the new board. There was much unemployment, even among persons who had had good salaries before the depression, and these board positions carried $10,000 salaries, but apparently there was no insistent clamor by anyone to get appointed to the new board.

I was, at the time, a teacher of Real Property at the University of Pittsburgh Law School. I knew no more about the Wagner Act than what was written in Pittsburgh newspapers and in Time magazine. By the sheerest of accidents, I had served in 1933 on a Pennsylvania Governor's Commission, appointed to investigate a remarkable Pennsylvania institution known as the Coal and Iron Police; and in 1934 I acted as arbitrator in a rather dull contract renewal arbitration between the Pittsburgh Street Car company and its employees. About August 20, 1935, I received a telephone call from the Solicitor of the Department of Labor, speaking for the Secretary [Frances Perkins] asking me to come to Washington that afternoon and talk about a place on the new Labor Board. My wife and children were excited, as was I. My visit with the Secretary before dinner occupied about a half-hour. She told me that she had discussed my qualifications with two good men who knew me. I told her that I was a teacher of Real Property and knew practically nothing about Labor Law. She said that was good; that I would have no prejudices. We agreed to meet again at ten that night at her house. At that meeting she told me she was authorized to offer me the chairmanship of the Board and the five year term. She also told me that my colleagues would be economists who had practical experience in labor relations. I accepted the Secretary's offer. * * *

The President sent the nominations to the Senate on the eve of adjournment, which had been delayed for a time by a one-man filibuster by Senator Huey Long. Since the names of my colleagues were favorably known, and mine was unknown, the Senate confirmed the nominations without debate.

The Board's first meeting was on August 27, 1935. There I became acquainted with the staff of people who had served the Resolution 44 Board and had, by statute, been assigned to serve the new Board if it desired to retain them. The Resolution 44 Board had set up Regional Offices in some 20 principal cities of the country. These holdover people knew the new statute thoroughly and had been busy making plans for its administration. Their knowledge was of great help to the Chairman. * * *

Just nine days after the Board's first meeting, the first of the slings and arrows, to which we were to become accustomed, arrived. The "National Lawyers Committee of the American Liberty League" called a press conference in Washington and distributed copies of its "Report on the Constitutionality of the National Labor Relations Act." [11] The committee members, whose names were printed in the report, were 58 in number, and the list was a real "who's who in American Law." A former Attorney General of the United States, two former Solicitors General, presidents of bar associations, lawyers for great business enterprises, and leaders of the bar in principal cities were among those who subscribed to the "Report."

This document is worthy of special mention because, I think, no such writing will ever occur again. It was in the form of a 132 page legal brief. Its introduction was a summary which concluded with this language:

> "Considering the Act in the light of our history, the established form of government and the decisions of our highest Court, we have no hesitancy in concluding that it is unconstitutional and that it constitutes a complete departure from our constitutional and traditional theories of government."

These fifty-eight lawyers had no client. The Board had not proceeded, nor even threatened to proceed, against anyone. So this definitive legal advice was just broadcast at large *pro bono publico.*

I have no doubt that the "Report" did great harm not only to the Board, in creating resistance to obedience to and enforcement of the law, but to clients of lesser lawyers who, relying on the dictum of the 58 distinguished lawyers, advised their clients that they could violate the law with impunity and thereby involved them in expensive litigation and charges for back pay. I think that had any one of these 58 lawyers had a paying client who sought advice on the question of whether the act was valid, the lawyer could not have given a definitive answer to his client's question. His research would have brought him to the conclusion that the act would probably be held unconstitutional, but there were precedents such as *Danbury Hatters, Second Coronado, Bedford Stone* and other cases which might lead to the opposite result. * * *

In spite of the condemnation of the new statute by important lawyers and editors, it was not for us to throw in the towel. But careful maneuvering was called for, lest we find ourselves in the United States Supreme Court with a weak case. That had happened to the Government in the *Schechter Poultry* case,[16] later known as the "sick chicken case," in which the Supreme Court had invalidated the National Industrial Recovery Act. The staff people of the board were able to settle unimpressive cases, or persuade unions not to press such cases, in order to protect our Supreme Court strategy. We were fortunate as well as careful, and in due time we reached the Supreme Court with five cases which fairly presented the constitutionality of our law as applied to a variety of situations.

Our cases were not argued in the Supreme Court until February, 1937, and in the meantime, that Court was making important decisions, some of

---

11. National Lawyers Committee of the American Liberty League, Constitutionality of the National Labor Relations Act (September 5, 1935).

16. Schechter Poultry Corp. v. United States, 295 U.S. 495, 55 S.Ct. 837, 79 L.Ed. 1570 (1935).

which were not at all promising for our project. In January, 1936, the Court held the important Agricultural Adjustment Act unconstitutional.[17] That case did not involve labor, and the Government was relying on the taxing power rather than the commerce power. But the decision did show that the Court was still relentless in narrowly interpreting the Constitution. In May of 1936, the Court decided the case of James Walter Carter v. The Carter Coal Company,[18] which did involve statutory wage-fixing and price-fixing in the depressed coal industry. The opinion repeated earlier statements of the Court that manufacturing was not interstate commerce but preceded such commerce, and applied the same rule to mining. We were greatly discouraged by the *Carter* decision.

Our activities proceeded on the assumption that the Wagner Act was our valid authority, but perhaps we were, as President Johnson said when describing the troubles which assail him from all directions, "in the position of a jack rabbit in a hailstorm, hunkered up and taking it." Some federal appellate courts had held, quite early, that our adversaries could not, by injunction, prevent us from holding hearings, but that they had to go through the statutorily provided procedure; and if they lost before the Board, they were required by statute to seek review in the United States Circuit Courts of Appeal. The Board and its hearing officers were frequently charged with being lax about the admission of evidence. Our statute, like most of the statutes creating administrative, quasi-judicial agencies, provided that we were not bound by the rules of evidence. On one occasion, the Board itself was hearing a case which involved an important manufacturer of truck trailers. The vice-president of the company was questioned by the Board counsel about the employment of a Pinkerton spy to undermine the union, which had lost all 29 of its members. The company counsel objected, urging that the relation between a labor spy and his employer is a privileged relation which is not subject to disclosure at a hearing. I forewent the opportunity, perhaps a unique one, of making this addition to the list of privileged relations. The story, when it was told, was not a pleasant one: the spy put the names of union members on pieces of paper which he deposited in agreed places; the vice-president picked them up, memorized them and burned the papers, and a day or two later discharged the union men for lingering overlong in the toilet or smoking in a forbidden place or some other infraction of company rules; when the union men were all discharged the spy was ostentatiously marched to the door and discharged, taking with him the contents of the union treasury, he being the treasurer.

*   *   *

The Supreme Court decisions in our cases came down on April 12, 1937. They were, of course, surprising. But it would be equally surprising to hear someone argue today that the federal government, given by the Constitution the power to foster and protect interstate commerce, must stand helpless in the face of an event which stops ore trains in Minnesota, ships on the Great Lakes, freight trains in Ohio, Pennsylvania and West Virginia and barges on the Ohio River, because the event occurred inside the gates of a steel mill in Aliquippa, Pennsylvania. I do not pursue this argument farther to include,

---

17. United States v. Butler, 297 U.S. 1, 56 S.Ct. 312, 80 L.Ed. 477 (1936).

18. 298 U.S. 238, 56 S.Ct. 855, 80 L.Ed. 1160 (1936).

for example, a barbecue stand in Alabama. But I can understand and sympathize with the Supreme Court's inability to draw a line anywhere short of *de minimis*.[23]

It gives one a good feeling to be held legitimate by the United States Supreme Court; to know, after all, that one has not been presiding over a kangaroo court. Our work increased, since unions and workmen naturally expected more of the Board after the Supreme Court decisions. The great mass-production industries of the country, now having good legal advice, came to terms with the law. But even before the Supreme Court decisions, the AFL–CIO civil war in the labor movement had occurred. It posed hard problems of statutory interpretation and many of our decisions made all of the involved parties unhappy. But these decisions were the first steps in the formation of legal doctrines, most of which are still the law. * * *

As I observe the Board's activities today, * * * I can only say that the work of the Board is voluminous and complex, which may be partly due to the 1947 and 1959 amendments and partly due to fine points in the statute which the Board and the labor bar of the 1930's were too unsophisticated to discover. * * * I am glad that I served with the Board during the 1930's and not more recently. In those days, there were very few gadgets on the instrument panel; we switched on the ignition, cranked up the machine and were off. * * *

23. In 1937 Professor Calvert Magruder sent me a poem written by the class poet of his Labor Law class at Harvard. The poem is based upon an actual decision of the Board. So it is good law. You may judge whether it is good poetry:

Alice in Labor Land (1937 Anonymous)

When Alice had decided that she was a silly ass
To waste her time exploring lands within the looking glass
While men like Warren Madden, Johnnie Lewis, Willie Green
At logical illogic far surpassed the King and Queen.

She tripped up to a factory which to her untutored gaze
Appeared just like a factory of the horse and buggy days
When stupid sort of people thought that laborers should work
And speeches should be given by such lads as Edmund Burke.
And other sorts of people had the charming naiveté
That made them think employers were entitled to last say.

Said Alice to the foreman: "How about a job for me?
For I would be a credit to your goddam company."
"Well really," said the foreman, "I'm afraid you'll have to go,

For I gather from your diction you espouse the C.I.O."
"Why, you economic royalist, you nasty so and so,"
Replied our lovely Alice, "I'll report to Uncle Joe."

So Joseph Warren Madden, at sweet Alice's behest,
Just took the little matter to his fond maternal breast.
But his milk of human kindness, at the outset, seemed to curdle
For he really hadn't reckoned on so difficult a hurdle.
The factory in question did not have a job to fill
Which to less resourceful bodies would have seemed a bitter pill.
The Board would not be beaten, they just all let down their hair
And solemnly they chanted "unfair, unfair, unfair."
So let there be created here a preferential list.
From hiring aught *but* Alice you must cease, you must desist.
It really doesn't matter, as a worker Alice stinks,
Or that she's rich as Croesus, or a stonehead like the Sphinx.
You'll take her in your factory so that by this you may know
You cannot take in vain the mystic letters, C.I.O.

Note

The constitutional validation of the Wagner Act in the Jones & Laughlin case, combined with the subsequent expansive interpretation of the Act under the "affecting commerce" standard (see Note 2, p. 122 supra), provided the setting for a head-on collision between that federal enactment and competing state regulatory schemes. The drama of this competition is traceable through a long line of Supreme Court decisions and has still not been fully played out. The rubric under which the contest has been conducted is "federal preemption," and the question in each case is whether the Supremacy Clause of the United States Constitution (Article VI) mandates, in the particular circumstances, a *federal* control and resolution of the controversy—"federal" not only in the sense of what law is to be applied but also of what agency or tribunal is to apply it.

The case which follows was the first to reach the United States Supreme Court in this crucial tug-of-war.

ALLEN–BRADLEY LOCAL NO. 1111 v. WISCONSIN EMPLOYMENT RELATIONS BOARD

Supreme Court of the United States, 1942.
315 U.S. 740, 62 S.Ct. 820, 86 L.Ed. 1154.

MR. JUSTICE DOUGLAS delivered the opinion of the Court.

The sole question presented by this case is whether an order of the Wisconsin Employment Relations Board entered under the Wisconsin Employment Peace Act, L. 1939, ch. 57, Wis.Stat.1939, ch. 111, pp. 1610–1618, is unconstitutional and void as being repugnant to the provisions of the National Labor Relations Act.

* * *

* * * Appellee, Allen-Bradley Co., is engaged in the manufacturing business in Wisconsin. Appellant union is a labor organization composed of the employees of that company. The union had a contract with the company governing terms and conditions of employment. The contract was cancelled by the union. Thereafter the union by secret ballot ordered a strike, which was called on May 11, 1939. The strike lasted about three months during which time the company continued to operate its plant. Differences arose between the employees who were on strike and the company and those employees who continued to work. The company thereupon filed a petition with the state Board charging the union and certain of its officers and members with unfair labor practices. The union answered and objected, inter alia, to the jurisdiction of the state Board on the ground that as respects the matters in controversy the company was subject exclusively to the provisions of the National Labor Relations Act and to the exclusive jurisdiction of the federal Board. The state Board made findings of fact and entered an order against the union and its officers and members. On a petition for review, the circuit court sustained and enforced the Board's order. The Supreme Court of Wisconsin affirmed that judgment. 237 Wis. 164, 295 N.W. 791. The case is here on appeal. Judicial Code, § 237(a), 28 U.S.C. § 344(a), 28 U.S.C.A. § 344(a).

The findings and order of the state Board as summarized by the Supreme Court (237 Wis. pages 168–170, 295 N.W. page 793) are as follows:

"Briefly, from the findings the following facts appear:

"(a) Appellants engaged in mass picketing at all entrances to the premises of the company for the purpose of hindering and preventing the pursuit of lawful work and employment by employees who desired to work.

"(b) They obstructed and interfered with the entrance to and egress from the factory and obstructed and interfered with the free and uninterrupted use of the streets and sidewalks surrounding the factory.

"(c) They threatened bodily injury and property damage to many of the employees who desired to continue their employment.

"(d) They required of persons desiring to enter the factory, to first obtain passes from the union. Persons holding such passes were admitted without interference.

* * *

"(f) That the union by its officers and many of its members injured the persons and property of employees who desired to continue their employment.

" * * *

"Based upon these findings the Board found as conclusions of law, that the union was guilty of unfair labor practices in the following respects:

"(a) Mass picketing for the purpose of hindering and preventing the pursuit of lawful work.

"(b) Threatening employees desiring to work with bodily injury and injury to their property.

"(c) Obstructing and interfering with entrance to and egress from the factory.

"(d) Obstructing and interfering with the free and uninterrupted use of the streets and public roads surrounding the factory.

* * *

"Based upon its findings of fact and conclusions of law the Board ordered that the union, its officers, agents, and members

"(1) Cease and desist from:

"(a) Mass picketing.

"(b) Threatening employees.

"(c) Obstructing or interfering with the factory entrances.

"(d) Obstructing or interfering with the free use of public streets, roads and sidewalks.

* * *

"The order required the union to post notices at its headquarters that it had ceased and desisted in the manner aforesaid and to notify the Board in writing of steps taken to comply with the order. * * *."

It was admitted that the company was subject to the National Labor Relations Act. The federal Board, however, had not undertaken in this case to exercise the jurisdiction which that Act conferred on it. Accordingly, the Supreme Court of Wisconsin upheld the order of the state Board stating that "there can be no conflict between the acts until they are applied to the same labor dispute." * * *

* * * [W]e confine our discussion to the precise facts of this case and intimate no opinion as to the validity of other types of orders in cases where the federal Board has not assumed jurisdiction.

* * *

The only employee or union conduct and activity forbidden by the state Board in this case was mass picketing, threatening employees desiring to work with physical injury or property damage, obstructing entrance to and egress from the company's factory, [and] obstructing the streets and public roads surrounding the factory * * *.

We agree with the statement of the United States as amicus curiae that the federal Act was not designed to preclude a State from enacting legislation limited to the prohibition or regulation of this type of employee or union activity. The Committee Reports [7] on the federal Act plainly indicate that it is not "a mere police court measure" and that authority of the several States may be exerted to control such conduct. Furthermore, this Court has long insisted that an "intention of Congress to exclude states from exerting their police power must be clearly manifested". Napier v. Atlantic Coast Line R. Co., 272 U.S. 605, 611, 47 S.Ct. 207, 209, 71 L.Ed. 432, * * *. Congress has not made such employee and union conduct as is involved in this case subject to regulation by the federal Board. * * * We will not lightly infer that Congress by the mere passage of a federal Act has impaired the traditional sovereignty of the several States in that regard.

* * * Sec. 7 of the federal Act, 29 U.S.C.A. § 157, guarantees labor its "fundamental right" (National Labor Relations Board v. Jones & Laughlin Steel Corp., 301 U.S. 1, 33, 57 S.Ct. 615, 622, 81 L.Ed. 893, 108 A.L.R. 1352) to self-organization and collective bargaining. Sec. 8 affords employees protection against unfair labor practices of employers including employer interference with the rights secured by § 7. Sec. 9 affords machinery for providing appropriate collective bargaining units. And § 10 grants the federal Board "exclusive" power of enforcement. * * * But, as we have said, the federal Act does not govern employee or union activity of the type here enjoined. And we fail to see how the inability to utilize mass picketing, threats, violence, and the other devices which were here employed impairs, dilutes, qualifies or in any respect subtracts from any of the rights guaranteed and protected by the federal Act. Nor is the freedom to engage in such conduct shown to be so essential or intimately related to a realization of the guarantees of the federal Act that its denial is an impairment of the federal policy. If the order of the state Board affected the status of the employees or if it caused a forfeiture of collective bargaining rights, a distinctly different question would arise. But since no such right is affected, we conclude that this case is not basically different from the common situation where a State takes steps to prevent breaches of the peace in connection with labor disputes. Since the state system of regulation, as construed and applied

7. S.Rep. No. 573, 74th Cong., 1st Sess., p. 16: "Nor can the committee sanction the suggestion that the bill should prohibit fraud or violence by employees or labor unions. The bill is not a mere police court measure. The remedies against such acts in the State and Federal courts and by the invocation of local police authorities are now adequate, as arrests and labor injunctions in industrial disputes throughout the country will attest. The Norris-LaGuardia Act does not deny to employers relief in the Federal courts against fraud, violence or threats of violence. See 29 U.S.C. § 104(e) and (i) [29 U.S.C.A. § 104 (e and i)]." * * *

here, can be reconciled with the federal Act and since the two as focused in this case can consistently stand together, the order of the state Board must be sustained under the rule which has long obtained in this Court. See Sinnot v. Davenport, 22 How. 227, 243, 16 L.Ed. 243.

In sum, we cannot say that the mere enactment of the National Labor Relations Act without more excluded state regulation of the type which Wisconsin has exercised in this case. * * *

Affirmed.

Note

The logic of the Supremacy Clause of the Constitution is that federal law is supreme when it wants to be supreme. This means, further analyzed, that congressional intent is the touchstone with regard to whether a given federal law preempts. Viewed with this perspective, do you agree with the decision in Allen-Bradley?

Suppose the following factual variation of Allen-Bradley: None of the union activities involved violence, threats of violence, or mass obstruction. Would, *should*, the state tribunal be authorized to ban the union activities, applying state law? Should it matter whether or not the National Labor Relations Board has been called upon to act in the case—i.e., should the preemption decision turn upon who wins the race to the most self-serving forum? If not, what tribunal should determine, in the first instance, whether the particular case should be governed by federal or state law?

All of the foregoing questions are subsumed under what has come to be called the "federal labor preemption doctrine." That doctrine is developed more fully infra pp. 330–372. For present purposes, it suffices to say that this preemption doctrine, together with the extreme reach of the "affecting commerce" jurisdictional standard of the Act, has provided the basis for a truly *national* labor policy under the control of the NLRB and the reviewing federal courts.

AMERICAN FEDERATION OF LABOR v. NATIONAL LABOR RELATIONS BOARD

Supreme Court of the United States, 1940.
308 U.S. 401, 60 S.Ct. 300, 84 L.Ed. 347.

MR. JUSTICE STONE delivered the opinion of the Court.

The question decisive of this case is whether a certification by the National Labor Relations Board under § 9(c) of the Wagner Act, * * * that a particular labor organization of longshore workers is the collective bargaining representative of the employees in a designated unit, composed of numerous employers of longshore workers at Pacific Coast ports, is reviewable by the Court of Appeals for the District of Columbia by the procedure set up in § 10(f) of the Act.

Petitioners, International Longshoremen's Association, and its affiliate, Pacific Coast District International Longshoremen's Association No. 38, are labor organizations, both affiliated with the petitioner, American Federation of Labor (A.F. of L.). In January, 1938, the International Longshoremen's & Warehousemen's Union, District No. 1, a labor organization affiliated with the Congress of Industrial Organization (C.I.O.) petitioned the Board for an investigation concerning the representation of longshoremen on the Pacific Coast, and that the Board certify the name of the appropriate representative for collective bargaining as provided in § 9(c) of the Wagner Act.

The Board directed an investigation with appropriate hearings, and a consolidation of the proceeding for purposes of hearing with two other proceedings already initiated by locals of the Longshoremen's Union. Petitioners were made parties to the consolidated proceedings and participated in the hearings, at the conclusion of which the Board made its findings of fact and of law and certified that the workers who do longshore work in the Pacific Coast ports for the employers which are members of five designated employer associations of Pacific Coast shipowners or of waterfront employers, constitute a unit appropriate for the purposes of collective bargaining within the meaning of § 9(b) of the Act. It also certified that the C.I.O. affiliate, Longshoremen's Union, District No. 1, is the exclusive bargaining representative of all the workers in such unit within the meaning of the Act. In the Matter of Shipowners' Association of the Pacific Coast et al., 7 N.L. R.B. 1002.

The effect of the certification, as petitioner alleges, is the inclusion in a single unit, for bargaining purposes, of all of the longshore employees of the members of the employer associations doing business at the west coast ports of the United States, and to designate the C.I.O. affiliate as their bargaining representative so that in the case of some particular employers, their workers who are not organized or represented by the C.I.O. affiliate have been deprived of opportunity to secure bargaining representatives of their own choice. Although the petitioners who are affiliated with the A.F. of L. assert that they have in fact been selected as bargaining representatives by a majority of the employees of their respective employers, petitioners allege that they have nevertheless been prevented from acting in that capacity by the Board's designation of the C.I.O. affiliate as the exclusive representative of such employees.

The present suit was begun by petition to the Court of Appeals of the District of Columbia in which the petitioners set forth, in addition to the facts already detailed, that they were aggrieved by the "decision and order of certification of the Board" in that the certificate is contrary to fact and to law; that the Wagner Act does not contemplate or authorize "the designation by the Board of an employee unit constituting all the employees of different employers in different and distant geographical districts of the United States." The petition prayed that the "order of certification" be set aside, in so far as it attempts to designate a single exclusive bargaining representative for longshore employees of many employers on the Pacific Coast and denies to a majority of the longshore employees of a single employer the right to select one of the petitioners as their exclusive bargaining representative.

The Court of Appeals dismissed the petition as not within the jurisdiction to review orders of the Board conferred upon it by § 10 of the Wagner Act. 70 App.D.C. 62, 103 F.2d 933. We granted certiorari * * * because of the importance of the question presented and to resolve an alleged conflict of the decision below with that of the Court of Appeals for the Sixth Circuit, in International Brotherhood of Electrical Workers v. National Labor Relations Board, 105 F.2d 598.

The Court of Appeals for the District of Columbia, like the several circuit courts of appeals, is without the jurisdiction over original suits conferred on district courts by § 24 of the Judicial Code, as amended. 28 U.S.C.A. § 41. Such jurisdiction as it has, to review directly the action of administrative agencies, is specially conferred by legislation relating specifically to the determinations of such agencies made subject to review, and prescribing the manner and extent of the review. Here, the provisions of the Wagner Act, § 10(f), which gives a right of review to "any person aggrieved by a final order of the Board", determines the nature and scope of the review by the court of appeals.

The <u>single issue</u> which we are now called on to decide is whether the certification by the Board is an "order" which, by related provisions of the statute, is made reviewable upon petition to the Court of Appeals of the District or in an appropriate case to a circuit court of appeals. The question is distinct from another much argued at the Bar, whether petitioners are precluded by the provisions of the Wagner Act from maintaining an independent suit in a district court to set aside the Board's action because contrary to the statute, and because it inflicts on petitioners an actionable injury otherwise irreparable.

By the provisions of the Wagner Act the Board is given two principal functions to perform. One, defined by § 9, which as enacted is headed "Representatives And Elections", is the certification, after appropriate investigation and hearing, of the name or names of representatives, for collective bargaining, of an appropriate unit of employees. The other, defined by § 10, which as enacted is headed "Prevention of Unfair Labor Practices", is the prevention by the Board's order after hearing and by a further appropriate proceeding in court, of the unfair labor practices enumerated in § 8. One of the outlawed practices is the refusal of an employer to bargain with the representative of his employees. § 8(5).

Certification involves, under § 9(b), decision by the Board whether "the unit appropriate for the purposes of collective bargaining shall be the employer unit, craft unit, plant unit, or subdivision thereof", and the ascertainment by the Board under § 9(c) of the bargaining representative who, under § 9(a) must be "designated or selected ∗ ∗ ∗ by the majority of the employees in a unit appropriate for such [bargaining] purposes". The Board is authorized by § 9(c) "whenever a question affecting commerce arises concerning the representation of employees" to investigate "such controversy" and to certify the names of the appropriate bargaining representatives. In conducting the investigation it is required to provide for appropriate hearing upon due notice "and may take a secret ballot of employees, or utilize any other suitable method" of ascertaining such representatives.[f] By § 9(d) whenever an order of the Board is made pursuant to § 10(c) directing any person to cease an unfair labor practice and there is a petition for enforcement or review of the order by a court, the Board's

---

f. In the Taft-Hartley amendments of 1947, Congress mandated an election whenever a "question of representation" exists: Section 9(c)(1) specifies that in such a case the Board "shall direct an election by secret ballot and shall certify the results thereof."

"certification and the record of such investigation" is to be included in the transcript of the entire record required to be filed under § 10(e) or (f), and the decree of the court enforcing, modifying or setting aside the order of the Board is to be made and entered upon the pleadings, testimony and proceedings set forth in the transcript.

It is to be noted that § 9, which is complete in itself, makes no provision, in terms, for review of a certification by the Board and authorizes no use of the certification or of the record in a certification proceeding, except in the single case where there is a petition for enforcement or review of an order restraining an unfair labor practice as authorized by § 10(c). In that event the record in the certification proceeding is included in the record brought upon review of the Board's order restraining an unfair labor practice. It then becomes a part of the record upon which the decree of the reviewing court is to be based.

All other provisions for review of any action of the Board are found in § 10 which as its heading indicates relates to the prevention of unfair labor practices. Nowhere in this section is there mention of investigations or certifications authorized and defined by § 9. Section 10(a) authorizes the Board "to prevent any person from engaging in any unfair labor practice (listed in section 8) affecting commerce". Section 10(b) prescribes the procedure of the Board when any person is charged with engaging in any unfair labor practice, and requires that the person so charged shall be served with a complaint and notice of hearing by the Board with opportunity to file an answer and be heard. Section 10(c) directs the Board, if it is of opinion, as the result of the proceedings before it, that any person named in the complaint has engaged in an unfair labor practice "to issue" "an order" directing that person to cease the practice and commanding appropriate affirmative action. If the Board is of opinion that there has been no unfair labor practice it is directed "to issue" "an order" dismissing the complaint. Section 10(e) authorizes a petition to the appropriate federal court of appeals by the Board for the enforcement of its order prohibiting an unfair labor practice.

This brings us to the provisions for review of action taken by the Board in § 10(f) which is controlling in the present proceeding. That subdivision appears as an integral part of § 10. All the other subdivisions relate exclusively to proceedings for the prevention of unfair labor practices. Both they and subdivision (f) are silent as to the proceedings or certifications authorized by § 9. Section 10(f), providing for review, speaks only of a "final order of the Board". It gives a right to review to persons aggrieved by a final order upon petition to a court of appeals in the circuit "wherein the unfair labor practice in question was alleged to have been engaged in or wherein such person resides or transacts business, or in the Court of Appeals of the District of Columbia". It directs that the order shall be reviewed on the entire record before the Board "including the pleading and testimony" upon which the order complained of was entered, although no complaint or other pleading is mentioned by § 9 relating to representation proceedings and certificates. Subdivision (f) provides that upon petition for review by an aggrieved person "the court shall proceed in the same manner as in the case of an application by the Board under subdivision [subsection] (e)", and it is given the same jurisdiction "to grant to the Board such temporary relief or restraining order as it deems just and proper, and in like manner to make and enter a decree enforcing, modifying, and enforcing as so modified, or setting aside in whole or in part the order of the Board." * * *

[I]t is evident that the entire structure of the Act emphasizes, for purposes of review, the distinction between an "order" of the Board restraining an unfair labor practice and a certification in representation proceedings. The one authorized by § 10 may be reviewed by the court on petition of the Board for enforcement of the order, or of a person aggrieved, in conformity to the procedure laid down in § 10, which says nothing of certifications. The other, authorized by § 9, is nowhere spoken of as an order, and no procedure is prescribed for its review apart from an order prohibiting an unfair labor practice. The exclusion of representation proceedings from the review secured by the provisions of § 10(f) is emphasized by the clauses of § 9(d), which provide for certification by the Board of a record of a representation proceeding only in the case when there is a petition for review of an order of the Board restraining an unfair labor practice. The statute on its face thus indicates a purpose to limit the review afforded by § 10 to orders of the Board prohibiting unfair labor practices, a purpose and a construction which its legislative history confirms.

Upon the introduction of the bill which was enacted as the Wagner Act, Congress had pointedly brought to its attention the experience under Public Resolution 44 of June 19, 1934, 48 Stat. 1183. That resolution authorized the National Labor Relations Board, predecessor of respondent, "to order and conduct an election" by employees of any employer to determine who were their representatives for bargaining purposes. Section 2 provided that any order of the Board should be reviewed in the same manner as orders of the Federal Trade Commission under the Federal Trade Commission Act. The reports of the Congressional committees upon the bill which became the Wagner Act refer to the long delays in the procedure prescribed by Resolution 44, resulting from applications to the federal appellate courts for review of orders for elections.[2] And in considering the provisions of § 9(d) the committee reports were emphatic in their declaration that the provisions of the bill for court review did not extend to proceedings under § 9 except as incidental to review of an order restraining an unfair labor practice under § 10.[3] The bill was similarly explained on the Senate floor by the committee

2. "Weaknesses in Existing Law. * * * (6) *Obstacles to elections.*—Under Public Resolution 44, any attempt by the Government to conduct an election of representatives may be contested ab initio in the courts, although such election is in reality merely a preliminary determination of fact. This means that the Government can be delayed indefinitely before it takes the first step toward industrial peace. After almost a year not a single case, in which a company has chosen to contest an election order of the Board, has reached decision in any circuit court of appeals." Sen. Rep. No. 573, Committee on Education and Labor, 74th Cong., 1st Sess., pp. 5, 6. * * *

3. "There is no more reason for court review prior to an election than for court review

prior to a hearing. But if subsequently the Board makes an order predicated upon the election, such as an order to bargain collectively with elected representatives, then the entire election procedure becomes part of the record upon which the order of the Board is based, and is fully reviewable by an aggrieved party in the Federal courts in the manner provided in section 10. And this review would include within its scope the action of the Board in determining the appropriate unit for purposes of the election. This provides a complete guarantee against arbitrary action by the Board." Sen.Rep. 573, Committee on Education and Labor, 74th Cong., 1st Sess., p. 14.

* * *

chairman who declared: "It provides for review in the courts only after the election has been held and the Board has ordered the employer to do something predicated upon the results of an election." 79 Cong.Rec., 7658. The conclusion is unavoidable that Congress, as the result of a deliberate choice of conflicting policies, has excluded representation certifications of the Board from the review by federal appellate courts authorized by the Wagner Act except in the circumstances specified in § 9(d).

An argument, much pressed upon us, is, in effect, that Congress was mistaken in its judgment that the hearing before the Board in proceedings under § 9(c), with review only when an order is made under § 10(c) directing the employer to do something "provides an appropriate safeguard and opportunity to be heard", House Rep., p. 23, and that "this provides a complete guarantee against arbitrary action by the Board," Sen.Rep., p. 14. It seems to be thought that this failure to provide for a court review is productive of peculiar hardships, which were perhaps not foreseen in cases where the interests of rival unions are affected. But these are arguments to be addressed to Congress and not the courts. The argument too that Congress has infringed due process by withholding from federal appellate courts a jurisdiction which they never possessed is similarly without force.

* * *

The Board argues that the provisions of the Wagner Act, particularly § 9(d), have foreclosed review of its challenged action by independent suit in the district court * * *. But that question is not presented for decision by the record before us. Its answer involves a determination whether the Wagner Act, in so far as it has given legally enforceable rights, has deprived the district courts of some portion of their original jurisdiction conferred by § 24 of the Judicial Code, 28 U.S.C.A. § 41. It can be appropriately answered only upon a showing in such a suit that unlawful action of the Board has inflicted an injury on the petitioners for which the law, apart from the review provisions of the Wagner Act, affords a remedy. This question can be properly and adequately considered only when it is brought to us for review upon a suitable record.

Affirmed.

Note

1. Could the AFL have obtained review of the NLRB's certification in the court of appeals by the means provided in the NLRA? What impact does Section 8(b)(7), subsequently added by the Landrum-Griffin Act of 1959, have on this question?

2. The question left open in AFL v. NLRB as to the propriety of review of a certification by an independent suit in the federal district court, invoking the original jurisdiction of that court under Section 24 of the Judicial Code, was answered by the Supreme Court in Leedom v. Kyne, 358 U.S. 184, 79 S.Ct. 180, 3 L.Ed.2d 210 (1958), infra p. 235. The limited circumstances under which judicial review of a certification may be had in such an independent suit are explored in the Leedom case and the Note which follows it.

3. The first formal step in any scheme of progression toward a collective bargaining relationship between an employer and employees is determination of the group of employees to be covered by that relationship. The second step is

the ascertainment of the employees' choice of bargaining representative, if any. These two steps are subsumed under the rubric "representation question." The first step, described as "unit determination," is fundamental to all that follows: Initially, it establishes what employees will be eligible to participate in the selection of the bargaining representative; the process of unit determination therefore entails, among other things, the likelihood of resort by all interested parties (employer, union or unions, and, on occasion, even the NLRB) to the logic and tactics of gerrymandering. Beyond that, the determination of the unit establishes what employees will have their terms and conditions of employment negotiated by the representative selected in the representation contest; therefore, the soundness of the collective bargaining relationship depends considerably upon the appropriateness of the unit.

What factors should be taken into account in determining the appropriateness of a bargaining unit? Are the pertinent factors political or economic in nature? Or both? On the basis of your own analysis, is the NLRB's unit determination in AFL v. NLRB sound? Is that determination consistent with the language of Section 9(b)? See Sections 2(2) and (1) of the Act.

It is interesting to note that in 1941 the Board reversed its decision in the AFL case to the extent of ordering separate elections in three of the ports encompassed in the coast-wide unit previously determined to be appropriate. These elections were won overwhelmingly by locals of the International Longshoremen's Association, AFL, which were accordingly certified as the representatives for the three units. The reopening of the unit question was prompted by the continued resistance of the longshoremen employed in those ports to representation by the CIO affiliate. 32 N.L.R.B. 668 (1941); 33 N.L.R.B. 845 (1941).

4. The AFL v. NLRB case suggests two prominent and related criticisms of the Board in its unit determinations under the Wagner Act. The Board was charged with (1) favoring large over small units where the extent of organization provided alternatives and (2) preferring industrial (CIO) over craft (AFL) unions. These criticisms were most strongly voiced by the AFL, gored by a quirk of history. When the Wagner Act was passed in 1935, there was yet no split in the labor movement, and such a split had not been foreseen by Congress. The Act and its predecessor, the NIRA, unwittingly occasioned the split by giving considerable impetus to the organization of millions of unskilled and little-skilled workers in the mass production industries. The AFL was confronted by a vast opportunity for organization of these workers but was inhibited in such an organizing effort by its tradition of craft jurisdiction. The potential recruits did not fit well into the pattern of craft organization, premised as the latter was upon the possession and compartmentalization of particular skills—e.g., electricians, plumbers, carpenters, each in their own craft union. As a consequence, the issue of industrial unionism boiled up within the AFL. Certain of the AFL affiliates, e.g., the United Mine Workers, had successfully engaged in industrial organization; they pressed for a vigorous effort at organizing the mass production industries along industrial lines. The alternative was to attempt to parcel out this tremendous group of noncraft, unorganized workers to the various craft unions within the AFL. Two obvious drawbacks to such an approach were that the task of delineating appropriate jurisdictional lines was difficult, if not impossible, and that, even if this could be done, the result would be a "Balkanization" of the industrial workers within a given plant and thus a weakening of their bargaining power.

The issue came to a head at the AFL Convention in 1935, when John L. Lewis, president of the Mine Workers, spoke out strongly in favor of industrial unionism. The president of the Carpenters' Union, William Hutcheson (lead player in U.S. v. Hutcheson, supra p. 92), objected to the point of fisticuffs, and the session ended abortively. In November of 1935 the presidents of eight disenchanted AFL unions formed the Committee for Industrial Organization, with John L. Lewis as chairman. The Executive Committee of the AFL ordered the Committee to dissolve. When this order was defied, the maverick unions were suspended from the Federation. Efforts to heal the breach failed, and in 1938 the charters of these unions were revoked. Thereafter, in the same year, the Committee for Industrial Organization transformed itself into the permanent Congress of Industrial Organizations. The first president of the CIO was Lewis, who was succeeded upon his resignation in 1940 by Philip Murray, president of the newly created Steelworkers Union. (For an interesting account of the "rise of the CIO," see Dulles, Labor in America 288–311 (3d ed. 1966).)

Since Congress had not anticipated the foregoing developments, it provided the NLRB with no guidance for confronting the intense rivalry produced by the split in the labor movement. The Board was forced to deal with the competition between AFL and CIO affiliates on the basis of such wisdom as it could muster and the evidence produced in particular cases. The unit-determination arena was the prime battleground.

A leading case illustrative of the jurisdictional struggle and loudly condemned by the AFL was AMERICAN CAN CO., 13 N.L.R.B. 1252 (1939). In that case a company in Brooklyn, engaged in the manufacture of tin containers, employed some 891 production and maintenance workers, of whom 135 were skilled craftsmen, including electricians, engineers, firemen and oilers. Four unions were contesting for the right to represent all or some of these employees. The Steel Workers' Organizing Committee (forerunner of the United Steelworkers of America), a CIO affiliate and therefore a union which organized on an industrial basis, sought certification as the bargaining representative of all 891 of the production and maintenance employees. The International Brotherhood of Electrical Workers, the Operating Engineers, and the Firemen and Oilers, all of which were craft unions affiliated with the AFL, sought to represent those craftsmen among the company's employees who fell within the jurisdiction of each of the three unions—i.e., the electricians, the engineers, and the firemen and oilers. The critical question was thus one of unit determination. The Steel Workers contended that the appropriate unit was an all-inclusive one, comprehending all 891 production and maintenance workers. The AFL unions contended for three small craft units, each one consisting of the skilled employees engaged in the particular craft. The question presented to the NLRB was therefore whether there should be only one comprehensive "industrial" unit, in which case the CIO union would be the exclusive bargaining representative for all of the employees, or, instead, separate units for each of the three crafts along with a larger unit for the non-craft production and maintenance workers, in which case there would be a different bargaining representative for each of the units.

For a year prior to the presentation of this representation question to the NLRB, the Steel Workers had been recognized by the employer as the exclusive bargaining representative of all 891 employees and had, indeed, negotiated a one-year collective bargaining agreement covering those employees. Moreover, that contract had been renewed by the Steel Workers and the company after the assertion by the AFL unions of their claim to bargaining rights on behalf of the craft employees.

The Board held in favor of the CIO union, establishing only the one comprehensive unit. It stated:

"We are of the opinion that the Board is not authorized by the Act to split the appropriate unit thus established by collective bargaining and embodied in a valid, exclusive bargaining contract. In any appropriate unit it is to be presumed that there will be dissatisfied groups from time to time. To permit such small groups to break up an appropriate unit established and maintained by a bona fide collective bargaining contract against the will of the majority of the employees who are bound by the contract would make stability and responsibility in collective bargaining impossible. Neither craft, plant, nor industrial units could maintain any unity in bargaining if any subordinate parts of established appropriate units were free to disregard contractual obligations and claim separate representation with separate contracts.

"If the Board certified separate representatives for the three small groups of employees in the present case, it would not only be setting aside a provision of a valid contract, but it would be substituting its own preferences for the preferences of the employees and the employer as to the appropriateness of a bargaining unit that they have voluntarily agreed in a contract is best for their purposes. We are of the opinion that the Board must look to established custom and practice as embodied in collective bargaining agreements for the appropriate units, and not to theoretical principles that appeal to the members of the Board as being fair.

"We therefore find that the separate bargaining units sought to be established by the Engineers, the Firemen & Oilers, and the I.B.E.W. in the present case are not appropriate for the purposes of collective bargaining." 13 N.L.R.B. at 1256–57.

The so-called "American Can doctrine," while not rigidly adhered to by the Board in all cases, drew the fire of the AFL and was one of the Board "abuses" upon which Congress focused in amending the Wagner Act in 1947.

5. A related "abuse," which also drew congressional attention in the Taft-Hartley Amendments of 1947 (Section 9(c)(5)), was the "extent of organization" criterion sometimes applied by the Board in unit determination. An example of this approach was Botany Worsted Mills, 27 N.L.R.B. 687 (1940), in which the Textile Workers Union, a CIO affiliate, sought bargaining rights for a department of "wool sorters or trappers." The company contested the appropriateness of such a unit on the ground that the "sorters or trappers work in merely one department of the entire company and, for this reason, cannot properly be set apart from the rest of the employees as a separate unit for the purposes of collective bargaining." The Board held in favor of the union, stating:

"Wherever possible, it is obviously desirable that, in a determination of the appropriate unit, we render collective bargaining of the Company's employees an immediate possibility. There is no evidence that the majority of the other employees of the Company belong to any union whatsoever; nor has any other labor organization petitioned the Board for certification as representative of the Company's employees on a plant-wide basis. Consequently, even if, under other circumstances, the wool sorters or trappers would not constitute the most effective bargaining unit, nevertheless, in the existing circumstances, unless they are recognized as a separate unit, there will be no collective bargaining agent whatsoever for these workers.

"At the present time, and in view of the existing state of labor organization among the employees of the Company, in order to insure to the sorters or trappers the full benefit of their right to self-organization and collective bargaining and otherwise to effectuate the policies of the Act, we find that the wool sorters or trappers of the Company, including the overlookers, constitute a unit appropriate for the purposes of collective bargaining with respect to rates of pay, wages, hours of employment, and other conditions of employment."   27 N.L.R.B. at 690.

NATIONAL LABOR RELATIONS BOARD v.
FANSTEEL METALLURGICAL CORP.

Supreme Court of the United States, 1939.
306 U.S. 240, 59 S.Ct. 490, 83 L.Ed. 627, 123 A.L.R. 599.

MR. CHIEF JUSTICE HUGHES delivered the opinion of the Court.

The Circuit Court of Appeals set aside an order of the National Labor Relations Board requiring respondent to desist from labor practices found to be in violation of the National Labor Relations Act and to offer reinstatement to certain discharged employees with back pay. While the other portions of the Board's order are under review, the principal question presented relates to the authority of the Board to require respondent to reinstate employees who were discharged because of their unlawful conduct in seizing respondent's property in what is called a "sit-down strike."

Respondent, Fansteel Metallurgical Corporation, is engaged at North Chicago, Illinois, in the manufacture and sale of products made from rare metals. * * * The findings of the Board show that in the summer of 1936 a group of employees organized Lodge 66 under the auspices of a committee of the Amalgamated Association of Iron, Steel and Tin Workers of North America; that respondent employed a "labor spy" to engage in espionage within the Union and his employment was continued until about December 1, 1936; that on September 10, 1936, respondent's superintendent was requested to meet with a committee of the union and the superintendent required that the committee should consist only of employees of five years' standing; that a committee, so constituted, presented a contract relating to working conditions; that the superintendent objected to "closed-shop and check-off provisions" and announced that it was respondent's policy to refuse recognition to "outside" unions; that on September 21, 1936, the superintendent refused to confer with the committee in which an "outside" organizer had been included; that meanwhile, and later, respondent's representatives sought to have a "company union" set up but the attempt proved abortive; that from November, 1936, to January, 1937, the superintendent required the president of the Union to work in a room adjoining the superintendent's office with the purpose of keeping him away from the other workers; that while in September, 1936, the Union did not have a majority of the production and maintenance employees, an appropriate unit for collective bargaining, by February 17, 1937, 155 of respondent's 229 employees in that unit had joined the Union and had designated it as their collective bargaining representative; that on that date, a committee of the Union met twice with the superintendent who refused to bargain with the Union as to rates of pay, hours and conditions of employment, the refusal being upon the ground that respondent would not deal with an "outside" union.

Shortly after the second meeting in the afternoon of February 17th the Union committee decided upon a "sit-down strike" by taking over and holding two of respondent's "key" buildings. These were thereupon occupied by about 95 employees. Work stopped and the remainder of the plant also ceased operations. Employees who did not desire to participate were permitted to leave, and a number of Union members who were on the night shift and did not arrive for work until after the seizure did not join their fellow members inside the buildings. At about six o'clock in the evening the superintendent accompanied by police officials and respondent's counsel, went to each of the buildings and demanded that the men leave. They refused and respondent's counsel "thereupon announced in loud tones that all the men in the plant were discharged for the seizure and retention of the buildings." The men continued to occupy the buildings until February 26, 1937. Their fellow members brought them food, blankets, stoves, cigarettes and other supplies.

On February 18th, respondent obtained from the state court an injunction order requiring the men to surrender the premises. The men refused to obey the order and a writ of attachment for contempt was served on February 19th. Upon the men's refusal to submit, a pitched battle ensued and the men successfully resisted the attempt by the sheriff to evict and arrest them. Efforts at mediation on the part of the United States Department of Labor and the Governor of Illinois proved unavailing. On February 26th the sheriff with an increased force of deputies made a further attempt and this time, after another battle, the men were ousted and placed under arrest. Most of them were eventually fined and given jail sentences for violating the injunction.

Respondent on regaining possession undertook to resume operations and production gradually began. By March 12th the restaffing was approximately complete. A large number of the strikers, including many who had participated in the occupation of the buildings, were individually solicited to return to work with back pay but without recognition of the Union. Some accepted the offer and were reinstated; others refused to return unless there were union recognition and mass reinstatement and were still out at the time of the hearing before the Board. New men were hired to fill the positions of those remaining on strike.

Meanwhile the Union was not inactive. On March 3d and 5th there were requests, which respondent refused, for meetings to consider the recognition of the Union for collective bargaining. There was no collective request for reinstatement of all the strikers. The position of practically all the strikers who did not go back, and who were named in the complaint filed with the Board, was "that they were determined to stay out until the Union reached a settlement with the respondent."

Early in April a labor organization known as Rare Metal Workers of America, Local No. 1, was organized among respondent's employees. There was a meeting in one of respondent's buildings on April 15th, which was attended by about 200 employees and the balloting resulted in a vote of 185 to 15 in favor of the formation of an "independent" organization. Another meeting was held soon after for the election of officers. Respondent accorded these efforts various forms of support. The Board concluded that the Rare Metal Workers of America, Local No. 1, was the result of the respondent's "antiunion campaign" and that respondent had dominated and interfered with its formation and administration.

Upon the basis of these findings and its conclusions of law, the Board made its order directing respondent to desist from interfering with its employees in the exercise of their right to self-organization and to bargain collectively through representatives of their own choosing as guaranteed in Section 7 of the Act; from dominating or interfering with the formation or administration of the Rare Metal Workers of America, Local No. 1, or any other labor organization of its employees or contributing support thereto; and from refusing to bargain collectively with the Amalgamated Association of Iron, Steel and Tin Workers of North America, Lodge 66, as the exclusive representative of the employees described. The Board also ordered the following affirmative action which it was found would "effectuate the policies" of the Act;—that is, upon request, to bargain collectively with the Amalgamated Association as stated above; to offer, upon application, to the employees who went on strike on February 17, 1937, and thereafter, "immediate and full reinstatement to their former positions," with back pay, dismissing, if necessary, all persons hired since that date; to withdraw all recognition from Rare Metal Workers of America, Local No. 1, as a representative of the employees for the purpose of dealing with respondent as to labor questions and to "completely disestablish" that organization as such representative; and to post notices of compliance. 5 N.L.R.B. 930. * * *

On respondent's petition, the Circuit Court of Appeals set aside the Board's order (7 Cir., 98 F.2d 375) and this Court granted certiorari * * *.

First.—The unfair labor practices. The Board concluded that by "the anti-union statements and actions" of the superintendent on September 10, 1936, and September 21, 1936, by "the campaign to introduce into the plant a company union," by "the isolation of the union president from contact with his fellow employees," and by the employment and use of a "labor spy," respondent had interfered with its employees, and restrained and coerced them, in the exercise of their right to self-organization guaranteed in Section 7 of the Act and thus had engaged in an unfair labor practice under Section 8(1) of the Act.

Owing to the fact that in September, 1936 the Union did not have a majority of the employees in the appropriate unit, the Board held that it was precluded from finding unfair labor practices in refusing to bargain collectively at that time, but the Board found that there was such a refusal on February 17, 1937, when the Union did have a majority of the employees in the appropriate unit, and that this constituted a violation of Section 8(5).

These conclusions are supported by the findings of the Board and the latter in this relation have substantial support in the evidence.

Second.—The discharge of the employees for illegal conduct in seizing and holding respondent's buildings. The Board does not now contend that there was not a real discharge on February 17th when the men refused to surrender possession. The discharge was clearly proved.

Nor is there any basis for dispute as to the cause of the discharge. Representatives of respondent demanded that the men leave and on their refusal announced that they were discharged "for the seizure and retention of the buildings." * * *

Nor is it questioned that the seizure and retention of respondent's property were unlawful. It was a high-handed proceeding without shadow of legal right. It became the subject of denunciation by the state court under the state law, resulting in fines and jail sentences for defiance of the court's order to vacate and in a final decree for respondent as the complainant in the injunction suit.

This conduct on the part of the employees manifestly gave good cause for their discharge unless the National Labor Relations Act abrogates the right of the employer to refuse to retain in his employ those who illegally take and hold possession of his property.

Third.—The authority of the Board to require the reinstatement of the employees thus discharged. The contentions of the Board in substance are these: (1) That the unfair labor practices of respondent led to the strike and thus furnished ground for requiring the reinstatement of the strikers; (2) That under the terms of the Act employees who go on strike because of an unfair labor practice retain their status as employees and are to be considered as such despite discharge for illegal conduct; (3) That the Board was entitled to order reinstatement or reemployment in order to "effectuate the policies" of the Act.

(1) For the unfair labor practices of respondent the Act provided a remedy. Interference in the summer and fall of 1936 with the right of self-organization could at once have been the subject of complaint to the Board. The same remedy was available to the employees when collective bargaining was refused on February 17, 1937. But reprehensible as was that conduct of the respondent, there is no ground for saying that it made respondent an outlaw or deprived it of its legal rights to the possession and protection of its property. The employees had the right to strike but they had no license to commit acts of violence or to seize their employer's plant. We may put on one side the contested questions as to the circumstances and extent of injury to the plant and its contents in the efforts of the men to resist eviction. The seizure and holding of the buildings was itself a wrong apart from any acts of sabotage. But in its legal aspect the ousting of the owner from lawful possession is not essentially different from an assault upon the officers of an employing company, or the seizure and conversion of its goods, or the despoiling of its property or other unlawful acts in order to force compliance with demands. To justify such conduct because of the existence of a labor dispute or of an unfair labor practice would be to put a premium on resort to force instead of legal remedies and to subvert the principles of law and order which lie at the foundations of society.

As respondent's unfair labor practices afforded no excuse for the seizure and holding of its buildings, respondent had its normal rights of redress. Those rights, in their most obvious scope, included the right to discharge the wrongdoers from its employ. To say that respondent could resort to the state court to recover damages or to procure punishment, but was powerless to discharge those responsible for the unlawful seizure, would be to create an anomalous distinction for which there is no warrant unless it can be found in the terms of the National Labor Relations Act. * * *

(2) * * *

We think that the true purpose of Congress is reasonably clear. Congress was intent upon the protection of the right of employees to self-organization and to the selection of representatives of their own choosing for collective bargaining without restraint or coercion. * * * To assure that protection, the employer is not permitted to discharge his employees because of union activity or agitation for collective bargaining. * * * The conduct thus protected is lawful conduct. Congress also recognized the right to strike,—that the employees could lawfully cease work at their own volition because of the failure of the employer to meet their demands. Section 13 provides that nothing in the Act "shall be construed so as to interfere with or impede or diminish in any way the right to strike." But this recognition of "the right to strike",—plainly contemplates a lawful strike,—the exercise of the unquestioned right to quit work.

Here the strike was illegal in its inception and prosecution. As the Board found, it was initiated by the decision of the Union committee "to take over and hold two of the respondent's 'key' buildings." It was pursuant to that decision that the men occupied the buildings and the work stopped. This was not the exercise of "the right to strike" to which the Act referred. It was not a mere quitting of work and statement of grievances in the exercise of pressure recognized as lawful. It was an illegal seizure of the buildings in order to prevent their use by the employer in a lawful manner and thus by acts of force and violence to compel the employer to submit. When the employees resorted to that sort of compulsion they took a position outside the protection of the statute and accepted the risk of the termination of their employment upon grounds aside from the exercise of the legal rights which the statute was designed to conserve.

(3) The Board contends that its order is valid under the terms of the Act "regardless of whether the men remained employees." The Board bases its contention on the general authority, conferred by Section 10(c), to require the employer to take such affirmative action as will "effectuate the policies" of the Act. Such action, it is argued, may embrace not only reinstatement of those whose status as employees has been continued by virtue of Section 2(3), but also a requirement of the "reemployment" of those who have ceased to be employed.

The authority to require affirmative action to "effectuate the policies" of the Act is broad but it is not unlimited. It has the essential limitations which inhere in the very policies of the Act which the Board invokes. Thus in Consolidated Edison Company v. National Labor Relations Board, 305 U.S. 197, 59 S.Ct. 206, 83 L.Ed. 126, decided December 5, 1938, we held that the authority to order affirmative action did not go so far as to confer a punitive jurisdiction enabling the Board to inflict upon the employer any penalty it may choose because he is engaged in unfair labor practices, even though the Board is of the opinion that the policies of the Act may be effectuated by such an order. We held that the power to command affirmative action is remedial, not punitive, and is to be exercised in aid of the Board's authority to restrain violations and as a means of removing or avoiding the consequences of violation where those consequences are of a kind to thwart the purposes of the Act.

* * * [T]he purpose of the Act is to promote peaceful settlements of disputes by providing legal remedies for the invasion of the employees' rights. * * * We are of the opinion that to provide for the reinstatement or reemployment of employees guilty of the acts which the Board finds to have been committed in this instance would not only not effectuate any policy of the Act but would directly tend to make abortive its plan for peaceable procedure.

What we have said also meets the point that the question whether reinstatement or reemployment would effectuate the policies of the Act is committed to the decision of the Board in the exercise of its discretion subject only to the limitation that its action may not be "arbitrary, unreasonable or capricious". The Board recognizes that in "many situations" reinstatement or reemployment after discharge for illegal acts would not be proper, but the Board insists that it was proper in this instance. For the reasons we have given we disagree with that view. We think that a clearer case could hardly be presented and that, whatever discretion may be deemed to be committed to the Board, its limits were transcended by the order under review. * * *

Sixth.—The requirement that respondents shall bargain collectively with Lodge 66 of the Amalgamated Association as the exclusive representative of the employees in the described unit.

Respondent resumed work about March 12, 1937. The Board's order was made on March 14, 1938. In view of the change in the situation by reason of the valid discharge of the "sit-down" strikers and the filling of positions with new men, we see no basis for a conclusion that after the resumption of work Lodge 66 was the choice of a majority of respondent's employees for the purpose of collective bargaining. The Board's order properly requires respondent to desist from interfering in any manner with its employees in the exercise of their right to self-organization and to bargain collectively through representatives of their own choosing. But it is a different matter to require respondent to treat Lodge 66 in the altered circumstances as such a representative. If it is contended that Lodge 66 is the choice of the employees, the Board has abundant authority to settle the question by requiring an election.

Seventh.—The requirement that respondent shall withdraw all recognition from Rare Metal Workers of America, Local No. 1.

While respondent presents a strong protest, insisting that Local No. 1 of the Rare Metal Workers was the free choice of the employees after work was resumed, we cannot say that there is not substantial evidence that the formation of this organization was brought about through promotion efforts of respondent contrary to the provision of Section 8(2), and we think that the order of the Board in this respect should be sustained. Whether Rare Metal Workers of America, Local No. 1, or any other organization, is the choice of the majority of the employees in the proper unit can be determined by proceedings open to the Board. * * *

The judgment of the Circuit Court of Appeals is modified accordingly and as modified is affirmed. * * *

Mr. Justice Frankfurter took no part in the consideration and decision of this case.

[The concurring opinion of Mr. Justice Stone is omitted.]

Mr. Justice Reed, dissenting in part.

* * * The issue while important is narrow. Can an employee, on strike or let out by an unfair labor practice, be discharged, finally, by an employer so as to be ineligible for reinstatement under the act?

* * * None on either side of the disputed issue need be suspected of "countenancing lawlessness," or of encouraging employees to resort to "violence in defiance of the law of the land." Disapproval of a sit-down does not logically compel the acceptance of the theory that an employer has the power to bar his striking employee from the protection of the Labor Act.

The Labor Act was enacted in an effort to protect interstate commerce from the interruptions of labor disputes. This object was sought through prohibition of certain practices deemed unfair to labor, and the sanctions adopted to enforce the prohibitions included reinstatement of employees. To assure that the status of strikers was not changed from employees to individuals beyond the protection of the act, the term employee was defined to include "any individual whose work has ceased as a consequence of, or in connection with, any current labor dispute or because of any unfair labor practice * * *." § 2(3) * * *. Without this assurance of the continued protection of the act, the striking employee would be quickly put beyond the pale of its protection by discharge. As now construed by the Court, the employer may discharge any striker, with or without cause, so long as the discharge is not used to interfere with self-organization or collective bargaining. Friction easily engendered by labor strife may readily give rise to conduct, from nose-thumbing to sabotage, which will give fair occasion for discharge on grounds other than those prohibited by the Labor Act.

The Congress sought by clear language to eliminate this prolific source of ill feeling by the provision just quoted which should be interpreted in accordance with its language as continuing the eligibility of a striker for reinstatement, regardless of conduct by the striker or action by the employer. The constitutional problem involved in such a conclusion is not different from the one involved in compelling an employer to reinstate an employee, discharged for union activity. There is here no protection for unlawful activity. Every punishment which compelled obedience to law still remains in the hands of the peace officers. It is only that the act of ceasing work in a current labor dispute involving unfair labor practices suspends for a period, not now necessary to determine, the right of an employer to terminate the relation. The interference with the normal exercise of the right to discharge extends only to the necessity of protecting the relationship in industrial strife.

The point is made that an employer should not be compelled to reemploy an employee guilty, perhaps, of sabotage. This depends upon circumstances. It is the function of the Board to weigh the charges and countercharges and determine the adjustment most conducive to industrial peace.

Courts certainly should not interfere with the normal action of administrative bodies in such circumstances. Here both labor and management had erred grievously in their respective conduct. It cannot be said to be unreasonable to restore both to their former status. Such restoration would apply to the sit-down strikers and those striking employees who aided and abetted them.

I am of the view that the provisions of the order of the Board ordering an offer of reinstatement to the employees discussed above should be sustained. * * *

MR. JUSTICE BLACK concurs in this dissent.

Note

1. What insight does Fansteel afford with regard to the NLRB's view of its function under the Wagner Act? Which decision—the Board's or the Court's— would, in your judgment, best "effectuate the policies of this Act"? For an absorbing argument in support of the Board's position, see Hart and Prichard, The Fansteel Case: Employee Misconduct and the Remedial Powers of the National Labor Relations Board, 52 Harv.L.Rev. 1275 (1939).

2. "Sit-down strikes first appeared as a major phenomenon in 1936 when employers and employers' lawyers were widely asserting that the Act was invalid—and when litigation over the validity of the Act was bringing the effort to enforce it to a stand-still. In that year there occurred 48 sit-down strikes, affecting 87,817 workers.[216] Early in 1937 when litigation concerning the Act reached its peak, so did the sit-down. In January of that year there were 25 such strikes, affecting 74,479 workers; in February, 47 strikes affecting 31,236 workers; in March, 170 strikes affecting 167,210 workers. The constitutionality of the National Labor Relations Act was upheld by the Supreme Court on April 12, 1937. Sit-down strikes in April declined to 52, affecting 33,339 workers. In May, there were 72 strikes, affecting 25,250 workers; in June, 29 strikes, affecting 18,804 workers; and in July, 20 strikes, affecting only 4,721 workers. The wage cuts of the fall of 1937 brought a slight recrudescence in the number of sit-down strikes. But in no month in 1938 were there more than 10 such strikes, and the average was only four and a fraction." Hart and Prichard, supra at pp. 1322–23.

Sit-down strikes played a major role in the unionizing of such industries as automobile and rubber, thus contributing to what most students of labor relations judge to be salutary change in the industrial environment of the United States. While violence was frequently associated with the sit-down strike, it was not a necessary component. In any event, few, if any, major industries in this country have been organized without bloodshed. All of this raises a basic and fascinating question of morality or social philosophy, indeed of "law": Is it ever "right" to engage in such conduct? Does the end ever justify the means?

The reader will perceive the relevance of the sit-down era in labor relations to the later developments in the civil rights and student-protest movements. Sit-ins, sit-downs, lock-ins, lie-ins—the whole spectrum of "civil disobedience"— became standard tactics for those who challenged, out of deeply held moral convictions, the "Establishment." "Participatory democracy" was the euphemism sometimes employed to describe and justify these actions. The basic

216. (1937) 46 Monthly Lab.Rev. 1233. In all the figures which follow, workers "affect- ed" means, not workers sitting down, but all workers idle as a result of the sit-down.

question recurs: Is such conduct "right"? Is "unlawful" conduct of this sort essential to the enhancement and refinement of basic human rights—i.e., "liberty," "justice," "equality," "democracy"? Or, on the other hand, does such conduct unreasonably threaten the *most* basic human rights—the very reason for civilized society—security of person and property?

Consider the following formulation of what might be called the generic problem: A fundamental dilemma of society, particularly of a "free" society, is that, while change is the law of life and must be accommodated, institutionally as well as otherwise, change is also traumatic. Without the necessary institutional accommodation to the inexorable change, a society runs the grave risk of ultimate explosion or collapse; but human institutions and the individuals who comprise them (particularly those most vested in interest) strongly fear and resist change. The art of government and leadership is adjustment to change at a pace which meets basic needs without *undue* trauma. Do you agree?

For an example of the degree and quality of societal resistance to change, consider the following statement of the Illinois court which cited the sit-downers for contempt in Fansteel, expressing a theme recurrent with minor variations from Socrates through Christ, Cordwainers, Fansteel, and Selma, Alabama:

"The evidence clearly reveals that the sit-down strike at the plant of the Fansteel company was conceived in sin and born in inequity [iniquity?]; that its origin sprang from the perverted minds of so-called organizers who wander from factory to factory throughout the country, having been sent by subversive designers under the guise of bettering the conditions of factory and other workers but, in reality, are only fomenters of strife, trouble and defiers of law and order, their aim by subversive means being to gain their point and reap the advantage to themselves by disorganizing orderly business.

"Many of the Company's employees have been with the Company for years; but the evidence does not reveal that there was ever any disharmony with the Company, or any unrest or dissatisfaction among the employees until after certain of those known peripatetic so-called organizers came into their midst and preached to them subversive doctrines of advantage by their joining hands and forming a chain with numerous other long-named groups and all dominated by some supreme Mogul having dictatorial propensities." Quoted in Hart and Prichard, supra at 1288–89.

3. Leon Green, then dean of the Northwestern University School of Law, only a few miles removed from the Fansteel plant, did not share the view of the judge in the foregoing quote that the sit-down strike was "conceived in sin." Indeed, he argued not merely its "rightness," but its legality. The gist of his argument is contained in the following excerpt from his contemporary article in the New Republic.

GREEN, THE CASE FOR THE SIT–DOWN STRIKE
The New Republic, March 24, 1937, 199–200.

* * *

The respective interests of employer and employee in their relations with each other have full recognition under the common law, statutes and constitutions of Anglo-American jurisdictions. Within the past century everything affecting their relations has changed completely. The personal master has become an industrial corporation, a conglomerate of thousands of stockholders, bondholders, directors, corporate officials, managers, superintendents and assistants of all sorts. The personal servant has become a labor union, itself a conglomerate of persons and organization almost as far-flung and equally as difficult to visualize as the corporation. The simple handcraft has become the highly coordinated mechanized mass-production processes of industry.

The industrial relation resulting from these changes differs as greatly from the simple relation of master and hired hand as does the modern industrial corporation from the personal master, the labor union from the personal servant, or industrial mechanization from simple handcraft. It is the result of a long, tedious, costly, evolutionary process. And the sit-down strike is but the latest step in the struggle between a large mass of employers operating under an institution known as an industrial corporation and an equally large or larger mass of employees operating or attempting to operate under a somewhat similar institution known as a labor union, to work out their respective rights, duties and privileges in industrial enterprise—enterprise resulting from the joint efforts of what we oversimplify as capital and labor.

The industrial enterprise is not made up merely of land, brick, mortar and machinery on the one hand, and personal services of many individuals on the other. These two great interests of property and personality are both essential to the enterprise, but each alone is meaningless to the industrial world. *It is their joinder that creates the third great interest, the industrial relation upon which industry is based.* It is their joinder that brings into existence this something distinct from its parental forebears as a child is distinct from its parents, or a corporation from its stockholders, a partnership from its members; about which cluster rights, duties, liabilities and immunities not yet clearly articulated in terms of legal theory except as they are recognized as relations equal in dignity and value to those of property or personality.

That this something which has been in the process of development for a century or more has an existence all its own, as much so as the family or the corporation, both of which in like manner are made up of an indefinite number of similar relational interests, is all too clear. And that it—as the family and corporation have come to be by a process of evolution in human affairs—is a usable, workable, recognizable concept, requires no demonstration further than common observation and experience.

The industrial relation in its initial or formative state is the result of a contractual nexus between the two parental organisms of industry—those who supply its property-capital on the one hand and those who supply its service-capital on the other. But as in the case of family, corporate, partnership, carrier, and all other important relations, the slender tie of the initial contract is overgrown by a network of tissue, nerves and tendons, as it were, which gives the relation its significance. The respective rights, duties, privileges and immunities of the parties to the industrial relation are too numerous to recite here, but they are well known.

Both participating groups have contributed heavily to the joint enterprise of industry. The contributions of those who make up the corporate organization on the one hand are visualized in plant, machinery, raw materials and the like. They can be seen, recorded and valued in dollars. We call them property. On the other side are hundreds of personalities who have spent years training their hands and senses to specialized skills; who have set up habitations conveniently located to their work; who have become obligated to families and for the facilities necessary for maintaining them; who have ordered their lives and developed disciplines; all to the end that the properties essential to industry may be operated for the profit of the owner group and for their own livelihoods. Their outlays are not so visible, nor so easily measured in dollars, but in gross they may equal or even exceed the contributions of the other group. Both groups are joint adventurers, as it were, in industrial enterprise. Both have and necessarily must have a voice in the matters of common concern. Both must have protection adequate to their interests as against the world at large as well as against the undue demands of each other. * * *

From such a background has come the sit-down strike. It is a refinement that could only result from years of struggle and bitter experience. Having found the walk-out ineffective and picketing, boycots, sympathetic strikes and other measures severely restricted by law, unions have used the sit-down strike to avoid the difficulties of them all, to be more effective. Instead of employees severing their relations and thereby automatically placing themselves outside as dissatisfied former employees, they now insist on maintaining their relations while they negotiate about their complaints. Once they sever the relations they become strangers to the enterprise and trespassers if they remain upon the employer's premises, but as employees they stay at their posts ready to work upon condition that the employer shall negotiate with them. Thus they retain their interest in and relation to the common enterprise.

Moreover, they deny the employer the power to discharge them and thereby sever the relations they have with the industry. They insist that by negotiation some basis be reached upon which work of the enterprise may be continued. The right to fire is an incident of the simplest form of contract, that of employment at the will of both parties; it has no place in a relation which is based upon infinitely more than mere contract. A wife cannot fire her husband, a parent his child, a corporate stockholder other stockholders, one partner another member of the firm, an insurer the insured, a carrier its passengers, with impunity. Neither can an employer fire his employees *en masse.* These other relations are at best only analogous but, they give point. All institutions built upon relational interests of the groups concerned must submit to the obligations which have grown up around the particular relation, and if it is to be destroyed it must be done subject to such obligations.

* * * It is thus that employees may peacefully sit and wait until their complaints are ironed out through negotiations between their representatives and the representatives of the corporate group of owners. They do not operate or do injury to the owner's property. They make no adverse claim of possession to the premises they occupy. They merely occupy them because they are an incident to the industry in which they have an interest. If more were needed they could well claim a license coupled with an interest in the

premises devoted to the enterprise. But they sit to negotiate some affair pertinent to their relation to industry.

And this is their right. If so, it is equally their right to protect themselves against attack. * * *

Note

Does Dean Green's thesis apply with equal force to tactics similar to the sit-down employed by civil rights and student-protest groups? Suppose the sit-down, in factory or academic building, were conceived and carried out by only a minority of the employees or students involved?

HUNT v. CRUMBOCH

Supreme Court of the United States, 1945.
325 U.S. 821, 65 S.Ct. 1545, 89 L.Ed. 1954.

MR. JUSTICE BLACK delivered the opinion of the Court.

The question here is whether an organization of laboring men [Local 107, International Brotherhood of Teamsters] violated the Sherman Act * * * by refusing to admit to membership petitioner's employees, and by refusing to sell their services to petitioner, thereby making it impossible for petitioner profitably to continue in business.

For about fourteen years prior to 1939, the petitioner, a business partnership engaged in motor trucking, carried freight under a contract with the Great Atlantic & Pacific Tea Co. (A & P). Eighty-five percent of the merchandise thus hauled by petitioner was interstate, from and to Philadelphia, Pennsylvania. * * * In 1937, the respondent union called a strike of the truckers and haulers of A & P in Philadelphia for the purpose of enforcing a closed shop. The petitioner, refusing to unionize its business, attempted to operate during the strike. Much violence occurred. One of the union men was killed near union headquarters, and a member of the petitioner partnership was tried for the homicide and acquitted. A & P and the union entered into a closed shop agreement, whereupon all contract haulers working for A & P, including the petitioner, were notified that their employees must join and become members of the union. All of the other contractor haulers except petitioner either joined the union or made closed shop agreements with it. The union, however, refused to negotiate with the petitioner, and declined to admit any of its employees to membership. Although petitioner's services had been satisfactory, A & P, at the union's instigation, cancelled its contract with petitioner in accordance with the obligations of its closed shop agreement with the union. Later, the petitioner obtained a contract with a different company, but again at the union's instigation, and upon the consummation of a closed shop contract by that company with the union, petitioner lost that contract and business. Because of the union's refusal to negotiate with the petitioner and to accept petitioner's employees as members, the petitioner was unable to obtain any further hauling contracts in Philadelphia. The elimination of the petitioner's service did not in any manner affect the interstate operations of A & P or other companies.

The petitioner then instituted this suit in a federal district court against respondents, the union and its representatives, praying for an injunction and asking for treble damages. Demurrers to the complaint were overruled, the case was tried, findings of fact were made, and the district court rendered a judgment for the respondents on the ground that petitioner had failed to prove a cause of action under the Anti-trust laws. Hunt v. Brotherhood of Transportation Workers, etc., D.C., 47 F.Supp. 571. The Circuit Court of Appeals affirmed, holding that the fact that respondents' actions had caused petitioner to go out of business was not such a restraint of interstate commerce as would be actionable under the Sherman and Clayton Acts. 3 Cir., 143 F.2d 902. We granted certiorari because of the questions involved concerning the responsibility of labor unions under the Anti-trust laws.

The "destruction" of petitioner's business resulted from the fact that the union members, acting in concert, refused to accept employment with the petitioner, and refused to admit to their association anyone who worked for petitioner. The petitioner's loss of business is therefore analogous to the case of a manufacturer selling goods in interstate commerce who fails in business because union members refuse to work for him. Had a group of petitioner's business competitors conspired and combined to suppress petitioner's business by refusing to sell goods and services to it, such a combination would have violated the Sherman Act. Binderup v. Pathé Exchange, 263 U.S. 291, 312, 44 S.Ct. 96, 100, 68 L.Ed. 308; Fashion Originators' Guild et al. v. Federal Trade Commission, 312 U.S. 457, 668, 61 S.Ct. 703, 85 L.Ed. 949. A labor union which aided and abetted such a group would have been equally guilty. Allen Bradley Co. et al. v. Local Union No. 3, I.B.E.W., 325 U.S. 797, 65 S.Ct. 1533. The only combination here, however, was one of the workers alone and what they refused to sell petitioner was their labor.

It is not a violation of the Sherman Act for laborers in combination to refuse to work. They can sell or not sell their labor as they please, and upon such terms and conditions as they choose, without infringing the Anti-trust laws. Apex Hosiery Co. v. Leader, 310 U.S. 469, 502, 503, 60 S.Ct. 982, 997, 998, 84 L.Ed. 1311, 128 A.L.R. 1044. A worker is privileged under congressional enactments, acting either alone or in concert with his fellow workers, to associate or to decline to associate with other workers, to accept, refuse to accept, or to terminate a relationship of employment, and his labor is not to be treated as "a commodity or article of commerce." Clayton Act, 38 Stat. 730, 731, 15 U.S.C.A. § 17; Norris-La Guardia Act, 47 Stat. 70, 29 U.S.C.A. § 101 et seq. * * *. It was the exercise of these rights that created the situation which caused the petitioner to lose its hauling contracts and its business.

It is argued that their exercise falls within the condemnation of the Sherman Act, because the union members' refusal to accept employment was due to personal antagonism against the petitioner arising out of the killing of a union man. But Congress in the Sherman Act and the legislation which followed it manifested no purpose to make any kind of refusal to accept personal employment a violation of the Anti-trust laws. Such an application of those laws would be a complete departure from their spirit and purpose. Cf. Apex Hosiery Co. v. Leader, supra, 310 U.S. 512, 60 S.Ct. 1002, 84 L.Ed. 1311, 128 A.L.R. 1044; Allen Bradley Co. v. Local Union No.

3, I.B.E.W., supra. Moreover "So long as a union acts in its self-interest and does not combine with non-labor groups, the licit and the illicit under § 20 are not to be distinguished by any judgment regarding the wisdom or unwisdom, the rightness or wrongness, the selfishness or unselfishness of the end of which the particular union activities are the means." United States v. Hutcheson, 312 U.S. 219, 232, 61 S.Ct. 463, 466, 85 L.Ed. 788. * * *

The controversy in the instant case, between a union and an employer, involves nothing more than a dispute over employment, and the withholding of labor services. It cannot therefore be said to violate the Sherman Act, as amended. That Act does not purport to afford remedies for all torts committed by or against persons engaged in interstate commerce. * * * Whether the respondents' conduct amounts to an actionable wrong subjecting them to liability for damages under Pennsylvania law is not our concern.

Affirmed.

MR. JUSTICE ROBERTS.

I think the judgment should be reversed.

The issue presented in this case, in my judgment, lies wholly outside and beyond any precedent to be found in the decisions of this court, and certainly so as to Apex Hosiery Co. v. Leader, 310 U.S. 469, 60 S.Ct. 982, 84 L.Ed. 1311, 128 A.L.R. 1044, on which the court relies.

There was a labor dispute as to unionization between motor carriers and the union representing employes. The record demonstrates that the dispute involved in this case was no part of that labor dispute but an off-shoot of it; not involving wages, unionization, closed shop, hours or other conditions of work.

The union, in an effort to organize the employes of motor carriers, resorted to a strike. The petitioners resisted unionization. During the ensuing disorder a man was shot. The union officials attributed the killing to one of the petitioners. In fact he was acquitted by a jury. The respondents having succeeded in unionizing the industry in Philadelphia the petitioners could continue in their business of interstate carriage only by having their men join the union and by signing a closed shop contract. The union determined to punish petitioners by refusing to sign a contract with them and by forbidding the members of the union to work for them. There is no suggestion in the record that they did so because of any labor conditions or considerations, or that petitioners' men would not join the union, or that union men would not work with them, if they did join. It is hardly an accurate description of their attitude to say that the union men decided not to sell their labor to the petitioners. They intended to drive petitioners out of business as interstate motor carriers, and they succeeded in so doing. * * *

The petitioners had been, and were at the time, in competition with other similar interstate carriers. The sole purpose of the respondents was to drive petitioners out of business in that field. This they accomplished. Thus they reduced competition between interstate carriers by eliminating one competitor from the field. The conspiracy, therefore, was clearly within the denunciation of the Sherman Act, as one intended and effective, to lessen competition in commerce, and not within any immunity conferred by the Clayton Act.

THE CHIEF JUSTICE, MR. JUSTICE FRANKFURTER and MR. JUSTICE JACKSON join in this opinion.

MR. JUSTICE JACKSON, dissenting. * * *

With this decision, the labor movement has come full circle. The working man has struggled long, the fight has been filled with hatred, and conflict has been dangerous, but now workers may not be deprived of their livelihood merely because their employers oppose and they favor unions. Labor has won other rights as well, unemployment compensation, old-age benefits and, what is most important and the basis of all its gains, the recognition that the opportunity to earn his support is not alone the concern of the individual but is the problem which all organized societies must contend with and conquer if they are to survive. This Court now sustains the claim of a union to the right to deny participation in the economic world to an employer simply because the union dislikes him. This Court permits to employees the same arbitrary dominance over the economic sphere which they control that labor so long, so bitterly and so rightly asserted should belong to no man.

Strikes aimed at compelling the employer to yield to union demands are not within the Sherman Act. Here the employer has yielded, and the union has achieved the end to which all legitimate union pressure is directed and limited. The union cannot consistently with the Sherman Act refuse to enjoy the fruits of its victory and deny peace terms to an employer who has unconditionally surrendered. * * *

THE CHIEF JUSTICE and MR. JUSTICE FRANKFURTER join in this opinion.

Note

1. Hunt v. Crumboch was a high-water mark of unchecked unionism in the federal scheme. The only federal law available for dealing with the union's conduct was the Sherman Act. But the decision in the Hutcheson case, "reading the Sherman Law and § 20 of the Clayton Act and the Norris-La Guardia Act as a harmonizing text of outlawry of labor conduct," precluded treating union conduct as a violation of the Sherman Act where the "union acts in its self-interest and does not combine with non-labor groups." This meant, as demonstrated in Hunt v. Crumboch, that union conduct of a highly questionable sort was beyond the reach of federal law.

Another flagrant example of the vacuum in the federal law pertaining to labor relations was Lauf v. E.G. Shinner & Co., 303 U.S. 323, 58 S.Ct. 578, 82 L.Ed. 872 (1938). A union demanded that an employer require its employees, as a condition of their continued employment, to become members of the union. The employer notified the employees that they were free to join the union, but the employees refused to join. The employer thereupon refused the union's demand. To enforce its demand, the union then picketed the employer and engaged in other pressure tactics, apparently peaceful. The employer obtained an injunction in the federal district court. The Supreme Court reversed, on the ground that a "labor dispute" within the meaning of Section 13 of the Norris-La Guardia Act was involved and that the District Court was therefore without jurisdiction to grant the requested relief.

Similarly, in Fur Workers Union, Local No. 72 v. Fur Workers Union, No. 21238, 105 F.2d 1 (D.C.Cir.1939), aff'd mem., 308 U.S. 522, 60 S.Ct. 292, 84 L.Ed. 443 (1939), an employer recognized an AFL union as bargaining representative of a group of eleven fur workers, nine of whom were members of the AFL union and had chosen it as their representative. The employer and the AFL union then negotiated a collective bargaining agreement. Notwithstanding the foregoing, a CIO union, which had also been seeking recognition as bargaining representative for the eleven fur workers, called a strike which was answered by the two of the eleven employees who were members of the CIO union. In support of the strike, the CIO union engaged in mass picketing of the employer's premises, and assaults were committed upon the fur workers who did not respond to the strike call. The employer obtained an injunction in the federal district court. The Court of Appeals for the District of Columbia reversed, on the ground that although a "labor dispute" entailing violence was present and therefore jurisdiction to grant an injunction was available under the Norris-LaGuardia Act, nonetheless the findings of fact stringently required by Section 7 of the Act as a condition precedent to the granting of an injunction had not been made. If the pressure tactics of the CIO union had been peaceful, no injunction could have been issued in any event because of Section 4 of the Act.

A particularly pernicious aspect of the last two cases (and others like them) was that the union's object in both cases was to compel the employer to engage in action constituting unfair labor practices under Sections 8(1), (2), and (3) of the Wagner Act. In the Fur Workers case, a violation of Section 8(5) would also have been involved.

2. Which of the following approaches would you deem most appropriate for regulating the union conduct involved in Hunt v. Crumboch, Lauf v. E.G. Shinner & Co., and the Fur Workers case: (1) reinterpretation or amendment of the Sherman Act and the Norris-LaGuardia Act so as to narrow the labor exemption under the former and/or the definition of a "labor dispute" under the latter, or (2) amendment of the Wagner Act so as to render such union actions unfair labor practices?

3. ALLEN BRADLEY v. LOCAL 3, IBEW, 325 U.S. 797, 65 S.Ct. 1533, 89 L.Ed. 1939 (1945), decided at the same time as Hunt v. Crumboch and discussed in it, demonstrated the one way in which a union, during the Wagner Act period, could run afoul of federal law while engaging in union conduct of a nonviolent and nonfraudulent character. In that case, as found by the Supreme Court, Local 3 of the International Brotherhood of Electrical Workers, having jurisdiction in the City of New York, combined with two "non-labor" groups—(1) New York City manufacturers of electrical equipment, (2) New York City electrical contractors—to establish a cozy monopoly on the production, sale, and installation of electrical equipment in the City of New York. Pursuant to the tripartite arrangement among them, the participating manufacturers and contractors agreed to employ only Local 3 members, Local 3 members agreed to work only for those manufacturers and contractors, the manufacturers agreed to sell only to the contractors, and the contractors agreed to buy only from the manufacturers. The consequence was a protected market for all three groups in New York City. Prices, profits, and wages soared. In a suit against Local 3 by manufacturers of electrical equipment who were not members of the combine, the arrangement was declared violative of the Sherman Act and the union enjoined from continuing to combine with the non-labor groups in the aforesaid manner. The Court conceded that the union might have achieved the same result by

extracting from each employer *separately* a contract by which the employer agreed to hire only Local 3 members and to deal only with manufacturers and contractors having similar closed-shop contracts with Local 3; in such a case, Local 3 would have been acting "in its self-interest" and not in combination "with non-labor groups."

The thinness of the line between licit and illicit union conduct as measured by the Sherman Act will be revealed more clearly (?) when the Allen Bradley case and its progeny are examined in detail in Chapter 9.

THE WAGNER ACT: A REQUIEM

The twelve years from 1935 to 1947 brought the most profound changes in labor relations of any era in the history of the United States. Union membership increased five-fold, from three million to almost fifteen million. Collective bargaining became ensconced in the major blue-collar industries, although the pattern of organization was spotty, with relatively little in the South, the Southwest, and other primarily agricultural areas. The third member of the triumvirate—Big Business, Big Government, Big Labor—was born. (Indeed, the second member also reached its majority.)

It oversimplifies to attribute this change solely to the protective policies introduced by the Wagner Act, but those policies were certainly the catalyst for the new mix. As a result of those policies, union organizers could and did say to prospective recruits: "FDR wants you to join a union!" The further circumstances, that the Wagner Act placed no controls on unions and that the Norris-LaGuardia Act relaxed existing controls in the federal law, contributed substantially to the environment for change. Another factor of considerable consequence was the federal government's World War II labor policy. In mobilizing the economy for war production, it was necessary to enlist the full cooperation of organized labor, now a major force in American industry. The War Labor Board, a tripartite agency composed of an equal number of representatives of the public, industry, and organized labor, was created to resolve labor disputes without loss of production and to establish wage-stabilization policies. Organized labor, in turn, pledged not to engage in strikes. Moreover, the Office of Production Management was established under the joint direction of William Knudsen, president of the General Motors Corporation, and Sidney Hillman, president of the Amalgamated Clothing Workers, CIO.[g] The policy of shared

g. Problems of some delicacy were encountered in the process of working out the manner in which the Office was to be administered: "The crux of the problem was the definition of the relationship between the Director-General [Knudsen] and the Associate Director-General [Hillman]. * * * Formulation of this relation defied the skills of the drafting experts, and the President pencilled into their version the following language: 'The Director-General, in association with the Associate Director-General, and serving under the direction and supervision of the President, shall discharge and perform the administrative responsibilities and duties * * * vested in the Office of Production Management.'

"The President's exposition of the positions of the Director-General and the Associate Director-General at his press conference of January 7, 1941, gave no satisfaction to those who

demanded a single-headed administration of the defense effort. * * *

"Q. Are they equals?

"THE PRESIDENT. That's not the point; they're a firm. Is a firm equals? I don't know. See what I mean? Roosevelt and O'Connor was a law firm in New York; there were just two partners. I don't know whether we were equal or not. Probably we might have disagreed in regard to a catch question of that kind; but we never had a dispute or an argument.

*   *   *   *   *

"Q. Why is it you don't want a single, responsible head?

"THE PRESIDENT. I have a single, responsible head; his name is Knudsen and Hillman."

authority was similarly implemented in other agencies concerned with war production.

Major change of the kind generated by the Wagner Act is invariably accompanied by strong protest on the part of those whose interests are adversely affected. Complaints fell into three major categories. First, the Act was criticized for its one-sidedness. It protected only employees, and through them their unions; it placed restraints only upon employers. The interests claimed to have been neglected were principally those of employers and of the public, although complaint was also made that big, strong, unregulated unions on occasion dealt perversely with individual and minority employee interests. Second, it was charged that this one-sided statute was administered in an over-zealous and one-sided fashion. The NLRB and its staff, in Washington and the regional offices around the country, were inveighed against as missionaries of a faith not entirely the creation of Congress—collective bargaining the message and evangelism the mood. A third category of complaint was the product of hard-core resistance on the part of many employers and their sympathizers to the central theme of the Wagner Act—the propriety and propagation of collective bargaining. Complaints against the Act at this basic level were frequently camouflaged in the garb of the first two categories of complaint.

No requiem for the Wagner Act would be complete without an additional commentary upon its impact. It enabled a largely peaceful revolution in the industrial relations of a capitalist society. The system of collective bargaining which it fostered constitutes a major oversight of socialist philosophers, such as Karl Marx, who failed to foresee the accommodating potential of a private-enterprise economy.[h] But organized labor, the new power center produced by the Act, like every other locus of power in a free society, invited and shortly received the disciplinary attention it now deserved.

Committee on Records of War Administration, The United States at War 53–54 (1946).

h. For an exposition of "the significance of collective bargaining to freedom of enterprise," see Frey, The Logic of Collective Bargaining and Arbitration, 12 Law & Contemp. Prob. 264 (1947).

Chapter 3

THE NEED FOR BALANCE: GOVERNMENT AS UMPIRE

INTRODUCTORY NOTE

The purpose of the present chapter is to continue the account of the search for balance in the law of labor relations in the United States, and to bring the story, in a general sense, up-to-date. The two remaining legislative efforts of consequence in that search are the Taft-Hartley Act of 1947 and the Landrum-Griffin Act of 1959. These enactments, with minor exceptions, are presently the law and will be the subject of much attention in Part II of this book. There is accordingly, no need to deal with them in detail at this point. The aim here is to capture moods and to sketch contours.

Title VII of the Civil Rights Act of 1964 is also introduced in this chapter. While not, strictly speaking, part of the "search for balance" between labor and management, Title VII does, along with a major portion of the Landrum-Griffin Act, focus upon the interests of individual and minority groups of employees vis-a-vis unions and employers. The protection of these interests within the collective bargaining system is a relatively recent concern of the law. Brief consideration of these interests and of the protection afforded them rounds out the overview of the law of American labor relations presented in Part I of this book.

The overview is concluded in Section D of the present chapter—"Government as Employer: The Umpire Unionized." The exportation of the notions and techniques of collective bargaining from the private into the public employment sector is a dramatic, still-current development in American labor relations.

A. THE TAFT–HARTLEY ACT OF 1947

The Taft-Hartley Act of 1947 constituted a major overhaul of the national labor policy. Whereas in the Wagner Act days union organizers could and did tell American workers that the President wanted them to join a union, under the Taft-Hartley Act the accurate paraphrase would be: "The President doesn't care whether or not you join a union." This change in policy is most basically demonstrated in the amendment of Section 7, the heart of the National Labor Relations Act. To the three Wagner Act rights there declared—the right to engage in self-organization, the right to engage in collective bargaining, and the right to engage in concerted activities in support thereof—Congress added a *fourth* right: "the right to *refrain* from any or all of such activities." (Emphasis added.)

The new role of government, that of umpire rather than paternal protector, was further manifested in related provisions of the Act. For example, a set of *union* unfair labor practices (Section 8(b)) was created, as a counterpart to the employer unfair labor practices (now Section 8(a)) carried over from the Wagner Act. Section 8(b)(1), by way of illustration, forbids a labor organization to "restrain or coerce * * * employees in the exercise of the rights guaranteed in Section 7," including, of course, the newly enacted right to refrain from union activities. Similarly, Section 8(b)(3) imposes upon unions the same duty to bargain in good faith as had been earlier imposed upon employers. The neutrality of the government in the new scheme was further evidenced in the so-called "free speech" provision, Section 8(c), which, in its most obvious application, encourages employers to compete more vigorously with unions for the loyalty of their employees than they had previously felt free to do.

Other important changes in policy were effectuated by the Taft-Hartley Act, most of them related in one way or another to the shift in the role of government from "drive" to "neutral." Before noting these changes, however, it will be helpful to outline the structure of the Act.

Officially entitled the "Labor Management Relations Act, 1947," the Act consists of five titles. Title I (Sections 101–104) amends the Wagner Act by reenacting it in altered form. Section 101 accordingly provides: "The National Labor Relations Act is hereby amended to read as follows." The entire Act, as amended, is then set forth, including Section 17, which reads: "This Act may be cited as the 'National Labor Relations Act'."

Title II (Sections 201–212) creates the Federal Mediation and Conciliation Service and establishes procedures for dealing with national emergency labor disputes.

Title III (Sections 301–305), in its major aspect, declares collective bargaining agreements enforceable in federal courts "without respect to the amount in controversy or without regard to the citizenship of the parties," and permits labor organizations to sue and be sued as legal entities in those courts. (Section 301.)

Title IV (Sections 401–407) created a joint congressional committee to study the entire field of labor-management relations and to report its findings and recommendations to Congress by January 2, 1949.

Title V (Sections 501–503) contains some miscellaneous provisions, including definitions of certain terms not defined in Title I.

The chief agency of government for the carrying out of the new labor policy continued to be the National Labor Relations Board, but with substantial changes in its structure and mode of operation. The changes were designed to better fit the Board for its new role as umpire. First, the membership of the Board was increased from three to five members, with staggered five-year terms. Each of these members was provided with a large and independent staff of attorneys. The purpose of this was to afford each Board member the wherewithal for independence of judgment in deciding cases, thereby permitting abolition of the much maligned "Review Section" which had been established during the administration of the Wagner Act. The Review Section was a group of approximately ninety lawyers employed by the Board, as an entity, to review transcripts of hearings and prepare drafts of opinions. This faceless group was charged with exerting undue influence upon Board policies and decisions without any accountability.

A second fundamental change in the Board's structure and functioning was the creation of the office of General Counsel, to be filled, as with the Board itself, by the President with the advice and consent of the Senate. The General Counsel, appointed for a four-year term, is charged with performing the prosecutorial function, i.e., investigating charges, issuing complaints, prosecuting cases. Accordingly, he has "general supervision over all attorneys employed by the Board (other than trial examiners [now "administrative law judges"] and legal assistants to Board members) and over the officers and employees in the regional offices." (Section 3(d).) The purpose of this change was to separate the prosecutorial function from the judicial one. Consistent with this purpose and demonstrating the degree of independence of the General Counsel from the Board, the statute vests in him final authority in the determination of whether or not a complaint should issue in unfair labor practice cases. (Ibid.)

Further changes of consequence wrought by the 1947 amendments—e.g., the broadening of the judicial review of Board decisions and the regulation of union security arrangements (such as the closed shop and union shop)—are encountered in the materials which follow. The first of these materials—the Dulles excerpt—describes, moreover, the environment which produced the Taft-Hartley Act.

DULLES, LABOR IN AMERICA
355–60 (3d ed. 1966).

While labor had come through the reconversion period with its wartime gains intact and the position of the nation's wage earners greatly improved, its very success had elements of danger. A public that had helplessly watched the great industrial unions threaten to paralyze the entire economy as they insisted on their rights and demanded ever higher wages for their members, was fearful of their vast economic power. The postwar strikes in the steel and coal industries, on the part of automobile workers, and on the railroads, for a time so gravely endangering the national welfare, intensified the powerful anti-union sentiment * * *. The feeling was widespread that in self-centered defense of its own interests, organized labor was totally ignoring those of the people as a whole. This latent hostility was fanned by reactionary, anti-labor forces within the business community which were basically opposed to all union organization. Yet the fact remained that repeated public opinion polls showed that the nation was deeply concerned over the militancy of labor's rank-and-file and the seeming lack of responsibility of its leaders.

In the past government had been compelled to assert its authority over Big Business. The question now arose as to whether it should not do so more rigorously over Big Labor. There was a growing popular conviction, strongly reflected in Congress, that it had become essential to prevent the arbitrary domination of the country's economic life by any minority, even though that minority might be as widely representative as the forces of labor.

At no time were there any suggestions from responsible quarters that the unions should be deprived of the basic rights guaranteed them under the terms of the National Labor Relations Act. A congressional majority was nevertheless convinced that the time had come when a measure which had been concerned only with unfair practices on the part of management, should be amended to single out and penalize unfair practices on the part of the unions. It was felt that something should be done, that is, to redress a balance which under the pro-labor administrations of the 1930's had been allowed to swing much too far in support of unions. The end result of this mounting agitation in favor of more restrictive legislation was the enactment, in June, 1947, of the Taft-Hartley Act. * * *

* * * The mid-term elections of 1946 strengthened [the anti-labor forces'] hand. The Republicans won decisive control of Congress and their landslide victory was interpreted as a direct popular mandate to take drastic action on the labor issue * * *. Some thirty states were to adopt various forms of restrictive legislation and in such circumstances it was hardly surprising that Congress should hasten to fall in line. The leaders of both the A.F. of L. and the C.I.O. assailed what they termed a "deliberate and monstrous movement * * * to cripple if not destroy, the labor movement," but they were unable to rally the support, either in Congress or in the country as a whole, to combat the anti-labor trend.

The Taft-Hartley Act had a stormy passage through Congress. The more severe provisions first incorporated in the measure by the House were to be somewhat liberalized by the Senate, but in its final form the bill very definitely reflected the conservative reaction. President Truman vetoed it * * *. He condemned it as primarily designed to weaken the unions, declared that it would in fact, encourage rather than discourage strikes, and deplored what he said would be its effect in making government "an unwanted participant at every bargaining table." The bill's provisions, he emphatically concluded, were "shocking—bad for labor, bad for management, bad for the country."

* * * Vehemently attacking the President for his pro-labor sympathies, the bill's proponents baldly charged that he had completely misrepresented its provisions. They succeeded in winning the necessary support in both the House and the Senate to override his veto and the Taft-Hartley Act duly became the law of the land.

It was a long and immensely complicated measure whose declared purpose was to restore that equality of bargaining power between employers and employees which it was contended had been sacrificed in the Wagner Act. The rights guaranteed labor in that earlier law were matched by specific safeguards for the rights of management. Employers were guaranteed full freedom of expression in respect to their views on union organization, short of threats of reprisal or promises of benefits, and they were authorized themselves to call for elections to determine the appropriate bargaining units in wage negotiations. At the same time it was declared an unfair labor practice for the unions in any way to attempt to coerce employers [employees?], engage in either secondary boycotts or jurisdictional strikes, or in their turn to refuse to bargain collectively.

These clauses might well be justified as more nearly equalizing the positions of management and labor, but the law also incorporated a number of provisions directly affecting union security. It expressly banned the closed shop * * * and, perhaps most significantly, left the door open to even more severe anti-union legislation by the states. In Section 14(b) it permitted the states to bypass federal legislation allowing the union shop by themselves banning it. This provision made possible the so-called state "right-to-work" laws which were to hamper further union organization more directly than anything in the Taft-Hartley Act itself.

There were further restrictions. Unions were required to give 60-day notice for the termination or modification of any agreement and were made suable in the federal courts for breach of contract. They were not allowed to make contributions or otherwise expend any of their funds in political campaigns. Their officers were required to file affidavits affirming that they were not members of the Communist Party or of any organization supporting it.

In Title II the Taft-Hartley Act broke entirely new ground with an elaborate formula for dealing with strikes that created a national emergency. It gave the President the authority, after making an investigation through a special board of inquiry, to apply for what in effect constituted an 80-day injunction against any strike that was found to be imperiling the national health or safety. Should negotiations during this period still fail to solve the controversy, the President was to submit a report to Congress "with such recommendations as he may see fit for consideration and appropriate action." * * *

The debate over the bill had been impassioned. The temper of the House was revealed in the report of its Committee on Education and Labor which declared that as a result of union activity, the individual worker's "mind, his soul, and his very life have been subjected to a tyranny more despotic than anyone could think possible in a free country." The committee would have abolished the National Labor Relations Board, eliminated the requirement of management obligation in collective bargaining, and required a vote of all workers involved before a strike could be called. The position of the Senate Committee on Labor and Public Welfare was a more moderate one. It recommended that the social gains which employees had received under previous legislation should be maintained and that Congress seek to remedy existing inequities between employers and employees by precise and carefully drawn legislation. The views of the Senate committee were more nearly to prevail, partly through common sense and partly to assure a majority that could override President Truman's expected veto. In the meantime, however, representatives of industry and of labor fought out their own battle in the public forum.

The full strength of employer associations, spearheaded by the National Association of Manufacturers, was thrown behind enactment of a stiff bill. The A.F. of L. and the C.I.O. opposed any new legislation whatsoever. Both industry and labor sent their spokesmen to the congressional hearings, inserted full-page advertisements in the country's newspapers presenting their contrasting philosophies, and bought radio time to air their views. While the bill's proponents maintained that the proposed legislation went no further than to equalize bargaining power, its opponents characterized it as a vindictive attack on unionism instigated by those who wished to do away with collective bargaining altogether.

In the light of the prevailing popular mood, labor's position was very weak. In refusing any compromise in respect to the proposed legislation and seeking to hold reactionary employees [employers?] wholly responsible for the drive to modify the pro-labor provisions of the Wagner Act, both the A.F. of L. and the C.I.O. were ignoring public opinion. Their leaders failed to take into consideration the almost universal sense of frustration among the people as a whole when industrywide strikes interfered with basic public services or otherwise threatened a breakdown in the national economy. And in refusing to suggest any alternative measure to meet the recognized inadequacies, if not unfairness, of the Wagner Act, they reinforced the widespread view that organized labor had become increasingly irresponsible in the exercise of monopolistic power. * * *

* * * In unjustified self-assurance, union leadership had failed to adjust itself to new times and new circumstances. At the peak of its economic power, labor had suffered a severe setback on the political front. * * *

UNIVERSAL CAMERA CORP. v. NATIONAL LABOR RELATIONS BOARD

Supreme Court of the United States, 1951.
340 U.S. 474, 71 S.Ct. 456, 95 L.Ed. 456.

MR. JUSTICE FRANKFURTER delivered the opinion of the Court.

The essential issue raised by this case and its companion, National Labor Relations Board v. Pittsburgh Steamship Co., 340 U.S. 498, 71 S.Ct. 453, infra, is the effect of the Administrative Procedure Act and the legislation colloquially known as the Taft-Hartley Act on the duty of Courts of Appeals when called upon to review orders of the National Labor Relations Board.

The Court of Appeals for the Second Circuit granted enforcement of an order directing, in the main, that petitioner reinstate with back pay an employee found to have been discharged because he gave testimony under the Wagner Act and cease and desist from discriminating against any employee who files charges or gives testimony under that Act. The court below, Judge Swan dissenting, decreed full enforcement of the order. 2 Cir., 179 F.2d 749. Because the views of that court regarding the effect of the new legislation on the relation between the Board and the courts of appeals in the enforcement of the Board's orders conflicted with those of the Court of Appeals for the Sixth Circuit [1] we brought both cases here. * * *

---

1. National Labor Relations Board v. Pittsburgh Steamship Co., 180 F.2d 731 * * *. The Courts of Appeals of five circuits have agreed with the Court of Appeals for the Second Circuit that no material change was made in the reviewing power. * * *

I.

Want of certainty in judicial review of Labor Board decisions partly reflects the intractability of any formula to furnish definiteness of content for all the impalpable factors involved in judicial review. But in part doubts as to the nature of the reviewing power and uncertainties in its application derive from history, and to that extent an elucidation of this history may clear them away.

The Wagner Act provided: "The findings of the Board as to the facts, if supported by evidence, shall be conclusive." * * * § 10(e) * * *. This Court read "evidence" to mean "substantial evidence," Washington, V. & M. Coach Co. v. Labor Board, 301 U.S. 142, 57 S.Ct. 648, 81 L.Ed. 965, and we said that "[s]ubstantial evidence is more than a mere scintilla. It means such relevant evidence as a reasonable mind might accept as adequate to support a conclusion." Consolidated Edison Co. v. National Labor Relations Board, 305 U.S. 197, 229, 59 S.Ct. 206, 217, 83 L.Ed. 126. Accordingly, it "must do more than create a suspicion of the existence of the fact to be established. * * * [I]t must be enough to justify, if the trial were to a jury, a refusal to direct a verdict when the conclusion sought to be drawn from it is one of fact for the jury." National Labor Relations Board v. Columbian Enameling & Stamping Co., 306 U.S. 292, 300, 59 S.Ct. 501, 505, 83 L.Ed. 660.

The very smoothness of the "substantial evidence" formula as the standard for reviewing the evidentiary validity of the Board's findings established its currency. But the inevitably variant applications of the standard to conflicting evidence soon brought contrariety of views and in due course bred criticism. Even though the whole record may have been canvassed in order to determine whether the evidentiary foundation of a determination by the Board was "substantial," the phrasing of this Court's process of review readily lent itself to the notion that it was enough that the evidence supporting the Board's result was "substantial" when considered by itself. It is fair to say that by imperceptible steps regard for the fact-finding function of the Board led to the assumption that the requirements of the Wagner Act were met when the reviewing court could find in the record evidence which, when viewed in isolation, substantiated the Board's findings. * * * This is not to say that every member of this Court was consciously guided by this view or that the Court ever explicitly avowed this practice as doctrine. What matters is that the belief justifiably arose that the Court had so construed the obligation to review.

Criticism of so contracted a reviewing power reinforced dissatisfaction felt in various quarters with the Board's administration of the Wagner Act in the years preceding the war. The scheme of the Act was attacked as an inherently unfair fusion of the functions of prosecutor and judge. Accusations of partisan bias were not wanting. The "irresponsible admission and weighing of hearsay, opinion, and emotional speculation in place of factual evidence" was said to be a "serious menace." [5] No doubt some, perhaps even

5. This charge was made by the majority of the Special Committee of the House appointed in 1939 to investigate the National Labor Relations Board. H.R.Rep. No. 1902, 76th Cong., 3d Sess. 76.

much, of the criticism was baseless and some surely was reckless.[6] What is here relevant, however, is the climate of opinion thereby generated and its effect on Congress. Protests against "shocking injustices" and intimations of judicial "abdication" with which some courts granted enforcement of the Board's orders stimulated pressures for legislative relief from alleged administrative excesses. * * *

* * * [D]issatisfaction with too restricted application of the "substantial evidence" test is reflected in the legislative history of the Taft-Hartley Act. * * * [A]s the Senate Committee Report relates, "it was finally decided to conform the statute to the corresponding section of the Administrative Procedure Act where the substantial evidence test prevails. In order to clarify any ambiguity * * *, however, the committee inserted the words 'questions of fact, if supported by substantial evidence *on the record considered as a whole* * * *." [21] * * *

It is fair to say that in all this Congress expressed a mood. And it expressed its mood not merely by oratory but by legislation. As legislation that mood must be respected, even though it can only serve as a standard for judgment and not as a body of rigid rules assuring sameness of application. Enforcement of such broad standards implies subtlety of mind and solidity of judgment. But it is not for us to question that Congress may assume such qualities in the federal judiciary.

From the legislative story we have summarized, two concrete conclusions do emerge. One is the identity of aim of the Administrative Procedure Act and the Taft-Hartley Act regarding the proof with which the Labor Board must support a decision. The other is that now Congress has left no room for doubt as to the kind of scrutiny which a court of appeals must give the record before the Board to satisfy itself that the Board's order rests on adequate proof. * * *

Whether or not it was ever permissible for courts to determine the substantiality of evidence supporting a Labor Board decision merely on the basis of evidence which in and of itself justified it, without taking into account contradictory evidence or evidence from which conflicting inferences could be drawn, the new legislation definitely precludes such a theory of review and bars its practice. The substantiality of evidence must take into account whatever in the record fairly detracts from its weight. This is clearly the significance of the requirement in both statutes that courts consider the whole record. * * *

To be sure, the requirement for canvassing "the whole record" in order to ascertain substantiality does not furnish a calculus of value by which a reviewing court can assess the evidence. Nor was it intended to negative the function of the Labor Board as one of those agencies presumably equipped or informed by experience to deal with a specialized field of knowledge, whose findings within that field carry the authority of an expertness which courts

---

6. Professor Gellhorn and Mr. Linfield reached the conclusion in 1939 after an extended investigation that "the denunciations find no support in fact." Gellhorn and Linfield, Politics and Labor Relations, 39 Col. L.Rev. 339, 394. See also Millis and Brown, From the Wagner Act to Taft-Hartley, 66–75.

21. * * * [I]t is to be noted that the phrase it italicized is indistinguishable in content from the requirement of § 10(e) of the Administrative Procedure Act that "the court shall review the whole record or such portions thereof as may be cited by any party * * *."

do not possess and therefore must respect. Nor does it mean that even as to matters not requiring expertise a court may displace the Board's choice between two fairly conflicting views, even though the court would justifiably have made a different choice had the matter been before it *de novo.* * * *

There remains * * * the question whether enactment of these two statutes has altered the scope of review other than to require that substantiality be determined in the light of all that the record relevantly presents. * * *

We conclude * * * that the Administrative Procedure Act, and, the Taft-Hartley Act direct that courts must now assume more responsibility for the reasonableness and fairness of Labor Board decisions than some courts have shown in the past. Reviewing courts must be influenced by a feeling that they are not to abdicate the conventional judicial function. Congress has imposed on them responsibility for assuring that the Board keeps within reasonable grounds. That responsibility is not less real because it is limited to enforcing the requirement that evidence appear substantial when viewed, on the record as a whole, by courts invested with the authority and enjoying the prestige of the Courts of Appeals. The Board's findings are entitled to respect; but they must nonetheless be set aside when the record before a Court of Appeals clearly precludes the Board's decision from being justified by a fair estimate of the worth of the testimony of witnesses or its informed judgment on matters within its special competence or both. * * *

Our power to review the correctness of application of the present standard ought seldom to be called into action. Whether on the record as a whole there is substantial evidence to support agency findings is a question which Congress has placed in the keeping of the Courts of Appeals. This Court will intervene only in what ought to be the rare instance when the standard appears to have been misapprehended or grossly misapplied.

II.

Our disagreement with the view of the court below that the scope of review of Labor Board decisions is unaltered by recent legislation does not of itself, as we have noted, require reversal of its decision. The court may have applied a standard of review which satisfies the present Congressional requirement.

The decision of the Court of Appeals is assailed on two grounds. It is said (1) that the court erred in holding that it was barred from taking into account the report of the examiner on questions of fact insofar as that report was rejected by the Board, and (2) that the Board's order was not supported by substantial evidence on the record considered as a whole, even apart from the validity of the court's refusal to consider the rejected portions of the examiner's report.

The latter contention is easily met. * * * [I]t is clear from the court's opinion in this case that it in fact did consider the "record as a whole," and did not deem itself merely the judicial echo of the Board's conclusion. The testimony of the company's witnesses was inconsistent, and there was clear evidence that the complaining employee had been discharged by an officer who was at one time influenced against him because of his appearance at the

Board hearing. On such a record we could not say that it would be error to grant enforcement.

The first contention, however, raises serious questions to which we now turn.

III.

The Court of Appeals deemed itself bound by the Board's rejection of the examiner's findings because the court considered these findings not "as unassailable as a master's." [24] 179 F.2d at 752. They are not. Section 10(c) of the Labor Management Relations Act provides that "If upon the preponderance of the testimony taken the Board shall be of the opinion that any person named in the complaint has engaged in or is engaging in any such unfair labor practice, then the Board shall state its findings of fact * * *." * * * The responsibility for decision thus placed on the Board is wholly inconsistent with the notion that it has power to reverse an examiner's findings only when they are "clearly erroneous." Such a limitation would make so drastic a departure from prior administrative practice that explicitness would be required. The Court of Appeals concluded from this premise "that, although the Board would be wrong in totally disregarding his findings, it is practically impossible for a court, upon review of those findings which the Board itself substitutes, to consider the Board's reversal as a factor in the court's own decision. This we say, because we cannot find any middle ground between doing that and treating such a reversal as error, whenever it would be such, if done by a judge to a master in equity." 179 F.2d at 753. Much as we respect the logical acumen of the Chief Judge of the Court of Appeals, we do not find ourselves pinioned between the horns of his dilemma.

We are aware that to give the examiner's findings less finality than a master's and yet entitle them to consideration in striking the account, is to introduce another and an unruly factor into the judgmatical process of review. But we ought not to fashion an exclusionary rule merely to reduce the number of imponderables to be considered by reviewing courts.

The Taft-Hartley Act provides that "The findings of the Board with respect to questions of fact if supported by substantial evidence on the record considered as a whole shall be conclusive." [§ 10(e).] Surely an examiner's report is as much a part of the record as the complaint or the testimony. According to the Administrative Procedure Act, "All decisions (including initial, recommended, or tentative decisions) shall become a part of the record * * *." § 8(b), 60 Stat. 242, 5 U.S.C.A. § 1007(b). We found that this Act's provision for judicial review has the same meaning as that in the Taft-Hartley Act. The similarity of the two statutes in language and purpose also requires that the definition of "record" found in the Administrative Procedure Act be construed to be applicable as well to the term "record" as used in the Taft-Hartley Act. * * * The conclusion is confirmed by the indications in the legislative history that enhancement of the

---

24. Rule 53(e)(2), Fed.Rules Civ.Proc., 28 U.S.C.A., gives finality to the findings of a master unless they are clearly erroneous.

The court's ruling excluding from consideration disagreement between the Board and the examiner was in apparent conflict with the views of three other circuits. * * *

status and function of the trial examiner was one of the important purposes of the movement for administrative reform. * * *

* * * Section 10(c) of the Labor Management Relations Act requires that examiners "shall issue * * * a proposed report, together with a recommended order". [It thus evinces] a purpose to increase the importance of the role of examiners in the administrative process. * * *

We do not require that the examiner's findings be given more weight than in reason and in the light of judicial experience they deserve. The "substantial evidence" standard is not modified in any way when the Board and its examiner disagree. We intend only to recognize that evidence supporting a conclusion may be less substantial when an impartial, experienced examiner who has observed the witnesses and lived with the case has drawn conclusions different from the Board's than when he has reached the same conclusion. The findings of the examiner are to be considered along with the consistency and inherent probability of testimony. The significance of his report, of course, depends largely on the importance of credibility in the particular case. To give it this significance does not seem to us materially more difficult than to heed the other factors which in sum determine whether evidence is "substantial." * * *

We therefore remand the cause to the Court of Appeals. On reconsideration of the record it should accord the findings of the trial examiner the relevance that they reasonably command in answering the comprehensive question whether the evidence supporting the Board's order is substantial. But the court need not limit its reexamination of the case to the effect of that report on its decision. We leave it free to grant or deny enforcement as it thinks the principles expressed in this opinion dictate.

Judgment vacated and cause remanded.

MR. JUSTICE BLACK and MR. JUSTICE DOUGLAS concur with parts I and II of this opinion but as to part III agree with the opinion of the court below, 2 Cir., 179 F.2d 749, 753.

LOCAL 357, INTERNATIONAL BROTHERHOOD OF TEAMSTERS v. NATIONAL LABOR RELATIONS BOARD

Supreme Court of the United States, 1961.
365 U.S. 667, 81 S.Ct. 835, 6 L.Ed.2d 11.

MR. JUSTICE DOUGLAS delivered the opinion of the Court.

Petitioner union (along with the International Brotherhood of Teamsters and a number of other affiliated local unions) executed a three-year collective bargaining agreement with California Trucking Associations, which represented a group of motor truck operators in California. The provisions of the contract relating to hiring of casual or temporary employees were as follows:

> "Casual employees shall, wherever the Union maintains a dispatching service, be employed only on a seniority basis in the Industry whenever such senior employees are available. An available list with seniority status will be kept by the Unions, and employees requested will be dispatched upon call to any employer who is a party to this Agreement. Seniority rating of such

employees shall begin with a minimum of three months service in the Industry, *irrespective of whether such employee is or is not a member of the Union.*

"Discharge of any employee by an employer shall be grounds for removal of any employee from seniority status. No casual employee shall be employed by any employer who is a party to this Agreement in violation of seniority status if such employees are available and if the dispatching service for such employees is available. The employer shall first call the Union or the dispatching hall designated by the Union for such help. In the event the employer is notified that such help is not available, or in the event the employees called for do not appear for work at the time designated by the employer, the employer may hire from any other available source." (Emphasis added.)

Accordingly the union maintained a hiring hall for casual employees. One Slater was a member of the union and had customarily used the hiring hall. But in August 1955 he obtained casual employment with an employer who was party to the hiring-hall agreement without being dispatched by the union. He worked until sometime in November of that year, when he was discharged by the employer on complaint of the union that he had not been referred through the hiring-hall arrangement.

Slater made charges against the union and the employer. Though, as plain from the terms of the contract, there was an express provision that employees would not be discriminated against because they were or were not union members, the Board found that the hiring-hall provision was unlawful *per se* and that the discharge of Slater on the union's request constituted a violation by the employer of § 8(a)(1) and § 8(a)(3) and a violation by the union of § 8(b)(2) and § 8(b)(1)(A) of the National Labor Relations Act, as amended by the Taft-Hartley Act * * *.[1] The Board ordered, *inter alia,* ~among other things~ that the company and the union cease giving any effect to the hiring-hall agreement; [and] that they jointly and severally reimburse Slater for any loss sustained by him as a result of his discharge * * *. 121 N.L.R.B. 1629.

The union petitioned the Court of Appeals for review of the Board's action, and the Board made a cross-application for enforcement. That court

---

1. Section 8 provides in relevant part:

"(a) It shall be an unfair labor practice for an employer—

"(1) to interfere with, restrain, or coerce employees in the exercise of the rights guaranteed in section 7;

* * * * *

"(3) by discrimination in regard to hire or tenure of employment or any term or condition of employment to encourage or discourage membership in any labor organization * * *

* * * * *

"(b) It shall be an unfair labor practice for a labor organization or its agents—

"(1) to restrain or coerce (A) employees in the exercise of the rights guaranteed in section 7 * * *

"(2) to cause or attempt to cause an employer to discriminate against an employee in violation of subsection (a)(3) * * *"

Section 7 provides:

"Employees shall have the right to self-organization, to form, join, or assist labor organizations, to bargain collectively through representatives of their own choosing, and to engage in other concerted activities for the purpose of collective bargaining or other mutual aid or protection, and shall also have the right to refrain from any or all of such activities except to the extent that such right may be affected by an agreement requiring membership in a labor organization as a condition of employment as authorized in section 8(a)(3)."

* * * by a divided vote upheld the Board in ruling that the hiring-hall agreement was illegal *per se.* 107 U.S.App.D.C. 188, 275 F.2d 646. * * *

The [problem] goes back to the Board's ruling in Mountain Pacific Chapter, 119 N.L.R.B. 883. That decision, rendered in 1958, departed from earlier rulings and held, Abe Murdock dissenting, that the hiring-hall agreement, despite the inclusion of a nondiscrimination clause, was illegal *per se:*

> "Here the very grant of work at all depends solely upon union sponsorship, and it is reasonable to infer that the arrangement displays and enhances the Union's power and control over the employment status. Here all that appears is unilateral union determination and subservient employer action with no above-board explanation as to the reason for it, and it is reasonable to infer that the Union will be guided in its concession by an eye towards winning compliance with a membership obligation or union fealty in some other respect. The Employers here have surrendered all hiring authority to the Union and have given advance notice via the established hiring hall to the world at large that the Union is arbitrary master and is contractually guaranteed to remain so. From the final authority over hiring vested in the Respondent Union by the three AGC chapters, the inference of the encouragement of union membership is inescapable." Id., 896.

The Board went on to say that a hiring-hall arrangement to be lawful must contain protective provisions. Its views were stated as follows:

> "We believe, however, that the inherent and unlawful encouragement of union membership that stems from unfettered union control over the hiring process would be negated, and we would find an agreement to be nondiscriminatory on its face, only if the agreement explicitly provided that:

> "(1) Selection of applicants for referral to jobs shall be on a nondiscriminatory basis and shall not be based on, or in any way affected by, union membership, bylaws, rules, regulations, constitutional provisions, or any other aspect or obligation of union membership, policies, or requirements.

> "(2) The employer retains the right to reject any job applicant referred by the union.

> "(3) The parties to the agreement post in places where notices to employees and applicants for employment are customarily posted, all provisions relating to the functioning of the hiring arrangement, including the safeguards that we deem essential to the legality of an exclusive hiring agreement." Id., 897.

The Board recognizes that the hiring hall came into being "to eliminate wasteful, time-consuming, and repetitive scouting for jobs by individual workmen and haphazard uneconomical searches by employers." Id., 896, n. 8. The hiring hall at times has been a useful adjunct to the closed shop.[3] But Congress may have thought that it need not serve that cause, that in fact it has served well both labor and management—particularly in the maritime field and in the building and construction industry. In the latter the contractor who frequently is a stranger to the area where the work is

3. Fenton, Union Hiring Halls Under the Taft-Hartley Act, 9 Lab.L.Jour. 505, 506 (1958).

done requires a "central source" for his employment needs;[5] and a man looking for a job finds in the hiring hall "at least a minimum guarantee of continued employment."[6]

Congress has not outlawed the hiring hall, though it has outlawed the closed shop except within the limits prescribed in the *provisos* to § 8(a)(3).[7] Senator Taft made clear his views that hiring halls are useful, that they are not illegal *per se*, that unions should be able to operate them so long as they are not used to create a closed shop:

> "In order to make clear the real intention of Congress, it should be clearly stated that the hiring hall is not necessarily illegal. The employer should be able to make a contract with the union as an employment agency. The union frequently is the best employment agency. The employer should be able to give notice of vacancies, and in the normal course of events to accept men sent to him by the hiring hall. He should not be able to bind himself, however, to reject non-union men if they apply to him; nor should he be able to contract to accept men on a rotary-hiring basis. * * *" S.Rep. No. 1827, 81st Cong., 2d Sess., pp. 13–14.

There being no express ban of hiring halls in any provisions of the Act, those who add one, whether it be the Board or the courts, engage in a legislative act. The Act deals with discrimination either by the employers or unions that encourages or discourages union membership. As respects § 8(a)(3) we said in Radio Officers, etc., v. National Labor Relations Board, 347 U.S. 17, 42–43, 74 S.Ct. 323, 337, 98 L.Ed. 455:

> "The language of § 8(a)(3) is not ambiguous. The unfair labor practice is for an employer to encourage or discourage membership by means of discrimination. Thus this section does not outlaw all encouragement or discouragement of membership in labor organizations; only such as is accomplished by discrimination is prohibited. Nor does this section outlaw discrimination in employment as such; only such discrimination as encourages or discourages membership in a labor organization is proscribed."

It is the "true purpose" or "real motive" in hiring or firing that constitutes the test. Id., 347 U.S. 43, 74 S.Ct. 337. Some conduct may by its very nature contain the implications of the required intent; the natural foreseeable consequences of certain action may warrant the inference. Id., 347 U.S. 45, 74 S.Ct. 338. * * * The existence of discrimination may at times be inferred by the Board, for "it is permissible to draw on experience in factual inquiries." Radio Officers' etc., v. National Labor Relations Board, supra, 347 U.S. 49, 74 S.Ct. 340.

---

5. Fenton, op. cit., supra, note 3, at 507.

6. Id., at 507.

7. Those *provisos* read:

"*Provided,* That nothing in this Act * * * shall preclude an employer from making an agreement with a labor organization (not established, maintained, or assisted by any action defined in section 8(a) of this Act as an unfair labor practice) to require as a condition of employment membership therein on or after the thirtieth day following the beginning of such employment or the effective date of such agreement, whichever is the later, * * * *Provided fur-* ther, That no employer shall justify any discrimination against an employee for nonmembership in a labor organization (A) if he has reasonable grounds for believing that such membership was not available to the employee on the same terms and conditions generally applicable to other members, or (B) if he has reasonable grounds for believing that membership was denied or terminated for reasons other than the failure of the employee to tender the periodic dues and the initiation fees uniformly required as a condition of acquiring or retaining membership * * *."

But surely discrimination cannot be inferred from the face of the instrument when the instrument specifically provides that there will be no discrimination against "casual employees" because of the presence or absence of union membership. The only complaint in the case was by Slater, a union member, who sought to circumvent the hiring-hall agreement. When an employer and the union enforce the agreement against union members, we cannot say without more that either indulges in the kind of discrimination to which the Act is addressed.

It may be that the very existence of the hiring hall encourages union membership. We may assume that it does. The very existence of the union has the same influence. When a union engages in collective bargaining and obtains increased wages and improved working conditions, its prestige doubtless rises and, one may assume, more workers are drawn to it. When a union negotiates collective bargaining agreements that include arbitration clauses and supervises the functioning of those provisions so as to get equitable adjustments of grievances, union membership may also be encouraged. The truth is that the union is a service agency that probably encourages membership whenever it does its job well. But, as we said in Radio Officers, etc., v. National Labor Relations Board, supra, the only encouragement or discouragement of union membership banned by the Act is that which is "accomplished by discrimination." 347 U.S. at page 43, 74 S.Ct. at page 337.

Nothing is inferable from the present hiring-hall provision except that employer and union alike sought to route "casual employees" through the union hiring hall and required a union member who circumvented it to adhere to it.

It may be that hiring halls need more regulation than the Act presently affords. As we have seen the Act aims at every practice, act, source or institution which in fact is used to encourage and discourage union membership by discrimination in regard to hire or tenure, term or condition of employment. Perhaps the conditions which the Board attaches to hiring-hall arrangements will in time appeal to the Congress. Yet, where Congress has adopted a selective system for dealing with evils, the Board is confined to that system. * * *

The present agreement for a union hiring hall has a protective clause in it, as we have said; and there is no evidence that it was in fact used unlawfully. We cannot assume that a union conducts its operations in violation of law or that the parties to this contract did not intend to adhere to its express language. Yet we would have to make those assumptions to agree with the Board that it is reasonable to infer the union will act discriminatorily.

Moreover, the hiring hall, under the law as it stands, is a matter of negotiation between the parties. The Board has no power to compel directly or indirectly that the hiring hall be included or excluded in collective agreements. * * * Its power, so far as here relevant, is restricted to the elimination of discrimination. Since the present agreement contains such a prohibition, the Board is confined to determining whether discrimination has in fact been practiced. * * *

[Reversed.]

MR. JUSTICE FRANKFURTER took no part in the consideration or decision of this case.

[The concurring opinion of MR. JUSTICE HARLAN, joined in by MR. JUSTICE STEWART, is omitted.]

MR. JUSTICE CLARK, dissenting * * *.

I cannot agree with the casual treatment the Court gives to the "casual employee" who is either unable to get employment or is fired therefrom because he has not been cleared by a union hiring hall. Inasmuch as the record, and the image of a hiring hall which it presents, are neglected by the Court, a short résumé of the facts is appropriate.

Lester Slater, the complainant, became a "casual employee" in the truck freight business in 1953 or early 1954. He approached an employer but was referred to the union hiring hall. There the dispatcher told him to see Barney Volkoff, an official of the union, whose office in the union headquarters building was some three miles away. Describing his visit to Volkoff, Slater stated that "[I] just give him [Volkoff] the money to send back East to pay up my dues back there for the withdrawal card, * * * and I went right to the [hiring] hall and went to work." However, this was but the beginning of Slater's trouble with the hall. After some difficulty with one of his temporary employers (Pacific Intermountain Express), the hall refused to refer Slater to other employers. In order to keep employed despite the union hall's failure to dispatch him, Slater relied on a letter from John Annand, an International Representative of the union, stating that "you may seek work wherever you can find it in the freight industry without working through the hiring hall." It was this letter that obtained Slater his employment with Los Angeles-Seattle Motor Express, where he was characterized by its dock foreman as being "a good worker." After a few months employment, the Business Agent of the union (Victor Karaty) called on the Los Angeles-Seattle Motor Express, advising that it could not hire Slater "any longer here without a referral card"; that the company would "have to get rid of Slater, and if [it] * * * didn't, that he was going to tie the place up in a knot, [that he] would pull the men off." Los Angeles-Seattle Motor Express fired Slater, telling him that "[We] * * * can't use you now until you get this straightened out with the union. Then come back; we will put you to work." He then went to the union, and was again referred to Volkoff who advised, "I can't do anything for you because you are out. You are not qualified for this job." Upon being shown the Annand letter, Volkoff declared "I am the union."

On later occasions when Slater attempted to get clearance from Volkoff he was asked "How come you weren't out on that—didn't go out on the picket line?" (Apparently the union had been on a strike.) Slater testified, "I told him that nobody asked me to. I was out a week. I thought the strike was on. The hall was closed. The guys told me there weren't no work." The landlady of Slater also approached Volkoff in an effort to get him cleared and she testified that "I asked Mr. Barney Volkoff what he had against Lester Slater and why he was doing this to him." And she quoted him as saying: "For a few reasons, one is about the P.I.E. [Pacific Intermountain Express] * * * [a]nother thing, he is an illiterate." She further testified that "he [Volkoff] didn't like the way he dressed. And he [Volkoff] fussed around and fussed around." He therefore refused to "route," as the Court calls it, Slater through the union hiring hall.

The Court finds that the National Labor Relations Act does not ban hiring halls *per se* and that therefore they are illegal only if they discriminate on the basis of union membership. It holds that no such actual discrimination was shown and that none is inferable from the face of the contract since it has a protective clause. Collaterally it holds, quoting Senator Taft, that hiring halls are "useful"; that they save time and eliminate waste and, finally, that the Court "cannot assume that a union conducts its operations in violation of law."

I do not doubt for a moment that men hired through such arrangements are saved the expense and delay of making the rounds of prospective employers on their own. Nor do I doubt their utility to employers with varying employee demands. And I accept the fact that Congress has outlawed only closed shops and allowed hiring halls to remain in operation. But just as those observations are not, in the final analysis, relied upon by the Court today in reaching its decision, my acquiescence in them is only a prologue to my dissent from the remaining considerations upon which its decision actually rests. These considerations are dependent upon the construction given § 8(a)(3) and I therefore first turn to that section.

Section 8(a)(3) provides, in part, that it shall be an unfair labor practice for an employer "*by discrimination* in regard to hire or tenure of employment or any term or condition of employment *to encourage or discourage* membership in any labor organization * * *." (Emphasis added.) As I view this prohibition, which by § 8(b)(2) is also applied to unions when causing or attempting to cause any employer to violate this section, two factors must be present before there is an unfair labor practice: (1) discrimination in the hiring or tenure of employees which is intended to, or inherently tends to, result in (2) encouragement or discouragement of membership in a union.

The word "discrimination" in the section, as the Board points out and I agree, includes not only distinctions contingent upon "the presence or absence of union membership," 365 U.S. at page 675, 81 S.Ct. at page 839, but all differences in treatment regardless of their basis. This is the "cause" portion of the section. But § 8(a)(3) also includes an "effect" clause which provides that the intended or inherent effect of the discrimination must be "to encourage or discourage [union] membership." The section has, therefore, a divided structure. Not all discriminations violate the section, but only those the effect of which is encouragement or discouragement of union membership. * * * [T]he union here contends, and the Court agrees, that there can be no "discrimination" within the section *unless it is based on* union membership, i.e., members treated one way, nonmembers another, with further distinctions, among members, based on good standing. Through this too superficial interpretation, the Court abuses the language of the Congress and unduly restricts the scope of the proscription so that it forbids only the most obvious "hard-sell" techniques of influencing employee exercise of § 7 rights.

[T]he plain and accepted meaning of the word "discrimination" supports my interpretation. In common parlance, the word means to distinguish or differentiate. * * *

Given that interpretation of the word "discrimination," it becomes necessary to determine the class of employee involved, and then whether *any* differences in treatment within that class are present. The Board found the class affected by the union hiring hall to be that group which was qualified, in the sense of ability, to do the work required by the employer and who had applied for work through the hiring hall. Obviously, not all of those who apply receive like treatment. Not all applicants receive referral cards. Clearly, then, the class applying to the hiring hall is itself divided into two groups treated differently—those cleared by the union and those who were not. The next question is whether the contract requiring and endorsing that discrimination or differentiation is designed to, or inherently tends to, encourage union membership. If it does, then § 8(a)(3) has been violated.

 * * * I therefore ask, "Does the ordinary applicant for casual employment, who walks into the union hall at the direction of his prospective employer, consider his chances of getting dispatched for work diminished because of his non-union status or default in dues payment?" Lester Slater testified—and it is uncontradicted—that "He [the applicant] had to be a union member; otherwise he wouldn't be working there * * * you got to have your dues paid up to date and so forth." When asked how he knew this, Slater replied, "I have always knew that." Such was the sum of his impressions gained from contact with the hall from 1953 or 1954 when he started to 1958 when he ended. The misunderstanding—if it is that—of this common worker, who had the courage to complain, is, I am sure, representative of many more who were afraid to protest or, worse, were unaware of their right to do so.

Of the gravity of such a situation the Board is the best arbiter and best equipped to find a solution. It is, after all, "permissible [for the Board] to draw on experience in factual inquiries." Radio Officers, supra, 347 U.S. at page 49, 74 S.Ct. at page 340. It has resolved the issue clearly, not only here, but also in its 1958 Report which, as I have said, repeated its Mountain Pacific position "that a union to which an employer has so delegated hiring powers will exercise its power with a view to securing compliance with membership obligations and union rules." At p. 68. In view of Slater's experience, for one, the idea is certainly not farfetched. Despite the contract provision as to equal treatment between union and nonunion men after a minimum amount of seniority is obtained, we find here that Slater had to "pay up" his dues in 1953. Despite the seniority rule,[3] dispatch was often made, the record shows, due to favoritism by the employer. Despite the contract's solemn words, the uncontradicted evidence is that lack of intellect, taste in dress and failure to appear on a union picket line prevented an employee from getting a job, although he was a "good worker." Likewise, approaching a union official (who indignantly asserts "I am the union") with a letter from a union "higher-up" may result in loss of work. Such factors

---

3. The employers did not receive any seniority lists from the union and were unaware   of whether this provision of the agreement was being properly administered.

are infinitely more persuasive than the self-serving declaration of a union hiring-hall agreement.

However, I need not go so far as to presume that the union has set itself upon an illegal course, conditioning referral on the unlawful criterion of union membership in good standing (which inference the majority today says cannot be drawn), to reach the same result. I need only assume that, by thousands of common workers like Slater, the contract and its conditioning of casual employment upon union referral will work a misunderstanding as to the significance of union affiliation unless the employer's abdication of his rule be made less than total and some note of the true function of the hiring hall be posted where all may see and read. The tide of encouragement may not be turned, but it will in part at least be stemmed. As an added dividend, the inherent probability of the free-wheeling operation of the union hiring hall resulting in arbitrary dispatching of job seekers would to some significant extent be diminished.

I would hold that there is not only a reasonable likelihood, but that it must inescapably be concluded under this record, that, without the safeguards at issue, a contract conditioning employment *solely upon union referral* encourages membership in the union by that very distinction itself.

* * *

Finally, let me say that the Board should not be hamstrung in its effort to enforce the mandate of the Congress that there shall be no closed shop. As Senator Taft stated on the floor of the Senate: [4]

"Perhaps [the closed shop] is best exemplified by the so-called hiring halls on the west coast, where shipowners cannot employ anyone unless the union sends him to them. * * * Such an arrangement gives the union tremendous power over the employees; furthermore, it abolishes a free labor market. A man cannot get a job where he wants to get it. He has to go to the union first; and if the union says that he cannot get in, then he is out of that particular labor field."

That is where Lester Slater finds himself today. I therefore dissent.

MR. JUSTICE WHITTAKER joins in * * * this dissent * * *.

SUMMERS, A SUMMARY EVALUATION OF THE TAFT–HARTLEY ACT

11 Industrial and Labor Relations Review 405, 409–10 (1958).

The individual is also given a degree of independence by the union security clauses of Sections 8(a)(3) and 8(b)(2). These were explicitly designed "to meet numerous examples of glaring disregard for the rights of minority members of unions"—exclusion of Negroes, admission only of sons of members, and expulsion of those who opposed the union leadership. Although the clause does give broad protection to job rights, it does not give the individual any right to participate in the affairs of his union. Negroes can still be relegated to subsidiary locals and have their contracts negotiated by all-white locals. Opponents can still be expelled and politically sterilized. Even job protection is not complete, for the union may induce the employer

4. 93 Cong.Rec. 3836; II Leg.Hist. of the Labor Management Relations Act, 1947, 1010.

to discharge individuals because they are "left-wingers," or because they don't drive a Studebaker. Union democracy is not encouraged or protected, and the individual is left helpless in the face of union-management cooperation.

These, however, suggest only the loopholes in the law—its gross failure to meet its stated objective. The real failure of the law is that it has not been obeyed. The closed shop and hiring hall are still standard practice in the construction industry and are only thinly disguised in printing, longshore, and maritime. In the building trades the established practice of the unions and employers is to ignore the law, pay any claims filed, and keep away from the courts. The very industries in which the abuses were most severe have not changed their ways.

The moral here again is that it is difficult to legislate against union-management cooperation, but the problem runs much deeper. The closed shop, closed union, and hiring hall—an inseparable trilogy—persist because of practical needs of both unions and employers. In industries where employment is short-term, seniority structures are impossible. Those workers who are established in the industry seek priority of job rights by requiring that new entrants wait until established workers are employed. The auto worker, the steel worker, and even the office worker has his seniority clause which gives him job priority. In these industries there is no "free labor market"; a man cannot get a job where he wants it. For the hodcarrier, the bricklayer, or the carpenter, the closed shop trilogy provides his substitute for seniority. The statute attempted to wipe out all this and substituted nothing in its place. This desperate need for job priority cannot thus be wished away with a wand of words. The employers' need is nearly as compelling. In these industries the employer needs a pool of labor on which to draw on short notice; he cannot advertise or even maintain an adequate personnel department. The hiring hall is a practical and proven solution.

The Taft-Hartley Act gave no recognition to these stubborn economic facts. Where there were genuine economic needs of the parties, it attempted to create a vacuum. It blandly assumed that, if the union were prohibited from having a closed shop, the employers would protect the individuals. The signal lesson of the Taft-Hartley Act is that when the union's needs are acute, and when the employer's needs or desires for cooperation are strong, legal measures must be carefully constructed to permit the creating of new institutions to meet the genuine needs. If the individual is to be protected, both unions and management need to be told clearly that they cannot interfere with his rights even though it is to their mutual advantage, and stringent measures must be provided to curb their interlocking interests.

Note

1. Given the functions of the hiring hall, on the one hand, and the congressional purpose in prohibiting the closed shop, on the other, with whom do you agree, Justice Douglas or Justice Clark? How do their interpretations of Section 8(a)(3) differ?

2. The variety of so-called "union security" arrangement expressly permitted in Section 8(a)(3) is known as the "union shop." With regard to the closed

shop and the union shop, it has been said: "In one of them, the boss determines who the union's members will be. In the other, the union determines who the boss's employees will be." Which is which?

3. What are the functions of union security arrangements such as the closed shop and the union shop? To what extent is there conflict between the interests of (1) union and union members, (2) nonunion members, and (3) employer, with regard to such arrangements? How did the Taft-Hartley amendments seek to accommodate these interests? In the hiring-hall context, does the Act rely too gullibly on the employer's incentive to police against the union's conversion of a permissible union shop into an impermissible closed shop?

4. The Local 357 case presents a classic tension between the NLRB and the reviewing courts, concerning how deeply the Board must immerse itself in relevant evidence in determining crucial questions of fact (or mixed questions of fact and law). The Board, in seeking to dispose of its large volume of cases as efficiently as possible, is driven to employ short cuts to decision, i.e., *"per se"* rules which have been distilled out of the Board's experience in dealing with the particular variety of case. In Local 357, for example, the Board sought to apply the *per se* rule which it had developed in Mountain Pacific for expeditious processing of hiring-hall cases; the application of that rule enabled the Board to resolve such cases through mere scrutiny of the face of the collective bargaining agreement, scanning for the three purging provisions required to be set forth therein. The majority of the Supreme Court rejected the Board's *per se* effort; on remand, the Board is required to consider all of the arguably relevant "yak-yak" (including that of the landlady and Barney Volkoff) with sufficient intensity to make the thus-mandated findings of fact with regard to the "discrimination" and "encouragement of union membership" elements of Section 8(a)(3).

The foregoing discussion may alert the reader to a more discerning insight into what is going on in the many later cases in this casebook in which the *per se* gambit is essayed by the Board. As will be noted, the effort is sometimes successful, sometimes not, the reasons for the difference in result being not always pellucid.

5. As stated at the outset of Chapter 3 (supra p. 159), the Taft-Hartley Act introduced a set of *union* unfair labor practices, in Section 8(b). Section 8(b)(1), in its principal application, prohibits a union from restraining or coercing employees in the exercise of their Section 7 rights (including the right to *refrain* from union activities). The meaning of "restrain or coerce" in this context, as compared with the meaning of Section 8(a)(1)'s *"interfere with,* restrain, or coerce," is dealt with infra p. 312, Note 1. Section 8(b)(2) was introduced in the Local 357 case. Section 8(b)(3), placing the same duty on the union to bargain in good faith as Section 8(a)(5) had previously placed upon employers, is dealt with in Chapter 6, infra. Section 8(b)(4), covering, most importantly, secondary boycotts, is treated in Chapter 5, Section C.

As experience divulged, not all union activity of an undesirable sort was reached by the Taft-Hartley Act. The major loopholes in that Act were in the areas of secondary boycotts and picketing for a recognitional and/or organizational purpose. The pressure generated to close these loopholes, as well as to deal with other forms of "unionitis" which had developed, culminated in the Landrum-Griffin Act of 1959. This Act is the subject of the next section.

B. THE LANDRUM–GRIFFIN ACT OF 1959

The Landrum-Griffin Act, officially entitled the Labor-Management Reporting and Disclosure Act of 1959, was the product of the second twelve-year cycle following the Wagner Act. More immediately, it was the consequence of the long investigation by the Senate's Select Committee on Improper Activities in the Labor or Management Field. The chairman of the committee was Senator John L. McClellan of Arkansas. Two other members of the committee were Senators John F. Kennedy and Barry Goldwater. Chief Counsel for the committee was Robert F. Kennedy. The so-called "McClellan Committee" began its hearings in 1957. Over the next three years it took 46,150 pages of testimony from 1,526 witnesses in well-publicized proceedings, frequently the subject of television coverage. The findings of the committee, with supporting evidence, were presented in a series of detailed reports which drew national attention.

It is no exaggeration to say that the committee uncovered shocking conditions in some American unions. In the process, it generated irresistible pressure for reform legislation. The central concern of this legislation was the regulation of internal union government so as to purge it of abuses highlighted in the hearings, including, in the case of a relatively small number of unions, outright corruption and, in the case of a much larger number, undemocratic practices. Titles I through VI of the Landrum-Griffin Act deal in various ways with these internal union problems.

Title VII, on the other hand, consists of a hodge-podge of amendments to the National Labor Relations Act. For present purposes, the most important of these amendments are two: first, the creation of an additional union unfair labor practice, rendering peaceful picketing for recognitional or organizational objectives illegal under certain circumstances (Section 8(b)(7)); second, the closing of some major loopholes in the secondary boycott provisions of Section 8(b)(4) (Sections 8(b)(4) and 8(e)).

The concern at this point in the book is for the internal union regulatory aspect of Landrum-Griffin, its major feature and the first substantial effort by the Federal Government to control internal union affairs. The materials which follow are intended to indicate the nature of the problems involved and to outline in very general fashion the manner in which the Act addresses them. Since, as others have observed, the Act might appropriately be named, giving due credit to those most responsible for it, the "*Hoffa*-Landrum-Griffin Act," it is not unfitting to give centerstage to the former president of the Teamsters Union.

UNITED STATES SENATE, SELECT COMMITTEE ON IMPROPER ACTIVITIES IN THE LABOR OR MANAGEMENT FIELD—INTERIM REPORT

85th Congress, 2d Session, Report No. 1417, pp. 211–16 (1958).

* * * [W]ith the background of the taxicab situation and the paper locals, the committee was able to draw a picture of continuing association, cooperation, and mutual assistance between Jimmy Hoffa, a top official of the teamsters union, and John Dioguardi, a convicted New York racketeer.

That the association between Hoffa and Dio was not a purely union affair became clearly evident in the closing hours of the first Hoffa hearing in August. As the committee attempted to probe deeper into the relationship between Hoffa and Dio, it ran into a stone wall of memory failure on Hoffa's part.

In one committee session alone, Hoffa claimed lack of memory in answers to committee questions 111 times. The teamster leader's classic answer to the question was:

> "I have run it through my mind during the lunch hour, and to the best of my recollection I cannot recall what you are talking about."

Senator Ives was moved to tell the teamster leader that he had "about the best forgettery of anyone I have ever known" * * *.

[T]he committee wanted to know whether or not Dio had ever sent any individual or group of individuals to Detroit to perform a job for Hoffa.
* * *

* * * Hoffa had denied to the committee knowing anything about Dio's sending any individual to Detroit. His attorney implied that the questions of the chief counsel touched on the area of a wiretapping indictment which had been returned against Hoffa in New York. In this indictment Hoffa was charged with conspiring with one Bernard Spindel, a notorious wiretapper, to "bug" the telephones of his associates and fellow teamster officials in Detroit. * * *

In an attempt to refresh Hoffa's memory, a tape recording of a phone conversation between Dio and Hoffa on June 2, 1953, was played: * * *

DIO. Well, I'm leaving Thursday morning around 8 o'clock in the morning.

HOFFA. What time do you arrive, Johnny? * * *

DIO. I should be there about 10:30–11 o'clock. * * *

HOFFA. I'll have a car pick you up. * * *

DIO. I got a couple of those things—

HOFFA. Good.

DIO. So, ah, maybe—maybe I'll have four of them tomorrow.

HOFFA. Fine. * * *

DIO. But two I got for sure—

HOFFA. Right.

DIO. But I may have four tomorrow. O.K.

HOFFA. Yeah, John.

DIO. All right, Jim.

HOFFA. O.K.

DIO. Bye, bye.

Hoffa was asked what "those things" were that Dio was talking about. Said the teamster leader—

> "I cannot refresh my memory from the notes, to the best of my recollection, I cannot understand what he would be talking about, 'four of

them' and I don't know whether or not he ever came to Detroit at that particular time."

Hoffa finally recalled that Dio had come to Detroit and was asked whether the "four of them" referred to Minifons, small German-built wire recorders which can be concealed on a person to record conversations. Hoffa said he could not remember whether Dio had brought the Minifons with him, but admitted he had purchased the Minifons. * * *

Hoffa finally recalled that the Minifons had been purchased from wiretapper Spindel in New York, with whom he was under indictment. * * *

The chairman then came to the major point involved in the Minifons purchased by Hoffa:

The CHAIRMAN. Let the Chair ask you a question. You say if we can suggest something it might remind you. Let me see if I can be of a little help.

At the time you bought these Minifons, you were under investigation by a grand jury, were you not?

(The witness conferred with his counsel.)

Mr. HOFFA. Mr. Fitzgerald reminds me that there was a grand jury.

The CHAIRMAN. Did you not buy them for the specific purpose, and did you not use them for the specific purpose, of placing them on witnesses who went into the grand jury room to testify so that when they came out you would have a recording of what they said?

(The witness conferred with his counsel.)

The CHAIRMAN. And did you not use them for that purpose?

(The witness conferred with his counsel.)

Mr. HOFFA. Mr. Chairman, I would like to answer that as a direct question, but again I am reminded in my own mind, listening to statements that have been made in this committee, attributed to myself, by other people, which I can't recall, and I have to say to the best of my recollection I cannot recall anybody being assigned or going into any grand jury chambers, and I may say, sir, that a certain judge that conducted that vigorously denied it when it appeared in the newspaper.

The CHAIRMAN. Let me ask you one more time. If you did this, this is certainly something you would not forget * * *.

Did you not procure these Minifons for the purpose of, and did you not use them to place on witnesses who went before the grand jury, so that when they came out you would have a recording of the testimony they had given?

Mr. HOFFA. May I consult with my attorney, sir?

The CHAIRMAN. Yes, sir.

(The witness conferred with his counsel.) * * *

Said Hoffa:

"To the best of my recollection, I must recall on my memory, I cannot remember."

UNITED STATES SENATE, SELECT COMMITTEE ON IMPROPER ACTIVITIES IN THE LABOR OR MANAGEMENT FIELD—SECOND INTERIM REPORT

86th Congress, 1st Session, Report No. 621, pp. 108–10 (1959).

FINDINGS—JAMES R. HOFFA

During 2 years of hearings, the committee has heard voluminous testimony relating to the conduct of the International Brotherhood of Teamsters, Chauffeurs, Warehousemen, and Helpers of America and that union's general president, James R. Hoffa. * * *

Ignominy was piled on ignominy as the testimony wove through stories of violence, financial manipulations, callous repression of democratic rights and racketeer control.

This is an ugly situation. The continuing attitude of Hoffa and other Teamster leaders that they are above the law can only serve to intensify the apprehensions of decent union members and decent people throughout the country.

It will serve no purpose to take each of Hoffa's acts and issue a list of condemnations. This the committee has done on numerous occasions. One point, however, must be made crystal clear. The understanding of this point is vital to the understanding of Hoffa's role as a labor leader, the head of the Nation's largest union.

On more occasions than we can recount, Hoffa has told the committee (and anyone else who would listen) that no matter what else can be said about him, he is first and foremost interested in the betterment of the working conditions of his union members. It is this point which the Teamster president repeatedly uses to justify his outrageous behavior. The fact is that nothing could be further from the truth.

Time and time again the committee has found Hoffa to be faithless to the members of his own union. He has betrayed these members so frequently that it has become abundantly clear that Hoffa's chief interest is his own advancement and that of his friends and cronies—a great number of whom are racketeers.

It is true that in many areas of the country wages paid to members of the Teamsters union are as high as or higher than those paid to other working people. This, however, has been historical with truckdrivers. It was so in the days of Dan Tobin and remained so during the administration of Dave Beck. The fact is, however, that Hoffa has permitted his close associates to sign contracts in other areas which are disgracefully low and in some cases even lower than the national minimum wage of $1 an hour. Such is certainly the case in Detroit, Hoffa's own backyard, where Teamster Union car washers work for as little as $2.50 a day for a 10-hour day.

In New York a number of Teamster locals brought into that union by Hoffa, with the help and assistance of John Dioguardi and Anthony "Tony Ducks" Corallo, executed contracts calling for low wages and poor working conditions. When this situation was brought to public light by the committee, Mr. Hoffa did nothing to clean up the situation. On the contrary, he permitted the corrupt union officials to leave the Teamsters and set up independent unions in the New York area, which today continue their faithless representation of the working people of that city. A number of other instances of sweetheart contracts, where directly participated in by Hoffa or his associates, have been placed in the committee record, including the contracts signed with the Englander Mattress Co. and the contract signed with the Midwest Burlap & Bag Co. in Des Moines, Iowa. These examples serve to destroy Hoffa's self-painted picture as a steadfast champion of working people.

In addition, Hoffa has used union funds for his own benefit and that of his friends.

Hoffa has consistently supported the interests of racketeer friends over those of his own members. * * *

Hoffa has connived with and maneuvered union insurance to racketeer friends, bringing these friends gigantic profits. While the cost of insurance has risen, the benefits to the members of his union were drastically reduced. * * *

If Hoffa is successful in combating the combined weight of the U.S. Government and public opinion, the cause of decent unionism is lost and labor-management relations in this country will return to the jungle era.

ROBERT F. KENNEDY, THE ENEMY WITHIN
126–28 (1960).

Another story our Committee heard begins with Clyde Buxton, of Joplin, Missouri. He was a member of Teamsters Local 823. In 1953 he and a number of his fellow Teamsters sent a petition to Jimmy Hoffa, protesting against the way their president, Floyd Webb, was administering the union. Webb, however, was a friend of Hoffa and Hoffa immediately sent him the petition. Within a few days Clyde Buxton was beaten and slugged into unconsciousness by an assailant with a ball-peen hammer. To an investigating committee of rank-and-file members, one of whom testified before the Senate Committee, Webb arrogantly admitted that he had ordered the attack. But he had been disappointed in the outcome.

"What I wanted was some funerals," he said, "and there are going to be some if you guys don't keep your nose out of it."

Webb showed he meant business. Three of the men who had signed the petition were told by their union steward to cross off their names or lose their jobs. Several weeks later a man who refused had his union book lifted.

Next Webb warned an official of the Roadway Express Company that the firm would catch "hell" unless it fired two particular employees—both of whom were signers of the anti-Webb petition. Twelve days later, after a twenty-four-hour strike, the two men were fired.

Now the rebel rank-and-filers went to court. Buxton filed an action in tort to recover damages for his slugging. In a settlement Webb paid him $4,000—which he took [along with funds to pay defense counsel] from the union treasury. * * *

Then Amos Reniker, a leading figure in the opposition group, filed suit asking that Webb be removed as union president. That night a bomb blast rocked Reniker's house. Damage was not serious but in the night Reniker's telephone rang and a voice warned: "The next time we will blow you to hell."

As Reniker's move to oust Webb gained momentum, the International used its old weapon, and placed the local in trusteeship, with Jimmy Hoffa as the trustee. Hoffa immediately put his old friend Floyd Webb back in charge to run the local union for him. Webb and Hoffa now had absolute control.

In the meantime, union members had filed suit, asking that an election be ordered. The court agreed and Reniker's group named a slate of officers to oppose the men Webb selected. A few days before the election word came from Hoffa: all Reniker's candidates were ineligible because of the provision requiring that they pay their dues by the first of the month. Reniker's group had paid their dues, but under the union-established check-off system. (As this arrangement is set up the company, which checks the dues off on the first day of the month, can't possibly get them to union headquarters before the second, third or fourth of the month. The Teamsters officers realize this and often use the gimmick to rule everyone ineligible but the incumbent officers, who work for the union and pay their own dues.)

Taking no chances, Hoffa and Harold Gibbons made special trips to Joplin to praise Webb and criticize Reniker before the membership. They made it clear that they expected this local to stay under their control.

The court then stepped in and blocked the election because of the undemocratic manner in which it was being handled. After prolonged litigation another election was set up for 1956. Again, in came Mr. Hoffa to inform the members that the officers under Webb's administration had done no wrong, and that Reniker and his group had cost the union $70,000 in litigation fees. He suggested that they throw Amos Reniker out of the union. Again the court delayed the election.

When Paul Tierney, an investigator for our Committee, went to Joplin to look into the situation, he of course talked with Amos Reniker. Immediately after Tierney left town, four men accosted Reniker and one grabbed him by the front of the shirt. They warned him: "Now if you don't quit talking about Mr. Hoffa and quit talking to those Senate investigators and quit talking about Mr. Webb we are going to make you awfully sorry, boy."

Amos Reniker was not intimidated. In September, 1958, he appeared before our Committee and told exactly how democracy in Joplin had suffered from the actions of Jimmy Hoffa and Floyd Webb. At the time of these hearings Webb and his men were still in power. Webb took the Fifth Amendment when he appeared before us.

Reniker told the Committee: "It looks to me like the situation has gotten so big that when the rank and file can't take care of their own problems and don't have any say in their own problems then there should be laws made to protect the rank and file."

Note

1. The foregoing account of the situation in Teamsters Local 823, Joplin, Missouri, brief though it is, contains the spectrum of abuses in the internal government of unions with which Titles I through VI of the Landrum-Griffin Act seek to cope.

Before considering these abuses, it may be well to examine the structure of the typical American labor union. The International Brotherhood of Teamsters, Chauffeurs, Warehousemen, and Helpers of America, for example, is an international labor organization, by which is meant that both Americans and Canadians are included in its membership. (If the membership were drawn entirely from the United States, the organization would be termed a "national" union.) Such an international union charters so-called local unions, the jurisdiction of which is established either on a geographic basis, an employer basis, a plant basis, or some variation thereof. Members of a local union are automatically members of the international union, and dues money is allocated between the local and the international on a basis specified in the constitution of the international union. The chief executive officer of the international is typically called the "international president." With the help of other international officers he administers the international's affairs, subject, in theory at least, to the control of an "international executive board" which the president himself chairs. Similarly, a local union is administered by a local president, other local officers, and a local executive board.

Ultimate power in the case of both the international and local union lies, in theory, with the membership—exercised in the case of the former through elected delegates at periodic international conventions, in the case of the latter through periodic and plenary membership meetings. In summary, most American unions are, on paper, democratic organizations. In practice, however, they strongly tend to exemplify, in one degree or another, Robert Michels' "Iron Law of Oligarchy." See Michels, Political Parties (1949).

2. The spectrum of internal union abuses revealed in the Joplin Teamsters case and the manner in which Titles I through VI of Landrum-Griffin address these abuses follow:

a. For his exercise of the democratic right to petition the president of his international union for a redress of grievances, Clyde Buxton was summarily "disciplined." Title I, entitled "Bill of Rights of Members of Labor Organizations," declares the rights of every union member to equal protection, freedom of speech and assembly, reasonable and uniform dues, and freedom to sue unions and their officers. (Sections 101(a)(1), (2), (3) and (4).) The effect of these provisions is to treat the union as a "government" within the government of society at large and to treat union members as free citizens in both governmental spheres. With these provisions in effect, Clyde Buxton could not lawfully be disciplined in any fashion for his act of petitioning the International President. And even for an act properly subject to discipline (e.g., violation of a "reasonable rule" in the union's constitution), he could be disciplined only in accordance with the requirements of due process of law, i.e., adequate notice of the charges, a reasonable time to prepare his defense, and a full and fair hearing. (Section 101(a)(5).) It should also be noted that *violent* interference with the exercise of any right protected by the Act is made a *criminal* offense. (Title VI, "Miscellaneous Provisions," Section 609.)

b. Floyd Webb paid Buxton, as well as Webb's attorney, out of the union till in settling the tort claim resulting from the attack upon Buxton with the ball-peen hammer. Conduct of this sort is dealt with in Titles II and V: Title II requires the periodic reporting and disclosure to the Secretary of Labor of financial transactions of unions, including "salary, allowances, and other direct and indirect disbursements * * * to each officer" and "direct and indirect loans made to any officer" (Sections 201(b)(3) and (4)); Title V imposes fiduciary responsibilities upon union officers, with sanctions for the non-fulfillment thereof (Section 501).

c. The placing of Local 823 in trusteeship, with Hoffa as trustee, was illustrative of a technique by which hundreds of recalcitrant local unions across the country were subjugated by national and international officers, their votes in national and international union elections controlled, and, on occasion, their treasuries milked. Title III ("Trusteeships") precludes such perversion of the otherwise legitimate device of trusteeships by establishing standards for their imposition and administration (Sections 302 and 303) and by requiring the filing of information pertinent for enforcement purposes with the Secretary of Labor. Section 302 sets forth the purposes for which a trusteeship may be established by "a labor organization over a subordinate body." These purposes include the elimination of corruption and other forms of financial malpractice and the restoration of democratic procedures. Section 303 makes it unlawful for the parent organization which established the trusteeship to manipulate either the votes or funds of the subordinate body in trusteeship.

d. Finagling with elections of union officials, as in the Joplin case, even if not a common practice, was sufficiently prevalent to call for and receive detailed attention in the Act. Title IV ("Elections") contains an elaborate regulatory scheme for union elections, specifying among other things election procedures and maximum terms of office.

Thus did Congress respond to the plaintive appeal of the Amos Renikers of the union world: " * * * there should be laws made to protect the rank and file."

C. RACIAL DISCRIMINATION IN LABOR RELATIONS: THE CIVIL RIGHTS ACT OF 1964

STEELE v. LOUISVILLE & NASHVILLE R.R.

Supreme Court of the United States, 1944.
323 U.S. 192, 65 S.Ct. 226, 89 L.Ed. 173.

MR. CHIEF JUSTICE STONE delivered the opinion of the Court.

The question is whether the Railway Labor Act * * * imposes on a labor organization, acting by authority of the statute as the exclusive bargaining representative of a craft or class of railway employees, the duty to represent all the employees in the craft without discrimination because of their race, and, if so, whether the courts have jurisdiction to protect the minority of the craft or class from the violation of such obligation.

The issue is raised by demurrer to the substituted amended bill of complaint filed by petitioner, a locomotive fireman, in a suit brought in the Alabama Circuit Court against his employer, the Louisville & Nashville

Railroad Company, the Brotherhood of Locomotive Firemen and Enginemen, an unincorporated labor organization, and certain individuals representing the Brotherhood. The Circuit Court sustained the demurrer, and the Supreme Court of Alabama affirmed. 245 Ala. 113, 16 So.2d 416. We granted certiorari, * * * the question presented being one of importance in the administration of the Railway Labor Act.

The allegations of the bill of complaint, so far as now material, are as follows: Petitioner, a Negro, is a locomotive fireman in the employ of respondent railroad, suing on his own behalf and that of his fellow employees who, like petitioner, are Negro firemen employed by the Railroad. Respondent Brotherhood, a labor organization, is as provided under § 2, Fourth of the Railway Labor Act, the exclusive bargaining representative of the craft of firemen employed by the Railroad and is recognized as such by it and the members of the craft. The majority of the firemen employed by the Railroad are white and are members of the Brotherhood, but a substantial minority are Negroes who, by the constitution and ritual of the Brotherhood, are excluded from its membership. As the membership of the Brotherhood constitutes a majority of all firemen employed on respondent Railroad, and as under § 2, Fourth, the members because they are the majority have the right to choose and have chosen the Brotherhood to represent the craft, petitioner and other Negro firemen on the road have been required to accept the Brotherhood as their representative for the purposes of the Act.

On March 28, 1940, the Brotherhood, purporting to act as representative of the entire craft of firemen, without informing the Negro firemen or giving them opportunity to be heard, served a notice on respondent Railroad and on twenty other railroads operating principally in the southeastern part of the United States. The notice announced the Brotherhood's desire to amend the existing collective bargaining agreement in such manner as ultimately to exclude all Negro firemen from the service. By established practice on the several railroads so notified only white firemen can be promoted to serve as engineers, and the notice proposed that only "promotable", i.e., white, men should be employed as firemen or assigned to new runs or jobs or permanent vacancies in established runs or jobs.

On February 18, 1941, the railroads and the Brotherhood, as representative of the craft, entered into a new agreement which provided that not more than 50% of the firemen in each class of service in each seniority district of a carrier should be Negroes; that until such percentage should be reached all new runs and all vacancies should be filled by white men; and that the agreement did not sanction the employment of Negroes in any seniority district in which they were not working. The agreement reserved the right of the Brotherhood to negotiate for further restrictions on the employment of Negro firemen on the individual railroads. On May 12, 1941, the Brotherhood entered into a supplemental agreement with respondent Railroad further controlling the seniority rights of Negro firemen and restricting their employment. The Negro firemen were not given notice or opportunity to be heard with respect to either of these agreements, which were put into effect before their existence was disclosed to the Negro firemen.

Until April 8, 1941, petitioner was in a "passenger pool", to which one white and five Negro firemen were assigned. These jobs were highly desirable in point of wages, hours and other considerations. Petitioner had performed and was performing his work satisfactorily. Following a reduction in the mileage covered by the pool, all jobs in the pool were, about April 1, 1941, declared vacant. The Brotherhood and the Railroad, acting under the agreement, disqualified all the Negro firemen and replaced them with four white men, members of the Brotherhood, all junior in seniority to petitioner and no more competent or worthy. As a consequence petitioner was deprived of employment for sixteen days and then was assigned to more arduous, longer, and less remunerative work in local freight service. In conformity to the agreement, he was later replaced by a Brotherhood member junior to him, and assigned work on a switch engine, which was still harder and less remunerative, until January 3, 1942. On that date, after the bill of complaint in the present suit had been filed, he was reassigned to passenger service.

Protests and appeals of petitioner and his fellow Negro firemen, addressed to the Railroad and the Brotherhood, in an effort to secure relief and redress, have been ignored. Respondents have expressed their intention to enforce the agreement of February 18, 1941, and its subsequent modifications. The Brotherhood has acted and asserts the right to act as exclusive bargaining representative of the firemen's craft. It is alleged that in that capacity it is under an obligation and duty imposed by the Act to represent the Negro firemen impartially and in good faith; but instead, in its notice to and contracts with the railroads, it has been hostile and disloyal to the Negro firemen, has deliberately discriminated against them, and has sought to deprive them of their seniority rights and to drive them out of employment in their craft, all in order to create a monopoly of employment for Brotherhood members.

The bill of complaint asks for discovery of the manner in which the agreements have been applied and in other respects; for an injunction against enforcement of the agreements made between the Railroad and the Brotherhood; for an injunction against the Brotherhood and its agents from purporting to act as representative of petitioner and others similarly situated under the Railway Labor Act, so long as the discrimination continues, and so long as it refuses to give them notice and hearing with respect to proposals affecting their interests; for a declaratory judgment as to their rights; and for an award of damages against the Brotherhood for its wrongful conduct.

The Supreme Court of Alabama took jurisdiction of the cause but held on the merits that petitioner's complaint stated no cause of action. It pointed out that the Act places a mandatory duty on the Railroad to treat with the Brotherhood as the exclusive representative of the employees in a craft, imposes heavy criminal penalties for willful failure to comply with its command, and provides that the majority of any craft shall have the right to determine who shall be the representative of the class for collective bargaining with the employer, see Virginian R. Co. v. System Federation, 300 U.S. 515, 545, 57 S.Ct. 592, 598, 81 L.Ed. 789. It thought that the Brotherhood was empowered by the statute to enter into the agreement of February 18, 1941, and that by virtue of the statute the Brotherhood has power by agreement with the Railroad both to create the seniority rights of petitioner and his fellow Negro employees and to destroy them. It construed the statute, not as creating the relationship of principal and agent between the members of the craft and the Brotherhood, but as conferring on the Brotherhood plenary authority to treat with the Railroad and enter into contracts fixing rates of pay and working conditions for the craft as a whole without any legal obligation or duty to protect the rights of minorities from discrimination or unfair treatment, however gross. Consequently it held that neither the Brotherhood nor the Railroad violated any rights of petitioner or his fellow Negro employees by negotiating the contracts discriminating against them.

If, as the state court has held, the Act confers this power on the bargaining representative of a craft or class of employees without any commensurate statutory duty toward its members, constitutional questions arise. For the representative is clothed with power not unlike that of a legislature which is subject to constitutional limitations on its power to deny, restrict, destroy or discriminate against the rights of those for whom it legislates and which is also under an affirmative constitutional duty equally to protect those rights. If the Railway Labor Act purports to impose on petitioner and the other Negro members of the craft the legal duty to comply with the terms of a contract whereby the representative has discriminatorily restricted their employment for the benefit and advantage of the Brotherhood's own members, we must decide the constitutional questions which petitioner raises in his pleading.

But we think that Congress, in enacting the Railway Labor Act and authorizing a labor union, chosen by a majority of a craft, to represent the craft, did not intend to confer plenary power upon the union to sacrifice, for the benefit of its members, rights of the minority of the craft, without imposing on it any duty to protect the minority. Since petitioner and the other Negro members of the craft are not members of the Brotherhood or eligible for membership, the authority to act for them is derived not from their action or consent but wholly from the command of the Act. Section 2, Fourth, provides: "Employees shall have the right to organize and bargain collectively through representatives of their own choosing. The majority of any craft or class of employees shall have the right to determine who shall be the representative of the craft or class for the purposes of this Act. * * *." * * * The use of the word "representative" * * * plainly implies that the representative is to act on behalf of all the employees which, by virtue of the statute, it undertakes to represent.

* * * The purposes of the Act declared by § 2 are the avoidance of "any interruption to commerce or to the operation of any carrier engaged therein," and this aim is sought to be achieved by encouraging "the prompt and orderly settlement of all disputes concerning rates of pay, rules, or working conditions." Compare Texas & N.O.R. Co. v. Brotherhood of Railway & S.S. Clerks, 281 U.S. 548, 569, 50 S.Ct. 427, 433, 74 L.Ed. 1034. These purposes would hardly be attained if a substantial minority of the craft were denied the right to have their interests considered at the conference table and if the final result of the bargaining process were to be the sacrifice of the interests of the minority by the action of a representative chosen by the

majority. The only recourse of the minority would be to strike, with the attendant interruption of commerce, which the Act seeks to avoid.

Section 2, Second, requiring carriers to bargain with the representative so chosen, operates to exclude any other from representing a craft. Virginian R. Co. v. System Federation, supra, 300 U.S. 545, 57 S.Ct. 598, 81 L.Ed. 789. The minority members of a craft are thus deprived by the statute of the right, which they would otherwise possess, to choose a representative of their own, and its members cannot bargain individually on behalf of themselves as to matters which are properly the subject of collective bargaining.

* * *

We think that the Railway Labor Act imposes upon the statutory representative of a craft at least as exacting a duty to protect equally the interests of the members of the craft as the Constitution imposes upon a legislature to give equal protection to the interests of those for whom it legislates. Congress has seen fit to clothe the bargaining representative with powers comparable to those possessed by a legislative body both to create and restrict the rights of those whom it represents, * * * but it has also imposed on the representative a corresponding duty. We hold that the language of the Act to which we have referred, read in the light of the purposes of the Act, expresses the aim of Congress to impose on the bargaining representative of a craft or class of employees the duty to exercise fairly the power conferred upon it in behalf of all those for whom it acts, without hostile discrimination against them.

This does not mean that the statutory representative of a craft is barred from making contracts which may have unfavorable effects on some of the members of the craft represented. Variations in the terms of the contract based on differences relevant to the authorized purposes of the contract in conditions to which they are to be applied, such as differences in seniority, the type of work performed, the competence and skill with which it is performed, are within the scope of the bargaining representation of a craft, all of whose members are not identical in their interest or merit. * * * Without attempting to mark the allowable limits of differences in the terms of contracts based on differences of conditions to which they apply, it is enough for present purposes to say that the statutory power to represent a craft and to make contracts as to wages, hours and working conditions does not include the authority to make among members of the craft discriminations not based on such relevant differences. Here the discriminations based on race alone are obviously irrelevant and invidious. Congress plainly did not undertake to authorize the bargaining representative to make such discriminations. * * *

The representative which thus discriminates may be enjoined from so doing, and its members may be enjoined from taking the benefit of such discriminatory action. No more is the Railroad bound by or entitled to take the benefit of a contract which the bargaining representative is prohibited by the statute from making. * * *

So long as a labor union assumes to act as the statutory representative of a craft, it cannot rightly refuse to perform the duty, which is inseparable from the power of representation conferred upon it, to represent the entire membership of the craft. While the statute does not deny to such a bargaining labor organization the right to determine eligibility to its membership, it does require the union, in collective bargaining and in making contracts with the carrier, to represent non-union or minority union members of the craft without hostile discrimination, fairly, impartially, and in good faith. Wherever necessary to that end, the union is required to consider requests of non-union members of the craft and expressions of their views with respect to collective bargaining with the employer and to give to them notice of and opportunity for hearing upon its proposed action.

* * *

In the absence of any available administrative remedy, the right here asserted, to a remedy for breach of the statutory duty of the bargaining representative to represent and act for the members of a craft, is of judicial cognizance. * * * [T]he statutory provisions which are in issue are stated in the form of commands. For the present command there is no mode of enforcement other than resort to the courts, whose jurisdiction and duty to afford a remedy for a breach of statutory duty are left unaffected. The right is analogous to the statutory right of employees to require the employer to bargain with the statutory representative of a craft, a right which this Court has enforced and protected by its injunction in Texas & N.O.R. Co. v. Brotherhood of Railway & S.S. Clerks, supra, 281 U.S. 556, 557, 560, 50 S.Ct. 429, 430, 74 L.Ed. 1034, and in Virginian R. Co. v. System Federation, supra, 300 U.S. 548, 57 S.Ct. 599, 81 L.Ed. 789, and like it is one for which there is no available administrative remedy.

We conclude that the duty which the statute imposes on a union representative of a craft to represent the interests of all its members stands on no different footing and that the statute contemplates resort to the usual judicial remedies of injunction and award of damages when appropriate for breach of that duty.

The judgment is accordingly reversed and remanded for further proceedings not inconsistent with this opinion.

Reversed.

MR. JUSTICE BLACK concurs in the result.

MR. JUSTICE MURPHY, concurring. * * *

The constitutional problem * * * is clear. Congress, through the Railway Labor Act, has conferred upon the union selected by a majority of a craft or class of railway workers the power to represent the entire craft or class in all collective bargaining matters. While such a union is essentially a private organization, its power to represent and bind all members of a class or craft is derived solely from Congress. The Act contains no language which directs the manner in which the bargaining representative shall perform its duties. But it cannot be assumed that Congress meant to authorize the representative to act so as to ignore rights guaranteed by the Constitution. Otherwise the Act would bear the stigma of unconstitutionality under the Fifth Amendment in this respect. * * *

The Constitution voices its disapproval whenever economic discrimination is applied under authority of law against any race, creed or color. A sound democracy cannot allow such discrimination to go unchallenged. Racism is far too virulent today to permit the slightest refusal, in the light of a Constitution that abhors it, to expose and condemn it wherever it appears in the course of a statutory interpretation.

Note

1. The "duty of fair representation," first declared in the Steele case with reference to the Railway Labor Act, was subsequently held to exist also under the National Labor Relations Act. Syres v. Oil Workers Union, 223 F.2d 739 (5th Cir.1955), rev'd and remanded per curiam, 350 U.S. 892, 76 S.Ct. 152, 100 L.Ed. 785 (1956); cf. Wallace Corp. v. NLRB, 323 U.S. 248, 65 S.Ct. 238, 89 L.Ed. 216 (1944).

2. What constitutional question was involved in the Steele case? If the legislative history had precluded the interpretation given the Railway Labor Act by the Court, how should this constitutional question have been answered?

3. If there had been no evidence of discrimination against the plaintiffs in Steele other than the denial of membership in the Brotherhood of Firemen and Enginemen, would any of their rights have been violated?

In Oliphant v. Brotherhood of Locomotive Firemen and Enginemen, 262 F.2d 359 (6th Cir.1958), cert. denied 359 U.S. 935, 79 S.Ct. 648, 3 L.Ed.2d 636 (1959), the foregoing question was answered in the negative on the ground that there was no "state action" present: "The Brotherhood is a private association whose membership policies are its own affair, and this is not an appropriate case for interposition of judicial control." 262 F.2d at 363. Contra Betts v. Easley, 161 Kan. 459, 169 P.2d 831 (1946). That Congress was of the same mind as the Oliphant court at about the same time is evidenced by its response to an amendment proposed by Representative Adam Clayton Powell when the bill which became the Landrum-Griffin Act was before the House. The amendment was that "no labor organization shall * * * refuse membership, segregate, or expel any person on the grounds of race, religion, color, sex, or national origin." It was rejected by a vote of 215 to 160. 2 Legislative History of the Labor-Management Reporting and Disclosure Act of 1959, at 1648, 1651 (1959) (published by the NLRB). The "Bill of Rights" ultimately incorporated as Title I in the Landrum-Griffin Act was, it may now be more meaningfully noted, a "Bill of Rights of *Members* of Labor Organizations." (Emphasis added.)

The narrow view of what constitutes government action reflected in Oliphant has been challenged by some constitutional scholars. A theory for "constitutionalizing" corporations, labor unions, and other private centers of power—i.e., subjecting them to the same constitutional restraints as apply to federal and state governments—has been articulated. It entails two elements: first, that in today's world some "private" organizations wield a degree of power over the lives of individuals, and therefore affect them in their liberty and property interests, to an extent comparable to government itself; second, that some of these "private governments"—e.g., General Motors, the United Steelworkers—obtain and exercise their power by reason of the grace of the state (the granting of the right to incorporate, the granting of the right to secure the status of exclusive bargaining representative). Therefore, the argument runs, the actions of these organizations should be treated as "state action" for such purposes as the application of due process provisions in federal and state constitutions. For elaboration of this theory, see Berle, The 20th Century Capitalist Revolution (1954); Miller, The Constitutional Law of the "Security State," 10 Stan.L.Rev. 620, 661 (1958). A dissenting view is expressed in

Wellington, The Constitution, The Labor Union, and "Governmental Action," 70 Yale L.J. 345 (1961).

The constitutional questions raised in this note were mooted by the enactment of the federal statute next discussed.

TITLE VII, CIVIL RIGHTS ACT, 1964
as amended by
Equal Employment Opportunity Act, 1972.

In 1964 Congress did what it had refused to do in 1959. It outlawed racial and certain other forms of discrimination in the admission to and expulsion from union membership. At the same time, Congress outlawed these forms of discrimination *by employers* in the hiring, treatment, and retention of employees. The central provisions of Title VII of the Civil Rights Act of 1964, as amended by the Equal Employment Opportunity Act of 1972, are the following:

"Sec. 703. (a) It shall be an unlawful employment practice for an employer—

"(1) to fail or refuse to hire or to discharge any individual, or otherwise to discriminate against any individual with respect to his compensation, terms, conditions, or privileges of employment, because of such individual's race, color, religion, sex, or national origin; or

"(2) to limit, segregate, or classify his employees or applicants for employment in any way which would deprive or tend to deprive any individual of employment opportunities or otherwise adversely affect his status as an employee, because of such individual's race, color, religion, sex, or national origin.

"(b) It shall be an unlawful employment practice for an employment agency to fail or refuse to refer for employment, or otherwise to discriminate against, any individual because of his race, color, religion, sex, or national origin, or to classify or refer for employment any individual on the basis of his race, color, religion, sex, or national origin.

"(c) It shall be an unlawful employment practice for a labor organization—

"(1) to exclude or to expel from its membership, or otherwise to discriminate against, any individual because of his race, color, religion, sex, or national origin;

"(2) to limit, segregate, or classify its membership or applicants for membership, or to classify or fail or refuse to refer for employment any individual, in any way which would deprive or tend to deprive any individual of employment opportunities, or would limit such employment opportunities or otherwise adversely affect his status as an employee or as an applicant for employment, because of such individual's race, color, religion, sex, or national origin; or

"(3) to cause or attempt to cause an employer to discriminate against an individual in violation of this section."

The administration of Title VII is in the charge of the Equal Employment Opportunities Commission (EEOC), which investigates complaints and attempts to secure voluntary compliance through conciliation. Under the 1964 Act, if the Commission was unable to achieve voluntary compliance, the "person aggrieved" was empowered to bring a civil action in the appropriate federal district court against the alleged offender. Under the 1972 amendments, the Commission may itself bring such an action in behalf of the "person aggrieved"; the latter, however, retains the right to sue where the Commission decides not to sue or delays unduly in making up its mind. The remedies available include injunctive relief and the recovery of lost wages.

More detailed consideration will be given to Title VII and the problems arising thereunder in Chapter 9, infra. For present purposes, it suffices to observe that Title VII represents a major step in the development of the national labor policy. Though anticipated in principle by a number of state "fair employment practice" codes, it constitutes the first legislative effort of the Federal Government to eliminate discriminatory practices of unions and employers based on race, color, religion, sex, or national origin. (Caveat: The Civil Rights Act of 1866, now 42 U.S.C.A. § 1981, was held in 1975 to prohibit racial discrimination in private employment. Johnson v. Railway Express Agency, 421 U.S. 454, 95 S.Ct. 1716, 44 L.Ed.2d 295 (1975). Though enacted almost a century before the Civil Rights Act of 1964, nobody knew what it really meant, insofar as here pertinent, until the 1970's.) The 1972 amendments made Title VII applicable to public, in addition to private, employees. As indicated supra, more of this too infra.

D. GOVERNMENT AS EMPLOYER: THE UMPIRE UNIONIZED

No attempted overview of the law of labor relations in the United States would be complete without mention of the most dramatic development of the last two decades—the mushrooming growth of collective bargaining in public employment. A major impetus for this "revolution" was President Kennedy's Executive Order 10988 [a] of January 17, 1962, entitled Employee-Management Cooperation in the Federal Service. That order provided a limited form of collective bargaining for federal employees. Of greater importance, the promulgation of Order 10988 triggered a tidal wave of organizational activity among employees of state and local government. In response, state after state enacted legislation providing, in one form or another, for greater employee participation in the determination of terms and conditions of public employment.

As of 1984, over forty states had passed public employment relations statutes, granting to some or all state and local public employees the right to organize and to engage in collective bargaining (sometimes called "collective negotiations"). The statutes typically declare strikes in public employment to be illegal, establish sanctions against such strikes, and create mediation and fact-finding procedures for the purpose of resolving impasses in collective bargaining without resort to strikes.

The importance of the aforesaid developments can be fully appreciated only with recognition of the explosive growth of public employment at all levels. The number of government employees rose from 5.4 million in 1947 to 15.8 million in 1982. The former figure represented 8.9% of a civilian

---

a. Since superseded by President Nixon's Executive Order 11491, effective January 1, 1970, the major provisions of which have now been recast into law by the Civil Service Reform Act of 1978 (discussed infra. p. 1146).

labor force of 60.2 million, the latter figure 17.7% of a civilian labor force of 89.5 million.

The case which follows presents a typical judicial handling of the most critical problem arising under the state collective bargaining statutes.

CITY OF NEW YORK v. DE LURY

Court of Appeals of New York, 1968.
23 N.Y.2d 175, 295 N.Y.S.2d 901, 243 N.E.2d 128.

FULD, CHIEF JUDGE. We recently decided, in Rankin v. Shanker, 23 N.Y.2d 111, 295 N.Y.S.2d 625, 242 N.E.2d 802, that public employees and labor organizations representing them were not entitled to a trial by jury in a criminal contempt proceeding for the violation of section 210 (subd. 1) of the Taylor Law.[1] In so holding, we concluded that a legislative classification "which differentiates between strikes by public employees and employees in private industry" is reasonable and does not offend against the constitutional guarantee of equal protection of the laws (23 N.Y.2d at p. 118, 295 N.Y.S.2d at p. 631, 242 N.E.2d at p. 806). The case now before us calls upon the court to determine, primarily, whether the Taylor Law's mandate that public employees shall not strike and that labor organizations representing them shall not cause or encourage a strike violates due process requirements of the State or Federal Constitution.

At about seven o'clock in the morning of February 2, 1968, virtually all of the sanitation men in the City of New York—employees of the Department of Sanitation—failed, without excuse, to report for work.[2] Later in the day, at a demonstration in front of City Hall, members of the Uniformed Sanitationmen's Association (referred to herein as the "Union") were addressed by their president, the defendant De Lury, in these words:

1. The Taylor Law was enacted in 1967 (L. 1967, ch. 392; Civil Service Law, Consol.Laws, c. 7, art. 14, §§ 200–212) to supersede the Condon-Wadlin Act (L.1947, ch. 391, adding Civil Service Law, former § 22–a, renum. by L.1958, ch. 790, as Civil Service Law, former § 108). Like its predecessor, the Taylor Law prohibits strikes by public employees (§ 210, subd. 1) but, unlike Condon-Wadlin, it does not mandate termination of employment for its violation. The Taylor Law grants to all public employees (which, broadly speaking, includes all employees in the service of the State or any subdivision thereof) rights which in the main they did not formerly possess, namely, the right to be represented by employee organizations of their own choosing and the right to negotiate collectively with public employers and, in addition, the right to require public employers to negotiate and to enter into collective agreements with them. It sets up a Public Employment Relations Board—known as PERB—to "resolve * * * disputes concerning the representation status of employee organizations" and to assist in the "voluntary resolution" of disputes between public employers and employee organizations. It also au-

thorizes, under the so-called "home rule" section (Civil Service Law § 212), the adoption by local governments of "provisions and procedures" which are "substantially equivalent" to those of the Taylor Law. The New York City equivalent of such law is Local Law No. 53 of 1967 but the parties did not utilize the machinery therein provided for resolving disputes between the city and municipal employee organizations. All public employees, whether or not covered by the "home rule" section (§ 212), are subject to the statutory mandate of section 210 (subd. 1) of the Civil Service Law prohibiting them from striking.

2. The City and the Uniformed Sanitationmen's Association had labored long in an attempt to arrive at a new collective agreement to replace one which expired on June 30, 1967. Bargaining between the parties, which commenced in December of 1966, had dragged along for the entire year of 1967 and through January, 1968. On January 31, 1968, a mutually agreed upon mediation panel formulated a settlement agreement which, though accepted by the City, was rejected by the Union stewards.

"Your sentiments before was go-go-go. I'd accept a motion for go-go-go (cheers). All in favor signify by saying yes (cheers). All opposed (boos). I didn't come here to bargain, I took a firm position with the City, I gave the members a final offer of this union. Now I want to show discipline here this morning—or this afternoon—I don't want to show where there is confusion in the members—You got a job at the locations to see that this is effective 100% (cheers)."

A nine-day strike, ending on the night of February 10, resulted. During that period, few, if any, of the sanitation men reported for work, in consequence of which garbage and refuse accumulated on the city streets at the rate of 10,000 tons a day. This constituted a serious health and fire threat; indeed, the Commissioner of Health characterized the "garbage situation" as a "serious one to the health of the city" and the Fire Commissioner declared that the Fire Department "experienced a marked increase in the number of outside rubbish fires." [3]

On February 2, the very day the work stoppage began, the City instituted the present action to enjoin the defendants from "striking" and moved for a preliminary injunction. A temporary restraining order was granted which enjoined the carrying on of the strike and required the leaders of the Union to instruct the members to return to work. Three days later, on February 5, the court at Special Term granted a preliminary injunction which again contained a directive to De Lury that he shall "forthwith instruct all members [of the Union] not to engage or participate in any strike, concerted stoppage of work or concerted slowdown against the plaintiff." Although, because of the health and fire hazards involved, immediate compliance with the orders was vital, the members of the Union, as previously noted, remained away from their jobs until February 10.

An application, brought on by order to show cause, to punish the Union and De Lury for criminal contempt for willfully disobeying the restraining order, came on for hearing before the court; the testimony adduced concerning the strike and its effects, as well as the conduct of De Lury, was substantially as outlined above. When the City, through its Corporation Counsel, stated that it was prepared to call witnesses to establish that the sanitation men "had [not] received instructions from Mr. De Lury to report back to work", defense counsel conceded that, if witnesses were called to the stand—as the Corporation Counsel proposed—"they would testify that they did not receive any instructions from Mr. De Lury to go back, because Mr. De Lury did not send them out, and Mr. De Lury did nothing to bring them back. These are the facts which are known to everybody."

At the conclusion of the hearings, the court, dismissing charges which had also been asserted against other officers, found De Lury and the Union guilty of criminal contempt for willfully disobeying its lawful mandate. It sentenced De Lury to 15 days in jail and fined him $250 and it fined the Union $80,000; in addition, the court ordered that the Union's right to dues check-off be forfeited for a period of 18 months.[5] The Appellate Division

---

3. On the sixth day of the strike, a volunteer group of some 500 men collected hospital refuse, the accumulation of which created an especially dangerous threat of disease.

5. The fines imposed, as well as the period for which the Union's dues check-off rights were forfeited, were the maximum authorized by the applicable statute (Judiciary Law, Con-

affirmed Special Term's orders and granted the defendants leave to appeal to our court on a certified question.

We consider, first, the defendants' contention that the Taylor Law is unconstitutional on the ground that, in prohibiting strikes by public employees, it deprives them of due process of law. Manifestly, neither the Fourteenth Amendment to the Federal Constitution nor the Bill of Rights of the State Constitution (art. I) grants to any individual an absolute right to strike. On the contrary, that right is subject to the qualification that, if a strike is for an illegal objective, it is enjoinable at the instance of an aggrieved party. To cull from the opinion of the Supreme Court in International Union, United Auto Workers, A.F. of L., Local 232 v. Wisconsin Employment Relations Bd. (336 U.S. 245, 259–260, 69 S.Ct. 516, 524, 93 L.Ed. 651), " 'the exercise of the unquestioned right to [strike]' * * * did not operate to legalize the sit-down strike, which state law made illegal and state authorities punished. [Case cited.] Nor, for example, did it make legal a strike that ran afoul of federal law [case cited]; nor one in violation of a contract made pursuant thereto [case cited]; nor one creating a national emergency [case cited]."

Although acknowledging that the right to strike is not absolute, the defendants would have us read the opinion in the *Auto Workers* case to mean that a prohibition against strikes will be upheld only where workers strike in violation of a no-strike clause or where there is a secondary boycott, violence or a trespass such as a sit-down. There is no basis for so narrowly viewing that decision. The Supreme Court did not limit the doctrine there applied to instances of illegal strikes mentioned by it. Rather, it laid down a general rule, applicable in all cases involving illegal strikes, namely, that the State, in governing its internal affairs, had the power to prohibit *any* strike if the prohibition was reasonably calculated to achieve a valid State policy in an area which was open to State regulation. (Cf. International Brotherhood of Teamsters Local 695 v. Vogt, Inc., 354 U.S. 284, 294–295, 77 S.Ct. 1166, 1 L.Ed.2d 1347.)

Our query must, therefore, be whether the condemnation of strikes by public employees, as provided in the Taylor Law, does effectuate a valid policy of our State.

For many years, strikes against the Government have been outlawed by special legislation and by common law. Today, no less than 20 States have statutes condemning strikes by some or all of its public employees and at least seven States have achieved the same result by the application of common-law principles. (See Rubin, A Summary of State Collective Bargaining Law in Public Employment, published by Cornell University in 1968.) In addition, a Federal statute specifically provides that strikes by Federal employees are illegal (U.S.Code, tit. 5, § 7311). Substantial reasons are at hand for this almost universal condemnation of strikes by public employees. As Professor George W. Taylor, an outstanding authority in the field of labor relations and one of the architects of the Taylor Law, put it

sol.Laws, c. 30, § 751, subds. 1, 2, par. [a]). [The ceilings on fines and dues check-off suspension were repealed in 1969, and both of these matters were consigned to the discretion of the courts. Laws of 1969, c. 24, § 12.]

(Public Employment: Strikes or Procedures?, 20 Industrial and Labor Relations Rev. 617, 619),

> "One of the vital interests of the public which should be considered in the government-employee relationship is the ability of representative government to perform the functions of levying taxes and, through the budgeting of governmental resources, of establishing priorities among the government services desired by the body politic."

Quite obviously, the ability of the Legislature to establish priorities among government services would be destroyed if public employees could, with impunity, engage in strikes which deprive the public of essential services. The striking employees, by paralyzing a city through the exercise of naked power, could obtain gains wholly disproportionate to the services rendered by them and at the expense of the public and other public employees. The consequence would be the destruction of democratic legislative processes because budgeting and the establishment of priorities would no longer result from the free choice of the electorate's representatives but from the coercive effect of paralyzing strikes of public employees. (See Final Report [March 31, 1966] of the Governor's Commission on Public Employment Relations [hereafter referred to as the Taylor Report], pp. 15–16).

It was undoubtedly because of such considerations that Governor Thomas E. Dewey, in his Memorandum approving the Condon-Wadlin Act (L.1947, ch. 391)—the predecessor of the Taylor Law—declared (N.Y.Legis. Ann., 1947, pp. 36–37):

> "The duty of public employees is to the whole of society. A strike of firemen could overnight permit the destruction of a whole city. A strike of police could endanger the safety of millions of people and all their possessions. A strike of sanitation workers could almost overnight produce an epidemic threatening the lives of other millions of people."

And President Franklin D. Roosevelt expressed himself in similar fashion in 1937, some 10 years earlier (Public Papers and Addresses for Year 1937 [1941] Letter of Aug. 16, 1937, p. 325):

> "Upon employees in the Federal service rests the obligation to serve the whole people, whose interests and welfare require orderliness and continuity in the conduct of Government activities. This obligation is paramount. Since their own services have to do with the functioning of the Government, a strike of public employees manifests nothing less than an intent on their part to prevent or obstruct the operations of Government until their demands are satisfied. Such action, looking toward the paralysis of Government by those who have sworn to support it, is unthinkable and intolerable."

The courts which have dealt with the constitutional question under discussion have concluded that no provision of either the Federal or State Constitution prevents the State from outlawing strikes by public employees.

* * *

In the case before us, the Legislature, after declaring (Civil Service Law § 200) that "it is the public policy of the state * * * to promote harmonious and cooperative relationships between government and its employees and to protect the public by assuring, at all times, the orderly and uninterrupted operations and functions of government", recited that such policy is best effectuated by "continuing the prohibition against strikes by public employees and providing remedies for violations of such prohibition." Furthermore, the Taylor Report, which preceded the enactment of the Taylor Law, found, after an exhaustive study of the matter, that the right of public employees to strike "is not compatible with the orderly functioning of our democratic form of representative government" (p. 19).

In view of the strong policy considerations which led to the enactment of the Taylor Law, it is our conclusion that the statutory prohibition against strikes by public employees is reasonably designed to effectuate a valid State policy in an area where it has authority to act and that the provisions of subdivision 1 of section 210 do not offend any due process rights of the defendants.

In view of our recent decision in the *Shanker* case (23 N.Y.2d 111, 295 N.Y.S.2d 625, 242 N.E.2d 802, supra), no extended discussion is required in addressing ourselves to the defendants' point that the prohibition against strikes by public employees (or their representative organizations) violates the equal protection clause of either the United States or the New York State Constitution. * * * As we had occasion to observe in Shanker (23 N.Y.2d, at p. 116, 295 N.Y.S.2d 629, 242 N.E.2d 805),

> "Ever since the enactment of the Norris-LaGuardia Act and our State's Little Norris-LaGuardia Act, the view has been uniformly and consistently held that a legitimate distinction between public and private employment is constitutionally permissible. This has been recognized * * * with regard not only to the prohibition against strikes but also to the issue, now confronting us, affecting jury trials."

There are a number of factual differences between employment in the public and private sectors which furnish reasonable justification for disparate treatment "vis-à-vis" the right to strike. Thus, for instance, the necessity for preventing goods or services being priced out of the market may have a deterrent effect upon collective bargaining negotiations in the private sector, whereas, in the public sector, the market place has no such restraining effect upon the negotiations and the sole constraint in terms of the negotiations is to be found in the budget allocation made by responsible legislators. Again, the orderly functioning of our democratic form of representative government and the preservation of the right of our representatives to make budgetary allocations—free from the compulsions of crippling strikes—require the regulation of strikes by public employees whereas there is no similar countervailing reason for a prohibition of strikes in the private sector. (See Taylor Report, pp. 15–16.) * * *

In view of the basic differences between public and private employment, it may not be said that a classification which prohibits strikes by public employees while failing to legislate against strikes by employees in the private sector is unreasonable, especially when it is considered that strikes by public employees, unlike private employees, have always been subject to injunctions by the courts. Consequently, we conclude here, just as we did in Rankin (p. 119, 295 N.Y.S.2d 632, 242 N.E.2d p. 629) that, "as of the present [time], legislative differentiation between public and private employees, insofar as restrictions on their right to strike and to jury trials are concerned, is reasonable." * * *

Nor is there any substance to the further contention that the city failed to prove * * * that De Lury disobeyed any mandate of the court. The strike was open and notorious. Its devastating impact on the City of New York and its inhabitants, including the danger of fire and the hazard to health, was known to the defendant, as it was to all New Yorkers. The court's order that the strike be terminated and that De Lury, as president of the Union, instruct his men "not to engage or participate in" the strike was clear beyond cavil. The defendant not only failed to obey that injunction but, going to the other extreme, actually urged the men to make the strike "effective 100%". What the proof convincingly demonstrated, the concession of the defendant's counsel rendered indisputable. We cannot accept the highly technical or hairsplitting arguments urged upon us in an attempt to evade compliance with the court's lawful mandates. Indeed, when confronted with a somewhat similar situation in United States v. Mine Workers (330 U.S. 258, 307, concurring opn., 67 S.Ct. 677, 91 L.Ed. 884)—a case in which an adjudication of criminal contempt was based on disobedience of an order enjoining a strike—MR. JUSTICE FRANKFURTER, after observing that we are " 'a government of laws and not of men' " (p. 307, 67 S.Ct. 677, p. 703), went on to say in language most appropriate here (p. 312, 67 S.Ct. 677, p. 705):

> "In our country law is not a body of technicalities in the keeping of specialists or in the service of any special interest. There can be no free society without law administered through an independent judiciary. If one man can be allowed to determine for himself what is law, every man can. That means first chaos, then tyranny. Legal process is an essential part of the democratic process. For legal process is subject to democratic control by defined, orderly ways which themselves are part of law. In a democracy, power implies responsibility. The greater the power that defies law the less tolerant can this Court be of defiance. As the Nation's ultimate judicial tribunal, this Court, beyond any other organ of society, is the trustee of law and charged with the duty of securing obedience to it."

We have considered each of the other arguments advanced by the defendants and find them so tenuous as to require no comment.

In conclusion, then—subdivision 1 of section 210 of the Civil Service Law, designed to prevent the paralysis of Government, offends against no constitutional guarantee or requirement. Self-interest of individual or organization may not be permitted to endanger the safety, health or public welfare of the State or any of its subdivisions. There was here indisputable proof not only of deliberate disobedience of the explicit provisions of the Taylor Law but willful defiance of the court's lawful mandates as well. Such defiance, the more egregious when committed by employees in the public sector, is not to be tolerated. The order appealed from should be affirmed, with costs, and the question certified answered in the affirmative.

All concur.

Note

1. Although the De Lury case emphasizes the Taylor Law's prohibition of strikes by public employees, other provisions of that statute accord to those employees rights incidental to collective bargaining other than the right to

strike. (See footnote 1, supra p. 196.) The degree and pace of change involved in this grant of rights may be seen by contrasting the present situation in the State of New York with that of not many years earlier, as revealed in the following passages from Railway Mail Ass'n v. Murphy, 180 Misc. 868, 875–876, 44 N.Y.S.2d 601, 607–608 (Sup.Ct.1943), reversed on other grounds, 267 A.D. 470 (1944), 293 N.Y. 315 (1944), 326 U.S. 88 (1945):

"To tolerate or recognize any combination of civil service employees of the government as a labor organization or union is not only incompatible with the spirit of democracy, but inconsistent with every principle upon which our government is founded. Nothing is more dangerous to public welfare than to admit that hired servants of the State can dictate to the government the hours, the wages and conditions under which they will carry on essential services vital to the welfare, safety and security of the citizen. To admit as true that government employees have power to halt or check the functions of government, unless their demands are satisfied, is to transfer to them all legislative, executive and judicial power. Nothing would be more ridiculous.

"The reasons are obvious which forbid acceptance of any such doctrine. Government is formed for the benefit of all persons, and the duty of all to support it is equally clear. Nothing is more certain than the indispensable necessity of government, and it is equally true that unless the people surrender some of their natural rights to the government it cannot operate. Much as we all recognize the value and the necessity of collective bargaining in industrial and social life, nonetheless, such bargaining is impossible between the government and its employees, by reason of the very nature of government itself. The formidable and familiar weapon in industrial strife and warfare—the strike—is without justification when used against the government. When so used, it is rebellion against constituted authority.

* * *

"Collective bargaining has no place in government service. The employer is the whole people. It is impossible for administrative officials to bind the Government of the United States or the State of New York by an agreement made between them and representatives of any union. Government officials and employees are governed and guided by laws which must be obeyed and which cannot be abrogated or set aside by an agreement of employees and officials."

2. In considering the wisdom of importing into the public sector the private sector's system for bilateral determination of terms and conditions of employment, relevant differences between the two sectors must be confronted. What importance would you assign to each of the following five asserted differences? (1) Public employees are public *servants* in the sense that they are employed by and serve the sovereign (the government, the people), and, in doing so, they implement the will of the people as expressed through their elected representatives; since the legislative representatives of the people must establish public programs and priorities, including those pertaining to public employment, "lobbying" is the only constitutionally permissible mode for public employees to influence their terms and conditions of employment. (2) In public employment it is often difficult to ascertain who the employer is; in a case like De Lury, for example, would the employer (the one to be bargained with) be the Sanitation Department, the Mayor, the City Council, the Governor or State Legislature because of the increasing amounts of state aid to municipalities, Congress

because of federal aid, the taxpayers of the city, of the state, of the nation? (3) Government services are typically monopolistic and essential in character; as a consequence, no ceiling is supplied by market forces on employee demands. (4) Government enterprise is nonprofit-seeking; public employers are therefore less inclined to exploit their employees. (5) A complex of paternalistic legislation (such as civil service tenure provisions) protects "public servants" in ways not provided for private employees.

3. The subject of collective bargaining in public employment will be examined in fuller detail in Chapter 9, infra. In the interests of early perspective, it should perhaps be noted that the question of the constitutionality of strike prohibitions in public employment was apparently put to rest in a three judge district court case, United Federation of Postal Clerks v. Blount, 325 F.Supp. 879 (D.D.C.1971), affirmed without opinion, 404 U.S. 802, 92 S.Ct. 80, 30 L.Ed.2d 38 (1971), reported infra p. 1069. Despite this and similar state decisions, a substantial degree of pressure against antistrike laws has been mounted by public employee organizations. A high point of success for this pressure is the position early adopted by the Supreme Court of Michigan in School District for City of Holland v. Holland Education Association, 380 Mich. 314, 157 N.W.2d 206 (1968), to the effect that the strike in public employment, even under a statute prohibiting strikes, is not *per se* enjoinable. The court stated: "We here hold it is insufficient merely to show that a concert of prohibited action by public employees has taken place and that *ipso facto* such a showing justifies injunctive relief. We so hold because it is basically contrary to public policy in this State to issue injunctions in labor disputes absent a showing of violence, irreparable injury, or breach of the peace." 380 Mich. at 326, 157 N.W.2d at 210. A more recent case, taking an even more liberal view of the strike in public employment is County Sanitation District No. 2 of Los Angeles v. Los Angeles County Employees' Association, Local 660, 38 Cal.3d 564, 214 Cal.Rptr. 424, 699 P.2d 835 (1985), reported infra p. 1075. Indeed, some 10 states have approved a qualified right to strike in public employment. See infra, p. 1077 fn. 8.

*

Part II

A LONG ANALYSIS OF PROBLEMS GLOSSED OVER IN THE SHORT HISTORY

POSTSCRIPT TO PART I

The reader, though perhaps not aware of it, has already completed a short course in labor law. The major conflicts have been identified, the evolution of the law in dealing with them outlined, the language learned. There is much to be said for approaching a subject as important and complex as the law of labor relations in historic manner. The student has an opportunity to grow with the subject; there is a "story line" which runs through the developments and holds them together, foreshadowing future developments. This approach to an understanding of society is known as "institutionalism." Practitioners of this method of ascertaining the past and discerning the future first seek to identify the "institutions" of a society (e.g., the system of labor relations) and then examine those institutions in their constantly changing internal and external relationships.

Just as the reader has already had a short course in labor law in Part I, a longer one will be developed in Part II. This time the approach will be more functional and analytical than historical and institutional. Legal problems of consequence in labor relations will be examined, area by area, the emphasis being on the current status of the law. The reader will discover that most of what follows has been previously encountered in one form or another in Part I; reencountered, in different contexts and from different angles of approach, legal problems acquire perspective.

Chapter 4

ESTABLISHING COLLECTIVE BARGAINING: THE COLLECTIVIZING OF THE EMPLOYMENT RELATION

PRELIMINARY NOTE: NLRB PROCEDURE IN "R" AND "C" CASES

Section 7 is the heart of the National Labor Relations Act in its protection of employee rights of self-organization and collective bargaining. The National Labor Relations Board administers this protection through the procedures of Sections 9 and 10 of the Act. The Board employs, in this process, a staff of approximately 2,600 persons, some at headquarters in Washington, D.C., and the rest at 33 Regional Offices. Each Regional Office is headed by a Regional Director who has the assistance of a Regional Attorney and a staff of "field attorneys" and "field examiners."

The Board's main task is to process two categories of cases: representation ("R") cases and unfair labor practice (complaint—"C") cases. In the discharge of these responsibilities, the Board is authorized under Section 3(b) of the Act "to delegate to any group of three or more [Board] members any or all of the power which it may itself exercise."

"R" cases arise under Section 9 and involve questions of representation affecting commerce. "C" cases arise under Section 10 and are concerned with the prevention of employer and union unfair labor practices affecting commerce.

Before summarizing the procedures employed in the disposition of these two categories of cases, a fundamental difference between them should be highlighted. "C" cases are typical adversary proceedings, quasi-judicial in nature, and not much different from ordinary civil litigation, except that the "plaintiff" (the charging party) is represented by a public prosecutor (the General Counsel or one of his representatives). "R" cases, by way of contrast, although sometimes involving contested issues such as appropriateness of unit, are treated by the Board as investigatory rather than adversary in nature.

206

"R" Case Procedure

A representation case is triggered by the filing of a petition in one of the Board's Regional Offices. The petition may be filed by an employee, a group of employees, a labor organization, or an employer. (Section 9(c).) The purpose of the petition is typically to ascertain whether an unrecognized labor organization should be certified as the majority representative of the employees involved, or whether a certified or otherwise recognized labor organization should be decertified. Petitions for certification or decertification, other than those filed by employers, must be supported by a "substantial number" (interpreted by the Board to be 30%) of the employees involved. (Section 9(c)(1)(A).)

A petition, once filed, is assigned to a field examiner for investigation. The examiner endeavors to bring about a voluntary resolution of the case by persuading the parties to agree on such questions as the appropriate unit and to "consent" to an election. A large proportion of cases are disposed of in this informal manner.

In the absence of such consent, a hearing is scheduled before a hearing officer who is either a field attorney or a field examiner from the Regional Office. At the hearing, testimony is taken on the questions at issue—most commonly related to unit determination. Decision on these contested matters is then made by the Regional Director, acting on behalf of the Board (pursuant to a delegation of power authorized by Congress in a 1959 Landrum-Griffin amendment to Section 3(b); the purpose of the amendment was to expedite the disposition of representation cases).

The Regional Director may either dismiss the petition or order an election in the unit he finds appropriate. His decision is subject to review by the Board, but only upon certain narrowly defined grounds. Section 102.67(c) of the Board's Rules and Regulations provides:

"The Board will grant a request for review only where compelling reasons exist therefor. Accordingly, a request for review may be granted only upon one or more of the following grounds:

"(1) That a substantial question of law or policy is raised because of (a) the absence of, or (b) a departure from, officially reported Board precedent.

"(2) That the regional director's decision on a substantial factual issue is clearly erroneous on the record and such error prejudicially affects the rights of a party.

"(3) That the conduct of the hearing or any ruling made in connection with the proceeding has resulted in prejudicial error.

"(4) That there are compelling reasons for reconsideration of an important Board rule or policy."

The Board has been sparing in the exercise of its review powers under these provisions.

If an election is directed, it is conducted by secret ballot, usually on the premises of the employer, under the supervision of one or more regional representatives of the Board. The parties involved are permitted to have observers at the polling places to check on the eligibility of voters and other matters affecting the fairness of the election. Following the election, the results are "certified."

The Board has adopted a procedure for the filing of objections to an election. Such objections generally involve alleged unfair labor practices on the part of employers or unions. If the objections are sustained, the election is set aside and a new election ordered. On the other hand, a valid election is a bar, under Section 9(c)(3), to any further election in the bargaining unit for a twelve-month period.

In view of the limited opportunities available for securing judicial review of Board decisions in representation cases, as seen in AFL v. NLRB, supra p. 132, and Leedom v. Kyne, infra p. 235, the authority of the Board and of its Regional Directors over representation matters is rather sweeping.

"C" Case Procedure

A "C" case is started in the same manner as an "R" case except that a "charge" is filed in the Regional Office instead of a petition. A charge (presented on a form provided by the Board) is an allegation that one or more unfair labor practices have been committed. Again, as in an "R" case, an investigation is conducted by the field examiner to whom the case is assigned. The examiner interviews the parties, gets written statements from witnesses,[a] and arranges an informal conference of the parties in an effort to settle the matter. Some ninety per cent of the unfair labor practice cases are disposed of informally—by withdrawal of the charge by the charging party, dismissal of the charge by the Regional Director, or voluntary adjustment of the charge by the parties. Dismissal of a charge (refusal to issue a complaint) is appealable to the General Counsel in Washington. Adverse action by the General Counsel is nonreviewable by the Board (Section 3(d)) and has also been held nonreviewable by the courts.[b]

If a charge is found to have merit and no settlement can be worked out informally, the Regional Director issues a complaint, the charged party (Respondent) files an answer, and a hearing is held before an Administrative

a. Employers have sought to obtain copies of these statements pursuant to the Freedom of Information Act, 5 U.S.C.A. § 552 (1977). The NLRB has refused to provide the information prior to the time the witness has testified, relying on Exemption 7(A) of that act which provides that disclosure is not required of "investigatory records compiled for law enforcement purposes, but only to the extent that the production of such records * * * would interfere with enforcement proceedings." 5 U.S.C.A. § 552(b)(7)(A) (1977). In NLRB v. Robbins Tire & Rubber Co., 437 U.S. 214, 98 S.Ct. 2311, 57 L.Ed.2d 159 (1978), the Court upheld the NLRB's position.

b. E.g., Lincourt v. NLRB, 170 F.2d 306 (1st Cir.1948); Hourihan v. NLRB, 201 F.2d 187 (D.C.Cir.1952), cert. denied 345 U.S. 930 (1953); United Electrical Contractors Ass'n v. Ordman, 366 F.2d 776 (2d Cir.1966), cert. denied 385 U.S. 1026 (1967). In the Hourihan case the court of appeals observed in a footnote: "We need not here canvass whether and if so under what circumstances, a court can correct an abuse of discretion by the General Counsel in failing to issue a complaint." 201 F.2d at 188 n. 4. By way of contrasting dictum, the Supreme Court has said that "the Board's General Counsel has unreviewable discretion to refuse to institute an unfair labor practice complaint." Vaca v. Sipes, 386 U.S. 171, 182, 87 S.Ct. 903, 912, 17 L.Ed.2d 842 (1967). (The Vaca case is reported infra p. 742.) See also NLRB v. Sears, Roebuck & Co., 421 U.S. 132, 138, 95 S.Ct. 1504, 1510, 44 L.Ed. 2d 28, 40 (1974). The rethinking of that dictum is strongly urged in McClintock, The Unreviewable Power of the General Counsel—Partial Enforcement of the Labor Act, 12 Gonz.L.Rev. 79 (1976); Rosenbloom, A New Look at the General Counsel's Unreviewable Discretion Not to Issue a Complaint Under the NLRA, 86 Yale L.J. 1349 (1977).

Law Judge (until 1972 called Trial Examiner). Administrative Law Judges, members of the Division of Judges of the Board, are independent of both the Board and the General Counsel. They are assigned to cases by the Chief Administrative Law Judge. Because they are subject to the rules of the Civil Service Commission governing appointment and tenure, they serve, in effect, for life and thus resemble federal district court judges. (Administrative Procedure Act, Section 11.)

The General Counsel is responsible for prosecuting the complaint and is customarily represented in this regard by an attorney from the Regional Office which issued the complaint. The charging party is also entitled to participate through counsel in the proceeding. The hearing resembles a trial in a court without a jury. It is conducted "so far as practicable * * * in accordance with the rules of evidence applicable in the district courts of the United States." (Section 10(b).)

After the close of the hearing and the filing of briefs, if any, the Administrative Law Judge submits his recommended decision to the Board, containing findings of fact, conclusions of law, underlying reasoning, and proposed order. The recommended decision becomes the decision of the Board unless exceptions to that decision are filed within 20 days. In the latter event the Board decides the case on the basis of the recommended decision, the exceptions and briefs of the parties, and the record made at the hearing. In rare instances, requests for oral argument are granted.

The Board obtains enforcement of its orders through petitioning an appropriate court of appeals. (Section 10(e).) If the court issues its order enforcing, in whole or in part, the order of the Board and there is still failure to comply, the court's order is enforced through contempt proceedings. Review of Board orders in an appropriate court of appeals is also available on the petition of any "person aggrieved by a final order of the Board." (Section 10(f).)

For an interesting and insightful description of the NLRB, pertinent to much of the foregoing, see Murphy, The National Labor Relations Board— An Appraisal, 52 Minn.L.Rev. 819 (1968).

A. THE PRINCIPLE OF EXCLUSIVITY

J.I. CASE CO. v. NATIONAL LABOR RELATIONS BOARD

Supreme Court of the United States, 1944.
321 U.S. 332, 64 S.Ct. 576, 88 L.Ed. 762.

MR. JUSTICE JACKSON delivered the opinion of the Court.

This cause was heard by the National Labor Relations Board on stipulated facts which so far as concern present issues are as follows:

The petitioner, J.I. Case Company, at its Rock Island, Illinois, plant, from 1937 offered each employee an individual contract of employment. The contracts were uniform and for a term of one year. The Company agreed to furnish employment as steadily as conditions permitted, to pay a specified rate, which the Company might redetermine if the job changed, and to maintain certain hospital facilities. The employee agreed to accept the provisions, to serve faithfully and honestly for the term, to comply with factory rules, and that defective work should not be paid for. About 75% of the employees accepted and worked under these agreements.

According to the Board's stipulation and finding, the execution of the contracts was not a condition of employment, nor was the status of individual employees affected by reason of signing or failing to sign the contracts. It is not found or contended that the agreements were coerced, obtained by any unfair labor practice, or that they were not valid under the circumstances in which they were made.

While the individual contracts executed August 1, 1941 were in effect, a C.I.O. union petitioned the Board for certification as the exclusive bargaining representative of the production and maintenance employees. On December 17, 1941 a hearing was held, at which the Company urged the individual contracts as a bar to representation proceedings. The Board, however, directed an election, which was won by the union. The union was thereupon certified as the exclusive bargaining representative of the employees in question in respect to wages, hours, and other conditions of employment.

The union then asked the Company to bargain. It refused, declaring that it could not deal with the union in any manner affecting rights and obligations under the individual contracts while they remained in effect. It offered to negotiate on matters which did not affect rights under the individual contracts, and said that upon the expiration of the contracts it would bargain as to all matters. Twice the Company sent circulars to its employees asserting the validity of the individual contracts and stating the position that it took before the Board in reference to them.

The Board held that the Company had refused to bargain collectively, in violation of § 8(5) of the National Labor Relations Act; and that the contracts had been utilized, by means of the circulars, to impede employees in the exercise of rights guaranteed by § 7 of the Act, with the result that the Company had engaged in unfair labor practices within the meaning of § 8(1) of the Act. It ordered the Company to cease and desist from giving effect to the contracts, from extending them or entering into new ones, from refusing to bargain and from interfering with the employees; and it required the Company to give notice accordingly and to bargain upon request.

The Circuit Court of Appeals, with modification not in issue here, granted an order of enforcement. The issues are unsettled ones important in the administration of the Act, and we granted certiorari. In doing so we asked counsel, in view of the expiration of the individual contracts and the negotiation of a collective contract, to discuss whether the case was moot. In view of the continuing character of the obligation imposed by the order we think it is not, and will examine the merits.

Contract in labor law is a term the implications of which must be determined from the connection in which it appears. Collective bargaining between employer and the representatives of a unit, usually a union, results in an accord as to terms which will govern hiring and work and pay in that unit. The result is not, however, a contract of employment except in rare cases; no one has a job by reason of it and no obligation to any individual ordinarily comes into existence from it alone. The negotiations between union and management result in what often has been called a trade agreement, rather than in a contract of employment. Without pushing the analogy too far, the agreement may be likened to the tariffs established by a carrier, to standard provisions prescribed by supervising authorities for insurance policies, or to utility schedules of rates and rules for service, which do not of themselves establish any relationships but which do govern the terms of the shipper or insurer or customer relationship whenever and with whomever it may be established. Indeed, in some European countries, contrary to American practice, the terms of a collectively negotiated trade agreement are submitted to a government department and if approved become a governmental regulation ruling employment in the unit.[1]

After the collective trade agreement is made, the individuals who shall benefit by it are identified by individual hirings. The employer, except as restricted by the collective agreement itself and except that he must engage in no unfair labor practice or discrimination, is free to select those he will employ or discharge. But the terms of the employment already have been traded out. There is little left to individual agreement except the act of hiring. This hiring may be by writing or by word of mouth or may be implied from conduct. In the sense of contracts of hiring, individual contracts between the employer and employee are not forbidden, but indeed are necessitated by the collective bargaining procedure.

But, however engaged, an employee becomes entitled by virtue of the Labor Relations Act somewhat as a third party beneficiary to all benefits of the collective trade agreement, even if on his own he would yield to less favorable terms. The individual hiring contract is subsidiary to the terms of the trade agreement and may not waive any of its benefits, any more than a shipper can contract away the benefit of filed tariffs, the insurer the benefit of standard provisions, or the utility customer the benefit of legally established rates.

Concurrent existence of these two types of agreement raises problems as to which the National Labor Relations Act makes no express provision. We have, however, held that individual contracts obtained as the result of an unfair labor practice may not be the basis of advantage to the violator of the Act nor of disadvantage to employees. National Licorice Co. v. National Labor Relations Board, 309 U.S. 350, 60 S.Ct. 569, 84 L.Ed. 799. But it is urged that where, as here, the contracts were not unfairly or unlawfully obtained, the court indicated a contrary rule in National Labor Relations Board v. Jones & Laughlin Steel Corp., 301 U.S. 1, 44, 45, 57 S.Ct. 615, 627, 628, 81 L.Ed. 893, 108 A.L.R. 1352, and Virginian R. Co. v. System Federation, 300 U.S. 515, 57 S.Ct. 592, 81 L.Ed. 789. Without reviewing those cases in detail, it may be said that their decision called for nothing and their opinions contain nothing which may be properly read to rule the case before us. The court in those cases recognized the existence of some scope for individual contracts, but it did not undertake to define it or to consider the relations between lawful individual and collective agreements, which is the problem now before us.

1. See Hamburger, "The Extension of Collective Agreements to Cover Entire Trade and Industries" (1939) 40 International Labor Review 153; Methods of Collaboration between Public Authorities, Workers' Organizations, and Employers' Organizations (International Labour Conference, 1940) p. 112.

Care has been taken in the opinions of the Court to reserve a field for the individual contract, even in industries covered by the National Labor Relations Act, not merely as an act or evidence of hiring, but also in the sense of a completely individually bargained contract setting out terms of employment, because there are circumstances in which it may legally be used, in fact, in which there is no alternative. Without limiting the possibilities, instances such as the following will occur: Men may continue work after a collective agreement expires and, despite negotiation in good faith, the negotiation may be deadlocked or delayed; in the interim express or implied individual agreements may be held to govern. The conditions for collective bargaining may not exist; thus a majority of the employees may refuse to join a union or to agree upon or designate bargaining representatives, or the majority may not be demonstrable by the means prescribed by the statute, or a previously existent majority may have been lost without unlawful interference by the employer and no new majority have been formed. As the employer in these circumstances may be under no legal obligation to bargain collectively, he may be free to enter into individual contracts.

Individual contracts, no matter what the circumstances that justify their execution or what their terms, may not be availed of to defeat or delay the procedures prescribed by the National Labor Relations Act looking to collective bargaining, nor to exclude the contracting employee from a duly ascertained bargaining unit; nor may they be used to forestall bargaining or to limit or condition the terms of the collective agreement. "The Board asserts a public right vested in it as a public body, charged in the public interest with the duty of preventing unfair labor practices." National Licorice Co. v. National Labor Relations Board, 309 U.S. 350, 364, 60 S.Ct. 569, 577, 84 L.Ed. 799. Wherever private contracts conflict with its functions, they obviously must yield or the Act would be reduced to a futility.

It is equally clear since the collective trade agreement is to serve the purpose contemplated by the Act, the individual contract cannot be effective as a waiver of any benefit to which the employee otherwise would be entitled under the trade agreement. The very purpose of providing by statute for the collective agreement is to supersede the terms of separate agreements of employees with terms which reflect the strength and bargaining power and serve the welfare of the group. Its benefits and advantages are open to every employee of the represented unit, whatever the type or terms of his pre-existing contract of employment.

But it is urged that some employees may lose by the collective agreement, that an individual workman may sometimes have, or be capable of getting, better terms than those obtainable by the group and that his freedom of contract must be respected on that account. We are not called upon to say that under no circumstances can an individual enforce an agreement more advantageous than a collective agreement, but we find the mere possibility that such agreements might be made no ground for holding generally that individual contracts may survive or surmount collective ones. The practice and philosophy of collective bargaining looks with suspicion on such individual advantages. Of course, where there is great variation in circumstances of employment or capacity of employees, it is possible for the collective bargain to prescribe only minimum rates or maximum hours or expressly to leave certain areas open to individual bargaining. But except as so provided, advantages to individuals may prove as disruptive of industrial peace as disadvantages. They are a fruitful way of intefering with organization and choice of representatives; increased compensation, if individually deserved, is often earned at the cost of breaking down some other standard thought to be for the welfare of the group, and always creates the suspicion of being paid at the long-range expense of the group as a whole. Such discriminations not infrequently amount to unfair labor practices. The workman is free, if he values his own bargaining position more than that of the group, to vote against representation: but the majority rules, and if it collectivizes the employment bargain, individual advantages or favors will generally in practice go in as a contribution to the collective result. We cannot except individual contracts generally from the operation of collective ones because some may be more individually advantageous. Individual contracts cannot subtract from collective ones, and whether under some circumstances they may add to them in matters covered by the collective bargain, we leave to be determined by appropriate forums under the laws of contracts applicable, and to the Labor Board if they constitute unfair labor practices.

It also is urged that such individual contracts may embody matters that are not necessarily included within the statutory scope of collective bargaining, such as stock purchase, group insurance, hospitalization, or medical attention. We know of nothing to prevent the employee's, because he is an employee, making any contract provided it is not inconsistent with a collective agreement or does not amount to or result from or is not part of an unfair labor practice. But in so doing the employer may not incidentally exact or obtain any diminution of his own obligation or any increase of those of employees in the matters covered by collective agreement.

Hence we find that the contentions of the Company that the individual contracts precluded a choice of representatives and warranted refusal to bargain during their duration were properly overruled. * * *

Affirmed.

MR. JUSTICE ROBERTS is of opinion that the judgment should be reversed.

Note

1. The principle of "exclusivity" (i.e., that the sole authority to bargain for employees in a bargaining unit resides in the union selected by a majority pursuant to Section 9(a) of the NLRA) is a fundamental premise of American labor policy. It is little employed in other countries, which leads to the question: What alternatives are there to exclusivity in unionized labor relations?

2. What are the implications of exclusivity's majority rule for the pursuit of excellence by employees in their work? Are there differences in this regard between assembly-line workers and college professors?

3. To what extent, if any, can individual bargaining coexist with collective bargaining under J.I. Case?

4. The principle of exclusive representation cannot function in a void; the group of employees eligible to participate in the selection of the representative,

and whose conditions of employment will be determined in the resultant bargaining, must be ascertained. This process, called unit determination, is the subject of the materials which follow. (The reader will profit from a re-examination at this time of the Note, supra pp. 137–141, following the AFL v. NLRB case.)

B. THE BARGAINING UNIT

PACIFIC INTERMOUNTAIN EXPRESS CO.
National Labor Relations Board, 1953.
105 N.L.R.B. 480.

Upon petitions duly filed under Section 9(c) of the National Labor Relations Act, a consolidated hearing was held before Shirley N. Bingham, hearing officer. The hearing officer's rulings made at the hearing are free from prejudicial error and are hereby affirmed.

Upon the entire record in this case, the Board finds:

1. The Employer is engaged in commerce within the meaning of the Act.

2. The labor organizations involved claim to represent certain employees of the Employer.

3. Questions affecting commerce exist concerning the representation of employees of the Employer within the meaning of Section 9(c)(1) and Section 2(6) and (7) of the Act.

4. The Employer is engaged in interstate trucking under an Interstate Commerce Commission certificate. Its central office is located in Oakland, California. It has terminal facilities located in Emoryville, California, 3 miles away, and in other cities in California. It also has terminal facilities in Nevada, Utah, Colorado, Kansas, Missouri, and Illinois.

The Association, Petitioner in Case No. 20–RC–2064, seeks a unit composed of all office clerical employees employed at the Oakland general office and at the Emoryville terminal. The AFL, Petitioner in Case No. 20–RC–2061, seeks a unit composed of all office clerical employees at the Emoryville terminal.

There are factors supporting the appropriateness of the unit sought by the Association. Thus, the skills required of the terminal employees and their duties are similar in nature to those required of the general office employees. The record indicates that wage rates between the 2 offices are comparable and that there is some interchange of employees between the 2 groups. The general office and the Emoryville terminal are located only 3 miles apart. The Employer testified that because of its proximity to the general office, the Emoryville terminal is used as a testing ground for new personnel and administrative techniques before they are introduced throughout the system. The two groups of employees are subject to the same ultimate supervision. Furthermore the general office personnel division oftentimes screens new employees to be hired at the Emoryville terminal.

On the other hand, certain other factors support the appropriateness of a separate unit confined to the office clerical employees at the Emoryville terminal. Thus, the terminal office clerical employees are concerned mainly with the movement of freight and the preparation of freight bills and bills of lading, whereas the general office clerical employees are engaged in administrative and clerical duties pertaining to all terminals, including the Emoryville terminal, and the overall operations of the Employer. The Employees of the two groups are under different immediate supervision. The district manager in charge of the terminal office has complete authority over the hiring and discharge of terminal employees. The terminal employees are required to work on Saturdays, Sundays, and on night shifts, whereas the general office employees are not. There is no history of collective bargaining on either a singleplant or multiplant basis.

In view of the foregoing and on the entire record, we are of the opinion that the Emoryville terminal office clerical employees may by themselves constitute an appropriate unit or that the office clerical employees of the Emoryville terminal and the general office may together constitute an appropriate unit.

However we shall make no final unit determination at this time, but shall direct that the questions concerning representation which have arisen be resolved by separate elections by secret ballot among the employees in the following voting groups:

1. All office clerical employees employed at the Employer's Oakland, California, general office, excluding supervisors as defined in the Act, guards, and all other employees.

2. All office clerical employees employed at the Employer's Emoryville, California, terminal, excluding supervisors as defined in the Act, guards, and all other employees.

Upon the results of these elections will depend, in part, our final unit determination. If the employees in group 2 select a bargaining representative different from that selected by the employees in group 1, the Board finds the group 2 employees constitute a separate appropriate unit; and in these circumstances if the employees in group 1 also select a bargaining representative the Board finds that the employees in group 1 also constitute an appropriate unit. If the employees in the two groups select the same bargaining representative, the Board finds that together they constitute an appropriate unit. The Regional Director conducting the elections directed herein is instructed to issue a certification of representatives to the union or unions in the unit or units which may result from the elections.

Our dissenting colleagues would have the Board adopt a new procedure for tallying the employees' votes in the elections hereinafter directed. Careful consideration has been given to their proposal and, although recognizing the equitable principles supporting it, we do not believe that the time is propitious for a change in administrative procedures that have operated successfully over a substantial period of time. The need for the proposed relief is likely to arise so rarely in practice that we doubt whether the theoretical arguments for changing the old practices are strong enough to override the mechanical complications which we would be inviting.

MEMBERS MURDOCK and PETERSON, dissenting in part.

We agree that the factors supporting the appropriateness of either a single-plant or a two-plant unit are sufficiently balanced to warrant the direction of a Globe-type election in this case. We, however, disagree with the majority opinion insofar as it perpetuates what, in our opinion, is an outmoded and impractical procedure for tallying the votes cast in Globe-type elections such as are directed herein. The Globe election has been employed by the Board since early in its history [7] as a means of assisting the Board to make appropriate unit findings in cases such as this where the factors favoring the appropriateness of two or more of the units requested are evenly balanced. In such circumstances, it has been the policy of the Board to consider the desires of the employees as the controlling factor in its unit determination. Accordingly, an election is held among the employees in the group which the Board has found may appropriately constitute a separate bargaining unit or part of a more comprehensive unit. At the time an election is also held among the remaining employees with whom, as found by the Board, the first group may be appropriately joined. The purpose of the election among the first group of employees (the Globed group) is to determine which type of unit representation they prefer. If they vote for the union seeking to represent them as a separate unit, they have thereby indicated their preference for separate representation and the Board finds such unit appropriate. On the other hand, if they vote for the union that seeks the more comprehensive unit, they are taken to have indicated their desire to be represented as part of that unit. Under the Board's current system of tallying the votes in such elections, and basing its unit determinations on the results thereof, the desires of the employees are often ignored. Thus, in this case for example, if the Association won in the group 2 election but lost the group 1 election, it would be certified for the group 2 employees as a separate bargaining unit, the very type of unit representation that they had plainly rejected. Moreover, under the current practice, even though the group 2 employees vote against separate representation, the Association must receive a majority of the votes cast in each election in order to be certified for the unit it is seeking. This is true regardless of the fact that a majority of all the employees involved may have voted for the Association. Thus, in such circumstances the will of the majority of the employees in a unit which the Board has said is appropriate is also thwarted.

We submit that such arbitrary results can be avoided simply by changing the present method of tallying the ballots cast in Globe-election cases to provide for pooling the votes in the event the globed group votes for inclusion in the larger unit. The pooled votes would then be counted to ascertain whether or not the union seeking the larger unit had received a majority of the votes cast in the two elections.

To illustrate, suppose in the instant case the results of the group 1 and group 2 elections were as follows:

Group 1

Votes for the Association 58

Votes against the Association 60

---

7. The first such election was conducted in The Globe Machine and Stamping Co., 3 NLRB 294. Hence the term "Globe election." In its decision in that case the Board said, "in such a case where the considerations are so evenly balanced, the determining factor is the desire of the men themselves."

Group 2

Votes for the Association 15
Votes for the AFL 10
Votes for no union 2

As a majority of the employees in the group 2 election have expressed their desire to be represented by the Association in a two-plant unit, the votes cast in both elections would be pooled as follows:

Votes for the Association 73
Votes for the AFL 10
Votes for no union 62
Total valid votes cast 145

As the number of votes cast for the Association constitutes a majority of the valid votes cast, the Association would be certified for the two-plant unit.

As illustrated above, in tallying the pooled votes, the votes cast against the participating labor organizations in the group 2 election would be counted as votes against the Association; the votes cast for the AFL would be counted as part of the valid votes cast but not as votes for or against the Association. Under this procedure a second election would be held if the tally of pooled votes showed that a majority of the valid votes were not cast for or against the Association. The Regional Director would be directed to conduct such further election among the employees in the two-plant unit to determine whether or not they desired to be represented by the Association.

To illustrate, suppose the results of the group 1 and group 2 elections were as follows:

Group 1

Votes for the Association 55
Votes against the Association 63

Group 2

Votes for the Association 15
Votes for the AFL 10
Votes for no union 2

As in the first illustration above, the votes cast in both elections will be pooled as follows:

Votes for the Association 70
Votes for the AFL 10
Votes for no union 65
Total valid votes cast 145

As neither the number of votes cast for the Association nor the number of votes cast for no union constitutes a majority of the total valid votes cast, a second election would be conducted among the eligible employees in the two-plant unit to determine whether or not they wish to be represented by the Association.

The practice of pooling the votes in Globe elections * * * would result in unit findings of the Board which conform to the desires of the employees and would therefore better effectuate the intent and purpose of the Globe election doctrine.

Note

1. Why did the two labor organizations in Pacific Intermountain seek the unit determinations they sought? Is Section 9(c)(5) of the NLRA relevant? What do you suppose the employer's unit preference was? Is its testimony a tip-off?

2. Reconsider the questions posed in Note 3 following AFL v. NLRB, supra p. 138. What factors should be taken into account in determining the appropriateness of a bargaining unit? Are the pertinent factors political or economic in nature?

The test generally applied in determining the appropriateness of a requested unit is whether or not the employees contained therein have a sufficient "community of interest." Therefore, one way to evaluate the relevance of a factor advanced in a particular unit dispute is to ascertain the extent to which it demonstrates or disproves "common employment interest of the group involved." [c] Perhaps a negative formulation of this general test is more easily understood: To what extent is there *conflict* of interest within the proposed unit?

3. As indicated in the Pacific Intermountain case, more than one unit configuration may be "appropriate" in a particular dispute. "On the question of the 'appropriate unit,' the policy of the National Labor Relations Board * * * appears to be well settled. In a representation proceeding there is no requirement that the unit in issue be found to be the *most* appropriate unit. Rather the question *simply* is whether it is *an* appropriate unit. Thus the fact that other groupings of employees would be as appropriate as the unit in issue, does not warrant a denial of the unit sought unless the unit itself is inappropriate." [d]

4. The recommendations of the dissenting Board members in Pacific Intermountain for changes in the method of tallying votes in "Globe elections," and of making unit determinations based thereon, were adopted by the Board in American Potash and Chemical Corp., 107 N.L.R.B. 1418, 1427 n. 12 (1954), a case otherwise dealt with infra p. 226.

5. Why were "supervisors" excluded from the unit definitions in Pacific Intermountain? What is a supervisor? What is the rationale of Sections 2(3) (so far as pertinent) and 2(11) of the NLRA?

EXCLUSION FROM COVERAGE UNDER THE NLRA

The statutory exclusion of "supervisors" from "employees" eligible for bargaining unit membership does not exhaust the categories of employees so excluded. Other workers expressly excluded from the definition of "employ-

---

c. NLRB, 23d Annual Report 30 (1958).

d. Crowley, The Resolution of Representation Status Disputes under the Taylor Law, 37 Ford.L.Rev. 517, 518 (1969), citing Metropolitan Life Ins. Co., 156 N.L.R.B. 1408 (1966). The author, a member of the Public Employment Relations Board of the State of New York, goes on to observe, by way of contrast: "The decisions of the PERB represent a substantial departure from the NLRB's policy. * * * [PERB decisions require] that the unit determined be the *most* appropriate unit." Id.

at 518–19. The explanation advanced by PERB for this difference in treatment is that the pertinent statute (N.Y.Civ.Serv.Law § 207.1) requires that "the unit shall be compatible with the joint responsibilities of the public employer and public employees to serve the public." The principal effect of the "most appropriate unit" approach has been larger units, thus avoiding the "administrative inconvenience" associated with "unwarranted fragmentation." 37 Ford.L.Rev. at 520.

ee" under Section 2(3), and therefore, by that same definition, excluded from membership in any "appropriate" unit, are: agricultural laborers, domestic servants, independent contractors, employees subject to the Railway Labor Act, and employees of any employer excluded from the definition of "employer" in Section 2(2). Among the employers so excluded are the United States and states or political subdivisions thereof.

Until 1974 nonprofit hospitals were also excluded from the definition of employer. P.L. 93–360 (July 24, 1974) deleted this exclusion, thereby according bargaining rights to employees of nonprofit hospitals. (The same Act amended Section 8(d) of the NLRA and added Section 213 to the Labor Management Relations Act, each change intended to render strikes in the health-care industry less likely to occur, because of the lengthening of notice requirements, and therefore the time for negotiations, and the strengthening of the role of the Federal Mediation and Conciliation Service in settlement efforts.)

To the foregoing *expressly* ineligible categories of workers have been added *impliedly* ineligible categories. "Confidential employees," i.e., those privy through the nature of their work to management secrets pertaining to collective bargaining strategy and tactics (therefore having a "labor nexus") are excluded from employee status and unit membership. Similarly, "managerial employees" are excluded—they being employees who formulate and implement management policy of a *non* supervisory sort, i.e., of a sort which does not have *direct* impact upon the conditions of employment of other employees (in the hiring, firing, promotion, discipline sense of Section 2(11); the analogy of *staff* officers, as opposed to *line* officers, in the military suggests itself). The reasons for excluding these two categories of employees from bargaining-unit eligibility are essentially the same, though more readily perceived in the confidential employee category: both are part of the management team for purposes of collective bargaining, and it would be unfair to management to deprive it of their undivided loyalty. Put otherwise, the congressional intent was neither to permit spies from the bargaining unit in the employer's councils, nor to provide collective bargaining rights to "executives." See NLRB v. Bell Aerospace, 416 U.S. 267, 94 S.Ct. 1757, 40 L.Ed.2d 134 (1974), and NLRB v. Hendricks County Rural Electric Membership Corp., 454 U.S. 170, 102 S.Ct. 216, 70 L.Ed.2d 323 (1981).

With regard to the "managerial" prong of the "impliedly excluded" categories of employees, the Supreme Court in NLRB v. Yeshiva University, 444 U.S. 672, 100 S.Ct. 856, 63 L.Ed.2d 115 (1980), held that faculty members who exercise significant decision-making power regarding curriculum, admissions, grading practices, etc., typical of a modern university, are "managerial" and thus excluded from the coverage of the Act.

In addition to the foregoing statutory exclusions from coverage by Congress through the definitions given to "employer" and "employee," the NLRB has itself *administratively* excluded many potential beneficiaries of the Act. From its inception the Board has had a larger *de jure* jurisdictional scope than it has in fact been able to exercise. As a consequence, the Board has had to develop standards by which to restrict its case load and, at the same time, to optimize the utilization of its limited resources. Since the basis of the Board's jurisdiction is the commerce clause, the Board has sought to establish and apply criteria which will screen out those cases least affecting commerce. Two methods of achieving this goal have been employed: (1) The Board has excluded entire industries which, for one reason or another, it concluded to be of insufficient consequence to interstate commerce. (2) The Board has adopted "dollar volume" standards for asserting jurisdiction in the remaining industries; the standards laid down vary with the nature of the enterprise (e.g., nonretail, retail, public utilities, hotels and motels, office buildings), but they are all designed to measure, in one way or another (e.g., gross annual volume of business, sales and purchases directly or indirectly in interstate commerce), the impact, in terms of dollars, of the particular activity on interstate commerce.

Some questions existed as to the Board's power to exercise its statutory jurisdiction in such selective fashion. Indeed, in 1957 the Supreme Court, in Office Employees Union v. NLRB, 353 U.S. 313, 77 S.Ct. 799, 1 L.Ed.2d 846, held that the Board could not refuse to assert jurisdiction over labor unions as a class, when acting as employers. Similarly, a year later, in Hotel Employees Union v. Leedom, 358 U.S. 99, 79 S.Ct. 150, 3 L.Ed.2d 143 (1958), the Court held that "the Board's 'long standing policy not to exercise jurisdiction over the hotel industry' as a class, is contrary to the principles expressed in" the Office Employees case. In the Landrum-Griffin Act of 1959, however, Congress put to rest any doubts as to the Board's authority to exercise its jurisdiction in a selective fashion by amending the NLRA so as to add Section 14(c)(1), which reads:

> "The Board, in its discretion, may, by rule of decision or by published rules adopted pursuant to the Administrative Procedure Act, decline to assert jurisdiction over any labor dispute involving any class or category of employers, where, in the opinion of the Board, the effect of such labor dispute on commerce is not sufficiently substantial to warrant the exercise of its jurisdiction: *Provided,* That the Board shall not decline to assert jurisdiction over any labor dispute over which it would assert jurisdiction under the standards prevailing upon August 1, 1959."

The jurisdictional standards in effect as of 1976 are succinctly set forth in How to Take a Case Before the National Labor Relations Board (4th ed. McGuiness 1976). The dollar volume standards technique for restricting jurisdiction is exemplified in the following excerpts (Id. at 34–38):

> "[*General Standards*]
>
> "1. GENERAL NONRETAIL CONCERNS: Sales of goods to consumers in other states, directly or indirectly (called outflow), or purchases of goods from suppliers in other states, directly or indirectly (called inflow), of at least $50,000 per year. *Direct Outflow* is defined as goods shipped or services furnished by the employer outside his home state. *Indirect Outflow* is defined as the sale of goods or services to users meeting any of the Board's jurisdictional standards, excepting the indirect outflow or indirect inflow standard. *Direct Inflow* is defined as goods or services furnished the employer directly from outside the state. *Indirect Inflow* is defined as goods or services which originated outside the state, but which the employer purchased from a seller or supplier within the state.

"In applying this standard, the Board will add direct and indirect outflow, or indirect and direct inflow; however, it will not add outflow and inflow.

"2. RETAIL CONCERNS: An annual volume of business of at least $500,000, including sales and excise taxes.

"3. RETAIL AND MANUFACTURING COMBINED: Either the retail or the nonretail standard, when a single, integrated enterprise manufactures a product as well as sells it directly to the public.

"4. RETAIL AND WHOLESALE COMBINED: The nonretail standard, when a company is involved in both retail and wholesale operations.

"5. INSTRUMENTALITIES, LINKS, AND CHANNELS OF INTERSTATE COMMERCE: An annual income of at least $50,000 from furnishing interstate transportation services or performing services valued at $50,000 or more for enterprises that meet any of the standards except indirect outflow or indirect inflow.

" * * *

"[*Specific Industries*]
" * * *

"2. AUTOMOBILE DEALERS: Treated as retail operations, even if the dealer has a franchise from a national manufacturer.
" * * *

"4. COLLEGES, UNIVERSITIES, AND SECONDARY SCHOOLS: At least $1 million total annual income from all sources except those designated by the grantor as not available for operating costs. This applies to both profit and nonprofit institutions.[21]
" * * *

"12. HOTELS AND MOTELS: At least $500,000 total annual volume of business, whether an establishment is residential or nonresidential.
" * * *

"17. RESTAURANTS: Treated as retail operations.
" * * *

"20. SYMPHONY ORCHESTRAS: At least $1 million annual income, compiled from all sources except those designated by the donor as not available for operating costs.
" * * * "

NATIONAL TUBE CO.

National Labor Relations Board, 1948.
76 N.L.R.B. 1199.

FINDINGS OF FACT

I. *The Business of the Employer*

National Tube Company * * * is engaged in the manufacture and sale of steel and tubular products at several plants located in various parts of the United States. * * *

---

21. Cornell University, 183 NLRB No. 41, 74 LRRM 1269 (1970); Windsor School Inc., 199 NLRB No. 54, 81 LRRM 1246 (1972). [The Cornell decision reversed a Board policy, established in Columbia University, 97 NLRB 424 (1951), of nonassertion of jurisdiction in the case of private schools. Public schools, including colleges and universities, are of course excluded from coverage by Sections 2(2) and (3) of the NLRA.]

II. The Organizations Involved

The Petitioner [Bricklayers, Masons and Plasterers International Union] is a labor organization, affiliated with the American Federation of Labor, claiming to represent employees of the Employer.

United Steelworkers of America, affiliated with the Congress of Industrial Organizations, is a labor organization claiming to represent employees of the Employer.

III. The Alleged Appropriate Unit

The issue before us is whether the amended Act requires or should induce the Board to conduct an election among certain bricklayers in order to afford them an opportunity to sever themselves from a long-established industrial unit in the basic steel industry.

The Petitioner seeks a craft unit of bricklayers and apprentices, employed at the Employer's Lorain, Ohio, plant. They are engaged primarily in the construction and repair of blast furnaces and related equipment used in the production of basic steel. In support of its position, the Petitioner contends that, regardless of prior decisions of the Board with respect to craft severance in this industry, the Board is now *required* under Section 9(b)(2) [2] of the amended Act, to grant an election to a group of craft employees seeking separate representation for the purposes of collective bargaining. The Petitioner also contends that, in any event, the Board should, upon the facts in the present record, find appropriate the unit it requests.

The Intervenor [United Steelworkers] and the Employer both oppose as inappropriate the unit sought by the Petitioner herein. * * * Both contend that the Board is not required by [the new Section 9(b)(2)] to grant craft severance to these bricklayers, because of the degree of integration in the basic steel manufacturing process and the history of collective bargaining by this Employer and by employers generally in the basic steel industry.

On July 30, 1942, the Intervenor was certified, in accordance with a stipulation for a consent election, as exclusive bargaining representative for a multiple-plant unit of the Employer's production and maintenance employees. Thereafter the Intervenor bargained for all such employees, including bricklayers, under a series of collective bargaining agreements, the most recent of which was executed as of April 22, 1947. The record indicates that the collective bargaining history of the Employer has followed the pattern of collective bargaining generally in the steel industry, which has been predominately on an industrial basis. No unit confined to bricklayers has ever been established among the employees in any operation controlled by the United States Steel Corporation, the parent of the Employer. The record further shows that the same situation exists at the plants of 65 other companies engaged in the production of basic steel. * * *

---

2. Section 9(b)(2) provides, in part, that the Board shall not "decide that any craft unit is inappropriate for such purposes on the ground that a different unit has been established by a prior Board determination unless a majority of the employees in the proposed craft unit vote against separate representation."

The Application of Section 9(b)(2) to the Present Proceeding

[Petitioner contends] that under Section 9(b)(2) the Board is *required* to establish a separate bargaining unit for a group of craft employees, unless there is a vote against separate representation by a majority of such employees. This contention is, in effect, that Section 9(b)(2), which precludes the Board from finding a craft unit inappropriate on the ground that a different unit has been established "*by a prior Board determination,*" removes from the Board's discretion not only the power to rely upon a prior decision as the basis for finding a proposed craft unit inappropriate, but also the power to find a craft unit inappropriate by reason either of any collective bargaining history or of other circumstances upon which we have customarily based a determination as to the appropriateness or inappropriateness of a proposed craft unit.

This argument asserts that no discretion exists, and is not directed to the Board's exercise of discretion.   *   *   *

The Petitioner urges, in support of its construction of Section 9(b)(2), various statements to be found in the legislative history preceding the passage of the Amendments to the Act. Consideration of legislative history to determine legislative intent is normally confined to those instances where the statutory language is not, on its face, susceptible of reasonable interpretation, or where it contains some patent ambiguity that cannot be resolved by a consideration of the statute as a whole. Here the statute clearly states that the Board's action in finding a craft unit inappropriate shall not be based upon the fact that a different unit has been established by a prior Board determination. Because the phrase "*a prior Board determination*" contains no substantial ambiguity, and because Section 9(b)(2) is a proviso, as distinguished from an affirmative statement of duties imposed by the statute, we believe that we should not strain to give this proviso an interpretation unwarranted by its express language. This conclusion is consistent with the general rule that a proviso must be the subject of strict construction. We find, therefore, that Section 9(b)(2) does not itself limit the Board's discretion to find a craft unit inappropriate in certain situations, so long as there is no reliance upon the fact that a different unit has already been established by a prior Board determination.[11]

Had Congress desired to deprive the Board of all discretion in matters of this sort, it had only to adopt language similar to the mandatory craft proviso contained in the New York State Labor Relations Act.[12] Although this was urged at the hearings on the bill, Congress saw fit not to enact it into law.

---

11. This construction *is* meaningful in limiting the Board's discretion, because, at the very least, the Board may no longer support administrative or other dismissal of craft petitions upon the sole ground of prior Board determination that a plant-wide unit was appropriate. The question of the appropriateness of the proposed craft grouping must be independently considered on its merits.

In this case, therefore, we have explored the entire situation *de novo*, without particular stress upon the certification issued in 1942 at 42 N.L.R.B. 1121.

12. The craft proviso of the New York Act (Section 705(2)) reads as follows:

"* * * provided, however, that in any case where the majority of employees of a particular craft shall so decide the board shall designate such craft as a unit appropriate for the purpose of collective bargaining."

Assuming, however, arguendo, that Section 9(b)(2) of the Act is sufficiently ambiguous to permit an examination of legislative history in an attempt to determine Congressional intent, it appears that such history is not conclusive. In the first place, it is clear that Section 9(b)(2) was enacted by the Congress with an eye directed toward the Board's earlier policy respecting craft severance under what became commonly known as the *American Can* doctrine.[13] The essence of that doctrine, as originally formulated, was that the bargaining history of a particular employer might, if conducted for a substantial period upon an over-all basis, provide sufficient basis for denying a later request for separate craft representation. The use of such bargaining history as a controlling factor under the *American Can* doctrine involved no distinction as to whether the bargaining history resulted from voluntary recognition of the Union by the Employer or from a prior Board determination. The *American Can* rule generally was not applied to questions of separate craft representation where the controlling factor relied upon by the Board was bargaining history in the industry, as distinguished from bargaining history at the plant of the particular employer concerned.

The legislative history preceding the enactment of Section 9(b)(2) discloses, at some points, a Congressional intent to overrule, by legislation, the *American Can* doctrine itself.[15] At other points, it indicates, consistently with the language ultimately adopted, that the only factor that the Congress desired to eliminate as a controlling element in considering a request for craft severance, was a prior Board determination.[16] Because, as indicated above, the *American Can* doctrine cannot be considered synonymous with the phrase "prior Board determination," we believe that the legislative history preceding the enactment of Section 9(b)(2) does not adequately establish a certain Congressional intent to eliminate the use of bargaining history by a particular employer as a controlling factor in determining the issue of separate craft representation. Accordingly, resort to legislative history does not, in our opinion, necessitate a construction contrary to that already adopted on the basis of the express language of the statute.

13. See Matter of American Can Company, 13 N.L.R.B. 1252 (1939), where the Board first gave expression to that doctrine. It was substantially modified by the Board itself in later years. See, for example, Matter of International Minerals, 71 N.L.R.B. 878 (1946). [The American Can case is also discussed supra pp. 139–140.]

15. The following reference to Section 9(b) in the majority report of the Senate Committee on Labor and Public Welfare concerning Senate Bill 1126 would indicate that the Board may no longer rely upon the bargaining history of a particular employer as the basis for finding a craft unit inappropriate in accordance with the *American Can* doctrine:

"Section 9(b): The several amendments to the subsection propose to limit the Board's discretion in determining the kind of unit appropriate for collective bargaining: * * * (2) In determining whether members of a craft may be separated from a larger unit the Board may not dismiss a craft petition on the ground that a different unit has been established by a prior determination. *This overrules the American Can rule, supra.*" (Emphasis supplied.)

16. The following, *and later,* statement by Senator Taft on the floor of the Senate in explaining the Senate bill to amend the National Labor Relations Act would indicate that Congress intended only to preclude the Board from relying exclusively upon a prior *determination* as the basis for finding a craft unit inappropriate:

"It (the bill) does not go the full way of giving them (craft employees) an absolute right in every case: *it simply provides that the Board shall have discretion and shall not bind itself by previous determination but that the subject shall always be open for further consideration by the Board.*" Congressional Record, Senate, April 23, 1947 (93 Cong.Rec., 3952). * * *

Even on the assumption, however, that the legislative history might be construed as indicating an intent on the part of Congress to eliminate the *American Can* doctrine altogether, so that neither a prior Board determination nor the bargaining history of a particular employer could be relied upon as the controlling factor in a decision finding a craft unit inappropriate, it is clear that the only restriction imposed by Section 9(b)(2) is that such prior determination or bargaining history may not be the *sole* ground upon which the Board may decide that a craft unit is inappropriate without an election. In other words, there is no basis for finding a Congressional intent to prohibit the use of a prior Board determination or any bargaining history based thereon as *a* factor to be considered in determining the issue of craft severance, so long as neither is made the sole ground upon which the Board predicates its decision. Regardless of any limitation on the use of the *bargaining history of a particular employer,* there is no suggestion, either in the provision itself or even in its legislative history, that the Board should be inhibited in using bargaining history in the industry concerned in determining the appropriateness of a proposed unit of craft employees. We conclude that bargaining history in an industry may be considered as a weighty factor in any Board decision affecting the issue of the appropriateness of separate craft representation.

     * * *

We find, therefore, that the appropriateness of the unit requested by the Petitioner is a matter that lies within the discretion of the Board, to be determined upon all the factors in the case, including those just mentioned. We turn now to those factors.

The Petitioner's contention that bricklayers and apprentices employed at the particular plant of this Employer constitute an appropriate unit, is based primarily upon craft considerations and the alleged inadequacy of their past representation as part of the present plant-wide bargaining unit. The record discloses that, unlike the usual craft maintenance employees whose work on any particular piece of production equipment occurs for the most part at irregular intervals, the bricklayers and apprentices for whom the Petitioner seeks separate representation are engaged in a definite program of replacing and repairing on regularly succeeding occasions, the instrumentalities used in the continuous production of basic steel.[19] Their functions are therefore intimately connected with the steelmaking process itself. The bricklayers and the steel production employees enjoy similar working conditions and, as already indicated, have been represented under a series of exclusive bargaining agreements between the Employer and the Intervenor, extending from 1942 through 1947, when the current collective bargaining agreement between the Employer and the Intervenor was executed.

The resultant integration of the bricklayers with the steel production employees has been further advanced by a job evaluation program recently completed pursuant to agreements between the Employer and the Intervenor. It covers all employees including bricklayers. The wage rates of

---

19. The bricklayers and apprentices herein concerned appear to have specialized skills with reference to the construction and repair of furnace linings and other equipment pecu- liar to the steel industry. Their work is, for the most part, entirely different from that of bricklayers normally employed in building construction.

production employees, including those of bricklayers and apprentices, have been integrated into a single coordinated wage structure. The experience of the Employer, as disclosed by its long history of collective bargaining with the Intervenor, is parallel to that of other employers in the steel industry, who generally have bargained upon the basis of an over-all unit in which craft employees, including bricklayers, have been included.

The Board is greatly impressed by the argument of the *Employer* that, due to the integrated nature of operations in the steel industry, any change in the unit governing the bargaining relations between the Employer and its employees would be detrimental to the basic wage rate structure underlying the Employer's present operations, and would necessarily have an adverse effect upon its productive capacity in an industry of vital national concern.

* * * We find, accordingly, that the unit sought by this Petitioner is inappropriate for the purposes of collective bargaining. We shall therefore order that the petition in the instant proceeding be dismissed. * * *

Note

1. Section 9(b)(2), added to the NLRA by the Taft-Hartley amendments, was the product of the long-continuing jurisdictional struggle between the AFL and CIO. This fight (the origin of which is described supra pp. 138–139) has been largely waged along unit-determination lines. The most frequent battleground has been the one defined by the "craft severance" issue. As intimated in National Tube, the Taft-Hartley Congress was concerned over the NLRB's propensity to favor large industrial units (CIO) to the prejudice of small craft units (AFL). Section 9(b)(2) represents the congressional effort to deal with this concern.

The interpretation given to that section in National Tube was sharply restricted in AMERICAN POTASH & CHEMICAL CORP., 107 N.L.R.B. 1418 (1954). In that case, a divided Board held (1) that the National Tube doctrine would not be extended beyond the four industries in which it had by that time been recognized (basic steel, basic aluminum, lumber, and wet milling), and (2) that for other industries the new test for craft severability would be whether the alleged craft was in fact a craft and whether the union seeking severance was one specially oriented to the representation of members of that craft. As the Board stated: "We find that the intent of Congress will best be effectuated by a finding, and we so find, that a craft group will be appropriate for severance purposes in cases where a true craft group is sought and where, in addition, the union seeking to represent it is one which traditionally represents that craft." Id. at 1422. The Board made it clear that the standards for "craftiness" would be demandingly applied and that the primary criterion would be the length of apprenticeship necessary to achieve journeyman status in the craft. At a more philosophical level, the Board observed:

> "* * * [I]t is not the province of this Board to dictate the course and pattern of labor organization in our vast industrial complex. If millions of employees today feel that their interests are better served by craft unionism, it is not for us to say that they can only be represented on an industrial basis or for that matter that they must bargain on strict craft lines. All that we are considering here is whether true craft groups should have an opportunity to decide the issue for themselves. We conclude that we must afford them that choice in order to give effect to the statute. Whatever may

be lost in maximum industrial efficiency, and experience has not shown that this loss is measurably greater than that which flowed from the rigid doctrine of *American Can,* is more than compensated for by the gain in industrial democracy and the freedom of employees to choose their own unions and their own form of collective bargaining." Id. at 1422–1423.

The approach adopted by the Board in American Potash provoked some strong criticism. In NLRB v. Pittsburgh Plate Glass Co., 270 F.2d 167 (4th Cir. 1959), the court refused to enforce a Board order directing an employer to bargain with a union which had successfully secured severance under the American Potash doctrine. The court characterized that doctrine as "arbitrary and discriminatory" in that it (1) gave disparate treatment to employees similarly situated (i.e., no severance in National Tube industries, severance in other industries under circumstances not differing in significant respect), (2) entailed an abdication by the Board of its duty to exercise its discretion under Section 9(b) to determine "*in each case* what unit would be most appropriate to effectuate the overall purpose of the Act to preserve industrial peace." Id. at 173. The abdication consisted of the Board's delegating to any qualified craft union which had organized a majority of the workers sought to be severed the power to decree severance by petitioning therefor.

Despite the foregoing criticism, the Board adhered to its American Potash position for a dozen years. In MALLINCKRODT CHEMICAL WORKS, 162 N.L. R.B. 387 (1966), however, the Board endorsed the view of the Fourth Circuit in Pittsburgh Plate Glass, overruled American Potash, and returned, in effect, to National Tube. Articulating its new approach, the Board stated: "[T]he *American Potash* tests do not effectuate the policies of the Act. We shall, therefore, no longer allow our inquiry to be limited by them. Rather, we shall, as the Board did prior to *American Potash,* broaden our inquiry to permit evaluation of all considerations relevant to an informed decision in this area. * * *." Id. at 397.

2. The "evolution" of the Board's position on the craft severance issue affords occasion for some cool reflection upon an aspect of the Board's nature and function which is often the subject of hot complaint. The Taft-Hartley Act of 1947, including, of course, Section 9(b)(2), was the product of the first Republican Congress following the New Deal. The Board which decided National Tube was appointed by Democratic presidents. American Potash was decided by a Board containing two Eisenhower appointees. By the time of the Mallinckrodt decision the Board had again been reconstituted, by two Democratic presidents.

As the foregoing may suggest, the charge is sometimes made that decisions of the Board are politically motivated. Labor representatives were considerably exercised by the performance of the so-called "Eisenhower Board." Management representatives were, in turn, agitated by the "Kennedy Board." Some critics of the Board advocate its replacement by a "labor court," manned by judges with life-tenure or long-term appointments. The obvious purpose of such proposals is to make the Board more impartial, less subject to political influence and pressures, more constant in its policies. While these arguments can be, indeed have been,[e] strongly made, there is another side, as persuasive. The kind of body Congress created in the NLRB is not intended to be as insulated as a

---

e. Various formulations of the arguments are reviewed and pertinent literature cited in Booker and Coe, The NLRB and Its Critics, 17 Lab.L.J. 522 (1966), and The Labor Board and Its Reformers, 18 Lab.L.J. 67 (1967).

court from the political environment. The five members of the Board each serve, in staggered terms, for five years. This means that the President (with the advice and consent of the Senate) has at least one vacancy each year to fill. As a consequence, a new President can by the third year of his term at the latest (sooner if the Board was previously split or if there are fortuitous vacancies) establish a new majority for the resolution or re-resolution of the perennial close questions of statutory interpretation. This gives a new administration a degree of control over labor policy (a major component of domestic policy) which would not be available were Board members appointed for longer terms or for life. Thus the national will, as expressed quadrennially, is more quickly reflected in those aspects of national labor policy over which the Board has control. The Board, in short, the argument runs, is not supposed to feel as politically invulnerable as a federal judge with life tenure or as a member of the Federal Reserve Board with a fourteen-year appointment. In the latter situations different considerations would be said to obtain.

Accepting, arguendo, this kind of "political jurisprudence," what light, if any, does it cast upon the National Tube, American Potash, Mallinckrodt circle?

3. As stated in Note 1 supra, the craft severance issue and the consequent enactment of Section 9(b)(2) were the product of the strife between the AFL, with its craft basis for organization, and the CIO, with its industrial basis. The heat of this controversy has been since reduced by the merger of the AFL and CIO in the mid-1950's and the "no-raiding" arrangements which resulted from, and substantially motivated, the merger. This development is discussed in the "Jurisdictional Disputes" section of Chapter 5, infra p. 461.

NATIONAL LABOR RELATIONS BOARD v. TRUCK DRIVERS LOCAL 449 ("BUFFALO LINEN")

Supreme Court of the United States, 1957.
353 U.S. 87, 77 S.Ct. 643, 1 L.Ed.2d 676.

MR. JUSTICE BRENNAN delivered the opinion of the Court.

The question presented by this case is whether the nonstruck members of a multi-employer bargaining association committed an unfair labor practice when, during contract negotiations, they temporarily locked out their employees as a defense to a union strike against one of their members which imperiled the employers' common interest in bargaining on a group basis.

The National Labor Relations Board determined that resort to the temporary lockout was not an unfair labor practice in the circumstances.[1] The Court of Appeals for the Second Circuit reversed.[2] This Court granted certiorari to consider this important question of the construction of the amended National Labor Relations Act, and also to consider an alleged conflict with decisions of Courts of Appeals of other circuits.

Eight employers in the linen supply business in and around Buffalo, New York, comprise the membership of the Linen and Credit Exchange. For approximately 13 years, the Exchange and the respondent Union, representing the truck drivers employed by the members, bargained on a multi-employer basis and negotiated successive collective bargaining agreements signed by the Union and by the eight employers. Sixty days before

1. 109 N.L.R.B. 447.   2. 231 F.2d 110.

such an agreement was to expire on April 30, 1953, the Union gave notice of its desire to open negotiations for changes.

The Exchange and the Union began negotiations some time before April 30, but the negotiations carried past that date and were continuing on May 26, 1953, when the Union put into effect a "whipsawing" plan [7] by striking and picketing the plant of one of the Exchange members, Frontier Linen Supply, Inc. The next day, May 27, the remaining seven Exchange members laid off their truck drivers after notifying the Union that the layoff action was taken because of the Frontier strike, advising the Union that the laid-off drivers would be recalled if the Union withdrew its picket line and ended the strike. Negotiations continued without interruption, however, until a week later when agreement was reached upon a new contract which the Exchange members and the Union approved and signed. Thereupon the Frontier strike was ended, the laid-off drivers were recalled, and normal operations were resumed at the plants of all Exchange members.

The Union filed with the National Labor Relations Board an unfair practice charge against the seven employers, alleging that the temporary lockout interfered with its rights guaranteed by § 7 thereby violating § 8(a) (1) and (3) of the Act. A complaint issued, and, after hearing, a trial examiner found the employers guilty of the unfair labor practice charged. The Board overruled the trial examiner, finding that "the more reasonable inference is that, although not specifically announced by the Union, the strike against the one employer necessarily carried with it an implicit threat of future strike action against any or all of the other members of the Association," with the "calculated purpose" of causing "successive and individual employer capitulations." The Board therefore found that "in the absence of any independent evidence of antiunion motivation, * * * the Respondent's [sic] action in shutting their plants until termination of the strike at Frontier was defensive and privileged in nature, rather than retaliatory and unlawful." * * *

Although, as the Court of Appeals correctly noted, there is no express provision in the law either prohibiting or authorizing the lockout, the Act does not make the lockout unlawful *per se*. Legislative history of the Wagner Act * * * indicates that there was no intent to prohibit strikes or lockouts as such. The unqualified use of the term "lock-out" in several sections of the Taft-Hartley Act [16] is statutory recognition that there are circumstances in which employers may lawfully resort to the lockout as an economic weapon. This conclusion is supported by the legislative history of the Act.

We are not concerned here with the cases in which the lockout has been held unlawful because designed to frustrate organizational efforts, to destroy or undermine bargaining representation, or to evade the duty to bargain.

---

7. "Whipsawing" is the process of striking one at a time the employer members of a multi-employer association.

16. 61 Stat. 140, 29 U.S.C.A. § 158(d)(4) (no resort to "strike or lock-out" during 60-day notice period); 61 Stat. 153, 29 U.S.C.A. § 173(c) (Director of Mediation Service to seek to induce parties to settle dispute peacefully

"without resort to strike, lock-out, or other coercion"); 61 Stat. 155, 29 U.S.C.A. § 176 (appointment of board of inquiry by President when "threatened or actual strike or lock-out" creates a national emergency); 61 Stat. 155, 29 U.S.C.A. § 178 (power to enjoin "strike or lock-out" in case of national emergency).

Nor are we called upon to define the limits of the legitimate use of the lockout.[19] The narrow question to be decided is whether a temporary lockout may lawfully be used as a defense to a union strike tactic which threatens the destruction of the employers' interest in bargaining on a group basis.

The Court of Appeals rejected the preservation of the integrity of the multi-employer bargaining unit as a justification for an employer lockout. The court founded this conclusion upon its interpretation of the Taft-Hartley Act and its legislative history. After stating that "[m]ulti-employer bargaining has never received the express sanction of Congress," the court reasoned that because at the time of the enactment of the Taft-Hartley Act the Board had never "gone to the extreme lengths to which it now seeks to go in order to maintain the 'stability of the employer unit,' " Congress cannot be said to have given legislative approval to the present Board action. * * *[22]

We cannot subscribe to this interpretation. Multi-employer bargaining long antedated the Wagner Act, both in industries like the garment industry, characterized by numerous employers of small work forces, and in industries like longshoring and building construction, where workers change employers from day to day or week to week. This basis of bargaining has had its greatest expansion since enactment of the Wagner Act because employers have sought through group bargaining to match increased union strength.[23] Approximately four million employees are now governed by collective bargaining agreements signed by unions with thousands of employer associations.[24] At the time of the debates on the Taft-Hartley amendments, proposals were made to limit or outlaw multi-employer bargaining. These proposals failed of enactment. They were met with a storm of protest that their adoption would tend to weaken and not strengthen the process of collective bargaining and would conflict with the national labor policy of promoting industrial peace through effective collective bargaining.

The debates over the proposals demonstrate that Congress refused to interfere with such bargaining because there was cogent evidence that in many industries the multi-employer bargaining basis was a vital factor in

19. We thus find it unnecessary to pass upon the question whether, as a general proposition, the employer lockout is the corollary of the employees' statutory right to strike.

22. * * * The opinion of the Court of Appeals may be interpreted as rejecting employer solidarity as a justification for a lockout on the ground that the Union strike constituted a withdrawal by the Union from the multi-employer bargaining unit. The Court of Appeals vigorously argued that a union should be accorded the same freedom of voluntary withdrawal from a multi-employer bargaining unit as the Board has accorded to individual employers. But that question is not presented by this case, and we expressly reserve decision until it is properly before us. The facts here clearly show that the Union strike was not an attempt to withdraw from the multi-employer bargaining unit. On the contrary, the Union continued to carry on

negotiations with the Exchange until an agreement was reached and signed.

23. Bahrs, The San Francisco Employers' Council; Chamberlain, Collective Bargaining, 178–179, 180, 182; Freidin, The Taft-Hartley Act and Multi-Employer Bargaining, 4–5; Garrett and Tripp, Management Problems Implicit in Multi-Employer Bargaining, 2–3; Kerr and Randall, Collective Bargaining in the Pacific Coast Pulp and Paper Industry, 3–4; Pierson, Multi-Employer Bargaining, 35–36; Wolman, Industry-Wide Bargaining.

24. 79 Monthly Labor Review 805 (1956). Based on collective bargaining agreements on file with the Bureau of Labor Statistics in 1951, approximately 80% of the unionized employees in the laundry industry were represented under multi-employer bargaining. B.L.S.Rep. No. 1 (1953), Collective Bargaining Structures: The Employer Bargaining Unit, 10.

the effectuation of the national policy of promoting labor peace through strengthened collective bargaining. The inaction of Congress with respect to multi-employer bargaining cannot be said to indicate an intention to leave the resolution of this problem to future legislation. Rather, the compelling conclusion is that Congress intended "that the Board should continue its established administrative practice of certifying multi-employer units, and intended to leave to the Board's specialized judgment the inevitable questions concerning multi-employer bargaining bound to arise in the future." [26]

Although the Act protects the right of the employees to strike in support of their demands, this protection is not so absolute as to deny self-help by employers when legitimate interests of employees and employers collide. Conflict may arise, for example, between the right to strike and the interest of small employers in preserving multi-employer bargaining as a means of bargaining on an equal basis with a large union and avoiding the competitive disadvantages resulting from nonuniform contractual terms. The ultimate problem is the balancing of the conflicting legitimate interests. The function of striking that balance to effectuate national labor policy is often a difficult and delicate responsibility, which the Congress committed primarily to the National Labor Relations Board, subject to limited judicial review.

* * * We hold that in circumstances of this case the Board correctly balanced the conflicting interests in deciding that a temporary lockout to preserve the multi-employer bargaining basis from the disintegration threatened by the Union's strike action was lawful.

Reversed.

MR. JUSTICE WHITTAKER took no part in the consideration or decision of this case.

Note

1. What considerations might prompt an employer to want to bargain on a multi-employer basis rather than individually? How about a union?

2. Assuming the desirability of a multiemployer bargaining unit in a particular case, what is the statutory basis therefor? Is not the Court of Appeals' observation in Buffalo Linen (as quoted by Justice Brennan), that "[m]ulti-employer bargaining has never received the express sanction of Congress," supported by the language of Section 9(b) to the effect that the "unit appropriate for the purposes of collective bargaining shall be the employer unit, craft unit, plant unit, or subdivision thereof"? (See Note 3, supra p. 137.)

EVENING NEWS ASS'N
National Labor Relations Board, 1965.
154 N.L.R.B. 1494.
Enforced, 372 F.2d 569 (6th Cir.1967).

Respondents [The Evening News Association, publisher of "The Detroit News," and Knight Newspapers, Inc., publisher of "The Detroit Free Press"] have bargained with the Union on a multiemployer basis, through the [Detroit Newspaper Publishers] Association, for about 25 years. The most

26. 231 F.2d at page 121 (dissenting opinion).

recent collective-bargaining contract between Respondents and the Union was effective to February 29, 1964, subject to automatic renewal unless either party served written notice of a desire to modify the contract at least 60 days before the terminal date. On December 27, 1963, the Union wrote each Respondent that it desired to terminate the contract as of its expiration date and to conduct negotiations for new contracts on an individual employer basis. Respondents replied that they would bargain only for a multiemployer unit and refused the request for individual employer bargaining. The Trial Examiner found that, by this refusal to bargain individually, Respondents had violated Section 8(a)(5) and (1) of the National Labor Relations Act, as amended.

Under existing law, if either Respondent had unequivocally sought to withdraw from multiemployer bargaining before negotiations had begun, as the Union did in this case, it would unquestionably have been permitted to do so without being required to demonstrate "good reason" for its withdrawal, that "the community of interest shared for 25 years by employees of the multiemployer unit no longer exists," or that there had been any "substantive change in the composition or operations of the multiemployer unit," and "without regard to the desires of the employees in the unit." [4] An employer can withdraw from a multiemployer bargaining unit at will, provided only that the withdrawal request is made before the date set by the contract for modification, or before the agreed-upon date to begin the multiemployer negotiations, and the withdrawal is unequivocal. Given compliance with these two conditions, neither the employer's motive for withdrawal nor the impact of the withdrawal upon the bargaining representative or other employer members of the multiemployer bargaining unit is considered relevant. There can be no question that the Union's withdrawal in this case was both timely and unequivocal. The issue here, therefore, is whether the Board can or should adopt different, more restrictive, rules to govern a union's withdrawal from multiemployer units than now exist to govern employer withdrawals. * * *

In principle, there is no basis for different treatment of union and employer withdrawals from multiemployer bargaining units. The Board does not find a multiemployer unit appropriate except where all parties clearly agree to such a unit or where there has been a history of bargaining on a multiemployer basis and the employers and either the incumbent or a rival union desire to continue bargaining on such a basis. In the absence of either of these two factors, the Board will not find appropriate a unit covering employees of more than one employer, regardless of the desirability of such a unit. It is because the multiemployer unit is rooted in consent that the Board has always permitted an employer to withdraw from such a unit for any reason at a proper time and by giving proper notice. The Board has considered material to permitting withdrawal only the "time and manner" of the withdrawal request. If, as is apparent, the basis of multiemployer bargaining unit is both original and continuing consent by both parties, the Board cannot logically deny the bargaining representative the same opportu-

4. The quotations are from the dissenting opinion.

nity it allows employers of withdrawing from the multiemployer unit by withdrawing its consent to such unit.

Respondents argue that the positions of employers and unions participating in multiemployer bargaining are dissimilar, and therefore more restrictive rules should be applied to union withdrawals from such units than to employer withdrawals. The basis arguments offered in support of differential treatment reduce themselves, upon analysis, to the proposition that when a union withdraws from multiemployer bargaining, its strength vis a vis the employer is substantially enhanced, whereas when an employer withdraws, his position is weakened. Without passing on the factual validity of this argument, we note that bargaining power of either union or employer is not a criterion used to determine the appropriateness of a bargaining unit. Section 9(b) of the Act says only that the Board shall decide the appropriateness of a unit in terms of what will "assure to employees the fullest freedom in exercising the rights guaranteed by this Act * * *." The Act nowhere says that, in determining the appropriateness of a unit, the Board shall consider relative bargaining power of the parties to the proceeding. It is beyond dispute that the Board does not consider bargaining power in deciding whether a multiemployer unit should be found appropriate in the first instance. Bargaining power should not therefore be a test in determining whether a multiemployer unit once created should be retained against the desires of one of the parties. As stated by the Supreme Court.[11]

> "[Our labor policy does not] contain a charter for the National Labor Relations Board to act at large in equalizing disparities of bargaining power between employer and union."

As an aspect of the power argument, Respondents assert that if unions are permitted the same freedom as employers to withdraw from multiemployer bargaining units, unions will also be free to utilize the so-called "whipsaw strike" and the employers will be left without the right to use the counterbalancing defensive lockout allowable under the decision in N.L.R.B. v. Truck Drivers Local Union No. 449, Teamsters, 353 U.S. 87. Even if this were the only union motivation for seeking withdrawal from such units—a desire to exercise more effectively its strike weapon—we agree with the Trial Examiner that it would not provide a legitimate basis for preventing withdrawals. In any event, we have no occasion to decide at this time whether a union's withdrawal from multiemployer bargaining followed by its striking fewer than all of the former employer-members of the larger unit would effectively deny to the employers who are not struck the right to engage in a lockout. That question, among others concerning lockouts, remains to be decided in light of the recent relevant Supreme Court decisions.[12]

11. N.L.R.B. v. Insurance Agents' International Union, AFL–CIO (Prudential Ins. Co.), 361 U.S. 477, 490. The Supreme Court has more recently made the same point just as forcefully, stating that "the Act's provisions are not indefinitely elastic, content-free forms to be shaped in whatever manner the Board might think best conforms to the proper balance of bargaining power." American Ship Building Company v. N.L.R.B., 380 U.S. 300.

12. N.L.R.B. v. Brown, et al., d/b/a Brown Food Store, 380 U.S. 278; American Ship Building Company v. N.L.R.B., 380 U.S. 300 * * *.

* * * [T]he dissent would give a right to the employer to withdraw from the unit at will, and deny the same right to the union. It is this proposed inequality of treatment which is at the root of our disagreement with the dissent. * * * Unlike our dissenting colleague, we believe that the rules for withdrawal from multiemployer bargaining units should be the same for unions as for employers because, unlike the dissenter, we perceive no material difference in the impact on the employing entity and on the union flowing from an employer's withdrawal from a multiemployer unit, on the one hand, and the union's withdrawal, on the other hand. In either case, the withdrawing party forces the other to forego bargaining in the established multiemployer unit, and in either case, the union may be faced with the possibility of having to demonstrate that it has been designated by a majority of the employees in the individual employer units resulting from the breakup of the multiemployer unit, if it is to retain its status as the bargaining representative of such employees.

* * * Unions, like employers, would understandably be reluctant to initiate multiemployer bargaining if the decision to do so were virtually irrevocable. Restricting union withdrawal might therefore in fact discourage multiemployer bargaining and not encourage it. Moreover, if a union remains bound to a multiemployer unit with which it has become dissatisfied while the employers are free to withdraw, the union's only recourse then is to seek to stimulate employer withdrawals in order to fragment the unit; e.g., by framing and insisting on demands which are far less acceptable to some employers than to others. Inequality of freedom to withdraw thus could become a means of producing, not stability, but friction and instability in the bargaining unit.

* * * As the notice of withdrawal served by the Union on Respondents would have been sufficient, if served by Respondents upon the Union, to terminate the obligation to bargain upon a multiemployer basis, we find that it had the same effect in this case, and that by Respondents' refusal thereafter to bargain individually and separately with the Union, the Respondents each violated Section 8(a)(5) and (1) of the Act.

[The dissenting opinion of Member Brown is omitted.]

Note

1. Should relative bargaining power be taken into account in the process of determining bargaining units? Or would this constitute an objectionable government thumb on the "free collective bargaining" scales?

2. What is the justification for laying down, as in Evening News, any formal requirements for union (or employer) withdrawal from multiemployer bargaining? Would it be preferable to permit union withdrawal by the mere calling of a whipsaw strike, as suggested by the Court of Appeals in Buffalo Linen (see footnote 22, supra p. 230)? May it fairly be said that in Buffalo Linen the union was trying to eat its cake and have it, too?

A related question was raised in Charles D. Bonanno Linen Service, Inc. v. NLRB, 454 U.S. 404, 102 S.Ct. 720, 70 L.Ed.2d 656 (1982): May an employer withdraw from a multiemployer unit once an impasse in bargaining has been reached. A divided Court held that it could not, agreeing with the Board that:

"Once negotiation for a new contract has commenced * * * withdrawal is permitted only if there is 'mutual consent' or 'unusual circumstances' exist * * *. [U]nusual circumstances will be found where an employer is subject to extreme financial pressure or a bargaining unit has become substantially fragmented * * *. [A]n impasse is not such an unusual circumstance * * *. [A] recurring feature in the bargaining process, impasse is only a temporary deadlock or hiatus in negotiations which in almost all cases is eventually broken either through a change of mind or the application of economic force * * *. Furthermore, an impasse may be brought about intentionally by one or both parties as a device to further, rather than destroy, the bargaining process * * *. [P]ermitting withdrawal at impasse would as a practical matter undermine the utility of multiemployer bargaining [because the parties would have to bargain under the threat of potential withdrawal by any party who was not completely satisfied with the results of the negotiations, thereby negating the stable, predictable bargaining relationship most needed at that point]." 454 U.S. at 411–12, 102 S.Ct. at 724–25, 70 L.Ed. at 663–64.

3. The question raised in footnote 19 of the Buffalo Linen case (supra p. 230), as to "whether, as a general proposition, the employer lockout is the corollary of the employees' statutory right to strike," has been further litigated, in one facet or another, in subsequent cases, including the two cited in footnote 12 of Evening News. These cases are considered in Chapter 6, infra.

LEEDOM v. KYNE

Supreme Court of the United States, 1958.
358 U.S. 184, 79 Sup.Ct. 180, 3 L.Ed.2d 210.

Mr. Justice Whittaker delivered the opinion of the Court.

Section 9(b)(1) of the National Labor Relations Act * * * provides that, in determining the unit appropriate for collective bargaining purposes, "the Board shall not (1) decide that any unit is appropriate for such purposes if such unit includes both professional employees and employees who are not professional employees unless a majority of such professional employees vote for inclusion in such unit." The Board, after refusing to take a vote among the professional employees to determine whether a majority of them would "vote for inclusion in such unit," included both professional and nonprofessional employees in the bargaining unit that it found appropriate. The sole and narrow question presented is whether a Federal District Court has jurisdiction of an original suit to vacate that determination of the Board because made in excess of its powers.

The facts are undisputed. Buffalo Section, Westinghouse Engineers Association, Engineers and Scientists of America, a voluntary unincorporated labor organization, hereafter called the Association, was created for the purpose of promoting the economic and professional status of the nonsupervisory professional employees of Westinghouse Electric Corporation at its plant in Cheektowaga, New York through collective bargaining with their employer. In October 1955, the Association petitioned the National Labor Relations Board for certification as the exclusive collective bargaining agent of all nonsupervisory professional employees, being then 233 in number, of the Westinghouse Company at its Cheektowaga plant * * *. A hearing was held by the Board upon that petition. A competing labor organization was permitted by the Board to intervene. It asked the Board to expand the unit to include employees in five other categories who performed technical work and were thought by it to be "professional employees" within the meaning of § 2(12) of the Act * * *. The Board found that they were not professional employees within the meaning of the Act. However, it found that nine employees in three of those categories should nevertheless be included in the unit because they "share a close community of employment interests with [the professional employees, and their inclusion would not] destroy the predominantly professional character of such a unit." The Board, after denying the Association's request to take a vote among the professional employees to determine whether a majority of them favored "inclusion in such unit," included the 233 professional employees and the nine nonprofessional employees in the unit and directed an election to determine whether they desired to be represented by the Association, by the other labor organization, or by neither. The Association moved the Board to stay the election and to amend its decision by excluding the nonprofessional employees from the unit. The Board denied that motion and went ahead with the election at which the Association received a majority of the valid votes cast and was thereafter certified by the Board as the collective bargaining agent for the unit.

Thereafter respondent, individually, and as president of the Association, brought this suit in the District Court against the members of the Board, alleging the foregoing facts and asserting that the Board had exceeded its statutory power in including the professional employees, without their consent, in a unit with nonprofessional employees in violation of § 9(b)(1) which commands that the Board "shall not" do so, and praying, among other things, that the Board's action be set aside. The defendants, members of the Board, moved to dismiss for want of jurisdiction and, in the alternative, for a summary judgment. The plaintiff also moved for summary judgment. The trial court found that the Board had disobeyed the express command of § 9(b)(1) in including nonprofessional employees and professional employees in the same unit without the latter's consent, and in doing so had acted in excess of its powers to the injury of the professional employees, and that the court had jurisdiction to grant the relief prayed. It accordingly denied the Board's motion and granted the plaintiff's motion and entered judgment setting aside the Board's determination of the bargaining unit and also the election and the Board's certification. 148 F.Supp. 597.

On the Board's appeal it did not contest the trial court's conclusion that the Board, in commingling professional with nonprofessional employees in the unit, had acted in excess of its powers and had thereby worked injury to the statutory rights of the professional employees. Instead, it contended only that the District Court lacked jurisdiction to entertain the suit. The Court of Appeals held that the District Court did have jurisdiction and affirmed its judgment. 101 App.D.C. 398, 249 F.2d 490. * * *

Petitioners, members of the Board, concede here that the District Court had jurisdiction of the suit under § 24(8) of the Judicial Code, 28 U.S.C.A. § 1337, unless the review provisions of the National Labor Relations Act destroyed it. In American Federation of Labor v. National Labor Relations Board, 308 U.S. 401, 60 S.Ct. 300, 303, 84 L.Ed. 347, this Court held that a

Board order in certification proceedings under § 9 is not "a final order" and therefore is not subject to judicial review except as it may be drawn in question by a petition for enforcement or review of an order, made under § 10(c) of the Act, restraining an unfair labor practice. But the Court was at pains to point out in that case that "[t]he question [there presented was] distinct from * * * whether petitioners are precluded by the provisions of the Wagner Act from maintaining an independent suit in a district court to set aside the Board's action because contrary to the statute * * *." Id., 308 U.S. at page 404, 60 S.Ct. at page 302. The Board argued there, as it does here, that the provisions of the Act, particularly § 9(d), have foreclosed review of its action by an original suit in a District Court. This Court said: "But that question is not presented for decision by the record before us. Its answer involves a determination whether the Wagner Act, in so far as it has given legally enforceable rights, has deprived the district courts of some portion of their original jurisdiction conferred by § 24 of the Judicial Code. It can be appropriately answered only upon a showing in such a suit that unlawful action of the Board has inflicted an injury on the petitioners for which the law, *apart from the review provisions of the Wagner Act,* affords a remedy. This question can be properly and adequately considered only when it is brought to us for review upon a suitable record." Id., 308 U.S. at page 412, 60 S.Ct. at page 305. (Emphasis added.)

The record in this case squarely presents the question found not to have been presented by the record in American Federation of Labor v. National Labor Relations Board, supra. This case, in this posture before us, involves "unlawful action of the Board [which] has inflicted an injury on the [respondent]." Does the law, "apart from the review provisions of the * * * Act," afford a remedy? We think the answer surely must be yes. This suit is not one to "review," in the sense of that term as used in the Act, a decision of the Board made within its jurisdiction. Rather it is one to strike down an order of the Board made in excess of its delegated powers and contrary to a specific prohibition in the Act. Section 9(b)(1) is clear and mandatory. It says that, in determining the unit appropriate for the purposes of collective bargaining, "the Board *shall not* (1) decide that any unit is appropriate for such purposes if such unit includes both professional employees and employees who are not professional employees unless a majority of such professional employees vote for inclusion in such unit." (Emphasis added.) Yet the Board included in the unit employees whom it found were not professional employees, after refusing to determine whether a majority of the professional employees would "vote for inclusion in such unit." Plainly, this was an attempted exercise of power that had been specifically withheld. It deprived the professional employees of a "right" assured to them by Congress. * * *

Where, as here, Congress has given a "right" to the professional employees it must be held that it intended that right to be enforced, and "the courts * * * encounter no difficulty in fulfilling its purpose." Texas & New Orleans R. Co. v. Brotherhood of Railway & S.S. Clerks, * * * 281 U.S. at page 568, 50 S.Ct. at page 433.

The Court of Appeals was right in holding, in the circumstances of this case, that the District Court had jurisdiction of this suit, and its judgment is affirmed. * * *

[The dissenting opinion of JUSTICE BRENNAN, whom JUSTICE FRANKFURTER joined, is omitted. It reiterated the policy considerations which moved Congress to limit judicial review of Board determinations in representation cases under Section 9. These considerations are expressed in the Court's opinion in AFL v. NLRB, page 132, supra. Simply stated, what they entail is the desire to preclude the delaying of the initiation of collective bargaining through dilatory challenges of Board certifications of collective bargaining representatives. The dissent found this rationale of AFL v. NLRB just as controlling in an independent action in a federal district court under Section 24(8) of the Judicial Code as in direct review proceedings in a court of appeals. "The Court today opens a gaping hole in this congressional wall," the dissent stated, adding: "There is nothing in the legislative history to indicate that the Congress intended any exception from the requirement that collective bargaining begin without awaiting judicial review of a Board certification or the investigation preceding it. Certainly nothing appears that an exception was intended where the attack upon the Board's action is based upon an alleged misinterpretation of the statute."]

Note

1. Was the Board wise in not contesting the trial court's conclusion that the Board had acted in excess of its powers? How would you have argued the Board's case?

2. Under Leedom v. Kyne, could the union which was denied craft severance in National Tube secure judicial review of the Board's interpretation of Section 9(b)(2) through an independent action in a federal district court? Is this the "gaping hole" referred to by the dissent?

At least some of the "gape" was closed in BOIRE v. GREYHOUND CORP., 376 U.S. 473, 84 S.Ct. 894, 11 L.Ed.2d 849 (1964). Floors, Inc., a corporation engaged in the business of providing maintenance services, had contracted with Greyhound to provide such services at four of Greyhound's terminals in Florida. A union filed a petition under Section 9(c), requesting a representation election among the porters, janitors, and maids who performed these maintenance services. The Board, concluding (1) that Greyhound and Floors were joint employers because they exercised common control over the employees, and (2) that the employees under the joint-employer relationship constituted an appropriate unit, directed an election to determine whether the employees desired to be represented by the union. Greyhound thereupon sued the NLRB Regional Director in a federal district court to set aside the decision of the Board and to enjoin the pending election. The court permanently enjoined the election, holding that the Board's findings were insufficient as a matter of law to establish a joint-employer relationship, that Floors was as a matter of law the sole employer, and that the board had therefore violated the Act by directing the aforesaid election. The court of appeals affirmed. The Supreme Court reversed, stating:

"* * * The argument is * * * that the present case is one which falls within the narrow limits of Kyne, as the District Court and the Court of Appeals held. The respondent points out that Congress has specifically excluded an independent contractor from the definition of 'employee' in § 2(3) of the Act. It is said that the Board's finding that Greyhound is an employer of employees who are hired, paid, transferred and promoted by an independent contractor is, therefore, plainly in excess of the statutory powers delegated to it by Congress. This argument, we think, misconceives both the import of the substantive federal law and the painstakingly delineated procedural boundaries of Kyne.

" * * * [W]hether Greyhound possessed sufficient indicia of control to be an 'employer' is essentially a factual issue, unlike the question in Kyne, which depended solely upon construction of the statute. The Kyne exception is a narrow one, not to be extended to permit plenary district court review of Board orders in certification proceedings whenever it can be said that an erroneous assessment of the particular facts before the Board has led it to a conclusion which does not comport with the law. Judicial review in such a situation has been limited by Congress to the courts of appeals, and then only under the conditions explicitly laid down in § 9(d) of the Act." 376 U.S. at 481–82, 84 S.Ct. at 898–99.

Leedom v. Kyne, Boire v. Greyhound, and other relevant cases are thoroughly analyzed in Goldberg, District Court Review of NLRB Representation Proceedings, 42 Ind.L.J. 455 (1967).

CONCLUDING COMMENT ON UNIT QUESTIONS

The fundamental principle of exclusive representation in the American scheme of collective bargaining in turn makes unit determination fundamental. Questions of the appropriateness of the bargaining unit are therefore threshold questions in that scheme.

Since collective bargaining is largely an institution for the consensual resolution of employer-employee conflict, it follows that unit determination by agreement of the parties themselves is the most desirable resolution. Many unit disputes are in fact resolved in this manner, with little or no Board involvement. Those which cannot be so resolved, and therefore come to the Board for decision, fall into typical categories. Several of these categories we have already encountered: plant versus multiplant (Pacific Intermountain), craft versus industrial (National Tube), single versus multiemployer (AFL v. NLRB, Buffalo Linen, Evening News), professional versus nonprofessional (Leedom v. Kyne).

Another variety of unit question may be characterized as "geographic" in nature. This type of problem is encountered, for example, in the insurance and chain-store industries. Two factors which distinguish these industries are (1) the way in which they are geographically dispersed, (2) the echelonned character of their management. In the insurance industry, for example, there may be a national office, regional office, state office, metropolitan-area office, district office, suburban and other local offices. Varying degrees of administrative authority may be held by management at each level of the structure. Dependent upon the mix of these factors, units appropriate for collective bargaining may be any of the following: nationwide, regional, statewide, metropolitan area, local district. For a case history providing further insight into much of the foregoing, see Metropolitan Life Insurance Co. v. NLRB, 327 F.2d 906 (1st Cir. 1964), NLRB v. Metropolitan Life Insurance Co., 380 U.S. 438, 85 S.Ct. 1061, 13 L.Ed.2d 951 (1965), Metropolitan Life Insurance Co., 156 N.L.R.B. 1408 (1966).

C. EMPLOYER CONDUCT IMPAIRING THE RIGHT TO ORGANIZE

EDWARD G. BUDD MFG. CO. v. NATIONAL LABOR RELATIONS BOARD

United States Court of Appeals, Third Circuit, 1943.
138 F.2d 86.

Certiorari denied, 321 U.S. 778 (1943).

BIGGS, CIRCUIT JUDGE. On charges filed by International Union, United Automobile, Aircraft and Agricultural Workers of America, an affiliate of the Congress of Industrial Organizations, with the National Labor Relations Board, a complaint issued dated November 26, 1941, alleging that the petitioner was engaging in unfair labor practices within the meaning of Section 8(1), (2), (3) of the National Labor Relations Act * * *. The complaint, as subsequently amended, alleges that the petitioner, in September, 1933, created and foisted a labor organization, known as the Budd Employee Representation Association, upon its employees and thereafter contributed financial support to the Association and dominated its activities. The amended complaint also alleges that in July, 1941, the petitioner discharged an employee, Walter Weigand, because of his activities on behalf of the union * * *. After extensive hearings before a trial examiner the Board on June 10, 1942 issued its decision and order, requiring the disestablishment of the Association and the reinstatement of Weigand * * *.

The case of Walter Weigand is extraordinary. If ever a workman deserved summary discharge it was he. He was under the influence of liquor while on duty. He came to work when he chose and he left the plant and his shift as he pleased. In fact, a foreman on one occasion was agreeably surprised to find Weigand at work and commented upon it. Weigand amiably stated that he was enjoying it.[6] He brought a woman (apparently generally known as the "Duchess") to the rear of the plant yard and introduced some of the employees to her. He took another employee to visit her and when this man got too drunk to be able to go home, punched his time-card for him and put him on the table in the representatives' meeting room in the plant in order to sleep off his intoxication. Weigand's immediate superiors demanded again and again that he be discharged, but each time higher officials intervened on Weigand's behalf because as was naively stated he was "a representative" [of the Association, determined by the Board in the omitted part of the opinion to be a "dominated" labor organization within the meaning of Section 8(2)]. In return for not working at the job for which he was hired, the petitioner gave him full pay and on five separate occasions raised his wages. One of these raises was general; that is to say, Weigand profited by a general wage increase throughout the plant, but the other four raises were given Weigand at times when other employees in the plant did not receive wage increases.

The petitioner contends that Weigand was discharged because of cumulative grievances against him. But about the time of the discharge it was

6. Weigand stated that he was carried on the payroll as a "rigger". He was asked what was a rigger. He replied: "I don't know; I am not a rigger."

suspected by some of the representatives that Weigand had joined the complaining CIO union. One of the representatives taxed him with this fact and Weigand offered to bet a hundred dollars that it could not be proven. On July 22, 1941 Weigand did disclose his union membership to the vice-chairman (Rattigan) of the Association and to another representative (Mullen) and apparently tried to persuade them to support the union. Weigand asserts that the next day he with Rattigan and Mullen, were seen talking to CIO organizer Reichwein on a street corner. The following day, according to Weigand's testimony, Mullen came to Weigand at the plant and stated that Weigand, Rattigan and himself had been seen talking to Reichwein and that he, Mullen, had just had an interview with Personnel Director McIlvain and Plant Manager Mahan. According to Weigand, Mullen said to him, "Maybe you didn't get me in a jam." And, "We were seen down there." The following day Weigand was discharged.

* * * [A]n employer may discharge an employee for a good reason, a poor reason or no reason at all so long as the provisions of the National Labor Relations Act are not violated. It is, of course, a violation to discharge an employee because he has engaged in activities on behalf of a union. Conversely an employer may retain an employee for a good reason, a bad reason or no reason at all and the reason is not a concern of the Board. But it is certainly too great a strain on our credulity to assert, as does the petitioner, that Weigand was discharged for an accumulation of offenses. We think that he was discharged because his work on behalf of the CIO had become known to the plant manager. That ended his sinecure at the Budd plant. The Board found that he was discharged because of his activities on behalf of the union. The record shows that the Board's finding was based on sufficient evidence.

The order of the Board will be enforced.

Note

1. Suppose Walter Weigand's discharge had been found by the Trial Examiner and the Board to have been motivated, in fact, by his poor work record. Would there then have been a violation of Section 8(3) (now 8(a)(3))? What are the elements of an 8(a)(3) violation? If the elements of an 8(a)(3) violation are (1) discrimination in regard to hire, tenure, or any term or condition of employment, (2) which encourages or discourages union membership, are not these elements present where an employee actively organizing for a union is discharged for incompetence?

If it were not clear as to why Walter Weigand had been discharged—whether for his CIO activities or for his poor work record—the allocation of the burdens of proof might be dispositive of his case. The problems presented in this commonly encountered discharge situation are discussed in Chapter 6, Section A, infra, most specifically in the Transportation Management case, p. 539.

2. In the Budd case a violation of Section 8(1) (now 8(a)(1)) was also found. Does a violation of 8(a)(3) necessarily entail a derivative violation of 8(a)(1)?

3. The part of the opinion discussing the Section 8(2) (now 8(a)(2)) violation has been omitted in the report of the Budd case. What conduct do you suppose constituted this violation?

4. What remedy should Walter Weigand receive from the Budd Manufacturing Company for his illegal discharge? He was terminated in July of 1941 and the case was finally decided in 1943. Remedies in such situations are described in 2 C. Morris, The Developing Labor Law 1657–1661 (2d ed. 1983) (supporting citations omitted):

> " * * * In the typical discrimination case, where an employee is discharged for union activity * * *, the Board normally orders reinstatement of the employee, with back pay, and issues a cease-and-desist order proscribing similar misconduct in the future. The Board also requires the posting of a notice in which the employer states that it will not engage in future unlawful activity and will comply with the affirmative action ordered. * * *

> "The make-whole provison of the back-pay order covers not only wages but also, where appropriate, other emoluments of employment, including vacation benefits, bonuses, shares in profit-sharing programs, pension coverage, health and medical coverage, employee-owned housing, and employee discounts on purchases. [The Board also requires the payment of interest on back pay found to be owing.] * * *

> "The Board deducts interim earnings from the back-pay award. * * *

> "As a corollary to the principle that interim earnings are deducted, the Board has held that back pay will not run during periods when the employee willfully chose not to seek interim earnings; thus, the employee must make a reasonable effort to secure and retain interim employment. However, the employee need not go beyond 'reasonable exertions' in an effort to mitigate back-pay liability. * * * "

NATIONAL LABOR RELATIONS BOARD v. BURNUP AND SIMS, INC.

Supreme Court of the United States, 1964.
379 U.S. 21, 85 S.Ct. 171, 13 L.Ed.2d 1.

MR. JUSTICE DOUGLAS delivered the opinion of the Court.

Two employees in respondent's plant, Davis and Harmon, undertook to organize the employees who worked there. The Superintendent was advised by another employee, one Pate, that Davis and Harmon while soliciting him for membership in the union, had told him the union would use dynamite to get in if the union did not acquire the authorizations. Respondent thereafter discharged Davis and Harmon because of these alleged statements. An unfair labor practice proceeding was brought. The Board held that the discharges violated §§ 8(a)(1) and 8(a)(3) of the Act * * *. It found that Pate's charges against Davis and Harmon were untrue and that they had actually made no threats against the company's property; and it concluded that respondent's honest belief in the truth of the statement was not a defense. 137 N.L.R.B. 766, 772–773.

The Court of Appeals refused reinstatement of Davis and Harmon, holding that since the employer acted in good faith, the discharges were not unlawful. 322 F.2d 57. We granted the petition for certiorari because of a conflict among the Circuits. Cf. with the opinion below National Labor Relations Board v. Industrial Cotton Mills, 4 Cir., 208 F.2d 87, 45 A.L.R.2d

880; National Labor Relations Board v. Cambria Clay Products Co., 6 Cir., 215 F.2d 48; Cusano v. National Labor Relations Board, 3 Cir., 190 F.2d 898.

We find it unnecessary to reach the questions raised under § 8(a)(3) for we are of the view that in the context of this record § 8(a)(1) was plainly violated, whatever the employer's motive. Section 7 grants employees, *inter alia,* "the right to self-organization, to form, join, or assist labor organizations." Defeat of those rights by employer action does not necessarily depend on the existence of an anti-union bias. Over and again the Board has ruled that § 8(a)(1) is violated if an employee is discharged for misconduct arising out of a protected activity, despite the employer's good faith, when it is shown that the misconduct never occurred. See, e.g., Mid-Continent Petroleum Corp., 54 N.L.R.B. 912, 932–934; Standard Oil Co., 91 N.L.R.B. 783, 790–791; Rubin Bros. Footwear, Inc., 99 N.L.R.B. 610, 611.[3] In sum, § 8(a)(1) is violated if it is shown that the discharged employee was at the time engaged in a protected activity, that the employer knew it was such, that the basis of the discharge was an alleged act of misconduct in the course of that activity, and that the employee was not, in fact, guilty of that misconduct.

That rule seems to us to be in conformity with the policy behind § 8(a)(1). Otherwise the protected activity would lose some of its immunity, since the example of employees who are discharged on false charges would or might have a deterrent effect on other employees. Union activity often engenders strong emotions and gives rise to active rumors. A protected activity acquires a precarious status if innocent employees can be discharged while engaging in it, even though the employer acts in good faith. It is the tendency of those discharges to weaken or destroy the § 8(a)(1) right that is controlling. We are not in the realm of managerial prerogatives. Rather we are concerned with the manner of soliciting union membership over which the Board has been entrusted with powers of surveillance. See International Ladies' Garment Workers' Union, AFL–CIO v. National Labor Relations Board, 366 U.S. 731, 738–739, 81 S.Ct. 1603, 1607–1608, 6 L.Ed.2d 762; National Labor Relations Board v. Erie Resistor Corp., 373 U.S. 221, 228–229, 83 S.Ct. 1139, 1145–1146, 10 L.Ed.2d 308. Had the alleged dynamiting threats been wholly disassociated from § 7 activities quite different considerations might apply.

Reversed.

MR. JUSTICE HARLAN, concurring in part and dissenting in part.

Both the rule adopted by the lower court and that now announced by this Court seem to me unacceptable. On the one hand, it impinges on the rights assured by §§ 7 and 8(a)(1) to hold, as the Court of Appeals did, that the employee must bear the entire brunt of his honest, but mistaken, discharge. On the other hand, it is hardly fair that the employer should be faced with the choice of risking damage to his business or incurring a penalty for taking honest action to thwart it.

---

3. The Rubin Bros. case made a qualification as to burden of proof. Prior thereto the burden was on the employer to prove that the discharged employee was in fact guilty of the misconduct. Rubin Bros. said that "once such an honest belief is established, the General Counsel must go forward with evidence to prove that the employees did not, in fact, engage in such misconduct." 99 N.L.R.B., at 611.

Between these two one-way streets lies a middle two-way course: a rule which would require reinstatement of the mistakenly discharged employee and back pay only as of the time that the employer learned, or should have learned, of his mistake, subject, however, to a valid business reason for refusing reinstatement.[1] Such a rule gives offense neither to any policy of the statute nor to the dictates of fairness to the employer, and in my opinion represents a reasonable accommodation between the two inflexible points of view evinced by the opinions below and here.

* * * I would vacate the judgment of the Court of Appeals and remand the case to the Board for further appropriate proceedings in light of what I believe to be the proper rule.

Note

1. Why did the Court "find it unnecessary to reach the questions raised under § 8(a)(3)," discrimination as to "tenure of employment" being clearly involved? To what extent is scienter (antiunion or antistatute state of mind) a requisite for employer liability under Section 8(a)(3)? Suppose an employer knows that his discharge of a union organizer will discourage union membership. Does he thereby have the violative state of mind? Consider the following:

"* * * Clear analysis requires that intent and motive be segregated with respect to 8(a)(3) in view of the Court's reliance upon the 'common-law rule that a man is held to intend the foreseeable consequences of his conduct,' a reliance first announced as to 8(a)(3) in [Radio Officers' Union v. NLRB, 347 U.S. 17, 74 S.Ct. 323, 98 L.Ed. 455 (1954)] and reiterated in [NLRB v. Erie Resistor Corp., 373 U.S. 221, 83 S.Ct. 1139, 10 L.Ed.2d 308 (1963)] and [NLRB v. Brown, 380 U.S. 278, 85 S.Ct. 980, 13 L.Ed.2d 839 (1965)].

"This common-law rule applies most classically to cases such as this: *A* points a gun which he knows to be loaded at a vital part of *B*'s anatomy and pulls the trigger, killing *B*. From this, without more, it may be presumed that A intended to kill *B*. However, it is open to A to seek to 'explain away' or 'justify' his act by showing, for example, that he shot in self-defense. If *A*'s motive *was* self-defense, then his intentional killing of B is justified or privileged; *A* has committed no offense.

"Similarly, if an employer discharges an employee who is actively engaged in seeking to organize the employer's plant, the employer may be presumed to *intend* to discourage union membership, since the latter follows not only foreseeably but, it would seem, inescapably from the employer's act, however much he might regret it, because of the loss of union leadership and the fear and suspicion generated among his employees. However, if the real *motive* for the discharge is shown to be a breach of shop rules by the employee, the discouragement of union membership is justified or privileged; the employer has committed no offense, despite the unavoidable, and hence *intended* (pursuant to the common-law presumption), consequence of discouraging union membership. * * *

"If the analogy to the common-law rule, as classically illustrated in the deadly-weapon example, is to hold true, the burden should fall upon the employer at least to raise the issue of his justifying motive by the presenta-

---

1. As for example, if a replacement had been hired and the discharged employee undu- ly delayed in apprising the employer of the mistake.

tion of supporting evidence. Otherwise the trier of fact (the Board) is entitled to find against him on the basis of what is at minimum a prima facie case." Oberer, The Scienter Factor in Sections 8(a)(1) and (3) of the Labor Act: Of Balancing, Hostile Motive, Dogs and Tails, 52 Cornell L.Q. 491, 505–06 (1967).

2. In Burnup and Sims the Court by-passed Section 8(a)(3) and its motive requirement by focusing upon Section 8(a)(1). The latter, the Court said, "was plainly violated, whatever the employer's motive. Section 7 grants employees, *inter alia,* 'the right to self-organization, to form, join, or assist labor organizations.' Defeat of those rights by employer action does not necessarily depend on the existence of an anti-union bias." This position gives rise to a question of sticky enough character never to have been squarely confronted by the Court: If a showing of X *plus* scienter is necessary to establish a violation of Section 8(a)(3) but a showing of X *alone* establishes a violation of Section 8(a)(1), is Section 8(a) (3) thus read out of the Act?

> "What we have in section 8(a)(1) is a blanket provision which protects all of the employee rights of section 7 against everything which the following four subdivisions of 8(a) more specifically protect against, and, in addition, affords independent protection against employer offenses not specifically covered by any of the other four subdivisions. When any one of the other four subdivisions is violated, 8(a)(1) is also violated; but a violation of 8(a)(1) does not necessarily entail a violation of any other subdivision.

> "A moment's reflection will demonstrate the problem of redundancy here. Either 8(a)(1) occupies the field, in which event, once its contours are established, the other four subdivisions become irrelevant, or each of the other four occupies its particular field, in which event 8(a)(1) becomes irrelevant in the areas of overlap. Neither of these alternatives has, as yet, established supremacy. Instead, the NLRB and the courts have rocked along in a kind of non-definitive approach to the line of demarcation between the blanket provision of 8(a)(1) and the narrower ambit of the other four subdivisions." Oberer, supra note 1, at 493–94 (1967).

3. In Phelps Dodge Corp. v. NLRB, 313 U.S. 177, 61 S.Ct. 845, 85 L.Ed. 1271 (1941), the Court held that the protection of Section 8[(a)] (3) reaches those who are not yet employed but merely seeking employment. *In*statement with back pay was granted to the discriminatees despite the provision in Section 10(c) empowering the Board to order "such affirmative action, including *re*instatement of employees with or without back pay, as will effectuate the policies of this Act." The "including" clause was held to be illustrative rather than restrictive. "Discrimination against union labor in the hiring of men is a dam to self-organization at the source of supply." 313 U.S. at 185, 61 S.Ct. at 848.

REPUBLIC AVIATION CORP. v. NATIONAL LABOR RELATIONS BOARD

Supreme Court of the United States, 1945.
324 U.S. 793, 65 S.Ct. 982, 89 L.Ed. 1372, 157 A.L.R. 1081.

MR. JUSTICE REED delivered the opinion of the Court.

In the Republic Aviation Corporation case, the employer, a large and rapidly growing military aircraft manufacturer, adopted, well before any union activity at the plant, a general rule against soliciting which read as follows:

"Soliciting of any type cannot be permitted in the factory or offices."

The Republic plant was located in a built-up section of Suffolk County, New York. An employee persisted after being warned of the rule in soliciting union membership in the plant by passing out application cards to employees on his own time during lunch periods. The employee was discharged for infraction of the rule and, as the National Labor Relations Board found, without discrimination on the part of the employer toward union activity.

Three other employees were discharged for wearing UAW–CIO union steward buttons in the plant after being requested to remove the insignia. The union was at that time active in seeking to organize the plant. The reason which the employer gave for the request was that as the union was not then the duly designated representative of the employees, the wearing of the steward buttons in the plant indicated an acknowledgment by the management of the authority of the stewards to represent the employees in dealing with the management and might impinge upon the employer's policy of strict neutrality in union matters and might interfere with the existing grievance system of the corporation.

The Board was of the view that wearing union steward buttons by employees did not carry any implication of recognition of that union by the employer where, as here, there was no competing labor organization in the plant. The discharges of the stewards, however, were found not to be motivated by opposition to the particular union, or we deduce, to unionism.

The Board determined that the promulgation and enforcement of the "no solicitation" rule violated Section 8(1) of the National Labor Relations Act as it interfered with, restrained and coerced employees in their rights under Section 7 and discriminated against the discharged employee under Section 8(3). It determined also that the discharge of the stewards violated Section 8(1) and 8(3). As a consequence of its conclusions as to the solicitation and the wearing of the insignia, the Board entered the usual cease and desist order and directed the reinstatement of the discharged employees with back pay and also the rescission of "the rule against solicitation in so far as it prohibits union activity and solicitation on company property during the employees' own time." 51 N.L.R.B. 1186, 1189. The Circuit Court of Appeals for the Second Circuit affirmed, 142 F.2d 193 * * *.

In the case of Le Tourneau Company of Georgia, two employees were suspended two days each for distributing union literature or circulars on the employees' own time on company owned and policed parking lots, adjacent to the company's fenced-in plant, in violation of a long standing and strictly enforced rule, adopted prior to union organization activity about the premises, which read as follows:

"In the future no Merchants, Concern, Company or Individual or Individuals will be permitted to distribute, post or otherwise circulate handbills or posters, or any literature of any description on company property without first securing permission from the Personnel Department."

The rule was adopted to control littering and petty pilfering from parked autos by distributors. The Board determined that there was no union bias or discrimination by the company in enforcing the rule.

The company's plant for the manufacture of earth moving machinery and other products for the war is in the country on a six thousand acre tract. The plant is bisected by one public road and built along another. There is one hundred feet of company-owned land for parking or other use between the highways and the employee entrances to the fenced enclosures where the work is done, so that contact on public ways or on non-company property with employees at or about the establishment is limited to those employees, less than 800 out of 2100, who are likely to walk across the public highway near the plant on their way to work, or to those employees who will stop their private automobiles, buses or other conveyances on the public roads for communications. The employees' dwellings are widely scattered.

The Board found that the application of the rule to the distribution of union literature by the employees on company property which resulted in the lay-offs was an unfair labor practice under Sections 8(1) and 8(3). Cease and desist, and rule rescission orders, with directions to pay the employees for their lost time followed. 54 N.L.R.B. 1253. The Circuit Court of Appeals for the Fifth Circuit reversed the Board, 143 F.2d 67 * * *.

These cases bring here for review the action of the National Labor Relations Board in working out an adjustment between the undisputed right of self-organization assured to employees under the Wagner Act and the equally undisputed right of employers to maintain discipline in their establishments. Like so many others, these rights are not unlimited in the sense that they can be exercised without regard to any duty which the existence of rights in others may place upon employer or employee. Opportunity to organize and proper discipline are both essential elements in a balanced society.

The Wagner Act did not undertake the impossible task of specifying in precise and unmistakable language each incident which would constitute an unfair labor practice. On the contrary that Act left to the Board the work of applying the Act's general prohibitory language in the light of the infinite combinations of events which might be charged as violative of its terms. Thus a "rigid scheme of remedies" is avoided and administrative flexibility within appropriate statutory limitations obtained to accomplish the dominant purpose of the legislation. * * * So far as we are here concerned that purpose is the right of employees to organize for mutual aid without employer interference. This is the principle of labor relations which the Board is to foster.

The gravamen of the objection of both Republic and Le Tourneau to the Board's orders is that they rest on a policy formulated without due administrative procedure. To be more specific it is that the Board cannot substitute its knowledge of industrial relations for substantive evidence. The contention is that there must be evidence before the Board to show that the rules and orders of the employers interfered with and discouraged union organization in the circumstances and situation of each company. Neither in the Republic nor the Le Tourneau cases can it properly be said that there was evidence or a finding that the plant's physical location made solicitation away from company property ineffective to reach prospective union members. Neither of these is like a mining or lumber camp where the employees pass their rest as well as their work time on the employer's premises, so that union organization must proceed upon the employer's premises or be seriously handicapped. * * *

* * * [The] statutory plan for an adversary proceeding requires that the Board's orders on complaints of unfair labor practices be based upon evidence which is placed before the Board by witnesses who are subject to cross-examination by opposing parties. Such procedure strengthens assurance of fairness by requiring findings on known evidence. * * * Such a requirement does not go beyond the necessity for the production of evidential facts, however, and compel evidence as to the results which may flow from such facts. * * * An administrative agency with power after hearings to determine on the evidence in adversary proceedings whether violations of statutory commands have occurred may infer within the limits of the inquiry from the proven facts such conclusions as reasonably may be based upon the facts proven. One of the purposes which lead to the creation of such boards is to have decisions based upon evidential facts under the particular statute made by experienced officials with an adequate appreciation of the complexities of the subject which is entrusted to their administration. * * *

In the Republic Aviation Corporation case the evidence showed that the petitioner was in early 1943 a non-urban manufacturing establishment for military production which employed thousands. It was growing rapidly. Trains and automobiles gathered daily many employees for the plant from an area on Long Island, certainly larger than walking distance. The rule against solicitation was introduced in evidence and the circumstances of its violation by the dismissed employee after warning was detailed.

As to the employees who were discharged for wearing the buttons of a union steward, the evidence showed in addition the discussion in regard to their right to wear the insignia when the union had not been recognized by the petitioner as the representative of the employees. Petitioner looked upon a steward as a union representative for the adjustment of grievances with the management after employer recognition of the stewards' union. Until such recognition petitioner felt that it would violate its neutrality in labor organization if it permitted the display of a steward button by an employee. From its point of view, such display represented to other employees that the union already was recognized.

No evidence was offered that any unusual conditions existed in labor relations, the plant location or otherwise to support any contention that conditions at this plant differed from those occurring normally at any other large establishment.

The Le Tourneau Company of Georgia case also is barren of special circumstances. The evidence which was introduced tends to prove the simple facts heretofore set out as to the circumstances surrounding the discharge of the two employees for distributing union circulars.

These were the facts upon which the Board reached its conclusions as to unfair labor practices. The Intermediate Report in the Republic Aviation case, 51 N.L.R.B. at 1195, set out the reason why the rule against solicitation was considered inimical to the right of organization.[6] This was approved by

6. 51 N.L.R.B. 1195:

the Board. Id., 1186. The Board's reasons for concluding that the petitioner's insistence that its employees refrain from wearing steward buttons appear at page 1187 of the report.[7] In the Le Tourneau Company case the discussion of the reasons underlying the findings was much more extended. 54 N.L.R.B. 1253, 1258, et seq. We insert in the note below a quotation which shows the character of the Board's opinion.[8] Furthermore, in both opinions of the Board full citation of authorities was given including Matter of Peyton Packing Company, 49 N.L.R.B. 828, 50 N.L.R.B. 355, hereinafter referred to.

The Board has fairly, we think, explicated in these cases the theory which moved it to its conclusions in these cases. The excerpts from its opinions just quoted show this. The reasons why it has decided as it has are sufficiently set forth. We cannot agree, as Republic urges, that in these present cases reviewing courts are left to "sheer acceptance" of the Board's conclusions or that its formulation of policy is "cryptic." * * *

Not only has the Board in these cases sufficiently expressed the theory upon which it concludes that rules against solicitation or prohibitions against the wearing of insignia must fall as interferences with union organization but in so far as rules against solicitation are concerned, it had theretofore succinctly expressed the requirements of proof which it considered appropriate to outweigh or overcome the presumption as to rules against solicitation. In the Peyton Packing Company case, 49 N.L.R.B. 828, at 843, hereinbefore referred to, the presumption adopted by the Board is set forth.[10]

"Thus, under the conditions obtaining in January 1943, the respondent's employees, working long hours in a plant engaged entirely in war production and expanding with extreme rapidity, were entirely deprived of their normal right to 'full freedom of association' in the plant on their own time, the very time and place uniquely appropriate and almost solely available to them therefor. The respondent's rule is therefore in clear derogation of the rights of its employees guaranteed by the Act."

7. We quote an illustrative portion. 51 N.L.R.B. 1187, 1188: "We do not believe that the wearing of a steward button is a representation that the employer either approves or recognizes the union in question as the representative of the employees, especially when, as here, there is no competing labor organization in the plant. Furthermore, there is no evidence in the record herein that the respondent's employees so understood the steward buttons or that the appearance of union stewards in the plant affected the normal operation of the respondent's grievance procedure. On the other hand, the right of employees to wear union insignia at work has long been recognized as a reasonable and legitimate form of union activity, and the respondent's curtailment of that right is clearly violative of the Act."

8. 54 N.L.R.B. at 1259, 1260: "As the Circuit Court of Appeals for the Second Circuit has held, 'It is not every interference with property rights that is within the Fifth Amendment and * * * [i]nconvenience or even some dislocation of property rights, may be necessary in order to safeguard the right to collective bargaining.' The Board has frequently applied this principle in decisions involving varying sets of circumstances, where it has held that the employer's right to control his property does not permit him to deny access to his property to persons whose presence is necessary there to enable the employees effectively to exercise their right to self-organization and collective bargaining, and in those decisions which have reached the courts, the Board's position has been sustained. Similarly, the Board has held that, while it was 'within the province of an employer to promulgate and enforce a rule prohibiting union solicitation during working hours,' it was 'not within the province of an employer to promulgate and enforce a rule prohibiting union solicitation by an employee outside of working hours, although on company property,' the latter restriction being deemed an unreasonable impediment to the exercise of the right to self-organization."

10. 49 N.L.R.B. at 843, 844: "The Act, of course, does not prevent an employer from making and enforcing reasonable rules covering the conduct of employees on company time. Working time is for work. It is therefore within the province of an employer to

* * * We perceive no error in the Board's adoption of this presumption. The Board had previously considered similar rules in industrial establishments and the definitive form which the Peyton Packing Company decision gave to the presumption was the product of the Board's appraisal of normal conditions about industrial establishments. Like a statutory presumption or one established by regulation, the validity, perhaps in a varying degree, depends upon the rationality between what is proved and what is inferred.

In the Republic Aviation case, petitioner urges that irrespective of the validity of the rule against solicitation, its application in this instance did not violate Section 8(3) * * * because the rule was not discriminatorily applied against union solicitation but was impartially enforced against all solicitors. It seems clear, however that if a rule against solicitation is invalid as to union solicitation on the employer's premises during the employee's own time, a discharge because of violation of that rule discriminates within the meaning of Section 8(3) in that it discourages membership in a labor organization.

Republic Aviation Corporation v. National Labor Relations Board is affirmed.

National Labor Relations Board v. Le Tourneau Company of Georgia is reversed.

MR. JUSTICE ROBERTS dissents in each case.

Note

Did the Court in Republic Aviation concern itself with scienter? Should scienter be required as an element of a Section 8(a)(1) violation, as in Section 8(a)(3)? Or, on the other hand, should the Board be allowed simply to weigh the Section 7 rights of the employees against the property rights of the employer and pronounce judgment accordingly, as in Republic Aviation, without detouring through the motive maze—the so-called "balancing test"? For further discussion, see infra p. 520.

NATIONAL LABOR RELATIONS BOARD v. BABCOCK & WILCOX CO.

Supreme Court of the United States, 1956.
351 U.S. 105, 76 S.Ct. 679, 100 L.Ed. 975.

MR. JUSTICE REED delivered the opinion of the Court.

In each of these cases the employer refused to permit distribution of union literature by nonemployee union organizers on company-owned parking lots. The National Labor Relations Board, in separate and unrelated

promulgate and enforce a rule prohibiting union solicitation during working hours. Such a rule must be presumed to be valid in the absence of evidence that it was adopted for a discriminatory purpose. It is no less true that time outside working hours, whether before or after work, or during luncheon or rest periods, is an employee's time to use as he wishes without unreasonable restraint, although the employee is on company property.

It is therefore not within the province of an employer to promulgate and enforce a rule prohibiting union solicitation by an employee outside of working hours, although on company property. Such a rule must be presumed to be an unreasonable impediment to self-organization and therefore discriminatory in the absence of evidence that special circumstances make the rule necessary in order to maintain production or discipline."

proceedings, found in each case that it was unreasonably difficult for the union organizer to reach the employees off company property and held that, in refusing the unions access to parking lots, the employers had unreasonably impeded their employees' right to self-organization in violation of § 8(a) (1) of the National Labor Relations Act. Babcock & Wilcox Co., 109 N.L.R.B. 485, 494; Ranco, Inc., id., 998, 1007, and Seamprufe, Inc., id., 24, 32.

The plant involved in No. 250, National Labor Relations Board v. Babcock & Wilcox Co., is a company engaged in the manufacture of tubular products such as boilers and accessories, located on a 100-acre tract about one mile from a community of 21,000 people. Approximately 40% of the 500 employees live in that town and the remainder live within a 30-mile radius. More than 90% of them drive to work in private automobiles and park on a company lot that adjoins the fenced in plant area. The parking lot is reached only by a driveway 100 yards long which is entirely on company property excepting for a public right-of-way that extends 31 feet from the metal of the highway to the plant's property. Thus, the only public place in the immediate vicinity of the plant area at which leaflets can be effectively distributed to employees is that place where this driveway crosses the public right-of-way. Because of the traffic conditions at that place the Board found it practically impossible for union organizers to distribute leaflets safely to employees in motors as they enter or leave the lot. The Board noted that the company's policy on such distribution had not discriminated against labor organizations and that other means of communication, such as the mail and telephones, as well as the homes of the workers, were open to the union.[1] The employer justified its refusal to allow distribution of literature on company property on the ground that it had maintained a consistent policy of refusing access to all kinds of pamphleteering and that such distribution of leaflets would litter its property.

The Board found that the parking lot and the walkway from it to the gatehouse, where employees punched in for work, were the only "safe and practicable" places for distribution of union literature. The Board viewed the place of work as so much more effective a place for communication of information that it held the employer guilty of an unfair labor practice for refusing limited access to company property to union organizers. It therefore ordered the employer to rescind its no-distribution order for the parking lot and walkway, subject to reasonable and nondiscriminating regulations "in the interest of plant efficiency and discipline, but not as to deny access to union representatives for the purpose of effecting such distribution." 109 N.L.R.B., at 486.

The Board petitioned the Court of Appeals for the Fifth Circuit for enforcement. That court refused enforcement on the ground the statute did not authorize the Board to impose a servitude on the employer's property

1. "Other union contacts with employees: In addition to distributing literature to some of the employees, as shown above, during the period of concern herein the Union has had other contacts with some of the employees. It has communicated with over 100 employees of Respondent on 3 different occasions by sending literature to them through the mails. Union representatives have communicated with many of Respondent's employees by talking with them on the streets of Paris, by driving to their homes and talking with them there, and by talking with them over the telephone. All of these contacts have been for the purpose of soliciting the adherence and membership of the employees in the Union." 109 N.L.R.B., at 492–493.

where no employee was involved. National Labor Relations Board v. Babcock & Wilcox Co., 5 Cir., 222 F.2d 316.

The conditions and circumstances involved in No. 251, National Labor Relations Board v. Seamprufe, Inc., and No. 422, Ranco, Inc., v. National Labor Relations Board, are not materially different. * * *

In each of these cases the Board found that the employer violated § 8(a) (1) of the National Labor Relations Act * * * making it an unfair labor practice for an employer to interfere with employees in the exercise of rights guaranteed in § 7 of that Act. * * * These holdings were placed on the Labor Board's determination in LeTourneau Company of Georgia, 54 N.L.R.B. 1253. In the *LeTourneau* case the Board balanced the conflicting interests of employees to receive information on self-organization on the company's property from fellow employees during nonworking time, with the employer's right to control the use of his property and found the former more essential in the circumstances of that case. Recognizing that the employer could restrict employees' union activities when necessary to maintain plant discipline or production, the Board said: "Upon all the above considerations, we are convinced, and find, that the respondent, in applying its 'no-distributing' rule to the distribution of union literature by its employees on its parking lots has placed an unreasonable impediment on the freedom of communication essential to the exercise of its employees' right to self-organization," LeTourneau Company of Georgia, 54 N.L.R.B. at page 1262. This Court affirmed the Board. Republic Aviation Corp. v. National Labor Relations Board, 324 U.S. 793, 801 et seq., 65 S.Ct. 982, 987, 89 L.Ed. 1372. The same rule had been earlier and more fully stated in Peyton Packing Co., 49 N.L.R.B. 828, 843–844.

The Board has applied its reasoning in the *LeTourneau* case without distinction to situations where the distribution was made, as here, by nonemployees. * * *

In these present cases the Board has set out the facts that support its conclusions as to the necessity for allowing nonemployee union organizers to distribute union literature on the company's property. In essence they are that nonemployee union representatives, if barred, would have to use personal contacts on streets or at home, telephones, letters or advertised meetings to get in touch with the employees. The force of this position in respect to employees isolated from normal contacts has been recognized by this Court and by others. * * * We recognize, too, that the Board has the responsibility of " 'applying the Act's general prohibitory language in the light of the infinite combinations of events which might be charged as violative of its terms.' " National Labor Relations Board v. Stowe Spinning Co., 336 U.S. 226, 231, 69 S.Ct. 541, 543. We are slow to overturn an administrative decision.

It is our judgment, however, that an employer may validly post his property against nonemployee distribution of union literature if reasonable efforts by the union through other available channels of communication will enable it to reach the employees with its message and if the employer's notice or order does not discriminate against the union by allowing other distribution. In these circumstances the employer may not be compelled to allow distribution even under such reasonable regulations as the orders in these cases permit.

This is not a problem of always open or always closed doors for union organization on company property. Organization rights are granted to workers by the same authority, the National Government, that preserves property rights. Accommodation between the two must be obtained with as little destruction of one as is consistent with the maintenance of the other. The employer may not affirmatively interfere with organization; the union may not always insist that the employer aid organization. But when the inaccessibility of employees makes ineffective the reasonable attempts by nonemployees to communicate with them through the usual channels, the right to exclude from property has been required to yield to the extent needed to permit communication of information on the right to organize.

The determination of the proper adjustments rests with the Board. Its rulings, when reached on findings of fact supported by substantial evidence on the record as a whole, should be sustained by the courts unless its conclusions rest on erroneous legal foundations. Here the Board failed to make a distinction between rules of law applicable to employees and those applicable to nonemployees.

The distinction is one of substance. No restriction may be placed on the employees' right to discuss self-organization among themselves, unless the employer can demonstrate that a restriction is necessary to maintain production or discipline. Republic Aviation Corp. v. National Labor Relations Board, 324 U.S. 793, 803, 65 S.Ct. 982, 988, 89 L.Ed. 1372. But no such obligation is owed nonemployee organizers. Their access to company property is governed by a different consideration. The right of self-organization depends in some measure on the ability of employees to learn the advantages of self-organization from others. Consequently, if the location of a plant and the living quarters of the employees place the employees beyond the reach of reasonable union efforts to communicate with them, the employer must allow the union to approach his employees on his property. No such conditions are shown in these records.

The plants are close to small well-settled communities where a large percentage of the employees live. The usual methods of imparting information are available. See, e.g., note 1, supra. The various instruments of publicity are at hand. Though the quarters of the employees are scattered they are in reasonable reach. The Act requires only that the employer refrain from interference, discrimination, restraint or coercion in the employees' exercise of their own rights. It does not require that the employer permit the use of its facilities for organization when other means are readily available. * * *

MR. JUSTICE HARLAN took no part in the consideration or decision of these cases.

Note

The phrase "no-solicitation rule" is, as the last two cases demonstrate, frequently used in generic fashion to encompass both oral solicitation and the distribution of literature. Is the balance of employer-employee interests the same with regard to each? Do you agree with the Board's disposition of this question in the following passage from STODDARD–QUIRK MFG. CO., 138 N.L. R.B. 615, 620–21 (1962):

"The distinguishing characteristic of literature as contrasted with oral solicitation—and a distinction too often overlooked—is that its message is of a permanent nature and that it is designed to be retained by the recipient for reading or rereading at his convenience. Hence, the purpose is satisfied so long as it is received.

"This purpose, however, can, absent special circumstances, be as readily and as effectively achieved at company parking lots, at plant entrances or exits, or in other nonworking areas, as it can be at the machines or work stations where the employer's interest in cleanliness, order, and discipline is undeniably greater than it is in nonworking areas. Granted that the distribution of union literature, even when it is limited to nonworking areas, is an intrusion upon an employer's acknowledged property rights, we believe that this limited intrusion is warranted if we are to accord a commensurate recognition to the statutory right of employees to utilize this organizational technique. On the other hand, opportunity for effective distribution of union literature is more easily afforded than opportunity for effective oral solicitation and the intrusion upon the employer's property rights can be correspondingly diminished without substantial prejudice to employee rights. Thus, in conformity with the Supreme Court mandate in Babcock & Wilcox, the limitation on the employer's property right in each situation is imposed only to the extent that it is necessary for the maintenance of the employees' organizational right.

"To sum up, we believe that to effectuate organizational rights through the medium of oral solicitation, the right of employees to solicit on plant premises must be afforded subject only to the restriction that it be on nonworking time. However, because distribution of literature is a different technique and poses different problems both from the point of view of the employees and from the point of view of management, we believe organizational rights in that regard require only that employees have access to nonworking areas of the plant premises."

CENTRAL HARDWARE CO. v. NATIONAL LABOR RELATIONS BOARD

Supreme Court of the United States, 1972.
407 U.S. 539, 92 S.Ct. 2238, 33 L.Ed.2d 122.

MR. JUSTICE POWELL delivered the opinion of the Court.

Petitioner, Central Hardware Co. (Central), owns and operates two retail hardware stores in Indianapolis, Indiana. Each store is housed in a large building, containing 70,000 square feet of floor space, and housing no other retail establishments. The stores are surrounded on three sides by ample parking facilities, accommodating approximately 350 automobiles. The parking lots are owned by Central, and are maintained solely for the use of Central's customers and employees. While there are other retail establishments in the vicinity of Central's stores, these establishments are not a part of a shopping center complex, and they maintain their own separate parking lots.

Approximately a week before Central opened its stores, the Retail Clerks Union, Local 725, Retail Clerks International Association, AFL–CIO (the

Union), began an organization campaign at both stores. The campaign consisted primarily of solicitation by nonemployee Union organizers on Central's parking lots. The nonemployee organizers confronted Central's employees in the parking lots and sought to persuade them to sign cards authorizing the Union to represent them in an appropriate bargaining unit. As a part of the organization campaign, an "undercover agent for the Union" was infiltrated into the employ of Central, receiving full-time salary from both the Union and the company. This agent solicited employees to join the Union, and obtained a list of the employees of the two stores which was about 80% complete.

Central had a no-solicitation rule which it enforced against all solicitational activities in its stores and on its parking lots. A number of employees complained to Central's local management that they were being harassed by the organizers, and these complaints were forwarded to Central's corporate headquarters in St. Louis, Missouri. The St. Louis officials directed the Indianapolis management to enforce the nonemployee no-solicitation rule and keep all Union organizers off the company premises, including the parking lots. Although most of the nonemployee Union organizers had either left Indianapolis or ceased work on the Central organization campaign, the Indianapolis management had occasion to assert the nonemployee no-solicitation rule on several occasions.

One arrest was made when a field organizer for the Union was confronted by the manager of one of the stores on its parking lot, and refused to leave after being requested to do so. The field organizer asserted that he was a "customer" and insisted upon entering the store. The police were called and when the organizer persisted in his refusal to leave, he was arrested.

Shortly after Central received complaints from its employees as to harassment by the organizers, Central filed unfair labor practice charges against the Union. The Union subsequently filed unfair labor practice charges against Central. After an investigation, the General Counsel of the National Labor Relations Board (the Board) dismissed Central's charges against the Union, and issued a complaint against Central on the Union's charges.

The Board held that Central's nonemployee no-solicitation rule was overly broad, and that its enforcement violated § 8(a)(1) of the National Labor Relations Act. The Board reasoned that the character and use of Central's parking lots distinguished the case from N.L.R.B. v. Babcock & Wilcox Co., 351 U.S. 105, 76 S.Ct. 679, 100 L.Ed. 975 (1956), and brought it within the principle of Amalgamated Food Employees Union Local 590 v. Logan Valley Plaza, Inc., 391 U.S. 308, 88 S.Ct. 1601, 20 L.Ed.2d 603 (1968). 181 N.L.R.B. 491 (1970). A divided Court of Appeals for the Eighth Circuit agreed, and ordered enforcement of the Board's order enjoining Central from enforcing any rule prohibiting nonemployee Union organizers from using its parking lots to solicit employees on behalf of the Union. 439 F.2d 1321 (1971). We granted certiorari to consider whether the principle of *Logan Valley* is applicable to this case. * * * We conclude that it is not.

I

Section 7 of the National Labor Relations Act, as amended, * * * guarantees to employees the right to "self-organization, to form, join, or assist labor organizations." This guarantee includes both the right of union officials to discuss organization with employees, and the right of employees to discuss organization among themselves. Section 8(a)(1) of the Act * * * makes it an unfair labor practice for an employer "to interfere with, restrain, or coerce employees in the exercise of the rights guaranteed" in § 7. But organization rights are not viable in a vacuum; their effectiveness depends in some measure on the ability of employees to learn the advantages and disadvantages of organization from others. Early in the history of the administration of the Act the Board recognized the importance of freedom of communication to the free exercise of organization rights. See Peyton Packing Co., 49 N.L.R.B. 828 (1943), enforced, 142 F.2d 1009 (C.A.5), cert. denied, 323 U.S. 730, 65 S.Ct. 66, 89 L.Ed. 585 (1944).

In seeking to provide information essential to the free exercise of organization rights, union organizers have often engaged in conduct inconsistent with traditional notions of private property rights. The Board and the courts have the duty to resolve conflicts between organization rights and property rights, and to seek a proper accommodation between the two. This Court addressed the conflict which often arises between organization rights and property rights in N.L.R.B. v. Babcock & Wilcox Co., 351 U.S. 105, 76 S.Ct. 679, 100 L.Ed. 975 (1956). * * *

The principle of Babcock is limited to [the] accommodation between organization rights and property rights. This principle requires a "yielding" of property rights only in the context of an organization campaign. Moreover, the allowed intrusion on property rights is limited to that necessary to facilitate the exercise of employees' § 7 rights. After the requisite need for access to the employer's property has been shown, the access is limited to (i) union organizers; (ii) prescribed nonworking areas of the employer's premises; and (iii) the duration of organization activity. In short, the principle of accommodation announced in Babcock is limited to labor organization campaigns, and the "yielding" of property rights it may require is both temporary and minimal.

II

The principle applied in Amalgamated Food Employees Union Local 590 v. Logan Valley Plaza, Inc., 391 U.S. 308, 88 S.Ct. 1601, 20 L.Ed.2d 603 (1968), is quite different. While it is true that Logan Valley involved labor picketing, the decision rests on constitutional grounds; it is not a § 7 case.

Logan Valley had its genesis in Marsh v. Alabama, 326 U.S. 501, 66 S.Ct. 276, 90 L.Ed. 265 (1946). Marsh involved a "company town," an economic anachronism rarely encountered today. The town was wholly owned by the Gulf Shipbuilding Corp., yet it had all of the characteristics of any other American town. Gulf Shipbuilding held title to all the land in the town, including that covered by streets and sidewalks. Gulf Shipbuilding also provided municipal services such as sewerage service and police protection to the residents of the town. A Jehovah's Witness undertook to distribute religious literature on a sidewalk near the post office in the "business block" of the town, and was arrested on a trespassing charge. She was subsequently convicted of the crime of trespassing, and the Alabama courts upheld the conviction on appeal. This Court reversed, holding that Alabama could not permit a corporation to assume the functions of a municipal government and at the same time deny First Amendment rights through the application of the State's criminal trespass law.

In *Logan Valley,* over a strong dissent by Mr. Justice Black, the author of *Marsh,* the Court applied the reasoning of *Marsh* to a modern economic phenomenon, the shopping center complex. The Logan Valley Mall was a complex of retail establishments, which the Court regarded under the factual circumstances as the functional equivalent of the "community business block" of the company town in *Marsh.* The corporate owner of Logan Valley Mall obtained a state court injunction against peaceful picketing on the shopping center property, and the Pennsylvania Supreme Court affirmed the issuance of the injunction on the ground that the picketing constituted a trespass on private property. This Court reversed, holding that Pennsylvania could not "delegate the power, through the use of its trespass laws, wholly to exclude those members of the public wishing to exercise their First Amendment rights on the premises in a manner and for a purpose generally consonant with the use to which the property is actually put." 391 U.S., at 319–320, 88 S.Ct., at 1609.

III

The Board and the Court of Appeals held that *Logan Valley* rather than *Babcock* controlled this case. The Board asserts that the distinguishing feature between these two cases is that in *Logan Valley* the owner had "diluted his property interest by opening his property to the general public for his own economic advantage."[4] The emphasis, both in the argument on behalf of the Board and in the opinion below, is on the opening of the property "to the general public."[5]

This analysis misconceives the rationale of *Logan Valley. Logan Valley* involved a large commercial shopping center which the Court found had displaced, in certain relevant respects, the functions of the normal municipal "business block." First and Fourteenth Amendment free-speech rights were deemed infringed under the facts of that case when the property owner invoked the trespass laws of the State against the pickets.

Before an owner of private property can be subjected to the commands of the First and Fourteenth Amendments the privately owned property must assume to some significant degree the functional attributes of public property devoted to public use. The First and Fourteenth Amendments are limitations on state action, not on action by the owner of private property used only for private purposes. The only fact relied upon for the argument that Central's parking lots have acquired the characteristics of a public municipal facility is that they are "open to the public." Such an argument could be made with respect to almost every retail and service establishment in the country, regardless of size or location. To accept it would cut *Logan Valley* entirely away from its roots in *Marsh.* It would also constitute an unwarranted infringement of long-settled rights of private property protect-

4. Brief for the NLRB 20.   5. 439 F.2d, at 1326–1328.

ed by the Fifth and Fourteenth Amendments. We hold that the Board and the Court of Appeals erred in applying *Logan Valley* to this case.

The Trial Examiner concluded that no reasonable means of communication with employees were available to the nonemployee Union organizers other than solicitation in Central's parking lots. The Board adopted this conclusion. Central vigorously contends that this conclusion is not supported by substantial evidence in the record as a whole. The Court of Appeals did not consider this contention, because it viewed *Logan Valley* as controlling rather than *Babcock*. The determination whether on the record as a whole there is substantial evidence to support agency findings is a matter entrusted primarily to the courts of appeals. Universal Camera Corp. v. N.L.R.B., 340 U.S. 474, 71 S.Ct. 456, 95 L.Ed. 456 (1951). Since the Court of Appeals has not yet considered this question in light of the principles of NLRB v. Babcock & Wilcox Co., supra, the judgment is vacated, and the case will be remanded to that court for such consideration.

It is so ordered.

Judgment vacated and case remanded.

[JUSTICE MARSHALL, joined by JUSTICES DOUGLAS and BRENNAN, dissented on the ground that the Court should not have answered the constitutional question of *Logan Valley* without first remanding the case to the Board for determination of the statutory question of *Babcock & Wilcox*.]

Note

1. The Board, having discovered the relative ease of deciding a trespassory labor issue on First Amendment (Logan Valley) grounds, as opposed to the more difficult-to-administer test of Babcock & Wilcox, continued to press the former approach after Central Hardware. In Hudgens v. NLRB, 424 U.S. 507, 96 S.Ct. 1029, 47 L.Ed.2d 196 (1976), a union peacefully picketed a retail store operated by the Butler Shoe Company, a lessee, on the premises of a shopping center, in support of an economic strike being waged against the Butler Company by the employees of its warehouse, located elsewhere. Hudgens, owner of the shopping center, threatened the picketers with arrest because of their trespass; they ceased picketing and filed an 8(a)(1) charge. The Board found Hudgens in violation. In its disposition of the case, the Supreme Court rejected the Board's effort to resolve the question on First Amendment grounds and remanded the case for decision under 8(a)(1) in accordance with the Babcock & Wilcox test. In so doing, the Court overruled Logan Valley, as an improper extension of Marsh v. Alabama, in the very *shopping center* context in which it had been conceived; Central Hardware, as a First Amendment issue, was thus rendered *a fortiori*.

2. Hudgens-type fact situations involve a potential conflict between the enforcement of state laws relating to trespass and the federal law protecting Section 7 rights. If a state court enjoined the trespassory picketing in Hudgens, or if arrests were made, employee conduct which might later be found by the Board (under the Babcock & Wilcox-8(a)(1) test) to be federally protected would have been wrongfully prohibited by the state. This and similar problems are the subject matter of Chapter 5, Section A, 2, infra p. 330; the trespassory picketing federal-state conflict is considered in Sears, Roebuck & Co. v. San Diego County District Council of Carpenters, 436 U.S. 180, 98 S.Ct. 1745, 56 L.Ed.2d 209 (1978), infra p. 359.

3. The extent to which peaceful picketing is equatable with speech and subject to protection under the First Amendment is further dealt with in Chapter 5, Section A, 1, infra p. 315.

4. The question as to which certiorari was granted in Central Hardware (i.e., whether by reason of the First Amendment as interpreted in Logan Valley the employer should be held to have violated Section 8(a)(1) on the facts presented) operated to keep the focus off an interesting aspect of the case. The no-solicitation rule in effect there was "enforced [by Central Hardware] against all solicitational activities in its stores and on its parking lots." (Supra p. 255.) As applied to *employees,* did that no-solicitation rule violate Section 8(a)(1) within the meaning of Republic Aviation? In other words, is a retail store the counterpart of an industrial plant for purposes of the application of such rules? What added factor is present in *selling* areas which should be taken into account in judging the propriety of employee solicitation even during nonwork time? Should the same considerations obtain in storage areas, employee lunchrooms, parking lots? Should it matter who uses the parking lots?

On the foregoing questions the Trial Examiner, Board, and Eighth Circuit all held in consonance with the following passages from the Trial Examiner's Decision:

"Unlike the situation obtaining in a factory, for example, where a rule forbidding solicitation during employees' off-duty time is presumptively invalid,[26] an operator of a retail store is 'privileged to promulgate a rule prohibiting all union solicitation within the selling areas of the store during both working and nonworking hours.' Montgomery Ward & Co., Inc., 145 N.L.R.B. 846, 848, modified in other respects 339 F.2d 889 (C.A. 6). However a retail store rule prohibiting 'solicitation in any form * * * on store premises' is 'unduly broad in scope' and therefore violative of Section 8(a)(1) of the Act because it forbids 'solicitation during nonworking time whether on or off the selling floor and in or out of work areas.' Mock Road Super Duper, Inc., 156 N.L.R.B. 983, 984.

"The validity of respondent's rule here under consideration turns, therefore, on whether it bans solicitation by employees off respondent's selling floors during their nonworking time. In this regard, even if the lunchroom in respondent's West Store, in which only employees eat, is considered as a selling area because customers enter it from time to time to buy the cigarettes and candy bars there offered for sale, there are other portions of respondent's premises, clearly not used for selling purposes, which would, nevertheless, fall within the rule's purview. Included among these are the lunchroom in the East Store, employees' locker-rooms, storage areas located off the sales floors, and the parking lots, in all of which the rule, on its face, forbids solicitation by employees regardless of whether they are actually working.

"Being thus unduly broad, respondent's employee 'no-solicitation' rule goes beyond the privilege set forth in *Montgomery Ward.* It is, therefore, invalid." Central Hardware Co., 181 N.L.R.B. 491, 497–98 (1970).

5. The 1974 extension of the coverage of the NLRA to include employees of non-profit hospitals (see supra p. 219) brought the problems of solicitation rules to hospital settings.

26. Stoddard-Quirk Manufacturing Co., 138 N.L.R.B. 615, 617.

In Beth Israel Hospital v. NLRB, 437 U.S. 483, 98 S.Ct. 2463, 57 L.Ed.2d 370 (1978), the employer hospital had a rule prohibiting solicitation and distribution of literature in all areas of the hospital other than employee locker rooms. The Board entered an order requiring the hospital to rescind its rule insofar as it prohibited solicitation and distribution in the hospital's cafeteria and coffee shop. The Supreme Court approved.

Beth Israel required that the Court consider only the validity of a hospital's no-solicitation rule in areas utilized negligibly by patients and extensively by employees. In NLRB v. Baptist Hospital, Inc., 442 U.S. 773, 99 S.Ct. 2598, 61 L.Ed.2d 251 (1979), the Court was confronted by the Board's invalidation of a rule which prohibited solicitation at all times "in any area of the hospital accessible to or used by the public." Thus, solicitation was prohibited in lobbies, the gift shop, the cafeteria, corridors, sitting rooms, and public restrooms. The Board order allowed the hospital to apply its rule only to employees soliciting during their work time and in "immediate patient care areas." The Supreme Court ruled that the record supported the invalidation of the solicitation rule as it applied to the cafeteria, gift shop, and lobbies, but that the hospital had justified its application to corridors and sitting rooms on the patients' floors.

NATIONAL LABOR RELATIONS BOARD v. VIRGINIA ELECTRIC & POWER CO.

Supreme Court of the United States, 1941.
314 U.S. 469, 62 S.Ct. 344, 86 L.Ed. 348.

Mr. Justice Murphy delivered the opinion of the Court.

Upon the usual proceedings [1] had pursuant to section 10 of the National Labor Relations Act, the Board made substantially the following findings of fact:

For years prior to the events in this case the Virginia Electric and Power Company (hereinafter called the Company) was hostile to labor organizations. From 1922, when a strike was unsuccessful by a nationally affiliated union, until the formation of the Independent Organization of Employees (hereinafter called the Independent) in 1937 there was no labor organization among its employees. Shortly after the enactment of the National Industrial Recovery Act in 1933, 48 Stat. 195, Holtzclaw, the president of the Company, spoke to the employees and stated that any organization among them was "entirely unnecessary". Until his death in May 1937 the Company utilized the services of one Walters, an employee of the Railway Audit and Inspection Company who prior to the effective date of the Act admittedly furnished a report on the labor activity of the employees to the Company. In 1936 Bishop, Superintendent of Transportation in Norfolk, interrogated employees concerning union activities. On April 26, 1937, shortly after the Act was upheld, and an A.F. of L. organizer had appeared, the Company posted a bulletin [5] throughout its operations appeal-

1. These proceedings were instituted • • • [by a CIO union and two AFL unions]. The complaint, as amended, charged that the employer • • • had engaged in unfair labor practices within the meaning of section 8(1), (2), and (3) of the Act • • •. The Independent Organization of Employees of the Virginia Electric and Power Company • • • was allowed to intervene with respect to the 8(2) charge, was represented by counsel and participated throughout the proceedings.

5.

"April 26, 1937.

To the Employees of the Company:

"As a result of recent national labor organization activities and the interpretation of the Wagner Labor Act by the Supreme Court,

ing to the employees to bargain with the Company directly without the intervention of an "outside" union, and thereby coerced its employees. In response to this bulletin several requests for increased wages and better working conditions were received. The Company decided to withhold action on those requests and directed its employees to select representatives to attend meetings at which Company officials would speak on the Wagner Act. These representatives met in Norfolk and Richmond on May 24 and were addressed by high Company officials who read identical speeches [7] stressing the desirability of forming a bargaining agency. At the Richmond meeting it was announced that any wage increase granted would be retroactive to June 1. By the substance of the speeches and the mechanics of the meetings the Company gave impetus to and assured the creation of an "inside" organization and coerced its employees in the exercise of their rights

employees of companies such as ours may be approached in the near future by representatives of one or more such labor organizations to solicit their membership. Such campaigns are now being pressed in various industries and in different parts of the country and strikes and unrest have developed in many localities. For the last fifteen years this company and its employees have enjoyed a happy relationship of mutual confidence and understanding with each other, and during this period there has not been any labor organization among our employees in any department, so far as the management is aware. Under these circumstances, we feel that our employees are entitled to know certain facts and have a statement as to the Company's attitude with reference to this matter.

"The Company recognizes the right of every employee to join any union that he may wish to join, and such membership will not affect his position with the company. On the other hand, we feel that it should be made equally clear to each employee that it is not at all necessary for him to join any labor organization, despite anything he may be told to the contrary. Certainly, there is no law which requires or is intended to compel you to pay dues to, or to join any organization.

"This company has always dealt with its employees in full recognition of the right of every individual employee, or group of employees, to deal directly with the Company with respect to matters affecting their interests. If any of you, individually or as a group, at any time, have any matter which you wish to discuss with us, any officer or department head will be glad, as they always have been, to meet with you and discuss them frankly and fully. It is our earnest desire to straighten out in a friendly manner, as we have done in the past, whatever questions you may have in mind. It is reasonable to believe that our interests are mutual and can best be promoted through confidence and cooperation.

(signed)

　　　　　　J.G. HOLTZCLAW,
　　　　　　　　"President."

7. "A substantial number of its employees representing various departments and various occupations have approached the Company with the request that the Company consider with them the matter of their working conditions and wages. In other words, they have requested collective bargaining. The Company's position with respect to this was recently stated in a posted bulletin.

"In a company such as ours, if an individual operator, for example, should ask for himself better working conditions or wages, this Company could not comply with his request without also making the same concessions to other similar operators. In such a case the operator who appealed individually would, as a practical matter, be bargaining collectively for all of his group, which is not the logical procedure.

"This Company is willing to consider the request mentioned above but feels that, in fairness to all of its employees and to itself, it should at the same time consider other groups who have not yet come to it. If the approaching negotiations are to be intelligent and fair to all properly concerned, they should be conducted in an orderly way, and all interested groups should be represented in these discussions by representatives of their own choosing, as provided in the Wagner National Labor Relations Act * * *.

"The Wagner Labor Act prohibits a company from 'dominating or interfering with the formation or administration of any labor organization or contribute (sic) financial or other support to it.'

"In view of your request to bargain directly with the Company and, in view of your right to self-organization as provided in the law, it will facilitate negotiations if you will proceed to set up your organization, select your own officers and adviser, adopt your own by-laws and rules, and select your representatives to meet with the Company officials whenever you desire."

guaranteed by section 7 of the Act. Meetings, arranged with the cooperation of Company supervisors, on Company property and, in some instances on Company time, followed, at which the May 24 speeches were reported to the men who voted to form an "inside" organization and selected committees for that purpose. These committees met on Company property until June 15 when the constitution of the Independent was adopted.

While the Independent was in the process of organization, Edwards, a supervisor, kept meetings of a rival C.I.O. union under surveillance and warned employees that they would be discharged for "messing with the C.I.O." On June 1 Mann, a member of the C.I.O., who had openly protested against an "inside" union at one of the May 11 meetings * * * attended by Superintendent Bishop's son, Warren, was discharged for union activities.

On June 17 application cards for the Independent were distributed throughout the entire system of the Company and many were signed on Company property and time. Within three weeks after the adoption of the constitution of the Independent a majority of the employees filled out application cards. By July 13 the organization was complete and permanent committeemen had been elected. A majority of those committeemen had been present at the May 24 meetings. On July 19 the Independent notified the Company that it represented a majority of the employees and submitted a proposed contract. Negotiations were begun on July 30 and agreement was reached by midnight of the following day. The contract was formally executed on August 5, and provided, inter alia, for a closed shop, a check-off, and a wage increase. On August 20 the Company paid $3,784.50 to the Independent although it had not yet deducted that entire amount from the employees' wages. On November 4, the date upon which the closed shop provision became effective, the Company discharged two employees, Staunton and Elliott, because they refused to join the Independent. In March, 1938, it discharged another employee, Harrell, for his membership and activity in an outside union.

Upon the basis of these findings and the entire record in the case the Board concluded that the Company had committed unfair labor practices within the meaning of section 8(1), (2) and (3) of the Act. Its order directed the Company to cease and desist from its unfair labor practices and from giving effect to its contract with the Independent, to withdraw recognition from and disestablish that organization, to reinstate with back pay the four wrongfully discharged employees, to reimburse each of its employees who was a member of the Independent in the amount of the dues and assessments checked off his wages by the Company on behalf of the Independent, and to post appropriate notices.

The Company and the Independent filed separate petitions in the court below to review and set aside the Board's order. The Board answered and requested enforcement of its order against the Company. The court below denied enforcement to any part of the Board's order, completely setting it aside. We granted the petition for writs of certiorari because the case was thought to present important questions in the administration of the Act.
* * *

Domination of the Independent

The command of section 10(e) of the Act that "the findings of the Board as to the facts, if supported by evidence, shall be conclusive" precludes an independent consideration of the facts. Bearing this in mind we must ever guard against allowing our views to be substituted for those of the agency which Congress has created to administer the Act. But here the Board's conclusion that the Independent was a Company dominated union seems based heavily upon findings which are not free from ambiguity and doubt. We believe that the Board, and not this Court, should undertake the task of clarification.

The Board specifically found that the bulletin of April 26 and the speeches of May 24 "interfered with, restrained and coerced" the Company's employees in the exercise of their rights guaranteed by section 7 of the Act. The Company strongly urges that such a finding is repugnant to the First Amendment. Neither the Act nor the Board's order here enjoins the employer from expressing its view on labor policies or problems, nor is a penalty imposed upon it because of any utterances which it has made. The sanctions of the Act are imposed not in punishment of the employer but for the protection of the employees. The employer in this case is as free now as ever to take any side it may choose on this controversial issue. But certainly conduct, though evidenced in part by speech, may amount in connection with other circumstances to coercion within the meaning of the Act. If the total activities of an employer restrain or coerce his employees in their free choice, then those employees are entitled to the protection of the Act. And in determining whether a course of conduct amounts to restraint or coercion, pressure exerted vocally by the employer may no more be disregarded than pressure exerted in other ways. For "Slight suggestions as to the employer's choice between unions may have telling effect among men who know the consequences of incurring that employer's strong displeasure." International Association of Machinists v. National Labor Relations Board, 311 U.S. 72, 78, 61 S.Ct. 83, 87, 88, 85 L.Ed. 50.

If the Board's order here may fairly be said to be based on the totality of the Company's activities during the period in question, we may not consider the findings of the Board as to the coercive effect of the bulletin and the speeches in isolation from the findings as respects the other conduct of the Company. If the Board's ultimate conclusion is based upon a complex of activities, such as the anti-union background of the Company, the activities of Bishop, Edwards' warning to the employees that they would be discharged for "messing with the C.I.O.", the discharge of Mann, the quick formation of the Independent, and the part which the management may have played in that formation, that conclusion would not be vitiated by the fact that the Board considered what the Company said in conjunction with what it did. The mere fact that language merges into a course of conduct does not put that whole course without the range of otherwise applicable administrative power. In determining whether the Company actually interfered with, restrained, and coerced its employees the Board has a right to look at what the Company has said as well as what it has done.

But from the Board's decision we are far from clear that the Board here considered the whole complex of activities, of which the bulletin and the speeches are but parts, in reaching its ultimate conclusion with regard to the Independent. The Board regarded the bulletin on its face as showing a marked bias against national unions by implying that strikes and unrest are caused by the organizational campaigns of such bodies, by stressing the "happy relationship of mutual confidence and understanding" prevailing in the absence of organization since the defeat of the Amalgamated in 1922, and by emphasizing the negative "right" of the employees to refrain from exercising their rights guaranteed under the Act after paying "lip service" to those rights. Summing up its conclusions the Board said: "We interpret the bulletin as an appeal to the employees to bargain with the respondent directly, without the intervention of any 'outside' union. We find that by posting the bulletin the respondent interfered with, restrained, and coerced its employees in the exercise of the rights guaranteed in Section 7 of the Act."

The Board was of the view that the speeches delivered in the meetings of May 24 provided the impetus for the formation of a system-wide organization, that they re-emphasized the Company's distaste for "outside" organizations by referring to the bulletin, and that, after quoting the provision of the Act forbidding employer domination of labor organizations, they suggested that the employees select their "own" officers, and adopt their "own" by-laws and rules. The Board's finding was: "We find that at the May 24 meetings the respondent urged its employees to organize and to do so independently of 'outside' assistance, and that it thereby interfered with, restrained, and coerced its employees in the exercise of the rights guaranteed in Section 7 of the Act."

It is clear that the Board specifically found that those utterances were unfair labor practices, and it does not appear that the Board raised them to the stature of coercion by reliance on the surrounding circumstances. If the utterances are thus to be separated from their background, we find it difficult to sustain a finding of coercion with respect to them alone. The bulletin and the speeches set forth the right of the employees to do as they please without fear of retaliation by the Company. Perhaps the purport of these utterances may be altered by imponderable subtleties at work which it is not our function to appraise. Whether there are sufficient findings and evidence of interference, restraint, coercion, and domination without reference to the bulletin and the speeches, or whether the whole course of conduct evidenced in part by the utterances was aimed at achieving objectives forbidden by the Act, are questions for the Board to decide upon the evidence.

Here we are not sufficiently certain from the findings that the Board based its conclusion with regard to the Independent upon the whole course of conduct revealed by this record. Rather it appears that the Board rested heavily upon findings with regard to the bulletin and the speeches the adequacy of which we regard as doubtful. We therefore remand the cause to the Circuit Court of Appeals with directions to remand it to the Board for a redetermination of the issues in the light of this opinion. We do not mean to intimate any views of our own as to whether the Independent was dominated or suggest to the Board what its conclusion should be when it reconsiders the case. Since the Board rested the remainder of its order in large part on its findings with respect to the domination of the Independent, we do not at this time reach the other parts of the Board's order, including the command that the checked-off dues and assessments should be refunded.

Reversed and remanded.

MR. JUSTICE ROBERTS and MR. JUSTICE JACKSON took no part in the consideration or decision of this case.

Note

1. Does Section 8(c), added to the NLRA by the Taft-Hartley amendments of 1947, overrule Virginia Electric's "totality of conduct" doctrine? Would such an interpretation of 8(c) render its protection broader than that of the First Amendment? See NLRB v. Gissel Packing Co., 395 U.S. 575, 89 S.Ct. 1918, 23 L.Ed.2d 547 (1969), infra p. 290 at 297. The legislative history of Section 8(c) is set forth, and the meaning of the section in the light of that history vigorously debated by majority and dissenting judges, in NLRB v. General Electric Co., 418 F.2d 736 (2d Cir.1969), cert. denied, 397 U.S. 965 (1970), discussed infra p. 603.

2. Is Section 8(c) a problem in both "C" and "R" cases? The Board confronted this question in two companion cases decided in 1953: LIVINGSTON SHIRT CORP., 107 N.L.R.B. 400, and PEERLESS PLYWOOD CO., 107 N.L.R.B. 427. Each entailed the "captive audience" problem—in which the employer delivers a noncoercive, antiunion speech to the employees on company time and premises and then refuses the union's demand for equal opportunity.

(a) In the Livingston Shirt case the union filed an 8(a)(1) charge by reason of the foregoing conduct, relying on Bonwit Teller, Inc., 96 N.L.R.B. 608 (1951), a consolidated "C" and "R" case in which the employer was found to have violated Section 8(a)(1) and the election was set aside. The Board refused to apply the Bonwit Teller doctrine, stating that:

> "＊ ＊ ＊ *Bonwit Teller* ＊ ＊ ＊ stemmed from the 'captive audience' concept of *Clark Bros.*[13] In that case, the majority of the Board found that it was an unfair labor practice for an employer to make a noncoercive speech to employees on his own premises during working hours. This doctrine was short lived. Congress specifically repudiated it, and said so, when it enacted Section 8(c) of the Act. But the concept was not so easily laid to rest, for the Board soon devised the *Bonwit Teller* doctrine. This latter case held that, while the speech was protected by 8(c), an employer who made a privileged speech was guilty of an unfair labor practice if he denied a request by the union to reply on his time and property. It requires little analysis to perceive that *Bonwit Teller* was the discredited *Clark Bros.* doctrine in scant disguise. It is equally contrary to the statute and congressional purpose.
>
> ＊ ＊ ＊
>
> "Accordingly, we are convinced that, absent special circumstances as hereinafter indicated, there is nothing improper in an employer refusing to grant to the union a right equal to his own in his plant. We rule therefore that, in the absence of either an unlawful broad no-solicitation rule (prohibiting union access to company premises on other than working time) or a privileged no-solicitation rule (broad, but not unlawful because of the charac-

---

13. Clark Bros., 70 N.L.R.B. 802.

ter of the business),[14] an employer does not commit an unfair labor practice if he makes a preelection speech on company time and premises to his employees and denies the union's request for an opportunity to reply." Livingston Shirt Corp., 107 N.L.R.B. at 407–09.

Why should the employer's denial of the union's request for equal opportunity to reply constitute, as the Board implies in the preceding paragraph, a violation of Section 8(a)(1) where "either an unlawful broad no-solicitation rule * * * or a privileged [broad] no-solicitation rule" is in effect? The Board solidified the implication into a holding against the employer in May Department Store, 136 N.L.R.B. 797 (1962), enforcement denied, 316 F.2d 797 (6th Cir. 1963).

(b) In the Peerless Plywood case, the Board set aside an election because of a noncoercive, antiunion speech by the employer to his employees, en masse, on company time and premises, less than twenty-four hours prior to the election. Explaining its action, the Board stated:

"We are now called upon to decide what our rule shall be in an election case in the light of our *Livingston Shirt* decision. We have abandoned the *Bonwit Teller* doctrine in complaint cases. But this does not however, dispose of the problem as it affects the conduct of an election. It is our considered view, based on experience with conducting representation elections, that last-minute speeches by either employers or unions delivered to massed assemblies of employees on company time have an unwholesome and unsettling effect and tend to interfere with that sober and thoughtful choice which a free election is designed to reflect. We believe that the real vice is in the last-minute character of the speech coupled with the fact that it is made on company time whether delivered by the employer or the union or both. Such a speech, because of its timing, tends to create a mass psychology which overrides arguments made through other campaign media and gives an unfair advantage to the party, whether employer or union, who in this manner obtains the last most telling word.

"When viewed in this light, it is plain that the situation is aggravated rather than equalized by an attempted application of the *Bonwit Teller* doctrine to elections. In an attempt to achieve equality, the effect of *Bonwit Teller* was to create a further imbalance by giving an advantage to the party who, by virtue of making a speech on company time only a few hours before the election, thereby was accorded the last most effective word.

"Accordingly, we now establish an election rule which will be applied in all election cases. This rule shall be that employers and unions alike will be prohibited from making election speeches on company time to massed assemblies of employees within 24 hours before the scheduled time for conducting an election. Violation of this rule will cause the election to be set aside whenever valid objections are filed.

"We institute this rule pursuant to our statutory authority and obligation to conduct elections in circumstances and under conditions which will insure employees a free and untrammeled choice. Implicit in this rule is our view that the combined circumstances of (1) the use of company time for preelection speeches and (2) the delivery of such speeches on the eve of the election tend to destroy freedom of choice and establish an atmosphere in

14. Marshall Field and Company, 93 N.L. R.B. 88 [a retail store case; see supra p. 259].

which a free election cannot be held. Also implicit in the rule is our judgment that noncoercive speeches made prior to the proscribed period will not interfere with a free election, inasmuch as our rule will allow time for their effect to be neutralized by the impact of other media of employee persuasion.

"This rule is closely akin to, and no more than an extension of, our longstanding rule prohibiting electioneering by either party at or near the polling place. We have previously prescribed space limitations, now we prescribe time limitations as well. * * *

"This rule will not interfere with the rights of unions or employers to circulate campaign literature on or off the premises at any time prior to an election, nor will it prohibit the use of any other legitimate campaign propaganda or media. It does not, of course, sanction coercive speeches or other conduct prior to the 24-hour period, nor does it prohibit an employer from making (without granting the union an opportunity to reply) campaign speeches on company time prior to the 24-hour period, provided, of course, such speeches are not otherwise violative of Section 8(a)(1). Moreover, the rule does not prohibit employers or unions from making campaign speeches on or off company premises during the 24-hour period if employee attendance is voluntary and on the employees' own time." 107 N.L.R.B. at 429–430.

3. Why was the focus in Virginia Electric on the 8(2) violation rather than the 8(1)? Consider the following:

(a) CARPENTER STEEL CO., 76 N.L.R.B. 670, 671–73 (1948):

"Section 10(c) of the original National Labor Relations Act directed the Board to order employers found to have engaged in conduct violative of the Act to cease and desist from their illegal conduct. It also gave the Board power to order employers to take affirmative action to remedy the unfair labor practices committed, a power limited only by the requirement that the remedy effectuate the policies of the Act. For 11 years, before the 1947 amendments were incorporated in the Act by the Labor Management Relations Act, the Board found that one particular type of affirmative action would most effectively remedy the consequences of an employer's illegal control of an unaffiliated labor organization, and make possible a free choice of representatives by the employees affected. That was the complete disestablishment of the subservient organization as a bargaining representative.[3] The Board invariably issued a disestablishment order, directing the employer to withhold all recognition in perpetuo, once it found a violation of Section 8(2) of the Act with respect to an unaffiliated organization. A disestablished union could never be certified by the Board. Such orders were approved by the courts as a valid exercise of the Board's remedial powers under Section 10(c).

"The Board did not, however, apply the full disestablishment remedy to employer-controlled or assisted labor organizations which were affiliated with a national or international federation. In such cases, the employer's conduct was complained against only as a violation of Section 8(1) of the Act rather than of Section 8(2). If a violation was found, the Board, in addition

---

3. See Matter of Pennsylvania Greyhound Lines, Inc., 1 N.L.R.B. 1, enforced 303 U.S. 261. [The fact that this *first* NLRB decision concerned a "company union" highlights the importance of Section 8(2) in the early application of the NLRA. The company-union problem has diminished with the widespread unionization of American industry.]

to directing the cessation of the illegal interference, merely ordered that recognition be withheld from the employer-controlled or assisted organization until it was certified by the Board. No certification would, of course, issue until the effects of the employer's illegal control or assistance had been dissipated, but thereafter it could issue to the same organization. This difference in treatment, as between affiliated and non-affiliated organizations, was based upon the Board's belief that a labor organization affiliated with a national or international federation that was outside the ambit of the employer's control could not be permanently and completely subjugated to the will of the employer. It was thought that complete disestablishment was therefore not required to remedy the effects of employer interference or to restore the employees' freedom of self-organization.

"That Congress disagreed with the distinction drawn by the Board became apparent when the Labor Management Relations Act of 1947 was passed. In reenacting Section 10(c) of the National Labor Relations Act, Congress qualified the Board's authority to direct affirmative action by adding a proviso which required that, in deciding cases involving unfair labor practices under Section 8(a)(1) or 8(a)(2), the Board should apply the 'same regulations and rules of decision * * * irrespective of whether or not the labor organization affected is affiliated with a labor organization national or international in scope.'[7] This proviso constitutes, in effect, Congressional rejection of the Board's prior view that mere affiliation with a national federation places a labor organization in such a different position from an organization not so affiliated as to warrant the use of different remedies when employer assistance or control has been found. There is no evidence, however, that the proviso was intended to abolish the disestablishment remedy itself; the target was discrimination in its use. Both the statutory language and the debates concerning the amendment make it wholly clear that Congress added this proviso to Section 10(c) in order to put an end to the disparity of treatment the Board had previously applied as between affiliated and unaffiliated organizations. The Board may no longer concern itself with the affiliation of a labor organization, or the lack thereof, in framing a remedy for violations of Section 8(a)(1) and 8(a)(2). So plain a mandate must be carried out without reservation or purpose of evasion, no matter how great the practical difficulties. Upon similar facts, the Board will hereafter apply the same remedy to both affiliated and unaffiliated labor organizations. Similarity of facts must be the test.

"Henceforth the Board's policy will be as follows:

"In all cases in which we find that an employer has dominated, or interfered with, or contributed support to a labor organization, or has committed any of these proscribed acts, we will find such conduct a violation of Section 8(a)(2) of the Act, as amended in 1947, regardless of whether the organization involved is affiliated. Where we find that an employer's unfair labor practices have been so extensive as to constitute *domination* of the organization, we shall order its disestablishment, whether or not it be

---

7. Section 9(c)(2) governs the impact of this proviso upon the Board's conduct of representation proceedings: "In determining whether or not a question of representation affecting commerce exists, the same regulations and rules of decision shall apply irrespective of the identity of the persons filing the petition or the kind of relief sought and in no case shall the Board deny a labor organization a place on the ballot by reason of an order with respect to such labor organization or its predecessor not issued in conformity with Section 10(c)."

affiliated. The Board believes that disestablishment is still necessary as a remedy, in order effectively to remove the consequences of an employer's unfair labor practices and to make possible a free choice of representatives, in those cases, perhaps few in number, in which an employer's control of *any* labor organization has extended to the point of actual domination. But when the Board finds that an employer's unfair labor practices were limited to interference and support and never reached the point of domination, we shall only order that recognition be withheld until certification, again without regard to whether or not the organization happens to be affiliated. Subsequent representation proceedings in such situations will be governed, of course, by the provisions of Section 9(c)(2).

"In the instant case we have made a finding * * * that the respondent's unfair labor practices exceeded the bounds of interference and support, and constituted *domination* of the Employees' Representation Committee, as well. Therefore, in accordance with our policy, modified to conform with the 1947 proviso to Section 10(c), we shall order the respondent to withdraw all recognition from the Employees' Representation Committee as the representative of any of its employees for the purpose of dealing with it concerning grievances, labor disputes, wages, rates of pay, hours of employment, or other conditions of employment, and completely to disestablish the Employees' Representation Committee as such representative."

(b) NLRB, Sixteenth Annual Report 155 (1951): "The Board customarily finds a labor organization to be dominated by the employer when its organization is directly instigated and encouraged, or directly participated in, by supervisors or other managerial employees and the employer provides financial or other direct support to the organization."

NATIONAL LABOR RELATIONS BOARD v. LORBEN CORP.

United States Court of Appeals, Second Circuit, 1965.
345 F.2d 346.

MARSHALL, CIRCUIT JUDGE. The National Labor Relations Board seeks enforcement of its order against The Lorben Corporation issued May 11, 1964 and reported at 146 N.L.R.B. No. 174.

The basic facts are simple and undisputed. On April 1, 1963 Local 1922, International Brotherhood of Electrical Workers, AFL–CIO, began organizing respondent's plant and secured the adherence of four of the 25 or 26 employees. On April 4 the union held a meeting to decide what to do about the discharge of one of the employees believed to have been discharged for union activities. A strike was decided upon and picketing began the next day with placards reading: "Employees of Lorben Electronics Corporation on Strike—Please help us maintain decent working conditions." About two days later the discharged employee asked respondent's president whether he wanted to have any discussions with the union's officials and the president said he did not want to do so. Subsequently, respondent's president, on advice of counsel, prepared a paper with a question: "Do you wish Local 1922 of the Electrical Workers to represent you?" Under this were two columns, "yes" and "no." The plant superintendent handed the sheet to each employee explaining to each that each was free to sign or not sign. This was done throughout the plant. All of the employees signed in the "no" column. There is no evidence of any employee [employer?] hostility to the union and the Trial Examiner found an absence of any "other unfair labor practices." However, the Examiner found that the respondent had violated the Act. While the Examiner mentioned the failure of respondent to advise the employees of the purpose of the interrogation and to assure them that no reprisals would follow, he based his decision primarily on his finding that the respondent had no legitimate purpose for the interrogation. The Board based its decision on the first two reasons and refused to rely on the third. We deny enforcement of the Board's order. *Court Decision*

Employer interrogation of employees as to their desire to be represented by a particular union is not coercive or intimidating on its face. It is extremely difficult to determine how often and under what circumstances threats will be inferred by the employees. The resulting confusion from efforts to set up basic ground rules in this field is carefully explored by Prof. Derek C. Bok, The Regulation of Campaign Tactics in Representation Elections under the National Labor Relations Act, 78 Harv.L.Rev. 38, 106 (1964).

The problem of delineating what is coercion by interrogation has resisted any set rules or specific limitations. The Board's original determination that interrogation by the employer was unlawful per se, Standard-Coosa-Thatcher Co., 85 N.L.R.B. 1358 (1949), was disapproved by the courts and the Board retreated to the position that interrogation would only be unlawful where it was found to be coercive in the light of all surrounding circumstances. As the Board stated in Blue Flash Express, Inc., 109 N.L.R.B. 591, 594 (1954): "We agree with and adopt the test laid down by the Court of Appeals for the Second Circuit in the Syracuse Color Press case [209 F.2d 596, cert. denied, 347 U.S. 966, 74 S.Ct. 777, 98 L.Ed. 1108 (1954)] which we construe to be that the answer to whether particular interrogation interferes with, restrains, and coerces employees must be found in the record as a whole." In Bourne v. NLRB, 332 F.2d 47, 48 (2 Cir.1964), this Circuit reaffirmed this comprehensive approach and we attempted to suggest some of the many factors that must be considered anew in each case to determine whether a particular interrogation is coercive:

"(1) The background, i.e. is there a history of employer hostility and discrimination?

"(2) The nature of the information sought, e.g. did the interrogator appear to be seeking information on which to base taking action against individual employees?

"(3) The identity of the questioner, i.e. how high was he in the company hierarchy?

"(4) Place and method of interrogation, e.g. was employee called from work to the boss's office? Was there an atmosphere of 'unnatural formality'?

"(5) Truthfulness of the reply." * * *

Recently the Board has withdrawn from this more comprehensive approach and has sought to establish the rule that employer interrogation is coercive in the absence of a showing that (1) there is a valid purpose for obtaining the information; (2) this purpose is communicated to the employees; and (3) the employees are assured that no reprisals will be taken, cf.

Johnnie's Poultry Co., 146 N.L.R.B. No. 98, p. 7 (April 17, 1964); Bok, supra, at 107. In the instant case, the Board applied this rule. It acknowledged that respondent had a valid purpose in conducting the poll, namely, to determine whether the union represented a majority of its employees for the purpose of deciding whether recognition should be extended. Yet the Board found that respondent had committed an unfair labor practice simply because of "the manner in which the poll was conducted, particularly the fact that Respondent did not explain the purpose of the poll to all of the employees, and did not offer or provide any assurances to the employees that their rights under the Act would not be infringed."

To enforce the Board's order which rests on this narrow ground alone, would be to depart from the line of decisions of this Circuit cited above, once approved by the Board, and we are not so inclined. While it is true that questioning can very well have a coercive effect where the purpose is not explained and there are no assurances against retaliation, * * * we hold that the absence of these two factors, without more and in the face of the undisputed facts in the record of this case, fails to show coercion within the meaning of section 8(a)(1).

The record of this case shows the following. Respondent owned a small plant of some 25 or 26 employees. A strike was called and a picket line had been set up after an employee had been discharged. The discharged employee asked management if it wanted to hold discussions with the union. The poll of employees followed. It was completed within the same day and this was the only poll that was taken. There was no showing of any employer hostility to the union nor any showing of any "other unfair labor practices." This record does not contain substantial evidence sufficient to support the Board's conclusion that the interrogation was coercive and enforcement must be denied.

FRIENDLY, CIRCUIT JUDGE (dissenting):

The Board supported its conclusion that Lorben "violated 8(a)(1) of the Act in polling the employees" by saying that it relied "principally on the manner in which the poll was conducted, particularly the fact that Respondent did not explain the purpose of the poll to all of the employees, and did not offer or provide any assurances to the employees that their rights under the Act would not be infringed."

I fail to understand on what basis, in a case like this, we may properly reject the conditions to permissible interrogation which the Board has developed and here enforced. The Board's adoption, in Blue Flash Express, Inc., 109 N.L.R.B. 591, 594 (1954), of language used by this court in granting enforcement in NLRB v. Syracuse Color Press, Inc., 209 F.2d 596, 599 (2 Cir.), cert. denied, 347 U.S. 966, 74 S.Ct. 777, 98 L.Ed. 1108 (1954), did not prevent it from later concluding, in the light of experience, that proper administration demanded working rules for reconciling the employer's desire to know what was afoot and the employees' need to be free from harassment, which would provide a test more definite, and more readily applicable, than "whether, under all the circumstances, the interrogation reasonably tends to restrain or interfere with the employees in the exercise of rights guaranteed by the Act," 109 N.L.R.B. at 593. * * * An agency receiving over 14,000 unfair labor practice charges a year, see 28 NLRB Ann.Rep. 161 (1963), ought not be denied the right to establish standards, appropriate to the statutory purpose, that are readily understandable by employers, regional directors and trial examiners, and be forced to determine every instance of alleged unlawful interrogation by an inquiry covering an employer's entire union history and his behavior during the particular crisis and to render decisions having little or no precedential value since "the number of distinct fact situations is almost infinite." See Bok, supra * * *, at 111, and also at 64–65. The Board's power to rule that certain types of conduct constitute unfair labor practices without further proof of motivation or effect has been sustained in cases too numerous for anything more than illustrative citation. Republic Aviation Corp. v. NLRB, 324 U.S. 793, 65 S.Ct. 982, 89 L.Ed. 1372 (1945) (prohibition of union solicitation on company premises outside of working hours); Brooks v. NLRB, 348 U.S. 96, 75 S.Ct. 176, 99 L.Ed. 125 (1954) (one-year rule on duty to bargain); NLRB v. Katz, 369 U.S. 736, 82 S.Ct. 1107, 8 L.Ed.2d 230 (1962) (*per se* violations of duty to bargain); NLRB v. Marcus Trucking Co., 286 F.2d 583 (2 Cir.1961) (contract bar rule).

It is true, as Professor Bok has also written, that one may well be "reluctant to find that he [an employer] has broken the law on the basis of inadvertent or uncalculating behavior which has created no more than a speculative risk of intimidating employees," and that in cases of that sort "one may justly question whether much can be done by faulting the employer long after the conduct in question has occurred." Bok, supra * * *, at 111. In such cases insistence on literal compliance with the three criteria stated in the majority opinion may appear to ignore the realities of industrial life. * * * But here we are dealing with employer conduct which was systematic and purposive, indeed taken after consultation with an attorney; the inquiry covered all the employees, and the answers were formalized by signatures on a list returned to the employer. Strict rules may not suit the casual question privately put to a few employees. But when the employer sets in motion a formal tabulation of this sort, it is not too much to ask that he provide some explanation and assure his employees against reprisal. Although my brothers condemn the Board's requirements, they do not explain why these rules are inappropriate or, more relevantly, why the Board may not reasonably think them so. * * *

While the Board relied "primarily" on the lack of explanation and assurance, the trial examiner's report which it adopted points to further circumstances supporting its conclusion. The interrogation occurred when several employees had been picketing the plant and one had been fired for what some workers apparently thought was pro-union activity; that this latter charge was not borne out cannot alter the cast thereby given to the inquiry into union support at that time. And one need not hold a doctoral degree in psychology to realize that the method of polling here utilized, in contrast to other methods of testing employee sentiment that were readily available, entailed serious risk that some employees would indicate a position quite different from that really held and would then feel obliged to adhere to it. Whether by design or by accident, the first workers to be questioned might be preponderantly against the union; the display of such votes would inevitably affect later voters who would be inclined to "follow the leader" and would see little use in bucking a trend; and all this could have a snowballing effect. I cannot believe that if the Board had utilized its rule-making power, under § 6 of the Act, see Peck, The Atrophied Rule-Making Powers of the National Labor Relations Board, 70 Yale L.J. 729 (1961), to prohibit such a means of ascertaining employee views as tending to "interfere with" rights guaranteed by § 7, and insisted on methods whereby each employee would indicate his sentiments without knowing those of others, any court would strike that down. I see no justification for a different result when the Board has followed the equally valid course of reaching its conclusion by the decision of a particular case. * * *

I would grant enforcement.

Note

In Struksnes Construction Co., 165 N.L.R.B. 1062 (1967), the Board, on remand from the Court of Appeals for the District of Columbia, 353 F.2d 852 (1965), in effect reiterated its Lorben approach with embellishment:

"Absent unusual circumstances, the polling of employees by an employer will be violative of Section 8(a)(1) of the Act unless the following safeguards are observed: (1) the purpose of the poll is to determine the truth of a union's claim of majority, (2) this purpose is communicated to the employees, (3) assurances against reprisal are given, (4) the employees are polled by secret ballot, and (5) the employer has not engaged in unfair labor practices or otherwise created a coercive atmosphere." 165 N.L.R.B. at 1063.

The Board went on to say:

"In accord with presumptive rules applied by the Board with court approval in other situations, this rule is designed to effectuate the purposes of the Act by maintaining a reasonable balance between the protection of employee rights and legitimate interests of employers.

"On the other hand, a poll taken while a petition for a Board election is pending does not, in our view, serve any legitimate interest of the employer that would not be better served by the forthcoming Board election. In accord with long-established Board policy, therefore, such polls will continue to be found violative of Section 8(a)(1) of the Act." Id.

How would these "Struksnes criteria" fare before the Second Circuit? What is "the law"?

With regard to this last question, the Board does not consider itself bound by Court of Appeals' rejection of the Board's perception of what "the law" is or should be as to a particular issue. If the Board is strongly enough minded on the issue, it persists in the application of its own point of view in *subsequent* cases, hoping to achieve approval by some other Court of Appeals, thus producing a conflict in decisions among the Court of Appeals which may lead to an authoritative resolution by the Supreme Court upon a grant of certiorari. The reader should be sensitized to this process; most of the Supreme Court decisions in this casebook exemplify a culmination of the foregoing type of conflict.

Indeed, the Board "flip flops," with its changing membership, in its own resolution of issues not yet decided by the Supreme Court, including the interrogation issue involved in the Lorben case. The Board vacillation on this issue continues to be between the per se approach of Standard-Coosa-Thatcher and the Blue Flash "totality of circumstances" test. The Board's Johnnie's

Poultry and Struksnes guidelines are way stations sometimes resorted to on this spectrum.

This Note is intended to sharpen insight on all questions of what "the law" is on issues which have not yet reached the Supreme Court. Has it?

NATIONAL LABOR RELATIONS BOARD v. WYMAN–GORDON CO.

Supreme Court of the United States, 1969.
394 U.S. 759, 89 S.Ct. 1426, 22 L.Ed.2d 709.

MR. JUSTICE FORTAS announced the judgment of the Court and delivered an opinion in which the CHIEF JUSTICE, MR. JUSTICE STEWART, and MR. JUSTICE WHITE join.

On the petition of the International Brotherhood of Boilermakers and pursuant to its powers under § 9 of the National Labor Relations Act * * *, the National Labor Relations Board ordered an election among the production and maintenance employees of the respondent company. At the election, the employees were to select one of two labor unions as their exclusive bargaining representative, or to choose not to be represented by a union at all. In connection with the election, the Board ordered the respondent to furnish a list of the names and addresses of its employees who could vote in the election, so that the unions could use the list for election purposes. The respondent refused to comply with the order, and the election was held without the list. Both unions were defeated in the election.

The Board upheld the unions' objections to the election because the respondent had not furnished the list, and the Board ordered a new election. The respondent again refused to obey a Board order to supply a list of employees, and the Board issued a subpoena ordering the respondent to provide the list or else produce its personnel and payroll records showing the employees' names and addresses. The Board filed an action in the United States District Court for the District of Massachusetts seeking to have its subpoena enforced or to have a mandatory injunction issued to compel the respondent to comply with its order.

The District Court held the Board's order valid and directed the respondent to comply. 270 F.Supp. 280 (1967). The United States Court of Appeals for the First Circuit reversed. 397 F.2d 394 (1968). The Court of Appeals thought that the order in this case was invalid because it was based on a rule laid down in an earlier decision by the Board, Excelsior Underwear Inc., 156 N.L.R.B. 1236 (1966), and the *Excelsior* rule had not been promulgated in accordance with the requirements that the Administrative Procedure Act prescribes for rule making, 5 U.S.C.A. § 553.* We granted certiorari to resolve a conflict among the circuits concerning the validity and effect of the *Excelsior* rule.

I.

The *Excelsior* case involved union objections to the certification of the results of elections that the unions had lost at two companies. The companies had denied the unions a list of the names and addresses of employees

---

* [Reporter's Note: The citations to the Administrative Procedure Act in the opinions in this case are to Supplement IV of the 1964 edition of the U.S. Code.]

eligible to vote. In the course of the proceedings, the Board "invited certain interested parties" to file briefs and to participate in oral argument of the issue whether the Board should require the employer to furnish lists of employees. 156 N.L.R.B., at 1238. Various employer groups and trade unions did so, as *amici curiae*. After these proceedings, the Board issued its decision in *Excelsior*. It purported to establish the general rule that such a list must be provided, but it declined to apply its new rule to the companies involved in the *Excelsior* case. Instead, it held that the rule would apply "only in those elections that are directed, or consented to, subsequent to 30 days from the date of [the] Decision." Id., at 1240, n. 5.

Specifically, the Board purported to establish "a requirement that will be applied in all election cases. That is, within 7 days after the Regional Director has approved a consent-election agreement entered into by the parties * * *, or after the Regional Director or the Board has directed an election * * *, the employer must file with the Regional Director an election eligibility list, containing the names and addresses of all the eligible voters. The Regional Director, in turn, shall make this information available to all parties in the case. Failure to comply with this requirement shall be grounds for setting aside the election whenever proper objections are filed." Id., at 1239–1240.

Section 6 of the National Labor Relations Act empowers the Board "to make * * *, in the manner prescribed by the Administrative Procedure Act, such rules and regulations as may be necessary to carry out the provisions of this Act." * * * The Administrative Procedure Act contains specific provisions governing agency rule making, which it defines as "an agency statement of general or particular applicability and future effect," 5 U.S.C.A. § 551(4). The Act requires among other things, publication in the Federal Register of notice of proposed rule making and of hearing; opportunity to be heard; a statement in the rule of its basis and purposes; and publication in the Federal Register of the rule as adopted. See 5 U.S.C.A. § 553. The Board asks us to hold that it has discretion to promulgate new rules in adjudicatory proceedings, without complying with the requirements of the Administrative Procedure Act.

The rule-making provisions of that Act, which the Board would avoid, were designed to assure fairness and mature consideration of rules of general application. * * * They may not be avoided by the process of making rules in the course of adjudicatory proceedings. There is no warrant in law for the Board to replace the statutory scheme with a rule-making procedure of its own invention. Apart from the fact that the device fashioned by the Board does not comply with statutory command, it obviously falls short of the substance of the requirements of the Administrative Procedure Act. The "rule" created in *Excelsior* was not published in the Federal Register, which is the statutory and accepted means of giving notice of a rule as adopted; only selected organizations were given notice of the "hearing," whereas notice in the Federal Register would have been general in character; under the Administrative Procedure Act, the terms or substance of the rule would have to be stated in the notice of hearing, and all interested parties would have an opportunity to participate in the rule making.

The Solicitor General does not deny that the Board ignored the rule-making provisions of the Administrative Procedure Act.[3] But he appears to argue that *Excelsior's* command is a valid substantive regulation, binding upon this respondent as such, because the Board promulgated it in the *Excelsior* proceeding, in which the requirements for valid adjudication had been met. This argument misses the point. There is no question that, in an adjudicatory hearing, the Board could validly decide the issue whether the employer must furnish a list of employees to the union. But that is not what the Board did in *Excelsior*. The Board did not even apply the rule it made to the parties in the adjudicatory proceeding, the only entities that could properly be subject to the order in that case. Instead, the Board purported to make a rule: i.e., to exercise its quasi-legislative power.

Adjudicated cases may and do, of course, serve as vehicles for the formulation of agency policies, which are applied and announced therein. See H. Friendly, The Federal Administrative Agencies 36–52 (1962).[4] They generally provide a guide to action that the agency may be expected to take in future cases. Subject to the qualified role of *stare decisis* in the administrative process, they may serve as precedents. But this is far from saying, as the Solicitor General suggests, that commands, decisions, or policies announced in adjudication are "rules" in the sense that they must, without more, be obeyed by the affected public.

In the present case, however, the respondent itself was specifically directed by the Board to submit a list of the names and addresses of its employees for use by the unions in connection with the election. This direction, which was part of the order directing that an election be held, is unquestionably valid. * * * Even though the direction to furnish the list was followed by citation to "Excelsior Underwear Inc., 156 NLRB No. 111," it is an order in the present case that the respondent was required to obey. Absent this direction by the Board, the respondent was under no compulsion to furnish the list because no statute and no validly adopted rule required it to do so.

Because the Board in an adjudicatory proceeding directed the respondent itself to furnish the list, the decision of the Court of Appeals for the First Circuit must be reversed.[6]

3. The Board has never utilized the Act's rule-making procedures. It has been criticized for contravening the Act in this manner. See, e.g., 1 K. Davis, Administrative Law Treatise § 6.13 (Supp.1965); Peck, The Atrophied Rule-Making Powers of the National Labor Relations Board, 70 Yale L.J. 729 (1961).

4. The Solicitor General argues that this Court has previously approved "rules" articulated by the Board in the adjudication of particular cases without questioning the propriety of that procedure. He cites Republic Aviation Corp. v. NLRB, 324 U.S. 793, 65 S.Ct. 982, 89 L.Ed. 1372 (1945); * * * and Brooks v. NLRB, 348 U.S. 96, 75 S.Ct. 176, 99 L.Ed. 125 (1954). In none of these cases has this Court ruled upon or sanctioned the exercise of quasi-legislative power—i.e., rule making—without compliance with § 6 of the NLRA and the rule-making provisions of the Administrative Procedure Act.

6. Mr. Justice Harlan's dissent argues that because the Board improperly relied upon the *Excelsior* "rule" in issuing its order, we are obliged to remand. * * * To remand would be an idle and useless formality. * * * [T]he substance of the Board's command is not seriously contestable. There is not the slightest uncertainty as to the outcome of a proceeding before the Board, whether the Board acted through a rule or an order. It would be meaningless to remand.

II.

The respondent also argues that it need not obey the Board's order because the requirement of disclosure of employees' names and addresses is substantively invalid. This argument lacks merit. The objections that the respondent raises to the requirement of disclosure were clearly and correctly answered by the Board in its *Excelsior* decision. All of the United States Courts of Appeals that have passed on the question have upheld the substantive validity of the disclosure requirement, and the court below strongly intimated a view that the requirement was substantively a proper one, 397 F.2d, at 396.

We have held in a number of cases that Congress granted the Board a wide discretion to ensure the fair and free choice of bargaining representatives. * * * The disclosure requirement furthers this objective by encouraging an informed employee electorate and by allowing unions the right of access to employees that management already possesses. It is for the Board and not for this Court to weigh against this interest the asserted interest of employees in avoiding the problems that union solicitation may present.

III.

The respondent contends that even if the disclosure requirement is valid, the Board lacks power to enforce it by subpoena. Section 11(1) of the National Labor Relations Act provides that the Board shall have access to "any evidence of any person being investigated or proceeded against that relates to any matter under investigation or in question," and empowers the Board to issue subpoenas "requiring the attendance and testimony of witnesses or the production of any evidence in such proceeding or investigation." Section 11(2) gives the district courts jurisdiction, upon application by the Board, to issue an order requiring a person who has refused to obey the Board's subpoena "to appear before the Board * * * there to produce evidence if so ordered, or there to give testimony touching the matter under investigation or in question * * *." * * *

The respondent takes the position that these statutory provisions do not give the Board authority to subpoena the list here in question because they are not "evidence" within the meaning of the statutory language. The District Court held, however, that "in the context of § 11 of the Act, 'evidence' means not only proof at a hearing but also books and records and other papers which will be of assistance to the Board in conducting a particular investigation." The courts of appeals that have passed on the question have construed the term "evidence" in a similar manner. * * *

We agree that the list here in issue is within the scope of § 11 so that the Board's subpoena power may be validly exercised.

The judgment of the Court of Appeals is reversed, and the case is remanded to that court with directions to enforce the Board's order against the respondent. * * * *Provide List of Names.*

MR. JUSTICE BLACK, with whom MR. JUSTICE BRENNAN and MR. JUSTICE MARSHALL join, concurring in the result.

I agree with Parts II and III of the prevailing opinion of MR. JUSTICE FORTAS, holding that the *Excelsior* requirement [1] that an employer supply the union with the names and addresses of its employees prior to an election is valid on its merits and can be enforced by a subpoena. But I cannot subscribe to the criticism in that opinion of the procedure followed by the Board in adopting that requirement in the *Excelsior* case, 156 N.L.R.B. 1236 (1966). Nor can I accept the novel theory by which the opinion manages to uphold enforcement of the *Excelsior* practice in spite of what it considers to be statutory violations present in the procedure by which the requirement was adopted. Although the opinion is apparently intended to rebuke the Board and encourage it to follow the plurality's conception of proper administrative practice, the result instead is to free the Board from all judicial control whatsoever regarding compliance with procedures specifically required by applicable federal statutes such as the National Labor Relations Act * * * and the Administrative Procedure Act * * *. Apparently, under the prevailing opinion, courts must enforce any requirement announced in a purported "adjudication" even if it clearly was not adopted as an incident to the decision of a case before the agency, and must enforce "rules" adopted in a purported "rule making" even if the agency materially violated the specific requirements that Congress has directed for such proceedings in the Administrative Procedure Act. I for one would not give judicial sanction to any such illegal agency action.

In the present case, however, I am convinced that the *Excelsior* practice was adopted by the Board as a legitimate incident to the adjudication of a specific case before it, and for that reason I would hold that the Board properly followed the procedures applicable to "adjudication" rather than "rule making." Since my reasons for joining in reversal of the Court of Appeals differ so substantially from those set forth in the prevailing opinion, I will spell them out at some length.

Most administrative agencies, like the Labor Board here, are granted two functions by the legislation creating them: (1) the power under certain conditions to make rules having the effect of laws, that is, generally speaking, quasi-legislative power; and (2) the power to hear and adjudicate particular controversies, that is quasi-judicial power. The line between these two functions is not always a clear one and in fact the two functions merge at many points. For example, in exercising its quasi-judicial function an agency must frequently decide controversies on the basis of new doctrines, not theretofore applied to a specific problem, though drawn to be sure from broader principles reflecting the purposes of the statutes involved and from the rules invoked in dealing with related problems. If the agency decision reached under the adjudicatory power becomes a precedent, it guides future conduct in much the same way as though it were a new rule promulgated under the rule-making power, and both an adjudicatory order

---

1. This requirement first announced in the *Excelsior* case, 156 N.L.R.B. 1236 (1966), has often been referred to by the Board, the lower courts, and the commentators as "the *Excelsior* rule." I understand the use of the word "rule" in this context to imply simply that the requirement is a rule of law such as would be announced in a court opinion and not neces-sarily that it is the kind of "rule" required to be promulgated in accordance with the "rule-making" procedures of the Administrative Procedure Act. For the sake of clarity, however, I have chosen in this opinion to avoid use of the word "rule" when referring to the procedure required by the *Excelsior* decision.

and a formal "rule" are alike subject to judicial review. Congress gave the Labor Board both of these separate but almost inseparably related powers.
* * *

In the present case there is no dispute that all the procedural safeguards required for "adjudication" were fully satisfied in connection with the Board's *Excelsior* decision * * *.

The prevailing opinion seems to hold that the *Excelsior* requirement cannot be considered the result of adjudication because the Board did not apply it to the parties in the *Excelsior* case itself, but rather announced that it would be applied only to elections called 30 days after the date of the *Excelsior* decision. But the *Excelsior* order was nonetheless an inseparable part of the adjudicatory process. The principal issue before the Board in the *Excelsior* case was whether the election should be set aside on the ground, urged by the unions, that the employer had refused to make the employee lists available to them. See 156 N.L.R.B., at 1236–1238. The Board decided that the election involved there should not be set aside and thus rejected the contention of the unions. In doing so, the Board chose to explain the reasons for its rejection of their claim, and it is this explanation, the Board's written opinion, which is the source of the *Excelsior* requirement. The Board's opinion should not be regarded as any less an appropriate part of the adjudicatory process merely because the reason it gave for rejecting the unions' position was not that the Board disagreed with them as to the merits of the disclosure procedure but rather, see 156 N.L.R.B., at 1239, 1240, n. 5, that while fully agreeing that disclosure should be required, the Board did not feel that it should upset the Excelsior Company's justified reliance on previous refusals to compel disclosure by setting aside this particular election.

Apart from the fact that the decisions whether to accept a "new" requirement urged by one party and, if so, whether to apply it retroactively to the other party are inherent parts of the adjudicatory process, I think the opposing theory accepted by the Court of Appeals and by the prevailing opinion today is a highly impractical one. In effect, it would require an agency like the Labor Board to proceed by adjudication only when it could decide, *prior* to adjudicating a particular case, that any new practice to be adopted would be applied retroactively. Obviously, this decision cannot properly be made until all the issues relevant to adoption of the practice are fully considered in connection with the final decision of that case. If the Board were to decide, after careful evaluation of all the arguments presented to it in the adjudicatory proceeding, that it might be fairer to apply the practice only prospectively, it would be faced with the unpleasant choice of either starting all over again to evaluate the merits of the question, this time in a "rule-making" proceeding, or overriding the considerations of fairness and applying its order retroactively anyway, in order to preserve the validity of the new practice and avoid duplication of effort. I see no good reason to impose any such inflexible requirement on the administrative agencies.

For all of the foregoing reasons I would hold that the Board acted well within its discretion in choosing to proceed as it did, and I would reverse the judgment of the Court of Appeals on this basis.

MR. JUSTICE DOUGLAS, dissenting, * * *

I am willing to assume that, if the Board decided to treat each case on its special facts and perform its adjudicatory function in the conventional way, we should have no difficulty in affirming its action. The difficulty is that it chose a different course in the *Excelsior* case and, having done so, it should be bound to follow the procedures prescribed in the Act * * *. When we hold otherwise, we let the Board "have its cake and eat it too." * * *

Rule making is no cure-all; but it does force important issues into full public display and in that sense makes for more responsible administrative action.

I would hold the agencies governed by the rule making procedure strictly to its requirements and not allow them to play fast and loose as the National Labor Relation Board apparently likes to do. * * *

MR. JUSTICE HARLAN, dissenting. * * *

* * * An agency chooses to apply a rule prospectively only because it represents such a departure from pre-existing understandings that it would be unfair to impose the rule upon the parties in pending matters. But it is precisely in these situations, in which established patterns of conduct are revolutionized, that rule-making procedures perform * * * vital functions * * *.

* * * Under today's prevailing approach, the agency may evade the commands of the Act whenever it desires and yet coerce the regulated industry into compliance. * * *

* * * The Regional Office that issued the order under review refused to consider the merits of the arguments against the *Excelsior* rule which were raised by Wyman-Gordon on the ground that they had been rejected by the Board in the *Excelsior* case itself:

> "[It] is well known that *Excelsior* issued only after oral argument and briefs, including *amicus curiae* briefs by interested parties. The Board has considered arguments such as those made here and nevertheless established the requirement embodied in *Excelsior* and the undersigned [Acting Regional Director] is bound by it." Appendix 33.

The Board denied review of this decision on the ground that "it raises no substantial issues warranting review." Appendix 35. * * *

Note

1. Should the Court, before approving the Excelsior "rule," have required the Board to meet the test laid down in Babcock & Wilcox and reiterated in NLRB v. United Steelworkers (Nutone, Inc.), 357 U.S. 357, 78 S.Ct. 1268, 2 L.Ed. 2d 1383 (1958),[f]—namely, that unless alternative means do not provide reasonable access to his employees, an employer may not be required to facilitate a

---

f. In the Nutone case the employer enforced against its employees a valid no-solicitation rule applicable to worktime only, while itself engaging in a noncoercive, antiunion campaign during worktime. The Court held this conduct not to be a violation of Section 8(a)(1), noting that the issue in such cases was whether "such conduct to any considerable degree created an imbalance in the opportunities for organizational communication." The Board had failed to make the necessary findings as to whether the union had reasonably adequate opportunity to communicate with the employees off the employer's premises.

union's effort to organize? Is the following passage from the Board's opinion in Excelsior persuasive on this point?

" *   *   * [A]s we read *Babcock* and *Nutone,* the existence of alternative channels of communication is relevant only when the opportunity to communicate made available by the Board would interfere with a significant employer interest—such as the employer's interest in controlling the use of property owned by him.   Here, *   *   * the employer has no significant interest in the secrecy of employee names and addresses.   Hence, there is no necessity for the Board to consider the existence of alternative channels of communication before requiring disclosure of that information.   Moreover, even assuming that there is some legitimate employer interest in nondisclosure, we think it relevant that the subordination of that interest which we here require is limited to a situation in which employee interests in self-organization are shown to be substantial.   For, whenever an election is directed (the precondition to disclosure) the Regional Director has found that a real question concerning representation exists; when the employer consents to an election, he has impliedly admitted this fact.   The opportunity to communicate on company premises sought in *Babcock* and *Nutone* was not limited to the situation in which employee organizational interests were substantial; i.e., in which an election had been directed; we think that on this ground also the cases are distinguishable.   Finally, both *Babcock* and *Nutone* dealt with the circumstances under which the Board might find an employer to have committed an unfair labor practice in violation of Section 8 of the Act, whereas the instant cases pose the substantially distinguishable issue of the circumstances under which the Board may set aside an election. '[T]he test of conduct which may interfere with the "laboratory conditions" for an election is considerably more restrictive than the test of conduct which amounts to interference, restraint, or coercion which violates Section 8(a)(1).'[24]   Whether or not an employer's refusal to disclose employee names and addresses after an election is directed would constitute 'interference, restraint, or coercion' within the meaning of Section 8(a)(1) of the Act, despite the existence of alternative channels of communication open to the union, is a question on which we express no view because it is not before us. However, we are persuaded, for the reasons previously stated, that disclosure is one of the 'safeguards necessary to insure the fair and free choice of bargaining representative by employees' and that an employer's refusal to disclose, regardless of the existence of alternative channels of communication, tends to interfere with a fair and free election.   Thus *Babcock* and *Nutone,* which dealt with the substantially different issue of whether the employers' conduct violated 8(a)(1), are, for this reason also, inapposite." Excelsior Underwear Inc., 156 N.L.R.B. 1236, 1245–46 (1966).

Do the *employees* have a "significant interest in the secrecy of employee names and addresses"?

2.   The Excelsior rule might be thought to have reduced union concern about "equal opportunity" in "captive audience" situations, the problem dealt with in Note 2(a), supra p. 265.   The Board apparently so thought.   In General Electric Co., 156 N.L.R.B. 1247 (1966), it declined to review its Livingston Shirt doctrine pending an opportunity to evaluate the impact of the Excelsior rule on

24. Dal-Tex Optical Company, Inc., 137 NLRB 1782, 1786–1787; see also General Shoe Corporation, 77 NLRB 124, 126–127.

employees' opportunities to make "a free and reasoned choice for or against unionization." No such review has yet occurred. The thinking of the unions has not paralleled that of the Board; they have sought another forum: the Labor Reform Bill of 1978, strongly supported by organized labor, contained a provision which, if enacted, would have overruled the Livingston Shirt doctrine.

3. With regard to the controversy concerning the manner in which the Board formulated the Excelsior "rule":

a. Which of the positions do you find most persuasive—that of the plurality, that of Justice Black, that of the dissenters?

b. How would you explain the Board's failure to exercise its substantive rulemaking power under Section 6? From the Board's point of view, what are the relative merits of rulemaking by adjudicatory and by quasi-legislative processes?

c. Was not the Wyman-Gordon Company denied the protection of *both* the adjudicatory and legislative processes? But is that not always true regarding a rule laid down by adjudication in one case and then applied in later cases?

NATIONAL LABOR RELATIONS BOARD v. EXCHANGE PARTS CO.

Supreme Court of the United States, 1964.
375 U.S. 405, 84 S.Ct. 457, 11 L.Ed.2d 435.

MR. JUSTICE HARLAN delivered the opinion of the Court.

This case presents a question concerning the limitations which § 8(a)(1) of the National Labor Relations Act * * * places on the right of an employer to confer economic benefits on his employees shortly before a representation election. The precise issue is whether that section prohibits the conferral of such benefits, without more, where the employer's purpose is to affect the outcome of the election. We granted the National Labor Relations Board's petition for certiorari * * * to clear up a possible conflict between the decision below and those of other Courts of Appeals on an important question of national labor policy. For reasons given in this opinion, we conclude that the judgment below must be reversed.

The respondent, Exchange Parts Company, is engaged in the business of rebuilding automobile parts in Fort Worth, Texas. Prior to November 1959 its employees were not represented by a union. On November 9, 1959, the International Brotherhood of Boilermakers, Iron Shipbuilders, Blacksmiths, Forgers and Helpers, AFL–CIO, advised Exchange Parts that the union was conducting an organizational campaign at the plant and that a majority of the employees had designated the union as their bargaining representative. On November 16 the union petitioned the Labor Board for a representation election. The Board conducted a hearing on December 29, and on February 19, 1960, issued an order directing that an election be held. The election was held on March 18, 1960.

At two meetings on November 4 and 5, 1959, C.V. McDonald, the Vice-President and General Manager of Exchange Parts, announced to the employees that their "floating holiday" in 1959 would fall on December 26 and that there would be an additional "floating holiday" in 1960. On February 25, six days after the Board issued its election order, Exchange Parts held a dinner for employees at which Vice-President McDonald told the employees that they could decide whether the extra day of vacation in 1960 would be a "floating holiday" or would be taken on their birthdays. The employees voted for the latter. McDonald also referred to the forthcoming representation election as one in which, in the words of the trial examiner, the employees would "determine whether * * * [they] wished to hand over their right to speak and act for themselves." He stated that the union had distorted some of the facts and pointed out the benefits obtained by the employees without a union. He urged all the employees to vote in the election.

On March 4 Exchange Parts sent its employees a letter which spoke of "the *Empty Promises* of the Union" and "the *fact* that *it is the Company that puts things in your envelope* * * *." After mentioning a number of benefits, the letter said: "The Union can't put any of those things in your envelope—*only the Company can do that.*" [2] Further on, the letter stated: "* * * [I]t didn't take a Union to get any of those things and * * * it won't take a Union to get additional improvements in the future." Accompanying the letter was a detailed statement of the benefits granted by the company since 1949 and an estimate of the monetary value of such benefits to the employees. Included in the statement of benefits for 1960 were the birthday holiday, a new system for computing overtime during holiday weeks which had the effect of increasing wages for those weeks, and a new vacation schedule which enabled employees to extend their vacations by sandwiching them between two weekends. Although Exchange Parts asserts that the policy behind the latter two benefits was established earlier, it is clear that the letter of March 4 was the first general announcement of the changes to the employees. In the ensuing election the union lost.

The Board, affirming the findings of the trial examiner, found that the announcement of the birthday holiday and the grant and announcement of overtime and vacation benefits were arranged by Exchange Parts with the intention of inducing the employees to vote against the union. It found that this conduct violated § 8(a)(1) of the National Labor Relations Act and issued an appropriate order. On the Board's petition for enforcement of the order, the Court of Appeals rejected the finding that the announcement of the birthday holiday was timed to influence the outcome of the election. It accepted the Board's findings with respect to the overtime and vacation benefits, and the propriety of those findings is not in controversy here. However, noting that "the benefits were put into effect unconditionally on a permanent basis, and no one has suggested that there was any implication the benefits would be withdrawn if the workers voted for the union," 304 F.2d 368, 375, the court denied enforcement of the Board's order. It believed that it was not an unfair labor practice under § 8(a)(1) for an employer to grant benefits to its employees in these circumstances.

* * * We think the Court of Appeals was mistaken in concluding that the conferral of employee benefits while a representation election is pending, for the purpose of inducing employees to vote against the union, does not "interfere with" the protected right to organize.

The broad purpose of § 8(a)(1) is to establish "the right of employes to organize for mutual aid without employer interference." Republic Aviation Corp. v. N.L.R.B., 324 U.S. 793, 798, 65 S.Ct. 982, 985, 89 L.Ed. 1372. We

2. The italics appear in the original letter.

have no doubt that it prohibits not only intrusive threats and promises but also conduct immediately favorable to employees which is undertaken with the express purpose of impinging upon their freedom of choice for or against unionization and is reasonably calculated to have that effect. In Medo Photo Supply Corp. v. N.L.R.B., 321 U.S. 678, 686, 64 S.Ct. 830, 834, 88 L.Ed. 1007, this Court said: "The action of employees with respect to the choice of their bargaining agents may be induced by favors bestowed by the employer as well as by his threats or domination." Although in that case there was already a designated bargaining agent and the offer of "favors" was in response to a suggestion of the employees that they would leave the union if favors were bestowed, the principles which dictated the result there are fully applicable here. The danger inherent in well-timed increases in benefits is the suggestion of a fist inside the velvet glove. Employees are not likely to miss the inference that the source of benefits now conferred is also the source from which future benefits must flow and which may dry up if it is not obliged.[3] The danger may be diminished if, as in this case, the benefits are conferred permanently and unconditionally. But the absence of conditions or threats pertaining to the particular benefits conferred would be of controlling significance only if it could be presumed that no question of additional benefits or renegotiation of existing benefits would arise in the future; and, of course, no such presumption is tenable.

* * * It is true, as the court below pointed out, that in most cases of this kind the increase in benefits could be regarded as "one part of an overall program of interference and restraint by the employer," 304 F.2d, at 372, and that in this case the questioned conduct stood in isolation. Other unlawful conduct may often be an indication of the motive behind a grant of benefits while an election is pending, and to that extent it is relevant to the legality of the grant; but when as here the motive is otherwise established, an employer is not free to violate § 8(a)(1) by conferring benefits simply because it refrains from other, more obvious violations. We cannot agree with the Court of Appeals that enforcement of the Board's order will have the "ironic" result of "discouraging benefits for labor." 304 F.2d, at 376. The beneficence of an employer is likely to be ephemeral if prompted by a threat of unionization which is subsequently removed. Insulating the right of collective organization from calculated good will of this sort deprives employees of little that has lasting value.

Reversed.

Note

Does Exchange Parts render every benefit bestowed by an employer upon his employees during a union's organizing campaign a violation of Section 8(a)(1)?

3. The inference was made almost explicit in Exchange Parts' letter to its employees of March 4, already quoted, which said: "The Union can't put any of those * * * [benefits] in your envelope—*only the Company can do that.*" (Original italics.) We place no reliance, however, on these or other words of the respondent disassociated from its conduct.

Section 8(c) of the Act * * * provides that the expression or dissemination of "any views, argument, or opinion" "shall not constitute or be evidence of an unfair labor practice under any of the provisions of this Act, if such expression contains no threat of reprisal or force of promise of benefit."

TEXTILE WORKERS UNION v. DARLINGTON MANUFACTURING CO.

Supreme Court of the United States, 1965.
380 U.S. 263, 85 S.Ct. 994, 13 L.Ed.2d 827.

Mr. Justice Harlan delivered the opinion of the Court.

We here review judgments of the Court of Appeals setting aside and refusing to enforce an order of the National Labor Relations Board which found respondent Darlington guilty of an unfair labor practice by reason of having permanently closed its plant following petitioner union's election as the bargaining representative of Darlington's employees.

Darlington Manufacturing Company was a South Carolina corporation operating one textile mill. A majority of Darlington's stock was held by Deering Milliken, a New York "selling house" marketing textiles produced by others. Deering Milliken in turn was controlled by Roger Milliken, president of Darlington, and by other members of the Milliken family. The National Labor Relations Board found that the Milliken family, through Deering Milliken, operated 17 textile manufacturers, including Darlington, whose products, manufactured in 27 different mills, were marketed through Deering Milliken.

In March 1956 petitioner Textile Workers Union initiated an organizational campaign at Darlington which the company resisted vigorously in various ways, including threats to close the mill if the union won a representation election.[3] On September 6, 1956, the union won an election by a narrow margin. When Roger Milliken was advised of the union victory, he decided to call a meeting of the Darlington board of directors to consider closing the mill. Mr. Milliken testified before the Labor Board:

> "I felt that as a result of the campaign that had been conducted and the promises and statements made in these letters that had been distributed [favoring unionization], that if before we had had some hope, possible hope of achieving competitive [costs] * * * by taking advantage of new machinery that was being put in, that this hope had diminished as a result of the election because a majority of the employees had voted in favor of the union * * *." (R. 457.)

The board of directors met on September 12 and voted to liquidate the corporation, action which was approved by the stockholders on October 17. The plant ceased operations entirely in November, and all plant machinery and equipment were sold piecemeal at auction in December.

The union filed charges with the Labor Board claiming that Darlington had violated §§ 8(a)(1) and (3) of the National Labor Relations Act by closing its plant, and § 8(a)(5) by refusing to bargain with the union after the election.[5] The Board, by a divided vote, found that Darlington had been

3. The Board found that Darlington had interrogated employees and threatened to close the mill if the union won the election. After the decision to liquidate was made (see infra), Darlington employees were told that the decision to close was caused by the election, and they were encouraged to sign a petition disavowing the union. These practices were held to violate § 8(a)(1) of the National

Labor Relations Act, * * * and that part of the Board decision is not challenged here.

5. The union asked for a bargaining conference on September 12, 1956 (the day that the board of directors voted to liquidate), but was told to await certification by the Board. The union was certified on October 24, and did meet with Darlington officials in November, but no actual bargaining took place. The

closed because of the antiunion animus of Roger Milliken, and held that to be a violation of § 8(a)(3).[6] The Board also found Darlington to be part of a single integrated employer group controlled by the Milliken family through Deering Milliken; therefore Deering Milliken could be held liable for the unfair labor practices of Darlington. Alternatively, since Darlington was a part of the Deering Milliken enterprise, Deering Milliken had violated the Act by closing part of its business for a discriminatory purpose. The Board ordered back pay for all Darlington employees until they obtained substantially equivalent work or were put on preferential hiring lists at the other Deering Milliken mills. Respondent Deering Milliken was ordered to bargain with the union in regard to details of compliance with the Board order. 139 N.L.R.B. 241.

On review, the Court of Appeals, sitting *en banc,* set aside the order and denied enforcement by a divided vote. 325 F.2d 682. The Court of Appeals held that even accepting *arguendo* the Board's determination that Deering Milliken had the status of a single employer, a company has the absolute right to close out a part or all of its business regardless of antiunion motives. The court therefore did not review the Board's finding that Deering Milliken was a single integrated employer. We granted certiorari * * * to consider the important questions involved. We hold that so far as the Labor Relations Act is concerned, an employer has the absolute right to terminate his entire business for any reason he pleases, but disagree with the Court of Appeals that such right includes the ability to close part of a business no matter what the reason. We conclude that the cause must be remanded to the Board for further proceedings.

Preliminarily it should be observed that both petitioners argue that the Darlington closing violated § 8(a)(1) as well as § 8(a)(3) of the Act. We think, however, that the Board was correct in treating the closing only under § 8(a)(3).[8] Section 8(a)(1) provides that it is an unfair labor practice for an employer "to interfere with, restrain, or coerce employees in the exercise of" § 7 rights. Naturally, certain business decisions will, to some degree, interfere with concerted activities by employees. But it is only when the interference with § 7 rights outweighs the business justification for the employer's action that § 8(a)(1) is violated. See, e.g., National Labor Relations Board v. United Steelworkers [Nutone], 357 U.S. 357, 78 S.Ct. 1268, 2 L.Ed.2d 1383; Republic Aviation Corp. v. National Labor Relations Board, 324 U.S. 793, 65 S.Ct. 982, 89 L.Ed. 1372. A violation of § 8(a)(1) alone therefore presupposes an act which is unlawful even absent a discriminatory motive. Whatever may be the limits of § 8(a)(1), some employer decisions are so peculiarly matters of management prerogative that they would never constitute violations of § 8(a)(1), whether or not they involved sound business judgment, unless they also violated § 8(a)(3). Thus it is not questioned in this case that an employer has the right to terminate his business, whatever

Board found this to be a violation of § 8(a)(5). Such a finding was in part based on the determination that the plant closing was an unfair labor practice * * *.

6. Since the closing was held to be illegal, the Board found that the gradual discharges of all employees during November and Decem-

ber constituted § 8(a)(1) violations. The propriety of this determination depends entirely on whether the decision to close the plant violated § 8(a)(3).

8. The Board did find that Darlington's discharges of employees following the decision to close violated § 8(a)(1). See n. 6, supra.

the impact of such action on concerted activities, if the decision to close is motivated by other than discriminatory reasons.[10] But such action, if discriminatorily motivated, is encompassed within the literal language of § 8(a)(3). We therefore deal with the Darlington closing under that section.

I.

We consider first the argument, advanced by the petitioner union but not by the Board, and rejected by the Court of Appeals, that an employer may not go completely out of business without running afoul of the Labor Relations Act if such action is prompted by a desire to avoid unionization.[11] Given the Board's findings on the issue of motive, acceptance of this contention would carry the day for the Board's conclusion that the closing of this plant was an unfair labor practice, even on the assumption that Darlington is to be regarded as an independent unrelated employer. A proposition that a single businessman cannot choose to go out of business if he wants to would represent such a startling innovation that it should not be entertained without the clearest manifestation of legislative intent or une- quivocal judicial precedent so construing the Labor Relations Act. We find neither.

So far as legislative manifestation is concerned, it is sufficient to say that there is not the slightest indication in the history of the Wagner Act or of the Taft-Hartley Act that Congress envisaged any such result under either statute.

As for judicial precedent, the Board recognized that "[t]here is no decided case directly dispositive of Darlington's claim that it had an absolute right to close its mill, irrespective of motive." 139 N.L.R.B., at 250. * * * The courts of appeals have generally assumed that a complete cessation of business will remove an employer from future coverage by the Act. Thus the Court of Appeals said in these cases: The Act "does not compel a person to become or remain an employee. It does not compel one to become or remain an employer. Either may withdraw from that status with immunity, so long as the obligations of any employment contract have been met." 325 F.2d at 685. * * *

The AFL–CIO suggests in its *amicus* brief that Darlington's action was similar to a discriminatory lockout, which is prohibited " 'because designed to frustrate organizational efforts, to destroy or undermine bargaining representation, or to evade the duty to bargain.' " One of the purposes of the Labor Relations Act is to prohibit the discriminatory use of economic weapons in an effort to obtain future benefits. The discriminatory lockout designed to destroy a union, like a "runaway shop," is a lever which has been used to discourage collective employee activities in the future. But a

---

10. It is also clear that the ambiguous act of closing a plant following the election of a union is not, absent an inquiry into the em- ployer's motive, inherently discriminatory. We are thus not confronted with a situation where the employer "must be held to intend the very consequences which foreseeably and inescapably flow from his actions * * *." (National Labor Relations Board v. Erie Resis- tor Corp., 373 U.S. 221, 228, 83 S.Ct. 1139, 1145, 10 L.Ed.2d 308), in which the Board could find a violation of § 8(a)(3) without an examination into motive. * * *

11. The Board predicates its argument on the finding that Deering Milliken was an inte- grated enterprise, and does not consider it necessary to argue that an employer may not go completely out of business for anti-union reasons. Brief for National Labor Relations Board, p. 3, n. 2.

complete liquidation of a business yields no such future benefit for the employer, if the termination is bona fide.[14] It may be motivated more by spite against the union than by business reasons, but it is not the type of discrimination which is prohibited by the Act. The personal satisfaction that such an employer may derive from standing on his beliefs and the mere possibility that other employers will follow his example are surely too remote to be considered dangers at which the labor statutes were aimed.[15] Although employees may be prohibited from engaging in a strike under certain conditions, no one would consider it a violation of the Act for the same employees to quit their employment *en masse,* even if motivated by a desire to ruin the employer. The very permanence of such action would negate any future economic benefit to the employees. The employer's right to go out of business is no different.

We are not presented here with the case of a "runaway shop," [16] whereby Darlington would transfer its work to another plant or open a new plant in another locality to replace its closed plant. Nor are we concerned with a shutdown where the employees, by renouncing the union, could cause the plant to reopen. Such cases would involve discriminatory employer action for the purpose of obtaining some benefit from the employees in the future. We hold here only that when an employer closes his entire business, even if the liquidation is motivated by vindictiveness toward the union, such action is not an unfair labor practice.[20]

II.

While we thus agree with the Court of Appeals that viewing Darlington as an independent employer the liquidation of its business was not an unfair labor practice, we cannot accept the lower court's view that the same conclusion necessarily follows if Darlington is regarded as an integral part of the Deering Milliken enterprise.

The closing of an entire business, even though discriminatory, ends the employer-employee relationship; the force of such a closing is entirely spent

---

14. The Darlington property and equipment could not be sold as a unit, and were eventually auctioned off piecemeal. ✱ ✱ ✱

15. Cf. NLRA § 8(c) ✱ ✱ ✱. Different considerations would arise were it made to appear that the closing employer was acting pursuant to some arrangement or understanding with other employers to discourage employee organizational activities in their businesses.

16. ✱ ✱ ✱ An analogous problem is presented where a department is closed for anti-union reasons but the work is continued by independent contractors.

20. Nothing we have said in this opinion would justify an employer's interfering with employee organizational activites by threatening to close his plant, as distinguished from announcing a decision to close already reached by the board of directors or other management authority empowered to make such a decision. We recognize that this safeguard does not wholly remove the possibility

that our holding may result in some deterrent effect on organizational activities independent of that arising from the closing itself. An employer may be encouraged to make a definitive decision to close on the theory that its mere announcement before a representation election will discourage the employees from voting for the union, and thus his decision may not have to be implemented. Such a possibility is not likely to occur, however, except in a marginal business; a solidly successful employer is not apt to hazard the possibility that the employees will call his bluff by voting to organize. We see no practical way of eliminating this possible consequence of our holding short of allowing the Board to order an employer who chooses so to gamble with his employees not to carry out his announced intention to close. We do not consider the matter of sufficient significance in the overall labor-management relations picture to require or justify a decision different from the one we have made.

as to that business when termination of the enterprise takes place. On the other hand, a discriminatory partial closing may have repercussions on what remains of the business, affording employer leverage for discouraging the free exercise of § 7 rights among remaining employees of much the same kind as that found to exist in the "runaway shop" and "temporary closing" cases. * * * Moreover, a possible remedy open to the Board in such a case, like the remedies available in the "runaway shop" and "temporary closing" cases, is to order reinstatement of the discharged employees in the other parts of the business. No such remedy is available when an entire business has been terminated. By analogy to those cases involving a continuing enterprise we are constrained to hold, in disagreement with the Court of Appeals, that a partial closing is an unfair labor practice under § 8(a)(3) if motivated by a purpose to chill unionism in any of the remaining plants of the single employer and if the employer may reasonably have foreseen that such closing would likely have that effect.

While we have spoken in terms of a "partial closing" in the context of the Board's finding that Darlington was part of a larger single enterprise controlled by the Milliken family, we do not mean to suggest that an organizational integration of plants or corporations is a necessary prerequisite to the establishment of such a violation of § 8(a)(3). If the persons exercising control over a plant that is being closed for antiunion reasons (1) have an interest in another business, whether or not affiliated with or engaged in the same line of commercial activity as the closed plant, of sufficient substantiality to give promise of their reaping a benefit from the discouragement of unionization in that business; (2) act to close their plant with the purpose of producing such a result; and (3) occupy a relationship to the other business which makes it realistically foreseeable that its employees will fear that such business will also be closed down if they persist in organizational activities, we think that an unfair labor practice has been made out.

Although the Board's single employer finding necessarily embraced findings as to Roger Milliken and the Milliken family which, if sustained by the Court of Appeals, would satisfy the elements of "interest" and "relationship" with respect to other parts of the Deering Milliken enterprise, that and the other Board findings fall short of establishing the factors of "purpose" and "effect" which are vital requisites of the general principles that govern a case of this kind.

Thus, the Board's findings as to the purpose and foreseeable effect of the Darlington closing pertained *only* to its impact on the Darlington employees. No findings were made as to the purpose and effect of the closing with respect to the employees in the other plants comprising the Deering Milliken group. It does not suffice to establish the unfair labor practice charged here to argue that the Darlington closing necessarily had an adverse impact upon unionization in such other plants. * * * In an area which trenches so closely upon otherwise legitimate employer prerogatives, we consider the absence of Board findings on this score a fatal defect in its decision. The Court of Appeals for its part did not deal with the question of purpose and effect at all, since it concluded that an employer's right to close down his entire business because of distaste for unionism, also embraced a partial closing so motivated. * * *

   * * * [W]e vacate the judgments of the Court of Appeals and remand the cases to that court with instructions to remand them to the Board for further proceedings consistent with this opinion. * * *

MR. JUSTICE STEWART took no part in the decision of these cases.

MR. JUSTICE GOLDBERG took no part in the consideration or decision of these cases.

[On remand, the Board, rejecting the contrary findings and recommendation of the Trial Examiner, held that the two tests laid down by the Court, as to the purpose and effect of the closing, were satisfied. The Board renewed its order that back wages be paid to the employees until they obtained substantially equivalent employment or were placed on a preferential hiring list by Deering Milliken. 165 N.L.R.B. 1074 (1967), enforced, 397 F.2d 760 (4th Cir.1968), cert. denied, 393 U.S. 1023 (1969).

[In 1980, 24 years after the incipience of the Darlington dispute, the backpay issue was settled for $5 million. Individual shares for the more than 500 employees (alive and dead) ranged from $50 to $36,000. N.Y. Times, Dec. 15, 1980, at A15, col. 1.]

Note

1. Why did the Court require the Board on remand in Darlington to find *both* that the employer liquidated Darlington for the purpose of chilling unionism in other segments of the corporate complex *and* that the employer had reason to foresee that the liquidation would have that effect? Is the purpose of the Court to curtail the Board's power to draw inferences as to the subjective motive from objective conduct? Or is it, rather, to protect possible lunatics who happen also to be employers intent upon liquidating their businesses?

2. Is Justice Harlan's interpretation of Section 8(a)(1) in Darlington consistent with his interpretation of that section in Exchange Parts? What does he mean in Darlington when he states, supra p. 286: "A violation of § 8(a)(1) alone therefore presupposes an act which is unlawful even absent a discriminatory motive"? Was not a "discriminatory motive" required in Exchange Parts? What does Justice Harlan mean by "discriminatory"?

3. In Burnup and Sims, supra p. 242, the Court disposed of an 8(a)(1) and (3) case on the basis of 8(a)(1) alone. In Darlington the Court does just the opposite. Can the cases be reconciled? This and related questions are discussed infra p. 520, where the argument is advanced that in 8(a)(3)–8(a)(1) "overlap" cases the analytical criteria of 8(a)(3) ought to control, making 8(a)(3) the "dog" and 8(a)(1) the "tail"; whereas in cases properly characterized as "independent" 8(a)(1) cases, the analytical criteria developed for 8(a)(1) ought to control.

NATIONAL LABOR RELATIONS BOARD v. GISSEL PACKING CO.

Supreme Court of the United States, 1969.
395 U.S. 575, 89 S.Ct. 1918, 23 L.Ed.2d 547.

MR. CHIEF JUSTICE WARREN delivered the opinion of the Court.

These [four] cases involve the extent of an employer's duty under the National Labor Relations Act to recognize a union that bases its claim to representative status solely on the possession of union authorization cards, and the steps an employer may take, particularly with regard to the scope and content of statements he may make, in legitmately resisting such card-based recognition. The specific questions facing us here are whether the duty to bargain can arise without a Board election under the Act; whether union authorization cards, if obtained from a majority of employees without misrepresentation or coercion, are reliable enough generally to provide a valid, alternate route to majority status; whether a bargaining order is an appropriate and authorized remedy where an employer rejects a card majority while at the same time committing unfair practices that tend to undermine the union's majority and make a fair election an unlikely possibility; and whether certain specific statements made by an employer to his employees constituted such an election-voiding unfair labor practice and thus fell outside the protection of the First Amendment and § 8(c) of the Act * * *. For reasons given below, we answer each of these questions in the affirmative.

[Three of the cases—*Gissel Packing Company, Heck's, Inc.,* and *General Steel Products, Inc.*—were decided by the Court of Appeals for the Fourth Circuit, and the fourth case—*Sinclair Company*—was decided by the First Circuit. All four cases presented similar fact patterns in that (a) the employers refused union requests to bargain on the basis of a claimed majority support premised upon authorization cards; (b) the employers engaged in coercive interrogation of employees, threats of reprisals and reprisals, including discharge, and promises of benefits in their efforts to thwart union organizing attempts and to dissipate the unions' claimed majority status; (c) the unions, either instead of pursuing an election under § 9(c) or after having lost an election, filed unfair labor practice charges with the NLRB; and (d) the NLRB found that the employers had undermined the unions' card-established majority status through violations of §§ 8(a)(1), (3), and (5) and, as a part of its remedy, ordered the employers to bargain with the unions. On appeal, the Fourth Circuit sustained the Board's findings as to § 8(a)(1) and (3) violations, but rejected the Board's findings as to § 8(a)(5) and that portion of the remedy directing the employers to bargain with the unions; the First Circuit sustained the Board's findings, conclusions, and order in full, thus creating a conflict among the circuits.]

* * *

III.

A.

The first issue facing us is whether a union can establish a bargaining obligation by means other than a Board election and whether the validity of alternate routes to majority status, such as cards, was affected by the 1947 Taft-Hartley amendments. The most commonly traveled [7] route for a union to obtain recognition as the exclusive bargaining representative of an unor-

---

7. In 1967, for instance, the Board conducted 8,116 elections but issued only 157 bargaining orders based on a card majority. Levi Strauss & Co., 172 N.L.R.B. No. 57, 68 L.R. R.M. 1338, 1342, in 9 (1968). See also Sheinkman, Recognition of Unions Through Authorization Cards, 3 Ga.L.Rev. 319 (1969).

The number of card cases that year, however, represents a rather dramatic increase over previous years from 12 such cases in 1964, 24 in 1965, and about 117 in 1966. Browne, Obligation to Bargain on Basis of Card Majority, 3 Ga.L.Rev. 334, 347 (1969).

ganized group of employees is through the Board's election and certification procedures under § 9(c) of the Act (29 U.S.C.A. § 159(c)); it is also, from the Board's point of view, the preferred route. A union is not limited to a Board election, however, for, in addition to § 9, the present Act provides in § 8(a)(5) * * *, as did the Wagner Act in § 8(5), that "[i]t shall be an unfair labor practice for an employer * * * to refuse to bargain collectively with the representatives of his employees, subject to the provisions of section 9(a)." Since § 9(a), in both the Wagner Act and the present Act, refers to the representative as the one "designated or selected" by a majority of the employees without specifying precisely how that representative is to be chosen, it was early recognized that an employer had a duty to bargain whenever the union representative presented "convincing evidence of majority support." [9] Almost from the inception of the Act, then, it was recognized that a union did not have to be certified as the winner of a Board election to invoke a bargaining obligation; it could establish majority status by other means under the unfair labor practice provision of § 8(a)(5)—by showing convincing support, for instance, by a union-called strike or strike vote, or, as here, by possession of cards signed by a majority of the employees authorizing the union to represent them for collective bargaining purposes.[11]

["Th[is] traditional approach utilized by the Board for many years has been known as the *Joy Silk* doctrine. Joy Silk Mills, Inc., 85 N.L.R.B. 1263 (1949), enforced, 87 U.S.App.D.C. 360, 185 F.2d 732 (1950). Under that rule, an employer could lawfully refuse to bargain with a union claiming representative status through possession of authorization cards if he had a 'good faith doubt' as to the union's majority status; instead of bargaining, he could insist that the union seek an election in order to test out his doubts. The Board, then, could find a lack of good faith doubt and enter a bargaining order in one of two ways. It could find (1) that the employer's independent unfair labor practices were evidence of bad faith, showing that the employer was seeking time to dissipate the union's majority. Or the Board could find (2) that the employer had come forward with no reasons for entertaining any doubt and therefore that he must have rejected the bargaining demand in bad faith. * * *

["The leading case codifying modifications to the *Joy Silk* doctrine was Aaron Brothers, 158 N.L.R.B. 1077 (1966). There the Board made it clear that it had shifted the burden to the General Counsel to show bad faith and that an employer 'will not be held to have violated his bargaining obligation * * * simply because he refuses to rely upon cards, rather than an election, as the method for determining the union's majority.' 158 N.L.R.B., at 1078. * * *

["Although the Board's brief before this Court generally followed the approach as set out in Aaron Brothers, supra, the Board announced at oral argument that it had virtually abandoned the *Joy Silk* doctrine altogether. Under the Board's current practice, an employer's good faith doubt is largely irrelevant, and the key to the issuance of a bargaining order is the commis-

9. NLRB v. Dahlstrom Metallic Door Co., 112 F.2d 756, 757 (C.A.2d Cir.1940).

11. The right of an employer lawfully to refuse to bargain if he had a good faith doubt as to the Union's majority status, even if in fact the Union did represent a majority, was recognized early in the administration of the Act, see NLRB v. Remington Rand, Inc., 94 F.2d 862, 868 (C.A.2d Cir.), cert. denied, 304 U.S. 576, 58 S.Ct. 1046, 82 L.Ed. 1540 (1938).

sion of serious unfair labor practices that interfere with the election processes and tend to preclude the holding of a fair election. Thus, an employer can insist that a union go to an election, regardless of his subjective motivation, so long as he is not guilty of misconduct; he need give no affirmative reasons for rejecting a recognition request, and he can demand an election with a simple 'no comment' to the union." *Gissel*, 395 U.S. at 592–94, 89 S.Ct. at 1929–30.] [g]

We have consistently accepted this interpretation of the Wagner Act and the present Act, particularly as to the use of authorization cards. See e.g., NLRB v. Bradford Dyeing Assn., 310 U.S. 318, 339–340, 60 S.Ct. 918, 929, 84 L.Ed. 122 (1940); Franks Bros. Co. v. NLRB, 321 U.S. 702, 64 S.Ct. 817, 88 L.Ed. 1020 (1944); United Mine Workers v. Arkansas Flooring Co., 351 U.S. 62, 76 S.Ct. 559, 100 L.Ed. 941 (1956). Thus, in *United Mine Workers,* supra, we noted that a "Board election is not the only method by which an employer may satisfy itself as to the union's majority status," 351 U.S. at 72, n. 8, 76 S.Ct. at 565, since § 9(a), "which deals expressly with employee representation, says nothing as to how the employees' representative shall be chosen," 351 U.S. at 71, 76 S.Ct. at 565. We therefore pointed out in that case, where the union had obtained signed authorization cards from a majority of the employees, that "[i]n the absence of any bona fide dispute as to the existence of the required majority of eligible employees, the employer's denial of recognition of the union would have violated § 8(a)(5) of the Act." 351 U.S. at 69, 76 S.Ct. at 563. We see no reason to reject this approach to bargaining obligations now, and we find unpersuasive the Fourth Circuit's view that the 1947 Taft-Hartley amendments, enacted some nine years before our decision in *United Mine Workers,* supra, require us to disregard that case. Indeed, the 1947 amendments weaken rather than strengthen the position taken by the employers here and the Fourth Circuit below. An early version of the bill in the House would have amended § 8(5) of the Wagner Act to permit the Board to find a refusal-to-bargain violation only where an employer had failed to bargain with a union "currently recognized by the employer or certified as such [through an election] under section 9." Section 8(a)(5) of H.R. 3020, 80th Cong., 1st Sess. (1947). The proposed change, which would have eliminated the use of cards, was rejected in Conference (H.R.Conf.Rep. No. 510, 80th Cong., 1st Sess., 41 (1947)), however, and we cannot make a similar change in the Act simply because, as the employers assert, Congress did not expressly approve the use of cards in rejecting the House amendment. Nor can we accept the Fourth Circuit's conclusion that the change was wrought when Congress amended § 9(c) to make election the sole basis for *certification* by eliminating the phrase "any other suitable method to ascertain such representatives," under which the Board had occasionally used cards as a certification basis. A certified union has the benefit of numerous special privileges which are not accorded unions recognized voluntarily or under a bargaining order [14] and which, Congress

---

g. The bracketed material is presented out of sequence by the editors in order to condense the lengthy opinion.

14. E.g., protection against the filing of new election petitions by rival unions or employees seeking decertification for 12 months (§ 9(c)(3)), protection for a reasonable period,

usually one year, against any disruption of the bargaining relationship because of claims that the union no longer represents a majority (see Brooks v. NLRB, 348 U.S. 96, 75 S.Ct. 176, 99 L.Ed. 125 (1954)), protection against recognitional picketing by rival unions (§ 8(b)(4)(C)), and freedom from the restrictions placed in

could determine, should not be dispensed unless a union has survived the crucible of a secret ballot election.

The employers rely finally on the addition to § 9(c) of subparagraph (B), which allows an employer to petition for an election whenever "one or more individuals or labor organizations have presented to him a claim [15] to be recognized as the representative defined in section 9(a)." That provision was not added, as the employers assert, to give them an absolute right to an election at any time; rather, it was intended, as the legislative history indicates, to allow them, after being asked to bargain, to test out their doubts as to a union's majority in a secret election which they would then presumably not cause to be set aside by illegal antiunion activity. We agree with the Board's assertion here that there is no suggestion that Congress intended § 9(c)(1)(B) to relieve any employer of his § 8(a)(5) bargaining obligation where, without good faith, he engaged in unfair labor practices disruptive of the Board's election machinery. And we agree that the policies reflected in § 9(c)(1)(B) fully support the Board's present administration of the Act * * *; for an employer can insist on a secret ballot election, unless in the words of the Board, he engages "in contemporaneous unfair labor practices likely to destroy the union's majority and seriously impede the election." Brief for Petitioner, the Board in No. 573, p. 36.

In short, we hold that the 1947 amendments did not restrict an employer's duty to bargain under § 8(a)(5) solely to those unions whose representative status is certified after a Board election.

B.

We next consider the question whether authorization cards are such inherently unreliable indicators of employee desires that, whatever the validity of other alternate routes to representative status, the cards themselves may never be used to determine a union's majority and to support an order to bargain. In this context, the employers urge us to take the step the 1947 amendments and their legislative history indicate Congress did not take, namely, to rule out completely the use of cards in the bargaining arena. Even if we do not unhesitatingly accept the Fourth Circuit's view in the matter, the employers argue, at the very least we should overrule the *Cumberland Shoe* doctrine * * * and establish stricter controls over the solicitation of the cards by union representatives.[18]

["Under the *Cumberland Shoe* doctrine [Cumberland Shoe Corp., 144 N.L.R.B. 1268 (1963)], if the card itself is unambiguous (i.e., states on its face

---

work assignments disputes by § 8(b)(4)(D), and on recognitional and organizational picketing by § 8(b)(7).

15. Under the Wagner Act, which did not prescribe who would file election petitions, the Board had ruled that an employer could seek an election only when two unions presented conflicting bargaining requests on the ground that if he were given the same election petition rights as the union, he could interrupt union drives by demanding an election before the union had obtained majority status. The 1947 amendments resolved the difficulty by providing that an employer could seek an elec-

tion only after he had been requested to bargain. See H.R.Rep No. 245, 80th Cong., 1st Sess., 35 (1947).

18. In dealing with the reliability of cards, we should re-emphasize what issues we are not confronting. * * * [A] union's right to rely on cards as a freely interchangeable substitute for elections where there has been no election interference is not put in issue here; we need only decide whether the cards are reliable enough to support a bargaining order where a fair election probably could not have been held, or where an election that was held was in fact set aside.

that the signer authorizes the Union to represent the employee for collective bargaining purposes and not to seek an election), it will be counted unless it is proved that the employee was told that the card was to be used *solely* for the purpose of obtaining an election." *Gissel,* 395 U.S. at 584, 89 S.Ct. at 1925.] [h]

The objections to the use of cards voiced by the employers and the Fourth Circuit boil down to two contentions: (1) that, as contrasted with the election procedure, the cards cannot accurately reflect an employee's wishes, either because an employer has not had a chance to present his views and thus a chance to insure that the employee choice was an informed one, or because the choice was the result of group pressures and not individual decision made in the privacy of a voting booth; and (2) that quite apart from the election comparison, the cards are too often obtained through misrepresentation and coercion which compound the cards' inherent inferiority to the election process. Neither contention is persuasive, and each proves too much. * * * The acknowledged superiority of the election process * * * does not mean that cards are thereby rendered totally invalid, for where an employer engages in conduct disruptive of the election process, cards may be the most effective—perhaps the only—way of assuring employee choice. As for misrepresentation, in any specific case of alleged irregularity in the solicitation of the cards, the proper course is to apply the Board's customary standards (to be discussed more fully below) and rule that there was no majority if the standards were not satisfied. It does not follow that because there are some instances of irregularity, the cards can never be used; otherwise, an employer could put off his bargaining obligation indefinitely through continuing interference with elections.

That the cards, though admittedly inferior to the election process, can adequately reflect employee sentiment when that process has been impeded, needs no extended discussion, for the employers' contentions cannot withstand close examination. The employers argue that their employees cannot make an informed choice because the card drive will be over before the employer has had a chance to present his side of the unionization issues. Normally, however, the union will inform the employer of its organization drive early in order to subject the employer to the unfair labor practice provisions of the Act; the union must be able to show the employer's awareness of the drive in order to prove that his contemporaneous conduct constituted unfair labor practices on which a bargaining order can be based if the drive is ultimately successful. * * * Further, the employers argue that without a secret ballot an employee may, in a card drive, succumb to group pressures or sign simply to get the union "off his back" and then be unable to change his mind as he would be free to do once inside a voting booth. But the same pressures are likely to be equally present in an election, for election cases arise most often with small bargaining units where virtually every voter's sentiments can be carefully and individually canvassed. And no voter, of course, can change his mind after casting a ballot in an election even though he may think better of his choice shortly thereafter.

h. The bracketed material is presented out of sequence by the editors in order to condense the lengthy opinion.

The employers' second complaint, that the cards are too often obtained through misrepresentation and coercion, must be rejected also in view of the Board's present rules for controlling card solicitation, which we view as adequate to the task where the cards involved state their purpose clearly and unambiguously on their face. We would be closing our eyes to obvious difficulties, of course, if we did not recognize that there have been abuses, primarily arising out of misrepresentations by union organizers as to whether the effect of signing a card was to designate the union to represent the employee for collective bargaining purposes or merely to authorize it to seek an election to determine that issue. * * *

We need make no decision as to * * * dual-purpose cards, for in each of the * * * organization campaigns in the four cases before us the cards used were single-purpose cards, stating clearly and unambiguously on their face that the signer designated the union as his representative.[4] * * * Thus, the sole question before us * * * is whether the *Cumberland Shoe* doctrine is an adequate rule under the Act for assuring employee free choice.

In resolving the conflict among the circuits in favor of approving the Board's *Cumberland* rule, we think it sufficient to point out that employees should be bound by the clear language of what they sign unless that language is deliberately and clearly canceled by a union adherent with words calculated to direct the signer to disregard and forget the language above his signature. There is nothing inconsistent in handing an employee a card that says the signer authorizes the union to represent him and then telling him that the card will probably be used first to get an election. Elections have been, after all, and will continue to be, held in the vast majority of cases; the union will still have to have the signatures of 30% of the employees when an employer rejects a bargaining demand and insists that the union seek an election. * * *

C.

Remaining before us is the propriety of a bargaining order as a remedy for a § 8(a)(5) refusal to bargain where an employer has committed independent unfair labor practices which have made the holding of a fair election unlikely or which have in fact undermined a union's majority and caused an election to be set aside. We have long held that the Board is not limited to a cease-and-desist order in such cases, but has the authority to issue a bargaining order without first requiring the union to show that it has been able to maintain its majority status. * * * And we have held the Board has the same authority even where it is clear that the union, which once had possession of cards from a majority of the employees, represents only a minority when the bargaining order is entered. Franks Bros. Co. v. NLRB, 321 U.S. 702, 64 S.Ct. 817, 88 L.Ed. 1020 (1944). We see no reason now to

---

4. [Presented out of sequence by the editors.] The cards used in all four campaigns * * * unambiguously authorized the Union to represent the signing employee for collective bargaining purposes; there was no reference to elections. Typical of the cards was the [following]:

"Desiring to become a member of the above Union of the International Brotherhood of Teamsters, Chauffeurs, Warehousemen and Helpers of America, I hereby make application for admission to membership. I hereby authorize you, your agents or representatives to act for me as collective bargaining agent on all matters pertaining to rates of pay, hours, or any other conditions of employment."

withdraw this authority from the Board. If the Board could enter only a cease-and-desist order and direct an election or a rerun, it would in effect be rewarding the employer and allowing him "to profit from [his] own wrongful refusal to bargain," Franks Bros., supra, at 704, 64 S.Ct. at 818, while at the same time severely curtailing the employees' right freely to determine whether they desire a representative. The employer could continue to delay or disrupt the election processes and put off indefinitely his obligation to bargain; [30] and any election held under these circumstances would not be likely to demonstrate the employees' true, undistorted desires.[31]   *   *   *

IV.

We consider finally petitioner Sinclair's First Amendment challenge to the holding of the Board and the Court of Appeals for the First Circuit. * * * [A]n employer's free speech right to communicate his views to his employees is firmly established and cannot be infringed by a union or the Board. Thus, § 8(c) * * * merely implements the First Amendment by requiring that the expression of "any views, argument, or opinion" shall not be "evidence of an unfair labor practice," so long as such expression contains "no threat of reprisal or force or promise of benefit" in violation of § 8(a)(1). Section 8(a)(1), in turn, prohibits interference, restraint or coercion of employees in the exercise of their right to self-organization.

Any assessment of the precise scope of employer expression, of course, must be made in the context of its labor relations setting. Thus, an employer's rights cannot outweigh the equal rights of the employees to associate freely, as those rights are embodied in § 7 and protected by § 8(a) (1) and the proviso to § 8(c). And any balancing of those rights must take into account the economic dependence of the employees on their employers, and the necessary tendency of the former, because of that relationship, to pick up intended implications of the latter that might be more readily dismissed by a more disinterested ear. * * *

Within this framework, we must reject the Company's challenge to the decision below and the findings of the Board on which it was based. The standards used below for evaluating the impact of an employer's statements are not seriously questioned by petitioner and we see no need to tamper with them here. Thus, an employer is free to communicate to his employees any

---

30. The Board indicates here that its records show that in the period between January and June 1968, the median time between the filing of an unfair labor practice charge and a Board decision in a contested case was 388 days. * * *

31. A study of 20,153 elections held between 1960 and 1962 shows that in the 267 cases where rerun elections were held over 30% were won by the party who caused the election to be set aside. See Pollitt, NLRB Re-Run Elections: A Study, 41 N.C.L.Rev. 209, 212 (1963). The study shows further that certain unfair labor practices are more effective to destroy election conditions for a longer period of time than others. For instance, in cases involving threats to close or transfer plant operations, the union won the rerun only 29% of the time, while threats to elimi-

nate benefits or refuse to deal with the union if elected seemed less irremediable with the union winning the rerun 75% of the time. Id., at 215–216. Finally, time appears to be a factor. The figures suggest that if a rerun is held too soon after the election before the effects of the unfair labor practices have worn off, or too long after the election when interest in the union may have waned, the chances for a changed result occurring are not as good as they are if the rerun is held sometime in between those periods. Thus, the study showed that if the rerun is held within 30 days of the election or over nine months after, the chances that a different result will occur are only one in five; when the rerun is held within 30–60 days after the election, the chances for a changed result are two in five. Id., at 221.

of his general views about unionism or any of his specific views about a particular union, so long as the communications do not contain a "threat of reprisal or force or promise of benefit." He may even make a prediction as to the precise effects he believes unionization will have on his company. In such a case, however, the prediction must be carefully phrased on the basis of objective fact to convey an employer's belief as to demonstrably probable consequences beyond his control or to convey a management decision already arrived at to close the plant in case of unionization. See Textile Workers v. Darlington Mfg. Co., 380 U.S. 263, 274, n. 20, 85 S.Ct. 994, 13 L.Ed.2d 827 (1965). If there is any implication that an employer may or may not take action solely on his own initiative for reasons unrelated to economic necessities and known only to him, the statement is no longer a reasonable prediction based on available facts but a threat of retaliation based on misrepresentation and coercion, and as such without the protection of the First Amendment. We therefore agree with the court below that "[c]onveyance of the employer's belief, even though sincere, that unionization will or may result in the closing of the plant is not a statement of fact unless, which is most improbable, the eventuality of closing is capable of proof." 397 F.2d 157, 160. As stated elsewhere, an employer is free only to tell "what he reasonably believes will be the likely economic consequences of unionization that are outside his control," and not "threats of economic reprisal to be taken solely on his own volition." NLRB v. River Togs, Inc., 382 F.2d 198, 202 (C.A.2d Cir.1967).

Equally valid was the finding by the court and the Board that petitioner's statements and communications were not cast as a prediction of "demonstrable 'economic consequences,'" 397 F.2d, at 160, but rather as a threat of retaliatory action. The Board found that petitioner's speeches, pamphlets, leaflets, and letters conveyed the following message: that the company was in a precarious financial condition; that the "strike-happy" union would in all likelihood have to obtain its potentially unreasonable demands by striking, the probable result of which would be a plant shutdown, as the past history of labor relations in the area indicated; and that the employees in such a case would have great difficulty finding employment elsewhere. In carrying out its duty to focus on the question: "[W]hat did the speaker intend and the listener understand?" (A. Cox, Law and the National Labor Policy 44 (1960)), the Board could reasonably conclude that the intended and understood import of that message was not to predict that unionization would inevitably cause the plant to close but to threaten to throw employees out of work regardless of the economic realities. In this connection, we need go no further than to point out (1) that petitioner had no support for its basic assumption that the union, which had not yet even presented any demands, would have to strike to be heard, and that it admitted at the hearing that it had no basis for attributing other plant closings in the area to unionism; and (2) that the Board has often found that employees, who are particularly sensitive to rumors of plant closings, take such hints as coercive threats rather than honest forecasts.

Petitioner argues that the line between so-called permitted predictions and proscribed threats is too vague to stand up under traditional First Amendment analysis and that the Board's discretion to curtail free speech rights is correspondingly too uncontrolled. It is true that a reviewing court must recognize the Board's competence in the first instance to judge the impact of utterances made in the context of the employer-employee relationship, see NLRB v. Virginia Electric & Power Co., 314 U.S. 469, 479, 62 S.Ct. 344, 349, 86 L.Ed. 348 (1941). But an employer, who has control over that relationship and therefore knows it best, cannot be heard to complain that he is without an adequate guide for his behavior. He can easily make his views known without engaging in " 'brinkmanship' " when it becomes all too easy to "overstep and tumble [over] the brink," Wausau Steel Corp. v. NLRB, 377 F.2d 369, 372 (C.A.7th Cir.1967). At the least he can avoid coercive speech simply by avoiding conscious overstatements he has reason to believe will mislead his employees.

For the foregoing reasons, we affirm the judgment of the Court of Appeals for the First Circuit * * * and we reverse the judgments of the Court of Appeals for the Fourth Circuit * * * insofar as they decline enforcement of the Board's orders to bargain * * *.

Note

1. How would you state the holding in the Gissel case as to bargaining orders based upon authorization cards?

Suppose there had been no independent (other than the alleged 8(a)(5)) unfair labor practices by the employer but, nonetheless, the union demanded that the employer either (1) recognize and bargain with it on the basis of a showing of majority support through valid authorization cards or (2) file an election petition under § 9(c)(1)(B). If the employer refuses to do either, should a bargaining order be issued by the Board without the holding of an election?

This was the problem in Linden Lumber Division, Summer & Co. v. NLRB, 419 U.S. 301, 95 S.Ct. 429, 42 L.Ed.2d 465 (1974). The Board held that the employer "should not be found guilty of a violation of Section 8(a)(5) solely upon the basis of refusal to accept evidence of majority status other than the results of a Board election." 190 N.L.R.B., at 721. The court of appeals reversed, concluding that if the employer had good faith doubts as to the union's majority status, the burden was on the employer to seek an answer to its doubts by petitioning for an election. A divided Supreme Court held with the Board, stating: "[W]e sustain the Board [as not having abused its discretion] in holding that, unless an employer has engaged in an unfair labor practice that impairs the electoral process, a union with authorization cards purporting to represent a majority of the employees, which is refused recognition, has the burden of taking the next step in invoking the Board's election procedure." 419 U.S. at 310, 95 S.Ct. at 434, 42 L.Ed.2d 471–72.

2. What is the test the Court lays down for distinguishing privileged from prohibited employer speech with regard to pre-election statements concerning cessation of business in the event of union victory? If, as Darlington holds, an employer may go out of business for any reason, including antiunion reasons, should he not also be permitted to threaten to do so?

BROOKS v. NATIONAL LABOR RELATIONS BOARD

Supreme Court of the United States, 1954.
348 U.S. 96, 75 S.Ct. 176, 99 L.Ed. 125.

MR. JUSTICE FRANKFURTER delivered the opinion of the Court.

The National Labor Relations Board conducted a representation election in petitioner's Chrysler-Plymouth agency on April 12, 1951. District Lodge No. 727, International Association of Machinists, won by a vote of eight to five, and the Labor Board certified it as the exclusive bargaining representative on April 20. A week after the election and the day before the certification, petitioner received a handwritten letter signed by 9 of the 13 employees in the bargaining unit stating: "We, the undersigned majority of the employees * * * are not in favor of being represented by Union Local No. 727 as a bargaining agent."

Relying on this letter and the decision of the Court of Appeals for the Sixth Circuit in National Labor Relations Board v. Vulcan Forging Co., 188 F.2d 927, petitioner refused to bargain with the union. The Labor Board found, 98 N.L.R.B. 976, that petitioner had thereby committed an unfair labor practice in violation of §§ 8(a)(1) and 8(a)(5) of the amended National Labor Relations Act * * *, and the Court of Appeals for the Ninth Circuit enforced the Board's order to bargain, 204 F.2d 899. In view of the conflict between the Circuits, we granted certiorari * * *.

The issue before us is the duty of an employer toward a duly certified bargaining agent if, shortly after the election which resulted in the certification, the union has lost, without the employer's fault, a majority of the employees from its membership.

Under the original Wagner Act, the Labor Board was given the power to certify a union as the exclusive representative of the employees in a bargaining unit when it had determined by election or "any other suitable method", that the union commanded majority support. § 9(c) * * *. In exercising this authority the Board evolved a number of working rules, of which the following are relevant to our purpose:

(a) A certification, if based on a Board-conducted election, must be honored for a "reasonable" period, ordinarily "one year," in the absence of "unusual circumstances."

(b) "Unusual circumstances" were found in at least three situations: (1) the certified union dissolved or became defunct; (2) as a result of a schism, substantially all the members and officers of the certified union transferred their affiliation to a new local or international; (3) the size of the bargaining unit fluctuated radically within a short time.

(c) Loss of majority support after the "reasonable" period could be questioned in two ways: (1) employer's refusal to bargain, or (2) petition by a rival union for a new election.

(d) If the initial election resulted in a majority for "no union," the election—unlike a certification—did not bar a second election within a year.

The Board uniformly found an unfair labor practice where, during the so-called "certification year," an employer refused to bargain on the ground that the certified union no longer possessed a majority. While the courts in the main enforced the Board's decisions, they did not commit themselves to one year as the determinate content of reasonableness. The Board and the courts proceeded along this line of reasoning:

(a) In the political and business spheres, the choice of the voters in an election binds them for a fixed time. This promotes a sense of responsibility in the electorate and needed coherence in administration. These considerations are equally relevant to healthy labor relations.

(b) Since an election is a solemn and costly occasion, conducted under safeguards to voluntary choice, revocation of authority should occur by a procedure no less solemn than that of the initial designation. A petition or a public meeting—in which those voting for and against unionism are disclosed to management, and in which the influences of mass psychology are present—is not comparable to the privacy and independence of the voting booth.

(c) A union should be given ample time for carrying out its mandate on behalf of its members, and should not be under exigent pressure to produce hot-house results or be turned out.

(d) It is scarcely conducive to bargaining in good faith for an employer to know that, if he dillydallies or subtly undermines, union strength may erode and thereby relieve him of his statutory duties at any time, while if he works conscientiously toward agreement, the rank and file may, at the last moment, repudiate their agent.

(e) In situations, not wholly rare, where unions are competing, raiding and strife will be minimized if elections are not at the hazard of informal and short-term recall.

Certain aspects of the Labor Board's representation procedures came under scrutiny in the Congress that enacted the Taft-Hartley Act in 1947 * * *. Congress was mindful that, once employees had chosen a union, they could not vote to revoke its authority and refrain from union activities, while if they voted against having a union in the first place, the union could begin at once to agitate for a new election. The National Labor Relations Act was amended to provide that (a) employees could petition the Board for a decertification election, at which they would have an opportunity to choose no longer to be represented by a union [§ 9(c)(1)(A)(ii)]; (b) an employer, if in doubt as to the majority claimed by a union without formal election or beset by the conflicting claims of rival unions, could likewise petition the Board for an election [§ 9(c)(1)(B)]; (c) after a valid certification or decertification election had been conducted, the Board could not hold a second election in the same bargaining unit until a year had elapsed [§ 9(c)(3)]; (d) Board certification could only be granted as the result of an election [§ 9(c)(1)], though an employer would presumably still be under a duty to bargain with an uncertified union that had a clear majority. * * *

The Board continued to apply its "one-year certification" rule after the Taft-Hartley Act came into force, except that even "unusual circumstances" no longer left the Board free to order an election where one had taken place within the preceding 12 months. Conflicting views became manifest in the

Courts of Appeals when the Board sought to enforce orders based on refusal to bargain in violation of its rule. * * *

The issue is open here. No case touching the problem has directly presented it. In Franks Bros. Co. v. National Labor Relations Board, 321 U.S. 702, 64 S.Ct. 817, 88 L.Ed. 1020, we held that where a union's majority was dissipated after an employer's unfair labor practice in refusing to bargain, the Board could appropriately find that such conduct had undermined the prestige of the union and require the employer to bargain with it for a reasonable period despite the loss of majority. * * *

Petitioner contends that whenever an employer is presented with evidence that his employees have deserted their certified union, he may forthwith refuse to bargain. In effect, he seeks to vindicate the rights of his employees to select their bargaining representative. * * * The underlying purpose of this statute is industrial peace. To allow employers to rely on employees' rights in refusing to bargain with the formally designated union is not conducive to that end, it is inimical to it. Congress has devised a formal mode for selection and rejection of bargaining agents and has fixed the spacing of elections, with a view of furthering industrial stability and with due regard to administrative prudence.

We find wanting the arguments against these controlling considerations. In placing a nonconsenting minority under the bargaining responsibility of an agency selected by a majority of the workers, Congress has discarded common-law doctrines of agency. It is contended that since a bargaining agency may be ascertained by methods less formal than a supervised election, informal repudiation should also be sanctioned where decertification by another election is precluded. This is to make situations that are different appear the same. * * *

To be sure, what we have said has special pertinence only to the period during which a second election is impossible. But the Board's view that the one-year period should run from the date of certification rather than the date of election seems within the allowable area of the Board's discretion in carrying out congressional policy. * * * Otherwise, encouragement would be given to management or a rival union to delay certification by spurious objections to the conduct of an election and thereby diminish the duration of the duty to bargain. Furthermore, the Board has ruled that one year after certification the employer can ask for an election or, if he has fair doubts about the union's continuing majority, he may refuse to bargain further with it.[18] This, too, is a matter appropriately determined by the Board's administrative authority.

We conclude that the judgment of the Court of Appeals enforcing the Board's order must be affirmed.

Note

1. Whereas in Brooks the employer was found to have violated Sections 8(a) (5) and 8(a)(1) for refusing to bargain with a union which once had a majority

---

18. Celanese Corp. of America, 95 N.L.R.B. 664. The Board has on several occasions intimated that even after the certification year has passed, the better practice is for an employer with doubts to keep bargaining and petition the Board for a new election * * *. Id., at 674 * * *.

and lost it, in International Ladies' Garment Workers' Union v. NLRB, 366 U.S. 731, 81 S.Ct. 1603, 6 L.Ed.2d 762 (1961), the employer was found to have violated Sections 8(a)(2) and 8(a)(1) for bargaining with a minority union which subsequently obtained majority support. In the ILGWU case the employer signed a memorandum of understanding recognizing the union as exclusive bargaining representative on August 30, 1957, at which time both the employer and union had a good faith belief that the union had obtained authorization cards from a majority of the employees. On October 10, 1957, the parties signed a collective bargaining agreement. At the later date the union had in fact majority support; at the earlier date, it was subsequently determined, the union had only minority support. In rejecting the defense of good faith, the Court stated: "We find nothing in the statutory language prescribing *scienter* as an element of the unfair labor practices here involved. The act made unlawful by § 8(a)(2) is employer support of a minority union. Here that support is an accomplished fact. More need not be shown, for, even if mistakenly, the employees' rights have been invaded. It follows that prohibited conduct cannot be excused by a showing of good faith." The union was similarly found to have violated Section 8(b)(1)(A).

Is the Brooks decision consistent with that in ILGWU?

2. At the end of the opinion in Brooks, Justice Frankfurter indicates that upon expiration of the "certification year" "the employer can ask for an election or, if he has fair doubts about the union's continuing majority, he may refuse to bargain further with it." Is the requirement of "fair doubts" in the second option consistent with Gissel?

3. Section 9(c)(3) poses a *statutory* bar to further representation proceedings in the affected unit for a twelve-month period. As demonstrated in Brooks, where the union *wins* the election, the twelve-month period is measured from the date the Board certifies the results of the election. The bar is, therefore, sometimes referred to as a "certification bar." Where, on the contrary, the vote is *against* collective bargaining, the twelve-month period begins to run from the date of the election and is consequently called an "election bar."

Another bar, *non*statutory in nature, to the initiation of representation proceedings—the so-called "contract bar"—is dealt with in the following materials.

AMERICAN SEATING CO.
National Labor Relations Board, 1953.
106 N.L.R.B. 250.

* * *

The facts in the case are undisputed. On September 20, 1949, following an election, the Board certified International Union, United Automobile, Aircraft and Agricultural Implement Workers of America, (UAW–CIO), and its Local No. 135, herein called the UAW–CIO, as bargaining representative of the Respondent's production and maintenance employees. On July 1, 1950, the Respondent and the UAW–CIO entered into a 3-year collective-bargaining contract covering all employees in the certified unit. Shortly before the expiration of 2 years from the date of signing of the contract, Pattern Makers' Association of Grand Rapids, Pattern Makers' League of North America, AFL, herein called the Union, filed a representation petition seeking to sever a craft unit of patternmakers from the existing production and maintenance unit. Both the Respondent and the UAW–CIO opposed the petition, contending that their 3-year contract which would not expire until July 1, 1953, was a bar. In a decision issued on September 4, 1952, the Board rejected this contention. It held that, as the contract had already been in existence for 2 years, and as the contracting parties had failed to establish that contracts for 3-year terms were customary in the seating industry, the contract was not a bar during the third year of its term. Accordingly, the Board directed an election in a unit of patternmakers which the Union won.

On October 6, 1952, the Board certified the Union as bargaining representative of the Respondent's patternmakers. Approximately 10 days later, the Union submitted to the Respondent a proposed collective-bargaining agreement covering terms and conditions of employment for patternmakers to be effective immediately. The Respondent replied that it recognized the Union as bargaining representative of the patternmakers and that it was willing to negotiate or discuss subjects properly open for discussion, but that the existing contract with the UAW–CIO was still in full force and effect and remained binding upon all employees, including patternmakers, until its July 1, 1953, expiration date.

There is no question raised as to the Board's power to direct an election upon its finding that the existing contract between the UAW–CIO and the Respondent was not a bar. The parties differ, however, as to the effect to be given to the new certification resulting from this election. The Respondent contends that the certification of the Pattern Makers merely resulted in the substitution of a new bargaining representative, for patternmakers in place of the old representative, with the substantive terms of the contract remaining unchanged.[3] In support of this position, the Respondent argues that the UAW–CIO was the agent of the patternmakers when it entered into the 1950 agreement with that organization, and that the patternmakers, as principals, are bound by that contract to the expiration date thereof, notwithstanding that they have changed their agent. The General Counsel, on the other hand, contends that the certification of the Pattern Makers resulted in making the existing contract with the UAW–CIO inoperative as to the employees in the unit of patternmakers.

The Respondent's principal agent argument assumes that common-law principles of agency control the relationship of exclusive bargaining representative to employees in an appropriate unit. We think that this assumption is unwarranted and overlooks the unique character of that relationship under the National Labor Relations Act.

Under the common law, agency is a consensual relationship.[4] On the other hand, the status of exclusive bargaining representative is a special one created and governed by statute * * *. A duly selected statutory representative is the representative of a shifting group of employees in an

---

3. In its brief, the Respondent concedes that the procedural aspects of the existing contract grievance procedure, the number of union stewards, and union security might be required subjects of negotiation with the newly certified bargaining representative.

4. "Agency is the relationship which results from the manifestation of consent by one person to another that the other shall act on his behalf and subject to his control, and consent by the other so to act." Restatement, Agency § 1 (1933).

appropriate unit which includes not only those employees who approve such relationship, but also those who disapprove and those who have never had an opportunity to express their choice. Under agency principles, a principal has the power to terminate the authority of his agent at any time. Not so in the case of a statutory bargaining representative. Thus, in its most important aspects the relationship of statutory bargaining representative to employees in an appropriate unit resembles a political rather than a private law relationship. In any event, because of the unique character of the statutory representative, a solution for the problem presented in this case must be sought in the light of that special relationship rather than by the device of pinning labels on the various parties involved and applying without change principles of law evolved to govern entirely different situations.

The National Labor Relations Act provides machinery for the selection and change of exclusive bargaining representatives. If, after the filing of a petition by employees, a labor organization, or an employer, and the holding of a hearing, the Board is convinced that a question of representation exists, it is directed by statute to conduct an election by secret ballot and certify the results thereof. The Act does not list the situations in which a "question of representation affecting commerce exists." That has been left to the Board to decide.[14] One of the problems in this connection arises from the claim that a collective-bargaining contract of fixed term should bar a new election during the entire term of such contract. In solving this problem, the Board has had to balance two separate interests: The interest of employees and society in the stability that is essential to the effective encouragement of collective bargaining, and the sometimes conflicting interest of employees in being free to change their representatives at will. Reconciling these two interests in the early days of the Act, the Board decided that it would not consider a contract of unreasonable duration a bar to an election to determine a new bargaining representative. The Board further decided that a contract of more than 1 year was of unreasonable duration and that it would direct an election after the first year of the existence of such a contract. In 1947, in the further interest of stability, the Board extended from 1 to 2 years the period during which a valid collective-bargaining contract would be considered a bar to a new determination of representatives. Contracts for periods longer than 2 years may be a bar, if such longer term contracts are customary in the industry * * *.

These contract-bar rules have been affirmed many times and have become an established part of the law of labor relations. They received the approval of Congress when it amended the Act in 1947, and have been "as it were, written into the statute." Therefore, when the Respondent and the UAW–CIO entered into their 3-year bargaining contract in 1950, they were on notice that, after the first 2 years of its term, unless it could be shown that longer term contracts were customary in the industry, the contract would not prevent the selection of a new bargaining representative for any group of employees who might constitute an appropriate unit. Neither the Board nor the courts have decided, however, the effect a new certification has upon an existing, collective-bargaining contract which has been held not

---

14. Except that no election may be directed in any bargaining unit or any subdivision within which, in the preceding 12-month period, a valid election has been held. Section 9(c) (3).

a bar to a new determination of representatives because it is of unreasonable duration.

In 1952, the Board decided that the Respondent's patternmakers, who constitute one of the most skilled craft groups, might, after 2 years of experience as part of a plantwide unit of approximately 1,500 employees, if they so desired, constitute a separate appropriate unit. Apparently dissatisfied with their representation by the UAW–CIO, all six patternmakers voted for a separate unit to be represented by the Pattern Makers, which is the labor organization that traditionally represents patternmakers in industry. The Board thereupon certified the Pattern Makers as bargaining representative for those employees. Although the certification of October 6, 1952, gave the Pattern Makers immediate status as exclusive representative for the purposes of collective bargaining "in respect to rates of pay, wages, and hours of employment," the Respondent would qualify the Pattern Makers' authority as to these subjects by adding "after July 1, 1953." If the Respondent's contention is sound, a certified bargaining representative might be deprived of effective statutory power as to the most important subjects of collective bargaining for an unlimited number of years as the result of an agreement negotiated by an unwanted and repudiated bargaining representative. There is no provision in the statute for this kind of emasculated certified bargaining representative. Moreover, the rule urged by the Respondent seems hardly calculated to reduce "industrial strife" by encouraging the "practice and procedure of collective bargaining," the declared purpose of the National Labor Relations Act, as amended.

The purpose of the Board's rule holding a contract of unreasonable duration not a bar to a new determination of representatives is the democratic one of insuring to employees the right at reasonable intervals of reappraising and changing, if they so desire, their union representation. Bargaining representatives are thereby kept responsive to the needs and desires of their constituents; and employees dissatisfied with their representatives know that they will have the opportunity of changing them by peaceful means at an election conducted by an impartial Government agency. Strikes for a change of representatives are thereby reduced and the effects of employee dissatisfaction with their representatives are mitigated. But, if a newly chosen representative is to be hobbled in the way proposed by the Respondent, a great part of the benefit to be derived from the no-bar rule will be dissipated. There is little point in selecting a new bargaining representative which is unable to negotiate new terms and conditions of employment for an extended period of time.

We hold that, for the reasons which led the Board to adopt the rule that a contract of unreasonable duration is not a bar to a new determination of representatives, such a contract may not bar full statutory collective bargaining, including the reduction to writing of any agreement reached, as to any group of employees in an appropriate unit covered by such contract, upon the certification of a new collective-bargaining representative for them. Accordingly, we find that by refusing on and after October 16, 1952, to bargain with the Pattern Makers concerning wages, hours, and other working conditions for employees in the unit of patternmakers, the Respondent violated Section 8(a)(5) and (1) of the Act.

Note

1. Collective bargaining has been described as a process for bringing democracy to the work place. Is there an analogy between the collective bargaining representative, on the one hand, and a legislative representative, on the other? Suppose, for example, that the Constitution provided for thirty-year terms for congressmen? Thirty-day terms?

The Board's effort to find the golden mean for contract-bar purposes underwent further evolution following American Seating. In 1958, in Pacific Coast Ass'n of Pulp and Paper Manufacturers, 121 N.L.R.B. 990, the Board established a flat two-year limit on the duration of the bar, eliminating the "customary in the industry" exception for longer contracts. In 1962, in General Cable Corp., 139 N.L.R.B. 1123, the bar was extended to three years. A succinct statement of the so-called "contract bar rule" as it currently exists is the following: *A valid, written contract of definite duration bars an election sought by an outside union for the length of the contract up to a maximum of three years. Contracts having no fixed duration constitute no bar at all.*

In support of the contract-bar rule the Board has developed a set of subsidiary rules designed to implement the policy of accommodating stability of bargaining relationship and employee freedom of choice. A challenging union should be afforded a reasonable opportunity to contest the incumbent's majority status; conversely, the disruption inherent in such a challenge should be minimized. Accordingly, the Board has established rules concerning the time for the filing of representation petitions in situations where there is an existing collective bargaining contract. In Deluxe Metal Furniture Co., 121 N.L.R.B. 995 (1958), the Board ruled that such a petition could not be filed more than 150 days, nor less than sixty-one days, prior to the contract's expiration. Subsequently, in Leonard Wholesale Meats, Inc., 136 N.L.R.B. 1000 (1962), the Board reduced the "open season" by requiring that petitions be filed no more than ninety days prior to the contract's expiration. The current situation is therefore that a representation petition is timely only if filed more than sixty days, but not more than ninety days, before the termination date of the contract. The Board has justified this limitation on representation challenges as follows:

> " * * * It will give rival unions a definite time-guide as to when to organize, and employees will know when to seek a change in representatives if they so desire. Thus, it will avoid as much disruption of labor relations as possible during the contract term. * * * It will also prevent the threat of overhanging rivalry and uncertainty during the [sixty-day insulated] bargaining period, and will eliminate the possibility for employees to wait and see how bargaining is proceeding and use another union as a threat to force their current representative into unreasonable demands." Deluxe Metal Furniture Co., supra at 1001.

2. Suppose Union B, seeking to oust Union A, the incumbent representative, files a timely Section 9(c) petition. Thereafter, and prior to the date for the representation election, Union A and the employer negotiate and execute a new contract to replace the old one. Has the employer committed an unfair labor practice? The most durable of the "leading" cases on this point, Midwest Piping and Supply Co., 63 N.L.R.B. 1060 (1945), held yes. The Board has vacillated in its position, departing from Midwest Piping in William D. Gibson Co., 110 N.L.R.B. 660 (1954), returning to it in Shea Chemical Corp., 121 N.L.R.B. 1027 (1958), and departing from it once again in RCA Del Caribe, Inc., 262 N.L.R.B. 963

(1982). The pendulum is likely to swing back. The important point is not that the Board vacillates on this issue, but why. What do you perceive to be the pros and cons and how do you evaluate them?

Is the problem the same where there is no incumbent representative and the employer bargains, nonetheless, with one of the competing unions prior to the election? The rule formerly laid down in Midwest Piping (still?) covers, *a fortiori*, this situation.

D. UNION CONDUCT IMPAIRING THE RIGHT TO ORGANIZE

The concern of the Wagner Act was to protect the employee rights declared in Section 7 from employer interference. By the time of the enactment of Taft-Hartley, it had become clear that those rights could also be impaired by unions. See, e.g., Lauf v. E.G. Shinner & Co., 303 U.S. 323, 58 S.Ct. 578, 82 L.Ed. 872 (1938), and Fur Workers Union, No. 21238 v. Fur Workers Union, Local No. 72, 105 F.2d 1 (D.C.Cir.1939), supra pp. 155–156. The congressional response was Section 8(b) and the addition to Section 7 of the right to *refrain* from union activity.

Much of the union conduct trespassing upon Section 7 rights consists of traditional concerted activities—strikes, picketing, boycotts. These activities have no peculiar relationship to the organizational stage of collective bargaining; they are also encountered in the course of bargaining itself. Accordingly, strikes, picketing, and boycotts are dealt with independently in the next chapter, sandwiched, as it were, between organization-stage problems (this chapter) and bargaining-stage problems (Chapter 6), to each of which they are relevant.

By way of contrast, the following case entails activity *peculiar to* the organizational stage.

NATIONAL LABOR RELATIONS BOARD v. SAVAIR MANUFACTURING CO.

Supreme Court of the United States, 1973.
414 U.S. 270, 94 S.Ct. 495, 38 L.Ed.2d 495.

MR. JUSTICE DOUGLAS delivered the opinion of the Court.

The National Labor Relations Board acting pursuant to § 9(c) of the Act * * * conducted an election by secret ballot among the production and maintenance employees of respondent at the request of the Mechanics Educational Society of America (the Union). * * * The Union won the election by a vote of 22–20.

Respondent filed objections to the election, but after an evidentiary hearing a hearing officer found against respondent and the Board certified the Union as the representative of the employees in that unit. Respondent, however, refused to bargain. The Union thereupon filed an unfair labor practice charge with the General Counsel who issued a complaint alleging that respondent had violated § 8(a)(1) and (5) of the Act. The Board sustained the allegations and ordered respondent to bargain with the Union. 194 N.L.R.B. 298. The Court of Appeals denied enforcement of the order. 470 F.2d 305. We granted the petition for certiorari, there apparently being a conflict between this decision in the Sixth Circuit with a decision in the Eighth Circuit (National Labor Relations Board v. DIT–MCO, 428 F.2d 775) and also with one in the Ninth Circuit. National Labor Relations Board v. G.K. Turner Associates, 457 F.2d 484. We affirm.   *COURT DECISION*

It appeared that prior to the election, "recognition slips" were circulated among employees. An employee who signed the slip before the election [4] became a member of the union and would not have to pay what at times was called an "initiation fee" and at times a "fine." If the Union was voted in, those who had not signed a recognition slip would have to pay.

* * * Under the by-laws of the Union, an initiation fee apparently was not to be higher than $10; but the employees who testified at the hearing (1) did not know how large the fee would be and (2) said that their understanding was that the fee was a "fine" or an "assessment."

* * *

The Board originally took the position that pre-election solicitation of memberships by a union with a promise to waive the initiation fee of the Union was not consistent with a fair and free choice of bargaining representatives. Lobue Bros., 109 N.L.R.B. 1182. Later in DIT–MCO, Inc., 163 N.L.R.B. 1019, the Board explained its changed position as follows:

> "We shall assume, *arguendo,* that employees who sign cards when offered a waiver of initiation fees do so solely because no cost is thus involved; that they in fact do not at that point really want the union to be their bargaining representative. The error of the *Lobue* premise can be readily seen upon a review of the consequences of such employees casting votes for or against union representation. Initially, it is obvious that employees who have received or been promised free memberships will not be required to pay an initiation fee, *whatever the outcome of the vote.* If the union wins the election, there is by postulate no obligation; and if the union loses, *there is still no obligation,* because compulsion to pay an initiation fee arises under the Act only when a union becomes the employees' representative and negotiates a valid union-security agreement. Thus, whatever kindly feeling toward the union may be generated by the cost-reduction offer, when consideration is given only to the question of initiation fees, it is completely illogical to characterize as improper inducement or coercion to vote 'Yes' a waiver of something that can be avoided simply by voting 'No.'

> "The illogic of *Lobue* does not become any more logical when other consequences of a vote for representation are considered. Thus, employees

---

4. The question for review presented by the Board is whether the "Board properly concluded that a union's offer to waive initiation fees for all employees who sign union authorization cards *before a Board representation election,* if the union wins the election, does not tend to interfere with employee free choice in the election." (Emphasis added.)

* * *

The Board argues that unions have a valid interest in waiving the initiation fee when the union has not yet been chosen as a bargaining representative, because "employees otherwise sympathetic to the union might well have been reluctant to pay out money before the union had done anything for them. Waiver of the [initiation fees] would remove this artificial obstacle to their endorsement of the union." See Amalgamated Clothing Workers v. National Labor Relations Board, 2 Cir., 345 F.2d 264, 268. While this union interest is legitimate, the Board's argument ignores the fact that this interest can be preserved as well by waiver of initiation fees available not only to those who have signed up with the union before an election but also to those who join after the election. The limitation imposed by the union in this case—to those joining before the election—is necessary only because it serves the additional purpose of affecting the union organizational campaign and the election.

know that if a majority vote for the union, it will be their exclusive representative, and, provided a valid union-security provision is negotiated, they will be obliged to pay dues as a condition of employment. Thus, viewed solely as a financial matter, a 'no' vote will help to avoid any subsequent obligations, a 'yes' may well help to incur such obligations. In these circumstances, an employee who did not want the union to represent him would hardly be likely to vote for the union just because there would be no initial cost involved in obtaining membership. Since an election resulting in the union's defeat would entail not only no initial cost, but also insure that no dues would have to be paid as a condition of employment, the financial inducement, if a factor at all, would be in the direction of a vote against the union, rather than for it." Id., at 1021–1022.

We are asked to respect the expertise of the Board on this issue, giving it leeway to alter or modify its policy in light of its ongoing experience with the problem. The difficulty is not in that principle but with the standards to govern the conduct of elections under § 9(c)(1)(A). We said in National Labor Relations Board v. Tower Co., 329 U.S. 324, 330, 67 S.Ct. 324, 327, 328, 91 L.Ed. 322, that the duty of the Board was to establish "the procedure and safeguards necessary to insure the fair and free choice of bargaining representatives by employees." * * *

* * * The Board in its DIT–MCO opinion says "it is completely illogical to characterize as improper inducement or coercion" a waiver of initiation fees for those who vote "yes" when the whole problem can be avoided by voting "no." But the Board's analysis ignores the realities of the situation.

Whatever his true intentions, an employee who signs a recognition slip prior to an election is indicating to other workers that he supports the Union. His outward manifestation of support must often serve as a useful campaign tool in the Union's hands to convince other employees to vote for the Union, if only because many employees respect their co-workers' views on the unionization issue. By permitting the Union to offer to waive an initiation fee for those employees signing a recognition slip prior to the election, the Board allows the Union to buy endorsements and paint a false portrait of employee support during its election campaign.

That influence may well have been felt here for * * * there were 28 who signed up with the Union before the election petition was filed with the Board and either seven or eight more who signed up before the election. We do not believe that the statutory policy of fair elections prescribed in the *Tower* case permits endorsements, whether for or against the Union, to be bought and sold in this fashion.

In addition, while it is correct that the employee who signs a recognition slip is not legally bound to vote for the Union and has not promised to do so in any formal sense, certainly there may be some employees who would feel obliged to carry through on their stated intention to support the Union. And on the facts of this case, the change of just one vote would have resulted in a 21–21 election rather than a 22–20 election.

Any procedure requiring a "fair" election must honor the right of those who oppose a union as well as those who favor it. The Act is wholly neutral when it comes to that basic choice. By § 7 of the Act employees have the right not only to "form, join, or assist" unions but also the right "to refrain from any or all of such activities." * * *

Congress has also listed in § 8(b) of the Act "unfair" labor practices of unions. * * * There is no explicit provision which makes "interference" by a union with the right of an employee to "refrain" from union activities an unfair labor practice.

Section 8(c), however, provides:

> "The expressing of any views, argument, or opinion, or the dissemination thereof, whether in written, printed, graphic, or visual form, shall not constitute or be evidence of an unfair labor practice under any of the provisions of this subchapter, *if such expression contains no threat of reprisal or force or promise of benefit."* * * * (emphasis added).

Whether it would be an "unfair" labor practice for a union to promise a special benefit to those who sign up for a union seems not to have been squarely resolved.[6] The right of a free choice is, however, inherent in the principles reflected in § 9(c)(1)(A).

When the dissent says that "The special inducement is to sign the card, not to vote for the union" and that treating the two choices as one is untenable, it overlooks cases like National Labor Relations Board v. Gissel Packing Co., 395 U.S. 575, 89 S.Ct. 1918, 23 L.Ed.2d 547. There we held that the gathering of authorization cards from a majority of the employees in the bargaining unit may entitle the union to represent the employees for collective bargaining purposes, even though there has been and will be no election * * *. The latent potential of that alternative use of authorization cards cautions us to treat the solicitation of authorization cards in exchange for consideration of fringe benefits granted by the union as a separate step protected by the same kind of moral standard that governs elections themselves. * * *

In the *Exchange Parts* case we said that although the benefits granted by the employer were permanent and unconditional, employees were "not likely to miss the inference that the source of benefits now conferred is also the source from which future benefits must flow and which may dry up if it

---

6. The lower courts have recognized that promising benefits or conferring benefits before representation elections may unduly influence the representational choices of employees where the offer is not across the board to all employees but, as here, only to those who sign up prior to the election. See, e.g., NLRB v. Gorbea, Perez & Morell, 328 F.2d 679, 681–682 and nn. 6–7 (CA1 1964) (promise to waive initiation fee for those joining union prior to election, but not after, may substantially influence election); Amalgamated Clothing Workers v. NLRB, 2 Cir., 345 F.2d 264, 268–269 (Friendly, J., concurring) (improper to waive fees for those joining union immediately while indicating that this is foreclosed to those joining later) (dicta). See also Collins & Aikman Corp. v. NLRB, 383 F.2d 722, 728–729 (CA4 1967) (paying employee $7 to be observer at election is an "unreasonable or excessive economic inducement" potentially influencing

other employees and is ground to set aside election); NLRB v. Commercial Letter, Inc., 455 F.2d 109 (CA8 1972) (disproportionate payments to employees attending union "hearings" prior to representation election).

The NLRB has itself recognized in other contexts that promising or conferring benefits may unduly influence representation elections. See, e.g., Wagner Electric Corp., 167 N.L.R.B. 532 (grant of life insurance policy to those who signed with union before representation election "subjects the donees to a constraint to vote for the donor union"); General Cable Corp., 170 N.L.R.B. 1682 ($5 gift to employees by union before election, even when not conditioned on outcome of election, was inducement to cast ballots favorable to union), Teletype Corp., 122 N.L.R.B. 1594 (payment of money by rival unions to those attending pre-election meetings).

is not obliged." 375 U.S., at 409, 84 S.Ct., at 460. If we respect, as we must, the statutory right of employees to resist efforts to unionize a plant, we cannot assume that unions exercising powers are wholly benign towards their antagonists whether they be nonunion protagonists or the employer. The failure to sign a recognition slip may well seem ominous to nonunionists who fear that if they do not sign they will face a wrathful union regime, should the union win. That influence may well have had a decisive impact in this case where a change of one vote would have changed the result.

Affirmed.

Mr. Justice White, with whom Mr. Justice Brennan and Mr. Justice Blackmun join, dissenting.

*   *   *

The majority places heavy reliance on the supposed analogy between the waiver of fees in this case and an actual increase in benefits made by an employer during the course of an election campaign. NLRB v. Exchange Parts, 375 U.S. 405, 84 S.Ct. 457, 11 L.Ed.2d 435 (1964). There the employer increased vacation-pay benefits during the course of the campaign. The Court agreed with the Board that this was coercive activity on the part of the employer, and *   *   * ordered enforcement of the Board's order. It was stated that "[t]he danger inherent in welltimed increases in benefits is the suggestion of a fist inside the velvet glove." Id., at 409, 84 S.Ct., at 460. A number of important differences exist between that case and the instant one. First, the employer actually gave his employees substantial increased benefits, whereas here the benefit is only contingent and small; the union glove is not very velvet. Secondly, in the union context, the fist is missing. When the employer increased benefits, the threat was made "that the source of benefits now conferred is also the source from which future benefits must flow and which may dry up if it is not obliged." Ibid. The union, on the other hand, since it was not the representative of the employees, and would not be if it were unsuccessful in the election, could not make the same threat by offering a benefit which it would take away if it *lost* the election. *   *   *

*   *   * There is certainly a conflicting interest between the union's right to make itself attractive to employees without misrepresentation and the employee's unfettered choice to vote for or against the union. I think it is rational [not an abuse of discretion] for the Board to conclude on the basis of the facts presented that the decision of the union to waive small fees was not coercive within the meaning of § 7. I, therefore, respectfully dissent.

Note

1. Should the union's tactic of "waiving" the initiation fee be considered a violation of Section 8(b)(1)(A) by analogy to Exchange Parts and Section 8(a)(1)? Did the Court resolve that issue?

The imperfect parallelism of Sections 8(a)(1) and 8(b)(1)(A) is *facially* evident: "*interfere with,* restrain, or coerce," as opposed to simply "restrain or coerce." In NLRB v. Drivers, Chauffeurs, Helpers, Local Union No. 639 ("Curtis Brothers"), 362 U.S. 274, 80 S.Ct. 706, 4 L.Ed.2d 710 (1960), it was held that peaceful picketing for recognitional or organizational purposes did not "restrain or coerce" within the meaning of Section 8(b)(1)(A). "[W]e hold," the Court said, "that § 8(b)(1)(A) is a grant of power to the Board limited to authority to proceed against union tactics involving violence, intimidation, and reprisal or threats thereof * * *" 362 U.S. at 290, 80 S.Ct. at 715, 4 L.Ed.2d at 721. "Reprisal" was further identified from the legislative history, as "violence, job reprisals and such repressive assertions as that double initiation fees would be charged those who delayed joining the union." 362 U.S. at 286, 80 S.Ct. at 713, 4 L.Ed.2d at 719.

If Section 8(b)(1)(A) was not the basis for the Court's decision in Savair, what was?

2. In Hollywood Ceramics, 140 N.L.R.B. 221 (1962), on the day before a representation election the union distributed a circular among the employees containing a material misrepresentation of the employer's wage rates as compared to those of competitors. The election, won by the union, was set aside on the ground that (1) the misrepresentation was of a sufficiently consequential order to have reasonably affected the election result, (2) the employees did not have independent means for recognizing the misrepresentation, (3) the misrepresentation was made at such a late moment in the election campaign as to preclude the employer from rebutting it through counter propaganda. This "Hollywood Ceramics rule" was applied to both union and employer election misrepresentation.

In Shopping Kart Market, Inc., 228 N.L.R.B. 1311 (1977), the union's vice president told the employees on the eve of the election that the employer had profits of $500,000 during the prior year. The uncontroverted evidence subsequently established that the employer's profits during that period amounted to only $50,000. In a 3–to–2 decision, the Board overruled Hollywood Ceramics, relying largely upon an empirical study of some 31 Board elections, involving pre-election and post-election interviews of employees to ascertain what moved the voters to decision. (Getman, Goldberg, and Herman, Union Representation Elections: Law and Reality (1976)[a]). The majority stated:

> "Our more than 20 years' experience with the rule of *Hollywood Ceramics* and its progenitor, The Gummed Products Company, 112 NLRB 1092 (1955), has revealed that although its adoption was premised on assuring employee free choice its administration has in fact tended to impede the attainment of that goal. The ill effects of the rule include extensive analysis of campaign propaganda, restriction of free speech, variance in application as between the Board and the courts, increasing litigation, and a resulting decrease in the finality of election results. * * *

> " * * * [O]ur fundamental disagreement with past Board regulation in this area lies in our unwillingness to embrace the completely unverified assumption that misleading campaign propaganda will interfere with employees' freedom of choice. Implicit in such an assumption is a view of employees as naive and unworldly whose decision on as critical an issue as union representation is easily altered by the self-serving campaign claims of the parties. If these postulates had any validity 20 years ago at the time of *Gummed Products*, they are surely anachronisms today. * * * [W]e believe that Board rules in this area must be based on a view of employees

---

a. The substance of this book can also be found in Getman, Goldberg and Herman, NLRB Regulation of Campaign Tactics: The Behavioral Assumptions on Which the Board Regulates, 27 Stan.L.Rev. 1465 (1975) and Getman and Goldberg, The Behavioral Assumptions Underlying NLRB Regulation of Campaign Misrepresentations: An Empirical Evaluation, 28 Stan.L.Rev. 263 (1976).

as mature individuals who are capable of recognizing campaign propaganda for what it is and discounting it. * * *

" * * * Accordingly, we decide today that we will no longer set elections aside on the basis of misleading campaign statements. * * *." 228 N.L.R.B. at 1312–1313.

The Board dissenters in Shopping Kart protested:

"In rationalizing their policy shift, our colleagues rely upon studies whose authors essentially conclude that employees do not attend closely to preelection campaigns, and that employee voting predilections are not easily changed by campaign information. * * *

"[If the Hollywood Ceramics standards are] relaxed—to the 'almost anything goes' standard proposed by our colleagues—one result can be fairly predicted. Campaign charges and countercharges would surely escalate. For the parties will campaign, and they will campaign on the assumption that what they say may make the difference. As 'bad money drives out the good,' so misrepresentation, if allowed to take the field unchallengeable as to its impact, will tend to drive out the responsible statement." 228 N.L.R.B. at 1316.

The Board continues to flip flop on Hollywood Ceramics. In General Knit of California, 239 N.L.R.B. 619 (1978), it returned to Hollywood Ceramics from Shopping Kart. In Midland National Life Insurance Co., 263 N.L.R.B. 127 (1982), it returned to Shopping Kart from Hollywood Ceramics.

Where are you?

For views pro and con, see Penello, Shopping Kart Food Market, Inc.: The Cure for the *Hollywood Ceramics* Malaise, 46 U.Cin.L.Rev. 464 (1977) and Phalen, The Demise of Hollywood Ceramics: Fact and Fantasy, 46 U.Cin.L.Rev. 450 (1977).

Chapter 5

UNION WEAPONS FOR ESTABLISH-ING COLLECTIVE BARGAINING AND ACHIEVING BARGAINING GOALS; OF STRIKES, PICKET-ING, AND BOYCOTTS

A. CONSTITUTIONAL CONSIDERATIONS

1. DUE PROCESS AND FREEDOM OF SPEECH

The materials in Chapter 1, supra, demonstrate the unimmaculate conception of the American labor movement. Combination by workers for the purpose of achieving the usual goals of concerted action was, as in the Philadelphia Cordwainers' Case of 1806, considered illegal. It is not uncommon for legal questions to run an ironic evolutionary gamut. Conduct which is viewed as criminal, and argued to be lawful, in one epoch, is later viewed as lawful, and argued to be constitutionally protected, in another. The purpose of the materials which follow is to consider the efforts to "constitutionalize" the right to strike and the right to picket.

DORCHY v. KANSAS

Supreme Court of the United States, 1926.
272 U.S. 306, 47 S.Ct. 86, 71 L.Ed. 248.

Mr. Justice Brandeis delivered the opinion of the Court.

Section 17 of the Court of Industrial Relations Act, Laws of Kansas, 1920, Special Session, c. 29, while reserving to the individual employee the right to quit his employment at any time, makes it unlawful to conspire "to induce others to quit their employment for the purpose and with the intent to hinder, delay, limit or suspend the operation of" mining. Section 19 makes it a felony for an officer of a labor union wilfully to use the power or influence incident to his office to induce another person to violate any provision of the Act. Dorchy was prosecuted criminally for violating § 19. The jury found him guilty through inducing a violation of § 17; the trial court sentenced him to fine and imprisonment; and its judgment was affirmed by the Supreme Court of the State, Kansas v. Howat, 112 Kan. 235. Dorchy duly claimed in both state courts that § 19 as applied was void

315

because it prohibits strikes; and that to do so is a denial of the liberty guaranteed by the Fourteenth Amendment. Because this claim was denied the case is here under § 237 of the Judicial Code as amended. * * *

* * * The question requiring decision is not, however, the broad one whether the legislature has power to prohibit strikes. It is whether the prohibition of § 19 is unconstitutional as here applied. * * * The special facts out of which the strike arose must, therefore, be considered.

Some years prior to February 3, 1921, the George H. Mackie Fuel Company had operated a coal mine in Kansas. Its employees were members of District No. 14, United Mine Workers of America. On that day, Howat, as president, and Dorchy, as vice-president, of the union, purporting to act under direction of its executive board, called a strike. So far as appears, there was no trade dispute. There had been no controversy between the company and the union over wages, hours or conditions of labor; over discipline or the discharge of an employee; concerning the observance of rules; or over the employment of non-union labor. Nor was the strike ordered as a sympathetic one in aid of others engaged in any such controversy. The order was made and the strike was called to compel the company to pay a claim of one Mishmash for $180. The men were told this; and they were instructed not to return to work until they should be duly advised that the claim had been paid. The strike order asserted that the claim had "been settled by the Joint Board of Miners and Operators but [that] the company refuses * * * to pay Brother Mishmash any part of the money that is due him." There was, however, no evidence that the claim had been submitted to arbitration, nor of any contract requiring that it should be. The claim was disputed. It had been pending nearly two years. So far as appears, Mishmash was not in the company's employ at the time of the strike order. The men went out in obedience to the strike order; and they did not return to work until after the claim was paid, pursuant to an order of the Court of Industrial Relations. While the men were out on strike this criminal proceeding was begun.

Besides these facts, which appear by the bill of exceptions, the State presents for our consideration further facts which appear by the record in Howat v. Kansas, 109 Kan. 376; 258 U.S. 181, one of the cases referred to by the Supreme Court of Kansas in its first opinion in the case at bar. These show that Dorchy called this strike in violation of an injunction issued by the State court; and that the particular controversy with Mishmash arose in this way. Under the contract between the company and the union, the rate of pay for employees under 19 was $3.65 a day and for those over 19 the rate was $5. Mishmash had been paid at the lower rate from August 31, 1917, to March 22, 1918, without protest. On that day he first demanded pay at the higher rate, and claimed back pay from August 31, 1917, at the higher rate. His contention was that he had been born August 31, 1898. The company paid him, currently at the higher rate beginning April 1, 1918. It refused him the back pay, on the ground that he was in fact less than nineteen years old. One entry in the Mishmash family Bible gave August 31, 1898, as the date of his birth, another August 31, 1899. Hence the dispute. These additional facts were not put in evidence in the case at bar. Howat v. Kansas, 109 Kan. 376, was a wholly independent proceeding. Mere reference to it by the court as a controlling decision did not incorporate its record into that of the case at bar.   *   *   * And it does not appear that the court treated these facts as matters of which it took judicial notice. We must dispose of the case upon the facts set forth in the bill of exceptions.

The right to carry on business—be it called liberty or property—has value. To interfere with this right without just cause is unlawful. The fact that the injury was inflicted by a strike is sometimes a justification. But a strike may be illegal because of its purpose, however orderly the manner in which it is conducted. To collect a stale claim due to a fellow member of the union who was formerly employed in the business is not a permissible purpose. In the absence of a valid agreement to the contrary, each party to a disputed claim may insist that it be determined only by a court.   *   *   * To enforce payment by a strike is clearly coercion. The legislature may make such action punishable criminally, as extortion or otherwise.   *   *   * And it may subject to punishment him who uses the power or influence incident to his office in a union to order the strike. Neither the common law, nor the Fourteenth Amendment, confers the absolute right to strike. *   *   *

Affirmed.

Note

If the purpose for which the union struck in Dorchy had been to obtain higher wages for present employees, would the decision have been the same? Would your answer be altered if the Kansas statute which prohibited the strike provided, as a substitute for the strike, compulsory arbitration of wage disputes?

The degree of constitutional protection, if any, of the right to strike has not yet been defined. The most obvious basis for an argument in support of constitutional protection might seem, at first impression, to be the Thirteenth Amendment. But the provision against involuntary servitude hardly shields a *concerted* refusal to work, assuming that refusal to be a "strike" rather than a permanent termination of employment. International Union, UAW–AFL. v. Wisconsin Employment Relations Board, 336 U.S. 245, 69 S.Ct. 516, 93 L.Ed. 651 (1949), so holds. A "strike," it should be noted, is a concerted work stoppage designed to bring economic pressure to bear upon the employer for the purpose of extracting better terms of employment; once the employer succumbs, work is resumed. A bona fide termination of the employment relation, however concerted, is, by way of contrast, a mere injury to the employer without correlative gain to the (former) employees responsible for the injury.

A more sophisticated and tenable effort to establish a constitutional root for the right to strike relies upon the concept of substantive due process under the Fifth and Fourteenth Amendments. The argument, as yet unvalidated by judicial imprimatur, runs as follows: A vital aspect of the concept of "liberty" or "property" in the case of employees is the freedom to take peaceful collective action against their employers concerning their conditions of employment. Without this freedom they lack the power, acting individually, to negotiate fair terms for the sale of their services; these services, representing in many instances the only significant economic asset, i.e., "property," employees possess, can, as a consequence, be said to be appropriated without just compensation, constituting a deprivation of property (and/or "liberty") without due process of law. (This line of argument is carried to its logical extreme in Green, The Case for the Sit-Down Strike, The New Republic, March 24, 1937, 199–200 (supra p. 149).)

The constitutional right to strike which would thus emerge would, of course, be subject to *reasonable* regulation; indeed, the right might accurately be articulated as a right against *un*reasonable restriction. Two inquiries would be relevant in assessing the reasonableness of any proposed restriction: (1) Does the interest served by the restriction sufficiently outweigh the loss suffered by the affected employees to justify the imposition of the restriction? (2) Is there an alternative method by which the social gain sought can be achieved at a lesser social cost? Under such an approach, those attacking the reasonableness of a legislative restriction of the right to strike would have to overcome a strong presumption of validity. At minimum, however, the right against unreasonable restriction would be constitutionally established. The posture of law which litigation along the foregoing lines would produce might prove quite similar to that produced by the much more voluminous litigation concerning the constitutional protection properly to be accorded to peaceful picketing. The evolution of the latter protection is the subject matter of the next two cases.

THORNHILL v. ALABAMA

Supreme Court of the United States, 1940.
310 U.S. 88, 60 S.Ct. 736, 84 L.Ed. 1093.

MR. JUSTICE MURPHY delivered the opinion of the Court.

Petitioner, Byron Thornhill, was convicted in the Circuit Court of Tuscaloosa County, Alabama, of the violation of Section 3448 of the State Code of 1923.[1] The Code Section reads as follows: "§ 3448. Loitering or picketing forbidden.—Any person or persons, who, without a just cause or legal excuse therefor, go near to or loiter about the premises or place of business of any other person, firm, corporation, or association of people, engaged in a lawful business, for the purpose, or with intent of influencing, or inducing other persons not to trade with, buy from, sell to, have business dealings with, or be employed by such persons, firm, corporation, or association, or who picket the works or place of business of such other persons, firms, corporations, or associations of persons, for the purpose of hindering, delaying, or interfering with or injuring any lawful business or enterprise of another, shall be guilty of a misdemeanor; but nothing herein shall prevent any person from soliciting trade or business for a competitive business."

The complaint against petitioner * * * is phrased substantially in the very words of the statute. The first and second counts charge that petitioner, without just cause or legal excuse, did "go near to or loiter about the premises" of the Brown Wood Preserving Company with the intent or purpose of influencing others to adopt one of the enumerated courses of conduct. In the third count, the charge is that petitioner "did picket" the works of the Company "for the purpose of hindering, delaying or interfering with or injuring [its] lawful business". Petitioner demurred to the complaint on the grounds, among others, that Section 3448 was repugnant to the Constitution of the United States (Amendment 1) in that it deprived him of "the right of peaceful assemblage", "the right of freedom of speech", and

---

1. * * * The Circuit Court sentenced pe-   for seventy-three days in default of payment
titioner, upon his conviction, to imprisonment   of a fine of one hundred dollars and costs.

"the right to petition for redress". The demurrer, so far as the record shows, was not ruled upon, and petitioner pleaded not guilty. The Circuit Court then proceeded to try the case without a jury, one not being asked for or demanded. At the close of the case for the State, petitioner moved to exclude all the testimony taken at the trial on the ground that Section 3448 was violative of the Constitution of the United States. The Circuit Court overruled the motion, found petitioner "guilty of Loitering and Picketing as charged in the complaint", and entered judgment accordingly. The judgment was affirmed by the Court of Appeals, which considered the constitutional question and sustained the section on the authority of two previous decisions in the Alabama courts. * * * A petition for certiorari was denied by the Supreme Court of the State. The case is here on certiorari granted because of the importance of the questions presented. * * *

The proofs consist of the testimony of two witnesses for the prosecution.[5] It appears that petitioner on the morning of his arrest was seen "in company with six or eight other men" "on the picket line" at the plant of the Brown Wood Preserving Company. Some weeks previously a strike order had been issued by a Union, apparently affiliated with The American Federation of Labor, which had as members all but four of the approximately one hundred employees of the plant. Since that time a picket line with two picket posts of six to eight men each had been maintained around the plant twenty-four hours a day. The picket posts appear to have been on Company property, "on a private entrance for employees, and not on any public road." One witness explained that practically all of the employees live on Company property and get their mail from a post office on Company property and that the Union holds its meetings on Company property. No demand was ever made upon the men not to come on the property. There is no testimony indicating the nature of the dispute between the Union and the Preserving Company, or the course of events which led to the issuance of the strike order, or the nature of the efforts for conciliation.

The Company scheduled a day for the plant to resume operations. One of the witnesses, Clarence Simpson, who was not a member of the Union, on reporting to the plant on the day indicated, was approached by petitioner who told him that "they were on strike and did not want anybody to go up there to work." None of the other employees said anything to Simpson, who testified: "Neither Mr. Thornhill nor any other employee threatened me on the occasion testified to. Mr. Thornhill approached me in a peaceful manner, and did not put me in fear; he did not appear to be mad." "I then turned and went back to the house, and did not go to work." The other witness, J.M. Walden, testified: "At the time Mr. Thornhill and Clarence Simpson were talking to each other, there was no one else present, and I heard no harsh words and saw nothing threatening in the manner of either man."[6] For engaging in some or all of these activities, petitioner was arrested, charged, and convicted as described.

5. No evidence was offered on behalf of petitioner.

6. Simpson and Walden are not in entire accord with respect to the number of persons present during the conversation between Simpson and petitioner. A possible inference from Simpson's testimony, considered by itself, is that petitioner was in the company of six or eight others when the conversation took place. This difference is not material in our view of the case.

First. The freedom of speech and of the press, which are secured by the First Amendment against abridgment by the United States, are among the fundamental personal rights and liberties which are secured to all persons by the Fourteenth Amendment against abridgment by a state.

The safeguarding of these rights to the ends that men may speak as they think on matters vital to them and that falsehoods may be exposed through the processes of education and discussion is essential to free government. Those who won our independence had confidence in the power of free and fearless reasoning and communication of ideas to discover and spread political and economic truth. Noxious doctrines in those fields may be refuted and their evil averted by the courageous exercise of the right of free discussion. Abridgment of freedom of speech and of the press, however, impairs those opportunities for public education that are essential to effective exercise of the power of correcting error through the processes of popular government. * * * Mere legislative preference for one rather than another means for combatting substantive evils, therefore, may well prove an inadequate foundation on which to rest regulations which are aimed at or in their operation diminish the effective exercise of rights so necessary to the maintenance of democratic institutions. It is imperative that, when the effective exercise of these rights is claimed to be abridged, the courts should "weigh the circumstances" and "appraise the substantiality of the reasons advanced" in support of the challenged regulations. Schneider v. State, 308 U.S. 147, 161, 162, 60 S.Ct. 146, 150, 151, 84 L.Ed. 155.

Second. The section in question must be judged upon its face.

The finding against petitioner was a general one. It did not specify the testimony upon which it rested.[8] The charges were framed in the words of the statute and so must be given a like construction. The courts below expressed no intention of narrowing the construction put upon the statute by prior State decisions. In these circumstances, there is no occasion to go behind the face of the statute or of the complaint for the purpose of determining whether the evidence, together with the permissible inferences to be drawn from it, could ever support a conviction founded upon different and more precise charges. * * *

Third. Section 3448 has been applied by the State courts so as to prohibit a single individual from walking slowly and peacefully back and forth on the public sidewalk in front of the premises of an employer, without speaking to anyone, carrying a sign or placard on a staff above his head stating only the fact that the employer did not employ union men affiliated with the American Federation of Labor; the purpose of the described activity was concededly to advise customers and prospective customers of the relationship existing between the employer and its employees and thereby to induce such customers not to patronize the employer. O'Rourke v. City of Birmingham, 27 Ala.App. 133, 168 So. 206, certiorari denied 232 Ala. 355, 168 So. 209.[14] The statute as thus authoritatively construed and applied

8. The trial court merely found petitioner "guilty of Loitering and Picketing as charged in the complaint."

14. Accused there asserted that the application of Section 3448 to the particular facts of his case deprived him of rights guaranteed to him by the Fourteenth Amendment. The Court of Appeals passed upon this constitutional question and decided it adversely to the contentions of accused.

leaves room for no exceptions based upon either the number of persons engaged in the proscribed activity, the peaceful character of their demeanor, the nature of their dispute with an employer, or the restrained character and the accurateness of the terminology used in notifying the public of the facts of the dispute.

The numerous forms of conduct proscribed by Section 3448 are subsumed under two offenses: the first embraces the activities of all who "without a just cause or legal excuse" "go near to or loiter about the premises" of any person engaged in a lawful business for the purpose of influencing or inducing others to adopt any of certain enumerated courses of action; the second, all who "picket" the place of business of any such person "for the purpose of hindering, delaying, or interfering with or injuring any lawful business or enterprise of another." It is apparent that one or the other of the offenses comprehends every practicable method whereby the facts of a labor dispute may be publicized in the vicinity of the place of business of an employer. The phrase "without a just cause or legal excuse" does not in any effective manner restrict the breadth of the regulation; the words themselves have no ascertainable meaning either inherent or historical. * * * The courses of action, listed under the first offense, which an accused—including an employee—may not urge others to take, comprehends those which in many instances would normally result from merely publicizing, without annoyance or threat of any kind, the facts of a labor dispute. An intention to hinder, delay or interfere with a lawful business, which is an element of the second offense, likewise can be proved merely by showing that others reacted in a way normally expectable of some upon learning the facts of a dispute. The vague contours of the term "picket" are nowhere delineated.[18] Employees or others, accordingly, may be found to be within the purview of the term and convicted for engaging in activities identical with those proscribed by the first offense. In sum, whatever the means used to publicize the facts of a labor dispute, whether by printed sign, by pamphlet, by word of mouth or otherwise, all such activity without exception is within the inclusive prohibition of the statute so long as it occurs in the vicinity of the scene of the dispute.

Fourth. We think that Section 3448 is invalid on its face.

18. See Hellerstein, Picketing Legislation and the Courts (1931), 10 No.Car.L.Rev. 158, 186n.:

"A picketer may: (1) Merely observe workers or customers. (2) Communicate information, e.g., that a strike is in progress, making either true, untrue or libelous statements. (3) Persuade employees or customers not to engage in relations with the employer: (a) through the use of banners, without speaking, carrying true, untrue or libelous legends; (b) by speaking, (i) in a calm, dispassionate manner, (ii) in a heated, hostile manner, (iii) using abusive epithets and profanity, (iv) yelling loudly, (v) by persisting in making arguments when employees or customers refuse to listen; (c) by offering money or similar inducements to strike breakers. (4) Threaten employees or customers: (a) by the mere presence of the picketer; the presence may be a threat of, (i) physical violence, (ii) social ostracism, being branded in the community as a 'scab', (iii) a trade or employees' boycott, i.e., preventing workers from securing employment and refusing to trade with customers, (iv) threatening injury to property; (b) by verbal threats. (5) Assaults and use of violence. (6) Destruction of property. (7) Blocking of entrances and interference with traffic.

"The picketer may engage in a combination of any of the types of conduct enumerated above. The picketing may be carried on singly or in groups; it may be directed to employees alone or to customers alone or to both. It may involve persons who have contracts with the employer or those who have not or both."

The freedom of speech and of the press guaranteed by the Constitution embraces at the least the liberty to discuss publicly and truthfully all matters of public concern without previous restraint or fear of subsequent punishment. * * * Freedom of discussion, if it would fulfill its historic function in this nation, must embrace all issues about which information is needed or appropriate to enable the members of society to cope with the exigencies of their period.

In the circumstances of our times the dissemination of information concerning the facts of a labor dispute must be regarded as within that area of free discussion that is guaranteed by the Constitution. * * * See Senn v. Tile Layers Union, 301 U.S. 468, 478, 57 S.Ct. 857, 862, 81 L.Ed. 1229. It is recognized now that satisfactory hours and wages and working conditions in industry and a bargaining position which makes these possible have an importance which is not less than the interests of those in the business or industry directly concerned. The health of the present generation and of those as yet unborn may depend on these matters, and the practices in a single factory may have economic repercussions upon a whole region and affect widespread systems of marketing. The merest glance at State and Federal legislation on the subject demonstrates the force of the argument that labor relations are not matters of mere local or private concern. Free discussion concerning the conditions in industry and the causes of labor disputes appears to us indispensable to the effective and intelligent use of the processes of popular government to shape the destiny of modern industrial society. The issues raised by regulations, such as are challenged here, infringing upon the right of employees effectively to inform the public of the facts of a labor dispute are part of this larger problem. We concur in the observation of Mr. Justice Brandeis, speaking for the Court in Senn's case (301 U.S. at page 478, 57 S.Ct. at page 862, 81 L.Ed. 1229): "Members of a union might, without special statutory authorization by a state, make known the facts of a labor dispute, for freedom of speech is guaranteed by the Federal Constitution."

It is true that the rights of employers and employees to conduct their economic affairs and to compete with others for a share in the products of industry are subject to modification or qualification in the interests of the society in which they exist. This is but an instance of the power of the State to set the limits of permissible contest open to industrial combatants. See Mr. Justice Brandeis in Duplex Printing Press Co. v. Deering, 254 U.S. 443, at page 488, 41 S.Ct. 172, 184, 65 L.Ed. 349, 16 A.L.R. 196. It does not follow that the State in dealing with the evils arising from industrial disputes may impair the effective exercise of the right to discuss freely industrial relations which are matters of public concern. A contrary conclusion could be used to support abridgment of freedom of speech and of the press concerning almost every matter of importance to society.

The range of activities proscribed by Section 3448, whether characterized as picketing or loitering or otherwise, embraces nearly every practicable, effective means whereby those interested—including the employees directly affected—may enlighten the public on the nature and causes of a labor dispute. The safeguarding of these means is essential to the securing of an informed and educated public opinion with respect to a matter which is of public concern. It may be that effective exercise of the means of advancing public knowledge may persuade some of those reached to refrain from entering into advantageous relations with the business establishment which is the scene of the dispute. Every expression of opinion on matters that are important has the potentiality of inducing action in the interests of one rather than another group in society. But the group in power at any moment may not impose penal sanctions on peaceful and truthful discussion of matters of public interest merely on a showing that others may thereby be persuaded to take action inconsistent with its interests. Abridgment of the liberty of such discussion can be justified only where the clear danger of substantive evils arises under circumstances affording no opportunity to test the merits of ideas by competition for acceptance in the market of public opinion. We hold that the danger of injury to an industrial concern is neither so serious nor so imminent as to justify the sweeping proscription of freedom of discussion embodied in Section 3448.

The State urges that the purpose of the challenged statute is the protection of the community from the violence and breaches of the peace, which, it asserts, are the concomitants of picketing. The power and the duty of the State to take adequate steps to preserve the peace and to protect the privacy, the lives, and the property of its residents cannot be doubted. But no clear and present danger of destruction of life or property, or invasion of the right of privacy, or breach of the peace can be thought to be inherent in the activities of every person who approaches the premises of an employer and publicizes the facts of a labor dispute involving the latter. We are not now concerned with picketing en masse or otherwise conducted which might occasion such imminent and aggravated danger to these interests as to justify a statute narrowly drawn to cover the precise situation giving rise to the danger. * * * Section 3448 in question here does not aim specifically at serious encroachments on these interests and does not evidence any such care in balancing these interests against the interest of the community and that of the individual in freedom of discussion on matters of public concern.

It is not enough to say that Section 3448 is limited or restricted in its application to such activity as takes place at the scene of the labor dispute. "[The] streets are natural and proper places for the dissemination of information and opinion; and one is not to have the exercise of his liberty of expression in appropriate places abridged on the plea that it may be exercised in some other place." Schneider v. State, 308 U.S. 147, 161, 60 S.Ct. 146, 150, 84 L.Ed. 155; Hague v. C.I.O., 307 U.S. 496, 515, 516, 59 S.Ct. 954, 963, 964, 83 L.Ed. 1423.[23] The danger of breach of the peace or serious invasion of rights of property or privacy at the scene of a labor dispute is not sufficiently imminent in all cases to warrant the legislature in determining that such place is not appropriate for the range of activities outlawed by Section 3448.

Reversed.

23. The fact that the activities for which petitioner was arrested and convicted took place on the private property of the Preserving Company is without significance. Petitioner and the other employees were never treated as trespassers, assuming that they could be where the Company owns such a substantial part of the town. * * * And Section 3448, in any event, must be tested upon its face.

MR. JUSTICE MCREYNOLDS is of opinion that the judgment below should be affirmed.

INTERNATIONAL BROTHERHOOD OF TEAMSTERS, LOCAL 695 v. VOGT, INC.

Supreme Court of the United States, 1957.
354 U.S. 284, 77 S.Ct. 1166, 1 L.Ed.2d 1347.

MR. JUSTICE FRANKFURTER delivered the opinion of the Court.

This is one more in the long series of cases in which this Court has been required to consider the limits imposed by the Fourteenth Amendment on the power of a State to enjoin picketing. The case was heard below on the pleadings and affidavits, the parties stipulating that the record contained "all of the facts and evidence that would be adduced upon a trial on the merits * * *." Respondent owns and operates a gravel pit in Oconomowoc, Wisconsin, where it employs 15 to 20 men. Petitioner unions sought unsuccessfully to induce some of respondent's employees to join the unions and commenced to picket the entrance to respondent's place of business with signs reading, "The men on this job are not 100% affiliated with the A.F.L." "In consequence," drivers of several trucking companies refused to deliver and haul goods to and from respondent's plant, causing substantial damage to respondent. Respondent thereupon sought an injunction to restrain the picketing.

The trial court did not make the finding, requested by respondent, "That the picketing of plaintiff's premises has been engaged in for the purpose of coercing, intimidating and inducing the employer to force, compel, or induce its employees to become members of defendant labor organizations, and for the purpose of injuring the plaintiff in its business because of its refusal to in any way interfere with the rights of its employees to join or not to join a labor organization." It nevertheless held that by virtue of Wis.Stat. § 103.535, prohibiting picketing in the absence of a "labor dispute," the petitioners must be enjoined from maintaining any pickets near respondent's place of business, from displaying at any place near respondent's place of business signs indicating that there was a labor dispute between respondent and its employees or between respondent and any of the petitioners, and from inducing others to decline to transport goods to and from respondent's business establishment.

On appeal, the Wisconsin Supreme Court at first reversed, relying largely on A.F.L. v. Swing, 312 U.S. 321, 61 S.Ct. 568, 85 L.Ed. 855, to hold § 103.535 unconstitutional, on the ground that picketing could not constitutionally be enjoined merely because of the absence of a "labor dispute." 270 Wis. 315, 71 N.W.2d 359.

Upon reargument, [270 Wis. 315, 74 N.W.2d 749, 753] however, the court withdrew its original opinion. Although the trial court had refused to make the finding requested by respondent, the Supreme Court, noting that the facts as to which the request was made were undisputed, drew the inference from the undisputed facts and itself made the finding. It canvassed the whole circumstances surrounding the picketing and held that "One would be credulous, indeed, to believe under the circumstances that the union had no thought of coercing the employer to interfere with its employees in their right to join or refuse to join the defendant union." Such picketing, the court held, was for "an unlawful purpose," since Wis.Stat. § 111.06(2)(b) made it an unfair labor practice for an employee individually or in concert with others to "coerce, intimidate or induce any employer to interfere with any of his employes in the enjoyment of their legal rights * * * or to engage in any practice with regard to his employes which would constitute an unfair labor practice if undertaken by him on his own initiative." Relying on Building Service Employees, etc. v. Gazzam, 339 U.S. 532, 70 S.Ct. 784, 94 L.Ed. 1045, and Pappas v. Stacey, 151 Me. 36, 116 A.2d 497, the Wisconsin Supreme Court therefore affirmed the granting of the injunction on this different ground. 270 Wis. 321a, 74 N.W.2d 749.

We are asked to reverse the judgment of the Wisconsin Supreme Court * * * and to restate the principles governing this type of case.

It is inherent in the concept embodied in the Due Process Clause that its scope be determined by a "gradual process of judicial inclusion and exclusion," Davidson v. New Orleans, 96 U.S. 97, 104, 24 L.Ed. 616. Inevitably, therefore, the doctrine of a particular case "is not allowed to end with its enunciation and * * * an expression in an opinion yields later to the impact of facts unforeseen." Jaybird Mining Co. v. Weir, 271 U.S. 609, 619, 46 S.Ct. 592, 595, 70 L.Ed. 1112 (Brandeis, J., dissenting). It is not too surprising that the response of States—legislative and judicial—to use of the injunction in labor controversies should have given rise to a series of adjudications in this Court relating to the limitations on state action contained in the provisions of the Due Process Clause of the Fourteenth Amendment. It is also not too surprising that examination of these adjudications should disclose an evolving, not a static, course of decision.

The series begins with Truax v. Corrigan, 257 U.S. 312, 42 S.Ct. 124, 66 L.Ed. 254, in which a closely divided Court found it to be violative of the Equal Protection Clause—not of the Due Process Clause—for a State to deny use of the injunction in the special class of cases arising out of labor conflicts. The considerations that underlay that case soon had to yield, through legislation and later through litigation, to the persuasiveness of undermining facts. Thus, to remedy the abusive use of the injunction in the federal courts, see Frankfurter and Greene, The Labor Injunction, the Norris-LaGuardia Act withdrew, subject to qualifications, jurisdiciton from the federal courts to issue injunctions in labor disputes to prohibit certain acts. Its example was widely followed by state enactments.

Apart from remedying the abuses of the injunction in this general type of litigation, legislatures and courts began to find in one of the aims of picketing an aspect of communication. This view came to the fore in Senn v. Tile Layers Union, 301 U.S. 468, 57 S.Ct. 857, 81 L.Ed. 1229, where the Court held that the Fourteenth Amendment did not prohibit Wisconsin from authorizing peaceful stranger picketing by a union that was attempting to unionize a shop and to induce an employer to refrain from working in his business as a laborer.

Although the Court had been closely divided in the Senn case, three years later, in passing on a restrictive instead of a permissive state statute, the Court made sweeping pronouncements about the right to picket in holding unconstitutional a statute that had been applied to ban all picketing, with "no exceptions based upon either the number of persons engaged in the proscribed activity, the peaceful character of their demeanor, the nature of their dispute with an employer, or the restrained character and the accurateness of the terminology used in notifying the public of the facts of the dispute." Thornhill v. Alabama, 310 U.S. 88, 99, 60 S.Ct. 736, 743, 84 L.Ed. 1093. As the statute dealt at large with all picketing, so the Court broadly assimilated peaceful picketing in general to freedom of speech, and as such protected against abridgment by the Fourteenth Amendment.

These principles were applied by the Court in A.F.L. v. Swing, 312 U.S. 321, 61 S.Ct. 568, 85 L.Ed. 855, to hold unconstitutional an injunction against peaceful picketing, based on a State's common-law policy against picketing when there was no immediate dispute between employer and employee.

Soon, however, the Court came to realize that the broad pronouncements, but not the specific holding, of Thornhill had to yield "to the impact of facts unforeseen," or at least not sufficiently appreciated. * * * Cases reached the Court in which a State had designed a remedy to meet a specific situation or to accomplish a particular social policy. These cases made manifest that picketing, even though "peaceful," involved more than just communication of ideas and could not be immune from all state regulation. "Picketing by an organized group is more than free speech, since it involves patrol of a particular locality and since the very presence of a picket line may induce action of one kind or another, quite irrespective of the nature of the ideas which are being disseminated." Bakery and Pastry Drivers Local v. Wohl, 315 U.S. 769, 776, 62 S.Ct. 816, 819, 86 L.Ed. 1178 (concurring opinion) * * *.

The implied reassessments of the broad language of the Thornhill case were finally generalized in a series of cases sustaining injunctions against peaceful picketing, even when arising in the course of a labor controversy, when such picketing was counter to valid state policy in a domain open to state regulation. The decisive reconsideration came in Giboney v. Empire Storage & Ice Co., 336 U.S. 490, 69 S.Ct. 684, 93 L.Ed. 834. A union, seeking to organize peddlers, picketed a wholesale dealer to induce it to refrain from selling to nonunion peddlers. The state courts, finding that such an agreement would constitute a conspiracy in restraint of trade in violation of the state antitrust laws, enjoined the picketing. This Court affirmed unanimously.

"It is contended that the injunction against picketing adjacent to Empire's place of business is an unconstitutional abridgment of free speech because the picketers were attempting peacefully to publicize truthful facts about a labor dispute. * * * But the record here does not permit this publicizing to be treated in isolation. For according to the pleadings, the evidence, the findings, and the argument of the appellants, the sole immediate object of the publicizing adjacent to the premises of Empire, as well as the other activities of the appellants and their allies, was to compel Empire to agree to stop selling ice to nonunion peddlers. Thus all of appellants' activities * * * constituted a single and integrated course of conduct, which was in violation of Missouri's valid law. In this situation, the injunction did no more than enjoin an offense against Missouri law, a felony." Id., 336 U.S. at pages 497–498, 69 S.Ct. at page 688.

The Court therefore concluded that it was "clear that appellants were doing more than exercising a right of free speech or press. * * * They were exercising their economic power together with that of their allies to compel Empire to abide by union rather than by state regulation of trade." Id., 336 U.S. at page 503, 69 S.Ct. at page 691.

The following Term, the Court decided a group of cases applying and elaborating on the theory of Giboney. In Hughes v. Superior Court, 339 U.S. 460, 70 S.Ct. 718, 94 L.Ed. 985, the Court held that the Fourteenth Amendment did not bar use of the injunction to prohibit picketing of a place of business solely to secure compliance with a demand that its employees be hired in percentage to the racial origin of its customers. "We cannot construe the Due Process Clause as prohibiting California from securing respect for its policy against involuntary employment on racial lines by prohibiting systematic picketing that would subvert such policy." Id., 339 U.S. at page 466, 70 S.Ct. at page 722. The Court also found it immaterial that the state policy had been expressed by the judiciary rather than by the legislature.

On the same day, the Court decided International Brotherhood of Teamsters Union v. Hanke, 339 U.S. 470, 70 S.Ct. 773, 94 L.Ed. 995, holding that a State was not restrained by the Fourteenth Amendment from enjoining picketing of a business, conducted by the owner himself without employees, in order to secure compliance with a demand to become a union shop. Although there was no one opinion for the Court, its decision was another instance of the affirmance of an injunction against picketing because directed against a valid public policy of the State.

A third case, Building Service Emp. Intern. Union v. Gazzam, 339 U.S. 532, 70 S.Ct. 784, 94 L.Ed. 1045, was decided the same day. Following an unsuccessful attempt at unionization of a small hotel and refusal by the owner to sign a contract with the union as bargaining agent, the union began to picket the hotel with signs stating that the owner was unfair to organized labor. The State, finding that the object of the picketing was in violation of its statutory policy against employer coercion of employees' choice of bargaining representative, enjoined picketing for such purpose. This Court affirmed, rejecting the argument that "the Swing case, supra, is controlling. * * * In that case this Court struck down the State's restraint of picketing based solely on the absence of an employer-employee relationship. An adequate basis for the instant decree is the unlawful objective of the picketing, namely, coercion by the employer of the employees' selection of a bargaining representative. Peaceful picketing for any lawful purpose is not prohibited by the decree under review." Id., 339 U.S. at page 539, 70 S.Ct. at page 788.

A similar problem was involved in Local Union No. 10, United Ass'n of Journeymen, Plumbers and Steamfitters, etc. v. Graham, 345 U.S. 192, 73 S.Ct. 585, 587, 97 L.Ed. 946, where a state court had enjoined, as a violation of its "Right to Work" law, picketing that advertised that nonunion men were being employed on a building job. This Court found that there was evidence in the record supporting a conclusion that a substantial purpose of the picketing was to put pressure on the general contractor to eliminate nonunion men from the job and, on the reasoning of the cases that we have just discussed, held that the injunction was not in conflict with the Four-teenth Amendment.

This series of cases, then established a broad field in which a State, in enforcing some public policy, whether of its criminal or its civil law, and whether announced by its legislature or its courts, could constitutionally enjoin peaceful picketing aimed at preventing effectuation of that policy.
* * *

* * * [T]he present case was tried without oral testimony. [T]he highest state court drew the inference from the facts that the picketing was to coerce the employer to put pressure on his employees to join the union, in violation of the declared policy of the State. (For a declaration of similar congressional policy, see § 8 of the National Labor Relations Act * * *.) The cases discussed above all hold that, consistent with the Fourteenth Amendment, a State may enjoin such conduct.

Of course, the mere fact that there is "picketing" does not automatically justify its restraint without an investigation into its conduct and purposes. State courts, no more than state legislatures, can enact blanket prohibitions against picketing. Thornhill v. Alabama and A.F.L. v. Swing, supra. The series of cases following Thornhill and Swing demonstrate that the policy of Wisconsin enforced by the prohibition of this picketing is a valid one. In this case, the circumstances set forth in the opinion of the Wisconsin Supreme Court afford a rational basis for the inference it drew concerning the purpose of the picketing. * * *

Affirmed.

MR. JUSTICE WHITTAKER took no part in the consideration or decision of this case.

MR. JUSTICE DOUGLAS, with whom THE CHIEF JUSTICE and MR. JUSTICE BLACK concur, dissenting.

The Court has now come full circle. In Thornhill v. Alabama, 310 U.S. 88, 102, 60 S.Ct. 736, 744, 84 L.Ed. 1093, we struck down a state ban on picketing on the ground that "the dissemination of information concerning the facts of a labor dispute must be regarded as within that area of free discussion that is guaranteed by the Constitution." Less than one year later, we held that the First Amendment protected organizational picketing on a factual record which cannot be distinguished from the one now before us. A.F.L. v. Swing, 312 U.S. 321, 61 S.Ct. 568, 85 L.Ed. 855. Of course, we have always recognized that picketing has aspects which make it more than speech. Bakery and Pastry Drivers Local v. Wohl, 315 U.S. 769, 776–777, 62 S.Ct. 816, 819, 820, 86 L.Ed. 1178 (concurring opinion). That difference underlies our decision in Giboney v. Empire Storage & Ice Co., 336 U.S. 490, 69 S.Ct. 684, 93 L.Ed. 834. There, picketing was an essential part of "a single and integrated course of conduct, which was in violation of Missouri's valid law." Id., 336 U.S. at page 498, 69 S.Ct. at page 688. And see National Labor Relations Board v. Virginia Elec. & Power Co., 314 U.S. 469, 477–478, 62 S.Ct. 344, 348, 86 L.Ed. 348. We emphasized that "there was clear danger, imminent and immediate, that unless restrained, appellants would succeed in making [the state] policy a dead letter * * *." 336 U.S. at page 503, 69 S.Ct. at page 691. Speech there was enjoined because it was an inseparable part of conduct which the State constitutionally could and did regulate.

But where, as here, there is no rioting, no mass picketing, no violence, no disorder, no fisticuffs, no coercion—indeed nothing but speech—the principles announced in Thornhill and Swing should give the advocacy of one side of a dispute First Amendment protection.

The retreat began when, in International Brotherhood of Teamsters Union v. Hanke, 339 U.S. 470, 70 S.Ct. 773, 94 L.Ed. 995, four members of the Court announced that all picketing could be prohibited if a state court decided that that picketing violated the State's public policy. The retreat became a rout in Local Union No. 10, United Ass'n of Journeymen, Plumbers and Steamfitters, etc. v. Graham, 345 U.S. 192, 73 S.Ct. 585, 97 L.Ed. 946. It was only the "purpose" of the picketing which was relevant. The state court's characterization of the picketers' "purpose" had been made wellnigh conclusive. Considerations of the proximity of picketing to conduct which the State could control or prevent were abandoned, and no longer was it necessary for the state court's decree to be narrowly drawn to prescribe a specific evil. Id., 345 U.S. at pages 201–205, 73 S.Ct. at pages 589–591 (dissenting opinion).

Today, the Court signs the formal surrender. State courts and state legislatures cannot fashion blanket prohibitions on all picketing. But, for practical purposes, the situation now is as it was when Senn v. Tile Layers Union, 301 U.S. 468, 57 S.Ct. 857, 81 L.Ed. 1229, was decided. State courts and state legislatures are free to decide whether to permit or suppress any particular picket line for any reason other than a blanket policy against all picketing. I would adhere to the principle announced in Thornhill. I would adhere to the result reached in Swing. I would return to the test enunciated in Giboney—that this form of expression can be regulated or prohibited only to the extent that it forms an essential part of a course of conduct which the State can regulate or prohibit. I would reverse the judgment below.

Note

1. With whom do you agree, the majority or the dissent? Is peaceful picketing "speech" or is it "speech plus"? Why is speech protected in the First Amendment? Does this rationale apply to peaceful picketing?

Would you accept, reject, or modify the following analysis: The effectiveness of peaceful picketing is not attributable to persuasion resulting from the communication of information or ideas. Its appeal is not to the reason. Rather, peaceful picketing constitutes a signal—like the flashing of a light or the raising of a fist—designed to cause (1) disciplined union members and sympathizers to refuse, in reflex fashion, to cross the picket line, and (2) timid persons, not subject to union discipline or sympathy, to refuse to cross the line out of subtly-induced fear.

2. If picketing, however peaceful, is really a form of economic pressure in which the resort to speech is, at best, incidental, at worst, mere empty form, should it not be dealt with under the Due Process Clause rather than the First Amendment? Picketing, the argument would run, is an economic weapon, largely supportive of the strike, and should therefore be subjected to the same

constitutional analysis as the strike itself. See Note following Dorchy v. Kansas, supra p. 317. Would such a shift in analysis produce any decisional change?

It should be noted that the foregoing observations are made with respect to picketing as known in the labor relations context. The term is occasionally employed with regard to what might more aptly be described as political demonstration. The terms "picket" and "picket line" are of military origin: The function of "pickets" in the military sense was to prevent, by force or alarm, the crossing by the enemy of the so-called "picket line" which surrounded and protected an encampment. The analogy of this to what has at times been called the "warfare" of labor relations is apparent. Political "picketing" does not usually have this military function of preventing the crossing of a line; its purpose is more clearly that of publicizing and dramatizing a point of view and of attracting new adherents to it. Do these two forms of "picketing"—labor and political—call for different constitutional analysis?

3. The reader should be cautioned that, for all of Vogt, the Thornhill doctrine may have regained some vitality in the case of NLRB v. Fruit and Vegetable Packers, Local 760, 377 U.S. 58, 12 L.Ed.2d 129, 84 S.Ct. 1063 (1964) ("Tree Fruits"), a secondary boycott case set forth infra p. 421.

Indeed, might the quiessence, but *non*death, of Thornhill be viewed as a healthy posture for a free society? The symphonic force of the First Amendment protection of peaceful picketing, though currently muted, remains in the background for constitutional appeal should a particular time and case persuade of its need.

4. For a consideration of peaceful picketing and the First Amendment in the shopping-center context, see the Hudgens case, supra Note 1, p. 258.

2. FEDERAL SUPREMACY

What the Supreme Court gave to the states under the Fourteenth Amendment in Vogt and its progenitors, it largely took away under the Supremacy Clause of Article VI. In substantially parallel developments, state jurisdiction, expanding under the First Amendment, as incorporated in the Fourteenth, was the subject of federal encroachment under Article VI. The materials which follow are concerned with the development of the doctrine of "federal preemption" under the national labor law—a development discussed previously, it may be recalled, in the 1942 decision of the Court in Allen-Bradley Local No. 1111 v. Wisconsin Employment Relations Board, supra p. 129.

SAN DIEGO BUILDING TRADES COUNCIL v. GARMON

Supreme Court of the United States, 1959.
359 U.S. 236, 79 S.Ct. 773, 3 L.Ed.2d 775.

MR. JUSTICE FRANKFURTER delivered the opinion of the Court.

This case is before us for the second time. The present litigation began with a dispute between the petitioning unions and respondents, co-partners in the business of selling lumber and other materials in California. Respondents began an action in the Superior Court for the County of San Diego, asking for an injunction and damages. Upon hearing, the trial court found the following facts. In March of 1953 the unions sought from respondents an agreement to retain in their employ only those workers who were already members of the unions, or who applied for membership within thirty days. Respondents refused, claiming that none of their employees had shown a desire to join a union, and that, in any event, they could not accept such an arrangement until one of the unions had been designated by the employees as a collective bargaining agent. The unions began at once peacefully to picket the respondents' place of business, and to exert pressure on customers and suppliers in order to persuade them to stop dealing with respondents. The sole purpose of these pressures was to compel execution of the proposed contract. The unions contested this finding, claiming that the only purpose of their activities was to educate the workers and persuade them to become members. On the basis of its findings, the court enjoined the unions from picketing and from the use of other pressures to force an agreement, until one of them had been properly designated as a collective bargaining agent. The court also awarded $1,000 damages for losses found to have been sustained.

At the time the suit in the state court was started, respondents had begun a representation proceeding before the National Labor Relations Board. The Regional Director declined jurisdiction, presumably because the amount of interstate commerce involved did not meet the Board's monetary standards in taking jurisdiction.

On appeal, the California Supreme Court sustained the judgment of the Superior Court, 45 Cal.2d 657, 291 P.2d 1, holding that, since the National Labor Relations Board had declined to exercise its jurisdiction, the California courts had power over the dispute. They further decided that the conduct of the union constituted an unfair labor practice under § 8(b)(2) of the National Labor Relations Act * * * and hence was not privileged under California law. As the California court itself later pointed out this decision did not specify what law, state or federal, was the basis of the relief granted. Both state and federal law played a part but, "[a]ny distinction as between those laws was not thoroughly explored." Garmon v. San Diego Bldg. Trades Council, 49 Cal.2d 595, 602, 320 P.2d 473, 477.

We granted certiorari * * * and decided the case together with Guss v. Utah Labor Relations Board, 353 U.S. 1, 77 S.Ct. 598, 609, 1 L.Ed.2d 601, and Amalgamated Meat Cutters, etc. v. Fairlawn Meats, Inc., 353 U.S. 20, 77 S.Ct. 604, 1 L.Ed.2d 613. In those cases, we held that the refusal of the National Labor Relations Board to assert jurisdiction did not leave with the States power over activities they otherwise would be preempted from regulating. Both Guss and Fairlawn involved relief of an equitable nature. In vacating and remanding the judgment of the California court in this case, we pointed out that those cases controlled this one, "in its major aspects." 353 U.S. 26, at page 28, 77 S.Ct. 607, at page 608, 1 L.Ed.2d 618. However, since it was not clear whether the judgment for damages would be sustained under California law, we remanded to the state court for consideration of that local law issue. The federal question, namely, whether the National Labor Relations Act * * * precluded California from granting an award for damages arising out of the conduct in question, could not be appropriately decided until the antecedent state law question was decided by the state court.

On remand, the California court, in accordance with our decision in Guss, set aside the injunction, but sustained the award of damages. Garmon v. San Diego Bldg. Trades Council, 49 Cal.2d 595, 320 P.2d 473 (three judges dissenting). After deciding that California had jurisdiction to award damages for injuries caused by the union's activities, the California court held that those activities constituted a tort based on an unfair labor practice under state law. In so holding the court relied on general tort provisions of the West's Ann. California Civil Code, §§ 1667, 1708, as well as state enactments dealing specifically with labor relations, West's Ann.Calif.Labor Code, § 923 (1937); ibid., §§ 1115–1118 (1947).

We again granted certiorari * * * to determine whether the California court had jurisdiction to award damages arising out of peaceful union activity which it could not enjoin.

The issue is a variant of a familiar theme. It began with Allen-Bradley Local No. 1111, etc. v. Wisconsin Employment Relations Board, 315 U.S. 740, 62 S.Ct. 820, 86 L.Ed. 1154, was greatly intensified by litigation flowing from the Taft-Hartley Act * * * and has recurred here in almost a score of cases during the last decade. The comprehensive regulation of industrial relations by Congress, novel federal legislation twenty-five years ago but now an integral part of our economic life, inevitably gave rise to difficult problems of federal-state relations. To be sure, in the abstract these problems came to us as ordinary questions of statutory construction. But they involved a more complicated and perceptive process than is conveyed by the delusive phrase, "ascertaining the intent of the legislature." Many of these problems probably could not have been, at all events were not, foreseen by the Congress. Others were only dimly perceived and their precise scope only vaguely defined. This Court was called upon to apply a new and complicated legislative scheme, the aims and social policy of which were drawn with broad strokes while the details had to be filled in, to no small extent, by the judicial process. Recently we indicated the task that was thus cast upon this Court in carrying out with fidelity the purposes of Congress, but doing so by giving application to congressional incompletion. What we said in Weber v. Anheuser-Busch, Inc., 348 U.S. 468, 75 S.Ct. 480, 99 L.Ed. 546, deserves repetition, because the considerations there outlined guide this day's decision:

> "By the Taft-Hartley Act, Congress did not exhaust the full sweep of legislative power over industrial relations given by the Commerce Clause. Congress formulated a code whereby it outlawed some aspects of labor activities and left others free for the operation of economic forces. As to both categories, the areas that have been pre-empted by federal authority and thereby withdrawn from state power are not susceptible of delimitation by fixed metes and bounds. Obvious conflict, actual or potential, leads to easy judicial exclusion of state action. Such was the situation in Garner v. Teamsters Union, supra [346 U.S. 485, 74 S.Ct. 161, 98 L.Ed. 228]. But as the opinion in that case recalled, the Labor Management Relations Act 'leaves much to the states, though Congress has refrained from telling us how much.' 346 U.S. at page 488, 74 S.Ct. at page 164. This penumbral area can be rendered progressively clear only by the course of litigation." 348 U.S. at pages 480–481, 75 S.Ct. at page 488.

The case before us concerns one of the most teasing and frequently litigated areas of industrial relations, the multitude of activities regulated by §§ 7 and 8 of the National Labor Relations Act. * * * These broad provisions govern both protected "concerted activities" and unfair labor practices. They regulate the vital, economic instruments of the strike and the picket line, and impinge on the clash of the still unsettled claims between employers and labor unions. The extent to which the variegated laws of the several States are displaced by a single uniform, national rule has been a matter of frequent and recurring concern. As we pointed out the other day, "the statutory implications concerning what has been taken from the States and what has been left to them are of a Delphic nature, to be translated into concreteness by the process of litigating elucidation." International Ass'n of Machinists v. Gonzales, 356 U.S. 617, 619, 78 S.Ct. 923, 924, 2 L.Ed.2d 1018.

In the area of regulation with which we are here concerned, the process thus described has contracted initial ambiguity and doubt and established guides for judgment by interested parties and certainly guides for decision. We state these principles in full realization that, in the course of a process of tentative, fragmentary illumination carried on over more than a decade during which the writers of opinions almost inevitably, because unconsciously, focus their primary attention on the facts of particular situations, language may have been used or views implied which do not completely harmonize with the clear pattern which the decisions have evolved. But it may safely be claimed that the basis and purport of a long series of adjudications have "translated into concreteness" the consistently applied principles which decide this case.

In determining the extent to which state regulation must yield to subordinating federal authority, we have been concerned with delimiting areas of potential conflict; potential conflict of rules of law, of remedy, and of administration. The nature of the judicial process precludes an *ad hoc* inquiry into the special problems of labor-management relations involved in a particular set of occurrences in order to ascertain the precise nature and degree of federal-state conflict there involved, and more particularly what exact mischief such a conflict would cause. Nor is it our business to attempt this. Such determinations inevitably depend upon judgments on the impact of these particular conflicts on the entire scheme of federal labor policy and administration. Our task is confined to dealing with classes of situations. To the National Labor Relations Board and to Congress must be left those precise and closely limited demarcations that can be adequately fashioned only by legislation and administration. We have necessarily been concerned with the potential conflict of two law-enforcing authorities, with the disharmonies inherent in two systems, one federal the other state, of inconsistent standards of substantive law and differing remedial schemes. But the unifying consideration of our decisions has been regard to the fact that Congress has entrusted administration of the labor policy for the Nation to a centralized administrative agency, armed with its own procedures, and equipped with its specialized knowledge and cumulative experience:

> "Congress did not merely lay down a substantive rule of law to be enforced by any tribunal competent to apply law generally to the parties. It

went on to confide primary interpretation and application of its rules to a specific and specially constituted tribunal and prescribed a particular procedure for investigation, complaint and notice, and hearing and decision, including judicial relief pending a final administrative order. Congress evidently considered that centralized administration of specially designed procedures was necessary to obtain uniform application of its substantive rules and to avoid these diversities and conflicts likely to result from a variety of local procedures and attitudes towards labor controversies. * * * A multiplicity of tribunals and a diversity of procedures are quite as apt to produce incompatible or conflicting adjudications as are different rules of substantive law. * * *" Garner v. Teamsters, etc. Union, 346 U.S. 485, 490–491, 74 S.Ct. 161, 165, 98 L.Ed. 228.

Administration is more than a means of regulation; administration is regulation. We have been concerned with conflict in its broadest sense; conflict with a complex and interrelated federal scheme of law, remedy, and administration. Thus, judicial concern has necessarily focused on the nature of the activities which the States have sought to regulate, rather than on the method of regulation adopted. When the exercise of state power over a particular area of activity threatened interference with the clearly indicated policy of industrial relations, it has been judicially necessary to preclude the States from acting. However, due regard for the presuppositions of our embracing federal system, including the principle of diffusion of power not as a matter of doctrinaire localism but as a promoter of democracy, has required us not to find withdrawal from the States of power to regulate where the activity regulated was a merely peripheral concern of the Labor Management Relations Act. See International Ass'n of Machinists v. Gonzales, 356 U.S. 617, 78 S.Ct. 923, 2 L.Ed.2d 1018.[a] Or where the regulated conduct touched interests so deeply rooted in local feeling and responsibility that, in the absence of compelling congressional direction, we could not infer that Congress had deprived the States of the power to act.[2]

When it is clear or may fairly be assumed that the activities which a State purports to regulate are protected by § 7 of the National Labor Relations Act, or constitute an unfair labor practice under § 8, due regard for the federal enactment requires that state jurisdiction must yield. To leave the States free to regulate conduct so plainly within the central aim of federal regulation involves too great a danger of conflict between power asserted by Congress and requirements imposed by state law. Nor has it mattered whether the States have acted through laws of broad general application rather than laws specifically directed towards the governance of industrial relations. Regardless of the mode adopted, to allow the States to control conduct which is the subject of national regulation would create potential frustration of national purposes.

At times it has not been clear whether the particular activity regulated by the States was governed by § 7 or § 8 or was, perhaps, outside both these

a. The *Gonzales* case is discussed infra pp. 347–348.

2. International Union, United Automobile, Aircraft and Agricultural Implement Workers, etc. v. Russell, 356 U.S. 634, 78 S.Ct. 932, 2 L.Ed.2d 1030; Youngdahl v. Rainfair, Inc., 355 U.S. 131, 78 S.Ct. 206, 2 L.Ed.2d 151; United Automobile, Aircraft and Agricultural Implement Workers, etc. v. Wisconsin Employment Relations Board, 351 U.S. 266, 76 S.Ct. 794, 100 L.Ed. 1162; United Construction Workers, etc. v. Laburnum Const. Corp., 347 U.S. 656, 74 S.Ct. 833, 98 L.Ed. 1025.

sections. But courts are not primary tribunals to adjudicate such issues. It is essential to the administration of the Act that these determinations be left in the first instance to the National Labor Relations Board. What is outside the scope of this Court's authority cannot remain within a State's power and state jurisdiction too must yield to the exclusive primary competence of the Board. *　*　*

The case before us is such a case. The adjudication in California has throughout been based on the assumption that the behavior of the petitioning unions constituted an unfair labor practice. This conclusion was derived by the California courts from the facts as well as from their view of the Act. It is not for us to decide whether the National Labor Relations Board would have, or should have, decided these questions in the same manner. When an activity is arguably subject to § 7 or § 8 of the Act, the States as well as the federal courts must defer to the exclusive competence of the National Labor Relations Board if the danger of state interference with national policy is to be averted.

To require the States to yield to the primary jurisdiction of the National Board does not ensure Board adjudication of the status of a disputed activity. If the Board decides, subject to appropriate federal judicial review, that conduct is protected by § 7, or prohibited by § 8, then the matter is at an end, and the States are ousted of all jurisdiction. Or, the Board may decide that an activity is neither protected nor prohibited, and thereby raise the question whether such activity may be regulated by the States.[4] However, the Board may also fail to determine the status of the disputed conduct by declining to assert jurisdiction, or by refusal of the General Counsel to file a charge, or by adopting some other disposition which does not define the nature of the activity with unclouded legal significance. This was the basic problem underlying our decision in Guss v. Utah Labor Relations Board, 353 U.S. 1, 77 S.Ct. 598, 609, 1 L.Ed.2d 601. In that case we held that the failure of the National Labor Relations Board to assume jurisdiction did not leave the States free to regulate activities they would otherwise be precluded from regulating. It follows that the failure of the Board to define the legal significance under the Act of a particular activity does not give the States the power to act. In the absence of the Board's clear determination that an activity is neither protected nor prohibited or of compelling precedent applied to essentially undisputed facts, it is not for this Court to decide whether such activities are subject to state jurisdiction. The withdrawal of this narrow area from possible state activity follows from our decisions in Weber and Guss. The governing consideration is that to allow the States to control activities that are potentially subject to federal regulation involves too great a danger of conflict with national labor policy.[5]

4. See International Union, United Auto Workers, etc. v. Wisconsin Employment Relations Board ["Briggs-Stratton"], 336 U.S. 245, 69 S.Ct. 516, 93 L.Ed. 651. The approach taken in that case, in which the Court undertook for itself to determine the status of the disputed activity, has not been followed in later decisions, and is no longer of general application. [The activity held to be "neither protected nor prohibited" consisted of intermittent, unannounced work stoppages ("quick-ie strikes"). The Briggs-Stratton case further held that such activity was not federally preempted; the case was overruled on this point in Lodge 76, International Association of Machinists v. Wisconsin Employment Relations Commission, 427 U.S. 132, 96 S.Ct. 2548, 49 L.Ed.2d 396 (1976), discussed infra p. 370.]

5. "When Congress has taken the particular subject-matter in hand, coincidence is as ineffective as opposition *　*　*." Charleston

In the light of these principles the case before us is clear. Since the National Labor Relations Board has not adjudicated the status of the conduct for which the State of California seeks to give a remedy in damages, and since such activity is arguably within the compass of § 7 or § 8 of the Act, the State's jurisdiction is displaced.

Nor is it significant that California asserted its power to give damages rather than to enjoin what the Board may restrain though it could not compensate. Our concern is with delimiting areas of conduct which must be free from state regulation if national policy is to be left unhampered. Such regulation can be as effectively exerted through an award of damages as through some form of preventive relief. The obligation to pay compensation can be, indeed is designed to be, a potent method of governing conduct and controlling policy. Even the States' salutary effort to redress private wrongs or grant compensation for past harm cannot be exerted to regulate activities that are potentially subject to the exclusive federal regulatory scheme. * * * It may be that an award of damages in a particular situation will not, in fact, conflict with the active assertion of federal authority. The same may be true of the incidence of a particular state injunction. To sanction either involves a conflict with federal policy in that it involves allowing two law-making sources to govern. In fact, since remedies form an ingredient of any integrated scheme of regulation, to allow the State to grant a remedy here which has been withheld from the National Labor Relations Board only accentuates the danger of conflict.

It is true that we have allowed the States to grant compensation for the consequences, as defined by the traditional law of torts, of conduct marked by violence and imminent threats to the public order. International Union, United Automobile, Aircraft and Agricultural Implement Workers, etc. v. Russell, 356 U.S. 634, 78 S.Ct. 932, 2 L.Ed.2d 1030; [b] United Construction Workers, etc. v. Laburnum Const. Corp., 347 U.S. 656, 74 S.Ct. 833, 98 L.Ed. 1025.[c] We have also allowed the States to enjoin such conduct. Youngdahl v. Rainfair, Inc., 355 U.S. 131, 78 S.Ct. 206, 2 L.Ed.2d 151; United Automobile, Aircraft and Agricultural Implement Workers, etc. v. Wisconsin Employment Relations Board, 351 U.S. 266, 76 S.Ct. 794, 100 L.Ed. 1162. State jurisdiction has prevailed in these situations because the compelling state interest, in the scheme of our federalism, in the maintenance of domestic peace is not overridden in the absence of clearly expressed congressional direction. We recognize that the opinion in United Construction Workers, etc. v. Laburnum Const. Corp., 347 U.S. 656, 74 S.Ct. 833, 835, 98 L.Ed. 1025, found support in the fact that the state remedy had no federal counterpart. But that decision was determined, as is demonstrated by the question to

and Western Carolina R. Co. v. Varnville Furniture Co., 237 U.S. 597, 604, 35 S.Ct. 715, 717, 59 L.Ed. 1137.

b. In the Russell case, plaintiff, a nonunion employee, was prevented from reaching his place of employment by the mass picketing of striking union adherents. This was held by the state courts of Alabama to constitute malicious interference with a lawful occupation. Plaintiff recovered a judgment in the amount of $10,000, of which $500 represented lost wages and the balance mental anguish and punitive damages.

c. The Laburnum Construction Corporation was forced to abandon certain construction projects because of threats of mass violence by a union seeking recognition without appreciable employee support. In a commonlaw tort action in the state courts of Virginia, the Corporation was awarded a judgment in the amount of $129,326.09, of which $100,000 was punitive damages.

which review was restricted, by the "type of conduct" involved, i.e., "intimidation and threats of violence." In the present case there is no such compelling state interest.

The judgment below is reversed.

MR. JUSTICE HARLAN whom MR. JUSTICE CLARK, MR. JUSTICE WHITTAKER and MR. JUSTICE STEWART join, concurring.

I concur in the result upon the narrow ground that the Unions' activities for which the State has awarded damages may fairly be considered protected under the Taft-Hartley Act, and that therefore state action is precluded until the National Labor Relations Board has made a contrary determination respecting such activities. As the Court points out, it makes no difference that the Board has declined to exercise its jurisdiction.

* * *

Were nothing more than this particular case involved, I would be content to rest my concurrence at this point without more. But as today's decision will stand as a landmark in future "pre-emption" cases in the labor field, I feel justified in particularizing why I cannot join the Court's opinion.

If it were clear that the Unions' conduct here was unprotected activity under Taft-Hartley, I think that United Construction Workers, etc. v. Laburnum Construction Corp., 347 U.S. 656, 74 S.Ct. 833, 98 L.Ed. 1025, and International Union, United Automobile, Aircraft and Agricultural Implement Workers, etc. v. Russell, 356 U.S. 634, 78 S.Ct. 932, 2 L.Ed.2d 1030 would require that the California judgment be sustained, even though such conduct might be deemed to be federally prohibited. In both these cases state tort damage judgments against unions were upheld in respect of conduct which this Court assumed was prohibited activity under the Federal Labor Act. The Court now says, however, that those decisions are not applicable here because they were premised on violence, which the States could also have enjoined, * * * whereas in this case the Unions' acts were peaceful. In this I think the Court mistaken.

The threshold question in every labor pre-emption case is whether the conduct with respect to which a State has sought to act is, or may fairly be regarded as, federally protected activity. Because conflict is the touchstone of pre-emption, such activity is obviously beyond the reach of all state power. Hill v. State of Florida, 325 U.S. 538, 65 S.Ct. 1373, 89 L.Ed. 1782 * * *. That threshold question was squarely faced in the Russell case, where the Court, 356 U.S. at page 640, 78 S.Ct. at page 936, said: "At the outset, we note that the union's activity in this case clearly was not protected by federal law." The same question was, in my view, necessarily faced in Laburnum.

In both cases it was possible to decide that question without prior reference to the National Labor Relations Board because the union conduct involved was violent, and as such was of course not protected by the federal Act. Thus in Laburnum, the pre-emption issue was limited to the "type of conduct" before the Court. 347 U.S. at page 658, 74 S.Ct. at page 834. Similarly in Russell, which was decided on Laburnum principles, the Court stated that the union's activity "clearly was not protected," and immediately went on to say (citing prior "violence" cases) that "the strike was conducted in such a manner that it could have been enjoined" by the State. 356 U.S. at page 640, 78 S.Ct. at page 936. In both instances the Court, in reliance on former "violence" cases involving injunctions, might have gone on to hold, as the Court now in effect says it did, that the state police power was not displaced by the federal Act, and thus disposed of the cases on the ground that state damage awards, like state injunctions, based on violent conduct did not conflict with the federal statute. The Court did not do this, however.

Instead the relevance of violence was manifestly deemed confined to rendering the Laburnum and Russell activities federally unprotected. So rendered, they could then only have been classified as prohibited or "neither protected nor prohibited." If the latter, state jurisdiction was beyond challenge. International Union, United Automobile Workers, etc. v. Wisconsin Employment Relations Board, 336 U.S. 245, 69 S.Ct. 516, 93 L.Ed. 651. Conversely, if the activities could have been considered prohibited, primary decision by the Board would have been necessary, if state damage awards were inconsistent with federal prohibitions. Garner v. Teamsters, etc. Union, 346 U.S. 485, 74 S.Ct. 161, 98 L.Ed. 228. To determine the need for initial reference to the Board, the Court assumed that the activities were unfair labor practices prohibited by the federal Act. Laburnum, supra, 347 U.S. at pages 660–663, 74 S.Ct. at pages 835–837; Russell, supra, 356 U.S. at page 641, 78 S.Ct. at page 936. It then considered the possibility of conflict and held that the state damage remedies were not pre-empted because the federal Act afforded no remedy at all for the past conduct involved in Laburnum, and less than full redress for that involved in Russell. The essence of the Court's holding, which made resort to primary jurisdiction unnecessary, is contained in the following passage from the opinion in Laburnum, supra, 347 U.S. at page 665, 74 S.Ct. at page 838 (also quoted in Russell, supra, 356 U.S. at page 644, 78 S.Ct. at page 938):

> "To the extent that Congress prescribed preventive procedure against unfair labor practices, that case [Garner v. Teamsters Union, supra,] recognized that the Act excluded conflicting state procedure to the same end. To the extent, however, that Congress has not prescribed procedure for dealing with the consequences of tortious conduct already committed, there is no ground for concluding that existing criminal penalties or liabilities for tortious conduct have been eliminated. The care we took in the Garner case to demonstrate the existing conflict between state and federal administrative remedies in that case was, itself, a recognition that if no conflict had existed, the state procedure would have survived."

Until today this holding of Laburnum has been recognized by subsequent cases. * * *

The Court's opinion in this case cuts deeply into the ability of States to furnish an effective remedy under their own laws for the redress of past nonviolent tortious conduct which is not federally protected, but which may be deemed to be, or is, federally prohibited. Henceforth the States must withhold access to their courts until the National Labor Relations Board has determined that such unprotected conduct is not an unfair labor practice, a course which, because of unavoidable Board delays, may render state redress ineffective. And in instances in which the Board declines to exercise its jurisdiction, the States are entirely deprived of power to afford any relief.

Moreover, since the reparation powers of the Board, as we observed in Russell, are narrowly circumscribed, those injured by nonviolent conduct will often go remediless even when the Board does accept jurisdiction.

* * *

In determining pre-emption in any given labor case, I would adhere to the Laburnum and Russell distinction between damages and injunctions and to the principle that state power is not precluded where the challenged conduct is neither protected nor prohibited under the federal Act. Solely because it is fairly debatable whether the conduct here involved is federally protected, I concur in the result of today's decision.

Note

1. How would you state the holding in the Garmon case? What, precisely, is the difference between the majority and the concurring Justices?

2. What is the statutory basis for finding federal preemption in a case like Garmon? Section 10(a)?

3. The "no-man's land" created by the Guss and Garmon cases was the subject of considerable indignation, culminating in an amendment to the NLRA in 1959: the Landrum-Griffin Act added Section 14(c) to the federal law. Section 14(c)(1), as we have already seen (supra p. 220), constitutes an express congressional grant of authority to the NLRB to continue doing that which the Board had long been doing anyway, viz., exercising its jurisdiction selectively, based upon the degree of impact of the activity involved on interstate commerce. Section 14(c)(2) then provides:

"Nothing in this Act shall be deemed to prevent or bar any agency or the courts of any State or Territory (including the Commonwealth of Puerto Rico, Guam, and the Virgin Islands), from assuming and asserting jurisdiction over labor disputes over which the Board declines, pursuant to paragraph (1) of this subsection, to assert jurisdiction."

Suppose a charging party seeks the issuance of a complaint which the General Counsel refuses to grant because of either (1) factual insufficiency (i.e., insufficiency of evidence to support the charge) or (2) legal insufficiency (i.e., insufficiency of the charge as measured by a proper interpretation of the statute). Would a state tribunal have jurisdiction under Section 14(c)(2)? Should it have jurisdiction?

APOLOGY

The problem: The blueprint drawn by the architects of the preemption doctrine is ill designed for casebook construction. Fragmenting the doctrine and dealing with it piecemeal throughout the book does not seem a happy choice, although that would be the "logical" result if preemption cases were positioned in accordance with the nonpreemption aspects of their subject matter. The topic does not lend itself readily to encompassing treatment in a chapter unto itself; the problems subsumed under the "preemption" rubric are quite disparate. The only remaining option is to put the core materials together as a section in the most appropriate chapter. Adopting the latter approach as the lesser of evils, the authors have elected to deal with preemption in the same chapter as picketing since the most frequent and important application of preemption is, á la Garmon, in state court suits involving picketing. The preemption doctrine which emerges from Garmon may be usefully styled the "Garmon preemption doctrine;" although rooted in the picketing cases, it has achieved, as the following cases demonstrate, a broader application.

The apology: Two of the next three cases deal not with picketing but with the aforesaid extension of the Garmon analysis to conceptually-related problems in the conflict between federal and state jurisdiction.

AMALGAMATED ASSOCIATION OF STREET, ELECTRIC RAILWAY AND MOTOR COACH EMPLOYEES v. LOCKRIDGE

Supreme Court of the United States, 1971.
403 U.S. 274, 91 S.Ct. 1909, 29 L.Ed.2d 473.

MR. JUSTICE HARLAN delivered the opinion of the Court.

San Diego Building Trades Council v. Garmon, 359 U.S. 236, 79 S.Ct. 773, 3 L.Ed.2d 775 (1959), established the general principle that the National Labor Relations Act pre-empts state and federal court jurisdiction to remedy conduct that is arguably protected or prohibited by the Act. That decision represents the watershed in this Court's continuing effort to mark the extent to which the maintenance of a general federal law of labor relations combined with a centralized administrative agency to implement its provisions necessarily supplants the operation of the more traditional legal processes in this field. We granted certiorari in this case because the divided decision of the Idaho Supreme Court demonstrated the need for this Court to provide a fuller explication of the premises upon which *Garmon* rests and to consider the extent to which that decision must be taken to have modified or superseded this Court's earlier efforts to treat with the knotty pre-emption problem.

I

Respondent, Wilson P. Lockridge, has obtained in the Idaho courts a judgment for $32,678.56 against petitioners, Northwest Division 1055 of the Amalgamated Association of Street, Electric Railway and Motor Coach Employees of America and its parent international association,[1] on the grounds that, in procuring Lockridge's discharge from employment, pursuant to a valid union security clause in the applicable collective-bargaining agreement, the Union breached a contractual obligation embodied in the Union's constitution and by-laws.

From May 1943 until November 2, 1959, Lockridge was a member of petitioner Union and employed within the State of Idaho as a bus driver for Western Greyhound Lines, or its predecessor. At the time of Lockridge's dismissal from the Union, § 3(a) of the collective-bargaining agreement in effect between the Union and Greyhound provided:

---

1. The local and its parent are, of course, separate legal entities for many purposes and were joined as codefendants below so that each appears as a petitioner in this Court. However both will be jointly described throughout this opinion as "the petitioner" or "the Union" since the parent was held liable on the theory that it was responsible for the acts of the local here involved, not on the basis of any separate acts committed only by the parent.

"All present employees covered by this contract shall become members of the ASSOCIATION [Union] not later than thirty (30) days following its effective date and shall remain members as a condition precedent to continued employment. This section shall apply to newly hired employees thirty (30) days from the date of their employment with the COMPANY." App. 88.

In addition, § 91 of the Union's Constitution and General Laws provided, in pertinent part, that:

"All dues * * * of the members of this Association are due and payable on the first day of each month for that month * * *. They must be paid by the fifteenth of the month in order to continue the member in good standing. * * * A member in arrears for his dues * * * after the fifteenth day of the month is not in good standing * * * and where a member allows his arrearage * * * to run into the second month before paying the same, he shall be debarred from benefits for one month after payment. Where a member allows his arrearage * * * to run over the last day of the second month without payment, he does thereby suspend himself from membership in this Association * * *. Where agreements with employing companies provide that members must be in continuous good financial standing, the member in arrears one month may be suspended from membership and removed from employment, in compliance with the terms of the agreement." App. 91–92.

Prior to September 1959, Lockridge's dues had been deducted from his paycheck by Greyhound, pursuant to a checkoff arrangement. During that year, however, Lockridge and a few other employees were released at their request from the checkoff, and thereby became obligated to pay their dues directly to the Union's office in Portland, Oregon. On November 2, 1959, C.A. Bankhead, the treasurer and financial secretary of the union local, suspended Lockridge from membership on the sole ground that since respondent had not yet paid his October dues he was therefore in arrears contrary to § 91. Bankhead simultaneously notified Greyhound of this determination and requested that Lockridge be removed from employment. Greyhound promptly complied. Lockridge's wife received notice of the suspension from membership in early November, while her husband was on vacation, and on November 10, 1959, tendered Bankhead a check to cover respondent's dues for October and November, which Bankhead refused to accept.

This chain of events, combined with the disparity between the above-quoted terms of the collective-bargaining agreement and the union constitution and general laws generated this lawsuit. Lockridge has contended, and the Idaho courts have so held, that because he was less than two months behind in his payment of dues, respondent had not yet "suspended himself from membership" within the meaning of the Union's rules, but instead had merely ceased to be a "member in good standing." And, because the collective-bargaining agreement required only that employees "remain members," those courts held that neither that agreement nor the final sentence of § 91 justified the Union's action in procuring Lockridge's discharge. Therefore, the Idaho courts have held, Lockridge's dismissal violated a promise, implied in law, that the Union would not seek termination of his employment unless he was sufficiently derelict in his dues payments to subject him to loss of his job under the terms of the applicable collective-bargaining agreement.

Although the trial court made no formal findings of fact on this score, it appears likely that the Union procured Lockridge's dismissal in the mistaken belief that the applicable union security agreement with Greyhound did, in fact, require employees to remain members in good standing and that the Union insisted on what it thought was a technically valid position because it was piqued by Lockridge's obtaining his release from the checkoff. The trial court did find specifically that "almost without exception" it had been the past practice of this local division of the Union merely to suspend delinquent members from service, rather than to strip them of membership, and to put them back to work without loss of seniority when their dues were paid.

Lockridge initially made some efforts, with Bankhead's assistance, to obtain reinstatement in the Union but these proved unsuccessful. No charges were filed before the National Labor Relations Board.[3] Instead, Lockridge filed suit in September 1960 in the Idaho State District Court against the Union and Greyhound, which was later dropped as a party. That court, on the Union's motion, dismissed the complaint in April 1961 on the grounds that it charged the Union with the commission of an unfair labor practice and consequently fell within the exclusive jurisdiction of the NLRB. A year later, the Idaho Supreme Court reversed, holding that the state courts had jurisdiction under this Court's decision in International Association of Machinists v. Gonzales, 356 U.S. 617, 78 S.Ct. 923, 2 L.Ed.2d 1018 (1958), and remanded for trial on the merits. Lockridge v. Amalgamated Assn. of St., El. Ry. & M.C. Emp., 84 Idaho 201, 369 P.2d 1006 (1962).

In 1965 Lockridge filed a second amended complaint which has since served as the basis for this lawsuit. Its first count alleged that

> "in suspending plaintiff from membership in the [Union] which resulted in plaintiff's loss of employment, the [Union] * * * acted wantonly, wilfully and wrongfully and without just cause, and * * * deprived plaintiff of his * * * employment with Greyhound Corporation that accrued to him and would accrue to him by reason of his employment, seniority and experience, and plaintiff has been harassed and subject to mental anguish * * *."
> App. 46–47.

Count Two, sounding squarely in contract, alleged that

> "in wrongfully suspending plaintiff from membership in the [Union], which resulted in plaintiff's discharge from employment with the Greyhound Corporation, the [Union] * * * acted wrongfully, wantonly, wilfully and maliciously and without just cause and violated the constitution and general laws of the [Union] which constituted a contract between the plaintiff as a

---

3. It appears that at least one other person, Elmer Day, was similarly suspended from membership in the Union and discharged from Greyhound. On November 12, 1959, he filed a formal charge with the Board's Regional Director. On December 15, 1959, the Director advised Day, by letter, that "it appears that, because there is insufficient evidence of violations, further proceedings are not warranted at this time. I am therefore refusing to issue Complaint in these matters." The Director further informed Day that "you may obtain a review of this action by filing a request for such review with the General Counsel of the National Labor Relations Board * * *." Day did not seek review. Instead, he filed suit against the Union in the Circuit Court of Multnomah County, Oregon, for tortious interference with employment, and obtained a jury award for general and punitive damages. On appeal, the Supreme Court of Oregon (two judges dissenting) reversed, holding the conduct complained of to be within the Board's exclusive jurisdiction. Day v. Northwest Division 1055, 238 Or. 624, 389 P.2d 42 (1964). (Some of these facts are taken from the dissenting opinion in that case.)

> member thereof and the [Union], and as a result of said breach of contract plaintiff has been deprived of his ＊ ＊ ＊ employment with ＊ ＊ ＊ Greyhound Corporation ＊ ＊ ＊ and plaintiff has been embarrassed and subjected to mental anguish ＊ ＊ ＊." App. 48.

The complaint sought damages in the amount of $212,000 "and such other and further relief as to the court may appear meet and equitable in the premises." Ibid.

After trial, the Idaho District Court found the facts as stated above and held that they did, indeed, amount to a breach of contract. The court felt itself bound by the prior determination of the Idaho Supreme Court to consider that it might properly exercise jurisdiction over the controversy and to "decide [the] case on the theories of" International Ass'n of Machinists v. Gonzales, supra. Consequently, the trial judge concluded that Lockridge was entitled to a decree restoring him to membership in the Union, "although plaintiff has never sought such remedy." Lockridge was also awarded $32,678.56 as compensation for wages actually lost due to his dismissal from Greyhound's employ, but his requests for future damages arising from continued loss of employment, compensation for loss of seniority or fringe benefits, and punitive damages were all denied. On appeal the Idaho Supreme Court affirmed, over one dissenting vote, except that it also ordered restoration of respondent's seniority rights. 93 Idaho 294, 460 P.2d 719 (1969). Having granted certiorari for the reasons stated at the outset of this opinion, we now reverse.

II

A

On the surface, this might appear to be a routine and simple case. Section 8(b)(2) of the National Labor Relations Act, as amended, 61 Stat. 141, 29 U.S.C.A. § 158(b)(2), makes it an unfair labor practice for a union

> "to cause or attempt to cause an employer to discriminate against an employee in violation of subsection (a)(3) ＊ ＊ ＊ or to discriminate against an employee with respect to whom membership in such organization has been denied or terminated on some ground other than his failure to tender the periodic dues and the initiation fees uniformly required as a condition of acquiring or retaining membership."

Section 8(b)(1)(A) makes it an unfair labor practice for a union "to restrain or coerce ＊ ＊ ＊ employees in the exercise of the rights guaranteed in section 7," which includes the right not only "to form, join, or assist labor organizations" but also "the right to refrain from any or all of such activities except to the extent that such right may be affected by an agreement requiring membership in a labor organization as a condition of employment as authorized in section 8(a)(3)." 61 Stat. 140, 29 U.S.C.A. § 157. Section 8(a)(3) makes it an unfair labor practice for an employer

> "by discrimination in regard to hire or tenure of employment ＊ ＊ ＊ to encourage or discourage membership in any labor organization: *Provided,* That nothing in this Act ＊ ＊ ＊ shall preclude an employer from making an agreement with a labor organization ＊ ＊ ＊ to require as a condition of employment membership therein on or after the thirtieth day following the beginning of such employment or the effective date of such agreement,

whichever is the later * * *: *Provided further,* That no employer shall justify any discrimination against an employee for nonmembership in a labor organization * * * if he has reasonable grounds for believing that membership was denied or terminated for reasons other than the failure of the employee to tender the periodic dues and the initiation fees uniformly required as a condition of acquiring or retaining membership * * *."

Further, in San Diego Building Trades Council v. Garmon we held that the National Labor Relations Act pre-empts the jurisdiction of state and federal courts to regulate conduct "arguably subject to § 7 or § 8 of the Act." On their face, the above-quoted provisions of the Act at least arguably either permit or forbid the union conduct dealt with by the judgment below. For the evident thrust of this aspect of the federal statutory scheme is to permit the enforcement of union security clauses, by dismissal from employment, only for failure to pay dues. Whatever other sanctions may be employed to exact compliance with those internal union rules unrelated to dues payment, the Act seems generally to exclude dismissal from employment. See Radio Officers' Union, etc. v. NLRB, 347 U.S. 17, 74 S.Ct. 323, 98 L.Ed. 455 (1954). Indeed, in the course of rejecting petitioner's pre-emption argument, the Idaho Supreme Court stated that, in its opinion, the Union "did most certainly violate 8(b)(1)(A), did most certainly violate 8(b)(2) * * * and probably caused the employer to violate 8(a)(3)." 93 Idaho, at 299, 460 P.2d, at 724. Thus, given the broad pre-emption principle enunciated in *Garmon*, the want of state court power to resolve Lockridge's complaint might well seem to follow as a matter of course.

The Idaho Supreme Court, however, concluded that it nevertheless possessed jurisdiction in these circumstances. That determination, as we understand it, rested upon three separate propositions, all of which are urged here by respondent. The first is that the Union's conduct was not only an unfair labor practice, but a breach of its contract with Lockridge as well. "Pre-emption is not established simply by showing that the same facts will sustain two different legal wrongs." 93 Idaho, at 300, 460 P.2d, at 725. In other words *Garmon*, the state court and respondent assert, states a principle applicable only where the state law invoked is designed specifically to regulate labor relations; it has no force where the State applies its general common law of contracts to resolve disputes between a union and its members. Secondly, it is urged that the facts that might be shown to vindicate Lockridge's claim in the Idaho state courts differ from those relevant to proceedings governed by the National Labor Relations Act. It is said that the conduct regulated by the Act is union and employer discrimination; general contract law takes into account only the correctness of competing interpretations of the language embodied in agreements.

Finally, there recurs throughout the state court opinion, and the arguments of respondent here, the theme that the facts of the instant case render it virtually indistinguishable from International Association of Machinists v. Gonzales, where this Court upheld the exercise of state court jurisdiction in an opinion written only one Term prior to *Garmon*, by the author of *Garmon* and which was approvingly cited in the *Garmon* opinion itself.

We do not believe that any of these arguments suffice to overcome the plain purport of *Garmon* as applied to the facts of this case. However, we have determined to treat these considerations at some length because of the understandable confusion, perhaps in a measure attributable to the previous opinions of this Court, they reflect over the jurisprudential bases upon which the *Garmon* doctrine rests.

B

The constitutional principles of pre-emption, in whatever particular field of law they operate, are designed with a common end in view: to avoid conflicting regulation of conduct by various official bodies which might have some authority over the subject matter. * * *

The course of events that eventuated in the enactment of a comprehensive national labor law, entrusted for its administration and development to a centralized, expert agency, as well as the very fact of that enactment itself, reveals that a primary factor in this development was the perceived incapacity of common-law courts and state legislatures, acting alone, to provide an informed and coherent basis for stabilizing labor relations conflict and for equitably and delicately structuring the balance of power among competing forces so as to further the common good. * * *

As it appears to us, nothing could serve more fully to defeat the congressional goals underlying the Act than to subject, without limitation, the relationships it seeks to create to the concurrent jurisdiction of state and federal courts free to apply the general local law. Nor would an approach suffice that sought merely to avoid disparity in the content of proscriptive behavioral rules. * * *

Conflict in technique can be fully as disruptive to the system Congress erected as conflict in overt policy. * * *

The rationale for pre-emption, then, rests in large measure upon our determination that when it set down a federal labor policy Congress plainly meant to do more than simply to alter the then-prevailing substantive law. It sought as well to restructure fundamentally the processes for effectuating that policy, deliberately placing the responsibility for applying and developing this comprehensive legal system in the hands of an expert administrative body rather than the federalized judicial system. Thus, that a local court, while adjudicating a labor dispute also within the jurisdiction of the NLRB, may purport to apply legal rules identical to those prescribed in the federal Act or may eschew the authority to define or apply principles specifically developed to regulate labor relations does not mean that all relevant potential for debilitating conflict is absent.

A second factor that has played an important role in our shaping of the pre-emption doctrine has been the necessity to act without specific congressional direction. The precise extent to which state law must be displaced to achieve those unifying ends sought by the national legislature has never been determined by the Congress. This has, quite frankly, left the Court with few available options. We cannot declare pre-empted all local regulation that touches or concerns in any way the complex interrelationships between employees, employers, and unions; obviously, much of this is left to the States. Nor can we proceed on a case-by-case basis to determine whether each particular final judicial pronouncement does, or might reasonably be thought to, conflict in some relevant manner with federal labor policy. This Court is ill-equipped to play such a role and the federal system dictates that this problem be solved with a rule capable of relatively easy application, so that lower courts may largely police themselves in this regard. Equally important, such a principle would fail to take account of the fact, as discussed above, that simple congruity of legal rules does not, in this area, prove the absence of untenable conflict. Further, it is surely not possible for this Court to treat the National Labor Relations Act section by section, committing enforcement of some of its provisions wholly to the NLRB and others to the concurrent domain of local law. Nothing in the language or underlying purposes of the Act suggests any basis for such distinctions. Finally, treating differently judicial power to deal with conduct protected by the Act from that prohibited by it would likewise be unsatisfactory.[6] Both areas equally involve conduct whose legality is governed by federal law, the application of which Congress committed to the Board, not courts.

This is not to say, however, that these inherent limitations on this Court's ability to state a workable rule that comports reasonably with apparent congressional objectives are necessarily self-evident. In fact, varying approaches were taken by the Court in initially grappling with this pre-emption problem. Thus, for example, some early cases suggested the true distinction lay between judicial application of general common law, which was permissible, as opposed to state rules specifically designed to regulate labor relations, which were pre-empted. See, e.g. International Union, United Automobile, etc., Workers v. Russell, 356 U.S. 634, 645, 78 S.Ct. 932, 939, 2 L.Ed.2d 1030 (1958). Others made pre-emption turn on whether the States purported to apply a remedy not provided for by the federal scheme, e.g., Weber v. Anheuser-Busch, Inc., 348 U.S. 468, 479–480, 75 S.Ct. 480, 487–488, 99 L.Ed. 546 (1955), while in still others the Court undertook a thorough scrutiny of the federal Act to ascertain whether the state courts had, in fact, arrived at conclusions inconsistent with its provisions, e.g., International Union, United Automobile Workers v. Wisconsin Employment Relations Bd., 336 U.S. 245, 69 S.Ct. 516, 93 L.Ed. 651 (1949). For the reasons outlined above none of these approaches proved satisfactory, however, and each was ultimately abandoned. It was, in short, experience—not pure logic—which initially taught that each of these methods sacrificed important federal interests in a uniform law of labor relations centrally administered by an expert agency without yielding anything in return by way of predictability or ease of judicial application.

The failure of alternative analyses and the interplay of the foregoing policy considerations, then, led this Court to hold in Garmon, 359 U.S., at 244, 79 S.Ct., at 779:

> "When it is clear or may fairly be assumed that the activities which a State purports to regulate are protected by § 7 of the National Labor Relations Act, or constitute an unfair labor practice under § 8, due regard for the federal enactment requires that state jurisdiction must yield. To

---

6. The objections raised to this latter point (White, J. dissenting), seem largely irrelevant to the case under review. This is not a situation where the sole argument for preemption is that the union's conduct was arguably pro- tected. Clearly, if the facts are as respondent believes them to be, there is ample reason to conclude that petitioner probably committed an unfair labor practice.

leave the States free to regulate conduct so plainly within the central aim of federal regulation involves too great a danger of conflict between power asserted by Congress and requirements imposed by state law."

C

Upon these premises, we think that *Garmon* rather clearly dictates reversal of the judgment below. * * *

Assuredly the proposition that Lockridge's complaint was not subject to the exclusive jurisdiction of the NLRB because it charged a breach of contract rather than an unfair labor practice is not tenable. Pre-emption, as shown above, is designed to shield the system from conflicting regulation of conduct. It is the conduct being regulated, not the formal description of governing legal standards, that is the proper focus of concern. * * *

[A] final strand of analysis underlies the opinion of the Idaho Supreme Court, and the position of respondent, in this case. Our decision in International Association of Machinists v. Gonzales, 356 U.S. 617, 78 S.Ct. 923, 2 L.Ed.2d 1018 (1958), it is argued, fully survived the subsequent reorientation of pre-emption doctrine effected by the *Garmon* decision, providing, in effect, an express exception for the exercise of judicial jurisdiction in cases such as this.

The fact situation in *Gonzales* does resemble in some relevant regards that of the instant case. There the California courts had entertained a complaint by an individual union member claiming he had been expelled from his union in violation of rights conferred upon him by the union's constitution and bylaws, which allegedly constituted a contract between him and his union. Gonzales prevailed on his breach-of-contract theory and was awarded damages for wages lost due to the revocation of membership [d] as well as a decree providing for his reinstatement in the union. This Court confirmed the California courts' power to award the monetary damages, the only aspect of the action below challenged in this Court. The primary rationale for the result reached was that California should be competent to "fill out" the reinstatement remedy by utilizing "the comprehensive relief of equity," which the Board did not fully possess. * * *

* * * *Garmon,* did not cast doubt upon the result reached in *Gonzales,* but cited it approvingly as an example of the fact that state court jurisdiction is not pre-empted "where the activity regulated was a merely peripheral concern of the * * * Act."

Against this background, we attempted to define more precisely the reach of *Gonzales* within the more comprehensive framework *Garmon* provided in the companion cases of Local 100 of United Ass'n of Journeymen and Apprentices v. Borden, 373 U.S. 690, 83 S.Ct. 1423, 10 L.Ed.2d 638 (1963), and Local No. 207, International Ass'n of Bridge, Structural and Ornamental Iron Workers v. Perko, 373 U.S. 701, 83 S.Ct. 1429, 10 L.Ed.2d 646 (1963).

Borden had sued his union in state courts, alleging that the union had arbitrarily refused to refer him to a particular job which he had lined up.

d. Gonzales was denied referrals from the union's hiring hall because he refused to pay a fine imposed pursuant to internal union disci- plinary proceedings, and was therefore expelled.

He recovered damages, based on lost wages, on the grounds that this conduct constituted both tortious interference with his right to contract for employment and a breach of promise, implicit in his membership arrangement with the union, not to discriminate unfairly against any member or deny him the right to work. Perko had obtained a large money judgment in the Ohio courts on proof that the union had conspired, without cause, to deprive him of employment as a foreman by demanding his discharge from one such position he had held and representing to others that his foreman's rights had been suspended. We held both Perko's and Borden's judgments inconsistent with the *Garmon* rule essentially for the same reasons we have concluded that Lockridge could not, consistently with the *Garmon* decision, maintain his lawsuit in the state courts. We further held there was no necessity to "consider the present vitality of [the *Gonzales*] rationale in the light of more recent decisions," because in those cases, unlike *Gonzales,* "the crux of the action[s] * * * concerned alleged interference with the plaintiff's existing or prospective employment relations and was not directed to internal union matters." Because no specific claim for restoration of membership rights had been advanced, "there was no permissible state remedy to which the award of consequential damages for loss of earnings might be subordinated." Perko, 373 U.S., at 705, 83 S.Ct., at 1431. See also Borden, 373 U.S., at 697, 83 S.Ct., at 1427.

In sum, what distinguished *Gonzales* from *Borden* and *Perko* was that the former lawsuit "was focused on purely internal union matters," Borden, supra, at 697, 83 S.Ct., at 1427, a subject the National Labor Relations Act leaves principally to other processes of law. The possibility that, in defining the scope of the union's duty to Gonzales the state courts would directly and consciously implicate principles of federal law was at best tangential and remote. In the instant case, however, this possibility was real and immediate. To assess the legality of his union's conduct toward Gonzales the California courts needed only to focus upon the union's constitution and by-laws. Here, however, Lockridge's entire case turned upon the construction of the applicable union security clause, a matter as to which, as shown above, federal concern is pervasive and its regulation complex. The reasons for Gonzales' deprivation of union membership had nothing to do with matters of employment, while Lockridge's cause of action and claim for damages were based solely upon the procurement of his discharge from employment. It cannot plausibly be argued, in any meaningful sense, that Lockridge's lawsuit "was focused on purely internal union matters." Although nothing said in *Garmon* necessarily suggests that States cannot regulate the general conditions which unions may impose on their membership, it surely makes crystal clear that *Gonzales* does not stand for the proposition that resolution of any union-member conflict is within state competence so long as one of the remedies provided is restoration of union membership. This much was settled by *Borden* and *Perko,* and it is only upon such an unwarrantably broad interpretation of *Gonzales* that the judgment below could be sustained. * * *

IV

Finally, we deem it appropriate to discuss briefly two other considerations underlying the conclusion we have reached in this case. First, our decision must not be taken as expressing any views on the substantive claims of the two parties to this controversy. Indeed, our judgment is, quite simply, that it is not the task of federal or state courts to make such determinations. Secondly, in our explication of the reasons for the *Garmon* rule, and the various exceptions to it, we noted that, although largely of judicial making, the labor relations pre-emption doctrine finds its basic justification in the presumed intent of Congress. While we do not assert that the *Garmon* doctrine is without imperfection, we do think that it is founded on reasoned principle and that until it is altered by congressional action or by judicial insights that are born of further experience with it, a heavy burden rests upon those who would, at this late date, ask this Court to abandon *Garmon* and set out again in quest of a system more nearly perfect. A fair regard for considerations of *stare decisis* and the coordinate role of the Congress in defining the extent to which federal legislation pre-empts state law strongly support our conclusion that the basic tenets of *Garmon* should not be disturbed.

For the reasons stated above, the judgment below is reversed.

Reversed.

MR. JUSTICE DOUGLAS, dissenting.

I would affirm this judgment on the basis of International Ass'n of Machinists v. Gonzales * * *. I would not extend San Diego Building Trades Council v. Garmon so as to make Lockridge, the employee, seek his relief in faraway Washington, D.C., from the National Labor Relations Board. * * *

Garmon involved a union-employer dispute. It should not be extended to the individual employee who seeks a remedy for his grievance against his union. * * *

Whether in the present case the discharge of Lockridge was "arguably" an unfair labor practice within the meaning of *Garmon* is irrelevant. The reason is that the Board would not have the power to supply the total remedy which Lockridge seeks even if the employer had committed an unfair labor practice. True, the Board has authority to award back pay [3] but it has no authority to award damages beyond back pay. * * *

While I joined the dissent in *Gonzales,* experience under *Garmon* convinces me that we should not apply its rule to the grievances of individual employees against a union. I would affirm the judgment below.

MR. JUSTICE WHITE, with whom THE CHIEF JUSTICE joins, dissenting.

Like MR. JUSTICE DOUGLAS, I would neither overrule nor eviscerate International Assn. of Machinists v. Gonzales. In light of present statutory law and congressional intention gleaned therefrom, state courts should not be foreclosed from extending relief for union deprivation of members' state law rights under the union constitution and bylaws. Even if I agreed that the doctrine of San Diego Building Trades Council v. Garmon properly pre-

---

3. Under § 10(c) of the Act, 29 U.S.C.A. § 160(c), the Board can award back pay against an employer, Phelps Dodge Corp. v. NLRB, 313 U.S. 177, 61 S.Ct. 845, 85 L.Ed. 1271 and the Board will order back pay against a union where it causes an employer to discriminate against an employee. See International Association of Heat & Frost Insulators, Local 84, 146 N.L.R.B. 660; United Mine Workers (Blue Diamond Coal Co.), 143 N.L.R.B. 795.

empts such union member actions based on state law where the challenged conduct is arguably an unfair labor practice, I could not join the opinion of the Court since it unqualifiedly applies the same doctrine where the conduct of the union is only arguably protected under the federal law. * * *

* * * The essential difference, for present purposes, between activity that is arguably prohibited and that which is arguably protected is that a hearing on the latter activity is virtually impossible unless one deliberately commits an unfair labor practice. In a typical unfair practice case, by alleging conduct arguably prohibited by § 8 the charging party can at least present the General Counsel with the facts, and if the General Counsel issues a complaint, the charging party can present the Board with the facts and arguments to support the claim. But for activity that is arguably protected, there is no provision for an authoritative decision by the Board in the first instance; yet the *Garmon* rule blindly pre-empts other tribunals. * * * The Assistant General Counsel of the NLRB has described the situation:

> "[A]pplication of the *Garmon* 'arguably protected' test in this situation leaves the employer's interests in an unsatisfactory condition. The employer cannot obtain relief from the state court with respect to activity that may in fact not be protected by section 7 of the Act, and the only way that he can obtain a Board determination of that question is by resorting to self-help measures; if he guesses wrong, this may subject him not only to a Board remedy but also to tort suits. That result is as undesirable as the 'no-man's land' created by the holding in *Guss* * * *." (Footnotes omitted.) Come, Federal Pre-emption of Labor-Management Relations: Current Problems in the Application of Garmon, 56 Va.L.Rev. 1435, 1444 (1970).

I believe that the considerations that justify exceptions to the rule of uniformity apply with greater force to § 7 situations and further, that basic concepts of fundamental fairness regardless of their effect on the model of uniformity, counsel against any rule that so inflexibly bars a hearing. * * *

* * * In terms of congressional intention I find it unsupportable to hold that one threatened by conduct illegal under state law may not proceed against it because it is arguably protected by federal law when he has absolutely no lawful method for determining whether that is actually, as well as arguably, the case. Particularly is this true where the dispute is between a union and its members and the latter are asserting claims under state law based on the union constitution. I would permit the state court to entertain the action and if the union defends on the ground that its conduct is protected by federal law, to pass on that claim at the outset of the proceeding. If the federal law immunizes the challenged union action, the case is terminated; but if not, the case is adjudicated under state law.

MR. JUSTICE BLACKMUN also dissents for the basic reasons set forth by MR. JUSTICE DOUGLAS and MR. JUSTICE WHITE in their respective dissenting opinions.

Note

1. Justice Harlan, concurring in Garmon, and Justice White, dissenting in Lockridge, mount a scissoring attack on the Garmon preemption doctrine:

Justice Harlan, carrying three colleagues, went along in Garmon only because the union activity there might "fairly be considered protected" under the NLRA; Justice White, joined in his Lockridge dissent by two other doubters, impugned from the opposite direction—federal law should preempt only when arguably *prohibited* conduct is involved. The Garmon doctrine survived each of these attacks by a bare 5-to-4 margin. Happily? Where are *you*? (With Harlan, 1959? 1971 (He changed his mind!)? Or White? In the Sears case, infra p. 359, the White view prevails, at least on the facts there involved.)

2. One way of rationalizing the Gonzales exception to the Garmon preemption doctrine is to say that in Gonzales the "dog" ("crux") was the reinstatement to union membership, a remedy not available from the NLRB, whereas the "tail" was the reimbursement of lost wages resulting from discriminatory treatment by the union; since the state court had jurisdiction over the dog, the tail went along as a matter of anatomical logic. Applying this figurative analysis, Borden and Perko may be characterized as "no dog, all tail," and Lockridge as "little [specious?] dog, big tail." The problem, of course, is one of characterization: What is "dog"? What is "tail"?

Does the Court in the Farmer case, which follows, do what it refused to do in Gonzales, i.e., separate the state dog from the federal tail by posterior surgery?

FARMER v. UNITED BROTHERHOOD OF CARPENTERS

Supreme Court of the United States, 1977.
430 U.S. 290, 97 S.Ct. 1056, 51 L.Ed.2d 338.

MR. JUSTICE POWELL delivered the opinion of the Court.

The issue in this case is whether the National Labor Relations Act, as amended, pre-empts a tort action brought in state court by a union member against the union and its officials to recover damages for the intentional infliction of emotional distress.

I

Petitioner Richard T. Hill [1] was a carpenter and a member of Local 25 of the United Brotherhood of Carpenters and Joiners of America. Local 25 (the Union) operates an exclusive hiring hall for employment referral of carpenters in the Los Angeles area. In 1965, Hill was elected to a three-year term as vice president of the Union. Shortly thereafter sharp disagreement developed between Hill and the Union Business Agent, Earl Daley, and other Union officials over various internal Union policies. According to Hill, the Union then began to discriminate against him in referrals to employers, prompting him to complain about the hiring hall operation within the Union and to the District Council and the International Union. Hill claims that as a result of these complaints he was subjected to a campaign of personal abuse and harassment in addition to continued discrimination in referrals from the hiring hall.[2]

---

1. Hill died after the petition for a writ of certiorari was granted. On June 1, 1976, Joy A. Farmer, special administrator of Hill's estate, was substituted as petitioner. We will refer to Hill as the petitioner.

2. According to Hill, the Union accomplished this discrimination by removing his name from the top of the out-of-work list and placing it at the bottom, by referring him to jobs of short duration when more desirable work was available, and by referring him to jobs for which he was not qualified.

In April of 1969 petitioner filed in Superior Court for the County of Los Angeles an action for damages against the Union, the District Council and the International with which the Union was affiliated, and certain officials of the Union, including Business Agent Daley. In count two of his amended complaint, Hill alleged that the defendants had intentionally engaged in outrageous conduct, threats, and intimidation, and had thereby caused him to suffer grievous emotional distress resulting in bodily injury. In three other counts, he alleged that the Union had discriminated against him in referrals for employment because of his dissident intra-Union political activities, that the Union had breached the hiring hall provisions of the collective-bargaining agreement between it and a contractors association by failing to refer him on a nondiscriminatory basis, and that the failure to comply with the collective-bargaining agreement also constituted a breach of his membership contract with the Union. He sought $500,000 in actual, and $500,000 in punitive, damages.

The Superior Court sustained a demurrer to the allegations of discrimination and breach of contract on the ground that federal law pre-empted state jurisdiction over them, but allowed the case to go to trial on the allegations in count two.[3] Hill attempted to prove that the Union's campaign against him included "frequent public ridicule," "incessant verbal abuse," and refusals to refer him to jobs in accordance with the rules of the hiring hall. The defendants countered with evidence that the hiring hall was operated in a nondiscriminatory manner. The trial court instructed the jury that in order to recover damages Hill had to prove by a preponderance of the evidence that the defendants intentionally and by outrageous conduct had caused him to suffer severe emotional distress. The court defined severe emotional distress as "any highly unpleasant mental reaction such as fright, grief, shame, humiliation, embarrassment, anger, chagrin, disappointment, or worr[y]." The injury had to be "severe," which in this context meant

> "substantial or enduring, as distinguished from transitory or trivial. It must be of such a substantial quantity or enduring quality that no reasonable man in a civilized society should be expected to endure it. Liability does not extend to mere insults, indignities, annoyances, petty or other trivialities."

The court also instructed that the National Labor Relations Board (the Board) would not have jurisdiction to compensate petitioner for injuries such as emotional distress, pain and suffering, and medical expenses, nor would it have authority to award punitive damages. The court refused to give a requested instruction to the effect that the jury could not consider any evidence regarding discrimination with respect to employment opportunities or hiring procedures.

The jury returned a verdict of $7,500 actual damages and $175,000 punitive damages against the Union, the District Council, and Business Agent Daley, and the trial court entered a judgment on the verdict.[4]

---

3. Hill did not appeal the Superior Court's ruling sustaining the demurrer with respect to the claims of discrimination and breach of contract, and we thus have no occasion to consider the applicability of the pre-emption doctrine to those counts.

4. Hill voluntarily dismissed the complaint against the International and one Union official, the trial court dismissed the complaint with respect to another Union official, and the jury entered a verdict in favor of two other Union officials.

The California Court of Appeal reversed. 49 Cal.App.3d 614, 122 Cal. Rptr. 722. Relying on this Court's decisions in Motor Coach Employees v. Lockridge, 403 U.S. 274, 91 S.Ct. 1909, 29 L.Ed.2d 473 (1971); Plumbers' Union v. Borden, 373 U.S. 690, 83 S.Ct. 1423, 10 L.Ed.2d 638 (1963); Iron Workers v. Perko, 373 U.S. 701, 83 S.Ct. 1429, 10 L.Ed.2d 646 (1963); and San Diego Building Trades Council v. Garmon, 359 U.S. 236, 79 S.Ct. 773, 3 L.Ed.2d 775 (1959), the Court of Appeal held that the state courts had no jurisdiction over the complaint since the "crux" of the action concerned employment relations and involved conduct arguably subject to the jurisdiction of the National Labor Relations Board. The Court remanded "with instructions to render judgment for the defendants and dismiss the action." 49 Cal.App.3d at 631, 122 Cal.Rptr., at 732. The California Supreme Court denied review.

We granted certiorari to consider the applicability of the pre-emption doctrine to cases of this nature. For the reasons set forth below we vacate the judgment of the Court of Appeal and remand for further proceedings.

II

The doctrine of pre-emption in labor law has been shaped primarily by two competing interests.[5] On the one hand, this Court has recognized that "the broad powers conferred by Congress upon the National Labor Relations Board to interpret and to enforce the complex Labor Management Relations Act * * * necessarily imply that potentially conflicting 'rules of law, of remedy, and of administration' cannot be permitted to operate." Vaca v. Sipes, 386 U.S. 171, 178–179, 87 S.Ct. 903, 910, 17 L.Ed.2d 842 (1967), quoting San Diego Building Trades Council v. Garmon, 359 U.S. 236, 242, 79 S.Ct. 773, 778, 3 L.Ed.2d 775 (1959). On the other hand, because Congress has refrained from providing specific directions with respect to the scope of pre-empted state regulation, the Court has been unwilling to "declare pre-empted all local regulation that touches or concerns in any way the complex interrelationships between employees, employers, and unions * * *." Motor Coach Employees v. Lockridge, 403 U.S. 274, 289, 91 S.Ct. 1909, 1919, 29 L.Ed.2d 473 (1971). Judicial experience with numerous approaches to the pre-emption problem in the labor law area eventually led to the general rule set forth in Garmon, 359 U.S., at 244, 79 S.Ct., at 779, and recently reaffirmed in both Lockridge, 403 U.S., at 291, 91 S.Ct., at 1920, and Lodge 76, International Association of Machinists and Aerospace Workers v. Wisconsin Employment Relations Comm'n, 427 U.S. 132, 138–141, 96 S.Ct. 2548, 2552–2553, 49 L.Ed.2d 396 (1976):

> "When it is clear or may fairly be assumed that the activities which a State purports to regulate are protected by § 7 of the National Labor Relations Act, or constitute an unfair labor practice under § 8, due regard for the federal enactment requires that state jurisdiction must yield. To leave the States free to regulate conduct so plainly within the central aim of

---

5. "[I]n referring to decisions holding state laws pre-empted by the NLRA, care must be taken to distinguish pre-emption based on federal protection of the conduct in question * * * from that based predominantly on the primary jurisdiction of the National Labor Relations Board * * *, although the two are often not easily separable." Brotherhood of Railroad Trainmen v. Jacksonville Terminal Co., 394 U.S. 369, 383 n. 19, 89 S.Ct. 1109, 1118, 22 L.Ed.2d 344 (1969). The branch of the pre-emption doctrine most applicable to the instant case concerns the primary jurisdiction of the National Labor Relations Board.

federal regulation involves too great a danger of conflict between power asserted by Congress and requirements imposed by state law." 359 U.S., at 244, 79 S.Ct., at 779.

But the same considerations that underlie the *Garmon* rule have led the Court to recognize exceptions in appropriate classes of cases.[7] We have refused to apply the pre-emption doctrine to activity that otherwise would fall within the scope of *Garmon* if that activity "was a merely peripheral concern of the Labor Management Relations Act * * * [or] touched interests so deeply rooted in local feeling and responsibility that, in the absence of compelling congressional direction, we could not infer that Congress had deprived the States of the power to act." Garmon, 359 U.S., at 243–244, 79 S.Ct., at 779. See, e.g., Linn v. Plant Guard Workers, 383 U.S. 53, 86 S.Ct. 657, 15 L.Ed.2d 582 (1966) (malicious libel); Automobile Workers v. Russell, 356 U.S. 634, 78 S.Ct. 932, 2 L.Ed.2d 1030 (1958) (mass picketing and threats of violence); International Association of Machinists v. Gonzales, 356 U.S. 617, 78 S.Ct. 923, 2 L.Ed.2d 1018 (1958) (wrongful expulsion from union membership). * * *[8]

These exceptions * * * highlight our responsibility in a case of this kind to determine the scope of the general rule by examining the state interests in regulating the conduct in question and the potential for interference with the federal regulatory scheme.

The nature of the inquiry is perhaps best illustrated by Linn v. Plant Guard Workers, 383 U.S. 53, 86 S.Ct. 657, 15 L.Ed.2d 582 (1966). Linn, an assistant manager of Pinkerton's Detective Agency, filed a diversity action in federal court against a union, two of its officers, and a Pinkerton employee, alleging that the defendants had circulated a defamatory statement about him in violation of state law. If unfair labor practice charges had been filed, the Board might have found that the union violated § 8 by intentionally circulating false statements during an organizational campaign, or that the issuance of the malicious statements during the campaign had such a significant effect as to require that the election be set aside. Under a formalistic application of *Garmon,* the libel suit could have been pre-empted.

But a number of factors influenced the Court to depart from the *Garmon* rule. First, the Court noted that the underlying conduct—the intentional

---

7. "[W]e [cannot] proceed on a case-by-case basis to determine whether each particular final judicial pronouncement does, or might reasonably be thought to, conflict in some relevant manner with federal labor policy. This Court is ill-equipped to play such a role and the federal system dictates that this problem be solved with a rule capable of relatively easy application, so that lower courts may largely police themselves in this regard." Motor Coach Employees v. Lockridge, 403 U.S., at 289–290, 91 S.Ct., at 1919.

8. In addition to the judicially developed exceptions referred to in the text, Congress itself has created exceptions to the Board's exclusive jurisdiction in other classes of cases. Section 303 of the Labor Management Relations Act, 1947, authorizes anyone injured in his business or property by activity violative

of § 8(b)(4) of the NLRA to recover damages in federal district court even though the underlying unfair labor practices are remediable by the Board. See Teamsters Union v. Morton, 377 U.S. 252, 84 S.Ct. 1253, 12 L.Ed.2d 280 (1964). Section 301 of that Act authorizes suits for breach of a collective-bargaining agreement even if the breach is an unfair labor practice within the Board's jurisdiction. See Smith v. Evening News Assn., 371 U.S. 195, 83 S.Ct. 267, 9 L.Ed.2d 246 (1962). Section 14 of the National Labor Relations Act, as amended by Title VII, § 701(a) of the Labor Management Reporting and Disclosure Act of 1959, permits state agencies and state courts to assert jurisdiction over "labor disputes over which the Board declines, pursuant to paragraph (1) of this subsection, to assert jurisdiction."

circulation of defamatory material known to be false—was not protected under the Act, 383 U.S., at 61, 86 S.Ct., at 662, and there was thus no risk that permitting the state cause of action to proceed would result in state regulation of conduct that Congress intended to protect. Second, the Court recognized that there was " 'an overriding state interest' " in protecting residents from malicious libels, and that this state interest was " 'deeply rooted in local feeling and responsibility.' " Id., at 61, 62, 86 S.Ct., at 663. Third, the Court reasoned that there was little risk that the state cause of action would interfere with the effective administration of national labor policy. The Board's § 8 unfair labor practice proceeding would focus only on whether the statements were misleading or coercive; whether the statements also were defamatory would be of no relevance to the Board's performance of its functions. Id., at 63, 86 S.Ct., at 663. Moreover, the Board would lack authority to provide the defamed individual with damages or other relief. Ibid. Conversely, the state law action would be unconcerned with whether the statements were coercive or misleading in the labor context, and in any event the court would have power to award Linn relief only if the statements were defamatory. Taken together, these factors justified an exception to the pre-emption rule.

The Court was careful, however, to limit the scope of that exception. To minimize the possibility that state libel suits would either dampen the free discussion characteristic of labor disputes or become a weapon of economic coercion, the Court adopted by analogy the standards enunciated in New York Times Co. v. Sullivan, 376 U.S. 254, 84 S.Ct. 710, 11 L.Ed.2d 686 (1964), and held that state damage actions in this context would escape pre-emption only if limited to defamatory statements published with knowledge or reckless disregard of their falsity. The Court also held that a complainant could recover damages only upon proof that the statements had caused him injury, including general injury to reputation, consequent mental suffering, alienation of associates, specific items of pecuniary loss, or any other form of harm recognized by state tort law. The Court stressed the responsibility of the trial judge to assure that damages were not excessive.

Similar reasoning underlies the exception to the pre-emption rule in cases involving violent tortious activity. Nothing in the federal labor statutes protects or immunizes from state action violence or the threat of violence in a labor dispute, Automobile Workers v. Russell, 356 U.S. 634, 640, 78 S.Ct. 932, 935, 2 L.Ed.2d 1030 (1958); id., at 649, 78 S.Ct., at 941 (Warren, C.J., dissenting); United Construction Workers v. Laburnum Construction Corp., 347 U.S. 656, 666, 74 S.Ct. 833, 838, 98 L.Ed. 1025 (1954), and thus there is no risk that state damage actions will fetter the exercise of rights protected by the NLRA. On the other hand, our cases consistently have recognized the historic state interest in "such traditionally local matters as public safety and order and the use of streets and highways." Allen-Bradley Local v. Wisconsin Employment Relations Board, 315 U.S. 740, 749, 62 S.Ct. 820, 825, 86 L.Ed. 1154 (1942). And, as with the defamation actions preserved by *Linn,* state court actions to redress injuries caused by violence or threats of violence are consistent with effective administration of the federal scheme: such actions can be adjudicated without regard to the merits of the underlying labor controversy. Automobile Workers v. Russell, supra, 356 U.S., at 649, 78 S.Ct., at 941 (Warren, C.J., dissenting).

Although cases like *Linn* and *Russell* involve state law principles with only incidental application to conduct occurring in the course of a labor dispute, it is well settled that the general applicability of a state cause of action is not sufficient to exempt it from pre-emption. "[I]t [has not] mattered whether the States have acted through laws of broad general application rather than laws specifically directed towards the governance of industrial relations." Garmon, 359 U.S., at 246, 79 S.Ct., at 779. Instead, the cases reflect a balanced inquiry into such factors as the nature of the federal and state interests in regulation and the potential for interference with federal regulation. * * *

III

In count two of his amended complaint Hill alleged that the defendants had intentionally engaged in "outrageous conduct, threats, intimidation, and words" which caused Hill to suffer "grievous mental and emotional distress as well as great physical damage." In the context of Hill's other allegations of discrimination in hiring hall referrals, these allegations of tortious conduct might form the basis for unfair labor practice charges before the Board. On this basis a rigid application of the *Garmon* doctrine might support the conclusion of the California courts that Hill's entire action was pre-empted by federal law. Our cases indicate, however, that inflexible application of the doctrine is to be avoided, especially where the state has a substantial interest in regulation of the conduct at issue and the State's interest is one that does not threaten undue interference with the federal regulatory scheme. With respect to Hill's claims of intentional infliction of emotional distress, we cannot conclude that Congress intended exclusive jurisdiction to lie in the Board.

No provision of the National Labor Relations Act protects the "outrageous conduct" complained of by petitioner Hill in the second count of the complaint. Regardless of whether the operation of the hiring hall was lawful or unlawful under federal statutes, there is no federal protection for conduct on the part of union officers which is so outrageous that "no reasonable man in a civilized society should be expected to endure it." Thus, as in Linn v. Plant Guard Workers, 383 U.S. 53, 86 S.Ct. 657, 15 L.Ed.2d 582 (1966), and Automobile Workers v. Russell, 356 U.S. 634, 78 S.Ct. 932, 2 L.Ed. 2d 1030 (1958), permitting the exercise of state jurisdiction over such complaints does not result in state regulation of federally protected conduct.

The State, on the other hand, has a substantial interest in protecting its citizens from the kind of abuse of which Hill complained. That interest is no less worthy of recognition because it concerns protection from emotional distress caused by outrageous conduct, rather than protection from physical injury, as in *Russell*, or damage to reputation, as in *Linn*. Although recognition of the tort of intentional infliction of emotional distress is a comparatively recent development in state law, see Prosser, Law of Torts, 49–50, 56 (4th ed.), our decisions permitting the exercise of state jurisdiction in tort actions based on violence or defamation have not rested on the history of the tort at issue, but rather on the nature of the State's interest in protecting the health and well-being of its citizens.

There is, to be sure, some risk that the state cause of action for infliction of emotional distress will touch on an area of primary federal concern.

Hill's complaint itself highlights this risk. In those counts of the complaint that the trial court dismissed, Hill alleged discrimination against him in hiring hall referrals, which were also alleged to be violations of both the collective-bargaining agreement and the membership contract. These allegations, if sufficiently supported before the National Labor Relations Board, would make out an unfair labor practice [11] and the Superior Court considered them pre-empted by the federal Act. Even in count two of the complaint Hill made allegations of discrimination in "job-dispatching procedures" and "work assignments" which, standing alone, might well be pre-empted as the exclusive concern of the Board. The occurrence of the abusive conduct, with which the state tort action is concerned, in such a context of federally prohibited discrimination suggests a potential for interference with the federal scheme of regulation.

Viewed, however, in light of the discrete concerns of the federal scheme and the state tort law, that potential for interference is insufficient to counterbalance the legitimate and substantial interest of the State in protecting its citizens. If the charges in Hill's complaint were filed with the Board, the focus of any unfair labor practice proceeding would be on whether the statements or conduct on the part of union officials discriminated or threatened discrimination against him in employment referrals for reasons other than failure to pay union dues. See n. 11, supra. Whether the statements or conduct of the respondents also caused Hill severe emotional distress and physical injury would play no role in the Board's disposition of the case, and the Board could not award Hill damages for pain, suffering, or medical expenses. Conversely, the state court tort action can be adjudicated without resolution of the "merits" of the underlying labor dispute. Recovery for the tort of emotional distress under California law requires proof that the defendant intentionally engaged in outrageous conduct causing the plaintiff to sustain mental distress. State Rubbish Collectors Assn. v. Siliznoff, 38 Cal.2d 330, 240 P.2d 282 (1952); Alcorn v. Anbro Engineering, Inc., 2 Cal.3d 493, 86 Cal.Rptr. 88, 468 P.2d 216 (1970). The state court need not consider, much less resolve, whether a union discriminated or threatened to discriminate against an employee in terms of employment opportunities. To the contrary, the tort action can be resolved without reference to any accommodation of the special interests of unions and members in the hiring hall context.

On balance, we cannot conclude that Congress intended to oust state court jurisdiction over actions for tortious activity such as that alleged in this case. At the same time, we reiterate that concurrent state court jurisdiction cannot be permitted where there is a realistic threat of interference with the federal regulatory scheme. Union discrimination in employment opportunities cannot itself form the underlying "outrageous" conduct

---

11. Discrimination in hiring hall referrals constitutes an unfair labor practice under §§ 8(b)(1)(A) and 8(b)(2) of the NLRA. See, e.g., Radio Officers' Union v. NLRB, 347 U.S. 17, 74 S.Ct. 323, 98 L.Ed. 455 (1954); Operating Engineers Local 18, 205 N.L.R.B. 901, enforced, 500 F.2d 48 (CA6 1974).

Prior to the filing of this suit, Hill filed an unfair labor practice charge with the Board with respect to one specific instance of alleged discrimination. He alleged that the Union violated §§ 8(b)(1)(A) and 8(b)(2) by refusing to honor an employer's request that he be referred for employment on a particular construction job. The Board awarded Hill $2,517 in backpay.

on which the state court tort action is based; to hold otherwise would undermine the pre-emption principle. Nor can threats of such discrimination suffice to sustain state court jurisdiction. It may well be that the threat, or actuality, of employment discrimination will cause a union member considerable emotional distress and anxiety. But something more is required before concurrent state court jurisdiction can be permitted. Simply stated, it is essential that the state tort be either unrelated to employment discrimination or a function of the particularly abusive manner in which the discrimination is accomplished or threatened rather than a function of the actual or threatened discrimination itself.[13]

Two further limitations deserve emphasis. Our decision rests in part on our understanding that California law permits recovery only for emotional distress sustained as a result of "outrageous" conduct. The potential for undue interference with federal regulation would be intolerable if state tort recoveries could be based on the type of robust language and clash of strong personalities that may be commonplace in various labor contexts. We also repeat that state trial courts have the responsibility in cases of this kind to assure that the damages awarded are not excessive. See Linn v. Plant Guard Workers, 383 U.S., at 65–66, 86 S.Ct., at 664.

IV

Although the second count of petitioner's complaint alleged the intentional infliction of emotional distress, it is clear from the record that the trial of that claim was not in accord with the standards discussed above. The evidence supporting the verdict in Hill's favor focuses less on the alleged campaign of harassment, public ridicule, and verbal abuse, than on the discriminatory refusal to dispatch him to any but the briefest and least desirable jobs;[14] and no appropriate instruction distinguishing the two categories of evidence was given to the jury. See n. 13, supra. The consequent risk that the jury verdict represented damages for employment discrimination rather than for instances of intentional infliction of emotional distress precludes reinstatement of the judgment of the Superior Court.

13. In view of the potential for interference with the federal scheme of regulation, the trial court should be sensitive to the need to minimize the jury's exposure to evidence of employment discrimination in cases of this sort. Where evidence of discrimination is necessary to establish the context in which the state claim arose, the trial court should instruct the jury that the fact of employment discrimination (as distinguished from attendant tortious conduct under state law) should not enter into the determination of liability or damages.

14. Almost the entire section of petitioner's brief summarizing the trial transcript, see Brief, at 4–10, is directed at instances of Union discrimination against Hill with respect to employment opportunities. Moreover, counsel for petitioner, who was also petitioner's trial counsel, indicated at oral argument that the focus of the trial was on employment discrimination rather than the intentional infliction of emotion distress: "We had to show simply two easy issues to the jury: one, what the [hiring hall] rules were; and two, were they fairly applied." Tr. of Oral Arg., at 69. It is plain that those two elements are more relevant to the issue of discriminatory referrals than to the issue of infliction of emotional distress.

Respondents concede that "[t]he allegations made in the plaintiff's second cause of action * * * sound in the state tort law of intentional infliction of emotional distress," but contend that the dominant focus of the evidence adduced at trial was on discriminatory hiring hall referrals. Brief, at 28.

The Judgment of the Court of Appeal is vacated, and the case is remanded to that court for further proceedings not inconsistent with this opinion.[15]

It is so ordered.

Note

1. Does Gonzales survive Farmer? If the state cause of action in Farmer cannot carry with it the recovery of damages for injuries dealt with under the National Labor Relations Act, how justify the "filling out" of the state remedy in Gonzales with damages for wages lost because of the union's discriminatory treatment? Does the distinction between Gonzales and Farmer (if there be any) lie in the fact that in Farmer the federal rights and duties were implicated in establishing *both* the cause of action and the remedy?

2. In Farmer the Court lists exceptions to the Garmon preemption doctrine (as indeed it did in Lockridge and Garmon itself), including activity which "touches interests so deeply rooted in local feeling and responsibility that, in the absence of compelling congressional direction, we could not infer that Congress had deprived the States of the power to act." Would *trespassory* peaceful picketing on private property constitute such an excepted activity? If not, what relief is available to the picketed employer? 8(b)(7)? 8(b)(1)? 8(b)(4)? Local police? National Guard? Baseball bat? Does the real problem in all this lie in a contradiction in terms: *peaceful trespass?* Suppose, for example, the employer were to perforate the "peace" with a baseball bat. Does a compelling local interest *thereupon* develop? These questions are addressed in the Sears case, which follows.

SEARS, ROEBUCK & CO. v. SAN DIEGO COUNTY DISTRICT COUNCIL OF CARPENTERS

Supreme Court of the United States, 1978.
436 U.S. 180, 98 S.Ct. 1745, 56 L.Ed.2d 209.

MR. JUSTICE STEVENS delivered the opinion of the Court.

The question in this case is whether the National Labor Relations Act as amended, deprives a state court of the power to entertain an action by an employer to enforce state trespass laws against picketing which is arguably—but not definitely—prohibited or protected by federal law.

I

On October 24, 1973, two business representatives of respondent Union visited the department store operated by petitioner (Sears) in Chula Vista, Cal., and determined that certain carpentry work was being performed by men who had not been dispatched from the Union hiring hall. Later that day, the Union agents met with the store manager and requested that Sears either arrange to have the work performed by a contractor who employed dispatched carpenters or agree in writing to abide by the terms of the Union's master labor agreement with respect to the dispatch and use of carpenters. The Sears manager stated that he would consider the request but he never accepted or rejected it.

15. We of course express no view on the question whether those aspects of the case that are not pre-empted are sufficient under state law to amount to conduct "that no reasonable man in a civilized society should be expected to endure."

Two days later the Union established picket lines on Sears' property. The store is located in the center of a large rectangular lot. The building is surrounded by walkways and a large parking area. A concrete wall at one end separates the lot from residential property; the other three sides adjoin public sidewalks which are adjacent to the public streets. The pickets patrolled either on the privately owned walkways next to the building or in the parking area a few feet away. They carried signs indicating that they were sanctioned by the "Carpenters Trade Union." The picketing was peaceful and orderly.

Sears' security manager demanded that the Union remove the pickets from Sears' property. The Union refused, stating that the pickets would not leave unless forced to do so by legal action. On October 29, Sears filed a verified complaint in the Superior Court of California seeking an injunction against the continuing trespass: the court entered a temporary restraining order enjoining the Union from picketing on Sears' property. The Union promptly removed the pickets to the public sidewalks.[2] On November 21, 1973, after hearing argument on the question whether the Union's picketing on Sears' property was protected by state or federal law, the court entered a preliminary injunction. The California Court of Appeals affirmed. While acknowledging the pre-emption guidelines set forth in San Diego Union v. Garmon, 359 U.S. 236, the court held that the Union's continuing trespass fell within the longstanding exception for conduct which touched interests so deeply rooted in local feeling and responsibility that pre-emption could not be inferred in the absence of clear evidence of congressional intent.

The Supreme Court of California reversed. It concluded that the picketing was arguably protected by § 7 because it was intended to secure work for Union members and to publicize Sears' undercutting of the prevailing area standards for the employment of carpenters. The court reasoned that the trespassory character of the picketing did not disqualify it from arguable protection, but was merely a factor which the National Labor Relations Board would consider in determining whether or not it was in fact protected. The court also considered it "arguable" that the Union had engaged in recognitional picketing subject to § 8(b)(7)(C) of the Act which could not continue for more than 30 days without petitioning for a representation election. Because the picketing was both arguably protected by § 7 and arguably prohibited by § 8, the court held that state jurisdiction was pre-empted under the *Garmon* guidelines.

Since the Wagner Act was passed in 1935, this Court has not decided whether, or under what circumstances, a state court has power to enforce local trespass laws against a union's peaceful picketing.[6] The obvious importance of this problem led us to grant certiorari in this case.[7]

---

2. Although Sears claimed that some delivery men and repairmen refused to cross the picket lines on the public sidewalks, the Union ultimately concluded that the picketing was then too far removed from the store to be effective. The picketing was discontinued on November 12.

6. The issue was left open by the Court in Amalgamated Meat Cutters v. Fairlawn Meat, 353 U.S. 20, 24–25. Cf. Taggart v. Weinack-

er's, Inc., 283 Ala. 171, 214 So.2d 913 (1968), cert. granted, 396 U.S. 813 (1969), cert. dismissed, 397 U.S. 223 (1970).

7. The state courts have divided on the question of state-court jurisdiction over peaceful trespassory activity. For cases in addition to this one in which pre-emption was found, see, e.g., Shirley v. Retail Store Employees Union, 22 Kan. 373, 565 P.2d 585 (1977); Freeman v. Retail Clerks Union Local 1207, 58

II

We start from the premise that the Union's picketing on Sears' property after the request to leave was a continuing trespass in violation of state law. We note, however, that the scope of the controversy in the state court was limited. Sears asserted no claim that the picketing itself violated any state or federal law. It sought simply to remove the pickets from its property to the public walkways, and the injunction issued by the state court was strictly confined to the relief sought. Thus, as a matter of state law, the location of the picketing was illegal but the picketing itself was unobjectionable.

As a matter of federal law, the legality of the picketing was unclear. Two separate theories would support an argument by Sears that the picketing was prohibited by § 8 of the NLRA and a third theory would support an argument by the Union that the picketing was protected by § 7. Under each of these theories the Union's purpose would be of critical importance.

If an object of the picketing was to force Sears into assigning the carpentry work away from its employees to Union members dispatched from the hiring hall, the picketing may have been prohibited by § 8(b)(4)(D).[9] Alternatively, if an object of the picketing was to coerce Sears into signing a prehire or members-only type agreement with the Union, the picketing was at least arguably subject to the prohibition on recognitional picketing contained in § 8(b)(7)(C).[10] Hence, if Sears had filed an unfair labor practice charge against the Union, the Board's concern would have been limited to the question whether the Union's picketing had an objective proscribed by the Act; the location of the picketing would have been irrelevant.

On the other hand, the Union contends that the sole objective of its action was to secure compliance by Sears with area standards,[e] and therefore the picketing was protected by § 7. Longshoremen v. Ariadne Co., 397 U.S.

Wash.2d 426, 363 P.2d 803 (1961). For cases reaching a contrary conclusion, see, e.g., May Department Stores Co. v. Teamsters Union Local No. 743, 64 Ill.2d 153, 355 N.E.2d 7 (1976); People v. Bush, 39 N.Y.2d 529, 349 N.E.2d 832 (1976); Hood v. Stafford, 213 Tenn. 684, 378 S.W.2d 766 (1964).

9. Section 8(b)(4)(D) provides in part that it shall be an unfair labor practice for a labor organization or its agents—

"to threaten, coerce, or restrain any person engaged in commerce or in an industry affecting commerce, where ⁕ ⁕ ⁕ an object thereof is—

⁕   ⁕   ⁕   ⁕   ⁕

"forcing or requiring any employer to assign particular work to employees in a particular labor organization or in a particular trade, craft, or class rather than to employees in another labor organization or in another trade, craft, or class, unless such employer is failing to conform to an order or certification of the Board determining the bargaining representative for employees performing such work." 29 U.S.C.A. § 158(b)(4)(D).

There are two provisos to 8(b)(4) which exempt certain conduct from its prohibitions,

but they appear to have no application in this case.

10. Section 8(b)(7)(C) provides in part that "[i]t shall be an unfair labor practice for a labor organization or its agents—

"to picket ⁕ ⁕ ⁕ any employer where an object thereof is forcing or requiring an employer to recognize or bargain with a labor organization as the representative of his employees ⁕ ⁕ ⁕ unless such labor organization is currently certified as the representative of such employees:

⁕   ⁕   ⁕   ⁕   ⁕

"where such picketing has been conducted without a petition ⁕ ⁕ ⁕ [for a representation election] being filed within a reasonable period of time not to exceed thirty days from the commencement of such picketing ⁕ ⁕ ⁕." 29 U.S.C.A. § 158(b)(7)(C).

e. [Ed. Note] "Area standards" picketing is the term commonly used to describe picketing aimed at "persuading" an employer to grant his employees a wage and benefit package equal to that of the employees of unionized businesses with which the target employer competes. If the picketing has, in addition to (or instead of) the purpose of maintaining area

195. Thus, if the Union had filed an unfair labor practice charge under § 8(a)(1) when Sears made a demand that the pickets leave its property, it is at least arguable that the Board would have found Sears guilty of an unfair labor practice.

Our second premise, therefore, is that the picketing was both arguably prohibited and arguably protected by federal law. The case is not, however, one in which "it is clear or may fairly be assumed" that the subject matter which the state court sought to regulate—that is, the location of the picketing—is either prohibited or protected by the Federal Act.

III

In San Diego Building Trades Council v. Garmon, 359 U.S. 236, the Court made two statements which have come to be accepted as the general guidelines for deciphering the unexpressed intent of Congress regarding the permissible scope of state regulation of activity touching upon labor-management relations. The first related to activity which is clearly protected or prohibited by the federal statute.[11] The second articulated a more sweeping prophylactic rule:

> "When an activity is arguably subject to § 7 or § 8 of the Act, the States as well as the federal courts must defer to the exclusive competence of the National Labor Relations Board if the danger of state interference with national policy is to be averted." Id., at 245.

While the *Garmon* formulation accurately reflects the basic federal concern with potential state interference with national labor policy, the history of the labor pre-emption doctrine in this Court does not support an approach which sweeps away state-court jurisdiction over conduct tradition-ally subject to state regulation without careful consideration of the relative impact of such a jurisdictional bar on the various interests affected. * * *

With this limitation in mind, we turn to the question whether pre-emption is justified in a case of this kind under either the arguably protected or the arguably prohibited branch of the *Garmon* doctrine. While the considerations underlying the two categories overlap, they differ in signifi-cant respects and therefore it is useful to review them separately. We therefore first consider whether the arguable illegality of the picketing as a matter of federal law should oust the state court of jurisdiction to enjoin its trespassory aspects. Thereafter, we consider whether the arguably protected character of the picketing should have that effect.

standards, an organizational or recognitional purpose, Section 8(b)(7)(C) is applicable. If it has the objective of requiring the employer to assign work to employees represented by the picketing union, Section 8(b)(4)(D)'s jurisdic-tional picketing prohibition may be applica-ble. Area standards picketing as it relates to Section 8(b)(7)(C) is treated in the "Claude Everett Construction" case infra p. 387. Sec-tion 8(b)(4)(D) is the subject of Section D of this chapter, infra p. 461.

11. As to conduct clearly protected or pro-hibited by the federal statute, the Court stat-ed:

"When it is clear or may fairly be as-sumed that the activities which a State pur-ports to regulate are protected by § 7 of the National Labor Relations Act, or constitute an unfair labor practice under § 8, due re-gard for the federal enactment requires that state jurisdiction must yield. To leave the States free to regulate conduct so plainly within the central aim of federal regulation involves too great a danger of conflict be-tween power asserted by Congress and re-quirements imposed by state law." 359 U.S., at 244.

IV

*   *   *

In *Farmer,* the Court held that a union member, who alleged that his union had engaged in a campaign of personal abuse and harassment against him, could maintain an action for damages against the union and its officers for the intentional infliction of emotional distress. One aspect of the alleged campaign was discrimination by the union in hiring hall referrals. Although such discrimination was arguably prohibited by §§ 8(b)(1)(A) and 8(b)(2) of the NLRA and therefore an unfair labor practice charge could have been filed with the Board, the Court permitted the state action to proceed.

The Court identified those factors which warranted a departure from the general pre-emption guidelines in the "local interest" cases. Two are relevant to the arguably *prohibited* branch of the *Garmon* doctrine. First, there existed a significant state interest in protecting the citizen from the challenged conduct. Second, although the challenged conduct occurred in the course of a labor dispute and an unfair labor practice charge could have been filed, the exercise of state jurisdiction over the tort claim entailed little risk of interference with the regulatory jurisdiction of the Labor Board. Although the arguable federal violation and the state tort arose in the same factual setting, the respective controversies presented to the state and federal forums would not have been the same.

The critical inquiry, therefore, is not whether the State is enforcing a law relating specifically to labor relations or one of general application but whether the controversy presented to the state court is identical to or different from that which could have been, but was not, presented to the Labor Board. For it is only in the former situation that a state court's exercise of jurisdiction necessarily involves a risk of interference with the unfair labor practice jurisdiction of the Board which the arguably prohibited branch of the *Garmon* doctrine was designed to avoid.

In the present case, the controversy which Sears might have presented to the Labor Board is not the same as the controversy presented to the state court. If Sears had filed a charge, the federal issue would have been whether the picketing had a recognitional or work reassignment objective; decision of that issue would have entailed relatively complex factual and legal determinations completely unrelated to the simple question whether a trespass had occurred. Conversely, in the state action, Sears only challenged the location of the picketing; whether the picketing had an objective proscribed by federal law was irrelevant to the state claim. Accordingly, permitting the state court to adjudicate Sears' trespass claim would create no realistic risk of interference with the Labor Board's primary jurisdiction to enforce the statutory prohibition against unfair labor practices.

The reasons why pre-emption of state jurisdiction is normally appropriate when union activity is arguably prohibited by federal law plainly do not apply to this situation; they therefore are insufficient to preclude a State from exercising jurisdiction limited to the trespassory aspects of that activity.

V

The question whether the arguably protected character of the Union's trespassory picketing provides a sufficient justification for pre-emption of the state court's jurisdiction over Sears' trespass claim involves somewhat different considerations.

Apart from notions of "primary jurisdiction," there would be no objection to state courts and the NLRB exercising concurrent jurisdiction over conduct prohibited by the Federal Act. But there is a constitutional objection to state court interference with conduct actually protected by the Act. Considerations of federal supremacy, therefore, are implicated to a greater extent when labor-related activity is protected than when it is prohibited. Nevertheless, several considerations persuade us that the mere fact that the Union's trespass was *arguably* protected is insufficient to deprive the state court of jurisdiction in this case.

The first is the relative unimportance in this context of the "primary jurisdiction" rationale articulated in *Garmon.* In theory, of course, that rationale supports pre-emption regardless of which section of the NLRA is critical to resolving a controversy which may be subject to the regulatory jurisdiction of the NLRB. Indeed, at first blush, the primary jurisdiction rationale provides stronger support for pre-emption in this case when the analysis is focused upon the arguably protected, rather than the arguably prohibited, character of the Union's conduct. For to the extent that the Union's picketing was arguably protected, there existed a potential overlap between the controversy presented to the state court and that which the Union might have brought before the NLRB. Prior to granting any relief from the Union's continuing trespass, the state court was obligated to decide that the trespass was not actually protected by federal law, a determination which might entail an accommodation of Sears' property rights and the Union's § 7 rights. In an unfair labor practice proceeding initiated by the Union, the Board might have been required to make the same accommodation.[32]

Although it was theoretically possible for the accommodation issue to be decided either by the state court or by the Labor Board, there was in fact no risk of overlapping jurisdiction in this case. The primary jurisdiction rationale justifies pre-emption only in situations in which an aggrieved party has a reasonable opportunity either to invoke the Board's jurisdiction himself or else to induce his adversary to do so. In this case, Sears could not directly obtain a Board ruling on the question whether the Union's trespass was federally protected. Such a Board determination could have been obtained only if the Union had filed an unfair labor practice charge alleging that Sears had interfered with the Union's § 7 right to engage in peaceful picketing on Sears' property. By demanding that the Union remove its pickets from the store's property, Sears in fact pursued a course of action which gave the Union the opportunity to file such a charge. But the Union's response to Sears' demand foreclosed the possibility of having the accommodation of § 7 and property rights made by the Labor Board; instead of filing

---

32. That accommodation would have been required only if the Board first found that the object of the picketing was to maintain area standards. [See footnote e supra p. 361.]

* * *

a charge with the Board, the Union advised Sears that the pickets would only depart under compulsion of legal process.

In the face of the Union's intransigence, Sears had only three options: permit the pickets to remain on its property; forcefully evict the pickets; or seek the protection of the State's trespass laws. Since the Union's conduct violated state law, Sears legitimately rejected the first option. Since the second option involved a risk of violence, Sears surely had the right— perhaps even the duty—to reject it. Only by proceeding in state court, therefore, could Sears obtain an orderly resolution of the question whether the Union had a federal right to remain on its property.

The primary jurisdiction rationale unquestionably requires that when the same controversy may be presented to the state court or the NLRB, it must be presented to the Board. But that rationale does not extend to cases in which an employer has no acceptable method of invoking, or inducing the Union to invoke, the jurisdiction of the Board.[33] We are therefore persuaded that the primary jurisdiction rationale does not provide a *sufficient* justification for pre-empting state jurisdiction over arguably protected conduct when the party who could have presented the protection issue to the Board has not done so and the other party to the dispute has no acceptable means of doing so.

This conclusion does not, however, necessarily foreclose the possibility that pre-emption may be appropriate. The danger of state interference with federally protected conduct is the principal concern of the second branch of the *Garmon* doctrine. To allow the exercise of state jurisdiction in certain contexts might create a significant risk of misinterpretation of federal law and the consequent prohibition of protected conduct. In those circumstances, it might be reasonable to infer that Congress preferred the costs inherent in a jurisdictional hiatus to the frustration of national labor policy which might accompany the exercise of state jurisdiction. Thus, the acceptability of "arguable protection" as a justification for pre-emption in a given class of cases is, at least in part, a function of the strength of the argument that § 7 does in fact protect the disputed conduct.

The Court has held that state jurisdiction to enforce its laws prohibiting violence,[35] defamation,[36] the intentional infliction of emotional distress,[37] or obstruction of access to property,[38] is not pre-empted by the NLRA. But none of those violations of state law involves protected conduct. In contrast,

---

33. Even if Sears had elected the self-help option, it could not have been assured that the Union would have invoked the jurisdiction of the Board. The Union may well have decided that the likelihood of success was remote and outweighed by the cost of the effort and the probability that Sears in turn would have charged the Union with violating § 8(b)(4)(D) or § 8(b)(7)(C) of the Act. Moreover, if Sears had elected this option, and the pickets were evicted with more force than reasonably necessary, it might have exposed itself to tort liability under state law. We are unwilling to presume that Congress intended to require employers to pursue such a risky course in order to ensure that issues involving the scope of § 7 rights be decided only by the Labor Board.

35. Youngdahl v. Rainfair, 355 U.S. 131; United Construction Workers v. Laburnum, 347 U.S. 656.

36. Linn v. Plant Guard Workers, 383 U.S. 53.

37. Farmer v. Carpenters Union, 430 U.S. 290.

38. United Automobile Workers v. Russell, 350 U.S. 634.

some violations of state trespass laws may be actually protected by § 7 of the Federal Act.

In NLRB v. Babcock & Wilcox, 351 U.S. 105, for example, the Court recognized that in certain circumstances non-employee union organizers may have a limited right of access to an employer's premises for the purpose of engaging in organization solicitation.[39] And the Court has indicated that *Babcock* extends to § 7 rights other than organizational activity, though the "locus" of the "accommodation of § 7 rights and the private property rights * * * may fall at differing points along the spectrum depending on the nature and strength of the respective § 7 rights and private property rights asserted in any given context." Hudgens v. NLRB, 424 U.S. 507.

For purpose of analysis we must assume that the Union could have proved that its picketing was, at least in the absence of a trespass, protected by § 7. The remaining question is whether under *Babcock* the trespassory nature of the picketing caused it to forfeit its protected status. Since it cannot be said with certainty that, if the Union had filed an unfair labor practice charge against Sears, the Board would have fixed the locus of the accommodation at the unprotected end of the spectrum, it is indeed "arguable" that the Union's peaceful picketing, though trespassory, was protected. Nevertheless, permitting state courts to evaluate the merits of an argument that certain trespassory activity is protected does not create an unacceptable risk of interference with conduct which the Board, and a court reviewing the Board's decision, would find protected. For while there are unquestionably examples of trespassory union activity in which the question whether it is protected is fairly debatable, experience under the Act teaches that such situations are rare and that a trespass is far more likely to be unprotected than protected.

Experience with trespassory organizational solicitation by nonemployees is instructive in this regard. While *Babcock* indicates that an employer may not always bar nonemployee union organizers from his property, his right to do so remains the general rule. To gain access, the union has the burden of showing that no other reasonable means of communicating its organizational message to the employees exists or that the employer's access rules discriminate against union solicitation. That the burden imposed on the Union is a heavy one is evidenced by the fact that the balance struck by the Board and the courts under the *Babcock* accommodation principle has rarely been in favor of trespassory organizational activity.[41]

Even on the assumption that picketing to enforce area standards is entitled to the same deference in the *Babcock* accommodation analysis as

---

39. As the Court stated:

"The employer may not affirmatively interfere with organization; the union may not always insist that the employer aid organization. But when the inaccessibility of employees makes ineffective the reasonable attempts by nonemployees to communicate with them through the usual channels, the right to exclude from property has been required to yield to the extent needed to permit communication of information on the right to organize." 351 U.S., at 112.

See also Central Hardware Co. v. NLRB, 407 U.S. 539.

41. In the absence of discrimination the union's asserted right of access for organizational activity has generally been denied except in cases involving unique obstacles to non-trespassory methods of communication with the employees. See, e.g., NLRB v. S & H Grossinger's, Inc., 372 F.2d 26 (CA2 1967); NLRB v. Lake Superior Lumber Corp., 167 F.2d 147 (CA6 1948).

organizational solicitation,[42] it would be unprotected in most instances. While there does exist some risk that state courts will on occasion enjoin a trespass that the Board would have protected, the significance of this risk is minimized by the fact that in the cases in which the argument in favor of protection is the strongest, the union is likely to invoke the Board's jurisdiction and thereby avoid the state forum. Whatever risk of an erroneous state court adjudication does exist is outweighed by the anomalous consequence of a rule which would deny the employer access to any forum in which to litigate either the trespass issue or the protection issue in those cases in which the disputed conduct is least likely to be protected by § 7.

If there is a strong argument that the trespass is protected in a particular case, a union can be expected to respond to an employer demand to depart by filing an unfair labor practice charge; the protection question would then be decided by the agency experienced in accommodating the § 7 rights of unions and the property rights of employers in the context of a labor dispute. But if the argument for protection is so weak that it has virtually no chance of prevailing, a trespassing union would be well advised to avoid the jurisdiction of the Board and to argue that the protected character of its conduct deprives the state court of jurisdiction.

As long as the union has a fair opportunity to present the protection issue to the Labor Board, it retains meaningful protection against the risk of error in a state tribunal. In this case the Union failed to invoke the jurisdiction of the Labor Board,[43] and Sears had no right to invoke that jurisdiction and could not even precipitate its exercise without resort to self-help. Because the assertion of state jurisdiction in a case of this kind does not create a significant risk of prohibition of protected conduct, we are unwilling to presume that Congress intended the arguably protected character of the Union's conduct to deprive the California courts of jurisdiction to entertain Sears' trespass action.[44]

42. This assumption, however, is subject to serious question. Indeed, several factors make the argument for protection of trespassory area standards picketing as a category of conduct less compelling than that for trespassory organizational solicitation. First, the right to organize is at the very core of the purpose for which the NLRA was enacted. Area standards picketing, in contrast, has only recently been recognized as a § 7 right. *Hod Carriers Local 41* (Calumet Contractors Assn.), 133 N.L.R.B. 512. Second, *Babcock* makes clear that the interests being protected by according limited access rights to nonemployee, union organizers are not those of the organizers but of the employees located on the employer's property. The Court indicated that "no * * * obligation is owed non-employee organizers"; any right they may have to solicit on an employer's property is a derivative of the right of that employer's employees to exercise their organization rights effectively. Area standards picketing, on the other hand, has no such vital link to the employees located on the employer's property. While such picketing may have a beneficial effect on the compensation of those employees, the rationale for protecting area standards picketing is that a union has a legitimate interest in protecting the wage standards of its members who are employed by competitors of the picketed employer.

43. Not only could the Union have filed an unfair labor practice charge pursuant to § 8(a) (1) of the Act at the time Sears demanded that the pickets leave its property, but the Board's jurisdiction could have been invoked and the protection of its remedial powers obtained even after the litigation in the state court had commenced or the state injunction issued. See Capital Service, Inc. v. NLRB, 347 U.S. 501; NLRB v. Nash-Finch Co., 404 U.S. 138.

44. The fact that Sears demanded that the Union discontinue the trespass before it initiated the trespass action is critical to our holding. While it appears that such a demand was a precondition to commencing a trespass action under California law, see Pet. for Cert. A–4, in order to avoid a valid claim of preemption it would have been required as a matter of federal law in any event.

The Board has taken the position that "a resort to court action * * * does not violate

The judgment of the Supreme Court of California is therefore reversed and the case is remanded to that court for further proceedings not inconsistent with this opinion.

[The concurring opinions of Justices Blackmun and Powell are omitted.

[Justice Blackmun expressed his view on a point not clearly confronted by the majority, viz., that the filing of an 8(a)(1) charge by the union should result in preemption of the state court jurisdiction "until such time as the General Counsel declines to issue a complaint or the Board, applying the standards of NLRB v. Babcock & Wilcox Co., 351 U.S. 105 (1956), rules against the union and holds the picketing to be unprotected. Similarly, if a union timely files a § 8(a)(1) charge, a state court would be bound to *stay* [emphasis added] any pending injunctive or damages suit brought by the employer until the Board has concluded, or the General Counsel by refusal to issue a complaint has indicated, that the picketing is not protected by § 7. As the Court also notes, the primary jurisdiction rationale articulated in *Garmon* 'unquestionably requires that when the same controversy may be presented to the state court or the NLRB, it must be presented to the Board.' Once the no-man's land has been bridged, as it is once a union files a charge, the importance of deferring to the Labor Board's case-by-case accommodation of employers' property rights and employees' § 7 rights mandates preemption of state court jurisdiction." 436 U.S. at 209–10, 98 S.Ct. at 1764, 56 L.Ed.2d at 233.

[Justice Powell in his concurring opinion, triggered by Justice Blackmun's foregoing assertion, expressed his opposing conclusion: "If a § 8(a)(1) charge is filed, nothing is likely to happen 'in a timely fashion.' * * * [I]t may take weeks for the General Counsel to decide whether to issue a complaint. Meanwhile, the 'no-man's land' prevents all recourse to the courts, and is an open invitation to self-help. I am unwilling to believe that Congress intended, by its silence in the Act, to create a situation where there is no forum to which the parties may turn for orderly interim relief in the face of a potentially explosive situation." 436 U.S. at 213, 98 S.Ct. at 1765–66, 56 L.Ed.2d at 235.]

[The dissenting opinion of Justice Brennan, joined by Justices Stewart and Marshall, is also omitted. The dissent lamented:

["That this Court's departure from *Garmon* creates a great risk that protected picketing will be enjoined is amply illustrated by the facts of this case and by the task that was assigned to the California Superior Court. To decide whether the location of the Union's picketing rendered it unlawful, the state court here had to address a host of exceedingly complex labor law questions, which implicated nearly every aspect of the Union's labor dispute with Sears and which were uniquely within the province of the Board. Because it had to assess the [relative strength of the § 7 right] * * * its first task necessarily was to determine the nature of the Union's picketing.

§ 8(a)(1)." NLRB v. Nash-Finch Co., 404 U.S., at 142. If the employer were not required to demand discontinuation of the trespass before proceeding in state court and the Board did not alter its position in cases of this kind, the union would be deprived of an opportunity to present the protection issue to the agency created by Congress to decide such questions. While the union's failure to invoke the Board's jurisdiction should not be a sufficient basis for pre-empting state jurisdiction, the employer should not be permitted to deprive the union of an opportunity to do so.

This picketing could have been characterized in one of three ways: as protected area standards picketing; as prohibited picketing to compel a reassignment of work; or as recognitional picketing that is protected at the outset but prohibited if no petition for a representative election is filed within a reasonable time, not to exceed 30 days. * * * Obviously, since even the Court admits that the characterization of the picketing 'entail[s] relatively complex factual and legal determinations,' there is a substantial danger that the state court, lacking the Board's expertise and specialized sensitivity to labor relations matters, would err at the outset and effectively deny [the Union] the right to engage in any effective § 7 communication.

[" * * * [T]he Court relies on *Babcock & Wilcox Co.,* for the proposition that there is a strong presumption against permitting trespasses by nonemployees. But the Court overlooks a critical distinction between *Babcock* and the case at bar. *Babcock* involved a trespass on industrial property which the employer had fenced off from the public at large, and it is a grave error to treat *Babcock* as having substantial implications for the generic situation presented by this case. To permit trespassory § 7 activities in the *Babcock* fact pattern entails far greater interference with an employer's business than does allowing peaceful nonobstructive picketing on a parking lot which is open to the public and which has been used for other types of solicitation. * * * [T]his Court's shortlived holding that picketing at shopping centers is protected by the Fourteenth Amendment, see Food Employees v. Logan Valley Plaza, 391 U.S. 308 (1968), overruled in Hudgens v. NLRB, [424 U.S. 507 (1976)], has resulted in a situation where * * * this Court * * * has [not] considered * * * the quite different question of the conditions under which union representatives may enter privately owned areas of shopping centers to engage in protected activities such as peaceful picketing. * * * Quite apart from the fact the Court has no basis for blithely assuming that all private property is fungible, that this Court would fail to appreciate so possibly vital a distinction in assessing the strength of a § 7 claim illustrates the danger of permitting lower courts, which lack even this Court's exposure to labor law, to rule on the question whether trespassory picketing by nonemployees is protected.

[" * * * Whatever the shortcomings of *Garmon,* none can deny the necessity for a rule in this complex area that is capable of uniform application by the lower courts. The Court's new exception to *Garmon* cannot be expected to be correctly applied by those courts and thus most inevitably will threaten erosion of the goal of uniform administration of the national labor laws.

[" * * * [T]he [trial] court must inquire whether the employer had a 'reasonable opportunity' to force a Board determination. What constitutes a 'reasonable opportunity'? I have to assume from today's decision that the employer can never be deemed to have an acceptable opportunity when nonemployees are engaged in the arguably protected activity. But what if employees are involved? Will the fact that the employer can provoke the filing of an unfair labor practice charge by disciplining the employee always constitute an acceptable alternative? Perhaps so, but the Court provides no guidance that can help the local judges. Some may believe that the fact that any discipline will enhance the seriousness of the unfair labor practice renders that course unacceptable.

[" * * * Because the Court has not demonstrated that *Garmon* produces an unacceptable accommodation of the conflicting state and federal interests, I respectfully dissent." 436 U.S. at 228–37, 98 S.Ct. at 1773–78, 56 L.Ed.2d at 245–50.]

Note

1.   There is no clear majority response in Sears to the question of whether the filing of a Section 8(a)(1) charge divests the state court's jurisdiction. Should it?

2.   (a) Suppose, in Sears (as hypothesized by Justice Brennan in his dissent), employees of Sears were doing the picketing? Should the fact that the employer could discipline the picketing employees, thus prompting 8(a)(1) and (3) charges and providing a forum for the employer before the NLRB, preclude the employer from obtaining relief in a state court?

(b) Suppose the foregoing employees were engaged in the trespassory picketing in support of their union's position vis-a-vis Sears in collective bargaining. Should Sears be precluded from obtaining relief in a state court?

(c) Applying the analytical approach specified by the majority in Sears, is the employer's argument for state relief stronger in case (a) or (b) above? The following note is relevant to this question.

3.   The Garmon rule, as modified by Sears, preempts with regard to activity arguably protected under Section 7 or prohibited under Section 8. What of activity *neither* protected nor prohibited? In UAW–AFL Local 232 v. Wisconsin Employment Relations Bd. (Briggs-Stratton), 336 U.S. 245, 69 S.Ct. 516, 93 L.Ed. 651 (1949), the Court held "quickie," on-again-off-again strike activity to be neither protected nor prohibited and, as a consequence, not federally preempted; state regulation of this activity was accordingly upheld. This was the posture of preemption for a quarter of a century—until the decision in Lodge 76, Int'l Ass'n of Machinists, v. Wisconsin Employment Relations Comm., 427 U.S. 132, 96 S.Ct. 2548, 49 L.Ed.2d 396 (1976). In the Lodge 76 case the employees, in support of their union's collective bargaining demand for a shorter workweek, concertedly refused to work overtime. Characterizing this activity as neither protected nor prohibited, the Court nonetheless held that Wisconsin could not regulate such conduct. Briggs-Stratton was overruled pursuant to the following line of reasoning: Activity which is neither protected (i.e., against employer retribution) nor prohibited (i.e., an unfair labor practice) may nonetheless be consistent with the national labor policy and therefore needful of insulation from state regulation. In a series of cases decided during the 27 years between Briggs-Stratton and Lodge 76 the Court had evolved a better understanding of the concept of *free* collective bargaining; union pressure neither prohibited by federal law nor protected by that law from employer retributive response was federally *permitted* activity—part of the free struggle of management and labor. Management was free to respond with its own permitted weaponry (including discharge or other disciplinary action), but state efforts to referee such contests impermissibly impeded the playing of a federally-sponsored nationally-uniform game.

A THEORY OF PREEMPTION: SEEKING
ORDER IN CHAOS

The federal labor preemption doctrine, introduced in Allen-Bradley Local No. 1111 v. Wisconsin Employment Relations Board, 315 U.S. 740, 62 S.Ct. 820, 86 L.Ed. 1154 (1942), supra p. 129, and culminating conceptually in the Garmon case (1958), had as its *raison d'etre* the establishment of a uniform national labor policy. But *why* such a uniform national labor policy? Speculation as to the answer to this question may afford helpful insight into the seeming (*and* confusing) erosion of the doctrine. Would you agree with the following analysis?

The underlying premise of the doctrine was to protect a nascent labor movement from potentially hostile and relatively uninformed state (and federal) tribunals. While the post-Wagner Act (1935) labor movement was in its relative infancy, it was more in need of such protection than later, after the policies favoring unionization and collective bargaining had taken secure root. Since Garmon, the felt need for protection of those policies, under the umbrella of a federal scheme of preemptive primary jurisdiction in the National Labor Relations Board, has attenuated. As a consequence, the early exceptions to that preemption were articulated in relatively strict language which made the exceptions less dangerously intrusive upon the federally declared policies—e.g., "compelling state interest" (violence: Laburnum, 1954; Russell, 1958), "merely peripheral federal concern" (reinstatement to union membership plus damages for lost wages: Gonzales, 1958). As a close reading of such cases as Farmer (1977) and Sears (1978) demonstrates, the exceptions have become less tightly articulated. What has evolved is a more loosely stated "balancing" of federal versus state interests and a concomitantly more relaxed accommodation of state interests within the federal scheme.

Problems under the Garmon doctrine arise in four categories: where state regulation is sought to be applied to (1) activity *clearly* (actually) federally protected; (2) activity *arguably* federally protected; (3) activity *clearly* federally prohibited; and (4) activity *arguably* federally prohibited.

The first category (*clearly* federally protected) is the clearest for operation of Article VI, the Supremacy Clause. By premise, state regulatory power with regard to such activity is preempted. Even the most compelling state interest, i.e., dealing with violence, would yield *if* the conduct had been accurately characterized as "federally protected." However, the more compelling the state interest, the more clear the federal protection would have to be in order to "outweigh" it.

As to the second category (*arguably* federally protected), state regulation of such activity is preempted except for the Sears exception, which operates where (a) the party aggrieved does not have access to the NLRB in order to have determined the actuality of the arguable protection, and (b) the union refuses itself to file an unfair labor practice charge, and (c) the strength of the argument for protection is not strong.

As to the third category (*clearly* federally prohibited), the preemption doctrine operates subject to two exceptions: (a) where a "compelling state interest" is involved, (b) where there is "merely peripheral federal concern."

The violence cases—Laburnum, Russell—are the primary examples of the first. Gonzales is the primary example of the second. Linn (state libel actions) and Farmer have been rationalized under both rubrics. What is evolving is a merging of the two categories of exceptions into a kind of balancing system where the federal and state interests are weighed against each other: where the state interest is compelling, that suggests a relatively light federal interest, and where the federal interest is merely peripheral, that suggests a weightier state interest. The new analysis is as follows: the first question is whether the state has a *substantial* interest in regulating the conduct involved. If so, the second question is whether that state regulation will pose a *serious* risk of interference with the administration of the national labor policy. In other words, what is now involved is a less *verbally-restricted* balancing of state interest against federal interest.

As to the fourth category (*arguably* federally prohibited), the most important question, as in the arguably federally *protected* category, is one of primary jurisdiction—i.e., what tribunal is to characterize the "arguable" as either actual or not. The preservation of a uniform federal labor policy calls ideally for the NLRB to have exclusive primary jurisdiction. However, the same exceptions operative in the "clearly prohibited" category are also operative here, with the reservation that the federal interest is obviously less strong in the "arguably prohibited" category than in the "clearly prohibited" category.

Note that where the characterization of the activity is in issue (i.e., where it is *arguable*), the question of what tribunal is to do the characterizing is fundamental. In the arguably protected area, that characterizing is the first and final step, assuming an affirmative characterization. In the arguably prohibited area, however, characterization of the activity as prohibited is only the first step; the second is the determination of the remedy, the sanction, for having engaged in that activity *and* the tribunal which should determine that sanction (the NLRB, unless the state interest outweighs the federal interest).

To repeat, what the Garmon preemption doctrine is mainly about is protecting organized labor from inexpert/unfriendly tribunals. The prime point of the "protected" prong (clearly or arguably) is to keep such tribunals off the union's back—i.e., from treating as unlawful that which should not be so treated. The prime point of the "prohibited" prong (clearly or arguably) is to assure that the remedy imposed for unlawful activity is that federally prescribed, i.e., not overly severe.

A fifth and final category of concern under the preemption doctrine should be noted in closing, activity *neither* federally protected nor prohibited. The Lodge 76 case, Note 3, p. 370 supra, deals with this category in the collective bargaining context, creating a federally *permitted* activity, though not federally protected and, of course, not federally prohibited.

B. ORGANIZATIONAL AND RECOGNITIONAL PICKETING

In the Landrum-Griffin Act of 1959, Congress sought to fill a void in the National Labor Relations Act with regard to the regulation of peaceful picketing by a minority union for recognitional or organizational purposes. Prior to that enactment, the only arguably relevant provisions in the Act were Section 8(b)(4)(C), which applied only where an incumbent union had been previously certified to represent the pertinent group of employees, and Section 8(b)(1)(A), which was held in the "Curtis Brothers" case (NLRB v. Drivers, Chauffeurs, Helpers, Local Union No. 639, 362 U.S. 274, 80 S.Ct. 706, 4 L.Ed.2d 710 (1960), discussed supra p. 311, Note 1) to be inapplicable to such picketing. Congress addressed this problem by adding Section 8(b)(7), the design of which was to preclude so-called "blackmail" picketing by a minority union for recognitional or organizational purposes. (See the discussion of Lauf v. E.G. Shinner & Co., 303 U.S. 323, 58 S.Ct. 578, 82 L.Ed. 872 (1938) and Fur Workers Union, Local No. 72 v. Fur Workers Union, No. 21238, 105 F.2d 1 (D.C.Cir.1939), affirmed mem., 308 U.S. 522, 60 S.Ct. 292, 84 L.Ed. 443 (1939), supra pp. 155–156.) The boundaries and content of Section 8(b)(7) are explored in the following materials.

INTERNATIONAL HOD CARRIERS BUILDING AND COMMON LABORERS UNION, LOCAL 840, AFL–CIO ("BLINNE CONSTRUCTION")

National Labor Relations Board, 1962.
135 N.L.R.B. 1153.

SUPPLEMENTAL DECISION AND ORDER

On February 20, 1961, the Board (Member Fanning dissenting) issued a Decision and Order in this case finding that Respondent Union had engaged in unfair labor practices in violation of Section 8(b)(7)(C) of the Act.[1] Thereafter, on or about April 3, 1961, Respondent Union filed with the Board a motion for reconsideration and for dismissal of the complaint * * *.

The Board * * * hereby grants the Union's motion insofar as it requests reconsideration. * * *

I.

The Decision and Order in the instant case is one of several issued on February 20, 1961, and immediately thereafter,[3] dealing with Section 8(b)(7)(C) of the Act, which became effective on November 13, 1959, pursuant to the Landrum-Griffin amendments. * * *

As indicated by its text, the thrust of Section 8(b)(7) is to deal with recognition and organization picketing, a matter not dealt with directly in the Taft-Hartley Act except to the limited extent provided in Section 8(b)(4)(C) of that Act. * * *

Even a cursory examination of the legislative history of the provisions here in issue reveals that, like the so-called "secondary boycott" provisions of

---

1. 130 NLRB 587.

3. The other decisions are: Chefs, Cooks, Pastry Cooks and Assistants, Local 89, etc., et al. (Stork Restaurant, Inc.), 130 NLRB 543; Local Joint Executive Board of Hotel and Restaurant Employees, etc., et al. (Leonard Smitley and Joseph W. Drown d/b/a Crown Cafeteria, a Co-partnership), 130 NLRB 570; Local 705 International Brotherhood of Teamsters, etc., et al. (Cartage and Terminal Management Corporation), 130 NLRB 558; International Typographical Union, et al. (Charlton-Press), 130 NLRB 727.

the Taft-Hartley Act, Section 8(b)(7) was also "to a marked degree, the result of conflict and compromise between strong contending forces and deeply held views on the role of organized labor in the free economic life of the Nation and the appropriate balance to be struck between the uncontrolled power of management and labor to further their respective interests." Local 1976, United Brotherhood of Carpenters and Joiners of America, AFL, et al. (Sand Door & Plywood Co.) v. N.L.R.B., 357 U.S. 93, 99–100.

In this context it could readily have been anticipated that the statutory language finally adopted, as applied to the myriad situations which arose, would create difficult problems of interpretation.   *   *   *

II.

Before proceeding to determine the application of Section 8(b)(7)(C) to the facts of the instant case, it is essential to note the interplay of the several subsections of Section 8(b)(7), of which subparagraph (C) is only a constitutent part.

The section as a whole, as is apparent from its opening phrases, prescribes limitations only on picketing for an object of "recognition" or "bargaining" (both of which terms will hereinafter be subsumed under the single term "recognition") or for an object of organization. Picketing for other objects is not proscribed by this section. Moreover, not all picketing for recognition or organization is proscribed. A "currently certified" union may picket for recognition or organization of employees for whom it is certified. And even a union which is not certified is barred from recognition or organization picketing only in three general areas. The first area, defined in subparagraph (A) of Section 8(b)(7), relates to situations where another union has been lawfully recognized and a question concerning representation cannot appropriately be raised.[5] The second area, defined in subparagraph (B), relates to situations where, within the preceding 12 months, a "valid election" has been held.

The intent of subparagraphs (A) and (B) is fairly clear. Congress concluded that where a union has been lawfully recognized and a question concerning representation cannot appropriately be raised, or where the employees within the preceding 12 months have made known their views concerning representation, both the employer and employees are entitled to immunity from recognition or organization picketing for prescribed periods.

Congress did not stop there, however. Deeply concerned with other abuses, most particularly "blackmail" picketing, Congress concluded that it would be salutary to impose even further limitations on picketing for recognition or organization. Accordingly, subparagraph (C) provides that even where such picketing is not barred by the provisions of (A) or (B) so that picketing for recognition or organization would otherwise be permissible, such picketing is limited to a reasonable period not to exceed 30 days unless

---

5. It will be noted, of course, that subparagraph (A) represents a substantial enlargement upon the prohibition already embodied in Section 8(b)(4)(C) of the Taft-Hartley Act which merely insulates certified unions from proscribed "raiding" by rival labor organizations. Subparagraph (A) affords protection to lawfully recognized unions which do not have certified status, and also incorporates, in effect, the Board's contract-bar rules relating to the existence of a question concerning representation.

a representation petition is filed prior to the expiration of that period.[7] Absent the filing of such a timely petition, continuation of the picketing beyond the reasonable period becomes an unfair labor practice. On the other hand, the filing of a timely petition stays the limitation and picketing may continue pending the processing of the petition. Even here, however, Congress by the addition of the first proviso to subparagraph (C) made it possible to foreshorten the period of permissible picketing by directing the holding of an expedited election pursuant to the representation petition.

The expedited election procedure is applicable, of course, only in a Section 8(b)(7)(C) proceeding, i.e., where an 8(b)(7)(C) unfair labor practice charge has been filed. Congress rejected efforts to amend the provisions of Section 9(c) of the Act so as to dispense generally with preelection hearings. Thus, in the absence of an 8(b)(7)(C) unfair labor practice charge, a union will not be enabled to obtain an expedited election by the mere device of engaging in recognition or organization picketing and filing a representation petition.[10] And on the other hand, a picketing union which files a representation petition pursuant to the mandate of Section 8(b)(7)(C) and to avoid its sanctions will not be propelled into an expedited election, which it may not desire, merely because it has filed such a petition. In both the above situations, the normal representation procedures are applicable; the showing of a substantial interest will be required, and the preelection hearing directed in Section 9(c)(1) will be held.

This, in our considered judgment, puts the expedited election procedure prescribed in the first proviso to subparagraph C in its proper and intended focus. That procedure was devised to shield aggrieved employers and employees from the adverse effects of prolonged recognition or organization picketing. * * *

Subparagraphs (B) and (C) serve different purposes. But it is especially significant to note their interrelationship. Congress was particularly concerned, even where picketing for recognition or organization was otherwise permissible, that the question concerning representation which gave rise to the picketing be resolved as quickly as possible. It was for this reason that it provided for the filing of a petition pursuant to which the Board could direct an expedited election in which the employees could freely indicate their desires as to representation. If, in the free exercise of their choice, they designate the picketing union as their bargaining representative, that union will be certified and it will by the express terms of Section 8(b)(7) be exonerated from the strictures of that section. If, conversely, the employees reject the picketing union, that union will be barred from picketing for 12 months thereafter under the provisions of subparagraph (B).

The scheme which Congress thus devised represents what that legislative body deemed a practical accommodation between the right of a union to

---

7. Section 9(c) of the Act permits such a petition to be filed "by an employee or group of employees or any individual or labor organization acting in their behalf" or "by an employer."

10. Congress plainly did not intend such a result. See Congressman Barden's statement (105 Daily Cong.Rec., A8062, September 2, 1959; 2 Legis.Hist.1813). And the Board has ruled further that a charge filed by a picketing union or a person "fronting" for it may not be utilized to invoke an expedited election. Claussen Baking Company, Case No. 11-RC-1329, May 5, 1960 (not published in NLRB volumes). * * *

engage in legitimate picketing for recognition or organization and abuse of that right. One caveat must be noted in that regard. The congressional scheme is, perforce, based on the premise that the election to be conducted under the first proviso to subparagraph (C) represents the free and un-coerced choice of the employee electorate. Absent such a free and uncoerced choice, the underlying question concerning representation is not resolved and, more particularly, subparagraph (B) which turns on the holding of a "valid election" does not become operative.

There remains to be considered only the second proviso to subparagraph (C). In sum, that proviso removes the time limitation imposed upon, and preserves the legality of, recognition or organization picketing falling within the ambit of subparagraph (C), where that picketing merely advises the public that an employer does not employ members of, or have a contract with, a union unless an effect of such picketing is to halt pickups or deliveries, or the performance of services.[11] Needless to add, picketing which meets the requirements of the proviso also renders the expedited election procedure inapplicable.

Except for the final clause in Section 8(b)(7) which provides that nothing in that section shall be construed to permit any act otherwise proscribed under Section 8(b) of the Act, the foregoing sums up the limitations imposed upon recognition or organization picketing by the Landrum-Griffin amendments. However, at the risk of laboring the obvious, it is important to note that structurally, as well as grammatically, subparagraphs (A), (B), and (C) are subordinate to and controlled by the opening phrases of Section 8(b)(7). In other words, the thrust of all the Section 8(b)(7) provisions is only upon picketing for an object of recognition or organization, and not upon picketing for other objects. Similarly, both structurally and grammatically, the two provisos in subparagraph (C) appertain only to the situation defined in the principal clause of that subparagraph.

Having outlined, in concededly broad strokes, the statutory framework of Section 8(b)(7) and particularly subparagraph (C) thereof, we may appropriately turn to a consideration of the instant case which presents issues going to the heart of that legislation.

The relevant facts may be briefly stated. On February 2, 1960, all three common laborers employed by Blinne at the Fort Leonard Wood jobsite signed cards designating the Union to represent them for purposes of collective bargaining. The next day the Union demanded that Blinne recognize the Union as the bargaining agent for the three laborers. Blinne not only refused recognition but told the Union it would transfer one of the laborers, Wann, in order to destroy the Union's majority.[13] Blinne carried out this threat and transferred Wann 5 days later, on February 8. Following this refusal to recognize the Union and the transfer of Wann the Union started picketing at Fort Wood. The picketing, which began on February 8, immediately following the transfer of Wann, had three announced objectives:

---

11. The scope and impact of that proviso are set forth in the dissenting opinion in Crown Cafeteria, 130 NLRB 570, which the majority of the Board this day adopted in its Supplemental Decision and Order in that case, 135 NLRB No. 124. * * *

13. Blinne's assumption that this transfer would destroy the Union's majority was in error. However, that error has no significance in this case.

(1) recognition of the Union; (2) payment of the Davis-Bacon scale of wages; [14] and (3) protest against Blinne's unfair labor practices in refusing to recognize the Union and in threatening to transfer and transferring Wann.

The picketing continued, with interruptions due to bad weather, until at least March 11, 1960, a period of more than 30 days from the date the picketing commenced. The picketing was peaceful, only one picket was on duty, and the picket sign he carried read "C.A. Blinne Construction Company, unfair." The three laborers on the job (one was the replacement for Wann) struck when the picketing started.

The Union, of course, was not the certified bargaining representative of the employees. Moreover, no representation petition was filed during the more than 30 days in which picketing was taking place. On March 1, however, about 3 weeks after the picketing commenced and well within the statutory 30-day period, the Union filed unfair labor practice charges against Blinne, alleging violations of Section 8(a)(1), (2), (3), and (5). On March 22, the Regional Director dismissed the 8(a)(2) and (5) charges, whereupon the Union forthwith filed a representation petition under Section 9(c) of the Act. Subsequently, on April 20, the Regional Director approved a unilateral settlement agreement with Blinne with respect to the Section 8(a)(1) and (3) charges which had not been dismissed. In the settlement agreement, Blinne neither admitted nor denied that it had committed unfair labor practices.

General Counsel argues that a violation of Section 8(b)(7)(C) has occurred within the literal terms of that provision because (1) the Union's picketing was concededly for an object of obtaining recognition; (2) the Union was not currently certified as the representative of the employees involved; and (3) no petition for representation was filed within 30 days of the commencement of the picketing. Inasmuch as the Union made no contention that its recognition picketing was "informational" within the meaning of the second proviso to subparagraph (C) or that it otherwise comported with the strictures of that proviso, General Counsel contends that a finding of unfair labor practice is required.

Respondent Union, for its part, points to the manifest inequity of such a finding and argues that Congress could not have intended so incongruous a result. In essence, its position is that it was entitled to recognition because it represented all the employees in the appropriate unit, that Blinne by a series of unfair labor practices deprived the Union and the employees it sought to represent of fundamental rights guaranteed by the Act, and that the impact of a finding adverse to the Union would be to punish the innocent and reward the wrongdoer. More specifically, Respondent argues that Section 8(b)(7)(C) was not intended to apply to picketing by a majority union and that, in any event, Blinne's unfair labor practices exonerated it from the statutory requirement of filing a timely representation petition.   *   *   *

IV.

     *   *   *

14. At the time of the request for recognition, the Union complained to Blinne that he was not paying the required Davis-Bacon rate for unskilled laborers. This dispute was settled after the picketing began. [The Davis-Bacon Act, 46 Stat. 1494 (1931), as amended, 40 U.S.C.A. § 276a et seq. requires that workers covered by federal construction contracts be paid, at a minimum, the wage rates determined by the Secretary of Labor to be prevailing on similar projects in the community.]

A. *The contention that Section 8(b)(7)(C) does not proscribe picketing for recognition or organization by a majority union*

Respondent, urging the self-evident proposition that a statute should be read as a whole, argues that Section 8(b)(7)(C) was not designed to prohibit picketing for recognition by a union enjoying majority status in an appropriate unit. Such picketing is for a lawful purpose inasmuch as Sections 8(a)(5) and 9(a) of the Act specifically impose upon an employer the duty to recognize and bargain with a union which enjoys that status. Accordingly, Respondent contends, absent express language requiring such a result, Section 8(b)(7)(C) should not be read in derogation of the duty so imposed.

* * * [W]e find [this argument] to be without merit. To be sure, the legislative history is replete with references that Congress in framing the 1959 amendments was primarily concerned with "blackmail" picketing where the picketing union represented none or few of the employees whose allegiance it sought. * * * Yet it cannot be gainsaid that Section 8(b)(7) by its explicit language exempts only "currently certified" unions from its proscriptions. Cautious as we should be to avoid a mechanical reading of statutory terms in involved legislative enactments, it is difficult to avoid giving the quoted words, essentially words of art, their natural construction. Moreover, such a construction is consonant with the underlying statutory scheme which is to resolve disputed issues of majority status, whenever possible, by the machinery of a Board election. Absent unfair labor practices or preelection misconduct warranting the setting aside of the election, majority unions will presumably not be prejudiced by such resolution. On the other hand, the admitted difficulties of determining majority status without such an election are obviated by this construction. * * *

B. *The contention that employer unfair labor practices are a defense to a charge of a Section 8(b)(7)(C) violation*

We turn now to the second issue, namely, whether employer unfair labor practices are a defense to an 8(b)(7)(C) violation. As set forth in the original Decision and Order, the Union argues that Blinne was engaged in unfair labor practices within the meaning of Section 8(a)(1) and (3) of the Act; that it filed appropriate unfair labor practice charges against Blinne within a reasonable period of time after the commencement of the picketing; that it filed a representation petition as soon as the 8(a)(2) and (5) allegations of the charges were dismissed; that the 8(a)(1) and (3) allegations were in effect sustained and a settlement agreement was subsequently entered into with the approval of the Board; and that, therefore, this sequence of events should satisfy the requirements of Section 8(b)(7)(C).

The majority of the Board in the original Decision and Order rejected this argument. Pointing out that the representation petition was concededly filed more than 30 days after the commencement of the picketing, the majority concluded that the clear terms of Section 8(b)(4)(C) [8(b)(7)(C)?] had been violated.

The majority also addressed itself specifically to the Union's contention that Section 8(b)(7)(C) could not have been intended by Congress to apply where an employer unfair labor practice had occurred. Its opinion alludes to the fact that the then Senator, now President, Kennedy had proposed statutory language to the effect that any employer unfair labor practice would be a defense to a charge of an 8(b)(7) violation both with respect to an application to the courts for a temporary restraining order and with respect to the unfair labor practice proceeding itself. The majority noted that the Congress did not adopt this proposal but instead limited itself merely to the insertion of a proviso in Section 10(l) prohibiting the application for a restraining order under Section 8(b)(7)(C) if there was reason to believe that a Section 8(a)(2) violation existed. Accordingly, the majority concluded that Congress had specifically rejected the very contention which Respondent urged.

The dissenting member in the original Decision and Order took sharp issue with the majority. * * * Conceding that Section 8(b)(7)(C) in terms outlawed recognition picketing for more than 30 days unless a representation petition was filed, he emphasized that the cited section also provided for an expedited election if such a petition was filed. The purpose of the election is to obtain a free and uncoerced expression of the employees' desires as to their representation. Where unfair labor practices have taken place, however, such a free and uncoerced expression is precluded and the filing of a representation petition would be a futility. Indeed, consistent Board practice, presumably known to Congress, is to stay representation proceedings and elections thereunder until the effect of existing unremedied unfair labor practices is dissipated. Accordingly, the dissenting member concluded that the failure of a picketing union to file a timely petition in the face of employer unfair labor practices should not be made the basis for a finding of a violation under Section 8(b)(7)(C) of the Act.

The dissenting opinion likewise did not find the majority's reliance upon the proviso to Section 10(l) persuasive. On the basis of the relevant legislative history, the dissent concluded that this proviso was intended merely to implement Section 8(b)(7)(A) of the Act, that is, to insure that a union which was the beneficiary of a "sweetheart agreement" with an employer could not derive the benefit of injunctive relief that would otherwise be accorded by virtue of the provisions of subparagraph (A).

In retrospect, both the majority and dissenting opinions are not without logic or respectable foundation. Certainly, the narrow proviso embodied in Section 10(l), and the failure to embrace a proposal that would exempt recognition and organization picketing from the Section 8(b)(7)(C) bar where employer unfair labor practices had been committed, suggest that Congress was reluctant to grant such an exemption. Conversely, as the dissenting opinion argues, to hold that employer unfair labor practices sufficient to affect the results of an election are irrelevant in an 8(b)(7)(C) context seems incongruous and inconsistent with the overall scheme of the Act.

Fortified by the advantages of hindsight and added deliberation as to the ramifications of the majority and minority opinions, we are now of the view that neither opinion affords a complete answer to the question here presented. It seems fair to say that Congress was unwilling to write an exemption into Section 8(b)(7)(C) dispensing with the necessity for filing a representation petition wherever employer unfair labor practices were alleged. * * * On the other hand, it strains credulity to believe that Congress proposed to make the rights of union and employees turn upon the results of an election which, because of the existence of unremedied unfair labor practices, is unlikely to reflect the true wishes of the employees.

We do not find ourselves impaled on the horns of this dilemma. Upon careful reappraisal of the statutory scheme we are satisfied that Congress meant to require, and did require, in an 8(b)(7)(C) situation, that a representation petition be filed within a reasonable period, not to exceed 30 days. By this device machinery can quickly be set in motion to resolve by a free and fair election the underlying question concerning representation out of which the picketing arises. This is the normal situation, and the situation which the statute is basically designed to serve.

There is legitimate concern, however, with the abnormal situation, that is, the situation where because of unremedied unfair labor practices a free and fair election cannot be held. We believe Congress anticipated this contingency also. Thus, we find no mandate in the legislative scheme to compel the holding of an election pursuant to a representation petition where, because of unremedied unfair labor practices or for other valid reason, a free and uncoerced election cannot be held. On the contrary, the interrelated provisions of subparagraphs (B) and (C), by their respective references to a "valid election" and to a "certif[ication of] results" presuppose that Congress contemplated only a fair and free election. Only after such an election could the Board certify the results and only after such an election could the salutary provisions of subparagraph (B) become operative.

In our view, therefore, Congress intended that, except to the limited extent set forth in the first proviso,[23] the Board in 8(b)(7)(C) cases follow the tried and familiar procedures it typically follows in representation cases where unfair labor practice charges are filed. That procedure, as already set forth, is to hold the representation case in abeyance and refrain from holding an election pending the resolution of the unfair labor practice charges. Thus, the fears that the statutory requirement for filing a timely petition will compel a union which has been the victim of unfair labor practices to undergo a coerced election are groundless. No action will be taken on that petition while unfair labor practice charges are pending, and until a valid election is held pursuant to that petition, the union's right to picket under the statutory scheme is unimpaired.

On the other side of the coin, it may safely be assumed that groundless unfair labor practice charges in this area, because of the statutory priority accorded Section 8(b)(7) violations, will be quickly dismissed. Following such dismissal an election can be directed forthwith upon the subsisting petition, thereby effectuating the congressional purpose. Moreover, the fact that a timely petition is on file will protect the innocent union, which through a mistake of fact or law has filed a groundless unfair labor practice charge, from a finding of an 8(b)(7)(C) violation. Thus, the policy of the entire Act is effectuated and all rights guaranteed by its several provisions are appropriately safeguarded. * * *

The facts of the instant case may be utilized to demonstrate the practical operation of the legislative scheme. Here the union had filed

---

23. As already noted, that proviso enables the Board to dispense with the preelection hearing prescribed in Section 9(c)(1), and to dispense also with the requirement of a showing of substantial interest.

unfair labor practice charges alleging violations by the employer of Section 8(a)(1), (2), (3), and (5) of the Act. General Counsel found the allegations of 8(a)(2) and (5) violations groundless. Hence had these allegations stood alone and had a timely petition been on file, an election could have been directed forthwith and the underlying question concerning representation out of which the picketing arose could have been resolved pursuant to the statutory scheme. The failure to file a timely petition frustrated that scheme.[24]

On the other hand, the Section 8(a)(1) and (3) charges were found meritorious. Under these circumstances, and again consistent with uniform practice, no election would have been directed notwithstanding the currency of a timely petition; the petition would be held in abeyance pending a satisfactory resolution of the unfair labor practice charges. The aggrieved union's right to picket would not be abated in the interim and the sole prejudice to the employer would be the delay engendered by its own unfair labor practices.[26] The absence of a timely petition, however, precludes disposition of the underlying question concerning representation which thus remains unresolved even after the Section 8(a)(1) and (3) charges are satisfactorily disposed of. * * *

Conclusion

Because we read Section 8(b)(7)(C) as requiring in the instant case the filing of a timely petition and because such a petition was admittedly not filed until more than 30 days after the commencement of the picketing, we find that Respondent violated Section 8(b)(7)(C) of the Act. As previously noted, it is undisputed that "an object" of the picketing was for recognition. It affords Respondent no comfort that its picketing was also in protest against the discriminatory transfer of an employee and against payment of wages at a rate lower than that prescribed by law. Had Respondent confined its picketing to these objectives rather than, as it did, include a demand for recognition, we believe none of the provisions of Section 8(b)(7) would be applicable. Under the circumstances here, however, Section 8(b)(7) (C) is applicable. * * *

[The "separate opinion" of Members Rodgers and Leedom and the "concurring and dissenting" opinion of Member Fanning are omitted.]

Note

1. According to Blinne, what should the union have done? Why? That is, what is the rationale of 8(b)(7)? What competing interests, held by whom, are sought to be balanced under the statutory scheme?

2. Can the union itself obtain an expedited election under 8(b)(7)(C) by engaging in organizational or recognitional picketing and also filing a petition under Section 9(c)? *Should* it be able to?

24. * * * [T]he filing of a representation petition will not be required of a union when it has filed a meritorious 8(a)(5) charge, but will be required where it has filed other 8(a) charges. The point of the distinction * * * is simply this: a meritorious 8(a)(5) case moots the question concerning representation which the petition is designed to resolve; other 8(a) charges merely delay the time when that un-resolved question can be submitted to a free election by the employees. * * *

26. To be sure, we would not permit a union to benefit by itself committing unfair labor practices to delay the holding of an election and thereby stay the sanctions of Section 8(b)(7).

3. What impact do Gissel, supra p. 290, and Linden, supra Note 1, p. 299, have on the substitutability of an 8(a)(5) charge for a 9(c) petition under 8(b)(7)(C) (See footnote 24, p. 381.)

LOCAL JOINT EXECUTIVE BOARD OF HOTEL AND RESTAURANT EMPLOYEES ("CROWN CAFETERIA")

National Labor Relations Board, 1961.
130 N.L.R.B. 570.

DECISION AND ORDER

* * * [U]nion representatives in April and May 1959 asked Crown to operate its cafeteria by hiring its employees through the union hiring hall and signing the standard union contract. Crown refused to do so, and employed nonunion employees instead. Beginning on May 5, 1959, the Respondents accordingly picketed the public entrance of Crown cafeteria, with signs addressed to "members of organized labor and their friends," stating that the cafeteria was nonunion, and asking them not to patronize the cafeteria. This recognitional or organizational picketing continued without the filing of a petition for more than a reasonable period of time after November 13, 1959, the effective date of Section 8(b)(7)(C).

On these facts the Trial Examiner concluded that the picketing, even though for an object of recognition or organization, fell within the protection of the publicity proviso to Section 8(b)(7)(C) because it did not have the effect of inducing any stoppage of goods or services.

We cannot agree with the Trial Examiner's unduly narrow construction of the Act. Congress in Section 8(b)(7) expressed the general objective of prohibiting picketing by uncertified labor organizations where *an* object was recognition or organization, even though the picketing may also have had other objects as well. * * *

We regard the Trial Examiner's and our dissenting colleagues' construction of the Act as undermining the carefully worked out program established by Congress in Section 8(b)(7). We cannot believe that Congress meant to permit recognition picketing merely because the picketing also takes the form of truthfully advising the public that the employer is nonunion, or does not have a union contract. Rather, we believe that Congress was careful to state that picketing will be permitted only if it is for "the" purpose of so advising the public. Indeed the ban against picketing is particularly applicable in the present situation, where the Union did not represent the majority of the employees, and the only lawful course for Crown to follow was to refuse to recognize the Union as it did. * * *

We are satisfied that Congress added the proviso only to make clear that purely informational picketing, which publicizes the lack of a union contract or the lack of union organization, and which has no present object of recognition, should not be curtailed "* * * unless an effect of such picketing is to induce any individual employed by any other person in the course of his employment not to pick up, deliver or transport any goods or not to perform any services." But that is not the situation in this case. As the Trial Examiner found, apart from the picketing, the Union was in fact demanding present recognition from Crown. Indeed, under established doctrine, even if the Union had disclaimed any object of recognition—which, of course, it did not do—but had engaged in the picketing here present, the Board would clearly have entertained a representation petition filed by Crown, apart from the specific provisions of Section 8(b)(7)(C). For a demand for recognition accompanied by picketing would not be deemed, under the Board's normal representation procedures, to have been removed by a disclaimer, where, as here, the picketing continues and the picket signs refer only to the lack of union organization.

Consideration of the result of the Trial Examiner's and our dissenting colleagues' contrary construction of the proviso convinces us of their error. They would permit present recognition picketing whenever the labor organization is careful to indicate by its picket signs only an ostensible purpose of advising the public. However, this would render meaningless, at the whim of a picketing union, the stated objective of Section 8(b)(7). The resulting nullification of the whole of Section 8(b)(7)(C) would most certainly result in an absurd situation. Clearly, under the established rules of statutory construction, the intention of the Congress to outlaw recognitional and organizational picketing is best effectuated by confining the second proviso of 8(b)(7)(C) to picketing where the sole object is dissemination of information divorced from a present object of recognition.

Moreover, the legislative history, if it were needed to explain what seems to us to be clear statutory language, supports this construction of the Act. As Senator Kennedy stated in the significant item of legislative history referred to by the Trial Examiner, the proviso applies only to "purely" informational picketing.

Accordingly, giving due weight to the terms of the proviso to Section 8(b)(7)(C), we find the instant picketing unlawful and not protected by the proviso because it was not for the sole purpose permitted in the proviso, namely, that of truthfully advising the public that Crown did not employ union members or have a union contract.

We conclude, contrary to the Trial Examiner, that the Respondent's picketing for more than a reasonable period of time after November 13, 1959, violated Section 8(b)(7)(C) of the Act, as alleged. * * *

MEMBERS JENKINS and FANNING, dissenting:

We would affirm the Trial Examiner and, in agreement with him, find that the picketing in this case falls squarely within the proviso to Section 8(b)(7)(C) which states that "nothing in this subparagraph (C) shall be construed to prohibit any picketing or other publicity for the purpose of truthfully advising the public (including consumers) that an employer does not employ members of, or have a contract with, a labor organization."

We are of the opinion that this proviso should be interpreted as having vitality rather than as a merely meaningless adjunct of a statutory enactment. To the extent that the proviso carves out a significant exception to the general ban on recognition and organizational picketing, it has a real meaning and effect in the statutory scheme. Our disagreement with our colleagues stems from the fact that their interpretation of the proviso renders it wholly ineffectual, as if indeed Congress had inserted mere language intended to serve as a useless appendage in an academic vacuum.

Section 8(b)(7)(C), in its present form, was proposed in conference as a compromise to the House version of the bill in this area of legislation. That version was substantially as enacted, but *without* the proviso. From the structure of the section as it emerged from conference, it seems clear that Congress intended to permit a kind of picketing which, but for the proviso, would have come within the prohibition of the section. It logically follows that the intent was to exclude from the ban picketing which, while it embraced the proscribed object of recognition or organization, was nonetheless permitted because it met two specific conditions. The first condition was, as already stated, "of truthfully advising the public (including consumers) that an employer does not employ members of, or have a contract with, a labor organization." The second condition was added immediately after the first, i.e., "unless an effect of such picketing is to induce any individual employed by any other person in the course of his employment not to pick up, deliver or transport any goods or not to perform any services."[6] In other words, Congress by way of compromise, excluded from its prohibition recognitional or organizational picketing that met these two conditions.

This reading of the proviso, we submit, gives life to its language. The interpretation our colleagues give it makes it, for all practical purposes, ineffectual and superfluous. * * *

To read the proviso the way our colleagues do would, it seems to us, have the patent effect of creating a new unfair labor practice not within the contemplation of Congress. For, if it is an unfair labor practice when a union does *not* engage in recognitional or organizational picketing if "an effect of such picketing is to induce any individual employed by any other person in the course of his employment not to pick up, deliver or transport any goods or not to perform any services," the prohibition obviously embraces an area wholly *outside* the statutory intendment. Even a casual reading of Section 8(b)(7) and its legislative history makes it abundantly clear that Congress was dealing solely with recognitional and organizational picketing. It could have dealt with other forms of picketing in that section, but did not. To hold that a work stoppage would convert nonrecognitional and nonorganizational picketing into an unfair labor practice under Section 8(b)(7)(C) is to write into the 1959 amendments an additional unfair labor practice. This, we feel is evident, Congress clearly did not do. We do not believe it is for the Board to rewrite the 1959 amendments.

Judge Swygert, in John C. Getreu v. Bartenders and Hotel and Restaurant Employees Union Local 58, etc. (Fowler Hotel, Inc.), 181 F.Supp. 738 (D.C.N.Ind.), accurately appraised the meaning of the proviso:

"It is difficult, if not impossible, to imagine any kind of informational picketing pertaining to an employer's failure or refusal to employ union members or to have a collective bargaining agreement where another object of such picketing would not be ultimate union recognition or bargaining. In most instances certainly the aim of such informational picketing could only

---

6. Our colleagues concede, and the record establishes, that Respondent's picketing did not have this "effect."

be to bring economic pressure upon the employer to recognize and bargain with the labor organization. To adopt petitioner's interpretation of subparagraph (C) would make the second proviso entirely meaningless."

Thus, he concluded that—

" * * * subparagraph (C) means that although 'an object' of picketing may be bargaining, * * * it is immunized from the statute if 'the purpose' of such picketing is also truthfully to inform the public that the employer does not have a contract with the union and further if the picketing does not curtail picking up, delivery or transportation of goods or the performance of services."

The legislative history fully supports our view. Immediately prior to the statement by Senator Kennedy that "purely informational picketing cannot be curtailed," to which our colleagues refer, he advised the Senate that the House bill had "unnecessarily restricted normal, legitimate trade union activity"; that the Senate conferees had "secured important changes in the restrictive provisions" of the House bill; that the House bill would have applied to virtually all recognitional and organizational picketing "even though the pickets did not stop truck deliveries," and that the Senate conferees agreed to a ban on picketing which appealed to the public *only if* the picketing resulted in the "refusal of other employees to cross the picket line." It was in *this* context that Senator Kennedy went on to state that publicity picketing which did not result in the refusal of any other employees to cross the picket line—"purely informational picketing"—was not prohibited by Section 8(b)(7)(C).[8] * * *

As the picketing in this case satisfied the proviso, we would dismiss the complaint.

SUPPLEMENTAL DECISION AND ORDER
135 N.L.R.B. 1183 (1962).
Affirmed, 327 F.2d 351 (9th Cir.1964).

On February 20, 1961, the Board (Members Jenkins and Fanning dissenting) issued a Decision and Order in this case finding that Respondent Unions had engaged in violations of Section 8(b)(7)(C) of the Act. Thereafter, on or about April 10, 1961, Respondent Unions filed a motion for reconsideration and General Counsel filed a motion for clarification. The Charging Parties filed an opposition to motion for reconsideration. * * *

1. For reasons indicated in our Supplemental Decision and Order in *International Hod Carriers, etc. (Charles A. Blinne, d/b/a C.A. Blinne Construction Company)*, 135 NLRB 1153, issued this day, we believe reconsideration is appropriate here. This is particularly true in the instant case where General Counsel, the prevailing party in the case, deems a motion for clarification appropriate. As General Counsel stated in his motion for clarification:

"The Decision and Order contains the Board's first direct interpretation concerning the scope and applicability of the second proviso to Section 8(b)(7) (C) of the Act. In view of its broad significance in the administration of the

---

8. See Legislative History of the Labor-Management Reporting and Disclosure Act of 1959 (vol. 2, p. 1431).

Act, it is important and desirable that the Board's position be explicit and readily ascertainable by the many parties and persons affected by the Board's interpretation."

2.   Because the facts and the issues in this case are clearly delineated in the majority and minority opinions heretofore rendered, we believe it would be profitless to restate them here.   After careful study of the two opinions, and in the light of our further reappraisal of the statutory scheme, set forth in greater detail in our Supplemental Decision and Order in *Blinne,* supra, we now conclude that the dissenting opinion more accurately reflects the congressional intent.   Accordingly, we adopt the dissenting opinion in the first decision.

3.   We note, however, that in the new dissenting opinion attached hereto, our colleagues espouse what appears to be a different position from that which they expounded in their original decision herein.   On that occasion they concluded that the "publicity" proviso immunized picketing only "where the sole object is dissemination of information divorced from a present object of recognition" (130 NLRB at 573).

This narrow interpretation made the proviso a contradiction in terms, for the express words of the proviso make it clear that the proviso applies where organization, recognition, or bargaining is an object.   Thus, "does not employ members of" clearly imports a present object of organization, and "[does not] have a contract with" just as clearly implies a recognition and bargaining object.

Departing from the illogic of their first construction, therefore, our colleagues now argue that the proviso saves picketing only if "there is no independent evidence of either a recognition or organizational object" (and there is, of course, an absence of stoppages).   But this new construction likewise imports into the statutory language a criterion with no foundation in the text, no basis in the legislative history, and no correlation with the legislative remedies devised to meet the actual problems presented.   Thus, in effect, our colleagues would read Congress as having said to the unions, "Only if you are *not* trying to organize, to secure recognition, or to get a contract, can you picket for the purpose of telling the public that the employer won't grant these objectives."[4]   Or, they would read Congress as saying, "You can picket only where the picketing does not coincide with any other union activity for recognition, bargaining, or organization."   Surely, we cannot assume that Congress, out of its hard-wrought legislative compromise, emerged with nothing more than such a sterile, untimely, and unrealistic license to carry on a traditional means of enlisting public sympathy.

The new basis for a narrow construction of the proviso is as unconvincing to us as the old.

4.   The dissenting opinion of our colleagues appears to suggest that picketing cannot be for "the purpose of truthfully advising the public" if subsumed in that activity is "an object" of recognition, bargaining, or organization.   We perceive no inconsistency and the text of Section 8(b)(7)(C) makes it obvious in our view that Congress perceived none.   We might note in passing, however, that while proviso picketing precludes the holding of an expedited election, nevertheless, if the proviso picketing is for recognition or bargaining, as distinguished from organization, a routine 9(c) representation petition would, if other necessary preconditions were satisfied, be entertained.

Accordingly, on the grounds set forth in the original dissenting opinion and for the additional reasons set forth herein, we direct dismissal of the complaint.

[The dissenting opinion of Member Rogers and Leedom is omitted.]

Note

Both the Crown Cafeteria case and the Claude Everett Construction case which follows may be pictorialized in pedagogically profitable fashion. The image is of a box or trap—"the 8(b)(7) trap." In order to fall into the trap, the union must engage in organizational or recognitional picketing. Once in the trap (but *only* then), the escape hatches ("provisos") of 8(b)(7)(C) may become relevant. In these terms, how are the two cases distinguishable?

HOUSTON BUILDING AND CONSTRUCTION TRADES COUNCIL ("CLAUDE EVERETT CONSTRUCTION")

National Labor Relations Board, 1962.
136 N.L.R.B. 321.

*   *   *

The facts as found by the Trial Examiner are not in dispute. The Respondent, a council of local unions in the building and construction industry in the Houston, Texas, area, inquired on March 8, 1961, about the wage rates of Claude Everett Construction Company, a general construction contractor in that area. The Respondent's representative was told by Wilson, the Company's construction superintendent, that it operated an "open shop", and that its wage rates were lower than those negotiated in the area by the local unions which were members of the Respondent. On March 10, 1961, the Respondent wrote to the Company protesting its "substandard" wages and threatening to picket its construction site on March 13, unless "prevailing" rates were paid. When this letter had not been answered by March 16, the Respondent began picketing the Company's jobsite with a sign which read as follows:

> "Houston Building and Construction Trades Council, AFL–CIO protests substandard wages and conditions being paid on this job by Claude Everett Company. Houston Building and Construction Trades Council does not intend by this picket line to induce or encourage the employees of any other employer to engage in a strike or a concerted refusal to work."

Such picketing continued for more than 30 days without the filing of a petition under Section 9(c) of the Act. The Respondent has never been certified as the representative of the Company's employees. The parties stipulated at the hearing that the picketing interfered with deliveries and services by inducing individuals employed by suppliers, service companies, and common carriers not to make pickups or deliveries or to perform services for the Company.

The Trial Examiner found that the Respondent picketed the Company to require it to conform its wage rates to those paid by employers having union contracts. Relying on the original Board decision in the *Calumet Contrac-*

tors case,[2] he concluded that such picketing violated Section 8(b)(7)(C) of the Act. Subsequent to the issuance of his Intermediate Report, however, the Board, having reconsidered the *Calumet Contractors* case,[3] found the picketing there involved not unlawful, and stated that:

"* * * Respondent's admitted objective to require the Association * * * to conform standards of employment to those prevailing in the area, is not tantamount to, nor does it have an objective of, recognition or bargaining. A union may legitimately be concerned that a particular employer is undermining area standards of employment by maintaining lower standards. It may be willing to forgo recognition and bargaining provided subnormal working conditions are eliminated from area considerations."

While the *Calumet Contractors* case arose under Section 8(b)(4)(C) of the Act, which prohibits only recognitional picketing, whereas the instant case arose under Section 8(b)(7)(C), which proscribes both recognitional and organizational picketing, the language of both subsections is similar, and the rationale in that case is equally applicable herein. The Respondent in the present case did not, in its conversation with the Company, its letter to the Company, or its picket sign, claim to represent the Company's employees, request recognition by the Company, or solicit employees of the Company to become members of any of the locals which are members of the Respondent. Moreover, the undisputed testimony of Executive Secretary Graham reveals that the Respondent Union has on numerous occasions in the past made similar protests against substandard wages paid by other employers without ever requesting recognition as the bargaining representative of their employees. Thus, it is clear, from the entire record, that the objective of the Respondent's picketing was to induce the Company to raise its wage rates to the union scale prevailing in the area. We cannot, as do our dissenting colleagues, equate this attempt to maintain area wage standards with conduct "forcing or requiring an employer to recognize or bargain with a labor organization as the representative of his employees, or forcing or requiring the employees * * * to accept or select such labor organization as their collective bargaining representative," the conduct proscribed by Section 8(b)(7).

Nor do we agree with our dissenting colleagues that the fact that the picketing interfered with deliveries and services in itself constitutes a violation of Section 8(b)(7)(C). To determine the effect of Section 8(b)(7)(C), we must look at the section in its entirety, in accord with the long-established principle of statutory construction that a legislative enactment is to be read in its entirety, not in bits and pieces. It is clear that this section, read as a whole, declares picketing by an uncertified union unlawful if it has a recognitional or organizational objective and if a petition has not been filed within a reasonable time, and that the interruption-of-deliveries clause does not enter into the picture unless the picketing can first be shown to have

2. International Hod Carriers, Building and Common Laborers' Union of America, Local No. 41, AFL–CIO (Calumet Contractors Association), 130 NLRB 78.

3. International Hod Carriers, Building and Common Laborers' Union of America, Local No. 41, AFL–CIO (Calumet Contractors Association), 133 NLRB 512 (Members Rodgers and Leedom dissenting).

such a prohibited objective. * * * Our dissenting colleagues interpret the second proviso of subparagraph (C) as though it creates a completely independent unfair labor practice, without reference to the fact that it is a subsidiary clause in a section which initially prohibits picketing with a recognitional or organizational objective. Such a reading would remove the proviso from its statutory setting, an interpretive result we feel constrained to avoid.

Accordingly, on the basis of the facts in the present case and of "the thrust of all the Section 8(b)(7) provisions," we find that the Respondent's picketing did not have a recognitional or organizational objective, and, therefore, that it did not violate the Act even though the picketing interfered with deliveries and services. Accordingly, we shall dismiss the complaint.

*   *   *

MEMBERS RODGERS and LEEDOM, dissenting:

We agree with the Trial Examiner's conclusion that the Respondent's picketing in this case was for "the proscribed object of 'forcing or requiring an employer to recognize or bargain with a labor organization as the representative of his employees, [and] forcing or requiring the employees of an employer to accept or select such labor organization as their collective bargaining representative,'" and that this picketing was therefore violative of Section 8(b)(7)(C).

Our colleagues of the majority deem controlling here the second decision in the *Calumet Contractors* case, which reversed the original decision. * * * Their holding does not withstand scrutiny in the light of industrial realities.

As to whether there was a recognitional objective in the present case, it is undenied that the Respondent Union was demanding a change in the Company's wage rates to conform to standards in the area. The alternative open to the Company was either to suffer a picket line or to comply with the Respondent Union's demand. Our colleagues, however, choose to view the problem unrealistically. For, they fail to take into consideration either the extent to which the standards of the Respondent Union are applicable to the Company's operations, the complications attendant upon changing a wage pattern, or the many factors that determine the pattern. Otherwise, they would readily concede that any effort on the part of the Company to adjust the Respondent's wage demand to its circumstances would have necessitated negotiations; that such negotiations would constitute bargaining with the Respondent Union as though it were the representative of the Company's employees; and that such recognition and bargaining would manifestly be the result of the Respondent forcing or requiring the Company by a picket line, to " * * * recognize or bargain with a labor organization as the representative of [its] employees * * * " in violation of Section 8(b)(7).

Nor can we lose sight of the organizational objective implicit in Respondent's picketing. We note further that the picket sign, after protesting the Company's "substandard wages and conditions," expressly disclaimed any intent of the Respondent that "the employees of any other employer" should engage in a work stoppage. The sign was silent as to the Respondent's intent with regard to the Company's employees. By dint of this omission, Respondent's real purpose is emphasized. For the Union was thereby calling upon the Company's employees to join with it in getting the Company to change its existing wage rates—clearly organizational and recognitional objectives.

Nor can the Respondent Union take refuge in the proviso to Section 8(b) (7)(C) to protect its recognitional or organizational picketing. In this regard, it is obvious that the picketing did not conform to the language of the proviso and the Respondent Union makes no claim to the contrary. * * *

Note

1. Since picketing or the threat thereof is a necessary element of a Section 8(b)(7) offense, the threshold question of what constitutes "picketing" may arise. In NLRB v. Local 182, International Brotherhood of Teamsters, 314 F.2d 53 (2d Cir.1963), union representatives planted two signs in a snowbank beside the entrance to the employer's premises, stationed themselves in heated autos parked on the shoulder of the adjacent highway, and, when trucks approached, emerged to speak with the drivers, after which the trucks would turn away. This conduct was held to constitute picketing; the Board's order against the union was enforced. On the other hand, in NLRB v. United Furniture Workers, 337 F.2d 936 (2d Cir.1964), enforcement was denied and the case remanded for additional findings and conclusions by the Board on the following facts: Union representatives affixed their signs to poles and trees in front of the employer's plant at 6 A.M. of each working day and then stationed themselves in autos in a parking lot across the street from the plant, where they remained until 3 P.M. when they removed the signs and departed. The court stated: "There is no indication whatever whether the men in parked cars were located in close proximity to Jamestown's premises so that they could be or were seen by employees, customers, or suppliers entering the plant. Nor does the record disclose whether the men in the cars were reasonably identifiable as union representatives." 337 F.2d at 940.

What should be the test for determining whether ambiguous conduct constitutes picketing? Is, for example, handbilling "picketing?"

2. A problem concerning the scope of protection accorded to informational picketing by the second proviso of Section 8(b)(7)(C) is demonstrated in Barker Brothers v. NLRB, 328 F.2d 431 (9th Cir.1964). In that case the picketing was carried out at eighteen of the employer's stores over a twelve-week period, and resulted in (1) three truckdrivers employed by other employers refusing to deliver one shipment of merchandise each, (2) the delay of other deliveries on at least three occasions, and (3) a few hours delay in the performance of window cleaning and window glazing services by employees of other employers. These refusals and delays occurred despite the strong efforts of the union to inform the Teamsters, other unions, and the public generally that the picketing was not intended to stop deliveries or services at the picketed stores. The picketing was confined to consumer entrances and directed at consumers only; no picketing occurred at delivery entrances. Both Board and court held the picketing to be protected under the second proviso of Section 8(b)(7)(C), rejecting the argument that the "unless" clause of the proviso, read literally, rendered the picketing unprotected under the proviso. The "unless" clause, the Board and court held, was not to be read in a fashion denying protection because of isolated stoppages not shown to have, in fact, injured the employer's business. The court explained:

> "[W]e do not think that the language is so clear as petitioners say it is. They interpret the words 'any goods' and 'any services' to mean one item of goods and one bit of service. Another possible, and we think, equally

reasonable interpretation of the language on its face could be that the proviso does not apply unless the effect of the picketing is to induce an individual 'not to pick up, deliver or transport *any* goods' at all, in other words, a total refusal to deliver while the picket line is there. The same, of course, would apply to the language referring to *'any* services.' There is no evidence whatever that would support a finding that anyone was so induced. We think that this suggested meaning is about as bizarre a reading of the statute as is petitioners'." 328 F.2d at 434.

3. How would you diagnose what Congress was trying to accomplish in Section 8(b)(7)(C) and its second proviso? Does explanation lie in the "peaceful picketing = free speech *plus*" equation? See the discussion supra pp. 329–330.

4. As observed in the Note following the Crown Cafeteria case, supra p. 387, and as demonstrated in the Claude Everett Construction case, the scope of protection afforded to informational picketing by the second proviso of Section 8(b)(7)(C) is an issue only where the charged union is engaging in organizational or recognitional picketing. Claude Everett excepts "area standards" picketing as being neither organizational nor recognitional in purpose. How far should this exception be carried? Suppose, for example, the picketing union were to demand that the picketed employer were to agree to honor *all* of the provisions of a collective bargaining agreement which the union had previously executed with competing employers in the industry, excepting only recognition of the union as collective bargaining representative of the subject employees. Should such picketing be characterized as "area standards" picketing or, instead, as "organizational or recognitional" picketing? In other words, how far should a union be permitted to press the area-standards exception before having crossed the line into recognitional picketing?

In NLRB v. Local Union No. 103, International Association of Bridge Workers, 434 U.S. 335, 98 S.Ct. 651, 54 L.Ed.2d 586 (1978), the Court accepted the Board's characterizing of such picketing as recognitional in character rather than area standards. The Court stated:

"Determining the object, or objects, of labor union picketing is a recurring and necessary function of the Board. Its resolution of these mixed factual and legal questions normally survives judicial review. A type of activity frequently found to violate § 8(b)(7) is picketing ostensibly for the purpose of forcing an employer to abide by terms incorporated into agreements between the union and other employers. Even in cases where the union expressly disavows any recognitional intent, acceptance of the uniform terms proposed by the union can have the 'net effect' of establishing the union 'as the negotiator of wage rates and benefits.' Centralia Building and Construction Trades Council v. NLRB, 124 U.S.App.D.C. 212, 214, 363 F.2d 699, 701 (1966). 'The Board has held that informing the public that an employer does not employ members of a labor organization indicates an organizational object, and that stating that an employer does not have a contract with a labor organization similarly implies an object of recognition and bargaining.' Carpenters Local 906, 204 N.L.R.B. 138, 139 (1973). Hence, picketing to enforce area standards, where an employer had been assured by notice from the union that 'while we expect you to observe the wages, hours, and other benefits set forth in these documents, we do not expect to seek any collective bargaining relationship with your firm,' has been held to violate § 8(b)(7). Hotel & Restaurant Employees, Local Joint Executive Board (Holiday Inns of America, Inc.), 169 N.L.R.B. 683 (1968).

"The Circuit Courts of Appeals have upheld the Board in these inferences. 'Though [the legend "Non-Union Conditions" on the picket signs] could be interpreted as merely a protest of the restaurant's working conditions, it was reasonable for the NLRB to conclude that the message * * * was at least in part that the union desired to alter a non-union working situation by obtaining recognition. In the absence of countervailing evidence, the NLRB could thus determine that the purpose of the picketing was recognitional.' San Francisco Local Joint Board v. NLRB, 163 U.S.App.D.C. 234, 239, 501 F.2d 794, 799 (1974). See also NLRB v. Carpenters Local 745, 450 F.2d 1255 (CA9 1971), and cases cited therein. * * *" 434 U.S. at 342 n. 7.

(The Bridge Workers case involved the application of Section 8(b)(7)(C) to picketing for enforcement of a Section 8(f) construction industry pre-hire agreement. For a fuller understanding of this context, see infra Note 4, p. 445.)

5. The Board's "reconsideration" of its original decisions in the Blinne and Crown Cafeteria cases offers dramatic example of the flip-flopping potential of an agency constituted like the NLRB—five members with five-year staggered terms of office. Those two key cases were among several of similar significance decided in February, 1961, in last-gasp fashion by the so-called "Eisenhower Board." Within a month and a half after these decisions, Fanning, a dissenting member of the Eisenhower Board, was joined by two new appointees (one of the vacancies was regular, one fortuitous), and the "Kennedy Board" was in being. The granting of the motions for reconsideration in the several key cases was one of its first orders of business. (For discussion of some of the pros and cons of this "political jurisprudence," see supra pp. 227–228.)

The foregoing developments are discussed and the pertinent cases analyzed in Meltzer, Organizational Picketing and the NLRB: Five on a Seesaw, 30 U.Chi. L.Rev. 78 (1962).

C. SECONDARY BOYCOTTS AND "HOT CARGO"

Secondary pressure—pressure brought to bear upon B in order to extract some concession from A—has long been frowned upon by the law. Loewe v. Lawlor, supra p. 55, and Duplex, supra p. 62, demonstrate early efforts to regulate such conduct by means of the common law and the Sherman Act. Not until 1947, however, did Congress make an express effort to regulate the application of secondary pressure. Section 8(b)(4)(A) of the Taft-Hartley Act specified certain kinds of such pressure to be unfair labor practices. This section is the subject of the next several cases. The reader will be saved some confusion if he understands at the outset that in the Landrum-Griffin Act of 1959 the structure of Section 8(b)(4) was amended by moving the main substance of the former Section 8(b)(4)(A) into Section 8(b)(4)(B) (see Statutory Supplement); as a consequence, cases arising after the 1959 amendments refer to Section 8(b)(4)(B) in situations where the prior cases referred to Section 8(b)(4)(A).

Section 8(b)(4) is, without question, the most involved and difficult provision in the Act. The section makes it illegal to seek to achieve certain objects through the use of certain means. Both a proscribed means and a proscribed object must be present for a violation to be made out. Simply stated, the proscribed means are strikes, picketing, and threats thereof (i and ii); the proscribed objects are forcing an employer or self-employed person to join a union or employer organization or to enter into an agreement to engage in secondary boycotts [so-called "hot cargo" agreements proscribed by Section 8(e)] (A); forcing a person to cease doing business with another person [secondary boycott] ((A) in Taft-Hartley; now (B)); forcing an employer to recognize one union when another union has been certified as the representative of its employees (C); forcing an employer to assign particular work to the members of one union instead of another [jurisdictional dispute] (D).

NATIONAL LABOR RELATIONS BOARD v. BUSINESS MACHINE AND OFFICE APPLIANCE MECHANICS CONFERENCE BOARD, LOCAL 459, IUE ("ROYAL TYPEWRITER")

United States Court of Appeals, Second Circuit, 1955.
228 F.2d 553.

Certiorari denied, 351 U.S. 962 (1956).

LUMBARD, CIRCUIT JUDGE. This case arose out of a labor dispute between the Royal Typewriter Company and the Business Machine and Office Appliance Mechanics Conference Board, Local 459, IUE–CIO, the certified bargaining agent of Royal's typewriter mechanics and other service personnel. The National Labor Relations Board now seeks enforcement of an order directing the Union to cease and desist from certain picketing and to post appropriate notices.

The findings of the Board, adequately supported by the record, disclose the following facts, about which there is no significant dispute. On about March 23, 1954, the Union, being unable to reach agreement with Royal on the terms of a contract, called the Royal service personnel out on strike. The service employees customarily repair typewriters either at Royal's branch offices or at its customers' premises. Royal has several arrangements under which it is obligated to render service to its customers. First, Royal's warranty on each new machine obligates it to provide free inspection and repair for one year. Second, for a fixed periodic fee Royal contracts to service machines not under warranty. Finally, Royal is committed to repairing typewriters rented from it or loaned by it to replace machines undergoing repair. Of course, in addition Royal provides repair services on call by non-contract users.

During the strike Royal differentiated between calls from customers to whom it owed a repair obligation and others. Royal's office personnel were instructed to tell the latter to call some independent repair company listed in the telephone directory. Contract customers, however, were advised to select such an independent from the directory, to have the repair made, and to send a receipted invoice to Royal for reimbursement for reasonable repairs within their agreement with Royal. Consequently many of Royal's contract customers had repair services performed by various independent repair companies. In most instances the customer sent Royal the unpaid repair bill and Royal paid the independent company directly. Among the independent companies paid directly by Royal for repairs made for such customers were Typewriter Maintenance and Sales Company and Tytell Typewriter Company.

On and after April 13, 1954 the Union picketed some of Royal's larger customers whom it had reason to believe were having independent companies do repair work on Royal contract machines. This picketing continued until restrained on June 15, 1954 by a temporary injunction issued by the District Court for the Southern District of New York, 122 F.Supp. 43. During this time the Union picketed some 37 customers of Royal at their principal offices in Manhattan and Brooklyn, usually in large office buildings. This picketing was in all cases peaceful and orderly. The Board found it unlawful with respect to six of Royal's customers: Electrolux Corporation, Royal Indemnity Insurance Co., Lily-Tulip Cup Corporation, Vick Chemical Co., New York Life Insurance Co., and American Can Co. With respect to these companies the Board found that the picketing took place before entrances "commonly used by members of the public, by employees of the picketed firm, and by employees of any other tenants of the building, and also by deliverymen making light deliveries." There was no evidence that the picketing took place at entrances used exclusively by employees. No violation was found with respect to the other customers because the Board found that there was no evidence that the picketing took place before entrances used or likely to be used by employees.

From April 13th until April 23rd, or shortly thereafter, the pickets carried signs reading (with minor variations and with the picketed customer's name inserted):

"Royal Business Machines In N.Y. Life Ins. Co.
are being repaired by Scab Labor Local 459, IUE–CIO"

Sometime after April 23rd the words "Notice to the Public Only" were added to the signs in large letters at the top. This was on advice of counsel after a conference with representatives of the Board who suggested that the picketing was unlawful. The picketing was carried on during ordinary business hours and during the time when at least some employees would be going to lunch. In at least one instance picketing began before the start of employees' working hours.

One of the picketed customers, Charles Pfizer, did agree to discontinue doing business with Royal and the Union withdrew its pickets. There is no evidence to indicate that this came about through any pressure on or from any of Pfizer's employees.

The Board found, and it is conceded, that an object of the picketing of Royal's customers was to induce the customers to cease doing business with Royal. The Union contended that it sought to do this only by embarrassing the firms picketed and bringing its grievance to the attention of the customers of those firms and the general public. The Trial Examiner found that the picketing constituted inducement and encouragement of employees, that the Union's professed intent not to influence employees was no defense, and that the picketing was therefore unlawful. These findings the Board adopted.

During May 1954 the Union also picketed four independent typewriter repair companies who had been doing work covered by Royal's contracts pursuant to the arrangement described above. The Board found this picketing unlawful with respect to Typewriter Maintenance and Tytell. Typewriter Maintenance was picketed for about three days and Tytell for several hours on one day. In each instance the picketing, which was peaceful and orderly, took place before entrances used in common by employees, deliverymen and the general public. The signs read substantially as follows (with the appropriate repair company name inserted):

"Notice To The Public Only
Employees Of Royal Typewriter Co. On Strike

Tytell Typewriter Company Employees Are Being Used As Strikebreakers

———

Business Machine & Office Appliance Mechanics Union, Local
459, IUE–CIO"

Both before and after this picketing, which took place in mid-May, Tytell and Typewriter Maintenance did work on Royal accounts and received payment directly from Royal. Royal's records show that Typewriter Maintenance's first voucher was passed for payment by Royal on April 20, 1954 and Tytell's first voucher was passed for payment on May 3, 1954. After these dates each independent serviced various of Royal's customers on numerous occasions and received payment directly from Royal.

With one exception there was no evidence that the picketing of either the customers or the repair companies resulted in a strike or refusal to work by any employee. Such evidence as there was indicated that no employee ceased work or refused to operate any Royal typewriter or other machine. The one exception was Gordon Speer, a repairman for Lewis Business Machines Service Company, who was sent on April 22nd to repair a Royal typewriter at the Royal Indemnity Insurance Company. On approaching the Royal Insurance office he saw pickets carrying signs as described above, without the words "Notice to the Public" as these were not added until a few days later. Not wishing to cross the picket line, he called his office, explained that because of the pickets he would not make the repair, and was instructed to return.

On the above facts the Trial Examiner and the Board found that both the customer picketing and the repair company picketing violated § 8(b)(4) of the National Labor Relations Act, * * * which provides:

"It shall be an unfair labor practice for a labor organization or its agents—

" * * * to induce or encourage the employees of any employer to engage in, a strike or a concerted refusal in the course of their employment * * * to perform any services, where an object thereof is: (A) forcing or requiring * * * any employer * * * to cease doing business with any other person; * * *."

With respect to each type of picketing the question before us is the same: Was there substantial evidence on the whole record to support the Board's finding that the Union's acts constituted an unfair labor practice under this section? Universal Camera Corp. v. N.L.R.B., 1951, 340 U.S. 474, 71 S.Ct. 456, 95 L.Ed. 456.

THE INDEPENDENT REPAIR COMPANY PICKETING

We are of the opinion that the Board's finding with respect to the repair company picketing cannot be sustained. The independent repair companies were so allied with Royal that the Union's picketing of their premises was not prohibited by § 8(b)(4)(A).

We approve the "ally" doctrine which had its origin in a well reasoned opinion by Judge Rifkind in the Ebasco case, Douds v. Metropolitan Federation of Architects, Engineers, Chemists & Technicians, Local 231, D.C.S.D. N.Y.1948, 75 F.Supp. 672, 676. Ebasco, a corporation engaged in the business of providing engineering services, had a close business relationship with Project, a firm providing similar services. Ebasco subcontracted some of its work to Project and when it did so Ebasco supervised the work of Project's employees and paid Project for the time spent by Project's employees on Ebasco's work plus a factor for overhead and profit. When Ebasco's employees went on strike, Ebasco transferred a greater percentage of its work to Project, including some jobs that had already been started by Ebasco's employees. When Project refused to heed the Union's requests to stop doing Ebasco's work, the Union picketed Project and induced some of Project's employees to cease work. On these facts Judge Rifkind found that Project was not "doing business" with Ebasco within the meaning of § 8(b)(4) (A) and that the Union had therefore not committed an unfair labor practice under that section. He reached this result by looking to the legislative history of the Taft-Hartley Act and to the history of the secondary boycotts which it sought to outlaw. He determined that Project was not a person " 'wholly unconcerned in the disagreement between an employer and his employees' " such as § 8(b)(4)(A) was designed to protect. This result has been described as a proper interpretation of the Act by its principal sponsor, Senator Taft, 95 Cong.Rec. (1949) 8709, and President Eisenhower in his January 1954 recommendations to Congress for revision of the Act included a suggestion which would make this rule explicit.

Here there was evidence of only one instance where Royal contacted an independent (Manhattan Typewriter Service, not named in the complaint) to see whether it could handle some of Royal's calls. Apart from that incident there is no evidence that Royal made any arrangement with an independent directly. It is obvious, however, that what the independents did would inevitably tend to break the strike. As Judge Rifkind pointed out in the Ebasco case: "The economic effect upon Ebasco's employees was precisely that which would flow from Ebasco's hiring strikebreakers to work on its own premises." And at 95 Cong.Rec. (1949) page 8709 Senator Taft said:

> "The spirit of the Act is not intended to protect a man who in the last case I mentioned is cooperating with a primary employer and taking his work and doing the work which he is unable to do because of the strike."

President Eisenhower's recommendation referred to above was to make it explicit "that concerted action against (1) an employer who is performing 'farmed-out' work for the account of another employer whose employees are on strike * * * will not be treated as a secondary boycott." Text of President's Message to Congress on Taft-Hartley Amendments, January 11, 1954. At least one commentator has suggested that the enactment of this change would add nothing to existing law. Cushman, Secondary Boycotts and the Taft-Hartley Law, 6 Syracuse L.Rev. 109, 121 (1954). Moreover, there is evidence that the secondary strikes and boycotts sought to be outlawed by § 8(b)(4)(A) were only those which had been unlawful at common law. 93 Cong.Rec. (1947) 3950, 4323 (Senator Taft), 2 Legislative History of the Labor-Management Relations Act, 1947, pp. 1006, 1106. And although secondary boycotts were generally unlawful, it has been held that the common law does not proscribe union activity designed to prevent employers from doing the farmed-out work of a struck employer. Iron Molders Union No. 125 of Milwaukee, Wis. v. Allis-Chalmers Co., 7 Cir., 1908, 166 F. 45, 51, 20 L.R.A.,N.S., 315. Thus the picketing of the independent typewriter companies was not the kind of secondary activity which § 8(b)(4)(A) of the Taft-Hartley Act was designed to outlaw. Where an employer is attempting to avoid the economic impact of a strike by securing the services of others to do his work, the striking union obviously has a great interest, and we think a proper interest in preventing those services from being rendered. This interest is more fundamental than the interest in bringing pressure on customers of the primary employer. Nor are those who render such services completely uninvolved in the primary strike. By doing the work of the primary employer they secure benefits themselves at the same time that they aid the primary employer. The ally employer may easily extricate himself from the dispute and insulate himself from picketing by refusing to do that work. A case may arise where the ally employer is unable to determine that the work he is doing is "farmed-out." We need not decide whether the picketing of such an employer would be lawful, for that is not the situation here. The existence of the strike, the receipt of checks from Royal, and the picketing itself certainly put the independents on notice that some of the work they were doing might be work farmed-out by Royal. Wherever they worked on new Royal machines they were probably aware that such machines were covered by a Royal warranty. But in any event, before working on a Royal machine they could have inquired of the customer whether it was covered by a Royal contract and refused to work on it if it was. There is no indication that they made any effort to avoid doing Royal's work. The Union was justified in picketing them in order to induce them to make such an effort. We therefore hold that an employer is not within the protection of § 8(b)(4)(A) when he knowingly does work which would otherwise be done by the striking employees of the primary employer and where this work is paid for by the primary employer pursuant to an arrangement devised and originated by him to enable him to meet his contractual obligations. The result must be the same whether or not the primary employer makes any direct arrangement with the employers providing the services.

THE CUSTOMER PICKETING

The picketing of Royal's customers was clearly secondary picketing with the object defined in § 8(b)(4)(A). The Union conceded that its aim was to force the customers to cease doing business with Royal and with the independent repair companies. But the Taft-Hartley Act does not proscribe all secondary activity. We have held that requests and threats addressed directly to secondary employers are not illegal, * * * and we have indicated that solicitation of customers of secondary employers is also lawful. * * * The only thing proscribed by § 8(b)(4) is inducement or encouragement of the employees of customers.

We turn then to the question of what constitutes such unlawful inducement and encouragement. We have recently decided that these words do not require a finding that the picketing was successful in convincing any employee to strike or cease performing services. * * * We based our reasoning partially on legislative history indicating that *attempts* to induce or encourage were proscribed. In the case now before us, however, the Trial Examiner found that the Union's intent not to induce employees was irrelevant if there was in fact inducement of the employees. Hence he made no finding that it was an object of the Union to influence employees, nor did the Board make any additional finding in this respect. We therefore have a situation where the Board found neither an attempt to affect employees nor any actual effect upon them from which the attempt could be inferred. The Trial Examiner went no further than to find that the "natural and probable consequence of" the picketing was to induce or encourage the employees to engage in concerted activity. We must therefore consider whether such a finding is a sufficient one upon which to predicate the conclusion that § 8(b)(4)(A) has been violated and if so whether the finding here was based upon substantial evidence.

The words of the statute, "to induce or encourage," do not necessarily carry with them a requirement that intent to induce or encourage be shown. It may be true that something less than a finding of specific intent to induce or encourage employees will suffice to support the Board's conclusion that § 8(b)(4)(A) has been violated. If it were shown that such inducement was the inevitable result or even the "natural and probable consequence" of the picketing this would perhaps be enough. Certainly if it were shown that the employees actually ceased work, no finding of intent would be necessary. But in this case there was insufficient evidence to support any of these findings. It was not shown that the picketing had any tendency to induce the employees to strike or cease performing services. The evidence showed, on the contrary, that no employee refused to work or to use a Royal machine.

* * * The Union picketed 37 of Royal's customers on many different days over a period of three months and the General Counsel was apparently unable to produce evidence of any effect upon a single one of the many thousands of employees of these customers. With respect to 31 of the firms no violation was found because it was not even shown that the Union picketed entrances "used or likely to be used" by employees. The Speer incident is not relevant because he was an employee of one of the repair companies whom we have found the Union had a right to picket. * * *

* * * Since we find in this case neither intent to induce, nor effective inducement, nor even probable inducement of employees, we conclude that there is no substantial evidence to support the Board's finding of unlawful inducement and encouragement of employees in violation of § 8(b)(4)(A).

Enforcement of the Board's order is therefore in all respects denied.
[The concurring opinions of Judges Hand and Medina are omitted.]

Note

1. One way to analyze the secondary boycott provision of Section 8(b)(4) is to ask whom Congress was trying to protect and why. What light does the Royal Typewriter case cast upon this question? (The reader may find it helpful to keep this line of analysis in mind in reading the next two cases.)

2. Section 8(b)(4) was substantially amended in the Landrum-Griffin Act of 1959. Would the picketing of the customers of the Royal Typewriter Company constitute an unfair labor practice under Section 8(b)(4)(B) in its amended form (i.e., under the (i) and (ii) dichotomy)?

NATIONAL LABOR RELATIONS BOARD v. DENVER BLDG. & CONST. TRADES COUNCIL

Supreme Court of the United States, 1951.
341 U.S. 675, 71 S.Ct. 943, 95 L.Ed. 1284.

MR. JUSTICE BURTON delivered the opinion of the Court.

The principal question here is whether a labor organization committed an unfair labor practice, within the meaning of § 8(b)(4)(A) of the National Labor Relations Act, * * * by engaging in a strike, an object of which was to force the general contractor on a construction project to terminate its contract with a certain subcontractor on that project. For the reasons hereafter stated, we hold that such an unfair labor practice was committed.

In September, 1947, Doose & Lintner was the general contractor for the construction of a commercial building in Denver, Colorado. It awarded a subcontract for electrical work on the building, in an estimated amount of $2,300, to Gould & Preisner, a firm which for 20 years had employed nonunion workmen on construction work in that city. The latter's employees proved to be the only nonunion workmen on the project. Those of the general contractor and of the other subcontractors were members of unions affiliated with the respondent Denver Building and Construction Trades Council (here called the Council). In November a representative of one of those unions told Gould that he did not see how the job could progress with Gould's nonunion men on it. Gould insisted that they would complete the electrical work unless bodily put off. The representative replied that the situation would be difficult for both Gould & Preisner and Doose & Lintner.

January 8, 1948, the Council's Board of Business Agents instructed the Council's representative "to place a picket on the job stating that the job was unfair" to it. In keeping with the Council's practice,[3] each affiliate was

---

3. The Council's by-laws provided in part:

"Article I–B

"Section 1. It shall be the duty of this Council to stand for absolute *closed shop* conditions on all jobs in the City of Denver and jurisdictional surroundings. * * * [Emphasis in original.]

"Section 2. The Board of Business Agents * * * shall have the power to declare a job unfair and remove all men from the job. They shall also have the power to place the men back on the job when satisfactory arrangements have been made.

"Section 3. Any craft refusing to leave a job which has been declared unfair or re-notified of that decision. That notice was a signal in the nature of an order to the members of the affiliated unions to leave the job and remain away until otherwise ordered. Representatives of the Council and each of the respondent unions visited the project and reminded the contractor that Gould & Preisner employed nonunion workmen and said that union men could not work on the job with nonunion men. They further advised that if Gould & Preisner's men did work on the job, the Council and its affiliates would put a picket on it to notify their members that nonunion men were working on it and that the job was unfair. All parties stood their ground.

January 9, the Council posted a picket at the project carrying a placard stating "This Job Unfair to Denver Building and Construction Trades Council." He was paid by the Council and his picketing continued from January 9 through January 22. During that time the only persons who reported for work were the nonunion electricians of Gould & Preisner. January 22, before Gould & Preisner had completed its subcontract, the general contractor notified it to get off the job so that Doose & Lintner could continue with the project. January 23, the Council removed its picket and shortly thereafter the union employees resumed work on the project. Gould & Preisner protested this treatment but its workmen were denied entrance to the job.

On charges filed by Gould & Preisner, the Regional Director of the National Labor Relations Board issued the complaint in this case against the Council and the respondent unions. It alleged that they had engaged in a strike or had caused strike action to be taken on the project by employees of the general contractor and of other subcontractors, an object of which was to force the general contractor to cease doing business with Gould & Preisner on that project.

* * * The Board adopted its examiner's findings, conclusions and recommendations * * * and ordered respondents to cease and desist from engaging in the activities charged. 82 N.L.R.B. 1195. Respondents petitioned the United States Court of Appeals for the District of Columbia Circuit for a review under § 10(f). The Board answered and asked for enforcement of its order. That court * * * set aside the order of the Board and said: "Convinced that the action in the circumstances of this case is primary and not secondary we are obliged to refuse to enforce the order based on § 8(b)(4) (A)." 87 U.S.App.D.C. 293, 304, 186 F.2d 326, 337. * * *

turning to the job before being ordered back by the Council or its Board of Agents shall be tried, and if found guilty, shall be fined the sum of $25.00.

"Section 4. Refusal of any organization to pay said fine shall be followed by expulsion from this Council. An organization so expelled shall pay said fine and one complete back quarter dues and per capita before being reinstated.

"Article XI-B

"Section 1. Strikes must be called by the Council or the Board of Agents in conformity with Article I-B, Sections 1-2. When strikes are called the Council shall have full jurisdiction over the same, and any contractor, who works on a struck job, or employs non-union men to work on a struck job, shall be declared unfair and all union men shall be called off from his work or shop.

"Section 2. The representative of the Council shall have the power to order all strikes when instructed to do so by the Council or Board of Agents. * * * All employees on a struck job shall leave the same when ordered to do so by the Council Agent and remain away from the same until such time as a settlement is made, or otherwise ordered." 82 N.L.R.B. at 1214–1215.

III. *The Secondary Boycott.* We now reach the merits. They require a study of the objectives of the strike and a determination whether the strike came within the definition of an unfair labor practice stated in § 8(b)(4)(A).

The language of that section which is here essential is as follows:

"(b) It shall be an unfair labor practice for a labor organization ∗ ∗ ∗

∗ ∗ ∗ ∗ ∗ ∗ ∗ ∗ ∗

"(4) to engage in ∗ ∗ ∗ a strike ∗ ∗ ∗ where an object thereof is: (A) forcing or requiring ∗ ∗ ∗ any employer or other person ∗ ∗ ∗ to cease doing business with any other person; ∗ ∗ ∗." ∗ ∗ ∗

While § 8(b)(4) does not expressly mention "primary" or "secondary" disputes, strikes or boycotts, that section often is referred to in the Act's legislative history as one of the Act's "secondary boycott sections." The other is § 303, ∗ ∗ ∗ which uses the same language in defining the basis for private actions for damages caused by these proscribed activities.

Senator Taft, who was the sponsor of the bill in the Senate and was the Chairman of the Senate Committee on Labor and Public Welfare in charge of the bill, said, in discussing this section: " ∗ ∗ ∗ [U]nder the provisions of the Norris-LaGuardia Act, it became impossible to stop a secondary boycott or any other kind of a strike, no matter how unlawful it may have been at common law. All this provision of the bill does is to reverse the effect of the law as to secondary boycotts. It has been set forth that there are good secondary boycotts and bad secondary boycotts. Our committee heard evidence for weeks and never succeeded in having anyone tell us any difference between different kinds of secondary boycotts. So we have so broadened the provision dealing with secondary boycotts as to make them an unfair labor practice." 93 Cong.Rec. 4198. ∗ ∗ ∗

At the same time that §§ 7 and 13 safeguard collective bargaining, concerted activities and strikes between the primary parties to a labor dispute, § 8(b)(4) restricts a labor organization and its agents in the use of economic pressure where an object of it is to force an employer or other person to boycott someone else.

A. We must first determine whether the strike in this case had a proscribed object. The conduct which the Board here condemned is readily distinguishable from that which it declined to condemn in the Rice Milling case [National Labor Relations Board v. International Rice Milling Co.], 341 U.S. 665, 71 S.Ct. 961. There the accused union sought merely to obtain its own recognition by the operator of a mill, and the union's pickets near the mill sought to influence two employees of a customer of the mill not to cross the picket line. In that case we supported the Board in its conclusion that such conduct was no more than was traditional and permissible in a primary strike. The union did not engage in a strike against the customer. It did not encourage concerted action by the customer's employees to force the customer to boycott the mill. It did not commit any unfair labor practice proscribed by § 8(b)(4).

In the background of the instant case there was a longstanding labor dispute between the Council and Gould & Preisner due to the latter's practice of employing nonunion workmen on construction jobs in Denver. The respondent labor organizations contend that they engaged in a primary dispute with Doose & Lintner alone, and that they sought simply to force Doose & Lintner to make the project an all-union job. If there had been no contract between Doose & Lintner and Gould & Preisner there might be substance in their contention that the dispute involved no boycott. If, for example, Doose & Lintner had been doing all the electrical work on this project through its own nonunion employees, it could have replaced them with union men and thus disposed of the dispute. However, the existence of the Gould & Preisner subcontract presented a materially different situation. The nonunion employees were employees of Gould & Preisner. The only way that respondents could attain their purpose was to force Gould & Preisner itself off the job. This, in turn, could be done only through Doose & Lintner's termination of Gould & Preisner's subcontract. The result is that the Council's strike, in order to attain its ultimate purpose, must have included among its objects that of forcing Doose & Lintner to terminate that subcontract. On that point, the board adopted the following finding: "That *an* object, if not the only object, of what transpired with respect to * * * Doose & Lintner was to force or require them to cease doing business with Gould & Preisner seems scarcely open to question, in view of all of the facts. And it is clear at least as to Doose & Lintner, that that purpose was achieved." (Emphasis supplied.) 82 N.L.R.B. at 1212.

We accept this crucial finding. It was an object of the strike to force the contractor to terminate Gould & Preisner's subcontract.

B. We hold also that a strike with such an object was an unfair labor practice within the meaning of § 8(b)(4)(A).

It is not necessary to find that the *sole* object of the strike was that of forcing the contractor to terminate the subcontractor's contract. This is emphasized in the legislative history of the section.[18] * * *

We agree with the Board also in its conclusion that the fact that the contractor and subcontractor were engaged on the same construction project, and that the contractor had some supervision over the subcontractor's work, did not eliminate the status of each as an independent contractor or make the employees of one the employees of the other. The business relationship between independent contractors is too well established in the law to be overridden without clear language doing so. The Board found that the relationship between Doose & Lintner and Gould & Preisner was one of "doing business" and we find no adequate reason for upsetting that conclusion.

Finally, § 8(c) safeguarding freedom of speech has no significant application to the picket's placard in this case. Section 8(c) does not apply to a mere signal by a labor organization to its members, or to the members of its affiliates, to engage in an unfair labor practice such as a strike proscribed by § 8(b)(4)(A). That the placard was merely such a signal, tantamount to a direction to strike, was found by the Board.

"* * * [T]he issues in this case turn upon acts by labor organizations which are tantamount to directions and instructions to their members to

---

18. Senator Taft, sponsor of the bill, stated in his supplementary analysis of it as passed: "Section 8(b)(4), relating to illegal strikes and boycotts, was amended in conference by strik-ing out the words 'for the purpose of' and inserting the clause 'where an object thereof is.'" 93 Cong.Rec. 6859.

engage in strike action. The protection afforded by Section 8(c) of the Act to the expression of 'any views, argument or opinion' does not pertain where, as here, the issues raised under Section 8(b)(4)(A) turn on official directions or instructions to a union's own members." 82 N.L.R.B. at 1213. * * *

Not only are the findings of the Board conclusive with respect to questions of fact in this field when supported by substantial evidence on the record as a whole, but the Board's interpretation of the Act and the Board's application of it in doubtful situations are entitled to weight. In the views of the Board as applied to this case we find conformity with the dual congressional objectives of preserving the right of labor organizations to bring pressure to bear on offending employers in primary labor disputes and of shielding unoffending employers and others from pressures in controversies not their own.

For these reasons we conclude that the conduct of respondents constituted an unfair labor practice within the meaning of § 8(b)(4)(A). The judgment of the Court of Appeals accordingly is reversed and the case is remanded to it for procedure not inconsistent with this opinion. * * *

MR. JUSTICE JACKSON would affirm the judgment of the Court of Appeals.

MR. JUSTICE DOUGLAS, with whom MR. JUSTICE REED joins, dissenting.

The employment of union and nonunion men on the same job is a basic protest in trade union history. That was the protest here. The union was not out to destroy the contractor because of his anti-union attitude. The union was not pursuing the contractor to other jobs. All the union asked was that union men not be compelled to work alongside nonunion men on the same job. As Judge Rifkind stated in an analogous case, "the union was not extending its activity to a front remote from the immediate dispute but to one intimately and indeed inextricably united to it." [1]

The picketing would undoubtedly have been legal if there had been no subcontractor involved—if the general contractor had put nonunion men on the job. The presence of a subcontractor does not alter one whit the realities of the situation; the protest of the union is precisely the same. In each the union was trying to protect the job on which union men were employed. If that is forbidden, the Taft-Hartley Act makes the right to strike, guaranteed by § 13, dependent on fortuitous business arrangements that have no significance so far as the evils of the secondary boycott are concerned. I would give scope to both § 8(b)(4) and § 13 by reading the restrictions of § 8(b)(4) to reach the case where an industrial dispute spreads from the job to another front.

Note

1. Why was Doose & Lintner not an "ally" of Gould & Preisner within the meaning of the Royal Typewriter case, as argued by Justice Douglas in his dissent?

2. Suppose the Denver Building and Construction Trades Council had formulated its demand to Doose & Lintner in the following fashion: "Our members refuse to work further for you on this project until you have succeeded

1. Douds v. Metropolitan Federation, D.C., 75 F.Supp. 672, 677.

in inducing Gould & Preisner to replace their nonunion employees with union members." Would this constitute "forcing or requiring any person * * * *to cease doing business with* any other person" within the meaning of Section 8(b)(4)(B)? This question was presented in NLRB v. Local 825, Operating Engineers, 400 U.S. 297, 91 S.Ct. 402, 27 L.Ed.2d 398 (1971). Local 825 was aggrieved because one of three subcontractors on a construction site employed members of the Iron Workers Union to perform work which Local 825 believed should be performed by operating engineers. Members of Local 825 who were employed on the project struck in support of their demand to the general contractor that he sign a contract which would be binding on all subcontractors, giving Local 825 jurisdiction over the disputed work (the running of all power equipment operated on the job site). The Board found a violation of both 8(b)(4)(B) and (D). The court of appeals approved the 8(b)(4)(D) determination, but reversed as to 8(b)(4)(B), concluding that the union's objective in its strike action was to force the general contractor "to use its influence with the subcontractor to change the subcontractor's conduct, not to terminate their relationship." The Supreme Court held, 7 to 2, that the court of appeals read the statutory language "to cease doing business with" too narrowly, "as requiring that the union demand nothing short of a complete termination of the business relationship between the neutral and the primary employer. * * * The clear implication of the demand was that [the general contractor] would be required either to force a change in [the subcontractor's] policy or to terminate [the subcontractor's] contract."

LOCAL 761, INTERNATIONAL UNION OF ELECTRICAL, RADIO AND MACHINE WORKERS, AFL–CIO v. NLRB ("GENERAL ELECTRIC")

Supreme Court of the United States, 1961.
366 U.S. 667, 81 S.Ct. 1285, 6 L.Ed.2d 592.

MR. JUSTICE FRANKFURTER delivered the opinion of the Court.

Local 761 of the International Union of Electrical, Radio and Machine Workers, AFL–CIO, was charged with a violation of § 8(b)(4)(A) of the National Labor Relations Act, as amended by the Taft-Hartley Act, * * * upon the following facts.

General Electric Corporation operates a plant outside of Louisville, Kentucky, where it manufactures washers, dryers, and other electrical household appliances. The square-shaped, thousand-acre, unfenced plant is known as Appliance Park. A large drainage ditch makes ingress and egress impossible except over five roadways across culverts, designated as gates.

Since 1954, General Electric sought to confine the employees of independent contractors, described hereafter, who work on the premises of the Park, to use of Gate 3–A and confine its use to them. The undisputed reason for doing so was to insulate General Electric employees from the frequent labor disputes in which the contractors were involved. Gate 3–A is 550 feet away from the nearest entrance available for General Electric employees, suppliers, and deliverymen. Although anyone can pass the gate without challenge,[1] the roadway leads to a guardhouse where identification must be presented. Vehicle stickers of various shapes and colors enable a guard to check on sight whether a vehicle is authorized to use Gate 3–A. Since

---

1. During the strike in question a guard was stationed at the gate.

January 1958, a prominent sign has been posted at the gate which states: "Gate 3–A for Employees Of Contractors Only—G.E. Employees Use Other Gates." On rare occasions, it appears, a General Electric employee was allowed to pass the guardhouse, but such occurrence was in violation of company instructions. There was no proof of any unauthorized attempts to pass the gate during the strike in question.

The independent contractors are utilized for a great variety of tasks on the Appliance Park premises. Some do construction work on new buildings; some install and repair ventilating and heating equipment; some engage in retooling and rearranging operations necessary to the manufacture of new models; others do "general maintenance work." These services are contracted to outside employers either because the company's employees lack the necessary skill or manpower, or because the work can be done more economically by independent contractors. The latter reason determined the contracting of maintenance work for which the Central Maintenance department of the company bid competitively with the contractors. While some of the work done by these contractors had on occasion been previously performed by Central Maintenance, the findings do not disclose the number of employees of independent contractors who were performing these routine maintenance services, as compared with those who were doing specialized work of a capital-improvement nature.

The Union, petitioner here, is the certified bargaining representative for the production and maintenance workers who constitute approximately 7,600 of the 10,500 employees of General Electric at Appliance Park. On July 27, 1958, the Union called a strike because of 24 unsettled grievances with the company. Picketing occurred at all the gates, including Gate 3–A, and continued until August 9 when an injunction was issued by a Federal District Court. The signs carried by the pickets at all gates read: "Local 761 On Strike G.E. Unfair." Because of the picketing, almost all of the employees of independent contractors refused to enter the company premises.

Neither the legality of the strike or of the picketing at any of the gates except 3–A nor the peaceful nature of the picketing is in dispute. The sole claim is that the picketing before the gate exclusively used by employees of independent contractors was conduct proscribed by § 8(b)(4)(A).

The Trial Examiner recommended that the Board dismiss the complaint. He concluded that the limitations on picketing which the Board had prescribed in so-called "common situs" cases were not applicable to the situation before him, in that the picketing at Gate 3–A represented traditional primary action which necessarily had a secondary effect of inconveniencing those who did business with the struck employer. He reasoned that if a primary employer could limit the area of picketing around his own premises by constructing a separate gate for employees of independent contractors, such a device could also be used to isolate employees of his suppliers and customers, and that such action could not relevantly be distinguished from oral appeals made to secondary employees not to cross a picket line where only a single gate existed.

The Board rejected the Trial Examiner's conclusion, 123 N.L.R.B. 1547. It held that, since only the employees of the independent contractors were allowed to use Gate 3–A, the Union's object in picketing there was "to enmesh these employees of the neutral employers in its dispute with the Company," thereby constituting a violation of § 8(b)(4)(A) because the independent employees were encouraged to engage in a concerted refusal to work "with an object of forcing the independent contractors to cease doing business with the Company." [2]

The Court of Appeals for the District of Columbia granted enforcement of the Board's order, 107 U.S.App.D.C. 402, 278 F.2d 282. Although noting that a fine line was being drawn, it concluded that the Board was correct in finding that the objective of the Gate 3–A picketing was to encourage the independent-contractor employees to engage in a concerted refusal to perform services for their employers in order to bring pressure on General Electric. Since the incidence of the problem involved in this case is extensive and the treatment it has received calls for clarification, we brought the case here ＊ ＊ ＊.

I.

Section 8(b)(4)(A) of the National Labor Relations Act provides that it shall be an unfair labor practice for a labor organization " ＊ ＊ ＊ to engage in, or to induce or encourage the employees of any employer to engage in, a strike or a concerted refusal in the course of their employment to use, manufacture, process, transport, or otherwise handle or work on any goods, articles, materials, or commodities or to perform any services, where an object thereof is: (A) forcing or requiring ＊ ＊ ＊ any employer or other person ＊ ＊ ＊ to cease doing business with any other person ＊ ＊ ＊." This provision could not be literally construed; otherwise it would ban most strikes historically considered to be lawful, so-called primary activity. "While § 8(b)(4) does not expressly mention 'primary' or 'secondary' disputes, strikes or boycotts, that section often is referred to in the Act's legislative history as one of the Act's 'secondary boycott sections.' " National Labor Relations Board v. Denver Building & Const. Trades Council, 341 U.S. 675, 686, 71 S.Ct. 943, 950, 95 L.Ed. 1284. "Congress did not seek by § 8(b)(4), to interfere with the ordinary strike ＊ ＊ ＊." National Labor Relations Board v. International Rice Milling Co., 341 U.S. 665, 672, 71 S.Ct. 961, 965, 95 L.Ed. 1277. The impact of the section was directed toward what is known as the secondary boycott whose "sanctions bear, not upon the employer who alone is a party to the dispute, but upon some third party who has no concern in it." International Brotherhood of Electrical Workers, Local 501 v. National Labor Relations Board, 2 Cir., 181 F.2d 34, 37. Thus the section "left a striking labor organization free to use persuasion, including picketing, not only on the primary employer and his employees but on numerous others. Among these were secondary employers who were customers or suppliers of the primary employer and persons dealing with them ＊ ＊ ＊ and even employees of secondary employers so long as the labor organization did not ＊ ＊ ＊ 'induce or encourage the employees of any employer to engage, in a strike or a concerted refusal in the course of their

---

2. Member Fanning concurred in the result, reasoning that the common-situs criteria set out by the Board in Sailors' Union of the Pacific (Moore Dry Dock), 92 N.L.R.B. 547, could be applied to situations where the primary employer owned the premises, and that the requirement that the picketing take place reasonably close to the situs of the labor dispute had therefore been violated by the picketing around Gate 3–A.

employment' * * *." National Labor Relations Board v. Local 294, International Brotherhood of Teamsters, 2 Cir., 284 F.2d 887, 889. * * *

Important as is the distinction between legitimate "primary activity" and banned "secondary activity," it does not present a glaringly bright line. * * *

However difficult the drawing of lines more nice than obvious, the statute compels the task. * * *

The nature of the problem, as revealed by unfolding variant situations, inevitably involves an evolutionary process for its rational response, not a quick, definitive formula as a comprehensive answer. And so, it is not surprising that the Board has more or less felt its way during the fourteen years in which it has had to apply § 8(b)(4)(A), and has modified and reformed its standards on the basis of accumulating experience. * * *

II.

The early decisions of the board following the Taft-Hartley amendments involved activity which took place around the secondary employer's premises. For example, in Wadsworth Building Co. [81 N.L.R.B. 802] the union set up a picket line around the situs of a builder who had contracted to purchase prefabricated houses from the primary employer. The Board found this to be illegal secondary activity. * * * In contrast, when picketing took place around the premises of the primary employer, the Board regarded this as valid primary activity. * * *

In United Electrical Workers (Ryan Construction Corp.), 85 N.L.R.B. 417, Ryan had contracted to perform construction work on a building adjacent to the Bucyrus plant and inside its fence. A separate gate was cut through the fence for Ryan's employees which no employee of Bucyrus ever used. The Board concluded that the union—on strike against Bucyrus—could picket the Ryan gate, even though an object of the picketing was to enlist the aid of Ryan employees, since Congress did not intend to outlaw primary picketing.

> "When picketing is wholly at the premises of the employer with whom the union is engaged in a labor dispute, it cannot be called 'secondary' even though, as is virtually always the case, an object of the picketing is to dissuade all persons from entering such premises for business reasons. It makes no difference whether 1 or 100 other employees wish to enter the premises. It follows in this case that the picketing of Bucyrus premises, which was primary because in support of a labor dispute *with Bucyrus,* did not lose its character and become 'secondary' at the so-called Ryan gate because Ryan employees were the only persons regularly entering Bucyrus premises at that gate." 85 N.L.R.B., at 418. * * *

Thus, the Board eliminated picketing which took place around the situs of the primary employer—regardless of the special circumstances involved—from being held invalid secondary activity under § 8(b)(4)(A).

However, the impact of the new situations made the Board conscious of the complexity of the problem by reason of the protean forms in which it appeared. This became clear in the "common situs" cases—situations where two employers were performing separate tasks on common premises. The Moore Dry Dock case [92 N.L.R.B. 547] laid out the Board's new standards in this area. There, the union picketed outside an entrance to a dock where a ship, owned by the struck employer, was being trained and outfitted. Although the premises picketed were those of the secondary employer, they constituted the only place where picketing could take place; furthermore, the objectives of the picketing were no more aimed at the employees of the secondary employer—the dock owner—than they had been in the * * * Ryan [case]. The Board concluded, however, that when the situs of the primary employer was "ambulatory" there must be a balance between the union's right to picket and the interest of the secondary employer in being free from picketing. It set out four standards for picketing in such situations which would be presumptive of valid primary activity: (1) that the picketing be limited to times when the situs of dispute was located on the secondary premises, (2) that the primary employer be engaged in his normal business at the situs, (3) that the picketing take place reasonably close to the situs, and (4) that the picketing clearly disclose that the dispute was only with the primary employer. These tests were widely accepted by reviewing federal courts. * * *

In Local 55 (PBM), 108 N.L.R.B. 363, the Board for the first time applied the Dry Dock test, although the picketing occurred at premises owned by the primary employer. There, an insurance company owned a tract of land that it was developing, and also served as the general contractor. A neutral subcontractor was also doing work at the site. The union, engaged in a strike against the insurance company, picketed the entire premises, characterizing the entire job as unfair, and the employees of the subcontractor walked off. The Court of Appeals for the Tenth Circuit enforced the Board's order which found the picketing to be illegal on the ground that the picket signs did not measure up to the Dry Dock standard that they clearly disclose that the picketing was directed against the struck employer only. 218 F.2d 226.

The Board's application of the Dry Dock standards to picketing at the premises of the struck employer was made more explicit in Retail Fruit & Vegetable Clerks (Crystal Palace Market), 116 N.L.R.B. 856. The owner of a large common market operated some of the shops within, and leased out others to independent sellers. The union, although given permission to picket the owner's individual stands, chose to picket outside the entire market. The Board held that this action was violative of § 8(b)(4)(A) in that the union did not attempt to minimize the effect of its picketing, as required in a common-situs case, on the operations of the neutral employers utilizing the market. "We believe * * * that the foregoing principles should apply to all common situs picketing, including cases where, as here, the picketed premises are owned by the primary employer." 116 N.L.R.B. at 859. The Ryan case, supra, was overruled to the extent it implied the contrary. * * *

* * * The application of the Dry Dock tests to limit the picketing effects to the employees of the employer against whom the dispute is directed carries out the "dual congressional objectives of preserving the right of labor organizations to bring pressure to bear on offending employers in primary labor disputes and of shielding unoffending employers and others from pressures in controversies not their own." National Labor Relations

Board v. Denver Building & Const. Trades Council, supra, 341 U.S. at page 692, 71 S.Ct. at page 953, 95 L.Ed. 1284.

III.

From this necessary survey of the course of the Board's treatment of our problem, the precise nature of the issue before us emerges. With due regard to the relation between the Board's function and the scope of judicial review of its rulings, the question is whether the board may apply the Dry Dock criteria so as to make unlawful picketing at a gate utilized exclusively by employees of independent contractors who work on the struck employer's premises. The effect of such a holding would not bar the union from picketing at all gates used by the employees, suppliers, and customers of the struck employer. * * *

The Union claims that, if the Board's ruling is upheld, employers will be free to erect separate gates for deliveries, customers, and replacement workers which will be immunized from picketing. This fear is baseless. The key to the problem is found in the type of work that is being performed by those who use the separate gate. It is significant that the Board has since applied its rationale, first stated in the present case, only to situations where the independent workers were performing tasks unconnected to the normal operations of the struck employer—usually construction work on his buildings. In such situations, the indicated limitations on picketing activity respect the balance of competing interests that Congress has required the Board to enforce. On the other hand, if a separate gate were devised for regular plant deliveries, the barring of picketing at that location would make a clear invasion on traditional primary activity of appealing to neutral employees whose tasks aid the employer's everyday operations. * * *

In a case similar to the one now before us, the Court of Appeals for the Second Circuit sustained the Board in its application of § 8(b)(4)(A) to a separate-gate situation. "There must be a separate gate marked and set apart from other gates; the work done by the men who use the gate must be unrelated to the normal operations of the employer and the work must be of a kind that would not, if done when the plant were engaged in its regular operations, necessitate curtailing those operations." United Steelworkers of America, AFL–CIO v. National Labor Relations Board, 2 Cir., 289 F.2d 591, 595. These seem to us controlling considerations.

IV.

The foregoing course of reasoning would require that the judgment below sustaining the Board's order be affirmed but for one consideration, even though this consideration may turn out not to affect the result. The legal path by which the Board and the Court of Appeals reached their decisions did not take into account that if Gate 3–A was in fact used by employees of independent contractors who performed conventional maintenance work necessary to the normal operations of General Electric, the use of the gate would have been a mingled one outside the bar of § 8(b)(4)(A). In short, such mixed use of this portion of the struck employer's premises would not bar picketing rights of the striking employees. While the record shows some such mingled use, it sheds no light on its extent. It may well turn out to be that the instances of these maintenance tasks were so insubstantial as to be treated by the Board as *de minimis*. We cannot here guess at the quantitative aspect of this problem. It calls for Board determination. For determination of the questions thus raised, the case must be remanded by the Court of Appeals to the Board.

Reversed.

THE CHIEF JUSTICE and MR. JUSTICE BLACK concur in the result.

MR. JUSTICE DOUGLAS.

I did not vote to grant certiorari in this case because it seemed to me that the problem presented was in the keeping of the Courts of Appeals within the meaning of Universal Camera Corp. v. National Labor Relations Board, 340 U.S. 474, 490, 71 S.Ct. 456, 95 L.Ed. 456. Since the Court of Appeals followed the guidelines of that case (see 107 U.S.App.D.C. 402, 278 F.2d 282, 286), I would leave the decision with it. I cannot say it made any egregious error, though I might have decided the case differently had I sat on the Labor Board or on the Court of Appeals.

Note

1. Does the Royal Typewriter case have relevance for the General Electric case?

2. The charging party in the GE case was GE itself, the primary employer. (The same was true in the Royal Typewriter and Denver cases.) What light does this cast upon the scope of protection afforded by Section 8(b)(4)(B), the "secondary boycott" provision?

3. The Board, on the remand to it of the GE case, determined that all of the affected independent contractors were engaged in work related to the normal operations of GE and that, as a consequence, the picketing at the reserved gate 3–A was primary. 138 N.L.R.B. 342, at 346 (1962). On these facts, if the labor dispute had been with one or more of the independent contractors, would picketing at gates other than 3–A have been lawful? In other words, may the relatedness test spread contagion from the independent contractors to GE as well as from GE to the independent contractors. In United Association of the Plumbing Industry, Local 60 and Circle, Inc., 202 N.L.R.B. 99, enforced, 486 F.2d 1401 (5th Cir. 1973), the Board refused to apply the relatedness test in that fashion. It applied instead the Moore Dry Dock criteria, found the picketing at the nonreserved gates not reasonably close to the situs of the labor dispute, and ordered the offending union to cease and desist. Query: What's sauce for the goose is *not* sauce for the gander? Is the rationale that the tail should not wag the dog—that the picketed premises in the GE case were those of the primary employer, while this was not so in Circle, Inc.?

MARKWELL AND HARTZ, INC. v. NATIONAL LABOR RELATIONS BOARD

United States Court of Appeals, Fifth Circuit, 1967.
387 F.2d 79.

Certiorari denied, 391 U.S. 914 (1968).

CONNALLY, DISTRICT JUDGE: * * *

Briefly stated, the facts are these. In September of 1963 Markwell and Hartz, Inc. was the general contractor for the expansion of a filtration plant at the East Jefferson Water Works, District No. 1, in Jefferson Parish, Louisiana. Prior to beginning construction, Markwell and Hartz entered into an agreement with District 50 of the United Mine Workers of America whereby District 50 became the recognized bargaining agent for Markwell and Hartz's employees. Also prior to beginning construction, Markwell and Hartz contracted with two subcontractors, Binnings Construction Company, Inc. ("Binnings") and Walter J. Barnes Electrical Company ("Barnes") to perform the pile driving and electrical work, respectively. It performed the remainder of the work, consisting of approximately 80%, itself. Employees of both Binnings and Barnes were represented by the respondent [Building and Construction] Trades Council [of New Orleans, AFL–CIO].

Immediately a dispute arose between Markwell and Hartz and the Trades Council. The latter sought to become the bargaining representative of the Markwell and Hartz employees. On October 17, 1963, the Council began to picket the project.

Shortly after the picket line appeared, Markwell and Hartz endeavored to insulate its subcontractors Binnings and Barnes, who were neutrals in the labor controversy, from the effects of the picketing. It did so by establishing four separate gates, three for the exclusive use of the subcontractors, their employees and suppliers; the fourth for the exclusive use of its own employees and suppliers. Despite the clear delineation by signs distinguishing between the subcontractors' gates and that for the use of the general contractor, the Council continued to picket all gates until enjoined by the District Court for the Eastern District of Louisiana on January 15, 1964. As a result of the picketing, the employees of Binnings and of Barnes refused to work on the project.

Acting on a complaint lodged by Markwell and Hartz, the National Labor Relations Board entered an order generally favorable to Markwell and Hartz, declaring that after November 16, 1963 (at which time the gates had been clearly marked) the Council had engaged in an unfair labor practice violative of Sections 8(b)(4)(i) and (ii)(B) of the Act. The Board found that one of the purposes of the picketing of the subcontractors' gates was to cause Binnings and Barnes (the neutrals) to cease doing business with Markwell and Hartz. The Board issued a typical cease and desist order.

The case is before this Court primarily on the Board's petition to enforce its order, while Markwell and Hartz seeks additional findings in its favor.

At the outset, it should be noted that the dispute that gave rise to the picketing was not between Markwell and Hartz and its employees. Nor was the dispute, in practical effect, between Markwell and Hartz and the Trades Council. The real adversaries were District 50 of the United Mine Workers and the Trades Council, the latter being the also-ran in the race to see who would be the bargaining representative of Markwell and Hartz's employees. District 50 has appeared as *amicus curiae*, urging enforcement of the Board's order. Hence the dispute was jurisdictional in nature.

It is the Trades Council's position that the facts of this case bring it within the ambit of Local 761, IUE, etc. v. NLRB, 366 U.S. 667, 81 S.Ct. 1285, 6 L.Ed.2d 592 (1961), popularly known as the *General Electric* case. The Trades Council further argues that the *General Electric* case and the *Carrier* case [United Steelworkers v. NLRB, 376 U.S. 492, 84 S.Ct. 899, 11 L.Ed.2d

863 (1964)], have, *sub silentio,* overruled the Supreme Court's decision in NLRB v. Denver Building & Construction Trades Council, 341 U.S. 675, 71 S.Ct. 943, 95 L.Ed. 1284 (1951). We do not agree with this position.

Attempts to distinguish between protected primary picketing and the forbidden secondary activity—particularly at a common situs where employees of the primary and of the secondary employers work side by side—have been the source of much litigation both before the Board and in the Courts. Much of the uncertainty which formerly shrouded this question has been clarified, we think, by *General Electric* wherein the question and the various authorities are reviewed at length, and by *Carrier* which follows and approves *General Electric.* These are the cases primarily relied upon by the Trades Council.   •

In *General Electric,* that company was the primary employer engaged in a dispute with its own employees at its own plant. A number of subcontractors were performing various services for General Electric at the plant site. Separate gates [sic] were clearly designated for the exclusive use of these subcontractors. The work performed by the subcontractors was of different types, the distinction being emphasized by the court as "routine maintenance service"—which at times was performed by General Electric's own employees, and occasionally subcontracted out—as distinguished from "specialized work of a capital-improvement nature" (366 U.S. at p. 669, 81 S.Ct. at p. 1287). There Mr. Justice Frankfurter, speaking for the Court, without dissent, rejected the argument of the Union that all picketing at the plant of the struck employer should be considered primary * * *.

Three years later in *Carrier* the Court, again without dissent, rejected the theory that ownership or control of the site of the picketing was controlling. There Carrier was engaged in a dispute with its employees, at its own plant. The picketing in question took place at a railroad spur track, owned by the railroad and used exclusively by the railroad and its employees, but located immediately adjacent to Carrier's plant and used for the delivery of supplies and removal of the manufactured products of Carrier. Approving and reaffirming the test of *General Electric,* the Court in *Carrier* held that the ownership of the railroad spur was immaterial, and that it was in fact, no more than another gate to the Carrier plant; hence the picketing at such gate to inform the railroad and its employees who were suppliers of Carrier of the existence of the dispute was primary and protected activity.

Thus the question posed here is whether the work of subcontractors Binnings and Barnes was "related to the normal operations" of Markwell and Hartz (as, for example, ordinary maintenance as in *General Electric*), in which event the picketing is primary; or whether it is unrelated to the normal operations (as "of a capital improvement nature").

While it would seem clear from a statement of this test that the work of Binnings and Barnes, consisting of specialized work for which Markwell and Hartz was unequipped and unable to perform itself, was of the unrelated variety, we need not speculate upon the answer to this question. It is answered authoritatively in *Denver,* supra. That case involved a construction project common situs where employees of the general and the subcontractors worked side by side. In a dispute with the subcontractor, picketing was likewise directed at the employees of the prime. There, as here, it was

found that an object of such picketing was to force or require the cessation of business, one with the other, and to force a termination of the subcontract.
*   *   *

The Trades Council argues that there is a conflict between *Denver,* on the one hand, and *General Electric* and *Carrier,* on the other. We find no such conflict. *Denver* is cited with approval in *General Electric.*

The Council further argues that *Denver* should be limited to its precise facts, that is, where the dispute is with a subcontractor and the general contractor is a neutral. Such a position is supported by neither logic nor authority. The statute, in condemning the secondary boycott, makes no such distinction and we are unable to say that it is less an unfair labor practice to bring economic pressure on a subcontractor to induce him to breach his contract and cease doing business with the prime, rather than where the parties are reversed.   *   *   *

Holding as we do that the subcontractors here were entitled to protection from the Trades Council's picketing, the Trades Council was obliged to restrict its picketing in conformity with the *Moore Dry Dock* criteria.[3] See Sailor's Union of the Pacific (*Moore Dry Dock*), 92 N.L.R.B. 547 (1950). The Board was warranted in concluding that the Trades Council's picketing was not in accord with *Moore Dry Dock* requirements and, therefore, an unfair labor practice.

On October 9, 1967, long after submission of this action, counsel for the N.L.R.B. filed with the clerk of this Court slip opinion of the Court of Appeals for the Sixth Circuit in N.L.R.B. v. Nashville Bldg. & Construction Trades Council, Oct. 5, 1967, 383 F.2d 562. This opinion deals with precisely the question considered here, in a similar controversy between Markwell & Hartz, the Nashville Council, and the United Mine Workers. We have considered that opinion as well as the brief filed October 27, 1967, by New Orleans Building and Trades Council in reply thereto. We cite the Sixth Circuit opinion in support of the views expressed above, and agree with the observation there made (last paragraph) that "if appellant's contention in this case is to prevail, it is a decision for the Supreme Court or for the Congress."

Enforcement of the Board's order is granted.

RIVES, CIRCUIT JUDGE (specially concurring):

It seems to me that the work of the subcontractors Binnings and Barnes was "related to the normal operation" of the general contractor Markwell and Hartz, Inc. (M & H). M & H was obligated by contract to complete the filtration plant expansion job. It decided to perform about four-fifths in cost of the project with its own employees and to subcontract the balance. The pile-driving contract was awarded to Binnings and the electrical work to Barnes. When Binnings' crews honored the picket line, M & H used its own employees to complete the pile driving. While Barnes' electrical work was more highly specialized, I do not find any contention that M & H could not have employed men to do that work.

---

3. The Board has often applied Moore Dry Dock standards to construction site picketing. See I.C.G. Elec. Inc., 142 N.L.R.B. 1418 (1963); Levitt Corp., 127 N.L.R.B. 900 (1960); St. Bridget's Catholic Congregation, Inc., 122 N.L.R.B. 1341 (1959).

The two dissenting members of the Board definitely stated that, "In applying the *General Electric* standards to the instant case, we find that the work of Binnings and Barnes was related to the normal operations of M & H, the general contractor." (R. 112.) The reasons for that finding were then elaborately stated. The three majority members of the Board agreed that " * * * the work of the neutral subcontractors in one sense is 'related to M & H's normal operations'," but nevertheless thought that the dissent's analysis "runs counter to firmly established principles governing common situs picketing in that (the construction) industry." (R. 96.)

When the work done by the secondary employees is related to the normal operations of the primary employer there remains a distinction between picketing at the situs of the primary employer and picketing at a common situs where two or more employers are performing separate tasks on common premises. It seems to me that the opinion in *General Electric* clearly recognizes that distinction and approves the four *Moore Dry Dock* standards as applicable to common situs picketing. (See 366 U.S. at 676–679, 81 S.Ct. 1285.) The *Carrier* case went no further than *General Electric* and continued to recognize the importance of the location of the picketing (376 U.S. at 497, 84 S.Ct. 899).

I agree that *General Electric* and *Carrier* are not inconsistent with *Denver*. *Denver* relates to common situs picketing. *General Electric* and *Carrier* involve illegal picketing at the premises of a struck manufacturer. Except for this difference in reasoning, I concur fully with Judge Connally.

WISDOM, CIRCUIT JUDGE (dissenting):

I respectfully dissent.

I agree with the Court that in this case the *General Electric* work-related standard should be applied. The difficulty I have with the majority opinion is that the Court accepts the Board's cavalier consideration of *General Electric* and enforces the Board order—although the Board rejected the work-related standard. The Board inferred an unlawful objective simply from the picketing of the reserved gate. I am with the dissenting Board members in their view that there should be an inquiry into whether the appeals through picketing to secondary employees constituted permissible primary activity. I would remand the case to the Board for a finding on the issue of relatedness with suggestions that the Board formulate criteria for determining relatedness in common situs cases, carrying out the principles expressed in *General Electric* and *Carrier*.

With deference, I must say that I am not as certain as the Court that *General Electric* and *Carrier* clarified *Denver* and do not conflict with that decision. *Denver* (which did not involve reserved gates) applied the *Moore Dry Dock* criteria—regardless of whether the secondary employer's work was related to the normal operations of the primary employer. In the Board's decision in N.L.R.B. v. Nashville Building and Construction Trades Council, 164 NLRB No. 50, enforced, 6 Cir. 1967, 383 F.2d 562, involving the same question at issue here in a controversy also involving Markwell & Hartz, the Board said:

"For in view of our holding in Building and Construction Trades Council of New Orleans, AFL–CIO (Markwell & Hartz, Inc.), 155 NLRB 319, that the legality of picketing at a common situs in the construction industry is to be determined under the *Moore Dry Dock* standards, rather than the special guidelines laid down by the Supreme Court in Local 761, IUE (General Electric Corporation v. N.L.R.B.), 366 U.S. 667 [81 S.Ct. 1285, 6 L.Ed.2d 592], the *work relationship test set forth in the latter is inapposite herein.*" (Emphasis added.)

In short, the Board's *Nashville* decision acknowledges explicitly that a majority of that Agency is of the view that the standards announced by the Supreme Court in *General Electric* and *Carrier* should not be applied in the context of construction industry picketing. * * *

The line between primary and secondary activity is relatively easy to draw where the primary and secondary employers have separate work-sites. Thus, union activity occurring at a manufacturer's own premises, and seeking no more than the disruption of his own normal operations, is considered primary and within the traditional area of protected union activity. On the other hand, activity extending beyond the premises of the primary employer to those of another employer, and designed to disrupt the operations of the latter employer, is secondary and prohibited. * * *

A more difficult problem is presented in the common situs cases— "situations where two employers were performing separate tasks on common premises". General Electric, 366 U.S. at 676, 81 S.Ct. at 1291. Early in the development of the law under section 8(b)(4), therefore, the Board evolved [the Moore Dry Dock] criteria to aid in determining whether picketing at a common situs was primary or secondary. * * * The Board has since applied these "*Moore Dry Dock* standards" in common situs situations generally, whether the premises were owned by the secondary employer (as in *Moore,* itself), the primary employer, or some third party, and whether the picketing union's dispute was with the general contractor or the subcontractor.

Common situs picketing in the construction industry raises special problems. The building trades unions have always contended that construction of a building is an integrated enterprise in which the subcontractors are interrelated allies of the prime contractor, not independent neutrals. In *Denver,* however, the Supreme Court rejected this contention. Instead, the Court looked to the traditional legal concept of the relationship between a prime contractor and his subcontractors: The subcontractors are independent contractors whose employees are not the employees of the prime contractors. As separate legal entities, they are entitled to protection from secondary boycotts. The construction industry, therefore, is subject to the same restrictions as are other industries in regard to common situs picketing. For purposes of the instant case, it is important to note that in *Denver* the Court did not consider the type of work performed by the subcontractor. The test was not the *relatedness* of the subcontractor's work to the normal operations of the prime contractor; the test was whether one of the *objects* of the picketing was to force the prime contractor to cease doing business with the subcontractor.

Denver has been criticized. Numerous bills have been introduced in Congress to overrule its holding. But *Denver* still stands. Here the Board rested its decision squarely on *Denver* and *Moore Dry Dock.*

The Trades Council and the dissenting members of the Board rely on *General Electric*. They contend that under *General Electric* the lawfulness of reserved gate picketing as a primary activity depends on "the type of work that is being performed by those who use the separate gate". 366 U.S. at 680, 81 S.Ct. at 1293. * * *

The Board attempts to distinguish away *General Electric* and *Carrier* on the ground that they were the product of the "lenient treatment * * * given to strike action taking place at the separate premises of a struck employer". Those decisions, so the Board and the Court here say, were not intended to upset the traditional approach to common situs problems in the construction industry. Relying therefore on *Denver* (although *Denver* did not involve a separate gate) and on the *Moore Dry Dock* criteria, the Board found that the timing and the picketing at the reserved gates were not intended to reach the employees of Markwell and Hartz but had the unlawful *object* of inducing strike action by the employees of neutral Binnings and Barnes.

General Electric and *Carrier* cannot be brushed off lightly. They represent an attempt to show in what circumstances picketing of a secondary employer is permissible. Under *General Electric,* not all independent contractors are neutrals: They lose their neutral status when their work is related ("necessary") to the normal or day-to-day operations of the primary employer.

Here the Board apparently limited the use of the term "common situs" to situations where the primary and secondary employers are engaged in operations on premises owned by a third person or by a secondary employer. But the Supreme Court in *General Electric* used the term "common situs" to refer to any location where both the primary and the secondary employers were present. 366 U.S. at 676, 81 S.Ct. 1285. The Board itself, in Crystal Palace Market, 116 NLRB 856, 859 (1956) stated: "[Moore Dry Dock] principles should apply to all common situs [picketing], including cases where, as here, the picketed premises are owned by the primary employer. We can see no logical reasons why the legality of such picketing should depend on title to property." The effect of the Board's decision is to apply more rigid standards to the construction industry than to the manufacturing industry. Any prime contractor would be able to frustrate the purposes of picketing by opening gates reserved for his subcontractors.

The Board assumes that if the related-work standard is applied to common construction situs, *General Electric* must be considered as having overruled *Denver sub silentio.* In *Denver,* however, the Court focused on the point that contractors and subcontractors on a construction project are not *necessarily* so interconnected that they should all be regarded as one entity. The Court did not hold that as a matter of law all independent contractors on a common situs must be considered as neutrals. In *General Electric* the Court accepted the *Denver* holding that subcontractors are separate legal entities and accepted the principle that the union may appeal to employees of a secondary employer. The Court then focused on the criteria for determining when and how the union may reach the employees of the secondary employer. The touchstone furnished by *Carrier* as well as by *General Electric* is relatedness of work. To the extent that the conclusions in *Denver* were arrived at independent of any consideration of relatedness, those conclusions must be considered as modified by application of the relatedness standard set down in *General Electric*. Here, therefore, the Board should have made a finding on the issue of relatedness. An unlawful object under Section 8(b)(4) cannot be inferred simply from the fact that the union has picketed at a gate reserved for the subcontractors' employees.

Since the Board has considered *General Electric* inapposite and has not made any finding on the issue of relatedness of work, the case should be remanded to the Board for such a finding. The Board should make the initial determination, not the Court. It is better able than this Court to formulate criteria in light of preserving the statutory balance between "the right of labor organizations to bring pressure to bear on offending employers in primary labor disputes and of shielding unoffending employers and others from pressures in controversies not their own." Denver, 341 U.S. at 692, 71 S.Ct. at 953. ＊　＊　＊

Note

1. With which of the three opinions do you agree?

2. Is Markwell and Hartz consistent with the Circle, Inc. decision, Note 3, supra p. 410?

3. Should, as a matter of sound public policy, picketing of the sort in issue in Markwell and Hartz be deemed lawful? Organized labor and its supporters have sought this goal by legislation since the Denver decision in 1951. Thus far, the efforts have aborted. The "construction industry proviso" to Section 8(e) does, however, afford some concession to the concerns of construction union members about having to work alongside of non- or other-union workers on common construction sites. Section 8(e) and this proviso are dealt with infra p. 436 et seq.

NATIONAL LABOR RELATIONS BOARD v. SERVETTE, INC.

Supreme Court of the United States, 1964.
377 U.S. 46, 84 S.Ct. 1098, 12 L.Ed.2d 121.

Mr. Justice Brennan delivered the opinion of the Court.

Respondent Servette, Inc., is a wholesale distributor of specialty merchandise stocked by retail food chains in Los Angeles, California. In 1960, during a strike which Local 848 of the Wholesale Delivery Drivers and Salesmen's Union was conducting against Servette, the Local's representatives sought to support the strike by asking managers of supermarkets of the food chains to discontinue handling merchandise supplied by Servette. In most instances the representatives warned that handbills asking the public not to buy named items distributed by Servette would be passed out in front of stores which refused to cooperate, and in a few cases handbills were in fact passed out.[2] A complaint was issued on charges by Servette that this

2. The handbill was as follows:

　"To the Patrons of This Store

"Wholesale Delivery Drivers & Salesmen's Local No. 848 urgently requests that you do

not buy the following products distributed by Servette, Inc.:

　"Brach's Candy

　"Servette Candy

conduct violated subsections (i) and (ii) of § 8(b)(4) of the National Labor Relations Act, as amended, which, in relevant part, provide that it is an unfair labor practice for a union

"(i) * * * to induce or encourage any individual employed by any person * * * to engage in * * * a refusal in the course of his employment to * * * handle * * * commodities or to perform any services; or

"(ii) to threaten, coerce, or restrain any person * * * where in either case an object thereof is—

*   *   *   *   *   *   *   *   *

"(B) forcing or requiring any person to cease * * * dealing in the products of any other producer, processor, or manufacturer, or to cease doing business with any other person * * *.

*   *   *   *   *   *   *   *   *

"*Provided further,* That for the purposes of this paragraph (4) only, nothing contained in such paragraph shall be construed to prohibit publicity, other than picketing, for the purpose of truthfully advising the public * * * that a product or products are produced by an employer with whom the labor organization has a primary dispute and are distributed by another employer * * *."

The National Labor Relations Board dismissed the complaint. The Board adopted the finding of the Trial Examiner that "the managers of McDaniels Markets were authorized to decide as they best could whether to continue doing business with Servette in the face of threatened or actual handbilling. This, a policy decision, was one for them to make. The evidence is persuasive that the same authority was vested in the managers of Kory." 133 N.L.R.B. 1506. The Board held that on these facts the Local's efforts to enlist the cooperation of the supermarket managers did not constitute inducement of an "individual" within the meaning of that term in subsection (i); the Board held further that the handbilling, even if constituting conduct which "threaten[s], coerce[s], or restrain[s] any person" under subsection (ii), was protected by the quoted proviso to amended § 8(b)(4). 133 N.L.R.B. 1501. The Court of Appeals set aside the Board's order, holding that the term "individual" in subsection (i) was to be read literally, thus including the supermarket managers, and that the distributed products were not "produced" by Servette within the meaning of the proviso, thus rendering its protection unavailable. 310 F.2d 659. * * * We reverse the judgment of the Court of Appeals.

The Court of Appeals correctly read the term "individual" in subsection (i) as including the supermarket managers,[4] but it erred in holding that the

"Good Season Salad Dressing

"Old London Products

"The Servette Company which distributes these products refuses to negotiate with the Union that represents its drivers. The Company is attempting to force the drivers to sign individual 'Yellow Dog' contracts.

"These contracts will destroy the wages and working conditions that the drivers now enjoy, and will set them back 20 years in their struggle for decent wages and working conditions.

"The drivers of Servette appreciate your cooperation in this fight."

4. The Board reached a contrary conclusion on the authority of its decision in Carolina Lumber Co., 130 N.L.R.B. 1438, 1443, which viewed the statute as distinguishing "low level" supervisors from "high level" supervisors, holding that inducement of "low level" supervisors is impermissible but inducement of "high level" supervisors is permitted. We hold today that this is not the distinction drawn by the statute; rather, the question of

Local's attempts to enlist the aid of the managers constituted inducement of the managers in violation of the subsection. The 1959 statute amended § 8(b)(4)(A) of the National Labor Relations Act, which made it unlawful to induce or encourage "the employees of any employer" to strike or engage in a "concerted" refusal to work. We defined the central thrust of that statute to be to forbid "a union to induce employees to strike against or to refuse to handle goods for their employer when an object is to force him or another person to cease doing business with some third party." Local 1976, United Brotherhood of Carpenters and Joiners of America, A.F.L. v. Labor Board, 357 U.S. 93, 98, 78 S.Ct. 1011, 1015, 2 L.Ed.2d 1186. In the instant case, however, the Local, in asking the managers not to handle Servette items, was not attempting to induce or encourage them to cease performing their managerial duties in order to force their employers to cease doing business with Servette. Rather, the managers were asked to make a managerial decision which the Board found was within their authority to make. Such an appeal would not have been a violation of § 8(b)(4)(A) before 1959, and we think that the legislative history of the 1959 amendments makes it clear that the amendments were not meant to render such an appeal an unfair labor practice.

The 1959 amendments were designed to close certain loopholes in the application of § 8(b)(4)(A) which had been exposed in Board and court decisions. Thus, it had been held that the term "the employees of any employer" limited the application of the statute to those within the statutory definitions of "employees" and "employer." Section 2(2) of the National Labor Relations Act defines "employer" to exclude the federal and state governments and their agencies or subdivisions, * * * and employers subject to the Railway Labor Act. * * * The definition of "employee" in § 2(3) excludes agricultural laborers, supervisors, and employees of an employer subject to the Railway Labor Act.[6] * * * Furthermore, since the section proscribed only inducement to engage in a strike or "concerted" refusal to perform services, it had been held that it was violated only if the inducement was directed at two or more employees. To close these loopholes, subsection (i) substituted the phrase "any individual employed by any person" for "the employees of any employer," and deleted the word "concerted." The first change was designed to make the provision applicable to refusals by employees who were not technically "employees" within the statutory definitions, and the second change was intended to make clear that inducement directed to only one individual was proscribed. But these changes did not expand the type of conduct which § 8(b)(4)(A) condemned, that is, union pressures calculated to induce the employees of a secondary employer to withhold their services in order to force their employer to cease dealing with the primary employer.

Moreover, the division of § 8(b)(4) into subsections (i) and (ii) by the 1959 amendments has direct relevance to the issue presented by this case. It had been held that § 8(b)(4)(A) did not reach threats of labor trouble made to the secondary employer himself. Congress decided that such conduct should be

the applicability of subsection (i) turns upon whether the union's appeal is to cease performing employment services, or is an appeal for the exercise of managerial discretion.

6. In view of these definitions, it was permissible for a union to induce work stoppages by minor supervisors, and farm, railway or public employees. * * *

made unlawful, but only when it amounted to conduct which "threaten[s], coerce[s] or restrain[s] any person"; hence the addition of subsection (ii). The careful creation of separate standards differentiating the treatment of appeals to the employees of the secondary employer not to perform their employment services, from appeals for other ends which are attended by threats, coercion or restraint, argues conclusively against the interpretation of subsection (i) as reaching the Local's appeals to the supermarket managers in this case. If subsection (i), in addition to prohibiting inducement of employees to withhold employment services, also reaches an appeal that the managers exercise their delegated authority by making a business judgment to cease dealing with the primary employer, subsection (ii) would be almost superfluous. Harmony between (i) and (ii) is best achieved by construing subsection (i) to prohibit inducement of the managers to withhold their services from their employer, and subsection (ii) to condemn an attempt to induce the exercise of discretion only if the inducement would "threaten, coerce, or restrain" that exercise.

We turn finally to the question whether the proviso to amended § 8(b)(4) protected the Local's handbilling. The Court of Appeals, following its decision in Great Western Broadcasting Corp. v. Labor Board, 310 F.2d 591 (C.A. 9th Cir.), held that the proviso did not protect the Local's conduct because, as a distributor, Servette was not directly involved in the physical process of creating the products, and thus "does not produce any products." The Board on the other hand followed its ruling in Lohman Sales Co., 132 N.L.R.B. 901, that products "produced by an employer" included products distributed, as here, by a wholesaler with whom the primary dispute exists. We agree with the Board. The proviso was the outgrowth of a profound Senate concern that the unions' freedom to appeal to the public for support of their case be adequately safeguarded. We elaborated the history of the proviso in National Labor Relations Board v. Fruit & Vegetable Packers, Local 760, 377 U.S. 58, 84 S.Ct. 1063. It would fall far short of achieving this basic purpose if the proviso applied only in situations where the union's labor dispute is with the manufacturer or processor. Moreover, a primary target of the 1959 amendments was the secondary boycotts conducted by the Teamsters Union, which ordinarily represents employees not of manufacturers, but of motor carriers. There is nothing in the legislative history which suggests that the protection of the proviso was intended to be any narrower in coverage than the prohibition to which it is an exception, and we see no basis for attributing such an incongruous purpose to Congress.

The term "produced" in other labor laws was not unfamiliar to Congress. Under the Fair Labor Standards Act, the term is defined as "produced, manufactured, mined, handled, or in any other manner worked on * * *," 29 U.S.C.A. § 203(j), and has always been held to apply to the wholesale distribution of goods. The term "production" in the War Labor Disputes Act has been similarly applied to a general retail department and mail-order business. The Court of Appeals' restrictive reading of "producer" was prompted in part by the language of § 8(b)(4)(B), which names as a proscribed object of the conduct defined in subsections (i) and (ii) "forcing or requiring any person to cease * * * dealing in the products of any other *producer, processor,* or *manufacturer.* " (Italics supplied.) In its decision in Great Western Broadcasting Corp. v. Labor Board, supra, the Court of

Appeals reasoned that since a "processor" and a "manufacturer" are engaged in the physical creation of goods, the word "producer" must be read as limited to one who performs similar functions. On the contrary, we think that "producer" must be given a broader reach, else it is rendered virtually superfluous.

Finally, the warnings that handbills would be distributed in front of noncooperating stores are not prohibited as "threats" within subsection (ii). The statutory protection for the distribution of handbills would be undermined if a threat to engage in protected conduct were not itself protected.

Reversed.

NATIONAL LABOR RELATIONS BOARD v. FRUIT AND VEGETABLE PACKERS, LOCAL 760 ("TREE FRUITS")

Supreme Court of the United States, 1964.
377 U.S. 58, 84 S.Ct. 1063, 12 L.Ed.2d 129.

MR. JUSTICE BRENNAN delivered the opinion of the Court.

Under § 8(b)(4)(ii)(B) of the National Labor Relations Act, as amended, it is an unfair labor practice for a union "to threaten, coerce, or restrain any person," with the object of "forcing or requiring any person to cease using, selling, handling, transporting, or otherwise dealing in the products of any other producer * * * or to cease doing business with any other person * * *." A proviso excepts, however, "publicity, *other than picketing*, for the purpose of truthfully advising the public * * * that a product or products are produced by an employer with whom the labor organization has a primary dispute and are distributed by another employer, as long as such publicity does not have an effect of inducing any individual employed by any person other than the primary employer in the course of his employment to refuse to pick up, deliver, or transport any goods, or not to perform any services, at the establishment of the employer engaged in such distribution." (Italics supplied.) The question in this case is whether the respondent unions violated this section when they limited their secondary picketing of retail stores to an appeal to the customers of the stores not to buy the products of certain firms against which one of the respondents was on strike.

Respondent Local 760 called a strike against fruit packers and warehousemen doing business in Yakima, Washington.[2] The struck firms sold Washington State apples to the Safeway chain of retail stores in and about Seattle, Washington. Local 760, aided by respondent Joint Council, instituted a consumer boycott against the apples in support of the strike. They placed pickets who walked back and forth before the customers' entrances of 46 Safeway stores in Seattle. The pickets—two at each of 45 stores and three at the 46th store—wore placards and distributed handbills which appealed to Safeway customers, and to the public generally, to refrain from buying Washington State apples, which were only one of numerous food

2. The firms, 24 in number, are members of the Tree Fruits Labor Relations Committee, Inc., which acts as the members' agent in labor disputes and in collective bargaining with unions which represent employees of the members. The strike was called in a dispute over the terms of the renewal of a collective bargaining agreement.

products sold in the stores.[3] Before the pickets appeared at any store, a letter was delivered to the store manager informing him that the picketing was only an appeal to his customers not to buy Washington State apples, and that the pickets were being expressly instructed "to patrol peacefully in front of the consumer entrances of the store, to stay away from the delivery entrances and not to interfere with the work of your employees, or with deliveries to or pickups from your store." A copy of written instructions to the pickets—which included the explicit statement that "you are also forbidden to request that the customers not patronize the store"—was enclosed with the letter. Since it was desired to assure Safeway employees that they were not to cease work, and to avoid any interference with pickups or deliveries, the pickets appeared after the stores opened for business and departed before the stores closed. At all times during the picketing, the store employees continued to work, and no deliveries or pickups were obstructed. Washington State apples were handled in normal course by both Safeway employees and the employees of other employers involved. Ingress and egress by customers and others was not interfered with in any manner.

A complaint issued on charges that this conduct violated § 8(b)(4) as amended.[5] The case was submitted directly to the National Labor Relations Board on a stipulation of facts and the waiver of a hearing and proceedings before a Trial Examiner. The Board held * * * that "by literal wording of the proviso [to Section 8(b)(4)] as well as through the interpretive gloss placed thereon by its drafters, consumer picketing in front of a secondary establishment is prohibited." 132 N.L.R.B. 1172, 1177. Upon respondents' petition for review and the Board's cross-petition for enforcement, the Court of Appeals for the District of Columbia Circuit set aside the Board's order and remanded. The court rejected the Board's construction and held that the statutory requirement of a showing that respondents' conduct would

---

3. The placard worn by each picket stated: "To the Consumer: Non-Union Washington State apples are being sold at this store. Please do not purchase such apples. Thank you. Teamsters Local 760, Yakima, Washington."

A typical handbill read:

"DON'T BUY
WASHINGTON STATE
APPLES

The 1960 Crop of Washington State Apples is Being Packed by Non-Union Firms

Included in this non-union operation are twenty-six firms in the Yakima Valley with which there is a labor dispute. These firms are charged with being

UNFAIR

by their employees who, with their union, are on strike and have been replaced by non-union strikebreaking workers employed under substandard wage scales and working conditions.

In justice to these striking union workers who are attempting to protect their living stan-

dards and their right to engage in good-faith collective bargaining, we request that you

DON'T BUY
WASHINGTON STATE
APPLES

Teamsters Union Local 760
Yakima, Washington

This is not a strike against any store or market.

(P.S.—PACIFIC FRUIT & PRODUCE CO. is the only firm packing Washington State Apples under a union contract.)"

5. The complaint charged violations of both subsections (i) and (ii) of § 8(b)(4). The Board held, however, that as the evidence indicated "that Respondents' picketing was directed at consumers only, and was not intended to 'induce or encourage' employees of Safeway or of its suppliers to engage in any kind of action, we find that by such picketing Respondents did not violate Section 8(b)(4)(i) (B) of the Act." 132 N.L.R.B., at 1177. See also National Labor Relations Board v. Servette, Inc., 377 U.S. 46, 84 S.Ct. 1098.

"threaten, coerce, or restrain" Safeway could only be satisfied by affirmative proof that a substantial economic impact on Safeway had occurred, or was likely to occur as a result of the conduct. Under the remand the Board was left "free to reopen the record to receive evidence upon the issue whether Safeway was in fact threatened, coerced, or restrained." 113 U.S.App.D.C. 356, 363, 308 F.2d 311, 318. * * *

The Board's reading of the statute—that the legislative history and the phrase "other than picketing" in the proviso reveal a congressional purpose to outlaw all picketing directed at customers at a secondary site—necessarily rested on the finding that Congress determined that such picketing always threatens, coerces or restrains the secondary employer. We therefore have a special responsibility to examine the legislative history for confirmation that Congress made that determination. Throughout the history of federal regulation of labor relations, Congress has consistently refused to prohibit peaceful picketing except where it is used as a means to achieve specific ends which experience has shown are undesirable. "In the sensitive area of peaceful picketing Congress has dealt explicitly with isolated evils which experience has established flow from such picketing." National Labor Relations Board v. Drivers etc. Local Union, 362 U.S. 274, 284, 80 S.Ct. 706, 712, 4 L.Ed.2d 710. We have recognized this congressional practice and have not ascribed to Congress a purpose to outlaw peaceful picketing unless "there is the clearest indication in the legislative history," ibid., that Congress intended to do so as regards the particular ends of the picketing under review. Both the congressional policy and our adherence to this principle of interpretation reflect concern that a broad ban against peaceful picketing might collide with the guarantees of the First Amendment.

We have examined the legislative history of the amendments to § 8(b) (4), and conclude that it does not reflect with the requisite clarity a congressional plan to proscribe all peaceful consumer picketing at secondary sites, and, particularly, any concern with peaceful picketing when it is limited, as here, to persuading Safeway customers not to buy Washington State apples when they traded in the Safeway stores. All that the legislative history shows in the way of an "isolated evil" believed to require proscription of peaceful consumer picketing at secondary sites was its use to persuade the customers of the secondary employer to cease trading with him in order to force him to cease dealing with, or to put pressure upon, the primary employer. This narrow focus reflects the difference between such conduct and peaceful picketing at the secondary site directed only at the struck product. In the latter case, the union's appeal to the public is confined to its dispute with the primary employer, since the public is not asked to withhold its patronage from the secondary employer, but only to boycott the primary employer's goods. On the other hand, a union appeal to the public at the secondary site not to trade at all with the secondary employer goes beyond the goods of the primary employer, and seeks the public's assistance in forcing the secondary employer to cooperate with the union in its primary dispute.[7] This is not to say that this distinction was

---

7. The distinction between picketing a secondary employer merely to "follow the struck goods," and picketing designed to result in a generalized loss of patronage, was well established in the state cases by 1940. The distinction was sometimes justified on the ground that the secondary employer, who was presumed to receive a competitive benefit from

expressly alluded to in the debates. It is to say, however, that the consumer picketing carried on in this case is not attended by the abuses at which the statute was directed.

The story of the 1959 amendments, which we have detailed at greater length in our opinion filed today in National Labor Relations Board v. Servette, Inc., 377 U.S. 46, 84 S.Ct. 1098, begins with the original § 8(b)(4) of the National Labor Relations Act. Its prohibition, in pertinent part, was confined to the inducing or encouraging of "the employees of any employer to engage in, a strike or a concerted refusal * * * to * * * handle * * * any goods * * * " of a primary employer. This proved to be inept language. Three major loopholes were revealed. Since only inducement of "employees" was proscribed, direct inducement of a supervisor or the secondary employer by threats of labor trouble was not prohibited. Since only a "strike or a concerted refusal" was prohibited, pressure upon a single employee was not forbidden. Finally, railroads, airlines and municipalities were not "employers" under the Act and therefore inducement or encouragement of their employees was not unlawful.

When major labor relations legislation was being considered in 1958 the closing of these loopholes was important to the House and to some members of the Senate. But the prevailing Senate sentiment favored new legislation primarily concerned with the redress of other abuses, and neither the Kennedy-Ives bill, which failed of passage in the House in the Eighty-fifth Congress, nor the Kennedy-Ervin bill, adopted by the Senate in the Eighty-sixth Congress, included any revision of § 8(b)(4). Proposed amendments of § 8(b)(4) offered by several Senators to fill the three loopholes were rejected. The Administration introduced such a bill, and it was supported by Senators Dirksen and Goldwater. Senator Goldwater, an insistent proponent of stiff boycott curbs, also proposed his own amendments. We think it is especially significant that neither Senator, nor the Secretary of Labor in testifying in support of the Administration's bill, referred to consumer picketing as making the amendments necessary. Senator McClellan, who also offered a bill to curb boycotts, mentioned consumer picketing but only such as was "pressure in the form of dissuading customers *from dealing with* secondary employers." (Emphasis supplied.) It was the opponents of the amendments who, in expressing fear of their sweep, suggested that they might proscribe consumer picketing. Senator Humphrey first sounded the warning early in April. Many months later, when the Conference bill was before the Senate, Senator Morse, a conferee, would not support the Conference bill on the express ground that it prohibited consumer picketing. But we have often cautioned against the danger, when interpreting a statute, of reliance upon the views of its legislative opponents. In their zeal to defeat a bill, they understandably tend to overstate its reach. "The fears and doubts of the opposition are no authoritative guide to the construction of legislation. It is

the primary employer's nonunion, and hence lower, wage scales, was in "unity of interest" with the primary employer, Goldfinger v. Feintuch, 276 N.Y. 281, 286, 11 N.E.2d 910, 913, 116 A.L.R. 477; Newark Ladder & Bracket Sales Co. v. Furniture Workers Union Local 66, 125 N.J.Eq. 99, 4 A.2d 49; Johnson v. Milk Drivers & Dairy Employees Union, Local 854, 195 So. 791 (Ct.App.La.), and sometimes on the ground that picketing restricted to the primary employer's product is "a primary boycott against the merchandise." Chiate v. United Cannery Agricultural Packing & Allied Workers of America, 2 CCH Lab.Cas. 125, 126 (Cal.Super.Ct.). See I Teller, Labor Disputes and Collective Bargaining § 123 (1940).

the sponsors that we look to when the meaning of the statutory words is in doubt." Schwegmann Bros. v. Calvert Distillers Corp., 341 U.S. 384, 394–395, 71 S.Ct. 745, 750, 95 L.Ed. 1035 * * *. The silence of the sponsors of amendments is pregnant with significance since they must have been aware that consumer picketing as such had been held to be outside the reach of § 8(b)(4). We are faithful to our practice of respecting the congressional policy of legislating only against clearly identified abuses of peaceful picketing when we conclude that the Senate neither specified the kind of picketing here involved as an abuse, nor indicated any intention of banning all consumer picketing.

The House history is similarly beclouded, but what appears confirms our conclusion. From the outset the House legislation included provisions concerning secondary boycotts. The Landrum-Griffin bill, which was ultimately passed by the House, embodied the Eisenhower Administration's proposals as to secondary boycotts. The initial statement of Congressman Griffin in introducing the bill which bears his name, contains no reference to consumer picketing in the list of abuses which he thought required the secondary boycott amendments. Later in the House debates he did discuss consumer picketing, but only in the context of its abuse when directed against shutting off the patronage of a secondary employer.

In the debates before passage of the House bill he stated that the amendments applied to consumer picketing of customer entrances to retail stores selling goods manufactured by a concern under strike, if the picketing were designed to "coerce or to restrain the employer of [the] second establishment, to get him not to do business with the manufacturer * * *," and further that, "of course, this bill and any other bill is limited by the constitutional right of free speech. If the purpose of the picketing is to *coerce the retailer not to do business* with the manufacturer"—then such a boycott could be stopped. (Italics supplied.)

The relevant changes in former § 8(b)(4) made by the House bill substituted "any individual employed by any person" for the Taft-Hartley wording, "the employees of any employer," deleted the requirement of a "concerted" refusal, and made it an unfair labor practice "to threaten, coerce, or restrain any person" where an object thereof was an end forbidden by the statute, e.g., forcing or requiring a secondary employer to cease handling the products of, or doing business with, a primary employer. There is thus nothing in the legislative history prior to the convening of the Conference Committee which shows any congressional concern with consumer picketing beyond that with the "isolated evil" of its use to cut off the business of a secondary employer as a means of forcing him to stop doing business with the primary employer. When Congress meant to bar picketing *per se,* it made its meaning clear; for example, § 8(b)(7) makes it an unfair labor practice, "to picket or cause to be picketed * * * any employer * * *." In contrast, the prohibition of § 8(b)(4) is keyed to the coercive nature of the conduct, whether it be picketing or otherwise.

Senator Kennedy presided over the Conference Committee. He and Congressman Thompson prepared a joint analysis of the Senate and House bills. This analysis pointed up the First Amendment implications of the broad language in the House revisions of § 8(b)(4) stating,

"The prohibition [of the House bill] reaches not only picketing but leaflets, radio broadcasts and newspaper advertisements, thereby interfering with freedom of speech.

*   *   *   *   *   *   *   *   *

" *   *   * one of the apparent purposes of the amendment is to prevent unions from appealing to the general public as consumers for assistance in a labor dispute. This is a basic infringement upon freedom of expression."

This analysis was the first step in the development of the publicity proviso, but nothing in the legislative history of the proviso alters our conclusion that Congress did not clearly express an intention that amended § 8(b)(4) should prohibit all consumer picketing. Because of the sweeping language of the House bill, and its implications for freedom of speech, the Senate conferees refused to accede to the House proposal without safeguards for the right of unions to appeal to the public, even by some conduct which might be "coercive." The result was the addition of the proviso. But it does not follow from the fact that some coercive conduct was protected by the proviso, that the exception "other than picketing" indicates that Congress had determined that all consumer picketing was coercive.

No Conference Report was before the Senate when it passed the compromise bill, and it had the benefit only of Senator Kennedy's statement of the purpose of the proviso. He said that the proviso preserved "the right to appeal to consumers by methods other than picketing asking them to refrain from buying goods made by nonunion labor *and* to refrain from trading with a retailer who sells such goods. *   *   * We were not able to persuade the House conferees to permit picketing in front of that secondary shop, but were able to persuade them to agree that the unions shall be free to conduct informational activity short of picketing. In other words, the union can hand out handbills at the shop *   *   * and can carry on all publicity short of having ambulatory picketing *   *   *." (Italics supplied.) This explanation does not compel the conclusion that the Conference Agreement contemplated prohibiting any consumer picketing at a secondary site beyond that which urges the public, in Senator Kennedy's words, to "refrain from trading with a retailer who sells such goods." To read into the Conference Agreement, on the basis of a single statement, an intention to prohibit all consumer picketing at a secondary site would depart from our practice of respecting the congressional policy not to prohibit peaceful picketing except to curb "isolated evils" spelled out by the Congress itself.

Peaceful consumer picketing to shut off all trade with the secondary employer unless he aids the union in its dispute with the primary employer, is poles apart from such picketing which only persuades his customers not to buy the struck product. The proviso indicates no more than that the Senate conferees' constitutional doubts led Congress to authorize publicity other than picketing which persuades the customers of a secondary employer to stop all trading with him, but not such publicity which has the effect of cutting off his deliveries or inducing his employees to cease work. On the other hand, picketing which persuades the customers of a secondary employer to stop all trading with him was also to be barred.

In sum, the legislative history does not support the Board's finding that Congress meant to prohibit all consumer picketing at a secondary site, having determined that such picketing necessarily threatened, coerced or restrained the secondary employer. Rather, the history shows that Congress was following its usual practice of legislating against peaceful picketing only to curb "isolated evils."

This distinction is opposed as "unrealistic" because, it is urged, all picketing automatically provokes the public to stay away from the picketed establishment. The public will, it is said, neither read the signs and handbills, nor note the explicit injunction that "This is not a strike against any store or market." Be that as it may, our holding today simply takes note of the fact that Congress has never adopted a broad condemnation of peaceful picketing, such as that urged upon us by petitioners, and an intention to do so is not revealed with that "clearest indication in the legislative history," which we require. National Labor Relations Board v. Drivers, etc. Local Union, supra.

We come then to the question whether the picketing in this case, confined as it was to persuading customers to cease buying the product of the primary employer, falls within the area of secondary consumer picketing which Congress did clearly indicate its intention to prohibit under § 8(b)(4) (ii). We hold that it did not fall within that area, and therefore did not "threaten, coerce, or restrain" Safeway. While any diminution in Safeway's purchases of apples due to a drop in consumer demand might be said to be a result which causes respondents' picketing to fall literally within the statutory prohibition, "it is a familiar rule that a thing may be within the letter of the statute and yet not within the statute, because not within its spirit nor within the intention of its makers." Holy Trinity Church v. United States, 143 U.S. 457, 459, 12 S.Ct. 511, 512, 36 L.Ed. 226. * * * When consumer picketing is employed only to persuade customers not to buy the struck product, the union's appeal is closely confined to the primary dispute. The site of the appeal is expanded to include the premises of the secondary employer, but if the appeal succeeds, the secondary employer's purchases from the struck firms are decreased only because the public has diminished its purchases of the struck product. On the other hand, when consumer picketing is employed to persuade customers not to trade at all with the secondary employer, the latter stops buying the struck product, not because of a falling demand, but in response to pressure designed to inflict injury on his business generally. In such case, the union does more than merely follow the struck product; it creates a separate dispute with the secondary employer.[20]

We disagree therefore with the Court of Appeals that the test of "to threaten, coerce, or restrain" for the purposes of this case is whether Safeway suffered or was likely to suffer economic loss. A violation of § 8(b) (4)(ii)(B) would not be established, merely because respondents' picketing was

20. For example: If a public appeal directed only at a product results in a decline of 25% in the secondary employer's sales of that product, the corresponding reduction of his purchases of the product is due to his inability to sell any more. But if the appeal is broadened to ask that the public cease all pa-tronage, and if there is a 25% response, the secondary employer faces this decision: whether to discontinue handling the primary product entirely, even though he might otherwise have continued to sell it at the 75% level, in order to prevent the loss of sales of other products.

effective to reduce Safeway's sales of Washington State apples, even if this led or might lead Safeway to drop the item as a poor seller.

The judgment of the Court of Appeals is vacated and the case is remanded with direction to enter judgment setting aside the Board's order.

* * *

MR. JUSTICE DOUGLAS took no part in the consideration or decision of this case.

MR. JUSTICE BLACK, concurring.

Because of the language of § 8(b)(4)(ii)(B) of the National Labor Relations Act and the legislative history set out in the opinions of the Court and of my Brother Harlan, I feel impelled to hold that Congress, in passing this section of the Act, intended to forbid the striking employees of one business to picket the premises of a neutral business where the purpose of the picketing is to persuade customers of the neutral business not to buy goods supplied by the struck employer. Construed in this way, as I agree with Brother Harlan that it must be, I believe, contrary to his view, that the section abridges freedom of speech and press in violation of the First Amendment.

"Picketing," in common parlance and in § 8(b)(4)(ii)(B), includes at least two concepts: (1) patrolling, that is, standing or marching back and forth or round and round on the street, sidewalks, private property, or elsewhere, generally adjacent to someone else's premises; (2) speech, that is, arguments, usually on a placard, made to persuade other people to take the picketers' side of a controversy. * * * While "the dissemination of information concerning the facts of a labor dispute must be regarded as within that area of free discussion that is guaranteed by the Constitution," Thornhill v. Alabama, 310 U.S. 88, 102, 60 S.Ct. 736, 744, 84 L.Ed. 1093, patrolling is, of course, conduct, not speech, and therefore is not directly protected by the First Amendment. It is because picketing includes patrolling that neither Thornhill nor cases that followed it lend "support to the contention that peaceful picketing is beyond legislative control." Giboney v. Empire Storage & Ice Co., 336 U.S. 490, 499–500, 69 S.Ct. 684, 690, 93 L.Ed. 834. Cf. Schneider v. State, 308 U.S. 147, 160–161, 60 S.Ct. 146, 150, 84 L.Ed. 155. However, when conduct not constitutionally protected, like patrolling, is intertwined, as in picketing, with constitutionally protected free speech and press, regulation of the non-protected conduct may at the same time encroach on freedom of speech and press. In such cases it is established that it is the duty of courts, before upholding regulations of patrolling, "to weigh the circumstances and to appraise the substantiality of the reasons advanced in support of the regulation of the free enjoyment of the rights" of speech and press. Schneider v. State, 308 U.S., supra, at 161, 60 S.Ct. at 150.

* * *

Even assuming that the Federal Government has power to bar or otherwise regulate patrolling by persons on local streets or adjacent to local business premises in the State of Washington, it is difficult to see that the section in question intends to do anything but prevent dissemination of information about the facts of a labor dispute—a right protected by the First Amendment. It would be different (again assuming federal power) if Congress had simply barred or regulated all patrolling of every kind for every purpose in order to keep the streets around interstate businesses open for movement of people and property. Schneider v. State, supra, 308 U.S. at 160–161, 60 S.Ct. at 150; or to promote the public safety, peace, comfort, or convenience, Cantwell v. Connecticut, 310 U.S. 296, 304, 60 S.Ct. 900, 903, 84 L.Ed. 1213; or to protect people from violence and breaches of the peace by those who are patrolling, Thornhill v. Alabama, supra, 310 U.S. at 105, 60 S.Ct. at 745. Here the section against picketing was not passed for any of these reasons. The statute in no way manifests any government interest against patrolling as such, since the only patrolling it seeks to make unlawful is that which is carried on to advise the public, including consumers, that certain products have been produced by an employer with whom the picketers have a dispute. All who do not patrol to publicize this kind of dispute are, so far as this section of the statute is concerned, left wholly free to patrol. Thus the section is aimed at outlawing free discussion of one side of a certain kind of labor dispute and cannot be sustained as a permissible regulation of patrolling. * * *

Nor can the section be sustained on the ground that it merely forbids picketers to help carry out an unlawful or criminal undertaking. Compare Giboney v. Empire Storage & Ice Co., supra. For the section itself contains a proviso which says that it shall not be construed "to prohibit publicity, other than picketing, for the purpose of truthfully advising the public, including consumers * * * that a product or products are produced by an employer with whom * * * [the picketers have] ᵃ a primary dispute * * *." Thus, it is clear that the object of the picketing was to ask Safeway customers to do something which the section itself recognizes as perfectly lawful. Yet, while others are left free to picket for other reasons, those who wish to picket to inform Safeway customers of their labor dispute with the primary employer, are barred from picketing—solely on the ground of the lawful information they want to impart to the customers.

In short, we have neither a case in which picketing is banned because the picketers are asking others to do something unlawful nor a case in which *all* picketing is, for reasons of public order, banned. Instead, we have a case in which picketing, otherwise lawful, is banned only when the picketers express particular views. The result is an abridgment of the freedom of these picketers to tell a part of the public their side of a labor controversy, a subject the free discussion of which is protected by the First Amendment.

I cannot accept my Brother Harlan's view that the abridgment of speech and press here does not violate the First Amendment because other methods of communication are left open. This reason for abridgment strikes me as being on a par with holding that governmental suppression of a newspaper in a city would not violate the First Amendment because there continue to be radio and television stations. First Amendment freedoms can no more validly be taken away by degrees than by one fell swoop.

For these reasons I concur in the judgment of the Court vacating the judgment of the Court of Appeals and remanding the case with directions to enter judgment setting aside the Board's order.

---

a. The bracketed phrase is Justice Black's. The statute actually reads "the labor organization has."

MR. JUSTICE HARLAN, whom MR. JUSTICE STEWART, joins, dissenting.
* * *

The Labor Board found the Union's picketing at Safeway stores, though peaceful, unlawful *per se* under § 8(b)(4)(ii)(B), and issued an appropriate order. The Court of Appeals reversed, holding the picketing lawful in the absence of any showing that Safeway had *in fact* been "threatened, coerced, or restrained" (113 U.S.App.D.C. 356, 360–363, 308 F.2d 311, at pp. 315–318), and remanded the case to the Board for further proceedings. This Court now rejects (correctly, I believe) the Court of Appeals' holding, but nevertheless refuses to enforce the Board's order. It holds that although § 8(b)(4)(ii)(B) does automatically outlaw peaceful secondary consumer picketing aimed at *all* products handled by a secondary employer, Congress has not, with "the requisite clarity" * * *, evinced a purpose to prohibit such picketing when directed *only* at the products of the primary employer. Here the Union's picketing related only to Washington apples, not to all products carried by Safeway.

Being unable to discern in § 8(b)(4)(ii)(B) or in its legislative history any basis for the Court's subtle narrowing of these statutory provisions, I must respectfully dissent.

I.

The Union's activities are plainly within the letter of subdivision (4)(ii) (B) of § 8(b), and indeed the Court's opinion virtually concedes that much * * *. Certainly Safeway is a "person" as defined in those subdivisions; indubitably "an object" of the Union's conduct was the "forcing or requiring" of Safeway, through the picketing of its customers, "to cease * * * selling, handling * * * or otherwise dealing in" Washington apples, "the products of" another "producer"; and consumer picketing is expressly excluded from the ameliorative provisions of the proviso. * * *

Nothing in the statute lends support to the fine distinction which the Court draws between general and limited product picketing. The enactment speaks pervasively of threatening, coercing, or restraining any person; the proviso differentiates only between modes of expression, not between types of secondary consumer picketing. For me, the Court's argument to the contrary is very unconvincing.

The difference to which the Court points between a secondary employer merely lowering his purchases of the struck product to the degree of decreased consumer demand and such an employer ceasing to purchase one product because of consumer refusal to buy any products, is surely too refined in the context of reality. It can hardly be supposed that in all, or even most, instances the result of the type of picketing involved here will be simply that suggested by the Court. Because of the very nature of picketing there may be numbers of persons who will refuse to buy at all from a picketed store, either out of economic or social conviction or because they prefer to shop where they need not brave a picket line. Moreover, the public can hardly be expected always to know or ascertain the precise scope of a particular picketing operation. Thus in cases like this, the effect on the secondary employer may not always be limited to a decrease in his sales of the struck product. And even when that is the effect, the employer may, rather than simply reducing purchases from the primary employer, deem it more expedient to turn to another producer whose product is approved by the union.

The distinction drawn by the majority becomes even more tenuous if a picketed retailer depends largely or entirely on sales of the struck product. If, for example, an independent gas station owner sells gasoline purchased from a struck gasoline company, one would not suppose he would feel less threatened, coerced, or restrained by picket signs which said "Do not buy X gasoline" than by signs which said "Do not patronize this gas station." To be sure Safeway is a multiple article seller, but it cannot well be gainsaid that the rule laid down by the Court would be unworkable if its applicability turned on a calculation of the relation between total income of the secondary employer and income from the struck product.

The Court informs us that "Peaceful consumer picketing to shut off all trade with the secondary employer unless he aids the union in its dispute with the primary employer, is poles apart from such picketing which only persuades his customers not to buy the struck product." The difference was, it is stated, "well established in the state cases by 1940," that is, before the present federal enactment. In light of these assertions, it is indeed remarkable that the Court not only substantially acknowledges that the statutory language does not itself support this distinction * * * but cites no report of Congress, no statement of a legislator, not even the view of any of the many commentators in the area, in any way casting doubt on the applicability of § 8(b)(4)(ii)(B) to picketing of the kind involved here.

II.

The Court's distinction fares no better when the legislative history of § 8(b)(4)(ii)(B) is examined. Even though there is no Senate, House, or Conference Report which sheds light on the matter, that hardly excuses the Court's blinding itself to what the legislative and other background materials do show. Fairly assessed they, in my opinion, belie Congress' having made the distinction upon which the Court's thesis rests. Nor can the Court find comfort in the generalization that " 'In the sensitive area of peaceful picketing Congress has dealt explicitly with isolated evils which experience has established flow from such picketing' " * * *; in enacting the provisions in question Congress *was* addressing itself to a particular facet of secondary boycotting not dealt with in prior legislation, namely, peaceful secondary consumer picketing. I now turn to the materials which illuminate what Congress had in mind.

It is clear that consumer picketing in connection with secondary boycotting was at the forefront of the problems which led to the amending of the Taft-Hartley Act by the Labor-Management Reporting and Disclosure Act of 1959. * * *

Reporting on the compromise reached by the Conference Committee on the Kennedy-Ervin and Landrum-Griffin bills, Senator Kennedy, who chaired the Conference Committee, stated:

"[T]he House bill prohibited the union from carrying on any kind of activity to disseminate informational material to secondary sites. They could not say that there was a strike in a primary plant. * * * Under the language of the conference [ultimately resulting in present § 8(b)(4)(ii)(B)], we agreed there would not be picketing at a secondary site. What was permitted was the giving out of handbills or information through the radio, and so forth." 105 Cong.Rec. 17720, II Leg.Hist. 1389.

Senator Morse, one day later, explained quite explicitly his objection to the relevant portion of the bill reported out of the Conference Committee, of which he was a member:

"This bill does not stop with threats and with illegalizing the hot cargo agreement. It also makes it illegal for a union to 'coerce, or restrain.' This prohibits consumer picketing. What is consumer picketing? A shoe manufacturer sells his product through a department store. The employees of the shoe manufacturer go on strike for higher wages. The employees, in addition to picketing the manufacturer, also picket at the premises of the department store with a sign saying, 'Do not buy X shoes.' This is consumer picketing, an appeal to the public not to buy the product of a struck manufacturer." 105 Cong.Rec. 17882, II Leg.Hist. 1426.

Later the same day, Senator Kennedy spoke further on the Conference bill and particularized the union rights protected by the Senate conferees:

"(c) The right to appeal to consumers by methods other than picketing asking them to refrain from buying goods made by nonunion labor and to refrain from trading with a retailer who sells such goods.

"Under the Landrum-Griffin bill it would have been impossible for a union to inform the customers of a secondary employer that that employer or store was selling goods which were made under racket conditions or sweatshop conditions, or in a plant where an economic strike was in progress. We were not able to persuade the House conferees to permit picketing in front of that secondary shop, but we were able to persuade them to agree that the union shall be free to conduct informational activity short of picketing. In other words, the union can hand out handbills at the shop, can place advertisements in newspapers, can make announcements over the radio, and can carry on all publicity short of having ambulatory picketing in front of a secondary site." 105 Cong.Rec. 17898–17899, II Leg.Hist. 1432.

The Court does not consider itself compelled by these remarks to conclude that the Conference Committee meant to prohibit *all* secondary consumer picketing. A fair reading of these comments, however, can hardly leave one seriously in doubt that Senator Kennedy believed this to be precisely what the Committee had done; the Court's added emphasis on the word "and" * * * is, I submit, simply grasping at straws, if indeed the phrase relied on does not equally well lend itself to a disjunctive reading. * * * The complicated role the Court assigns to the publicity proviso * * * makes even less understandable its failure to accord to the remarks of Senator Kennedy their proper due. The proviso, according to the Court's interpretation, is unnecessary in regard to picketing designed to effect a boycott of the primary product and comes into play only if a complete boycott of the secondary employer is sought. Had this ingenious interpretation been intended, would not Senator Kennedy, who was at pains to emphasize the scope of activities still left to unions, have used it to refute the criticisms of Senator Morse made only shortly before?

Further, Senator Goldwater spoke in favor of the Conference bill and pointed out that in contrast to the Senate bill, which he had opposed, "[t]he House bill * * * closed up every loophole in the boycott section of the law including the use of a secondary consumer picket line * * *." 105 Cong. Rec. 17904, II Leg.Hist. 1437. * * *

A reading of proceedings in the House of Representatives leads to a similar conclusion regarding the intent of that body. * * *

Indicative of the contemporaneous understanding is an analysis of the bill prepared by Congressmen Thompson and Udall and inserted in the Congressional Record, in which a hypothetical case, as directly in point as the department store example used by Senator Morse, is suggested:

> "Suppose that the employees of the Coors Brewery were to strike for higher wages and the company attempted to run the brewery with strike-breakers. Under the present law, the union can ask the public not to buy Coors beer during the strike. It can picket the bars and restaurants which sold Coors beer with the signs asking the public not to buy the product. It can broadcast the request over the radio or in newspaper advertisements.

> "The Landrum bill forbids this elementary freedom to appeal to the general public for assistance in winning fair labor standards." 105 Cong. Rec. 15540, II Leg.Hist. 1576. * * *

In the light of the foregoing, I see no escape from the conclusion that § 8(b)(4)(ii)(B) does prohibit *all* consumer picketing. * * *

III.

Under my view of the statute the constitutional issue is therefore reached. Since the Court does not discuss it, I am content simply to state in summary form my reasons for believing that the prohibitions of § 8(b)(4)(ii) (B), as applied here, do not run afoul of constitutional limitations. This Court has long recognized that picketing is "inseparably something more [than] and different" from simple communication. Hughes v. Superior Court, 339 U.S. 460, 464, 70 S.Ct. 718, 721, 94 L.Ed. 985 * * *. Congress has given careful and continued consideration to the problems of labor-management relations, and its attempts to effect an accommodation between the right of unions to publicize their position and the social desirability of limiting a form of communication likely to have effects caused by something apart from the message communicated, are entitled to great deference. The decision of Congress to prohibit secondary consumer picketing during labor disputes is, I believe, not inconsistent with the protections of the First Amendment, particularly when, as here, other methods of communication are left open.[5]

Contrary to my Brother Black, I think the fact that Congress in prohibiting secondary consumer picketing has acted with a discriminating eye is the very thing that renders this provision invulnerable to constitutional attack. That Congress has permitted other picketing which is likely to have effects beyond those resulting from the "communicative" aspect of picketing does not, of course, in any way lend itself to the conclusion that

---

5. I mean to intimate no view on the constitutionality of the regulation or prohibition of picketing which publicizes something other than a grievance in a labor-management dispute.

Congress here has aimed to "prevent dissemination of information about the facts of a labor dispute" * * *. Even on the highly dubious assumption that the "non-speech" aspect of picketing is always the same whatever the particular context, the social consequences of the "non-communicative" aspect of picketing may certainly be thought desirable in the case of "primary" picketing and undesirable in the case of "secondary" picketing, a judgment Congress has indeed made in prohibiting secondary but not primary picketing.

I would enforce the Board's order.

Note

1. May it fairly be charged that the Supreme Court in the Tree Fruits case abdicated its judicial function of laying the constitutional yardstick alongside a congressional enactment and usurped the legislative function by rewriting Section 8(b)(4)(ii)? Is the charge a serious one? For a critical analysis, see Lewis, Consumer Picketing and the Court—The Questionable Yield of Tree Fruits, 49 Minn.L.Rev. 479 (1965).

2. Under the interpretation of Section 8(b)(4) in Tree Fruits, what room for operation is afforded the publicity proviso?

3. As with Section 8(b)(7) (see Note, p. 387 supra), Section 8(b)(4) may profitably be pictorialized as a box or trap—"the 8(b)(4) trap." In order to fall into the trap, the union must engage in activity satisfying either (i) (strike inducement) or (ii) (threat, coercion, restraint) and (A), (B), (C), or (D). Once in the trap (but only then), the escape hatch of the "publicity proviso" becomes relevant. Did the union in Tree Fruits ever make it into the trap? In Servette?

4. Justice Harlan, in his dissent in Tree Fruits, focused upon a potential conundrum in the application of the Tree Fruits doctrine which has since borne its own confounding fruit. As Justice Harlan stated supra. p. 431:

> "The distinction drawn by the majority becomes even more tenuous if a picketed retailer depends largely or entirely on sales of the struck product. If, for example, an independent gas station owner sells gasoline purchased from a struck gasoline company, one would not suppose he would feel less threatened, coerced, or restrained by picket signs which said 'Do not buy X gasoline' than by signs which said 'Do not patronize this gas station.' To be sure Safeway is a multiple article seller, but it cannot well be gainsaid that the rule laid down by the Court would be unworkable if its applicability turned on a calculation of the relation beween total income of the secondary employer and income from the struck product."

This issue came home to the Supreme Court's roost in NLRB v. Retail Store Employees Union, Local 1001 ("Safeco"), 447 U.S. 607, 100 S.Ct. 2372, 65 L.Ed.2d 377 (1980), a case in which the union, seeking a collective bargaining agreement with Safeco Title Insurance Co., an underwriter of real estate title insurance in the State of Washington, struck against Safeco and extended its supportive picketing to the premises of five local title companies which did business with Safeco. The picket signs, read in the context of accompanying handbilling, constituted product boycotting of the kind protected in Tree Fruits. However, the five local title companies derived over 90% of their gross incomes from the sale of Safeco title insurance. The National Labor Relations Board found a violation of Section 8(b)(4)(ii)(B), concluding that since the sale of the Safeco policies accounted for substantially all of the title companies' business, the

Union's action was "reasonably calculated to induce customers not to patronize the neutral parties at all." 226 N.L.R.B. at 757. The D.C. Court of Appeals set aside the Board's order on the ground that, though the title companies were neutral parties entitled to the benefit of Section 8(b)(4)(ii)(B), the Tree Fruits doctrine nonetheless applied. 627 F.2d 1133 (D.C.Cir.1979).

The Supreme Court, in a 6–3 decision, reversed the Court of Appeals and remanded to enforce the Board's order. The Court stated:

> "Although *Tree Fruits* suggested that secondary picketing against a struck product and secondary picketing against a neutral party were 'poles apart,' * * * the courts soon discovered that product picketing could have the same effect as an illegal secondary boycott. In Hoffman ex rel. NLRB v. Cement Masons Local 337, 468 F.2d 1187 (CA9 1972), cert. denied., 411 U.S. 986, 93 S.Ct. 2269, 36 L.Ed.2d 964 (1973), for example, a union embroiled with a general contractor picketed the housing subdivision that he had constructed for a real estate developer. Pickets sought to persuade prospective purchasers not to buy the contractor's houses. The picketing was held illegal because purchasers 'could reasonably expect that they were being asked not to transact any business whatsoever' with the neutral developer. Id., at 1192. '[W]hen a union's interest in picketing a primary employer at a "one product" site, [directly conflicts] with the need to protect * * * neutral employers from the labor disputes of others,' Congress has determined that the neutrals' interests should prevail. Id., at 1191.[7]

> "*Cement Masons* highlights the critical difference between the picketing in this case and the picketing at issue in *Tree Fruits*. The product picketed in *Tree Fruits* was but one item among the many that made up the retailer's trade. * * * If the appeal against such a product succeeds, the Court observed, it simply induces the neutral retailer to reduce his orders for the product or 'to drop the item as a poor seller.' * * * The decline in sales attributable to consumer rejection of the struck product puts pressure upon the primary employer, and the marginal injury to the neutral retailer is purely incidental to the product boycott. The neutral therefore has little reason to become involved in the labor dispute. In this case, on the other hand, the title companies sell only the primary employer's product and perform the services associated with it. Secondary picketing against consumption of the primary product leaves responsive consumers no realistic option other than to boycott the title companies altogether. If the appeal succeeds, each company 'stops buying the struck product, not because of a falling demand, but in response to pressure designed to inflict injury on [its] business generally.' Thus, 'the union does more than merely follow the struck product; it creates a separate dispute with the secondary employer.' * * * Such an expansion of labor discord was one of the evils that Congress intended § 8(b)(4)(ii)(B) to prevent." 447 U.S. at 612–14, 100 S.Ct. at 2376–77, 65 L.Ed.2d at 383–84.

Recognizing the difficulty thus produced in the line-drawing between Tree Fruits and Safeco, the Court observed in footnote 11 of the Safeco opinion (the Court seems increasingly to secrete its ultimate wisdom in footnotes):

7. The so-called merged product cases also involve situations where an attempt to follow the struck product inevitably encourages an illegal boycott of the neutral party. See K & K Construction Co. v. NLRB, 592 F.2d 1228, 1231–1234 (3d Cir.1979); American Bread Co. v. NLRB, 411 F.2d 147, 154–155 (6th Cir.1969); Honolulu Typographical Union No. 37 v. NLRB, 131 U.S.App.D.C. 1, 4–5, 401 F.2d 952, 954–955 (1968); Note, Consumer Picketing and the Single-Product Secondary Employer, 47 U.Chi.L.Rev. 112, 132–136 (1979).

"The picketing in *Tree Fruits* and the picketing in this case are relatively extreme examples of the spectrum of conduct that the Board and the courts will encounter in complaints charging violations of § 8(b)(4)(ii)(B). If secondary picketing were directed against a product representing a major portion of a neutral's business, but significantly less than that represented by a single dominant product, neither *Tree Fruits* nor today's decision necessarily would control. The critical question would be whether, by encouraging customers to reject the struck product, the secondary appeal is reasonably likely to threaten the neutral party *with ruin or substantial loss.* Resolution of the question in each case will be entrusted to the Board's expertise." 447 U.S. at 615–16, 100 S.Ct. at 2378, 65 L.Ed.2d at 385 n. 11 (emphasis supplied.)

Justice Brennan, joined by Justices White and Marshall dissented. In so doing, he framed the fundamental issue involved in the Tree Fruits-Safeco dichotomy, namely, the proper interpretation to be given to the word "coerce" in Section 8(b)(4)(ii)(B). The dissent's definition would exclude as non-coercive *any* secondary pressure resulting from the primary-product boycotting endorsed in Tree Fruits.

With whom do you agree, the majority or dissent?

THE PRIMARY–SECONDARY DISTINCTION CARRIED TO DISTRACTION

A line has classically been drawn between primary and secondary activity in determining the lawfulness of union conduct. As with all line-drawing in the law, the gray area does not self-divide. Whether the activity under scrutiny shields employee interests which have matured to the point of acceptability or, instead, reaches out in sword-like fashion to seek fresh advantage through pressure applied remotely from its target is an inquiry and concern of the law of labor relations as enduring as this sentence. We are about to see how attenuated the line between primary and secondary activity can become in a technological society where business relationships are complex and all sides are creatively organized for the protection of their own self-interests.

NATIONAL WOODWORK MANUFACTURERS ASSOCIATION v. NATIONAL LABOR RELATIONS BOARD

Supreme Court of the United States, 1967.
386 U.S. 612, 87 S.Ct. 1250, 18 L.Ed.2d 357.

MR. JUSTICE BRENNAN delivered the opinion of the Court.

Under the Landrum-Griffin Act amendments enacted in 1959, * * * § 8(b)(4)(A) of the National Labor Relations Act * * * became § 8(b)(4)(B) and § 8(e) was added. The questions here are whether, in the circumstances of these cases, the Metropolitan District Council of Philadelphia and Vicinity of the United Brotherhood of Carpenters and Joiners of America, AFL–CIO (hereafter the Union), committed the unfair labor practices prohibited by §§ 8(e) and 8(b)(4)(B).

Frouge Corporation, a Bridgeport, Connecticut, concern was the general contractor on a housing project in Philadelphia. Frouge had a collective bargaining agreement with the Carpenters' International Union under which Frouge agreed to be bound by the rules and regulations agreed upon by local unions with contractors in areas in which Frouge had jobs. Frouge was therefore subject to the provisions of a collective bargaining agreement between the Union and an organization of Philadelphia contractors, the General Building Contractors Association, Inc. A sentence in a provision of that agreement entitled Rule 17 provides that " * * * No member of this District Council will handle * * * any doors * * * which have been fitted prior to being furnished on the job. * * * " [2] Frouge's Philadelphia project called for 3,600 doors. Customarily, before the doors could be hung on such projects, "blank" or "blind" doors would be mortised for the knob, routed for the hinges, and beveled to make them fit between jambs. These are tasks traditionally performed in the Philadelphia area by the carpenters employed on the jobsite. However, precut and prefitted doors ready to hang may be purchased from door manufacturers. Although Frouge's contract and job specifications did not call for premachined doors, and "blank" or "blind" doors could have been ordered, Frouge contracted for the purchase of premachined doors from a Pennsylvania door manufacturer which is a member of the National Woodwork Manufacturers Association, petitioner in No. 110 and respondent in No. 111. The Union ordered its carpenter members not to hang the doors when they arrived at the jobsite. Frouge thereupon withdrew the prefabricated doors and substituted "blank" doors which were fitted and cut by its carpenters on the jobsite.

The National Woodwork Manufacturers Association and another filed charges with the National Labor Relations Board against the Union alleging that by including the "will not handle" sentence of Rule 17 in the collective bargaining agreement the Union committed the unfair labor practice under § 8(e) of entering into an "agreement * * * whereby [the] employer * * * agrees to cease or refrain from handling * * * any of the products of any other employer * * *," and alleging further that in enforcing the sentence against Frouge, the Union committed the unfair labor practice under § 8(b)(4)(B) of "forcing or requiring any person to cease using * * * the products of any other * * * manufacturer * * *." The National Labor Relations Board dismissed the charges, 149 N.L.R.B. 646.[3] The Board adopted the findings of the Trial Examiner that the "will not handle"

2. The full text of Rule 17 is as follows:

"No employer shall work on any job on which cabinet work, fixtures, millwork, sash, doors, trim or other detailed millwork is used unless the same is Union-made and bears the Union Label of the United Brotherhood of Carpenters and Joiners of America. No member of this District Council will handle material coming from a mill where cutting out and fitting has been done for butts, locks, letter plates, or hardware on any description, nor any doors or transoms which have been fitted prior to being furnished on job, including base, chair, rail, picture moulding, which has been previously fitted. This section to exempt partition work furnished in sections." The National Labor Relations Board determined that the first sentence violated § 8(e), 149 N.L.R.B.

646, 655–656, and the Union did not seek judicial review of that determination.

3. There were also charges of violation of §§ 8(e) and 8(b)(4)(B) arising from the enforcement of the Rule 17 provision against three other contractors whose contracts with the owners of the construction projects involved specified that the contractors should furnish and install precut and prefinished doors. The Union refused to permit its members to hang these doors. The Board held that this refusal violated § 8(b)(4)(B). The Board reasoned that, since these contractors (in contrast to Frouge) did not have "control" over the work that the Union sought to preserve for its members, the Union's objective was secondary—to compel the project owners to stop specifying precut doors in their contracts with the employer-contractors. 149 N.L.R.B., at

sentence in Rule 17 was language used by the parties to protect and preserve cutting out and fitting as unit work to be performed by the jobsite carpenters. The Board also adopted the holding of the Trial Examiner that both the sentence of Rule 17 itself and its maintenance against Frouge were therefore "primary" activity outside the prohibitions of §§ 8(e) and 8(b)(4)(B). The following statement of the Trial Examiner was adopted by the Board:

> "I am convinced and find that the tasks of cutting out and fitting millwork, including doors, has, at least customarily, been performed by the carpenters employed on the jobsite. Certainly, this provision of rule 17 is not concerned with the nature of the employer with whom the contractor does business nor with the employment conditions of other employers or employees, nor does it attempt to control such other employers or employees. The provision guards against encroachments on the cutting out and fitting work of the contract unit employees who have performed that work in the past. Its purpose is plainly to regulate the relations between the general contractor and his own employees and to protect a legitimate economic interest of the employees by preserving their unit work. Merely because it incidentally also affects other parties is no basis for invalidating this provision.

> "I find that * * * [the provision] is a lawful work-protection or work-preservation provision and that Respondents have not violated Section 8(e) of the Act by entering into agreements containing this provision and by thereafter maintaining and enforcing this provision." 149 N.L.R.B., at 657.

The Court of Appeals for the Seventh Circuit reversed the Board in this respect. 354 F.2d 594, 599. The Court held that the "will not handle" agreement violated § 8(e) without regard to any "primary" or "secondary" objective, and remanded to the Board with instructions to enter an order accordingly. In the court's view, the sentence was designed to effect a product boycott like the one condemned in Allen Bradley Co. v. Local Union No. 3, etc., 325 U.S. 797, 65 S.Ct. 1533, 89 L.Ed. 1939, and Congress meant, in enacting § 8(e) and § 8(b)(4)(B), to prohibit such agreements and conduct forcing employers to enter into them.

The Court of Appeals sustained, however, the dismissal of the § 8(b)(4) (B) charge. The court agreed with the Board that the Union's conduct as to Frouge involved only a primary dispute with it, and held that the conduct was therefore not·prohibited by that section but expressly protected by the proviso "[t]hat nothing contained in this Clause (B) shall be construed to make unlawful, where not otherwise unlawful, any primary strike or primary picketing * * *." 354 F.2d at 597.

We granted certiorari on the petition of the Woodwork Manufacturers Association in No. 110 and on the petition of the Board in No. 111. * * * We affirm in No. 110 and reverse in No. 111.

---

658. The Union petitioned the Court of Appeals to set aside the remedial order issued by the Board on this finding, but the court sustained the Board. 354 F.2d 594, 597. The Union did not seek review of the question here. Not before us, therefore, is the issue argued by the AFL–CIO in its brief *amicus curiae,* namely, whether the Board's "right-to-control doctrine—that employees can never strike against their own employer about a matter over which he lacks the legal power to grant their demand"—is an incorrect rule of law inconsistent with the Court's decision in National Labor Relations Board v. Insurance Agents' International Union, AFL–CIO, 361 U.S. 477, 497–498, 80 S.Ct. 419, 431–432.

I.

Even on the doubtful premise that the words of § 8(e) unambiguously embrace the sentence of Rule 17,[4] this does not end inquiry into Congress' purpose in enacting the section. It is a "familiar rule, that a thing may be within the letter of the statute and yet not within the statute, because not within its spirit nor within the intention of its makers." Holy Trinity Church v. United States, 143 U.S. 457, 459, 12 S.Ct. 511, 512, 36 L.Ed. 226. * * *

Strongly held opposing views have invariably marked controversy over labor's use of the boycott to further its aims by involving an employer in disputes not his own. But congressional action to deal with such conduct has stopped short of proscribing identical activity having the object of pressuring the employer for agreements regulating relations between him and his own employees. That Congress meant §§ 8(e) and 8(b)(4)(B) to prohibit only "secondary" objectives clearly appears from an examination of the history of congressional action on the subject. * * *

The history begins with judicial application of the Sherman Act * * * to labor activities. Federal court injunctions freely issued against all manner of strikes and boycotts under rulings that condemned virtually every collective activity of labor as an unlawful restraint of trade.[6] The first congressional response to vehement labor protests came with § 20 of the Clayton Act in 1914. That section purported drastically to limit the injunction power of federal courts in controversies "involving, or growing out of, a dispute concerning terms or conditions of employment." * * * Labor hailed the law as a charter immunizing its activities from the antitrust laws. This expectation was disappointed when Duplex Printing Press Co. v. Deering, 254 U.S. 443, 41 S.Ct. 172, 65 L.Ed. 349, and Bedford Cut Stone Co. v. Journeymen Stone Cutters' Assn., 274 U.S. 37, 47 S.Ct. 522, 71 L.Ed. 916, held that § 20 immunized only trade union activities directed against an employer by his own employees. * * *

Thus "primary" but not "secondary" pressures were excepted from the antitrust laws. * * *

In 1932 Congress enacted the Norris-LaGuardia Act and tipped the scales the other way. Its provisions "established that the allowable area of union activity was not to be restricted, as it had been in the *Duplex* case, to an immediate employer-employee relation." United States v. Hutcheson, 312 U.S. 219, 231, 61 S.Ct. 463, 466, 85 L.Ed. 788.[9] Congress abolished, for purposes of labor immunity, the distinction between primary activity be-

---

4. The statutory language of § 8(e) is far from unambiguous. It prohibits agreements to "cease * * * from handling * * * any of the products *of any other employer* * * *." (Emphasis supplied.) Since both the product and its source are mentioned, the provision might be read not to prohibit an agreement relating solely to the nature of the product itself, such as a work-preservation agreement, but only to prohibit one arising from an objection to the other employers or a definable group of employers who are the source of the product, for example, their nonunion status.

6. See Loewe v. Lawlor, 208 U.S. 274, 28 S.Ct. 301, 52 L.Ed. 488 and 235 U.S. 522, 35 S.Ct. 170, 59 L.Ed. 341 (*Danbury Hatters' Case*). The history of this development under the Sherman Act is traced in Duplex Printing Press Co. v. Deering, 254 U.S. 443, 41 S.Ct. 172; Allen Bradley Co. v. Local Union No. 3, etc., Electrical Workers, 325 U.S. 797, 800–803, 65 S.Ct. 1533, 1535–1537. * * *

9. Section 13(c) of the Norris-LaGuardia Act provided that the term labor dispute and thus the scope of immunity "includes any controversy concerning terms or conditions of

tween the "immediate disputants" and secondary activity in which the employer disputants and the members of the union do not stand "in the proximate relation of employer and employee. * * *" H.R.Rep.No. 669, 72d Cong., 1st Sess., 8 (1932). * * *

Labor abuses of the broad immunity granted by the Norris-LaGuardia Act resulted in the Taft-Hartley Act prohibitions against secondary activities enacted in § 8(b)(4)(A), which, as amended in 1959, is now § 8(b)(4)(B). As will appear, the basic thrust of the accommodation there effected by Congress was not expanded by the Landrum-Griffin amendments. The congressional design in enacting § 8(b)(4)(A) is therefore crucial to the determination of the scope of §§ 8(e) and 8(b)(4)(B). Senator Taft said of its purpose: * * *

> "This provision makes it unlawful to resort to a *secondary boycott to injure the business of a third person who is wholly unconcerned in the disagreement between an employer and his employees.* * * * [U]nder the provisions of the Norris-LaGuardia Act, it became impossible to stop a secondary boycott or any other kind of a strike, no matter how unlawful it may have been at common law. *All this provision of the bill does is to reverse the effect of the law as to secondary boycotts."* [11] (Emphasis supplied.)
> * * *

Judicial decisions interpreting the broad language of § 8(b)(4)(A) of the Act uniformly limited its application to such "secondary" situations. * * * This Court accordingly refused to read § 8(b)(4)(A) to ban traditional primary strikes and picketing having an impact on neutral employers even though the activity fell within its sweeping terms. National Labor Relations Board v. International Rice Milling Co., 341 U.S. 665, 71 S.Ct. 961. * * *

The literal terms of § 8(b)(4)(A) also were not applied in the so-called "ally doctrine" cases, in which the union's pressure was aimed toward employers performing the work of the primary employer's striking employees. The rationale, again, was the inapplicability of the provision's central theme, the protection of neutrals against secondary pressure, where the secondary employer against whom the union's pressure is directed has entangled himself in the vortex of the primary dispute. * * *

In effect Congress, in enacting § 8(b)(4)(A) of the Act, returned to the regime of *Duplex Printing Press Co.* and *Bedford Cut Stone Co.,* supra, and barred as a secondary boycott union activity directed against a neutral employer, including the immediate employer when in fact the activity directed against him was carried on for its effect elsewhere. * * *

II.

The Landrum-Griffin Act amendments in 1959 were adopted only to close various loopholes in the application of § 8(b)(4)(A) which had been exposed in Board and court decisions. We discussed some of these loopholes, and the particular amendments adopted to close them, in National Labor Relations Board v. Servette, Inc., 377 U.S. 46, 51–54, 84 S.Ct. 1098, 1102, 12

employment, or concerning the association or representation of persons in negotiating, fixing, maintaining, changing, or seeking to arrange terms or conditions of employment, *regardless of whether or not the disputants stand in the proximate relation of employer*

and employee." 47 Stat. 73. (Emphasis supplied.)

11. 93 Cong.Rec. 4198, II Legislative History of the Labor Management Relations Act, 1947 (hereafter 1947 Leg.Hist.), 1106.

L.Ed.2d 121. We need not repeat that discussion here, except to emphasize, as we there said, that "these changes did not expand the type of conduct which § 8(b)(4)(A) condemned, that is, union pressures calculated to induce the employees of a secondary employer to withhold their services in order to force their employer to cease dealing with the primary employer." Id., at 52–53, 84 S.Ct. at 1103.

Section 8(e) simply closed still another loophole. In Local 1976, United Brotherhood of Carpenters, etc., v. National Labor Relations Board (Sand Door), 357 U.S. 93, 78 S.Ct. 1011, the Court held that it was no defense to an unfair labor practice charge under § 8(b)(4)(A) that the struck employer had agreed, in a contract with the union, not to handle nonunion material. However, the Court emphasized that the mere execution of such a contract provision (known as a "hot cargo" clause because of its prevalence in Teamsters Union contracts), or its voluntary observance by the employer, was not unlawful under § 8(b)(4)(A). Section 8(e) was designed to plug this gap in the legislation by making the "hot cargo" clause itself unlawful. The *Sand Door* decision was believed by Congress not only to create the possibility of damage actions against employers for breaches of "hot cargo" clauses, but also to create a situation in which such clauses might be employed to exert subtle pressures upon employers to engage in "voluntary" boycotts. Hearings in late 1958 before the Senate Select Committee explored seven cases of "hot cargo" clauses in Teamsters Union contracts, the use of which the Committee found conscripted neutral employers in Teamsters organizational campaigns.[24]

This loophole-closing measure likewise did not expand the type of conduct which § 8(b)(4)(A) condemned. Although the language of § 8(e) is sweeping, it closely tracks that of § 8(b)(4)(A), and just as the latter and its successor § 8(b)(4)(B) did not reach employees' activity to pressure their employer to preserve for themselves work traditionally done by them, § 8(e) does not prohibit agreements made and maintained for that purpose.

The legislative history of § 8(e) confirms this conclusion. * * *

[P]rovisos were added to § 8(e) to preserve the *status quo* in the construction industry, and exempt the garment industry from the prohibitions of §§ 8(e) and 8(b)(4)(B). This action of the Congress is strong confirmation that Congress meant that both §§ 8(e) and 8(b)(4)(B) reach only secondary pressures. If the body of § 8(e) applies only to secondary activity, the garment industry proviso is a justifiable exception which allows what the legislative history shows it was designed to allow, secondary pressures to counteract the effects of sweatshop conditions in an industry with a highly integrated process of production between jobbers, manufacturers, contractors and subcontractors. [T]his motivation for the proviso sheds light on the central theme of the body of § 8(e), to which the proviso is an exception. * * * [Similarly], if the heart of § 8(e) is construed to be directed only to

---

24. See Final Report of the Senate Select Committee on Improper Activities in the Labor or Management Field, S.Rep. No. 1139, 86th Cong., 2d Sess., 3 (1960). The Final Report, ordered to be printed after enactment of the Landrum-Griffin Act, defined a "hot cargo" clause as "an agreement between a union and a unionized employer that his employees shall not be required to work on or handle 'hot goods' or 'hot cargo' being manufactured or transferred by another employer with whom the union has a labor dispute or whom the union considers and labels as being unfair to organized labor." Ibid.

secondary activities, the construction proviso becomes, as it was intended to be, a measure designed to allow agreements pertaining to certain secondary activities on the construction site because of the close community of interests there, but to ban secondary-objective agreements concerning nonjobsite work, in which respect the construction industry is no different from any other. The provisos are therefore substantial probative support that primary work preservation agreements were not to be within the ban of § 8(e).
* * *

In addition to all else, [b]efore we may say that Congress meant to strike from workers' hands the economic weapons traditionally used against their employers' efforts to abolish their jobs, that meaning should plainly appear. "[I]n this era of automation and onrushing technological change, no problems in the domestic economy are of greater concern than those involving job security and employment stability. Because of the potentially cruel impact upon the lives and fortunes of the working men and women of the Nation, these problems have understandably engaged the solicitous attention of government, of responsible private business, and particularly of organized labor." Fibreboard Paper Prods. Corp. v. Labor Board, 379 U.S. 203, 225, 13 L.Ed.2d 233, 247, 85 S.Ct. 398, 6 A.L.R.2d 1130 (concurring opinion of Stewart, J.). We would expect that legislation curtailing the ability of management and labor voluntarily to negotiate for solutions to these significant and difficult problems would be preceded by extensive congressional study and debate, and consideration of voluminous economic, scientific, and statistical data. The silence regarding such matters in the Eighty-sixth Congress is itself evidence that Congress, in enacting § 8(e), had no thought of prohibiting agreements directed to work preservation. * * *

The Woodwork Manufacturers Association and *amici* who support its position advance several reasons, grounded in economic and technological factors, why "will not handle" clauses should be invalid in all circumstances. Those arguments are addressed to the wrong branch of government.
* * *

III.

The determination whether the "will not handle" sentence of Rule 17 and its enforcement violated § 8(e) and § 8(b)(4)(B) cannot be made without an inquiry into whether, under all the surrounding circumstances, the Union's objective was preservation of work for Frouge's employees, or whether the agreements and boycott were tactically calculated to satisfy union objectives elsewhere. Were the latter the case, Frouge, the boycotting employer, would be a neutral bystander, and the agreement or boycott would, within the intent of Congress, become secondary. There need not be an actual dispute with the boycotted employer, here the door manufacturer, for the activity to fall within this category, so long as the tactical object of the agreement and its maintenance is that employer, or benefits to other than the boycotting employees or other employees of the primary employer thus making the agreement or boycott secondary in its aim. The touchstone is whether the agreement or its maintenance is addressed to the labor relations of the contracting employer *vis-à-vis* his own employees. * * *

That the "will not handle" provision was not an unfair labor practice in these cases is clear. The finding of the Trial Examiner, adopted by the

Board, was that the objective of the sentence was preservation of work traditionally performed by the jobsite carpenters. This finding is supported by substantial evidence, and therefore the Union's making of the "will not handle" agreement was not a violation of § 8(e).

Similarly, the Union's maintenance of the provision was not a violation of § 8(b)(4)(B). The Union refused to hang prefabricated doors whether or not they bore a union label, and even refused to install prefabricated doors manufactured off the jobsite by members of the Union. This and other substantial evidence supported the finding that the conduct of the Union on the Frouge jobsite related solely to preservation of the traditional tasks of the jobsite carpenters.

*   *   *

MR. JUSTICE STEWART, whom MR. JUSTICE BLACK, MR. JUSTICE DOUGLAS, and MR. JUSTICE CLARK join, dissenting.

The Union's boycott of the prefitted doors clearly falls within the express terms of the federal labor law, which makes such conduct unlawful when "an object thereof" is "forcing or requiring any person to cease using *   *   * the products of any other *   *   * manufacturer *   *   *." And the collective bargaining provision that authorizes such a boycott likewise stands condemned by the law's prohibition of any agreement whereby an employer "agrees to cease or refrain from handling *   *   * any of the products of any other employer *   *   *." The Court undertakes a protracted review of legislative and decisional history in an effort to show that the clear words of the statute should be disregarded in these cases. But the fact is that the relevant history fully confirms that Congress meant what it said, and I therefore dissent.

The Court concludes that the Union's conduct in these cases falls outside the ambit of § 8(b)(4) because it had an ultimate purpose that the Court characterizes as "primary" in nature—the preservation of work for union members. But § 8(b)(4) is not limited to boycotts that have as their only purpose the forcing of any person to cease using the products of another; it is sufficient if that result is "an object" of the boycott. *   *   * Without question, preventing Frouge from using prefitted doors was "an object" of the Union's conduct here. *   *   *

Note

1. Houston Insulation Contractors Association v. NLRB, 386 U.S. 664, 87 S.Ct. 1278, 18 L.Ed.2d 389 (1967), a companion case to National Woodwork, differed from the latter in that the boycotting employees were not members of the same bargaining unit nor represented by the same local union as the employees who benefited from the boycott; they were, however, employed by the same employer. In a 5 to 4 decision finding no Section 8(b)(4) violation, the Court stated:

> "Armstrong Company, a member of the Contractors Association, was engaged in a construction project in Victoria, Texas, within the jurisdiction of Local 113 of the Heat and Frost Insulators and Asbestos Workers. The cutting and mitering of asbestos fittings for such jobs was customarily performed at Armstrong's Houston shop, which was within Local 22's jurisdiction. Armstrong purchased from Thorpe Company, a manufacturer

of insulation materials, asbestos fittings upon which the cutting and mitering work had already been performed. Agents of Local 113 informed
Armstrong that fittings would not be installed unless the cutting and
mitering had been performed by its sister Local 22 as provided by Local 22's
bargaining agreement. The Board found * * * that the object of this
refusal was primary—the preservation of work customarily performed by
Armstrong's own employees. 148 N.L.R.B., at 869. The Court of Appeals
reversed on the ground that Local 113 'had no economic interest in Local
22's claim of breach of contract,' and that therefore 'it was coercing Armstrong not for its own benefit but for the benefit of another local at the
expense of a neutral employer [Thorpe].' 357 F.2d, at 189. We disagree.
* * *

"A boycott cannot become secondary because engaged in by primary
employees not directly affected by the dispute, or because only engaged in by
some of the primary employees, and not the entire group. Since that
situation does not involve the employer in a dispute not his own, his
employees' conduct in support of their fellow employees is not secondary
and, therefore, not a violation of § 8(b)(4)(B)." 386 U.S. at 667–69, 87 S.Ct.
at 1280–81.

2. Is the following provision void under Section 8(e): "The Employer agrees
to refrain from using the services of any person who does not observe the wages,
hours and conditions of employment established by labor unions having jurisdiction over the types of services performed"? In Truck Drivers Union, Local 413 v.
NLRB, 334 F.2d 539 (D.C.Cir.1964), cert. denied, 379 U.S. 916 (1964), the Board
had held that this provision was secondary in nature and therefore invalid under
Section 8(e). The D.C. Court of Appeals, Judge Skelly Wright writing, reversed
the Board, explaining:

"This Board position groups together, as secondary, contract clauses
which impose boycotts on subcontractors not signatory to union agreements,
and those which merely require subcontractors to meet the equivalent of
union standards in order to protect the work standards of the employees of
the contracting employer. But the distinction between these two types of
clauses is vital. Union-signatory subcontracting clauses are secondary, and
therefore within the scope of § 8(e), while union-standards subcontracting
clauses are primary as to the contracting employer. * * *

"This clause would be a union-signatory clause if it required subcontractors to have collective bargaining agreements with petitioner unions or their
affiliates, or with unions generally. We interpret it, however, as merely
requiring that subcontractors observe the equivalent of union wages, hours,
and the like. Since we find that this clause only requires union standards,
and not union recognition, we * * * rule it primary, and thus outside
§ 8(e)'s prohibitions." 334 F.2d at 548.

Which position is more persuasive, that of the Board or of the court of
appeals?

3. Is the following provision void under Section 8(e) and its construction
industry proviso: "The general contractor agrees to refrain from subcontracting
any work to be done on this construction project to any non-unionized contractor"? If the provision is valid, would it be legal for the union beneficiary to seek
to enforce it by conduct falling within Section 8(b)(4)(i) or (ii)? Are the two
questions the same? See the Sand Door discussion in the Pipefitters case, infra
p. 448.

In Connell Constr. Co. v. Plumbers Local 100, 421 U.S. 616, 95 S.Ct. 1830, 44 L.Ed.2d 418 (1975), reported infra p. 1038, the union had elicited agreement to the inclusion of the following provision in a contract with a general contractor:

"[T]he contractor and the union mutually agree with respect to work falling within the scope of this agreement [plumbing and pipefitting] that is to be done at the site of the construction, alteration, painting or repair of any building, structure, or other works, that if the contractor should contract or subcontract any of the aforesaid work falling within the normal trade jurisdiction of the union, said contractor shall contract or subcontract such work only to firms that are parties to an executed, current, collective bargaining agreement with Local Union 100 of the United Association of Journeymen and Apprentices of the Plumbing and Pipefitting Industry."

Is this provision protected by the construction industry proviso of Section 8(e)? Would it make a difference if, as was the case in Connell, the union neither represented nor sought to represent employees of the general contractor, but instead represented only potential employees of the subcontractors? *Should it?*

4. The legislation and the litigation involving construction industry labor relations reflect, in part, a desire to accommodate the labor laws to the practical realities of the construction industry while, at the same time, not unduly restricting employee Section 7 rights. The Supreme Court has been reluctant to sanction interpretations of those laws which appear to give support to "top-down organizing" in the absence of unambiguous congressional intent to permit the questioned conduct. The 1959 amendments to the NLRA, which included Section 8(e) and its construction industry proviso, also included Section 8(f), which permits employers and unions in the construction industry to enter into *pre-hire* agreements. (A pre-hire agreement is a collective bargaining agreement, including union security and hiring hall clauses, entered into before the hiring of a construction force occurs.) Section 8(f) also provides that a pre-hire agreement, entered into pursuant to that section, is not a bar to a petition for an election under Section 9. The Board has interpreted Section 8(f) as merely insulating pre-hire agreements from the principle, exemplified in International Ladies' Garment Workers' v. NLRB, Note 1, supra p. 302, that Sections 8(a)(1) and (2) and 8(b)(1)(A) of the Act are violated if an employer enters into a collective bargaining agreement with other than a majority union. Consequently, the pre-hire agreement merely sets the stage for an enforceable collective bargaining agreement when, and if, the union achieves majority status. Therefore, the employer who repudiates the pre-hire agreement and hires a non-union construction force has not committed a Section 8(a)(5) unfair labor practice, and a union's picketing to enforce the agreement is governed by the organizational and recognitional picketing limitations of Section 8(b)(7).

In NLRB v. Local Union No. 103, International Ass'n of Bridge Workers, 434 U.S. 335, 98 S.Ct. 651, 54 L.Ed.2d 586 (1978), the Court, overruling the D.C. Circuit and stressing the dangers of top-down organizing, approved the Board's interpretation of Section 8(f) and held that picketing for longer than 30 days to enforce a Section 8(f) pre-hire agreement constituted a violation of Section 8(b)(7) (C).

NATIONAL LABOR RELATIONS BOARD v. ENTERPRISE ASSOCIATION OF STEAM AND GENERAL PIPEFITTERS OF NEW YORK

Supreme Court of the United States, 1977.
429 U.S. 507, 97 S.Ct. 891, 51 L.Ed.2d 1.

MR. JUSTICE WHITE delivered the opinion of the Court.

* * * The question now before us is whether a union seeking the kind of work traditionally performed by its members at a construction site violates § 8(b)(4)(B) when it induces its members to engage in a work stoppage against an employer who does not have control over the assignment of the work sought by the union. More specifically, the issue is whether a union-instigated refusal of a subcontractor's employees to handle or install factory-piped climatic control units, which were included in the general contractor's job specifications and delivered to the construction site, was primary activity beyond the reach of § 8(b)(4)(B) or whether it was secondary activity prohibited by the statute. As we shall see, this issue turns on whether the boycott was "addressed to the labor relations of the contracting employer *vis-à-vis* his own employees," National Woodwork, supra, 386 U.S., at 645, 87 S.Ct., at 1268, and is therefore primary conduct, or whether the boycott was "tactically calculated to satisfy union objectives elsewhere," id., at 644, 87 S.Ct., at 1268, in which event the boycott would be prohibited secondary activity.

I

Austin Company, Incorporated (Austin), was the general contractor and engineer on a construction project known as the Norwegian Home for the Aged. As the result of competitive bidding, Austin awarded a subcontract to Hudik-Ross Company, Incorporated (Hudik), to perform the heating, ventilation, and air conditioning work for the Norwegian Home construction. Hudik employs a regular complement of about 10 to 20 steamfitters. For many years, these employees have been represented by respondent Enterprise Association (Enterprise), a plumbing and pipefitting union. Over the years Hudik and Enterprise have entered into successive collective-bargaining agreements, and such an agreement was in force at the time that the dispute involved in the present litigation arose. Austin had no agreement with Enterprise regarding the work to be done on the Norwegian Home project.

The subcontract between Austin and Hudik incorporated Austin's job specifications. These specifications provided that Austin would purchase certain climate control units manufactured by Slant/Fin Corporation (Slant/Fin) to be installed in the Norwegian Home. The specifications further provided that the internal piping in the climate control units was to be cut, threaded, and installed at the Slant/Fin factory. At the time that Hudik entered into the subcontract with Austin, Hudik was aware that its employees would be called upon to install the Slant/Fin units but not to do the internal piping work for the units on the jobsite.

Traditionally, members of respondent union have performed the internal piping on heating and air conditioning units on the jobsite. Also, Rule

IX of the then-current collective-bargaining contract between Hudik and Enterprise provided that pipe threading and cutting were to be performed on the jobsite in accordance with Rule V, which in turn specified that the work would be performed by units of two employees.[4] There had been similar or identical provisions in previous collective-bargaining contracts. There is no dispute that the work designated by Austin's specifications to be performed at the Slant/Fin factory was the kind of cutting and threading work referred to in Rule IX.

When the Slant/Fin units arrived on the job, the union steamfitters refused to install them. The business agent of the union told Austin's superintendent that the steamfitters "would not install the Slant/Fin units because the piping inside the units was steamfitters' work." Enterprise Association of Steam Pipefitters, 204 N.L.R.B. 760, 762 (1973). Hudik was informed that the factory-installed internal piping in the units was in violation of Rule IX of the union contract and "that such piping was Local 638's work." Ibid. When the union persisted in its refusal to install the units, thereby interfering with the completion of the Norwegian Home job, Austin filed a complaint with the Board, alleging that Enterprise had committed an unfair labor practice under § 8(b)(4)(B) of the National Labor Relations Act by engaging in a strike and encouraging Hudik employees to refuse to install the Slant/Fin units in furtherance of an impermissible object. Specifically, Austin charged that the union's action was taken to force Hudik to cease doing business with Austin and to force Hudik and Austin to cease dealing with the products of Slant/Fin. The union's position before the administrative law judge was that it was merely seeking to enforce its contract with Hudik and to preserve the jobsite cutting and threading work covered by Rule IX.

The administrative law judge found that because Austin had specified factory-piped units, there was no internal threading and cutting work to be done on the jobsite of the kind covered by Rule IX and that no such work at the Norwegian Home project could be obtained through pressure on Hudik alone, even if Hudik was forced to abandon its contract, unless and until Austin changed its job specifications so as to provide the piping the union members had traditionally performed for Hudik as a subcontractor. The administrative law judge thus concluded that the union had violated § 8(b)(4)(B) because in seeking to enforce its contract and to obtain the work at the Norwegian Home jobsite, the union's object was in reality to influence Austin by exerting pressure on Hudik, an employer who had no power to award the work to the union.

The Board agreed. 204 N.L.R.B. 760 (1973). It noted first that the steamfitters' refusal to install the Slant/Fin units "was based on a valid work preservation clause in the agreement with Hudik, the subcontractor,

---

4. Rule IX provided in relevant part:

"Radiator branches, convector branches and coil connections shall be cut and threaded by hand on the job in accordance with Rule V." Rule V provided:

"MEN TO WORK IN UNITS OF TWO

"All work to be performed within the jurisdiction of Enterprise Association must be performed by journeymen steamfitters or apprentices working in units of two, one of whom must be a steamfitter. A unit shall be composed of:

"A. Steamfitter with a steamfitter, or

"B. Steamfitter with an apprentice."

and was for the purpose of preserving work they had traditionally performed." 204 N.L.R.B. 760. This did not settle the legality of the work stoppage under § 8(b)(4)(B), however; for "Hudik was incapable of assigning its employees this work; such work was never Hudik's to assign in the first place * * *. Respondent was exerting prohibited pressure on Hudik with an object of either forcing a change in Austin's manner of doing business or forcing Hudik to terminate its subcontract with Austin. Since the pressure exerted by the respondent on Hudik was undertaken for its effect on other employers, this pressure was secondary and prohibited by § 8(b)(4)(B)." Ibid.
* * *

A divided Court of Appeals for the District of Columbia, sitting en banc, set aside the Board's order. Enterprise Association of Steam Pipefitters v. NLRB, 521 F.2d 885 (1975). We granted certiorari because of an apparent conflict between the circuits.[5] * * *

II

In setting aside the Board's order, the Court of Appeals disagreed with the Board on both legal and factual grounds. We deal first with the Court of Appeals' proposition that "an employer who is struck by his own employees for the purpose of requiring him to do what he has lawfully contracted to do to benefit those employees can [n]ever be considered a neutral bystander in a dispute not his own." 521 F.2d, at 903 (footnote omitted). Under this view, a strike or refusal to handle undertaken to enforce such a contract would not itself warrant an inference that the union sought to satisfy secondary, rather than primary, objectives, whatever the impact on the immediate employer or on other employers might be. Thus, where a union seeks to enforce a work preservation agreement by a strike or work stoppage, the existence of the agreement would always provide an adequate defense to a § 8(b)(4) unfair labor practice charge. This approach is untenable under the Act and our cases construing it.

Local 1976, United Brotherhood of Carpenters v. NLRB (*Sand Door*), 357 U.S. 93, 78 S.Ct. 1011, 2 L.Ed.2d 1186 (1958), involved a collective-bargaining contract containing a provision, then quite legal, that "workmen shall not be required to handle non-union material." 357 U.S., at 95, 78 S.Ct., at 1014. The case arose when certain nonunion doors arrived at a construction site and the union notified the contractor that the doors would not be hung. The Board found that the union had committed an unfair practice by encouraging employees to strike or refuse to handle the disputed doors in order to force the contractor to cease doing business with the door manufacturer. The union stood squarely on the contract; and as the case arrived here the sole question was whether the collective-bargaining provision was a "defense to a charge of an unfair labor practice under § 8(b)(4)(A) when, in the absence of such a provision, the conduct would unquestionably be a violation."[6] 357 U.S., at 101, 78 S.Ct., at 1017.

5. For a discussion of the decisions of the courts of appeals on the issues presented in this case see n. 15, infra.

6. Section 8(b)(4)(A) was renumbered as § 8(b)(4)(B) in 1959. As we shall see, no sub- stantive changes made by the 1959 amendments had any effect on the rule established in *Sand Door.*

The union argued that if the statute was aimed at protecting neutral employers from becoming involuntarily involved in the labor disputes of others, "protection should not extend to an employer who has agreed to a hot cargo provision, for such an employer is not in fact involuntarily involved in the dispute," especially "when the employer takes no steps at the time of the boycott to repudiate the contract and to order his employees to handle the goods." In such circumstances, "[t]he union does no more than inform the employees of their contractual rights and urge them to take the only action effective to enforce them." 357 U.S., at 105, 78 S.Ct., at 1019. These arguments were squarely rejected:

> "Nevertheless, it seems most probable that the freedom of choice for the employer contemplated by § 8(b)(4)(A) is a freedom of choice at the time the question whether to boycott or not arises in a concrete situation calling for the exercise of judgment on a particular matter of labor and business policy. Such a choice, free from the prohibited pressures—whether to refuse to deal with another or to maintain normal business relations on the ground that the labor dispute is no concern of his—must as a matter of federal policy be available to the secondary employer notwithstanding any private agreement entered into between the parties. * * * This is so because by the employer's intelligent exercise of such a choice under the impact of a concrete situation when judgment is most responsible, and not merely at the time a collective bargaining agreement is drawn up covering a multitude of subjects, often in a general and abstract manner, Congress may rightly be assumed to have hoped that the scope of industrial conflict and the economic effects of the primary dispute might be effectively limited." 357 U.S., at 105–106, 78 S.Ct., at 1019.

The Court went on to hold that inducements of employees that are prohibited by § 8(b)(4) in the absence of a contractual provision countenancing them "are likewise prohibited when there is such a provision," id., at 106, 78 S.Ct., at 1020. This was true even though the making and voluntary observance of such contracts were not contrary to law at the time that *Sand Door* was decided; however lawful, these contracts could not be enforced "by means specifically prohibited" by the section. Id., at 108, 78 S.Ct., at 1020. The Court held that the legality of the union's conduct is to be viewed at the time of the boycott.

Sand Door's holding that employer promises in a collective-bargaining contract provide no defense to a § 8(b)(4) charge against a union has not been disturbed. In contemplating the 1959 amendments to the Landrum-Griffin Act, Congress viewed that part of *Sand Door* in which the Court suggested that contractual provisions having secondary objectives were not forbidden by law as creating a loophole in the Act. Section 8(e) was enacted to close that loophole. See National Woodwork, supra, 386 U.S., at 634, 87 S.Ct., at 1262. Section 8(e) makes it an unfair labor practice, with provisos, for unions and employers to enter into collective-bargaining contracts whereby the employer ceases or agrees to cease doing business with any other person. Although on its face not limited to agreements having secondary objectives, the section was construed by the Board and this Court as only closing the loophole left by *Sand Door* and as having no broader reach than § 8(b)(4) itself. Section 8(e) does not prohibit agreements made for "primary" purposes, including the purpose of preserving for the contracting employees themselves work traditionally done by them. Id., at 635, 87 S.Ct. 1262.

By no stretch of the imagination, however, can it be thought, that in enacting § 8(e) Congress intended to disagree with or ease *Sand Door's* construction of § 8(b)(4), under which a perfectly legal collective-bargaining contract may not be enforced by a strike or refusal to handle which in the absence of such a provision would be a violation of the statute. * * * To hold, as the Court of Appeals did, that a work stoppage is necessarily primary and not an unfair practice when it aims at enforcing a legal promise in a collective-bargaining contract is inconsistent with the statute as construed in *Sand Door,* a construction that was accepted and that has never been abandoned by Congress.

Nor did we modify *Sand Door* in *National Woodwork.* * * *

In reversing the Court of Appeals' § 8(e) holding and agreeing that § 8(b)(4)(B) had not been violated, we held that neither the Frouge contract nor its maintenance was illegal. Our rationale was *not* that the work preservation provision was valid under § 8(e) and that *therefore* it could be enforced by striking or picketing without violating § 8(b)(4)(B). Expressly recognizing the continuing validity of the *Sand Door* decision that a valid contract does not immunize conduct otherwise violative of § 8(b)(4), 386 U.S., at 634, we held that neither § 8(b)(4)(B) nor § 8(e) forbade primary activity by employees designed to preserve for themselves work traditionally done by them and that on this basis the union's conduct violated neither section. * * * We went on to rule that there was substantial evidence to sustain the finding of the Board that both the agreement and the union activity at the Frouge jobsite related solely to the preservation of the traditional tasks of the jobsite carpenters. In consequence, we agreed that there was neither a § 8(b)(4)(B) nor a § 8(e) unfair labor practice.

There is thus no doubt that the collective-bargaining provision that pipes be cut by hand on the job and that the work be conducted by units of two is not itself a sufficient answer to a § 8(b)(4)(B) charge. The substantial question before us is whether, with or without the collective-bargaining contract, the union's conduct at the time it occurred was proscribed secondary activity within the meaning of the section. If it was, the collective-bargaining provision does not save it. If it was not, the reason is that § 8(b)(4)(B) did not reach it, not that it was immunized by the contract. Thus, regardless of whether an agreement is valid under § 8(e), it may not be enforced by means that would violate § 8(b)(4).[8]

III

The Court of Appeals was also of the view that the Board's "control" test, under which the union commits an unfair practice under § 8(b)(4)(B) when it coerces an employer in order to obtain work that the employer has

---

8. The validity of the will-not-handle provision in this case was not challenged by the charging party, and the Board referred to it as a valid provision. Because the scope of the prohibitions in §§ 8(b)(4)(B) and 8(e) are essentially identical, except where the proscriptions in § 8(e) are limited by the provisos in that section, the Court of Appeals regarded as anomalous that a valid provision in a collective-bargaining contract could not be enforced through economic pressure exerted by the union. This conclusion ignores the substance of our decision in *Sand Door.* * * *

not power to assign, is invalid as a matter of law because it fails to comply with the *National Woodwork* standard that the union's conduct be judged in light of all the relevant circumstances. Again, we think the Court of Appeals was in error.

* * *

Here, the administrative law judge, cognizant of *National Woodwork* and the Board's own precedents, examined the history both of the relevant jobsite work traditionally done by the steamfitters and of the contractual provision calling for jobsite cutting and threading of pipe, assessed the agreement and refusal to handle in the light of the actual conditions in the New York market, and concluded that "under all the surrounding circumstances," Hudik was "only a means or instrumentality for exerting pressure against Slant/Fin and Austin with whom the Union has its primary dispute." [10] It thus does not appear to us that either the administrative law judge or the Board, in agreeing with him, articulated a different standard from that which this Court recognized as the proper test in *National Woodwork*.

Nor is it the case that the Board, in applying its control standard, failed to consider all of the relevant circumstances. Surely the fact that the Board distinguishes between two otherwise identical cases because in the one the employer has control of the work and in the other he has no power over it does not indicate that the Board has ignored any material circumstance. The contrary might more rationally be inferred. Of course, the Board may assign to the presence or absence of control much more weight than would the Court of Appeals, but this far from demonstrates a departure from the totality-of-the-circumstances test recognized in *National Woodwork*. [12]

There is little or no basis in the statute, its legislative history, or our cases for the Court of Appeals' conclusion that the distinction the Board has

10. 204 N.L.R.B., at 764. The administrative law judge concluded that Austin and Slant/Fin were primary employers. The Board, while adopting the remainder of the administrative law judge's report, did not reach this question.

12. The Board also adopted the administrative law judge's discussion of the economic context in which the dispute arose.

The administrative law judge was of the view that union pressure on Austin and other contractors who preferred factory-piped units could effectively foreclose Slant/Fin and similar producers from the market. The Board did not disturb the administrative law judge's findings that

"If prepaid units cannot be installed in the large commercial, public, and industrial buildings in the New York area or in other areas effectively organized by the Union and other building trades unions, the manufacture will be materially affected and Austin and other engineers and general contractors will not specify their purchase and use in buildings." 204 N.L.R.B., at 764.

"In my opinion, it is an appropriate subject of official notice that in New York City,

and probably in all or most of the major cities in this country, the building and construction industry is unionized, certainly with respect to major industrial, commercial, and public construction. Unionized in this context means that craft unions affiliated with the AFL–CIO represent and have contracts for the employees who work on such projects and, in fact, the unions are the source of the labor supply and furnish the employees to the employer-contractors. The strategic position of the unions in the industry is confirmed by the fact that governmental efforts to increase the number of minority employees in the industry are concentrated on the unions and not on the employers. In most industries, if it is desired to increase the number of minority employees, governmental pressure is effectively directed to the employers. But in the construction industry it is the unions that control the labor supply and if the union steamfitter employees of Hudik on the Norwegian job refuse to work, other steamfitters will not be available to Hudik or to anyone else to perform work on the job." Id., n. 10.

drawn between those cases where the struck employer is in position to deliver the work to the union and those where the work is controlled by others is erroneous as a matter of law. The Board has taken this approach in applying § 8(b)(4) at least since 1958 * * *.

Since that time, as its decision in *National Woodwork* exemplifies, the Board has continued to interpret and apply § 8(b)(4)(B) to find an unfair practice at least where the union employs a product boycott to claim work that the immediate employer is not in a position to award, and it has declined to find a violation where the employer has such power, even if awarding the work might cause him to terminate contractual relations with another employer. In the latter circumstances, the cease-doing-business consequences are merely incidental to primary activity, but not in the former where the union, if it is to obtain work, must intend to exert pressure on one or more other employers.

No legislative disagreement with the Board's interpretation of § 8(b)(4) was expressed in 1959 when Congress amended the section. On the contrary, in adding the primary-secondary proviso to the section, as the relevant reports clearly show, Congress intended merely to reflect the existing law. "This provision does not eliminate, restrict, or modify the limitations on picketing at the site of a primary labor dispute that are in existing law." H.R.Conf.Rep. No. 1147, 86th Cong., 1st Sess., 38, in I 1959 Leg.Hist. 942, U.S.Code Cong. & Admin.News 1959, p. 2510.

Furthermore, the courts of appeals regularly sustained the relevant Board interpretations of § 8(b)(4), and we did not question the Board's approach in *National Woodwork*, let alone overrule it *sub silentio*. It is true that since our decision in that case some courts of appeals, like the Court of Appeals for the District of Columbia, have concluded that the Board's interpretation of the statute is in error.[15] The Board's reading and application of the statute involved in this case, however, are long established, have remained undisturbed by Congress, and fall well within that category of situations in which the courts should defer to the agency's understanding of the statute which it administers. See Bayside Enterprises, Inc. v. NLRB, 429

---

15. Prior to this Court's decision in *National Woodwork*, the courts of appeals had uniformly held that it was a violation of § 8(b)(4)(B) for a union to use economic pressures to obtain work that was not within the struck employer's power to award. * * * Generally, the courts of appeals did not treat the Board's control test as a *per se* rule, reasoning instead that the absence of the right to control the work sought is strong evidence that the objective of the economic pressure being applied by the union is to affect someone other than the struck employer.

In many of the pre-*National Woodwork* cases the unions argued that their activity was primary on the ground that they were merely enforcing valid work preservation agreements. The courts of appeals uniformly rejected this argument * * *.

Since this Court's decision in *National Woodwork*, six circuits have addressed the

control issue. The Fourth Circuit in a well-reasoned opinion has expressly sustained the Board's control test. George Koch Sons, Inc. v. NLRB, 490 F.2d 323 (C.A.4 1973). The Ninth Circuit has done the same. See Associated General Contractors of California v. NLRB, 514 F.2d 433 (C.A.9 1975). * * *

The Third, Eighth, and District of Columbia Circuits have rejected the Board's control theory. In addition to the District of Columbia Circuit's opinion in the present case, see Local Union No. 636, United Association of Journeymen v. NLRB, 139 U.S.App.D.C. 165, 430 F.2d 906 (1970); American Boiler Manufacturers Association v. NLRB, 404 F.2d 556 (C.A.8 1968); NLRB v. Local 164, International Brotherhood of Electrical Workers, 388 F.2d 105 (C.A.3 1968). The First Circuit has said the same thing in dictum. Beacon Castle Square Building Corp. v. NLRB, 406 F.2d 188 (C.A.1 1969).

U.S. 298, 302–304, 97 S.Ct. 576, 580–581, 50 L.Ed.2d 494 (1977); NLRB v. Boeing Co., 412 U.S. 67, 75, 93 S.Ct. 1952, 1957, 36 L.Ed.2d 752 (1973); NLRB v. United Insurance Co. of America, 390 U.S. 254, 260, 88 S.Ct. 988, 991, 19 L.Ed.2d 1083 (1968); * * * Sand Door, supra, 356 U.S., at 107, 78 S.Ct., at 1020.

IV

Wholly apart from its determination that the union's conduct was justified as a measure to enforce its collective-bargaining contract and that the Board applied an incorrect standard for determining liability, the Court of Appeals held that since there was "no substantial evidence * * * in this record that the union's purpose was also 'to satisfy union objectives elsewhere,' the Board's decision holding the union guilty of a Section 8(b)(4)(B) violation may not stand." 521 F.2d, at 904. We disagree.

That there existed inducement and coercion within the meaning of § 8(b)(4) is not disputed. The issue is whether "an object" of the inducement and the coercion was to cause the cease-doing-business consequences prohibited by § 8(b)(4), the resolution of which in turn depends on whether the product boycott was "addressed to the labor relations of [Hudik] * * * vis-à-vis his own employees," National Woodwork, supra, 386 U.S., at 645, 87 S.Ct., at 1268, or whether the union's conduct was "tactically calculated to satisfy [its] objectives elsewhere," id., at 644, 87 S.Ct., at 1268.

There is ample support in the record for the Board's resolution of this question. The union sought to enforce its contract with Hudik by a jobsite product boycott by which the steamfitters asserted their rights to the cutting and threading work on the Norwegian Home project. It is uncontrovertible that the work at this site could not be secured by pressure on Hudik alone and that the union's work objectives could not be obtained without exerting pressure on Austin as well. That the union may also have been seeking to enforce its contract and to convince Hudik that it should bid on no more jobs where prepiped units were specified does not alter the fact that the union refused to install the Slant/Fin units and asserted that the piping work on the Norwegian Home job belonged to its members.[17] It was not error for the Board to conclude that the union's objectives were not confined to the employment relationship with Hudik but included the object of influencing Austin in a manner prohibited by § 8(b)(4)(B).

The Court of Appeals was of the view that other inferences from the facts were possible. The court, for example, could "clearly see that it was possible for Hudik-Ross to settle the labor dispute which it had created. The record is void of any suggestion that Hudik-Ross attempted to negotiate a compromise with the union under which the union would have agreed to install the climate control units in exchange for extra pay or other special benefits." 521 F.2d, at 899. How this observation impugns the Board's finding with respect to the union's object is not clear. The union simply refused to handle the Slant/Fin units and asserted that under the contract

---

17. "It is not necessary to find that the *sole* object of the strike" was secondary so long as one of the union's objectives was to influence another employer by inducing the struck employer to cease doing business with that other employer. See NLRB v. Denver Building and Construction Trades Council, 341 U.S. 675, 689, 71 S.Ct. 943, 951, 95 L.Ed. 1284 (1951). * * *

the cutting and threading work belonged to them. The commonsense inference from these facts is that the product boycott was in part aimed at securing the cutting and threading work at the Norwegian Home job, which could only be obtained by exerting pressure on Austin.

The statutory standard under which the Court of Appeals was obliged to review this case was not whether the Court of Appeals would have arrived at the same result as the Board did, but whether the Board's findings were "supported by substantial evidence on the record considered as a whole." 29 U.S.C.A. § 160(e). * * * It appears to us that in reweighing the facts and setting aside the Board's order, the Court of Appeals improperly substituted its own views of the facts for those of the Board.

The judgment of the Court of Appeals is *Reversed*.

MR. JUSTICE BRENNAN, with whom MR. JUSTICE STEWART and MR. JUSTICE MARSHALL join, dissenting. * * *

The Court's result cannot be squared with National Woodwork Manufacturers Assn. v. NLRB, supra, whose totality-of-the-circumstances test the Court purports to apply. * * * That case and this are virtually indistinguishable in relevant respects. * * *

* * * For here, as in *National Woodwork*, the Board found that the Union's actions were taken "for the purpose of preserving work [its members] had traditionally performed." 204 N.L.R.B., at 760. Cf. 386 U.S., at 645–646, 87 S.Ct., at 1268–1269. It defies reality to deny that the Union's principal dispute was with Hudik, the immediate employer of its members. It was Hudik which had acceded to the Union's demand for the work-preservation clause particularly desired by its employees for their own protection. And it was Hudik which breached that clause. Nothing whatever in the record even remotely suggests that the Union had any quarrel with Slant/Fin or Austin. Those companies were simply the vehicles used by Hudik to effect the breach which created the primary dispute between it and its own employees and their Union. Nor is there the slightest basis for a suggestion that the true purpose of the work-preservation clause or the pressure applied to enforce it was to benefit employees "other than the boycotting employees or other employees of [Hudik]." 386 U.S., at 645, 87 S.Ct., at 1268. * * *

Nor is *National Woodwork* distinguishable, as contended, because Austin, and not Hudik, had the "right to control" the assignment of the work of cutting and threading the internal piping. Any conclusion from this that the Union's pressure must have been directed at Austin and not Hudik is totally inconsistent with the premises and conclusion of *National Woodwork*. First, Hudik was by no means a "neutral" in the sense contemplated by Congress as warranting or requiring protection. * * *

Second, it is not true that Hudik was a neutral because it was powerless to deal with the union demands. As the Court of Appeals pointed out, if the Union's purpose is truly work preservation for the benefit of its own members, it presumably would be willing to negotiate some substitute for full compliance, such as premium pay, to replace the lost work. Nothing in this record indicates that Hudik made any attempt to reach that or any other compromise solution, and there is no reason to think that the Union would not have been satisfied with such a result.[4]   *   *   *

The Court is wholly in error in treating the case as one of a factual finding by the Board—to be treated with deference by us—that Austin was the target of the Union's pressure.   *   *   * "Right to control" may, in some circumstances, be relevant to the "inquiry into whether, in all the surrounding circumstances, the [u]nion's objective was preservation of work for [the pressured employer's] employees, or whether the [union pressure was] tactically calculated to satisfy union objectives elsewhere." National Woodwork, supra, 386 U.S., at 644, 87 S.Ct., at 1268. But once the Board determined that the Union's object was preservation of work its members had traditionally performed for Hudik, its factfinding task was completed. The Board concluded that despite this finding, Austin's "right to control" the disputed work required the conclusion that Austin was the Union's target. This was an error of law, not a factual finding.

    *   *   *

Note

1. Perhaps the most fundamental question distillable out of the National Woodwork-Pipefitters sequence is: Has the primary-secondary test for lawfulness of union pressure been stretched beyond its reach? Answering this question requires analysis of the underlying rationale of that test. The rationale is that union pressure should be confined to parties immediately involved in the pertinent controversy so as to protect "neutrals" ("innocent bystanders," "unoffending employers"). The current problem is that the primary-secondary dichotomy no longer provides an apt criterion for distinguishing proper combatants from proper noncombatants. In the Pipefitters case, for example, while Hudik can, on primary-secondary analysis, be fairly allocated to the secondary category, Hudik is nonetheless most difficultly consigned to the role of innocent victim. The problem is the product of technological advance, complexity of business relationships, and ingenuity of organizational strategy and tactics of the various categories of interest groups involved in the pertinent labor disputes. This problem is aggravated in the construction industry by the fact that conflicting contractual obligations are negotiated, in varying time sequence, between 1) owners and general contractors, 2) general contractors and subcontractors, 3) general/subcontractors and unions. (The contractor-union contracting is frequently the product of multiemployer bargaining between associations of contractors (general and/or sub) and building trades unions or regional councils of such unions.) The dominant interests at each of these levels of contracting differ; the contractual provisions accordingly clash; the resolution of the clashes is left to the subsequent decisional processes of the NLRB, reviewing courts, contractual grievance and arbitration procedures, and self-help.

Against this backdrop, both the majority and dissenting positions in Pipefitters are tenable under the primary-secondary analysis. Indeed, that analysis may be said to be irrelevant. Which is to say that the present state of federal

---

4. The Court purports to fail to see "[h]ow this observation impugns the Board's finding with respect to the union's object."   *   *   * That "finding" is based exclusively on the inference that because only Austin could satisfy the Union's demands, Austin must have been the real target of the union pressure. But since there were means by which Hudik could have satisfied the Union's protest, and it did not attempt to take advantage of them, the premise of the Board's argument falls.   *   *   *

labor relations law is inadequate to cope with these sophisticated problems, produced, as they are, by the underlying sophisticated institutional arrangements described above. Two solutions suggest themselves: 1) amendment of the federal labor code so as to define in more refined fashion the licit and the illicit; 2) consignment, by default, of the anticompetitive problems involved to the federal antitrust law—a sufficiently shorthanded body of proscriptions to allow enough judicial elbowroom for federal judges to "enact" their own version of social justice as these questions of labor policy are litigated.

The above analysis is presented provocatively. Has it?

A harbinger of an antitrust-type approach to these problems may lie in Connell Constr. Co. v. Plumbers Local 100, 421 U.S. 616, 95 S.Ct. 1830, 44 L.Ed. 2d 418 (1975), reported infra p. 1038. (While deeper analysis of the labor-code-versus-antitrust-law competition in this area may be comfortably postponed at this point, preliminary show of intellectual curiosity is encouraged.)

2.   A case which dramatizes a dilemma described in Note 1 in an industry other than construction and which poses an even more difficult problem is NLRB v. INTERNATIONAL LONGSHOREMEN'S ASS'N, 447 U.S. 490, 100 S.Ct. 2305, 65 L.Ed.2d 289 (1980), known in the trade as the "CONTAINER CASE" (now, in view of a later return of the case to the Supreme Court, "CONTAINER I"). There, the longshoremen, represented by the ILA, had traditionally performed "on the pier" loading and unloading of ships. The employer organizations in the East Coast shipping industry had introduced over a period of time the use of containers, evolving ultimately to a length of 20 to 40 feet and capable of carrying upwards of 30,000 pounds of freight, which could be moved on and off an ocean vessel unopened. These employers also introduced "container ships" specially designed to carry the containers affixed to their holds. The containers could also be attached to a truck chassis and transported intact to and from the pier like a conventional trailer. The result was a loss of much "on the pier" work for the longshoremen. Responding to this technological innovation, the ILA demanded provisions in the collective bargaining agreement protecting its members against this loss of work. The ILA did not, however, stand adamantly against this innovation, as had the Carpenters in National Woodwork and the Pipefitters in NLRB v. Enterprise Ass'n, but instead accepted, after lengthy strikes, an arrangement encompassing "Rules on Containers." These Rules (so complex as they have evolved over many years of renegotiation and refinement as to defy complete report; the editors have sought in the following to distill them in pedagogically manageable form) required the employers to permit the longshoremen to "strip and stuff" (unload and reload) the containers on the pier in situations where origin or destination of the containerized goods occurred within a 50-mile radius of the subject port, despite the fact that the work was unnecessary (a re-doing of work already done by non-longshoremen off the pier in the case of containers moving from land to sea and a pre-doing of work much of which subsequently had to be redone by non-longshoremen off the pier in the case of containers moving from sea to land). In the alternative, for the violation of these Rules, the employers were to pay $1,000 per container (variously defined as "royalty," "fine," "liquidated damages") to an ILA fund for the welfare of its members. The containers, owned by the employers (shipping-lines), were leased to trucking companies which delivered the loaded containers to and/or picked them up at the dock-site. Violations of the collective bargaining provisions with regard to the "make work" (on-the-pier unloading and reloading) provoked strikes and threats of strikes by the ILA to enforce the "penalty" provisions of

the contract. This union pressure forced the employers of the longshoremen to pay substantial sums of money to the ILA fund, and to demand similar payments by way of reimbursement from the trucking companies, themselves responsible for the violations of the "make work" provisions in the Rules (through their misrepresentations that the origin or destination of the containers was *outside* of the 50-mile radius). Upon the refusal of the trucking companies to so reimburse or in some cases without providing that alternative, the employers ceased furnishing them with containers (i.e., ceased doing business with them within the meaning of 8(b)(4)(B)). The truckers then filed 8(e) and 8(b)(4)(B) charges against the ILA.

The real dispute was thus over whether the containers were to be analogized to the hold of a ship, the unloading and loading of which was traditional work of the longshoremen, or the trailer of a truck, the loading and unloading of which was the traditional work of trucking employees, i.e., teamsters. The NLRB held the loading and unloading of the containers within the 50-mile radius to be "off pier" and therefore not traditionally the work of the longshoremen. Consequently, it found the pertinent Rules and the ILA strike pressure in support thereof to be for the purpose of work acquisition rather than work preservation, and accordingly secondary pressure in violation of both 8(e) and 8(b)(4)(B).

The D.C. Court of Appeals denied enforcement of the Board's order, holding that the Board had erred as a matter of law in defining the work in controversy. 613 F.2d 890 (D.C.Cir.1979).

The Supreme Court, 5–4, agreed with the Court of Appeals, explaining:

"The Board's approach reflects a fundamental misconception of the work preservation doctrine as it has been applied in our previous cases. Identification of the work at issue in a complex case of technological displacement requires a careful analysis of the traditional work patterns that the parties are allegedly seeking to preserve, and of how the agreement seeks to accomplish that result under the changed circumstances created by the technological advance. The analysis must take into account 'all the surrounding circumstances,' *National Woodwork,* supra at 644, 87 S.Ct., at 1268, including the nature of the work both before and after the innovation. In a relatively simple case, such as *National Woodwork* or *Pipefitters,* the inquiry may be of rather limited scope. Other, more complex cases will require a broader view, taking into account the transformation of several interrelated industries or types of work; this is such a case. Whatever its scope, however, the inquiry must be carefully focused: to determine whether an agreement seeks no more than to preserve the work of bargaining unit members, the Board must focus on the work of the bargaining unit employees, not on the work of other employees who may be doing the same or similar work,[22] and examine the relationship between the work as it existed before the innovation and as the agreement proposes to preserve it.

"The Board, by contrast, focused on the work done by the employees of the charging parties [the trucking companies] * * * after the introduction of containerized shipping. It found that work was similar to work those employees had done before the innovation, and concluded that ILA was

---

22. The effect of work preservation agreements on the employment opportunities of employees not represented by the union, no matter how severe, is of course irrelevant to the validity of the agreement so long as the union had no forbidden secondary purpose to affect the employment relations of the neutral employer. See *Pipefitters,* supra, 429 U.S. at 510, 526, 97 S.Ct. at 894, 902.

trying to acquire the traditional work of those employees. That conclusion ignores the fact that the impact of containerization occurred at the interface between ocean and motor transport; not surprisingly, the work of stuffing and stripping containers in similar to work previously done by both long-shoremen and truckers. The Board's approach would have been entirely appropriate in considering an agreement to preserve the work of truckers' employees, but it misses the point when applied to judge this contract between the ILA and the shipowner employers.

"By focusing on the work as performed after the innovation took place, by the employees who allegedly have displaced the longshoremen's work, the Board foreclosed—by definition—any possibility that the longshoremen could negotiate an agreement to permit them to continue to play any part in the loading or unloading of containerized cargo. For the very reason the rules were negotiated was that longshoremen do not perform that work away from the pier, and never have. Thus it is apparent that under the Board's approach, in the words of the Court of Appeals, the 'work preservation doctrine is sapped of all life.' 198 U.S. App.D.C., at 176, 613 F.2d, at 909.

"That this is so is vividly demonstrated by considering how different would have been the results in *National Woodwork* and *Pipefitters* if we had adopted the approach now chosen by the Board. In *National Woodwork* we held that carpenters could seek to preserve their traditional work of finishing blank doors at the construction jobsite by prohibiting the employer, a general contractor, from purchasing prefinished doors from the factory. If we had followed the Board's current approach in analyzing the agreement, we would have defined the work in controversy as 'the finishing of blank doors away from the construction site.' That work, of course, had never been done by the carpenters employed by the general contractor, but had been performed by the employees of the door manufacturers since before the adoption of the agreement. We would perforce have determined that the object of the agreement was work acquisition, not work preservation.

"Similarly, *Pipefitters* involved an agreement between a subcontractor and a pipefitters' union that pipe threading and cutting were to be performed on the jobsite. Relying on the agreement, the union refused to install climate-control units whose internal piping had been cut, threaded, and installed at the factory. The Board held that the provision was a lawful work preservation agreement, but that the refusal to handle the prepiped units was an unfair labor practice because the units had been specified by the general contractor and the subcontractor had no power to assign the employees the work they sought. Neither the Court of Appeals nor this court questioned the validity of the work preservation clause but for the fact that it was enforced against an employer who could not control the work. Under the Board's current approach, however, the 'work' would have been 'cutting, threading, and installing pipe in climate-control units at the factory.' Since the bargaining unit employees had never performed that work, there would have been no reason to reach the 'right of control' issue.

"Thus the Board's determination that the work of longshoremen had historically been the loading and unloading of ships should be only the beginning of the analysis. * * * This case presents a much more difficult problem than either *National Woodwork* or *Pipefitters* because the union did not simply insist on doing the work as it had always been done and try to prevent the employers from using container ships at all—though such an approach would have been consistent with *National Woodwork* and *Pipefitters*. Instead, ILA permitted the great majority of containers [80%] to pass over the piers intact, reserving the right to stuff and strip only those containers that would otherwise have been stuffed or stripped locally [i.e., within the 50-mile radius] by anyone except the beneficial owner's employees. The legality of the agreement turns, as an initial matter, on whether the historical and functional relationship between this retained work and traditional longshore work can support the conclusion that the objective of the agreement was work preservation rather than the satisfaction of union goals elsewhere.[24] * * *

"* * * We emphasize that neither our decision nor that of the Court of Appeals implies that the result of the Board's reconsideration of this case is foreordained. Viewing the work allegedly to be preserved by the Rules from the proper perspective, the Board will be free to determine whether the Rules represent a lawful attempt to preserve traditional longshore work, or whether, instead, they are 'tactically calculated to satisfy union objectives elsewhere,' *National Woodwork* supra 386 U.S., at 644, 87 S.Ct., at 1268. This determination will, of course, be informed by an awareness of the congressional preference for collective bargaining as the method for resolving disputes over dislocations caused by the introduction of technological innovations in the workplace, see id., at 641–642, 87 S.Ct., at 1266–67. Thus, in judging the legality of a thoroughly bargained and apparently reasonable accommodation to technological change, the question is not whether the Rules represent the most rational or efficient response to innovation but whether they are a legally permissible effort to preserve jobs." 447 U.S. at 507–011, 1100 S.Ct. at 2315–17, 65 L.Ed.2d at 304–07.

One way of viewing the Container case is to conclude that the collective bargaining provisions alleged to have violated Section 8(e) were for the purpose of enlarging "the pier," for "work preservation" analysis, to a radius of 50 miles. Creative lawyering or chicanery? In any event, collective bargaining!

[On remand, the Board found the "work in controversy" to be, indeed, traditional longshoremen work and therefore subject to "preservation" by the Rules on Containers, except for certain aspects of the traditional work which the Board found to have been "eliminated" by containerization; efforts to capture the latter work were deemed to be "work acquisition" in character and therefore to entail unlawful secondary pressure. As to the latter work, the Board focused on the effect that the Rules might have on truckers and warehousers, in depriving them of work they now performed, as opposed to the effect of the Rules on longshoremen in restoring to them work now "eliminated." 266 N.L.R.B. 230 (1980). The Fourth Circuit Court of Appeals, 743 F.2d 966 (4th Cir.1984), enforced the Board's order except with respect to this "eliminated" work, holding that an agreement that preserved "technologically 'eliminated' work" does not constitute unlawful "work acquisition." The Supreme Court agreed, 6–3, with the Fourth Circuit, reasoning that: " 'Elimination' of work in the sense that it is made unnecessary by innovation is not of itself a reason to condemn

---

24. Obviously, the result will depend on how closely the parties have tailored their agreement to the objective of preserving the essence of the traditional work patterns. Thus the claim that if the Rules were upheld the union would be able to follow containers around the country and assert the right to stuff and strip them far inland is groundless. That work would bear an entirely different relation to traditional longshore work, and would require a wholly different analysis.

work-preservation agreements under §§ 8(b)(4)(B) and 8(e); to the contrary, such elimination provides the very premise for such agreements." NLRB v. International Longshoreman's Ass'n, ___ U.S. ___, ___, 105 S.Ct. 3045, 3057, 87 L.Ed.2d 47, 59 (1985). ("CONTAINER II").]

POSTSCRIPT

Two other aspects of the federal law dealing with secondary boycotts bear mention in conclusion.

First. Section 303 of the LMRA provides an additional remedy for persons injured by conduct which violates Section 8(b)(4)(A), (B), (C), or (D). It authorizes actions for damages by such injured persons in any federal district court or state court having jurisdiction of the parties. In Local 20, Teamsters Union v. Morton, 377 U.S. 252, 84 S.Ct. 1253, 12 L.Ed.2d 280 (1964), the question of the relationship between federal and state law in the application of Section 303 arose. The Teamsters Union brought secondary pressure to bear upon the primary employer by (1) encouraging employees of a supplier and of certain customers of the primary employer to force their employers to cease doing business with the primary, and (2) persuading, by direct request, the management of another customer to refrain from doing business with the primary. The primary sued the union in a federal district court under Section 303 and under the common law of Ohio, claiming damages for business losses caused by the union's unlawful conduct. The district court (200 F.Supp. 653 (N.D.Ohio 1961)) found that the conduct described in (1) above violated Section 303, and awarded $1,600 in damages for business losses caused by this violation of federal law. The court also determined that the conduct described in (2) above, while permissible activity under federal law, violated the common law of Ohio, which, the court said, prohibits "making direct appeals to a struck employer's customers or suppliers to stop doing business with the struck employer * * *." 377 U.S. at 255, 84 S.Ct. at 1256. The plaintiff was awarded $9,000 as compensatory damages for this violation of Ohio law. Moreover, the court awarded punitive damages in the amount of $15,000. The court of appeals affirmed in all respects. 320 F.2d 505 (6th Cir.1963). The Supreme Court affirmed the award of $1,600 for business losses caused by the violation of federal law, but reversed as to the award of $9,000 as compensatory damages for the violation of Ohio law and as to the award of $15,000 as punitive damages. As to both of the latter, Section 303 was held to preempt the state law: Section 303 (like Section 8(b)(4) upon which it builds) permits peaceful persuasion (as opposed to coercion) of secondary employers to refrain from dealing with a primary employer; similarly, Section 303 permits the recovery of actual damages only ("the damages by him *sustained*"), thus precluding punitive damages.

While the competition in the Morton case was between federal and state law, every Section 303 case carries with it a potential conflict between the court in which action is brought (federal or state) and the NLRB. Whose determination of the basic question of liability—whether 8(b)(4) has been violated—should control, the court's or the Board's? Two hypothetical cases may be put: (1) At the time of decision by the court in the action for damages under Section 303, the Board has not yet rendered a decision under

Section 8(b)(4); (2) at the time the decision is rendered by the court, the Board has already issued its 8(b)(4) decision. As for the first category, the Morton case demonstrates that the court may decide the question of liability under Section 303 even though the Board has not yet passed upon the conduct involved under Section 8(b)(4). (Is this consistent with the Garmon decision, supra p. 330?) As to the second, nice questions of res judicata and collateral estoppel may arise. In Painters District Council No. 38 v. Edgewood Contracting Co., 416 F.2d 1081 (5th Cir.1969), the court applied the doctrine of res judicata in a 303 proceeding by adopting the Board's previous finding of an 8(b)(4) violation involving the same parties and on the same facts. This approach was approved in Wickham Contracting Co., Inc. v. Board of Educ. of the City of New York, 715 F.2d 21 (2d Cir.1983).

Second. The Railway Labor Act, in contrast to the National Labor Relations Act, contains no express prohibitions against the use of secondary pressure. Its philosophy has been held to be that of permitting both management and labor the full panoply of peaceful economic pressure, both primary and secondary, provided only that no resort to any such pressure be had unless and until the full gamut of impasse-resolving procedures prescribed by the Act (bargaining, mediation, voluntary arbitration, emergency board proceedings, "cooling off" periods) has been exhausted. In Brotherhood of Railroad Trainmen v. Jacksonville Terminal Co., 394 U.S. 369, 89 S.Ct. 1109, 22 L.Ed.2d 344 (1969), a state court injunction against union conduct alleged to be secondary in nature, and accepted as such, *arguendo,* by the Court, was set aside, in a 4 to 3 decision, by reason of the failure of the state court to apply the preempting and permissive federal law. The Court explained:

> "In short, we have been furnished by Congress neither usable standards nor access to administrative expertise in a situation where both are required. In these circumstances there is no really satisfactory judicial solution to the problem at hand. However, we conclude that the least unsatisfactory one is to allow parties who have unsuccessfully exhausted the Railway Labor Act's procedures for resolution of a major dispute to employ the full range of whatever peaceful economic power they can muster, so long as its use conflicts with no other obligation imposed by federal law. Hence, until Congress acts, picketing—whether characterized as primary or secondary—must be deemed conduct protected against state proscription." 394 U.S. at 392–93, 89 S.Ct. at 1123.

D. JURISDICTIONAL DISPUTES

NATIONAL LABOR RELATIONS BOARD v. PLASTERERS' INTERNATIONAL ASS'N, LOCAL 79

Supreme Court of the United States, 1971.
404 U.S. 116, 92 S.Ct. 360, 30 L.Ed.2d 312.

MR. JUSTICE WHITE delivered the opinion of the Court.

When a charge is filed under § 8(b)(4)(D) of the National Labor Relations Act, as amended, the provision banning so-called jurisdictional disputes, the Board must under § 10(k) "hear and determine the dispute out of which [the] unfair labor practice shall have arisen, unless * * * the parties to such dispute" adjust or agree upon a method for the voluntary adjustment of the dispute. The issue here is whether an employer, picketed to force reassignment of work, is a "party" to the "dispute" for purposes of § 10(k). When the two unions involved, but not the employer, have agreed upon a method of settlement, must the Board dismiss the § 10(k) proceedings or must it proceed to determine the dispute with the employer being afforded a chance to participate?

I

Texas State Tile & Terrazzo Co. (Texas State) and Martini Tile & Terrazzo Co. (Martini) are contractors in Houston, Texas, engaged in the business of installing tile and terrazzo. Both have collective-bargaining agreements with the Tile, Terrazzo and Marble Setters Local Union No. 20 (Tile Setters) and have characteristically used members of the Tile Setters union for laying tile and also for work described in the collective-bargaining contract as applying "a coat or coats of mortar, prepared to proper tolerance to receive tile on floors, walls and ceiling regardless of whether the mortar coat is wet or dry at the time the tile is applied to it."

This case arose when Plasterers' Local Union No. 79, Operative Plasterers' and Cement Masons' International Association of Houston, Texas (Plasterers), picketed the job sites of Texas State and Martini claiming that the work of applying the mortar to receive tile was the work of the Plasterers' union and not of the Tile Setters.[4] Neither Texas State nor Martini had a collective-bargaining contract with the Plasterers or regularly employed workers represented by that union.

Before the Texas State picketing began, the Plasterers submitted their claim to the disputed work to the National Joint Board for Settlement of Jurisdictional Disputes (Joint Board), a body established by the Building Trades Department, AFL–CIO, and by certain employer groups.[5] Both the Plasterers' and the Tile Setters' locals were bound by Joint Board decisions because their international unions were members of the AFL–CIO's Building Trades Department. Neither Texas State nor Martini had agreed to be bound by Joint Board procedures and decisions, however. The Joint Board found the work in dispute to be covered by an agreement of August 1917, between the two international unions, and awarded the work to the Plasterers.[6] When Texas State and the Tile Setters refused to acquiesce in the

---

4. This dispute grew out of a new method of applying tile that was developed in the mid-1950's. R. 111, 123, 135.

5. The National Joint Board for the Settlement of Jurisdictional Disputes is an arbitration panel established by a 1948 agreement between the Building and Construction Trades Department, AFL–CIO, and the Associated General Contractors of America and several specialty contractors' associations. The Joint Board consists of an equal number of representatives of employers and unions and a neutral chairman. An employer may become a party to a Joint Board proceeding by signing a stipulation agreeing to be bound by the results of the proceeding. Art. III, § 7, AFL–CIO, Bldg. & Constr. Trades Dept., Plan for Settling

Jurisdictional Disputes Nationally and Locally 10 (1970). Member unions of the AFL–CIO's Building Trades Department do not have to agree formally to abide by Joint Board decisions, because they are bound by virtue of provisions contained in their constitutions. AFL–CIO, Bldg. & Constr. Trades Dept., Procedural Rules and Regulations of the National Joint Board 2 (1970). See generally K. Strand, Jurisdictional Disputes in Construction: The Causes, the Joint Board, and the NLRB 89–104 (1961). In the cases here, both the Tile Setters and the Plasterers were members of the Building Trades Department.

6. In the Texas State case, the Joint Board on November 9, 1966, awarded all of the disputed work to the Plasterers except "any coat

Joint Board decision and change the work assignment, the Plasterers began the picketing of Texas State which formed the basis for the § 8(b)(4)(D) charges. The Plasterers also picketed a jobsite where Martini employees, members of the Tile Setters, were installing tile, although this dispute had not been submitted to the Joint Board.

Martini and Southwestern Construction Co., the general contractor that had hired Texas State, filed § 8(b)(4)(D) unfair labor practice charges against the Plasterers, and the NLRB's Regional Director noticed a consolidated § 10(k) hearing to determine the dispute. Southwestern, Texas State, Martini, and the two unions participated in the hearing. A panel of the Board noted that the Tile Setters admitted being bound by Joint Board procedures, but deemed the Joint Board decision to lack controlling weight, and "after taking into account and balancing all relevant factors" awarded the work to the Tile Setters.[9] When the Plasterers refused to indicate that they would abide by the Board's award, a § 8(b)(4)(D) complaint was issued against them, and they were found to have committed an unfair labor practice by picketing to force Texas State and Martini to assign the disputed work to them.[10] In

to be applied wet the same day under tile." App. 316. The Tile Setters refused to give up the work of laying the plaster undercoat to which the dry mortar was applied, claiming that the Joint Board decision gave this work to them. The Plasterers established a picket line on January 24, 1967; on March 15, 1967, the Joint Board issued a clarification of its decision, stating that the final smooth plaster coat was to be done by the Plasterers unless it was laid the same day as the tile and dry-set mortar were applied, in which case it was to be done by the Tile Setters.

9. The NLRB considered the collective-bargaining agreements among the parties, industry and area practice, relative skills and efficiency of operation, past practices of the employers, agreements between the Plasterers and the Tile Setters, the Joint Board award (the NLRB refused to give this controlling weight because of its "ambiguous nature," App. 22), and concluded:

"Tile setters are at least as skilled in the performance of the work as plasterers, and both Texas Tile and Martini, which assigned them to the work, have been satisfied with both the quality of their work and the cost of employing them. Moreover, the instant assignments of the disputed work to tile setters are consistent with the explicit provisions of the collective-bargaining agreement between the Tile Setters and Texas Tile and Martini, are consistent with the past practice of the Employers, and are not inconsistent with area or industry practice * * *." App. 23.

The Board's decision in the § 10(k) proceeding is reported at 167 N.L.R.B. 185 (1967) and its decision and order in the unfair labor practice proceeding are reported at 172 N.L.R.B. Nos. 70, 72 (1968).

[The following passage from footnote 26, deleted, is pertinent here:]

[The Joint Board award in this case was based solely on the Joint Board's interpretation of a 1917 agreement between the two international unions and a 1924 decision interpreting that agreement. * * * At the time of the dispute, the criteria used by the Joint Board in making awards were: "Decisions and agreements of record as set forth in the Green Book [the Building Trades Department's book of precedents], valid agreements between affected International Unions attested by the Chairman of the Joint Board, established trade practice and prevailing practice in the locality." Art. III, § 1(a), AFL–CIO Bldg. & Constr. Trades Dept., Plan for Settling Jurisdictional Disputes Nationally and Locally (1965). These criteria were broadened in 1970 by the addition of Art. III, § 1(f), which provides: "Because efficiency, cost and good management are essential to the well-being of the industry, the Joint Board should not ignore the interests of the consumer in settling jurisdictional disputes." AFL–CIO Bldg. & Constr. Trades Dept., Plan for Settling Jurisdictional Disputes Nationally and Locally 8 (1970).]

10. The § 10(k) determination is not binding as such even on the striking union. If that union continues to picket despite an adverse § 10(k) decision, the Board must prove the union guilty of a § 8(b)(4)(D) violation before a cease-and-desist order can issue. The findings and conclusions in a § 10(k) proceeding are not *res judicata* on the unfair labor practice issue in the later § 8(b)(4)(D), determination. International Typographical Union, 125 N.L.R.B. 759, 761 (1959). Both parties may put in new evidence at the § 8(b)(4)(D) stage, although often, as in the present cases, the parties agree to stipulate the record

making both the § 10(k) and § 8(b)(4)(D) decisions, the Board rejected the Plasterers' contention that even though the employer had not agreed to be bound by the Joint Board decision, the provisions of § 10(k) precluded a subsequent Board decision because the competing unions had agreed upon a voluntary method of adjustment.

On petition to review by the Plasterers and cross petition to enforce by the Board, a divided panel of the Court of Appeals set aside the order of the Board.[11] It held that: "It is not the employer but the rival unions (or other employee groups) who are the parties to the jurisdictional dispute contesting which employees are entitled to seek the work in question."[12] It concluded that the Board may not make a § 10(k) determination of a jurisdictional dispute where the opposing unions have agreed to settle their differences through binding arbitration. Both the Board and the employers petitioned for certiorari, and we granted the petitions.

II

Section 8(b)(4)(D) makes it an unfair labor practice for a labor organization to strike or threaten or coerce an employer or other person in order to force or require an employer to assign particular work to one group of employees rather than to another, unless the employer is refusing to honor a representation order of the Board. On its face, the section would appear to cover any union challenge to an employer work assignment where the prohibited means are employed. National Labor Relations Board v. Radio & Television Broadcast Engineers Union, Local 1212, 364 U.S. 573, 576, 81 S.Ct. 330, 332, 5 L.Ed.2d 302 (1961) (hereinafter CBS). As the charging or intervening party, the employer would normally be a party to any proceedings under that section. Section 8(b)(4)(D), however, must be read in light of § 10(k) with which it is interlocked. CBS, supra, at 576, 81 S.Ct., at 332. When a § 8(b)(4)(D) charge is filed and there is reasonable cause to believe that an unfair labor practice has been committed, issuance of the complaint is withheld until the provisions of § 10(k) have been satisfied. That section directs the Board to "hear and determine" the dispute out of which the alleged unfair labor practice arose; the Board is required to decide which union or group of employees is entitled to the disputed work in accordance with acceptable, Board-developed standards, unless the parties to the underlying dispute settle the case or agree upon a method for settlement. Whether the § 8(b)(4)(D) charge will be sustained or dismissed is thus dependent on the outcome of the proceeding. The Board allows an employer to fully participate in a § 10(k) proceeding as a party. If the employer prefers the employees to whom he has assigned the work, his right to later relief against the other union's picketing is conditioned upon his ability to convince the

of the § 10(k) hearing as a basis for the Board's determination of the unfair labor practice. Finally, to exercise its powers under § 10(k), the Board need only find that there is reasonable cause to believe that a § 8(b)(4)(D) violation has occurred, while in the § 8(b)(4)(D) proceeding itself the Board must find by a preponderance of the evidence that the picketing union has violated § 8(b)(4)(D). International Typographical Union, supra, at 761 n. 5 (1959).

11. 142 U.S.App.D.C. 146, 440 F.2d 174 (1970).

12. Id., at 152, 440 F.2d, at 180. Although the dispute at the Martini worksite had not been submitted to the Joint Board, the Court of Appeals nevertheless held that, because the two unions had agreed to be bound by the procedures and decisions of the Joint Board, the NLRB was precluded from hearing and determining the Martini dispute under § 10(k).

Board in the § 10(k) proceeding that his original assignment is valid under the criteria employed by the Board.

The alleged unfair labor practice in this cause was the picketing of the job-sites by the Plasterers, and the dispute giving rise to this picketing was the disagreement over whether Plasterers or Tile Setters were to lay the final plaster coat. This dispute was a three-cornered one. The Plasterers made demands on both Texas State and the Tile Setters and on both Martini and the Tile Setters. In both cases, the employers' refusal to accede to the Plasterers' demands inevitably and inextricably involved them with the Tile Setters against the Plasterers. It was this triangular dispute that the § 10(k) proceeding was intended to resolve.

It may be that in some cases employers have no stake in how a jurisdictional dispute is settled and are interested only in prompt settlement. Other employers, as shown by this cause, are not neutral and have substantial economic interests in the outcome of the § 10(k) proceeding. A change in work assignment may result in different terms or conditions of employment, a new union to bargain with, higher wages or costs, and lower efficiency or quality of work. In the construction industry, in particular, where employers frequently calculate bids on very narrow margins, small cost differences are likely to be extremely important.[15] In the present cause, both employers had collective-bargaining contracts with the Tile Setters specifically covering the work at issue; neither had contracts with the Plasterers nor employed Plasterers regularly. Both employers determined it to be in their best interests to participate vigorously in the Board's § 10(k) proceedings. The employers contended it was more efficient and less costly to use the same craft for applying the last coat of plaster, putting on the bonding coat, and laying the tile and that it was more consistent with industry practice to use the Tile Setters as they did. Both companies claimed that their costs would be substantially increased if the award went to the Plasterers, and that without collective-bargaining contracts with the Plasterers, they would lose 30%–40% of their work to plastering contractors. It is obvious, therefore, that both Texas State and Martini had substantial stakes in the outcome of the § 10(k) proceeding.

The phrase "parties to the dispute" giving rise to the picketing must be given its commonsense meaning corresponding to the actual interests involved here. * * * Section 10(k) does not expressly or impliedly deny party status to an employer, and since the section's adoption in 1947, the Board has regularly accorded party status to the employer and has refused to dismiss the proceeding when the unions, but not the employer, have agreed to settle.

The Court of Appeals rejected this construction of § 10(k). Its reasoning, which we find unpersuasive, was that because the employer is not bound by the § 10(k) decision, he should have no right to insist upon participation. But the § 10(k) decision standing alone, binds no one. No cease-and-desist order against either union or employer results from such a proceeding; the impact of the § 10(k) decision is felt in the § 8(b)(4)(D) hearing because for all practical purposes the Board's award determines who will prevail in the

---

15. See Comment, The Employer as a Necessary Party to Voluntary Settlement of Work Assignment Disputes Under Section 10(k) of the NLRA, 38 U.Chi.L.Rev. 389, 400 (1971).

unfair labor practice proceeding. If the picketing union persists in its conduct despite a § 10(k) decision against it, a § 8(b)(4)(D) complaint issues and the union will likely be found guilty of an unfair labor practice and be ordered to cease and desist. On the other hand, if that union wins the § 10(k) decision and the employer does not comply, the employer's § 8(b)(4)(D) case evaporates and the charges he filed against the picketing union will be dismissed. Neither the employer nor the employees to whom he has assigned the work are legally bound to observe the § 10(k) decision, but both will lose their § 8(b)(4)(D) protection against the picketing which may, as it did here, shut down the job. The employer will be under intense pressure, practically, to conform to the Board's decision. This is the design of the Act; Congress provided no other way to implement the Board's § 10(k) decision.

* * *

Nothing in CBS, supra, mandates a different conclusion. Until that case, the Board's practice had been to decide against the striking or picketing union unless it was entitled to the work pursuant to a Board certification or a collective-bargaining contract. The Court found the Board to have taken too narrow a view of its task and held that the Board, employing broader, more inclusive criteria with respect to entitlement, must make an affirmative award to one union or the other. * * * The Court in CBS did not have before it a case in which the employer was particularly interested in which union did the work, since it had collective-bargaining contracts with both unions and since both unions were able to do the disputed work with equal skill, expense, and efficiency. The Court recognized that there, "*as in most instances*" the quarrel was of "so little interest to the employer that he seems perfectly willing to assign work to either [union] if the other will just let him alone." Ibid. (emphasis added). We have no doubt, therefore, that the Court had no intention of deciding the case now before us.

If employers must be considered parties to the dispute that the Board must decide under § 10(k), absent private agreement, they must also be deemed parties to the adjustment or agreement to settle that will abort the § 10(k) proceedings. * * *

Reversed.

Note

1. "Jurisdictional dispute" is an ambiguous rubric in that it may be used to characterize two similar but quite different types of controversy. The first type is the "work assignment" dispute. The Plasterers' case is a good example of this type of dispute; its essence is: which of two or more contesting groups of employees (whether organized or unorganized) is to have certain work assigned to it. The second type of "jurisdictional dispute" arises where two or more unions contest for the right to represent an employee or group of employees performing a certain variety of work. This is a "representation," as opposed to a "work assignment," dispute. Only "work assignment" disputes are dealt with under Sections 8(b)(4)(D), 10(k), and 303. "Representation" disputes, on the other hand, are dealt with through the procedures and machinery of Section 9.

2. The two most ambitious schemes for the voluntary adjustment of jurisdictional disputes are (1) the National Joint Board for the Settlement of Jurisdictional Disputes, discussed in the Plasterers' case (see footnote 5), and (2) the

jurisdictional dispute adjustment machinery incorporated since 1961 in the AFL–CIO constitution. The provisions in the AFL–CIO constitution are the culmination of the No-Raiding Pact signed in 1954 by several, but not all, of the unions composing the then separate AFL and CIO. This pact constituted an important step toward the merger of the two organizations in 1955. Since employers are not subject to the provisions of the AFL–CIO constitution, they are not bound by the jurisdictional dispute determinations which are the product of the constitutional machinery (featuring mediation, hearing and determination by an impartial umpire, right of appeal to the Executive Council of the AFL–CIO).

Comment on Preliminary Injunctive Relief Under The NLRA

While an employer aggrieved by union activity falling within the ambit of Section 8(b)(4)(A), (B), (C), or (D) may seek relief before a court in a Section 303 proceeding or before the Board in a Section 10 proceeding (or, indeed, before both concurrently), there is an aspect to the *Board* option which holds considerable appeal. Under Section 10(*l*), where the Board officer handling the case has "reasonable cause to believe" that the 8(b)(4) charge is true, he "shall" petition the federal district court for "appropriate injunctive relief pending the final adjudication of the Board with respect to such matter. Upon the filing of any such petition the district court shall have jurisdiction to grant such injunctive relief or temporary restraining order as it deems just and proper, notwithstanding any other provision of law [i.e., the Norris-LaGuardia Act]." Moreover, upon the filing of an 8(b)(4) charge in a regional office of the NLRB, "the preliminary investigation of such charge shall be made forthwith and given priority over all other cases except cases of like character * * *."

This expedited preliminary injunctive relief under Section 10(*l*), at the instance of the Board, is also available for employers aggrieved by union conduct falling within Sections 8(b)(7) and 8(e).

Preliminary injunctive relief is available, under Section 10(j), also at the instance of the Board, in the case of any other unfair labor practice charge (against union *or* employer), but the Board is not mandated to seek such relief, expeditiously or otherwise. Section 10(j) states simply that the Board "shall have power" to petition the federal district court for appropriate temporary relief and that the court "shall have jurisdiction to grant to the Board such temporary relief * * * as it deems just and proper." The Board's discretion to seek preliminary injunctive relief under 10(j) has been little used, in contrast to the nondiscretionary resort mandated under 10(*l*). The sparing use of 10(j) has occasioned some criticism (including, not surprisingly, complaints from unions over the imbalance between 10(j) and 10(*l*). For an analysis of 10(j) and 10(*l*) and an argument in favor of more frequent and liberal application of the former by Board and courts, see Note, Temporary Injunctions under Section 10(j) of the Taft-Hartley Act, 44 N.Y.U.L.Rev. 181 (1969). The difficulties encountered by the Board in obtaining a Section 10(j) injunction are discussed in Lubbers, Discretionary Injunction Authority under Section 10(j), 35 Lab.L.J. 259 (1984); Schatzki, Some Observations About Standards Applied to Labor Injunction Litigation Under Sections 10(j) and 10(*l*) of the National Labor Relations Act, 59 Ind.L.J. 565 (1984); Comment, The Use of Section 10(j) of the Labor Management Relations Act in Employer Refusal to Bargain Cases, 1976 Ill.L.F. 845.

E. FEATHERBEDDING

AMERICAN NEWSPAPER PUBLISHERS ASS'N v. NATIONAL LABOR RELATIONS BOARD.

Supreme Court of the United States, 1953.
345 U.S. 100, 73 S.Ct. 552, 97 L.Ed. 852.

MR. JUSTICE BURTON delivered the opinion of the Court.

The question here is whether a labor organization engages in an unfair labor practice, within the meaning of § 8(b)(6) of the National Labor Relations Act, as amended by the Labor Management Relations Act, 1947, when it insists that newspaper publishers pay printers for reproducing advertising matter for which the publishers ordinarily have no use. For the reasons hereafter stated, we hold that it does not.

Petitioner, American Newspaper Publishers Association, is a New York corporation the membership of which includes more than 800 newspaper publishers. They represent over 90% of the circulation of the daily and Sunday newspapers in the United States and carry over 90% of the advertising published in such papers.

In November, 1947, petitioner filed with the National Labor Relations Board charges that the International Typographical Union, here called ITU, and its officers were engaging in unfair labor practices within the meaning of § 8(b)(1), (2) and (6) of the National Labor Relations Act, as amended by the Labor Management Relations Act, 1947, here called the Taft-Hartley Act. The Regional Director of the Board issued its complaint, including a charge of engaging in an unfair labor practice as defined in § 8(b)(6), popularly known as the "anti-featherbedding" section of the Act. It is not questioned that the acts complained of affected interstate commerce.

The trial examiner recommended that ITU be ordered to cease and desist from several of its activities but that the "featherbedding" charges under § 8(b)(6) be dismissed. 86 N.L.R.B. 951, 964, 1024–1033. The Board dismissed those charges. 86 N.L.R.B., at pages 951, 963. Petitioner then filed the instant proceeding in the Court of Appeals for the Seventh Circuit seeking review and modification of the Board's orders. That court upheld the Board's dismissal of all charges under § 8(b)(6). 193 F.2d 782, 796, 802. See also, 190 F.2d 45. A comparable view was expressed in Rabouin v. National Labor Relations Board, 2 Cir., 195 F.2d 906, 912–913, but a contrary view was taken in Gamble Enterprises v. National Labor Relations Board, 6 Cir., 196 F.2d 61. Because of this claimed conflict upon an important issue of first impression, we granted certiorari in the instant case * * * and in National Labor Relations Board v. Gamble Enterprises, 344 U.S. 814, 73 S.Ct. 43, Id., 344 U.S. 872, 73 S.Ct. 165. Our decision in the Gamble case (National Labor Relations Board v. Gamble Enterprises, Inc.) follows this, 345 U.S. 117, 73 S.Ct. 560.[4]

Printers in newspaper composing rooms have long sought to retain the opportunity to set up in type as much as possible of whatever is printed by

4. For a general discussion of the problems in these cases, see Cox, Some Aspects of the Labor Management Relations Act, 1947, 61 Harv.L.Rev. 274, 288–290; Featherbedding and Taft-Hartley, 52 Col.L.Rev. 1020–1033.

their respective publishers. In 1872, when printers were paid on a piece-work basis, each diversion of composition was at once reflected by a loss in their income. Accordingly, ITU, which had been formed in 1852 from local typographical societies, began its long battle to retain as much typesetting work for printers as possible.

With the introduction of the linotype machine in 1890, the problem took on a new aspect. When a newspaper advertisement was set up in type, it was impressed on a cardboard matrix, or "mat." These mats were used by their makers and also were reproduced and distributed, at little or no cost, to other publishers who used them as molds for metal castings from which to print the same advertisement. This procedure by-passed all compositors except those who made up the original form. Facing this loss of work, ITU secured the agreement of newspaper publishers to permit their respective compositors, at convenient times, to set up duplicate forms for all local advertisements in precisely the same manner as though the mat had not been used. For this reproduction work the printers received their regular pay. The doing of this "made work" came to be known in the trade as "setting bogus." It was a wasteful procedure. Nevertheless, it has become a recognized idiosyncrasy of the trade and a customary feature of the wage structure and work schedule of newspaper printers.

By fitting the "bogus" work into slack periods, the practice interferes little with "live" work. The publishers who set up the original compositions find it advantageous because it burdens their competitors with costs of mat making comparable to their own. Approximate time limits for setting "bogus" usually have been fixed by agreement at from four days to three weeks. On rare occasions the reproduced compositions are used to print the advertisements when rerun, but, ordinarily, they are promptly consigned to the "hell box" and melted down. Live matter has priority over reproduction work but the latter usually takes from 2 to 5% of the printers' time.[5] By 1947, detailed regulations for reproduction work were included in the "General Laws" of ITU. They thus became a standard part of all employment contracts signed by its local unions. The locals were allowed to negotiate as to foreign language publications, time limits for setting "bogus" and exemptions of mats received from commercial compositors or for national advertisements.

Before the enactment of § 8(b)(6), the legality and enforceability of payment for setting "bogus," agreed to by the publisher, was recognized. Even now the issue before us is not what policy should be adopted by the Nation toward the continuance of this and other forms of featherbedding. The issue here is solely one of statutory interpretation: Has Congress made setting "bogus" an unfair labor practice?

While the language of § 8(b)(6) is claimed by both sides to be clear, yet the conflict between the views of the Seventh and Sixth Circuits amply

5. In metropolitan areas, only the printers on the "ad side" of a composing room, as contrasted with those on the "news side," take part in the reproduction work and never on a full-time basis. Such work is not done at overtime rates but when there is an accumulation of it, the newspaper is not permitted to reduce its work force or decline to hire suitable extra printers applying for employment. The trial examiner, in the instant case, found that reproduction work at the Rochester Democrat & Chronical cost over $5,000 a year, at the Chicago Herald-American, about $50,000, and at the New York Times, about $150,000.

justifies our examination of both the language and the legislative history of the section. The section reads:

"Sec. 8.   *   *   *

*   *   *   *   *   *   *   *   *

"(b) It shall be an unfair labor practice for a labor organization or its agents—

*   *   *   *   *   *   *   *   *

"(6) to cause or attempt to cause an employer to pay or deliver or agree to pay or deliver any money or other thing of value, in the nature of an exaction, for services which are not performed or not to be performed."
*   *   *

From the above language and its history, the court below concluded that the insistence by ITU upon securing payment of wages to printers for setting "bogus" was not an unfair labor practice. It found that the practice called for payment only for work which actually was done by employees of the publishers in the course of their employment as distinguished from payment "for services which are not performed or not to be performed." Setting "bogus" was held to be service performed and it remained for the parties to determine its worth to the employer.   *   *   *

However desirable the elimination of all industrial featherbedding practices may have appeared to Congress, the legislative history of the Taft-Hartley Act demonstrates that when the legislation was put in final form Congress decided to limit the practice but little by law.

A restraining influence throughout this congressional consideration of featherbedding was the fact that the constitutionality of the Lea Act penalizing featherbedding in the broadcasting industry was in litigation. That Act, known also as the Petrillo Act, had been adopted April 16, 1946, as an amendment to the Communications Act of 1934, 47 U.S.C.A. § 151 et seq. Its material provisions are stated in the margin.[6] December 2, 1946, the United States District Court for the Northern District of Illinois held that it

---

6. "§ 506. (a) It shall be unlawful, by the use or express or implied threat of the use of force, violence, intimidation, or duress, or by the use or express or implied threat of the use of other means, to coerce, compel or constrain or attempt to coerce, compel, or constrain a licensee—

"(1) to employ or agree to employ, in connection with the conduct of the broadcasting business of such licensee, any person or persons in excess of the number of employees needed by such licensee to perform actual services; or

"(2) to pay or give or agree to pay or give any money or other thing of value in lieu of giving, or on account of failure to give, employment to any person or persons, in connection with the conduct of the broadcasting business of such licensee, in excess of the number of employees needed by such licensee to perform actual services; or

"(3) to pay or agree to pay more than once for services performed in connection with the conduct of the broadcasting business of such licensee; or

"(4) to pay or give or agree to pay or give any money or other thing of value for services, in connection with the conduct of the broadcasting business of such licensee, which are not to be performed;   *   *   *

*   *   *   *   *

"(c) The provisions of subsection (a) or (b) of this section shall not be held to make unlawful the enforcement or attempted enforcement, by means lawfully employed, of any contract right heretofore or hereafter existing or of any legal obligation heretofore or hereafter incurred or assumed.

"(d) Whoever willfully violates any provision of subsection (a) or (b) of this section shall, upon conviction thereof, be punished by imprisonment for not more than one year or by a fine of not more than $1,000, or both.   *   *   *" 60 Stat. 89, 90, 47 U.S.C.A. § 506(a, c, d).

violated the First, Fifth and Thirteenth Amendments to the Constitution of the United States. United States v. Petrillo, D.C., 68 F.Supp. 845. The case was pending here on appeal throughout the debate on the Taft-Hartley bill. Not until June 23, 1947, on the day of the passage of the Taft-Hartley bill over the President's veto, was the constitutionality of the Lea Act upheld. United States v. Petrillo, 332 U.S. 1, 67 S.Ct. 1538, 91 L.Ed. 1877.[7]

The purpose of the sponsors of the Taft-Hartley bill to avoid the controversial features of the Lea Act is made clear in the written statement which Senator Taft, co-sponsor of the bill and Chairman of the Senate Committee on Labor and Public Welfare, caused to be incorporated in the proceedings of the Senate, June 5, 1947. Referring to the substitution of § 8(b)(6) in place of the detailed featherbedding provisions of the House bill that statement said:

> "The provisions in the Lea Act from which the House language was taken are now awaiting determination by the Supreme Court, partly because of the problem arising from the term 'in excess of the number of employees reasonably required.' Therefore, the conferees were of the opinion that general legislation on the subject of featherbedding was not warranted at least until the joint study committee proposed by this bill could give full consideration to the matter." 93 Cong.Rec. 6443.

On the same day this was amplified in the Senator's oral statement on the floor of the Senate:

> "There is one further provision which may possibly be of interest, which was not in the Senate bill. The House had rather elaborate provisions prohibiting so-called feather-bedding practices and making them unlawful labor practices. The Senate conferees, while not approving of feather-bedding practices, felt that it was impracticable to give to a board or a court the power to say that so many men are all right, and so many men are too many. It would require a practical application of the law by the courts in hundreds of different industries, and a determination of facts which it seemed to me would be almost impossible. So we declined to adopt the provisions which are now in the Petrillo Act. After all, that statute applies to only one industry. Those provisions are now the subject of court procedure. Their constitutionality has been questioned. We thought that probably we had better wait and see what happened, in any event, even though we are in favor of prohibiting all feather-bedding practices. However, we did accept one provision which makes it an unlawful-labor practice for a union to accept money for people who do not work. That seemed to be a fairly clear case, easy to determine, and we accepted that additional unfair labor practice on the part of unions, which was not in the Senate bill." 93 Cong. Rec. 6441. * * *

As indicated above, the Taft-Hartley bill, H.R. 3020, when it passed the House, April 17, 1947, contained in §§ 2(17) and 12(a)(3)(B) an explicit condemnation of featherbedding. Its definition of featherbedding was based upon that in the Lea Act. For example, it condemned practices which required an employer to employ "persons in excess of the number of employees reasonably required by such employer to perform actual services,"

7. For a report of the subsequent trial and acquittal on the merits, see United States v. Petrillo, D.C., 75 F.Supp. 176.

as well as practices which required an employer to pay "for services * * * which are not to be performed."

The substitution of the present § 8(b)(6) for that definition compels the conclusion that § 8(b)(6) means what the court below has said it means. The Act now limits its condemnation to instances where a labor organization or its agents exact pay from an employer in return for services not performed or not to be performed. * * *

We do not have here a situation comparable to that mentioned by Senator Taft as an illustration of the type of featherbedding which he would consider an unfair labor practice within the meaning of § 8(b)(6). June 5, 1947, in a colloquy on the floor of the Senate he said in reference to § 8(b)(6):

> "[I]t seems to me that it is perfectly clear what is intended. It is intended to make it an unfair labor practice for a man to say, 'You must have 10 musicians, and if you insist that there is room for only 6, you must pay for the other 4 anyway.' That is in the nature of an exaction from the employer for services which he does not want, does not need, and is not even willing to accept." 93 Cong.Rec. 6446.

In that illustration the service for which pay was to be exacted was not performed and was not to be performed by anyone.[10] The last sentence of the above quotation must be read in that context. There was no room for more than six musicians and there was no suggestion that the excluded four did anything or were to do anything for their pay. Section 8(b)(6) leaves to collective bargaining the determination of what, if any, work, including bona fide "made work," shall be included as compensable services and what rate of compensation shall be paid for it.

Accordingly, the judgment of the Court of Appeals sustaining dismissal of the complaint, insofar as it was based upon § 8(b)(6), is affirmed.

MR. JUSTICE DOUGLAS, dissenting.

I fail to see how the reproduction of advertising matter which is never used by a newspaper but which indeed is set up only to be thrown away is a service performed for the newspaper. The practice of "setting bogus" is old and deeply engrained in trade union practice. But so are other types of "feather-bedding." Congress, to be sure, did not outlaw all "feather-bedding" by the Taft-Hartley Act. That Act leaves unaffected the situation where two men are employed to do one man's work. It also, in my view, leaves unaffected the situation presented in National Labor Relations Board v. Gamble Enterprises, Inc., 345 U.S. 117, 73 S.Ct. 560.

Mr. Justice Jackson labels the services tendered in that case as "useless and unwanted work." Certainly it was "unwanted" by the employer—as much unwanted as putting on two men to do one man's work. But there is no basis for saying that those services were "useless." They were to be performed in the theatres, providing music to the audiences. The Gamble

---

10. Section 8(b)(6) does not relate to union requests for, or insistence upon, such types of payments as employees' wages during lunch rest, waiting or vacation periods; payments for service on relief squads; or payments for reporting for duty to determine whether work is to be done. Such practices are recognized to be incidental to the employee's general employment and are given consideration in fixing the rate of pay for it. They are not in the nature of exactions of pay for something not performed or not to be performed. See 93 Cong.Rec. 6859.

Enterprises case is not one where the employer was forced to hire musicians who were not used. They were to be used in the theatrical program offered the public. Perhaps the entertainment would be better without them. But to conclude with Mr. Justice Jackson that it would be better would be to rush in where Congress did not want to tread.   *   *   *

But the situation in this case is to me quite different. Here the typesetters, while setting the "bogus," are making no contribution whatsoever to the enterprise. Their "work" is not only unwanted, it is indeed wholly useless. It does not add directly or indirectly to the publication of the newspaper nor to its contents. It does not even add an "unwanted" page or paragraph. In no sense that I can conceive is it a "service" to the employer. To be sure, the employer has agreed to pay for it. But the agreement was under compulsion. The statute does not draw the distinction Mr. Justice Jackson tenders. No matter how time-honored the practice, it should be struck down if it is not a service performed for an employer.

The outlawry of this practice under § 8(b)(6) of the Taft-Hartley Act might be so disruptive of established practices as to be against the public interest. But the place to obtain relief against the new oppression is in the Congress, not here.

Mr. Justice Clark, with whom The Chief Justice joins, dissenting.

Today's decision twists the law by the tail. If the employees had received pay for staying home, conserving their energies and the publisher's material, the Court concedes, as it must, that § 8(b)(6) of the National Labor Relations Act would squarely apply. Yet in the Court's view these printers' peculiar "services" snatch the transaction from the reach of the law. Those "services," no more and no less, consist of setting "bogus" type, then proofread and reset for corrections, only to be immediately discarded and never used. Instead, this type is consigned as waste to a "hell box" which feeds the "melting pot"; that, in turn, oozes fresh lead then molded into "pigs" which retravel the same Sisyphean journey. The Court thus holds that an "anti-featherbedding" statute designed to hit wasteful labor practices in fact sanctions additional waste in futile use of labor, lead, machines, proofreading, "hell-boxing," etc. Anomalously, the more wasteful the practice the less effectual the statute is.

*   *   * [T]he printers' doing solely that which then must be undone passes for "work." An imaginative labor organization need not strain far to invent such "work." With that lethal definition to stifle § 8(b)(6), this Court's first decision on "featherbedding" may well be the last.   *   *   *

Note

1. In NLRB v. GAMBLE ENTERPRISES, 345 U.S. 117, 73 S.Ct. 560, 97 L.Ed. 864 (1953), the companion case to American Newspaper Publishers, the question was whether a local of the American Federation of Musicians had violated Section 8(b)(6) by insisting that a theater employ a local orchestra which it did not need or want to employ. The union "opened negotiations with respondent for the latter's employment of a pit orchestra of local musicians whenever a traveling band performed on the stage. The pit orchestra was to play overtures, intermissions, and 'chasers' (the latter while patrons were leaving the theater). The union required acceptance of this proposal as a condition

of its consent to local appearances of traveling bands." 345 U.S. at 120, 73 S.Ct. at 562. The NLRB held for the union, stating: "In our opinion, Section 8(b)(6) was not intended to reach cases where a labor organization seeks actual employment for its members, even in situations where the employer does not want, does not need, and is not willing to accept such services." 92 N.L.R.B. 1528, 1533 (1951). The court of appeals disagreed. 196 F.2d 61 (6th Cir.1952). The Supreme Court agreed with the Board:

> "We are not dealing here with offers of mere 'token' or nominal services. The proposals before us were appropriately treated by the Board as offers in good faith of substantial performances by competent musicians. There is no reason to think that sham can be substituted for substance under § 8(b)(6) any more than under any other statute. Payments for 'standing-by,' or for the substantial equivalent of 'standing-by,' are not payments for services performed, but when an employer receives a bona fide offer of competent performance of relevant services, it remains for the employer, through free and fair negotiation, to determine whether such offer shall be accepted and what compensation shall be paid for the work done." 345 U.S. at 123–24, 73 S.Ct. at 563.

Interestingly, while both of the Court's decisions in the featherbedding cases were by a vote of 6 to 3, it was not the same 6 and 3. Justice Douglas, who dissented so vigorously in the American Newspaper Publishers case, joined the majority in Gamble Enterprises: There was no "service" whatsoever to the employer in the first case, whereas in the second there *was* a "service," albeit unwanted. Justice Jackson flipped the other way: "Setting bogus" was an old custom in the printing industry, long predating Section 8(b)(6), whereas prior to Section 8(b)(6) the American Federation of Musicians had extracted compensation for local musicians for merely "standing-by" when traveling bands performed within their jurisdiction; the union, he said, had "substituted for the practice specifically condemned by the statute a new device for achieving the same result."

2. The hoariness of the custom in the printing trade upon which Justice Jackson relied is evidenced in the following passage from Jacobs, Dead Horse and the Featherbird 8–9 (1962):

> "By 1557 the master printers of London had banded together as the London Stationers' Company and carried on their trade under a charter from the Crown. The Company, controlled by twenty-odd master printers, was among the most rigidly operated of guilds. By 1587, the work rules of the Company provided that type, once having been set and used, could not be used against without first being broken up and put back in the type box. Rule 1 decreed: 'Ffyrst that no formes of letters be kept standinge to the prejudice of Woorkemen at any time.' Rule 2 imposed a limit ranging from 1250 to 1500 on the number of impressions that might be made from any one form of type, except for 'Grammars Accidences Prymers and Catechisms' when '3000 at the moste' were permitted. There were a few additional exemptions—'the statutes and proclamacons with all other bookes belonging to ye office of her maiesties printer which by reason of her maiesties affayres are to be limited to no numbers,' 'all Calendars printed Red and black,' and, finally, 'all Almanaches and prognosticatons.'

> "By 1635, the Stationers' Company had issued a new set of rules governing the operations of print shops and presses. An increase was granted in the number of impressions that might be drawn from a single

form and the old rule that 'no formes of letters be kept standinge' was modified to permit the use of the standing form, provided that if a compositor in the shop wanted work, he would be paid for the form that was used just as if he had composed it himself. * * *

"In the course of many years, another rule emerged: the printers in a shop or newspaper had a right to set all the type in that shop or be paid for any type or drawing that was actually used even if the master printer had borrowed it or purchased it already set up from another shop. There seemed to be no other way to handle the interchange of type and other materials, and the rule was accepted by both journeymen and masters."

3. Which approach to the problems usually characterized as "featherbedding" do you deem to be the sounder—that contained in Section 8(b)(6) as enacted, that adopted in the Petrillo Act (footnote 6, supra p. 470) and the House version of the Taft-Hartley bill (supra p. 471) or some intermediate approach?

Chapter 6

NEGOTIATION OF THE COLLECTIVE AGREEMENT

INTRODUCTORY NOTE

Collective bargaining is at base a power relationship. This is most manifest at the negotiation stage, where collective agreement is sought. The strategy and tactics of the negotiation process—the demands that are made, the counterproposals, the timing—are oriented to an appraisal by each side of the balance of power between them. This appraisal determines the credibility to be accorded to threats to use economic leverage. The crucial questions are: (1) Can the union afford to take the employees out on strike or subject them to a lockout? (2) If so, what is the staying power of the employees? (3) Can the employer afford a strike or lockout? (4) If so, what is the employer's staying power? The willingness to concede an important demand is more likely to be the product of such a power analysis than it is of objective rationality, although the latter has its role to play.

The materials in this chapter have been selected and arranged in accordance with the foregoing view of the negotiation process. The economic weaponry of the parties relative to that process will be examined, the thrust-parry relationship considered, and the legal frame of reference brought into focus. It will be seen that the major effort of the law governing the negotiation process has been to domesticate the economic strife involved, while at the same time allowing sufficient play to the vital, therapeutic, and, to a large extent, inevitable forces of "free" collective bargaining. With regard to the union weapons—strikes, picketing, and boycotts—the civilizing force of the law has already been seen at work in the preceding chapter. The story now continues, with the additive of *employer* exercise of power and the resulting action and reaction between the contestants.

A. HEREIN OF EMPLOYEE BARGAINING PRESSURES, PROTECTED AND UNPROTECTED, AND OF EMPLOYER COUNTER–PRESSURES, LEGAL AND ILLEGAL

NATIONAL LABOR RELATIONS BOARD v. WASHINGTON ALUMINUM CO.

Supreme Court of the United States, 1962.
370 U.S. 9, 82 S.Ct. 1099, 8 L.Ed.2d 298.

MR. JUSTICE BLACK delivered the opinion of the Court.

The Court of Appeals for the Fourth Circuit, with Chief Judge Sobeloff dissenting, refused to enforce an order of the National Labor Relations Board directing the respondent Washington Aluminum Company to reinstate and make whole seven employees whom the company had discharged for leaving their work in the machine shop without permission on claims that the shop was too cold to work in. * * *

The Board's order, as shown by the record and its findings, rested upon these facts and circumstances. The respondent company is engaged in the fabrication of aluminum products in Baltimore, Maryland, a business having interstate aspects that subject it to regulation under the National Labor Relations Act. The machine shop in which the seven discharged employees worked was not insulated and had a number of doors to the outside that had to be opened frequently. An oil furnace located in an adjoining building was the chief source of heat for the shop, although there were two gas-fired space heaters that contributed heat to a lesser extent. The heat produced by these units was not always satisfactory and, even prior to the day of the walkout involved here, several of the eight machinists who made up the day shift at the shop had complained from time to time to the company's foreman "over the cold working conditions."

January 5, 1959, was an extraordinarily cold day for Baltimore, with unusually high winds and a low temperature of 11 degrees followed by a high of 22. When the employees on the day shift came to work that morning, they found the shop bitterly cold, due not only to the unusually harsh weather, but also to the fact that the large oil furnace had broken down the night before and had not as yet been put back into operation. As the workers gathered in the shop just before the starting hour of 7:30, one of them, a Mr. Caron, went into the office of Mr. Jarvis, the foreman, hoping to warm himself but, instead, found the foreman's quarters as uncomfortable as the rest of the shop. As Caron and Jarvis sat in Jarvis' office discussing how bitingly cold the building was, some of the other machinists walked by the office window "huddled" together in a fashion that caused Jarvis to exclaim that "[i]f those fellows had any guts at all, they would go home." When the starting buzzer sounded a few moments later, Caron walked back to his working place in the shop and found all the other machinists "huddled there, shaking a little, cold." Caron then said to these workers, " * * * Dave [Jarvis] told me if we had any guts, we would go home. * * * I am going home, it is too damned cold to work." Caron asked the other workers what they were going to do and, after some discussion among themselves, they decided to leave with him. One of these workers, testifying before the Board, summarized their entire discussion this way: "And we had all got together and thought it would be a good idea to go home; maybe we could get some heat brought into the plant that way." As they started to leave, Jarvis approached and persuaded one of the workers to remain at the job. But Caron and the other six workers on the day shift left practically in a body in a matter of minutes after the 7:30 buzzer.

When the company's general foreman arrived between 7:45 and 8 that morning, Jarvis promptly informed him that all but one of the employees had left because the shop was too cold. The company's president came in at approximately 8:20 a.m. and, upon learning of the walkout, immediately said to the foreman, " * * * if they have all gone, we are going to terminate them." After discussion "at great length" between the general foreman and the company president as to what might be the effect of the walkout on employee discipline and plant production, the president formalized his discharge of the workers who had walked out by giving orders at 9 a.m. that the affected workers should be notified about their discharge immediately, either by telephone, telegram or personally. This was done.

On these facts the Board found that the conduct of the workers was a concerted activity to protest the company's failure to supply adequate heat in its machine shop, that such conduct is protected under the provision of § 7 of the National Labor Relations Act * * *, and that the discharge of these workers by the company amounted to an unfair labor practice under § 8(a)(1) of the Act. * * * Acting under the authority of § 10(c) of the Act, * * * the Board then ordered the company to reinstate the discharged workers to their previous positions and to make them whole for losses resulting from what the Board found to have been the unlawful termination of their employment.

In denying enforcement of this order, the majority of the Court of Appeals took the position that because the workers simply "summarily left their place of employment" without affording the company an "opportunity to avoid the work stoppage by granting a concession to a demand," their walkout did not amount to a concerted activity protected by § 7 of the Act. On this basis, they held that there was no justification for the conduct of the workers in violating the established rules of the plant by leaving their jobs without permission and that the Board had therefore exceeded its power in issuing the order involved here because § 10(c) declares that the Board shall not require reinstatement or back pay for an employee whom an employer has suspended or discharged "for cause."

We cannot agree that employees necessarily lose their right to engage in concerted activities under § 7 merely because they do not present a specific demand upon their employer to remedy a condition they find objectionable. The language of § 7 is broad enough to protect concerted activities whether they take place before, after, or at the same time such a demand is made. To compel the Board to interpret and apply that language in the restricted fashion suggested by the respondent here would only tend to frustrate the policy of the Act to protect the right of workers to act together to better their working conditions. Indeed, as indicated by this very case, such an interpretation of § 7 might place burdens upon employees so great that it would effectively nullify the right to engage in concerted activities which that section protects. The seven employees here were part of a small group of employees who were wholly unorganized. They had no bargaining representative and, in fact, no representative of any kind to present their grievances to their employer. Under these circumstances, they had to speak for themselves as best they could. As pointed out above, prior to the day they left the shop, several of them had repeatedly complained to company officials about the cold working conditions in the shop. These had been more or less spontaneous individual pleas, unsupported by any threat of concerted protest, to which the company apparently gave little consideration and which it now says the Board should have treated as nothing more than "the same sort of gripes as the gripes made about the heat in the summertime." The bitter cold of January 5, however, finally brought these workers' individual complaints into concert so that some more effective action could be considered. Having no bargaining representative and no established procedure by which they could take full advantage of their unanimity of opinion in negotiations with the company, the men took the most direct course to let the company know that they wanted a warmer place in which to work. So, after talking among themselves, they walked out together in the hope that this action might spotlight their complaint and bring about some improvement in what they considered to be the "miserable" conditions of their employment. This we think was enough to justify the Board's holding that they were not required to make any more specific demand than they did to be entitled to the protection of § 7.

Although the company contends to the contrary, we think that the walkout involved here did grow out of a "labor dispute" within the plain meaning of the definition of that term in § 2(9) of the Act, which declares that it includes "any controversy concerning terms, tenure or *conditions of employment* * * *." The findings of the Board, which are supported by substantial evidence and which were not disturbed below, show a running dispute between the machine shop employees and the company over the heating of the shop on cold days—a dispute which culminated in the decision of the employees to act concertedly in an effort to force the company to improve that condition of their employment. The fact that the company was already making every effort to repair the furnace and bring heat into the shop that morning does not change the nature of the controversy that caused the walkout. At the very most, that fact might tend to indicate that the conduct of the men in leaving was unnecessary and unwise, and it has long been settled that the reasonableness of workers' decisions to engage in concerted activity is irrelevant to the determination of whether a labor dispute exists or not.[12] Moreover, the evidence here shows that the conduct of these workers was far from unjustified under the circumstances. The company's own foreman expressed the opinion that the shop was so cold that the men should go home. This statement by the foreman but emphasizes

12. "The wisdom or unwisdom of the men, their justification or lack of it, in attributing to respondent an unreasonable or arbitrary attitude in connection with the negotiations, cannot determine whether, when they struck, they did so as a consequence of or in connection with, a current labor dispute." National Labor Relations Board v. Mackay Radio & Telegraph Co., 304 U.S. 333, 344, 58 S.Ct. 904, 910, 82 L.Ed. 1381.

the obvious—that is, that the conditions of coldness about which complaint had been made before had been so aggravated on the day of the walkout that the concerted action of the men in leaving their jobs seemed like a perfectly natural and reasonable thing to do.

Nor can we accept the company's contention that because it admittedly had an established plant rule which forbade employees to leave their work without permission of the foreman, there was justifiable "cause" for discharging these employees, wholly separate and apart from any concerted activities in which they engaged in protest against the poorly heated plant. Section 10(c) of the Act does authorize an employer to discharge employees for "cause" and our cases have long recognized this right on the part of an employer. But this, of course, cannot mean that an employer is at liberty to punish a man by discharging him for engaging in concerted activities which § 7 of the Act protects. And the plant rule in question here purports to permit the company to do just that for it would prohibit even the most plainly protected kinds of concerted work stoppages until and unless the permission of the company's foreman was obtained.

It is of course true that § 7 does not protect all concerted activities, but that aspect of the section is not involved in this case. The activities engaged in here do not fall within the normal categories of unprotected concerted activities such as those that are unlawful,[14] violent [15] or in breach of contract.[16] Nor can they be brought under this Court's more recent pronouncement which denied the protection of § 7 to activities characterized as "indefensible" because they were there found to show a disloyalty to the workers' employer which this Court deemed unnecessary to carry on the workers' legitimate concerted activities.[17] The activities of these seven employees cannot be classified as "indefensible" by any recognized standard of conduct. Indeed, concerted activities by employees for the purpose of trying to protect themselves from working conditions as uncomfortable as the testimony and Board findings showed them to be in this case are unquestionably activities to correct conditions which modern labor-management legislation treats as too bad to have to be tolerated in a humane and civilized society like ours.

Holding

We hold therefore that the Board correctly interpreted and applied the Act to the circumstances of this case and it was error for the Court of Appeals to refuse to enforce its order. The judgment of the Court of Appeals is reversed and the cause is remanded to that court with directions to enforce the order in its entirety.

Reversed and remanded.

14. Southern Steamship Co. v. National Labor Relations Board, 316 U.S. 31, 62 S.Ct. 886, 86 L.Ed. 1246.

15. National Labor Relations Board v. Fansteel Metallurgical Corp., 306 U.S. 240, 59 S.Ct. 490, 83 L.Ed. 627.

16. National Labor Relations Board v. Sands Manufacturing Co., 306 U.S. 332, 59 S.Ct. 508, 83 L.Ed. 682.

17. National Labor Relations Board v. Local Union No. 1229, International Brotherhood of Electrical Workers, [Jefferson Standard], 346 U.S. 464, 477, 74 S.Ct. 172, 179, 98 L.Ed. 195.

Note

1. The Court states that "[t]he language of § 7 is broad enough to protect concerted activities whether they take place before, after, or at the same time such a demand [for employer action] is made" (supra p. 478) and that "it has long been settled that the reasonableness of workers' decisions to engage in concerted activity is irrelevant to the determination of whether a labor dispute exists or not" (supra p. 479). Is this a sound position? Does it license economic strife of an unnecessary nature? Is it too much to ask that employees, as a condition precedent to their right to engage in economic warfare, first make known to their employer what they want him to do in order to afford him an opportunity to render the employee action unnecessary by responding to the demand?

2. Suppose after the discussion with Jarvis, the foreman, and after talking with the other employees, Caron had gone home alone and had been fired for this action. Should Caron's lone cessation of work be deemed a "concerted activity" within the meaning of Section 7? Would your judgment be altered if Caron went home without first discussing the matter with his colleagues? What, indeed, *is* "concerted activity"? If the Washington Aluminum plant were unionized and a collective bargaining provision existed that the temperature in the plant should be "reasonably tolerable" for the workers, would your judgment as to the last question be altered? *Should* it be?

In NLRB v. City Disposal Systems, Inc., 465 U.S. 822, 104 S.Ct. 1505, 79 L.Ed.2d 839 (1984), a 5–4 decision, the majority stated:

"James Brown, a truck driver employed by respondent, was discharged when he refused to drive a truck that he honestly and reasonably believed to be unsafe because of faulty brakes. Article XXI of the collective-bargaining agreement between respondent and Local 247 of the Teamsters which covered Brown provides: '[t]he Employer should not require employees to take out on the streets or highways any vehicle that is not in safe operating condition or equipped with safety appliances prescribed by law. It shall not be a violation of the Agreement where employees refuse to operate such equipment unless such refusal is unjustified.'

"The question to be decided is whether Brown's honest and reasonable assertion of his right to be free of the obligation to drive unsafe trucks constituted 'concerted activit[y]' within the meaning of § 7 of the National Labor Relations Act * * *. The National Labor Relations Board * * * held that Brown's refusal was concerted activity within § 7, and that his discharge was, therefore, an unfair labor practice under § 8(a)(1) of the Act, 29 U.S.C. § 158(a). 256 N.L.R.B. 451 (1981). The Court of Appeals disagreed and declined enforcement. 683 F.2d 1005 (CA6 1982). At least three other Courts of Appeals, however, have accepted the Board's interpretation of 'concerted activities' as including the assertion by an individual employee of a right grounded in a collective-bargaining agreement. We granted certiorari to resolve the conflict, 460 U.S. 1050, 103 S.Ct. 1496, 75 L.Ed.2d 928 (1983), and now reverse.

" * * * Section 7 * * * provides that '[e]mployees shall have the right to * * * join or assist labor organizations, to bargain collectively through representatives of their own choosing, and to engage in other concerted activities for the purpose of collective bargaining or other mutual aid or protection.' * * *. The NLRB's decision in this case applied the

Board's longstanding 'Interboro doctrine,' under which an individual's assertion of a right grounded in a collective-bargaining agreement is recognized
as 'concerted activit[y]' and therefore accorded the protection of § 7. See
Interboro Contractors, Inc., 157 N.L.R.B. 1295, 1298 (1966), enforced, 388
F.2d 495 (CA2 1967); Bunney Bros. Construction Co., 139 N.L.R.B. 1516,
1519 (1962). The Board has relied on two justifications for the doctrine:
First, the assertion of a right contained in a collective-bargaining agreement
is an extension of the concerted action that produced the agreement, *Bunney
Bros. Construction,* supra, at 1519; and second, the assertion of such a right
affects the rights of all employees covered by the collective-bargaining
agreement. *Interboro Contractors,* supra, at 1298. * * *.

" *   *   *

"The term 'concerted activit[y]' is not defined in the Act but it clearly
enough embraces the activities of employees who have joined together in
order to achieve common goals. See, e.g., Meyer Industries, 268 N.L.R.B.
No. 73, at 3 (1984). What is not self-evident from the language of the Act,
however, and what we must elucidate, is the precise manner in which
particular actions of an individual employee must be linked to the actions of
fellow employees in order to permit it to be said that the individual is
engaged in concerted activity. We now turn to consider the Board's analysis
of that question as expressed in the *Interboro* doctrine.

"Although one could interpret the phrase, 'to engage in concerted
activities,' to refer to a situation in which two or more employees are
working together at the same time and the same place toward a common
goal, the language of § 7 does not confine itself to such a narrow meaning.
In fact, § 7 itself defines both joining and assisting labor organizations—
activities in which a single employee can engage—as concerted activities.
Indeed, even the courts that have rejected the *Interboro* doctrine recognize
the possibility that an individual employee may be engaged in concerted
activity when he acts alone. They have limited their recognition of this type
of concerted activity, however, to two situations: (1) that in which the lone
employee intends to induce group activity, and (2) that in which the
employee acts as a representative of at least one other employee. See, e.g.,
Aro, Inc. v. NLRB, 596 F.2d, at 713, 717 (CA6 1979); NLRB v. Northern
Metal Co., 440 F.2d 881, 884 (CA3 1971). The disagreement over the
Interboro doctrine, therefore, merely reflects differing views regarding the
nature of the relationship that must exist between the action of the individual employee and the actions of the group in order for § 7 to apply. We
cannot say that the Board's view of that relationship, as applied in the
Interboro doctrine, is unreasonable." 465 U.S. at 824–31, 104 S.Ct. at 1507–
11, 79 L.Ed.2d at 845–49.

What definition of "concerted activity" do you understand the Court to have
endorsed in City Disposal?

3. The dissent in City Disposal was premised on the notion that James
Brown should have filed a grievance under the grievance-arbitration provisions
of the collective bargaining agreement instead of acting unilaterally. To understand this position, assume that in Washington Aluminum the plant had been
unionized and a collective bargaining agreement executed containing grievance-
arbitration provisions and a promise on the part of the union not to strike over
issues covered by those provisions. Would the walkout, by the seven employees,
even conceding it be a concerted activity, be a *protected* activity? How should a

sensible code of labor relations treat such a "wildcat" (i.e., unauthorized by the union) strike? [a]

4. What effect, if any, would Section 502 of the Labor Management Relations Act of 1947 have in the hypothetical variation of Washington Aluminum described in Note 3?

NATIONAL LABOR RELATIONS BOARD v. LOCAL 1229, IBEW ("JEFFERSON STANDARD")

Supreme Court of the United States, 1953.
346 U.S. 464, 74 S.Ct. 172, 98 L.Ed. 195.

MR. JUSTICE BURTON delivered the opinion of the Court.

The issue before us is whether the discharge of certain employees by their employer constituted an unfair labor practice, within the meaning of §§ 8(a)(1) and 7 of the Taft-Hartley Act, justifying their reinstatement by the National Labor Relations Board. For the reason that their discharge was "for cause" within the meaning of § 10(c) of that Act, we sustain the Board in not requiring their reinstatement.

In 1949, the Jefferson Standard Broadcasting Company (here called the company) was a North Carolina corporation engaged in interstate commerce. Under a license from the Federal Communications Commission, it operated, at Charlotte, North Carolina, a 50,000-watt radio station, with call letters WBT. It broadcast 10 to 12 hours daily by radio and television. The television service, which it started July 14, 1949, representing an investment of about $500,000, was the only such service in the area. Less than 50% of the station's programs originated in Charlotte. The others were piped in over leased wires, generally from New York, California or Illinois from several different networks. Its annual gross revenue from broadcasting operations exceeded $100,000 but its television enterprise caused it a monthly loss of about $10,000 during the first four months of that operation, including the period here involved. Its rates for television advertising were geared to the number of receiving sets in the area. Local dealers had large inventories of such sets ready to meet anticipated demands.

The company employed 22 technicians. In December 1948, negotiations to settle the terms of their employment after January 31, 1949, were begun between representatives of the company and of the respondent Local Union No. 1229, International Brotherhood of Electrical Workers, American Federation of Labor (here called the union). The negotiations reached an impasse in January 1949, and the existing contract of employment expired January 31. The technicians, nevertheless, continued to work for the company and their collective-bargaining negotiations were resumed in July, only to break down again July 8. The main point of disagreement arose from the union's

a. Various facets of the wildcat problem are dealt with in the following articles: Atleson, Work Group Behavior and Wildcat Strikes: The Causes and Functions of Industrial Civil Disobedience, 34 Ohio St.L.J. 750 (1973); Fishman & Brown, Union Responsibility for Wildcat Strikes, 21 Wayne L.Rev. 1017 (1975); Handsaker & Handsaker, Remedies and Penalties for Wildcat Strikes: How Arbitrators and Federal Courts Have Ruled, 22 Cath.U.L.Rev. 279 (1973); Shearer, Legal Remedies and Practical Considerations in Dealing with a Wildcat Strike, 22 Drake L.Rev. 36 (1972); Whitman, Wildcat Strikes: The Unions' Narrowing Path to Rectitude?, 50 Ind.L.J. 472 (1972).

demand for the renewal of a provision that all discharges from employment be subject to arbitration and the company's counter-proposal that such arbitration be limited to the facts material to each discharge, leaving it to the company to determine whether those facts gave adequate cause for discharge.

July 9, 1949, the union began daily peaceful picketing of the company's station. Placards and handbills on the picket line charged the company with unfairness to its technicians and emphasized the company's refusal to renew the provision for arbitration of discharges. The placards and handbills named the union as the representative of the WBT technicians. The employees did not strike. They confined their respective tours of picketing to their off-duty hours and continued to draw full pay. There was no violence or threat of violence and no one has taken exception to any of the above conduct.

But on August 24, 1949, a new procedure made its appearance. Without warning, several of its technicians launched a vitriolic attack on the quality of the company's television broadcasts. Five thousand handbills were printed over the designation "WBT TECHNICIANS."

These were distributed on the picket line, on the public square two or three blocks from the company's premises, in barber shops, restaurants and busses. Some were mailed to local businessmen. The handbills made no reference to the union, to a labor controversy or to collective bargaining. They read:

"IS CHARLOTTE A SECOND-CLASS CITY?

"You might think so from the kind of Television programs being presented by the Jefferson Standard Broadcasting Co. over WBTV. Have you seen one of their television programs lately? Did you know that all the programs presented over WBTV are on film and may be from one day to five years old. There are no local programs presented by WBTV. You cannot receive the local baseball games, football games or other local events because WBTV does not have the proper equipment to make these pickups. Cities like New York, Boston, Philadelphia, Washington receive such programs nightly. Why doesn't the Jefferson Standard Broadcasting Company purchase the needed equipment to bring you the same type of programs enjoyed by other leading American cities? Could it be that they consider Charlotte a second-class community and only entitled to the pictures now being presented to them?

"WBT TECHNICIANS"

This attack continued until September 3, 1949, when the company discharged ten of its technicians, whom it charged with sponsoring or distributing these handbills. The company's letter discharging them tells its side of the story.[4]

4. "Dear Mr. * * *,

   "* * *

   "Now, however, you have turned from trying to persuade the public that we are unfair *to you* and are trying to persuade the public that we give inferior service *to them*. While we are struggling to expand into and develop a new field, and incidentally losing large sums of money in the process, you are busy trying to turn customers and the public against us in every possible way, even handing out leaflets on the public streets advertising that our operations are 'second-class,' and endeavoring in various ways to hamper and totally destroy our business. Certainly we are not required by law or common sense to keep you in our

September 4, the union's picketing resumed its original tenor and, September 13, the union filed with the Board a charge that the company, by discharging the above-mentioned ten technicians, had engaged in an unfair labor practice. The General Counsel for the Board filed a complaint based on those charges and, after hearing, a trial examiner made detailed findings and a recommendation that all of those discharged be reinstated with back pay. * * * The Board found that one of the discharged men had neither sponsored nor distributed the "Second-Class City" handbill and ordered his reinstatement with back pay. It then found that the other nine had sponsored or distributed the handbill and held that the company, by discharging them for such conduct, had not engaged in an unfair labor practice. The Board, accordingly, did not order their reinstatement. One member dissented. * * * Under § 10(f) of the Taft-Hartley Act, the union petitioned the Court of Appeals for the District of Columbia Circuit for a review of the Board's order and for such a modification of it as would reinstate all ten of the discharged technicians with back pay. That court remanded the cause to the Board for further consideration and for a finding as to the "unlawfulness" of the conduct of the employees which had led to their discharge. We granted certiorari because of the importance of the case in the administration of the Taft-Hartley Act.

In its essence, the issue is simple. It is whether these employees, whose contracts of employment had expired, were discharged "for cause." They were discharged solely because, at a critical time in the initiation of the company's television service, they sponsored or distributed 5,000 handbills making a sharp, public disparaging attack upon the quality of the company's product and its business policies, in a manner reasonably calculated to harm the company's reputation and reduce its income. The attack was made by them expressly as "WBT TECHNICIANS." It continued ten days without indication of abatement. The Board found that—

"It [the handbill] occasioned widespread comment in the community, and caused Respondent to apprehend a loss of advertising revenue due to dissatisfaction with its television broadcasting service.

"In short, the employees in this case deliberately undertook to alienate their employer's customers by impugning the technical quality of his product. As the Trial Examiner found, they did not misrepresent, at least wilfully, the facts they cited to support their disparaging report. And their ultimate purpose—to extract a concession from the employer with respect to the terms of their employment—was lawful. That purpose, however, was undisclosed; the employees purported to speak as experts, in the interest of

employment and pay you a substantial salary while you thus do your best to tear down and bankrupt our business.

"You are hereby discharged from our employment. Although there is nothing requiring us to do so, and the circumstances certainly do not call for our doing so, we are enclosing a check payable to your order for two weeks' advance or severance pay.

"Very truly yours,

"Jefferson Standard Broadcasting Company

"By: Charles H. Crutchfield

"*Vice President*

"Enclosure"

consumers and the public at large. They did not indicate that they sought to secure any benefit for themselves, *as employees,* by casting discredit upon their employer." 94 N.L.R.B., at 1511.

The company's letter shows that it interpreted the handbill as a demonstration of such detrimental disloyalty as to provide "cause" for its refusal to continue in its employ the perpetrators of the attack. We agree.

Section 10(c) of the Taft-Hartley Act expressly provides that "No order of the Board shall require the reinstatement of any individual as an employee who has been suspended or discharged, or the payment to him of any back pay, if such individual was suspended or discharged for cause." There is no more elemental cause for discharge of an employee than disloyalty to his employer. It is equally elemental that the Taft-Hartley Act seeks to strengthen, rather than to weaken, that co-operation, continuity of service and cordial contractual relation between employer and employee that is born of loyalty to their common enterprise.

Congress, while safeguarding, in § 7, the right of employees to engage in "concerted activities for the purpose of collective bargaining or other mutual aid or protection," did not weaken the underlying contractual bonds and loyalties of employer and employee. * * *

* * * The legal principle that insubordination, disobedience or disloyalty is adequate cause for discharge is plain enough. The difficulty arises in determining whether, in fact, the discharges are made because of such a separable cause or because of some other concerted activities engaged in for the purpose of collective bargaining or other mutual aid or protection which may not be adequate cause for discharge. * * *

In the instant case the Board found that the company's discharge of the nine offenders resulted from their sponsoring and distributing the "Second-Class City" handbills of August 24—September 3, issued in their name as the "WBT TECHNICIANS." Assuming that there had been no pending labor controversy, the conduct of the "WBT TECHNICIANS" from August 24 through September 3 unquestionably would have provided adequate cause for their disciplinary discharge within the meaning of § 10(c). Their attack related itself to no labor practice of the company. It made no reference to wages, hours or working conditions. The policies attacked were those of finance and public relations for which management, not technicians, must be responsible. The attack asked for no public sympathy or support. It was a continuing attack, initiated while off duty, upon the very interests which the attackers were being paid to conserve and develop. Nothing could be further from the purpose of the Act than to require an employer to finance such activities. Nothing would contribute less to the Act's declared purpose of promoting industrial peace and stability.[12]

The fortuity of the coexistence of a labor dispute affords these technicians no substantial defense. While they were also union men and leaders in the labor controversy, they took pains to separate those categories. In

12. " * * * An employee can not work and strike at the same time. He can not continue in his employment and openly or secretly refuse to do his work. He can not collect wages for his employment, and, at the same time, engage in activities to injure or destroy his employer's business." Hoover Co. v. National Labor Relations Board, 6 Cir., 191 F.2d 380, 389 * * *.

contrast to their claims on the picket line as to the labor controversy, their handbill of August 24 omitted all reference to it. The handbill diverted attention from the labor controversy. It attacked public policies of the company which had no discernible relation to that controversy. The only connection between the handbill and the labor controversy was an ultimate and undisclosed purpose or motive on the part of some of the sponsors that, by the hoped-for financial pressure, the attack might extract from the company some future concession. A disclosure of that motive might have lost more public support for the employees that it would have gained, for it would have given the handbill more the character of coercion than of collective bargaining. Referring to the attack, the Board said "In our judgment, these tactics, in the circumstances of this case, were hardly less 'indefensible' than acts of physical sabotage." 94 N.L.R.B., at 1511. In any event, the findings of the Board effectively separate the attack from the labor controversy and treat it solely as one made by the company's technical experts upon the quality of the company's product. As such, it was as adequate a cause for the discharge of its sponsors as if the labor controversy had not been pending. The technicians, themselves, so handled their attack as thus to bring their discharge under § 10(c).

The Board stated "We * * * do not decide whether the disparagement of product involved here would have justified the employer in discharging the employees responsible for it, had it been uttered in the context of a conventional appeal for support of the union in the labor dispute." Id., at 1512, n. 18. This underscored the Board's factual conclusion that the attack of August 24 was not part of an appeal for support in the pending dispute. It was a concerted separable attack purporting to be made in the interest of the public rather than in that of the employees.

We find no occasion to remand this cause to the Board for further specificity of findings. Even if the attack were to be treated, as the Board has not treated it, as a concerted activity wholly or partly within the scope of those mentioned in § 7, the means used by the technicians in conducting the attack have deprived the attackers of the protection of that section, when read in the light and context of the purpose of the Act.

Accordingly, the order of the Court of Appeals remanding the cause to the National Labor Relations Board is set aside, and the cause is remanded to the Court of Appeals with instructions to dismiss respondent's petition to modify the order of the Board. * * *

MR. JUSTICE FRANKFURTER, whom MR. JUSTICE BLACK and MR. JUSTICE DOUGLAS join, dissenting.

The issue before us is not whether this Court would have sustained the Board's order in this case had we been charged by Congress, as we could not have been, "with the normal and primary responsibility for granting or denying enforcement of Labor Board orders." National Labor Relations Board v. Pittsburgh S.S. Co., 340 U.S. 498, 502, 71 S.Ct. 453, 456, 95 L.Ed. 479. The issue is whether we should reverse the Court of Appeals, which is so charged, because that court withheld immediate decision on the Board's order and asked the Board for further light. That court found that the Board employed an improper standard as the basis for its decision. The Board judged the conduct in controversy by finding it "indefensible." The

Court of Appeals held that by "giving 'indefensible' a vague content different from 'unlawful,' the Board misconceived the scope of the established rule." 91 U.S.App.D.C. 333, 202 F.2d 186, 188. Within "unlawful" that court included activities which "contravene * * * basic policies of the Act". The Court of Appeals remanded the case for the Board's judgment whether the conduct of the employees was protected by § 7 under what it deemed "the established rule."

On this central issue—whether the Court of Appeals rightly or wrongly found that the Board applied an improper criterion—this Court is silent. It does not support the Board in using "indefensible" as the legal litmus nor does it reject the Court of Appeals' rejection of that test. This Court presumably does not disagree with the assumption of the Court of Appeals that conduct may be "indefensible" in the colloquial meaning of that loose adjective, and yet be within the protection of § 7.

Instead, the Court, relying on § 10(c) which permits discharges "for cause," points to the "disloyalty" of the employees and finds sufficient "cause" regardless of whether the handbill was a "concerted activity" within § 7. Section 10(c) does not speak of discharge "for disloyalty." If Congress had so written that section, it would have overturned much of the law that had been developed by the Board and the courts in the twelve years preceding the Taft-Hartley Act. The legislative history makes clear that Congress had no such purpose but was rather expressing approval of the construction of "concerted activities" adopted by the Board and the courts. Many of the legally recognized tactics and weapons of labor would readily be condemned for "disloyalty" were they employed between man and man in friendly personal relations. In this connection it is significant that the ground now taken by the Court, insofar as it is derived from the provision of § 10(c) relating to discharge "for cause," was not invoked by the Board in justification of its order.

To suggest that all actions which in the absence of a labor controversy might be "cause"—or, to use the words commonly found in labor agreements, "just cause"—for discharge should be unprotected, even when such actions were undertaken as "concerted activities for the purpose of collective bargaining", is to misconstrue legislation designed to put labor on a fair footing with management. Furthermore, it would disregard the rough and tumble of strikes, in the course of which loose and even reckless language is properly discounted.

"Concerted activities" by employees and dismissal "for cause" by employers are not dissociated legal criteria under the Act. They are like the two halves of a pair of shears. Of course, as the Conference Report on the Taft-Hartley Act said, men on strike may be guilty of conduct "in connection with a concerted activity" which properly constitutes "cause" for dismissal and bars reinstatement. But § 10(c) does not obviate the necessity for a determination whether the distribution of the handbill here was a legitimate tool in a labor dispute or was so "improper," as the Conference Report put it, as to be denied the protection of § 7 and to constitute a discharge "for cause." It is for the Board, in the first instance, to make these evaluations, and a court of appeals does not travel beyond its proper bounds in asking the

Board for greater explicitness in light of the correct legal standards for judgment.

The Board and the courts of appeals will hardly find guidance for future cases from this Court's reversal of the Court of Appeals, beyond that which the specific facts of this case may afford. More than that, to float such imprecise notions as "discipline" and "loyalty" in the context of labor controversies, as the basis of the right to discharge, is to open the door wide to individual judgment by Board members and judges. One may anticipate that the Court's opinion will needlessly stimulate litigation.

Section 7 of course only protects "concerted activities" in the course of promoting legitimate interests of labor. But to treat the offensive handbills here as though they were circulated by the technicians as interloping outsiders to the sustained dispute between them and their employer is a very unreal way of looking at the circumstances of a labor controversy. Certainly there is nothing in the language of the Act or in the legislative history to indicate that only conventional placards and handbills, headed by a trite phrase such as "Unfair To Labor," are protected. In any event, on a remand the Board could properly be asked to leave no doubt whether the technicians, in distributing the handbills, were, so far as the public could tell, on a frolic of their own or whether this tactic, however unorthodox, was no more unlawful than other union behavior previously found to be entitled to protection.

It follows that the Court of Appeals should not be reversed.

Note

1. Suppose the picketing employees in Jefferson Standard had carried signs which read: "The Jefferson Standard Broadcasting Company is unfair to its employees because it denies them arbitration rights and is unfair to the TV viewers of Charlotte because of inferior programming. You help us and we'll help you. Local 1229, IBEW." Would such picketing be protected under Section 7? Should it be?

The union would apparently lose in the foregoing circumstances under the decision in Patterson-Sargent Co., 115 N.L.R.B. 1627 (1956). In that case, striking employees passed out handbills in front of retail hardware stores which sold paint manufactured by Patterson-Sargent, the struck employer. The handbills warned prospective buyers of the employer's paint products that the paint "could peel, crack, blister, scale or any one of many undesirable things that would cause you inconvenience, lost time and money" because not made by the "regular employees," the "well trained, experienced employees who have made the paint you have always bought" and who were now on strike. The Board, interpreting and following the Jefferson Standard decision, held the conduct to be unprotected. Is this a sound application of Jefferson Standard?

2. Would organizing a consumer boycott against one's employer, while still on the job as in Jefferson Standard, constitute a protected activity? The Board held yes and ordered the reinstatement of employees discharged for promoting such a boycott; the Sixth Circuit, however, refused to enforce the Board's order, observing that "an employer is not required, under the Act, to finance a boycott against himself." Hoover Co. v. NLRB, 191 F.2d 380 (6th Cir.1951), denying enforcement of 90 N.L.R.B. 1614 (1950).

With whom do you agree, the Board or the Sixth Circuit? How does the Hoover case differ from Jefferson Standard? From Patterson-Sargent?

3. The four most frequently cited examples of the proposition that the protection of concerted activities in Section 7 is not absolute are: NLRB v. Fansteel Metallurgical Corp., 306 U.S. 240, 59 S.Ct. 490, 83 L.Ed. 627, 123 A.L.R. 599 (1939), supra p. 141, denying protection to a sit-down strike; NLRB v. Sands Mfg. Co., 306 U.S. 332, 59 S.Ct. 508, 83 L.Ed. 682 (1939), denying protection to a strike in violation of a collective bargaining agreement; Southern S.S. Co. v. NLRB, 316 U.S. 31, 62 S.Ct. 886, 86 L.Ed. 1246 (1942), denying protection to a peaceful strike by seamen on shipboard in violation of federal laws against mutiny; and International Union, UAW, AFL v. Wisconsin Employment Relations Board (Briggs-Stratton), 336 U.S. 245, 69 S.Ct. 516, 93 L.Ed. 651 (1949), discussed infra p. 499, denying protection to intermittent and unannounced work stoppages.

While in each of these cases the denial of protection was occasioned by the nature of the concerted activity (i.e., the *means* used), activity may also be denied protection because of the *purpose* it seeks to achieve. An example of the latter is American News Co., 55 N.L.R.B. 1302 (1944), in which protection was denied to a strike designed to force an employer to grant a wage increase prior to approval by the National War Labor Board and therefore in violation of the wartime Wage Stabilization Act. Board Chairman Millis, dissenting in American News, warned against "a revival of the discredited legality-of-object test" and contended that a happier accommodation of the Wage Stabilization Act and the NLRA would be achieved by ordering the reinstatement of the discharged strikers while denying them, in the exercise of the Board's remedial discretion under Section 10(c) of the NLRA, back pay. One way of examining the concern expressed by Chairman Millis is to confront the issue in the form in which it most frequently arises—i.e., is a strike for the purpose of compelling the employer to make a change in supervisory personnel (e.g., foremen) within the protection of Section 7? The decisions, going both ways, are discussed in Getman, The Protection of Economic Pressure by Section 7 of the National Labor Relations Act, 115 U.Pa.L. Rev. 1195, 1211–18 (1967).

NATIONAL LABOR RELATIONS BOARD v. INSURANCE AGENTS' INTERNATIONAL UNION

Supreme Court of the United States, 1960.
361 U.S. 477, 80 S.Ct. 419, 4 L.Ed.2d 454.

Mr. Justice Brennan delivered the opinion of the Court.

This case presents an important issue of the scope of the National Labor Relations Board's authority under § 8(b)(3) of the National Labor Relations Act, which provides that "It shall be an unfair labor practice for a labor organization or its agents * * * to refuse to bargain collectively with an employer, provided it is the representative of his employees * * *." The precise question is whether the Board may find that a union, which confers with an employer with the desire of reaching agreement on contract terms, has nevertheless refused to bargain collectively, thus violating that provision, solely and simply because during the negotiations it seeks to put economic pressure on the employer to yield to its bargaining demands by sponsoring on-the-job conduct designed to interfere with the carrying on of the employer's business.

Since 1949 the respondent Insurance Agents' International Union and the Prudential Insurance Company of America have negotiated collective bargaining agreements covering district agents employed by Prudential in 35 States and the District of Columbia. The principal duties of a Prudential district agent are to collect premiums and to solicit new business in an assigned locality known in the trade as his "debit." He has no fixed or regular working hours except that he must report at his district office two mornings a week and remain for two or three hours to deposit his collections, prepare and submit reports, and attend meetings to receive sales and other instructions. He is paid commissions on collections made and on new policies written; his only fixed compensation is a weekly payment of $4.50 intended primarily to cover his expenses.

In January 1956 Prudential and the union began the negotiation of a new contract to replace an agreement expiring in the following March. Bargaining was carried on continuously for six months before the terms of the new contract were agreed upon on July 17, 1956. It is not questioned that, if it stood alone, the record of negotiations would establish that the union conferred in good faith for the purpose and with the desire of reaching agreement with Prudential on a contract.

However, in April 1956, Prudential filed a § 8(b)(3) charge of refusal to bargain collectively against the union. The charge was based upon actions of the union and its members outside the conference room, occurring after the old contract expired in March. The union had announced in February that if agreement on the terms of the new contract was not reached when the old contract expired, the union members would then participate in a "Work Without a Contract" program—which meant that they would engage in certain planned, concerted on-the-job activities designed to harass the company.

A complaint of violation of § 8(b)(3) issued on the charge and hearings began before the bargaining was concluded. It was developed in the evidence that the union's harassing tactics involved activities by the member agents such as these: refusal for a time to solicit new business, and refusal (after the writing of new business was resumed) to comply with the company's reporting procedures; refusal to participate in the company's "May Policyholders' Month Campaign"; reporting late at district offices the days the agents were scheduled to attend them, and refusing to perform customary duties at the offices, instead engaging there in "sit-in-mornings," "doing what comes naturally" and leaving at noon as a group; absenting themselves from special business conferences arranged by the company; picketing and distributing leaflets outside the various offices of the company on specified days and hours as directed by the union; distributing leaflets each day to policyholders and others and soliciting policyholders' signatures on petitions directed to the company; and presenting the signed policyholders' petitions to the company at its home office while simultaneously engaging in mass demonstrations there.

The hearing examiner filed a report recommending that the complaint be dismissed. * * *

However, the Board * * * rejected the trial examiner's recommendation, and entered a cease-and-desist order, 119 N.L.R.B. 768. The Court of

Appeals for the District of Columbia Circuit * * * set aside the Board's order. 104 U.S.App.D.C. 218, 260 F.2d 736. We granted the Board's petition for certiorari to review the important question presented. * * *

The hearing examiner found that there was nothing in the record, apart from the mentioned activities of the union during the negotiations, that could be relied upon to support an inference that the union had not fulfilled its statutory duty; in fact nothing else was relied upon by the Board's General Counsel in prosecuting the complaint. The hearing examiner's analysis of the congressional design in enacting the statutory duty to bargain led him to conclude that the Board was not authorized to find that such economically harassing activities constituted a § 8(b)(3) violation. The Board's opinion answers flatly "We do not agree" and proceeds to say " * * * the Respondent's reliance upon harassing tactics during the course of negotiations for the avowed purpose of compelling the Company to capitulate to its terms is the antithesis of reasoned discussion it was duty-bound to follow. Indeed, it clearly revealed an unwillingness to submit its demands to the consideration of the bargaining table where argument, persuasion, and the free interchange of views could take place. In such circumstances, the fact that the Respondent continued to confer with the Company and was desirous of concluding an agreement does not *alone* establish that it fulfilled its obligation to bargain in good faith * * *." 119 N.L.R.B., at 769, 770–771. Thus the Board's view is that irrespective of the union's good faith in conferring with the employer at the bargaining table for the purpose and with the desire of reaching agreement on contract terms, its tactics during the course of the negotiations constituted *per se* a violation of § 8(b)(3).[5] * * *

First. The bill which became the Wagner Act included no provision specifically imposing a duty on either party to bargain collectively. Senator Wagner thought that the bill required bargaining in good faith without such a provision. However, the Senate Committee in charge of the bill concluded that it was desirable to include a provision making it an unfair labor practice for an *employer* to refuse to bargain collectively in order to assure that the Act would achieve its primary objective of requiring an employer to recognize a union selected by his employees as their representative. It was believed that other rights guaranteed by the Act would not be meaningful if the employer was not under obligation to confer with the union in an effort to arrive at the terms of an agreement. * * *

However, the nature of the duty to bargain in good faith thus imposed upon employers by § 8(5) of the original Act was not sweepingly conceived. The Chairman of the Senate Committee declared: "When the employees have chosen their organization, when they have selected their representatives, all the bill proposes to do is to escort them to the door of their employer and say, 'Here they are, the legal representatives of your employ-

---

5. The Board observed that the union's continued participation in negotiations and desire to reach an agreement only indicated that it "was prepared to go through the motions of bargaining while relying upon a campaign of harassing tactics to disrupt the Company's business to achieve acceptance of its contractual demands." 119 N.L.R.B., at 771. The only apparent basis for the conclusion that the union was only going through the "motions" of bargaining is the Board's own postulate that the tactics in question were inconsistent with the statutorily required norm of collective bargaining, and the Board's opinion, and its context, reveal that this was all that it meant. * * *

ees.' What happens behind those doors is not inquired into, and the bill does not seek to inquire into it."

The limitation implied by the last sentence has not been in practice maintained—practically, it could hardly have been—but the underlying purpose of the remark has remained the most basic purpose of the statutory provision. That purpose is the making effective of the duty of management to extend recognition to the union; the duty of management to bargain in good faith is essentially a corollary of its duty to recognize the union. Decisions under this provision reflect this. For example, an employer's unilateral wage increase during the bargaining processes tends to subvert the union's position as the representative of the employees in matters of this nature, and hence has been condemned as a practice violative of this statutory provision. See National Labor Relations Board v. Crompton-Highland Mills, Inc., 337 U.S. 217, 69 S.Ct. 960, 93 L.Ed. 1320. And as suggested, the requirement of collective bargaining, although so premised, necessarily led beyond the door of, and into, the conference room. * * * Collective bargaining, then, is not simply an occasion for purely formal meetings between management and labor, while each maintains an attitude of "take it or leave it"; it presupposes a desire to reach ultimate agreement, to enter into a collective bargaining contract. See Heinz Co. v. National Labor Relations Board, 311 U.S. 514, 61 S.Ct. 320, 85 L.Ed. 309. This was the sort of recognition that Congress, in the Wagner Act, wanted extended to labor unions, recognition as the bargaining agent of the employees in a process that looked to the ordering of the parties' industrial relationship through the formation of a contract. * * *

But at the same time, Congress was generally not concerned with the substantive terms on which the parties contracted. * * * Obviously there is tension between the principle that the parties need not contract on any specific terms and a practical enforcement of the principle that they are bound to deal with each other in a serious attempt to resolve differences and reach a common ground. And in fact criticism of the Board's application of the "good-faith" test arose from the belief that it was forcing employers to yield to union demands if they were to avoid a successful charge of unfair labor practice. Thus, in 1947 in Congress the fear was expressed that the Board had "gone very far, in the guise of determining whether or not employers had bargained in good faith, in setting itself up as the judge of what concessions an employer must make and of the proposals and counterproposals that he may or may not make." H.R.Rep. No. 245, 80th Cong., 1st Sess., p. 19. Since the Board was not viewed by Congress as an agency which should exercise its powers to arbitrate the parties' substantive solutions of the issues in their bargaining, a check on this apprehended trend was provided by writing the good-faith test of bargaining into § 8(d) of the Act. * * *

The same problems as to whether positions taken at the bargaining table violate the good-faith test continue to arise under the Act as amended. * * * But it remains clear that § 8(d) was an attempt by Congress to prevent the Board from controlling the settling of the terms of collective bargaining agreements. * * *

Second. At the same time as it was statutorily defining the duty to bargain collectively, Congress, by adding § 8(b)(3) of the Act through the Taft-Hartley amendments, imposed that duty on labor organizations. Unions obviously are formed for the very purpose of bargaining collectively; but the legislative history makes it plain that Congress was wary of the position of some unions, and wanted to ensure that they would approach the bargaining table with the same attitude of willingness to reach an agreement as had been enjoined on management earlier. It intended to prevent employee representatives from putting forth the same "take it or leave it" attitude that had been condemned in management. 93 Cong.Rec. 4135, 4363, 5005.

Third. It is apparent from the legislative history of the whole Act that the policy of Congress is to impose a mutual duty upon the parties to confer in good faith with a desire to reach agreement, in the belief that such an approach from both sides of the table promotes the over-all design of achieving industrial peace. * * * But apart from this essential standard of conduct, Congress intended that the parties should have wide latitude in their negotiations, unrestricted by any governmental power to regulate the substantive solution of their differences. * * *

We believe that the Board's approach in this case—unless it can be defended, in terms of § 8(b)(3), as resting on some unique character of the union tactics involved here—must be taken as proceeding from an erroneous view of collective bargaining. It must be realized that collective bargaining, under a system where the Government does not attempt to control the results of negotiations, cannot be equated with an academic collective search for truth—or even with what might be thought to be the ideal of one. The parties—even granting the modification of views that may come from a realization of economic interdependence—still proceed from contrary and to an extent antagonistic viewpoints and concepts of self-interest. The system has not reached the ideal of the philosophic notion that perfect understanding among people would lead to perfect agreement among them on values. The presence of economic weapons in reserve, and their actual exercise on occasion by the parties, is part and parcel of the system that the Wagner and Taft-Hartley Acts have recognized. Abstract logical analysis might find inconsistency between the command of the statute to negotiate toward an agreement in good faith and the legitimacy of the use of economic weapons, frequently having the most serious effect upon individual workers and productive enterprises, to induce one party to come to the terms desired by the other. But the truth of the matter is that at the present statutory stage of our national labor relations policy, the two factors—necessity for good-faith bargaining between parties, and the availability of economic pressure devices to each to make the other party incline to agree on one's terms—exist side by side. One writer recognizes this by describing economic force as "a prime motive power for agreements in free collective bargaining."[14] Doubtless one factor influences the other; there may be less need to apply economic pressure if the areas of controversy have been defined through discussion; and at the same time, negotiation positions are apt to be weak or

14. G.W. Taylor, Government Regulation of Industrial Relations, p. 18.

strong in accordance with the degree of economic power the parties possess.
* * *

[W]e think the Board's approach involves an intrusion into the substantive aspects of the bargaining process—again, unless there is some specific warrant for its condemnation of the precise tactics involved here. The scope of § 8(b)(3) and the limitations on Board power which were the design of § 8(d) are exceeded, we hold, by inferring a lack of good faith not from any deficiencies of the union's performance at the bargaining table by reason of its attempted use of economic pressure, but solely and simply because tactics designed to exert economic pressure were employed during the course of the good-faith negotiations. Thus the Board in the guise of determining good or bad faith in negotiations could regulate what economic weapons a party might summon to its aid. And if the Board could regulate the choice of economic weapons that may be used as part of collective bargaining, it would be in a position to exercise considerable influence upon the substantive terms on which the parties contract. As the parties' own devices became more limited, the Government might have to enter even more directly into the negotiation of collective agreements. Our labor policy is not presently erected on a foundation of government control of the results of negotiations. See S.Rep. No. 105, 80th Cong., 1st Sess., p. 2. Nor does it contain a charter for the National Labor Relations Board to act at large in equalizing disparities of bargaining power between employer and union.

Fourth. The use of economic pressure, as we have indicated, is of itself not at all inconsistent with the duty of bargaining in good faith. * * * The Board freely (and we think correctly) conceded here that a "total" strike called by the union would not have subjected it to sanctions under § 8(b)(3), at least if it were called after the old contract, with its no-strike clause, had expired. * * *

(a) The Board contends that the distinction between a total strike and the conduct at bar is that a total strike is a concerted activity protected against employer interference by §§ 7 and 8(a)(1) of the Act, while the activity at bar is not a protected concerted activity. We may agree *arguendo* with the Board that this Court's decision in the Briggs-Stratton case, International Union, U.A.W., A.F. of L., Local 232 v. Wisconsin Employment Relations Board, 336 U.S. 245, 69 S.Ct. 516, 93 L.Ed. 651, establishes that the employee conduct here was not a protected concerted activity.[23] On this assumption the employer could have discharged or taken other appropriate disciplinary action against the employees participating in these "slow-down," "sit-in," and arguably unprotected disloyal tactics. See National Labor Relations Board v. Fansteel Metallurgical Corp., 306 U.S. 240, 59 S.Ct. 490, 83 L.Ed. 627; National Labor Relations Board v. Local No. 1229, Intern. B. of Electrical Workers [Jefferson Standard], 346 U.S. 464, 74 S.Ct. 172, 98 L.Ed. 195. But surely that a union activity is not protected against disciplinary action does not mean that it constitutes a refusal to bargain in good faith. The reason why the ordinary economic strike is not evidence of a failure to bargain in good faith is not that it constitutes a protected activity but that,

23. Briggs-Stratton held, among other things, that employee conduct quite similar to the conduct at bar was neither protected by § 7 of the Act, nor prohibited (made an unfair labor practice) by § 8. * * *

as we have developed, there is simply no inconsistency between the application of economic pressure and good-faith collective bargaining. The Board suggests that since (on the assumption we make) the union members' activities here were unprotected, and they could have been discharged, the activities should also be deemed unfair labor practices, since thus the remedy of a cease-and-desist order, milder than mass discharges of personnel and less disruptive of commerce, would be available. The argument is not persuasive. There is little logic in assuming that because Congress was willing to allow employers to use self-help against union tactics, if they were willing to face the economic consequences of its use, it also impliedly declared these tactics unlawful as a matter of federal law. Our problem remains that of construing § 8(b)(3)'s terms, and we do not see how the availability of self-help to the employer has anything to do with the matter.

(b) The Board contends that because an orthodox "total" strike is "traditional" its use must be taken as being consistent with § 8(b)(3); but since the tactics here are not "traditional" or "normal," they need not be so viewed. Further, the Board cites what it conceives to be the public's moral condemnation of the sort of employee tactics involved here. But again we cannot see how these distinctions can be made under a statute which simply enjoins a duty to bargain in good faith. Again, these are relevant arguments when the question is the scope of the concerted activities given affirmative protection by the Act. But as we have developed, the use of economic pressure by the parties to a labor dispute is not a grudging exception to some policy of completely academic discussion enjoined by the Act; it is part and parcel of the process of collective bargaining. On this basis, we fail to see the relevance of whether the practice in question is time-honored or whether its exercise is generally supported by public opinion. It may be that the tactics used here deserve condemnation, but this would not justify attempting to pour that condemnation into a vessel not designed to hold it. The same may be said for the Board's contention that these activities, as opposed to a "normal" strike, are inconsistent with § 8(b)(3) because they offer maximum pressure on the employer at minimum economic cost to the union. One may doubt whether this was so here, but the matter does not turn on that. Surely it cannot be said that the only economic weapons consistent with good-faith bargaining are those which minimize the pressure on the other party or maximize the disadvantage to the party using them. The catalog of union and employer weapons that might thus fall under ban would be most extensive.[28]

---

28. There is a suggestion in the Board's opinion that it regarded the union tactics as a unilateral setting of the terms and conditions of employment and hence also on this basis violative of § 8(b)(3), just as an employer's unilateral setting of employment terms during collective bargaining may amount to a breach of its duty to bargain collectively. National Labor Relations Board v. Crompton-Highland Mills, Inc., 337 U.S. 217, 69 S.Ct. 960, 93 L.Ed. 1320. See 119 N.L.R.B., at 772. Prudential, as *amicus curiae* here, renews this point though the Board does not make it here. It seems baseless to us. There was no indication that the practices that the union was engag-ing in were designed to be permanent conditions of work. They were rather means to another end. The question whether union conduct could be treated, analogously to employer conduct, as unilaterally establishing working conditions, in a manner violative of the duty to bargain collectively, might be raised for example by the case of a union, anxious to secure a reduction of the working day from eight to seven hours, which instructed its members, during the negotiation process, to quit work an hour early daily. Cf. Note, 71 Harv.L.Rev. 502, 509. But this situation is not presented here, and we leave the question open.

Fifth. These distinctions essayed by the Board here, and the lack of relationship to the statutory standard inherent in them, confirm us in our conclusion that the judgment of the Court of Appeals, setting aside the order of the Board, must be affirmed. For they make clear to us that when the Board moves in this area, with only § 8(b)(3) for support, it is functioning as an arbiter of the sort of economic weapons the parties can use in seeking to gain acceptance of their bargaining demands. It has sought to introduce some standard of properly "balanced" bargaining power, or some new distinction of justifiable and unjustifiable, proper and "abusive" economic weapons into the collective bargaining duty imposed by the Act. The Board's assertion of power under § 8(b)(3) allows it to sit in judgment upon every economic weapon the parties to a labor contract negotiation employ, judging it on the very general standard of that section, not drafted with reference to specific forms of economic pressure. We have expressed our belief that this amounts to the Board's entrance into the substantive aspects of the bargaining process to an extent Congress has not countenanced.

* * * Congress has been rather specific when it has come to outlaw particular economic weapons on the part of unions. See § 8(b)(4) * * * § 8(b)(7) * * *. But the activities here involved have never been specifically outlawed by Congress. To be sure, the express prohibitions of the Act are not exclusive. * * * But it is clear to us that the Board needs a more specific charter than § 8(b)(3) before it can add to the Act's prohibitions here. * * *

* * * Where Congress has in the statute given the Board a question to answer, the courts will give respect to that answer; but they must be sure the question has been asked. We see no indication here that Congress has put it to the Board to define through its processes what economic sanctions might be permitted negotiating parties in an "ideal" or "balanced" state of collective bargaining. * * *

Affirmed.

Separate opinion of MR. JUSTICE FRANKFURTER, which MR. JUSTICE HARLAN and MR. JUSTICE WHITTAKER join. * * *

I agree that the position taken by the Board here is not tenable. In enforcing the duty to bargain the Board must find the ultimate fact whether, in the case before it and in the context of all its circumstances, the respondent has engaged in bargaining without the sincere desire to reach agreement which the Act commands. I further agree that the Board's action in this case is not sustainable as resting upon a determination that respondent's apparent bargaining was in fact a sham, because the evidence is insufficient to justify that conclusion even giving the Board, as we must, every benefit of its right to draw on its experience in interpreting the industrial significance of the facts of a record. See Universal Camera Corp. v. National Labor Relations Board, 340 U.S. 474, 71 S.Ct. 456, 95 L.Ed. 456. What the Board has in fact done is lay down a rule of law that such conduct as was involved in carrying out the "Work Without a Contract" program necessarily betokens bad faith in the negotiations.

The Court's opinion rests its conclusion on the generalization that "the ordinary economic strike is not evidence of a failure to bargain in good faith * * * [because] there is simply no inconsistency between the application of economic pressure and good-faith collective bargaining." * * * But in determining the state of mind of a party to collective bargaining negotiations the Board does not deal in terms of abstract "economic pressure." It must proceed in terms of specific conduct which it weighs as a more or less reliable manifestation of the state of mind with which bargaining is conducted. No conduct in the complex context of bargaining for a labor agreement can profitably be reduced to such an abstraction as "economic pressure." An exertion of "economic pressure" may at the same time be part of a concerted effort to evade or disrupt a normal course of negotiations. Vital differences in conduct, varying in character and effect from mild persuasion to destructive, albeit "economic," violence are obscured under cover of a single abstract phrase. * * *

Moreover, conduct designed to exert and exerting "economic pressure" may not have the shelter of § 8(b)(3) even in isolation. Unlawful violence, whether to person or livelihood, to secure acceptance of an offer, is as much a withdrawal of included statutory subjects from bargaining as the "take it or leave it" attitude which the statute clearly condemns. One need not romanticize the community of interest between employers and employees, or be unmindful of the conflict between them, to recognize that utilization of what in one set of circumstances may only signify resort to the traditional weapons of labor may in another and relevant context offend the attitude toward bargaining commanded by the statute. Section 8(b)(3) is not a specific direction, but an expression of a governing viewpoint or policy to which, by the process of specific application, the Board and the courts must give concrete, not doctrinaire content. * * *

[N]o reason is manifest why the respondent's nuisance tactics here should be thought a sufficient basis for the conclusion that all its bargaining was in reality a sham. On this record it does not appear that respondent merely stalled at the bargaining table until its conduct outside the negotiations might force Prudential to capitulate to its demands, nor does any other evidence give the color of pretence to its negotiating procedure. From the conduct of its counsel before the Trial Examiner, and from its opinion, it is apparent that the Board proceeded upon the belief that respondent's tactics were, without more, sufficient evidence of a lack of a sincere desire to reach agreement to make other consideration of its conduct unnecessary. For that reason the case should be remanded to the Board for further opportunity to introduce pertinent evidence, if any there be, of respondent's lack of good faith.

Viewed as a determination by the Board that it could, quite apart from respondent's state of mind, proscribe its tactics because they were not "traditional," or were thought to be subject to public disapproval, or because employees who engaged in them may have been subject to discharge, the Board's conclusion proceeds from the application of an erroneous rule of law.

The decision of the Court of Appeals should be vacated, and the case remanded to the Board for further proceedings consistent with these views.

Note

1. As you read the Insurance Agents case, does it hold that a slowdown cannot be *evidence* of a union's bad faith in collective bargaining?

2. Suppose the insurance agents, as part of their "Work Without a Contract" program, had sabotaged a number of Prudential office machines while continuing to conduct themselves at the bargaining table in the same manner as described in the case. Should this, without more, be held to constitute a violation of 8(b)(3)?

3. What are the legal consequences of categorizing a concerted activity as neither prohibited nor protected, as the Court apparently does in Insurance Agents, endorsing, at least arguendo, its prior decision in International Union, UAW, AFL v. Wisconsin Employment Relations Board (Briggs-Stratton)? If the activity is neither protected nor prohibited under federal law, is it not free of federal preemption and a proper object for state jurisdiction on a common law or statutory tort basis? In the Briggs-Stratton case, the Supreme Court held that engaging in "intermittent and unannounced work stoppages" was neither a protected activity within the meaning of Section 7 nor prohibited by Section 8 and that a state court was therefore free to enjoin such conduct.

Briggs-Stratton was, however, overruled in Lodge 76, International Ass'n of Machinists v. Wisconsin Employment Relations Comm., 427 U.S. 132, 96 S.Ct. 2548, 49 L.Ed.2d 396 (1976), for the reasons set forth in Note 3, supra p. 370. In essence, the rationale of Lodge 76 is that activity which is neither federally protected nor prohibited is nonetheless federally preempted and thus *permitted* to the extent of being insulated from state regulation. Such activity is thus relegated to the "forum" of free economic self-help.

4. Whereas the cases in the present section to this point have involved union weaponry in the collective bargaining process, the remaining cases address themselves to the legality of countering pressures by employers.

NATIONAL LABOR RELATIONS BOARD v. MACKAY RADIO & TELEGRAPH CO.

Supreme Court of the United States, 1938.
304 U.S. 333, 58 S.Ct. 904, 82 L.Ed. 1381.

[Employees struck in an effort to obtain a collective bargaining agreement. There was no allegation or evidence that the employer had failed to bargain in good faith. During the strike, the company employed several replacements for the strikers, five of them on a permanent basis. After the strike, in deciding which five of the strikers were not to get their jobs back, the company singled out those who had been most active in the union's activities.]

MR. JUSTICE ROBERTS delivered the opinion of the Court. [After stating the facts and the disposition below, the Court said:]

Fourth. It is contended that the board lacked jurisdiction because respondent [employer] was at no time guilty of any unfair labor practice. Section 8 of the act denominates as such practice action by an employer to interfere with, restrain, or coerce employees in the exercise of their rights to organize, to form, join, or assist labor organizations, and to engage in concerted activities for the purpose of collective bargaining or other mutual aid or protection, or "by discrimination in regard to * * * tenure of employment or any term or condition of employment to encourage or discourage membership in any labor organization. * * *" There is no evidence and no finding that the respondent was guilty of any unfair labor practice in connection with the negotiations * * *. On the contrary, it affirmatively appears that the respondent was negotiating with the authorized representatives of the union. Nor was it an unfair labor practice to replace the striking employees with others in an effort to carry on the business. Although section 13 of the act provides, "Nothing in this Act shall be construed so as to interfere with or impede or diminish in any way the right to strike," it does not follow that an employer, guilty of no act denounced by the statute, has lost the right to protect and continue his business by supplying places left vacant by strikers. And he is not bound to discharge those hired to fill the places of strikers, upon the election of the latter to resume their employment, in order to create places for them. The assurance by respondent to those who accepted employment during the strike that if they so desired their places might be permanent was not an unfair labor practice, nor was it such to reinstate only so many of the strikers as there were vacant places to be filled. But the claim put forward is that the unfair labor practice indulged by the respondent was discrimination in reinstating striking employees by keeping out certain of them for the sole reason that they had been active in the union. As we have said, the strikers retained, under the act, the status of employees. Any such discrimination in putting them back to work is, therefore, prohibited by section 8.

[The Court directed that the Board's order of reinstatement of the five strikers, with back pay, be enforced.]

Note

1. The Mackay doctrine—that permanent replacement of economic strikers is lawful—is examined and criticized in Note, Replacement of Workers During Strikes, 75 Yale L.J. 630 (1966). As there stated: "The Labor Board in *Mackay* did not discuss the basis of the permanent replacement rule and, in fact, did not even focus on the general question of replacement. Instead, the Board inquired into only the narrow issue of discriminatory employment. However, in a reply brief to the Supreme Court, the Board accepted Mackay's assertion that as a public utility it had a right and duty to hire permanent replacements. The rule which emanated from the *Mackay* case was not litigated before the Board and was inadequately argued before the Court. Despite this lack of consideration, the dictum has been followed blindly. In view of its background and its continuing impact in economic strikes the permanent replacement rule should now be reconsidered." Id. at 631–32.

2. Can the Mackay rule be squared with Sections 7, 13, 8(a)(1) and (3)? How would you argue in justification of the rule? Is it consistent with Insurance Agents?

What effect, if any, should the availability of *temporary* replacements have upon the application of the Mackay doctrine?

Suppose the striking employees in Mackay had been first discharged and sometime thereafter permanently replaced? Such sequence was held in NLRB v. International Van Lines, 409 U.S. 48, 93 S.Ct. 74, 34 L.Ed.2d 201 (1972), to constitute a violation of Section 8(a)(3), and the strikers were ordered reinstated with back pay. Is this case consistent with Mackay?

3. The rights of strikers who have been replaced by their employers while on strike are described in 2 C. Morris, The Developing Labor Law 1007–15 (2d ed. 1983) (supporting citations omitted):

"Section 2(3) of the Act provides that strikers retain their employee status while on strike. Whether they have an absolute right to reinstatement, however, depends primarily upon whether the stoppage is determined to be an Unfair labor practice strike or an economic strike. An *unfair labor practice strike* is strike activity initiated in whole or in part in response to unfair labor practices committed by the employer. An *economic strike* is one that is neither caused nor prolonged by an unfair labor practice on the part of the employer. * * *

"The most significant aspect of an unfair labor practice strike is that strikers who have been engaged in such a strike are entitled to reinstatement to their former jobs upon an unconditional offer to return to work. [Unfair labor practice] strikers must be reinstated even if the employer has hired permanent replacements and even if permanent replacements must be discharged. * * * Strikers who have been guilty of strike misconduct * * * need not be reinstated, notwithstanding the fact that the work stoppage was an unfair labor practice strike. * * * [H]owever, it is for the Board to determine 'whether under the circumstances there was cause for the respondent's refusal to rehire the particular strikers involved in the non-Section 7 activity, and if not whether reinstatement of these employees would effectuate the policies of the Act.' * * * Unfair labor practice strikers are entitled to vote in elections; temporary replacements are not.

"Under the *Mackay* doctrine, when an economic strike occurs, the employer is free to hire permanent replacements for the strikers, and may lawfully refuse a striker's request for reinstatement if he or she has been permanently replaced by the time the strike is ended. * * *

"If economic strikers are guilty of misconduct, the employer is under no duty to reinstate them regardless of whether replacements have been hired. * * *

"Although economic strikers may lose their right to reinstatement [because of the hiring of permanent replacements for them], they remain eligible to vote in a representation election held within 12 months of the commencement of the strike. [§ 9(c)(3).] Strikers who have been discharged because of misconduct, however, are denied the right to vote.

"* * * [A] strike which begins as an economic strike may be converted into an unfair labor practice strike by acts of the employer, thereby changing the status of the participants to unfair labor practice strikers and entitling them to reinstatement. To illustrate, since the existence of a strike does not suspend the obligation to bargain in good faith, if during an economic strike the employer refuses to bargain with the employee's representative, the strike [thereafter] becomes an unfair labor practice strike."

4. As Note 1 above presages, there has been a continuing assault on the Mackay doctrine as too intrusive upon the rights of employees to engage in concerted activities in support of collective bargaining. See, e.g., Atleson, Values and Assumptions in American Labor Law 19–34 (1983); Weiler, Striking a New Balance: Freedom of Contract and the Prospects for Union Representation, 98 Harv.L.Rev. 351, 387–394 (1984).

In Belknap, Inc. v. Hale, 463 U.S. 491, 103 S.Ct. 3172, 77 L.Ed.2d 798 (1983), a tangential attack upon the Mackay doctrine reached the Supreme Court. The employer, confronted by an economic strike, had hired replacements to whom it had assured permanency of employment. However, other action by the employer resulted in the union's filing pertinent unfair labor practice charges with the Board. Upon an agreement between the employer and the union settling the strike, the unfair labor practice complaint which had been issued by the Board was dismissed. The strike settlement agreement required the employer to reinstate the strikers, thus displacing the "permanent" substitutes. The latter then sued the employer in a state court to recover damages for misrepresentation and breach of contract. The issue thus presented to the Supreme Court was whether the asserted causes of action were preempted pursuant to the Mackay doctrine. The Court held, 6–3, against preemption, rejecting both the contention that (1) the state court action impermissibly impinged upon the federal system of free collective bargaining in violation of the Lodge 76 principle (see Note 3, supra p. 370) and (2) the Garmon doctrine (see supra p. 330) granting primary jurisdiction to the NLRB for the resolution of activity arguably protected or prohibited under the National Labor Relations Act.

The Court stated:

"Arguments that entertaining suits by innocent third parties for breach of contract or for misrepresentation will 'burden' the employer's right to hire permanent replacements are no more than arguments that 'this is war,' that 'anything goes,' and that promises of permanent employment that under federal law the employer is free to keep, if it so chooses, are essentially meaningless. It is one thing to hold that the federal law intended to leave the employer and the union free to use their economic weapons against one another, but it is quite another to hold that either the employer or the union is also free to injure innocent third parties without regard to the normal rules of law governing those relationships. We cannot agree with the dissent that Congress intended such a lawless regime.

"The argument that entertaining suits like this will interfere with the asserted policy of the federal law favoring settlement of labor disputes fares no better. This is just another way of asserting that the employer need not answer for its repeated assurances of permanent employment or for its otherwise actionable misrepresentations to secure permanent replacements. We do not think that the normal contractual rights and other usual legal interests of the replacements can be so easily disposed of by broad-brush assertions that no legal rights may accrue to them during a strike because the federal law has privileged the 'permanent' hiring of replacements and encourages settlement.

"In defense of this position, Belknap, supported by the Board in an amicus brief, urges that permitting the state suit where employers may, after the beginning of a strike, either be ordered to reinstate strikers or find it advisable to sign agreements providing for reinstatement of strikers, will deter employers from making permanent offers of employment or at the very least force them to condition their offer by stating the circumstances under which replacements must be fired. This would considerably weaken the employer's position during the strike, it is said, because without assuring permanent employment, it would be difficult to secure sufficient replacements to keep the business operating. Indeed, as the Board interprets the law, the employer must reinstate strikers at the conclusion of even a purely economic strike unless it has 'permanent' replacements, that is, hired in a manner that would 'show that the men [and women] who replaced the strikers were regarded by themselves and the [employer] as having received their jobs on a permanent basis.' *Georgia Highway Express, Inc.,* 165 NLRB 514, 516 (1967), affirmed *sub nom., Truck Drivers and Helpers Local No. 728 v. NLRB,* 403 F.2d 921 (CADC), cert. denied, 393 U.S. 935, 89 S.Ct. 296, 21 L.Ed.2d 272 (1968).

"We remain unconvinced. If serious detriment will result to the employer from conditioning offers so as to avoid a breach of contract if the employer is forced by Board order to reinstate strikers or if the employer settles on terms requiring such reinstatement, much the same result would follow from Belknap's and the Board's construction of the Act. Their view is that, as a matter of federal law, an employer may terminate replacements, without liability to them, in the event of settlement or Board decision that the strike is an unfair labor practice strike. Any offer of permanent employment to replacements is thus necessarily conditional and nonpermanent. This view of the law would inevitably become widely known and would deter honest employers from making promises that they know they are not legally obligated to keep. Also, many putative replacements would know that the proffered job is, in important respects, non-permanent and may not accept employment for that reason. It is doubtful, with respect to the employer's ability to hire, that there would be a substantial difference between the effect of the Board's preferred rule and a rule that would subject the employer to damages liability unless it suitably conditions its offers of employment to replacements.7" 463 U.S. at 500–02, 103 S.Ct. at 3178–79, 77 L.Ed.2d at 808–09.

NATIONAL LABOR RELATIONS BOARD v. ERIE RESISTOR CORP.

Supreme Court of the United States, 1963.
373 U.S. 221, 83 S.Ct. 1139, 10 L.Ed.2d 308, 94 A.L.R.2d 1147.

MR. JUSTICE WHITE delivered the opinion of the Court.

The question before us is whether an employer commits an unfair labor practice under § 8(a) of the National Labor Relations Act ＊ ＊ ＊ when he extends a 20-year seniority credit to strike replacements and strikers who leave the strike and return to work. ＊ ＊ ＊

Erie Resistor Corporation and Local 613 of the International Union of Electrical Radio and Machine Workers were bound by a collective bargaining agreement which was due to expire on March 31, 1959. In January 1959, both parties met to negotiate new terms but, after extensive bargaining, they were unable to reach agreement. Upon expiration of the contract, the union, in support of its contract demands, called a strike which was joined by all of the 478 employees in the unit.[2]

7. The dissent's argument that state causes of action such as this must be preempted because they make it more difficult for the employer to hire replacements proves entirely too much. For example, it might be easier for an employer to obtain replacements by misstating the wages or fringe benefits that it would provide. But if the employer did so, surely the employees affected could seek protection in the state courts.

2. In addition to these employees, 450 employees in the unit were on layoff status.

The company, under intense competition and subject to insistent demands from its customers to maintain deliveries, decided to continue production operations. Transferring clerks, engineers and other nonunit employees to production jobs, the company managed to keep production at about 15% to 30% of normal during the month of April. On May 3, however, the company notified the union members that it intended to begin hiring replacements and that strikers would retain their jobs until replaced. The plant was located in an area classified by the United States Department of Labor as one of severe unemployment and the company had in fact received applications for employment as early as a week or two after the strike began.

Replacements were told that they would not be laid off or discharged at the end of the strike. To implement that assurance, particularly in view of the 450 employees already laid off on March 31, the company notified the union that it intended to accord the replacements some form of super-seniority. At regular bargaining sessions between the company and union, the union made it clear that, in its view, no matter what form the super-seniority plan might take, it would necessarily work an illegal discrimination against the strikers. As negotiations advanced on other issues, it became evident that super-seniority was fast becoming the focal point of disagreement. On May 28, the company informed the union that it had decided to award 20 years' additional seniority both to replacements and to strikers who returned to work, which would be available only for credit against future layoffs and which could not be used for other employee benefits based on years of service. The strikers, at a union meeting the next day, unanimously resolved to continue striking now in protest against the proposed plan as well.

The company made its first official announcement of the super-seniority plan on June 10, and by June 14, 34 new employees, 47 employees recalled from layoff status and 23 returning strikers had accepted production jobs. The union, now under great pressure, offered to give up some of its contract demands if the company would abandon super-seniority or go to arbitration on the question, but the company refused. In the following week, 64 strikers returned to work and 21 replacements took jobs, bringing the total to 102 replacements and recalled workers and 87 returned strikers. When the number of returning strikers went up to 125 during the following week, the union capitulated. A new labor agreement on the remaining economic issues was executed on July 17, and an accompanying settlement agreement was signed providing that the company's replacement and job assurance policy should be resolved by the National Labor Relations Board and the federal courts but was to remain in effect pending final disposition.

Following the strike's termination, the company reinstated those strikers whose jobs had not been filled (all but 129 were returned to their jobs). At about the same time, the union received some 173 resignations from membership. By September of 1959, the production unit work force had reached a high of 442 employees, but by May of 1960, the work force had gradually slipped back to 240. Many employees laid off during this cut back period were reinstated strikers whose seniority was insufficient to retain their jobs as a consequence of the company's super-seniority policy.

The union filed a charge with the National Labor Relations Board alleging that awarding super-seniority during the course of the strike constituted an unfair labor practice and that the subsequent layoff of the recalled strikers pursuant to such a plan was unlawful. The Trial Examiner found that the policy was promulgated for legitimate economic reasons,[4] not for illegal or discriminatory purposes, and recommended that the union's complaint be dismissed. The Board could not agree with the Trial Examiner's conclusion that specific evidence of subjective intent to discriminate against the union was necessary to finding that super-seniority granted during a strike is an unfair labor practice. Its consistent view, the Board said, had always been that super-seniority, in circumstances such as these, was an unfair labor practice. The Board rejected the argument that super-seniority granted during a strike is a legitimate corollary of the employer's right of replacement under National Labor Relations Board v. Mackay Radio & Tel. Co., 304 U.S. 333, 58 S.Ct. 904, 82 L.Ed. 1381, and detailed at some length the factors which to it indicated that "superseniority is a form of discrimination extending far beyond the employer's right of replacement sanctioned by Mackay, and is, moreover, in direct conflict with the express provisions of the Act prohibiting discrimination." Having put aside Mackay, the Board went on to deny "that specific evidence of Respondent's discriminatory motivation is required to establish the alleged violations of the Act," * * *. Moreover, in the Board's judgment, the employer's insistence that its overriding purpose in granting super-seniority was to keep its plant open and that business necessity justified its conduct was unacceptable since "to excuse such conduct would greatly diminish, if not destroy, the right to strike guaranteed by the Act, and would run directly counter to the guarantees of Sections 8(a)(1) and (3) that employees shall not be discriminated against for engaging in protected concerted activities."[5] Accordingly, the Board declined to make findings as to the specific motivation of the plan or its business necessity in the circumstances here.

The Court of Appeals rejected as unsupportable the rationale of the Board that a preferential seniority policy is illegal however motivated.

> "We are of the opinion that inherent in the right of an employer to replace strikers during a strike is the concomitant right to adopt a preferential seniority policy which will assure the replacements some form of tenure, provided the policy is adopted SOLELY to protect and continue the business of the employer. We find nothing in the Act which proscribes such a policy.

---

4. The Examiner had relied upon the company's employment records for his conclusion that the replacement program was ineffective until the announcement of the super-seniority awards. The General Counsel, to show that such a plan was not necessary for that purpose, pointed to the facts that the company had 300 unprocessed job applications when the strike ended, that the company declared to the union that it could have replaced all the strikers and that the company did not communicate its otherwise well-publicized policy to replacements before they were hired but only after they accepted jobs.

5. In addition, the Board held that continued insistence on this or a similar proposal as a condition to negotiating an agreement constituted a refusal to bargain in good faith under § 8(a)(5). See National Labor Relations Board v. Wooster Division of Borg-Warner Corp., 356 U.S. 342, 78 S.Ct. 718, 2 L.Ed.2d 823.

The Board also concluded that on May 29, when the union voted to continue striking in protest against the super-seniority plan, the strike was converted into an unfair labor practice strike. All strikers not replaced at that date, the Board held, were entitled to reinstatement as of the date of their unconditional abandonment of the strike regardless of replacements.

Whether the policy adopted by the Company in the instant case was illegally motivated we do not decide. The question is one of fact for decision by the Board." 303 F.2d, at 364.

It consequently denied the Board's petition for enforcement and remanded the case for further findings. * * *

We think the Court of Appeals erred in holding that, in the absence of a finding of specific illegal intent, a legitimate business purpose is always a defense to an unfair labor practice charge. Cases in this Court dealing with unfair labor practices have recognized the relevance and importance of showing the employer's intent or motive to discriminate or to interfere with union rights. But specific evidence of such subjective intent is "not an indispensable element of proof of violation." Radio Officers Union of Commercial Telegraphers Union, A.F.L. v. National Labor Relations Board, 347 U.S. 17, 44, 74 S.Ct. 323, 98 L.Ed. 455. "Some conduct may by its very nature contain the implications of the required intent; the natural foreseeable consequences of certain action may warrant the inference. * * * The existence of discrimination may at times be inferred by the Board, for 'it is permissible to draw on experience in factual inquiries.'" Local 357, International Brotherhood of Teamsters, Chauffeurs, Warehousemen and Helpers of America v. National Labor Relations Board, 365 U.S. 667, 675, 81 S.Ct. 835, 839, 6 L.Ed.2d 11.

Though the intent necessary for an unfair labor practice may be shown in different ways, proving it in one manner may have far different weight and far different consequences than proving it in another. When specific evidence of a subjective intent to discriminate or to encourage or discourage union membership is shown, and found, many otherwise innocent or ambiguous actions which are normally incident to the conduct of a business may, without more, be converted into unfair labor practices. * * * Such proof itself is normally sufficient to destroy the employer's claim of a legitimate business purpose, if one is made, and provides strong support to a finding that there is interference with union rights or that union membership will be discouraged. Conduct which on its face appears to serve legitimate business ends in these cases is wholly impeached by the showing of an intent to encroach upon protected rights. The employer's claim of legitimacy is totally dispelled.

The outcome may well be the same when intent is founded upon the inherently discriminatory or destructive nature of the conduct itself. The employer in such cases must be held to intend the very consequences which foreseeably and inescapably flow from his actions and if he fails to explain away, to justify or to characterize his actions as something different than they appear on their face, an unfair labor practice charge is made out. Radio Officers Union of Commercial Telegraphers Union, A.F.L. v. National Labor Relations Board, supra. But, as often happens, the employer may counter by claiming that his actions were taken in the pursuit of legitimate business ends and that his dominant purpose was not to discriminate or to invade union rights but to accomplish business objectives acceptable under the Act. Nevertheless, his conduct *does* speak for itself—it *is* discriminatory and it *does* discourage union membership and whatever the claimed overriding justification may be, it carries with it unavoidable consequences which the employer not only foresaw but which he must have intended. As is not uncommon in human experience, such situations present a complex of motives and preferring one motive to another is in reality the far more delicate task, reflected in part in decisions of this Court, of weighing the interests of employees in concerted activity against the interest of the employer in operating his business in a particular manner and of balancing in the light of the Act and its policy the intended consequences upon employee rights against the business ends to be served by the employer's conduct. This essentially is the teaching of the Court's prior cases dealing with this problem and, in our view, the Board did not depart from it.

The Board made a detailed assessment of super-seniority and, to its experienced eye, such a plan had the following characteristics:

(1) Super-seniority affects the tenure of all strikers whereas permanent replacement, proper under Mackay, affects only those who are, in actuality, replaced. It is one thing to say that a striker is subject to loss of his job at the strike's end but quite another to hold that in addition to the threat of replacement, all strikers will at best return to their jobs with seniority inferior to that of the replacements and of those who left the strike.

(2) A super-seniority award necessarily operates to the detriment of those who participated in the strike as compared to nonstrikers.

(3) Super-seniority made available to striking bargaining unit employees as well as to new employees is in effect offering individual benefits to the strikers to induce them to abandon the strike.

(4) Extending the benefits of super-seniority to striking bargaining unit employees as well as to new replacements deals a crippling blow to the strike effort. At one stroke, those with low seniority have the opportunity to obtain the job security which ordinarily only long years of service can bring, while conversely, the accumulated seniority of older employees is seriously diluted. This combination of threat and promise could be expected to undermine the strikers' mutual interest and place the entire strike effort in jeopardy. The history of this strike and its virtual collapse following the announcement of the plan emphasize the grave repercussions of super-seniority.

(5) Super-seniority renders future bargaining difficult, if not impossible, for the collective bargaining representative. Unlike the replacement granted in Mackay which ceases to be an issue once the strike is over, the plan here creates a cleavage in the plant continuing long after the strike is ended. Employees are henceforth divided into two camps: those who stayed with the union and those who returned before the end of the strike and thereby gained extra seniority. This breach is reemphasized with each subsequent layoff and stands as an ever-present reminder of the dangers connected with striking and with union activities in general.

In the light of this analysis, super-seniority by its very terms operates to discriminate between strikers and nonstrikers, both during and after a strike, and its destructive impact upon the strike and union activity cannot be doubted. The origin of the plan, as respondent insists, may have been to keep production going and it may have been necessary to offer super-seniority to attract replacements and induce union members to leave the strike. But if this is true, accomplishment of respondent's business purpose inexorably was contingent upon attracting sufficient replacements and strikers by offering preferential inducements to those who worked as opposed to those who struck. We think the Board was entitled to treat this case as involving conduct which carried its own indicia of intent and which is barred by the Act unless saved from illegality by an overriding business purpose justifying the invasion of union rights. The Board concluded that the business purpose asserted was insufficient to insulate the super-seniority plan from the reach of § 8(a)(1) and § 8(a)(3), and we turn now to a review of that conclusion.

The Court of Appeals and respondent rely upon Mackay as precluding the result reached by the Board but we are not persuaded. Under the decision in that case an employer may operate his plant during a strike and at its conclusion need not discharge those who worked during the strike in order to make way for returning strikers. It may be, as the Court of Appeals said, that "such a replacement policy is obviously discriminatory and may tend to discourage union membership." But Mackay did not deal with super-seniority, with its effects upon all strikers, whether replaced or not, or with its powerful impact upon a strike itself. Because the employer's interest must be deemed to outweigh the damage to concerted activities caused by permanently replacing strikers does not mean it also outweighs the far greater encroachment resulting from super-seniority in addition to permanent replacement.

We have no intention of questioning the continuing vitality of the Mackay rule, but we are not prepared to extend it to the situation we have here. To do so would require us to set aside the Board's considered judgment that the Act and its underlying policy require, in the present context, giving more weight to the harm wrought by super-seniority than to the interest of the employer in operating its plant during the strike by utilizing this particular means of attracting replacements. We find nothing in the Act or its legislative history to indicate that super-seniority is necessarily an acceptable method of resisting the economic impact of a strike, nor do we find anything inconsistent with the result which the Board reached. On the contrary, these sources are wholly consistent with, and lend full support to, the conclusion of the Board.

Section 7 guarantees, and § 8(a)(1) protects from employer interference the rights of employees to engage in concerted activities, which, as Congress has indicated, * * * include the right to strike. Under § 8(a)(3), it is unlawful for an employer by discrimination in terms of employment to discourage "membership in any labor organization," which includes discouraging participation in concerted activities * * * such as a legitimate strike. * * * Section 13 makes clear that although the strike weapon is not an unqualified right, nothing in the Act except as specifically provided is to be construed to interfere with this means of redress, * * * and § 2(3) preserves to strikers their unfilled positions and status as employees during the pendency of a strike. * * * This repeated solicitude for the right to strike is predicated upon the conclusion that a strike when legitimately employed is an economic weapon which in great measure implements and supports the principles of the collective bargaining system.

While Congress has from time to time revamped and redirected national labor policy, its concern for the integrity of the strike weapon has remained constant. Thus when Congress chose to qualify the use of the strike, it did so by prescribing the limits and conditions of the abridgment in exacting detail, e.g., §§ 8(b)(4), 8(d), by indicating the precise procedures to be followed in effecting the interference, e.g., § 10(j), (k), (l); §§ 206–210, Labor Management Relations Act, and by preserving the positive command of § 13 that the right to strike is to be given a generous interpretation within the scope of the labor Act. The courts have likewise repeatedly recognized and effectuated the strong interest of federal labor policy in the legitimate use of the strike. * * *

Accordingly, in view of the deference paid the strike weapon by the federal labor laws and the devastating consequences upon it which the Board found was and would be precipitated by respondent's inherently discriminatory super-seniority plan, we cannot say the Board erred in the balance which it struck here. Although the Board's decisions are by no means immune from attack in the courts as cases in this Court amply illustrate, * * * its findings here are supported by substantial evidence, * * * its explication is not inadequate, irrational or arbitrary, * * * and it did not exceed its powers or venture into an area barred by the statute. * * * The matter before the Board lay well within the mainstream of its duties. It was attempting to deal with an issue which Congress had placed in its hands and "[w]here Congress has in the statute given the Board a question to answer, the courts will give respect to that answer." National Labor Relations Board v. Insurance Agents, supra, 361 U.S. at 499, 80 S.Ct. at 433. Here, as in other cases, we must recognize the Board's special function of applying the general provisions of the Act to the complexities of industrial life. * * * "The ultimate problem is the balancing of the conflicting legitimate interests. The function of striking that balance to effectuate national labor policy is often a difficult and delicate responsibility, which the Congress committed primarily to the National Labor Relations Board, subject to limited judicial review." National Labor Relations Board v. Truck Drivers Local Union, 353 U.S. 87, 96, 77 S.Ct. 643, 648, 1 L.Ed.2d 676.

Consequently, because the Board's judgment was that the claimed business purpose would not outweigh the necessary harm to employee rights—a judgment which we sustain—it could properly put aside evidence of respondent's motive and decline to find whether the conduct was or was not prompted by the claimed business purpose. * * *

Reversed and remanded.

MR. JUSTICE HARLAN, concurring.

I agree with the Court that the Board's conclusions respecting this 20-year "superseniority" plan were justified without inquiry into the respondents' motives. However, I do not think that the same thing would necessarily be true in all circumstances, as for example with a plan providing for a much shorter period of extra seniority. Being unsure whether the Court intends to hold that the Board has power to outlaw *all* such plans, irrespective of the employer's motives and other circumstances, or only to sustain its action in the particular circumstances of *this* case, I concur in the judgment.

AMERICAN SHIP BUILDING CO. v. NATIONAL LABOR RELATIONS BOARD

Supreme Court of the United States, 1965.
380 U.S. 300, 85 S.Ct. 955, 13 L.Ed.2d 855.

MR. JUSTICE STEWART delivered the opinion of the Court.

The American Ship Building Company seeks review of a decision of the United States Court of Appeals for the District of Columbia enforcing an order of the National Labor Relations Board which found that the company had committed an unfair labor practice under §§ 8(a)(1) and 8(a)(3) of the National Labor Relations Act. The question presented is that expressly reserved in National Labor Relations Board v. Truck Drivers Local Union, etc. [Buffalo Linen—supra p. 228], 353 U.S. 87, 93, 77 S.Ct. 643, 646, 1 L.Ed. 2d 676; namely, whether an employer commits an unfair labor practice under these sections of the Act when he temporarily lays off or "locks out" his employees during a labor dispute to bring economic pressure in support of his bargaining position.

The American Ship Building Company operates four shipyards on the Great Lakes—at Chicago, at Buffalo, and at Toledo and Lorain, Ohio. The company is primarily engaged in the repairing of ships, a highly seasonal business concentrated in the winter months when the freezing of the Great Lakes renders shipping impossible. What limited business is obtained during the shipping season is frequently such that speed of execution is of the utmost importance to minimize immobilization of the ships.

Since 1952 the employer has engaged in collective bargaining with a group of eight unions. Prior to the negotiations here in question, the employer had contracted with the unions on five occasions, each agreement having been preceded by a strike. The particular chapter of the collective bargaining history with which we are concerned opened shortly before May 1, 1961, when the unions notified the company of their intention to seek modification of the current contract, due to expire on August 1.

At the initial bargaining meeting on June 6, 1961, the company took the position that its competitive situation would not allow increased compensation. The unions countered with demands for increased fringe benefits and some unspecified wage increase. Several meetings were held in June and early July during which negotiations focussed upon the fringe benefit questions without any substantial progress. At the last meeting, the parties resolved to call in the Federal Mediation and Conciliation Service, which set the next meeting for July 19. At this meeting, the unions first unveiled their demand for a 20-cent-an-hour wage increase and proposed a six-month extension of the contract pending continued negotiations. The employer rejected the proposed extension because it would have led to expiration during the peak season.

Further negotiations narrowed the dispute to five or six issues, all involving substantial economic differences. On July 31, the eve of the contract's expiration, the employer made a proposal; the unions countered with another, revived their proposal for a six-month extension, and proposed in the alternative that the existing contract, with its no-strike clause, be extended indefinitely with the terms of the new contract to be made retroactive to August 1. After rejection of the proposed extensions, the employer's proposal was submitted to the unions' membership; on August 8 the unions announced that this proposal had been overwhelmingly rejected. The following day, the employer made another proposal which the unions refused to submit to their membership; the unions made no counteroffer and the parties separated without setting a date for further meetings, leaving this to the discretion of the conciliator.

Thus on August 9, after extended negotiations, the parties separated without having resolved substantial differences on the central issues dividing them and without having specific plans for further attempts to resolve them—a situation which the trial examiner found was an impasse. Throughout the negotiations, the employer displayed anxiety as to the unions' strike plans, fearing that the unions would call a strike as soon as a ship entered the Chicago yard or delay negotiations into the winter to increase strike leverage. The union negotiator consistently insisted that it was his intention to reach an agreement without calling a strike; however, he did concede incomplete control over the workers—a fact borne out by the occurrence of a wildcat strike in February 1961. Because of the danger of an unauthorized strike and the consistent and deliberate use of strikes in prior negotiations, the employer remained apprehensive of the possibility of a work stoppage.

In light of the failure to reach an agreement and the lack of available work, the employer decided to lay off certain of his workers. On August 11 the employees received a notice which read: "Because of the labor dispute which has been unresolved since August 1, 1961, you are laid off until further notice." The Chicago yard was completely shut down and all but two employees laid off at the Toledo yard. A large force was retained at Lorain to complete a major piece of work there and the employees in the Buffalo yard were gradually laid off as miscellaneous tasks were completed. Negotiations were resumed shortly after these layoffs and continued for the following two months until a two-year contract was agreed upon on October 27. The employees were recalled the following day.

Upon claims filed by the unions, the General Counsel of the Board issued a complaint charging the employer with violations of §§ 8(a)(1), (a)(3), and (a)(5). The trial examiner found that although there had been no work in the Chicago yard since July 19, its closing was not due to lack of work. Despite similarly slack seasons in the past, the employer had for 17 years retained a nucleus crew to do maintenance work and remain ready to take such work as might come in. The examiner went on to find that the employer was reasonably apprehensive of a strike at some point. Although the unions had given assurances that there would be no strike, past bargaining history was thought to justify continuing apprehension that the unions would fail to make good their assurances. It was further found that the employer's primary purpose in locking out his employees was to avert peculiarly harmful economic consequences which would be imposed on him and his customers if a strike were called either while a ship was in the yard during the shipping season or later when the yard was fully occupied. The examiner concluded that the employer:

"was economically justified and motivated in laying off its employees when it did, and the fact that its judgment was partially colored by its intention to break the impasse which existed is immaterial in the peculiar and special circumstances of this case. Respondent, by its actions, therefore, did not violate sections 8(a)(1), (3), and (5) of the Act."

A three-to-two majority of the Board rejected the trial examiner's conclusion that the employer could reasonably anticipate a strike. Finding the unions' assurances sufficient to dispel any such apprehension, the Board was able to find only one purpose underlying the layoff: a desire to bring economic pressure to secure prompt settlement of the dispute on favorable terms. The Board did not question the examiner's finding that the layoffs had not occurred until after a bargaining impasse had been reached. Nor did the Board remotely suggest that the company's decision to lay off its employees was based either on union hostility or on a desire to avoid its bargaining obligations under the Act. The Board concluded that the employer "by curtailing its operations at the South Chicago yard with the consequent layoff of the employees, coerced employees in the exercise of their bargaining rights in violation of Section 8(a)(1) of the Act, and discriminated against its employees within the meaning of Section 8(a)(3) of the Act." [5] 142 N.L.R.B., at 1364–1365.

The difference between the Board and the trial examiner is thus a narrow one turning on their differing assessments of the circumstances which the employer claims gave it reason to anticipate a strike. Both the Board and the examiner assumed, within the established pattern of Board analysis, that if the employer had shut down its yard and laid off its workers solely for the purpose of bringing to bear economic pressure to break an impasse and secure more favorable contract terms, an unfair labor practice would be made out. "The Board has held that, absent special circumstances, an employer may not during bargaining negotiations either threaten to lock out or lock out his employees in aid of his bargaining position. Such conduct the Board has held presumptively infringes upon the collective-bargaining rights of employees in violation of Section 8(a)(1) and the lockout, with its consequent layoff, amounts to discrimination within the meaning of Section 8(a)(3). In addition, the Board has held that such conduct subjects the Union and the employees it represents to unwarranted and illegal pressure and creates an atmosphere in which the free opportunity for negotiation contemplated by Section 8(a)(5) does not exist." Quaker State Oil Refining Corp., 121 N.L.R.B. 334, 337.

The Board has, however, exempted certain classes of lockouts from proscription. "Accordingly, it has held that lockouts are permissible to safeguard against * * * loss where there is reasonable ground for believing that a strike was threatened or imminent." Ibid. Developing this distinction in its rulings, the Board has approved lockouts designed to prevent seizure of a plant by a sitdown strike, Link-Belt Co., 26 N.L.R.B. 227;

---

5. Although the complaint stated a violation of § 8(a)(5) as well, the Board made no findings as to this claim, believing that there would have been no point in entering a bargaining order because the parties had long since executed an agreement. The passage quoted below in the text of this opinion from National Labor Relations Board v. Insurance Agents' International Union, 361 U.S. 477, 80 S.Ct. 419, 4 L.Ed.2d 454, has even more direct application to the § 8(a)(5) question. * * *

to forestall repetitive disruptions of an integrated operation by "quickie" strikes, International Shoe Co., 93 N.L.R.B. 907; to avoid spoilage of materials which would result from a sudden work stoppage, Duluth Bottling Assn., 48 N.L.R.B. 1335; and to avert the immobilization of automobiles brought in for repair, Betts Cadillac Olds, Inc., 96 N.L.R.B. 268. In another distinct class of cases the Board has sanctioned the use of the lockout by a multiemployer bargaining unit as a response to a whipsaw strike against one of its members. Buffalo Linen Supply Co., 109 N.L.R.B. 447, rev'd sub nom. Truck Drivers Local Union, etc. v. National Labor Relations Board, 2 Cir., 231 F.2d 110, rev'd, 353 U.S. 87, 77 S.Ct. 643, 1 L.Ed.2d 676.

In analyzing the status of the bargaining lockout under §§ 8(a)(1) and (3) of the National Labor Relations Act, it is important that the practice with which we are here concerned be distinguished from other forms of temporary separation from employment. * * * What we are here concerned with is the use of a temporary layoff of employees solely as a means to bring economic pressure to bear in support of the employer's bargaining position, after an impasse has been reached. This is the only issue before us, and all that we decide.

To establish that this practice is a violation of § 8(a)(1), it must be shown that the employer has interfered with, restrained, or coerced employees in the exercise of some right protected by § 7 of the Act. The Board's position is premised on the view that the lockout interferes with two of the rights guaranteed by § 7: the right to bargain collectively and the right to strike. In the Board's view, the use of the lockout "punishes" employees for the presentation of and adherence to demands made by their bargaining representatives and so coerces them in the exercise of their right to bargain collectively. It is important to note that there is here no allegation that the employer used the lockout in the service of designs inimical to the process of collective bargaining. There was no evidence and no finding that the employer was hostile to its employees' banding together for collective bargaining or that the lockout was designed to discipline them for doing so. It is therefore inaccurate to say that the employer's intention was to destroy or frustrate the process of collective bargaining. What can be said is that it intended to resist the demands made of it in the negotiations and to secure modification of these demands. We cannot see that this intention is in any way inconsistent with the employees' rights to bargain collectively.

Moreover, there is no indication, either as a general matter or in this specific case, that the lockout will necessarily destroy the unions' capacity for effective and responsible representation. The unions here involved have vigorously represented the employees since 1952, and there is nothing to show that their ability to do so has been impaired by the lockout. Nor is the lockout one of those acts which are demonstrably so destructive of collective bargaining that the Board need not inquire into employer motivation, as might be the case, for example, if an employer permanently discharged his unionized staff and replaced them with employees known to be possessed of a violent antiunion animus. Cf. National Labor Relations Board v. Erie Resistor Corp., 373 U.S. 221, 83 S.Ct. 1139, 10 L.Ed.2d 308. The lockout may well dissuade employees from adhering to the position which they initially adopted in the bargaining, but the right to bargain collectively does not entail any "right" to insist on one's position free from economic disadvantage. Proper analysis of the problem demands that the simple intention to support the employer's bargaining position as to compensation and the like be distinguished from a hostility to the process of collective bargaining which could suffice to render a lockout unlawful. See National Labor Relations Board v. Brown, 380 U.S. 278, 85 S.Ct. 980.

The Board has taken the complementary view that the lockout interferes with the right to strike protected under §§ 7 and 13 of the Act in that it allows the employer to pre-empt the possibility of a strike and thus leave the union with "nothing to strike against." Insofar as this means that once employees are locked out, they are deprived of their right to call a strike against the employer because he is already shut down, the argument is wholly specious, for the work stoppage which would have been the object of the strike has in fact occurred. It is true that recognition of the lockout deprives the union of exclusive control of the timing and duration of work stoppages calculated to influence the result of collective bargaining negotiations, but there is nothing in the statute which would imply that the right to strike "carries with it" the right exclusively to determine the timing and duration of all work stoppages. The right to strike as commonly understood is the right to cease work—nothing more. No doubt a union's bargaining power would be enhanced if it possessed not only the simple right to strike but also the power exclusively to determine when work stoppages should occur, but the Act's provisions are not indefinitely elastic, content-free forms to be shaped in whatever manner the Board might think best conforms to the proper balance of bargaining power.

Thus, we cannot see that the employer's use of a lockout solely in support of a legitimate bargaining position is in any way inconsistent with the right to bargain collectively or with the right to strike. Accordingly, we conclude that on the basis of the findings made by the Board in this case, there has been no violation of § 8(a)(1).

Section 8(a)(3) prohibits discrimination in regard to tenure or other conditions of employment to discourage union membership. Under the words of the statute there must be both discrimination and a resulting discouragement of union membership. It has long been established that a finding of violation under this section will normally turn on the employer's motivation. * * * Thus when the employer discharges a union leader who has broken shop rules, the problem posed is to determine whether the employer has acted purely in disinterested defense of shop discipline or has sought to damage employee organization. It is likely that the discharge will naturally tend to discourage union membership in both cases, because of the loss of union leadership and the employees' suspicion of the employer's true intention. But we have consistently construed the section to leave unscathed a wide range of employer actions taken to serve legitimate business interests in some significant fashion, even though the act committed may tend to discourage union membership. See, e.g., National Labor Relations Board v. Mackay Radio & Telegraph Co., 304 U.S. 333, 347, 58 S.Ct. 904, 911, 82 L.Ed. 1381. Such a construction of § 8(a)(3) is essential if due protection is to be accorded the employer's right to manage his enterprise. See Textile Workers' Union v. Darlington Mfg. Co., 380 U.S. 263, 85 S.Ct. 994.

This is not to deny that there are some practices which are inherently so prejudicial to union interests and so devoid of significant economic justification that no specific evidence of intent to discourage union membership or other antiunion animus is required. In some cases, it may be that the employer's conduct carries with it an inference of unlawful intention so compelling that it is justifiable to disbelieve the employer's protestations of innocent purpose. Radio Officers' Union v. National Labor Relations Board, * * * 347 U.S. at 44–45, 74 S.Ct. at 337–338; National Labor Relations Board v. Erie Resistor Corp., supra. Thus where many have broken a shop rule, but only union leaders have been discharged, the Board need not listen too long to the plea that shop discipline was simply being enforced. In other situations, we have described the process as the "far more delicate task * * * of weighing the interests of employees in concerted activity against the interest of the employer in operating his business in a particular manner * * *." National Labor Relations Board v. Erie Resistor Corp., supra, 373 U.S. at 229, 83 S.Ct. at 1145.

But this lockout does not fall into that category of cases arising under § 8(a)(3) in which the Board may truncate its inquiry into employer motivation. As this case well shows use of the lockout does not carry with it any necessary implication that the employer acted to discourage union membership or otherwise discriminate against union members as such. The purpose and effect of the lockout were only to bring pressure upon the union to modify its demands. Similarly, it does not appear that the natural tendency of the lockout is severely to discourage union membership while serving no significant employer interest. In fact, it is difficult to understand what tendency to discourage union membership or otherwise discriminate against union members was perceived by the Board. There is no claim that the employer locked out only union members, or locked out any employee simply because he was a union member; nor is it alleged that the employer conditioned rehiring upon resignation from the union. It is true that the employees suffered economic disadvantage because of their union's insistence on demands unacceptable to the employer, but this is also true of many steps which an employer may take during a bargaining conflict, and the existence of an arguable possibility that someone may feel himself discouraged in his union membership or discriminated against by reason of that membership cannot suffice to label them violations of § 8(a)(3) absent some unlawful intention. The employer's permanent replacement of strikers (National Labor Relations Board v. Mackay Radio & Telegraph Co., supra), his unilateral imposition of terms (National Labor Relations Board v. Tex-Tan, Inc., 5 Cir., 318 F.2d 472, 479–482), or his simple refusal to make a concession which would terminate a strike—all impose economic disadvantage during a bargaining conflict, but none is necessarily a violation of § 8(a)(3).

To find a violation of § 8(a)(3), then, the Board must find that the employer acted for a proscribed purpose. Indeed, the Board itself has always recognized that certain "operative" or "economic" purposes would justify a lockout. But the Board has erred in ruling that only these purposes will remove a lockout from the ambit of § 8(a)(3), for that section requires an intention to discourage union membership or otherwise discriminate against the union. There was not the slightest evidence and there was no finding that the employer was actuated by a desire to discourage membership in the union as distinguished from a desire to affect the outcome of the particular negotiations in which it was involved. We recognize that the "union membership" which is not to be discouraged refers to more than the payment of dues and that measures taken to discourage participation in protected union activities may be found to come within the proscription. Radio Officers' Union v. National Labor Relations Board, supra, 347 U.S. at 39–40, 74 S.Ct. at 335. However, there is nothing in the Act which gives employees the right to insist on their contract demands, free from the sort of economic disadvantage which frequently attends bargaining disputes. Therefore, we conclude that where the intention proven is merely to bring about a settlement of a labor dispute on favorable terms, no violation of § 8(a)(3) is shown. * * *

The conclusions which we draw from analysis of §§ 8(a)(1) and (3) are consonant with what little of relevance can be drawn from the balance of the statute and its legislative history. In the original version of the Act, the predecessor of § 8(a)(1) declared it an unfair labor practice "[t]o attempt, by interference, influence, restraint, favor, coercion, or lockout, or by any other means, to impair the right of employees guaranteed in section 4." Prominent in the criticism leveled at the bill in the Senate Committee hearings was the charge that it did not accord evenhanded treatment to employers and employees because it prohibited the lockout while protecting the strike. In the face of such criticism, the Committee added a provision prohibiting employee interference with employer bargaining activities and deleted the reference to the lockout. A plausible inference to be drawn from this history is that the language was deleted to mollify those who saw in the bill an inequitable denial of resort to the lockout, and to remove any language which might give rise to fears that the lockout was being proscribed *per se.* It is in any event clear that the Committee was concerned with the status of the lockout and that the bill, as reported and as finally enacted, contained no prohibition on the use of the lockout as such.

Although neither § 8(a)(1) nor § 8(a)(3) refers specifically to the lockout, various other provisions of the National Labor Relations Act do refer to the lockout, and these references can be interpreted as a recognition of the legitimacy of the device as a means of applying economic pressure in support of bargaining positions. Thus 29 U.S.C.A. § 158(d)(4) prohibits the use of a strike or lockout unless requisite notice procedures have been complied with; 29 U.S.C.A. § 173(c) directs the Federal Mediation and Conciliation Service to seek voluntary resolution of labor disputes without resort to strikes or lockouts; and 29 U.S.C.A. §§ 176, 178 authorize procedures whereby the President can institute a board of inquiry to forestall certain strikes or lockouts. The correlative use of the terms "strike" and "lockout" in these sections contemplates that lockouts will be used in the bargaining process in some fashion. This is not to say that these provisions serve to define the permissible scope of a lockout by an employer. That, in the context of the present case, is a question ultimately to be resolved by analysis of §§ 8(a)(1) and (3).

The Board has justified its ruling in this case and its general approach to the legality of lockouts on the basis of its special competence to weigh the competing interests of employers and employees and to accommodate these interests according to its expert judgment. "The Board has reasonably concluded that the availability of such a weapon would so substantially tip the scales in the employer's favor as to defeat the Congressional purpose of placing employees on a par with their adversary at the bargaining table." [15] To buttress its decision as to the balance struck in this particular case, the Board points out that the employer has been given other weapons to counterbalance the employees' power of strike. The employer may permanently replace workers who have gone out on strike, or, by stockpiling and subcontracting, maintain his commercial operations while the strikers bear the economic brunt of the work stoppage. Similarly, the employer can institute unilaterally the working conditions which he desires once his contract with the union has expired. Given these economic weapons, it is argued, the employer has been adequately equipped with tools of economic self-help.

There is of course no question that the Board is entitled to the greatest deference in recognition of its special competence in dealing with labor problems. In many areas its evaluation of the competing interests of employer and employee should unquestionably be given conclusive effect in determining the application of §§ 8(a)(1), (3), and (5). However, we think that the Board construes its functions too expansively when it claims general authority to define national labor policy by balancing the competing interests of labor and management.

While a primary purpose of the National Labor Relations Act was to redress the perceived imbalance of economic power between labor and management, it sought to accomplish that result by conferring certain affirmative rights on employees and by placing certain enumerated restrictions on the activities of employers. * * * The central purpose of these provisions was to protect employee self-organization and the process of collective bargaining from disruptive interferences by employers. Having protected employee organization in countervailance to the employers' bargaining power, and having established a system of collective bargaining whereby the newly coequal adversaries might resolve their disputes, the Act also contemplated resort to economic weapons should more peaceful measures not avail. Sections 8(a)(1) and (3) do not give the Board a general authority to assess the relative economic power of the adversaries in the bargaining process and to deny weapons to one party or the other because of its assessment of that party's bargaining power. National Labor Relations Board v. Brown, 380 U.S. 278, 85 S.Ct. 980. In this case the Board has, in essence, denied the use of the bargaining lockout to the employer because of its conviction that use of this device would give the employer "too much power." In so doing, the Board has stretched §§ 8(a)(1) and (3) far beyond their functions of protecting the rights of employee organization and collective bargaining. What we have recently said in a closely related context is equally applicable here:

> "[W]hen the Board moves in this area * * * it is functioning as an arbiter of the sort of economic weapons the parties can use in seeking to gain acceptance of their bargaining demands. It has sought to introduce

15. Respondent's Brief 17.

some standard of properly 'balanced' bargaining power, or some new distinction of justifiable and unjustifiable, proper and 'abusive' economic weapons into * * * the Act. * * * We have expressed our belief that this amounts to the Board's entrance into the substantive aspects of the bargaining process to an extent Congress has not countenanced." National Labor Relations Board v. Insurance Agents' International Union, 361 U.S. 477, 497–498, 80 S.Ct. 419, 431.

We are unable to find that any fair construction of the provisions relied on by the Board in this case can support its finding of an unfair labor practice. Indeed, the role assumed by the Board in this area is fundamentally inconsistent with the structure of the Act and the function of the sections relied upon. The deference owed to an expert tribunal cannot be allowed to slip into a judicial inertia which results in the unauthorized assumption by an agency of major policy decisions properly made by Congress. Accordingly, we hold that an employer violates neither § 8(a)(1) nor § 8(a)(3) when, after a bargaining impasse has been reached, he temporarily shuts down his plant and lays off his employees for the sole purpose of bringing economic pressure to bear in support of his legitimate bargaining position.

Reversed.

[The concurring opinions of Justices White and Goldberg are omitted.]

Note

✳ 1. May an employer lock out his employees *before* an impasse is reached in collective bargaining? The court answered yes in Lane v. NLRB, 418 F.2d 1208 (D.C.Cir.1969), under circumstances establishing the employer's good faith in bargaining and the seasonal nature of the employer's business. Similarly, in Detroit Newspaper Publishers Ass'n v. NLRB, 346 F.2d 527 (6th Cir.1965), a case *not* involving a seasonal business, the court held a pre-impasse lockout to be lawful, explaining that "where the intention proven is merely to bring about a settlement of a labor dispute on favorable terms, no violation of § 8(a)(3) is shown." Id. at 531. This judgment of the Sixth Circuit was vacated by the Supreme Court with direction that the case be remanded to the Board "for further consideration in light of American Ship." 382 U.S. 374, 86 S.Ct. 543, 15 L.Ed.2d 423 (1966). On remand, the Board found the negotiations to have been "deadlocked" at the time of the lockout, thus mooting the pre-impasse question. 404 F.2d 1159 (6th Cir.1968). How does one ascertain whether negotiations have reached an impasse?

2. Would the Mackay doctrine permit an employer to replace permanently the employees he has locked out pursuant to American Ship? In NLRB v. BROWN, 380 U.S. 278, 85 S.Ct. 980, 13 L.Ed.2d 839 (1965), the companion case to American Ship, the nonstruck members of a multiemployer bargaining unit locked out their employees in response to a whipsaw strike. When the struck employer member hired temporary replacements, the members who had locked out their employees also hired temporary replacements. The Board, two members dissenting, found the case not controlled by Buffalo Linen (supra p. 228) for the reason that, since the struck employer was operating through replacements, no need existed for the nonstruck employers to lock out in defense of the multiemployer bargaining unit. John Brown (d/b/a Brown Food Store), 137 N.L. R.B. 73 (1962). The Tenth Circuit, in a 2 to 1 decision, reversed the Board on the ground that there was no independent evidence of unlawful motivation and the

Board could not reasonably infer that "the act of hiring replacements per se" was retaliatory rather than defensive. NLRB v. Brown, 319 F.2d 7, 10 (10th Cir. 1963). The Supreme Court affirmed the court of appeals, 8 to 1, holding that neither the lockout nor the continued operations by the nonstruck employers through the use of temporary replacements, whether "viewed separately or as a single act," constituted, per se, a violation of the statute.

However, in Inland Trucking Co. v. NLRB, 440 F.2d 562 (7th Cir.1971), it was held that an employer who engages in a so-called "offensive" lockout, à la American Ship, and also employs temporary replacements thereby commits a *per se* violation of Sections 8(a)(1) and (3). By way of contrast, in Inter-Collegiate Press, Graphic Arts Div. v. NLRB, 486 F.2d 837 (8th Cir.1973), cert. denied, 416 U.S. 938 (1974), the per se approach was rejected by the Board (3 to 2) and the circuit court in favor of a case by case analysis pursuant to the tests set forth by the Supreme Court in NLRB v. Great Dane Trailers, Inc., reported infra p. 528. Applying that analysis, the court found no violations of Sections 8(a)(1) and (3) by an employer who (1) was engaged in a seasonal business (Inland Trucking Co. was also engaged in a seasonal business), (2) continued its operations with temporary replacements after a post-impasse lockout, (3) made an offer to terminate the lockout conditioned on the union's agreement not to strike during the busy season, and (4) made an unconditional offer of reinstatement at the end of the busy season. This combination of factors was held to constitute a "legitimate and substantial business justification" for the hiring of temporary replacements for the locked-out employees; there was no evidence of antiunion animus.

The foregoing and related questions are discussed at some length in Oberer, Lockouts and the Law: The Impact of *American Ship Building* and *Brown Food,* 51 Cornell L.Q. 193 (1966); Bernhardt, Lockouts: An Analysis of Board and Court Decisions Since *Brown* and *American Ship,* 57 Cornell L.Rev. 211 (1972); Comment, Lockouts and Replacements in Bargaining—Management on the Offensive, 9 Loy.U.L.Rev. 67 (1975).

3. Does the Court in American Ship equate the lockout with the strike? *Should* they be equated? Should, for example, the pre-impasse *strike* be made unlawful?

4. The decision and language in the American Ship case, like that in Insurance Agents, purport to deny to the Board the authority to assess and "balance" the parties' bargaining power and weapons. Is such balancing avoidable? Is not the Court itself "balancing" bargaining power in American Ship? If balancing is unavoidable, who, under the statutory scheme, should be doing it? The Board first, the courts in review?

Indeed, does the Court in American Ship equate Sections 8(a)(1) and 8(a)(3), so as to read the anti-union motive requirement of the latter into the former as well, thus qualifying the Board's balancing power in *each*? The following article addresses this issue.

OBERER, SECTIONS 8(a)(1) AND (3) OF THE LABOR ACT IN THE WAKE OF THE LOCKOUT DECISIONS: OF BALANCING, HOSTILE MOTIVE, DOGS AND TAILS [b]

Proceedings of the Nineteenth Annual Winter Meeting, Industrial Relations Research Association 76–87 (1967).

THE PROBLEM OF REDUNDANCY

More than thirty years have elapsed since the passage of the Wagner Act in 1935. It is somewhat surprising, therefore, to find that a fundamental problem implicit in its structure has not yet been resolved. Indeed, the problem has only recently been confronted.

The problem is one of redundancy. In constructing the employer unfair labor practices of section 8, Congress was astute to protect against erosion by the courts of the section 7 rights of employees. It sought to accomplish this by enacting both a blanket protection, now section 8(a)(1), which makes unlawful any "interference with, restraint, or coercion" of employees in the exercise of their section 7 rights, and, at the same time, the particularized protections in what are now sections 8(a)(2), (3), (4), and (5).

The legislative history of the Wagner Act makes clear the congressional purpose in this double protection of employee rights. The purpose was to shore up the general protection with the particularizations and to shore up the particularized protections with the general. The particularized protections were necessary, in Senator Wagner's words, because "long experience has proved * * * that courts and administrative agencies have difficulties in enforcing * * * general declarations of right in the absence of greater statutory particularity." [3] Conversely, as stated elsewhere in the legislative history, the "blanket unfair labor practice" of section 8(1) "is necessary, since the courts may emasculate or construe very narrowly some one of the following specific unfair practices." [4] The legislative history is, moreover, replete with assertions that the four specific unfair practice provisions were not intended to limit "in any way * * * the broadest reasonable interpretation" of the "omnibus guaranty of freedom" contained in the first.[5]

A moment's reflection will demonstrate the problem of redundancy here. Either 8(a)(1) occupies the field, in which event, once its contours are established, the other four subsections become irrelevant, or each of the other four occupies its particular field, in which event 8(a)(1) becomes irrelevant in the areas of overlap. Neither of these alternatives has, as yet,

b. An expanded version of this article is The Scienter Factor in Sections 8(a)(1) and (3) of the Labor Act: Of Balancing, Hostile Motive, Dogs and Tails, 52 Cornell L.Q. 491 (1967).

3. Hearings on H.R. 6288 Before the House Committee on Labor, 74th Cong., 1st Sess. 13 (1935), reproduced in 2 Legislative History of the National Labor Relations Act 1935 (published by the NLRB) 2487 (1949) (hereinafter cited as "Legislative History").

4. Comparison of S. 2926 (73rd Cong., 2d Sess.) and S. 1958 (74th Cong., 1st Sess): Memorandum of March 11, 1935, Prepared for Senate Committee on Education and Labor, 74th Cong., 1st Sess. 26–27 (Comm. Print 1935), reproduced in 1 Legislative History 1351–52.

5. The language quoted is from Senator Wagner's statement before the House Committee on Labor, supra note 3. See also H.R. Rep. No. 969, 74th Cong., 1st Sess. 15 (1935), reproduced in 2 Legislative History 2924; S.Rep.No. 573, 74th Cong., 1st Sess. 9 (1935), reproduced in 2 Legislative History 2309.

established supremacy. But the problems inherent in a blanket provision which covers all that particularized provisions cover, and then some, have been brought into a sharpening focus.

THE CONFUSING LESSON OF THE LOCKOUT CASES [6]

The focus has never been sharper than in three cases decided by the Supreme Court in March of 1965—the lockout cases, *American Ship Building* [7] and *Brown Food,* [8] and their companion case, *Darlington.* [9]

In *American Ship Building* the employer had locked out its employees for bargaining leverage after an impasse had been reached in negotiations for a contract renewal. In *Brown Food* the nonstruck members of a multiemployer bargaining unit had locked out their employees in response to a whipsaw strike; when the struck employer hired temporary replacements, the locking-out employers did likewise. In both of these cases the NLRB found violations of 8(a)(1) and (3). In both cases the Supreme Court denied enforcement of the Board's orders.

The basis of the Court's action in each case was the same. Both 8(a)(1) and (3) require, the Court indicated, a "hostile motive" on the employer's part for a violation to be found. This hostile motive must be proved by affirmative evidence *except where* the action of the employer is "inherently destructive of employee rights and is not justified by the service of important business ends."[11] In the latter situation the necessary motive may be inferred or presumed from the employer's act, without more. Sections 8(a) (1) and (3) were thus equated with respect to the state-of-mind element.

This hostile-motive requirement (sometimes described as "antiunion" or "antistatutory") makes more sense as applied to 8(a)(3) than as applied to 8(a)(1). What 8(a)(3) proscribes is discrimination in terms or tenure of employment to encourage or discourage union membership. Both discrimination and discouragement of union membership are present where an employer discharges an active union organizer. If, however, the discharge is motivated by the employee's incompetent performance of his job, the discharge should obviously not be treated as an unfair labor practice. Thus, the employer's motive for the discharge is necessarily in issue. Both legislative history and a substantial body of precedent support this interpretation of 8(a)(3).

The opposite is the case with respect to 8(a)(1). Its very purpose, as illuminated in the legislative history, is to afford the Board a vehicle for dealing with employer practices which "interfere with, restrain, or coerce" employees in the exercise of their statutory rights *without* running afoul of any of the other, more particularized subsections of 8(a). It undercuts this purpose to saddle 8(a)(1) with a state-of-mind requirement appropriate for 8(a)(3). In no case prior to *American Ship Building* and *Brown Food* has the

---

6. For a fuller discussion of the lockout cases in respects pertinent to this paper, see Oberer, Lockouts and the Law: The Impact of American Ship Building and Brown Food, 51 Cornell L.Q. 193 (1966).

7. American Ship Bldg. Co. v. NLRB, 380 U.S. 300 (1965).

8. NLRB v. Brown (d/b/a Brown Food Store), 380 U.S. 278 (1965).

9. Textile Workers v. Darlington Mfg. Co., 380 U.S. 263 (1965).

11. NLRB v. Brown, 380 U.S. 278, 287 (1965).

Supreme Court sought so clearly to engraft the hostile-motive requirement on 8(a)(1).

The lockout cases demonstrate the dilemma confronting the Court in dealing with section 8(a)(1) as it relates to section 8(a)(3). From the standpoint of judicial review, an amorphously stated blanket provision, particularized in narrower provisions but not delimited by them, is a legislative bull in a judicial china shop. The tendency is to deal with the narrower standard at the expense of the broader. In cases of overlap between 8(a)(3) and 8(a)(1), the focus is typically on 8(a)(3). Where 8(a)(3) is found to have been violated, 8(a)(1) is accorded perfunctory, derivative treatment. Even where 8(a)(3) is found not to have been violated, a tendency is discernible in some cases of overlap to deny any independent force to 8(a)(1).[15] While this development is understandable in cases of overlap, the danger inheres that the derivative content given to 8(a)(1) in such cases will qualify it even where there is no overlap.

Carried to the latter length, this development conflicts with the Supreme Court's still viable precedents dealing with independent 8(a)(1) violations. Thus, in *Republic Aviation*,[16] a no-solicitation-rule case, the Court recognized the necessity for the Board to balance the conflicting interests of the employees in their section 7 rights and of the employer in his property rights. Hostile motive was not a required element of the Board's finding of a violation. Similarly, in *Burnup & Sims*,[17] a 1964 case in which union activists were discharged in the honestly mistaken belief that they had threatened to dynamite the employer's property, the Court found it "unnecessary to reach the questions raised under § 8(a)(3) for we are of the view that * * * § 8(a)(1) was plainly violated, whatever the employer's motive." [18]

AN INTERPRETATION: SEEKING ORDER IN DISORDER

How, then can we justify the *American Ship Building* and *Brown Food* equation of 8(a)(1) and (3) with respect to the hostile-motive requirement? At the risk of over-simplification, I intend to essay this task. What the Court was concerned about in the lockout cases was a Board thumb on the collective bargaining scales. While the cases reached the Court under sections 8(a)(1) and (3) only, what really was at issue were the rights and duties of the parties in the process of collective bargaining. The fundamental 8(a)(5) charges had been mooted by the execution of new contracts while the cases were pending before the Board. In contrast, what was involved in *Republic Aviation* and *Burnup & Sims* was the right of self-organization. This seminal right requires a stronger degree of protection.

What the Court has been striving to develop is a formula which facilitates a circumscribing of the Board's power where circumscription is in order. The old balancing test was too loose a standard for accomplishing

15. See, e.g., Local 357, Int'l. Bhd. of Teamsters v. NLRB, 365 U.S. 667 (1961); Textile Workers v. Darlington Mfg. Co., 380 U.S. 263 (1965); Getman, Section 8(a)(3) of the NLRA and the Effort to Insulate Free Employee Choice, 32 U. of Chi.L.Rev. 735, 759 (1965). *Burnup & Sims*, 379 U.S. 21 (1964), is an obvious departure from the pattern.

16. Republic Aviation Corp. v. NLRB, 324 U.S. 793 (1945).

17. NLRB v. Burnup & Sims, 379 U.S. 21 (1964).

18. Id. at 22–33.

this in collective bargaining situations. It provided the Board with a kind of blank check. The Board could weigh the right to engage in self-organization against the employer's right to run his business, as in the "no solicitation" rule cases, and achieve the purposes of the Act, which are, most basically, to encourage collective bargaining. But when the Board applied the same balancing test to collective bargaining pressures, as in the lockout cases, it thwarted collective bargaining.

The new formula which the Court is evolving seeks to preserve what is good in the balancing test, while weeding out what is bad. At the same time it seeks to accommodate prior decisions of the Court, premised upon the balancing approach, by means of a new rationalization of the "true" basis for such decisions. The new rationalization may entail two correlative theses. The first is that where 8(a)(1) and (3) overlap in their application to a problem presented, the more particular criteria of 8(a)(3) control. 8(a)(3) is the dog, and 8(a)(1) the tail. The second is that in cases where mere balancing produces an unsatisfactory result because too invasive of free collective bargaining or of management prerogatives, independent evidence of a hostile motive is an essential ingredient of the unfair labor practice.

The Dog-and-Tail Thesis

In cases of overlap between 8(a)(1) and (3)—indeed, between 8(a)(1) and any other subsection of 8(a)—there is strong reason for equating the general provision with the particular. Otherwise, the particular is read out of the statute. If, for example, the elements of 8(a)(3) properly include scienter, the same scienter must be required for 8(a)(1) in cases of overlap. Otherwise, the reason justifying the requirement of scienter in 8(a)(3) would be defeated; all prosecutions in such cases of overlap would be under 8(a)(1), the requirements of which would be satisfied by proof of the elements necessary under 8(a)(3) with the exception of the scienter element. Having found the commission of an unfair labor practice under 8(a)(1), the Board could grant the same relief as under 8(a)(3), since the Court has scotched any notion that the Board's remedial power under 8(a)(3) is greater than under 8(a)(1).[21]

Darlington is particularly instructive on the dog-and-tail point. The Board found the employer's closing of a plant in which a union had just won a representation election to be a violation of 8(a)(1) and (3).[22] The Supreme Court reviewed the case on the basis of 8(a)(3) alone.[23] In so doing, however, the Court made it quite clear that its decision would have been the same under 8(a)(1), through what may be characterized as an application of the dog-and-tail principle. Mr. Justice Harlan, writing for the Court, stated:

"Whatever may be the limits of § 8(a)(1), some employer decisions are so peculiarly matters of management prerogative that they would never consti-

---

21. See NLRB v. Burnup & Sims, 379 U.S. 21 (1964).

22. Darlington Mfg. Co., 139 N.L.R.B. 241, 252 (1962).

23. The Court stated: "Preliminarily it should be observed that both petitioners argue that the Darlington closing violated § 8(a)(1) as well as § 8(a)(3) of the Act. We think, however, that the Board was correct in treat-

ing the closing only under § 8(a)(3)." Textile Workers v. Darlington Mfg. Co., 380 U.S. 263, 268 (1965). Actually, the Board found the closing to violate both 8(a)(3) and 8(a)(1), although the former received the focus of the Board's attention. 8(a)(1) was given the derivative, "tag-on" treatment so frequently accorded it. See note 22 supra.

tute violations of § 8(a)(1) * * * unless they also violated § 8(a)(3). * * * We therefore deal with the Darlington closing under [the latter] section." [24]

It should be noted that the Court did *not* uphold the Board's finding of a violation under 8(a)(3), thus rendering consideration under 8(a)(1) mere surplusage. The case was, instead, remanded to the Board for further findings on the "chilling unionism" issues under 8(a)(3).[25]

A definitional problem exists, to be sure, in determining when "overlap" between 8(a)(1) and (3) is really present—in determining, that is, when the dog-and-tail principle is operative. But this is a problem of line-drawing, inherent in the law. Where the determination is properly made that the criteria of 8(a)(3) are applicable to a given case, strong reason exists to give those criteria preemptive force.

The logic which supports the equation of 8(a)(1) and (3) in areas of overlap likewise supports the equating of 8(a)(1) and the other subsections of 8(a) in areas of overlap.[26] Again, unless the particularized dogs of 8(a)(2), (4), and (5) wag the generalized tail of 8(a)(1), the former will be read out of the statute. The Board will proceed along the line of least resistance, and this will be 8(a)(1).

The alternative to the dog-and-tail interpretation of the lockout cases is that the Court has embarked upon an across-the-board equation of 8(a)(1) and (3) with respect to the hostile motive requirement, intending to apply the latter in independent 8(a)(1) cases as well as in cases of overlap with 8(a)(3). While the Court may, indeed, have started down this path, there is reason to question the propriety of such a course. In any event, the contours of the hostile-motive doctrine must be examined.

The Hostile-Motive Doctrine (with Escape Hatch)

The hostile-motive doctrine had its genesis in the first 8(a)(3) cases to reach the Supreme Court—*Jones & Laughlin*[27] and *Associated Press.*[28] The "true motive" of the employer was held to be the key to an 8(a)(3) violation.[29] The *Radio Officers*[30] case in 1954 provided the first occasion for the Court to clarify in definitive fashion the motive requirement of 8(a)(3). The Court held that while it is essential for a violation of 8(a)(3) that the employer's motive in discriminating against an employee be to encourage or discourage union membership, "specific evidence of intent to encourage or discourage is not an indispensable element of proof. * * *"[31] The Court stated that "specific proof of intent is unnecessary where employer conduct inherently

24. Id. at 269.

25. If the Court had considered the 8(a)(1) question open to the Board despite the overlap with 8(a)(3), it is reasonable to conclude that its remand would have left the Board free to reconsider the case under *both* sections. The fact that the Court limited the remand to the 8(a)(3) questions suggests that the Board cannot control whether a given case is to be reviewed under 8(a)(3) or 8(a)(1) by the choice it makes of the section to proceed under.

26. See, e.g., Getman, Section 8(a)(3) of the NLRA and the Effort to Insulate Free Em-

ployee Choice, 32 U. of Chi.L.Rev. 735, 758–59 (1965).

27. NLRB v. Jones & Laughlin, 301 U.S. 1 (1937).

28. Associated Press v. NLRB, 301 U.S. 103 (1937).

29. Jones & Laughlin, supra note 27, at 45–46; Associated Press, supra note 28, at 132.

30. Radio Officers Union v. NLRB, 347 U.S. 17 (1954).

31. Id. at 45.

encourages or discourages union membership," observing that this was "but an application of the common-law rule that a man is held to intend the foreseeable consequences of his conduct." [32]

Interestingly, while the hostile-motive doctrine was being developed and refined under 8(a)(3), the so-called "balancing test" was also being formulated and approved under both 8(a)(1) and (3).[33] The two developments traveled a collision course.

Erie Resistor,[34] the superseniority case of 1963, provided the Supreme Court an opportunity to attempt a reconciliation of the hostile-motive doctrine and the balancing test under 8(a)(3). The balancing process, the Court indicated, is a means for establishing motive—for "preferring one motive to another." [35] The necessary "hostile motive" could be inferred by the Board through the process of "weighing the interests of employees in concerted activity against the interest of the employer in operating his business in a particular manner. * * * " [36] Whether one judges this "reconciliation" to be a laborious exercise in judicial obfuscation or an ingenious clarification, it set the stage for the "hostile-motive-doctrine-with-escape-hatch" which emerges, full blown, in the lockout cases.

[The "hostile motive" element of 8(a)(3) need not be established by independent evidence in all cases. In some cases (the "escape hatch") the employer conduct will, without more, support an inference of hostile motive.] One way of describing, then, what the Court has done in the lockout decisions is to say that it has merely redefined the balancing test. The purpose of the balancing under the new test is to ascertain whether independent evidence of hostile motive is necessary. The new definition requires, apparently, that the scales be more out of balance than was previously required for a violation to be found without independent evidence of hostile motive, sufficiently so that an inference of hostile motive is solidly based. In such cases the employer's conduct will carry "its own indicia of improper intent." [38]

As I read the lockout cases, employer conduct will carry such indicia in two situations: (1) where the employer has no significant legitimate business reason for actions which undercut the section 7 rights of his employees (*Republic Aviation* is the prime example); (2) where the employer does have a significant business purpose, but his actions, nevertheless, are so "inherently destructive" of employee rights as not to be "tolerated consistently with the Act" [40] (*Erie Resistor* is the prime example).

---

32. Id. at 46.

33. See, e.g., Republic Aviation Corp. v. NLRB, 324 U.S. 793 (1945); NLRB v. Babcock & Wilcox Co., 351 U.S. 105 (1956); NLRB v. Truck Drivers Union, 353 U.S. 87 (1957) ("Buffalo Linen").

34. NLRB v. Erie Resistor Corp., 373 U.S. 221 (1963).

35. Id. at 228.

36. Id. at 229. [Confronted by a bargaining strike and desiring to continue operating, the employer offered the incentive of twenty years of unearned seniority to replacements and defecting strikers. He sought to justify this grant of superseniority on the ground that replacements could not otherwise be obtained. The Court held that the Board did not err in refusing to inquire into the validity of this employer contention since, in any event, the "claimed business purpose would not outweigh the necessary harm to employee rights."]

38. [NLRB v. Brown, 380 U.S. 278, 287 (1965).]

40. NLRB v. Brown, 380 U.S. 278, 287 (1965).

INDEPENDENT 8(a)(1) VIOLATIONS

A question arises as to whether this new balancing test or hostile-motive-doctrine-with-escape-hatch applies not only to 8(a)(3) cases and to 8(a)(1) charges which fall in the area of overlap with 8(a)(3), but also to independent 8(a)(1) cases. Since the 8(a)(1) charges involved in the lockout cases were of the overlap variety—i.e., the factual circumstances to which 8(a)(1) was sought to be applied were the same as the factual circumstances to which 8(a)(3) was sought to be applied—the holding of the Court, narrowly interpreted, reaches only overlapping 8(a)(1) cases.

The propriety of extending the doctrine in mechanical fashion to all 8(a)(1) cases, in the interests of symmetry and ease of review, is subject to question. What is right for section 8(a)(3) is not necessarily right for section 8(a)(1). The legislative history would seem to make this clear, as would the very language of 8(a)(1). What that section proscribes is "interference with, restraint, or coercion of" employees in the exercise of their section 7 rights. In contrast to section 8(a)(3), no hint of a scienter requirement is present here. As stated by the Supreme Court in the *International Ladies' Garment Workers* [41] case in 1961: "We find nothing in the statutory language prescribing scienter as an element of the unfair labor practices [8(a)(1) and (2)] here involved." [42] *Burnup & Sims*, as previously seen, is to the same express effect.

This is not to say that motive is, or should be deemed, irrelevant in all independent 8(a)(1) cases. It is clearly relevant where it operates, for example, to deprive an employer of a privilege he would otherwise have to interfere with section 7 activities, as in the case of an apparently valid no-solicitation rule which is vitiated by evidence of an antiunion purpose in its promulgation or application. Similarly, in those independent 8(a)(1) cases which analogize closely to 8(a)(3), the motive apparatus of 8(a)(3), replete with escape hatch, becomes relevant, despite the absence of overlap, usually because discharges or related disciplinary action is involved and a significant management prerogative therefore at stake. An example of such an independent 8(a)(1) case is where an employer discharges employees for engaging in concerted protected activities which are unrelated to any union or unionizing effort.

Despite these reservations, what 8(a)(1) protects independently, with few exceptions, is the right to organize. Since this right is the bedrock of the national labor policy, it merits particularly sensitive protection by the Board. Legitimate employer interest in such cases is so slight, and illegitimate employer interest so strong, as to deny any valid function to a hostile-motive requirement here. The old balancing-of-conflicting-legitimate-interests test has worked reasonably well in these cases. What that test amounts to is the rule of reason. It affords adequate protection to the employer interests on the scales and has the virtue of relative simplicity. No need exists for the engrafting of a hostile-motive requirement, the real purpose of which is to circumscribe Board power; if the Board finds the employer conduct to be violative, the remedy is merely a cease and desist order which protects the section 7 right with minimal invasion of any legitimate employ-

41. ILGWU v. NLRB, 366 U.S. 731 (1961).   42. Id. at 739.

er interest. Typically, where the employer conduct reaches the stage of discharge or related disciplinary action, section 8(a)(3), with its prerogative-protecting motive paraphernalia, becomes involved.

Indeed, because of this minimal impact upon management prerogatives, even if the hostile-motive doctrine is extended to such independent 8(a)(1) cases, they should fall in the escape-hatch area where no independent evidence of hostility is required. This is another way of saying that the doctrine, soundly applied, would have no function here, other than to obscure analysis and lengthen opinions. Unsoundly applied, it would have a most mischievous potential, endangering the protection traditionally accorded the seminal right of self-organization.

In summary, then, while motive is relevant in some independent 8(a)(1) cases, hostility to employee rights should not be a required element in all such cases. Perhaps the simplest and safest way to deal with motive in independent 8(a)(1) cases is to treat it as *presumptively irrelevant,* in contrast to 8(a)(3) cases and overlapping 8(a)(1) cases where it may be said to be *presumptively relevant.* If this approach were adopted, the extension of the hostile-motive doctrine, so modified, to independent 8(a)(1) cases would be subject to little objection. The Board, courts, labor bar, employers, and unions would know where they stand, since the traditional handling of such cases would be reaffirmed. No necessity would arise for a tortured "accommodation" of precedents, such as *Republic Aviation,* on the basis of a dubious inference or presumption of hostile employer purpose.

CONCLUSION

The hostile-motive doctrine is the product of section 8(a)(3), as to which it makes some sense. Application of the doctrine to overlapping 8(a)(1) cases makes sense also, since the alternative is to read 8(a)(3) out of the statute. On the basis of the legislative history of section 8(a)(1) and a textual reading of its language, the generic engrafting of the hostile-motive requirement on independent 8(a)(1) charges does not make sense.

Withal, extension of the hostile-motive doctrine to independent 8(a)(1) cases, pursuant to an interpretation of the lockout cases which gives the doctrine generic 8(a)(1) application, need have no substantial effect upon existing Board policy *if* proper play is judicially afforded to the "escape hatch" of the doctrine. If a re-rationalization by the Board in such cases is the sole cost for circumscribing the Board's power to place a thumb on the bargaining scales in situations akin to the lockout cases, and for protecting significant management prerogatives in 8(a)(3) cases where 8(a)(1) has merely redundant applicability, as in *Darlington,* the Supreme Court's price is not too steep to pay. But mere symmetry is hardly a compelling reason for extending a cumbersome doctrine developed for other cases and purposes to cases where it serves no legitimate function—where, indeed, it may do violence to legislative intent, statutory language, substantial precedent, and clarity of analysis.

In any event, the Court has still before it the problem of coming explicitly to grips with the scope of 8(a)(1), as related to 8(a)(3).

NATIONAL LABOR RELATIONS BOARD v. GREAT DANE TRAILERS, INC.

Supreme Court of the United States, 1967.
388 U.S. 26, 87 S.Ct. 1792, 18 L.Ed.2d 1027.

MR. CHIEF JUSTICE WARREN delivered the opinion of the Court.

The issue here is whether, in the absence of proof of an antiunion motivation, an employer may be held to have violated §§ 8(a)(3) and (1) of the National Labor Relations Act when it refused to pay striking employees vacation benefits accrued under a terminated collective bargaining agreement while it announced an intention to pay such benefits to striker replacements, returning strikers, and non-strikers who had been at work on a certain date during the strike.

The respondent company and the union entered into a collective bargaining agreement which was effective by its terms until March 31, 1963. The agreement contained a commitment by the company to pay vacation benefits to employees who met certain enumerated qualifications. In essence, the company agreed to pay specified vacation benefits to employees who, during the preceding year, had worked at least 1,525 hours. It was also provided that, in the case of a "lay-off, termination or quitting," employees who had served more than 60 days during the year would be entitled to pro rata shares of their vacation benefits. Benefits were to be paid on the Friday nearest July 1 of each year.

The agreement was temporarily extended beyond its termination date, but on April 30, 1963, the union gave the required 15 days' notice of intention to strike over issues which remained unsettled at the bargaining table. Accordingly, on May 16, 1963, approximately 350 of the company's 400 employees commenced a strike which lasted until December 26, 1963. The company continued to operate during the strike, using nonstrikers, persons hired as replacements for strikers, and some original strikers who had later abandoned the strike and returned to work.[4] On July 12, 1963, a number of the strikers demanded their accrued vacation pay from the company. The company rejected this demand, basing its response on the assertion that all contractual obligations had been terminated by the strike and, therefore, none of the company's employees had a right to vacation pay. Shortly thereafter, however, the company announced that it would grant vacation pay—in the amounts and subject to the conditions set out in the expired agreement—to all employees who had reported for work on July 1, 1963. The company denied that these payments were founded on the agreement and stated that they merely reflected a new "policy" which had been unilaterally adopted.

The refusal to pay vacation benefits to strikers, coupled with the payments to nonstrikers, formed the bases of an unfair labor practice complaint filed with the Board while the strike was still in progress. Violations of §§ 8(a)(3) and (1) were charged. A hearing was held before a trial examiner who found that the company's action in regard to vacation pay constituted a discrimination in terms and conditions of employment

---

4. All strikers had been replaced by October 8, 1963. After their replacement, some strikers were rehired by the company, apparently as new employees.

which would discourage union membership, as well as an unlawful interference with protected activity. He held that the company had violated §§ 8(a) (3) and (1) and recommended that it be ordered to cease and desist from its unfair labor practice and to pay the accrued vacation benefits to strikers. The Board, after reviewing the record, adopted the Trial Examiner's conclusions and remedy.

A petition for enforcement of the order was filed in the Court of Appeals for the Fifth Circuit. That court first dealt with the company's contention that the Board had lacked jurisdiction and that the union should have been relegated either to the bargaining table or to a lawsuit under § 301 of the Act, since the basic question was one of contract interpretation and application. It noted that the company's announced policy relating to vacation pay clearly concerned a "term or condition of employment"; since it was alleged that the company had discriminated between striking and nonstriking employees in regard to that term or condition of employment, the complaint stated "an unfair labor practice charge in simplest terms" and the Board had properly exercised its jurisdiction.[7]

Reviewing the substantive aspects of the Board's decision next, the Court of Appeals held that, although discrimination between striking and nonstriking employees had been proved, the Board's conclusion that the company had committed an unfair labor practice was not well-founded inasmuch as there had been no affirmative showing of an unlawful motivation to discourage union membership or to interfere with the exercise of protected rights. Despite the fact that the company itself had not introduced evidence of a legitimate business purpose underlying its discriminatory action, the Court of Appeals speculated that it might have been motivated by a desire "(1) to reduce expenses; (2) to encourage longer tenure among present employees; or (3) to discourage early leaves immediately before vacation periods." Believing that the possibility of the existence of such motives was sufficient to overcome the inference of an improper motive which flowed from the conduct itself, the court denied enforcement of the order. 363 F.2d 130 (1966). * * *

The unfair labor practice charged here is grounded primarily in § 8(a)(3) which requires specifically that the Board find a discrimination and a resulting discouragement of union membership. American Ship Building Co. v. National Labor Relations Board, 380 U.S. 300, 311, 85 S.Ct. 955, 963, 13 L.Ed.2d 855 (1965). There is little question but that the result of the company's refusal to pay vacation benefits to strikers was discrimination in its simplest form. * * * Some employees who met the conditions specified

---

7. In this Court the company apparently abandoned the argument under § 301. In any event, we agree with the Court of Appeals that the complaint, alleging as it did a discrimination in regard to a term or condition of employment, stated an unfair labor practice charge. The fact that the conduct complained of might also have supported an action under § 301 did not deprive the Board of jurisdiction. NLRB v. C & C Plywood Corp., 385 U.S. 421, 87 S.Ct. 559, 17 L.Ed.2d 486 (1967); Mastro Plastics Corp. v. National Labor Relations Board, 350 U.S. 270, 76 S.Ct. 349, 100 L.Ed. 309 (1956). Cf. Smith v. Evening News Assn., 371 U.S. 195, 83 S.Ct. 267, 9 L.Ed.2d 246 (1962). This, of course, is not to say that every breach of a collective bargaining agreement may be the subject of an unfair labor practice proceeding. But when the elements of an unfair labor practice are present in a breach of contract, the injured party is not automatically deprived by § 301 of his right to proceed before the Board where his remedy may be speedier and less expensive than a lawsuit. NLRB v. C & C Plywood Corp., supra, 385 U.S. at 429–430, 87 S.Ct. at 564, 565.

in the expired collective bargaining agreement were paid accrued vacation benefits in the amounts set forth in that agreement, while other employees who also met the conditions but who had engaged in protected concerted activity were denied such benefits. Similarly, there can be no doubt but that the discrimination was capable of discouraging membership in a labor organization within the meaning of the statute. Discouraging membership in a labor organization "includes discouraging participation in concerted activities * * * such as a legitimate strike." National Labor Relations Board v. Erie Resistor Corp., 373 U.S. 221, 233, 83 S.Ct. 1139, 1148, 10 L.Ed. 2d 308 (1963). The act of paying accrued benefits to one group of employees while announcing the extinction of the same benefits for another group of employees who are distinguishable only by their participation in protected concerted activity surely may have a discouraging effect on either present or future concerted activity.

But inquiry under § 8(a)(3) does not usually stop at this point. The statutory language "discrimination * * * to * * * discourage" means that the finding of a violation normally turns on whether the discriminatory conduct was motivated by an antiunion purpose. American Ship Building Co. v. National Labor Relations Board, 380 U.S. 300, 85 S.Ct. 955 (1965). It was upon the motivation element that the Court of Appeals based its decision not to grant enforcement, and it is to that element which we now turn. In three recent opinions we considered employer motivation in the context of asserted § 8(a)(3) violations. American Ship Building Co. v. National Labor Relations Board, supra; National Labor Relations Board v. Brown, 380 U.S. 278, 85 S.Ct. 980, 13 L.Ed.2d 839 (1965); and National Labor Relations Board v. Erie Resistor Corp., supra. We noted in *Erie Resistor,* supra, 373 U.S. at 227, 83 S.Ct. at 1144, that proof of an antiunion motivation may make unlawful certain employer conduct which would in other circumstances be lawful. Some conduct, however, is so "inherently destructive of employee interests" that it may be deemed proscribed without need for proof of an underlying improper motive. National Labor Relations Board v. Brown, supra, 380 U.S., at 287, 85 S.Ct. at 986, American Ship Building Co. v. National Labor Relations Board, supra, 380 U.S. at 311, 85 S.Ct. at 963. That is, some conduct carries with it "unavoidable consequences which the employer not only foresaw but which he must have intended" and thus bears "its own indicia of intent." National Labor Relations Board v. Erie Resistor Corp., supra, at 228, 231, 83 S.Ct. at 1145–1147. If the conduct in question falls within this "inherently destructive" category, the employer has the burden of explaining away, justifying or characterizing "his actions as something different than they appear on their face," and if he fails, "an unfair labor practice charge is made out." Id., at 228, 83 S.Ct. at 1145. And even if the employer does come forward with counter explanations for his conduct in this situation, the Board may nevertheless draw an inference of improper motive from the conduct itself and exercise its duty to strike the proper balance between the asserted business justifications and the invasion of employee rights in light of the Act and its policy. Id., at 229, 83 S.Ct. at 1145. On the other hand, when "the resulting harm to employee rights is * * * comparatively slight, and a substantial and legitimate business end is served, the employers' conduct is prima facie lawful," and an affirmative showing of improper motivation must be made. National Labor Relations Board v. Brown, supra, 380 U.S. at 289, 85 S.Ct. at 987; American Ship Building Co. v. National Labor Relations Board, supra, 380 U.S. at 311–313, 85 S.Ct. at 963–964.

From this review of our recent decisions, several principles of controlling importance here can be distilled. First, if it can reasonably be concluded that the employer's discriminatory conduct was "inherently destructive" of important employee rights, no proof of an antiunion motivation is needed and the Board can find an unfair labor practice even if the employer introduces evidence that the conduct was motivated by business considerations. Second, if the adverse effect of the discriminatory conduct on employee rights is "comparatively slight," an antiunion motivation must be proved to sustain the charge *if* the employer has come forward with evidence of legitimate and sustantial business justifications for the conduct. Thus, in either situation, once it has been proved that the employer engaged in discriminatory conduct which could have adversely affected employee rights to *some* extent, the burden is upon the employer to establish that he was motivated by legitimate objectives since proof of motivation is most accessible to him.

Applying the principles to this case then, it is not necessary for us to decide the degree to which the challenged conduct might have affected employee rights. As the Court of Appeals correctly noted, the company came forward with no evidence of legitimate motives for its discriminatory conduct. 363 F.2d at 134. The company simply did not meet the burden of proof, and the Court of Appeals misconstrued the function of judicial review when it proceeded nonetheless to speculate upon what *might have* motivated the company. Since discriminatory conduct carrying a potential for adverse effect upon employee rights was proved and no evidence of a proper motivation appeared in the record, the Board's conclusions were supported by substantial evidence, Universal Camera Corp. v. National Labor Relations Board, 340 U.S. 474, 71 S.Ct. 456, 95 L.Ed. 456 (1951), and should have been sustained. * * *

Reversed and remanded with directions.

MR. JUSTICE HARLAN, whom MR. JUSTICE STEWART joins, dissenting.
* * *

* * * In the Court's view an employer must "come forward with evidence of legitimate and substantial business justifications" whenever any of his actions are challenged in a § 8(a)(3) proceeding. Prior to today's decision, § 8(a)(3) violations could be grouped into two general categories: those based on actions serving no legitimate business purposes or actions inherently severely destructive of employee rights where improper motive could be inferred from the actions themselves, and, in the latter instance, even a legitimate business purpose could be held by the Board not to justify the employer's conduct, National Labor Relations Board v. Erie Resistor Corp., 373 U.S. 221, 83 S.Ct. 1139, and those not based on actions "demonstrably so destructive of employee rights and so devoid of significant service to any legitimate business end," where independent evidence evincing the employer's antiunion animus would be required to find a violation. National Labor Relations Board v. Brown, 380 U.S. 278, 286, 85 S.Ct. 980, 985. The Court is unable to conclude that the employer's conduct in this case falls into

the first category, and has proposed its rule as an added gloss on the second whose contours were fixed only two years ago in *Brown*.

Under today's formulation, the Board is required to find independent evidence of the employer's antiunion motive only when the employer has overcome the presumption of unlawful motive which the Court raises. This alteration of the burden in § 8(a)(3) cases may either be a rule of convenience important to the resolution of this case alone or may, more unfortunately, portend an important shift in the manner of deciding employer unfair labor practice cases under § 8(a)(3). In either event, I believe it is unwise.

The "legitimate and substantial business justifications" test may be interpreted as requiring only that the employer come forward with a nonfrivolous business purpose in order to make operative the usual requirement of proof of antiunion motive. If this is the result of today's decision, then the Court has merely penalized Great Dane for not anticipating this requirement when arguing before the Board. Such a penalty seems particularly unfair in view of the clarity of our recent pronouncements that "the Board must find from evidence independent of the mere conduct involved that the conduct was primarily motivated by an antiunion animus," National Labor Relations Board v. Brown, 380 U.S., at 288, 85 S.Ct. at 986, and that "the Board must find that the employer acted for a proscribed purpose." American Ship Building Co. v. National Labor Relations Board, 380 U.S. 300, 313, 85 S.Ct. 955, 965.

On the other hand, the use of the word "substantial" in the burden of proof formulation may give the Board a power which it formerly had only in § 8(a)(3) cases like *Erie Resistor*, supra. The Board may seize upon that term to evaluate the merits of the employer's business purposes and weigh them against the harm that befalls the union's interests as a result of the employer's action. If this is the Court's meaning, it may well impinge upon the accepted principle that "the right to bargain collectively does not entail any 'right' to insist on one's position free from economic disadvantage." American Ship Building Co. v. National Labor Relations Board, supra, at 309, 85 S.Ct. at 962. Employers have always been free to take reasonable measures which discourage a strike by pressuring the economic interests of employees, including the extreme measure of hiring permanent replacements, without having the Board inquire into the "substantiality" of their business justifications. National Labor Relations Board v. Mackay Radio & Telegraph Co., 304 U.S. 333, 58 S.Ct. 904, 82 L.Ed. 1381. If the Court means to change this rule, though I assume it does not, it surely should not do so without argument of the point by the parties and without careful discussion.

In my opinion, the Court of Appeals correctly held that this case fell into the category in which independent evidence of antiunion motive is required to sustain a violation. As was pointed out in the Court of Appeals opinion, a number of legitimate motives for the terms of the vacation policy could be inferred, * * * and an unlawful motive is not the sole inference to be drawn from the conduct. Nor is the employer's conduct here, like the superseniority plan in *Erie Resistor*, * * * such that an unlawful motive can be found by "an application of the common law rule that a man is held to intend the foreseeable consequences of his conduct." Radio Officers, Union of Comm. Telegraphers Union, AFL v. National Labor Relations Board, 347 U.S. 17, 45, 74 S.Ct. 323, 338, 98 L.Ed. 455. The differences between the facts of this case and those of *Erie Resistor* * * * are, as the parties recognize, so significant as to preclude analogy. Unlike the granting of super-seniority, the vacation pay policy here had no potential long-term impact on the bargaining situation. The vacation policy was not employed as a weapon against the strike as was the super-seniority plan. Notice of the date of required presence for vacation pay eligibility was not given until after the date had passed. The record shows clearly that Great Dane had no need to employ any such policy to combat the strike, since it had successfully replaced almost all of the striking employees.[4] The Trial Examiner rejected all union claims that particular actions by Great Dane demonstrated anti-union animus. In these circumstances, the Court of Appeals correctly found no substantial evidence of a violation of § 8(a)(3).

Plainly the Court is concerned lest the strikers in this case be denied their "rights" under the collective bargaining agreement that expired at the commencement of the strike. Equally plainly, a suit under § 301 is the proper manner by which to secure these "rights," if they indeed exist. I think it inappropriate to becloud sound prior interpretations of § 8(a)(3) simply to reach what seems a sympathetic result.

Note

1. In what respects is the Great Dane doctrine different from and similar to the old "balancing" test, most clearly exemplified and described in Buffalo Linen (supra p. 231; quoted in Erie Resistor, supra p. 509)?

2. How would the Mackay question (Should an employer be permitted to hire permanent replacements for economic strikers?) be answered under the Great Dane formula?

NATIONAL LABOR RELATIONS BOARD v. FLEETWOOD TRAILER CO.

Supreme Court of the United States, 1967.
389 U.S. 375, 88 S.Ct. 543, 19 L.Ed.2d 614.

MR. JUSTICE FORTAS delivered the opinion of the Court.

Respondent is a manufacturer of mobile homes. On August 5, 1964, it employed about 110 persons. On August 6, 1964, as a result of a breakdown in collective bargaining negotiations between respondent and the Union, about half of the employees struck. Respondent cut back its production schedule from the prestrike figure of 20 units to 10 units per week, and curtailed its orders for raw materials correspondingly. On August 18, the Union accepted the respondent's last contract offer, terminated the strike, and requested reinstatement of the strikers.

Respondent explained that it could not reinstate the strikers "right at that moment" because of the curtailment of production caused by the strike. The evidence is undisputed that it was the company's intention "at all

---

4. By July 1, 1963, almost 75% of the striking employees had been replaced. By August 1, 1963, when the dispute over vaca- tion pay was coming to a head almost 90% had been replaced. All strikers had been re- placed by October 8, 1963.

times" to increase production to the full prestrike volume "as soon as possible." [2]

The six strikers involved in this case applied for reinstatement on August 20 and on a number of occasions thereafter. On that date, no jobs were available, and their applications were rejected. However, between October 8 and 16, the company hired six new employees, who had not previously worked for it, for jobs which the striker-applicants were qualified to fill. Later, in the period from November 2 through December 14, the six strikers were reinstated.

An NLRB complaint was issued upon charges filed by the six employees. As amended, the complaint charged respondent with unfair labor practices within the meaning of §§ 8(a)(1) and (3) * * * because of the hiring of new employees instead of the six strikers. After hearing, the Trial Examiner concluded that respondent had discriminated against the strikers by failing to accord them their rights to reinstatement as employees in October when respondent hired others to fill the available jobs. Accordingly, the Examiner recommended that respondent should make each of the six whole for loss of earnings due to its failure to return them to employment at the time of the October hirings and until they were reemployed. A three-member panel of the Board adopted the findings, conclusions and recommendations of the Trial Examiner.

The Board filed a petition for enforcement of the order. The Court of Appeals for the Ninth Circuit, one judge dissenting, denied enforcement. 366 F.2d 126 (1966). It held that the right of the strikers to jobs must be judged as of the date when they apply for reinstatement. Since the six strikers applied for reinstatement on August 20, and since there were no jobs available on that date, the court concluded that the respondent had not committed an unfair labor practice by failing to employ them. We granted certiorari on petition of the Board. * * *

We reverse.

Section 2(3) of the Act * * * provides that an individual whose work has ceased as a consequence of a labor dispute continues to be an employee if he has not obtained regular and substantially equivalent employment. If, after conclusion of the strike, the employer refuses to reinstate striking employees, the effect is to discourage employees from exercising their rights to organize and to strike guaranteed by §§ 7 and 13 of the Act * * *. Under §§ 8(a)(1) and (3) * * * it is an unfair labor practice to interfere with the exercise of these rights. Accordingly, unless the employer who refuses to reinstate strikers can show that his action was due to "legitimate and substantial business justifications," he is guilty of an unfair labor practice. NLRB v. Great Dane Trailers, 388 U.S. 26, 34, 87 S.Ct. 1792, 1798, 18 L.Ed.2d 1027 (1967). The burden of proving justification is on the employer. Ibid. It is the primary responsibility of the Board and not of the courts "to strike the proper balance between the asserted business justifications and the invasion of employee rights in light of the Act and its policy."

---

2. Respondent's production program was consistent with this intention. During a period of about 18 weeks after the strike, the number of units scheduled per week increased in a steady progression from 10 to 12 to 14 to 16 to 18 to 19 and, finally, to 20 for the week ending December 13, 1964.

Id., at 33–34, 87 S.Ct., at 1797. See also NLRB v. Erie Resistor Corp., 373 U.S. 221, 228–229, 235–236, 83 S.Ct. 1139, 1145, 1149, 10 L.Ed.2d 308 (1963). Universal Camera Corp. v. NLRB, 340 U.S. 474, 71 S.Ct. 456, 95 L.Ed. 456 (1951), is not an invitation to disregard this rule.[4]

In some situations, "legitimate and substantial business justifications" for refusing to reinstate striking employees who engaged in an economic strike, have been recognized. One is when the jobs claimed by the strikers are occupied by workers hired as permanent replacements during the strike in order to continue operations. NLRB v. Mackay Radio & Telegraph Co., 304 U.S. 333, 345–346, 58 S.Ct. 904, 910–911, 82 L.Ed. 1381 (1938); NLRB v. Plastilite Corp., 375 F.2d 343 (C.A.8th Cir.1967); Brown & Root, 132 N.L.R.B. 486 (1961).[5] In the present case, respondent hired 21 replacements during the strike, compared with about 55 strikers; and it is clear that the jobs of the six strikers were available after the strike. Indeed, they were filled by new employees.[6]

A second basis for justification is suggested by the Board—when the striker's job has been eliminated for substantial and bona fide reasons other than considerations relating to labor relations: for example, "the need to adapt to changes in business conditions or to improve efficiency."[7] We need not consider this claimed justification because in the present case no changes in methods of production or operation were shown to have been instituted which might have resulted in eliminating the strikers' jobs.

The Court of Appeals emphasized in the present case the absence of any antiunion motivation for the failure to reinstate the six strikers. But in NLRB v. Great Dane Trailers, supra, which was decided after the Court of Appeals' opinion in the present case, we held that proof of antiunion motivation is unnecessary when the employer's conduct "could have adversely affected employee rights to *some* extent" and when the employer does not meet his burden of establishing "that it was motivated by legitimate objectives." Id., 388 U.S. at 34, 87 S.Ct., at 1798. *Great Dane Trailers* determined that payment of vacation benefits to nonstrikers and denial of those payments to strikers carried "a potential for adverse effect upon employee rights." Because "no evidence of a proper motivation appeared in the record," we agreed with the Board that the employer had committed an unfair labor practice. Id., at 35, 87 S.Ct., at 1798. A refusal to reinstate striking employees, which is involved in this case, is clearly no less destructive of important employee rights than a refusal to make vacation payments.

4. Although the decision of the Court of Appeals, as we read it, resulted from its erroneous holding that the right of the strikers to jobs depends upon the date of their (first) application for reinstatement, it recited that the Board's General Counsel had failed to show "that the jobs of complainants had not been absorbed or that they were still available." Such proof is not essential to establish an unfair labor practice. It relates to justification, and the burden of such proof is on the employer. NLRB v. Great Dane Trailers, supra, 388 U.S. at 34, 87 S.Ct. at 1798. Cf. also NLRB v. Plastilite Corp., 375 F.2d 343, 348 (C.A. 8th Cir.1967).

5. Unfair labor practice strikers are ordinarily entitled to reinstatement even if the employer has hired permanent replacements. See Mastro Plastics Corp. v. NLRB, 350 U.S. 270, 278, 76 S.Ct. 349, 355, 100 L.Ed. 309 (1956).

6. The Trial Examiner found that "the six job openings in October could have been filled by the striker applicants and, had the Respondent considered them as employees rather than as mere applicants for hire, would have been so filled."

7. Brief on behalf of NLRB 15.

And because the employer here has not shown "legitimate and substantial business justifications," the conduct constitutes an unfair labor practice without reference to intent.

The Court of Appeals, however, held that the respondent did not discriminate against the striking employees because on the date when they applied for work, two days after the end of the strike, respondent had no need for their services. But it is undisputed that the employees continued to make known their availability and desire for reinstatement, and that "at all times" respondent intended to resume full production to reactivate the jobs and to fill them.

It was clearly error to hold that the right of the strikers to reinstatement expired on August 20, when they first applied. This basic right to jobs cannot depend upon job availability as of the moment when the applications are filed. The right to reinstatement does not depend upon technicalities relating to application. On the contrary, the status of the striker as an employee continues until he has obtained "other regular and substantially equivalent employment." (29 U.S.C.A. § 152(3).) Frequently a strike affects the level of production and the number of jobs. It is entirely normal for striking employees to apply for reinstatement immediately after the end of the strike and before full production is resumed. If and when a job for which the striker is qualified becomes available, he is entitled to an offer of reinstatement. The right can be defeated only if the employer can show "legitimate and substantial business justifications." NLRB v. Great Dane Trailers, supra.

Accordingly, the judgment of the Court of Appeals is vacated and the cause is remanded for further proceedings consistent with this opinion.

*   *   *

MR. JUSTICE MARSHALL took no part in the consideration or decision of this case.

[The concurring opinion of Justice Harlan, joined in by Justice Stewart, is omitted.]

Note

1. If an employer has permanently replaced all of the strikers and has a full force of workers, do the strikers still have a preferred reinstatement position? Three courts of appeals have agreed with the Board that permanently replaced strikers have rights of reinstatement when the replacements depart from their jobs. Laidlaw v. NLRB, 414 F.2d 99 (7th Cir.1969), cert. denied, 397 U.S. 920 (1970); American Machinery Corp. v. NLRB, 424 F.2d 1321 (5th Cir. 1970); Soule Glass and Glazing Co. v. NLRB, 652 F.2d 1055 (1st Cir.1981). The Board has also held that there is no time limit on this obligation of the employer to reinstate such strikers preferentially. Brooks Research & Mfg., 202 N.L.R.B. 634 (1973); Lincoln Hills Nursing Home, 257 N.L.R.B. 1145 (1981).

2. The Great Dane resolution of the scienter problem of Section 8(a)(3) is less difficult of formulation than of application. The universe of transgressions is divided into (1) "inherently destructive" and (2) "comparatively slight." This is hardly a self-executing dichotomy, and neither Great Dane nor Fleetwood Trailer cast light upon criteria for differentiation.

Some light, however dim, was cast in Metropolitan Edison Co. v. NLRB, 460 U.S. 693, 103 S.Ct. 1467, 75 L.Ed.2d 387 (1983). There the employer had disciplined employees who had engaged in a wildcat strike by imposing 5 to 10-day suspensions; two of the employees, the president and vice-president of the union, were more severely punished with 25-day suspensions. The Board found that this "selective discipline" of the union officials constituted a violation of Sections 8(a)(1) and 8(a)(3), reasoning that "in the absence of a clear contractual duty, requiring a union official to take affirmative steps to end an illegal work stoppage would place him in an intolerable position. If he failed to follow the company's directions, he would place his job in jeopardy. If he complied with the company's demands and crossed the picket line, he would lose the respect and support of the union members." 460 U.S. at 698, 103 S.Ct. at 1472, 75 L.Ed. 2d at 394.

The Supreme Court endorsed the Board's position, stating:

"Neither the union nor the Board has argued that union officials who fail to honor a no-strike clause are immunized from being disciplined in the same manner as other strike participants. The narrow question presented is whether an employer unilaterally may define the actions a union official is required to take to enforce a no-strike clause and penalize him for his failure to comply. * * *

"Section 8(a)(3) * * * requires proof that disparate treatment has been accorded union members and that the employer's action is likely to discourage participation in union activities. * * * Congress, however, did not intend to make unlawful all acts that might have the effect of discouraging union membership. Rather, the intention was to forbid only those acts that are motivated by an antiunion animus. * * *

" * * * [T]he Court has divided an employer's conduct into two classes. See NLRB v. Great Dane Trailers, Inc., 388 U.S., at 33–34, 87 S.Ct., at 1797–98. Some conduct is so 'inherently destructive of employee interests' that it carries with it a strong inference of impermissible motive. * * * In such a situation, even if an employer comes forward with a nondiscriminatory explanation for its actions, the Board 'may nevertheless draw an inference of improper motive from the conduct itself and exercise its duty to strike the proper balance between the asserted business justifications and the invasion of employee rights in light of the Act and its policy.' 388 U.S., at 33–34, 87 S.Ct., at 1797. On the other hand, if the adverse effect of the discriminatory conduct on employee rights is 'comparatively slight,' an antiunion motivation must be proved to sustain the charge *if* the employer has come forward with evidence of legitimate and substantial business justifications for the conduct.' Id., at 34, 87 S.Ct., at 1798 (emphasis in original). Congress has entrusted this determination in the first instance to the Board * * *.

"The Board has found that disciplining union officials more severely than other employees for participating in an unlawful work stoppage 'is contrary to the plain meaning of Section 8(a)(3) and would frustrate the policies of the Act if allowed to stand.' Precision Castings Co., 233 N.L.R.B., at 184. This conduct, in the Board's view, is 'inherently destructive' of protected individual rights because it discriminates solely on the basis of union status. * * * The Board has concluded that an employer's contractual right to be free of unauthorized strikes does not counterbalance the 'discriminatory effects of singling out union officers for especially harsh treatment.' Consolidation Coal Co., 263 N.L.R.B., at 1309. Disciplining union officials discriminatorily may have only an indirect effect on the rank and file's decision to strike, but it may well deter qualified employees from seeking union office. * * *

"We defer to the Board's conclusion that conduct such as Metropolitan Edison's adversely affects protected employee interests. Section 8(a)(3) not only proscribes discrimination that affects union membership, it also makes unlawful discrimination against employees who participate in concerted activities protected by § 7 of the Act. * * * Holding union office clearly falls within the activities protected by § 7 * * *, and there can be little doubt that an employer's unilateral imposition of discipline on union officials inhibits qualified employees from holding office * * *.

"Determining that such conduct adversely affects protected employee interests does not conclude the inquiry. If the employer comes forward with a legitimate explanation for its conduct, the Board must 'strike the proper balance between the asserted business justifications and the invasion of employee rights.' NLRB v. Great Dane Trailers, Inc., supra, 388 U.S., at 33–34, 87 S.Ct., at 1797. In this case the company has argued that its actions were justified because there is an implied duty on the part of the union officials to uphold the terms of the collective-bargaining agreement. Unquestionably there is support for the proposition that union officials, as leaders of the rank and file, have a legal obligation to support the terms of the contract and to set a responsible example for their members. * * * and in view of the disruptive effects of wildcat strikes, the importance of ensuring compliance with no-strike clauses is self-evident. * * * But it does not follow that an employer may assume that a union official is required to attempt to enforce a no-strike clause by complying with the employer's directions and impose a penalty on the official for declining to comply. As the Board has concluded, the imposition of such a penalty would violate § 8(a)(3).

"We think the Board's view is consistent with the policies served by the Act. 'The entire process of collective bargaining is structured and regulated on the assumption that "[t]he parties * * * proceed from contrary and to an extent antagonistic viewpoints and concepts of self-interest." ' General Building Contractors Assn. v. Pennsylvania, 458 U.S. 375, 394, 102 S.Ct. 3141, 3152, 73 L.Ed.2d 835 (1982) (quoting NLRB v. Insurance Agents, 361 U.S. 477, 488, 80 S.Ct. 419, 426, 4 L.Ed.2d 454 (1960)). Congress has sought to ensure the integrity of this process by preventing both management and labor's representatives from being coerced in the performance of their official duties. * * * If, as the company urges, an employer could define unilaterally the actions that a union official is required to take, it would give the employer considerable leverage over the manner in which the official performs his union duties. Failure to comply with the employer's directions would place the official's job in jeopardy. But compliance might cause him to take actions that would diminish the respect and authority necessary to perform his job as a union official. This is the dilemma Congress sought to avoid. We believe the Board's decision furthers these policies and upholds its determination." 460 U.S. at 699–705, 103 S.Ct. at 1472–75, 395–98, 75 L.Ed. 2d at 395–98.

Metropolitan Edison also casts light on the relationship between sections 8(a)(1) and (3) in "overlap" situations. In a footnote (460 U.S. at 698, 103 S.Ct. at

1472, 75 L.Ed.2d 394 n. 4), the Court observed: "Although §§ 8(a)(1) and (a)(3) are not coterminous, a violation of § 8(a)(3) constitutes a derivative violation of § 8(a)(1). * * * Because the Board has not suggested that there is an independent violation of § 8(a)(1), we consider only the § 8(a)(3) charge."

NATIONAL LABOR RELATIONS BOARD v. TRANSPORTATION MANAGEMENT CORP.

Supreme Court of the United States, 1983.
462 U.S. 393, 103 S.Ct. 2469, 76 L.Ed.2d 667.

JUSTICE WHITE delivered the opinion of the Court.

The National Labor Relations Act * * * makes unlawful the discharge of a worker because of union activity, [§ 8(a)(1), (3)], but employers retain the right to discharge workers for any number of other reasons unrelated to the employee's union activities. When the General Counsel of the National Labor Relations Board (Board) files a complaint alleging that an employee was discharged because of his union activities, the employer may assert legitimate motives for his decision. In Wright Line, 251 N.L.R.B. 1083 (1980), enforced 662 F.2d 899 (CA1 1981), cert. denied 455 U.S. 989, 102 S.Ct. 1612, 71 L.Ed.2d 848 (1982), the National Labor Relations Board reformulated the allocation of the burden of proof in such cases. It determined that the General Counsel carried the burden of persuading the Board that an antiunion animus contributed to the employer's decision to discharge an employee, a burden that does not shift, but that the employer, even if it failed to meet or neutralize the General Counsel's showing, could avoid the finding that it violated the statute by demonstrating by a preponderance of the evidence that the worker would have been fired even if he had not been involved with the union. The question presented in this case is whether the burden placed on the employer in *Wright Line* is consistent with §§ 8(a)(1) and 8(a)(3), as well as with § 10(c) of the NLRA * * * which provides that the Board must find an unfair labor practice by a "preponderance of the testimony."

Prior to his discharge, Sam Santillo was a busdriver for respondent Transportation Management Corp. On March 19, 1979, Santillo talked to officials of the Teamster's Union about organizing the drivers who worked with him. Over the next four days Santillo discussed with his fellow drivers the possibility of joining the Teamsters and distributed authorization cards. On the night of March 23, George Patterson, who supervised Santillo and the other drivers, told one of the drivers that he had heard of Santillo's activities. Patterson referred to Santillo as two-faced, and promised to get even with him.

Later that evening Patterson talked to Ed West, who was also a busdriver for respondent. Patterson asked, "What's with Sam and the Union?" Patterson said that he took Santillo's actions personally, recounted several favors he had done for Santillo, and added that he would remember Santillo's activities when Santillo again asked for a favor. On Monday, March 26, Santillo was discharged. Patterson told Santillo that he was being fired for leaving his keys in the bus and taking unauthorized breaks.

Santillo filed a complaint with the Board alleging that he had been discharged because of his union activities, contrary to §§ 8(a)(1) and 8(a)(3) of the NLRA. The General Counsel issued a complaint. The Administrative Law Judge (ALJ) determined by a preponderance of the evidence that Patterson clearly had an antiunion animus and that Santillo's discharge was motivated by a desire to discourage union activities. The ALJ also found that the asserted reasons for the discharge could not withstand scrutiny. Patterson's disapproval of Santillo's practice of leaving his keys in the bus was clearly a pretext, for Patterson had not known about Santillo's practice until after he had decided to discharge Santillo; moreover, the practice of leaving keys in buses was commonplace among respondent's employees. Respondent identified two types of unauthorized breaks, coffeebreaks and stops at home. With respect to both coffeebreaks and stopping at home, the ALJ found that Santillo was never cautioned or admonished about such behavior, and that the employer had not followed its customary practice of issuing three written warnings before discharging a driver. The ALJ also found that the taking of coffeebreaks during working hours was normal practice, and that respondent tolerated the practice unless the breaks interfered with the driver's performance of his duties. In any event, said the ALJ, respondent had never taken any adverse personnel action against an employee because of such behavior. While acknowledging that Santillo had engaged in some unsatisfactory conduct, the ALJ was not persuaded that Santillo would have been fired had it not been for his union activities.

The Board affirmed, adopting with some clarification the ALJ's findings and conclusions and expressly applying its *Wright Line* decision. It stated that respondent had failed to carry its burden of persuading the Board that the discharge would have taken place had Santillo not engaged in activity protected by the Act. The Court of Appeals for the First Circuit relying on its previous decision rejecting the Board's *Wright Line* test, NLRB v. Wright Line, 662 F.2d 899 (CA1 1981), refused to enforce the Board's order and remanded for consideration of whether the General Counsel had proved by a preponderance of the evidence that Santillo would not have been fired had it not been for his union activities. 674 F.2d 130. We granted certiorari, 459 U.S. 1014, 103 S.Ct. 372, 74 L.Ed.2d 506 (1982), because of conflicts on the issue among the Courts of Appeals.[3] We now reverse.

Employees of an employer covered by the NLRA have the right to form, join, or assist labor organizations. NLRA § 7 * * *. It is an unfair labor practice to interfere with, restrain, or coerce the exercise of those rights, NLRA § 8(a)(1), * * * or by discrimination in hire or tenure "to encourage or discourage membership in any labor organization," NLRA § 8(a)(3) * * *.

Under these provisions it is undisputed that if the employer fires an employee for having engaged in union activities and has no other basis for the discharge, or if the reasons that he proffers are pretextual, the employer commits an unfair labor practice. He does not violate the NLRA, however,

---

3. The Board's *Wright Line* decision has been rejected by the Second and Third Circuits, see NLRB v. New York University Medical Center, 702 F.2d 284 (CA2 1983), cert. pending, No. 82–1705; Behring International, Inc. v. NLRB, 675 F.2d 83 (CA3 1982), cert. pending, No. 82–438, as well as by the First.

Several Circuits have expressly approved the *Wright Line* test. See NLRB v. Senftner Volkswagen Corp., 681 F.2d 557, 560 (CA8 1982); NLRB v. Nevis Industries, Inc., 647 F.2d 905, 909 (CA9 1981); Peavey Co. v. NLRB, 648 F.2d 460 (CA7 1981).

if any antiunion animus that he might have entertained did not contribute at all to an otherwise lawful discharge for good cause. Soon after the passage of the Act, the Board held that it was an unfair labor practice for an employer to discharge a worker where antiunion animus actually contributed to the discharge decision. Consumers Research, Inc., 2 N.L.R.B. 57, 73 (1936); Louisville Refining Co., 4 N.L.R.B. 844, 861 (1938), enforced, 102 F.2d 678 (CA6), cert. denied, 308 U.S. 568, 60 S.Ct. 81, 84 L.Ed. 477 (1939); Dow Chemical Co., 13 N.L.R.B. 993, 1023 (1939), enforced in relevant part, 117 F.2d 455 (CA6 1941); Republic Creosoting Co., 19 N.L.R.B. 267, 294 (1940). In *Consumers Research,* the Board rejected the position that "antecedent to a finding of violation of the Act, it must be found that the *sole* motive for discharge was the employee's union activity." It explained that "[s]uch an interpretation is repugnant to the purpose and meaning of the Act, and * * * may not be made." 2 N.L.R.B., at 73. In its Third Annual Report, the Board stated: "Where the employer has discharged an employee for two or more reasons, and one of them is union affiliation or activity, the Board has found a violation [of § 8(a)(3)]." 3 NLRB Ann. Rep. 70 (1938). In the following year in *Dow Chemical Co.,* supra, the Board stated that a violation could be found where the employer acted out of antiunion bias "whether or not the [employer] may have had some other motive * * * and without regard to whether or not the [employer's] asserted motive was lawful." 13 N.L.R.B., at 1023. This construction of the Act—that to establish an unfair labor practice the General Counsel need show by a preponderance of the evidence only that a discharge is in any way motivated by a desire to frustrate union activity—was plainly rational and acceptable. The Board has adhered to that construction of the Act since that time.

At the same time, there were decisions indicating that the presence of an antiunion motivation in a discharge case was not the end of the matter. An employer could escape the consequences of a violation by proving that without regard to the impermissible motivation, the employer would have taken the same action for wholly permissible reasons. See, e.g., Eagle-Picher Mining & Smelting Co., 16 N.L.R.B. 727, 801 (1939), enforced in relevant part, 119 F.2d 903 (CA8 1941); Borden Mills, Inc., 13 N.L.R.B. 459, 474–475 (1939); Robbins Tire & Rubber Co., 69 N.L.R.B. 440, 454, n. 21 (1946), enforced, 161 F.2d 798 (CA5 1947).

The Courts of Appeals were not entirely satisfied with the Board's approach to dual-motive cases. The Board's *Wright Line* decision in 1980 was an attempt to restate its analysis in a way more acceptable to the Courts of Appeals. The Board held that the General Counsel of course had the burden of proving that the employee's conduct protected by § 7 was a substantial or a motivating factor in the discharge.[5] Even if this was the case, and the employer failed to rebut it, the employer could avoid being held in violation of §§ 8(a)(1) and 8(a)(3) by proving by a preponderance of the evidence that the discharge rested on the employee's unprotected conduct as well and that the employee would have lost his job in any event. It thus became clear, if it was not clear before, that proof that the discharge would

---

5. The Board has not purported to shift the burden of persuasion on the question of whether the employer fired Santillo at least in part because he engaged in protected activi-ties. The General Counsel satisfied his burden in this respect and no one disputes it. * * *

have occurred in any event and for valid reasons amounted to an affirmative defense on which the employer carried the burden of proof by a preponderance of the evidence. "The shifting burden merely requires the employer to make out what is actually an affirmative defense * * *." Wright Line, 251 N.L.R.B., at 1088, n. 11; see also *id.*, at 1084, n. 5.

The Court of Appeals for the First Circuit refused enforcement of the *Wright Line* decision because in its view it was error to place the burden on the employer to prove that the discharge would have occurred had the forbidden motive not been present. The General Counsel, the Court of Appeals held, had the burden of showing not only that a forbidden motivation contributed to the discharge but also that the discharge would not have taken place independently of the protected conduct of the employee. The Court of Appeals was quite correct, and the Board does not disagree, that throughout the proceedings, the General Counsel carries the burden of proving the elements of an unfair labor practice. Section 10(c) * * * expressly directs that violations may be adjudicated only "upon the preponderance of the testimony" taken by the Board. The Board's rules also state that "[t]he Board's attorney has the burden of pro[ving] violations of Section 8." 29 CFR § 101.10(b) (1982). We are quite sure, however, that the Court of Appeals erred in holding that § 10(c) forbids placing the burden on the employer to prove that absent the improper motivation he would have acted in the same manner for wholly legitimate reasons.

As we understand the Board's decisions, they have consistently held that the unfair labor practice consists of a discharge or other adverse action that is based in whole or in part on antiunion animus—or as the Board now puts it, that the employee's protected conduct was a substantial or motivating factor in the adverse action. The General Counsel has the burden of proving these elements under § 10(c). But the Board's construction of the statute permits an employer to avoid being adjudicated a violator by showing what his actions would have been regardless of his forbidden motivation. It extends to the employer what the Board considers to be an affirmative defense but does not change or add to the elements of the unfair labor practice that the General Counsel has the burden of proving under § 10(c).[6] We assume that the Board could reasonably have construed the Act in the

---

6. The language of the NLRA requiring that the Board act on a preponderance of the testimony taken was added by the LMRA, 61 Stat. 136, in 1947. A closely related provision directed that no order of the Board reinstate or compensate any employee who was fired for cause. Section 10(c) places the burden on the General Counsel only to prove the unfair labor practice, not to disprove an affirmative defense. Furthermore, it is clear from the legislative history of the LMRA that the drafters of § 10(c) were not thinking of the mixed-motive case. Their discussions reflected the assumption that discharges were either "for cause" or punishment for protected activity. Read fairly, the legislative history does not indicate whether, in mixed-motive cases, the employer or the General Counsel has the burden of proof on the issue of what would have happened if the employer had not been influ-

enced by his unlawful motives; on that point the legislative history is silent.

The "for cause" proviso was not meant to apply to cases in which both legitimate and illegitimate causes contributed to the discharge, see *infra*. The amendment was sparked by a concern over the Board's perceived practice of inferring from the fact that someone was active in a union that he was fired because of antiunion animus even though the worker had been guilty of gross misconduct. The House Report explained the change in the following terms:

"A third change forbids the Board to reinstate an individual unless the weight of the evidence shows that the individual was not suspended or discharged for cause. In the past, the Board, admitting that an employee was guilty of gross misconduct, nevertheless

manner insisted on by the Court of Appeals. We also assume that the Board might have considered a showing by the employer that the adverse action would have occurred in any event as not obviating a violation adjudication but as going only to the permissible remedy, in which event the burden of proof could surely have been put on the employer. The Board has instead chosen to recognize, as it insists it has done for many years, what it designates as an affirmative defense that the employer has the burden of sustaining. We are unprepared to hold that this is an impermissible construction of the Act. "[T]he Board's construction here, while it may not be required by the Act, is at least permissible under it * * *," and in these circumstances its position is entitled to deference. NLRB v. J. Weingarten, Inc., 420 U.S. 251, 266–267, 95 S.Ct. 959, 968, 43 L.Ed.2d 171 (1975); NLRB v. Erie Resistor Corp., 373 U.S. 221, 236, 83 S.Ct. 1139, 1149, 10 L.Ed.2d 308 (1963).

The Board's allocation of the burden of proof is clearly reasonable in this context, for the reason stated in NLRB v. Remington Rand, Inc., 94 F.2d 862, 872 (CA2), cert. denied, 304 U.S. 576, 58 S.Ct. 1046, 82 L.Ed. 1540 (1938), a case on which the Board relied when it began taking the position that the burden of persuasion could be shifted. E.g., Eagle-Picher Mining & Smelting, 16 N.L.R.B., at 801. The employer is a wrongdoer; he has acted out of a motive that is declared illegitimate by the statute. It is fair that he bear the risk that the influence of legal and illegal motives cannot be separated, because he knowingly created the risk and because the risk was created not by innocent activity but by his own wrongdoing.

In Mount Healthy City Board of Education v. Doyle, 429 U.S. 274, 97 S.Ct. 568, 50 L.Ed.2d 471 (1977), we found it prudent, albeit in a case implicating the Constitution, to set up an allocation of the burden of proof which the Board heavily relied on and borrowed from in its *Wright Line* decision. There, we held that the plaintiff had to show that the employer's disapproval of his First Amendment protected expression played a role in the employer's decision to discharge him. If that burden of persuasion were carried, the burden would be on the defendant to show by a preponderance of the evidence that he would have reached the same decision even if, hypothetically, he had not been motivated by a desire to punish plaintiff for exercising his First Amendment rights. The analogy to *Mount Healthy* drawn by the Board was a fair one.

For these reasons, we conclude that the Court of Appeals erred in refusing to enforce the Board's orders, which rested on the Board's *Wright Line* decision.

The Board was justified in this case in concluding that Santillo would not have been discharged had the employer not considered his efforts to establish a union. At least two of the transgressions that purportedly would

frequently reinstated him, 'inferring' that, because he was a member or an official of a union, this, not his misconduct, was *the* reason for his discharge." H.R.Rep. No. 245, 80th Cong., 1st Sess., 42 (1947) (emphasis added).

The proviso was thus a reaction to the Board's readiness to infer antiunion animus from the fact that the discharged person was active in the union, and thus has little to do with the situation in which the Board has soundly concluded that the employer had an antiunion animus and that such feelings played a role in a worker's discharge.

have in any event prompted Santillo's discharge were commonplace, and yet no transgressor had ever before received any kind of discipline. Moreover, the employer departed from its usual practice in dealing with rules infractions; indeed, not only did the employer not warn Santillo that his actions would result in being subjected to discipline, it also never even expressed its disapproval of his conduct. In addition, Patterson, the person who made the initial decision to discharge Santillo, was obviously upset with Santillo for engaging in such protected activity. It is thus clear that the Board's finding that Santillo would not have been fired if the employer had not had an antiunion animus was "supported by substantial evidence on the record considered as a whole," 29 U.S.C. § 160(f).

Accordingly, the judgment is reversed.

Note

Transportation Management, endorsing the Board's Wright Line doctrine, coexists with Great Dane and its progeny. No authoritative delineation of the proper area of function of each has yet been declared. Can they be reconciled?

The Board attempted such a delineation in its Wright Line decision, observing:

"In the final analysis, the applicability of the *Mt. Healthy* test [discussed in Transportation Management, supra p. 543] to the NLRA depends upon its compatibility with established labor law principles and the extent to which the test reaches an accommodation between conflicting legitimate interests. For, as the Supreme Court noted, in unfair labor practice cases:

'The ultimate problem is the balancing of the conflicting legitimate interests. The function of striking that balance to effectuate national labor policy is often a difficult and delicate responsibility, which the Congress committed primarily to the National Labor Relations Board, subject to limited judicial review. [N.L.R.B. v. Truck Drivers Local Union No. 449, International Brotherhood of Teamsters, Chauffeurs, Warehousemen and Helpers of America, AFL, 353 U.S. 87, 96 (1957).] [Ed. note: "Buffalo Linen," supra p. 228.]'

"Initially, support for the *Mt. Healthy* test of shifting burdens is found in the 1947 amendment of Section 10(c). That amendment provided that:

'No order of the Board shall require the reinstatement of any individual as employee who has been suspended or discharged, or the payment to him of any backpay, if such individual was suspended or discharged for cause.'

While the amendment itself does not address the 'in part' or 'dominant motive' analysis [with regard to the required degree of proof of the hostile motive] or the allocation of burdens, the legislative history does. In explaining the amendment Senator Taft stated:

'The original House provision was that no order of the Board could require the reinstatement of any individual or employee who had been suspended or discharged, unless the weight of the evidence showed that such individual was not suspended or discharged for cause. In other words, it was turned around so as to put the entire burden on the employee to show he was not discharged for cause. Under provision of the conference report, the employer has to make the proof. That is the present rule and the present practice of the Board. [93 Cong.Rec. 6678; 2 Leg.Hist. 1595 (1947).]'

The principle that 'the employer has to make the proof' is also found in the Supreme Court's decision in N.L.R.B. v. Great Dane Trailers, Inc., 388 U.S. 26 (1967). In that case the Court was concerned with the burden of proof in 8(a)(3) cases. It first noted that certain employer actions are inherently destructive of employee rights and, therefore, no proof of antiunion motive is required. Of course, the discharge of an employee, in and of itself, is not normally an inherently destructive act which would obviate the requirement of showing an improper motive. In this context, the Court in *Great Dane* stated that:

> '[I]f the adverse effect of the discriminatory conduct on employee rights is 'comparatively slight,' an antiunion motivation must be proved to sustain the charge *if* the employer has come forward with evidence of legitimate and substantial business justifications for the conduct. Thus * * * once it has been proved that the employer engaged in discriminatory conduct which could have adversely affected employee rights to *some* extent, the burden is upon the employer to establish that he was motivated by legitimate objectives since proof of motivation is most accessible to him. [388 U.S. at 34.]'

Thus, both Congress and the Supreme Court have implicitly sanctioned the shift of burden called for in *Mt. Healthy* in the context of Section 8(a)(3).

"Indeed, as is indicated by the above quotation of legislative history and the citation of *Great Dane,* the shifting burden process in *Mt. Healthy* is consistent with the process envisioned by Congress and the Supreme Court to resolve discrimination cases, although the process has not been articulated formally in the manner set forth in *Mt. Healthy.* Similarly, it is the process used by the Board. Thus, the Board's decisional process traditionally has involved, first, an inquiry as to whether protected activities played a role in the employer's decision. If so, the inquiry then focuses on whether any 'legitimate business reason' asserted by the employer is sufficiently proven to be the cause of the discipline to negate the General Counsel's showing of prohibited motivation.[12] Thus, while the Board's process has not been couched in the language of *Mt. Healthy,* the two methods of analysis are essentially the same.

"Perhaps most important for our purposes, however, is the fact that the *Mt. Healthy* procedure accommodates the legitimate competing interests inherent in dual motivation cases, while at the same time serving to effectuate the policies and objectives of Section 8(a)(3) of the Act. As the Supreme Court noted in N.L.R.B. v. Erie Resistor Corp., 373 U.S. 221 (1963), it is fundamental in 'situations present[ing] a complex of motives' that the decisional body be able to accomplish the 'delicate task' of:

> 'weighing the interests of employees in concerted activity against the interest of the employer in operating his business in a particular manner and of balancing in the light of the Act and its policy the

---

12. The absence of any legitimate basis for an action, of course, may form part of the proof of the General Counsel's case. See, e.g., Shattuck Denn Mining Company v. N.L.R.B., 362 F.2d 466 (9th Cir.1966).

intended consequences upon employee rights against the business ends to be served by the employer's conduct. [373 U.S. at 229.]'

Mt. Healthy achieves this goal.

"Under the *Mt. Healthy* test, the aggrieved employee is afforded protection since he or she is only required initially to show that protected activities played a role in the employer's decision. Also, the employer is provided with a formal framework within which to establish its asserted legitimate justification. In this context, it is the employer which has 'to make the proof.' Under this analysis, should the employer be able to demonstrate that the discipline or other action would have occurred absent protected activities, the employee cannot justly complain if the employer's action is upheld. Similarly, if the employer cannot make the necessary showing, it should not be heard to object to the employee's being made whole because its action will have been found to have been motivated by an unlawful consideration in a manner consistent with congressional intent, Supreme Court precedent, and established Board processes.

"Finally, we find it to be of substantial importance that our explication of this test of causation will serve to alleviate the intolerable confusion in the 8(a)(3) area. In this regard, we believe that this test will provide litigants and the decisionmaking bodies with a uniform test to be applied in these 8(a)(3) cases.

"Thus, for the reasons set forth above, we shall henceforth employ the following causation test in all cases alleging violation of Section 8(a)(3) or violations of Section 8(a)(1) turning on employer motivation. First, we shall require that the General Counsel make a *prima facie* showing sufficient to support the inference that protected conduct was a 'motivating factor' in the employer's decision. Once this is established, the burden will shift to the employer to demonstrate that the same action would have taken place even in the absence of the protected conduct.[14]

"Finally, inherent in the adoption of the foregoing analysis is our recognition of the advantage of clearing the air by abandoning the 'in part' language in expressing our conclusion as to whether the Act was violated. Yet, our abandonment of this familiar phraseology should not be viewed as a repudiation of the well-established principles and concepts which we have applied in the past. For, as noted at the outset of this Decision, our task in resolving cases alleging violations which turn on motivation is to determine whether a causal relationship existed between employees engaging in union or other protected activities and actions on the part of their employer which detrimentally affect such employees' employment. Indeed, it bears repeating that the 'in part' test, the 'dominant motive' test, and the *Mt. Healthy* test all share a fundamental common denominator in that the objective of each is to determine the relationship, if any, between employer action and protected employee conduct. Until now, in making this determination we frequently have employed the term 'in part.' But in so doing it only was a term used in pursuit of our goal which is to analyze thoroughly and

14. In this regard we note that in those instances where, after all the evidence has been submitted, the employer has been unable to carry its burden, we will not seek to quantitatively analyze the effect of the unlawful cause once it has been found. It is enough that the employees' protected activities are causally related to the employer action which is the basis of the complaint. Whether that "cause" was the straw that broke the camel's back or a bullet between the eyes, if it were enough to determine events, it is enough to come within the proscription of the Act.

completely the justification presented by the employer. It is, however, our considered view that adoption of the *Mt. Healthy* test, with its more precise and formalized framework for making this analysis, will serve to provide the necessary clarification of our decisional processes while continuing to advance the fundamental purposes and objectives of the Act." 251 N.L.R.B. at 1088–89.

Is it plausible to read between the lines of the Board's foregoing explanation a desire to avoid the difficulty implicit in the first analytical step of the Great Dane doctrine, i.e., the characterizing of the subject employer conduct as either "inherently destructive" or "comparatively slight" in its impact on employee rights? Is it further fair to conclude that the Wright Line-Mt. Healthy doctrine telescopes the entire Great Dane analysis into a simpler, more manageable formula, at least in discharge cases? In this connection, is it significant that none of the Supreme Court decisions giving rise to the Great Dane doctrine— Erie Resistor, American Ship, Brown Food, Great Dane itself, Fleetwood—can fairly be described as a discharge case?

NATIONAL LABOR RELATIONS BOARD v. KATZ

Supreme Court of the United States, 1962.
369 U.S. 736, 82 S.Ct. 1107, 8 L.Ed.2d 230.

MR. JUSTICE BRENNAN delivered the opinion of the Court.

Is it a violation of the duty "to bargain collectively" imposed by § 8(a)(5) of the National Labor Relations Act for an employer, without first consulting a union with which it is carrying on bona fide contract negotiations, to institute changes regarding matters which are subjects of mandatory bargaining under § 8(d) and which are in fact under discussion? The National Labor Relations Board answered the question affirmatively in this case, in a decision which expressly disclaimed any finding that the totality of the respondents' conduct manifested bad faith in the pending negotiations. 126 N.L.R.B. 288. A divided panel of the Court of Appeals for the Second Circuit denied enforcement of the Board's cease-and-desist order, finding in our decision in National Labor Relations Board v. Insurance Agents' Union, 361 U.S. 477, 80 S.Ct. 419, 4 L.Ed.2d 454, a broad rule that the statutory duty to bargain cannot be held to be violated, when bargaining is in fact being carried on, without a finding of the respondent's subjective bad faith in negotiating. 2 Cir., 289 F.2d 700. The Courts of Appeals said:

> "We are of the opinion that the unilateral acts here complained of, occurring as they did during the negotiating of a collective bargaining agreement, do not *per se* constitute a refusal to bargain collectively and *per se* are not violative of § 8(a)(5). While the subject is not generally free from doubt, it is our conclusion that in the posture of this case a necessary requisite of a Section 8(a)(5) violation is a finding that the employer failed to bargain in good faith." 2 Cir., 289 F.2d, at 702–703.

We granted certiorari * * * in order to consider whether the Board's decision and order were contrary to Insurance Agents. We find nothing in the Board's decision inconsistent with Insurance Agents and hold that the Court of Appeals erred in refusing to enforce the Board's order.

The respondents are partners engaged in steel fabricating under the firm name of Williamsburg Steel Products Company. Following a consent election in a unit consisting of all technical employees at the company's plant, the Board, on July 5, 1956, certified as their collective bargaining representative Local 66 of the Architectural and Engineering Guild, American Federation of Technical Engineers, AFL–CIO. The Board simultaneously certified the union as representative of similar units at five other companies which, with the respondent company, were members of the Hollow Metal Door & Buck Association. The certifications related to separate units at the several plants and did not purport to establish a multi-employer bargaining unit.

On July 11, 1956, the union sent identical letters to each of the six companies, requesting collective bargaining. Negotiations were invited on either an individual or "association wide" basis, with the reservation that wage rates and increases would have to be discussed with each employer separately. A follow-up letter of July 19, 1956, repeated the request for contract negotiations and enumerated proposed subjects for discussion. Included were merit increases, general wage levels and increases, and a sick-leave proposal.

The first meeting between the company and the union took place on August 30, 1956. On this occasion, as at the ten other conferences held between October 2, 1956, and May 13, 1957, all six companies were in attendance and represented by the same counsel. It is undisputed that the subject of merit increases was raised at the August 30, 1956, meeting although there is an unresolved conflict as to whether an agreement was reached on joint participation by the company and the union in merit reviews, or whether the subject was simply mentioned and put off for discussion at a later date. It is also clear that proposals concerning sick leave were made. Several meetings were held during October and one in November, at which merit raises and sick leave were each discussed on at least two occasions. It appears, however, that little progress was made.

On December 5, a meeting was held at the New York State Mediation Board attended by a mediator of that agency, who was at that time mediating a contract negotiation between the union and Aetna Steel Products Corporation, a member of the Association bargaining separately from the others; and a decision was reached to recess the negotiations involved here pending the results of the Aetna negotiation. When the mediator called the next meeting on March 29, 1957, the completed Aetna contract was introduced into the discussion. At a resumption of bargaining on April 4, the company, along with the other employers, offered a three-year agreement with certain initial and prospective automatic wage increases. The offer was rejected. Further meetings with the mediator on April 11, May 1, and May 13, 1957, produced no agreement, and no further meetings were held.

Meanwhile, on April 16, 1957, the union had filed the charge upon which the General Counsel's complaint later issued. As amended and amplified at the hearing and construed by the Board, the complaint's charge of unfair labor practices particularly referred to three acts by the company: unilaterally granting numerous merit increases in October 1956 and January 1957; unilaterally announcing a change in sick-leave policy in March

1957; and unilaterally instituting a new system of automatic wage increases during April 1957. * * *

[The Company argues] that the Board could not hinge a conclusion that § 8(a)(5) had been violated on unilateral actions alone, without making a finding of the employer's subjective bad faith at the bargaining table; and that the unilateral actions were merely evidence relevant to the issue of subjective good faith. This argument prevailed in the Court of Appeals which remanded the cases [sic] to the Board saying:

> "Although we might * * * be justified in denying enforcement without remand, * * * since the Board's finding of an unfair labor practice impliedly proceeds from an erroneous view that specific unilateral acts, regardless of bad faith, may constitute violations of § 8(a)(5), the case should be remanded to the Board in order that it may have an opportunity to take additional evidence, and make such findings as may be warranted by the record." 2 Cir., 289 F.2d, at 709.

The duty "to bargain collectively" * * * may be violated without a general failure of subjective good faith; for there is no occasion to consider the issue of good faith if a party has refused even to negotiate *in fact*—"to meet * * * and confer"—about any of the mandatory subjects. A refusal to negotiate *in fact* as to any subject which is within § 8(d), and about which the union seeks to negotiate, violates § 8(a)(5) though the employer has every desire to reach agreement with the union upon an over-all collective agreement and earnestly and in all good faith bargains to that end. We hold that an employer's unilateral change in conditions of employment under negotiation is similarly a violation of § 8(a)(5), for it is a circumvention of the duty to negotiate which frustrates the objectives of § 8(a)(5) much as does a flat refusal.[11]

The unilateral actions of the respondent illustrate the policy and practical considerations which support our conclusion.

We consider first the matter of sick leave. A sick-leave plan had been in effect since May 1956, under which employees were allowed ten paid sick-leave days annually and could accumulate half the unused days, or up to five days each year. Changes in the plan were sought and proposals and counterproposals had come up at three bargaining conferences. In March

---

11. Compare Medo Photo Supply Corp. v. National Labor Relations Board, 321 U.S. 678, 64 S.Ct. 830, 88 L.Ed. 1007; May Department Stores v. National Labor Relations Board, 326 U.S. 376, 66 S.Ct. 203, 90 L.Ed. 145; National Labor Relations Board v. Crompton-Highland Mills, 337 U.S. 217, 69 S.Ct. 960, 93 L.Ed. 1320.

In Medo, the Court held that the employer interfered with his employees' right to bargain collectively through a chosen representative, in violation of § 8(1) * * * (now § 8(a)(1)), when it treated directly with employees and granted them a wage increase in return for their promise to repudiate the union they had designated as their representative. It further held that the employer violated the statutory duty to bargain when he refused to nego-

tiate with the union after the employees had carried out their promise.

May held that the employer violated § 8(1) when, after having unequivocally refused to bargain with a certified union on the ground that the unit was inappropriate, it announced that it had applied to the War Labor Board for permission to grant a wage increase to all its employees except those whose wages had been fixed by "closed shop agreements."

Crompton-Highland Mills sustained the Board's conclusion that the employer's unilateral grant of a wage increase substantially greater than any it had offered to the union during negotiations which had ended in impasse clearly manifested bad faith and violated the employer's duty to bargain.

1957, the company, without first notifying or consulting the union, announced changes in the plan, which reduced from ten to five the number of paid sick-leave days per year, but allowed accumulation of twice the unused days, thus increasing to ten the number of days which might be carried over. This action plainly frustrated the statutory objective of establishing working conditions through bargaining. Some employees might view the change to be a diminution of benefits. Others, more interested in accumulating sick-leave days, might regard the change as an improvement. If one view or the other clearly prevailed among the employees, the unilateral action might well mean that the employer had either uselessly dissipated trading material or aggravated the sick-leave issue. On the other hand, if the employees were more evenly divided on the merits of the company's changes the union negotiators, beset by conflicting factions, might be led to adopt a protective vagueness on the issue of sick leave, which also would inhibit the useful discussion contemplated by Congress in imposing the specific obligation to bargain collectively.

Other considerations appear from consideration of the respondents' unilateral action in increasing wages. At the April 4, 1957, meeting the employers offered, and the union rejected, a three-year contract with an immediate across-the-board increase of $7.50 per week, to be followed at the end of the first year and again at the end of the second by further increases of $5 for employees earning less than $90 at those times. Shortly thereafter, without having advised or consulted with the union the company announced a new system of automatic wage increases whereby there would be an increase of $5 every three months up to $74.99 per week; an increase of $5 every six months between $75 and $90 per week; and a merit review every six months for employees earning over $90 per week. It is clear at a glance that the automatic wage increase system which was instituted unilaterally was considerably more generous than that which had shortly theretofore been offered to and rejected by the union. Such action conclusively manifested bad faith in the negotiations, National Labor Relations Board v. Crompton-Highland Mills, 337 U.S. 217, 69 S.Ct. 960, 93 L.Ed. 1320, and so would have violated § 8(a)(5) even on the Court of Appeals' interpretation, though no additional evidence of bad faith appeared. An employer is not required to lead with his best offer; he is free to bargain. But even after an impasse is reached he has no license to grant wage increases greater than any he has ever offered the union at the bargaining table, for such action is necessarily inconsistent with a sincere desire to conclude an agreement with the union.

The respondents' third unilateral action related to merit increases, which are also a subject of mandatory bargaining. National Labor Relations Board v. J.H. Allison & Co., 6 Cir., 165 F.2d 766. The matter of merit increases had been raised at three of the conferences during 1956 but no final understanding had been reached. In January 1957, the company, without notice to the union, granted merit increases to 20 employees out of the approximately 50 in the unit, the increases ranging between $2 and $10. This action too must be viewed as tantamount to an outright refusal to negotiate on that subject, and therefore as a violation of § 8(a)(5), unless the fact that the January raises were in line with the company's long-standing practice of granting quarterly or semiannual merit reviews—in effect, were a mere continuation of the status quo—differentiates them from the wage increases and the changes in the sick-leave plan. We do not think it does. Whatever might be the case as to so-called "merit raises" which are in fact simply automatic increases to which the employer has already committed himself, the raises here in question were in no sense automatic, but were informed by a large measure of discretion. There simply is no way in such case for a union to know whether or not there has been a substantial departure from past practice, and therefore the union may properly insist that the company negotiate as to the procedures and criteria for determining such increases.

It is apparent from what we have said why we see nothing in Insurance Agents contrary to the Board's decision. The union in that case had not in any way whatever foreclosed discussion of any issue, by unilateral actions or otherwise.[15] The conduct complained of consisted of partial-strike tactics designed to put pressure on the employer to come to terms with the union negotiators. We held that Congress had not, in § 8(b)(3), the counterpart of § 8(a)(5), empowered the Board to pass judgment on the legitimacy of any particular economic weapon used in support of genuine negotiations. But the Board *is* authorized to order the cessation of behavior which is in effect a refusal to negotiate, or which directly obstructs or inhibits the actual process of discussion, or which reflects a cast of mind against reaching agreement. Unilateral action by an employer without prior discussion with the union does amount to a refusal to negotiate about the affected conditions of employment under negotiation, and must of necessity obstruct bargaining, contrary to the congressional policy. It will often disclose an unwillingness to agree with the union. It will rarely be justified by any reason of substance. It follows that the Board may hold such unilateral action to be an unfair labor practice in violation of § 8(a)(5), without also finding the employer guilty of over-all subjective bad faith. While we do not foreclose the possibility that there might be circumstances which the Board could or should accept as excusing or justifying unilateral action, no such case is presented here.

The judgment of the Court of Appeals is reversed and the case is remanded with direction to the court to enforce the Board's order. * * *

Note

1. Do you agree with the Court's conclusion that the denial to the employer of the right to exercise his economic power in the Katz case is consistent with Insurance Agents? Is such denial consistent with American Ship?

2. If the employer may lock his employees out as in American Ship, should he not also be permitted to stop short of this and merely reduce wages or other benefits as a bargaining pressure—i.e., engage in a "partial lockout"? In Local 155, Molders v. NLRB, 442 F.2d 742 (D.C.Cir.1971), the employer was engaged in a seasonal business, that of the manufacture and sale of soil pipe. The months

---

15. The Court expressly left open the question which would be raised by a union's attempt to impose new working conditions unilaterally. 361 U.S., at 496–497, n. 28, 80 S.Ct. at 430, 431.

of peak demand were in the summer, those of lowest demand in the winter. By December 12 an impasse had developed in the negotiations for renewal of an expired collective bargaining agreement. The union obtained strike authorization through a vote of its members, but advised the employer that it did not intend or want to strike (at least not at that time!). Effective December 19, the company cancelled a wage increase which it had granted with union acquiescence upon the expiration of the old contract, after first having offered the same increase to the union during negotiations prior to impasse, and also cancelled certain other employee benefits contained in the expired contract, including paid holidays, premium pay for Sundays, and vacation pay. The purpose of the reduction in benefits was admittedly to pressure the employees to accept the employer's proposals for a new contract or, alternatively, to provoke a strike at that time rather than risk a later strike when business would be better. Bargaining continued under the new conditions of employment, but the impasse persisted; the employer's tactics did not provoke a strike. Accordingly, on January 31, the employer locked out all employees in the bargaining unit. The lockout continued until May 13, when a new contract was signed, substantially similar to that proposed earlier by the employer.

The NLRB held the lockout itself to be lawful, but found (applying the doctrine of Great Dane Trailers, supra p. 528) the *pre-lockout reduction in benefits* to constitute a violation of Sections 8(a)(1) and (3) on the ground that the reduction was "inherently destructive" of the employees' right to strike. The Board also found that the reduction of employee benefits constituted a violation of Section 8(a)(5) on the theory that a bargaining tactic designed to provoke a strike was inconsistent with the duty to bargain in good faith. The court of appeals enforced the Board's order in all respects, one judge dissenting.

By way of contrast, in NLRB v. Great Falls Employers' Council, 277 F.2d 772 (9th Cir.1960), the nonstruck members of an employers' association had locked out their employees in response to a whipsaw strike against one of the members. When the locked-out employees attempted to collect unemployment benefits,[c] their employers recalled them to work to the extent of earning sixteen dollars per week, thereby disqualifying them under the applicable law from receiving those benefits. The NLRB had found this conduct to violate Sections 8(a)(1) and (3). The court of appeals denied enforcement of the Board's order.

Is the following conclusion aptly drawn from such cases as Insurance Agents (partial strike not a protected activity under Section 7), Molders, and the Board decision in Great Falls Employers' Council: "Economic weapons must be used on an all-or-nothing basis; the whole does not encompass the part"? Is light cast by this excerpt from Member Zagoria's dissent in the Molders case at the Board level, sub nom. United States Pipe & Foundry Co., 180 N.L.R.B. 325, 325–26 (1969):

> "The Employer's temporary reduction in employee benefits, reasons the Trial Examiner, was unlawful because it put pressure upon them while not at the same time subjecting the Employer to the pressures inherent in a full lockout; i.e., his employees' absence from work and the consequent impediment to his own operations. Furthermore, Trial Examiner Reel points out, the employees wishing to protest the temporary changes by striking against

c. For a discussion of the factors determining the eligibility for unemployment compensation of employees out of work by reason of a labor dispute, see Williams, The Labor Dispute Disqualification—A Primer and Some Problems, 8 Vand.L.Rev. 338 (1955).

them would be subject to replacement, and hence in a worse position than had they been locked out. The Trial Examiner does point out that "it may be argued that had the employees stopped work altogether to protest the loss of holiday pay, etc., the law would view them as protesting a partial lockout and not as strikers vulnerable to replacement.' He concludes, however, that he 'know[s] of no authority to that effect,' and that it would be harsh 'to expect such foresight from employees. * * *' * * * Since we are writing on a clean slate, I feel free to consider the desirability of the various approaches.

"I find it preferable to permit an employer temporarily to reduce benefits for the purpose of putting economic pressure on employees in aid of good-faith bargaining, and at the same time to give the employees the choice of going on strike when this happens without incurring the risk of replacement. In effect, the employees who struck would be constructively (though lawfully) locked out. This approach would have several effects: First, it permits the employer to use a form of economic pressure much less drastic than a full lockout. Second, it permits a continued production flow, thus benefiting not only the general public, but also all employees of other companies whose welfare is tied to that of the company involved. Third, and most significantly, it gives the employees the effective choice of whether to continue to work with reduced benefits, or to stop work, without the risk of replacement, once the employer has fired the first shot in the economic warfare. My colleagues' result also permits the employees to strike without fear of replacement, by making the temporary reduction an unfair labor practice and hence a strike to protect it an unfair labor practice strike. But none of the other beneficial purposes of my proposal are achieved by their solution, for once it is held, as it is by the majority here, that the temporary reduction is unlawful, and the employer has to reimburse the employees *pro tanto*, that is the end of this particular economic weapon. Complete lockout will henceforth be the employer's only legitimate weapon. Anything less will be banned. And both sides will suffer. Indeed, under the majority view employees will not even have a choice. Had the employer here told his employees that he could lock them out, but if they *chose*, would instead adopt the lesser economic pressure of reducing benefits and continuing in operation, that would obviously be lawful. My suggestion would accomplish this. For these reasons, I would dismiss the complaint."

3. Another question for the would-be labor lawyer: Why is a "partial lockout" a violation of Section 8(a)(5), as held in the Molders case, while a partial strike is not a violation of Section 8(b)(3), as held in Insurance Agents? Is it relevant that union conduct can be relegated to any one of *three* categories—protected, unprotected, prohibited—while employer activity can be relegated to only *two*—lawful and unlawful?

4. The Great Falls case, discussed in Note 2, supra, raises a question of profound importance in the federal refereeing of the otherwise "free" fight between employer and union engaged in economic warfare: to what extent, if any, should a state be permitted to support the Union through subsidizing striking employees via unemployment compensation? Put otherwise: is the state interest in cushioning the impact of unemployment stronger than the federal interest in *free* collective bargaining?

The Supreme Court confronted this issue in NEW YORK TELEPHONE COMPANY v. NEW YORK STATE DEPT. OF LABOR, 440 U.S. 519, 99 S.Ct. 1328, 59 L.Ed.2d 553 (1979), a case arising out of the 1971–72 Communication Workers strike against the Bell System companies. The strike, national in scope, began on July 14, 1971, and lasted only a week for most workers. However, as reported by the Court:

"[T]he 38,000 CWA members employed by petitioners [New York State Bell System affiliates] remained on strike for seven months.

"New York's unemployment insurance law normally authorizes the payment of benefits after approximately one week of unemployment. If a claimant's loss of employment is caused by 'a strike, lockout, or other industrial controversy in the establishment in which he was employed,' * * * the law suspends the payment of benefits for an additional 7-week period. In 1971, the maximum weekly benefit of $75 was payable to an employee whose base salary was at least $149 per week.

"After the 8-week waiting period, petitioners' striking employees began to collect unemployment compensation. During the ensuing five months more than $49 million in benefits were paid to about 33,000 striking employees at an average rate of somewhat less than $75 per week. Because New York's unemployment insurance system is financed primarily by employer contributions based on the benefits paid to former employees of each employer in past years, a substantial part of the cost of these benefits was ultimately imposed on petitioners.

"Petitioners brought suit in the United States District Court for the Southern District of New York against the state officials responsible for the administration of the unemployment compensation fund. They sought a declaration that the New York statute authorizing the payment of benefits to strikers conflicts with federal law and is therefore invalid, an injunction against the enforcement of [the statute], and an award recouping the increased taxes paid in consequence of the disbursement of funds to their striking employees. * * * [T]he District Court granted the requested relief, [concluding] that the availability of unemployment compensation is a substantial factor in the worker's decision to remain on strike, and that in this case, as in others, it had a measurable impact on the progress of the strike. The court held that the payment of such compensation by the State conflicted 'with the policy of free collective bargaining established in the federal labor laws and is therefore invalid under the supremacy clause of the United States Constitution.' * * *.

"The Court of Appeals for the Second Circuit reversed. It did not, however, question the District Court's finding that the New York statute 'alters the balance in the collective bargaining relationship and therefore conflicts with the federal labor policy favoring the free play of economic forces in the collective bargaining process' [but rather] the court inferred from the legislative history of the National Labor Relations Act, and * * * of the Social Security Act, as well as from later developments, that the omission [see below] was deliberate. Accordingly, without questioning the premise that federal law generally requires that 'State statutes which touch or concern labor relations should be neutral,' the Court of Appeals concluded that 'th[is] conflict is one which Congress has decided to tolerate.' * * *.

"The importance of the question led us to grant certiorari. * * *. We now affirm. Our decision is ultimately governed by our understanding of the intent of the Congress that enacted the National Labor Relations Act on July 5, 1935, and the Social Security Act on August 14 of the same year.

* * *

"* * * The omission of any direction concerning payment to strikers in either the National Labor Relations Act or the Social Security Act implies that Congress intended that the States be free to authorize, or to prohibit, such payments.

"Subsequent events confirm our conclusion that the congressional silence in 1935 was not evidence of an intent to pre-empt the States' power to make this policy choice. On several occasions since the 1930's Congress has expressly addressed the question of paying benefits to strikers, and especially the effect of such payments on federal labor policy.[44] On none of these occasions has it suggested that such payments were already prohibited by an implicit federal rule of law. Nor, on any of these occasions has it been willing to supply the prohibition. The fact that the problem has been discussed so often supports the inference that Congress was well aware of the issue when the Wagner Act was passed in 1935, and that it chose, as it has done since, to leave this aspect of unemployment compensation eligibility to the States." 440 U.S. at 522–27, 544–45, 99 S.Ct. at 1331–34, 1343, 59 L.Ed.2d at 558–60, 571–72.

Quite apart from congressional intent, is it sound labor policy to permit a state or the federal government to subsidize one side of a collective bargaining dispute which has been carried to a test of economic strength?

The dissent in the New York Telephone case (the decision was 6–3) gave a resounding answer to this question, observing:

"The Court's decision substantially alters, in the State of New York, the balance of advantage between management and labor prescribed by the National Labor Relations Act. It sustains a New York law that requires the employer, after a specified time, to pay striking employees as much as 50% of their normal wages. In so holding, the Court substantially rewrites the principles of pre-emption that have been developed to protect the free collective bargaining which is the essence of federal labor law." 440 U.S. at 551, 99 S.Ct. at 1346–47, 59 L.Ed.2d 575–76.

5. The payment of welfare benefits, as distinguished from unemployment compensation, by states to strikers, raises questions of similar import: the area

---

44. * * *

In 1969, the Nixon Administration proposed an amendment to the Social Security Act that would have excluded strikers from unemployment compensation eligibility. Speaking in opposition to the proposal, Congressman Mills made the following comment:

"We have tried to keep from prohibiting the States from doing the things the States believe are in the best interest of their people. There are a lot of decisions in this whole program which are left to the States.

"For example, there are two States [New York and Rhode Island] which will pay unemployment benefits when employees are on strike, but only two out of 50 make that decision. That is their privilege to do so. * * * I would not vote for it * * *, but

if the State wants to do it we believe they ought to be given latitude to enable them to write the program they want." 115 Cong. Rec. 34106 (1969).

Congress rejected the proposal.

On two other occasions, Congress has confronted the problem of providing purely federal unemployment and welfare benefits to persons involved in labor disputes. In both instances, it has drawn the eligibility criteria broadly enough to encompass strikers. 45 U.S.C. § 354(a–2)(iii) (Railroad Unemployment Insurance Act); 7 U.S.C. § 2014(c) (Food Stamp Act). It thereby rejected the argument that such eligibility forces the Federal Government "to take sides in labor disputes." H.R.Rep. No. 91–1402, p. 11 (1970), U.S.Code Cong. & Admin.News, pp. 6025, 6035.

of impact, however, is much broader since *every* state (not just New York and Rhode Island, see supra fn. 44, p. 555) and the federal government (through programs such as Aid to Families with Dependent Children) maintain welfare programs which hold the potential of succor for strikers and their families. The various forms of public assistance to strikers and their families and the impact of such programs on the collective bargaining process are discussed in Carney, The Forgotten Man on the Welfare Roll: A Study of Public Subsidies for Strikers, 1973 Wash.U.L.Q. 469.

B. HEREIN OF THE SCOPE AND MEANING OF THE DUTY TO BARGAIN IN GOOD FAITH

NATIONAL LABOR RELATIONS BOARD v. AMERICAN NATIONAL INSURANCE CO.

Supreme Court of the United States, 1952.
343 U.S. 395, 72 S.Ct. 824, 96 L.Ed. 1027.

Mr. Chief Justice Vinson delivered the opinion of the Court.

This case arises out of a complaint that respondent refused to bargain collectively with the representatives of its employees as required under the National Labor Relations Act, as amended.

The Office Employees International Union A.F. of L., Local No. 27, certified by the National Labor Relations Board as the exclusive bargaining representative of respondent's office employees, requested a meeting with respondent for the purpose of negotiating an agreement governing employment relations. At the first meetings, beginning on November 30, 1948, the Union submitted a proposed contract covering wages, hours, promotions, vacations and other provisions commonly found in collective bargaining agreements, including a clause establishing a procedure for settling grievances arising under the contract by successive appeals to management with ultimate resort to an arbitrator.

On January 10, 1949, following a recess for study of the Union's contract proposals, respondent objected to the provisions calling for unlimited arbitration. To meet this objection, respondent proposed a so-called management functions clause listing matters such as promotions, discipline and work scheduling as the responsibility of management and excluding such matters from arbitration. The Union's representative took the position "as soon as [he] heard [the proposed clause]" that the Union would not agree to such a clause so long as it covered matters subject to the duty to bargain collectively under the Labor Act.

Several further bargaining sessions were held without reaching agreement on the Union's proposal or respondent's counterproposal to unlimited arbitration. As a result, the management functions clause was "by-passed" for bargaining on other terms of the Union's contract proposal. On January 17, 1949, respondent stated in writing its agreement with some of the terms proposed by the Union and, where there was disagreement, respondent offered counterproposals, including a clause entitled "Functions and Prerogatives of Management" along the lines suggested at the meeting of January 10th. The Union objected to the portion of the clause providing:

"The right to select and hire, to promote to a better position, to discharge, demote or discipline for cause, and to maintain discipline and efficiency of employees and to determine the schedules of work is recognized by both union and company as the proper responsibility and prerogative of management to be held and exercised by the company, and while it is agreed that an employee feeling himself to have been aggrieved by any decision of the company in respect to such matters, or the union in his behalf, shall have the right to have such decision reviewed by top management officials of the company under the grievance machinery hereinafter set forth, it is further agreed that the final decision of the company made by such top management officials shall not be further reviewable by arbitration."

At this stage of the negotiations, the National Labor Relations Board filed a complaint against respondent based on the Union's charge that respondent had refused to bargain as required by the Labor Act and was thereby guilty of interfering with the rights of its employees guaranteed by Section 7 of the Act and of unfair labor practices under Sections 8(a)(1) and 8(a)(5) of the Act. While the proceeding was pending, negotiations between the Union and respondent continued with the management functions clause remaining an obstacle to agreement. During the negotiations, respondent established new night shifts and introduced a new system of lunch hours without consulting the Union.

On May 19, 1949, a Union representative offered a second contract proposal which included a management functions clause containing much of the language found in respondent's second counterproposal, quoted above, with the vital difference that questions arising under the Union's proposed clause would be subject to arbitration as in the case of other grievances. Finally, on January 13, 1950, after the Trial Examiner had issued his report but before decision by the Board, an agreement between the Union and respondent was signed. The agreement contained a management functions clause that rendered nonarbitrable matters of discipline, work schedules and other matters covered by the clause. The subject of promotions and demotions was deleted from the clause and made the subject of a special clause establishing a union-management committee to pass upon promotion matters.

While these negotiations were in progress, the Board's Trial Examiner conducted hearings on the Union's complaint. The Examiner held that respondent had a right to bargain for inclusion of a management functions clause in a contract. However, upon review of the entire negotiations, including respondent's unilateral action in changing working conditions during the bargaining, the Examiner found that from and after November 30, 1948, respondent had refused to bargain in a good faith effort to reach agreement. The Examiner recommended that respondent be ordered in general terms to bargain collectively with the Union.

The Board agreed with the Trial Examiner that respondent had not bargained in a good faith effort to reach an agreement with the Union. But the Board rejected the Examiner's views on an employer's right to bargain for a management functions clause and held that respondent's action in bargaining for inclusion of any such clause "constituted, quite [apart from] Respondent's demonstrated bad faith, per se violations of Section 8(a)(5) and

(1)." Accordingly, the Board not only ordered respondent in general terms to bargain collectively with the union (par. 2(a)), but also included in its order a paragraph designed to prohibit bargaining for any management functions clause covering a condition of employment. (Par. 1(a)). 89 N.L. R.B. 185.

On respondent's petition for review and the Board's cross-petition for enforcement, the Court of Appeals for the Fifth Circuit agreed with the Trial Examiner's view that the Act does not preclude an employer from bargaining for inclusion of any management functions clause in a labor agreement. The Court of Appeals further found that the evidence does not support the view that respondent failed to bargain collectively in good faith by reason of its bargaining for a management functions clause. As a result, enforcement of the portion of the Board's order directed to the management functions clause (par. 1(a)) was denied. Other portions of the Board's order (pars. 1(b) and 2(a)) were enforced because respondent's unilateral action in changing working conditions during bargaining does support a finding that respondent had not bargained collectively in good faith as required by the Act. 5 Cir., 187 F.2d 307. We granted certiorari on petition of the Board for review of the denial of enforcement as to paragraph 1(a) of the Board's order. * * *

First. The National Labor Relations Act is designed to promote industrial peace by encouraging the making of voluntary agreements governing relations between unions and employers. The Act does not compel any agreement whatsoever between employees and employers. Nor does the Act regulate the substantive terms governing wages, hours and working conditions which are incorporated in an agreement. The theory of the Act is that the making of voluntary labor agreements is encouraged by protecting employees' rights to organize for collective bargaining and by imposing on labor and management the mutual obligation to bargain collectively.

Enforcement of the obligation to bargain collectively is crucial to the statutory scheme. And, as has long been recognized, performance of the duty to bargain requires more than a willingness to enter upon a sterile discussion of union-management differences. Before the enactment of the National Labor Relations Act, it was held that the duty of an employer to bargain collectively required the employer "to negotiate in good faith with his employees' representatives * * *." [9] The duty to bargain collectively, implicit in the Wagner Act as introduced in Congress, was made express by the insertion of the fifth employer unfair labor practice accompanied by an explanation of the purpose and meaning of [§ 8(5)].[10] This understanding of

---

9. Houde Engineering Corp., 1 N.L.R.B. (old) 35 (1934), decided by the National Labor Relations Board organized under 48 Stat. 1183 (1934) [i.e., Resolution 44 discussed in the Madden article supra, pp. 124–125].

10. Before the addition of Section 8(5), now Section 8(a)(5), to the bill, Senator Wagner described the bill as imposing the duty to bargain in good faith, citing the Houde Engineering case, note 9, supra. Hearings before the Senate Committee on Education and Labor on S. 1958, 74th Cong., 1st Sess. 43 (1935). Section 8(5) was inserted at the suggestion of the Chairman of the Board that decided

Houde. Id., at 79, 136–137. The insertion of Section 8(5) was described by the Senate Committee as follows:

"* * *

"[T]he committee has concluded that this fifth unfair labor practice should be inserted in the bill. It seems clear that a guarantee of the right of employees to bargain collectively through representatives of their own choosing is mere delusion if it is not accompanied by the correlative duty on the part of the other party to recognize such representatives as they have been designated * * *

the duty to bargain collectively has been accepted and applied throughout the administration of the Wagner Act by the National Labor Relations Board and the Courts of Appeal.

In 1947, the fear was expressed in Congress that the Board "has gone very far, in the guise of determining whether or not employers had bargained in good faith, in setting itself up as the judge of what concessions an employer must make and of the proposals and counter-proposals that he may or may not make." Accordingly, the Hartley Bill, passed by the House, eliminated the good faith test and expressly provided that the duty to bargain collectively did not require submission of counterproposals. As amended in the Senate and passed as the Taft-Hartley Act, the good faith test of bargaining was retained and written into Section 8(d) of the National Labor Relations Act. That Section contains the express provision that the obligation to bargain collectively does not compel either party to agree to a proposal or require the making of a concession.

Thus it is now apparent from the statute itself that the Act does not encourage a party to engage in fruitless marathon discussions at the expense of frank statement and support of his position. And it is equally clear that the Board may not, either directly or indirectly, compel concessions or otherwise sit in judgment upon the substantive terms of collective bargaining agreements.

Second. The Board offers in support of the portion of its order before this Court a theory quite apart from the test of good faith bargaining prescribed in Section 8(d) of the Act, a theory that respondent's bargaining for a management functions clause as a counterproposal to the Union's demand for unlimited arbitration was, "*per se,*" a violation of the Act.

Counsel for the Board do not contend that a management functions clause covering some conditions of employment is an illegal contract term.[15] As a matter of fact, a review of typical contract clauses collected for convenience in drafting labor agreements shows that management functions clauses similar in essential detail to the clause proposed by respondent have been included in contracts negotiated by national unions with many employers. The National War Labor Board, empowered during the last war "[t]o decide the dispute, and provide by order the wages and hours and all other terms and conditions (customarily included in collective-bargaining agreements)," ordered management functions clauses included in a number of agreements. Several such clauses ordered by the War Labor Board provided for arbitration in case of union dissatisfaction with the exercise of management functions, while others, as in the clause proposed by respondent in this case, provided that management decisions would be final. Without intimating any opinion as to the form of management functions clause proposed by respondent in this case or the desirability of including any such clause in a labor agreement, it is manifest that bargaining for management functions clauses is common collective bargaining practice.

and to negotiate with them in a bona fide effort to arrive at a collective bargaining agreement. * * * " S.Rep. No. 573, 74th Cong., 1st Sess. 12 (1935). * * *

15. Thus we put aside such cases as National Labor Relations Board v. National Mar-itime Union, 2 Cir., 1949, 175 F.2d 686 (bargaining for discriminatory hiring hall clause), where a party bargained for a clause violative of an express provision of the Act.

If the Board is correct, an employer violates the Act by bargaining for a management functions clause touching any condition of employment without regard to the traditions of bargaining in the particular industry or such other evidence of good faith as the fact in this case that respondent's clause was offered as a counterproposal to the Union's demand for unlimited arbitration. The Board's argument is a technical one for it is conceded that respondent would not be guilty of an unfair labor practice if, instead of proposing a clause that removed some matters from arbitration, it simply refused in good faith to agree to the Union proposal for unlimited arbitration. The argument starts with a finding, not challenged by the court below or by respondent, that at least some of the matters covered by the management functions clause proposed by respondent are "conditions of employment" which are appropriate subjects of collective bargaining under Sections 8(a)(5), 8(d) and 9(a) of the Act. The Board considers that employer bargaining for a clause under which management retains initial responsibility for work scheduling, a "condition of employment," for the duration of the contract is an unfair labor practice because it is "in derogation of" employees' statutory rights to bargain collectively as to conditions of employment.[22]

Conceding that there is nothing unlawful in including a management functions clause in a labor agreement, the Board would permit an employer to "propose" such a clause. But the Board would forbid bargaining for any such clause when the Union declines to accept the proposal, even where the clause is offered as a counterproposal to a Union demand for unlimited arbitration. Ignoring the nature of the Union's demand in this case, the Board takes the position that employers subject to the Act must agree to include in any labor agreement provisions establishing fixed standards for work schedules or any other condition of employment. An employer would be permitted to bargain as to the content of the standard so long as he agrees to freeze a standard into a contract. Bargaining for more flexible treatment of such matters would be denied employers even though the result may be contrary to common collective bargaining practice in the industry. The Board was not empowered so to disrupt collective bargaining practices. On the contrary, the term "bargain collectively" as used in the Act "has been considered to absorb and give statutory approval to the philosophy of bargaining as worked out in the labor movement in the United States." Order of Railroad Telegraphers v. Railway Express Agency, 1944, 321 U.S. 342, 346, 64 S.Ct. 582, 585, 88 L.Ed. 788.

Congress provided expressly that the Board should not pass upon the desirability of the substantive terms of labor agreements. Whether a contract should contain a clause fixing standards for such matters as work scheduling or should provide for more flexible treatment of such matters is an issue for determination across the bargaining table, not by the Board. If the latter approach is agreed upon, the extent of union and management

---

22. The Board's argument would seem to prevent an employer from bargaining for a "no-strike" clause, commonly found in labor agreements, requiring a union to forego for the duration of the contract the right to strike expressly granted by Section 7 of the Act. However, the Board has permitted an employer to bargain in good faith for such a clause. Shell Oil Co., 77 N.L.R.B. 1306 (1948). This result is explained by referring to the "salutary objective" of such a clause. Bethlehem Steel Co., 89 N.L.R.B. 341, 345 (1950).

participation in the administration of such matters is itself a condition of employment to be settled by bargaining.

Accordingly, we reject the Board's holding that bargaining for the management functions clause proposed by respondent was, *per se,* an unfair labor practice. Any fears the Board may entertain that use of management functions clauses will lead to evasion of an employer's duty to bargain collectively as to "rates of pay, wages, hours and conditions of employment" do not justify condemning all bargaining for management functions clauses covering any "condition of employment" as *per se* violations of the Act. The duty to bargain collectively is to be enforced by application of the good faith bargaining standards of Section 8(d) to the facts of each case rather than by prohibiting all employers in every industry from bargaining for management functions clauses altogether.

Third. The court below correctly applied the statutory standard of good faith bargaining to the facts of this case. It held that the evidence, viewed as a whole does not show that respondent refused to bargain in good faith by reason of its bargaining for a management functions clause as a counterproposal to the Union's demand for unlimited arbitration. Respondent's unilateral action in changing working conditions during bargaining, now admitted to be a departure from good faith bargaining, is the subject of an enforcement order issued by the court below and not challenged in this Court.

*   *   *

Affirmed.

MR. JUSTICE MINTON, with whom MR. JUSTICE BLACK and MR. JUSTICE DOUGLAS join, dissenting:

I do not see how this case is solved by telling the National Labor Relations Board that since *some* "management functions" clauses are valid (which the Board freely admits), respondent was not guilty of an unfair labor practice *in this case.* The record is replete with evidence that respondent insisted on a clause which would classify the control over certain conditions of employment as a management prerogative, and that the insistence took the form of a refusal to reach a settlement unless the Union accepted the clause. The Court of Appeals agreed that respondent was "steadfast" in this demand. Therefore, *this case* is one where the employer came into the bargaining room with a demand that certain topics upon which it had a duty to bargain were to be removed from the agenda—that was the price the Union had to pay to gain a contract. There is all the difference between the hypothetical "management functions" clauses envisioned by the majority and this "management functions" clause as there is between waiver and coercion. No one suggests that an employer is guilty of an unfair labor practice when it proposes that it be given unilateral control over certain working conditions and the union accepts the proposal in return for various other benefits. But where, as here, the employer tells the union that the only way to obtain a contract as to wages is to agree not to bargain about certain other working conditions, the employer has refused to bargain about those other working conditions. There is more than a semantic difference between a proposal that the union waive certain rights and a demand that the union give up those rights as a condition precedent to enjoying other rights.

I need not and do not take issue with the Court of Appeals' conclusion that there was no absence of good faith. Where there is a refusal to bargain, the Act does not require an inquiry as to whether that refusal was in good faith or bad faith. The duty to bargain about certain subjects is made absolute by the Act. The majority seems to suggest that an employer could be found guilty of bad faith if it used a "management functions" clause to close off bargaining about all topics of discussion. Whether the employer closes off all bargaining or, as in this case, only a certain area of bargaining, he has refused to bargain as to whatever he has closed off, and any discussion of his good faith is pointless.

That portion of § 8(d) of the Act which declares that an employer need not agree to a proposal or make concessions does not dispose of this case. Certainly the Board lacks power to compel concessions as to the substantive terms of labor agreements. But the Board in this case was seeking to compel the employer to bargain about subjects properly within the scope of collective bargaining. That the employer has such a duty to bargain and that the Board is empowered to enforce the duty is clear.

An employer may not stake out an area which is a proper subject for bargaining and say, "As to this we will not bargain." To do so is a plain refusal to bargain in violation of § 8(a)(5) of the Act. If employees' bargaining rights can be cut away so easily, they are indeed illusory. I would reverse.

NATIONAL LABOR RELATIONS BOARD v. WOOSTER DIVISION OF BORG–WARNER CORP.

Supreme Court of the United States, 1958.
356 U.S. 342, 78 S.Ct. 718, 2 L.Ed.2d 823.

MR. JUSTICE BURTON delivered the opinion of the Court.

In these cases an employer insisted that its collective-bargaining contract with certain of its employees include: (1) a "ballot" clause calling for a pre-strike secret vote of those employees (union and non-union) as to the employer's last offer, and (2) a "recognition" clause which excluded, as a party to the contract, the International Union which had been certified by the National Labor Relations Board as the employees' exclusive bargaining agent, and substituted for it the agent's uncertified local affiliate. [The union took the position that neither of these proposals was acceptable "under any conditions." An impasse was reached, and the union struck.] The Board held that the employer's insistence upon either of such clauses amounted to a refusal to bargain, in violation of § 8(a)(5) of the National Labor Relations Act, as amended. The issue turns on whether either of these clauses comes within the scope of mandatory collective bargaining as defined in § 8(d) of the Act. For the reasons hereafter stated, we agree with the Board that neither clause comes within that definition. * * *

* * * Section 8(a)(5) makes it an unfair labor practice for an employer "to refuse to bargain collectively with the representatives of his employees * * *." Section 8(d) defines collective bargaining. * * *

Read together, these provisions establish the obligation of the employer and the representative of its employees to bargain with each other in good faith with respect to "wages, hours, and other terms and conditions of employment * * *." The duty is limited to those subjects, and within that area neither party is legally obligated to yield. National Labor Relations Board v. American National Insurance Co., 343 U.S. 395, 72 S.Ct. 824, 96 L.Ed. 1027. As to other matters, however, each party is free to bargain or not to bargain, and to agree or not to agree.

The company's good faith has met the requirements of the statute as to the subjects of mandatory bargaining. But that good faith does not license the employer to refuse to enter into agreements on the ground that they do not include some proposal which is not a mandatory subject of bargaining. We agree with the Board that such conduct is, in substance, a refusal to bargain about the subjects that are within the scope of mandatory bargaining. This does not mean that bargaining is to be confined to the statutory subjects. Each of the two controversial clauses is lawful in itself. Each would be enforceable if agreed to by the unions. But it does not follow that, because the company may propose these clauses, it can lawfully insist upon them as a condition to any agreement.

Since it is lawful to insist upon matters within the scope of mandatory bargaining and unlawful to insist upon matters without, the issue here is whether either the "ballot" or the "recognition" clause is a subject within the phrase "wages, hours, and other terms and conditions of employment" which defines mandatory bargaining. The "ballot" clause is not within that definition. It relates only to the procedure to be followed by the employees among themselves before their representative may call a strike or refuse a final offer. It settles no term or condition of employment—it merely calls for an advisory vote of the employees. It is not a partial "no-strike" clause. A "no-strike" clause prohibits the employees from striking during the life of the contract. It regulates the relations between the employer and the employees. See National Labor Relations Board v. American National Insurance Co., supra, 343 U.S. at page 408, n. 22, 72 S.Ct. at page 831, 96 L.Ed. 1027. The "ballot" clause, on the other hand, deals only with relations between the employees and their unions. It substantially modifies the collective-bargaining system provided for in the statute by weakening the independence of the "representative" chosen by the employees. It enables the employer, in effect, to deal with its employees rather than with their statutory representative. Cf. Medo Photo Corp. v. National Labor Relations Board, 321 U.S. 678, 64 S.Ct. 830, 88 L.Ed. 1007.

The "recognition" clause likewise does not come within the definition of mandatory bargaining. The statute requires the company to bargain with the certified representative of its employees. It is an evasion of that duty to insist that the certified agent not be a party to the collective-bargaining contract. The Act does not prohibit the voluntary addition of a party, but that does not authorize the employer to exclude the certified representative from the contract.

Accordingly, the judgment of the Court of Appeals in No. 53 [setting aside the Board's order as to the ballot clause] is reversed and the cause remanded for disposition consistent with this opinion. In No. 78, the judgment [upholding the Board's order as to the recognition clause] is affirmed.

MR. JUSTICE FRANKFURTER joins this opinion insofar as it holds that insistence by the company on the "recognition" clause, in conflict with the provisions of the Act requiring an employer to bargain with the representative of his employees, constituted an unfair labor practice. He agrees with the views of MR. JUSTICE HARLAN regarding the "ballot" clause. The subject matter of that clause is not so clearly outside the reasonable range of industrial bargaining as to establish a refusal to bargain in good faith, and is not prohibited simply because not deemed to be within the rather vague scope of the obligatory provisions of § 8(d).

MR. JUSTICE HARLAN, whom MR. JUSTICE CLARK and MR. JUSTICE WHITTAKER join, concurring in part and dissenting in part.

I agree that the company's insistence on the "recognition" clause constituted an unfair labor practice, but reach that conclusion by a different route from that taken by the Court. However, in light of the finding below that the company bargained in "good faith," I dissent from the view that its insistence on the "ballot" clause can support the charge of an unfair labor practice.

Over twenty years ago this Court said in its first decision under the Wagner Act: "The theory of the act is that *free opportunity for negotiation* with accredited representatives of employees is likely to promote industrial peace and may bring about the adjustments and agreements which the act in itself does not attempt to compel." National Labor Relations Board v. Jones & Laughlin Steel Corp., 301 U.S. 1, 45, 57 S.Ct. 615, 628, 81 L.Ed. 893. (Italics added.) Today's decision proceeds on assumptions which I deem incompatible with this basic philosophy of the original labor Act, which has retained its vitality under the amendments effected by the Taft-Hartley Act. See National Labor Relations Board v. American National Insurance Co., 343 U.S. 395, 401–404, 72 S.Ct. 824, 828–829, 96 L.Ed. 1027. I fear that the decision may open the door to an intrusion by the Board into the substantive aspects of the bargaining process which goes beyond anything contemplated by the National Labor Relations Act or suggested in this Court's prior decisions under it.

The Court considers both the "ballot" and "recognition" clauses to be outside the scope of the mandatory bargaining provisions of § 8(d) of the Act, which in connection with §§ 8(a)(5) and 8(b)(3) imposes an obligation on an employer and a union to " * * * confer in good faith with respect to wages, hours, and other terms and conditions of employment * * *." From this conclusion it is said to follow that although the company was free to "propose" these clauses and "bargain" over them, it could not "insist" on their inclusion in the collective bargaining contract as the price of agreement, and that such insistence was a *per se* unfair labor practice because it was tantamount to a refusal to bargain on "mandatory" subjects. At the same time the Court accepts the Trial Examiner's unchallenged finding that the company had bargained in "good faith," both with reference to these clauses and all other subjects, and holds that the clauses are lawful in themselves and " * * * would be enforceable if agreed to by the unions."

Preliminarily, I must state that I am unable to grasp a concept of "bargaining" which enables one to "propose" a particular point, but not to "insist" on it as a condition to agreement. The right to bargain becomes illusory if one is not free to press a proposal in good faith to the point of insistence. Surely adoption of so inherently vague and fluid a standard is apt to inhibit the entire bargaining process because of a party's fear that strenuous argument might shade into forbidden insistence and thereby produce a charge of an unfair labor practice. This watered-down notion of "bargaining" which the Court imports into the Act with reference to matters not within the scope of § 8(d) appears as foreign to the labor field as it would be to the commercial world. To me all of this adds up to saying that the Act limits *effective* "bargaining" to subjects within the three fields referred to in § 8(d), that is "wages, hours, and other terms and conditions of employment," even though the Court expressly disclaims so holding.

I shall discuss my difficulties with the Court's opinion in terms of the "ballot" clause. The "recognition" clause is subject in my view to different considerations.

I.

At the start, I question the Court's conclusion that the "ballot" clause does not come within the "other terms and conditions of employment" provision of § 8(d). The phrase is inherently vague and prior to this decision has been accorded by the Board and courts an expansive rather than a grudging interpretation. Many matters which might have been thought to be the sole concern of management are now dealt with as compulsory bargaining topics. E.g. National Labor Relations Board v. J.H. Allison & Co., 6 Cir., 165 F.2d 766, 3 A.L.R.2d 990 (merit increases). And since a "no-strike" clause is something about which an employer can concededly bargain to the point of insistence, see Shell Oil Co., 77 N.L.R.B. 1306, I find it difficult to understand even under the Court's analysis of this problem why the "ballot" clause should not be considered within the area of bargaining described in § 8(d). It affects the employer-employee relationship in much the same way, in that it may determine the timing of strikes or even whether a strike will occur by requiring a vote to ascertain the employees' sentiment prior to the union's decision.

Nonetheless I shall accept the Court's holding that this clause is not a condition of employment, for even though the union would accordingly not be *obliged* under § 8(d) to bargain over it, in my view it does not follow that the company was *prohibited* from insisting on its inclusion in the collective bargaining agreement. In other words, I think the clause was a permissible, even if not an obligatory, subject of good faith bargaining.

The legislative history behind the Wagner and Taft-Hartley Acts persuasively indicates that the Board was never intended to have power to prevent good faith bargaining as to any subject not violative of the provisions or policies of those Acts. As a leading proponent for the Wagner Act explained:

> "When the employees have chosen their organization, when they have selected their representatives, all the bill proposes to do is to escort them to the door of their employer and say, 'Here they are, the legal representatives of your employees.' What happens behind those doors is not inquired into, and the bill does not seek to inquire into it." 79 Cong.Rec. 7660.

The Wagner Act did not contain the "good faith" qualification now written into the bargaining requirements of § 8(d), although this lack was remedied by early judicial interpretation which implied from former § 8(5) * * * the requirement that an employer bargain in good faith. * * * But apart from this essential check on the bargaining process, the Board possessed no statutory authority to regulate the *substantive* scope of the bargaining process insofar as lawful demands of the parties were concerned. Nevertheless, the Board engaged occasionally in the practice of determining that certain contract terms urged by unions were conditions of employment and thereby imposing on employers an affirmative duty to bargain as to such terms rather than insist upon their unilateral determination * * * or conversely of determining that certain clauses were not conditions of employment and thereby prohibiting an employer from bargaining over them. * * *

These early intrusions of the Board into the substantive aspects of the bargaining process became a matter of concern to Congress, and in the 1947 Taft-Hartley amendments to the Wagner Act, Congress took steps to curtail them by writing into § 8(d) the particular fields as to which it considered bargaining *should* be required. * * *

The decision of this Court in 1952 in National Labor Relations Board v. American National Insurance Co. * * * was fully in accord with this legislative background in holding that the Board lacked power to order an employer to cease bargaining over a particular clause because such bargaining under the Board's view, entirely apart from a showing of bad faith, constituted *per se* an unfair labor practice. * * *

[T]his Court, in reversing the Board, emphasized that flexibility was an essential characteristic of the process of collective bargaining, and that whether the topics contained in the disputed clause should be allocated exclusively to management or decided jointly by management and union " * * * is an issue for determination across the bargaining table, not by the Board." 343 U.S. at page 409, 72 S.Ct. at page 832, 96 L.Ed. 1027. It is true that the disputed clause related to matters which concededly were "terms and conditions of employment," but the broad rationale of the Court's opinion undercuts an attempt to distinguish the case on any such ground. "Congress provided expressly that the Board should not pass upon the desirability of the substantive terms of labor agreements. * * * The duty to bargain collectively is to be enforced by application of the good faith bargaining standards of Section 8(d) to the facts of each case * * *." 343 U.S. at pages 408–409, 72 S.Ct. at pages 831–832, 96 L.Ed. 1027.

I therefore cannot escape the view that today's decision is deeply inconsistent with legislative intention and this Court's precedents. The Act sought to compel management and labor to meet and bargain in good faith as to certain topics. This is the *affirmative* requirement of § 8(d) which the Board is specifically empowered to enforce, but I see no warrant for inferring from it any power in the Board to *prohibit* bargaining in good faith as to lawful matters not included in § 8(d). The Court reasons that such conduct on the part of the employer, when carried to the point of insistence, is in substance equivalent to a refusal to bargain as to the statutory subjects, but I cannot understand how this can be said over the Trial Examiner's unequivocal finding that the employer did in fact bargain in "good faith," not only over the disputed clauses but also over the statutory subjects.

It must not be forgotten that the Act requires bargaining, *not* agreement, for the obligation to bargain " * * * does not compel either party to agree to a proposal or require the making of a concession." § 8(d). Here the employer concededly bargained but simply refused to *agree* until the union would accept what the Court holds would have been a lawful contract provision. It may be that an employer or union, by adamant insistence in good faith upon a provision which is not a statutory subject under § 8(d), does in fact require the other party to bargain over it. But this effect is traceable to the economic power of the employer or union in the circumstances of a given situation and should not affect our construction of the Act. If one thing is clear, it is that the Board was not viewed by Congress as an agency which should exercise its powers to aid a party to collective bargaining which was in an economically disadvantageous position.

The most cursory view of decisions of the board and the circuit courts under the National Labor Relations Act reveals the unsettled and evolving character of collective bargaining agreements. Provisions which two decades ago might have been thought to be the exclusive concern of labor or management are today commonplace in such agreements. The bargaining process should be left fluid, free from intervention of the Board leading to premature crystallization of labor agreements into any one pattern of contract provisions, so that these agreements can be adapted through collective bargaining to the changing needs of our society and to the changing concepts of the responsibilities of labor and management. What the Court does today may impede this evolutionary process. Under the facts of this case, an employer is precluded from attempting to limit the likelihood of a strike. But by the same token it would seem to follow that unions which bargain in good faith would be precluded from insisting upon contract clauses which might not be deemed statutory subjects within § 8(d).

As unqualifiedly stated in Labor Board v. American National Insurance Co., * * * it is through the "good faith" requirement of § 8(d) that the Board is to enforce the bargaining provisions of § 8. A determination that a party bargained as to statutory or nonstatutory subjects in good or bad faith must depend upon an evaluation of the total circumstances surrounding any given situation. I do not deny that there may be instances where unyielding insistence on a particular item may be a relevant consideration in the overall picture in determining "good faith," for the demands of a party might in the context of a particular industry be so extreme as to constitute some evidence of an unwillingness to bargain. But no such situation is presented in this instance by the "ballot" clause. "No-strike" clauses, and other provisions analogous to the "ballot" clause limiting the right to strike, are hardly novel to labor agreements [2]. And in any event the uncontested finding of "good faith" by the Trial Examiner forecloses that issue here.

2. It was stipulated by the parties during hearings on the charge of unfair labor practices that collective bargaining agreements between several unions and companies have incorporated clauses requiring, in one form or another, secret ballots of employees before the union is able to call a strike. The clauses varied in defining employees to include only union members or all those working in the unit represented by the union and gave varying effect to the employee vote. The clause here involved does not purport to make the vote of the employees binding on the union.

Of course an employer or union cannot insist upon a clause which would be illegal under the Act's provisions * * * or conduct itself so as to contravene specific requirements of the Act. Medo Photo Supply Corp. v. Labor Board, 321 U.S. 678, 64 S.Ct. 830, 88 L.Ed. 1007. But here the Court recognizes, as it must, that the clause is lawful under the Act, and I think it clear that the company's insistence upon it violated no statutory duty to which it was subject. The fact that the employer here *did* bargain with the union over the inclusion of the "ballot" clause in the proposed agreement distinguishes this case from a situation involved in the Medo Photo Supply Corp. case, * * * where an employer, without the sanction of a labor agreement contemplating such action, negotiated *directly* with its employees in reference to wages. This Court upheld the finding of an unfair labor practice, observing that the Act " * * * makes it the duty of the employer to *bargain collectively with the chosen representatives* of his employees. The obligation being exclusive * * *, it exacts 'the negative duty to treat with no other.' " 321 U.S., at pages 683–684, 64 S.Ct. at page 833, 88 L.Ed. 1007. (Italics added.) Bargaining directly with employees " * * * would be subversive of the mode of collective bargaining which the statute has ordained * * *." 321 U.S. at page 684, 64 S.Ct. at page 833. The important consideration is that the Act does not purport to define the terms of an agreement but simply secures the representative status of the union for purposes of bargaining. The controlling distinction from Medo Photo is that the employer here has not sought to bargain with anyone else over the terms of the agreement being negotiated.

II.

The company's insistence on the "recognition" clause, which had the effect of excluding the International Union as a party signatory to agreement and making Local 1239 the sole contracting party on the union side, presents a different problem. In my opinion the company's action in this regard did constitute an unfair labor practice since it contravened specific requirements of the Act.

Section 8(a)(5) makes it an unfair labor practice for an employer not to bargain collectively "with the representatives of his employees." Such representatives are those who have been chosen by a majority of the employees of the appropriate unit, and they constitute " * * * the exclusive representatives of all the employees in such unit for the purposes of collective bargaining * * *." § 9(a). The Board under § 9(c) is authorized to direct a representation election and certify its results. The employer's duty to bargain with the representatives includes not merely the obligation to confer in good faith, but also " * * * the execution of a written contract incorporating any agreement reached if requested * * * " by the employees' representatives. § 8(d). I think it hardly debatable that this language must be read to require the company, if so requested, to sign any agreement reached with the same representative with which it is required to bargain. By conditioning agreement upon a change in signatory from the certified exclusive bargaining representative, the company here in effect violated this duty.

I would affirm the judgment of the Court of Appeals in both cases and require the Board to modify its cease and desist order so as to allow the company to bargain over the "ballot" clause.

Note

1. Suppose a union calls a strike: *case 1,* because of the employer's refusal to bargain over the union's demand that a joint committee be established to discuss the employer's merchandising policies, including pricing, markets, and advertising; *case 2,* because of the employer's refusal to abandon a demand that grievances be signed by aggrieved employees rather than, as previously, by the union alone (in order to reduce the number of grievances filed by increasing the degree of personal responsibility felt by potential grievants). What lawful action could the company take in each case?

2. What does the doctrine of Borg-Warner mean for what actually transpires at the bargaining table? In the case of a subject which is neither mandatory nor illegal (and is therefore "voluntary" or "permissible"), which of the following four postures on the part of the proposing party would be lawful? (1) "This proposal is the sine qua non of agreement." (2) "This proposal is the most important issue in these negotiations." (3) "All proposals are part of a total package—everything affects everything else." (4) "This proposal is very important, but we will not insist."

Would it be better simply to leave nonmandatory issues to the bargaining power of the parties, as maintained by Justice Harlan in Borg-Warner—assuming, of course, that the particular proposal, if agreed upon, could lawfully be incorporated in the resulting contract?

3. The case immediately following is highly pertinent to the questions posed in this Note.

INTERNATIONAL UNION OF MARINE WORKERS v. NATIONAL LABOR RELATIONS BOARD ("BETHLEHEM STEEL")

United States Court of Appeals, Third Circuit, 1963.
320 F.2d 615.

Certiorari denied, 375 U.S. 984 (1964).

STALEY, CIRCUIT JUDGE. The National Labor Relations Board has found that the Bethlehem Steel Company (Shipbuilding Division) violated § 8(a)(5) and (1) of the National Labor Relations Act. The case is here on petitions for review filed by both the company and the charging union, Industrial Union of Marine and Shipbuilding Workers of America, AFL–CIO, and on the cross-petition of the Board for enforcement of its order. The employer asserts that the Board's findings are unwarranted, while the union contends that the Board should have found additional violations.

The circumstances giving rise to this proceeding occurred during the summer of 1959 when Bethlehem and the union were negotiating a new collective bargaining agreement to cover hourly-paid employees at the company's east coast shipyards. A prior agreement, executed in 1956, had an expiration date of July 31, 1959. The union made an oral presentation of its bargaining demands on July 7, 1959. These included, among others, a proposed change in the formula for adjusting wages to the cost of living, increases in premium pay and vacation benefits, an extension of the scope of the arbitration clause, and changes which would give an increased emphasis to seniority in determining layoffs. The following day the company presented its proposed new contract (described as the White Book in the record), together with a written statement explaining its position. This detailed plan included elimination of the cost of living adjustment, a reduction in premium pay, limitations on the scope of the arbitration clause, and alterations in the grievance procedure. The latter contained a clause requiring the signature of each employee involved before a grievance could be processed. The reason assigned for this was that "under our current agreement we have been flooded with grievances." The thrust of the company's explanatory statement was that competitive conditions necessitated these proposals. Discussion of the basic wage structure was postponed pending resolution of these issues. * * *

The trial examiner found that Bethlehem had violated § 8(a)(5) and (1) by insisting on the clause requiring the signature of individual employees on grievances. * * *

[T]he Board adopted the conclusions and recommendations of the trial examiner. * * *

With respect to the grievance-signatory plan, the company advances two arguments: (1) there is no evidence that this was made a condition of reaching agreement; and (2) the proposal is a mandatory subject of bargaining. The record and the findings of the trial examiner make it abundantly clear that Bethlehem vigorously insisted that the substance of this proposal be incorporated in any new labor contract. But the employer urges that at no time did it state that this was a *sine qua non* of agreement. It says that since, as hereinafter more fully discussed, the Board found that there was an impasse on all disputed matters, it could not have concluded that insistence on this particular clause barred an accord.

The argument does not withstand analysis. It was not necessary for the Board to find that the company's insistence on this proposal was the sole cause of the failure to reach agreement. If the proposal is not a mandatory bargaining subject, insistence upon it was a per se violation of the duty to bargain. NLRB v. Wooster Division of Borg-Warner Corp., 356 U.S. 342, 78 S.Ct. 718, 2 L.Ed.2d 823 (1958); NLRB v. Davison, 318 F.2d 550 (C.A.4, 1963). Any other rule would permit insistence upon a non-mandatory item so long as there were any dispute as to mandatory topics. As the Supreme Court held in Borg-Warner, 356 U.S. at 349, 78 S.Ct. at 722:

> "We agree with the Board that such conduct [insistence on a non-mandatory topic] is, in substance, a refusal to bargain about the subjects that are within the scope of mandatory bargaining."

We turn now to the second aspect of the employer's argument on this point, i.e., the proposal is a mandatory bargaining subject. In accordance with § 8(d) of the Act, the Supreme Court has defined mandatory subjects as those within the phrase "wages, hours, and other terms and conditions of employment." NLRB v. Katz, 369 U.S. 736, 82 S.Ct. 1107, 8 L.Ed.2d 230 (1962); NLRB v. Wooster Division of Borg-Warner Corp., supra. It is clear to us that Bethlehem's proposal does not come within the scope of that phrase. Although at first glance it might appear to be a "condition of employment," actually the effect of the proposal is to limit the union's representation of the employees and not to condition the employees' employment. Cf. NLRB v. Davison, supra.

Under § 9(a) the union is the exclusive representative of the employees "in respect to rates of pay, wages, hours of employment, or other conditions of employment." * * * Bethlehem's proposal which would restrict the union's role in the prosecution of grievances to those complaints which had been signed by individual employees clearly limits this representation. The company acknowledges the union's rights with respect to the prosecution of grievances, but seeks solace in the proviso to § 9(a) which grants individual employees the right to adjust grievances without the intervention of the representative so long as the adjustment is not inconsistent with the collective bargaining contract.

We find nothing in this section to support the company's position. Indeed, the proviso itself requires that the union be given opportunity to be present at the adjustment. In short, the fact that individual employees have the right to adjust their own grievances does not mean that an employer can restrict the union's statutory rights by requiring that each grievance be signed by the employee involved. Such a limitation is not within the statutory definition of mandatory bargaining subjects. Like the pre-strike ballot clause in Borg-Warner, "it substantially modifies the collective-bargaining system provided for in the statute by weakening the independence of the 'representative' chosen by the employees. It enables the employer, in effect, to deal with its employees rather than with their statutory representatives." 356 U.S. at 350, 78 S.Ct. at 723. As the Board cogently points out in its brief, such a clause would preclude the union from prosecuting flagrant violations of the contract merely because the employee involved, due to fear of employer reprisals, or for similar reasons, chose not to sign a grievance. Hence, redress for a violation would be made contingent upon the intrepidity of the individual employee.

The fact that there are other labor contracts in this industry requiring employee signatures on grievances is not significant. Non-mandatory subjects may lawfully be included in collective bargaining contracts if the parties agree to them. NLRB v. Wooster Division of Borg-Warner Corp., 356 U.S. at 349, 78 S.Ct. at 722. * * *

Note

1. Do you understand the court to base its decision on Section 8(d) or on Section 9(a)? *Both?*

2. Would the decision be the same if the employer's demand were for a ceiling on the number of grievances filed each month?

3. Do you think you could devise a method which would allow the employer in Bethlehem Steel to make the grievance-signatory proposal, never reach agreement without the union's agreeing to the proposal, but nonetheless appear not to be conditioning agreement upon the union's acceptance of the proposal? Would you feel yourself in an uncomfortable ethical position? Does subterfuge make for sound collective bargaining? What is sound collective bargaining—playing poker in good faith?(!)

4. Do the questions raised in the foregoing Notes give you cause for reconsideration of the wisdom of the Borg-Warner decision?

FIBREBOARD PAPER PRODUCTS CORP. v. NATIONAL LABOR RELATIONS BOARD

Supreme Court of the United States, 1964.
379 U.S. 203, 85 S.Ct. 398, 13 L.Ed.2d 233.

MR. CHIEF JUSTICE WARREN delivered the opinion of the Court.

This case involves the obligation of an employer and the representative of his employees under §§ 8(a)(5), 8(d) and 9(a) of the National Labor Relations Act to "confer in good faith with respect to wages, hours, and other terms and conditions of employment." The primary issue is whether the "contracting out" of work being performed by employees in the bargaining unit is a statutory subject of collective bargaining under those sections.

Petitioner, Fibreboard Paper Products Corporation (the Company), has a manufacturing plant in Emeryville, California. Since 1937 the East Bay Union Machinists, Local 1304, United Steelworkers of America, AFL–CIO (the Union) has been the exclusive bargaining representative for a unit of the Company's maintenance employees. In September 1958, the Union and the Company entered the latest of a series of collective bargaining agreements which was to expire on July 31, 1959. The agreement provided for automatic renewal for another year unless one of the contracting parties gave 60 days' notice of a desire to modify or terminate the contract. On May 26, 1959, the Union gave timely notice of its desire to modify the contract and sought to arrange a bargaining session with Company representatives. On June 2, the Company acknowledged receipt of the Union's notice and stated: "We will contact you at a later date regarding a meeting for this purpose." As required by the contract, the Union sent a list of proposed modifications on June 15. Efforts by the Union to schedule a bargaining session met with no success until July 27, four days before the expiration of the contract, when the Company notified the Union of its desire to meet.

The Company, concerned with the high cost of its maintenance operation, had undertaken a study of the possibility of effecting cost savings by engaging an independent contractor to do the maintenance work. At the July 27, meeting, the Company informed the Union that it had determined that substantial savings could be effected by contracting out the work upon expiration of its collective bargaining agreements with the various labor organizations representing its maintenance employees. The Company delivered to the Union representatives a letter which stated in pertinent part:

"For some time we have been seriously considering the question of letting out our Emeryville maintenance work to an independent contractor, and have now reached a definite decision to do so effective August 1, 1959.

"In these circumstances, we are sure you will realize that negotiation of a new contract would be pointless. However, if you have any questions, we will be glad to discuss them with you."

After some discussion of the Company's right to enter a contract with a third party to do the work then being performed by employees in the bargaining unit, the meeting concluded with the understanding that the parties would meet again on July 30.

By July 30, the Company had selected Fluor Maintenance, Inc., to do the maintenance work. Fluor had assured the Company that maintenance costs could be curtailed by reducing the work force, decreasing fringe benefits and overtime payments, and by preplanning and scheduling the services to be performed. The contract provided that Fluor would:

> "furnish all labor, supervision and office help required for the performance of maintenance work * * * at the Emeryville plant of Owner as Owner shall from time to time assign to Contractor during the period of this contract; and shall also furnish such tools, supplies and equipment in connection therewith as Owner shall order from Contractor, it being understood however that Owner shall ordinarily do its own purchasing of tools, supplies and equipment."

The contract further provided that the Company would pay Fluor the costs of the operation plus a fixed fee of $2,250 per month.

At the July 30 meeting the Company's representative, in explaining the decision to contract out the maintenance work, remarked that during bargaining negotiations in previous years the Company had endeavored to point out through the use of charts and statistical information "just how expensive and costly our maintenance work was and how it was creating quite a terrific burden upon the Emeryville plant." He further stated that unions representing other Company employees "had joined hands with management in an effort to bring about an economical and efficient operation," but "we had not been able to attain that in our discussions with this particular Local." The Company also distributed a letter stating that "since we will have no employees in the bargaining unit covered by our present Agreement, negotiation of a new or renewed Agreement would appear to us to be pointless." On July 31, the employment of the maintenance employees represented by the Union was terminated and Fluor employees took over. That evening the Union established a picket line at the Company's plant.

The Union filed unfair labor practice charges against the Company, alleging violations of §§ 8(a)(1), 8(a)(3) and 8(a)(5). After hearings were held upon a complaint issued by the National Labor Relations Board's Regional Director, the Trial Examiner filed an Intermediate Report recommending dismissal of the complaint. The Board accepted the recommendation and dismissed the complaint. 130 N.L.R.B. 1558.

Petitions for reconsideration, filed by the General Counsel and the Union, were granted. Upon reconsideration, the Board adhered to the Trial Examiner's finding that the Company's motive in contracting out its maintenance work was economic rather than antiunion but found nonetheless that the Company's "failure to negotiate with * * * [the Union] concerning its decision to subcontract its maintenance work constituted a violation of Section 8(a)(5) of the Act."[2] This ruling was based upon the doctrine established in Town & Country Mfg. Co., 136 N.L.R.B. 1022, 1027, enforcement granted, 316 F.2d 846 (C.A. 5th Cir.1963), that contracting out work,

2. The Board did not disturb its original holding that the Company had not violated § 8(a)(1) or § 8(a)(3), or its holding that the Company had satisfied its obligation to bargain about termination pay.

"albeit for economic reasons, is a matter within the statutory phrase 'other terms and conditions of employment' and is a mandatory subject of collective bargaining within the meaning of Section 8(a)(5) of the Act."

The Board ordered the Company to reinstate the maintenance operation previously performed by the employees represented by the Union, to reinstate the employees to their former or substantially equivalent positions with back pay computed from the date of the Board's supplemental decision, and to fulfill its statutory obligation to bargain.

On appeal, the Court of Appeals for the District of Columbia Circuit granted the Board's petition for enforcement. 116 U.S.App.D.C. 198, 322 F.2d 411. Because of the importance of the issues and because of an alleged conflict among the courts of appeals, we granted certiorari limited to a consideration of the following questions:

"1. Was petitioner required by the National Labor Relations Act to bargain with a union representing some of its employees about whether to let to an independent contractor for legitimate business reasons the performance of certain operations in which those employees had been engaged?

"3. Was the Board, in a case involving only a refusal to bargain, empowered to order the resumption of operations which had been discontinued for legitimate business reasons and reinstatement with back pay of the individuals formerly employed therein?"

We agree with the Court of Appeals that, on the facts of this case, the "contracting out" of the work previously performed by members of an existing bargaining unit is a subject about which the National Labor Relations Act requires employers and the representatives of their employees to bargain collectively. We also agree with the Court of Appeals that the Board did not exceed its remedial powers in directing the Company to resume its maintenance operations, reinstate the employees with back pay, and bargain with the Union.

I.

Section 8(a)(5) of the National Labor Relations Act provides that it shall be an unfair labor practice for an employer "to refuse to bargain collectively with the representatives of his employees." Collective bargaining is defined in § 8(d) as "the performance of the mutual obligation of the employer and the representative of the employees to meet at reasonable times and confer in good faith with respect to wages, hours, and other terms and conditions of employment."

"Read together, these provisions establish the obligation of the employer and the representative of its employees to bargain with each other in good faith with respect to 'wages, hours, and other terms and conditions of employment * * *.' The duty is limited to those subjects, and within that area neither party is legally obligated to yield. National Labor Relations Board v. American [Nat.] Ins. Co., 343 U.S. 395, 72 S.Ct. 824, 96 L.Ed. 1027. As to other matters, however, each party is free to bargain or not to bargain * * *." National Labor Relations Board v. Wooster Div. of Borg-Warner Corp., 356 U.S. 342, 349, 78 S.Ct. 718, 722, 2 L.Ed.2d 823. Because of the limited grant of certiorari, we are concerned here only with whether the subject upon which the employer allegedly refused to bargain—contracting out of plant maintenance work previously performed by employees in the bargaining unit, which the employees were capable of continuing to perform—is covered by the phrase "terms and conditions of employment" within the meaning of § 8(d).

The subject matter of the present dispute is well within the literal meaning of the phrase "terms and conditions of employment." See Order of Railroad Telegraphers v. Chicago & N.W.R. Co., 362 U.S. 330, 80 S.Ct. 761, 4 L.Ed.2d 774. A stipulation with respect to the contracting out of work performed by members of the bargaining unit might appropriately be called a "condition of employment." The words even more plainly cover termination of employment which, as the facts of this case indicate, necessarily results from the contracting out of work performed by members of the established bargaining unit.

The inclusion of "contracting out" within the statutory scope of collective bargaining also seems well designed to effectuate the purposes of the National Labor Relations Act. One of the primary purposes of the Act is to promote the peaceful settlement of industrial disputes by subjecting labor-management controversies to the mediatory influence of negotiation. The Act was framed with an awareness that refusals to confer and negotiate had been one of the most prolific causes of industrial strife. * * * To hold, as the Board has done, that contracting out is a mandatory subject of collective bargaining would promote the fundamental purpose of the Act by bringing a problem of vital concern to labor and management within the framework established by Congress as most conducive to industrial peace.

The conclusion that "contracting out" is a statutory subject of collective bargaining is further reinforced by industrial practices in this country. While not determinative, it is appropriate to look to industrial bargaining practices in appraising the propriety of including a particular subject within the scope of mandatory bargaining. National Labor Relations Board v. American Nat. Ins. Co., 343 U.S. 395, 408, 72 S.Ct. 824, 831, 96 L.Ed. 1027. Industrial experience is not only reflective of the interests of labor and management in the subject matter but is also indicative of the amenability of such subjects to the collective bargaining process. Experience illustrates that contracting out in one form or another has been brought, widely and successfully, within the collective bargaining framework. Provisions relating to contracting out exist in numerous collective bargaining agreements, and "[c]ontracting out work is the basis of many grievances; and that type of claim is grist in the mills of the arbitrators." United Steelworkers of America, etc. v. Warrior & Gulf Nav. Co., 363 U.S. 574, 584, 80 S.Ct. 1347, 1354, 4 L.Ed.2d 1409.

The situation here is not unlike that presented in Local 24, of Intern. Broth. of Teamsters, etc. v. Oliver, 358 U.S. 283, 79 S.Ct. 297, 3 L.Ed.2d 312, where we held that conditions imposed upon contracting out work to prevent possible curtailment of jobs and the undermining of conditions of employment for members of the bargaining unit constituted a statutory subject of collective bargaining. The issue in that case was whether state antitrust laws could be applied to a provision of a collective bargaining agreement which fixed the minimum rental to be paid by the employer motor carrier who leased vehicles to be driven by their owners rather than the carrier's employees. We held that the agreement was upon a subject matter as to which federal law directed the parties to bargain and hence that state antitrust laws could not be applied to prevent the effectuation of the agreement. We pointed out that the agreement was a "direct frontal attack upon a problem thought to threaten the maintenance of the basic wage structure established by the collective bargaining contract. The inadequacy of a rental which means that the owner makes up his excess costs from his driver's wages not only clearly bears a close relation to labor's efforts to improve working conditions but is in fact of vital concern to the carrier's employed drivers; an inadequate rental might mean the progressive curtailment of jobs through withdrawal of more and more carrier-owned vehicles from service." Id., at 294, 79 S.Ct. at 304.

Thus, we concluded that such a matter is a subject of mandatory bargaining under § 8(d). Id., at 294–295, 79 S.Ct. at 303–304. The only difference between that case and the one at hand is that the work of the employees in the bargaining unit was let out piecemeal in Oliver, whereas here the work of the entire unit has been contracted out. ＊ ＊ ＊

The facts of the present case illustrate the propriety of submitting the dispute to collective negotiation. The Company's decision to contract out the maintenance work did not alter the Company's basic operation. The maintenance work still had to be performed in the plant. No capital investment was contemplated; the Company merely replaced existing employees with those of an independent contractor to do the same work under similar conditions of employment. Therefore, to require the employer to bargain about the matter would not significantly abridge his freedom to manage the business.

The Company was concerned with the high cost of its maintenance operation. It was induced to contract out the work by assurances from independent contractors that economies could be derived by reducing the work force, decreasing fringe benefits, and eliminating overtime payments. These have long been regarded as matters peculiarly suitable for resolution within the collective bargaining framework, and industrial experience demonstrates that collective negotiation has been highly successful in achieving peaceful accommodation of the conflicting interests. Yet, it is contended that when an employer can effect cost savings in these respects by contracting the work out, there is no need to attempt to achieve similar economies through negotiation with existing employees or to provide them with an opportunity to negotiate a mutually acceptable alternative. The short answer is that, although it is not possible to say whether a satisfactory solution could be reached, national labor policy is founded upon the congressional determination that the chances are good enough to warrant subjecting such issues to the process of collective negotiation.

The appropriateness of the collective bargaining process for resolving such issues was apparently recognized by the Company. In explaining its decision to contract out the maintenance work, the Company pointed out that in the same plant other unions "had joined hands with management in an effort to bring about an economical and efficient operation," but "we had not been able to attain that in our discussions with this particular Local."

Accordingly, based on past bargaining experience with this union, the Company unilaterally contracted out the work. While "the Act does not encourage a party to engage in fruitless marathon discussions at the expense of frank statement and support of his position," National Labor Relations Board v. American Nat. Ins. Co., 343 U.S. 395, 404, 72 S.Ct. 824, 829, it at least demands that the issue be submitted to the mediatory influence of collective negotiations. As the Court of Appeals pointed out, "[i]t is not necessary that it be likely or probable that the union will yield or supply a feasible solution but rather that the union be afforded an opportunity to meet management's legitimate complaints that its maintenance was unduly costly."

We are thus not expanding the scope of mandatory bargaining to hold, as we do now, that the type of "contracting out" involved in this case—the replacement of employees in the existing bargaining unit with those of an independent contractor to do the same work under similar conditions of employment—is a statutory subject of collective bargaining under § 8(d). Our decision need not and does not encompass other forms of "contracting out" or "subcontracting" which arise daily in our complex economy.

II.

The only question remaining is whether, upon a finding that the Company had refused to bargain about a matter which is a statutory subject of collective bargaining, the Board was empowered to order the resumption of maintenance operations and reinstatement with back pay. We believe that it was so empowered.

Section 10(c) * * * "charges the Board with the task of devising remedies to effectuate the policies of the Act." National Labor Relations Board v. Seven-Up Bottling Co., 344 U.S. 344, 346, 73 S.Ct. 287, 289, 97 L.Ed. 377. The Board's power is a broad discretionary one, subject to limited judicial review. Ibid. "[T]he relation of remedy to policy is peculiarly a matter for administrative competence * * *." Phelps Dodge Corp. v. National Labor Relations Board, 313 U.S. 177, 194, 61 S.Ct. 845, 852, 85 L.Ed. 1271. "In fashioning remedies to undo the effects of violations of the Act, the Board must draw on enlightenment gained from experience." National Labor Relations Board v. Seven-Up Bottling Co., 344 U.S. 344, 346, 73 S.Ct. 287, 289. The Board's order will not be disturbed "unless it can be shown that the order is a patent attempt to achieve ends other than those which can fairly be said to effectuate the policies of the Act." Virginia Elec. & Power Co. v. National Labor Relations Board, 319 U.S. 533, 540, 63 S.Ct. 1214, 1218, 87 L.Ed. 1568. Such a showing has not been made in this case.

There has been no showing that the Board's order restoring the status quo ante to insure meaningful bargaining is not well designed to promote the policies of the Act. Nor is there evidence which would justify disturbing the Board's conclusion that the order would not impose an undue or unfair burden on the Company.[10]

10. The Board stated: "We do not believe that requirement [restoring the status quo ante] imposes an undue or unfair burden on Respondent. The record shows that the maintenance operation is still being performed in much the same manner as it was prior to the subcontracting arrangement. Respondent has a continuing need for the services of maintenance employees; and Respondent's subcon-

It is argued, nonetheless, that the award exceeds the Board's powers under § 10(c) in that it infringes the provision that "[n]o order of the Board shall require the reinstatement of any individual as an employee who has been suspended or discharged, or the payment to him of any back pay, if such individual was suspended or discharged for cause. * * *" The legislative history of that provision indicates that it was designed to preclude the Board from reinstating an individual who had been discharged because of misconduct. There is no indication, however, that it was designed to curtail the Board's power in fashioning remedies when the loss of employment stems directly from an unfair labor practice as in the case at hand.

The judgment of the Court of Appeals is affirmed.

MR. JUSTICE GOLDBERG took no part in the consideration or decision of this case.

MR. JUSTICE STEWART, with whom MR. JUSTICE DOUGLAS and MR. JUSTICE HARLAN join, concurring.

Viewed broadly, the question before us stirs large issues. The Court purports to limit its decision to "the facts of this case." But the Court's opinion radiates implications of such disturbing breadth that I am persuaded to file this separate statement of my own views. * * *

* * * The question posed is whether the particular decision sought to be made unilaterally by the employer in this case is a subject of mandatory collective bargaining within the statutory phrase "terms and conditions of employment." That is all the Court decides. The Court most assuredly does not decide that every managerial decision which necessarily terminates an individual's employment is subject to the duty to bargain. Nor does the Court decide that subcontracting decisions are as a general matter subject to that duty. The Court holds no more than that this employer's decision to subcontract this work, involving "the replacement of employees in the existing bargaining unit with those of an independent contractor to do the same work under similar conditions of employment," is subject to the duty to bargain collectively. Within the narrow limitations implicit in the specific facts of this case, I agree with the Court's decision.

Fibreboard had performed its maintenance work at its Emeryville manufacturing plant through its own employees, who were represented by a local of the United Steelworkers. Estimating that some $225,000 could be saved annually by dispensing with internal maintenance, the company contracted out this work, informing the union that there would be no point in negotiating a new contract since the employees in the bargaining unit had been replaced by employees of the independent contractor, Fluor. Maintenance work continued to be performed within the plant, with the work ultimately supervised by the company's officials and "functioning as an integral part" of the company. Fluor was paid the cost of operations plus $2,250 monthly. The savings in costs anticipated from the arrangement derived largely from the elimination of fringe benefits, adjustments in work scheduling, enforcement of stricter work quotas, and close supervision of the new personnel. Under the cost-plus arrangement, Fibreboard remained responsible for what-

tract is terminable at any time upon 60 days' notice." 138 N.L.R.B., at 555, n. 19.

ever maintenance costs were actually incurred. On these facts, I would agree that the employer had a duty to bargain collectively concerning the replacement of his internal maintenance staff by employees of the independent contractor.   *   *   *

    *   *   * I do not believe that an employer's subcontracting practices are, as a general matter, in themselves conditions of employment. Upon any definition of the statutory terms short of the most expansive, such practices are not conditions—tangible or intangible—of any person's employment. The question remains whether this particular kind of subcontracting decision comes within the employer's duty to bargain. On the facts of this case, I join the Court's judgment, because all that is involved is the substitution of one group of workers for another to perform the same task in the same plant under the ultimate control of the same employer. The question whether the employer may discharge one group of workers and substitute another for them is closely analogous to many other situations within the traditional framework of collective bargaining. Compulsory retirement, layoffs according to seniority, assignment of work among potentially eligible groups within the plant—all involve similar questions of discharge and work assignment, and all have been recognized as subjects of compulsory collective bargaining.

Analytically, this case is not far from that which would be presented if the employer had merely discharged all its employees and replaced them with other workers willing to work on the same job in the same plant without the various fringe benefits so costly to the company. While such a situation might well be considered a § 8(a)(3) violation upon a finding that the employer discriminated against the discharged employees because of their union affiliation, it would be equally possible to regard the employer's action as a unilateral act frustrating negotiation on the underlying questions of work scheduling and remuneration, and so an evasion of its duty to bargain on these questions, which are concededly subject to compulsory collective bargaining. Similarly, had the employer in this case chosen to bargain with the union about the proposed subcontract, negotiations would have inevitably turned to the underlying questions of cost, which prompted the subcontracting. Insofar as the employer frustrated collective bargaining with respect to these concededly bargaining issues by its unilateral act of subcontracting this work, it can properly be found to have violated its statutory duty under § 8(a)(5).

This kind of subcontracting falls short of such larger entrepreneurial questions as what shall be produced, how capital shall be invested in fixed assets, or what the basic scope of the enterprise shall be. In my view, the Court's decision in this case has nothing to do with whether any aspects of those larger issues could under any circumstances be considered subjects of compulsory collective bargaining under the present law.

I am fully aware that in this era of automation and onrushing technological change, no problems in the domestic economy are of greater concern than those involving job security and employment stability. Because of the potentially cruel impact upon the lives and fortunes of the working men and women of the Nation, these problems have understandably engaged the solicitous attention of government, of responsible private business, and particularly of organized labor. It is possible that in meeting these problems

Congress may eventually decide to give organized labor or government a far heavier hand in controlling what until now have been considered the prerogatives of private business management. That path would mark a sharp departure from the traditional principles of a free enterprise economy. Whether we should follow it is, within constitutional limitations, for Congress to choose. But it is a path which Congress certainly did not choose when it enacted the Taft-Hartley Act.

Note

1. Fibreboard holds that the *termination* of employment in the bargaining unit is a "condition of employment" and therefore a mandatory subject for bargaining. How far can this be carried? Are the pension and health-care benefits of *previously retired* employees also conditions of employment and therefore mandatory subjects? This was the issue posed in Allied Chemical Workers v. Pittsburgh Plate Glass Co., 404 U.S. 157, 92 S.Ct. 383, 30 L.Ed.2d 341 (1971). The employer made unilateral changes in the retirees' portion of a health insurance program contained in an existing collective bargaining agreement. The union filed an 8(a)(5) charge. The Court held for the employer on the grounds (1) that retired employees are not "employees" within the meaning of Section 2(3), and (2) that, accordingly, the terms of such retirees' retirement benefits, though permissible subjects of bargaining, are not mandatory.

2. Suppose Fibreboard and the union representing its maintenance workers had bargained to impasse with regard to renewal of the collective bargaining agreement, that thereupon, the union had called a strike, and that, thereafter, Fibreboard had, without prior discussion with the union, contracted out the maintenance work to Fluor. Would Fibreboard be guilty of an 8(a)(5) violation for failure to bargain over this decision? Or, on the contrary, should this ploy on the part of Fibreboard be deemed a lawful variation of the Mackay doctrine (supra p. 499)? This was the situation presented in Hawaii Meat Co. v. NLRB, 321 F.2d 397 (9th Cir.1963). The Board found a violation of Section 8(a)(5) in the employer's failure to bargain over the decision to contract out the struck work. The Ninth Circuit refused enforcement, stating:

> "An employer is under no duty to offer to bargain, after a strike starts, about a decision to hire replacements for strikers, even on a permanent basis. (See NLRB v. Mackay Radio * * *).

> "We think it no more proper for the Board to intrude upon the decision of the employer, in a strike situation, to keep going by subcontracting, than to intrude upon a decision to replace, permanently, individual strikers. This, we think, is consistent with the philosophy expressed by the Supreme Court in NLRB v. Insurance Agents * * *." 321 F.2d at 400.

The court left open, as not presented, the question of the employer's duty to bargain "about the question of whether, when the strike is over, he will continue the subcontract arrangement." 321 F.2d at 399.

Is Hawaii Meat a sound extension of the Mackay principle? Consistent with Fibreboard? Should a struck employer be permitted to subcontract the struck work for the duration of the strike only?

3. Is Bethlehem Steel consistent with Fibreboard? Should not a union's decision to process a grievance (and also the standards by which that decision is to be made) be deemed as much a mandatory subject of bargaining as an employer's decision to contract out?

What is involved in such analysis is an effort to draw the line between, on the one hand, the areas in which a party should be free to make *unilateral* decisions and, on the other hand, the areas in which decision-making should be *bilateral*. By way of obvious example, should not each party have unilateral control over the selection of its own president? Would *any* value be served by requiring bilateralism as to such decisions? Does the mandatory-voluntary distinction serve a useful function, then, in determining when one party must give notice to the other, and accordant opportunity to demand bargaining, before initiating a change?

FIRST NATIONAL MAINTENANCE CORP. v. NATIONAL LABOR RELATIONS BOARD

Supreme Court of the United States, 1981.
452 U.S. 666, 101 S.Ct. 2573, 69 L.Ed.2d 318.

JUSTICE BLACKMUN delivered the opinion of the Court.

Must an employer, under its duty to bargain in good faith "with respect to wages, hours, and other terms and conditions of employment," §§ 8(d) and 8(a)(5) * * * negotiate with the certified representative of its employees over its decision to close a part of its business? In this case, the National Labor Relations Board (the Board) imposed such a duty on petitioner with respect to its decision to terminate a contract with a customer, and the United States Court of Appeals, although differing over the appropriate rationale, enforced its order.

I

Petitioner, First National Maintenance Corporation (FNM), is a New York corporation engaged in the business of providing housekeeping, cleaning, maintenance, and related services for commercial customers in the New York City area. It supplies each of its customers, at the customer's premises, contracted-for labor force and supervision in return for reimbursement of its labor costs (gross salaries, FICA and FUTA taxes, and insurance) and payment of a set fee. It contracts for and hires personnel separately for each customer, and it does not transfer employees between locations.

During the Spring of 1977, petitioner was performing maintenance work for the Greenpark Care Center, a nursing home in Brooklyn. Its written agreement dated April 28, 1976, with Greenpark specified that Greenpark "shall furnish all tools, equipment [sic], materials, and supplies," and would pay petitioner weekly "the sum of five hundred dollars plus the gross weekly payroll and fringe benefits." App. in No. 79–4167 (CA2), pp. 43, 44. Its weekly fee, however, had been reduced to $250 effective November 1, 1976. Id., at 46. The contract prohibited Greenpark from hiring any of petitioner's employees during the term of the contract and for 90 days thereafter. Id., at 44. Petitioner employed approximately 35 workers in its Greenpark operation.

Petitioner's business relationship with Greenpark, seemingly, was not very remunerative or smooth. In March 1977, Greenpark gave petitioner the 30 days' written notice of cancellation specified by the contract, because of "lack of efficiency." Id., at 52. This cancellation did not become effective, for FNM's work continued after the expiration of that 30-day period. Petitioner, however, became aware that it was losing money at Greenpark. On June 30, by telephone, it asked that its weekly fee be restored at the $500 figure and, on July 6, it informed Greenpark in writing that it would discontinue its operations there on August 1 unless the increase were granted.[2] Id., at 47. By telegram on July 25, petitioner gave final notice of termination. Id., at 48.

While FNM was experiencing these difficulties, District 1199, National Union of Hospital and Health Care Employees, Retail, Wholesale and Department Store Union, AFL–CIO (the union) was conducting an organization campaign among petitioner's Greenpark employees. On March 31, 1977, at a Board-conducted election, a majority of the employees selected the union as their bargaining agent. On July 12, the union's vice president, Edward Wecker, wrote petitioner, notifying it of the certification and of the union's right to bargain, and stating: "We look forward to meeting with you or your representative for that purpose. Please advise when it will be convenient." Id., at 49. Petitioner neither responded nor sought to consult with the union.

On July 28, petitioner notified its Greenpark employees that they would be discharged 3 days later. Wecker immediately telephoned petitioner's secretary-treasurer, Leonard Marsh, to request a delay for the purpose of bargaining. Marsh refused the offer to bargain and told Wecker that the termination of the Greenpark operation was purely a matter of money, and final, and that the 30-days' notice provision of the Greenpark contract made staying on beyond August 1 prohibitively expensive. Id., at 79–81, 83, 85–86, 94. Wecker discussed the matter with Greenpark's management that same day, but was unable to obtain a waiver of the notice provision. Id., at 91–93, 98–99. Greenpark also was unwilling itself to hire the FNM employees because of the contract's 90-day limitation on hiring. Id., at 100–101, 106–107. With nothing but perfunctory further discussion, petitioner on July 31 discontinued its Greenpark operation and discharged the employees. Id., at 110–116.

The union filed an unfair labor practice charge against petitioner, alleging violations of the Act's §§ 8(a)(1) and (5). After a hearing held upon the Regional Director's complaint, the administrative law judge made findings in the union's favor. Relying on Ozark Trailers, Inc., 161 N.L.R.B. 561 (1966), he ruled that petitioner had failed to satisfy its duty to bargain concerning both the decision to terminate the Greenpark contract and the effect of that change upon the unit employees.[4] The judge reasoned:

"That the discharge of a man is a change in his conditions of employment hardly needs comment. In these obvious facts, the law is clear. When an employer's work complement is represented by a union and he wishes to alter the hiring arrangements, be his reason lack of money or a mere desire to become richer, the law is no less clear that he must first talk to the union about it. * * * If Wecker had been given an opportunity to talk, something might have been worked out to transfer these people to other parts of [petitioner's] business. * * * Entirely apart from whether open discussion

2. The record does not disclose how the contract's 30-day written notice provision was satisfied. In any event, the parties make no point of any shortage in the notice.

4. The administrative law judge rejected petitioner's contention that it had satisfied, by that single phone call to [from?] Wecker, its duty to bargain about the termination.

between the parties—with the Union speaking on behalf of the employees as was its right—might have persuaded [petitioner] to find a way of continuing this part of its operations, there was always the possibility that Marsh might have persuaded Greenpark to use these same employees to continue doing its maintenance work, either as direct employees or as later hires by a replacement contractor." 242 N.L.R.B. 462, 465 (1979).

The administrative law judge recommended an order requiring petitioner to bargain in good faith with the union about its decision to terminate its Greenpark service operation and its consequent discharge of the employees, as well as the effects of the termination. He recommended, also, that petitioner be ordered to pay the discharged employees backpay from the date of discharge until the parties bargained to agreement, or the bargaining reached impasse, or the union failed timely to request bargaining, or the union failed to bargain in good faith.

The National Labor Relations Board adopted the administrative law judge's findings without further analysis, and additionally required petitioner, if it agreed to resume its Greenpark operations, to offer the terminated employees reinstatement to their former jobs or substantial equivalents; conversely, if agreement was not reached, petitioner was ordered to offer the employees equivalent positions, to be made available by discharge of subsequently-hired employees, if necessary, at its other operations. Id., at 463.

The United States Court of Appeals for the Second Circuit, with one judge dissenting in part, enforced the Board's order, although it adopted an analysis different from that espoused by the Board. 627 F.2d 596 (1980). The Court of Appeals' reasoned that no *per se* rule could be formulated to govern an employer's decision to close part of its business. Rather, the court said, § 8(d) creates a *presumption* in favor of mandatory bargaining over such a decision, a presumption that is rebuttable "by showing that the purposes of the statute would not be furthered by imposition of a duty to bargain," for example, by demonstrating that "bargaining over the decision would be futile," or that the decision was due to "emergency financial circumstances," or that the "custom of the industry, shown by the absence of such an obligation from typical collective bargaining agreements, is not to bargain over such decisions." Id., at 601–602.

The Court of Appeals' decision in this case appears to be at odds with decisions of other Courts of Appeals, some of which decline to require bargaining over any management decision involving "a major commitment of capital investment" or a "basic operational change" in the scope or direction of an enterprise,[8] and some of which indicate that bargaining is not mandated unless a violation of § 8(a)(3) (a partial closing motivated by antiunion animus) is involved.[9] The Court of Appeals for the Fifth Circuit has imposed a duty to bargain over partial closing decisions. See NLRB v.

8. See, e.g., NLRB v. International Harvester Co., 618 F.2d 85 (CA9 1980); NLRB v. Adams Dairy, Inc., 350 F.2d 108 (CA8 1965), cert. denied, 382 U.S. 1011, 86 S.Ct. 619, 15 L.Ed.2d 526 (1966); NLRB v. Transmarine Navigation Corp., 380 F.2d 933 (CA10 1967); Royal Typewriter Co. v. NLRB, 533 F.2d 1030 (CA8 1976); NLRB v. Rapid Bindery, Inc., 293 F.2d 170 (CA2 1961); NLRB v. Thompson Transport Co., 406 F.2d 698 (CA10 1969).

9. See, e.g., Morrison Cafeterias Consolidated, Inc. v. NLRB, 431 F.2d 254 (CA8 1970); NLRB v. Drapery Mfg. Co., 425 F.2d 1026 (CA8 1970); NLRB v. William J. Burns International Detective Agency, Inc., 346 F.2d 897 (CA8 1965).

Winn-Dixie Stores, Inc., 361 F.2d 512, cert. denied, 385 U.S. 935, 87 S.Ct. 295, 17 L.Ed.2d 215 (1966). The Board itself has not been fully consistent in its rulings applicable to this type of management decision.[10]

Because of the importance of the issue and the continuing disagreement between and among the Board and the Courts of Appeals, we granted certiorari. * * *

II

A fundamental aim of the National Labor Relations Act is the establishment and maintenance of industrial peace to preserve the flow of interstate commerce. NLRB v. Jones & Laughlin Steel Corp., 301 U.S. 1, 57 S.Ct. 615, 81 L.Ed. 893 (1937). Central to achievement of this purpose is the promotion of collective bargaining as a method of defusing and channeling conflict between labor and management. Section 1 of the Act, as amended, 29 U.S.C. § 151. Congress ensured that collective bargaining would go forward by creating the National Labor Relations Board and giving it the power to condemn as unfair labor practices certain conduct by unions and employers that it deemed deleterious to the process, including the refusal "to bargain collectively." §§ 3 and 8, 29 U.S.C. §§ 153 and 158.

Although parties are free to bargain about any legal subject, Congress has limited the mandate or duty to bargain to matters of "wages, hours, and other terms and conditions of employment." * * * Congress deliberately left the words "wages, hours, and other terms and conditions of employment" without further definition, for it did not intend to deprive the Board of power further to define those terms in light of specific industrial practices.

Nonetheless, in establishing what issues must be submitted to the process of bargaining, Congress had no expectation that the elected union representative would become an equal partner in the running of the business enterprise in which the union's members are employed. Despite the deliberate open-endedness of the statutory language, there is an undeniable limit to the subjects about which bargaining must take place * * *.

Some management decisions, such as choice of advertising and promotion, product type and design, and financing arrangements, have only an indirect and attenuated impact on the employment relationship. See *Fibreboard*, 379 U.S., at 223, 85 S.Ct., at 409 (Stewart, J., concurring). Other management decisions, such as the order of succession of layoffs and recalls, production quotas, and work rules, are almost exclusively "an aspect of the relationship" between employer and employee. *Chemical Workers*, 404 U.S.,

10. Compare National Car Rental System, Inc., 252 N.L.R.B. No. 27, p. 15 (1980) (employer's decision to terminate car leasing operations at one location not a mandatory subject because " 'essentially financial and managerial in nature,' involving a 'significant investment or withdrawal of capital, affecting the scope and ultimate direction of an enterprise,' " quoting from General Motors Corp., GMC Truck & Coach Div., 191 N.L.R.B., at 952), and Summit Tooling Co., 195 N.L.R.B. 479, 480 (1972) (decision to close a subsidiary not a mandatory subject because "its practical effect was to take the Respondent out of the business of manufacturing tool and tooling products"), with Ozark Trailers, Inc., 161 N.L.R.B. 561, 567, 568 (1966) (employer's decision to shut down one of multiple plants was a mandatory subject because it was "a decision directly affecting terms and conditions of employment" and "interests of employees are of sufficient importance that their representatives ought to be consulted in matters affecting them"). See also Kingwood Mining Co., 210 N.L.R.B. 844 (1974), aff'd, sub nom. United Mine Workers v. NLRB, 169 U.S.App.D.C. 301, 515 F.2d 1018 (1975).

at 178, 92 S.Ct., at 397. The present case concerns a third type of management decision, one that had a direct impact on employment, since jobs were inexorably eliminated by the termination, but had as its focus only the economic profitability of the contract with Greenpark, a concern under these facts wholly apart from the employment relationship. This decision, involving a change in the scope and direction of the enterprise, is akin to the decision whether to be in business at all, "not in [itself] primarily about conditions of employment, though the effect of the decision may be necessarily to terminate employment." *Fibreboard*, 379 U.S., at 223, 85 S.Ct., at 409 (Stewart, J., concurring). Cf. Textile Workers v. Darlington Co., 380 U.S. 263, 268, 85 S.Ct. 994, 998, 13 L.Ed.2d 827 (1965) ("an employer has the absolute right to terminate his entire business for any reason he pleases"). At the same time, this decision touches on a matter of central and pressing concern to the union and its member employees: the possibility of continued employment and the retention of the employees' very jobs. See Brockway Motor Trucks, Etc. v. NLRB, 582 F.2d 720, 735–736 (CA3 1978); Ozark Trailers, Inc., 161 N.L.R.B. 561, 566–568 (1966).

Petitioner contends it had no duty to bargain about its decision to terminate its operations at Greenpark. This contention requires that we determine whether the decision itself should be considered part of petitioner's retained freedom to manage its affairs unrelated to employment.[15] The aim of labeling a matter a mandatory subject of bargaining, rather than simply permitting, but not requiring, bargaining, is to "promote the fundamental purpose of the Act by bringing a problem of vital concern to labor and management within the framework established by Congress as most conducive to industrial peace," *Fibreboard*, 379 U.S., at 211, 85 S.Ct., at 403. The concept of mandatory bargaining is premised on the belief that collective discussions backed by the parties' economic weapons will result in decisions that are better for both management and labor and for society as a whole. * * * This will be true, however, only if the subject proposed for discussion is amenable to resolution through the bargaining process. Management must be free from the constraints of the bargaining process to the extent essential for the running of a profitable business. It also must have some degree of certainty beforehand as to when it may proceed to reach decisions without fear of later evaluations labeling its conduct an unfair labor practice. Congress did not explicitly state what issues of mutual concern to union and management it intended to exclude from mandatory bargaining. Nonetheless, in view of an employer's need for unencumbered decisionmaking, bargaining over management decisions that have a substantial impact on the continued availability of employment should be required only if the benefit, for labor-management relations and the collective bargaining process, outweighs the burden placed on the conduct of the business.

The Court in *Fibreboard* implicitly engaged in this analysis with regard to decision to subcontract for maintenance work previously done by unit employees. Holding the employer's decision a subject of mandatory bargain-

---

15. There is no doubt that petitioner was under a duty to bargain about the results or effects of its decision to stop the work at Greenpark, or that it violated that duty. Peti-tioner consented to enforcement of the Board's order concerning bargaining over the effects of the closing and has reached agreement with the union on severance pay. * * *

ing, the Court relied not only on the "literal meaning" of the statutory words, but also reasoned:

> "The Company's decision to contract out the maintenance work did not alter the Company's basic operation. The maintenance work still had to be performed in the plant. No capital investment was contemplated; the Company merely replaced existing employees with those of an independent contractor to do the same work under similar conditions of employment. Therefore, to require the employer to bargain about the matter would not significantly abridge his freedom to manage the business." 379 U.S., at 213, 85 S.Ct., at 404.

The Court also emphasized that a desire to reduce labor costs, which it considered a matter "peculiarly suitable for resolution within the collective bargaining framework," id., at 214, 85 S.Ct., at 404, was at the base of the employer's decision to subcontract:

> "It was induced to contract out the work by assurances from independent contractors that economies could be derived by reducing the work force, decreasing fringe benefits, and eliminating overtime payments. These have long been regarded as matters peculiarly suitable for resolution within the collective bargaining framework, and industrial experience demonstrates that collective negotiation has been highly successful in achieving peaceful accommodation of the conflicting interests." Id., at 213–214, 85 S.Ct., at 404.

The prevalence of bargaining over "contracting out" as a matter of industrial practice generally was taken as further proof of the "amenability of such subjects to the collective bargaining process." Id., at 211, 85 S.Ct., at 403.

With this approach in mind, we turn to the specific issue at hand: an economically-motivated decision to shut down part of a business.

III

A

Both union and management regard control of the decision to shut down an operation with the utmost seriousness. As has been noted, however, the Act is not intended to serve either party's individual interest, but to foster in a neutral manner a system in which the conflict between these interests may be resolved. It seems particularly important, therefore, to consider whether requiring bargaining over this sort of decision will advance the neutral purposes of the Act.

A union's interest in participating in the decision to close a particular facility or part of an employer's operations springs from its legitimate concern over job security. The Court has observed: "The words of [§ 8(d)] * * * plainly cover termination of employment which * * * necessarily results" from closing an operation. *Fibreboard*, 379 U.S., at 210, 85 S.Ct., at 402. The union's practical purpose in participating, however, will be largely uniform: it will seek to delay or halt the closing. No doubt it will be impelled, in seeking these ends, to offer concessions, information, and alternatives that might be helpful to management or forestall or prevent the termination of jobs. It is unlikely, however, that requiring bargaining over the decision itself, as well as its effects, will augment this flow of information and suggestions. There is no dispute that the union must be given a significant opportunity to bargain about these matters of job security as part of the "effects" bargaining mandated by § 8(a)(5). See, e.g., NLRB v. Royal Plating & Polishing Co., 350 F.2d 191, 196 (CA3 1965); NLRB v. Adams Dairy, Inc., 350 F.2d 108 (CA8 1965), cert. denied, 382 U.S. 1011, 86 S.Ct. 619, 15 L.Ed.2d 256 (1966). And, under § 8(a)(5), bargaining over the effects of a decision must be conducted in a meaningful manner and at a meaningful time, and the Board may impose sanctions to insure its adequacy. A union, by pursuing such bargaining rights, may achieve valuable concessions from an employer engaged in a partial closing. It also may secure in contract negotiations provisions implementing rights to notice, information, and fair bargaining. See BNA, Basic Patterns in Union Contracts 62–64 (9th ed., 1979).

Moreover, the union's legitimate interest in fair dealing is protected by § 8(a)(3), which prohibits partial closing motivated by anti-union animus, when done to gain an unfair advantage. Textile Workers v. Darlington Co., 380 U.S. 263, 85 S.Ct. 994, 13 L.Ed.2d 827 (1965). Under § 8(a)(3) the Board may inquire into the motivations behind a partial closing. An employer may not simply shut down part of its business and mask its desire to weaken and circumvent the union by labeling its decision "purely economic."

Thus, although the union has a natural concern that a partial closing decision not be hastily or unnecessarily entered into, it has some control over the effects of the decision and indirectly may ensure that the decision itself is deliberately considered. It also has direct protection against a partial closing decision that is motivated by an intent to harm a union.

Management's interest in whether it should discuss a decision of this kind is much more complex and varies with the particular circumstances. If labor costs are an important factor in a failing operation and the decision to close, management will have an incentive to confer voluntarily with the union to seek concessions that may make continuing the business profitable. Cf. U.S. News & World Report, Feb. 9, 1981, p. 74; BNA, Labor Relations Yearbook–1979, p. 5 (UAW agreement with Chrysler Corp. to make concessions on wages and fringe benefits). At other times, management may have great need for speed, flexibility, and secrecy in meeting business opportunities and exigencies. It may face significant tax or securities consequences that hinge on confidentiality, the timing of a plant closing, or a reorganization of the corporate structure. The publicity incident to the normal process of bargaining may injure the possibility of a successful transition or increase the economic damage to the business. The employer also may have no feasible alternative to the closing, and even good-faith bargaining over it may be both futile and cause the employer additional loss.

There is an important difference, also, between permitted bargaining and mandated bargaining. Labeling this type of decision mandatory could afford a union a powerful tool for achieving delay, a power that might be used to thwart management's intentions in a manner unrelated to any feasible solution the union might propose. See Comment, "Partial Terminations"—A Choice between Bargaining Equality and Economic Efficiency, 14 U.C.L.A.L.Rev. 1089, 1103–1105 (1967). In addition, many of the cases before the Board have involved, as this one did, not simply a refusal to bargain over the decision, but a refusal to bargain at all, often coupled with other unfair labor practices. See, e.g., Electrical Products Div. of Midland-

Ross Corp. v. NLRB, 617 F.2d 977 (CA3 1980), cert. denied, 449 U.S. 871, 101 S.Ct. 210, 66 L.Ed.2d 91 (1981); NLRB v. Amoco Chemicals Corp., 529 F.2d 427 (CA5 1976); Royal Typewriter Co. v. NLRB, 533 F.2d 1030 (CA8 1976); NLRB v. American Mfg. Co., 351 F.2d 74 (CA5 1965) (subcontracting); Smyth Mfg. Co., 247 N.L.R.B. No. 164 (1980). In these cases, the employer's action gave the Board reason to order remedial relief apart from access to the decisionmaking process. It is not clear that a union would be equally dissatisfied if an employer performed all its bargaining obligations apart from the additional remedy sought here.

While evidence of current labor practice is only an indication of what is feasible through collective bargaining, and not a binding guide, see *Chemical Workers,* 404 U.S., at 176, 92 S.Ct., at 396, that evidence supports the apparent imbalance weighing against mandatory bargaining. We note that provisions giving unions a right to participate in the decisionmaking process concerning alteration of the scope of an enterprise appear to be relatively rare. Provisions concerning notice and "effects" bargaining are more prevalent. See II BNA, Collective Bargaining Negotiations and Contracts § 65:201–233 (1981); U.S. Dept. of Labor, Bureau of Labor Statistics, Bull. 2065, Characteristics of Major Collective Bargaining Agreements, January 1, 1978, pp. 96, 100, 101, 102–103 (charting provisions giving interplant transfer and relocation allowances; advance notice of layoffs, shutdowns, and technological changes; and wage-employment guarantees; no separate tables on decision-bargaining, presumably due to rarity). See also U.S. Dept. of Labor, Bull. No. 1425–10, Major Collective Bargaining Agreements, Plant Movement, Transfer, and Relocation Allowances (July 1969).

Further, the presumption analysis adopted by the Court of Appeals seems ill-suited to advance harmonious relations between employer and employee. An employer would have difficulty determining beforehand whether it was faced with a situation requiring bargaining or one that involved economic necessity sufficiently compelling to obviate the duty to bargain. If it should decide to risk not bargaining, it might be faced ultimately with harsh remedies forcing it to pay large amounts of backpay to employees who likely would have been discharged regardless of bargaining, or even to consider reopening a failing operation. See e.g., Electrical Products Div. of Midland-Ross Corp., 239 N.L.R.B. 323 (1978), enf'd, 617 F.2d 977 (CA3 1980), cert. denied, 449 U.S. 871, 101 S.Ct. 210, 66 L.Ed.2d 91 (1981). Cf. Lever Brothers Co. v. International Chemical Workers Union, 554 F.2d 115 (CA4 1976) (enjoining plant closure and transfer to permit negotiations). Also, labor costs may not be a crucial circumstance in a particular economically-based partial termination. See e.g., NLRB v. International Harvester Co., 618 F.2d 85 (CA9 1980) (change in marketing structure); NLRB v. Thompson Transport Co., 406 F.2d 698 (CA10 1969) (loss of major customer). And in those cases, the Board's traditional remedies may well be futile. See ABC Trans-National Transport, Inc. v. NLRB, 642 F.2d 675 (CA3 1981) (although employer violated its "duty" to bargain about freight terminal closing, court refused to enforce order to bargain). If the employer intended to try to fulfill a court's direction to bargain, it would have difficulty determining exactly at what stage of its deliberations the duty to bargain would arise and what amount of bargaining would suffice before it could implement its decision. Compare Burns Ford, Inc., 182 N.L.

R.B. 753 (1970) (one week's notice of layoffs sufficient), and Hartmann Luggage Co., 145 N.L.R.B. 1572 (1964) (entering into executory subcontracting agreement before notifying union not a violation since contract not yet final), with Royal Plating & Polishing Co., 148 N.L.R.B. 545, 555 (1964), enf. denied, 350 F.2d 191 (CA3 1965) (two weeks' notice before final closing of plant inadequate). If an employer engaged in some discussion, but did not yield to the union's demands, the Board might conclude that the employer had engaged in "surface bargaining," a violation of its good faith. See NLRB v. Reed & Prince Mfg. Co., 205 F.2d 131 (CA1), cert. denied, 346 U.S. 887, 74 S.Ct. 139, 98 L.Ed. 391 (1953). A union, too, would have difficulty determining the limits of its prerogatives, whether and when it could use its economic powers to try to alter an employer's decision, or whether, in doing so, it would trigger sanctions from the Board. See, e.g., International Offset Corp., 210 N.L.R.B. 854 (1974) (union's failure to realize that shutdown was imminent, in view of successive advertisements, sales of equipment, and layoffs, held a waiver of right to bargain); Shell Oil Co., 149 N.L.R.B. 305 (1965) (union waived its right to bargain by failing to request meetings when employer announced intent to transfer a few days before implementation).

We conclude that the harm likely to be done to an employer's need to operate freely in deciding whether to shut down part of its business purely for economic reasons outweighs the incremental benefit that might be gained through the union's participation in making the decision,[22] and we hold that the decision itself is not part of § 8(d)'s "terms and conditions" * * * over which Congress has mandated bargaining.

B

In order to illustrate the limits of our holding, we turn again to the specific facts of this case. First, we note that when petitioner decided to terminate its Greenpark contract, it had no intention to replace the discharged employees or to move that operation elsewhere. Petitioner's sole purpose was to reduce its economic loss, and the union made no claim of anti-union animus. In addition, petitioner's dispute with Greenpark was solely over the size of the management fee Greenpark was willing to pay. The union had no control or authority over that fee. The most that the union could have offered would have been advice and concessions that Greenpark, the third party upon whom rested the success or failure of the contract, had no duty even to consider. These facts in particular distinguish this case from the subcontracting issue presented in Fibreboard. Further, the union was not selected as the bargaining representative or certified until well after petitioner's economic difficulties at Greenpark had begun. We thus are not faced with an employer's abrogation of ongoing negotiations or

---

22. In this opinion we of course intimate no view as to other types of management decisions, such as plant relocations, sales, other kinds of subcontracting, automation, etc., which are to be considered on their particular facts. See, e.g., International Ladies' Garment Workers Union v. NLRB, 150 U.S.App. D.C. 71, 463 F.2d 907 (1972) (plant relocation predominantly due to labor costs); Weltronic Co. v. NLRB, 419 F.2d 1120 (CA6 1969), cert. denied, 398 U.S. 938, 90 S.Ct. 1841, 26 L.Ed.2d 270 (1970) (decision to move plant three miles); Dan Dee West Virginia Corp., 180 N.L.R.B. 534 (1970) (decision to change method of distribution, under which employee-drivers became independent contractors); Young Motor Truck Service, Inc., 156 N.L.R.B. 661 (1966) (decision to sell major portion of business). See also Schwarz, Plant Relocation or Partial Termination—The Duty to Decision-Bargain, 39 Ford.L.Rev. 8–1, 100–102, (1970).

an existing bargaining agreement. Finally, while petitioner's business enterprise did not involve the investment of large amounts of capital in single locations, we do not believe that the absence of "significant investment or withdrawal of capital," General Motors Corp., GMC Truck & Coach Div., 191 N.L.R.B. at 952, is crucial. The decision to halt work at this specific location represented a significant change in petitioner's operations, a change not unlike opening a new line of business or going out of business entirely.

The judgment of the Court of Appeals, accordingly, is reversed and the case is remanded to that court for further proceedings consistent with this opinion.

It is so ordered.

JUSTICE BRENNAN, with whom JUSTICE MARSHALL joins, dissenting.

*   *   * In the exercise of its congressionally-delegated authority and accumulated expertise, the Board has determined that an employer's decision to close part of its operations affects the "terms and conditions of employment" within the meaning of the Act, and is thus a mandatory subject for collective bargaining. Ozark Trailers, Inc., 161 N.L.R.B. 561 (1966). Nonetheless, the Court today declines to defer to the Board's decision on this sensitive question of industrial relations, and on the basis of pure speculation reverses the judgment of the Board and of the Court of Appeals. I respectfully dissent.

The Court bases its decision on a balancing test. It states that "bargaining over management decisions that have a substantial impact on the continued availability of employment should be required only if the benefit, for labor-management relations and the collective-bargaining process, outweighs the burden placed on the conduct of the business." *   *   * I cannot agree with this test, because it takes into account only the interests of *management;* it fails to consider the legitimate employment interests of the workers and their Union. Cf. Brockway Motor Trucks v. NLRB, 582 F.2d 720, 734–740 (CA3 1978) (balancing of interests of workers in retaining their jobs against interests of employers in maintaining unhindered control over corporate direction). This one-sided approach hardly serves "to foster in a neutral manner" a system for resolution of these serious, two-sided controversies. *   *   *

Even if the Court's statement of the test were accurate, I could not join in its application, which is based solely on speculation. Apparently, the Court concludes that the benefit to labor-management relations and the collective-bargaining process from negotiation over partial closings is minimal, but it provides no evidence to that effect. The Court acknowledges that the Union might be able to offer concessions, information, and alternatives that might obviate or forestall the closing, but it then asserts that "[i]t is unlikely, however, that requiring bargaining over the decision *   *   * will augment this flow of information and suggestions." *   *   * Recent experience, however, suggests the contrary. Most conspicuous, perhaps, were the negotiations between Chrysler Corporation and the United Auto Workers, which led to significant adjustments in compensation and benefits, contributing to Chrysler's ability to remain afloat. See Wall St. Journal, Oct. 26, 1979, at 3, col. 1. Even where labor costs are not the direct cause of a company's financial difficulties, employee concessions can often enable the company to continue in operation—if the employees have the opportunity to offer such concessions.*

The Court further presumes that management's need for "speed, flexibility, and secrecy" in making partial closing decisions would be frustrated by a requirement to bargain. * * * In some cases the Court might be correct. In others, however, the decision will be made openly and deliberately, and considerations of "speed, flexibility, and secrecy" will be inapposite. Indeed, in view of management's admitted duty to bargain over the effects of a closing, see ante, n. 15, it is difficult to understand why additional bargaining over the closing itself would necessarily unduly delay or publicize the decision.

I am not in a position to judge whether mandatory bargaining over partial closings *in all cases* is consistent with our national labor policy, and neither is the Court. The primary responsibility to determine the scope of the statutory duty to bargain has been entrusted to the NLRB, which should not be reversed by the courts merely because they might prefer another view of the statute. Ford Motor Co. v. NLRB, 441 U.S. 488, 495–497, 99 S.Ct. 1842, 1848–1849, 60 L.Ed.2d 420 (1979); see NLRB v. Erie Resistor Corp., 373 U.S. 221, 236, 83 S.Ct. 1139, 1149, 10 L.Ed.2d 308 (1963). I therefore agree with the Court of Appeals that employers presumptively have a duty to bargain over a decision to close an operation, and that this presumption can be rebutted by a showing that bargaining would be futile, that the closing was due to emergency financial circumstances, or that, for some other reason, bargaining would not further the purposes of the National Labor Relations Act. 627 F.2d 596, 601 (CA2 1980). I believe that this approach is amply supported by recent decisions of the Board. E.g., Brooks-Scanlon, Inc., 246 N.L.R.B. No. 76, 102 L.R.R.M. 1606 (1979); Raskin Packing Co., 246 N.L.R.B. No. 15, 102 L.R.R.M. 1489 (1979); M. & M. Transportation Co., 239 N.L.R.B. 73 (1978). With respect to the individual facts of this case, however, I would vacate the judgment of the Court of Appeals, and remand to the Board for further examination of the evidence. See SEC v. Chenery Corp., 318 U.S. 80, 94–95, 63 S.Ct. 454, 462, 87 L.Ed. 626 (1943).

Note

What is the holding of First National Maintenance? Put otherwise, where does it draw the line between issues properly the subject of the bilateral decision-making of collective bargaining and issues wisely left to unilateral entrepreneurial control? Where would *you* draw the line?

For a discussion of the scope-of-bargaining problems generated by Fibreboard and its progeny, see Rabin, Fibreboard and the Termination of Bargaining Unit Work: The Search for Standards in Defining the Scope of the Duty to Bargain, 71 Colum. L. Rev. 803 (1971); Rabin, Limitations on Employer Independent Action, 27 Vand. L. Rev. 133 (1974); Swift, Plant Relocation:

---

* Indeed, in this case, the Court of Appeals found: "On the record, * * * there is sufficient reason to believe that, given the opportunity, the union might have made concessions, by accepting reduction in wages or benefits (take-backs) or a reduction in the work force, which would in part or in whole have enabled Greenpark to give FNM an increased management fee. At least, if FNM had bargained over its decision to close, that possibility would have been tested, and management would still have been free to close the Greenpark operation if bargaining did not produce a solution." 627 F.2d 596, 602 (CA2 1980).

Catching Up With the Runaway Shop, 14 B.C. Indus.&Com. L. Rev. 1135 (1973); Heinsz, The Partial-Closing Conundrum: The Duty of Employers and Unions to Bargain in Good Faith, 1981 Duke L.J. 71; Harper, Leveling the Road from Borg-Warner to First National Maintenance: The Scope of Mandatory Bargaining, 68 Va. L. Rev. 1447 (1982); George, To Bargain or Not to Bargain: A New Chapter in Work Relocation Decisions, 69 Minn. L. Rev. 667 (1985).

NATIONAL LABOR RELATIONS BOARD v. TRUITT MANUFACTURING CO.

Supreme Court of the United States, 1956.
351 U.S. 149, 76 S.Ct. 753, 100 L.Ed. 1027.

MR. JUSTICE BLACK delivered the opinion of the Court.

* * * The question presented by this case is whether the National Labor Relations Board may find that an employer has not bargained in good faith where the employer claims it cannot afford to pay higher wages but refuses requests to produce information substantiating its claim.

The dispute here arose when a union representing certain of respondent's employees asked for a wage increase of 10 cents per hour. The company answered that it could not afford to pay such an increase, it was undercapitalized, had never paid dividends, and that an increase of more than 2½ cents per hour would put it out of business. The union asked the company to produce some evidence substantiating these statements, requesting permission to have a certified public accountant examine the company's books, financial data, etc. This request being denied, the union asked that the company submit "full and complete information with respect to its financial standing and profits," insisting that such information was pertinent and essential for the employees to determine whether or not they should continue to press their demand for a wage increase. A union official testified before the trial examiner that "[W]e were wanting anything relating to the Company's position, any records or what have you, books, accounting sheets, cost expenditures, what not, anything to back the Company's position that they were unable to give any more money." The company refused all the requests, relying solely on the statement that "the information * * * is not pertinent to this discussion and the company declines to give you such information; You have no legal right to such."

On the basis of these facts the National Labor Relations Board found that the company had "failed to bargain in good faith with respect to wages in violation of Section 8(a)(5) of the Act." 110 N.L.R.B. 856. The Board ordered the company to supply the union with such information as would "substantiate the Respondent's position of its economic inability to pay the requested wage increase." The Court of Appeals refused to enforce the Board's order, agreeing with respondent that it could not be held guilty of an unfair labor practice because of its refusal to furnish the information requested by the union. 4 Cir., 224 F.2d 869. In National Labor Relations Board v. Jacobs Mfg. Co., 196 F.2d 680, the Second Circuit upheld a Board finding of bad-faith bargaining based on an employer's refusal to supply financial information under circumstances similar to those here. Because of the conflict and the importance of the question we granted certiorari.
* * *

The company raised no objection to the Board's order on the ground that the scope of information required was too broad or that disclosure would put an undue burden on the company. Its major argument throughout has been that the information requested was irrelevant to the bargaining process and related to matters exclusively within the province of management. Thus we lay to one side the suggestion by the company here that the Board's order might be unduly burdensome or injurious to its business. In any event, the Board has heretofore taken the position in cases such as this that "It is sufficient if the information is made available in a manner not so burdensome or time-consuming as to impede the process of bargaining." And in this case the Board has held substantiation of the company's position requires no more than "reasonable proof."

We think that in determining whether the obligation of good-faith bargaining has been met the Board has a right to consider an employer's refusal to give information about its financial status. While Congress did not compel agreement between employers and bargaining representatives, it did require collective bargaining in the hope that agreements would result. Section 204(a)(1) of the Act admonishes both employers and employees to "exert every reasonable effort to make and maintain agreements concerning rates of pay, hours, and working conditions * * *." In their effort to reach an agreement here both the union and the company treated the company's ability to pay increased wages as highly relevant. The ability of an employer to increase wages without injury to his business is a commonly considered factor in wage negotiations. Claims for increased wages have sometimes been abandoned because of an employer's unsatisfactory business condition; employees have even voted to accept wage decreases because of such conditions.

Good-faith bargaining necessarily requires that claims made by either bargainer should be honest claims. This is true about an asserted inability to pay an increase in wages. If such an argument is important enough to present in the give and take of bargaining, it is important enough to require some sort of proof of its accuracy. And it would certainly not be farfetched for a trier of fact to reach the conclusion that bargaining lacks good faith when an employer mechanically repeats a claim of inability to pay without making the slightest effort to substantiate the claim. Such has been the holding of the Labor Board since shortly after the passage of the Wagner Act. In Pioneer Pearl Button Co., decided in 1936, where the employer's representative relied on the company's asserted "poor financial condition," the Board said: "He did no more than take refuge in the assertion that the respondent's financial condition was poor; he refused either to prove his statement, or to permit independent verification. This is not collective bargaining." 1 N.L.R.B. 837, 842–843. This was the position of the Board when the Taft-Hartley Act was passed in 1947 and has been its position ever since. We agree with the Board that a refusal to attempt to substantiate a claim of inability to pay increased wages may support a finding of a failure to bargain in good faith.

The Board concluded that under the facts and circumstances of this case the respondent was guilty of an unfair labor practice in failing to bargain in good faith. We see no reason to disturb the findings of the Board. We do not hold, however, that in every case in which economic inability is raised as an argument against increased wages it automatically follows that the employees are entitled to substantiating evidence. Each case must turn upon its particular facts. The inquiry must always be whether or not under the circumstances of the particular case the statutory obligation to bargain in good faith has been met. Since we conclude that there is support in the record for the conclusion of the Board here that respondent did not bargain in good faith, it was error for the Court of Appeals to set aside the Board's order and deny enforcement.

Reversed.

MR. JUSTICE FRANKFURTER, whom MR. JUSTICE CLARK and MR. JUSTICE HARLAN join, concurring in part and dissenting in part. * * *

[The Act] obligate[s] the parties to make an honest effort to come to terms; they are required to try to reach an agreement in good faith. "Good faith" means more than merely going through the motions of negotiating; it is inconsistent with a predetermined resolve not to budge from an initial position. But it is not necessarily incompatible with stubbornness or even with what to an outsider may seem unreasonableness. A determination of good faith or of want of good faith normally can rest only on an inference based upon more or less persuasive manifestations of another's state of mind. The previous relations of the parties, antecedent events explaining behavior at the bargaining table, and the course of negotiations constitute the raw facts for reaching such a determination. The appropriate inferences to be drawn from what is often confused and tangled testimony about all this makes a finding of absence of good faith one for the judgment of the Labor Board, unless the record as a whole leaves such judgment without reasonable foundation. See Universal Camera Corp. v. National Labor Relations Board, 340 U.S. 474, 71 S.Ct. 456, 95 L.Ed. 456.

An examination of the Board's opinion and the position taken by its counsel here disclose that the Board did not so conceive the issue of good-faith bargaining in this case. The totality of the conduct of the negotiation was apparently deemed irrelevant to the question; one fact alone disposed of the case. "[I]t is settled law [the Board concluded], that when an employer seeks to justify the refusal of a wage increase upon an economic basis, as did the Respondent herein, good-faith bargaining under the Act requires that upon request the employer attempt to substantiate its economic position by reasonable proof." 110 N.L.R.B. 856.

This is to make a rule of law out of one item—even if a weighty item—of the evidence. * * *

The Labor Board itself has not always approached "good faith" and the disclosure question in such a mechanical fashion. In Southern Saddlery Co., 90 N.L.R.B. 1205, the Board also found that § 8(a)(5) had been violated. But how differently the Board there considered its function.

"Bargaining in good faith is a duty on both sides to enter into discussions with an open and fair mind and a sincere purpose to find a basis for agreement touching wages and hours and conditions of labor. In applying this definition of good faith bargaining to any situation, the Board examines the Respondent's conduct as a whole for a clear indication as to whether the latter has refused to bargain in good faith, and the Board usually does not rely upon any one factor as conclusive evidence that the Respondent did not genuinely try to reach an agreement." 90 N.L.R.B. 1205, 1206.

The Board found other factors in the Southern Saddlery case. The employer had made no counter-proposals or efforts to "compromise the controversy." Compare, McLean-Arkansas Lumber Co., Inc., 109 N.L.R.B. 1022. Such specific evidence is not indispensable, for a study of all the evidence in a record may disclose a mood indicative of a determination not to bargain. That is for the Board to decide. It is a process of inference-drawing, however, very different from the *ultra vires* law-making of the Board in this case.

Since the Board applied the wrong standard here, by ruling that Truitt's failure to supply financial information to the union constituted *per se* a refusal to bargain in good faith, the case should be returned to the Board. There is substantial evidence in the record which indicates that Truitt tried to reach an agreement. It offered a 2½ cent wage increase, it expressed willingness to discuss with the union "at any time the problem of how our wages compare with those of our competition," and it continued throughout to meet and discuss the controversy with the union.

Because the record is not conclusive as a matter of law, one way or the other, I cannot join in the Court's disposition of the case. To reverse the Court of Appeals without remanding the case to the Board for further proceedings, implies that the Board would have reached the same conclusion in applying the right rule of law that it did in applying a wrong one. I cannot make such a forecast. I would return the case to the Board so that it may apply the relevant standard for determining "good faith."

Note

1. What, precisely, is the holding in the Truitt case? Why does Justice Frankfurter charge the Board with "*ultra vires* law-making"?

2. Justice Black states, writing for the Court: "Good-faith bargaining necessarily requires that claims made by either bargainer should be honest claims." What does this mean? Suppose a union negotiator asserts at the bargaining table: "My people have to have a $1.00 an hour increase or they'll go on strike," when the truth of the matter is that the employees would be happy with a $.50 increase and would not want to go on strike if they got as much as a $.25 increase. Is this a violation of Section 8(b)(3)? If your answer is no, how does that union "claim" differ from the employer's responding assertion: "My God! That kind of wage increase would bankrupt me," when the truth of the matter is that a wage increase of twice that amount would still leave him a profit and that in no event could he be bankrupted, because of a personal fortune?

Is Justice Black's ultimate point that good-faith bargaining is, like good-faith poker playing (a close relative of collective bargaining, in the latter's more benign form), for *losers* only?

3. The Truitt principle—i.e., that under certain circumstances the employer must disclose information to the bargaining representative—was expanded in a per curiam opinion in NLRB v. F.W. Woolworth Co., 352 U.S. 938, 77 S.Ct. 261, 1 L.Ed.2d 235 (1956) (reversing 235 F.2d 319 (9th Cir.1956)), holding that an employer must divulge wage information (names, hours, and wages of employees)

essential to the representative's discharge of its bargaining function. The employer's duty to disclose was further extended in NLRB v. Acme Industrial Co., 385 U.S. 432, 87 S.Ct. 565, 17 L.Ed.2d 495 (1967), holding that an employer violated Section 8(a)(5) by refusing to divulge information necessary to the union for the purpose of ascertaining whether or not to process a grievance. (The Acme case is reported infra p. 718.)

For an analysis of Truitt and of the employer's broad obligation to supply data relevant to the bargaining process, see Bartosic & Hartley, The Employer's Duty to Supply Information to the Union, 58 Cornell L.Rev. 23 (1972).

WHITE v. NATIONAL LABOR RELATIONS BOARD

United States Court of Appeals, Fifth Circuit, 1958.
255 F.2d 564.

TUTTLE, CIRCUIT JUDGE. This is a petition by the individual petitioners, doing business as White's Uvalde Mines, to review and set aside an order of the National Labor Relations Board, and a cross-request by the Board that the order be enforced.

Although the petitioners seek also to have set aside orders of the Board finding they had violated Section 8(a)(1) of the Act by making threats and promises to their employees and that they violated Section 8(a)(5) and (1) of the Act by instituting minor wage increases without prior negotiations with the employee's bargaining representative, the principal issue is whether there was substantial evidence on the record as a whole to support the Board's finding that petitioners failed to bargain in good faith and that the strike which occurred was therefore an unfair labor practice strike.

Without outlining the evidence as to the 8(a)(1) violations, we find that there was evidence which supported the finding of the Board that there was conduct on behalf of the company which interfered with, restrained and coerced employees in the exercise of their right to engage in union and concerted activities, and that petitioners thus violated Section 8(a)(1) of the Act. We think, however, the unilateral increase of pay of five of the sixty members of the bargaining unit, each of which was accounted for as being appropriate to the particular individual in relation to his job, and all of which occurred before the bargaining sessions commenced did not amount to violations of either Section 8(a)(1) or 8(a)(5) of the Act. These were not such general increases as were criticized in N.L.R.B. v. Crompton-Highland Mills, 337 U.S. 217, 69 S.Ct. 960, 93 L.Ed. 1320 and May Department Stores Co. v. N.L.R.B., 326 U.S. 376, 66 S.Ct. 203, 90 L.Ed. 145, or in Armstrong Cork Co. v. N.L.R.B., 5 Cir., 211 F.2d 843. In the subsequent bargaining sessions petitioners were willing at all times to bargain with respect to wages and classifications, but they adhered to their insistence on the inclusion in any contract of their right to make merit increases. These particular increases were simply in line with their custom and practice and could not be said to be either restraint or coercion under 8(a)(1) or a refusal to bargain in good faith under 8(a)(5).

Coming to the remaining issue, we find that we are at last required to determine whether, in an otherwise unassailable attitude of collective bargaining, the employer may nevertheless be found guilty of a failure to bargain in good faith solely upon a consideration of the content of the proposals and counter proposals of the parties. In other words may the charge of refusal to bargain in good faith be sustained solely by reference to the terms of the employment contract which management finally says it is willing to sign if such proposed contract could fairly be found to be one which would leave the employees in no better state than they were without it. For the purpose of considering this question we may assume that the Board could find that the terms of the contract insisted on by the company requiring the surrender by the employees of their right to strike and their agreeing to leave to management the right to hire and fire and fix wages in return for agreements by the company respecting grievances and security that gave the union little, if any, real voice in these important aspects of employment relations would in fact have left the union in no better position than if it had no contract. It is perfectly apparent that the company representatives approached the bargaining table with a full understanding of their obligations to meet with, and discuss with, representatives of the employees any terms and conditions of employment that either party put forward; that they must at least expose themselves to such argument and persuasion as could be put forward, and that they must try to seek an area of agreement at least as to some of the terms of employment; that if they were able to arrive at such agreement they must be willing to reduce it to writing and sign it. It is of some significance that at the fourth of the six bargaining sessions, when challenged by the employees' bargaining agent [1] the company's managing partner signed the company's proposed complete contract and tendered it to the union, which declined to accept it. The question is: Can the company's insistence on terms overall favorable to it in net result be taken as proof that it did not approach the bargaining table in good faith, but that it approached the bargaining table only to give the outward sign of compliance when it had already excluded the possibility of agreement?

We think it quite significant that neither the Board itself nor the general counsel places any reliance on the 8(a)(1) violations, other than the unilateral wage increases, as affording any evidence of absence of good faith bargaining. The trial examiner did comment in his findings on the testimony of an employee to the effect that a company foreman, Evetts, attempted to secure his aid to destroy the Union. The Board adopted the findings, recommendations and conclusions of the examiner, but neither in the Board's opinion nor in the General Counsel's brief is this matter mentioned. Having eliminated the wage increases as 8(a)(5) violations we find that there is therefore nothing to support the Board's finding of a failure to bargain in good faith aside from the proposals and counter proposals of the parties and their attitudes as reflected at the bargaining table.

We start with the statute which states specifically that the "obligation [to bargain collectively] does not compel either party to agree to a proposal or require the making of a concession." The Board, in its brief, recognizes this but fails to give effect to it in stating its contention. * * * Immediately after outlining nine different points of difference between the parties,[3] the brief says:

1. Burton, the union representative, said: "I told him personally I didn't believe they would sign their own contract. He called my bluff and had John White sign it."

3. It would extend this opinion too greatly to outline in detail the proposals and counter proposals and the responses of the parties to them at the seven different bargaining ses-

"We do not contend that any one of the foregoing specifications * * * would standing alone constitute a refusal to bargain. We do urge, however, that on the record as a whole,[5] and in accord with such authorities as Majure v. N.L.R.B., 5 Cir., 198 F.2d 735; N.L.R.B. v. Denton, 5 Cir., 217 F.2d 567,

sions. However, it would seem that the statement of the criticized actions of the company, as enumerated by counsel for the Board in its brief, is as strong a presentation of the Board's views as is available. With some comments added by the Court, the brief says:

"A fair summary of the Company's bargaining in this case reveals the following:

"1. The Company, while insisting on a 'no strike' clause with provisions for union liability in the case of breach, at first resisted a corresponding 'no lockout' clause, and after agreeing to such a clause refused at all times to agree to a provision calling for corresponding liability in the event of its breach.

"2. As the courts have recognized, a union's contractual waiver of its statutory right to strike is normally accompanied by a provision that disputes between the parties will be settled by grievance procedures and arbitration rather than by such 'self-help' measures as strikes. But the Company in this case coupled its insistence on a no-strike clause with an insistence that matters going to arbitration must be decided in the Company's favor if there was any evidence that the Company's position was not arbitrary or capricious. Such limited arbitration would leave the Union 'hamstrung' in a dispute with the Company, unable to strike or to secure a review on the merits by the arbitrators.

"3. The Company at no time acceded to any proposal for the selection of a neutral arbitrator, in the event the arbitrators chosen by the Union and the Company could not agree. [The company proposal was that the two arbitrators select the third.]

"4. In the absence of any contract, the Company could not lawfully change its wage rates or grant merit increases or alter shop rules relating to working conditions without first bargaining with the Union over those changes. But the Company insisted, as a condition of the contract, that the Union surrender its right to bargain about those matters, and leave the Company free to act in a manner which, but for the contract, would be violative of the law.

"5. Although the Company professed to find the matters of house rentals and physical examinations 'of no importance', it insisted that the contract contain no provision as to the Union's right to bargain over the rental rates of Company houses, and further insisted that the contract require the employees to submit to a physical examination by the Company doctor, whose word as to employment would be final. The Company's intransigent attitude over matters which it regarded as unimportant is itself suggestive of a want of good faith. [The company insisted that these matters were important to it, but not to the employees, because in neither respect had there been any complaint as to the company's attitude.]

"6. The Company rejected the Union's request that the contract provide for bargaining over the annual bonus, although in the absence of a contract such bonuses are matters over which bargaining is required. N.L.R.B. v. Niles-Bement-Pond Co., 2 Cir., 199 F.2d 713.

"7. Admitting that its minimum wage rate was substantially lower than comparable rates in the area, the Company at first 'stood pat' on wages, and eventually offered an increase to less than that embodied in the amendment to the federal wage and hour law, then being debated in Congress. [The statement that the Company admitted its minimum rate was substantially lower than comparable rates is strongly contested by the Company. The proposed increase was a minimum of 90 cents per hour, which was the minimum actually enacted months later].

"8. Notwithstanding substantial concessions by the Union in the course of the negotiations, the Company characterized the Union's second proposal as 'about the same' as its first one, and the Union's third proposal as 'not substantially different'. Such a denial of the realities of the Union's efforts to compromise differences hardly comports with a good faith desire to bargain.

"9. Granting little beyond such bare requirements as a provision against discrimination, the Company took the attitude, expressed by its chief negotiator, that 'we are giving the contract, and that is something.' This attitude, we submit falls far short of what this Court has described as 'a duty * * * to enter into discussion with an open and fair mind, and a sincere purpose to find a basis of agreement touching wages and hours and conditions of employment, and if found to embody it in a contract as specific as possible * * *' Globe Cotton Mills v. N.L.R.B. [5 Cir.], 103 F.2d 91, 94."

5. We assume by this is meant "all nine of them together with the unilateral increase of wages" heretofore eliminated by us.

570, certiorari denied 348 U.S. 981 [75 S.Ct. 572, 99 L.Ed. 764]; N.L.R.B. v. Reed & Prince Mfg. Co., 1 Cir., 205 F.2d 131, certiorari denied 346 U.S. 887 [74 S.Ct. 139, 98 L.Ed. 391], and N.L.R.B. v. Century Cement Mfg. Co., 2 Cir., 208 F.2d 84, the Board could reasonably find that the Company had not approached the bargaining in the good faith spirit required by the Act."

Thus the Board is saying that although the statute says no concession need be made and no item need be agreed upon, if a company fails to concede *anything* substantial,[6] then this is too much, and such failure amounts to bad faith.

The language of the Courts is not, as it cannot be, in construing this difficult statute, entirely clear, but we find no case which precisely supports the proposition here asserted by the Board. The principal basis of the Board's attack here is the broad management function clause and the failure to agree to a real arbitration clause in which the arbitrators have final powers. The remaining provisions criticized by the Board could not conceivably be considered as proof of bad faith by the petitioners. As to the inclusion of a broad management functions clause and thus a refusal to permit matters relating to hiring, discharging, hours and working conditions to be subject to grievance procedures and arbitration, the Supreme Court has said:

"Congress provided expressly that the Board should not pass upon the desirability of the substantive terms of labor agreements. Whether a contract should contain a clause fixing standards for such matters as work scheduling or should provide for more flexible treatment of such matters is an issue for determination across the bargaining table, not by the Board. If the latter approach is agreed upon, the extent of union and management participation in the administration of such matters is itself a condition of employment to be settled by bargaining.

"Accordingly, we reject the Board's holding that bargaining for the management functions clause proposed by respondent was, per se, an unfair labor practice." National Labor Relations Board v. American National Insurance Co., 343 U.S. 395, 72 S.Ct. 824, 832, 96 L.Ed. 1027.

If such a clause is not per se proof of failure to bargain in good faith then *a fortiori* insistence on physical examination by the company's own doctor, refusal to include terms of a Christmas bonus, a refusal to grant specified wage increases, refusal to "freeze" rent and utility charges on company-owned houses and like issues could not either separately or collectively constitute such proof.

In Majure v. National Labor Relations Board, 5 Cir., 198 F.2d 735, 737, in addition to insisting during the entire negotiations on an agreement wholly "favorable to its position," which we may assume occurred in the case before us, the employer there specifically refused to consider during the negotiations requests for increased compensation and paid vacations, whereas within a month after the negotiations broke down following a bargaining session at which the company contended "there was no place for a contract at Majure" because the men worked on commission and had "no right to be in the union," the company voluntarily granted a raise from 18% to 20%

---

6. Although it is here assumed that no net substantial concessions were made, the compa-ny vigorously asserts it made some of substance during the negotiations.

commission and granted paid vacations. This Court held that although it was not easy in that case to draw the dividing line, "we place our acceptance of the Board's order upon a consideration of the entire circumstances of the case," including what we have above outlined.

In N.L.R.B. v. Denton, 5 Cir., 217 F.2d 567, 570, also decided by this Court, we considered as part of the record which we found supported a finding of failure to bargain in good faith repeated statements by the employer and his supervisors that Denton "would never sign a contract with any union." This was coupled with the affirmed finding of discriminatory discharge of several employees to support a finding by the Board that the resulting strike was an unfair labor strike.

In addition to these Fifth Circuit cases the Board cites, in support of its position, N.L.R.B. v. Reed & Prince Mfg. Co., 1 Cir., 205 F.2d 131, certiorari denied 346 U.S. 887, 74 S.Ct. 139, 98 L.Ed. 391, and N.L.R.B. v. Century Cement Mfg. Co., 2 Cir., 208 F.2d 84. In both of these cases it is apparent that there were additional facts in the record which, when coupled with the absence of any concessions by the employer, warranted the Board, in the opinion of the respective Courts of Appeals to find failure to bargain in good faith.

We do not hold that under no possible circumstances can the mere content of the various proposals and counter proposals of management and union be sufficient evidence of a want of good faith to justify a holding to that effect. We can conceive of one party to such bargaining procedure suggesting proposals of such a nature or type or couched in such objectionable language that they would be calculated to disrupt any serious negotiations. A careful study of the record before us, and viewed with all the adverse emphasis the Board has placed upon the challenged actions of the company in its brief, footnote 3 supra, leaves us with the clear impression that the Board erred in finding adequate proof of a failure to bargain in good faith.

The petition will be granted to the extent that the findings and order of the Board relate to a Section 8(a)(5) violation and to a refusal to bargain in good faith, and to the determination that the strike was an unfair labor practice strike. It is denied so far as it relates to the finding and order of the Board as to the Section 8(a)(1) violation based on the findings other than as to the minor wage increase.

RIVES, CIRCUIT JUDGE. I respectfully dissent. The nature of the 8(a)(1) violations, which we all agree are supported by substantial evidence on the record as a whole, seems to me to have a bearing upon the other claimed violations. They were accurately described in the Board's brief, as quoted in the margin.[1] From those violations, along with the other evidence, both

1. "A. Interference, restraint, and coercion

"As developed more fully, infra, the Union called a strike in May 1955 over what it regarded as the Company's failure to bargain in good faith. Shortly before the strike Foreman Evetts asked Employee Lopez 'to help [Evetts] destroy the Union,' adding, 'If we destroy it, I will give you a raise' (R. 203; B.A.

30). In response to Lopez' questions, Evetts went on to say: 'I am authorized by Mr. Johnny White [petitioner's managing partner] to do this. You and I can destroy this if you will only help me ＊ ＊ ＊ I will go bring a paper and get signatures and we will destroy it' (R. 203; B.A. 30). In similar vein, Evetts told Employee Vara after the strike started that if Vara signed a certain paper, Evetts

positive and negative, the Trial Examiner arrived at a carefully reasoned finding, "that at the time Respondent was meeting with the Union it was also seeking to destroy it." * * * The Board adopted that finding.

The Union won a Board-conducted representation election 50 votes to 10. On October 8, 1954, the Union was certified as the bargaining representative of the employees. Within a month, without any attempt at bargaining, or even notice to the Union, the Company raised the wages of five employees. I do not agree that only "general increases" were criticized in N.L.R.B. v. Crompton-Highland Mills, 337 U.S. 217, 69 S.Ct. 960, 93 L.Ed. 1320; May Department Stores Co. v. N.L.R.B., 326 U.S. 376, 66 S.Ct. 203, 90 L.Ed. 145; Armstrong Cork Co. v. N.L.R.B., 5 Cir., 211 F.2d 843. Granting merit increases to five out of sixty employees, without consulting the Union, constituted, I think, unilateral action which naturally tended to undermine the authority of the certified bargaining representative for each and all of the employees, and violated Sections 8(a)(5) and (1) of the Act.

Certainly, against the background evidenced by the other violations, the record as a whole discloses a rational basis, a reasonable foundation for the Board's conclusion that the Company failed to bargain in good faith. This Court should not substitute its judgment for that of the Board.

Collective bargaining is at the very heart and core of the Labor Management Relations Act. If, in any particular case, effective collective bargaining is not had and cannot be required, then in that case the Act is nothing. It follows that there must be some protection against "merely going through the motions of negotiating," [2] "a predetermined resolve not to budge from an initial position," [3] "surface bargaining" accompanied by "a purpose to defeat it and wilful obstruction of it," [4] "shadow boxing to a draw," [5] "giving the Union a runaround while purporting to be meeting with the Union for the purpose of collective bargaining." [6]

Nowhere has the rule been better stated than by Judge Russell for this Circuit in Majure v. National Labor Relations Board, 5 Cir., 1952, 198 F.2d 735, 739:

> "* * * It is true, of course, that the employer was not required to accept the union's proposal, nor to make any concession, or counter-proposal. However, the employer was required to bargain in good faith. This Court held in American National Insurance Co. v. N.L.R.B., 5 Cir., 187 F.2d 307, affirmed by the Supreme Court in N.L.R.B. v. American National Insurance Co., 343 U.S. 395, 72 S.Ct. 824 [96 L.Ed. 1027], that the obligation of the employer to bargain in good faith does not require the yielding of positions

---

'would raise [Vara's] salary' and if they 'could find a few more that would sign, he could destroy the Union' (R. 202–203; B.A. 27). Also after the strike started, Evetts went to the homes of Employees Lopez and Hernandez and offered each a raise in pay if he would abandon the strike and return to work (R. 202, 203–204; B.A. 20, 31). The day the strike began, Superintendent Tracey asked Employee Norred if he was going on strike, and on receiving an affirmative answer warned Norred, who lived in a Company-owned house, that he 'better start looking' for another house (R. 201–202; B.A. 13–14). * * *'"

2. Dissenting opinion in N.L.R.B. v. Truitt Mfg. Co., 1956, 351 U.S. 149, 154, 76 S.Ct. 753, 100 L.Ed. 1027.

3. Ibid.

4. N.L.R.B. v. Whittier Mills Co., 5 Cir., 1940, 111 F.2d 474, 478, per Judge Sibley.

5. Stonewall Cotton Mills v. N.L.R.B., 5 Cir., 1942, 129 F.2d 629, 631, per Judge Hutcheson.

6. N.L.R.B. v. Athens Mfg. Co., 5 Cir., 1947, 161 F.2d 8.

fairly maintained, nor permit the Board, under the guise of a finding of bad faith, to require the employer to contract in a way which the Board might deem proper. Nevertheless, the requirement of good faith in such bargaining is imposed by the statute. The dividing line between the right to the exercise of good faith and independent judgment and to maintain the resultant position with firmness, with no obligation of retreat, and nevertheless obey the statutory command to bargain in good faith must, in the nature of such right, and yet obligation, be frequently difficult of ascertainment and establishment. It has not been easy in the present case. In such cases there is danger that the negotiating parties may have their freedom of contract as to substance restricted or destroyed by a construction of their conduct as an evidence of bad faith. However, judicial ingenuity has devised but one standard, or test, which, recognizing the problem, yet seeks to insure reconciliation of privilege and obligation. This rule requires fair appraisal of the circumstances and the particular facts of the particular case. N.L.R.B. v. American National Insurance Company, supra.

"Applying the rule here, we think the circumstances of this case support the Board's finding that the employer, while freely conferring, did not approach the bargaining table with an open mind and purpose to reach an agreement consistent with the respective rights of the parties."

Chief Judge Magruder, speaking for the First Circuit in N.L.R.B. v. Reed & Prince Mfg. Co., 1953, 205 F.2d 131, 134, 135, made an admirable expression of the same principle:

"It is true, as stated in N.L.R.B. v. American National Ins. Co., 1952, 343 U.S. 395, 404, 72 S.Ct. 824, 829, 96 L.Ed. 1027, that the Board may not 'sit in judgment upon the substantive terms of collective bargaining agreements.' But at the same time it seems clear that if the Board is not to be blinded by empty talk and by the mere surface motions of collective bargaining, it must take some cognizance of the reasonableness of the positions taken by an employer in the course of bargaining negotiations. See Wilson & Co., Inc., v. N.L.R.B., 8 Cir., 1940, 115 F.2d 759, 763. See also Smith, The Evolution of the 'Duty to Bargain' Concept in American Law, 39 Mich.L.Rev. 1065, 1108 (1941). Thus if an employer can find nothing whatever to agree to in an ordinary current-day contract submitted to him, or in some of the union's related minor requests, and if the employer makes not a single serious proposal meeting the union at least part way, then certainly the Board must be able to conclude that this is at least some evidence of bad faith, that is, of a desire not to reach an agreement with the union. In other words, while the Board cannot force an employer to make a 'concession' on any specific issue or to adopt any particular position, the employer is obliged to make *some* reasonable effort in *some* direction to compose his differences with the union, if § 8(a)(5) is to be read as imposing any substantial obligation at all."

Chief Judge Chase, speaking for the Second Circuit in N.L.R.B. v. Century Cement Mfg. Co., 1953, 208 F.2d 84, 86, said:

"* * * The respondent made no proposals of its own as a basis for negotiation on such subjects. They were all, however, proper subjects for collective bargaining and while the respondent was, indeed, free to reject the union's demands in the exercise of its business judgment the failure to do little more than reject them was indicative of a failure to comply with its statutory requirement to bargain in good faith."

Under all of the authorities, in determining whether *either* an employer or a labor organization has failed to bargain in good faith, the Board must necessarily consider its conduct at the bargaining table, and whether it has acted reasonably or arbitrarily.

In the present case, the Company insisted on a no-strike clause with provisions for Union liability in the case of breach. It further insisted that matters going to arbitration must be decided in the Company's favor if there is any evidence that the Company's position was not arbitrary or capricious. It declined to accede to any proposal for the selection of a neutral arbitrator in the event the arbitrators chosen by the Union and the Company could not agree. While thus insisting that the Union waive its statutory right to strike, the Company declined to give any substitute, such as effective arbitration. In the recent case of Textile Workers Union of America v. Lincoln Mills, 1957, 353 U.S. 448, 455, 77 S.Ct. 912, 917, 1 L.Ed.2d 972, the Supreme Court said: "Plainly the agreement to arbitrate grievance disputes is the *quid pro quo* for an agreement not to strike."

Even without a contract, the Company could not lawfully change its wage rates, grant merit increases, or alter shop rules relating to working conditions without first bargaining with the Union. Nevertheless, the Company insisted that the Union surrender its right to bargain about those matters and leave the Company free to act as it saw fit. There are many other instances of arbitrary and unreasonable action set forth in the fair and careful intermediate report of the Trial Examiner and the decision of the Board, which leave me convinced that the Board had a rational basis for its conclusion that the Company failed to bargain in good faith. The other violations on the part of the Company make that conclusion all the more reasonable. In my opinion, that is a conclusion peculiarly within the province of the Board and which the Board is more competent to arrive at than is this Court. I, therefore, respectfully dissent.

Note

1. Do you consider the White decision to be outrageous or sound policy? If the former, is it your assumption that collective bargaining means that the union should always get "more"? Or only if it is strong enough? Is it the function of the good-faith requirement to enable the Government to aid the weaker party (traditionally the union?) by putting a thumb on the scales? How does all of this square with the emergence of "concession bargaining"?

2. Perhaps the most "celebrated" case of employer intransigence testing the outer limits of good-faith bargaining is NLRB v. General Electric Co., 418 F.2d 736 (2d Cir.1969), cert. denied 397 U.S. 965, 90 S.Ct. 995, 25 L.Ed.2d 257 (1970). In this "GE Case," a vice-president of the company, one Lemuel R. Boulware, had developed a collective bargaining strategy designed to disabuse the company's employees of the notion that "good things" in an employment sense come from the union rather than the employer. The strategy, which came to be called "Boulwarism," entailed three elements. The first was a careful study by the employer of employee desires, of union demands, and of the competitive market, for the purpose of constructing an attractive offer. The second element was the presentation to the union of a "fair, firm" offer, from which the employer made clear it would not deviate because of union pressure, but only upon being persuaded that it had made a mistake of fact in any of its

calculations. The third element was a "merchandising" of the offer directly to its employees and to the public at large, seeking to win support for this "product" in much the same fashion as it sold its other products. The union, unsettled by this strategy, called a national strike which aborted some three weeks later in capitulation by the union.

In the meantime, the union had filed Section 8(a)(5) charges against the employer. The Board found a refusal by the employer to bargain in good faith. The Second Circuit granted enforcement of the Board's order on the ground that, by its pronouncements that it could not be moved off its "firm, fair" offer through union strike pressure and by its extravagant "merchandising" of that offer, GE had painted itself into a corner deemed to be inconsistent with the duty to bargain in good faith.

Judge Friendly dissented forcefully from this conclusion on the grounds of (1) Section 8(d)'s provision that the obligation to bargain "does not compel either party to agree to a proposal or require the making of a concession," (2) that Section 8(c) protected the employer in its campaign to "sell" its offer directly to the employees and the public, and (3) that there was no showing that the employer did not sincerely desire to reach agreement, albeit, with minor concessions, upon the basis of its own terms.

The case, for all of its long-drawn-out litigation (almost four years before the Board and an additional five years before the Second Circuit Court of Appeals), did not reach the Supreme Court. The question of whether the strategy of Boulwarism is consistent with the duty to bargain in good faith has, as a consequence, never been ultimately answered. That strategy builds upon the employer position in the White case. How would *you* decide this question under our system of free collective bargaining? Was GE simply exercising to the maximum its bargaining power, as proclaimed by the dissent in the Second Circuit? Or did the Boulware strategy of first, full, fair, firm, final offer (arguably "take-it-or-leave-it"), with its potential for locking the employer into its initial stance, constitute bargaining in bad faith, as determined by the Board and the majority of the Second Circuit? Should, in other words, a model labor code require a stategy which does not *lead* with the final offer but rather "haggles" up to it through a process of give and take? Did GE, as its detractors claimed, seek "to deal with the Union through the employees rather than with the employees through the Union"? If so, *so what* —assuming, as was conceded in the case, GE was not seeking to rid itself of the union but was sincerely desirous of reaching agreement, although on its own terms?

What the White case and GE literally *provoke* is a bedrock analysis of the meaning of "good faith" in a system of "free collective bargaining." For pertinent comment (almost as widely split on the spelling of Boulwarism/ Boulwareism as over its merits), see H.R. Northrup, Boulwarism (1964); Note, Boulwareism: Legality and Effect, 76 Harv.L.Rev. 807 (1963); Cooper, Boulwarism and the Duty to Bargain in Good Faith, 20 Rutgers L.Rev. 653 (1966); Gross, Cullen & Hanslowe, Good Faith in Labor Negotiations: Tests and Remedies, 53 Corn.L.Rev. 1009 (1969); Forkosch, Boulwarism: Will Labor-Management Relations Take It or Leave It?, 19 Cath.U.L.Rev. 311 (1970); Abramson, The Anatomy of Boulwarism With A Discussion of Forkosch, 19 Cath.U.L.Rev. 459 (1970).

3. Is not the GE case a pellucid example of the way in which *law* may limit the *freedom* to bargain collectively? By the finding of bad faith in GE's overall bargaining posture, the Board and Court of Appeals simultaneously limited the freedom of GE to bring to bear on the union the totality of its bargaining power.

On the other hand, if GE were allowed full flex of its economic power, might not the result be that GE's freedom to bargain collectively would devour the employees' freedom to bargain collectively, and thereby restore the imbalance of individual bargaining? In other words, is this not but another example of the reciprocity between freedom and law? In the words of the late Justice Wiley Rutledge: "I believe in law. At the same time I believe in freedom. And I know that each of these * * * may destroy the other. But I know too that, without both, neither can long endure." Rutledge, A Declaration of Legal Faith 6 (1947).

4. An interesting procedural aspect of the judicial review of the Board's decisions in the courts of appeals is noted in the Second Circuit's majority opinion in the GE case. As there observed, the long-delayed Board decision was followed by:

> "[T]he race to the courthouse that is an unhappy feature too often encoun-
> tered in these matters. See Carrington, Crowded Dockets and the Courts of
> Appeals: The Threat to the Function of Review and the National Law, 82
> Harv.L.Rev. 542, 598–600 (1969). Since GE does business in every state,
> every court of appeals has [potential] jurisdiction, [see sections 10(e) and
> 10(f)] * * *. The IUE [International Union of Electrical Workers]
> claimed that it filed in the District of Columbia Circuit 14 seconds before GE
> handed its petition to the clerk in the Seventh Circuit. GE's version of
> course differed. The NLRB, admitting its confusion (not without reasons, it
> would seem), suggested that since the question of timing was incapable of
> rational solution, the Second Circuit, where the unfair labor practices
> complained of occurred, would be the logical place to begin. The District of
> Columbia and Seventh Circuits agreed. IUE v. NLRB, 120 U.S.App.D.C. 45,
> 343 F.2d 327 (1965); GE v. NLRB, 58 LRRM 2694 (7th Cir.1965)." 418 F.2d
> at 739.

C. HEREIN OF THE NONREMEDIAL REMEDY: EFFORTS AT "MAKE–WHOLE" RELIEF

The traditional remedy for a violation of Section 8(a)(5) is an order directing the employer to perform its statutory duty to bargain collectively. This order is enforceable through the contempt power of the federal courts. But what incentive does such a remedy provide for an employer to bargain early, rather than late—to obey its statutory duty when the conditions to its invocation have first been satisfied, instead of delaying until an instant before the fall of the sword of contempt? Indeed, how much edge does that "sword" really have? If the incentive to bargain provided by the traditional remedy is weak, what alternatives might better "effectuate the policies of the Act"?

These are the questions of this section.

H.K. PORTER CO. v. NATIONAL LABOR RELATIONS BOARD

Supreme Court of the United States, 1970.
397 U.S. 99, 90 S.Ct. 821, 25 L.Ed.2d 146.

MR. JUSTICE BLACK delivered the opinion of the Court.

After an election respondent United Steelworkers Union was, on October 5, 1961, certified by the National Labor Relations Board as the bargaining agent for certain employees at the Danville, Virginia, plant of the petitioner, H.K. Porter Co. Thereafter negotiations commenced for a collective-bargaining agreement. Since that time the controversy has see-sawed between the Board, the Court of Appeals for the District of Columbia Circuit, and this Court. This delay of over eight years is not because the case is exceedingly complex but appears to have occurred chiefly because of the skill of the company's negotiators in taking advantage of every opportunity for delay in an act more noticeable for its generality than for its precise prescriptions. The entire lengthy dispute mainly revolves around the union's desire to have the company agree to "check off" the dues owed to the union by its members, that is, to deduct those dues periodically from the company's wage payments to the employees. The record shows, as the Board found, that the company's objection to a checkoff was not due to any general principle or policy against making deductions from employees' wages. The company does deduct charges for things like insurance, taxes, and contributions to charities, and at some other plants it has a checkoff arrangement for union dues. The evidence shows, and the court below found, that the company's objection was not because of inconvenience, but solely on the ground that the company was "not going to aid and comfort the union." Efforts by the union to obtain some kind of compromise on the checkoff request were all met with the same staccato response to the effect that the collection of union dues was the "union's business" and the company was not going to provide any assistance. Based on this and other evidence the Board found, and the Court of Appeals approved the finding, that the refusal of the company to bargain about the checkoff was not made in good faith, but was done solely to frustrate the making of any collective-bargaining agreement. In May 1966, the Court of Appeals upheld the Board's order requiring the company to cease and desist from refusing to bargain in good faith and directing it to engage in further collective bargaining, if requested by the union to do so, over the checkoff. United Steelworkers of America v. NLRB, 124 U.S.App.D.C. 143, 363 F.2d 272, cert. denied, H.K. Porter, Inc., Disston Division-Danville Works v. N.L.R.B., 385 U.S. 851, 87 S.Ct. 90, 17 L.Ed.2d 80.

In the course of that opinion, the Court of Appeals intimated that the Board conceivably might have required petitioner to agree to a checkoff provision as a remedy for the prior bad-faith bargaining, although the order enforced at that time did not contain any such provision. 124 U.S.App.D.C., at 146–147, and n. 16, 363 F.2d, at 275–276, and n. 16. In the ensuing negotiations the company offered to discuss alternative arrangements for collecting the union's dues, but the union insisted that the company was required to agree to the checkoff proposal without modification. Because of this disagreement over the proper interpretation of the court's opinion, the union, in February 1967, filed a motion for clarification of the 1966 opinion. The motion was denied by the court on March 22, 1967, in an order suggesting that contempt proceedings by the Board would be the proper avenue for testing the employer's compliance with the original order. A request for the institution of such proceedings was made by the union, and, in June 1967, the Regional Director of the Board declined to prosecute a contempt charge, finding that the employer had "satisfactorily complied with the affirmative requirements of the Order." App. 111. The union then filed in the Court of Appeals a motion for reconsideration of the earlier motion to clarify the 1966 opinion. The court granted that motion and issued a new opinion in which it held that in certain circumstances a "checkoff may be imposed as a remedy for bad faith bargaining." United Steelworkers of America v. NLRB, 128 U.S.App.D.C. 344, 347, 389 F.2d 295, 298 (1967). The case was then remanded to the Board and on July 3, 1968, the Board issued a supplemental order requiring the petitioner to "[g]rant to the Union a contract clause providing for the checkoff of union dues." 172 N.L.R.B. No. 72, 68 L.R.R.M. 1337. The Court of Appeals affirmed this order, H.K. Porter Co. v. NLRB, 134 U.S.App.D.C. 227, 414 F.2d 1123 (1969). We granted certiorari to consider whether the Board in these circumstances has the power to remedy the unfair labor practice by requiring the company to agree to check off the dues of the workers. * * * For reasons to be stated we hold that while the Board does have power under the National Labor Relations Act, * * * as amended, to require employers and employees to negotiate, it is without power to compel a company or a union to agree to any substantive contractual provision of a collective-bargaining agreement.

Since 1935 the story of labor relations in this country has largely been a history of governmental regulation of the process of collective bargaining. * * *

The objective of [the Wagner] Act was not to allow governmental regulation of the terms and conditions of employment, but rather to ensure that employers and their employees could work together to establish mutually satisfactory conditions. The basic theme of the Act was that through collective bargaining the passions, arguments, and struggles of prior years would be channeled into constructive, open discussions leading, it was hoped, to mutual agreement. But it was recognized from the beginning that agreement might in some cases be impossible, and it was never intended that the Government would in such cases step in, become a party to the negotiations and impose its own views of a desirable settlement. This fundamental limitation was made abundantly clear in the legislative reports accompanying the 1935 Act. * * *

In 1947 Congress reviewed the experience under the Act and concluded that certain amendments were in order. In the House committee report accompanying what eventually became the Labor Management Relations Act, 1947, the committee * * * said:

"[T]he present Board has gone very far, in the guise of determining whether or not employers had bargained in good faith, in setting itself up as the judge of what concessions an employer must make and of the proposals and counterproposals that he may or may not make. * * *

"[U]nless Congress writes into the law guides for the Board to follow, the Board may attempt to carry this process still further and seek to control more and more the terms of collective-bargaining agreements.'[3]

Accordingly Congress amended the provisions defining unfair labor practices and said in § 8(d) that:

3. H.R.Rep. No. 245, 80th Cong., 1st Sess., 19–20 (1947).

"[The duty to bargain] *does not compel either party to agree to a proposal or require the making of a concession*" [emphasis added].

In discussing the effect of that amendment, this Court said it is "clear that the Board may not, either directly or indirectly, compel concessions or otherwise sit in judgment upon the substantive terms of collective bargaining agreements." N.L.R.B. v. American Nat. Ins. Co., 343 U.S. 395, 404, 72 S.Ct. 824, 829, 96 L.Ed. 1027 (1952). Later this Court affirmed that view stating that "it remains clear that § 8(d) was an attempt by Congress to prevent the Board from controlling the settling of the terms of collective bargaining agreements." N.L.R.B. v. Insurance Agents' Inter. Union, 361 U.S. 477, 487, 80 S.Ct. 419, 426, 4 L.Ed.2d 454 (1960). The parties to the instant case are agreed that this is the first time in the 35-year history of the Act that the Board has ordered either an employer or a union to agree to a substantive term of a collective-bargaining agreement.

Recognizing the fundamental principle "that the National Labor Relations Act is grounded on the premise of freedom of contract," 128 U.S.App. D.C., at 349, 389 F.2d, at 300, the Court of Appeals in this case concluded that nevertheless in the circumstances presented here the Board could properly compel the employer to agree to a proposed checkoff clause. The Board had found that the refusal was based on a desire to frustrate agreement and not on any legitimate business reason. On the basis of that finding the Court of Appeals approved the further finding that the employer had not bargained in good faith, and the validity of that finding is not now before us. Where the record thus revealed repeated refusals by the employer to bargain in good faith on this issue, the Court of Appeals concluded that ordering agreement to the checkoff clause "may be the only means of assuring the Board, and the court, that [the employer] no longer harbors an illegal intent." 128 U.S.App.D.C., at 348, 389 F.2d, at 299.

In reaching this conclusion the Court of Appeals held that § 8(d) did not forbid the Board from compelling agreement. That court felt that "[s]ection 8(d) defines collective bargaining and relates to a determination of *whether* a * * * violation has occurred and not to the *scope* of the remedy which may be necessary to cure violations which have already occurred." 128 U.S.App. D.C., at 348, 389 F.2d, at 299. We may agree with the Court of Appeals that as a matter of strict, literal interpretation that section refers only to deciding when a violation has occurred, but we do not agree that that observation justifies the conclusion that the remedial powers of the Board are not also limited by the same considerations that led Congress to enact § 8(d). It is implicit in the entire structure of the Act that the Board acts to oversee and referee the process of collective bargaining, leaving the results of the contest to the bargaining strengths of the parties. It would be anomalous indeed to hold that while § 8(d) prohibits the Board from relying on a refusal to agree as the sole evidence of bad-faith bargaining, the Act permits the Board to compel agreement in that same dispute. The Board's remedial powers under § 10 of the Act are broad, but they are limited to carrying out the policies of the Act itself. One of these fundamental policies is freedom of contract. While the parties' freedom of contract is not absolute under the Act, allowing the Board to compel agreement when the parties themselves are unable to agree would violate the fundamental premise on which the Act is based—private bargaining under governmental supervision of the procedure alone, without any official compulsion over the actual terms of the contract.

In reaching its decision the Court of Appeals relied extensively on the equally important policy of the Act that workers' rights to collective bargaining are to be secured. In this case the court apparently felt that the employer was trying effectively to destroy the union by refusing to agree to what the union may have considered its most important demand. Perhaps the court, fearing that the parties might resort to economic combat, was also trying to maintain the industrial peace that the Act is designed to further. But the Act as presently drawn does not contemplate that unions will always be secure and able to achieve agreement even when their economic position is weak, or that strikes and lockouts will never result from a bargaining impasse. It cannot be said that the Act forbids an employer or a union to rely ultimately on its economic strength to try to secure what it cannot obtain through bargaining. It may well be true, as the Court of Appeals felt, that the present remedial powers of the board are insufficiently broad to cope with important labor problems. But it is the job of Congress, not the Board or the courts, to decide when and if it is necessary to allow governmental review of proposals for collective-bargaining agreements and compulsory submission to one side's demands. The present Act does not envision such a process.

The judgment is reversed and the case is remanded to the Court of Appeals for further action consistent with this opinion.

MR. JUSTICE WHITE took no part in the decision of this case.

MR. JUSTICE MARSHALL took no part in the consideration or decision of this case.

MR. JUSTICE HARLAN, concurring.

I join in the Court's opinion on the understanding that nothing said therein is meant to disturb or question the primary determination made by the Board and sustained by the Court of Appeals, that petitioner did not bargain in "good faith," and thus may be subjected to a bargaining order enforceable by a citation for contempt if the Board deems such a proceeding appropriate.

MR. JUSTICE DOUGLAS, with whom MR. JUSTICE STEWART concurs, dissenting.

The Court correctly describes the general design and main thrust of the Act. It does not encompass compulsory arbitration; the Board does not sit to impose what it deems to be the best conditions for the collective-bargaining agreement * * *.

Yet the Board has the power, where one party does not bargain in good faith, "to take such affirmative action * * * as will effectuate the policies" of the Act. § 10(c) of the Act.

Here the employer did not refuse the checkoff for any business reason, whether cost, inconvenience, or what not. Nor did the employer refuse the checkoff as a factor in its bargaining strategy, hoping that delay and denial might bring it in exchange favorable terms and conditions. Its reason was a resolve to avoid reaching any agreement with the union.

In those narrow and specialized circumstances, I see no answer to the power of the Board in its discretion to impose the checkoff as "affirmative action" necessary to remedy the flagrant refusal of the employer to bargain in good faith.

The case is rare, if not unique, and will seldom arise. I realize that any principle once announced may in time gain a momentum not warranted by the exigencies of its creation. But once there is any business consideration that leads to a denial of a demand or any consideration of bargaining strategy that explains the refusal, the Board has no power to act. Its power is narrowly restricted to the clear case where the refusal is aimed solely at avoidance of any agreement. Such is the present case. Hence, with all respect for the strength of the opposed view, I dissent.

Note

1. The tension in H.K. Porter is classical in nature: between the elusive imperatives of "good faith bargaining" and the more tangible imperatives of rational (i.e., tough, self-serving) exercise of bargaining strength in "free collective bargaining." While it was perhaps true that the checkoff of union dues would have proved no more onerous than the checkoff of charitable contributions and therefore it might fairly be said that the employer's basis for objection was in that sense "antiunion" in nature, is not such antiunionism inherent in hard-nosed assertion of employer interest? "The evidence shows, and the court below found, that the company's objection was not because of inconvenience, but solely on the ground that the company was 'not going to aid and comfort the union.'" (Supra p. 606.) Why was not the collection of dues indeed the "union's business," as the company contended?

Against this backdrop, what *was* the rationale of the bad faith determination of the Board, the Court of Appeals, and the dissent? The focus on this question is tightened by Justice Black's assertion that "the record thus revealed repeated refusals to bargain in good faith on *this* issue." (Supra, p. 608; emphasis added.) Justice Black's apparent acceptance of the Board's and Court of Appeals' finding of bad faith by reason of the refusal of the employer to grant the checkoff, while mooting the bad faith issue in order to reach decision on the affirmative-remedy ground, does not answer the bad faith issue. (*Indeed*, that issue was not before the Court for decision.)

A fundamental question distillable out of H.K. Porter with regard to the meaning of the duty to bargain in good faith is this: May a finding of lack of good faith be premised on the intransigence of a party as to *one mandatory* subject of bargaining (here the checkoff provision)? For such intransigence to preclude the reaching of agreement on an overall contract, is not counter-intransigence by the other party an essential element? Under such circumstances, is the onus of bad faith fairly castable on either?

2. Accepting the finding of bad faith, do you agree that the affirmative remedy granted was beyond the Board's power? Is *all* affirmative ("make-whole") relief for an 8(a)(5) violation beyond the Board's power?

3. A helpful way of approaching the foregoing question and the conflicting decisions concerning it is to ask why the Board does not "effectuate the policies of the Act" by express assessment of penalties against wilful transgressors of those policies. The confines within which the Board and the reviewing courts must seek "effectuation" may be better perceived in the light of REPUBLIC

STEEL CORP. v. NLRB, 311 U.S. 7, 61 S.Ct. 77, 85 L.Ed. 6 (1940). There, the Board, in providing back pay for employees discriminatorily discharged, directed the employer "to deduct from the payments to the reinstated employees the amounts they had received for work performed upon 'work relief projects' [WPA] and to pay over such amounts to the appropriate governmental agencies." In holding that this order exceeded the Board's authority, the Court stated:

"The payments to the Federal, State, County, or other governments concerned are thus conceived as being required for the purpose of redressing, not an injury to the employees, but an injury to the public,—an injury thought to be not the less sustained although here the respective governments have received the benefit of the services performed. So conceived, these required payments are in the nature of penalties imposed by law upon the employer,—the Board acting as the legislative agency in providing that sort of sanction by reason of public interest. * * * The question is,—Has Congress conferred the power upon the Board to impose such requirements.

"We think that the theory advanced by the Board proceeds upon a misconception of the National Labor Relations Act * * *. The Act is essentially remedial. It does not carry a penal program declaring the described unfair labor practices to be crimes. The Act does not prescribe penalties or fines in vindication of public rights or provide indemnity against community losses as distinguished from the protection and compensation of employees. Had Congress been intent upon such a program, we cannot doubt that Congress would have expressed its intent and would itself have defined its retributive scheme.

"The remedial purposes of the Act are quite clear. * * *

"As the sole basis for the claim of authority to go further and to demand payments to governments, the Board relies on the language of Section 10(c) * * *.

"This language should be construed in harmony with the spirit and remedial purposes of the Act. * * * We have said that the power to command affirmative action is remedial, not punitive. Consolidated Edison Company v. National Labor Relations Board, 305 U.S. 197, 235, 236, 59 S.Ct. 206, 219, 83 L.Ed. 126. * * * We adhere to that construction.

"In that view, it is not enough to justify the Board's requirements to say that they would have the effect of deterring persons from violating the Act. That argument proves too much, for if such a deterrent effect is sufficient to sustain an order of the Board, it would be free to set up any system of penalties which it would deem adequate to that end.

"We think that affirmative action to 'effectuate the policies of this Act' is action to achieve the remedial objectives which the Act sets forth. Thus the employer may be required not only to end his unfair labor practices; he may also be directed affirmatively to recognize an organization which is found to be the duly chosen bargaining-representative of his employees; he may be ordered to cease particular methods of interference, intimidation or coercion, to stop recognizing and to disestablish a particular labor organization which he dominates or supports, to restore and make whole employees who have been discharged in violation of the Act, to give appropriate notice of his compliance with the Board's order, and otherwise to take such action as will assure to his employees the rights which the statute undertakes to safeguard. These are all remedial measures. To go further and to require the employer to pay to governments what they have paid to employees for services rendered to them is an exaction neither to make the employees whole nor to assure that they can bargain collectively with the employer through representatives of their own choice. We find no warrant in the policies of the Act for such an exaction." 311 U.S. at 9–13, 61 S.Ct. at 78–80.

EX–CELL–O CORP.

National Labor Relations Board, 1970.
185 N.L.R.B. 107.

Decision and Order

On March 2, 1967, Trial Examiner Owsley Vose issued his Decision in the above-entitled proceeding, finding that Respondent Ex-Cell-O Corporation had engaged in and was engaging in certain unfair labor practices within the meaning of the National Labor Relations Act, as amended, and recommending that it cease and desist therefrom and take certain affirmative action, including an order directing the Respondent to make whole its employees for any losses suffered on account of its unlawful refusal to bargain with the UAW (the Charging Party).[a] Thereafter, the Respondent filed exceptions to the Trial Examiner's Decision and a supporting brief, together with a request for oral argument. As the compensatory remedy adopted by the Trial Examiner in this case poses several novel issues of importance, the National Labor Relations Board granted oral argument and consolidated this matter for purposes of said argument with three other cases involving the same or related issues (*Zinke's Foods, Inc.,* 30–CA–372; *Herman Wilson Lumber Company,* 26–CA–2536; *Rasco Olympia, Inc. d/b/a Rasco 5–10–25 cents,* 19–CA–3187).

The Board granted a number of motions for permission to file briefs *amicus curiae* and also invited certain other interested parties to file them and to participate in the oral argument which was held on July 12 and 13, 1967. The parties who submitted *amicus* briefs and participated as such in the argument were: The Chamber of Commerce of the United States, the National Association of Retail Merchants, The American Federation of Labor and Congress of Industrial Organizations, and The International Brotherhood of Teamsters, Chauffeurs, Warehousemen and Helpers of America. *Amicus* briefs were also submitted by the National Association of Manufacturers, Preston Products Company, Inc., and The NAACP Legal Defense and Educational Fund, Inc.

The Board has reviewed the rulings of the Trial Examiner made at the hearing and finds that no prejudicial error was committed. The rulings are hereby affirmed. The Board has considered the Trial Examiner's Decision, the exceptions, cross-exceptions, the briefs of the parties and those submitted

---

a. The Trial Examiner's pertinent recommendation read: "After giving considerable thought to the precise form a remedial provision would take which would help solve the delay problem in refusal-to-bargain situations, I propose for consideration the following provision:

'Compensate ∗ ∗ ∗ each of its employees for the monetary value of the minimum additional benefits, if any, including wages, which it is reasonable to conclude that the Union would have been able to obtain through collective bargaining with the Respondent, for the period commencing with the date of the Respondent's formal refusal to bargain collectively, October 25, 1965, and continuing until paid.'"

amicus curiae, the oral arguments made before the Board, and the record in the proceeding, and adopts the findings, conclusions, and recommendations of the Trial Examiner, as modified herein.

This case began with the UAW's request for recognition on August 3, 1964. Ex-Cell-O refused the Union's request on August 10, 1964, and the Union immediately filed a petition for Certification of Representative. After a hearing the Regional Director ordered an election, which was held on October 22, 1964, and a majority of the employees voted for the Union. The Company, however, filed objections to the conduct of the election, alleging that the Union made certain misrepresentations which assertedly interfered therewith, but the Acting Regional Director, in a Supplemental Decision of December 29, 1964, overruled them. The Company then requested review of that decision, which the Board granted, and a hearing was held on May 18 and 19, 1965. The Hearing Officer issued his Report on Objections on July 15, 1965, and recommended that the objections be overruled. The Company filed exceptions thereto, but on October 28, 1965, the Board adopted the Hearing Officer's findings and recommendations and affirmed the Regional Director's certification of the Union.

The day after the Board's certification was issued, the Company advised the Union that it would refuse to bargain in order to secure a court review of the Board's action[2] and later reiterated this position after receiving the Union's request for a bargaining meeting. The Union thereupon filed the 8(a)(1) and (5) charge in this case and the complaint was issued on November 23, 1965. The Respondent's answer admitted the factual allegations of the complaint but denied the violation on the ground that the Board's certification was invalid. The hearing herein, originally scheduled for February 15, 1966, commenced on June 1, 1966;[3] it was adjourned until June 29, 1966, to permit the Union to offer evidence supporting its request for a compensatory remedy for the alleged refusal to bargain; the hearing was postponed again until July 28, 1966.[4] The Company also petitioned the United States District Court for an injunction against the Regional Director and the Trial Examiner to restrain the latter from closing the hearing until the Regional Director had produced the investigative records in the representation case. The court issued a summary judgment denying the injunction on December 13, 1966, and on December 21, 1966, the Trial Examiner formally closed his hearing. On March 2, 1967, the Trial Examiner issued his Decision, finding that the Company had unlawfully refused to bargain in violation of Section 8(a)(5) and (1) of the Act and recommended the standard bargaining order as a remedy. In addition the Trial Examiner ordered the Company to compen-

2. The Company's letter stated that:

"We have received the Labor Board's decision concerning our objections to the conduct of the union election held October 22, 1964. As you know, the only way the Labor Board's decision in this case can be reviewed is through a technical refusal to bargain, and consequently we are unable to meet with you and bargain until the review procedure is carried out."

3. This delay was caused by Respondent's unsuccessful attempt to subpena the Regional Director's files in the representation case.

4. This postponement grew out of the Company's objections to the authenticity of certain collective-bargaining contracts offered by the Union to substantiate its request for a compensatory remedy. The Company later withdrew its objection. It also refused to comply with a *subpoena duces tecum* requesting production of certain records relating to wage increases and fringe benefits.

sate its employees for monetary losses incurred as a result of its unlawful conduct.

It is not disputed that Respondent refused to bargain with the Union, and we hereby affirm the Trial Examiner's conclusion that Respondent thereby violated Section 8(a)(1) and (5) of the Act. The compensatory remedy which he recommends, however, raises important issues concerning the Board's powers and duties to fashion appropriate remedies in its efforts to effectuate the policies of the National Labor Relations Act.

It is argued that such a remedy exceeds the Board's general statutory powers. In addition, it is contended that it cannot be granted because the amount of employee loss, if any, is so speculative that an order to make employees whole would amount to the imposition of a penalty. And the position is advanced that the adoption of this remedy would amount to the writing of a contract for the parties, which is prohibited by Section 8(d).

We have given most serious consideration to the Trial Examiner's recommended financial reparations Order, and are in complete agreement with his finding that current remedies of the Board designed to cure violations of Section 8(a)(5) are inadequate. A mere affirmative order that an employer bargain upon request does not eradicate the effects of an unlawful delay of 2 or more years in the fulfillment of a statutory bargaining obligation. It does not put the employees in the position of bargaining strength they would have enjoyed if their employer had immediately recognized and bargained with their chosen representative. It does not dissolve the inevitable employee frustration or protect the Union from the loss of employee support attributable to such delay. The inadequacy of the remedy is all the more egregious where, as in the recent N.L.R.B. v. Tiidee Products, Inc.,[6] case, the court found that the employer had raised "frivolous" issues in order to postpone or avoid its lawful obligation to bargain. We have weighed these considerations most carefully. For the reasons stated below, however, we have reluctantly concluded that we cannot approve Trial Examiner's Recommended Order that Respondent compensate its employees for monetary losses incurred as a consequence of Respondent's determination to refuse to bargain until it had tested in court the validity of the Board's certification.

Section 10(c) of the Act directs the Board to order a person found to have committed an unfair labor practice to cease and desist and "to take such affirmative action including reinstatement of employees with or without back pay, as will effectuate the policies of this Act." This authority, as our colleagues note with full documentation, is extremely broad and was so intended by Congress. It is not so broad, however, as to permit the punishment of a particular respondent or a class of respondents. Nor is the statutory direction to the Board so compelling that the Board is without discretion in exercising the full sweep of its power, for it would defeat the purposes of the Act if the Board imposed an otherwise proper remedy that resulted in irreparable harm to a particular respondent and hampered rather than promoted meaningful collective bargaining. Moreover, as the Supreme Court recently emphasized, the Board's grant of power does not extend to compelling agreement. (H.K. Porter Co., Inc., v. N.L.R.B., 397 U.S.

6.　426 F.2d 1243 (C.A.D.C.).

99.) It is with respect to these three limitations upon the Board's power to remedy a violation of Section 8(a)(5) that we examine the UAW's requested remedy in this case.

The Trial Examiner concluded that the proposed remedy was not punitive, that it merely made the employees partially whole for losses occasioned by the Respondent's refusal to bargain, and was much less harsh than a backpay order for discharged employees, which might require the Respondent to pay wages to these employees as well as their replacements. Viewed solely in the context of an assumption of employee monetary losses resulting directly from the Respondent's violation of Section 8(a)(5), as finally determined in court, the Trial Examiner's conclusion appears reasonable. There are, however, other factors in this case which provide counterweights to that rationale. In the first place, there is no contention that this Respondent acted in a manner flagrantly in defiance of the statutory policy. On the contrary, the record indicates that this Respondent responsibly fulfills its legally established collective-bargaining obligations. It is clear that Respondent merely sought judicial affirmance of the Board's decision that the election of October 22, 1964, should not be set aside on the Respondent's objections. In the past, whenever an employer has sought court intervention in a representation proceeding the Board has argued forcefully that court intervention would be premature, that the employer had an unquestioned right under the statute to seek court review of any Board order before its bargaining obligation became final. Should this procedural right in 8(a)(5) cases be tempered by a large monetary liability in the event the employer's position in the representation case is ultimately found to be without merit? Of course, an employer or a union which engages in conduct later found in violation of the Act, does so at the peril of ultimate conviction and responsibility for a make-whole remedy. But the validity of a particular Board election tried in an unfair labor practice case is not, in our opinion, an issue on the same plane as the discharge of employees for union activity or other conduct in flagrant disregard of employee rights. There are wrongdoers and wrongdoers. Where the wrong in refusing to bargain is, at most, a debatable question, though ultimately found a wrong, the imposition of a large financial obligation on such a respondent may come close to a form of punishment for having elected to pursue a representation question beyond the Board and to the courts. The desirability of a compensatory remedy in a case remarkably similar to the instant case was recently considered by the Court of Appeals for the District of Columbia in United Steelworkers [Quality Rubber Manufacturing Company, Inc.] v. N.L.R.B., 430 F.2d 519. There the court, distinguishing *Tiidee Products'* supra indicated that the Board was warranted in refusing to grant such a remedy in an 8(a)(5) case where the employer "desired only to obtain an authoritative determination of the validity of the Board's decision." It is not clear whether the court was of the opinion that the requested remedy was within the Board's discretion or whether it would have struck down such a remedy as punitive in view of the technical nature of the respondent's unfair labor practice. In any event, we find ourselves in disagreement with the Trial Examiner's view that a compensatory remedy as applied to the Respondent in the instant case is not punitive "in any sense of the Word."

In *Tiidee Products* the court suggested that the Board need not follow a uniform policy in the application of a compensatory remedy in 8(a)(5) cases. Indeed, the court noted that such uniformity in this area of the law would be unfair when applied "to unlike cases." The court was of the opinion that the remedy was proper where the employer had engaged in a "manifestly unjustifiable refusal to bargain" and where its position was "palpably without merit." [7] As in *Quality Rubber,* the court in *Tiidee Products* distinguished those cases in which the employer's failure to bargain rested on a "debatable question." With due respect for the opinion of the Court of Appeals for the District of Columbia, we cannot agree that the application of a compensatory remedy in 8(a)(5) cases can be fashioned on the subjective determination that the position of one respondent is "debatable" while that of another is "frivolous." What is debatable to the Board may appear frivolous to a court, and vice versa. Thus, the debatability of the employer's position in an 8(a)(5) case would itself become a matter of intense litigation.

We do not believe that the critical question of the employer's motivation in delaying bargaining should depend so largely on the expertise of counsel, the accident of circumstances, and the exigencies of the moment.

In our opinion, however, the crucial question to be determined in this case relates to the policies which the requested order would effectuate. The statutory policy as embodied in Section 8(a)(5) and (d) of the Act was considered at some length by the Supreme Court in H.K. Porter Co., Inc. v. N.L.R.B., supra. There the Court held that the Board has power to require employers and employees "to negotiate" but that the Board was without power to compel a company or a union "to agree to any substantive contractual provision of a collective bargaining agreement." The purpose of the Act, the Court held, was to ensure that employers and their employees "work together to establish mutually satisfactory conditions." The Court noted that Congress was aware that agreement between employers and unions might not always be reached, that agreement might in some cases be impossible, or thwarted by strikes and lockouts. But it was never intended, the Court held, that the Government in such cases step in and become a party to the negotiations. Recognizing that the Board's remedial powers might be insufficient to cope with important labor problems, the Supreme Court nevertheless struck down an order requiring the respondent employer involuntarily to agree to a specific contractual provision. It was the job of Congress, not the Board or the courts, Justice Black wrote, "to decide when and if it is necessary to allow governmental review of proposals for collective bargaining agreements and compulsory submission to one side's demands."

It is argued that the instant case is distinguishable from *H.K. Porter* in that here the requested remedy merely would require an employer to compensate employees for losses they incurred as a consequence of their employer's *failure to agree* to a contract he *would* have agreed to if he had bargained in good faith. In our view, the distinction is more illusory than real. The remedy in *H.K. Porter* operates prospectively to bind an employer to a specific contractual term. The remedy in the instant case operates

---

7. In these cases, at least, it would seem incumbent on the Board to utilize to the fullest extent its authority under Sec. 10(j) and (e) of the Act, thereby minimizing the pernicious delay in collective bargaining and consequent loss of benefits to the employees affected. See also Justice Harlan's concurrence in *H.K. Porter,* supra.

retroactively to impose financial liability upon an employer flowing from a *presumed* contractual agreement. The Board [dissent or Union?] infers that the latter contract, though it never existed and does not and need not exist, was *denied* existence by the employer because of his refusal to bargain. In either case the employer has not agreed to the contractual provision for which he must accept full responsibility *as though he had agreed to it.* Our colleagues contend that a compensatory remedy is not the "writing of a contract" because it does not "specify new or continuing terms of employment and does not prohibit changes in existing terms and conditions." But there is no basis for such a remedy unless the Board finds, as a matter of fact, that a contract would have resulted from bargaining. The fact that the contract, so to speak, is "written in the air" does not diminish its financial impact upon the recalcitrant employer who, willy-nilly, is forced to accede to terms never mutually established by the parties. Despite the admonition of the Supreme Court that Section 8(d) was intended to mean what it says, i.e., that the obligation to bargain "does not compel either party to agree to a proposal or require the making of a concession," one of the parties under this remedy is forced by the Government to submit to the other side's demands. It does not help to argue that the remedy could not be applied unless there was substantial evidence that the employer would have yielded to these demands during bargaining negotiations. Who is to say in a specific case how much an employer is prepared to give and how much a union is willing to take? Who is to say that a favorable contract would, in any event, result from the negotiations? And it is only the employer of such good will as to whom the Board might conclude that he, at least, would have given his employees a fair increase, who can be made subject to a financial reparations order; should such an employer be singled out for the imposition of such an order? To answer these questions the Board would be required to engage in the most general, if not entirely speculative, inferences to reach the conclusion that employees were deprived of specific benefits as a consequence of their employer's refusal to bargain.

Much as we appreciate the need for more adequate remedies in 8(a)(5) cases, we believe that, as the law now stands, the proposed remedy is a matter for Congress, not the Board. In our opinion, however, substantial relief may be obtained immediately through procedural reform, giving the highest possible priority to 8(a)(5) cases combined with full resort to the injunctive relief provisions of Section 10(j) and (e) of the Act.

Members McCulloch and Brown, dissenting in part:

* * *

The present remedies for unlawful refusals to bargain often fall short, as in the present case, of adequately protecting the employees' right to bargain. Recent court decisions, congressional investigations, and scholarly studies have concluded that, in the present remedial framework, justice delayed is often justice denied.

In N.L.R.B. v. Tiidee Products, Inc., the Court of Appeals for the District of Columbia Circuit recently stated that:

" * * * Employee interest in a union can wane quickly as working conditions remain apparently unaffected by the union or collective bargaining. When the company is finally ordered to bargain with the union some years later, the union may find that it represents only a small fraction of the employees. See Ross, Analysis of Administrative Process Under Taft-Hartley, 1966 Labor Relations Yearbook 299, 302–303; Note, An Assessment of the Proposed 'Make-Whole' Remedy in Refusal-To-Bargain Cases, 67 Mich.L. Rev. 374, 378 (1968). Thus the employer may reap a second benefit from his original refusal to comply with the law: He may continue to enjoy lower labor expenses after the order to bargain either because the union is gone or because it is too weak to bargain effectively."

A study by Professor Philip Ross shows that a contract is signed in most situations where the employer honors its duty to bargain without delay,[47] but that the chance of a contract being signed is cut in half if the case must go to court enforcement of a bargaining order.[48] In the interim, of course, the employees are deprived of their rightful union representation and the opportunity to bargain over their terms and conditions of employment, while at the same time their employers may gain a monetary advantage over their competitors who have complied with their legal duty.

The present case is but another example of a situation where a bargaining order by itself is not really adequate to remedy the effects of an unlawful refusal to bargain. * * * While a bargaining order at this time, operating prospectively, may insure the exercise of that right in the future, it clearly does not repair the injury to the employees here, caused by the Respondent's denial of their rights during the past 5 years.

* * * [T]he injury suffered by employees is predicated upon the employees' being deprived of the right to collective bargaining as required by the Act. The burden of proof would be upon the General Counsel at the compliance stage to translate that legal injury into terms of measurable

---

47. An independent study of UAW experience in obtaining first bargaining contracts during a 6-month period was made by Professor Ross, and the results were appended to the UAW's brief. The study indicates that the UAW succeeded in obtaining contracts in 97 percent of the cases following a Board-conducted election. The contracts resulted in average percentage wage increases of 7.9 percent and an average increase in the value of fringe benefits amounting to 3.9 percent.

48. A study made of 1960 cases in five Board Regional Offices revealed that unions succeeded in gaining contracts in 84 to 90 percent of the cases following their winning Board-conducted elections. Ross, The Government as a Source of Union Power 251 (1965). Professor Ross' more recent study, The Labor Law in Action: An Analysis of the Administrative Process Under the Taft-Hartley Act (1966), considered all 8(a)(5) cases during a 5-year period. Cases concerning first bargaining situations yielded the following conclusions:

"By far, the most significant influence on bargaining consequences was the stage of case disposition. The facts speak for themselves. About two-thirds of cases closed before issuance of complaints resulted in execution of first contracts. * * *

"With the exception of a handful of cases which required Supreme Court action prior to closing, the longer the litigation the less likely was the prospect of the signing of a first contract. Only about half (approximately 57 percent) of all cases closed after a Board order resulted in such contracts and less than 36 percent of the cases closed after circuit court enforcement ended up with agreements.

"The explanation for these results which comes most readily to mind is the factor of time. The long, drawn out process of administrative investigation, hearing and findings and, ultimately adjudication, bring two, three or four years of delay and a weakening of the charging union through the effects of the unexpunged unfair labor practices upon the employees. * * *"

Professor Ross' earlier study revealed that on the average nearly 2½ years elapse between the filing of an unfair labor practice charge and the issuance of a judicial decree. Ross, The Government as a Source of Union Power, at 171.

financial loss, if any, which the employees might reasonably be found to have suffered as a consequence of that injury.

A showing at the compliance stage by the General Counsel or Charging Party by acceptable and demonstrable means that the employees could have reasonably expected to gain a certain amount of compensation by bargaining would establish a *prima facie* loss, and the Respondent would then be afforded an opportunity to rebut such a showing. This might be accomplished, for example, by adducing evidence to show that a contract would probably not have been reached, or that there would have been less or no increase in compensation as a result of any contract which might have been signed.

Accordingly, uncertainty as to the amount of loss does not preclude a make-whole order proposed here, and some reasonable method or basis of computation can be worked out as part of the compliance procedure. These cannot be defined in advance, but there are many methods for determining the measurable financial gain which the employees might reasonably have expected to achieve, had the Respondent fulfilled its statutory obligation to bargain collectively. The criteria which prove valid in each case must be determined by what is pertinent to the facts. Nevertheless, the following methods for measuring such loss do appear to be available, although these are neither exhaustive nor exclusive. Thus, if the particular employer and union involved have contracts covering other plants of the employer, possibly in the same or a relevant area, the terms of such agreements may serve to show what the employees could probably have obtained by bargaining.[68] The parties could also make comparisons with compensation patterns achieved through collective bargaining by other employees in the same geographic area and industry. Or the parties might employ the national average percentage changes in straight time hourly wages computed by the Bureau of Labor Statistics. * * *

For the reasons set out above, we would order the Employer to make its employees whole for their measurable losses, if any, resulting from the unlawful refusal to bargain. We dissent from the Decision of the Board to the extent that it fails to direct such a remedy.

Note

1. The D.C. Court of Appeals had the later word. In a 2 to 1 decision, it remanded the Ex-Cell-O case to the Board, stating testily: "We * * * grant the Union's motion for summary reversal of the NLRB's decision insofar as it denies 'make-whole' compensation to the Union on the ground that the denial was in direct conflict with this Court's Tiidee Products * * * decision, and remand the case to the Board for further proceedings * * *, including express determinations whether Ex-Cell-O's objections to the certification were frivolous or fairly debatable, and whether 'make-whole' compensation or some other special remedy is appropriate." Sub nom. International Union, UAW v. NLRB, 449 F.2d 1046, 1050 (D.C.Cir.1971).

2. The Ex-Cell-O case is symptomatic of an incredible amount of yo-yoing between the Board and the D.C. Court of Appeals over the make-whole relief

---

68. As an example, the Union here presented evidence of the collective-bargaining agreements it had negotiated with Ex-Cell-O at five of its other plants in nearby States.

issue in one or another of its facets.[b] In the Heck's case, which follows, the Supreme Court seeks to snip the string.

NATIONAL LABOR RELATIONS BOARD v. FOOD STORE EMPLOYEES UNION, LOCAL 347 ["HECK'S"]

Supreme Court of the United States, 1974.
417 U.S. 1, 94 S.Ct. 2074, 40 L.Ed.2d 612.

MR. JUSTICE BRENNAN delivered the opinion of the Court.

The National Labor Relations Board refused to include in a cease and desist order against Heck's Inc. a provision sought by respondent union, as charging party, that Heck's reimburse respondent's litigation expenses and excess organizational costs incurred as a result of Heck's unlawful conduct. The Board's stated reason was that "it would not on balance effectuate the policies of the [National Labor Relations] Act to require reimbursement with respect to such costs in the circumstances here." 191 N.L.R.B. 886, 889 (1971). Respondent prevailed, however, in enforcement and review proceedings in the Court of Appeals for the District of Columbia Circuit. That court enlarged the Board's order by adding a provision, paragraph 2(f), that Heck's "Pay to the Board and the Union the costs and expenses incurred by them in the investigation, preparation, presentation, and conduct of these cases before the National Labor Relations Board and the courts, such costs to be determined at the compliance stage of these proceedings." See 155 U.S.App. D.C. 101, 476 F.2d 546 (1973). We granted certiorari to consider whether the enlargement of this order was a proper exercise of the authority of courts of appeals under § 10(e) and (f) of the Act * * * to "make and enter a decree * * * modifying, and enforcing as so modified" the order of the Board * * *. We reverse. *Supreme Ct.*

Heck's Inc. operates a chain of discount stores in the Southeast section of the country. Its resistance to union organization has resulted in some 11 proceedings before the National Labor Relations Board. This case grew out of its efforts to prevent organization by respondent union of Heck's employees at its store in Clarksburg, West Virginia. The case was twice before the

---

b. The history of the Tiidee Products cases exemplifies: In 1969, the Board found violations of Sections 8(a)(1), (3), and (5) on the basis of pre- and post-election conduct, including a refusal to bargain until "all litigation" had been resolved; the Board, however, denied "make-whole" relief. Tiidee I, 174 N.L. R.B. 705 (1969). The court enforced the Board orders but remanded for further consideration of make-whole relief. 426 F.2d 1243, cert. denied, 400 U.S. 950 (1970). In the meantime, conduct of the employer subsequent to the original Board hearing had resulted in a second unfair labor practice proceeding in which the Board again found Section 8(a)(1), (3), and (5) violations, and again refused make-whole relief. Tiidee II, 176 N.L.R.B. 969 (1969). The court again remanded for reconsideration of remedy. 440 F.2d 298 (1970). In 1972, the Board reconsidered both cases and denied make-whole relief in each, but ordered the employer to reimburse the union and the Board for their expenses in the unfair labor practice proceedings since the expenses resulted from the employer's "frivolous" refusals to bargain. Tiidee I, 194 N.L.R.B. 1234 (1972); Tiidee II, 196 N.L.R.B. 158 (1972). In 1974, both cases were again heard in the D.C. Circuit and the Board's orders enforced. However, the remedy was modified to restrict the litigation expenses payable by the employer to those incurred by the union in the initial Board proceedings because subsequent proceedings related to the "non-frivolous" issue of appropriate remedy, and also to eliminate the imposition of the Board's expenses on the employer. International Union of Electrical Workers v. NLRB ("Tiidee I & II"), 163 U.S. App.D.C. 347, 502 F.2d 349 (1974), cert. denied, 421 U.S. 991, 95 S.Ct. 1997, 44 L.Ed.2d 481 (1975).

Board. In its first decision, the Board determined that Heck's violated § 8(a) (1) of the Act * * * by threatening and coercively interrogating employees during respondent's organizational campaign, and by conducting a nonsecret poll to ascertain employee support for the union. Further, the Board found that Heck's "flagrant repetition" of similar unfair labor practices at its other stores, and its "extensive violations of the Act" in the Clarksburg store justified an inference that Heck's did not entertain any good-faith doubt concerning majority support for respondent union when the company refused to recognize and bargain with the union on the basis of authorization cards signed by a majority of employees. Accordingly, the Board found that Heck's violated § 8(a)(5) and (1) of the Act * * *. Finally, because Heck's extensive violations were found to have made a free and fair election impossible, an order directing Heck's to bargain with the union was entered. The Board rejected, however, the union's argument that adequate relief required certain additional remedies, including reimbursement of litigation expenses and excess organizational costs incurred as a result of Heck's unlawful behavior.[2] Heck's Inc., 172 N.L.R.B. 2231, at n. 2 (1968).

The Court of Appeals for the District of Columbia Circuit enforced the Board's order, but remanded to the Board for further consideration of additional remedies including reimbursement of litigation expenses and excess organizational costs. 139 U.S.App.D.C. 383, 433 F.2d 541 (1970).[3] On remand, the Board amended its original order to encompass certain supplemental remedies,[4] but again refused to order reimbursement of litigation expenses and excess organizational costs.[5] Heck's Inc., supra, 191 N.L.R.B. 886. Although the Board found that Heck's unfair labor practices were "aggravated and pervasive" and that its intransigence had probably caused the union to incur greater litigation expenses and organizational costs, the Board's rationale, previously mentioned, was that the provision would not effectuate the policies of the Act. The Board reasoned that its "orders must be remedial, not punitive, and collateral losses are not considered in framing

2. The Board also rejected respondent's requests for provisions directing the mailing of notices to employees; either a company-wide bargaining order or a shifting of the burden of proof in future cases to require Heck's to demonstrate its good faith in rejecting authorization cards; injunctions under § 10(j) of the Act; increased access to employees; and a "make-whole" provision directing compensation to employees for collective-bargaining benefits lost as a result of the employer's unlawful conduct.

3. The remand was ordered in light of the Court of Appeals' intervening decision in International Union of Elec., Radio and Mach. Workers v. NLRB, 138 U.S.App.D.C. 249, 426 F.2d 1243 (1970), known as the Tiidee Products case, in which the court had remanded for further Board consideration a union's submission that similar supplementary remedies were necessary where an employer's refusal to bargain was found to be "a clear and flagrant violation of the law," and its objections to a representation election were determined to be "patently frivolous." Id., at 1248.

4. The Board directed Heck's to mail notices of the Board's amended order to the homes of all employees at each of Heck's store locations; to provide the union with reasonable access for a one-year period to bulletin boards and other places where union notices are normally posted; and to provide the union with a list of names and addresses of all employees at all locations, to be kept current for one year.

5. The Board also refused to order, as sought by respondent, that notices of the Board's decision be read to assembled groups of employees; that a companywide bargaining order be issued; that the company be required to bargain whenever the union obtained an authorization card majority at other locations; that greater access to employees on company property be granted; and that a "make-whole" provision for reimbursement of dues and fees, and collective-bargaining benefits, lost as a result of the unlawful refusal to bargain, be ordered.

a reimbursement order." Id., at 889 (footnotes omitted).[6] Moreover, a charging party's participation in the case is, the Board found, primarily for the purpose of protecting its private interests, whereas the Board has the primary responsibility for protecting the public interest. The Board therefore concluded that, although the public interest might also arguably be served "in allowing the Charging Party to recover the costs of its participation in this litigation," that consideration did not "override the general and well-established principle that litigation expenses are ordinarily not recoverable." Ibid. * * *

Prior to review of its supplementary decision in the Court of Appeals, the Board issued its decision in Tiidee Products, Inc., 194 N.L.R.B. 1234 (1972), in which the Board ordered reimbursement of litigation expenses in the context of a finding that an employer had engaged in "frivolous litigations."[7] The Board's opinion in *Tiidee* reasoned that industrial peace could be best achieved if "speedy access to uncrowded Board and court dockets [were] available" and therefore that an assessment of legal fees would serve the public interest by "discourag[ing] future frivolous litigation," 194 N.L.R.B., at 1236. The Board did not explain why those considerations had not led it to order similar relief in this case. The Court of Appeals therefore concluded in the present case that the Board had abandoned its policy against award of litigation expenses and excess organizational costs,[8] stating

"Although the Board in its Supplemental Decision in this case has nowhere characterized the litigation as frivolous, it has used the language of 'clearly aggravated and pervasive' misconduct; and in its original opinion it questioned Heck's good faith because of its 'flagrant repetition of conduct previously found unlawful' at other Heck's stores. It would appear that the Board has now recognized that employers who follow a pattern of resisting union organization, and who to that end unduly burden the processes of the Board and the courts, should be obliged, at the very least, to respond in terms of making good the legal expenses to which they have put the charging parties and the Board. We hold that the case before us is an appropriate one for according such relief." 476 F.2d, at 551.

The Court of Appeals also viewed *Tiidee* as the signal of a shift in the Board's attitude toward excess organizational costs. In *Tiidee,* the Board refused to order reimbursement of excess organizational costs because " 'no

---

6. In support of this proposition, the Board relied upon Republic Steel Corp. v. NLRB, 311 U.S. 7, 11–12, 61 S.Ct. 77, 79, 85 L.Ed. 6 (1940) * * *. [Discussed supra p. 610, Note 3.]

7. The Board's decision in *Tiidee* was issued after supplementary proceedings following a remand from the Court of Appeals. See n. 3, supra. In an opinion filed April 25, 1974, the Court of Appeals, on review of the Board's supplementary decision in *Tiidee,* enforced as modified the Board's amended order. International Union of Elec., Radio and Mach. Workers v. NLRB, 502 F.2d 349.

8. The Court of Appeals made clear that the enlargement of the Board order was based squarely on the Board's change of policy perceived to have been made by *Tiidee.* The court refused to decide the question argued by

respondent union that, independently of *Tiidee,* an order of reimbursement should be directed. The Court of Appeals said:

"There are, it seems to us, obvious difficulties [in relying upon the subsidiary role of the charging party as a basis for denial of litigation expenses] * * *, certainly in the case of an employer who appears to look upon litigation as a convenient means of delaying—and thereby perhaps avoiding—the fatal day of union recognition and collective bargaining. *We need not pursue those difficulties in detail,* however, for the reason that the Board itself has subsequently departed from the rationale upon which its refusal of litigation expenses in this case is based." 476 F.2d, at 550 (emphasis added).

nexus between [the employer's] unlawful conduct * * * and the Union's pre-election organizational expenses' " had been proved. 476 F.2d, at 551. Since, in the instant case, the Board had indicated that Heck's violations had probably caused respondent to incur excess organizational costs, a nexus was proved and accordingly the court held that respondent was entitled to an order directing reimbursement of organizational costs.

In the circumstances of this case, the Court of Appeals, in our view improperly exercised its authority under § 10(e) and (f) to modify Board orders, and the case must therefore be returned to the Board.[9] Congress has invested the Board, not the courts, with broad discretion to order a violator "to take such affirmative action * * * as will effectuate the policies of this Act." 29 U.S.C.A. § 160(c) * * *. This case does not present the exceptional situation in which crystal clear Board error renders a remand an unnecessary formality. * * * For it cannot be gainsaid that the finding here that Heck's asserted at least "debatable" defenses to the unfair labor practice charges, whereas objections to the representation election in *Tiidee* were "patently frivolous," might have been viewed by the Board as putting the question of remedy in a different light. We cannot say that the Board, in performing its appointed function of balancing conflicting interests, could not reasonably decide that where "debatable" defenses are asserted, the public and private interests in affording the employer a determination of his "debatable" defenses, unfettered by the prospect of bearing his adversary's litigation costs, outweigh the public interest in uncrowded dockets.

There are, however, facial inconsistencies between the Board's opinion in this case and the *Tiidee* decision, and the Court of Appeals therefore correctly declined to resolve those inconsistencies by substituting Board counsel's rationale for that of the Board. 476 F.2d, at 552 n. 8; see NLRB v. Metropolitan Life Ins. Co., 380 U.S. 438, 444, 85 S.Ct. 1061, 1064, 13 L.Ed.2d 951 (1965) * * *. The integrity of the administrative process demands no less than that the Board, not its legal representative, exercise the discretionary judgment which Congress has entrusted to it. But since a plausible reconciliation by the Board of the seeming inconsistency was reasonably possible, it was "incompatible with the orderly function of the process of judicial review," NLRB v. Metropolitan Life Ins. Co., supra, 380 U.S. at 444, 85 S.Ct. at 1064, for the Court of Appeals to enlarge the Heck's order without first affording the Board an opportunity to clarify the inconsistencies.

It is a guiding principle of administrative law, long recognized by this Court, that "an administrative determination in which is imbedded a legal question open to judicial review does not impliedly foreclose the administrative agency, after its error has been corrected, from enforcing the legislative policy committed to its charge." FCC v. Pottsville Broadcasting Co., 309 U.S. 134, 145, 60 S.Ct. 437, 442 84 L.Ed. 656 (1940) * * *. Thus, when a reviewing court concludes that an agency invested with broad discretion to fashion remedies has apparently abused that discretion by omitting a remedy justified in the court's view by the factual circumstances, remand to the agency for reconsideration, and not enlargement of the agency order, is

---

9. We thus have no occasion at this time to address the question whether the Board's broad powers under § 10(c) * * * to fashion remedies includes power to order reimbursement of litigation expenses and excess organizational costs.

ordinarily the reviewing court's proper course. Application of that general principle in this case best respects the congressional scheme investing the Board and not the courts with broad powers to fashion remedies that will effectuate national labor policy. It also affords the Board the opportunity, through additional evidence or findings, to reframe its order better to effectuate that policy. * * * Moreover, in this case, if the Court of Appeals correctly read *Tiidee* as having signalled a change of policy in respect of reimbursement, a remand was necessary, because the Board should be given the first opportunity to determine whether the new policy should be applied retroactively.

The judgment of the Court of Appeals is reversed insofar as paragraph 2(f) was added to the Board's order, and the case is remanded to the Court of Appeals with direction that it be remanded to the Board for further proceedings.

Note

1. On remand, the Board stood pat on its remedial order, explaining the difference in its Heck's and Tiidee remedies on the ground that in the former the employer's position was at least "debatable," whereas in the latter the employer's position was "frivolous":

> "Thus, those cases, when read together, indicated our intent to refrain from assessing litigation expenses against a respondent, notwithstanding that the respondent may be found to have engaged in 'clearly aggravated and pervasive misconduct' or in the 'flagrant repetition of conduct previously found unlawful,' where the defenses raised by that respondent are 'debatable' rather than 'frivolous.' Likewise, it was our intention, under similar circumstances, to refrain from ordering reimbursement of excess organizational costs although a nexus has been shown between such excess costs incurred by a union and the unfair labor practices committed by an employer." Heck's Inc., 215 N.L.R.B. 765, at 767 (1974).

Lest the reader find over-solace in the foregoing, the Board added: "[W]e [do not] intend to lock in concrete any past precedent, nor to appear to make this Decision the authoritative expression of future remedial policy." Id. at 768.

Is "debatability" of defense a satisfactory standard as applied to "flagrant repetition of conduct previously found unlawful"?

2. Does adequate answer to the inadequate remedy question lie ultimately with Congress? What legislative reform would you suggest? The Labor Reform Bill of 1978, passed by the House but not by the Senate, contained the following provision:

> "Sec. 8. Section 10(c) [of the NLRA] is amended * * *
>
> "(3) by adding at the end thereof the following new paragraphs.
>
> * * *
>
> " '(3) * * * In a case in which the Board determines that an unlawful refusal to bargain prior to the entry into the first collective-bargaining contract between the employer and the representative selected or designated by a majority of the employees in the bargaining unit has taken place, the Board may award to the employees in that unit compensation for the delay in bargaining caused by the unfair labor practice which shall be measured by the difference between (i) the wages and other benefits received by such

employees during the period of delay, and (ii) the wages and fringe benefits such employees were receiving at the time of the unfair labor practice multiplied by the percentage change in wages and other benefits stated in the Bureau of Labor Statistics' average wage and benefit settlements, quarterly report of major collective-bargaining settlements, for the quarter in which the delay began.   *   *   * ' "

Chapter 7

PROBLEMS ARISING UNDER
THE COLLECTIVE AGREEMENT

A. ENFORCEMENT OF THE COLLECTIVE AGREEMENT

TEXTILE WORKERS UNION v. LINCOLN MILLS

Supreme Court of the United States, 1957.
353 U.S. 448, 77 S.Ct. 912, 1 L.Ed.2d 972.

MR. JUSTICE DOUGLAS delivered the opinion of the Court.

Petitioner-union entered into a collective bargaining agreement in 1953 with respondent-employer, the agreement to run one year and from year to year thereafter, unless terminated on specified notices. The agreement provided that there would be no strikes or work stoppages and that grievances would be handled pursuant to a specified procedure. The last step in the grievance procedure—a step that could be taken by either party—was arbitration.

This controversy involves several grievances that concern work loads and work assignments. The grievances were processed through the various steps in the grievance procedure and were finally denied by the employer. The union requested arbitration, and the employer refused. Thereupon the union brought this suit in the District Court to compel arbitration.

The District Court concluded that it had jurisdiction and ordered the employer to comply with the grievance arbitration provisions of the collective bargaining agreement. The Court of Appeals reversed by a divided vote. 230 F.2d 81. It held that, although the District Court had jurisdiction to entertain the suit, the court had no authority founded either in federal or state law to grant the relief. The case is here on a petition for a writ of certiorari which we granted because of the importance of the problem and the contrariety of views in the courts. * * *

The starting point of our inquiry is § 301 of the Labor Management Relations Act of 1947, * * * which provides:

"(a) Suits for violation of contracts between an employer and a labor organization representing employees in an industry affecting commerce as defined in this chapter, or between any such labor organizations, may be brought in any district court of the United States having jurisdiction of the parties, without respect to the amount in controversy or without regard to the citizenship of the parties.

"(b) Any labor organization which represents employees in an industry affecting commerce as defined in this chapter and any employer whose activities affect commerce as defined in this chapter shall be bound by the acts of its agents. Any such labor organization may sue or be sued as an entity and in behalf of the employees whom it represents in the courts of the United States. Any money judgment against a labor organization in a district court of the United States shall be enforceable only against the organization as an entity and against its assets, and shall not be enforceable against any individual member or his assets."

There has been considerable litigation involving § 301 and courts have construed it differently. There is one view that § 301(a) merely gives federal district courts jurisdiction in controversies that involve labor organizations in industries affecting commerce, without regard to diversity of citizenship or the amount in controversy. Under that view § 301(a) would not be the source of substantive law; it would neither supply federal law to resolve these controversies nor turn the federal judges to state law for answers to the questions. Other courts—the overwhelming number of them—hold that § 301(a) is more than jurisdictional—that it authorizes federal courts to fashion a body of federal law for the enforcement of these collective bargaining agreements and includes within that federal law specific performance of promises to arbitrate grievances under collective bargaining agreements. * * * That is our construction of § 301(a), which means that the agreement to arbitrate grievance disputes, contained in this collective bargaining agreement, should be specifically enforced.

From the face of the Act it is apparent that § 301(a) and § 301(b) supplement one another. Section 301(b) makes it possible for a labor organization, representing employees in an industry affecting commerce, to sue and be sued as an entity in the federal courts. Section 301(b) in other words provides the procedural remedy lacking at common law. Section 301(a) certainly does something more than that. Plainly, it supplies the basis upon which the federal district courts may take jurisdiction and apply the procedural rule of § 301(b). The question is whether § 301(a) is more than jurisdictional.

The legislative history of § 301 is somewhat cloudy and confusing. But there are a few shafts of light that illuminate our problem.

The bills, as they passed the House and the Senate, contained provisions which would have made the failure to abide by an agreement to arbitrate an unfair labor practice. S.Rep. No. 105, 80th Cong., 1st Sess., pp. 20–21, 23; H.R. Rep. No. 245, 80th Cong., 1st Sess., p. 21. This feature of the law was dropped in Conference. As the Conference Report stated, "Once parties have made a collective bargaining contract, the enforcement of that contract should be left to the usual processes of the law and not to the National Labor Relations Board." H.R.Conf.Rep. No. 510, 80th Cong., 1st Sess., p. 42.

* * * Both the Senate Report and the House Report indicate a primary concern that unions as well as employees [employers?] should be bound to collective bargaining contracts. But there was also a broader

concern—a concern with a procedure for making such agreements enforceable in the courts by either party. At one point the Senate Report, supra p. 15, states, "We feel that the aggrieved party should also have a right of action in the Federal courts. Such a policy is completely in accord with the purpose of the Wagner Act which the Supreme Court declared was 'to compel employers to bargain collectively with their employees to the end that an employment contract, binding on both parties, should be made * * *.' "

Congress was also interested in promoting collective bargaining that ended with agreements not to strike. * * *

Plainly the agreement to arbitrate grievance disputes is the *quid pro quo* for an agreement not to strike. Viewed in this light, the legislation does more than confer jurisdiction in the federal courts over labor organizations. It expresses a federal policy that federal courts should enforce these agreements on behalf of or against labor organizations and that industrial peace can be best obtained only in that way.

To be sure, there is a great medley of ideas reflected in the hearings, reports, and debates on this Act. Yet, to repeat, the entire tenor of the history indicates that the agreement to arbitrate grievance disputes was considered as *quid pro quo* of a no-strike agreement. And when in the House the debate narrowed to the question whether § 301 was more than jurisdictional, it became abundantly clear that the purpose of the section was to provide the necessary legal remedies. Section 302 of the House bill, the substantial equivalent of the present § 301, was being described by Mr. Hartley, the sponsor of the bill in the House:

> "MR. BARDEN. Mr. Chairman, I take this time for the purpose of asking the Chairman a question, and in asking the question I want it understood that it is intended to make a part of the record that may hereafter be referred to as history of the legislation.

> "It is my understanding that section 302, the section dealing with equal responsibility under collective bargaining contracts in strike actions and proceedings in district courts contemplates not only the ordinary lawsuits for damages but also such other remedial proceedings, both legal and equitable, as might be appropriate in the circumstances; in other words, proceedings could, for example, be brought by the employers, the labor organizations, or interested individual employees under the Declaratory Judgments Act in order to secure declarations from the Court of legal rights under the contract.

> "MR. HARTLEY. The interpretation the gentleman has just given of that section is absolutely correct." 93 Cong.Rec. 3656–3657.

It seems, therefore, clear to us that Congress adopted a policy which placed sanctions behind agreements to arbitrate grievance disputes, by implication rejecting the common-law rule, discussed in Red Cross Line v. Atlantic Fruit Co., 264 U.S. 109, 44 S.Ct. 274, 68 L.Ed. 582, against enforcement of executory agreements to arbitrate.[7] We would undercut the Act

---

7. We do not reach the question, which the Court reserved in Red Cross Line v. Atlantic Fruit Co., supra, 264 U.S. at page 125, 44 S.Ct. at page 278, whether as a matter of federal law executory agreements to arbitrate are enforceable, absent congressional approval.

and defeat its policy if we read § 301 narrowly as only conferring jurisdiction over labor organizations.

The question then is, what is the substantive law to be applied in suits under § 301(a)? We conclude that the substantive law to apply in suits under § 301(a) is federal law, which the courts must fashion from the policy of our national labor laws. See Mendelsohn, Enforceability of Arbitration Agreements Under Taft-Hartley Section 301, 66 Yale L.J. 167. The Labor Management Relations Act expressly furnishes some substantive law. It points out what the parties may or may not do in certain situations. Other problems will lie in the penumbra of express statutory mandates. Some will lack express statutory sanction but will be solved by looking at the policy of the legislation and fashioning a remedy that will effectuate that policy. The range of judicial inventiveness will be determined by the nature of the problem. * * * Federal interpretation of the federal law will govern, not state law. * * * But state law, if compatible with the purpose of § 301, may be resorted to in order to find the rule that will best effectuate the federal policy. * * * Any state law applied, however, will be absorbed as federal law and will not be an independent source of private rights.

It is not uncommon for federal courts to fashion federal law where federal rights are concerned. * * * Congress has indicated by § 301(a) the purpose to follow that course here. There is no constitutional difficulty. Article III, § 2, extends the judicial power to cases "arising under * * * the Laws of the United States * * *." The power of Congress to regulate these labor-management controversies under the Commerce Clause is plain. * * * National Labor Relations Board v. Jones & Laughlin Corp., 301 U.S. 1, 57 S.Ct. 615, 81 L.Ed. 893. A case or controversy arising under § 301(a) is, therefore, one within the purview of judicial power as defined in Article III.

The question remains whether jurisdiction to compel arbitration of grievance disputes is withdrawn by the Norris-LaGuardia Act * * *. Section 7 of that Act prescribes stiff procedural requirements for issuing an injunction in a labor dispute. The kinds of acts which had given rise to abuse of the power to enjoin are listed in § 4. The failure to arbitrate was not a part and parcel of the abuses against which the Act was aimed. Section 8 of the Norris-LaGuardia Act does, indeed, indicate a congressional policy toward settlement of labor disputes by arbitration, for it denies injunctive relief to any person who has failed to make "every reasonable effort" to settle the dispute by negotiation, mediation, or "voluntary arbitration." Though a literal reading might bring the dispute within the terms of the Act (see Cox, Grievance Arbitration in the Federal Courts, 67 Harv.L. Rev. 591, 602–604), we see no justification in policy for restricting § 301(a) to damage suits, leaving specific performance of a contract to arbitrate grievance disputes to the inapposite procedural requirements of that Act. Moreover, we held in Virginian R. Co. v. System Federation, 300 U.S. 515, 57 S.Ct. 592, 81 L.Ed. 789, and in Graham v. Brotherhood of Firemen, 338 U.S. 232, 237, 70 S.Ct. 14, 17, 94 L.Ed. 22, that the Norris-LaGuardia Act does not deprive federal courts of jurisdiction to compel compliance with the mandates of the Railway Labor Act * * *. The mandates there involved concerned racial discrimination. Yet those decisions were not based on any peculiarities of the Railway Labor Act. We followed the same course in

Syres v. Oil Workers International Union, 350 U.S. 892, 76 S.Ct. 152, 100 L.Ed. 785, which was governed by the National Labor Relations Act * * *. There an injunction was sought against racial discrimination in application of a collective bargaining agreement; and we allowed the injunction to issue. The congressional policy in favor of the enforcement of agreements to arbitrate grievance disputes being clear,[9] there is no reason to submit them to the requirements of § 7 of the Norris-LaGuardia Act.

A question of mootness was raised on oral argument. It appears that since the date of the decision in the Court of Appeals respondent has terminated its operations and has contracted to sell its mill properties. All work in the mill ceased in March, 1957. Some of the grievances, however, ask for back pay for increased work loads; and the collective bargaining agreement provides that "the Board of Arbitration shall have the right to adjust compensation retroactive to the date of the change." Insofar as the grievances sought restoration of workloads and job assignments, the case is, of course, moot. But to the extent that they sought a monetary award, the case is a continuing controversy.

The judgment of the Court of Appeals is reversed and the cause is remanded to that court for proceedings in conformity with this opinion.

MR. JUSTICE BLACK took no part in the consideration or decision of this case.

MR. JUSTICE BURTON, whom MR. JUSTICE HARLAN joins, concurring in the result.

This suit was brought in a United States District Court under § 301 of the Labor Management Relations Act of 1947, * * * seeking specific enforcement of the arbitration provisions of a collective-bargaining contract. The District Court had jurisdiction over the action since it involved an obligation running to a union—a union controversy—and not uniquely personal rights of employees sought to be enforced by a union. Cf. Association of Westinghouse Salaried Employees v. Westinghouse Elec. Corp., 348 U.S. 437, 75 S.Ct. 489, 99 L.Ed. 510. Having jurisdiction over the suit, the court was not powerless to fashion an appropriate federal remedy. The power to decree specific performance of a collectively bargained agreement to arbitrate finds its source in § 301 itself, and in a Federal District Court's inherent equitable powers, nurtured by a congressional policy to encourage and enforce labor arbitration in industries affecting commerce.

I do not subscribe to the conclusion of the Court that the substantive law to be applied in a suit under § 301 is federal law. At the same time, I agree with Judge Magruder in International Brotherhood v. W.L. Mead, Inc., 1 Cir., 230 F.2d 576, that some federal rights may necessarily be involved in a § 301 case, and hence that the constitutionality of § 301 can be upheld as a congressional grant to Federal District Courts of what has been called "protective jurisdiction."

[The dissenting opinion of JUSTICE FRANKFURTER is omitted. He argued that section 301 only created jurisdiction in the federal courts and did not

---

9. Whether there are situations in which individual employees may bring suit in an appropriate state or federal court to enforce grievance rights under employment contracts where the collective bargaining agreement provides for arbitration of those grievances is a question we do not reach in this case. * * *

create a new federal substantive law. Accordingly, he concluded that Section 301 was unconstitutional since it purported to create federal jurisdiction where there was neither a federal question nor diversity of citizenship.]

Note

1. The following passage from Gregory, The Collective Bargaining Agreement: Its Nature and Scope, 1949 Wash.U.L.Q. 3, 11, briefly describes the legal status of collective agreements prior to enactment of Section 301:

"The legal significance of a collective agreement has always been uncertain. Some courts have called it a mere gentlemen's agreement, unenforcible at law; and the treaty analogy is still made. Our Supreme Court has said it is not a contract of employment at all. It is, rather, merely a schedule of terms and commitments, which become part of the individual workers' contracts of employment, whether or not they belong to the union. Insofar as the collective agreement is a contract at all, it has to be one between the employer and the union. This has led to much confusion, since most unions are not incorporated and thus cannot be legal parties to contracts. And if they are not legally recognized parties, they cannot act as plaintiffs in law suits to enforce these so-called contracts; nor can they be sued on them. Traditionally, only individual employees could enforce the terms of collective agreements, in some states only the members of the unions.

"In recent years, however, our courts are beginning to recognize collective agreements as legally binding contracts. This development means that unions may secure rights for themselves in contracts, over and above the rights secured for their constituents, with the legal power to sue for the enforcement of these rights. This recognition of unions as legal persons, capable of acting as parties to contracts and law-suits, has largely been the result of legislation. And now the Taft-Hartley Act permits unions to sue and be sued in the federal arena on their collective agreements."

2. The Supreme Court, in its first exposure to Section 301, a case prior to Lincoln Mills, had fragmented over the meaning to be given the section. A majority could be rallied only for the proposition that it was not, in any event, the intent of Congress to permit suits by employees or by unions in their behalf to enforce "uniquely personal rights of employees" (e.g., to unpaid wages) arising under collective bargaining agreements. Association of Westinghouse Salaried Employees v. Westinghouse Electric Corp., 348 U.S. 437, 75 S.Ct. 489, 99 L.Ed. 510 (1955) (discussed in the concurring opinion in Lincoln Mills, supra). Justice Frankfurter, writing for the Court (but joined by only two of his colleagues), justified the narrow interpretation of Section 301 in part by observing that "Congress, at a time when its attention was directed to congestion in the federal courts, particularly in the heavy industrial areas, [had not] intended to open the doors of the federal courts to a potential flood of grievances ＊　＊　＊." 348 U.S. at 460, 75 S.Ct. at 500.

The dike protecting the federal courts from these floodwaters was, of course, breached in Lincoln Mills.

The next four cases demonstrate the ingenuity of the Court in constructing sluices to divert from federal courthouse doors the waters of Section 301. The first three cases lead to one reservoir, the fourth to another.

UNITED STEELWORKERS v. AMERICAN MANUFACTURING CO.

Supreme Court of the United States, 1960.
363 U.S. 564, 80 S.Ct. 1343, 4 L.Ed.2d 1403.

Opinion of the Court by MR. JUSTICE DOUGLAS, announced by MR. JUSTICE BRENNAN.

This suit was brought by petitioner union in the District Court to compel arbitration of a "grievance" that petitioner, acting for one Sparks, a union member, had filed with the respondent, Sparks' employer. The employer defended on the ground (1) that Sparks is estopped from making his claim because he had a few days previously settled a workmen's compensation claim against the company on the basis that he was permanently partially disabled, (2) that Sparks is not physically able to do the work, and (3) that this type of dispute is not arbitrable under the collective bargaining agreement in question.

The agreement provided that during its term there would be "no strike," unless the employer refused to abide by a decision of the arbitrator. The agreement sets out a detailed grievance procedure with a provision for arbitration (regarded as the standard form) of all disputes between the parties "as to the meaning, interpretation and application of the provisions of this agreement." [1]

The agreement reserves to the management power to suspend or discharge any employee "for cause." [2] It also contains a provision that the employer will employ and promote employees on the principle of seniority "where ability and efficiency are equal." [3] Sparks left his work due to an injury and while off work brought an action for compensation benefits. The case was settled, Sparks' physician expressing the opinion that the injury had made him 25% "permanently partially disabled." That was on September 9. Two weeks later the union filed a grievance which charged that

1. The relevant arbitration provisions read as follows:

"Any disputes, misunderstandings, differences or grievances arising between the parties as to the meaning, interpretation and application of the provisions of this agreement, which are not adjusted as herein provided, may be submitted to the Board of Arbitration for decision. ✳ ✳ ✳

"The arbitrator may interpret this agreement and apply it to the particular case under consideration but shall, however, have no authority to add to, subtract from, or modify the terms of the agreement. Disputes relating to discharges or such matters as might involve a loss of pay for employees may carry an award of back pay in whole or in part as may be determined by the Board of Arbitration.

"The decision of the Board of Arbitration shall be final and conclusively binding upon both parties, and the parties agree to observe and abide by same. ✳ ✳ ✳ "

2. "The Management of the works, the direction of the working force, plant lay-out and routine of work, including the right to hire, suspend, transfer, discharge or otherwise discipline any employee for cause, such cause being: infraction of company rules, inefficiency, insubordination, contagious disease harmful to others, and any other ground or reason that would tend to reduce or impair the efficiency of plant operation; and to lay off employees because of lack of work, is reserved to the Company, provided it does not conflict with this agreement. ✳ ✳ ✳ "

3. This provision provides in relevant part:

"The Company and the Union fully recognize the principle of seniority as a factor in the selection of employees for promotion, transfer, lay-off, re-employment, and filling of vacancies, where ability and efficiency are equal. It is the policy of the Company to promote employees on that basis."

Sparks was entitled to return to his job by virtue of the seniority provision of the collective bargaining agreement. Respondent refused to arbitrate and this action was brought. The District Court held that Sparks, having accepted the settlement on the basis of permanent partial disability, was estopped to claim any seniority or employment rights and granted the motion for summary judgment. The Court of Appeals affirmed, 264 F.2d 624, for different reasons. After reviewing the evidence it held that the grievance is "a frivolous, patently baseless one, not subject to arbitration under the collective bargaining agreement." Id., at page 628. The case is here on a writ of certiorari.

Section 203(d) of the Labor Management Relations Act states, "Final adjustment by a method agreed upon by the parties is hereby declared to be the desirable method for settlement of grievance disputes arising over the application or interpretation of an existing collective-bargaining agreement. * * *" That policy can be effectuated only if the means chosen by the parties for settlement of their differences under a collective bargaining agreement is given full play.

A state decision that held to the contrary announced a principle that could only have a crippling effect on grievance arbitration. The case was International Ass'n of Machinists v. Cutler-Hammer, Inc., 271 App.Div. 917, 67 N.Y.S.2d 317, affirmed 297 N.Y. 519, 74 N.E.2d 464. It held that "If the meaning of the provision of the contract sought to be arbitrated is beyond dispute, there cannot be anything to arbitrate and the contract cannot be said to provide for arbitration." 271 App.Div. at page 918, 67 N.Y.S.2d at page 318. The lower courts in the instant case had a like preoccupation with ordinary contract law. The collective agreement requires arbitration of claims that courts might be unwilling to entertain. In the context of the plant or industry the grievance may assume proportions of which judges are ignorant. Yet, the agreement is to submit all grievances to arbitration, not merely those that a court may deem to be meritorious. There is no exception in the "no strike" clause and none therefore should be read into the grievance clause, since one is the *quid pro quo* for the other. The question is not whether in the mind of the court there is equity in the claim. Arbitration is a stabilizing influence only as it serves as a vehicle for handling any and all disputes that arise under the agreement.

The collective agreement calls for the submission of grievances in the categories which it describes, irrespective of whether a court may deem them to be meritorious. In our role of developing a meaningful body of law to govern the interpretation and enforcement of collective bargaining agreements, we think special heed should be given to the context in which collective bargaining agreements are negotiated and the purpose which they are intended to serve. * * * The function of the court is very limited when the parties have agreed to submit all questions of contract interpretation to the arbitrator. It is confined to ascertaining whether the party seeking arbitration is making a claim which on its face is governed by the contract. Whether the moving party is right or wrong is a question of contract interpretation for the arbitrator. In these circumstances the moving party should not be deprived of the arbitrator's judgment, when it was his judgment and all that it connotes that was bargained for.

The courts, therefore, have no business weighing the merits of the grievance, considering whether there is equity in a particular claim, or determining whether there is particular language in the written instrument which will support the claim. The agreement is to submit all grievances to arbitration, not merely those which the court will deem meritorious. The processing of even frivolous claims may have therapeutic values of which those who are not a part of the plant environment may be quite unaware.

The union claimed in this case that the company had violated a specific provision of the contract. The company took the position that it had not violated that clause. There was, therefore, a dispute between the parties as to "the meaning, interpretation and application" of the collective bargaining agreement. Arbitration should have been ordered. When the judiciary undertakes to determine the merits of a grievance under the guise of interpreting the grievance procedure of collective bargaining agreements, it usurps a function which under that regime is entrusted to the arbitration tribunal.

Reversed.

[JUSTICES FRANKFURTER and WHITTAKER concurred in the result. JUSTICE BLACK took no part in the case. JUSTICE BRENNAN'S concurring opinion in Warrior and Gulf, the next case, applies also to this case.]

UNITED STEELWORKERS v. WARRIOR AND GULF NAVIGATION CO.

Supreme Court of the United States, 1960.
363 U.S. 574, 80 S.Ct. 1347, 4 L.Ed.2d 1409.

Opinion of the Court by MR. JUSTICE DOUGLAS, announced by MR. JUSTICE BRENNAN.

Respondent transports steel and steel products by barge and maintains a terminal at Chickasaw, Alabama, where it performs maintenance and repair work on its barges. The employees at that terminal constitute a bargaining unit covered by a collective bargaining agreement negotiated by petitioner union. Respondent between 1956 and 1958 laid off some employees, reducing the bargaining unit from 42 to 23 men. This reduction was due in part to respondent contracting maintenance work, previously done by its employees, to other companies. The latter used respondent's supervisors to lay out the work and hired some of the laid-off employees of respondent (at reduced wages). Some were in fact assigned to work on respondent's barges. A number of employees signed a grievance which petitioner presented to respondent, the grievance reading:

"We are hereby protesting the Company's actions, of arbitrarily and unreasonably contracting out work to other concerns, that could and previously has been performed by Company employees.

"This practice becomes unreasonable, unjust and discriminatory in lieu [sic] of the fact that at present there are a number of employees that have been laid off for about 1 and ½ years or more for allegedly lack of work.

"Confronted with these facts we charge that the Company is in violation of the contract by inducing a partial lock-out, of a number of the employees who would otherwise be working were it not for this unfair practice."

The collective agreement had both a "no strike" and a "no lockout" provision. It also had a grievance procedure which provided in relevant part as follows:

"Issues which conflict with any Federal statute in its application as established by Court procedure or matters which are strictly a function of management shall not be subject to arbitration under this section.

"Should differences arise between the Company and the Union or its members employed by the Company as to the meaning and application of the provisions of this Agreement, or should any local trouble of any kind arise, there shall be no suspension of work on account of such differences but an earnest effort shall be made to settle such differences immediately in the following manner:

"A. For Maintenance Employees:

"First, between the aggrieved employees, and the Foreman involved;

"Second, between a member or members of the Grievance Committee designated by the Union, and the Foreman and Master Mechanic.

*   *   *   *   *   *   *   *   *

"Fifth, if agreement has not been reached the matter shall be referred to an impartial umpire for decision. The parties shall meet to decide on an umpire acceptable to both. If no agreement on selection of an umpire is reached, the parties shall jointly petition the United States Conciliation Service for suggestion of a list of umpires from which selection shall be made. The decision of the umpire will be final."

Settlement of this grievance was not had and respondent refused arbitration. This suit was then commenced by the union to compel it.

The District Court granted respondent's motion to dismiss the complaint. 168 F.Supp. 702. It held after hearing evidence, much of which went to the merits of the grievance, that the agreement did not "confide in an arbitrator the right to review the defendant's business judgment in contracting out work." Id., at page 705. It further held that "the contracting out of repair and maintenance work, as well as construction work, is strictly a function of management not limited in any respect by the labor agreement involved here." Ibid. The Court of Appeals affirmed by a divided vote, 269 F.2d 633, 635, the majority holding that the collective agreement had withdrawn from the grievance procedure "matters which are strictly a function of management" and that contracting out fell in that exception. The case is here on a writ of certiorari. *   *   *

We held in Textile Workers v. Lincoln Mills, 353 U.S. 448, 77 S.Ct. 912, 923, 1 L.Ed.2d 972, that a grievance arbitration provision in a collective agreement could be enforced by reason of § 301(a) of the Labor Management Relations Act and that the policy to be applied in enforcing this type of arbitration was that reflected in our national labor laws. *   *   * The present federal policy is to promote industrial stabilization through the collective bargaining agreement. *   *   * A major factor in achieving industrial peace is the inclusion of a provision for arbitration of grievances in the collective bargaining agreement.[4]

4. Complete effectuation of the federal policy is achieved when the agreement contains both an arbitration provision for all unresolved grievances and an absolute prohibition of strikes, the arbitration agreement being the *"quid pro quo"* for the agreement not

Thus the run of [commercial] arbitration cases, illustrated by Wilko v. Swan, 346 U.S. 427, 74 S.Ct. 182, 98 L.Ed. 168, becomes irrelevant to our problem. There the choice is between the adjudication of cases or controversies in courts with established procedures or even special statutory safeguards on the one hand and the settlement of them in the more informal arbitration tribunal on the other. In the commercial case, arbitration is the substitute for litigation. Here arbitration is the substitute for industrial strife. Since arbitration of labor disputes has quite different functions from arbitration under an ordinary commercial agreement, the hostility evinced by courts toward arbitration of commercial agreements has no place here. For arbitration of labor disputes under collective bargaining agreements is part and parcel of the collective bargaining process itself.

The collective bargaining agreement states the rights and duties of the parties. It is more than a contract; it is a generalized code to govern a myriad of cases which the draftsmen cannot wholly anticipate. See Shulman, Reason, Contract, and Law in Labor Relations, 68 Harv.L.Rev. 999, 1004–1005. The collective agreement covers the whole employment relationship.[5] It calls into being a new common law—the common law of a particular industry or of a particular plant. As one observer has put it:[6]

"* * * [I]t is not unqualifiedly true that a collective-bargaining agreement is simply a document by which the union and employees have imposed upon management limited, express restrictions of its otherwise absolute right to manage the enterprise, so that an employee's claim must fail unless he can point to a specific contract provision upon which the claim is founded. There are too many people, too many problems, too many unforeseeable contingencies to make the words of the contract the exclusive source of rights and duties. One cannot reduce all the rules governing a community like an industrial plant to fifteen or even fifty pages. Within the sphere of collective bargaining, the institutional characteristics and the governmental nature of the collective-bargaining process demand a common law of the shop which implements and furnishes the context of the agreement. We must assume that intelligent negotiators acknowledged so plain a need unless they stated a contrary rule in plain words."

A collective bargaining agreement is an effort to erect a system of industrial self-government. When most parties enter into contractual relationship they do so voluntarily, in the sense that there is no real compulsion to deal with one another, as opposed to dealing with other parties. This is

to strike. Textile Workers v. Lincoln Mills, 353 U.S. 448, 455, 77 S.Ct. 912, 917.

5. "Contracts which ban strikes often provide for lifting the ban under certain conditions. Unconditional pledges against strikes are, however, somewhat more frequent than conditional ones. Where conditions are attached to no-strike pledges, one or both of two approaches may be used: certain *subjects* may be exempted from the scope of the pledge, or the pledge may be lifted after certain *procedures* are followed by the union. (Similar qualifications may be made in pledges against lockouts.)

"Most frequent conditions for lifting no-strike pledges are: (1) The occurrence of a deadlock in wage reopening negotiations; and (2) violation of the contract, especially non-compliance with the grievance procedure and failure to abide by an arbitration award.

"No-strike pledges may also be lifted after compliance with specified procedures. Some contracts permit the union to strike after the grievance procedure has been exhausted without a settlement, and where arbitration is not prescribed as the final recourse. Other contracts permit a strike if mediation efforts fail, or after a specified cooling-off period." Collective Bargaining, Negotiations and Contracts, Bureau of National Affairs, Inc., 77:101.

6. Cox, Reflections Upon Labor Arbitration, 72 Harv.L.Rev. 1482, 1498–1499 (1959).

not true of the labor agreement. The choice is generally not between entering or refusing to enter into a relationship, for that in all probability pre-exists the negotiations. Rather it is between having that relationship governed by an agreed-upon rule of law or leaving each and every matter subject to a temporary resolution dependent solely upon the relative strength, at any given moment, of the contending forces. The mature labor agreement may attempt to regulate all aspects of the complicated relationship, from the most crucial to the most minute over an extended period of time. Because of the compulsion to reach agreement and the breadth of the matters covered, as well as the need for a fairly concise and readable instrument, the product of negotiations (the written document) is, in the words of the late Dean Shulman, "a compilation of diverse provisions: some provide objective criteria almost automatically applicable; some provide more or less specific standards which require reason and judgment in their application; and some do little more than leave problems to future consideration with an expression of hope and good faith." Shulman, supra, at 1005. Gaps may be left to be filled in by reference to the practices of the particular industry and of the various shops covered by the agreement. Many of the specific practices which underlie the agreement may be unknown, except in hazy form, even to the negotiators. Courts and arbitration in the context of most commercial contracts are resorted to because there has been a breakdown in the working relationship of the parties; such resort is the unwanted exception. But the grievance machinery under a collective bargaining agreement is at the very heart of the system of industrial self-government. Arbitration is the means of solving the unforeseeable by molding a system of private law for all the problems which may arise and to provide for their solution in a way which will generally accord with the variant needs and desires of the parties. The processing of disputes through the grievance machinery is actually a vehicle by which meaning and content are given to the collective bargaining agreement.

Apart from matters that the parties specifically exclude, all of the questions on which the parties disagree must therefore come within the scope of the grievance and arbitration provisions of the collective agreement. The grievance procedure is, in other words, a part of the continuous collective bargaining process. It, rather than a strike, is the terminal point of a disagreement.

The labor arbitrator performs functions which are not normal to the courts; the considerations which help him fashion judgments may indeed be foreign to the competence of courts.

"A proper conception of the arbitrator's function is basic. He is not a public tribunal imposed upon the parties by superior authority which the parties are obliged to accept. He has no general charter to administer justice for a community which transcends the parties. He is rather part of a system of self-government created by and confined to the parties. * * *" Shulman, supra, at 1016.

The labor arbitrator's source of law is not confined to the express provisions of the contract, as the industrial common law—the practices of the industry and the shop—is equally a part of the collective bargaining agreement although not expressed in it. The labor arbitrator is usually chosen because of the parties' confidence in his knowledge of the common law of the shop and their trust in his personal judgment to bring to bear considerations which are not expressed in the contract as criteria for judgment. The parties expect that his judgment of a particular grievance will reflect not only what the contract says but, insofar as the collective bargaining agreement permits, such factors as the effect upon productivity of a particular result, its consequence to the morale of the shop, his judgment whether tensions will be heightened or diminished. For the parties' objective in using the arbitration process is primarily to further their common goal of uninterrupted production under the agreement, to make the agreement serve their specialized needs. The ablest judge cannot be expected to bring the same experience and competence to bear upon the determination of a grievance, because he cannot be similarly informed.

The Congress, however, has by § 301 of the Labor Management Relations Act, assigned the courts the duty of determining whether the reluctant party has breached his promise to arbitrate. For arbitration is a matter of contract and a party cannot be required to submit to arbitration any dispute which he has not agreed so to submit. Yet, to be consistent with congressional policy in favor of settlement of disputes by the parties through the machinery of arbitration, the judicial inquiry under § 301 must be strictly confined to the question whether the reluctant party did agree to arbitrate the grievance or did agree to give the arbitrator power to make the award he made. An order to arbitrate the particular grievance should not be denied unless it may be said with positive assurance that the arbitration clause is not susceptible of an interpretation that covers the asserted dispute. Doubts should be resolved in favor of coverage.[7]

We do not agree with the lower courts that contracting-out grievances were necessarily excepted from the grievance procedure of this agreement. To be sure, the agreement provides that "matters which are strictly a function of management shall not be subject to arbitration." But it goes on to say that if "differences" arise or if "any local trouble of any kind" arises, the grievance procedure shall be applicable.

Collective bargaining agreements regulate or restrict the exercise of management functions; they do not oust management from the performance of them. Management hires and fires, pays and promotes, supervises and plans. All these are part of its function, and absent a collective bargaining agreement, it may be exercised freely except as limited by public law and by the willingness of employees to work under the particular, unilaterally imposed conditions. A collective bargaining agreement may treat only with certain specific practices, leaving the rest to management but subject to the possibility of work stoppages. When, however, an absolute no-strike clause is included in the agreement, then in a very real sense everything that management does is subject to the agreement, for either management is

---

7. It is clear that under both the agreement in this case and that involved in American Manufacturing Co., 363 U.S. 564, 80 S.Ct. 1343, the question of arbitrability is for the courts to decide. Cf. Cox, Reflections Upon Labor Arbitration, 72 Harv.L.Rev. 1482, 1508–1509. Where the assertion by the claimant is that the parties excluded from court determination not merely the decision of the merits of the grievance but also the question of its arbitrability, vesting power to make both decisions in the arbitrator, the claimant must bear the burden of a clear demonstration of that purpose.

prohibited or limited in the action it takes, or if not, it is [not?] protected from interference by strikes. This comprehensive reach of the collective bargaining agreement does not mean, however, that the language, "strictly a function of management," has no meaning.

"Strictly a function of management" might be thought to refer to any practice of management in which, under particular circumstances prescribed by the agreement, it is permitted to indulge. But if courts, in order to determine arbitrability, were allowed to determine what is permitted and what is not, the arbitration clause would be swallowed up by the exception. Every grievance in a sense involves a claim that management has violated some provision of the agreement. Accordingly, "strictly a function of management" must be interpreted as referring only to that over which the contract gives management complete control and unfettered discretion. Respondent claims that the contracting out of work falls within this category. Contracting out work is the basis of many grievances; and that type of claim is grist in the mills of the arbitrators. A specific collective bargaining agreement may exclude contracting out from the grievance procedure. Or a written collateral agreement may make clear that contracting out was not a matter for arbitration. In such a case a grievance based solely on contracting out would not be arbitrable. Here, however, there is no such provision. Nor is there any showing that the parties designed the phrase "strictly a function of management" to encompass any and all forms of contracting out. In the absence of any express provision excluding a particular grievance from arbitration, we think only the most forceful evidence of a purpose to exclude the claim from arbitration can prevail, particularly where, as here, the exclusion clause is vague and the arbitration clause quite broad. Since any attempt by a court to infer such a purpose necessarily comprehends the merits, the court should view with suspicion an attempt to persuade it to become entangled in the construction of the substantive provisions of a labor agreement, even through the back door of interpreting the arbitration clause, when the alternative is to utilize the services of an arbitrator.

The grievance alleged that the contracting out was a violation of the collective bargaining agreement. There was, therefore, a dispute "as to the meaning and application of the provisions of this Agreement" which the parties had agreed would be determined by arbitration.

The judiciary sits in these cases to bring into operation an arbitral process which substitutes a regime of peaceful settlement for the older regime of industrial conflict. Whether contracting out in the present case violated the agreement is the question. It is a question for the arbiter, not for the courts.

Reversed.

MR. JUSTICE BRENNAN, with whom MR. JUSTICE HARLAN joins, concurring.

*   *   *

In each of these two cases [American Manufacturing and Warrior and Gulf] the issue concerns the enforcement of but one promise—the promise to arbitrate in the context of an agreement dealing with a particular subject matter, the industrial relations between employers and employees. Other promises contained in the collective bargaining agreements are beside the point unless, by the very terms of the arbitration promise, they are made relevant to its interpretation. And I emphasize this, for the arbitration promise is itself a contract. The parties are free to make that promise as broad or as narrow as they wish, for there is no compulsion in law requiring them to include any such promises in their agreement. The meaning of the arbitration promise is not to be found simply by reference to the dictionary definitions of the words the parties use, or by reference to the interpretation of commercial arbitration clauses. Words in a collective bargaining agreement, rightly viewed by the Court to be the charter instrument of a system of industrial self-government, like words in a statute, are to be understood only by reference to the background which gave rise to their inclusion. The Court therefore avoids the prescription of inflexible rules for the enforcement of arbitration promises. Guidance is given by identifying the various considerations which a court should take into account when construing a particular clause—considerations of the milieu in which the clause is negotiated and of the national labor policy. It is particularly underscored that the arbitral process in collective bargaining presupposes that the parties wanted the informed judgment of an arbitrator, precisely for the reason that judges cannot provide it. Therefore, a court asked to enforce a promise to arbitrate should ordinarily refrain from involving itself in the interpretation of the substantive provisions of the contract.

To be sure, since arbitration is a creature of contract, a court must always inquire, when a party seeks to invoke its aid to force a reluctant party to the arbitration table, whether the parties have agreed to arbitrate the particular dispute. In this sense, the question of whether a dispute is "arbitrable" is inescapably for the court.

On examining the arbitration clause, the court may conclude that it commits to arbitration any "dispute, difference, disagreement, or controversy of any nature or character." With that finding the court will have exhausted its function, except to order the reluctant party to arbitration. Similarly, although the arbitrator may be empowered only to interpret and apply the contract, the parties may have provided that any dispute as to whether a particular claim is within the arbitration clause is itself for the arbitrator. Again the court, without more, must send any dispute to the arbitrator, for the parties have agreed that the construction of the arbitration promise itself is for the arbitrator, and the reluctant party has breached his promise by refusing to submit the dispute to arbitration.

In American, the Court deals with a request to enforce the "standard" form of arbitration clause, one that provides for the arbitration of "[a]ny disputes, misunderstandings, differences or grievances arising between the parties as to the meaning, interpretation and application of * * * this agreement * * *." Since the arbitration clause itself is part of the agreement, it might be argued that a dispute as to the meaning of that clause is for the arbitrator. But the Court rejects this position, saying that the threshold question, the meaning of the arbitration clause itself, is for the judge unless the parties clearly state to the contrary. However, the Court finds that the meaning of that "standard" clause is simply that the parties have agreed to arbitrate any dispute which the moving party asserts to involve construction of the substantive provisions of the contract, because such a dispute necessarily does involve such a construction.

The issue in the Warrior case is essentially no different from that in American, that is, it is whether the company agreed to arbitrate a particular grievance. In contrast to American, however, the arbitration promise here excludes a particular area from arbitration—"matters which are strictly a function of management." Because the arbitration promise is different, the scope of the court's inquiry may be broader. Here, a court may be required to examine the substantive provisions of the contract to ascertain whether the parties have provided that contracting out shall be a "function of management." If a court may delve into the merits to the extent of inquiring whether the parties have expressly agreed whether or not contracting out was a "function of management," why was it error for the lower court here to evaluate the evidence of bargaining history for the same purpose? Neat logical distinctions do not provide the answer. The Court rightly concludes that appropriate regard for the national labor policy and the special factors relevant to the labor arbitral process, admonish that judicial inquiry into the merits of this grievance should be limited to the search for an explicit provision which brings the grievance under the cover of the exclusion clause since "the exclusion clause is vague and arbitration clause quite broad." The hazard of going further into the merits is amply demonstrated by what the courts below did. On the basis of inconclusive evidence, those courts found that Warrior was in no way limited by any implied covenants of good faith and fair dealing from contracting out as it pleased—which would necessarily mean that Warrior was free completely to destroy the collective bargaining agreement by contracting out all the work.

The very ambiguity of the Warrior exclusion clause suggests that the parties were generally more concerned with having an arbitrator render decisions as to the meaning of the contract than they were in restricting the arbitrator's jurisdiction. The case might of course be otherwise were the arbitration clause very narrow, or the exclusion clause quite specific, for the inference might then be permissible that the parties had manifested a greater interest in confining the arbitrator; the presumption of arbitrability would then not have the same force and the Court would be somewhat freer to examine into the merits.

The Court makes reference to an arbitration clause being the *quid pro quo* for a no-strike clause. I do not understand the Court to mean that the application of the principles announced today depends upon the presence of a no-strike clause in the agreement.

Mr. Justice Frankfurter joins these observations.

Mr. Justice Whittaker, dissenting.

Until today, I have understood it to be the unquestioned law, as this Court has consistently held, that arbitrators are private judges chosen by the parties to decide particular matters specifically submitted; that the contract under which matters are submitted to arbitrators is at once the source and limit of their authority and power; and that their power to decide issues with finality, thus ousting the normal functions of the courts, must rest upon a clear, definitive agreement of the parties, as such powers can never be implied. United States v. Moorman, 338 U.S. 457, 462, 70 S.Ct. 288, 291, 94

L.Ed. 256; [3] Mercantile Trust Co. v. Hensey, 205 U.S. 298, 309, 27 S.Ct. 535, 539, 51 L.Ed. 811. See also Fernandez & Hnos. v. Rickert Rice Mills, 1 Cir., 119 F.2d 809, 815, 136 A.L.R. 351; Marchant v. Mead-Morrison Mfg. Co., 252 N.Y. 284, 299, 169 N.E. 386, 391; [6] Continental Milling & Feed Co. v. Doughnut Corp., 186 Md. 669, 676, 48 A.2d 447, 450; Jacob v. Weisser, 207 Pa. 484, 489, 56 A. 1065, 1067. I believe that the Court today departs from the established principles announced in these decisions.

Here, the employer operates a shop for the normal maintenance of its barges, but it is not equipped to make major repairs, and accordingly the employer has, from the beginning of its operations more than 19 years ago, contracted out its major repair work. During most, if not all, of this time the union has represented the employees in that unit. The District Court found that "[t]hroughout the successive labor agreements between these parties, including the present one, * * * [the union] has unsuccessfully sought to negotiate changes in the labor contracts, and particularly during the negotiation of the present labor agreement, * * * which would have limited the right of the [employer] to continue the practice of contracting out such work." 168 F.Supp. 702, 704–705.

The labor agreement involved here provides for arbitration of disputes respecting the interpretation and application of the agreement and, arguably, also some other things. But the first paragraph of the arbitration section says: "[M]atters which are strictly a function of management shall not be subject to arbitration under this section." Although acquiescing for 19 years in the employer's interpretation that contracting out work was "strictly a function of management," and having repeatedly tried—particularly in the negotiation of the agreement involved here—but unsuccessfully, to induce the employer to agree to a covenant that would prohibit it from contracting out work, the union, after having agreed to and signed the contract involved, presented a "grievance" on the ground that the employer's contracting out work, at a time when some employees in the unit were laid off for lack of work, constituted a partial "lockout" of employees in violation of the antilockout provision of the agreement. * * *

The Court now * * * holds that the arbitrator's source of law is "not confined to the express provisions of the contract," that arbitration should be ordered "unless it may be said with positive assurance that the arbitration clause is not susceptible of an interpretation that covers the asserted dispute," that "[d]oubts [of arbitrability] should be resolved in favor of coverage," and that when, as here, "an absolute no-strike clause is included in the agreement, then * * * everything that management does is subject to [arbitration]." I understand the Court thus to hold that the arbitrators are not confined to the express provisions of the contract, that arbitration is

---

3. "It is true that *the intention of parties to submit their contractual disputes to final determination outside the courts should be made manifest by plain language.*" (Emphasis added.) United States v. Moorman, 338 U.S. 457, 462, 70 S.Ct. 288, 291, 94 L.Ed. 256.

6. In this leading case, Judge, later Mr. Justice, Cardozo said:

"The question is one of intention, to be ascertained by the same tests that are ap-

plied to contracts generally. * * * No one is under a duty to resort to these conventional tribunals, however helpful their processes, *except to the extent that he has signified his willingness.* Our own favor or disfavor of the cause of arbitration is not to count as a factor in the appraisal of the thought of others." (Emphasis added.) Marchant v. Mead-Morrison Mfg. Co., 252 N.Y. 284, 299, 169 N.E. 386, 391.

to be ordered unless it may be said with positive assurance that arbitration of a particular dispute is excluded by the contract, that doubts of arbitrability are to be resolved in favor of arbitration, and that when, as here, the contract contains a no-strike clause, everything that management does is subject to arbitration.

This is an entirely new and strange doctrine to me. I suggest, with deference, that it departs from both the contract of the parties and the controlling decisions of this Court. I find nothing in the contract that purports to confer upon arbitrators any such general breadth of private judicial power. The Court cites no legislative or judicial authority that creates for or gives to arbitrators such broad general powers. * * *

* * * [T]he interpretation given by the parties over 19 years to the phrase "matters which are strictly a function of management" should logically have some significance here. By their contract, the parties agreed that "matters which are strictly a function of management shall not be subject to arbitration." The union over the course of many years repeatedly tried to induce the employer to agree to a covenant prohibiting the contracting out of work, but was never successful. The union again made such an effort in negotiating the very contract involved here, and, failing of success, signed the contract, knowing, of course, that it did not contain any such covenant, but that, to the contrary, it contained, just as had the former contracts, a covenant that "matters which are strictly a function of management shall not be subject to arbitration." Does not this show that, instead of signifying a willingness to submit to arbitration the matter of whether the employer might continue to contract out work, the parties fairly agreed to exclude at least that matter from arbitration? * * *

Surely the question whether a particular subject or class of subjects is or is not made arbitrable by a contract is a judicial question, and if, as the concurring opinion suggests, "the court may conclude that [the contract] commits to arbitration any [subject or class of subjects]," it may likewise conclude that the contract does not commit such subject or class of subjects to arbitration, and "[w]ith that finding the court will have exhausted its function" no more nor less by denying arbitration than by ordering it. Here the District Court found, and the Court of Appeals approved its finding, that by the terms of the contract, as interpreted by the parties over 19 years, the contracting out of work was "strictly a function of management" and "not subject to arbitration." That finding, I think, should be accepted here. Acceptance of it requires affirmance of the judgment.

Note

1. How would you formulate the test or tests laid down in American Manufacturing and Warrior and Gulf for determining arbitrability? What should the court look to: (1) Arbitration provision only? (2) Other parts of the contract to which the parties direct attention? (3) The entire contract? (4) Bargaining history?

2. The Court makes it clear that the question of arbitrability is for a court to answer rather than for the arbitrator. This holding was reaffirmed in AT&T Technologies, Inc. v. Communications Workers, ___ U.S. ___, 106 S.Ct. 1415, 89 L.Ed.2d 648 (1986). In that case the company claimed that a union's grievance

protesting the company's decision to lay off certain employees was not arbitrable. The federal district court and the court of appeals determined that the issue of arbitrability was for the arbitrator to decide rather than the court since the agreement contained a standard arbitration clause, there was no express exclusion of the arbitrability issue from arbitration, and deciding the arbitrability issue might entangle the court in the merits of the dispute. The Supreme Court unanimously reversed, stating:

> "The principles necessary to decide this case * * * were set out by this Court over 25 years ago in * * * *Steelworkers v. American Mfg. Co.* [and] *Steelworkers v. Warrior & Gulf Navigation Co.* * * *. These precepts have served the industrial relations community well * * *.

> "[T]he question of arbitrability—whether a collective-bargaining agreement creates a duty for the parties to arbitrate the particular grievance—is undeniably an issue for judicial determination. Unless the parties clearly and unmistakably provide otherwise, the question of whether the parties agreed to arbitrate is to be decided by the court, not the arbitrator. * * *

> "[I]n deciding whether the parties have agreed to submit a particular grievance to arbitration, a court is not to rule on the potential merits of the underlying claims. Whether 'arguable' or not, indeed even if it appears to the court to be frivolous, the union's claim that the employer has violated the collective-bargaining agreement is to be decided, not by the court asked to order arbitration, but as the parties have agreed, by the arbitrator. * * *" __ U.S. at __, 106 S.Ct. at 1418–1419, 39 L.Ed.2d at 655–656.

Why should the court rather than the arbitrator decide the issue of arbitrability? Does this not derogate from the premise of American Manufacturing and Warrior and Gulf, that arbitration is therapeutic and analgesic?

Would it be open to the arbitrators who are called upon to hear and decide the grievances in American Manufacturing, Warrior and Gulf, and AT&T, as an aftermath of the Supreme Court decisions, to reconsider the question of arbitrability? If not, has *any* tribunal really considered that question—given it other than the superficial, "face of the contract" appraisal prescribed for the judiciary by the Court?

Where the parties expressly provide that the question of arbitrability is itself to be decided by the arbitrator, is there not still a threshold question for the court?

In Warrior and Gulf, the dissent points out that the company had been contracting out for nineteen years without protest by the union; that the union had attempted to obtain in a succession of collective agreements, including the existing one, a limitation on the employer's authority to contract out; that the union had never succeeded in getting such a concession from management. The dissent concludes from this that the matter of contracting out is not within the reach of the arbitration clause. Is this persuasive? Or is the argument directed more at the result the arbitrator ought to reach *on the merits?* While in the Warrior situation the employer will, in all likelihood, win on the merits before the arbitrator, this need not always be the case. Can you construct a set of facts in which the question of arbitrability would, on the contrary, be crucial?

3. Whereas in the first two cases of what has come to be called the "arbitration trilogy" the courts look ahead to a sought arbitration and are concerned with the degree of their own involvement in the determination of the underlying dispute, in the third case, Enterprise Wheel, which follows, the

judicial view is backward, upon an arbitration award already rendered, and is concerned over the extent to which the arbitrator should be second-guessed. Is it accurate, nonetheless, to say that the core problem in each is the same, with only the chronology different? (For a relevant observation, see infra p. 649 footnote 6. Persuaded?)

UNITED STEELWORKERS v. ENTERPRISE WHEEL AND CAR CORP.

Supreme Court of the United States, 1960.
363 U.S. 593, 80 S.Ct. 1358, 4 L.Ed.2d 1424.

Opinion of the Court by MR. JUSTICE DOUGLAS, announced by MR. JUSTICE BRENNAN.

Petitioner union and respondent during the period relevant here had a collective bargaining agreement which provided that any differences "as to the meaning and application" of the agreement should be submitted to arbitration and that the arbitrator's decision "shall be final and binding on the parties." Special provisions were included concerning the suspension and discharge of employees. The agreement stated:

"Should it be determined by the Company or by an arbitrator in accordance with the grievance procedure that the employee has been suspended unjustly or discharged in violation of the provisions of this Agreement, the Company shall reinstate the employee and pay full compensation at the employee's regular rate of pay for the time lost."

The agreement also provided:

"* * * It is understood and agreed that neither party will institute *civil suits or legal proceedings* against the other for alleged violation of any of the provisions of this labor contract; instead all disputes will be settled in the manner outlined in this Article III—Adjustment of Grievances."

A group of employees left their jobs in protest against the discharge of one employee. A union official advised them at once to return to work. An official of respondent at their request gave them permission and then rescinded it. The next day they were told they did not have a job any more "until this thing was settled one way or the other."

A grievance was filed; and when respondent finally refused to arbitrate, this suit was brought for specific enforcement of the arbitration provisions of the agreement. The District Court ordered arbitration. The arbitrator found that the discharge of the men was not justified, though their conduct, he said, was improper. In his view the facts warranted at most a suspension of the men for 10 days each. After their discharge and before the arbitration award the collective bargaining agreement had expired. The union, however, continued to represent the workers at the plant. The arbitrator rejected the contention that expiration of the agreement barred reinstatement of the employees. He held that the provision of the agreement above quoted imposed an unconditional obligation on the employer. He awarded reinstatement with back pay, minus pay for a 10-day suspension and such sums as these employees received from other employment.

Respondent refused to comply with the award. Petitioner moved the District Court for enforcement. The District Court directed respondent to comply.   168 F.Supp. 308.   The Court of Appeals, while agreeing that the District Court had jurisdiction to enforce an arbitration award under a collective bargaining agreement, held that the failure of the award to specify the amounts to be deducted from the back pay rendered the award unenforceable.   That defect, it agreed, could be remedied by requiring the parties to complete the arbitration.   It went on to hold, however, that an award for back pay subsequent to the date of termination of the collective bargaining agreement could not be enforced.   It also held that the requirement for reinstatement of the discharged employees was likewise unenforceable because the collective bargaining agreement had expired.   269 F.2d 327.   We granted certiorari.   *   *   *

The refusal of courts to review the merits of an arbitration award is the proper approach to arbitration under collective bargaining agreements.   The federal policy of settling labor disputes by arbitration would be undermined if courts had the final say on the merits of the awards.   As we stated in United Steelworkers of America v. Warrior & Gulf Navigation Co., 363 U.S. 574, 80 S.Ct. 1347, the arbitrators under these collective agreements are indispensable agencies in a continuous collective bargaining process.   They sit to settle disputes at the plant level—disputes that require for their solution knowledge of the custom and practices of a particular factory or of a particular industry as reflected in particular agreements.[2]

When an arbitrator is commissioned to interpret and apply the collective bargaining agreement, he is to bring his informed judgment to bear in order to reach a fair solution of a problem.   This is especially true when it comes to formulating remedies.   There the need is for flexibility in meeting a wide variety of situations.   The draftsmen may never have thought of what specific remedy should be awarded to meet a particular contingency.   Nevertheless, an arbitrator is confined to interpretation and application of the collective bargaining agreement; he does not sit to dispense his own brand of industrial justice.   He may of course look for guidance from many sources, yet his award is legitimate only so long as it draws its essence from the collective bargaining agreement.   When the arbitrator's words manifest an infidelity to this obligation, courts have no choice but to refuse enforcement of the award.

---

2. "Persons unfamiliar with mills and factories—farmers or professors, for example— often remark upon visiting them that they seem like another world.   This is particularly true if, as in the steel industry, both tradition and technology have strongly and uniquely molded the ways men think and act when at work.   The newly hired employee, the 'green hand,' is gradually initiated into what amounts to a miniature society.   There he finds himself in a strange environment that assaults his senses with unusual sounds and smells and often with different 'weather conditions' such as sudden drafts of heat, cold, or humidity.   He discovers that the society of which he only gradually becomes a part has of course a formal government of its own—the rules which management and the union have laid down—but that it also differs from or parallels the world outside in social classes, folklore, ritual, and traditions.

"Under the process in the old mills a very real 'miniature society' had grown up, and in important ways the technological revolution described in this case history shattered it.   But a new society or work community was born immediately, though for a long time it developed slowly.   As the old society was strongly molded by the *discontinuous* process of making pipe, so was the new one molded by the *continuous* process and strongly influenced by the characteristics of new high-speed automatic equipment."   Walker, Life in the Automatic Factory, 36 Harv.Bus.Rev. 111, 117.

The opinion of the arbitrator in this case, as it bears upon the award of back pay beyond the date of the agreement's expiration and reinstatement, is ambiguous. It may be read as based solely upon the arbitrator's view of the requirements of enacted legislation, which would mean that he exceeded the scope of the submission. Or it may be read as embodying a construction of the agreement itself, perhaps with the arbitrator looking to "the law" for help in determining the sense of the agreement. A mere ambiguity in the opinion accompanying an award, which permits the inference that the arbitrator may have exceeded his authority, is not a reason for refusing to enforce the award. Arbitrators have no obligation to the court to give their reasons for an award. To require opinions free of ambiguity may lead arbitrators to play it safe by writing no supporting opinions. This would be undesirable for a well-reasoned opinion tends to engender confidence in the integrity of the process and aids in clarifying the underlying agreement. Moreover, we see no reason to assume that this arbitrator has abused the trust the parties confided in him and has not stayed within the areas marked out for his consideration. It is not apparent that he went beyond the submission. The Court of Appeals' opinion refusing to enforce the reinstatement and partial back pay portions of the award was not based upon any finding that the arbitrator did not premise his award on his construction of the contract. It merely disagreed with the arbitrator's construction of it.

The collective bargaining agreement could have provided that if any of the employees were wrongfully discharged, the remedy would be reinstatement and back pay up to the date they were returned to work. Respondent's major argument seems to be that by applying correct principles of law to the interpretation of the collective bargaining agreement it can be determined that the agreement did not so provide, and that therefore the arbitrator's decision was not based upon the contract. The acceptance of this view would require courts, even under the standard arbitration clause, to review the merits of every construction of the contract. This plenary review by a court of the merits would make meaningless the provisions that the arbitrator's decision is final, for in reality it would almost never be final. This underlines the fundamental error which we have alluded to in United Steelworkers of America v. American Manufacturing Co., 363 U.S. 564, 80 S.Ct. 1343. As we there emphasized, the question of interpretation of the collective bargaining agreement is a question for the arbitrator. It is the arbitrator's construction which was bargained for; and so far as the arbitrator's decision concerns construction of the contract, the courts have no business overruling him because their interpretation of the contract is different from his.

We agree with the Court of Appeals that the judgment of the District Court should be modified so that the amounts due the employees may be definitely determined by arbitration. In all other respects we think the judgment of the District Court should be affirmed. Accordingly, we reverse the judgment of the Court of Appeals, except for that modification, and remand the case to the District Court for proceedings in conformity with this opinion. * * *

[JUSTICE FRANKFURTER concurred in the result. JUSTICE BLACK took no part in the case.]

Mr. Justice Whittaker, dissenting. ⁎ ⁎ ⁎

That the propriety of the discharges, under the collective agreement, was arbitrable under the provisions of that agreement, even after its expiration, is not in issue. Nor is there any issue here as to the power of the arbitrator to award reinstatement status and back pay to the discharged employees to the date of expiration of the collective agreement. It is conceded, too, that the collective agreement expired by its terms on April 4, 1957, and was never extended or renewed.

The sole question here is whether the arbitrator exceeded the submission and his powers in awarding reinstatement and back pay for any period after expiration of the collective agreements. Like the Court of Appeals, I think he did. I find nothing in the collective agreement that purports to so authorize. Nor does the Court point to anything in the agreement that purports to do so. Indeed, the union does not contend that there is any such covenant in the contract. Doubtless all rights that accrued to the employees under the collective agreement during its term, and that were made arbitrable by its provisions, could be awarded to them by the arbitrator, even though the period of the agreement had ended. But surely no rights *accrued* to the employees under the agreement after it had expired. Save for the provisions of the collective agreement, and in the absence, as here, of any applicable rule of law or contrary covenant between the employer and the employees, the employer had the legal right to discharge the employees at will. The collective agreement, however, protected them against discharge, for specified reasons, during its continuation. But when that agreement expired, it did not continue to afford rights *in futuro* to the employees—as though still effective and governing. After the agreement expired, the employment status of these 11 employees was terminable at the will of the employer, as the Court of Appeals quite properly held, ⁎ ⁎ ⁎ and the announced discharge of these 11 employees then became lawfully effective.

Once the contract expired, no rights continued to accrue under it to the employees. Thereafter they had no contractual right to demand that the employer continue to employ them, and *a fortiori* the arbitrator did not have power to order the employer to do so; nor did the arbitrator have power to order the employer to pay wages to them after the date of termination of the contract, which was also the effective date of their discharges. ⁎ ⁎ ⁎

Note

1. Would any of the following formulations of the arbitrator's award be denied judicial enforcement under the Enterprise Wheel standard?

a. "I find for the aggrieved employees on the basis of my interpretation of the provisions of the contract."

b. "I find for the aggrieved employees on the basis of my interpretation of the provisions of the contract read in the light of Section 7 of the NLRA."

c. "I find for the aggrieved employees on the basis of my interpretation of Section 7 of the NLRA."

2. Another variation of the problem treated in Note 1, supra, is posed in the following: "I find for the aggrieved employees on the basis of a promise not dealt with at all in the written contract but found by me, by reason of past

practice and bargaining history, to be an implied provision of the contract between the parties." In TORRINGTON CO. v. METAL PRODUCTS WORKERS UNION, 362 F.2d 677 (2d Cir.1966), that was the problem presented. For some twenty years the employer's practice had been to permit employees time off with pay to vote on election days. This practice had been unilaterally instituted by the employer and was not mentioned in the present or any preceding collective bargaining agreement. The bargaining history with respect to this benefit was muddy. Prior to the grievance at issue, the employer had unilaterally announced discontinuance of the election-day policy. The arbitration section of the contract contained the following standard provision:

> "The arbitrator shall be bound by and must comply with all of the terms of this agreement and he shall have no power to add to, delete from, or modify, in any way, any of the provisions of this agreement." 362 F.2d at 678 n. 2.

The arbitrator found that the election-day benefit was an implied part of the contract and decided in favor of the union.

The Second Circuit, in a 2 to 1 decision, affirmed the district court's vacating of the award on the ground that the arbitrator had acted in excess of the jurisdiction conferred upon him by the contract. The court stated: "In our opinion, the Union by pressing this grievance has attempted to have 'added' to the 1964 agreement a benefit which it did not think sufficiently vital to insist upon during negotiations for the contract which ended a long and costly strike. We find this sufficiently clear from the facts as found by the arbitrator to agree with the district court that the arbitrator exceeded his authority by ruling that such a benefit was implied in the terms of that agreement." Id. at 682.

The court further observed:

> "In some cases, it may be appropriate exercise of an arbitrator's authority to resolve ambiguities in the scope of a collective bargaining agreement on the basis of prior practice, since no agreement can reduce all aspects of the labor-management relationship to writing. However, while courts should be wary of rejecting the arbitrator's interpretation of the implications of the parties' prior practice, the mandate that the arbitrator stay within the confines of the collective bargaining agreement * * * requires a reviewing court to pass upon whether the agreement authorizes the arbitrator to expand its express terms on the basis of the parties' prior practice. Therefore, we hold that the question of an arbitrator's authority is subject to judicial review, and that the arbitrator's decision that he has authority should not be accepted where the reviewing court can clearly perceive that he has derived that authority from sources outside the collective bargaining agreement at issue. * * * [6]" Id. at 680–81.

6. Of course, it can be argued that our decision authorizes an impermissible review of the "merits" in a case where the principal issue was whether the arbitrator should find an implied substantive obligation in the contract, see Meltzer, The Supreme Court, Arbitrability, and Collective Bargaining, 28 U.Chi. L.Rev. 464, 484–85 (1961), but we think this position is contrary to *Enterprise Wheel.* * * * The question of the arbitrator's authority is really one of his contractual jurisdiction, and the courts cannot be expected to place their stamp of approval upon his action without making some examination of his jurisdiction to act. As stated above, we think more exhaustive judicial review of this question is appropriate after the award has been made than before the award in a suit to compel arbitration; in this way, the court receives the benefit of the arbitrator's interpretive skills as to the matter of his contractual authority. See Livingston v. John Wiley & Sons, Inc., 313 F.2d 52, 59 n. 5 (2 Cir.1963), aff'd, 376 U.S. 543, 84 S.Ct. 909, 11 L.Ed.2d 898 (1964).

The dissent in Torrington argued:

"I start with the proposition, accepted by the majority, that an arbitrator's award may be reviewed by the courts only to see if 'it draws its essence from the collective bargaining agreement' and whether 'the arbitrator's words manifest an infidelity to this obligation.' See United Steelworkers of America v. Enterprise Wheel & Car Corp., 363 U.S. 593, 597, 80 S.Ct. 1358, 1361, 4 L.Ed.2d 1424 (1960). But this inquiry is a very limited one and, so limited, should lead to reversal of the court below. * * *

"The arbitrator assumed that a collective bargaining agreement can include terms or conditions not made explicit in the written contract. This proposition is correct. * * * In United Steelworkers of America v. Warrior & Gulf Nav. Co., 363 U.S. 574, 580, 80 S.Ct. 1347, 1352, 4 L.Ed.2d 1409 (1960), the Supreme Court said: 'Gaps [in the "written document"] may be left to be filled in by reference to the practices of the particular industry and of the various shops covered by the agreement.' * * *

"Thus, the arbitrator looked to prior practice, the conduct of the negotiation for the new contract and the agreement reached at the bargaining table to reach his conclusion that paid time off for voting was 'an implied part of the contract.' From all of this, I conclude that the arbitrator's award 'draws its essence from the collective bargaining agreement' and his words do not 'manifest an infidelity to this obligation.' Once that test is met, the inquiry ends. Whether the arbitrator's conclusion was correct is irrelevant because the parties agreed to abide by it, right or wrong. Nevertheless, the majority has carried the inquiry further and concerned itself with a minute examination of the merits of the award, which we are enjoined not to do. * * *" Id. at 682–83.

The Torrington decision is criticized in Aaron, Judicial Intervention in Labor Arbitration, 20 Stan.L.Rev. 41 (1967); Jones, The Name of the Game is Decision—Some Reflections on "Arbitrability" and "Authority" in Labor Arbitration, 46 Tex.L.Rev. 865 (1968); Meltzer, Ruminations About Ideology, Law, and Labor Arbitration, 34 U.Chi.L.Rev. 545 (1967).

3. The position of the employer in Enterprise Wheel was that the arbitrator lacked power to grant relief (in the form of reinstatement and back pay) relative to the period *after* the expiration of the contract. Suppose, by way of carrying the issue to its ultimate, an employer were to contend no arbitrability *at all* on the following facts: (1) the union during contract renewal negotiations exercised an option to cancel the existing contract through the giving of a seven-day notice; (2) the employer thereafter went out of business; (3) the union presented a claim for severance pay for the thus-terminated employees under the cancelled contract and, when the employer refused, demanded arbitration; (4) the employer again refused on the ground that, since the contract had expired, there was no obligation to arbitrate; (5) the union sued under Section 301 to compel the employer to arbitrate the severance pay issue, or, in the alternative, for judgment for the severance pay due. How should the court rule?

The foregoing facts are as in Nolde Brothers, Inc. v. Local 358, Bakery Workers, 430 U.S. 243, 97 S.Ct. 1067, 51 L.Ed.2d 300 (1977). The Court held the issue to be arbitrable. Justices Stewart and Rehnquist dissented, observing that doubts as to arbitrability, giving rise to a presumption of arbitrability, could not survive "when the contract providing for arbitration had terminated and the rights in dispute, though claimed to arise under the contract, ripened only after the contract had expired and the employment relationship had terminated."

LOCAL 174, TEAMSTERS v. LUCAS FLOUR CO.

Supreme Court of the United States, 1962.
369 U.S. 95, 82 S.Ct. 571, 7 L.Ed.2d 593.

MR. JUSTICE STEWART delivered the opinion of the Court.

The petitioner and the respondent (which we shall call the union and the employer) were parties to a collective bargaining contract within the purview of the National Labor Relations Act * * *. The contract contained the following provisions, among others:

"ARTICLE II

"The Employer reserves the right to discharge any man in his employ if his work is not satisfactory.

*   *   *   *   *   *   *   *   *

"ARTICLE XIV

"Should any difference as to the true interpretation of this agreement arise, same shall be submitted to a Board of Arbitration of two members, one representing the firm, and one representing the Union. If said members cannot agree, a third member, who must be a disinterested party shall be selected, and the decision of the said Board of Arbitration shall be binding. It is further agreed by both parties hereto that during such arbitration, there shall be no suspension of work.

"Should any difference arise between the employer and the employee, same shall be submitted to arbitration by both parties. Failing to agree, they shall mutually appoint a third person whose decision shall be final and binding."

In May of 1958 an employee named Welsch was discharged by the employer after he had damaged a new fork-lift truck by running it off a loading platform and onto some railroad tracks. When a business agent of the union protested, he was told by a representative of the employer that Welsch had been discharged because of unsatisfactory work. The union thereupon called a strike to force the employer to rehire Welsch. The strike lasted eight days.[1] After the strike was over, the issue of Welsch's discharge was submitted to arbitration. Some five months later the Board of Arbitration rendered a decision, ruling that Welsch's work had been unsatisfactory, that his unsatisfactory work had been the reason for his discharge, and that he was not entitled to reinstatement as an employee.

In the meantime, the employer had brought this suit against the union in the Superior Court of King County, Washington, asking damages for business losses caused by the strike. After a trial that court entered a judgment in favor of the employer in the amount of $6,501.60. On appeal the judgment was affirmed by Department One of the Supreme Court of Washington. 57 Wash.2d 95, 356 P.2d 1. The reviewing court held that the preemption doctrine of San Diego Building Trades Council, etc. v. Garmon, 359 U.S. 236, 79 S.Ct. 773, 3 L.Ed.2d 775, did not deprive it of jurisdiction over the controversy. The court further held that § 301 of the Labor

---

1. The strike was terminated by a temporary injunction issued by the state court.

Management Relations Act of 1947 * * * could not "reasonably be interpreted as pre-empting state jurisdiction, or as affecting it by limiting the substantive law to be applied." 57 Wash.2d at 102, 356 P.2d at 5. Expressly applying principles of state law, the court reasoned that the strike was a violation of the collective bargaining contract, because it was an attempt to coerce the employer to forego his contractual right to discharge an employee for unsatisfactory work. We granted certiorari to consider questions of federal labor law which this case presents. * * *

One of those issues—whether § 301(a) of the Labor Management Relations Act of 1947 deprives state courts of jurisdiction over litigation such as this—we have decided this Term in Charles Dowd Box Co. v. Courtney, 368 U.S. 502, 82 S.Ct. 519, 7 L.Ed.2d 483. For the reasons stated in our opinion in that case, we hold that the Washington Supreme Court was correct in ruling that it had jurisdiction over this controversy.[9] There remain for consideration two other issues, one of them implicated but not specifically decided in Dowd Box. Was the Washington court free, as it thought, to decide this controversy within the limited horizon of its local law? If not, does applicable federal law require a result in this case different from that reached by the state court?

In Dowd Box we proceeded upon the hypothesis that state courts would apply federal law in exercising jurisdiction over litigation within the purview of § 301(a), although in that case there was no claim of any variance in relevant legal principles as between the federal law and that of Massachusetts. In the present case, by contrast, the Washington court held that there was nothing in § 301 "limiting the substantive law to be applied," and the court accordingly proceeded to dispose of this litigation exclusively in terms of local contract law. The union insists that the case was one to be decided by reference to federal law, and that under applicable principles of national labor law the strike was not a violation of the collective bargaining contract. We hold that in a case such as this, incompatible doctrines of local law must give way to principles of federal labor law. We further hold, however, that application of such principles to this case leads to affirmance of the judgment before us.

It was apparently the theory of the Washington court, that, although Textile Workers Union v. Lincoln Mills, 353 U.S. 448, 77 S.Ct. 912, 1 L.Ed.2d 972, requires the federal courts to fashion, from the policy of our national labor laws, a body of federal law for the enforcement of collective bargaining agreements, nonetheless, the courts of the States remain free to apply individualized local rules when called upon to enforce such agreements. This view cannot be accepted. The dimensions of § 301 require the conclusion that substantive principles of federal labor law must be paramount in

---

9. Since this was a suit for violation of a collective bargaining contract within the purview of § 301(a) of the Labor Management Relations Act of 1947, the pre-emptive doctrine of cases such as San Diego Building Trades Council, etc. v. Garmon, 359 U.S. 236, 79 S.Ct. 773, 3 L.Ed.2d 775, based upon the exclusive jurisdiction of the National Labor Relations Board, is not relevant. * * * It is, of course, true that conduct which is a violation of a contractual obligation may also be conduct constituting an unfair labor practice, and what has been said is not to imply that enforcement by a court of a contract obligation affects the jurisdiction of the N.L.R.B. to remedy unfair labor practices, as such. See generally Dunau, Contractual Prohibition of Unfair Labor Practices: Jurisdictional Problems, 57 Col.L.Rev. 52.

the area covered by the statute. Comprehensiveness is inherent in the process by which the law is to be formulated under the mandate of Lincoln Mills, requiring issues raised in suits of a kind covered by § 301 to be decided according to the precepts of federal labor policy.

More important, the subject matter of § 301(a) "is peculiarly one that calls for uniform law." Pennsylvania R. Co. v. Public Service Comm., 250 U.S. 566, 569, 40 S.Ct. 36, 37, 64 L.Ed. 1142 * * *. The possibility that individual contract terms might have different meanings under state and federal law would inevitably exert a disruptive influence upon both the negotiation and administration of collective agreements. Because neither party could be certain of the rights which it had obtained or conceded, the process of negotiating an agreement would be made immeasurably more difficult by the necessity of trying to formulate contract provisions in such a way as to contain the same meaning under two or more systems of law which might someday be invoked in enforcing the contract. Once the collective bargain was made, the possibility of conflicting substantive interpretation under competing legal systems would tend to stimulate and prolong disputes as to its interpretation. Indeed, the existence of possibly conflicting legal concepts might substantially impede the parties' willingness to agree to contract terms providing for final arbitral or judicial resolution of disputes.

The importance of the area which would be affected by separate systems of substantive law makes the need for a single body of federal law particularly compelling. The ordering and adjusting of competing interests through a process of free and voluntary collective bargaining is the keystone of the federal scheme to promote industrial peace. State law which frustrates the effort of Congress to stimulate the smooth functioning of that process thus strikes at the very core of federal labor policy. With due regard to the many factors which bear upon competing state and federal interests in this area, * * * we cannot but conclude that in enacting § 301 Congress intended doctrines of federal labor law uniformly to prevail over inconsistent local rules.

Whether, as a matter of federal law, the strike which the union called was a violation of the collective bargaining contract is thus the ultimate issue which this case presents. It is argued that there could be no violation in the absence of a no-strike clause in the contract explicitly covering the subject of the dispute over which the strike was called. We disagree.

The collective bargaining contract expressly imposed upon both parties the duty of submitting the dispute in question to final and binding arbitration.

In a consistent course of decisions the Courts of Appeals of at least five Federal Circuits have held that a strike to settle a dispute which a collective bargaining agreement provides shall be settled exclusively and finally by compulsory arbitration constitutes a violation of the agreement. The National Labor Relations Board has reached the same conclusion. W.L. Mead, Inc., 113 N.L.R.B. 1040. We approve that doctrine. To hold otherwise would obviously do violence to accepted principles of traditional contract law. Even more in point, a contrary view would be completely at odds with the basic policy of national labor legislation to promote the arbitral process as a substitute for economic warfare. See United Steelworkers v. Warrior & Gulf Nav. Co., 363 U.S. 574, 80 S.Ct. 1347, 4 L.Ed.2d 1409.

What has been said is not to suggest that a no-strike agreement is to be implied beyond the area which it has been agreed will be exclusively covered by compulsory terminal arbitration. Nor is it to suggest that there may not arise problems in specific cases as to whether compulsory and binding arbitration has been agreed upon, and, if so, as to what disputes have been made arbitrable. But no such problems are present in this case. The grievance over which the union struck was, as it concedes, one which it had expressly agreed to settle by submission to final and binding arbitration proceedings. The strike which it called was a violation of that contractual obligation.

Affirmed.

Mr. Justice Black, dissenting.

The petitioner local union and the respondent company entered into a written collective bargaining agreement containing an express provision for the arbitration of disputes growing out of differences as to the proper application of the agreement in the following terms:

> "Should any difference arise between the employer and the employee, same shall be submitted to arbitration by both parties. Failing to agree, they shall mutually appoint a third person whose decision shall be final and binding."

The Court now finds—out of clear air, so far as I can see—that the union, without saying so in the agreement, not only agreed to arbitrate such differences, but also promised that there would be no strike while arbitration of a dispute was pending under this provision. And on the basis of its "discovery" of this additional unwritten promise by the union, the Court upholds a judgment awarding the company substantial damages for a strike in breach of contract.

That the Court's decision actually vacates and amends the contract that the parties themselves had made and signed is shown, I think, by the very face of that original contract. The arbitration provision covering disputes growing out of the application of the contract immediately follows another quite different arbitration provision—one covering disputes "as to the true interpretation of this agreement" in the following terms:

> "Should any difference as to the true interpretation of this agreement arise, same shall be submitted to a Board of Arbitration of two members, one representing the firm, and one representing the Union. If said members cannot agree, a third member, who must be a disinterested party shall be selected, and the decision of the said Board of Arbitration shall be binding. *It is further agreed by both parties hereto that during such arbitration, there shall be no suspension of work.*" (Emphasis supplied.)

In view of the fact that this latter provision contains an explicit promise by the union "that during such arbitration, there shall be no suspension of work," it seems to me plain that the parties to this contract, knowing how to write a provision binding a union not to strike, deliberately included a no-strike clause with regard to disputes over broad questions of contractual interpretation and deliberately excluded such a clause with regard to the essentially factual disputes arising out of the application of the contract in particular instances. And there is not a word anywhere else in this agreement which indicates that this perfectly sensible contractual framework for handling these two different kinds of disputes was not intended to operate in the precise manner dictated by the express language of the two arbitration provisions.

The defense offered for the Court's rewriting of the contract which the parties themselves made is that to allow the parties' own contract to stand "would obviously do violence to accepted principles of traditional contract law" and "be completely at odds with the basic policy of national labor legislation to promote the arbitral process." I had supposed, however—though evidently the Court thinks otherwise—that the job of courts enforcing contracts was to give legal effect to what the contracting parties actually agree to do, not to what courts think they ought to do. In any case, I have been unable to find any accepted principle of contract law—traditional or otherwise—that permits courts to change completely the nature of a contract by adding new promises that the parties themselves refused to make in order that the new court-made contract might better fit into whatever social, economic, or legal policies the courts believe to be so important that they should have been taken out of the realm of voluntary contract by the legislative body and furthered by compulsory legislation. * * *

The additional burden placed upon the union by the Court's writing into the agreement here a promise not to strike is certainly not a matter of minor interest to this employer or to the union. * * * It is difficult to believe that the desire of employers to get such a promise and the desire of the union to avoid giving it are matters which are not constantly in the minds of those who negotiate these contracts. In such a setting, to hold—on the basis of no evidence whatever—that a union, without knowing it, impliedly surrendered the right to strike by virtue of "traditional contract law" or anything else is to me just fiction. It took more than 50 years for unions to have written into federal legislation the principle that they have a right to strike. I cannot understand how anyone familiar with that history can allow that legislatively recognized right to be undercut on the basis of the attenuated implications the Court uses here.

I do not mean to suggest that an implied contractual promise cannot sometimes be found where there are facts and circumstances sufficient to warrant the conclusion that such was the intention of the parties. But there is no factual basis for such a conclusion in this case and the Court does not even claim to the contrary. The implication of a no-strike clause which the Court purports to find here—an implication completely at war with the language the parties used in making this contract as well as with the normal understanding of the negotiation process by which such contracts are made—has not been supported by so much as one scrap of evidence in this record. The implication found by the Court thus flows neither from the contract itself nor, so far as this record shows, from the intention of the parties. In my judgment, an "implication" of that nature would better be described as a rigid rule of law that an agreement to arbitrate has precisely the same effect as an agreement not to strike—a rule of law which introduces revolutionary doctrine into the field of collective bargaining.

* * * That approach is certainly contrary to the industrial and labor philosophy of the Taft-Hartley Act. Whatever else may be said about that Act, it seems plain that it was enacted on the view that the best way to bring about industrial peace was through voluntary, not compelled, labor agreements. Section 301 is torn from its roots when it is held to require the sort of compulsory arbitration imposed by this decision. I would reverse this case and relegate this controversy to the forum in which it belongs—the collective bargaining table.

Note

Do you think the proposition of Dowd Box and Lucas Flour to be sound: that state courts may, indeed shall, assist the federal courts in creating a body of *federal* substantive law concerning collective bargaining agreements?

BOYS MARKETS, INC. v. RETAIL CLERKS UNION

Supreme Court of the United States, 1970.
398 U.S. 235, 90 S.Ct. 1583, 26 L.Ed.2d 199.

MR. JUSTICE BRENNAN delivered the opinion of the Court.

In this case we re-examine the holding of Sinclair Refining Co. v. Atkinson, 370 U.S. 195, 82 S.Ct. 1328, 8 L.Ed.2d 440 (1962), that the anti-injunction provisions of the Norris-LaGuardia Act preclude a federal district court from enjoining a strike in breach of a no-strike obligation under a collective bargaining agreement, even though that agreement contains provisions, enforceable under § 301(a) of the Labor Management Relations Act, 1947, for binding arbitration of the grievance dispute concerning which the strike was called. The Court of Appeals for the Ninth Circuit, considering itself bound by *Sinclair,* reversed the grant by the District Court for the Central District of California of petitioner's prayer for injunctive relief. 416 F.2d 368 (1969). We granted certiorari. * * * Having concluded that *Sinclair* was erroneously decided and that subsequent events have undermined its continuing validity, we overrule that decision and reverse the judgment of the Court of Appeals.

I

In February 1969, at the time of the incidents that produced this litigation, petitioner and respondent were parties to a collective-bargaining agreement which provided, *inter alia,* that all controversies concerning its interpretation or application should be resolved by adjustment and arbitration procedures set forth therein and that, during the life of the contract, there should be "no cessation or stoppage of work, lock-out, picketing or boycotts * * *." The dispute arose when petitioner's frozen foods supervisor and certain members of his crew who were not members of the bargaining unit began to rearrange merchandise in the frozen food cases of one of petitioner's supermarkets. A union representative insisted that the food cases be stripped of all merchandise and be restocked by union personnel. When petitioner did not accede to the union's demand, a strike was called and the union began to picket petitioner's establishment. Thereupon petitioner demanded that the union cease the work stoppage and picketing and sought to invoke the grievance and arbitration procedures specified in the contract.

The following day, since the strike had not been terminated, petitioner filed a complaint in California Superior Court seeking a temporary restraining order, a preliminary and permanent injunction, and specific performance of the contractual arbitration provision. The state court issued a temporary restraining order forbidding continuation of the strike and also an order to show cause why a preliminary injunction should not be granted. Shortly thereafter, the union removed the case to the Federal District Court and there made a motion to quash the state court's temporary restraining order. In opposition, petitioner moved for an order compelling arbitration and enjoining continuation of the strike. Concluding that the dispute was subject to arbitration under the collective-bargaining agreement and that the strike was in violation of the contract, the District Court ordered the parties to arbitrate the underlying dispute and simultaneously enjoined the strike, all picketing in the vicinity of petitioner's supermarket, and any attempts by the union to induce the employees to strike or to refuse to perform their services.

II

At the outset, we are met with respondent's contention that *Sinclair* ought not to be disturbed because the decision turned on a question of statutory construction which Congress can alter at any time. Since Congress has not modified our conclusions in *Sinclair,* even though it has been urged to do so,[5] respondent argues that principles of *stare decisis* should govern the present case.

We do not agree that the doctrine of *stare decisis* bars a re-examination of *Sinclair* in the circumstances of this case. We fully recognize that important policy considerations militate in favor of continuity and predictability in the law. Nevertheless, as Mr. Justice Frankfurter wrote for the Court, "*[S]tare decisis* is a principle of policy and not a mechanical formula of adherence to the latest decision, however recent and questionable, when such adherence involves collision with a prior doctrine more embracing in its scope, intrinsically sounder, and verified by experience." Helvering v. Hallock, 309 U.S. 106, 119, 60 S.Ct. 444, 451, 84 L.Ed. 604 (1940). * * * It is precisely because *Sinclair* stands as a significant departure from our otherwise consistent emphasis upon the congressional policy to promote the peaceful settlement of labor disputes through arbitration [6] and our efforts to accommodate and harmonize this policy with those underlying the anti-injunction provisions of the Norris-LaGuardia Act that we believe *Sinclair* should be reconsidered. Furthermore, in light of developments subsequent to *Sinclair,* in particular our decision in Avco Corp. v. Aero Lodge 735, 390

---

5. See, e.g., Report of Special Atkinson-Sinclair Committee, A.B.A. Labor Relations Law Section—Proceedings 226 (1963) [hereinafter cited as A.B.A. *Sinclair* Report].

6. See, e.g., United Steelworkers of America v. American Mfg. Co., 363 U.S. 564, 80 S.Ct. 1343, 4 L.Ed.2d 1403 (1960); United Steelworkers of America v. Warrior & Gulf

Nav. Co., 363 U.S. 574, 80 S.Ct. 1347, 4 L.Ed. 2d 1409 (1960); United Steelworkers of America v. Enterprise Wheel & Car Corp., 363 U.S. 593, 80 S.Ct. 1358, 4 L.Ed.2d 1424 (1960); Textile Workers Union of America v. Lincoln Mills, 353 U.S. 448, 77 S.Ct. 912, 1 L.Ed.2d 972 (1957).

U.S. 557, 88 S.Ct. 1235, 20 L.Ed.2d 126 (1968), it has become clear that the *Sinclair* decision does not further but rather frustrates realization of an important goal of our national labor policy.

Nor can we agree that conclusive weight should be accorded to the failure of Congress to respond to *Sinclair* on the theory that congressional silence should be interpreted as acceptance of the decision. The Court has cautioned that "[i]t is at best treacherous to find in congressional silence alone the adoption of a controlling rule of law." Girouard v. United States, 328 U.S. 61, 69, 66 S.Ct. 826, 830, 90 L.Ed. 1084 (1946). Therefore, in the absence of any persuasive circumstances evidencing a clear design that congressional inaction be taken as acceptance of *Sinclair,* the mere silence of Congress is not a sufficient reason for refusing to reconsider the decision.

* * *

III

From the time Textile Workers Union of America v. Lincoln Mills, 353 U.S. 448, 77 S.Ct. 912 (1957), was decided, we have frequently found it necessary to consider various substantive and procedural aspects of federal labor contract law and questions concerning its application in both state and federal courts. *Lincoln Mills* held generally that "the substantive law to apply in suits under § 301(a) is federal law, which the courts must fashion from the policy of our national labor laws," 353 U.S., at 456, 77 S.Ct., at 918, and more specifically that a union can obtain specific performance of an employer's promise to arbitrate grievances. We rejected the contention that the anti-injunction proscriptions of the Norris-LaGuardia Act prohibited this type of relief, noting that a refusal to arbitrate was not "part and parcel of the abuses against which the Act was aimed," id., at 458, 77 S.Ct. at 918, and that the Act itself manifests a policy determination that arbitration should be encouraged. * * * Subsequently in the *Steelworkers Trilogy* we emphasized the importance of arbitration as an instrument of federal policy for resolving disputes between labor and management and cautioned the lower courts against usurping the functions of the arbitrator.

Serious questions remained, however, concerning the role that state courts were to play in suits involving collective-bargaining agreements. Confronted with some of these problems in Charles Dowd Box Co. v. Courtney, 368 U.S. 502, 82 S.Ct. 519, 7 L.Ed.2d 483 (1962), we held that Congress clearly intended *not* to disturb the pre-existing jurisdiction of the state courts over suits for violations of collective-bargaining agreements. We noted that the "clear implication of the entire record of the congressional debates in both 1946 and 1947 is that the purpose of conferring jurisdiction upon the federal district courts was not to displace, but to supplement, the thoroughly considered jurisdiction of the courts of the various States over contracts made by labor organizations." Id., at 511, 82 S.Ct. at 525.

Shortly after the decision in *Dowd Box,* we sustained, in Local 174, Teamsters, etc. v. Lucas Flour Co., 369 U.S. 95, 82 S.Ct. 571, 7 L.Ed.2d 593 (1962), an award of damages by a state court to an employer for a breach by the union of a no-strike provision in its contract. While emphasizing that "in enacting § 301 Congress intended doctrines of federal labor law uniformly to prevail over inconsistent local rules," id., at 104, 82 S.Ct. at 577, we did not consider the applicability of the Norris-LaGuardia Act to state court proceedings because the employer's prayer for relief sought only damages and not specific performance of a no-strike obligation.

Subsequent to the decision in *Sinclair,* we held in Avco Corp. v. Aero Lodge 735, supra, that § 301(a) suits initially brought in state courts may be removed to the designated federal forum under the federal question removal jurisdiction delineated in 28 U.S.C. § 1441. In so holding, however, the Court expressly left open the questions whether state courts are bound by the anti-injunction proscription of the Norris-LaGuardia Act and whether federal courts, after removal of a § 301(a) action, are required to dissolve any injunctive relief previously granted by the state courts. See generally General Electric Co. v. Local Union 191, 413 F.2d 964 (C.A. 5th Cir.1969) (dissolution of state injunction required). Three Justices who concurred expressed the view that *Sinclair* should be reconsidered "upon an appropriate future occasion." 390 U.S., at 562, 88 S.Ct. at 1238 (Stewart, J., concurring).[10]

The decision in *Avco,* viewed in the context of *Lincoln Mills* and its progeny, has produced an anomalous situation which, in our view, makes urgent the reconsideration of *Sinclair.* The principal practical effect of *Avco* and *Sinclair* taken together is nothing less than to oust state courts of jurisdiction in § 301(a) suits where injunctive relief is sought for breach of a no-strike obligation. Union defendants can, as a matter of course, obtain removal to a federal court,[11] and there is obviously a compelling incentive for them to do so in order to gain the advantage of the strictures upon injunctive relief which *Sinclair* imposes on federal courts. The sanctioning of this practice, however, is wholly inconsistent with our conclusion in *Dowd Box* that the congressional purpose embodied in § 301(a) was to *supplement,* and not to encroach upon, the pre-existing jurisdiction of the state courts. It is ironic indeed that the very provision that Congress clearly intended to provide additional remedies for breach of collective-bargaining agreements has been employed to displace previously existing state remedies. We are not at liberty thus to depart from the clearly expressed congressional policy to the contrary.

On the other hand, to the extent that widely disparate remedies theoretically remain available in state, as opposed to federal, courts, the federal policy of labor law uniformity elaborated in *Lucas Flour Co.,* is seriously offended. This policy, of course, could hardly require, as a practical matter, that labor law be administered identically in all courts, for undoubtedly a certain diversity exists among the state and federal systems in matters of procedural and remedial detail, a fact that Congress evidently took into

10. Shortly after *Sinclair* was decided, an erosive process began to weaken its underpinnings. Various authorities suggested methods of mitigating the absolute rigor of the *Sinclair* rule. For example, the Court of Appeals for the Fifth Circuit held that *Sinclair* does not prevent a federal district court from enforcing an arbitrator's order directing a union to terminate work stoppages in violation of a no-strike clause. New Orleans Steamship Assn. v. General Longshore Workers, 389 F.2d 369, cert. denied, 393 U.S. 828, 89 S.Ct. 92, 21 L.Ed. 2d 99 (1968); see Pacific Maritime Assn. v.

International Longshoremen's and Warehousemen's Union, 304 F.Supp. 1315 (D.C.N.D. Cal.1969). See generally Keene, The Supreme Court, Section 301 and No-Strike Clauses: From Lincoln Mills to Avco and Beyond, 15 Vill.L.Rev. 32 (1969).

11. Section 301(a) suits require neither the existence of diversity of citizenship nor a minimum jurisdictional amount in controversy. All § 301(a) suits may be removed pursuant to 28 U.S.C.A. § 1441.

account in deciding not to disturb the traditional jurisdiction of the States. The injunction, however, is so important a remedial device, particularly in the arbitration context, that its availability or non-availability in various courts will not only produce rampant forum shopping and maneuvering from one court to another but will also greatly frustrate any relative uniformity in the enforcement of arbitration agreements.

Furthermore, the existing scheme, with the injunction remedy technically available in the state courts but rendered inefficacious by the removal device, assigns to removal proceedings a totally unintended function. While the underlying purposes of Congress in providing for federal question removal jurisdiction remain somewhat obscure,[13] there has never been a serious contention that Congress intended that the removal mechanism be utilized to foreclose completely remedies otherwise available in the state courts. Although federal question removal jurisdiction may well have been intended to provide a forum for the protection of federal rights where such protection was deemed necessary or to encourage the development of expertise by the federal courts in the interpretation of federal law, there is no indication that Congress intended by the removal mechanism to effect a wholesale dislocation in the allocation of judicial business between the state and federal courts. * * *

It is undoubtedly true that each of the foregoing objections to *Sinclair-Avco* could be remedied either by overruling *Sinclair* or by extending that decision to the States. While some commentators have suggested that the solution to the present unsatisfactory situation does lie in the extension of the *Sinclair* prohibition to state court proceedings, we agree with Chief Justice Traynor of the California Supreme Court that "whether or not Congress could deprive state courts of the power to give such [injunctive] remedies when enforcing collective bargaining agreements, it has not attempted to do so either in the Norris-LaGuardia Act or section 301." McCarroll v. Los Angeles County Dist. Council of Carpenters, 49 Cal.2d 45, 63, 315 P.2d 322, 332 (1957), cert. denied, 355 U.S. 932, 78 S.Ct. 413, 2 L.Ed. 2d 415 (1958). * * *

An additional reason for not resolving the existing dilemma by extending *Sinclair* to the States is the devastating implications for the enforceability of arbitration agreements and their accompanying no-strike obligations if equitable remedies were not available.[15] As we have previously indicated, a no-strike obligation, express or implied, is the *quid pro quo* for an undertaking by the employer to submit grievance disputes to the process of arbitration. * * * Any incentive for employers to enter into such an

---

13. The legislative history of the federal question removal provision is meager, but it has been suggested that its purpose was the same as original federal question jurisdiction, enacted at the same time in the Judiciary Act of 1875, 18 Stat. 470, namely, to protect federal rights, see H. Hart & H. Wechsler, The Federal Courts and the Federal System 727–733 (1953), and to provide a forum that could more accurately interpret federal law, see Mishkin, The Federal "Question" in the District Courts, 53 Col.L.Rev. 157, 159 (1953). 113 U.Pa.L.Rev. 1096, 1098 and n. 17 (1965).

15. It is true that about one-half of the States have enacted so-called "little Norris-LaGuardia Acts" that place various restrictions upon the granting of injunctions by state courts in labor disputes. However, because many States do not bar injunctive relief for violations of collective-bargaining agreements, in only about 14 jurisdictions is there a significant Norris-LaGuardia-type prohibition against equitable remedies for breach of no-strike obligations. * * *

arrangement is necessarily dissipated if the principal and most expeditious method by which the no-strike obligation can be enforced is eliminated. While it is of course true, as respondent contends, that other avenues of redress, such as an action for damages, would remain open to an aggrieved employer, an award of damages after a dispute has been settled is no substitute for an immediate halt to an illegal strike. Furthermore, an action for damages prosecuted during or after a labor dispute would only tend to aggravate industrial strife and delay an early resolution of the difficulties between employer and union.[17]

Even if management is not encouraged by the unavailability of the injunction remedy to resist arbitration agreements, the fact remains that the effectiveness of such agreements would be greatly reduced if injunctive relief were withheld. Indeed, the very purpose of arbitration procedures is to provide a mechanism for the expeditious settlement of industrial disputes without resort to strikes, lockouts, or other self-help measures. This basic purpose is obviously largely undercut if there is no immediate, effective remedy for those very tactics that arbitration is designed to obviate. Thus, because *Sinclair,* in the aftermath of *Avco,* casts serious doubt upon the effective enforcement of a vital element of stable labor-management relations—arbitration agreements with their attendant no-strike obligations—we conclude that *Sinclair* does not make a viable contribution to federal labor policy.

IV

We have also determined that the dissenting opinion in *Sinclair* states the correct principles concerning the accommodation necessary between the seemingly absolute terms of the Norris-LaGuardia Act and the policy considerations underlying § 301(a).[18] 370 U.S., at 215, 82 S.Ct., at 1339. Although we need not repeat all that was there said, a few points should be emphasized at this time.

The literal terms of § 4 of the Norris-LaGuardia Act must be accommodated to the subsequently enacted provisions of § 301(a) of the Labor Management Relations Act and the purposes of arbitration. Statutory interpretation requires more than concentration upon isolated words; rather, consideration must be given to the total corpus of pertinent law and the policies that inspired ostensibly inconsistent provisions. See ＊ ＊ ＊ United States v. Hutcheson, 312 U.S. 219, 235, 61 S.Ct. 463, 467, 85 L.Ed. 788 (1941).

---

17. As the neutral members of the A.B.A. committee on the problems raised by *Sinclair* noted in their report:

"Under existing laws, employers may maintain an action for damages resulting from a strike in breach of contract and may discipline the employees involved. In many cases, however, neither of these alternatives will be feasible. Discharge of the strikers is often inexpedient because of a lack of qualified replacements or because of the adverse effect on relationships within the plant. The damage remedy may also be unsatisfactory because the employer's losses are often hard to calculate and because the employer may hesitate to exacerbate relations with the union by bringing a damage action. Hence, injunctive relief will often be the only effective means by which to remedy the breach of the no-strike pledge and thus effectuate federal labor policy." A.B.A. *Sinclair* Report 242.

18. Scholarly criticism of *Sinclair* has been sharp, and it appears to be almost universally recognized that *Sinclair,* particularly after *Avco,* has produced an untenable situation. The commentators are divided, however, with respect to proposed solutions, some favoring reconsideration of *Sinclair,* others suggesting extension of *Sinclair* to the States, and still others recommending that any action in this area be left to Congress. ＊ ＊ ＊

The Norris-LaGuardia Act was responsive to a situation totally different from that which exists today. In the early part of this century, the federal courts generally were regarded as allies of management in its attempt to prevent the organization and strengthening of labor unions; and in this industrial struggle the injunction became a potent weapon that was wielded against the activities of labor groups. The result was a large number of sweeping decrees, often issued *ex parte*, drawn on an *ad hoc* basis without regard to any systematic elaboration of national labor policy. ＊ ＊ ＊

In 1932 Congress attempted to bring some order out of the industrial chaos that had developed and to correct the abuses that had resulted from the interjection of the federal judiciary into union-management disputes on the behalf of management. See declaration of public policy, Norris-LaGuardia Act, § 2 ＊ ＊ ＊. Congress, therefore, determined initially to limit severely the power of the federal courts to issue injunctions "in any case involving or growing out of any labor dispute ＊ ＊ ＊." Even as initially enacted, however, the prohibition against federal injunctions was by no means absolute. See Norris-LaGuardia Act, §§ 7, 8, 9 ＊ ＊ ＊. Shortly thereafter Congress passed the Wagner Act, designed to curb various management activities that tended to discourage employee participation in collective action.

As labor organizations grew in strength and developed toward maturity, congressional emphasis shifted from protection of the nascent labor movement to the encouragement of collective bargaining and to administrative techniques for the peaceful resolution of industrial disputes. This shift in emphasis was accomplished, however, without extensive revision of many of the older enactments, including the anti-injunction section of the Norris-LaGuardia Act. Thus it became the task of the courts to accommodate, to reconcile the older statutes with the more recent ones.

A leading example of this accommodation process is Brotherhood of Railroad Trainmen v. Chicago River & Ind. R. Co., 353 U.S. 30, 77 S.Ct. 635, 1 L.Ed.2d 622 (1957). There we were confronted with a peaceful strike which violated the statutory duty to arbitrate imposed by the Railway Labor Act. The Court concluded that a strike in violation of a statutory arbitration duty was not the type of situation to which the Norris-LaGuardia Act was responsive, that an important federal policy was involved in the peaceful settlement of disputes through the statutorily mandated arbitration procedure, that this important policy was imperiled if equitable remedies were not available to implement it, and hence that Norris-LaGuardia's policy of nonintervention by the federal courts should yield to the overriding interest in the successful implementation of the arbitration process.

The principles elaborated in *Chicago River* are equally applicable to the present case. To be sure, *Chicago River* involved arbitration procedures established by statute. However, we have frequently noted, in such cases as *Lincoln Mills*, the *Steelworkers Trilogy*, and *Lucas Flour*, the importance that Congress has attached generally to the voluntary settlement of labor disputes without resort to self-help and more particularly to arbitration as a means to this end. ＊ ＊ ＊

The *Sinclair* decision, however, seriously undermined the effectiveness of the arbitration technique as a method peacefully to resolve industrial disputes without resort to strikes, lockouts, and similar devices. Clearly employers will be wary of assuming obligations to arbitrate specifically enforceable against them when no similarly efficacious remedy is available to enforce the concomitant undertaking of the union to refrain from striking. On the other hand, the central purpose of the Norris-LaGuardia Act to foster the growth and viability of labor organizations is hardly retarded—if anything, this goal is advanced—by a remedial device that merely enforces the obligation that the union freely undertook under a specifically enforceable agreement to submit disputes to arbitration. We conclude therefore, that the unavailability of equitable relief in the arbitration context presents a serious impediment to the congressional policy favoring the voluntary establishment of a mechanism for the peaceful resolution of labor disputes, that the core purpose of the Norris-LaGuardia Act is not sacrificed by the limited use of equitable remedies to further this important policy, and consequently that the Norris-LaGuardia Act does not bar the granting of injunctive relief in the circumstances of the instant case.

V

Our holding in the present case is a narrow one. We do not undermine the vitality of the Norris-LaGuardia Act. We deal only with the situation in which a collective-bargaining contract contains a mandatory grievance adjustment or arbitration procedure. Nor does it follow from what we have said that injunctive relief is appropriate as a matter of course in every case of a strike over an arbitrable grievance. The dissenting opinion in *Sinclair* suggested the following principles for the guidance of the district courts in determining whether to grant injunctive relief—principles that we now adopt:

> "A District Court entertaining an action under § 301 may not grant injunctive relief against concerted activity unless and until it decides that the case is one in which an injunction would be appropriate despite the Norris-LaGuardia Act. When a strike is sought to be enjoined because it is over a grievance which both parties are contractually bound to arbitrate, the District Court may issue no injunctive order until it first holds that the contract *does* have that effect; and the employer should be ordered to arbitrate, as a condition of his obtaining an injunction against the strike. Beyond this, the District Court must, of course, consider whether issuance of an injunction would be warranted under ordinary principles of equity— whether breaches are occurring and will continue, or have been threatened and will be committed; whether they have caused or will cause irreparable injury to the employer; and whether the employer will suffer more from the denial of an injunction than will the union from its issuance." 370 U.S., at 228, 82 S.Ct., at 1346. (Emphasis in original.)

In the present case there is no dispute that the grievance in question was subject to adjustment and arbitration under the collective-bargaining agreement and that the petitioner was ready to proceed with arbitration at the time an injunction against the strike was sought and obtained. The District Court also concluded that, by reason of respondent's violations of its no-strike obligation, petitioner "has suffered irreparable injury and will continue to suffer irreparable injury." Since we now overrule *Sinclair,* the holding of the Court of Appeals in reliance on *Sinclair* must be reversed.

Accordingly, we reverse the judgment of the Court of Appeals and remand the case with directions to enter a judgment affirming the order of the District Court. * * *

MR. JUSTICE MARSHALL took no part in the decision of this case.

[The concurring opinion of MR. JUSTICE STEWART is omitted.]

MR. JUSTICE BLACK, dissenting.

Congress in 1932 enacted the Norris-LaGuardia Act, § 4 of which, * * * with exceptions not here relevant, specifically prohibited federal courts in the broadest and most comprehensive language from issuing any injunctions, temporary or permanent, against participation in a labor dispute. Subsequently, in 1947, Congress gave jurisdiction to the federal courts in "[s]uits for violation of contracts between an employer and a labor organization." Although this subsection, § 301(a) of the Taft-Hartley Act * * * explicitly waives the diversity and amount-in-controversy requirements for federal jurisdiction, it says nothing at all about granting injunctions. Eight years ago this Court considered the relation of these two statutes: after full briefing and argument, relying on the language and history of the Acts, the Court decided that Congress did not wish this later statute to impair in any way Norris-LaGuardia's explicit prohibition against injunctions in labor disputes. Sinclair Refining Co. v. Atkinson, 370 U.S. 195, 82 S.Ct. 1328, 8 L.Ed.2d 440 (1962).

Although Congress has been urged to overrule our holding in *Sinclair,* it has steadfastly refused to do so. Nothing in the language or history of the two Acts has changed. Nothing at all has changed, in fact, except the membership of the Court and the personal views of one Justice [Stewart]. I remain of the opinion that *Sinclair* was correctly decided, and, moreover, that the prohibition of the Norris-LaGuardia Act is close to the heart of the entire federal system of labor regulation. In my view *Sinclair* should control the disposition of this case.

Even if the majority were correct, however, in saying that *Sinclair* misinterpreted the Taft-Hartley and Norris-LaGuardia Acts, I should be compelled to dissent. I believe that both the making and the changing of laws which affect the substantial rights of the people are primarily for Congress, not this Court. Most especially is this so when the laws involved are the focus of strongly held views of powerful but antagonistic political and economic interests. The Court's function in the application and interpretation of such laws must be carefully limited to avoid encroaching on the power of Congress to determine policies and make laws to carry them out. * * *

* * * Of course, when this Court first interprets a statute, then the statute becomes what this court has said it is. * * * Such an initial interpretation is proper, and unavoidable, in any system in which courts have the task of applying general statutes in a multitude of situations. B. Cardozo, The Nature of the Judicial Process 112–115 (1921). The Court undertakes the task of interpretation, however, not because the Court has any special ability to fathom the intent of Congress, but rather because interpretation is unavoidable in the decision of the case before it. When the law has been settled by an earlier case then any subsequent "reinterpreta-

tion" of the statute is gratuitous and neither more nor less than an amendment; it is no different in effect from a judicial alteration of language that Congress itself placed in the statute.

Altering the important provisions of a statute is a legislative function. * * * It is Congress, not this Court, that has the capacity to investigate the divergent considerations involved in the management of a complex national labor policy. And it is Congress, not this Court, that is elected by the people. This Court should, therefore, interject itself as little as possible into the law-making and law-changing process. Having given our view on the meaning of a statute, our task is concluded, absent extraordinary circumstances. * * *

* * * Bills were introduced in Congress seeking to effect a legislative change. * * * Congress, however, did not act, thus indicating at least a willingness to leave the law as *Sinclair* had construed it. It seems to me highly inappropriate for this Court now, eight years later, in effect to enact the amendment that Congress has refused to adopt. * * *

I do not believe that the principle of *stare decisis* forecloses all reconsiderations of earlier decisions. In the area of constitutional law, for example, where the only alternative to action by this Court is the laborious process of constitutional amendment and where the ultimate responsibility rests with this Court, I believe reconsideration is always proper. * * * Even on statutory questions the appearance of new facts or changes in circumstances might warrant re-examination of past decisions in exceptional cases under exceptional circumstances. In the present situation there are no such circumstances. * * *

The only "subsequent event" to which the Court can point is our decision in Avco Corp. v. Aero Lodge 735, 390 U.S. 557, 88 S.Ct. 1235, 20 L.Ed.2d 126 (1968). The Court must recognize that the holding of *Avco* is in no way inconsistent with *Sinclair*. As we said in *Avco,* supra, at 561, 88 S.Ct., at 1237: "The nature of the relief available after jurisdiction attaches is, of course, different from the question whether there is jurisdiction to adjudicate the controversy." The Court contends, however, that the result of the two cases taken together is the "anomalous situation" that no-strike clauses become unenforceable in state courts, and this is inconsistent with "an important goal of our national labor policy."

Avco does make any effort to enforce a no-strike clause in a state court removable to a federal court, but it does not follow that the no-strike clause is unenforceable. Damages may be awarded; the union may be forced to arbitrate. And the employer may engage in self-help. The Court would have it that these techniques are less effective than an injunction. That is doubtless true. But the harshness and effectiveness of injunctive relief—and opposition to "government by injunction"—were the precise reasons for the congressional prohibition in the Norris-LaGuardia Act. The effect of the *Avco* decision is, indeed, to highlight the limited remedial powers of federal courts. But if the Congress is unhappy with these powers as this Court defined them, then the Congress may act; this Court should not. The members of the majority have simply decided that they are more sensitive to the "realization of an important goal of our national labor policy" than the Congress or their predecessors on this Court.

The correct interpretation of the Taft-Hartley Act, and even the goals of "our national labor policy," are less important than the proper division of functions between the branches of our Federal Government. The Court would do well to remember the words of John Adams, written in the Declaration of Rights in the Constitution of the Commonwealth of Massachusetts:

"The judicial [department] shall never exercise the legislative and executive powers, or either of them: to the end it may be a government of laws and not of men."

I dissent.

MR. JUSTICE WHITE dissents for the reasons stated in the majority opinion in Sinclair Refining Co. v. Atkinson, 370 U.S. 195, 82 S.Ct. 1328, 8 L.Ed.2d 440 (1962).

Note

1. The following passage from the majority opinion in SINCLAIR, written by (surprise) Justice Black, may better manifest the strength of the then majority position than Justice Black's dissent in Boys Markets:

"The language of § 301 itself seems to us almost if not entirely conclusive of this question. It is especially significant that the section contains no language that could by any stretch of the imagination be interpreted to constitute an explicit repeal of the anti-injunction provisions of the Norris-LaGuardia Act in view of the fact that the section does expressly repeal another provision of the Norris-LaGuardia Act dealing with union responsibility for the acts of agents.[17] If Congress had intended that § 301 suits should also not be subject to the anti-injunction provisions of the Norris-LaGuardia Act, it certainly seems likely that it would have made its intent known in this same express manner. That is indeed precisely what Congress did do in § 101, amending § 10(h) of the National Labor Relations Act, and § 208(b) of the Taft-Hartley Act, by permitting injunctions to be obtained, not by private litigants, but only at the instance of the National Labor Relations Board and the Attorney General, and in § 302(e), by permitting private litigants to obtain injunctions in order to protect the integrity of employees' collective bargaining representatives in carrying out their responsibilities.[19] Thus the failure of Congress to include a provision in § 301 expressly repealing the anti-injunction provisions of the Norris-LaGuardia Act must be evaluated in the context of a statutory pattern that

17. Section 301(e) of the Act provides: "For the purposes of this section, in determining whether any person is acting as an 'agent' of another person so as to make such other person responsible for his acts, the question of whether the specific acts performed were actually authorized or subsequently ratified shall not be controlling." This, of course, was designed to and did repeal for purposes of suits under § 301 the previously controlling provisions of § 6 of the Norris-LaGuardia Act * * *: "No officer or member of any association or organization, and no association or organization participating or interested in a labor dispute, shall be held responsible or liable in any court of the United States for the unlawful acts of individual officers, members, or agents, except upon clear proof of actual participation in, or actual authorization of, such acts, or of ratification of such acts after actual knowledge thereof."

19. That this section, which stands alone in expressly permitting suits for injunctions previously proscribed by the Norris-LaGuardia Act to be brought in the federal courts by private litigants under the Taft-Hartley Act, deals with an unusually sensitive and important problem is shown by the fact that § 186 makes the conduct so enjoinable a crime punishable by both fine and imprisonment.

indicates not only that Congress was completely familiar with those provisions but also that it regarded an express declaration of inapplicability as the normal and proper manner of repealing them in situations where such repeal seemed desirable.

"When the inquiry is carried beyond the language of § 301 into its legislative history, whatever small doubts as to the congressional purpose could have survived consideration of the bare language of the section should be wholly dissipated. For the legislative history of § 301 shows that Congress actually considered the advisability of repealing the Norris-LaGuardia Act insofar as suits based upon breach of collective bargaining agreements are concerned and deliberately chose not to do so. The section as eventually enacted was the product of a conference between Committees of the House and Senate, selected to resolve the differences between conflicting provisions of the respective bills each had passed. * * *

"* * * Senator Taft, Chairman of the Conference Committee and one of the authors of this legislation that bore his name, was * * * explicit in explaining the results of the Conference to the Senate: 'The Conferees * * * rejected the repeal of the Norris-LaGuardia Act.' [27]

"We cannot accept the startling argument made here that even though Congress did not itself want to repeal the Norris-LaGuardia Act, it was willing to confer a power upon the courts to 'accommodate' that Act out of existence whenever they might find it expedient to do so in furtherance of some policy they had fashioned under § 301." 370 U.S. at 204–09, 82 S.Ct. at 1333–36.

2. The key to the problem involved in the Sinclair and Boys Markets cases would seem to lie in the last paragraph of the above-quoted passage from Justice Black's opinion for the majority in Sinclair. The "policy" which the Supreme Court "had fashioned under § 301" had taken the provision so far beyond the congressional analysis at the time of enactment that head-on collision with Norris-LaGuardia was the unforeseen, though inevitable, result. Sinclair, Avco, and Boys Markets were the natural offspring, however unfraternal the first and the third, of Lincoln Mills. Against this backdrop, Justice Frankfurter's dissent in Lincoln Mills, summarized supra pp. 630–631, may seem both sensitive and prophetic.

3. In the Sinclair case the company sued the union in three counts, the third of which sought the injunction denied in Sinclair Refining Co. v. Atkinson. Counts I and II sought damages against the international and local unions and against 24 individual employees, each of whom was alleged to be a committeeman of the local union and an agent of the international. These two counts were decided in ATKINSON v. SINCLAIR REFINING CO., 370 U.S. 238, 82 S.Ct. 1318, 8 L.Ed.2d 462 (1962). The Court held that while the company could recover damages from the union under Section 301, it could not recover from the individual union members. The Court observed:

"When Congress passed § 301, it declared its view that only the union was to be made to respond for union wrongs, and that the union members were not to be subject to levy. Section 301(b) has three clauses. One makes unions suable in the courts of the United States. Another makes unions bound by the acts of their agents according to conventional principles of

27. 93 Cong.Rec. 6445–6446, II Leg.Hist.
1544. * * *

agency law (cf. § 301(e)). At the same time, however, the remaining clause exempts agents and members from personal liability for judgments against the union (apparently even when the union is without assets to pay the judgment). The legislative history of § 301(b) makes it clear that this third clause was a deeply felt congressional reaction against the Danbury Hatters case (Loewe v. Lawlor, 208 U.S. 274, 28 S.Ct. 301, 52 L.Ed. 488; Lawlor v. Loewe, 235 U.S. 522, 35 S.Ct. 170, 59 L.Ed. 341), and an expression of legislative determination that the aftermath (Loewe v. Savings Bank of Danbury, 236 F. 444 (C.A.2d Cir.)) of that decision was not to be permitted to recur. In that case, an antitrust treble damage action was brought against a large number of union members, including union officers and agents, to recover from them the employer's losses in a nationwide, union-directed boycott of his hats. The union was not named as a party, nor was judgment entered against it. A large money judgment was entered, instead, against the individual defendants for participating in the plan 'emanating from headquarters' (235 U.S., at 534, 35 S.Ct., at 172), by knowingly authorizing and delegating authority to the union officers to do the acts involved. In the debates, Senator Ball, one of the Act's sponsors, declared that § 301, 'by providing that the union may sue and be sued as a legal entity, for a violation of contract, and that liability for damages will lie against union assets only, will prevent a repetition of the Danbury Hatters case, in which many members lost their homes' (93 Cong.Rec. 5014). * * *

"* * * We have already said in another context that § 301(b) at least evidences 'a congressional intention that the union as an entity, like a corporation, should in the absence of agreement be the sole source of recovery for injury inflicted by it' (Lewis v. Benedict Coal Corp., 361 U.S. 459, 470, 80 S.Ct. 489, 496, 4 L.Ed.2d 442). This policy cannot be evaded or truncated by the simple device of suing union agents or members, whether in contract or tort, or both, in a separate count or in a separate action for damages for violation of a collective bargaining contract for which damages the union itself is liable. The national labor policy requires and we hold that when a union is liable for damages for violation of the no-strike clause, its officers and members are not liable for these damages." 370 U.S. at 247–49, 82 S.Ct. at 1324–25.

As subsequently noted in Complete Auto Transit, Inc. v. Reis, 451 U.S. 401, 101 S.Ct. 1836, 68 L.Ed.2d 248 (1981), the Atkinson decision "expressly reserved the question whether an employer might maintain a suit for damages against 'individual defendants acting not in behalf of the union but in their personal and non-union capacity' where their unauthorized, individual action violated the no-strike provision of the collective-bargaining agreement" (i.e., a wildcat strike). 451 U.S. at 402, 101 S.Ct. at 1838. In Complete Auto Transit, the Court answered this question: "[W]hile § 301(b) explicitly addresses only union-authorized violations of a collective-bargaining agreement, the legislative history establishes that Congress meant to exclude individual strikers from damages liability, whether or not they were authorized by their union to strike. The legislative debates and the process of legislative amendment demonstrate that Congress deliberately chose to allow a damages remedy for breach of the no-strike provision of a collective-bargaining agreement only against *unions*, not *individuals*, and, as to unions, only when they participated in or authorized the strike. See Carbon Fuel Co. v. United Mine Workers, 444 U.S. 212, 216, 100 S.Ct. 410, 413, 62 L.Ed.2d 394 (1979) [holding that a parent union, signatory to a bargaining agreement containing an implied no-strike clause, was not liable for damages resulting from a wildcat strike by a local union, despite the parent's failure to use "all reasonable means" to terminate the strike; such failure did not constitute participation in or authorization of the strike]." 451 U.S. at 406, 101 S.Ct. at 1840.

BUFFALO FORGE CO. v. UNITED STEELWORKERS

Supreme Court of the United States, 1976.
428 U.S. 397, 96 S.Ct. 3141, 49 L.Ed.2d 1022.

MR. JUSTICE WHITE delivered the opinion of the Court.

The issue for decision is whether a federal court may enjoin a sympathy strike pending the arbitrator's decision as to whether the strike is forbidden by the express no-strike clause contained in the collective-bargaining contract to which the striking union is a party.

I

The Buffalo Forge Company (the employer) operates three separate plant and office facilities in the Buffalo, New York area. For some years production and maintenance (P & M) employees at the three locations have been represented by the United Steelworkers of America, AFL–CIO, and its Local Unions No. 1874 and No. 3732 (the Union). The United Steelworkers is a party to the two separate collective-bargaining agreements between the locals and the employer. The contracts contain identical no-strike clauses,[1] as well as grievance and arbitration provisions for settling disputes over the interpretation and application of each contract. The latter provide:

> "26. Should differences arise between the [employer] and any employee covered by this Agreement as to the meaning and application of the provisions of this Agreement, or should any trouble of any kind arise in the plant, there shall be no suspension of work on account of such differences, but an earnest effort shall be made to settle such differences immediately [under the six-step grievance and arbitration procedure provided in sections 27 through 32.]"[2]

Shortly before this dispute arose, the United Steelworkers and two other locals not parties to this litigation were certified to represent the employer's "office clerical-technical" (O & T) employees at the same three locations. On November 16, 1974, after several months of negotiations looking toward their first collective-bargaining agreement, the O & T employees struck and established picket lines at all three locations. On November 18, P & M

---

1. Section 14.b. of each agreement provides:

"There shall be no strikes, work stoppages or interruption or impeding of work. No Officers or representatives of the Union shall authorize, instigate, aid or condone any such activities. No employee shall participate in any such activity. The Union recognizes its possible liabilities for violation of this provision and will use its influence to see that work stoppages are prevented. Unsuccessful efforts by Union officers or Union representatives to prevent and terminate conduct prohibited by this paragraph, will not be construed as 'aid' or 'con-

donation' of such conduct and shall not result in any disciplinary actions against the Officers, committeemen or stewards involved."

2. The final step in the six-part grievance procedure is provided for in § 32:

"In the event the grievance involves a question as to the meaning and application of the provisions of this Agreement, and has not been previously satisfactorily adjusted, it may be submitted to arbitration upon written notice of the Union or the Company."

employees at one plant refused to cross the O & T picket line for the day. Two days later, the employer learned that the P & M employees planned to stop work at all three plants the next morning. In telegrams to the Union, the employer stated its position that a strike by the P & M employees would violate the no-strike clause and offered to arbitrate any dispute which had led to the planned strike. The next day, at the Union's direction, the P & M employees honored the O & T picket line and stopped work at the three plants. They did not return to work until December 16, the first regular working day after the District Court denied the employer's prayer for a preliminary injunction.

The employer's complaint under § 301(a) of the Labor Management Relations Act, filed in District Court on November 26, claimed the work stoppage was in violation of the no-strike clause. Contending in the alternative that the work strike was caused by a specific incident involving P & M truck drivers' refusal to follow a supervisor's instructions to cross the O & T picket line, and that the question whether the P & M employees' work stoppage violated the no-strike clause was itself arbitrable, the employer requested damages, a temporary restraining order and a preliminary injunction against the strike and an order compelling the parties to submit any "underlying dispute" to the contractual grievance and arbitration procedures. The Union's position was that the work stoppage did not violate the no-strike clause. It offered to submit that question to arbitration "on one day's notice," but opposed the prayer for injunctive relief.

After denying the temporary restraining order and finding that the P & M work stoppage was not the result of the specific refusal to cross the O & T picket line, the District Court concluded that the P & M employees were engaged in a sympathy action in support of the striking O & T employees. The District Court then held itself forbidden to issue an injunction by § 4 of the Norris-LaGuardia Act because the P & M employees' strike was not over an "arbitrable grievance" and hence was not within the "narrow" exception to the Norris-LaGuardia Act established in Boys Markets, Inc. v. Retail Clerks Union, 398 U.S. 235, 90 S.Ct. 1583, 26 L.Ed.2d 199 (1970). Buffalo Forge Co. v. United Steelworkers of America, 386 F.Supp. 405 (WDNY 1974).

On the employer's appeal from the denial of a preliminary injunction, the parties stipulated that the District Court's findings of fact were correct, that the Union had authorized and directed the P & M employees' work stoppage, that the O & T employees' strike and picket line were bona fide, primary and legal, and that the P & M employees' work stoppage, though ended, might "be resumed at any time in the near future at the direction of the International Union, or otherwise."

The Court of Appeals affirmed. It held that enjoining this strike, which was not "over a grievance which the union has agreed to arbitrate," was not permitted by the *Boys Markets* exception to the Norris-LaGuardia Act. Buffalo Forge Co. v. United Steelworkers of America, 517 F.2d 1207, 1210 (CA2 1975). Because the Courts of Appeals are divided on the question whether such a strike may be enjoined,[9] we granted the employer's petition for a writ of certiorari and now affirm the judgment of the Court of Appeals.

9. The decision of the Second Circuit in this case is in accord with decisions of the Fifth and Sixth Circuits, Amstar Corp. v. Amalgamated Meat Cutters, 468 F.2d 1372

II

As a preliminary matter, certain elements in this case are not in dispute. The Union has gone on strike not by reason of any dispute it or any of its members has with the employer but in support of other local unions, of the same international organization, that were negotiating a contract with the employer and were out on strike. The parties involved here are bound by a collective-bargaining contract containing a no-strike clause which the Union claims does not forbid sympathy strikes. The employer has the other view, its complaint in the District Court asserting that the work stoppage violated the no-strike clause. The contract between the parties also has an arbitration clause broad enough to reach not only disputes between the Union and the employer about other provisions in the contract but also as to the meaning and application of the no-strike clause itself. Whether the sympathy strike the Union called violated the no-strike clause, and the appropriate remedies if it did, are subject to the agreed-upon dispute-settlement procedures of the contract and are ultimately issues for the arbitrator. United Steelworkers of America v. American Mfg. Co., 363 U.S. 564, 80 S.Ct. 1343, 4 L.Ed.2d 1403 (1960); United Steelworkers of America v. Warrior & Gulf Navigation Co., 363 U.S. 574, 80 S.Ct. 1347, 4 L.Ed.2d 1409 (1960); United Steelworkers of America v. Enterprise Wheel & Car Corp., 363 U.S. 593, 80 S.Ct. 1358, 4 L.Ed.2d 1424 (1960). The employer thus was entitled to invoke the arbitral process to determine the legality of the sympathy strike and to obtain a court order requiring the Union to arbitrate if the Union refused to do so. Gateway Coal Co. v. United Mine Workers, 414 U.S. 368, 94 S.Ct. 629, 38 L.Ed.2d 583 (1974). Furthermore, were the issue arbitrated and the strike found illegal, the relevant federal statutes as construed in our cases would permit an injunction to enforce the arbitral decision. United Steelworkers of America v. Enterprise Wheel & Car Corp., supra.

The issue in this case arises because the employer not only asked for an order directing the Union to arbitrate but prayed that the strike itself be enjoined pending arbitration and the arbitrator's decision whether the strike was permissible under the no-strike clause. Contrary to the Court of Appeals, the employer claims that despite the Norris-LaGuardia Act's ban

(CA5 1972); Plain Dealer Publishing Co. v. Cleveland Typographical Union #53, 520 F.2d 1220 (CA6 1975), cert. pending, No. 75–565; see United States Steel Corp. v. United Mine Workers, 519 F.2d 1236 (1975), reh. denied, 526 F.2d 376 (CA5 1976), cert. pending, No. 75–1562, but at odds with decisions of the Third, Fourth, and Eighth Circuits, NAPA Pittsburgh, Inc. v. Automotive Chauffeurs, Local Union No. 926, 502 F.2d 321 (CA3) (en banc), cert. denied, 419 U.S. 1049, 96 S.Ct. 625, 42 L.Ed.2d 644 (1974); Island Creek Coal Co. v. United Mine Workers, 507 F.2d 650 (CA3), cert. denied, 423 U.S. 877, 96 S.Ct. 150, 46 L.Ed.2d 110 (1975); Armco Steel Corp. v. United Mine Workers, 505 F.2d 1129 (CA4 1974), cert. denied, 423 U.S. 877, 96 S.Ct. 150, 46 L.Ed.2d 110 (1975); Pilot Freight Carriers, Inc. v. International Brotherhood of Teamsters, 497 F.2d 311 (CA4), cert. denied, 419 U.S. 869, 95 S.Ct. 127, 42 L.Ed.2d 107 (1974); Wilmington Shipping Co. v. International Longshoremen's Assn., 86 LRRM 2846 (CA4 1974), cert. denied, 419 U.S. 1022, 95 S.Ct. 498, 42 L.Ed.2d 296 (1974); Monongahela Power Co. v. Local No. 2332, IBEW, 484 F.2d 1209 (CA4 1973); Valmac Industries v. Food Handlers Local 425, 519 F.2d 263 (CA8 1975), cert. pending, No. 75–647; Associated General Contractors v. International Union of Operating Engineers, 519 F.2d 269 (CA8 1975). The Seventh Circuit has adopted an intermediate position. Hyster Co. v. Independent Towing Assn., 519 F.2d 89 (CA7 1975), cert. pending, No. 75–524; Gary Hobart Water Corp. v. NLRB, 511 F.2d 284 (CA7), cert. denied, 423 U.S. 925, 96 S.Ct. 269, 46 L.Ed.2d 252 (1975). But cf. Inland Steel Co. v. Local Union No. 1545, United Mine Workers, 505 F.2d 293 (CA7 1974).

on federal court injunctions in labor disputes the District Court was empowered to enjoin the strike by § 301 of the Labor Management Relations Act as construed by Boys Markets, Inc. v. Retail Clerks Union, supra. This would undoubtedly have been the case had the strike been precipitated by a dispute between union and management that was subject to binding arbitration under the provisions of the contract. In *Boys Markets*, the union demanded that supervisory employees cease performing tasks claimed by the union to be union work. The union struck when the demand was rejected. The dispute was of the kind subject to the grievance and arbitration clauses contained in the collective-bargaining contract, and it was also clear that the strike violated the no-strike clause accompanying the arbitration provisions. The Court held that the union could be enjoined from striking over a dispute which it was bound to arbitrate at the employer's behest.

The holding in *Boys Markets* was said to be a "narrow one," dealing only with the situation in which the collective-bargaining contract contained mandatory grievance and arbitration procedures. 398 U.S., at 253, 90 S.Ct., at 1594. "[F]or the guidance of the district courts in determining whether to grant injunctive relief," the Court expressly adopted the principles enunciated in the dissent in Sinclair Refining Co. v. Atkinson, 370 U.S. 195, 228, 82 S.Ct. 1328, 1346, 8 L.Ed.2d 440 (1962), including the proposition that:

> " 'When a strike is sought to be enjoined because it is over a grievance which both parties are contractually bound to arbitrate, the District Court may issue no injunctive order until it first holds that the contract *does* have that effect; and the employer should be ordered to arbitrate, as a condition of his obtaining an injunction against the strike.' " 398 U.S., at 254, 90 S.Ct., at 1594 (emphasis in *Sinclair*).

The driving force behind *Boys Markets* was to implement the strong congressional preference for the private dispute settlement mechanisms agreed upon by the parties. Only to that extent was it held necessary to accommodate § 4 of the Norris-LaGuardia Act to § 301 of the Labor Management Relations Act and to lift the former's ban against the issuance of injunctions in labor disputes. Striking over an arbitrable dispute would interfere with and frustrate the arbitral processes by which the parties had chosen to settle a dispute. The *quid pro quo* for the employer's promise to arbitrate was the union's obligation not to strike over issues that were subject to the arbitration machinery. Even in the absence of an express no-strike clause, an undertaking not to strike would be implied where the strike was over an otherwise arbitrable dispute. Gateway Coal Co. v. United Mine Workers, supra; Teamsters Local v. Lucas Flour Co., 369 U.S. 95, 82 S.Ct. 571, 7 L.Ed. 2d 593 (1962). Otherwise, the employer would be deprived of his bargain and the policy of the labor statutes to implement private resolution of disputes in a manner agreed upon would seriously suffer.

Boys Markets plainly does not control this case. The District Court found, and it is not now disputed, that the strike was not *over* any dispute between the Union and the employer that was even remotely subject to the arbitration provisions of the contract. The strike at issue was a sympathy strike in support of sister unions negotiating with the employer; neither its causes nor the issue underlying it were subject to the settlement procedures provided by the contract between the employer and respondents. The strike had neither the purpose nor the effect of denying or evading an obligation to arbitrate or of depriving the employer of his bargain. Thus, had the contract not contained a no-strike clause or had the clause expressly excluded sympathy strikes, there would have been no possible basis for implying from the existence of an arbitration clause a promise not to strike that could have been violated by the sympathy strike in this case. Gateway Coal Co. v. Mine Workers, supra, 414 U.S. at 382, 94 S.Ct., at 639.

Nor was the injunction authorized solely because it was alleged that the sympathy strike called by the Union violated the express no-strike provision of the contract. Section 301 of the Act assigns a major role to the courts in enforcing collective bargaining agreements, but aside from the enforcement of the arbitration provisions of such contracts, within the limits permitted by *Boys Markets,* the Court has never indicated that the courts may enjoin actual or threatened contract violations despite the Norris-LaGuardia Act. In the course of enacting the Taft-Hartley Act, Congress rejected the proposal that the Norris-LaGuardia Act's prohibition against labor-dispute injunctions be lifted to the extent necessary to make injunctive remedies available in federal courts for the purpose of enforcing collective bargaining agreements. * * * The allegation of the complaint that the Union was breaching its obligation not to strike did not in itself warrant an injunction. * * *

The contract here at issue, however, also contained grievance and arbitration provisions for settling disputes over the interpretation and application of the provisions of the contract, including the no-strike clause. That clause, like others, was subject to enforcement in accordance with the procedures set out in the contract. Here the Union struck, and the parties were in dispute whether the sympathy strike violated the Union's no-strike undertaking. Concededly, that issue was arbitrable. It was for the arbitrator to determine whether there was a breach, as well as the remedy for any breach, and the employer was entitled to an order requiring the Union to arbitrate if it refused to do so. But the Union does not deny its duty to arbitrate; in fact, it denies that the employer ever demanded arbitration. However that may be, it does not follow that the District Court was empowered not only to order arbitration but to enjoin the strike pending the decision of the arbitrator, despite the express prohibition of § 4(a) of the Norris-LaGuardia Act against injunctions prohibiting any person from "ceasing or refusing to perform any work or to remain in any relation of employment." If an injunction could issue against the strike in this case, so in proper circumstances could a court enjoin any other alleged breach of contract pending the exhaustion of the applicable grievance and arbitration provisions even though the injunction would otherwise violate one of the express prohibitions of § 4. The court in such cases would be permitted, if the dispute was arbitrable, to hold hearing, make findings of fact, interpret the applicable provisions of the contract and issue injunctions so as to restore the status quo ante or to otherwise regulate the relationship of the parties pending exhaustion of the arbitration process. This would cut deeply into the policy of the Norris-LaGuardia Act and make the courts potential participants in a wide range of arbitrable disputes under the many existing and future collective-bargaining contracts, not just for the purpose of enforcing promises to arbitrate, which was the limit of *Boys Markets,* but for the purpose of preliminary dealing with the merits of the factual and legal issues that are subjects for the arbitrator and of issuing injunctions that would otherwise be forbidden by the Norris-LaGuardia Act.

This is not what the parties have bargained for. Surely it cannot be concluded here, as it was in *Boys Markets*, that such injunctions pending arbitration are essential to carry out promises to arbitrate and to implement the private arrangements for the administration of the contract. As is typical, the agreement in this case outlines the prearbitration settlement procedures and provides that if the grievance "has not been * * * satisfactorily adjusted," arbitration may be had. Nowhere does it provide for coercive action of any kind, let alone judicial injunctions, short of the terminal decision of the arbitrator. The parties have agreed to grieve and arbitrate, not to litigate. They have not contracted for a judicial preview of the facts and the law. Had they anticipated additional regulation of their relationships pending arbitration, it seems very doubtful that they would have resorted to litigation rather than to private arrangements. The unmistakable policy of Congress stated in § 203(d) 29 U.S.C. § 173(d) * * * is that "Final adjustment by a method agreed upon by the parties is declared to be the desirable method for settlement of grievance disputes arising over the application or interpretation of an existing collective-bargaining agreement." Gateway Coal Co. v. United Mine Workers, supra, 414 U.S. at 377, 94 S.Ct., at 636. But the parties' agreement to adjust or to arbitrate their differences themselves would be eviscerated if the courts for all practical purposes were to try and decide contractual disputes at the preliminary injunction stage.

The dissent suggests that injunctions should be authorized in cases such as this at least where the violation, in the court's view, is clear and the court is sufficiently sure that the parties seeking the injunction will win before the arbitrator. But this would still involve hearings, findings and judicial interpretations of collective-bargaining contracts. It is incredible to believe that the courts would always view the facts and the contract as the arbitrator would; and it is difficult to believe that the arbitrator would not be heavily influenced or wholly preempted by judicial views of the facts and the meaning of contracts if this procedure is to be permitted. Injunctions against strikes, even temporary injunctions, very often permanently settle the issue; and in other contexts time and expense would be discouraging factors to the losing party in court in considering whether to relitigate the issue before the arbitrator.

With these considerations in mind, we are far from concluding that the arbitration process will be frustrated unless the courts have the power to issue interlocutory injunctions pending arbitration in cases such as this or in others in which an arbitrable dispute awaits decision. We agree with the Court of Appeals that there is no necessity here such as was found to be the case in *Boys Markets*, to accommodate the policies of the Norris-LaGuardia Act to the requirements of § 301 by empowering the District Court to issue the injunction sought by the employer.

The judgment of the Court of Appeals is affirmed.

* * *

Mr. Justice Stevens, with whom Mr. Justice Brennan, Mr. Justice Marshall, and Mr. Justice Powell join, dissenting.

A contractual undertaking not to strike is the union's normal *quid pro quo* for the employer's undertaking to submit grievances to binding arbitration. The question in this case is whether that *quid pro quo* is severable into two parts—one which a federal court may enforce by injunction and another which it may not. * * *

The Court today holds that only a part of the union's *quid pro quo* is enforceable by injunction. The principal bases for the holding are (1) the Court's literal interpretation of the Norris-LaGuardia Act; and (2) its fear that the federal judiciary would otherwise make a "massive" entry into the business of contract interpretation heretofore reserved for arbitrators. [Justice Stevens' discussion of (1) is omitted.]

* * * In this case, the question whether the sympathy strike violates the no-strike clause is an arbitrable issue. If the court had the benefit of an arbitrator's resolution of the issue in favor of the employer, it could enforce that decision just as it could require the parties to submit the issue to arbitration. And if the agreement were so plainly unambiguous that there could be no bona fide issue to submit to the arbitrator, there must be the same authority to enforce the parties' bargain pending the arbitrator's final decision.

The Union advances three arguments against this conclusion: (1) that interpretation of the collective-bargaining agreement is the exclusive province of the arbitrator; (2) that an injunction erroneously entered pending arbitration will effectively deprive the union of the right to strike before the arbitrator can render his decision; and (3) that it is the core purpose of the Norris-LaGuardia Act to eliminate the risk of an injunction against a lawful strike.[21] Although I acknowledge the force of these arguments, I think they are insufficient to take this case outside the rationale of *Boys Markets*.

The *Steelworkers Trilogy* establishes that a collective-bargaining agreement submitting all questions of contract interpretation to the arbitrator deprives the courts of almost all power to interpret the agreement to prevent submission of a dispute to arbitration or to refuse enforcement of an arbitrator's award. *Boys Markets* itself repeated the warning that it was not for the courts to usurp the functions of the arbitrator. * * * And *Gateway Coal* held that an injunction may issue to protect the arbitration process even if a "substantial question of contractual interpretation" must be answered to determine whether the strike is over an arbitrable grievance. Id.,

---

21. The Union also argues that an injunction should be barred because the party seeking arbitration is usually required to accept the condition of which he complains pending the decision of the arbitrator. The employer normally receives the benefit of this rule, since it is the union that initiates most grievances. The Union contends that fairness dictates that it receive the same benefit pending the outcome of employer grievances. However, the rule has its origins in the need for production to go forward under the employer's control pending clarification of the agreement

through arbitration. See Feller, A General Theory of the Collective Bargaining Agreement, 61 Calif.L.Rev. 663, 737–740 (1973). This justification hardly supports, but rather undermines, the Union's position.

The Court advances the same argument as a threat of "massive preliminary injunction litigation" by both employers and unions over all arbitrable disputes. * * * This argument simply ignores the special status of the no-strike clause as the *quid pro quo* of the arbitration clause.

at 382–384, 94 S.Ct. at 639–640. In each of these cases, however, the choice was between interpretation of the agreement by the court or interpretation by the arbitrator; a decision that the dispute was not arbitrable, or not properly arbitrated, would have precluded an interpretation of the agreement according to the contractual grievance procedure. In the present case, an interim determination of the no-strike question by the court neither usurps nor precludes a decision by the arbitrator. By definition, issuance of an injunction pending the arbitrator's decision does not supplant a decision that he otherwise would have made. Indeed it is the ineffectiveness of the damage remedy for strikes pending arbitration that lends force to the employer's argument for an injunction. The court does not oust the arbitrator of his proper function but fulfills a role that he never served.

The Union's second point, however, is that the arbitrator will rarely render his decision quickly enough to prevent an erroneously issued injunction from effectively depriving the union of its right to strike. The Union relies particularly upon decisions of this Court that recognize that even a temporary injunction can quickly end a strike. But this argument demonstrates only that arbitration, to be effective, must be prompt, not that the federal courts must be deprived entirely of jurisdiction to grant equitable relief. Denial of an injunction when a strike violates the agreement may have effects just as devastating to an employer as the issuance of an injunction may have to the union when the strike does not violate the agreement. Furthermore, a sympathy strike does not directly further the economic interests of the members of the striking local or contribute to the resolution of any dispute between that local, or its members, and the employer. On the contrary, it is the source of a new dispute which, if the strike goes forward, will impose costs on the strikers, the employer, and the public without prospect of any direct benefit to any of these parties. A rule that authorizes postponement of a sympathy strike pending an arbitrator's clarification of the no-strike clause will not critically impair the vital interests of the striking local even if the right to strike is upheld, and will avoid the costs of interrupted production if the arbitrator concludes that the no-strike clause applies.

Finally, the Norris-LaGuardia Act cannot be interpreted to immunize the union from all risk of an erroneously issued injunction. *Boys Markets* itself subjected the union to the risk of an injunction entered upon a judge's erroneous conclusion that the dispute was arbitrable and that the strike was in violation of the no-strike clause * * *. *Gateway Coal* subjected the union to a still greater risk for the court there entered an injunction to enforce an implied no-strike clause despite the fact that the arbitrability of the dispute, and hence the legality of the strike over the dispute, presented a "substantial question of contractual interpretation." Id., 414 U.S. at 384, 94 S.Ct., at 640 * * *. The strict reading that the Union would give the Norris-LaGuardia Act would not have permitted this result.[26]

26. The Court emphasizes the risk of conflicting determinations in this case, but ignores the risk of conflicting determinations in *Boys Markets* and *Gateway Coal.* In *Boys Markets,* the District Court was required to determine the arbitrability of the dispute and the legality of the strike, clear or not, and in *Gateway Coal,* the District Court need only have found that the arbitrability of the dispute and the legality of the strike were "a substantial question of contractual interpretation," and hence not clear at all. The likelihood of an injunction against a lawful strike was vastly larger under the standard of *Gate-*

These considerations, however, do not support the conclusion that a sympathy strike should be temporarily enjoined whenever a collective-bargaining agreement contains a no-strike clause and an arbitration clause. The accommodation between the Norris-LaGuardia Act and § 301(a) of the Labor Management Relations Act allows the judge to apply "the usual processes of the law" but not to take the place of the arbitrator. Because of the risk that a federal judge, less expert in labor matters than an arbitrator, may misconstrue general contract language, I would agree that no injunction or temporary restraining order should issue without first giving the union an adequate opportunity to present evidence and argument, particularly upon the proper interpretation of the collective-bargaining agreement; the judge should not issue an injunction without convincing evidence that the strike is clearly within the no-strike clause.[27] Furthermore, to protect the efficacy of arbitration, any such injunction should require the parties to submit the issue immediately to the contractual grievance procedure, and if the union so requests, at the last stage and upon an expedited schedule that assures a decision by the arbitrator as soon as practicable. Such stringent conditions would insure that only strikes in violation of the agreement would be enjoined and that the union's access to the arbitration process would not be foreclosed by the combined effect of a temporary injunction and protracted grievance procedures. Finally, as in *Boys Markets,* the normal conditions of equitable relief would have to be met.[28]

Like the decision in *Boys Markets,* this opinion reflects, on the one hand, my confidence that experience during the decades since the Norris-LaGuardia Act was passed has dissipated any legitimate concern about the impartiality of federal judges in disputes between labor and management, and on the other, my continued recognition of the fact that judges have less familiarity and expertise than arbitrators and administrators who regularly work in this specialized area. The decision in *Boys Markets* requires an accommodation between the Norris-LaGuardia Act and the Labor Management Relations Act. I would hold only that the terms of that accommoda-

---

way Coal than under a standard requiring the District Court to find a clear violation of the no-strike clause.

The Court obscures the latter point by misreading *Gateway Coal* to hold that an injunction was properly issued because the dispute in that case was arbitrable. Ante, at n. 10. But *Gateway Coal* expressly held that the question whether the union properly invoked a provision for work stoppages because of unsafe mine conditions was "a substantive question of contractual interpretation, and the collective-bargaining agreement explicitly commits to resolution by an impartial umpire all disagreements 'as to the meaning and application of the provisions of this agreement.' " Id., at 384, 94 S.Ct., at 640 (footnote omitted). Consistently with this holding, the arbitrator remained free to decide that the underlying dispute was not arbitrable and hence that the enjoined strike was not in violation of the agreement.

27. Of course, it is possible that an arbitrator would disagree with the court even when

the latter finds the strike to be clearly prohibited. But in that case, the arbitrator's determination would govern, provided it withstands the ordinary standard of review for arbitrator's awards. See United Steelworkers of America v. Enterprise Wheel & Car Corp., 363 U.S. 593, 597–599, 80 S.Ct. 1358, 1361–1362, 4 L.Ed.2d 1424.

28. " '[T]he District Court must, of course, consider whether issuance of an injunction would be warranted under ordinary principles of equity—whether breaches are occurring and will continue, or have been threatened and will be committed; whether they have caused or will cause irreparable injury to the employer; and whether the employer will suffer more from the denial of an injunction than will the union from its issuance.' " 398 U.S., at 254, 90 S.Ct., at 1594, quoting Sinclair, supra, 370 U.S., at 228, 82 S.Ct., at 1346 (Brennan, J., dissenting).

tion do not entirely deprive the federal courts of all power to grant any relief to an employer, threatened with irreparable injury from a sympathy strike clearly in violation of a collective bargaining agreement, regardless of the equities of his claim for injunctive relief pending arbitration.

Since in my view the Court of Appeals erroneously held that the District Court had no jurisdiction to enjoin the Union's sympathy strike, I would reverse and remand for consideration of the question whether the employer is entitled to an injunction.

Note

1. What is *the* difference in circumstance between Boys Markets and Buffalo Forge which prompts the refusal to grant the preliminary injunction in the latter? Does this difference in circumstance justify the difference in result?

Suppose the P & M employees had struck (refused to cross the O & T picket line) for the sole purpose of testing out their right to engage in a sympathy strike despite the no-strike clause contained in the collective bargaining agreement to which they were subject; what result under Boys Markets?

2. The problem of Buffalo Forge may be structured as follows: (1) The Norris-LaGuardia Act precludes federal courts from issuing injunctions in labor disputes, broadly defined (excepting only cases of violence or fraud; for a succinct outline of the Act, see supra pp. 90–91). (2) Boys Markets created an exception to the anti-injunction rule for the purpose of the resolution of disputes through arbitration (a goal favored by the Norris-LaGuardia Act itself). (3) This exception entails the requirement that what is struck over be also arbitrable so that the union is accorded the remedy of arbitration in substitution for the right to strike. (4) Pursuant to this requirement, the originally amorphous notion of the relationship of the employer's arbitration promise and the union's no-strike promise as one of "quid pro quo" takes on a harder meaning for Boys Markets purposes: if the matter struck over is not resoluble by arbitration, the union cannot be federally enjoined from striking. (5) In Buffalo Forge what the P & M workers struck over (sympathetically—by refusing to cross the picket line) were the bargaining demands of the O & T workers, a matter quite clearly not resoluble by arbitration under the P & M workers' collective bargaining agreement. (6) Which leads to the question: Would enjoining the breach of the no-strike promise in the Buffalo Forge circumstances constitute a proper extension of the Boys Markets exception since it would also support, albeit in a less direct fashion, the resolution of disputes by arbitration?

The argument would run as follows: The promise not to strike elicits the promise by the employer to arbitrate. In this sense the promises are quid pro quo; each elicits the other. But quids and quos need not be of exactly equal scope—a strong employer might obtain a no-strike promise of broader coverage than his own arbitration commitment. Enforcement of the no-strike promise by injunction, even in areas not also covered by the employer's promise to arbitrate, would further the cause of arbitration through giving effective remedy for breach of the counterpromise constituting the consideration for the employer's promise to arbitrate—i.e., the union's promise not to strike. Unions which make such broad no-strike promises in order to elicit whatever they are willing to accept in the way of contractual "goodies" (not limited to the employer's promise to arbitrate) ought to be held effectively to that bargain if free collective bargaining "sense" is to be made.

If the Norris-LaGuardia Act precludes the extension of the arbitration-supporting principle of Boys Markets to the sympathy strike situation, as held in Buffalo Forge, is not that Act in need of amendment? Sympathy strikes, it should be remembered, are at best questionable activities under any discerning analysis of the scope of the arena and the propriety of the weaponry in labor-management disputes. (See Justice Brandeis dissenting in the Duplex case, supra p. 69, and Note 3, supra p. 74.) Perhaps a countering point should be made: the activity involved in Buffalo Forge may not have been characterized as a "sympathy strike" at common law since there is only one employer involved; the use of the term "sympathy" here is the product of the development of the sophisticated concept of "bargaining unit," a product of the unique American (Wagner Act) labor relations premise of "exclusivity."

3. How do you react to the following suggested resolution of the Buffalo Forge problem, different from that of Justice White and Justice Stevens and faithful to the Steelworkers (Arbitration) Trilogy but taking a relaxed view of Boys Markets: the court would determine arbitrability in the Trilogy-prescribed fashion, and if it found the issue (whether or not there was a breach of the no-strike clause) to be arbitrable, the strike would be temporarily enjoined, with appropriate conditions for expediting the arbitration process? This was the course adopted by the Third Circuit, sitting en banc, in NAPA Pittsburgh, Inc. v. Automotive Chauffeurs Employees, Local 926, cited in footnote 9 of Justice White's opinion in Buffalo Forge.

4. A problem with the NAPA Pittsburgh approach in Note 3 above, found in *all* Boys Markets cases, not merely in the Buffalo Forge variety, is the tension between the Trilogy and the Boys Markets doctrines. For an injunction to issue under the latter, the grievance struck over must be arbitrable. But under the Trilogy the judicial inquiry as to arbitrability is shallow. As a consequence, a Boys Markets injunction might well be granted in circumstances where the arbitrator, making the first real examination of the arbitrability question, subsequently determines the grievance to be nonarbitrable.

Both Justice White and Justice Stevens evince the same concern over the foregoing tension, without speaking directly to it. Each assumed that the judicial scrutiny of the arbitrability question as presented in Buffalo Forge would have to be deeper than that prescribed in the Trilogy, but each used the concern for opposite purposes of advocacy. Justice Stevens would have plunged the trial judge deeply into the merits of the issue to be arbitrated; in his words, "the judge should not issue an injunction without convincing evidence that the strike is clearly within the no-strike clause." See supra, p. 677. Justice White feared that such would result in a "judicial preview of the facts and the law," constituting judicial invasion of the province of the arbitrator. See supra, p. 674.

Somewhat ironically, in the 1974 Gateway Coal case, discussed in Buffalo Forge, the Court applied the Trilogy presumption of arbitrability to a collective bargaining agreement calling for arbitration of "any local trouble of any kind arising at the mine," concluded that the continued employment of two foremen who had previously been found to have violated federal mine safety regulations was an arbitrable issue, further found that the union was accordingly subject to an implied promise not to strike (à la Lucas Flour, supra p. 651), and upheld the issuance of a preliminary injunction ordering "the union to end the strike and to submit the dispute to an impartial umpire without delay."

For a study of the Trilogy-Boys Markets tension, see Note, Labor Injunctions, Boys Markets, and the Presumption of Arbitrability, 85 Harv.L.Rev. 636

(1972); and for analysis of the impact of Buffalo Forge on that tension see Gould, On Labor Injunctions Pending Arbitration: Recasting *Buffalo Forge,* 30 Stan.L. Rev. 533 (1978), and Lowden & Flaherty, Sympathy Strikes, Arbitration Policy, and the Enforceability of No-Strike Agreements: An Analysis of Buffalo Forge, 45 Geo.Wash.L.Rev. 633 (1977).

5. In Jacksonville Bulk Terminals, Inc. v. International Longshoremen's Association, 457 U.S. 702, 102 S.Ct. 2673, 73 L.Ed.2d 327 (1982), the Court reaffirmed both Boys Markets and Buffalo Forge. The question was whether a federal court had power to enjoin the ILA's boycott of cargos bound to and from the Soviet Union. The employer, alleging a violation of the no-strike clause, sought to compel arbitration under the agreement, and requested a preliminary injunction pending arbitration. The Court held, 6 to 3, that the underlying dispute was, despite its political character, a labor dispute within the meaning of the Norris-LaGuardia Act. The Court concluded, however, that the case was governed by Buffalo Forge rather than Boys Markets, because the dispute underlying the work stoppage, i.e., the union's protest over the invasion of Afghanistan by the Soviet Union, was plainly not arbitrable under the collective bargaining agreement. Injunctive relief was therefore not available.

MASTRO PLASTICS CORP. v. NATIONAL LABOR RELATIONS BOARD

Supreme Court of the United States, 1956.
350 U.S. 270, 76 S.Ct. 349, 100 L.Ed. 309.

MR. JUSTICE BURTON delivered the opinion of the Court.

This case presents two principal questions: (1) whether, in the collective-bargaining contract before us, the union's undertaking "to refrain from engaging in any strike or work stoppage during the term of this agreement" waives not only the employees' right to strike for economic benefits but also their right to strike solely against unfair labor practices of their employers, and (2) whether § 8(d) of the National Labor Relations Act, as amended, deprives individuals of their status as employees if, within the waiting period prescribed by § 8(d)(4), they engage in a strike solely against unfair labor practices of their employers. For the reasons hereafter stated, we answer each in the negative.

Mastro Plastics Corp. and French-American Reeds Manufacturing Co., Inc., petitioners herein, are New York corporations which, in 1949 and 1950, were engaged in interstate commerce, manufacturing, selling and distributing plastic articles, including reeds and other accessories for musical instruments. They operated in the City of New York within the same plant, under the same management and with the same employees. For collective bargaining, their employees were represented by * * * Local 3127, United Brotherhood of Carpenters and Joiners of America, AFL. * * *

In August 1950, Local 65 of the Wholesale and Warehouse Workers Union began a campaign among petitioners' employees in an effort to become their collective-bargaining representative. Petitioners bitterly opposed the movement, believing Local 65 to be Communist-controlled. Feeling that the Carpenters were too weak to cope successfully with Local 65, petitioners asked the Carpenters to transfer their bargaining rights to Local 318, International Brotherhood of Pulp, Sulphite and Paper Mill Workers,

AFL. When the Carpenters declined to do so, petitioners selected a committee of employees to visit 318, obtain membership cards and seek members for that union. The cards were distributed during working hours and petitioners paid their employees for time spent in the campaign, including attendance at a meeting of 318. Petitioners' officers and supervisors instructed employees to sign these cards and indicated that those refusing to do so would be "out." * * *

November 10, 1950, a crisis developed when the president of petitioners summarily discharged Frank Ciccone, an employee of over four years' standing, because of the latter's activity in support of the Carpenters and his opposition to 318. We accept the finding of the National Labor Relations Board that petitioners "discriminatorily discharged, and thereafter refused to reinstate, Frank Ciccone because of his organizational activities in support of the * * * [Carpenters]." This discharge at once precipitated the strike which is before us and which the Board found "was clearly caused and prolonged by the cumulative effects of the [petitioners'] unfair labor practices culminating in the discriminatory discharge of Ciccone." There was no disorder but the plant was virtually shut down until December 11 and it was March 9, 1951, before the Carpenters, on behalf of petitioners' employees, made an unconditional request to return to work. Petitioners ignored that request and neither Ciccone nor any of the other 76 striking employees has been reinstated.

While the strike against petitioners' unfair labor practices continued, the collective-bargaining contract between petitioners and the Carpenters approached its expiration date of November 30, 1950, and * * * the Carpenters had taken timely steps to secure modification of their agreement. October 10, they had delivered to petitioners a notice (dated September 29, 1950) "requesting modification" of the contract. They thus had started the statutory negotiating period running as prescribed by the above-mentioned § 8(d). The Carpenters met several times with petitioners and pressed their demands for changes in the contract but the expiration date passed without any agreement being reached.

In January 1951, the Carpenters initiated the present proceedings before the National Labor Relations Board by charging petitioners with unfair labor practices. Acting on those charges, the Board's general counsel filed a complaint alleging petitioners' support of Local 318 and discharge of numerous employees, including Ciccone, as violations of § 8(a)(1), (2) and (3) of the Act.

Petitioners admitted that they had discharged the employees in question and had not rehired them. They denied, however, that in so doing they had committed any unfair labor practices. Their first affirmative defense was that the waiver of the right to strike, expressed by their employees in their collective-bargaining contract, applied to strikes not only for economic benefits but to any and all strikes by such employees, including strikes directed solely against unfair labor practices of the employer.

Petitioners' other principal defense was that the existing strike began during the statutory waiting period initiated by the employees' request for modification of the contract and that, by virtue of § 8(d) of the Act, the strikers had lost their status as employees. That defense turned upon petitioners' interpretation of § 8(d), applying it not only to strikes for economic benefits but to any and all strikes occurring during the waiting period, including strikes solely against unfair labor practices of the employer.

The trial examiner made findings of fact sustaining the complaint and recommended that petitioners be ordered to cease and desist from the interference complained of and be required to offer to Ciccone and the 76 other discharged employees full reinstatement, together with back pay for Ciccone from November 10, 1950, and for the other employees from March 9, 1951. See 103 N.L.R.B. 511, 526–563. With minor modifications, the Board adopted the examiner's findings and conclusions and issued the recommended order. 103 N.L.R.B. 511. The chairman and one member dissented in part.

The Court of Appeals, with one judge dissenting in part, accepted the Board's findings of fact and conclusions of law and enforced the Board's order. 214 F.2d 462. * * * Because of the importance of the issues in industrial relations and in the interpretation of the National Labor Relations Act, as amended, we granted certiorari. * * *

Apart from the issues raised by petitioners' affirmative defenses, the proceedings reflect a flagrant example of interference by the employers with the expressly protected right of their employees to select their own bargaining representative. The findings disclose vigorous efforts by the employers to influence and even to coerce their employees to abandon the Carpenters as their bargaining representatives and to substitute Local 318. Accordingly, unless petitioners sustain at least one of their affirmative defenses, they must suffer the consequences of their unfair labor practices violating § 8(a) (1), (2) or (3) of the Act, as amended.

In the absence of some contractual or statutory provision to the contrary, petitioners' unfair labor practices provide adequate ground for the orderly strike that occurred here. Under those circumstances, the striking employees do not lose their status and are entitled to reinstatement with back pay, even if replacements for them have been made. Failure of the Board to enjoin petitioners' illegal conduct or failure of the Board to sustain the right to strike against that conduct would seriously undermine the primary objectives of the Labor Act. * * * While we assume that the employees, by explicit contractual provision, could have waived their right to strike against such unfair labor practices and that Congress, by explicit statutory provision, could have deprived strikers, under the circumstances of this case, of their status as employees, the questions before us are whether or not such a waiver was made by the Carpenters in their 1949–1950 contract and whether or not such a deprivation of status was enacted by Congress in § 8(d) of the Act, as amended in 1947.

I. *Does the collective-bargaining contract waive the employees' right to strike against the unfair labor practices committed by their employers?* The answer turns upon the proper interpretation of the particular contract before us. * * *

The waiver in the contract before us, upon which petitioners rely, is as follows:

"5. The Union agrees that during the term of this agreement, there shall be no interference of any kind with the operations of the Employers, or any interruptions or slackening of production of work by any of its members. The Union further agrees to refrain from engaging in any strike or work stoppage during the term of this agreement."

That clause expresses concern for the continued operation of the plant and has a natural application to strikes and work stoppages involving the subject matter of the contract.

Conceding that the words "in any strike or work stoppage during the [one-year] term of this agreement," if read in complete isolation, may include all strikes and work stoppages of every nature, yet the trial examiner, the Board and the Court of Appeals agree that those words do not have that scope when read in their context and in the light of the law under which the contract was made. This unanimity of interpretation is entitled to much weight.

Petitioners argue that the words "any strike" leave no room for interpretation and necessarily include all strikes, even those against unlawful practices destructive of the foundation on which collective bargaining must rest. We disagree. We believe that the contract, taken as a whole, deals solely with the economic relationship between the employers and their employees. It is a typical collective-bargaining contract dealing with terms of employment and the normal operations of the plant. It is for one year and assumes the existence of a lawfully designated bargaining representative. Its strike and lockout clauses are natural adjuncts of an operating policy aimed at avoiding interruptions of production prompted by efforts to change existing economic relationships. The main function of arbitration under the contract is to provide a mechanism for avoiding similar stoppages due to disputes over the meaning and application of the various contractual provisions.

To adopt petitioners' all-inclusive interpretation of the clause is quite a different matter. That interpretation would eliminate, for the whole year, the employees' right to strike, even if petitioners, by coercion, ousted the employees' lawful bargaining representative and, by threats of discharge, caused the employees to sign membership cards in a new union. Whatever may be said of the legality of such a waiver when explicitly stated, there is no adequate basis for implying its existence without a more compelling expression of it than appears in § 5 of this contract.   *   *   *

For the reasons stated above and those given by the Board and the court below, we conclude that the contract did not waive the employees' right to strike solely against the unfair labor practices of their employers.

II. *Does § 8(d) of the National Labor Relations Act, as amended, deprive individuals of their status as employees if, within the waiting period prescribed by § 8(d)(4), they engage in a strike solely against unfair labor practices of their employers?*   *   *   * Section 8(d) seeks to bring about the termination and modification of collective-bargaining agreements without interrupting the flow of commerce or the production of goods, while §§ 7 and 8(a) seek to insure freedom of concerted action by employees at all times.

The language in § 8(d) especially relied upon by petitioners is as follows: "Any employee who engages in a strike within the sixty-day period specified in this subsection shall lose his status as an employee of the employer engaged in the particular labor dispute, for the purposes of sections 8, 9, and 10 of this Act, as amended * * *."

Petitioners contend that the above words must be so read that employees who engage in any strike, regardless of its purpose, within the 60-day waiting period, thereby lose their status as employees. That interpretation would deprive Ciccone and his fellow strikers of their rights to reinstatement and would require the reversal of the judgment of the Court of Appeals. If the above words are read in complete isolation from their context in the Act, such an interpretation is possible. * * *

Reading the clause in conjunction with the rest of § 8, the Board points out that "the sixty-day period" referred to is the period mentioned in paragraph (4) of § 8(d). That paragraph requires the party giving notice of a desire to *"terminate or modify"* such a contract, as part of its obligation to bargain under § 8(a)(5) or § 8(b)(3), to continue "in full force and effect, without resorting to strike or lockout, all the terms and conditions of the existing contract for a period of sixty days after such notice is given or until the expiration date of such contract, whichever occurs later". Section 8(d) thus seeks, during this natural renegotiation period, to relieve the parties from the economic pressure of a strike or lockout in relation to the subjects of negotiation. The final clause of § 8(d) also warns employees that, if they join a proscribed strike, they shall thereby lose their status as employees and, consequently, their right to reinstatement.

The Board reasons that the words which provide the key to a proper interpretation of § 8(d) with respect to this problem are "termination or modification". Since the Board expressly found that the instant strike was *not to terminate or modify* the contract, but was designed instead to protest the unfair labor practices of petitioners, the loss-of-status provision of § 8(d) is not applicable. We sustain that interpretation. Petitioners' construction would produce incongruous results. It concedes that prior to the 60-day negotiating period, employees have a right to strike against unfair labor practices designed to oust the employees' bargaining representative, yet petitioners' interpretation of § 8(d) means that if the employees give the 60-day notice of their desire to modify the contract, they are penalized for exercising that right to strike. This would deprive them of their most effective weapon at a time when their need for it is obvious. Although the employees' request to modify the contract would demonstrate their need for the services of their freely chosen representative, petitioners' interpretation would have the incongruous effect of cutting off the employees' freedom to strike against unfair labor practices aimed at that representative. This would relegate the employees to filing charges under a procedure too slow to be effective. The result would unduly favor the employers and handicap the employees during negotiation periods contrary to the purpose of the Act. There also is inherent inequity in any interpretation that penalizes one party to a contract for conduct induced solely by the unlawful conduct of the other, thus giving advantage to the wrongdoer.

Petitioners contend that, unless the loss-of-status clause is applicable to unfair labor practice strikes, as well as to economic strikes, it adds nothing to the existing law relating to loss of status. Assuming that to be so, the clause is justifiable as a clarification of the law and as a warning to employees against engaging in economic strikes during the statutory waiting period. Moreover, in the face of the affirmative emphasis that is placed by the Act upon freedom of concerted action and freedom of choice of representatives, any limitation on the employees' right to strike against violations of §§ 7 and 8(a), protecting those freedoms, must be more explicit and clear than it is here in order to restrict them at the very time they may be most needed. * * *

As neither the collective-bargaining contract nor § 8(d) of the National Labor Relations Act, as amended, stands in the way, the judgment of the Court of Appeals is affirmed. * * *

[The dissenting opinion of JUSTICE FRANKFURTER, joined in by JUSTICES HARLAN and MINTON, is omitted.]

Note

1. If the Mastro contract had contained an express waiver of the right to strike over unfair labor practices, would the Court have held the other way?

2. If the loss-of-status clause of Section 8(d) is not applicable to an unfair-labor-practice strike, does it have any force at all since an economic strike in violation of 8(d)(4) would, in any event, be unprotected under Section 7? (The dissenting opinion of Justice Frankfurter was premised upon the analysis here involved.)

JOHN WILEY & SONS, INC. v. LIVINGSTON

Supreme Court of the United States, 1964.
376 U.S. 543, 84 S.Ct. 909, 11 L.Ed.2d 898.

MR. JUSTICE HARLAN delivered the opinion of the Court.

This is an action by a union, pursuant to § 301 of the Labor Management Relations Act, * * * to compel arbitration under a collective bargaining agreement. The major questions presented are (1) whether a corporate employer must arbitrate with a union under a bargaining agreement between the union and another corporation which has merged with the employer, and, if so, (2) whether the courts or the arbitrator is the appropriate body to decide whether procedural prerequisites which, under the bargaining agreement, condition the duty to arbitrate have been met. Because of the importance of both questions to the realization of national labor policy, we granted certiorari * * * to review a judgment of the Court of Appeals directing arbitration (313 F.2d 52), in reversal of the District Court which had refused such relief (203 F.Supp. 171). We affirm the judgment below, but, with respect to the first question above, on grounds which may differ from those of the Court of Appeals, whose answer to that question is unclear.

I.

District 65, Retail, Wholesale and Department Store Union, AFL–CIO, entered into a collective bargaining agreement with Interscience Publishers,

Inc., a publishing firm, for a term expiring on January 31, 1962. The agreement did not contain an express provision making it binding on successors of Interscience. On October 2, 1961, Interscience merged with the petitioner, John Wiley & Sons, Inc., another publishing firm, and ceased to do business as a separate entity. There is no suggestion that the merger was not for genuine business reasons.

At the time of the merger Interscience had about 80 employees, of whom 40 were represented by this Union. It had a single plant in New York City, and did an annual business of somewhat over $1,000,000. Wiley was a much larger concern, having separate office and warehouse facilities and about 300 employees, and doing an annual business of more than $9,000,000. None of Wiley's employees was represented by a union.

In discussions before and after the merger, the Union and Interscience (later Wiley) were unable to agree on the effect of the merger on the collective bargaining agreement and on the rights under it of those covered employees hired by Wiley. The Union's position was that despite the merger it continued to represent the covered Interscience employees taken over by Wiley, and that Wiley was obligated to recognize certain rights of such employees which had "vested" under the Interscience bargaining agreement. Such rights, more fully described below, concerned matters typically covered by collective bargaining agreements, such as seniority status, severance pay, etc. The Union contended also that Wiley was required to make certain pension fund payments called for under the Interscience bargaining agreement.

Wiley, though recognizing for purposes of its own pension plan the Interscience service of the former Interscience employees, asserted that the merger terminated the bargaining agreement for all purposes. It refused to recognize the Union as bargaining agent or to accede to the Union's claims on behalf of Interscience employees. All such employees, except a few who ended their Wiley employment with severance pay and for whom no rights are asserted here, continued in Wiley's employ.

No satisfactory solution having been reached, the Union, one week before the expiration date of the Interscience bargaining agreement, commenced this action to compel arbitration.

II.

The threshold question in this controversy is who shall decide whether the arbitration provisions of the collective bargaining agreement survived the Wiley-Interscience merger, so as to be operative against Wiley. Both parties urge that this question is for the courts. Past cases leave no doubt that this is correct. * * * The duty to arbitrate being of contractual origin, a compulsory submission to arbitration cannot precede judicial determination that the collective bargaining agreement does in fact create such a duty. Thus, just as an employer has no obligation to arbitrate issues which it has not agreed to arbitrate, so *a fortiori*, it cannot be compelled to arbitrate if an arbitration clause does not bind it at all.

The unanimity of views about who should decide the question of arbitrability does not, however, presage the parties' accord about what is the correct decision. Wiley, objecting to arbitration, argues that it never was a party to the collective bargaining agreement, and that, in any event, the Union lost its status as representative of the former Interscience employees when they were mingled in a larger Wiley unit of employees. The Union argues that Wiley, as successor to Interscience, is bound by the latter's agreement, at least sufficiently to require it to arbitrate. The Union relies on § 90 of the N.Y. Stock Corporation Law, McKinney's Consol. Laws, c. 59, which provides, among other things, that no "claim or demand for any cause" against a constituent corporation shall be extinguished by a consolidation. Alternatively, the Union argues that, apart from § 90, federal law requires that arbitration go forward, lest the policy favoring arbitration frequently be undermined by changes in corporate organization.

Federal law, fashioned "from the policy of our national labor laws," controls. Textile Workers Union of America v. Lincoln Mills, 353 U.S. 448, 456, 77 S.Ct. 912, 918, 1 L.Ed.2d 972. State law may be utilized so far as it is of aid in the development of correct principles or their application in a particular case, * * * but the law which ultimately results is federal. We hold that the disappearance by merger of a corporate employer which has entered into a collective bargaining agreement with a union does not automatically terminate all rights of the employees covered by the agreement, and that, in appropriate circumstances, present here, the successor employer may be required to arbitrate with the union under the agreement.

This Court has in the past recognized the central role of arbitration in effectuating national labor policy. Thus, in Warrior & Gulf Navigation Co., * * * 363 U.S. at 578, 80 S.Ct. 1347, 1351, 4 L.Ed.2d 1409, arbitration was described as "the substitute for industrial strife," and as "part and parcel of the collective bargaining process itself." It would derogate from "[t]he federal policy of settling labor disputes by arbitration," United Steelworkers of America v. Enterprise Wheel & Car Corp., 363 U.S. 593, 596, 80 S.Ct. 1358, 1360, 4 L.Ed.2d 1424, if a change in the corporate structure or ownership of a business enterprise had the automatic consequence of removing a duty to arbitrate previously established; this is so as much in cases like the present, where the contracting employer disappears into another by merger, as in those in which one owner replaces another but the business entity remains the same.

Employees, and the union which represents them, ordinarily do not take part in negotiations leading to a change in corporate ownership. The negotiations will ordinarily not concern the well-being of the employees, whose advantage or disadvantage, potentially great, will inevitably be incidental to the main considerations. The objectives of national labor policy, reflected in established principles of federal law, require that the rightful prerogative of owners independently to rearrange their businesses and even eliminate themselves as employers be balanced by some protection to the employees from a sudden change in the employment relationship. The transition from one corporate organization to another will in most cases be eased and industrial strife avoided if employees' claims continue to be resolved by arbitration rather than by "the relative strength * * * of the contending forces," Warrior & Gulf, * * * 363 U.S. at 580, 80 S.Ct. at 1352, 4 L.Ed.2d 1409.

The preference of national labor policy for arbitration as a substitute for tests of strength between contending forces could be overcome only if other considerations compellingly so demanded. We find none. While the principles of law governing ordinary contracts would not bind to a contract an unconsenting successor to a contracting party,[3] a collective bargaining agreement is not an ordinary contract. " * * * [I]t is a generalized code to govern a myriad of cases which the draftsmen cannot wholly anticipate * * *. The collective agreement covers the whole employment relationship. It calls into being a new common law—the common law of a particular industry or of a particular plant." Warrior & Gulf, * * * 363 U.S. at 578–579, 80 S.Ct. at 1351, 4 L.Ed.2d 1409 (footnotes omitted). Central to the peculiar status and function of a collective bargaining agreement is the fact, dictated both by circumstance * * * and by the requirements of the National Labor Relations Act, that it is not in any real sense the simple product of a consensual relationship. Therefore, although the duty to arbitrate * * * must be founded on a contract, the impressive policy considerations favoring arbitration are not wholly overborne by the fact that Wiley did not sign the contract being construed.[4] This case cannot readily be assimilated to the category of those in which there is no contract whatever, or none which is reasonably related to the party sought to be obligated. There was a contract, and Interscience, Wiley's predecessor, was party to it. We thus find Wiley's obligation to arbitrate this dispute in the Interscience contract construed in the context of a national labor policy.

We do not hold that in every case in which the ownership or corporate structure of an enterprise is changed the duty to arbitrate survives. As indicated above, there may be cases in which the lack of any substantial continuity of identity in the business enterprise before and after a change would make a duty to arbitrate something imposed from without, not reasonably to be found in the particular bargaining agreement and the acts of the parties involved. So too, we do not rule out the possibility that a union might abandon its right to arbitration by failing to make its claims known. Neither of these situations is before the Court. Although Wiley was substantially larger than Interscience, relevant similarity and continuity of operation across the change in ownership is adequately evidenced by the wholesale transfer of Interscience employees to the Wiley plant, apparently without difficulty. The Union made its position known well before the merger and never departed from it. In addition, we do not suggest any view on the questions surrounding a certified union's claim to continued representative status following a change in ownership. * * * This Union does not assert that it has any bargaining rights independent of the Interscience agreement; it seeks to arbitrate claims based on that agreement, now expired, not to negotiate a new agreement.[5]

3. But cf. the general rule that in the case of a merger the corporation which survives is liable for the debts and contracts of the one which disappears. 15 Fletcher, Private Corporations (1961 rev. ed.), § 7121.

4. Compare the principle that when a contract is scrutinized for evidence of an intention to arbitrate a particular kind of dispute, *national labor policy* requires, within reason, that "an interpretation that covers the asserted dispute," Warrier & Gulf, supra, 363 U.S. pp. 582–583, 80 S.Ct. pp. 1352, 1353, 4 L.Ed.2d 1409, be favored.

5. The fact that the Union does not represent a majority of an appropriate bargaining unit in Wiley does not prevent it from representing those employees who are covered by the agreement which is in dispute and out of

III.

Beyond denying its obligation to arbitrate at all, Wiley urges that the Union's grievances are not within the scope of the arbitration clause. The issues which the Union sought to arbitrate, as set out in the complaint, are:

"(a) Whether the seniority rights built up by the Interscience employees must be accorded to said employees now and after January 30, 1962.

"(b) Whether, as part of the wage structure of the employees, the Company is under an obligation to continue to make contributions to District 65 Security Plan and District 65 Security Plan Pension Fund now and after January 30, 1962.

"(c) Whether the job security and grievance provisions of the contract between the parties shall continue in full force and effect.

"(d) Whether the Company must obligate itself to continue liable now and after January 30, 1962 as to severance pay under the contract.

"(e) Whether the Company must obligate itself to continue liable now and after January 30, 1962 for vacation pay under the contract."

Section 16.0 of the collective bargaining agreement provides for arbitration as the final stage of grievance procedures which are stated to be the "sole means of obtaining adjustment" of "any differences, grievance or dispute between the Employer and the Union arising out of or relating to this agreement, or its interpretation or application, or enforcement * * *." There are a number of specific exceptions to the coverage of the grievance procedures, none of which is applicable here.[6] Apart from them, the intended wide breadth of the arbitration clause is reflected by § 16.9 of the agreement which provides, with an irrelevant exception:

"* * * [T]he arbitration procedure herein set forth is the sole and exclusive remedy of the parties hereto and the employees covered hereby, for any claimed violations of this contract, and for any and all acts or omissions claimed to have been committed by either party during the term of this agreement, and such arbitration procedure shall be (except to enforce,

which Wiley's duty to arbitrate arises. Retail Clerks Int'l Ass'n., Local Unions Nos. 128 and 633, v. Lion Dry Goods, Inc., 369 U.S. 17, 82 S.Ct. 541, 7 L.Ed.2d 503. There is no problem of conflict with another union, cf. L.B. Spear & Co., 106 N.L.R.B. 687, since Wiley had no contract with any union covering the unit of employees which received the former Interscience employees.

Problems might be created by an arbitral award which required Wiley to give special treatment to the former Interscience employees because of rights found to have accrued to them under the Interscience contract. But the mere possibility of such problems cannot cut off the Union's right to press the employees' claims in arbitration. While it would be premature at this stage to speculate on how to avoid such hypothetical problems, we have little doubt that within the flexible procedures of arbitration a solution can be reached which

would avoid disturbing labor relations in the Wiley plant.

6. Section 16.5 provides:

"It is agreed that, in addition to other provisions elsewhere contained in this agreement which expressly deny arbitration to specific events, situations or contract provisions, the following matters shall not be subject to the arbitration provisions of this agreement:

"(1) the amendment or modification of the terms and provisions of this agreement;

"(2) salary or minimum wage rates as set forth herein;

"(3) matters not covered by this agreement; and

"(4) any dispute arising out of any question pertaining to the renewal or extension of this agreement." * * *

vacate or modify awards) in lieu of any and all other remedies, forums at law, in equity or otherwise which will or may be available to either of the parties * * *."

All of the Union's grievances concern conditions of employment typically covered by collective bargaining agreements and submitted to arbitration if other grievance procedures fail. Specific provision for each of them is made in the Interscience agreement. There is thus no question that had a dispute concerning any of these subjects, such as seniority rights or severance pay, arisen between the Union and Interscience prior to the merger, it would have been arbitrable. Wiley argues, however, that the Union's claims are plainly outside the scope of the arbitration clause: first, because the agreement did not embrace post-merger claims, and, second, because the claims relate to a period beyond the limited term of the agreement.

In all probability, the situation created by the merger was one not expressly contemplated by the Union or Interscience when the agreement was made in 1960. Fairly taken, however, the Union's demands collectively raise the question which underlies the whole litigation: What is the effect of the merger on the rights of covered employees? It would be inconsistent with our holding that the obligation to arbitrate survived the merger were we to hold that the fact of the merger, without more, removed claims otherwise plainly arbitrable from the scope of the arbitration clause.

It is true that the Union has framed its issues to claim rights not only "now"—after the merger but during the term of the agreement—but also after the agreement expired by its terms. Claimed rights during the term of the agreement, at least, are unquestionably within the arbitration clause; we do not understand Wiley to urge that the Union's claims to all such rights have become moot by reason of the expiration of the agreement.[8] As to claimed rights "after January 30, 1962," it is reasonable to read the claims as based solely on the Union's construction of the Interscience agreement in such a way that, had there been no merger, Interscience would have been required to discharge certain obligations notwithstanding the expiration of the agreement. We see no reason why parties could not if they so chose agree to the accrual of rights during the term of an agreement and their realization after the agreement had expired. Of course, the Union may not use arbitration to acquire new rights against Wiley any more than it could have used arbitration to negotiate a new contract with Interscience, had the existing contract expired and renewal negotiations broken down.

Whether or not the Union's demands have merit will be determined by the arbitrator in light of the fully developed facts. It is sufficient for present purposes that the demands are not so plainly unreasonable that the subject matter of the dispute must be regarded as nonarbitrable because it can be seen in advance that no award to the Union could receive judicial sanction.

* * *

IV.

Wiley's final objection to arbitration raises the question of so-called "procedural arbitrability." The Interscience agreement provides for arbitration as the third stage of the grievance procedure.

---

8. Wiley apparently concedes the possibility that a right to severance pay might accrue before the expiration of the contract but be payable "at some future date." Brief, p. 38.

"Step 1" provides for "a conference between the affected employee, a Union Steward and the Employer, officer or exempt supervisory person in charge of his department." In "Step 2," the grievance is submitted to "a conference between an officer of the Employer, or the Employer's representative designated for that purpose, the Union Shop Committee and/or a representative of the Union." Arbitration is reached under "Step 3" "in the event that the grievance shall not have been resolved or settled in 'Step 2.' " Wiley argues that since Steps 1 and 2 have not been followed, and since the duty to arbitrate arises only in Step 3, it has no duty to arbitrate this dispute.[11] Specifically, Wiley urges that the question whether "procedural" conditions to arbitration have been met must be decided by the court and not the arbitrator.

We think that labor disputes of the kind involved here cannot be broken down so easily into their "substantive" and "procedural" aspects. Questions concerning the procedural prerequisites to arbitration do not arise in a vacuum; they develop in the context of an actual dispute about the rights of the parties to the contract or those covered by it. In this case, for example, the Union argues that Wiley's consistent refusal to recognize the Union's representative status after the merger made it "utterly futile—and a little bit ridiculous to follow the grievance steps as set forth in the contract." Brief, p. 41. In addition, the Union argues that time limitations in the grievance procedure are not controlling because Wiley's violations of the bargaining agreement were "continuing." These arguments in response to Wiley's "procedural" claim are meaningless unless set in the background of the merger and the negotiations surrounding it.

Doubt whether grievance procedures or some part of them apply to a particular dispute, whether such procedures have been followed or excused, or whether the unexcused failure to follow them avoids the duty to arbitrate cannot ordinarily be answered without consideration of the merits of the dispute which is presented for arbitration. In this case, one's view of the Union's responses to Wiley's "procedural" arguments depends to a large extent on how one answers questions bearing on the basic issue, the effect of the merger; e.g., whether or not the merger was a possibility considered by Wiley [sic] and the Union during the negotiation of the contract. It would be a curious rule which required that intertwined issues of "substance" and "procedure" growing out of a single dispute and raising the same questions on the same facts had to be carved up between two different forums, one deciding after the other. Neither logic nor considerations of policy compel such a result.

Once it is determined, as we have, that the parties are obligated to submit the subject matter of a dispute to arbitration, "procedural" questions which grow out of the dispute and bear on its final disposition should be left to the arbitrator. Even under a contrary rule, a court could deny arbitration only if it could confidently be said not only that a claim was strictly

---

11. In addition to the failure to follow the procedures of Steps 1 and 2, Wiley objects to the Union's asserted failure to comply with § 16.6, which provides: "Notice of any grievance must be filed with the Employer and with the Union Shop Steward within four (4) weeks after its occurrence or latest existence. The failure by either party to file the grievance within this time limitation shall be construed and be deemed to be an abandonment of the grievance."

"procedural," and therefore within the purview of the court, but also that it should operate to bar arbitration altogether, and not merely limit or qualify an arbitral award. In view of the policies favoring arbitration and the parties' adoption of arbitration as the preferred means of settling disputes, such cases are likely to be rare indeed. In all other cases, those in which arbitration goes forward, the arbitrator would ordinarily remain free to reconsider the ground covered by the court insofar as it bore on the merits of the dispute, using the flexible approaches familiar to arbitration. Reservation of "procedural" issues for the courts would thus not only create the difficult task of separating related issues, but would also produce frequent duplication of effort.

In addition, the opportunities for deliberate delay and the possibility of well-intentioned but no less serious delay created by separation of the "procedural" and "substantive" elements of a dispute are clear. While the courts have the task of determining "substantive arbitrability," there will be cases in which arbitrability of the subject matter is unquestioned but a dispute arises over the procedures to be followed. In all of such cases, acceptance of Wiley's position would produce the delay attendant upon judicial proceedings preliminary to arbitration. * * *

No justification for such a generally undesirable result is to be found in a presumed intention of the parties. Refusal to order arbitration of subjects which the parties have not agreed to arbitrate does not entail the fractionating of disputes about subjects which the parties do wish to have submitted. Although a party may resist arbitration once a grievance has arisen, as does Wiley here, we think it best accords with the usual purposes of an arbitration clause and with the policy behind federal labor law to regard procedural disagreements not as separate disputes but as aspects of the dispute which called the grievance procedures into play. * * *

Affirmed.

MR. JUSTICE GOLDBERG took no part in the consideration or decision of this case.

Note

If you were the arbitrator charged with hearing and deciding the grievances ordered to arbitration in the Wiley case, on what basis would you resolve the substantive issues presented? The arbitrator's award is summarized in footnote 4 of the Howard Johnson case, reported infra p. 709.

NATIONAL LABOR RELATIONS BOARD v. BURNS INTERNATIONAL SECURITY SERVICES

Supreme Court of the United States, 1972.
406 U.S. 272, 92 S.Ct. 1571, 32 L.Ed.2d 61.

MR. JUSTICE WHITE delivered the opinion of the Court.

Burns International Security Services, Inc. (Burns), replaced another employer, the Wackenhut Corp. (Wackenhut), which had previously provided plant protection services for the Lockheed Aircraft Service Co. (Lockheed) located at the Ontario International Airport in California. When Burns began providing security service, it employed 42 guards; 27 of them had been employed by Wackenhut. Burns refused, however, to bargain with the United Plant Guard Workers of America (UPG) which had been certified after a National Labor Relations Board (Board) election as the exclusive bargaining representative of Wackenhut's employees less than four months earlier. The issues presented in this case are whether Burns refused to bargain with a union representing a majority of employees in an appropriate unit and whether the National Labor Relations Board could order Burns to observe the terms of a collective-bargaining contract signed by the union and Wackenhut that Burns had not voluntarily assumed. Resolution turns to a great extent on the precise facts involved here.

I

The Wackenhut Corp. provided protection services at the Lockheed plant for five years before Burns took over this task. On February 28, 1967, a few months before the changeover of guard employers, a majority of the Wackenhut guards selected the union as their exclusive bargaining representative in a Board election after Wackenhut and the union had agreed that the Lockheed plant was the appropriate bargaining unit. On March 8 the Regional Director certified the union as the exclusive bargaining representative for these employees, and, on April 29, Wackenhut and the union entered into a three-year collective-bargaining contract.

Meanwhile, since Wackenhut's one-year service agreement to provide security protection was due to expire on June 30, Lockheed had called for bids from various companies supplying these services, and both Burns and Wackenhut submitted estimates. At a pre-bid conference attended by Burns on May 15, a representative of Lockheed informed the bidders that Wackenhut's guards were represented by the union, that the union had recently won a Board election and been certified, and that there was in existence a collective-bargaining contract between Wackenhut and the union. Lockheed then accepted Burns' bid, and on May 31 Wackenhut was notified that Burns would assume responsibility for protection services on July 1. Burns chose to retain 27 of the Wackenhut guards, and it brought in 15 of its own guards from other Burns locations.

During June, when Burns hired the 27 Wackenhut guards, it supplied them with membership cards of the American Federation of Guards (AFG), another union with which Burns had collective-bargaining contracts at other locations, and informed them that they had to become AFG members to work for Burns, that they would not receive uniforms otherwise, and that Burns "could not live with" the existing contract between Wackenhut and the union. On June 29, Burns recognized the AFG on the theory that it had obtained a card majority. On July 12, however, the UPG demanded that Burns recognize it as the bargaining representative of Burns' employees at Lockheed and that Burns honor the collective-bargaining agreement between it and Wackenhut. When Burns refused, the UPG filed unfair labor practice charges, and Burns responded by challenging the appropriateness of the unit and by denying its obligation to bargain.

The Board, adopting the trial examiner's findings and conclusions, found the Lockheed plant an appropriate unit and held that Burns had violated

§§ 8(a)(2) and 8(a)(1) of the National Labor Relations Act by unlawfully recognizing and assisting the AFG, a rival of the UPG; and that it had violated §§ 8(a)(5) and 8(a)(1) by failing to recognize and bargain with the UPG and by refusing to honor the collective-bargaining agreement that had been negotiated between Wackenhut and UPG.

Burns did not challenge the § 8(a)(2) unlawful assistance finding in the Court of Appeals but sought review of the unit determination and the order to bargain and observe the pre-existing collective-bargaining contract. The Court of Appeals accepted the Board's unit determination and enforced the Board's order insofar as it related to the finding of unlawful assistance of a rival union and the refusal to bargain, but it held that the Board had exceeded its powers in ordering Burns to honor the contract executed by Wackenhut. Both Burns and the Board petitioned for certiorari, Burns challenging the unit determination and the bargaining order and the Board maintaining its position that Burns was bound by the Wackenhut contract, and we granted both petitions, though we declined to review the propriety of the bargaining unit, a question which was presented in No. 71–198. 404 U.S. 822, 92 S.Ct. 99, 30 L.Ed.2d 49 (1971).

II

We address first Burns' alleged duty to bargain with the union ＊ ＊ ＊.

The trial examiner first found that the unit designated by the regional director was an appropriate unit for bargaining. ＊ ＊ ＊

The trial examiner then found, *inter alia,* that Burns "had in its employ a majority of Wackenhut's former employees," and that these employees had already expressed their choice of a bargaining representative in an election held a short time before. Burns was therefore held to have a duty to bargain, which arose when it selected as its work force the employees of the previous employer to perform the same tasks at the same place they had worked in the past.

The Board, without revision, accepted the trial examiner's findings and conclusions with respect to the duty to bargain, and we see no basis for setting them aside. In an election held but a few months before, the union had been designated bargaining agent for the employees in the unit and a majority of these employees had been hired by Burns for work in the identical unit. It is undisputed that Burns knew all the relevant facts in this regard and was aware of the certification and of the existence of a collective-bargaining contract. In these circumstances, it was not unreasonable for the Board to conclude that the union certified to represent all employees in the unit still represented a majority of the employees and that Burns could not reasonably have entertained a good-faith doubt about that fact. Burns' obligation to bargain with the union over terms and conditions of employment stemmed from its hiring of Wackenhut's employees and from the recent election and Board certification. It has been consistently held that a mere change of employers or of ownership in the employing industry is not such an "unusual circumstance" as to affect the force of the Board's certification within the normal operative period if a majority of employees after the change of ownership or management were employed by the preceding employer. NLRB v. Downtown Bakery Corp., 330 F.2d 921, 925 (CA6 1964) * * *.[3]

It would be a wholly different case if the Board had determined that because Burns' operational structure and practices differed from those of Wackenhut, the Lockheed bargaining unit was no longer an appropriate one.[4] Likewise, it would be different if Burns had not hired employees already represented by a union certified as a bargaining agent,[5] and the Board recognized as much at oral argument.[6] But where the bargaining unit remains unchanged and a majority of the employees hired by the new employer are represented by a recently certified bargaining agent there is little basis for faulting the Board's implementation of the express mandates of § 8(a)(5) and § 9(a) by ordering the employer to bargain with the incumbent union. This is the view of several courts of appeals, and we agree with those courts. NLRB v. Zayre Corp., 424 F.2d 1159, 1162 (CA5 1970); Tom-A-Hawk Transit, Inc. v. NLRB, 419 F.2d 1025, 1026–1027 (CA7 1969); S.S. Kresge Co. v. NLRB, 416 F.2d 1225, 1234 (CA6 1969); NLRB v. McFarland, 306 F.2d at 220.

3. Cf. § 9(c)(3) of the NLRA, 29 U.S.C.A. § 159(c)(3), which provides that "[n]o election shall be directed in any bargaining unit or any subdivision within which in the preceding twelve-month period a valid election shall have been held." See NLRB v. Gissel Packing Co., 395 U.S. 575, 599 n. 14, 89 S.Ct. 1918, 1932, 23 L.Ed.2d 547 (1969).

Where an employer remains the same, a Board certification carries with it an almost conclusive presumption that the majority representative status of the union continues for a reasonable time, usually a year. See Brooks v. NLRB, 348 U.S. 96, 98–99, 75 S.Ct. 176, 178–179, 99 L.Ed. 125 (1954). After this period, there is a rebuttable presumption of majority representation. Celanese Corp. of America, 95 N.L.R.B. 664, 672 (1951). If there is a change of employers, however, and an almost complete turnover of employees, the certification may not bar a challenge if the successor employer is not bound by the collective-bargaining contract, particularly if the new employees are represented by another union or if the old unit is ruled an accretion to another unit. Cf. McGuire v. Humble Oil & Refining Co., 355 F.2d 352 (CA2), cert. denied, 384 U.S. 988, 86 S.Ct. 1889, 16 L.Ed.2d 1004 (1966). See n. 5, infra.

4. The Court of Appeals was unimpressed with the asserted differences between Burns' and Wackenhut's operations: "All of the important factors which the Board has used and the courts have approved are present in the instant case: 'continuation of the same types of product lines, departmental organization, employee identity and job functions.' * * * Both Burns and Wackenhut are nationwide organizations; both performed the identical services at the same facility; although Burns used its own supervisors, their functions and responsibilities were similar to those performed by their predecessors; and finally, and perhaps most significantly, Burns commenced performance of the contract with 27 former Wackenhut employees out of its total complement of 42." 441 F.2d 911, 915 (1971) (citation omitted). Although the labor policies of the two companies differed somewhat, the Board's determination that the bargaining unit remained appropriate after the changeover meant that Burns would face essentially the same labor relations environment as Wackenhut: it would confront the same union representing most of the same employees in the same unit.

5. The Board has never held that the National Labor Relations Act itself requires that an employer who submits the winning bid for a service contract or who purchases the assets of a business be obligated to hire all of the employees of the predecessor though it is possible that such an obligation might be assumed by the employer. But cf. Chemrock Corp., 151 N.L.R.B. 1074 (1965). However, an employer who declines to hire employees solely because they are members of a union commits a § 8(a)(3) unfair labor practice. * * *

6. "Q. But [counsel for the Union], when he argued, said that even if [Burns] hadn't taken over any [employees of Wackenhut], even if they hadn't taken over a single employee, the legal situation would be the same.

"Mr. Come [for the NLRB]. We do not go that far. We don't think that you have to go that far in—

"Q. Do you think it has to be a majority?

"Mr. Come. I wouldn't say that it has to be a majority, I think it has to be a substantial number. It has to be enough to give you a continuity of employment conditions in the bargaining unit." Tr. of Oral Arg. 64–65.

III

It does not follow, however, from Burns' duty to bargain that it was bound to observe the substantive terms of the collective-bargaining contract the union had negotiated with Wackenhut and to which Burns had in no way agreed. Section 8(d) of the Act expressly provides that the existence of such bargaining obligation "does not compel either party to agree to a proposal or require the making of a concession." Congress has consistently declined to interfere with free collective bargaining and has preferred that device, or voluntary arbitration, to the imposition of compulsory terms as a means of avoiding or terminating labor disputes. * * *

This history was reviewed in detail and given controlling effect in H.K. Porter Co. v. NLRB, 397 U.S. 99, 90 S.Ct. 821, 25 L.Ed.2d 146 (1970). * * *

[T]he Board's prior decisions * * * until now have consistently held that, although successor employers may be bound to recognize and bargain with the union, they are not bound by the substantive provisions of a collective-bargaining contract negotiated by their predecessors but not agreed to or assumed by them. * * *

The Board, however, has now departed from this view and argues that the same policies which mandate a continuity of bargaining obligation also require that successor employers be bound to the terms of a predecessor's collective-bargaining contract. It asserts that the stability of labor relations will be jeopardized and that employees will face uncertainty and a gap in the bargained-for terms and conditions of employment, as well as the possible loss of advantages gained by prior negotiations, unless the new employer is held to have assumed, as a matter of federal labor law, the obligations under the contract entered into by the former employer. Recognizing that under normal contract principles a party would not be bound to a contract in the absence of consent, the Board notes that in John Wiley & Sons, Inc. v. Livingston, 376 U.S. 543, 550, 84 S.Ct. 909, 914, 11 L.Ed.2d 898 (1964), the Court declared that "a collective bargaining agreement is not an ordinary contract" but is, rather, an outline of the common law of a particular plant or industry. * * *

We do not find *Wiley* controlling in the circumstances here. *Wiley* arose in the context of a § 301 suit to compel arbitration, not in the context of an unfair labor practice proceeding where the Board is expressly limited by the provisions of § 8(d). That decision emphasized "[t]he preference of national labor policy for arbitration as a substitute for tests of strength before contending forces" and held only that the agreement to arbitrate, "construed in the context of a national labor policy," survived the merger and left to the arbitrator, subject to judicial review, the ultimate question of the extent to which, if any, the surviving company was bound by other provisions of the contract. Id., at 549, 551, 84 S.Ct., at 914, 915.

Wiley's limited accommodation between the legislative endorsement of freedom of contract and the judicial preference for peaceful arbitral settlement of labor disputes does not warrant the Board's holding that the employer commits an unfair labor practice unless he honors the substantive terms of the pre-existing contract. The present case does not involve a § 301 suit; nor does it involve the duty to arbitrate. Rather, the claim is that

Burns must be held bound by the contract executed by Wackenhut, whether Burns has agreed to it or not and even though Burns made it perfectly clear that it had no intention of assuming that contract. *Wiley* suggests no such open-ended obligation. Its narrower holding dealt with a merger occurring against a background of state law that embodied the general rule that in merger situations the surviving corporation is liable for the obligations of the disappearing corporation. See N.Y. Stock Corporation Law § 90 (1951); 15 W. Fletcher, Private Corporations, § 7121 (1961 rev. ed.). Here there was no merger or sale of assets, and there were no dealings whatsoever between Wackenhut and Burns. On the contrary, they were competitors for the same work, each bidding for the service contract at Lockheed. Burns purchased nothing from Wackenhut and became liable for none of its financial obligations. Burns merely hired enough of Wackenhut's employees to require it to bargain with the union as commanded by § 8(a)(5) and § 9(a). But this consideration is a wholly insufficient basis for implying either in fact or in law that Burns had agreed or must be held to have agreed to honor Wackenhut's collective-bargaining contract. * * *

We also agree with the Court of Appeals that holding either the union or the new employer bound to the substantive terms of an old collective-bargaining contract may result in serious inequities. A potential employer may be willing to take over a moribund business only if he can make changes in corporate structure, composition of the labor force, work location, task assignment, and nature of supervision. Saddling such an employer with the terms and conditions of employment contained in the old collective-bargaining contract may make these changes impossible and may discourage and inhibit the transfer of capital. On the other hand, a union may have made concessions to a small or failing employer that it would be unwilling to make to a large or economically successful firm. The congressional policy manifest in the Act is to enable the parties to negotiate for any protection either deems appropriate, but to allow the balance of bargaining advantage to be set by economic power realities. Strife is bound to occur if the concessions that must be honored do not correspond to the relative economic strength of the parties. * * *

* * * We accordingly set aside the Board's finding of a § 8(a)(5) unfair labor practice insofar as it rested on a conclusion that Burns was required to but did not honor the collective-bargaining contract executed by Wackenhut.

IV

It therefore follows that the Board's order requiring Burns to "give retroactive effect to all the clauses of said [Wackenhut] contract and, with interest of 6 percent, make whole its employees for any losses suffered by reason of Respondent's [Burns'] refusal to honor, adopt and enforce said contract" must be set aside. We note that the regional director's charge instituting this case asserted that "[o]n or about July 1, 1967, Respondent [Burns] unilaterally changed existing wage rates, hours of employment, overtime wage rates, differentials for swing shift and graveyard shift, and other terms and conditions of employment of the employees in the appropriate unit * * *," App. 113, and that the Board's opinion stated that "[t]he obligation to bargain imposed on a successor-employer includes the negative injunction to refrain from unilaterally changing wages and other benefits established by a prior collective-bargaining agreement even though that agreement had expired. In this respect, the successor-employer's obligations are the same as those imposed upon employers generally during the period between collective-bargaining agreements." App. 8–9. This statement by the Board is consistent with its prior and subsequent cases that hold that whether or not a successor employer is bound by its predecessor's contract, it must not institute terms and conditions of employment different from those provided in its predecessor's contract, at least without first bargaining with the employees' representative. * * * Thus, if Burns without bargaining to impasse with the union, had paid its employees on and after July 1 at a rate lower than Wackenhut had paid under its contract, or otherwise provided terms and conditions of employment different from those provided in the Wackenhut collective-bargaining agreement, under the Board's view, Burns would have committed a § 8(a)(5) unfair labor practice and would have been subject to an order to restore to employees what they had lost by this so-called unilateral change. * * *

Although Burns had an obligation to bargain with the union concerning wages and other conditions of employment when the union requested it to do so, this case is not like a § 8(a)(5) violation where an employer unilaterally changes a condition of employment without consulting a bargaining representative. It is difficult to understand how Burns could be said to have *changed* unilaterally any pre-existing term or condition of employment without bargaining when it had no previous relationship whatsoever to the bargaining unit and, prior to July 1, no outstanding terms and conditions of employment from which a change could be inferred. The terms on which Burns hired employees for service after July 1 may have differed from the terms extended by Wackenhut and required by the collective-bargaining contract, but it does not follow that Burns changed *its* terms and conditions of employment when it specified the initial basis on which employees were hired on July 1.

Although a successor employer is ordinarily free to set initial terms on which it will hire the employees of a predecessor, there will be instances in which it is perfectly clear that the new employer plans to retain all of the employees in the unit and in which it will be appropriate to have him initially consult with the employees' bargaining representative before he fixes terms. In other situations, however, it may not be clear until the successor employer has hired his full complement of employees that he has a duty to bargain with a union, since it will not be evident until then that the bargaining representative represents a majority of the employees in the unit as required by § 9(a) of the Act. Here, for example, Burns' obligation to bargain with the union did not mature until it had selected its force of guards late in June. The Board quite properly found that Burns refused to bargain on July 12 when it rejected the overtures of the union. It is true that the wages it paid when it began protecting the Lockheed plant on July 1 differed from those specified in the Wackenhut collective-bargaining agreement, but there is no evidence that Burns ever unilaterally changed the terms and conditions of employment it had offered to potential employees in June after its obligation to bargain with the union became apparent. If the union had made a request to bargain after Burns had completed its hiring and if Burns had negotiated in good faith and had made offers to the union which the union rejected, Burns could have unilaterally initiated such proposals as the opening terms and conditions of employment on July 1 without committing an unfair labor practice. Cf. NLRB v. Katz, 369 U.S. 736, 745, n. 12, 82 S.Ct. 1107, 1113, 8 L.Ed.2d 230 (1962) ＊ ＊ ＊. The Board's order requiring Burns to make whole its employees for any losses suffered by reason of Burns' refusal to honor and enforce the contract, cannot therefore be sustained on the ground that Burns unilaterally changed existing terms and conditions of employment, thereby committing an unfair labor practice which required monetary restitution in these circumstances.

Affirmed.

MR. JUSTICE REHNQUIST, with whom THE CHIEF JUSTICE, MR. JUSTICE BRENNAN, and MR. JUSTICE POWELL join, concurring in No. 71–123 and dissenting in No. 71–198.

Although the Court studiously avoids using the term "successorship" in concluding that Burns did have a statutory obligation to bargain with the union, it affirms the conclusions of the Board and the Court of Appeals to that effect which were based entirely on the successorship doctrine. Because I believe that the Board and the Court of Appeals stretched that concept beyond the limits of its proper application, I would enforce neither the Board's bargaining order nor its order imposing upon Burns the terms of the contract between the union and Wackenhut. I therefore concur in No. 71–123 and dissent in No. 71–198.

＊ ＊ ＊

The Court concludes that because the trial examiner and the Board found the Lockheed facility to be an appropriate bargaining unit for Burns' employees, and because Burns hired a majority of Wackenhut's previous employees who had worked at that facility, Burns should have bargained with the union, even though the union never made any showing to Burns of majority representation. There is more than one difficulty with this analysis.

First, it is by no means mathematically demonstrable that the union was the choice of a majority of the 42 employees with which Burns began the performance of its contract with Lockheed. True, 27 of the 42 had been represented by the union when they were employees of Wackenhut, but there is nothing in the record before us to indicate that all 27 of these employees chose the union as their bargaining agent even at the time of negotiations with Wackenhut. There is obviously no evidence whatever that the remaining 15 employees of Burns, who had never been employed by Wackenhut, had ever expressed their views one way or the other about the union as a bargaining representative. It may be that, if asked, all would have designated the union. But they were never asked. Instead, the trial examiner concluded that because Burns was a "successor" employer to Wackenhut, it was obligated by that fact alone to bargain with the union.

The second problem with the Court's reasoning is that it relies on the Board's approval of the Lockheed plant as an appropriate unit to support its conclusion that Burns must bargain with the union. While it is true, as the Court notes, that the trial examiner and the Board found the Lockheed facility to be an appropriate bargaining unit for Burns' employees, it is equally true that the trial examiner's finding to this effect was clearly dependent upon the previous stipulation between Wackenhut and the union. One of the reasons asserted by Burns for declining to recognize the union was its belief that the single Lockheed facility was not an appropriate bargaining unit. This was more than a colorable claim. Unlike Wackenhut, Burns had never bargained with a union consisting of its employees in a single job location. One of the reasons for this difference was that Burns made a practice of transferring employees from one job to another, on a temporary or permanent basis. Both Burns and Wackenhut had numerous security guard jobsites in Southern California; for administrative purposes, Wackenhut treated each jobsite as a separate unit, while Burns treated large numbers of them together.

* * *

Thus, in a situation where there was no evidence at the time as to the preference of a majority of the employees at the Lockheed facility as to a bargaining agent, and there was no independent finding that the employees at that facility were an appropriate unit as to Burns, the Board nonetheless imposed the duty to bargain. This result is sustainable, if at all, only on the theory that Burns was a "successor" to Wackenhut. The imposition of successorship in this case is unusual because the successor instead of purchasing business or assets from or merging with Wackenhut was in direct competition with Wackenhut for the Lockheed contract. I believe that a careful analysis of the admittedly imprecise concept of successorship indicates that important rights of both the employee and the employer to independently order their own affairs are sacrificed needlessly by the application of that doctrine to this case.

It has been aptly observed that the doctrine of "successor" employer in the field of labor law is "shrouded in somewhat impressionist approaches." [3] In John Wiley & Sons, Inc. v. Livingston, 376 U.S. 543, 84 S.Ct. 909, 11 L.Ed. 2d 898 (1964), we employed a form of the "successor" doctrine to impose upon an employer an obligation to arbitrate disputes under an arbitration clause in an agreement entered into between a predecessor employer and the bargaining representative of the latter's employees. The doctrine has been applied by the Board and by the courts of appeals to impose upon the successor employer a duty to bargain with representatives of the employees of his predecessor, NLRB v. Auto Ventshade, Inc., 276 F.2d 303, 304 (CA5 1960); Makela Welding, Inc. v. NLRB, 387 F.2d 40, 46 (CA6 1967), to support a finding of unfair labor practices from a course of conduct engaged in by both the predecessor and the successor, NLRB v. Blair Quarries, Inc., 152 F.2d 25 (CA4 1945), and to require the successor to remedy unfair labor practices committed by a predecessor employer, United States Pipe & Foundry Co. v. NLRB, 398 F.2d 544 (CA5 1968). The consequences of the application of the "successor" doctrine in each of these cases has been that the "successor" employer has been subjected to certain burdens or obligations to which a similarly situated employer who is not a "successor" would not be subject.

The various decisions that have applied the successor doctrine exhibit more than one train of reasoning in support of its application. There is

3. International Assn. of Machinists, etc. v. NLRB, 134 U.S.App.D.C. 239, 243, 414 F.2d 1135, 1139 (1969) (Leventhal, J., concurring).

authority for the proposition that it rests in part at least upon the need for continuity in industrial labor relations, and the concomitant avoidance of industrial strife that presumably follows from such continuity. NLRB v. Colten, 105 F.2d 179 (CA6 1939); Tom-A-Hawk Transit, Inc. v. NLRB, 419 F.2d 1025 (CA7 1969). On examination, however, this proposition may more accurately be described as a statement of the result of a finding of successorship, rather than a reason for making that finding.

Other cases have stated the guiding principle to be whether the "employing industry" remains essentially the same after the change in ownership. NLRB v. Tempest Shirt Mfg. Co., 285 F.2d 1 (CA5 1960); NLRB v. Alamo White Truck Service, Inc., 273 F.2d 238 (CA5 1959). Under this approach a variety of facts relating to the "employing industry" have been examined to see whether a sufficient number remain unchanged to warrant the imposition of successorship. While it cannot be doubted that a determination as to successorship will vary with different fact situations, some general concept of the reason for the successorship doctrine is essential in order to determine the importance of the various factual combinations and permutations that may or may not call for its application.

This Court's opinion in *Wiley* makes it clear that one of the bases for a finding of successorship is the need to grant some protection to employees from a sudden transformation of their employer's business that results in the substitution of a new legal entity, not bound by the collective-bargaining contract under contract law, as the employer, but leaves intact significant elements of the employer's business. The Court said there:

> "The objectives of national labor policy, reflected in established principles of federal law, require that the rightful prerogative of owners independently to rearrange their businesses and even eliminate themselves as employers be balanced by some protection to the employees from a sudden change in the employment relationship. The transition from one corporate organization to another will in most cases be eased and industrial strife avoided if employees' claims continue to be resolved by arbitration rather than by 'the relative strength * * * of the contending forces,' * * *." 376 U.S., at 549, 84 S.Ct., at 914.

But other language in *Wiley* makes it clear that the considerations favoring the continuity of existing bargaining relationships are not without their limits:

> "We do not hold that in every case in which the ownership or corporate structure of an enterprise is changed the duty to arbitrate survives. As indicated above, there may be cases in which the lack of any substantial continuity of identity in the business enterprise before and after a change would make a duty to arbitrate something imposed from without, not reasonably to be found in the particular bargaining agreement and the acts of the parties involved." 376 U.S., at 551, 84 S.Ct., at 915.

The conflicting implications in these portions of the opinion in *Wiley* suggest that employees are indeed entitled to a measure of protection against change in the employing entity where the new employer continues to make use of tangible or intangible assets used in carrying on the business of the first employer. They also make clear that the successorship doctrine, carried to its ultimate limits, runs counter to other equally well-established principles of labor law. Industrial peace is an important goal of the Labor Management Relations Act. But Congress has time and again refused to sacrifice free collective bargaining between representatives of the employees and the employer for a system of compulsory arbitration. * * *

There is also a natural tension between the constraints imposed on employers by the Labor Management Relations Act, and the right of those employers in competition with one another "independently to rearrange their businesses and even eliminate themselves as employers." *Wiley*, 376 U.S., at 549, 84 S.Ct., at 914. An employer's ability to compete in his market is affected, of course, by the terms of whatever collective-bargaining agreement he negotiates with the representative of his employees. Aside from the direct influence on price brought about by the terms of a collective-bargaining agreement, the collective-bargaining process itself presents a certain cost factor that may affect competition between employers in the market. The national commitment to collective bargaining embodied in the Labor Management Relations Act either requires or permits many of these constraints. But quite reasonable expectations of the employees in a particular collective-bargaining unit may be disappointed by a voluntary change in the condition of the employer that is quite incapable of being remedied by any rational application of the successorship doctrine. An employer is free to cease doing business, even though he chooses to do so wholly because of anti-union animus. Textile Workers Union of America v. Darlington Mfg. Co., 380 U.S. 263, 85 S.Ct. 994, 13 L.Ed.2d 827 (1965). An employer may adamantly refuse, at the expiration of the period covered by a collective-bargaining agreement, to again consent to a particular term of the agreement that the employees regarded as significant. NLRB v. American National Insurance Co., 343 U.S. 395, 72 S.Ct. 824, 96 L.Ed. 1027 (1952). These examples of permissible employer conduct for which the Labor Management Relations Act provides no remedy, notwithstanding that the conduct results in the disappointment of legitimate expectations of employees, suggest that the successorship principle, like every other principle of law, has limits beyond which it may not be expanded.

Wiley, supra, speaks in terms of a change in the "ownership or corporate structure of an enterprise" as bringing into play the obligation of the successor employer to perform an obligation voluntarily undertaken by the predecessor employer. But while the principle enunciated in *Wiley* is by no means limited to the corporate merger situation present there, it cannot logically be extended to a mere naked shifting of a group of employees from one employer to another without totally disregarding the basis for the doctrine. The notion of a change in the "ownership or corporate structure of an enterprise" connotes at the very least that there is continuity in the enterprise, as well as change; and that that continuity be at least in part on the employer's side of the equation, rather than only on that of the employees. If we deal with the legitimate expectations of employees that the employer who agreed to the collective-bargaining contract perform it, we can require another employing entity to perform the contract only when he has succeeded to some of the tangible or intangible assets by the use of which the employees might have expected the first employer to have performed his contract with them.

Phrased another way, the doctrine of successorship in the federal common law of labor relations accords to employees the same general protection against transfer of assets by an entity against which they have a claim as is accorded by other legal doctrines to nonlabor-related claimants against the same entity. Nonlabor-related claimants in such transfer situations may be protected not only by assumption agreements resulting from the self-interest of the contracting parties participating in a merger or sale of assets but also by state laws imposing upon the successor corporation of any merger the obligations of the merged corporation (see, e.g., § 90 of the New York Stock Corporation Law (1951), cited in *Wiley,* supra), and by bulk sales acts found in numerous States.[6] These latter are designed to give the nonlabor-related creditor of the predecessor entity some claim, either as a matter of contract right against the successor, or as a matter of property right to charge the assets that pass from the predecessor to the successor. The implication of *Wiley* is that the federal common law of labor relations accords the same general type and degree of protection to employees claiming under a collective-bargaining contract.

Cases from the courts of appeals have found successorship, consistently with these principles, where the new employer purchases a part or all of the assets of the predecessor employer, NLRB v. Interstate 65 Corp., 453 F.2d 269 (CA6 1971); where the entire business is purchased by the new employer, NLRB v. McFarland, 306 F.2d 219 (CA10 1962); and where there is merely a change in the ownership interest in a partnership that operates the employing entity, NLRB v. Colten, 105 F.2d 179 (CA6 1939). Other courts of appeals have, equally consistently with these principles, refused to find successorship where there have been no contractual dealings between the two employers, and all that has taken place is a shift in employees. Tri State Maintenance Corp. v. NLRB, 132 U.S.App.D.C. 368, 408 F.2d 171 (1968); International Assn. of Machinists, District Lodge 94 v. NLRB, 134 U.S.App.D.C. 239, 414 F.2d 1135 (1969).

The rigid imposition of a prior-existing labor relations environment on a new employer whose only connection with the old employer is the hiring of some of the latter's employees and the performance of some of the work which was previously performed by the latter, might well tend to produce industrial peace of a sort. But industrial peace in such a case would be produced at a sacrifice of the determination by the Board of the appropriateness of bargaining agents and of the wishes of the majority of the employees which the Act was designed to preserve. These latter principles caution us against extending successorship, under the banner of industrial peace, step by step to a point where the only connection between the two employing entities is a naked transfer of employees. Justice Holmes in Hudson County Water Co. v. McCarter, 209 U.S. 349, 355, 28 S.Ct. 529, 531, 52 L.Ed. 828 (1908), summarized the general problem this way:

> "All rights tend to declare themselves absolute to their logical extreme. Yet all in fact are limited by the neighborhood of principles of policy which are other than those on which the particular right is founded, and which become strong enough to hold their own when a certain point is reached."

6. Uniform Commercial Code §§ 6–101 to 6–111.

Burns acquired not a single asset, tangible or intangible, by negotiation or transfer from Wackenhut. It succeeded to the contractual rights and duties of the plant protection service contract with Lockheed, not by reason of Wackenhut's assignment or consent, but over Wackenhut's vigorous opposition. I think the only permissible conclusion is that Burns is not a successor to Wackenhut. * * *

To conclude that Burns was a successor to Wackenhut in this situation, with its attendant consequences under the Board's order imposing a duty to bargain with the bargaining representative of Wackenhut's employees, would import unwarranted rigidity into labor-management relations. The fortunes of competing employers inevitably ebb and flow, and an employer who has currently gained production orders at the expense of another may well wish to hire employees away from that other. There is no reason to think that the best interests of the employees, the employers, and ultimately of the free market are not served by such movement. Yet inherent in the expanded doctrine of successorship that the Board urges in this case is the notion that somehow the "labor relations environment" comes with the new employees if the new employer has but obtained orders or business that previously belonged to the old employer. The fact that the employees in the instant case continued to perform their work at the same situs, while not irrelevant to the analysis, cannot be deemed controlling. For the rigidity that would follow from the Board's application of successorship to this case would not only affect competition between Wackenhut and Burns, but would also affect Lockheed's operations. In effect, it would be saddled, as against its competitors, with the disadvantageous consequences of a collective-bargaining contract unduly favorable to Wackenhut's employees, even though Lockheed's contract with Wackenhut was set to expire at a given time. By the same token, it would be benefited, at the expense of its competitors, as a result of a "sweetheart" contract negotiated between Wackenhut and its employees. * * *

This is not to say that Burns would be unilaterally free to mesh into its previously recognized Los Angeles County bargaining unit a group of employees such as were involved here who already have designated a collective-bargaining representative in their previous employment. Burns' actions in this regard would be subject to the commands of the Labor Management Relations Act, and to the regulation of the Board under proper application of governing principles. The situation resulting from the addition of a new element of the component work force of an employer has been dealt with by the Board in numerous cases, and various factors are weighed in order to determine whether the new workforce component should be itself a separate bargaining unit, or whether the employees in this component shall be "accreted" to the bargaining unit already in existence. See, e.g., NLRB v. Food Employers Council, Inc., 399 F.2d 501 (CA9 1968); Northwest Galvanizing Co., 168 N.L.R.B. 26 (1967). Had the Board made the appropriate factual inquiry and determinations required by the Act, such inquiry might have justified the conclusion that Burns was obligated to recognize and bargain with the union as a representative of its employees at the Lockheed facility.

But the Board, instead of applying this type of analysis to the union's complaints here, concluded that because Burns was a "successor" it was absolutely bound to the mold that had been fashioned by Wackenhut and its employees at Lockheed. Burns was thereby precluded from challenging the designation of Lockheed as an appropriate bargaining unit for a year after the original certification. 61 Stat. 144, 29 U.S.C.A. § 159(c)(3).

I am unwilling to follow the Board this far down the successorship road, since I believe to do so would substantially undercut the principle of free choice of bargaining representatives by the employees and designation of the appropriate bargaining unit by the Board that are guaranteed by the Act.

HOWARD JOHNSON CO. v. DETROIT LOCAL JOINT EXECUTIVE BOARD, HOTEL EMPLOYEES INTERNATIONAL UNION

Supreme Court of the United States, 1974.
417 U.S. 249, 94 S.Ct. 2236, 41 L.Ed.2d 46.

MR. JUSTICE MARSHALL delivered the opinion of the Court.

Once again we are faced with the problem of defining the labor law obligations of a "successor" employer to the employees of its predecessors. In this case, petitioner Howard Johnson Co. is the bona fide purchaser of the assets of a restaurant and motor lodge. Respondent Union was the bargaining representative of the employees of the previous operators, and had successfully concluded collective-bargaining agreements with them. In commencing its operation of the restaurant, Howard Johnson hired only a small fraction of the predecessors' employees. The question presented in this case is whether the Union may compel Howard Johnson to arbitrate, under the arbitration provisions of the collective-bargaining agreements signed by its predecessors, the extent of its obligations under those agreements to the predecessors' employees.

Prior to the sale at issue here, the Grissoms—Charles T. Grissom, P.L. Grissom, Ben Bibb, P.L. Grissom & Son, Inc., and the Belleville Restaurant Co., a corporation wholly owned by P.L. Grissom & Son—had operated a Howard Johnson's Motor Lodge and an adjacent Howard Johnson's Restaurant in Belleville, Michigan, under franchise agreements with the petitioner. Employees at both the restaurant and motor lodge were represented by the respondent Hotel & Restaurant Employees & Bartenders International Union. The Grissoms had entered into separate collective-bargaining agreements with the Union covering employees at the two establishments. Both agreements contained dispute settlement procedures leading ultimately to arbitration. Both agreements also provided that they would be binding upon the employer's "successors, assigns, purchasers, lessees or transferees."

On June 16, 1972, the Grissoms entered into an agreement with Howard Johnson to sell it all of the personal property used in connection with operation of the restaurant and motor lodge. The Grissoms retained ownership of the real property, leasing both premises to Howard Johnson. Howard Johnson did not agree to assume any of the Grissoms' obligations, except for four specific contracts relating to operation of the restaurant and motor lodge. On June 28, Howard Johnson mailed the Grissoms a letter, which they later acknowledged and confirmed, clarifying that "[i]t was understood and agreed that the Purchaser * * * would not recognize and assume any labor agreements between the Sellers * * * and any labor organizations," and that it was further agreed that "the Purchaser does not assume any obligations or liabilities of the Sellers resulting from any labor agreements * * *."

Transfer of operation of the restaurant and motor lodge was set for midnight, July 23, 1972. On July 9, the Grissoms notified all of their employees that their employment would terminate as of that time. The Union was also notified of the termination of the Grissoms' business. On July 11, Howard Johnson advised the Union that it would not recognize the Union or assume any obligations under the existing collective-bargaining agreements.

After reaching agreement with the Grissoms, Howard Johnson began hiring its own work force. It placed advertisements in local newspapers, and posted notices in various places, including the restaurant and motor lodge. It began interviewing prospective employees on July 10, hired its first employees on July 18, and began training them at a Howard Johnson facility in Ann Arbor on July 20. Prior to the sale, the Grissoms had 53 employees. Howard Johnson commenced operations with 45 employees, 33 engaged in the restaurant and 12 in the motor lodge. Of these, only nine of the restaurant employees and none of the motor lodge employees had previously been employed by the Grissoms. None of the supervisory personnel employed by the Grissoms were hired by Howard Johnson.

The Union filed this action in the state courts on July 21. Characterizing Howard Johnson's failure to hire all of the employees of the Grissoms as a "lockout" in violation of the collective-bargaining agreements, the Union sought a temporary restraining order enjoining this "lockout" and an order compelling Howard Johnson and the Grissoms to arbitrate the extent of their obligations to the Grissom employees under the bargaining agreements. The state court granted an *ex parte* temporary restraining order, but the Company refused to honor it, claiming that it had not received adequate notice or service, and the order was dissolved after a hearing on July 24.

The defendants subsequently removed this action to the federal courts on the ground that it was brought under § 301 of the Labor Management Relations Act. At a hearing before the District Court on August 7, the Grissoms admitted that they were required to arbitrate in accordance with the terms of the collective-bargaining agreement they had signed and that an order compelling arbitration should issue. On August 22, the District Court, in a memorandum opinion unofficially reported at 81 L.R.R.M. 2329 (E.D.Mich.1972), held that Howard Johnson was also required to arbitrate the extent of its obligations to the former Grissom employees. The court denied, however, the Union's motion for a preliminary injunction requiring the Company to hire all the former Grissom employees, and granted a stay of its arbitration order pending appeal. Howard Johnson appealed the order compelling arbitration, but the Court of Appeals affirmed. 482 F.2d 489 (CA6 1973). We granted certiorari to consider the important labor law question presented. We reverse.

Both courts below relied heavily on this Court's decision in John Wiley & Sons v. Livingston, 376 U.S. 543, 84 S.Ct. 909, 11 L.Ed.2d 898 (1964). In *Wiley,* the union representing the employees of a corporation which had disappeared through a merger sought to compel the surviving corporation, which had hired all of the merged corporation's employees and continued to operate the enterprise in a substantially identical form after the merger, to arbitrate under the merged corporation's collective-bargaining agreement. As *Wiley* was this Court's first experience with the difficult "successorship" question, its holding was properly cautious and narrow:

> "We hold that the disappearance by merger of a corporate employer which has entered into a collective bargaining agreement with a union does not automatically terminate all rights of the employees covered by the agreement, and that, in appropriate circumstances, present here, the successor employer may be required to arbitrate with the union under the agreement." Id., at 548, 84 S.Ct., at 914.

Mr. Justice Harlan, writing for the Court, emphasized "the central role of arbitration in effectuating national labor policy" and preventing industrial strife, and the need to afford some protection to the interests of the employees during a change of corporate ownership. Id., at 549, 84 S.Ct., at 914.

The courts below recognized that the reasoning of *Wiley* was to some extent inconsistent with our more recent decision in NLRB v. Burns International Security Services, 406 U.S. 272, 92 S.Ct. 1571, 32 L.Ed.2d 61 (1972).

*   *   *

The courts below held that *Wiley* rather than *Burns* was controlling here on the ground that *Burns* involved an NLRB order holding the employer bound by the substantive terms of the collective-bargaining agreement, whereas this case, like *Wiley,* involved a § 301 suit to compel arbitration. Although this distinction was in fact suggested by the Court's opinion in *Burns,* see id., at 285–286, 92 S.Ct., at 1581–1582, we do not believe that the fundamental policies outlined in *Burns* can be so lightly disregarded. In Textile Workers Union v. Lincoln Mills, 353 U.S. 448, 77 S.Ct. 912, 1 L.Ed.2d 972 (1957), this Court held that § 301 of the Labor Management Relations Act authorized the federal courts to develop a federal common law regarding enforcement of collective-bargaining agreements. But *Lincoln Mills* did not envision any freewheeling inquiry into what the federal courts might find to be the most desirable rule, irrespective of congressional pronouncements. Rather, *Lincoln Mills* makes clear that this federal common law must be "fashion[ed] from the policy of our national labor laws." Id., at 456, 77 S.Ct., at 918, Mr. Justice Douglas described the process of analysis to be employed:

> "The Labor Management Relations Act expressly furnishes some substantive law. It points out what the parties may or may not do in certain situations. Other problems will lie in the penumbra of express statutory mandates. Some will lack express statutory sanction but will be solved by looking at the policy of the legislation and fashioning a remedy that will effectuate that policy." Id., at 457, 77 S.Ct., at 918.

It would be plainly inconsistent with this view to say that the basic policies found controlling in an unfair labor practice context may be disregarded by the courts in a suit under § 301, and thus to permit the rights enjoyed by the new employer in a successorship context to depend upon the forum in which the union presses its claims.[2] Clearly the reasoning of *Burns* must be taken into account here.

We find it unnecessary, however, to decide in the circumstances of this case whether there is any irreconcilable conflict between *Wiley* and *Burns*. We believe that even on its own terms, *Wiley* does not support the decision of the courts below. The Court in *Burns* recognized that its decision "turn[ed] to a great extent on the precise facts involved here." 406 U.S., at 274, 92 S.Ct., at 1575. The same observation could have been made in *Wiley*, as indeed it could be made in this case. In our development of the federal common law under § 301, we must necessarily proceed cautiously, in the traditional case-by-case approach of the common law. Particularly in light of the difficulty of the successorship question, the myriad factual circumstances and legal contexts in which it can arise, and the absence of congressional guidance as to its resolution, emphasis on the facts of each case as it arises is especially appropriate. The Court was obviously well aware of this in *Wiley*, as its guarded, almost tentative statement of its holding amply demonstrates.

When the focus is placed on the facts of these cases, it becomes apparent that the decision below is an unwarranted extension of *Wiley* beyond any factual context it may have contemplated. Although it is true that both *Wiley* and this case involve § 301 suits to compel arbitration, the similarity ends there. *Wiley* involved a merger, as a result of which the initial employing entity completely disappeared. In contrast, this case involves only a sale of some assets, and the initial employers remain in existence as viable corporate entities, with substantial revenues from the lease of the motor lodge and restaurant to Howard Johnson. Although we have recognized that ordinarily there is no basis for distinguishing among mergers, consolidations, or purchases of assets in the analysis of successorship problems, see Golden State Bottling Co. v. NLRB, 414 U.S. 168, 182–183, n. 5, 94 S.Ct. 414, 424, 38 L.Ed.2d 388 (1973), we think these distinctions are relevant here for two reasons. First, the merger in *Wiley* was conducted "against a background of state law that embodied the general rule that in merger situations the surviving corporation is liable for the obligations of the disappearing corporation," *Burns*, 406 U.S., at 286, 92 S.Ct., at 1581, which suggests that holding Wiley bound to arbitrate under its predecessor's collective-bargaining agreement may have been fairly within the reasonable expectations of the parties. Second, the disappearance of the original employing entity in the *Wiley* merger meant that unless the union were afforded some remedy against Wiley, it would have no means to enforce the obligations voluntarily undertaken by the merged corporation, to the extent that those obligations vested prior to the merger or to the extent that its promises were intended to survive a change of ownership. Here, in contrast, because the Grissom corporations continue as viable entities with substantial retained assets, the Union does have a realistic remedy to enforce their contractual obligations. Indeed, the Grissoms have agreed to arbitrate the extent of their liability to the Union and their former employees; presumably this arbitration will explore the question whether the Grissoms breached

2. See The Supreme Court, 1971 Term, 86 Harv.L.Rev. 1, 255–256 (1972); Christensen, Successorships, Unit Changes, and the Bar- gaining Table, in Southwestern Leg.Found., 19th Institute on Labor Law, Labor Law Developments 1973, pp. 197, 205–206.

the successorship provisions of their collective-bargaining agreements, and what the remedy for this breach might be.[3]

Even more important, in *Wiley* the surviving corporation hired *all* of the employees of the disappearing corporation. Although, under *Burns,* the surviving corporation may have been entitled to make substantial changes in its operation of the enterprise, the plain fact is that it did not. As the arbitrator in *Wiley* subsequently stated:

> "Although the Wiley merger was effective on October 2, 1961, the former Interscience employees continued to perform the same work on the same products under the same management at the same work place as before the change in the corporate employer." Interscience Encyclopedia, Inc., 55 Lab. Arb. 210, 218 (1970).[4]

The claims which the union sought to compel Wiley to arbitrate were thus the claims of Wiley's employees as to the benefits they were entitled to receive in connection with their employment. It was on this basis that the Court in *Wiley* found that there was the "substantial continuity of identity in the business enterprise," 376 U.S., at 551, 84 S.Ct., at 915, which it held necessary before the successor employer could be compelled to arbitrate.

Here, however, Howard Johnson decided to select and hire its own independent work force to commence its operation of the restaurant and motor lodge.[5] It therefore hired only nine of the 53 former Grissom

3. The Union apparently did not explore another remedy which might have been available to it prior to the sale, i.e., moving to enjoin the sale to Howard Johnson on the ground that this was a breach by the Grissoms of the successorship clauses in the collective-bargaining agreements. See National Maritime Union v. Commerce Tankers Corp., 325 F.Supp. 360 (S.D.N.Y.1971), vacated, 457 F.2d 1127 (CA2 1972). The mere existence of the successorship clauses in the bargaining agreements between the Union and the Grissoms, however, cannot bind Howard Johnson either to the substantive terms of the agreements or to the arbitration clauses thereof, absent the continuity required by *Wiley,* when it is perfectly clear the Company refused to assume any obligations under the agreements.

4. Subsequently, the Interscience plant was closed and the former Interscience employees were integrated into Wiley's work force. The arbitrator, relying in part on the NLRB's decision in *Burns,* held that the provisions of the Interscience collective-bargaining agreement remained in effect for as long as Wiley continued to operate the former Interscience enterprise as a unit in substantially the same manner as prior to the merger, but that the integration of the former Interscience employees into Wiley's operations destroyed this continuity of identity and terminated the effectiveness of the bargaining agreement. 55 Lab.Arb., at 218–220.

5. It is important to emphasize that this is not a case where the successor corporation is the "alter ego" of the predecessor, where it is

"merely a disguised continuance of the old employer." Southport Petroleum Co. v. NLRB, 315 U.S. 100, 106, 62 S.Ct. 452, 456, 86 L.Ed. 718 (1942). Such cases involve a mere technical change in the structure or identity of the employing entity, frequently to avoid the effect of the labor laws, without any substantial change in its ownership or management. In these circumstances, the courts have had little difficulty holding that the successor is in reality the same employer and is subject to all the legal and contractual obligations of the predecessor. See Southport Petroleum Co. v. NLRB, supra; NLRB v. Herman Bros. Pet Supply, 325 F.2d 68 (CA6 1963); NLRB v. Ozark Hardwood Co., 282 F.2d 1 (CA8 1960); NLRB v. Lewis, 246 F.2d 886 (CA9 1957).

There is not the slightest suggestion in this case that the sale of the restaurant and motor lodge by the Grissoms to Howard Johnson was in any sense a paper transaction without meaningful impact on the ownership or operation of the enterprise. Howard Johnson had no ownership interest in the restaurant or motor lodge prior to this transaction. Although the Grissoms' operation of the enterprise as Howard Johnson's franchisee was subject to substantial restraints imposed by the franchise agreements on some aspects of the business, the franchise agreements imposed no restrictions on the Grissoms' hiring or labor relations policies. There is nothing in the record to indicate that Howard Johnson had had any previous dealings with the Union, or had participated in any way in negotiating or

employees and none of the Grissom supervisors. The primary purpose of the Union in seeking arbitration here with Howard Johnson is not to protect the rights of Howard Johnson's employees; rather, the Union primarily seeks arbitration on behalf of the former Grissom employees who were *not* hired by Howard Johnson. It is the Union's position that Howard Johnson was bound by the pre-existing collective-bargaining agreement to employ all of these former Grisson employees, except those who could be dismissed in accordance with the "just cause" provision or laid off in accordance with the seniority provision. It is manifest from the Union's efforts to obtain injunctive relief requiring the Company to hire all of these employees that this is the heart of the controversy here. Indeed, at oral argument, the Union conceded that it would be making the same argument here if Howard Johnson had not hired any of the former Grissom employees, and that what was most important to the Union was the prospect that the arbitrator might order the Company to hire all of these employees.

What the Union seeks here is completely at odds with the basic principles this Court elaborated in *Burns*. We found there that nothing in the federal labor laws "requires that an employer * * * who purchases the assets of a business be obligated to hire all of the employees of the predecessor though it is possible that such an obligation might be assumed by the employer." 406 U.S., at 280 n. 5, 92 S.Ct., at 1578. See also Golden State Bottling Co. v. NLRB, 414 U.S., at 184 n. 6, 94 S.Ct., at 425. *Burns* emphasized that "[a] potential employer may be willing to take over a moribund business only if he can make changes in corporate structure, composition of the labor force, * * * and nature of supervision." 406 U.S., at 287–288, 92 S.Ct., at 1582. * * *

Clearly, *Burns* establishes that Howard Johnson had the right not to hire any of the former Grissom employees, if it so desired.[8] The Union's effort to circumvent this holding by asserting its claims in a § 301 suit to compel arbitration rather than in an unfair labor practice context cannot be permitted.

We do not believe that *Wiley* requires a successor employer to arbitrate in the circumstances of this case.[9] The Court there held that arbitration

approving the collective-bargaining agreements.

8. See Crotona Service Corp., 200 N.L.R.B. 738 (1972). Of course, it is an unfair labor practice for an employer to discriminate in hiring or retention of employees on the basis of union membership or activity under § 8(a) (3) of the National Labor Relations Act, 29 U.S.C.A. § 158(a)(3). Thus, a new owner could not refuse to hire the employees of his predecessor solely because they were union members or to avoid having to recognize the union. See NLRB v. Burns International Security Services, 406 U.S. 272, 280–281, n. 5, 92 S.Ct. 1571, 1578–1579, 32 L.Ed.2d 61 (1972); K.B. & J. Young's Super Markets v. NLRB, 377 F.2d 463 (CA9), cert. denied, 389 U.S. 841, 88 S.Ct. 71, 19 L.Ed.2d 105 (1967); Tri State Maintenance Corp. v. NLRB, 132 U.S.App.D.C. 368, 408 F.2d 171 (1968). There is no suggestion in this case that Howard Johnson in any way discriminated in its hiring against the former Grissom employees because of their union membership, activity, or representation.

9. The Court of Appeals stated that "[t]he first question we must face is whether Howard Johnson is a successor employer," 482 F.2d, at 492, and, finding that it was, that the next question was whether a successor is required to arbitrate under the collective-bargaining agreement of its predecessor, id., at 494, which the court found was resolved by *Wiley*. We do not believe that this artificial division between these questions is a helpful or appropriate way to approach these problems. The question whether Howard Johnson is a "successor" is simply not meaningful in the abstract. Howard Johnson is of course a successor employer in the sense that it succeeded to operation of a restaurant and motor lodge formerly operated by the Grissoms. But the real question in each of these "successorship"

could not be compelled unless there was "substantial continuity of identity in the business enterprise" before and after a change of ownership, for otherwise the duty to arbitrate would be "something imposed from without, not reasonably to be found in the particular bargaining agreement and the acts of the parties involved." 376 U.S., at 551, 84 S.Ct., at 915. This continuity of identity in the business enterprise necessarily includes, we think, a substantial continuity in the identity of the work force across the change in ownership. The *Wiley* Court seemingly recognized this, as it found the requisite continuity present there in reliance on the "wholesale transfer" of Interscience employees to Wiley. Ibid. This view is reflected in the emphasis most of the lower courts have placed on whether the successor employer hires a majority of the predecessor's employees in determining the legal obligations of the successor in § 301 suits under *Wiley*.[10] This interpretation of *Wiley* is consistent also with the Court's concern with affording protection to those employees who are in fact retained in "[t]he transition from one corporate organization to another" from sudden changes in the terms and conditions of their employment, and with its belief that industrial strife would be avoided if these employees' claims were resolved by arbitration rather than by " 'the relative strength * * * of the contending forces.' " Id., at 549, 84 S.Ct., at 914 quoting United Steelworkers v. Warrior & Gulf Navigation Co., 363 U.S. 574, 580, 80 S.Ct. 1347, 1351, 4 L.Ed.2d 1409 (1960). At the same time, it recognizes that the employees of the terminating employer have no legal right to continued employment with the new employer, and avoids the difficulties inherent in the Union's position in this case. This holding is compelled, in our view, if the protection afforded employee interests in a change of ownership by *Wiley* is to be reconciled with the new employer's right to operate the enterprise with his own independent labor force.

Since there was plainly no substantial continuity of identity in the work force hired by Howard Johnson with that of the Grissoms, and no express or

cases is, on the particular facts, what are the legal obligations of the new employer to the employees of the former owner or their representative? The answer to this inquiry requires analysis of the interests of the new employer and the employees and of the policies of the labor laws in light of the facts of each case and the particular legal obligation which is at issue, whether it be the duty to recognize and bargain with the union, the duty to remedy unfair labor practices, the duty to arbitrate, etc. There is, and can be, no single definition of "successor" which is applicable in every legal context. A new employer, in other words, may be a successor for some purposes and not for others. See Golden State Bottling Co. v. NLRB, 414 U.S. 168, 181, 94 S.Ct. 414, 423, 38 L.Ed.2d 388 (1973); International Ass'n of Machinists v. NLRB, 134 U.S.App.D.C. 239, 244, 414 F.2d 1135, 1140 (1969) (Leventhal, J., concurring); Goldberg, The Labor Law Obligations of a Successor Employer, 63 Nw.U.L.Rev. 735 (1969); Comment, Contractual Successorship: The Impact of Burns, 40 U.Chi.L.Rev. 617, 619 n. 10 (1973).

Thus, our holding today is that Howard Johnson was not required to arbitrate with the Union representing the former Grissom employees in the circumstances of this case. We necessarily do not decide whether Howard Johnson is or is not a "successor employer" for any other purpose.

10. See Printing Specialties Union v. Pride Papers Aaronson Bros. Paper Corp., 445 F.2d 361, 363–364 (CA2 1971); Wackenhut Corp. v. Plant Guard Workers, 332 F.2d 954, 958 (CA9 1964); International Ass'n of Machinists v. NLRB, 134 U.S.App.D.C., at 244 n. 4, 414 F.2d at 1140 n. 4 (Leventhal, J., concurring); Boeing Co. v. International Ass'n of Machinists, 351 F.Supp. 813 (M.D.Fla.1972); Owens-Illinois, Inc. v. District 65, Retail, Wholesale & Department Store Union, 276 F.Supp. 740 (S.D.N.Y.1967); Local Joint Executive Board, Hotel & Restaurant Employees v. Joden, Inc., 262 F.Supp. 390 (D.C.Mass.1966). See also Comment, supra, n. 9, at 621.

implied assumption of the agreement to arbitrate, the courts below erred in compelling the Company to arbitrate the extent of its obligations to the former Grissom employees. Accordingly, the judgment of the Court of Appeals must be reversed.

Reversed.

MR. JUSTICE DOUGLAS, dissenting.

* * * I believe that the principles of successorship laid down in John Wiley & Sons v. Livingston, 376 U.S. 543, 84 S.Ct. 909, 11 L.Ed.2d 898, and NLRB v. Burns International Security Services, Inc., 406 U.S. 272, 92 S.Ct. 1571, 32 L.Ed.2d 61, require affirmance, and thus I dissent.

Wiley was also a § 301 suit, to compel arbitration. There the company had merged with Interscience, another and smaller publisher, 40 of whose employees were represented by the union. The union contended that the merger did not affect its right to represent these employees in negotiations with Wiley, and that Wiley was bound to recognize certain rights of these employees which had been guaranteed in the collective-bargaining agreement signed by Interscience. Wiley contended that the merger terminated the collective-bargaining agreement for all purposes and refused to bargain with the union. We held that the union could compel arbitration of this dispute under the arbitration provision of the collective-bargaining agreement even though Wiley had never signed the agreement. We pointed out that the duty to arbitrate will not in every case survive a change of ownership, as when "the lack of any substantial continuity of identity in the business enterprise before and after a change would make a duty to arbitrate something imposed from without, not reasonably to be found in the particular bargaining agreement and the acts of the parties involved." *Wiley,* supra, 376 U.S. 551, 84 S.Ct. 915. But that was not the case in *Wiley:* "[T]he impressive policy considerations favoring arbitration are not wholly overborne by the fact that Wiley did not sign the contract being construed. This case cannot readily be assimilated to the category of those in which there is no contract whatever, or none which is reasonably related to the party sought to be obligated." Id., at 550, 84 S.Ct. at 915.

It must follow *a fortiori* that it is also not the case here. The contract between the Grissoms and the Union explicitly provided that successors of the Grissoms would be bound, and certainly there can be no question that there was a substantial continuity—indeed identity—of the business operation under Howard Johnson, the successor employer. Under its franchise agreement Howard Johnson had substantial control over the Grissoms' operation of the business;[2] it was no stranger to the enterprise it took over. The business continued without interruption at the same location, offering the same products and services to the same public, under the same name and in the same manner, with almost the same number of employees. The only change was Howard Johnson's replacement of the Union members with new

---

2. The motel franchise agreement provided, for example, that Howard Johnson would determine and approve standards of construction, operation, and service, and would have the right at any time to enter the premises for that purpose; that prior approval would be required for equipment and supplies bearing the name "Howard Johnson"; that Howard Johnson would have the first option to purchase if the business were to be sold, and that in any event Howard Johnson must approve any successor. See the District Court opinion, 81 L.R.R.M. 2329, 2330, and App. 50a et seq.

personnel, but as the court below pointed out, petitioner's reliance upon that fact is sheer "bootstrap":

> "[Howard Johnson] argues that it need not arbitrate the refusal to hire Grissoms' employees because it is not a successor. It is not a successor, because it did not hire a majority of Grissoms' employees." 482 F.2d 489, 493.

As we said in *Wiley,* "[i]t would derogate from 'the federal policy of settling labor disputes by arbitration,' * * * if a change in the corporate structure or ownership of a business enterprise had the automatic consequence of removing a duty to arbitrate previously established * * *." 376 U.S., at 549, 84 S.Ct., at 914.

NLRB v. Burns International Security Services, supra, does not require any different result. * * * In distinguishing *Wiley,* we pointed out in *Burns* that unlike *Wiley,* it did not involve a § 301 suit to compel arbitration, and thus was without the support of the national policy favoring arbitration. Moreover, in *Burns* "there was no merger or sale of assets, and there were no dealings whatsoever between Wackenhut and Burns. On the contrary, they were competitors for the same work, each bidding for the service contract at Lockheed. Burns purchased nothing from Wackenhut and became liable for none of its financial obligations." Ibid.

All of the factors distinguishing *Burns* and *Wiley* call here for affirmance of the order to arbitrate. This is a § 301 suit, and Howard Johnson did purchase the assets from the Grissoms. As a matter of federal labor law, when Howard Johnson took over the operation that had been conducted by its franchisee, it seems clear that it also took over the duty to arbitrate under the collective-bargaining agreements which expressly bound the Grissoms' successors. Any other result makes nonsense of the principles laid down in *Wiley.* The majority, by making the number of prior employees retained by the successor the sole determinative factor, accepts petitioner's bootstrap argument. The effect is to allow any new employer to determine for himself whether he will be bound, by the simple expedient of arranging for the termination of all of the prior employer's personnel. I cannot accept such a rule especially when, as here, all of the other factors point so compellingly to the conclusion that petitioner is a successor employer who should be bound by the arbitration agreement.

Note

1. Based upon Wiley, Burns, and Howard Johnson, is it fair to say that the "successorship" problem is primarily one of doing justice to the employees of the predecessor employer who are continued on in the employ of the successor employer to an extent consistent with the conditions necessary to make business transfers economically feasible? If that is, indeed, the teaching of these cases, do you agree with it?

What employees were benefited or sought to be benefited by invocation of the successorship "doctrine," and in what ways, in Wiley, in Burns, in Howard Johnson? To what extent would a change, either up or down (try both), in the number of predecessor employees hired by the successor affect the result in each of the three cases?

2. In Golden State Bottling Co. v. NLRB, 414 U.S. 168, 94 S.Ct. 414, 38 L.Ed.2d 388 (1973), a "bona fide" successor (not a successor for union-defeating purposes) was held liable for an unfair labor practice committed by the predecessor employer under the following circumstances: (1) the successor purchased the entire business of the predecessor and continued it without substantial change in operations or in the complement of employees; (2) the successor purchased the business with knowledge of an outstanding NLRB order directing the reinstatement with back pay of an employee of the predecessor who had been discharged in violation of Section 8(a)(3). The Court also affirmed the Board's order that the successor reinstate the employee and that the successor and predecessor "jointly or severally" pay him the earnings lost by reason of the wrongful discharge.

Does Golden State Bottling fit into the rationale of Wiley, Burns, and Howard Johnson advanced in Note 1 above?

NATIONAL LABOR RELATIONS BOARD v. C & C PLYWOOD CORP.

Supreme Court of the United States, 1967.
385 U.S. 421, 87 S.Ct. 559, 17 L.Ed.2d 486.

MR. JUSTICE STEWART delivered the opinion of the Court.

The respondent employer was brought before the National Labor Relations Board to answer a complaint that its inauguration of a premium pay plan during the term of a collective agreement, without prior consultation with the union representing its employees, violated the duties imposed by § 8(a)(5) and (1) of the National Labor Relations Act. The Board issued a cease-and-desist order, rejecting the claim that the respondent's action was authorized by the collective agreement.[2] The Court of Appeals for the Ninth Circuit refused, however, to enforce the Board's order. It reasoned that a provision in the agreement between the union and the employer, which "arguably" allowed the employer to institute the premium pay plan, divested the Board of jurisdiction to entertain the union's unfair labor practice charge. 351 F.2d 224. We granted certiorari to consider a substantial question of federal labor law. * * *

In August 1962, the Plywood, Lumber, and Saw Mill Workers Local No. 2405 was certified as the bargaining representative of the respondent's production and maintenance employees. The agreement which resulted from collective bargaining contained the following provision:

"Article XVII

"WAGES

"A. A classified wage scale has been agreed upon by the Employer and Union, and has been signed by the parties and thereby made a part of the written agreement. The Employer reserves the right to pay a premium rate over and above the contractual classified wage rate to reward any particular employee for some special fitness, skill, aptitude or the like. The payment of such a premium rate shall not be consid-

2. The NLRB's order directed respondent to bargain with the union upon the latter's request and similarly to rescind any payment plan which it had unilaterally instituted.

ered a permanent increase in the rate of that position and may, at sole option of the Employer, be reduced to the contractual rate * * *."

The agreement also stipulated that wages should be "closed" during the period it was effective and that neither party should be obligated to bargain collectively with respect to any matter not specifically referred to in the contract. Grievance machinery was established, but no ultimate arbitration of grievances or other disputes was provided.

Less than three weeks after this agreement was signed, the respondent posted a notice that all members of the "glue spreader" crews would be paid $2.50 per hour if their crews met specified bi-weekly (and later weekly) production standards, although under the "classified wage scale" referred to in the above quoted Art. XVII of the agreement, the members of these crews were to be paid hourly wages ranging from $2.15 to $2.29, depending upon their function within the crew. When the union learned of this premium pay plan through one of its members, it immediately asked for a conference with the respondent. During the meetings between the parties which followed this request, the employer indicated a willingness to discuss the terms of the plan, but refused to rescind it pending those discussions.

It was this refusal which prompted the union to charge the respondent with an unfair labor practice in violation of §§ 8(a)(5) and (1). The trial examiner found that the respondent had instituted the premium pay program in good-faith reliance upon the right reserved to it in the collective agreement. He, therefore, dismissed the complaint. The Board reversed. Giving consideration to the history of negotiations between the parties,[6] as well as the express provisions of the collective agreement, the Board ruled the union had not ceded power to the employer unilaterally to change the wage system as it had. For while the agreement specified different hourly pay for different members of the glue spreader crews and allowed for merit increases for "particular employee[s]," the employer had placed all the members of these crews on the same wage scale and had made it a function of the production output of the crew as a whole.

In refusing to enforce the Board's order, the Court of Appeals did not decide that the premium pay provision of the labor agreement had been misinterpreted by the Board. Instead, it held the Board did not have jurisdiction to find the respondent had violated § 8(a) of the Labor Act, because the "existence * * * of an unfair labor practice [did] not turn entirely upon the provisions of the Act, but arguably upon a good-faith dispute as to the correct meaning of the provisions of the collective-bargaining agreement * * *." 351 F.2d at 228.

The respondent does not question the proposition that an employer may not unilaterally institute merit increases during the term of a collective agreement unless some provision of the contract authorizes him to do so.

6. The trial examiner found that "quite some time prior" to the execution of the contract, the respondent's general manager had proposed an "incentive bonus system" within the department where the glue spreader crews worked. The union's representative, however, declared that the union would not agree to such a plan. Sometime later in the negotiations, the respondent again made reference to the fact that it was "giving thought" to incentive pay, but the trial examiner was unable to conclude that this reference was related to the premium pay provision that eventually appeared in the contract.

* * *[7] The argument is, rather, that since the contract contained a provision which *might* have allowed the respondent to institute the wage plan in question, the Board was powerless to determine whether that provision *did* authorize the respondent's action, because the question was one for a state or federal court under § 301 of the Act.

In evaluating this contention, it is important first to point out that the collective bargaining agreement contained no arbitration clause. The contract did provide grievance procedures, but the end result of those procedures, if differences between the parties remained unresolved was economic warfare, not "the therapy of arbitration." Carey v. Westinghouse Electric Corp., 375 U.S. 261, 272, 84 S.Ct. 401, 409, 11 L.Ed.2d 320. Thus, the Board's action in this case was in no way inconsistent with its previous recognition of arbitration as "an instrument of national labor policy for composing contractual differences." International Harvester Co., 138 N.L.R.B. 923, 926 (1962), aff'd sub nom. Ramsey v. National Labor Relations Board, 327 F.2d 784 (C.A.7th Cir.), cert. denied, 377 U.S. 1003, 84 S.Ct. 1938, 12 L.Ed.2d 1052.

The respondent's argument rests primarily upon the legislative history of the 1947 amendments to the National Labor Relations Act. It is said that the rejection by Congress of a bill which would have given the Board unfair labor practice jurisdiction over all breaches of collective bargaining agreements shows that the Board is without power to decide any case involving the interpretation of a labor contract. We do not draw that inference from this legislative history.

When Congress determined that the Board should not have general jurisdiction over all alleged violations of collective bargaining agreements[11] and that such matters should be placed within the jurisdiction of the courts, it was acting upon a principle which this Court had already recognized:

> "The Railway Labor Act, like the National Labor Relations Act, does not undertake governmental regulation of wages, hours, or working conditions. Instead it seeks to provide a means by which agreement may be reached with respect to them." Terminal Railroad Ass'n v. Brotherhood of Railroad Trainmen, 318 U.S. 1, 6, 63 S.Ct. 420, 423, 87 L.Ed. 571.

To have conferred upon the National Labor Relations Board generalized power to determine the rights of parties under all collective agreements would have been a step toward governmental regulation of the terms of those agreements. We view Congress' decision not to give the Board that broad power as a refusal to take this step.

But in this case the Board has not construed a labor agreement to determine the extent of the contractual rights which were given the union

---

7. For illustrations of the limited discretion which the Labor Act allows employers concerning the wages of employees represented by certified unions, see National Labor Relations Board v. Katz, 369 U.S. 736, 82 S.Ct. 1107, 8 L.Ed.2d 230; National Labor Relations Board v. Crompton-Highland Mills, Inc., 337 U.S. 217, 69 S.Ct. 960, 93 L.Ed. 1320.

11. An earlier version of the Senate bill contained the following provision:

"Sec. 8. (a) It shall be an unfair labor practice for an employer—

* * * * *

"(6) to violate the terms of a collective-bargaining agreement or the terms of an agreement to submit a labor dispute to arbitration * * *."

Section 8(b)(5) of the same bill imposed a similar limitation upon labor organizations. S. 1126, 80th Cong., 1st Sess., 1 Legis.History of LMRA 109–111, 114. Neither of these provisions was in the bill enacted into law.

by the employer. It has not imposed its own view of what the terms and conditions of the labor agreement should be. It has done no more than merely enforce a statutory right which Congress considered necessary to allow labor and management to get on with the process of reaching fair terms and conditions of employment—"to provide a means by which agreement may be reached." The Board's interpretation went only so far as was necessary to determine that the union did not agree to give up these statutory safeguards. Thus, the Board, in necessarily construing a labor agreement to decide this unfair labor practice case, has not exceeded the jurisdiction laid out for it by Congress.

This conclusion is reinforced by previous judicial recognition that a contractual defense does not divest the Labor Board of jurisdiction. For example, in Mastro Plastics Corp. v. National Labor Relations Board, 350 U.S. 270, 76 S.Ct. 349, 100 L.Ed. 309, the legality of an employer's refusal to reinstate strikers was based upon the Board's construction of a "no strike" clause in the labor agreement, which the employer contended allowed it to refuse to take back workers who had walked out in protest over its unfair labor practice. The strikers applied to the Board for reinstatement and back pay. In giving the requested relief, the Board was forced to construe the scope of the "no strike" clause. This Court, in affirming, stressed that the whole case turned "upon the proper interpretation of the particular contract * * *." 350 U.S., at 279, 76 S.Ct., at 356. Thus, *Mastro Plastics* stands squarely against the respondent's theory as to the Board's lack of power in the present case.

If the Board in a case like this had no jurisdiction to consider a collective agreement prior to an authoritative construction by the courts, labor organizations would face inordinate delays in obtaining vindication of their statutory rights. Where, as here, the parties have not provided for arbitration, the union would have to institute a court action to determine the applicability of the premium pay provision of the collective bargaining agreement.[15] If it succeeded in court, the union would then have to go back to the Labor Board to begin an unfair labor practice proceeding. It is not unlikely that this would add years to the already lengthy period required to gain relief from the Board.[16] Congress cannot have intended to place such obstacles in the way of the Board's effective enforcement of statutory duties. For in the labor field, as in few others, time is crucially important in obtaining relief.

The legislative history of the Labor Act, the precedents interpreting it, and the interest of its efficient administration thus all lead to the conclusion that the Board had jurisdiction to deal with the unfair labor practice charge in this case. We hold that the Court of Appeals was in error in deciding to the contrary.

The remaining question, not reached by the Court of Appeals, is whether the Board was wrong in concluding that the contested provision in the

15. The precise nature of the union's case in court is not readily apparent. If damages for breach of contract were sought, the union would have difficulty in establishing the amount of injury caused by respondent's action. For the real injury in this case is to the union's status as bargaining representative, and it would be difficult to translate such damage into dollars and cents. * * *

16. The instant charge, for example, was filed July 31, 1963.

collective agreement gave the respondent no unilateral right to institute its premium pay plan. In reaching this conclusion, the Board relied upon its experience with labor relations and the Act's clear emphasis upon the protection of free collective bargaining. We cannot disapprove of the Board's approach. For the law of labor agreements cannot be based upon abstract definitions unrelated to the context in which the parties bargained and the basic regulatory scheme underlying that context. See Cox, The Legal Nature of Collective Bargaining Agreements, 57 Mich.L.Rev. 1 (1958). Nor can we say that the Board was wrong in holding that the union had not forgone its statutory right to bargain about the pay plan inaugurated by the respondent. For the disputed contract provision referred to increases for "particular employee[s]," not groups of workers. And there was nothing in it to suggest that the carefully worked out wage differentials for various members of the glue spreader crew could be invalidated by the respondent's decision to pay all members of the crew the same wage. * * *

Reversed and remanded.

Note

1. Would the decision have been the same if the collective bargaining agreement had contained an arbitration provision covering the matter at issue? In such a case, should the Board defer decision on the 8(a)(5) complaint pending disposition by arbitration of the contract-interpretation question? (This is the subject of the Collyer case, reported infra p. 725.)

2. Putting aside the effect of the presence or absence of an arbitration provision, what is the basis for concern over Board exercise of jurisdiction to interpret collective bargaining agreements? Could the Board not in short order develop an expertise in contract interpretation comparable to that of courts and arbitrators? Is this really the problem?

If there is a sound policy reason for denying to the Board, as Congress did, the authority to treat mere breaches of contract as unfair labor practices, does not the decision in C & C Plywood fly in the face of that policy?

NATIONAL LABOR RELATIONS BOARD v. ACME INDUSTRIAL CO.

Supreme Court of the United States, 1967.
385 U.S. 432, 87 S.Ct. 565, 17 L.Ed.2d 495.

MR. JUSTICE STEWART delivered the opinion of the Court.

In NLRB v. C & C Plywood Corp., 385 U.S. 421, 87 S.Ct. 559, 17 L.Ed.2d 486, decided today, we dealt with one aspect of an employer's duty to bargain during the term of a collective bargaining agreement. In this case we deal with another—involving the obligation to furnish information that allows a union to decide whether to process a grievance.

In April 1963, at the conclusion of a strike, the respondent entered into a collective bargaining agreement with the union which was the certified representative of its employees. The agreement contained two sections relevant to this case. Article I, § 3, provided, "It is the Company's general policy not to subcontract work which is normally performed by employees in the bargaining unit where this will cause the layoff of employees or prevent the recall of employees who would normally perform this work ∗ ∗ ∗." In Art. VI, § 10, the respondent agreed that "[i]n the event the equipment of the plant ∗ ∗ ∗ is hereafter moved to another location of the Company, employees working in the plant ∗ ∗ ∗ who are subject to reduction in classification or layoff as a result thereof may transfer to the new location with full rights and seniority, unless there is then in existence at the new location a collective bargaining agreement covering ∗ ∗ ∗ employees at such location." A grievance procedure culminating in compulsory and binding arbitration was also incorporated into the collective agreement.

The present controversy began in January 1964, when the union discovered that certain machinery was being removed from the respondent's plant. When asked by union representatives about this movement, the respondent's foremen replied that there had been no violation of the collective agreement and that the company, therefore, was not obliged to answer any questions regarding the machinery. After this rebuff, the union filed 11 grievances charging the respondent with violations of the above quoted clauses of the collective agreement. The president of the union then wrote a letter to the respondent, requesting "the following information at the earliest possible date:

"1. The approximate dates when each piece of equipment was moved out of the plant.

"2. The place to which each piece of equipment was moved and whether such place is a facility which is operated or controlled by the Company.

"3. The number of machines or equipment that was moved out of the plant.

"4. What was the reason or purpose of moving the equipment out of the plant.

"5. Is this equipment used for production elsewhere."

The company replied by letter that it had no duty to furnish this information since no layoffs or reductions in job classification had occurred within five days (the time limitation set by the contract for filing grievances) prior to the union's formal request for information.

This refusal prompted the union to file unfair labor practice charges with the National Labor Relations Board. A complaint was issued, and the Board, overruling its trial examiner, held the respondent had violated § 8(a) (5) of the Act by refusing to bargain in good faith. Accordingly, it issued a cease-and-desist order. The Board found that the information requested was "necessary in order to enable the Union to evaluate intelligently the grievances filed" and pointed out that the agreement contained no "clause by which the Union waives its statutory right to such information."

The Court of Appeals for the Seventh Circuit refused to enforce the Board's order. 351 F.2d 258. It did not question the relevance of the information nor the finding that the union had not expressly waived its right to the information. The court ruled, however, that the existence of a provision for binding arbitration of differences concerning the meaning and application of the agreement foreclosed the Board from exercising its statutory power. The court cited United Steelworkers v. Warrior & Gulf Navig.

Co., 363 U.S. 574, 80 S.Ct. 1347, 4 L.Ed.2d 1409, and United Steelworkers v. American Mfg. Co., 363 U.S. 564, 80 S.Ct. 1343, 4 L.Ed.2d 1403, as articulating a national labor policy favoring arbitration and requiring the Board's deference to an arbitrator when construction and application of a labor agreement are in issue. We granted certiorari to consider the substantial question of federal labor law thus presented. * * *

There can be no question of the general obligation of an employer to provide information that is needed by the bargaining representative for the proper performance of its duties. National Labor Relations Board v. Truitt Mfg. Co., 351 U.S. 149, 76 S.Ct. 753, 100 L.Ed. 1027. Similarly, the duty to bargain unquestionably extends beyond the period of contract negotiations and applies to labor-management relations during the term of an agreement. National Labor Relations Board v. C & C Plywood Corp., 385 U.S. 421, 87 S.Ct. 559, 17 L.Ed.2d 486; National Labor Relations Board v. F.W. Woolworth Co., 352 U.S. 938, 77 S.Ct. 261, 1 L.Ed.2d 235. The only real issue in this case, therefore, is whether the Board must await an arbitrator's determination of the relevancy of the requested information before it can enforce the union's statutory rights under § 8(a)(5).

The two cases upon which the court below relied, and the third of the Steelworkers trilogy, United Steelworkers of America v. Enterprise Wheel & Car Corp., 363 U.S. 593, 80 S.Ct. 1358, 4 L.Ed.2d 1424, do not throw much light on the problem. For those cases dealt with the relationship of courts to arbitrators when an arbitration award is under review or when the employer's agreement to arbitrate is in question. The weighing of the arbitrator's greater institutional competency, which was so vital to those decisions, must be evaluated in that context. * * * The relationship of the Board to the arbitration process is of a quite different order. See Cary v. Westinghouse Corp., 375 U.S. 261, 269–272, 84 S.Ct. 401, 407–409, 11 L.Ed.2d 320. Moreover, in assessing the Board's power to deal with unfair labor practices, provisions of the Labor Act which do not apply to the power of the courts under § 301, must be considered. [The Court cited and quoted from Sections 8(a)(5), 8(d), and, most significantly, 10(a), the latter providing that the Board's power to prevent "any unfair labor practice"] "shall not be affected by any other means of adjustment or prevention that has been or may be established by agreement, law, or otherwise * * *." Thus, to view the *Steelworkers* decisions as automatically requiring the Board in this case to defer to the primary determination of an arbitrator is to overlook important distinctions between those cases and this one.

But even if the policy of the *Steelworkers* Cases were thought to apply with the same vigor to the Board as to the courts, that policy would not require the Board to abstain here. For when it ordered the employer to furnish the requested information to the union, the Board was not making a binding construction of the labor contract. It was only acting upon the probability that the desired information was relevant, and that it would be of use to the union in carrying out its statutory duties and responsibilities. This discovery-type standard decided nothing about the merits of the union's contractual claims. When the respondent furnishes the requested information, it may appear that no subcontracting or work transfer has occurred, and, accordingly, that the grievances filed are without merit. On the other hand, even if it appears that such activities have taken place, an arbitrator might uphold the respondent's contention that no breach of the agreement occurred because no employees were laid off or reduced in grade within five days prior to the filing of any grievance. Such conclusions would clearly not be precluded by the Board's threshold determination concerning the potential relevance of the requested information. Thus, the assertion of jurisdiction by the Board in this case in no way threatens the power which the parties have given the arbitrator to make binding interpretations of the labor agreement.[7]

Far from intruding upon the preserve of the arbitrator, the Board's action was in aid of the arbitral process. Arbitration can function properly only if the grievance procedures leading to it can sift out unmeritorious claims. For if all claims originally initiated as grievances had to be processed through to arbitration, the system would be woefully overburdened. Yet, that is precisely what the respondent's restrictive view would require. It would force the union to take a grievance all the way through to arbitration without providing the opportunity to evaluate the merits of the claim. The expense of arbitration might be placed upon the union only for it to learn that the machines had been relegated to the junk heap. Nothing in federal labor law requires such a result.   *   *   *

Reversed and remanded.

Note

1. By extension of the Acme rationale, should a refusal to arbitrate a particular grievance constitute a violation of the duty to bargain? Or would such an extension put the Board in the business of determining the threshold question of arbitrability, declared in the trilogy to be for the courts? The Board has held that a mere refusal to arbitrate is *not* a violation of the duty to bargain despite a contractual commitment to submit to arbitration. E.g., Sucesion Mario Mercado E. Hijos, 161 N.L.R.B. 696, 700 (1966); GAF Corp., 265 N.L.R.B. 1361, 1364–65 (1982).

2. Is the following effort to rationalize Acme and C & C Plywood persuasive: The common denominator running through these companion holdings is support of arbitration. In Acme, that support is obvious: the Board supplies a discovery service facilitating the arbitral process. In C & C Plywood, less obviously, the Board provides a substitute for arbitration, i.e., Board interpretation of the contract, thereby encouraging employers to agree to the incorporation of arbitration provisions in their collective bargaining agreements. If the employer wants to avoid the C & C Plywood fate, the way is readily available to him; in the meantime, the sluices are still carrying 301 water away from federal courthouse doors.

3. There are limits, however, to the duty of the employer to disclose requested information to the union, even in an arbitration proceeding. In Detroit Edison Co. v. NLRB, 440 U.S. 301, 99 S.Ct. 1123, 59 L.Ed.2d 333 (1979), the collective bargaining agreement provided that promotions were to be based on seniority "whenever the reasonable qualifications and abilities of the employ-

---

7. This case, therefore, differs from N.L.R.B. v. C & C Plywood Corp., 385 U.S. 421, 87 S.Ct. 559, 17 L.Ed.2d 486, where the Board's determination that the employer did not have a contractual right to institute a premium pay plan was a determination on the merits. See *C & C Plywood*, at 426 of 385 U.S., at 563 of 87 S.Ct. and n. 10.

ee[s] being considered are not significantly different." The employer utilized standardized tests, administered by professional psychologists in its employ, to measure ability. The union filed grievances on behalf of employees who failed the tests. During arbitration, the union demanded information relating to the testing program. The company provided copies of test validation studies and a report by an outside consultant on the entire testing program, but refused to provide the actual tests, the applicants' test papers, or (without their consent) their scores. At the outset of the hearing on the Section 8(a)(5) charge which the union then filed, the company offered to turn the disputed material over to an industrial psychologist (bound by professional ethics to preserve the confidentiality of the data) selected by the union. The Board, in an order enforced by the Court of Appeals, required the employer to give the disputed material to the union. The Supreme Court, disagreeing, upheld the employer's contention that such disclosure would undermine the future usability of the tests and would violate the privacy of the employees who took the tests. The Court said:

"A union's bare assertion that it needs information to process a grievance does not automatically oblige the employer to supply all the information in the manner requested. The duty to supply information under § 8(a)(5) turns upon 'the circumstances of the particular case,' NLRB v. Truitt Mfg. Co., 351 U.S. 149, 153, 76 S.Ct. 753, 756, 100 L.Ed. 1027, and much the same may be said for the type of disclosure that will satisfy that duty. * * * Throughout this proceeding, the reasonableness of the Company's concern for test secrecy has been essentially conceded. The finding by the Board that this concern did not outweigh the Union's interest in exploring the fairness of the Company's criteria for promotion did not carry with it any suggestion that the concern itself was not legitimate and substantial. Indeed, on this record—which has established the Company's freedom under the collective contract to use aptitude tests as a criterion for promotion, the empirical validity of the tests, and the relationship between secrecy and test validity—the strength of the Company's concern has been abundantly demonstrated. The Board has cited no principle of national labor policy to warrant a remedy that would unnecessarily disserve this interest, and we are unable to identify one.

* * *

"[Regarding] the dispute over Union access to the actual scores received by named employees * * * the Company argues that even if the scores were relevant to the Union's grievance (which it vigorously disputes), the Union's need for the information was not sufficiently weighty to require breach of the promise of confidentiality to the examinees, breach of its industrial psychologists' code of professional ethics, and potential embarrassment and harassment of at least some of the examinees. The Board responds that this information does satisfy the appropriate standard of 'relevance,' * * * and that the Company having 'unilaterally' chosen to make a promise of confidentiality to the examinees, cannot rely on that promise to defend against a request for relevant information. The professional obligations of the Company's psychologists, it argues, must give way to paramount federal law. * * *

"We may accept for the sake of this discussion the finding that the employee scores were of potential relevance to the Union's grievance, as well as the position of the Board that the federal statutory duty to disclose relevant information cannot be defeated by the ethical standards of a private group. * * * Nevertheless we agree with the Company that its willingness to disclose these scores only upon receipt of consents from the examinees satisfied its statutory obligations under § 8(a)(5).

"The Board's position appears to rest on the proposition that union interests in arguably relevant information must always predominate over all other interests, however legitimate. But such an absolute rule has never been established, and we decline to adopt such a rule here. There are situations in which an employer's conditional offer to disclose [is] warranted." 440 U.S. at 314, 99 S.Ct. at 1131.

THE DUTY TO BARGAIN DURING THE LIFE OF THE COLLECTIVE AGREEMENT

Three important and interlocking questions arise with regard to the duty to bargain during the life of a collective agreement:

(1) What is the duty to bargain with regard to matters within the scope of mandatory bargaining but already "contained in" the contract?

(2) What is the duty to bargain with regard to matters within the scope of mandatory bargaining but *not* "contained in" the contract?

(3) Is adherence to the grievance and arbitration provisions of a contract a discharge of the duty, if any, to bargain with regard to matters *arguably* "contained in" the contract?

The first two questions were answered as follows in the leading case of NLRB v. JACOBS MFG. CO., 196 F.2d 680, 683–84 (2d Cir.1952):

"Before the National Labor Relations Act was amended by the Taft-Hartley Act an employer was under a duty, upon request, to bargain with the representatives of his employees as to terms and conditions of employment whether or not an existing collective bargaining agreement bound the parties as to the subject matter to be discussed. See N.L.R.B. v. Sands Mfg. Co., 306 U.S. 332, 342, 59 S.Ct. 508, 83 L.Ed. 682. However, § 8(d) of the amended Act ＊ ＊ ＊ narrowed this requirement by providing that the duty to bargain collectively ' ＊ ＊ ＊ shall not be construed as requiring either party to discuss or agree to any modification of the terms and conditions *contained in* a contract for a fixed period, if such modification is to become effective before such terms and conditions can be reopened under the provisions of the contract ＊ ＊ ＊.' The respondent's position is that, except as to subjects expressly reserved for further negotiations in a reopening clause, any fixed period contract creates a static period in the entire industrial relationship between the employer and his employees, for the term of the contract, even as to aspects of that relationship which were not covered by that contract or even discussed in the negotiations leading up to it.

"We, however, agree with the Board that § 8(d) cannot fairly be given such a broad effect. The purpose of this provision is, apparently, to give stability to agreements governing industrial relations. But, the exception thus created necessarily conflicts with the general purpose of the Act, which is to require employers to bargain as to employee demands whenever made to the end that industrial disputes may be resolved peacefully without resort to drastic measures likely to have an injurious effect upon commerce, and the general purpose should be given effect to the extent there is no contrary provision. Since the language chosen to describe this exception is precise and explicit, 'terms and conditions contained in a contract for a fixed period,' we do not think it relieves an employer of the duty to bargain as to subjects which were neither discussed nor embodied in any of the terms and conditions of the contract." (Emphasis supplied.)

The Board itself, in the Jacobs case (94 N.L.R.B. 1214 (1951)), was interestingly, instructively, and sharply divided on the meaning to be given to the "contained in" clause of Section 8(d). One of the five members took the position of the respondent employer, summarized in the foregoing excerpt—that everything is "contained in" the contract, and therefore no longer subject to bargaining during its term, except matters *expressly excluded,* as, for example, in a "reopening" clause. Two other Board members took the opposite position—that nothing is "contained in" the contract except those matters *expressly included.* For reasons not necessary to recapitulate, it fell to the Chairman of the Board, Paul Herzog, to produce a "swing" position—that the pivotal question is: What was the *total* "bargain" struck by the parties in the negotiation and execution of the contract, including trade-offs (demands withdrawn because of other concessions) agreed upon but not incorporated in the written instrument?

The hazards in the Herzog position became apparent in cases such as BEACON PIECE DYEING AND FINISHING CO., 121 N.L.R.B. 953 (1958), in which the union had, during negotiations, made a demand for freezing a workload ceiling into the contract, then later abandoned this demand in return for employer concessions elsewhere. The Trial Examiner found that the union had, as a consequence, "bargained away" or "waived" its right to bargain on that matter, so that a unilateral increase in the workload by the employer during the term of the contract did not violate Section 8(a)(5). The Board, by a divided vote, rejected the Trial Examiner's recommended decision, stating:

"In our opinion, the basic fallacy in our dissenting colleague's position is that he has lost sight of the crucial fact that more often than not, as here, an employer will resist inclusion of a certain provision in a contract simply because he is opposed to the provision *on its merits,* and not because he is seeking the right to act unilaterally on the subject as a matter of 'management prerogative'; and the union, as here, also with no thought in mind that a possible relinquishment of its statutory bargaining rights on the subject are involved, will trade off its demands on the subject in return for concessions on other demands as a part of the normal and everyday collective-bargaining process. Is our dissenting colleague prepared to say that the Board should find a 'waiver' of statutory bargaining rights in this common 'give and take' bargaining situation? To read into such an essential and basic part of the collective-bargaining process, as our dissenting colleague would do, an *implied* 'management prerogative' position by the employer, an *implied* agreement thereon by the union, and a resulting *implied* waiver of the union's statutory bargaining rights on the subject, would have the following results: (1) It would be *contra* to the Board's established test for waiver of a collective-bargaining right * * * that such a waiver 'will not readily be inferred'; (2) without meeting that test, it would not only deprive the union of a statutory right it never intended to relinquish, but would give the employer a right of unilateral action on the subject which even he never intended to acquire; (3) it would encourage employers to firmly resist inclusion in contracts of as many subjects as possible, with a view to such resistance giving them a right of unilateral action thereafter on all subjects excluded from the contract, thereby impeding the collective-bargaining process and creating an atmosphere which inevitably would lead to more strikes; and (4) it would discourage unions from presenting *any* subject in negotiations, for a simple refusal by the employer to agree to the demand on the subject would leave the union in the unhappy dilemma of either giving up the demand and thereby losing its bargaining rights on the subject, or striking in support of the demand—this too would seriously impede the collective-bargaining process and lead to more strikes." 121 N.L. R.B. at 960.

The waiver problem is further explored after the next case. The third question posed at the outset of this Note, namely, the effect of the presence of contractual grievance-arbitration procedures upon the statutory duty to bargain, is the subject of that case. As to a matter arguably "contained in" the contract, does an employer satisfy his statutory duty to bargain by honoring the grievance and arbitration provisions in the collective agreement, without more? Suppose the following: *Case One*—the arbitrator holds that the matter *is* "contained in" the contract; *Case Two*—the arbitrator holds that the matter is *not* "contained in" the contract.

COLLYER INSULATED WIRE CO.

National Labor Relations Board, 1971.
192 N.L.R.B. 837.

DECISION AND ORDER

*   *   *

The complaint alleges and the General Counsel contends that Respondent violated Section 8(a)(5) and (1) of the National Labor Relations Act, as amended, by making assertedly unilateral changes in certain wages and working conditions. Respondent contends that its authority to make those changes was sanctioned by the collective-bargaining contract between the parties and their course of dealing under that contract. Respondent further contends that any of its actions in excess of contractual authorization should properly have been remedied by grievance and arbitration proceeding as provided in the contract. We agree with Respondent's contention that this dispute is essentially a dispute over the terms and meaning of the contract between the Union and the Respondent. For that reason, we find merit in Respondent's exceptions [to the Trial Examiner's Decision] that the dispute should have been resolved pursuant to the contract and we shall dismiss the complaint.

I. The Alleged Unilateral Changes

Respondent manufactures unsulated electrical wiring at its plant in Lincoln, Rhode Island. The Union has represented Respondent's production and maintenance employees under successive contracts since 1937. The contract in effect when this dispute arose resulted from lengthy negotiations commencing in December 1968 and concluding with the execution of the contract of September 16, 1969. The contract was made effective from April 1, 1969, until July 2, 1971.

Respondent's production employees have historically been compensated on an incentive basis. The contract provides for a job evaluation plan and for the adjustment of rates, subject to the grievance procedure, during the term of the contract. Throughout the bargaining relationship, Respondent has routinely made adjustments in incentive rates to accommodate new or changed production methods. The contract establishes nonincentive rates for skilled maintenance tradesmen but provides for changes in those rates, also, pursuant to the job evaluation plan, upon changes in or additions to the duties of the classifications. The central issue here is whether these contract provisions permitted certain midcontract wage rate changes which Respondent made in November 1969.

A. The Rate Increase for Skilled Maintenance Tradesmen

Since early 1968, Respondent's wage rates for skilled tradesmen have not been sufficiently high to attract and retain the numbers of skilled maintenance mechanics and electricians required for the efficient operation of the plant. The record clearly establishes, and the Trial Examiner found, that other employers in the same region paid "substantially higher rates than those paid by Respondent." In consequence, the number of skilled maintenance workers had declined from about 40 in January 1968 to about 30 in mid-1969, and Respondent had been unable to attract employees to fill the resulting vacancies.

During negotiations, Respondent several times proposed wage raises for maintenance employees over and above those being negotiated for the production and maintenance unit generally. The Union rejected those proposals and the contract did not include any provision for such raises. It is clear, nevertheless, that the matter of the "skill factor" increase was left open, in *some* measure, for further negotiations after the execution of the agreement. The parties sharply dispute, however, the extent to which the matter remained open and the conditions which were to surround further discussions. The Union asserts, and the Trial Examiner found, that the Union was willing, and made known its willingness, to negotiate further wage adjustments only on a plantwide basis, consistent with the job evaluation system. Respondent insists that it understood the Union's position to be that wage increases for maintenance employees only might still be agreed to by the Union after the signing of the contract, if such increases could be justified under the job evaluation system.

At monthly meetings following conclusion of the contract negotiations, Respondent and the Union continued to discuss the Respondent's desire to raise the rates for maintenance employees. Finally, on November 12, 1969, Respondent informed the Union that 5 days thence, on November 17, Respondent would institute an upward adjustment of 20 cents per hour. The Union protested and restated its desire for a reevaluation of all jobs in the plant. Respondent's representative agreed to consider such an evaluation on a plantwide basis, upon union agreement to the increase for the skilled tradesmen. The Trial Examiner found that the Union did not agree. The rate increase became effective November 17, 1969. * * *

II. Relevant Contract Provisions

The contract now in effect between the parties makes provision for adjustment by Respondent in the wages of its employees during the contract term. Those provisions appear to contemplate changes in rates in both incentive and nonincentive jobs. * * *

* * * The Union, if dissatisfied, may then challenge the propriety of the rate by invoking the grievance procedure which culminates in arbitration.

[T]he breadth of the arbitration provision makes clear that the parties intended to make the grievance and arbitration machinery the exclusive forum for resolving contract disputes. By article IV of the contract the parties agree that the grievance machinery "shall be adopted for any complaint or dispute * * * which may arise between any employee or group of employees and the Corporation. * * *" That intent is further evidenced by the no-strike, no-lockout provision, article XI, which declares, in part: "All questions, disputes or controversies under this Agreement shall be settled and determined solely and exclusively by the conciliation and arbitration procedures provided in this Agreement. * * *" A grievance is defined as any controversy between an employee and his supervisor or any controversy between the Union and the Respondent involving "the interpretation, application or violation of any provision of this agreement or supplement thereto." The arbitration clause, article V, provides that "any grievance" may be submitted to an impartial arbitrator for decision and that the decision of the arbitrator "shall be final and binding upon the parties" if not contrary to law.

III. The Trial Examiner's Decision

The Decision of the Trial Examiner reviews in careful detail the Respondent's actions which gave rise to this proceeding. He finds that the subject of the skill factor increase for maintenance tradesmen was discussed at September and October meetings and that Respondent's decision to grant such an increase was announced on November 12. The Trial Examiner found that despite these discussions, the Union did not accede to the proposed change. He further found that the contract did not authorize Respondent to act unilaterally in the matter and that by so acting Respondent had sought to escape from the basic wage framework established in the contract. This, the Trial Examiner concluded, had been in violation of Section 8(a)(5). * * *

IV. Discussion

We find merit in Respondent's exceptions that because this dispute in its entirety arises from the contract between the parties, and from the parties' relationship under the contract, it ought to be resolved in the manner which that contract prescribes. We conclude that the Board is vested with authority to withhold its processes in this case, and that the contract here made available a quick and fair means for the resolution of this dispute including, if appropriate, a fully effective remedy for any breach of contract which occurred. We conclude, in sum, that our obligation to advance the purposes of the Act is best discharged by the dismissal of this complaint.

In our view, disputes such as these can better be resolved by arbitrators with special skill and experience in deciding matters arising under established bargaining relationships than by the application by this Board of a particular provision of our statute. * * * The determination of these issues, we think, is best left to discussions in the grievance procedure by the parties who negotiated the applicable provisions or, if such discussions do not resolve them, then to an arbitrator chosen under the agreement and authorized by it to resolve such issues.

The Board's authority, in its discretion, to defer to the arbitration process has never been questioned by the courts of appeals,[2] or by the Supreme Court. Although Section 10(a) of the Act clearly vests the Board with jurisdiction over conduct which constitutes a violation of the provisions of Section 8, notwithstanding the existence of methods of "adjustment or prevention that might be established by agreement," nothing in the Act intimates that the Board must exercise jurisdiction where such methods exist. On the contrary in Carey v. Westinghouse Electric Corporation, 375 U.S. 261, 271 (1964), the Court indicated that it favors our deference to such agreed methods by quoting at length with obvious approval the following language from the Board's decision in International Harvester Co.:[4]

"There is no question that the Board is not precluded from adjudicating unfair labor practice charges even though they might have been the subject of an arbitration proceeding and award. Section 10(a) of the Act expressly makes this plain, and the courts have uniformly so held. However, it is equally well established that *the Board has considerable discretion to respect an arbitration award and decline to exercise its authority over alleged unfair labor practices if to do so will serve the fundamental aims of the Act.*

"The Act, as has repeatedly been stated, is primarily designed to promote industrial peace and stability by encouraging the practice and procedure of collective bargaining. Experience has demonstrated that collective-bargaining agreements that provide for final and binding arbitration of grievance and disputes arising thereunder, 'as a substitute for industrial strife,' contribute significantly to the attainment of this statutory objective." [Emphasis supplied.] * * *

The policy favoring voluntary settlement of labor disputes through arbitral processes finds specific expression in Section 203(d) of the LMRA, in which Congress declared:

"Final adjustment by a method agreed upon by the parties is hereby declared to be the desirable method for settlement of grievance disputes arising over the application or interpretation of an existing collective-bargaining agreement."

2. Indeed, some courts have gone so far as to hold that the Board is required, in certain circumstances, to defer to the arbitration process. See, e.g., Sinclair Refining Company v. N.L.R.B., 306 F.2d 569 (C.A.5); Timken Roller Bearing Co. v. N.L.R.B., 161 F.2d 949 (C.A.6).

denied 377 U.S. 1003. In enforcing the Board's decision, the Seventh Circuit stated at p. 787, "Thus, the Supreme Court has held that the Board has the discretion to defer to the decision of an arbitrator." As indicated, the Supreme Court denied certiorari.

4. 138 NLRB 923, 925–926, enfd. sub nom. Ramsey v. N.L.R.B., 327 F.2d 784 (C.A.7), cert.

And, of course, disputes under Section 301 of the LMRA called forth from the Supreme Court the celebrated affirmation of that national policy in the *Steelworkers* trilogy.

Admittedly, neither Section 203 nor Section 301 applies specifically to the Board. However, labor law as administered by the Board does not operate in a vacuum isolated from other parts of the Act, or, indeed, from other acts of Congress. In fact, the legislative history suggests that at the time the Taft-Hartley amendments were being considered, Congress anticipated that the Board would "develop by rules and regulations, a policy of entertaining under these provisions only such cases * * * as cannot be settled by resort to the machinery established by the contract itself, voluntary arbitration. * * *"[8]

The question whether the Board should withhold its process arises, of course, only when a set of facts may present not only an alleged violation of the Act but also an alleged breach of the collective-bargaining agreement subject to arbitration. Thus, this case like each such case compels an accommodation between, on the one hand, the statutory policy favoring the fullest use of collective bargaining and the arbitral process and, on the other, the statutory policy reflected by Congress' grant to the Board of exclusive jurisdiction to prevent unfair labor practices.

We address the accommodation required here with the benefit of the Board's full history of such accommodations in similar cases. From the start the Board has, case by case, both asserted jurisdiction and declined, as the balance was struck on particular facts and at various stages in the long ascent of collective bargaining to its present state of wide acceptance. Those cases reveal that the Board has honored the distinction between two broad but distinct classes of cases, those in which there has been an arbitral award, and those in which there has not.

In the former class of cases the Board has long given hospitable acceptance to the arbitral process. In Timken Roller Bearing Company,[9] the Board refrained from exercising jurisdiction, in deference to an arbitrator's decision, despite the fact that the Board would otherwise have found that an unfair labor practice had been committed. The Board explained "[I]t would not comport with the sound exercise of our administrative discretion to permit the Union to seek redress under the Act after having initiated arbitration proceedings which, at the Union's request, resulted in a determination upon the merits." Id. at 501. The Board's policy was refined in Spielberg Manufacturing Company,[10] where the Board established the now settled rule that it would limit its inquiry, in the presence of an arbitrator's award, to whether the procedures were fair and the results not repugnant to the Act.

In those cases in which no award had issued, the Board's guidelines have been less clear. At times the Board has dealt with the unfair labor practice, and at other times it has left the parties to their contract remedies. In an early case, Consolidated Aircraft Corporation,[11] the Board, after pointing out that the charging party had failed to utilize the grievance procedures, stated:

8. S.Rep. No. 105, 80th Cong., 1st Sess. 23; Leg.Hist. of the LMRA 1947, p. 429.

9. 70 NLRB 500.

10. 112 NLRB 1080, 1082.

11. 47 NLRB 694, enfd. in pertinent part 141 F.2d 785 (C.A.9).

"[I]t will not effectuate the statutory policy of encouraging the practice and procedure of collective bargaining for the Board to assume the role of policing collective contracts between employers and labor organizations by attempting to decide whether disputes as to the meaning and administration of such contracts constitute unfair labor practices under the Act. On the contrary, we believe that parties to collective contracts would thereby be encouraged to abandon their efforts to dispose of disputes under the contracts through collective bargaining or through the settlement procedures mutually agreed upon by them, and to remit the interpretation and administration of their contracts to the Board. We therefore do not deem it wise to exercise our jurisdiction in such a case, where the parties have not exhausted their rights and remedies under the contract as to which this dispute has arisen."

The Board has continued to apply the doctrine enunciated in *Consolidated Aircraft*, although not consistently.

Jos. Schlitz Brewing Company,[13] is the most significant recent case in which the Board has exercised its discretion to defer. The underlying dispute in *Schlitz* was strikingly similar to the one now before us. In *Schlitz* the respondent employer decided to halt its production line during employee breaks. That decision was a departure from an established practice of maintaining extra employees, relief men, to fill in for regular employees during breaktime. The change resulted in, among other things, elimination of the relief man job classification. The change elicited a union protest leading to an unfair labor practice proceeding in which the Board ruled that the case should be "left for resolution within the framework of the agreed upon settlement procedures." The majority there explained its decision in these words:

"Thus, we believe that where, as here, the contract clearly provides for grievance and arbitration machinery, where the unilateral action taken is not designed to undermine the Union and is not patently erroneous but rather is based on a substantial claim of contractual privilege, and it appears that the arbitral interpretation of the contract will resolve both the unfair labor practice issue and the contract interpretation issue in a manner compatible with the purposes of the Act, then the Board should defer to the arbitration clause conceived by the parties. This particular case is indeed an appropriate one for just such deferral. The parties have an unusually long established and successful bargaining relationship; they have a dispute involving substantive contract interpretation almost classical in its form, each party asserting a reasonable claim in good faith in a situation wholly devoid of unlawful conduct or aggravated circumstances of any kind; they have a clearly defined grievance-arbitration procedure which Respondent has urged the Union to use for resolving their dispute; and, significantly, the Respondent, the party which in fact desires to abide by the terms of its contract, is the same party which, although it firmly believed in good faith in its right under the contract to take the action it did take, offered to discuss the entire matter with the Union prior to taking such action. Accordingly, under the principles above stated, and the persuasive facts in this case we believe that the policy of promoting industrial peace and stability through collective bargaining obliges us to defer [sic] the parties to

13. 175 NLRB No. 23.

the grievance-arbitration procedures they themselves have voluntarily established." [175 NLRB No. 23. * * * Footnotes omitted.]

The circumstances of this case, no less than those in *Schlitz,* weigh heavily in favor of deferral. Here, as in *Schlitz,* this dispute arises within the confines of a long and productive collective-bargaining relationship. The parties before us have, for 35 years, mutually and voluntarily resolved the conflicts which inhere in collective bargaining. Here, as there no claim is made of enmity by Respondent to employees' exercise of protected rights. Respondent here has credibly asserted its willingness to resort to arbitration under a clause providing for arbitration in a very broad range of disputes and unquestionably broad enough to embrace this dispute.

Finally, here, as in *Schlitz,* the dispute is one eminently well suited to resolution by arbitration. The contract and its meaning in present circumstances lie at the center of this dispute. In contrast, the Act and its policies become involved only if it is determined that the agreement between the parties, examined in the light of its negotiating history and the practices of the parties thereunder, did not sanction Respondent's right to make the disputed changes, subject to review if sought by the Union, under the contractually prescribed procedure. That threshold determination is clearly within the expertise of a mutually agreed-upon arbitrator. In this regard we note especially that here, as in *Schlitz,* the dispute between these parties is the very stuff of labor contract arbitration. The competence of a mutually selected arbitrator to decide the issue and fashion an appropriate remedy, if needed, can no longer be gainsaid.

We find no basis for the assertion of our dissenting colleagues that our decision here modifies the standards established in *Spielberg* for judging the acceptability of an arbitrator's award. *Spielberg* established that such awards would not be contravened by this Board where:

> "[T]he proceedings appear to have been fair and regular, all parties had agreed to be bound, and the decision of the arbitration panel is not clearly repugnant to the purposes and policies of the Act."

As already noted, the contract between Respondent and the Union unquestionably obligates each party to submit to arbitration any dispute arising under the contract and binds both parties to the result thereof. It is true, manifestly, that we cannot judge the regularity or statutory acceptability of the result in an arbitration proceeding which has not occurred. However, we are unwilling to adopt the presumption that such a proceeding will be invalid under *Spielberg* and to exercise our decisional authority at this juncture on the basis of a mere possibility that such a proceeding might be unacceptable under *Spielberg* standards. That risk is far better accommodated, we believe, by the result reached here of retaining jurisdiction against an event which years of experience with labor arbitration have now made clear is a remote hazard.

Member Fanning's dissenting opinion incorrectly characterizes this decision as instituting "compulsory arbitration" and as creating an opportunity for employers and unions to "strip parties of statutory rights."

We are not compelling any party to agree to arbitrate disputes arising during a contract term, but are merely giving full effect to their own voluntary agreements to submit all such disputes to arbitration, rather than permitting such agreements to be sidestepped and permitting the substitution of our processes, a forum not contemplated by their own agreement.

Nor are we "stripping" any party of "statutory rights." The courts have long recognized that an industrial relations dispute may involve conduct which, at least arguably, may contravene both the collective agreement and our statute. When the parties have contractually committed themselves to mutually agreeable procedures for resolving their disputes during the period of the contract, we are of the view that those procedures should be afforded full opportunity to function. The long and successful functioning of grievance and arbitration procedures suggests to us that in the overwhelming majority of cases, the utilization of such means will resolve the underlying dispute and make it unnecessary for either party to follow the more formal, and sometimes lengthy, combination of administrative and judicial litigation provided for under our statute. At the same time, by our reservation of jurisdiction, infra, we guarantee that there will be no sacrifice of statutory rights if the parties' own processes fail to function in a manner consistent with the dictates of our law. * * *

V. Remedy

Without prejudice to any party and without deciding the merits of the controversy, we shall order that the complaint herein be dismissed, but we shall retain jurisdiction for a limited purpose. Our decision represents a developmental step in the Board's treatment of these problems and the controversy here arose at a time when the Board decisions may have led the parties to conclude that the Board approved dual litigation of this controversy before the Board and before an arbitrator. We are also aware that the parties herein have not resolved their dispute by the contractual grievance and arbitration procedure and that, therefore, we cannot now inquire whether resolution of the dispute will comport with the standards set forth in *Spielberg,* supra. In order to eliminate the risk of prejudice to any party we shall retain jurisdiction over this dispute solely for the purpose of entertaining an appropriate and timely motion for further consideration upon a proper showing that either (a) the dispute has not, with reasonable promptness after the issuance of this decision, either been resolved by amicable settlement in the grievance procedure or submitted promptly to arbitration, or (b) the grievance or arbitration procedures have not been fair and regular or have reached a result which is repugnant to the Act.

[The concurring opinion of Member Brown is omitted.]

MEMBER FANNING, dissenting:

* * * I believe the majority's policy is contrary to the intent of Congress and, indeed, beyond the power of the Board. Section 10(a) of the Act clearly states that the Board's power to prevent unfair labor practices "shall not be *affected* by other means of adjustment or prevention that has been or may be established by agreement, law, or otherwise." (Emphasis supplied.) Moreover, under Section 14(c)(1), Congress in the amended Act specifically limited the extent to which the Board may exercise its discretion to refuse jurisdiction over any "class or category of employers" by providing: "That the Board shall not decline to assert jurisdiction over any labor

dispute over which it would assert jurisdiction under the standards prevailing upon August 1, 1959."

Assuming *arguendo* the power of the Board to refuse to entertain charges in cases of this type, the policy of embarking upon such a program is open to serious question. Arbitrators are employed to interpret and apply a specific collective-bargaining agreement. Generally, they are loath to intrude into the area of public rights or national labor policy. These questions historically have been the prime concern of the Board, which was established by Congress exclusively for this purpose. Understandably, an arbitrator, paid jointly by a union and an employer to adjudicate their private rights and obligations, may be unwilling to suggest that one of them is in violation of the National Labor Relations Act and to direct a remedy appropriate to such a finding. The function of good arbitration involves not only the resolution of a particular dispute, but the fostering of a harmonious relationship between the parties to collective bargaining. To endow the arbitrator's award in all cases involving contract interpretation with the prior *imprimatur* of Board approval is, in my opinion, a disservice to the arbitrator, the parties before him, and the effectuation of a sound national labor policy.

*   *   *

MEMBER JENKINS, dissenting:

*   *   *

The majority is reading out of our jurisdiction the statutory protection against all unfair labor practices which may involve in part, and perhaps distantly, the interpretation of a contract provision, where the contract contains an arbitration clause. Most unfair labor practices can be connected somehow to contract terms or existing practices, by broad construction of general clauses, by the necessary inquiry into existing practices, by "waiver," or otherwise. This decision will, of course, encourage the creation of such clauses where they do not now exist. It will also permit unions and employers to contract themselves almost entirely out of the Act by writing into their agreements a provision that neither will violate any provision of the Act, and any alleged such violation will be arbitrated.[48]

Note

1. The concern expressed by dissenting Member Jenkins over the application of the Collyer deferral policy to alleged unfair labor practices other than those under Section 8(a)(5) was well founded. The policy was expanded so as to encompass 8(a)(3) charges in National Radio, 198 N.L.R.B. 527 (1972), another 3-to-2 decision. In General American Transportation Corp., 228 N.L.R.B. No. 102 (1977), however, again by a vote of 3-to-2, the Board deflated the doctrine so as to encompass only 8(a)(5). Chairman Murphy, concurring and thereby providing the swing vote (she joined Members Fanning and Jenkins, who continued to

---

48. This possibility is hardly farfetched, for Member Brown states that he would defer also in 8(a)(1) and 8(a)(3) cases, involving employer interference and coercion, and discriminatory discharge. There is no way to relate a discharge for union activity to a contract term except by a provision of the kind we have mentioned. A "discharge for just cause" could not justify deferral to arbitration, because "just cause" might exist though the true reason for the firing was union activity, which insofar as protected by the Act, cannot be limited by the contract.

oppose Collyer in any of its applications; the two dissenting Members supported Collyer all the way), explained her position thusly:

"[T]he Board should stay its processes in favor of the parties' grievance arbitration machinery only in those situations where the dispute is essentially between the contracting parties and where there is no alleged interference with individual employees' basic rights under Section 7 of the Act. Complaints alleging violations of Sections 8(a)(5) and 8(b)(3) fall squarely into this category, while complaints alleging violations of Sections 8(a)(3), 8(a)(1), 8(b)(1)(A), and 8(b)(2) clearly do not. * * * [I]n the former category the dispute is principally between the contracting parties—the employer and the union—while in the latter the dispute is between the employee on the one hand and the employer and/or the union on the other. In cases alleging violations of Sections 8(a)(5) and 8(b)(3), based upon conduct assertedly in derogation of the contract, the principal issue is whether the complained-of conduct is permitted by the parties' contract. Such issues are eminently suited to the arbitral process, and resolution of the contract issue by an arbitrator will, as a rule, dispose of the unfair labor practice issue. On the other hand, in cases alleging violations of Sections 8(a)(1), 8(a)(3), 8(b)(1)(A), and 8(b)(2), although arguably also involving a contract violation, the determinative issue is not whether the conduct is permitted by the contract, but whether the conduct was unlawfully motivated or whether it otherwise interfered with, restrained, or coerced employees in the exercise of the rights guaranteed them by Section 7 of the Act. In these situations, an arbitrator's resolution of the contract issue will not dispose of the unfair labor practice allegation. * * * Accordingly, * * * I find that our decision in National Radio, [198 N.L.R.B. 527 (1972)] was an unwise extension of the Collyer deferral policy into an area in which the Board should retain its preeminence. That decision and its progeny must, therefore, be reversed."

Lest the reader mistakenly conclude that the 8(a)(1), 8(a)(3), 8(b)(1)(A), and 8(b)(2) issues were thus put to rest by General American Transportation Corp., the Board, in United Technologies Corp., 269 N.L.R.B. 557 (1984), by a 3–1 margin (there was one vacancy at the time), returned to the National Radio view, again manifesting the "flip-flop" potential of this politically-designed body.

2. Member Jenkins also manifested concern over the use to which "waiver" clauses might be put in connection with efforts to broaden the impact of the Collyer decision. The all-inclusive waiver clause (sometimes called a "zipper" clause) set forth below as paragraph 116 was centrally involved in Unit Drop Forge Division, Eaton Yale & Towne, Inc., 171 N.L.R.B. 600, enforced 412 F.2d 108 (7th Cir.1969). Can you figure out the logical progression by which such a clause (or some less inclusive one) might be contended to expand the applicability of the Collyer rule? (Hint: the route lies through Section 8(d).)

"116. The Company and the Union, for the life of this Agreement, each voluntarily and unqualifiedly waives the right, and each agrees that the other shall not be obligated, to bargain collectively with respect to any subject or matter referred to, or covered in this Agreement, or with respect to any subject or matter not specifically referred to or covered in this Agreement even though such subject or matter may not have been within the knowledge or contemplation of either or both of the parties at the time that they negotiated or signed this Agreement."

In Unit Drop Forge, the Board, again 3-to-2, reversed the Trial Examiner in adjudging the foregoing provision as follows:

"As the Trial Examiner correctly states, a union's statutory right to be notified and consulted concerning any substantial change in employment may be waived by contract, but such waiver must be expressed in clear and unmistakable terms, and will not lightly be inferred. We also agree with the Trial Examiner that the mere existence of contractual grievance and arbitration procedures will not by itself warrant a finding that the union waived its right to bargain on changes planned by the employer. However, we do not agree with the Trial Examiner that paragraph 116 or other provisions of the contract in the instant case constitute a clear waiver of the Union's right to be consulted about Respondent's change in the mode of operating its shipping room.

"In *Rockwell-Standard,* [8] which involved a waiver provision identical to the one herein, the Board adopted the Trial Examiner's finding that even when a 'waiver' is expressed in a contract in such broad, sweeping terms * * * it must appear from an evaluation of * * * negotiations that the particular matter [in issue] was fully discussed or consciously explored and the union consciously yielded or clearly and unmistakably waived its interest in the matter. Applying this test to the situation herein, it does not appear from the record or the various contractual provisions alluded to by the Trial Examiner and analyzed herein that the Union consciously yielded or clearly waived its interest in changes such as the one in dispute herein." 171 N.L.R.B. at 601.

With whom do you agree, Trial Examiner or Board? From the standpoint of the application of the Collyer doctrine, what difference does it make which view prevails?

THE IMPACT OF BANKRUPTCY ON THE DUTY TO BARGAIN DURING THE LIFE OF THE COLLECTIVE AGREEMENT

Suppose that an employer during the existence of a collective bargaining agreement feels forced to file a petition for reorganization under Chapter 11 of the Bankruptcy Code.[a] What impact should this have on the employer's duty to bargain (i.e., continue to honor an existing collective bargaining agreement)? In NLRB v. Bildisco and Bildisco, 465 U.S. 513, 104 S.Ct. 1188, 79 L.Ed.2d 482 (1984), the following sequence of events occurred: (1) The employer filed a petition under Chapter 11 of the Bankruptcy Code. (2) The employer repudiated an existing collective bargaining agreement. (3) Thereafter, the employer requested and received permission from the bankruptcy court to "reject" (rid itself of) the agreement. (4) The union filed a section 8(a)(5) charge, premised upon the employer's refusal to honor the agreement, which charge the Board upheld. (5) The union's appeal from affirmance by the federal district court of the bankruptcy court's ruling and the Board's petition for enforcement of its 8(a)(5) ruling were consolidated for review by the Third Circuit Court of Appeals. (6) The Third Circuit refused to enforce the Board's ruling and ordered the case remanded to the bankruptcy court

---

8. Rockwell-Standard Corporation, Transmission and Axle Division, Forge Division, 166 NLRB 124.

a. Chapter 11 was part of the Bankruptcy Reform Act of 1978, Pub.L. No. 95–598, 92 Stat. 2549 (1978), and allows an enterprise in economic difficulty to reorganize so as to continue in business, while at the same time affording protection to creditors and the public interest. 11 U.S.C.A. §§ 1101–1174 (1982).

for reconsideration, applying a standard more stringent than the "usual business judgment rule" applicable to the rejection-in-bankruptcy of other contracts. (7) The Supreme Court granted certiorari and affirmed the decision of the Third Circuit, holding (a) (by a 9–0 vote) that a bankruptcy court may authorize the rejection of a collective bargaining agreement when the court is persuaded that reasonable efforts to negotiate a voluntary modification have been made by the company and union and that these efforts are not likely to produce a prompt and satisfactory resolution, and (b) (by a 5–4 vote) that the employer does not commit an unfair labor practice when it unilaterally rejects or modifies a collective bargaining agreement before formal rejection is approved by the bankruptcy court.

Congress reacted promptly to the pressures created by the Bildisco decision by enacting the Bankruptcy Amendments and Federal Judgeship Act of 1984, Pub.L. No. 98–353, 98 Stat. 390 (1984), which requires bankruptcy court approval as a condition precedent to rejection of a collective bargaining agreement. 11 U.S.C.A. § 1113 (West Supp.1985). In order to satisfy that condition, an employer filing for bankruptcy must, before rejection of the agreement, make a proposal to the union of "necessary" contract modifications. The bankruptcy court must then find that the proposal meets the statutory requirements, that the employer has conferred "in good faith" with the union concerning the proposal, that the union has refused to accept it "without good cause," and that the "balance of the equities" among "all creditors, the debtor [employer], and all of the affected parties" "clearly favors rejection" of the existing collective bargaining agreement.

Does not the process imposed by Congress in the 1984 Act balance as nicely as possible the competing values of the labor and bankruptcy policies? If your answer is no, how would *you* adjust the balance?

B. INDIVIDUAL RIGHTS UNDER THE COLLECTIVE AGREEMENT

1. INDIVIDUAL RIGHTS AND THE DUTY OF FAIR REPRESENTATION: CONGRUENCE AND CONFLICT

The duty of fair representation was declared by the Supreme Court in the seminal Steele case of 1944, supra p. 187. The duty was found to be the reverse side, so to speak, of the coin of exclusivity. A union elevated by the standards, procedures, and agencies of the federal law to the status of exclusive bargaining representative of all of the employees in a bargaining unit was held to owe to each employee a duty of representation comparable to that owed by a legislative body to its constituents.

The materials which follow are intended to explore the scope and manner of enforcement of the duty. As will be seen when the course has been fully run, the doctrine of fair representation not only creates, but also circumscribes, individual rights.

LOCAL 12, UNITED RUBBER WORKERS v.
NATIONAL LABOR RELATIONS BOARD

United States Court of Appeals, Fifth Circuit, 1966.
368 F.2d 12.

Certiorari denied, 389 U.S. 837 (1967).

THORNBERRY, CIRCUIT JUDGE.

Petitioner, United Rubber, Cork, Linoleum & Plastic Workers of America, AFL–CIO, Local Union No. 12 (hereinafter referred to as Local 12), initiated these proceedings to review a determination by the National Labor Relations Board that Local 12 had engaged in unfair labor practices within the purview of sections 8(b)(1)(A), 8(b)(2), and 8(b)(3) of the Labor Management Relations Act ∗ ∗ ∗ by refusing to process certain grievances of eight Negro employees in its bargaining unit at Goodyear Tire & Rubber Company of East Gadsden, Alabama. The facts underlying the controversy are virtually undisputed.

Local 12 has been the exclusive collective bargaining representative of Goodyear's East Gadsden plant employees since 1943. Until March 1962, three separate seniority rolls—white male, Negro male, and female—were maintained, although the bargaining contract between Goodyear and Local 12 appeared to provide for plantwide seniority without regard to race or sex. As a matter of custom and interpretation during this period, Negro employees with greater seniority had no rights over white employees with less seniority, and vice versa, with respect to promotions, transfers, layoffs, and recalls. Also as a matter of custom, racially separate plant facilities such as lunchrooms, restrooms and showers were maintained, although no provision in the bargaining contract dealt with such matters.

The eight complainants were laid off in August or September 1960, and were recalled approximately one year later. In October 1961, Buckner, one of the eight complainants, having been notified that he was to be again laid off, inquired why a white employee with less seniority continued to remain employed. He was informed by the assistant manager of Goodyear's labor department that the posted job was a "white job." Thereupon, Buckner and the other complainants, who were also in layoff status, executed affidavits that during their period of layoff subsequent to August or September 1960, new workers had been hired in violation of plant seniority rules. These affidavits were forwarded to the President of Local 12, requesting that Local 12 investigate the alleged grievances and take remedial action. The complainants appeared before the grievance committee on December 8, 1961, and presented a more complete "Statement of Complaint" which charged (1) that the original layoff and recall had not been in accordance with contract-stated seniority and that complainants demanded reinstatement with back wages, (2) that upon recall complainants wanted all transfer privileges as set forth in the contract, and (3) that complainants demanded the right to all plant privileges without color barriers. The committee concluded that "no contract violation exists, therefore, the Union has no ground on which to base a complaint against the company." Subsequent appeals to the union executive board and the full union membership were likewise denied. In March 1962, complainants appealed the action of Local 12 to George Burdon, the union's International President. In light of the information requested by Burdon, and provided by the complainants and Local 12, he concluded that the decision refusing to process the grievances should be reversed.

While Local 12 continued to refrain from filing a formal grievance, the record reflects that in the latter part of March 1962 union representatives met with company officials and a representative of the President's Committee on Equal Employment Opportunity to discuss the racially segregated employment practices. These discussions apparently culminated in a verbal agreement between Local 12 and Goodyear to discontinue any application of the bargaining contract which confined Negro and white employees to particular jobs and restricted opportunities for upgrading, recall, and transfer to jobs theretofore separated on racial lines. Complainants were reinstated and there is no evidence that any racially discriminatory practices with regard to job opportunities, transfer, promotion, layoff, or participation in Goodyear's training program existed after March 1962. It is further clear from the record, however, that Local 12 continued to refuse to process the grievances concerning back wages for the period of layoff occasioned by application of the seniority system in effect prior to March 1962, as well as those concerning the continued segregated nature of plant facilities. Accordingly, on October 22, 1962, the initial unfair labor practice charges were filed against Local 12.

In reversing the trial examiner's determination that no unfair labor practice had been established, the Board concluded that petitioner, by refusing to process the grievances concerning back wages and segregated plant facilities, had thereby (1) restrained or coerced complainants in their section 7 right to be represented without invidious discrimination, (2) caused or attempted to cause Goodyear to discriminate against complainants, and (3) refused to bargain in complainants' behalf, thus violating sections 8(b)(1) (A), 8(b)(2), and 8(b)(3) of the act. Petitioner was accordingly ordered to process the grievances through arbitration and to propose to Goodyear specific contractual provisions prohibiting racial discrimination in terms and conditions of employment pursuant to the oral agreement of March 1962. From that order Local 12 petitions this Court for review.

The facts of this controversy once again present the critical challenge of striking a meaningful balance, consistent with existing labor policy, between individual employee rights and the continued effectiveness of the collective bargaining process. Essential to an adequate analysis of any issue involving the scope of union responsibility to those it represents is the recognition that administration of internal union affairs constitutes a significant element in the collective bargaining process. Accordingly, the vital issue in this area resolves itself into that of determining at what point the exclusive bargaining agent's duty to represent fairly the interests of each individual employee must bow to the equally comprehensive obligation of negotiating and administering the bargaining contract in accordance with the act's primary policy of fostering union-employer relations. While the Supreme Court has declared that an exclusive bargaining agent "is responsible to, and owes complete loyalty to, the interests of all whom it represents," Ford Motor Co. v. Huffman, 1953, 345 U.S. 330, 338, 73 S.Ct. 681, 686, 97 L.Ed. 1048, 1058, it has at the same time recognized the inherent burden this mandate serves to impose upon a union obliged to exercise good faith in adjusting the numerous competing interests of its individual members:

"Inevitably differences will arise in the manner and degree to which the terms of any negotiated agreement affect individual employees and classes of employees. The mere existence of such differences does not make them invalid. The complete satisfaction of all who are represented is hardly to be expected. A wide range of reasonableness must be allowed a statutory bargaining representative in serving the unit it represents, subject always to complete good faith and honesty of purpose in the exercise of its discretion." Ibid.

Nevertheless, when the individual employee, pursuant to federal law aimed at preserving industrial harmony, is required to surrender completely his right of self-representation in deference to an "exclusive" bargaining agent designated by a majority of his coworkers, both logic and equity dictate that such agent be impressed with a reciprocal duty to "represent all its members, the majority as well as the minority, and * * * to act for and not against those whom it represents." Steele v. Louisville & N.R.R., 1944, 323 U.S. 192, 202, 65 S.Ct. 226, 232, 89 L.Ed. 173, 183; see Hughes Tool Co. v. N.L.R.B., 5th Cir.1945, 147 F.2d 69, 74, 158 A.L.R. 1165. Indeed, the Supreme Court has indicated that any statute purporting to bestow upon a union the exclusive right to represent all employees would be unconstitutional if it failed to impose upon the union this reciprocal duty of fair representation. Steele v. Louisville & N.R.R., supra, 323 U.S. at 198–199, 65 S.Ct. at 230, 89 L.Ed. at 180–181.

Although the concept of "fair representation" is generally thought of as having arisen initially in Steele v. Louisville & N.R.R., which involved a controversy under the Railway Labor Act, * * * the Supreme Court on that same day declared an identical duty to be implicit in section 9(a) of the National Labor Relations Act. Wallace Corp. v. NLRB, 1944, 323 U.S. 248, 65 S.Ct. 238, 89 L.Ed. 216. * * *

Therefore, we are not here called upon to establish such duty but rather to face the issue of what conduct represents a breach of that duty, together with its appropriate remedy. More specifically, we must determine whether a breach of the duty of fair representation in itself constitutes an unfair labor practice within contemplation of the National Labor Relations Act, as amended. We are convinced that the duty of fair representation implicit in the exclusive-representation requirement in section 9(a) of the act comprises an indispensable element of the right of employees "to bargain collectively through representatives of their own choosing" as guaranteed in section 7. We therefore conclude that by summarily refusing to process the complainants' grievances concerning back wages and segregated plant facilities, petitioner thereby violated section 8(b)(1)(A) of the act by restraining those employees in the exercise of their section 7 rights.

At the outset it must be reiterated that every union decision which may in some way result in overriding the wishes or disappointing the expectations of an individual employee, or even an appreciable number of employees, does not in and of itself constitute a breach of the fiduciary duty of fair representation. Even in the administration stage of the bargaining contract, when the necessity of adjusting competing employee claims may not be as pressing as during the negotiation stage where rigorous scrutiny of each compromise might frustrate the act's policy of encouraging industrial peace, the union must necessarily retain a broad degree of discretion in processing individual grievances. Thus, where the union, after a good faith investigation of the merits of a grievance, concludes that the claim is insubstantial and refuses to encumber further its grievance channels by continuing to process the unmeritorious claim, its duty of fair representation may well be satisfied. Such good-faith effort to represent fairly the interests of individual employees, however, is not evidenced in this controversy. To the contrary, Local 12 in open disregard of the recommendations of its International President has continued to refuse to represent the vital interests of a segment of its membership. The claims with regard to back pay and segregation of plant facilities clearly concern meritorious issues involving wages and conditions of employment, issues with respect to which these employees have relinquished to the union as exclusive bargaining agent their individual rights to negotiate. See J.I. Case Co. v. NLRB, 1944, 321 U.S. 332, 64 S.Ct. 576, 88 L.Ed. 762. Neither does the mere fact that the act provides that an individual employee may present his claim directly to the employer diminish the union's duty of fair representation, for admittedly the grievance of a single employee can have little force in the absence of support from his bargaining representative. Conley v. Gibson, 1957, 355 U.S. 41, 45, 78 S.Ct. 99, 102, 2 L.Ed.2d 80, 84. Undoubtedly, the duty of fair representation can be breached by discriminatory inaction in refusing to process a grievance as well as by active conduct on the part of the union. Conley v. Gibson, supra; Steele v. Louisville & N.R.R., supra, 323 U.S. at 204, 65 S.Ct. at 226, 89 L.Ed. at 184 * * *.

In defense of its refusal to process the claims for back wages arising during the period when seniority was applied on a racial basis, the union argues that since those practices have been abandoned, recognition of the back wage claims for that period would in effect render its decision to abandon the practices retroactive. It thus contends that its choice to reject the claims in order to avoid such effect was not based upon considerations of an arbitrary or unfair nature. Significantly, however, from 1943 to March 1962 the union consistently adhered to the practice of applying seniority on a racial basis, conduct which manifested a patent breach of its duty of fair representation. * * * As the Board properly concluded, had the claims been allowed to proceed to arbitration, an arbitrator would not have been bound by the prior invalid interpretation of the contract and might well have awarded back wages. We thus conclude that where the record demonstrates that a grievance would have been processed to arbitration but for arbitrary and discriminatory reasons, the refusal to so process it constitutes a violation of the union's duty to represent its members "without hostile discrimination, fairly, impartially, and in good faith." Steele v. Louisville & N.R.R., supra, 323 U.S. at 204, 65 S.Ct. at 233, 89 L.Ed. at 184.

Similarly, with respect to the grievances concerning the segregated nature of plant facilities, the union not only refused to process such claims but actively opposed desegregation of shower and toilet facilities. It is impossible for us to look upon such conduct as anything other than an effort to discriminate against Negro employees with respect to conditions of employment. As exclusive representative of all employees in the bargaining unit, Local 12's statutory obligation required it "to make an honest effort to serve the interests of all of those members, without hostility to any." Ford Motor Co. v. Huffman, supra, 345 U.S. at 337, 73 S.Ct. at 686, 97 L.Ed. at 1057. In summarily refusing to consider in good faith the merits of these grievances, the union's conduct inarguably failed to meet this standard. As the Board properly concluded, "whatever may be the bases on which a statutory representative may properly decline to process grievances, the bases must bear a reasonable relation to the Union's role as bargaining representative or its functioning as a labor organization; manifestly racial discrimination bears no such relationship." 150 N.L.R.B. at 312, 317.

We have been able to find but one appellate decision on the specific issue of whether a breach of the union's duty of fair representation constitutes an unfair labor practice. NLRB v. Miranda Fuel Co., 2d Cir.1963, 326 F.2d 172. That decision, moreover, was comprised of three separate opinions. Careful study of those opinions and the briefs in this case * * * convinces us that Local 12, in refusing to represent the complainants in a fair and impartial manner, thereby violated section 8(b)(1)(A) by restraining them in the exercise of their section 7 right to bargain collectively through their chosen representatives. The mere fact that Local 12's conduct may not have directly resulted in encouraging or discouraging union membership does not persuade us to alter our determination, for the language of section 8(b)(1)(A), unlike certain other provisions of section 8, is not restricted to discrimination which encourages or discourages union membership.

* * *

Moreover, the Board's recent assertions that fair representation constitutes an essential element of section 7 employee rights are even more convincing in light of the similarity in language between section 7 and section 2 of the Railway Labor Act, from which the Supreme Court in *Steele* perceived congressional intent to impose such duty of fair representation upon the bargaining representative. In that case, the court reasoned that since the jurisdiction of the Railway Adjustment Board did not encompass disputes between employees and unions, the remedy must necessarily be sought in the courts. Since the National Labor Relations Board has, however, been given jurisdiction over employee-union disputes, the Court's logic in *Steele*, reinforced by the Board's express desire to assume jurisdiction, further supports our conclusion that unfair representation cases are properly subject to Board jurisdiction. Significantly, the violation of every other duty imposed by the act, including the general duty to bargain collectively, has been designated an unfair labor practice, and we find no compelling reason to conclude that a breach of the duty of fair representation was intended to represent a single, narrow exception to Board jurisdiction.

[The court concluded that the Garmon preemption doctrine would not preclude parallel judicial enforcement of the duty of fair representation. This conclusion is endorsed and fully discussed by the Supreme Court in Vaca v. Sipes, infra p. 742.]

In thus concluding that a breach of the duty of fair representation constitutes an unfair labor practice, we are not unmindful that Title VII of the Civil Rights Act of 1964, effective July 2, 1965, makes it an "unlawful employment practice" for a union to discriminate against "any individual because of his race, color, religion, sex, or national origin" or to cause or attempt to cause an employer to do so. Section 703(c)(1)–(3) * * *. Since the claims before us arose fully three years prior to the effective date of Title VII, its pertinent provisions are clearly inapplicable in this controversy. Nevertheless, it is equally clear that had these claims arisen after July 2, 1965, the complainants under our holding today would be at liberty to seek redress under the enforcement provisions of Title VII or to assert unfair labor practice charges before the Board. This problem of overlapping remedies, however, would exist even in the absence of recognition of a breach of the duty of fair representation as an unfair labor practice, for undeniably unfair labor practice charges arising under many provisions of section 8 will also involve union and employer conduct proscribed by Title VII. We recognize that while Title VII represents an appreciable addition to the protection afforded employee rights in the specific areas of discrimination covered by the Civil Rights Act, there continues to exist a broad potential range of arbitrary union conduct not specifically covered by Title VII which may also violate the union's duty of fair representation. The comprehensive right of an employee to be represented fairly and in good faith by his exclusive bargaining agent clearly encompasses more than freedom from union discrimination based solely upon race, religion, and sex. The mere fact, therefore, that Congress has seen fit to provide specific protection to employees from union and employer discrimination in the area of civil rights in no way detracts from the legal and practical bases of our determination that a breach of the union's duty of fair representation constitutes a violation of section 8(b)(1)(A).

Having thus concluded that petitioner's breach of the duty of fair representation constitutes an unfair labor practice under section 8(b)(1)(A) of the act, we need not consider the Board's additional contentions that such conduct also violated sections 8(b)(2) and 8(b)(3). We also conclude that under the circumstances the Board did not exceed the scope of its remedial powers in ordering petitioner to process the grievances in question through arbitration and to propose to the employer contractual provisions aimed at prohibiting continued racial discrimination in terms and conditions of employment as expressed in the oral agreement of March 1962.

Enforcement granted.

Note

Title VII of the Civil Rights Act of 1964, referred to by Judge Thornberry, is the subject of Chapter 9, Section A, infra p. 927.

VACA v. SIPES

Supreme Court of the United States, 1967.
386 U.S. 171, 87 S.Ct. 903, 17 L.Ed.2d 842.

MR. JUSTICE WHITE delivered the opinion of the Court.

On February 13, 1962, Benjamin Owens filed this class action against petitioners, as officers and representatives of the National Brotherhood of Packinghouse Workers and of its Kansas City Local No. 12 (the Union), in the Circuit Court of Jackson County, Missouri. Owens, a Union member, alleged that he had been discharged from his employment at Swift & Company's (Swift) Kansas City Meat Packing Plant in violation of the collective bargaining agreement then in force between Swift and the Union, and that the Union had "arbitrarily, capriciously and without just or reasonable reason or cause" refused to take his grievance with Swift to arbitration under the fifth step of the bargaining agreement's grievance procedures.

Petitioners' answer included the defense that the Missouri courts lacked jurisdiction because the gravamen of Owens' suit was "arguably and basically" an unfair labor practice under § 8(b) of the National Labor Relations Act * * * within the exclusive jurisdiction of the National Labor Relations Board (NLRB). After a jury trial, a verdict was returned awarding Owens $7,000 compensatory and $3,300 punitive damages. The trial judge set aside the verdict and entered judgment for petitioners on the ground that the NLRB had exclusive jurisdiction over this controversy, and the Kansas City Court of Appeals affirmed. The Supreme Court of Missouri reversed and directed reinstatement of the jury's verdict,[2] relying on this Court's decisions in International Assn. of Machinists v. Gonzales, 356 U.S. 617, 78 S.Ct. 923, 2 L.Ed.2d 1018, and in International Union, United Automobile, etc. Workers of America v. Russell, 356 U.S. 634, 78 S.Ct. 932, 2 L.Ed.2d 1030. 397 S.W.2d 658. During the appeal, Owens died and respondent, the administrator of Owens' estate, was substituted. We granted certiorari to consider whether exclusive jurisdiction lies with the NLRB and, if not, whether the finding of Union liability and the relief afforded Owens are consistent with governing principles of federal labor law. * * * The American Federation of Labor and Congress of Industrial Organizations (AFL–CIO), Swift, and the United States have filed *amicus* briefs supporting petitioners. Although we conclude that state courts have jurisdiction in this type of case, we hold that federal law governs, that the governing federal standards were not applied here, and that the judgment of the Supreme Court of Missouri must accordingly be reversed.

I.

In mid-1959, Owens, a long-time high blood pressure patient, became sick and entered a hospital on sick leave from his employment with Swift. After a long rest during which his weight and blood pressure were reduced, Owens was certified by his family physician as fit to resume his heavy work in the packing plant. However, Swift's company doctor examined Owens upon his return and concluded that his blood pressure was too high to permit reinstatement. After securing a second authorization from another outside doctor, Owens returned to the plant, and a nurse permitted him to resume work on January 6, 1960. However, on January 8, when the doctor discovered Owens' return, he was permanently discharged on the ground of poor health.

Armed with his medical evidence of fitness, Owens then sought the Union's help in securing reinstatement, and a grievance was filed with Swift on his behalf. By mid-November 1960, the grievance had been processed

2. Punitive damages were reduced to $3,000, the amount claimed by Owens in his complaint.

through the third and into the fourth step of the grievance procedure established by the collective bargaining agreement.[3] Swift adhered to its position that Owens' poor health justified his discharge, rejecting numerous medical reports of reduced blood pressure proffered by Owens and by the Union. Swift claimed that these reports were not based upon sufficiently thorough medical tests.

On February 6, 1961, the Union sent Owens to a new doctor at Union expense "to see if we could get some better medical evidence so that we could go to arbitration with his case." R., at 107. This examination did not support Owens' position. When the Union received the report, its executive board voted not to take the Owens grievance to arbitration because of insufficient medical evidence. Union officers suggested to Owens that he accept Swift's offer of referral to a rehabilitation center, and the grievance was suspended for that purpose. Owens rejected this alternative and demanded that the Union take his grievance to arbitration, but the Union refused. With his contractual remedies thus stalled at the fourth step, Owens brought this suit. The grievance was finally dismissed by the Union and Swift shortly before trial began in June 1964.[4]

In his charge to the jury, the trial judge instructed that petitioners would be liable if Swift had wrongfully discharged Owens and if the Union had "arbitrarily * * * and without just cause or excuse * * * refused" to press Owens' grievance to arbitration. Punitive damages could also be awarded, the trial judge charged, if the Union's conduct was "willful, wanton and malicious." However, the jury must return a verdict for the defendants, the judge instructed, "if you find and believe from the evidence that the union and its representatives acted reasonably and in good faith in the handling and processing of the grievance of the plaintiff." R., at 161–162. The jury then returned the general verdict for Owens which eventually was reinstated by the Missouri Supreme Court.

II.

Petitioners challenge the jurisdiction of the Missouri courts on the ground that the alleged conduct of the Union was arguably an unfair labor practice and within the exclusive jurisdiction of the NLRB. Petitioners rely on Miranda Fuel Co., 140 N.L.R.B. 181 (1962), enforcement denied, 326 F.2d 172 (C.A.2d Cir.1963), where a sharply divided Board held for the first time that a union's breach of its statutory duty of fair representation violates N.L. R.A. § 8(b), as amended. With the NLRB's adoption of *Miranda Fuel*, petitioners argue, the broad pre-emption doctrine defined in San Diego Building Trades Council v. Garmon, 359 U.S. 236, 79 S.Ct. 773, 3 L.Ed.2d

---

3. The agreement created a five-step procedure for the handling of grievances. In steps one and two, either the aggrieved employee or the Union's representative presents the grievance first to Swift's department foreman, and then in writing to the division superintendent. In step three, grievance committees of the Union and management meet, and the company must state its position in writing to the Union. Step four is a meeting between Swift's general superintendent and represent-

atives of the National Union. If the grievance is not settled in the fourth step, the National Union is given power to refer the grievance to a specified arbitrator.

4. No notice of the dismissal was given to Owens, who by that time had filed a second suit against Swift for breach of contract. The suit against Swift is still pending in a pretrial stage.

775, becomes applicable. For the reasons which follow, we reject this argument.

It is now well established that, as the exclusive bargaining representative of the employees in Owens' bargaining unit, the Union had a statutory duty fairly to represent all of those employees, both in its collective bargaining with Swift, see Ford Motor Co. v. Huffman, 345 U.S. 330, 73 S.Ct. 681, 97 L.Ed. 1048; Syres v. Oil Workers International Union, 350 U.S. 892, 76 S.Ct. 152, 100 L.Ed. 785, and in its enforcement of the resulting collective bargaining agreement, see Humphrey v. Moore, 375 U.S. 335, 84 S.Ct. 363, 11 L.Ed.2d 370. The statutory duty of fair representation was developed over 20 years ago in a series of cases involving alleged racial discrimination by unions certified as exclusive bargaining representatives under the Railway Labor Act * * * and was soon extended to unions certified under the N.L.R.A. * * *. Under this doctrine, the exclusive agent's statutory authority to represent all members of a designated unit includes a statutory obligation to serve the interests of all members without hostility or discrimination toward any, to exercise its discretion with complete good faith and honesty, and to avoid arbitrary conduct. * * * It is obvious that Owens' complaint alleged a breach by the Union of a duty grounded in federal statutes, and that federal law therefore governs his cause of action. * * *

Although N.L.R.A. § 8(b) was enacted in 1947, the NLRB did not until *Miranda Fuel* interpret a breach of a union's duty of fair representation as an unfair labor practice. * * *

The Board's *Miranda Fuel* decision was denied enforcement by a divided Second Circuit, 326 F.2d 172 (1963). However, in Local Union No. 12, United Rubber, etc., Workers of America v. N.L.R.B., 368 F.2d 12, the Fifth Circuit upheld the Board's *Miranda Fuel* doctrine * * *. In light of these developments, petitioners argue that Owens' state court action was based upon Union conduct that is arguably proscribed by N.L.R.A. § 8(b), was potentially enforceable by the NLRB, and was therefore pre-empted under the *Garmon* line of decisions.

A. * * *

This pre-emption doctrine, however, has never been rigidly applied to cases where it could not fairly be inferred that Congress intended exclusive jurisdiction to lie with the NLRB. * * *

A primary justification for the pre-emption doctrine—the need to avoid conflicting rules of substantive law in the labor relations area and the desirability of leaving the development of such rules to the administrative agency created by Congress for that purpose—is not applicable to cases involving alleged breaches of the union's duty of fair representation. The doctrine was judicially developed in *Steele* and its progeny, and suits alleging breach of the duty remained judicially cognizable long after the NLRB was given unfair labor practice jurisdiction over union activities by the L.M.R.A. Moreover when the Board declared in *Miranda Fuel* that a union's breach of its duty of fair representation would henceforth be treated as an unfair labor practice, the Board adopted and applied the doctrine as it had been developed by the federal courts. * * * Finally, as the dissenting Board members in *Miranda Fuel* have pointed out, fair representation duty suits often require review of the substantive positions taken and policies pursued by a union in its negotiation of a collective bargaining agreement and in its handling of the grievance machinery; as these matters are not normally within the Board's unfair labor practice jurisdiction, it can be doubted whether the Board brings substantially greater expertise to bear on these problems than do the courts, which have been engaged in this type of review since the *Steele* decision. In addition to the above considerations, the unique interests served by the duty of fair representation doctrine have a profound effect, in our opinion, on the applicability of the pre-emption rule to this class of cases. The federal labor laws seek to promote industrial peace and the improvement of wages and working conditions by fostering a system of employee organization and collective bargaining. * * * The collective bargaining system as encouraged by Congress and administered by the NLRB of necessity subordinates the interests of an individual employee to the collective interests of all employees in a bargaining unit. See e.g., J.I. Case Co. v. N.L.R.B., 321 U.S. 332, 64 S.Ct. 576, 88 L.Ed. 762. This Court recognized in *Steele* that the congressional grant of power to a union to act as exclusive collective bargaining representative, with its corresponding reduction in the individual rights of the employees so represented, would raise grave constitutional problems if unions were free to exercise this power to further racial discrimination. * * * Since that landmark decision, the duty of fair representation has stood as a bulwark to prevent arbitrary union conduct against individuals stripped of traditional forms of redress by the provisions of federal labor law. Were we to hold, as petitioners and the Government urge, that the courts are foreclosed by the NLRB's *Miranda Fuel* decision from this traditional supervisory jurisdiction, the individual employee injured by arbitrary or discriminatory union conduct could no longer be assured of impartial review of his complaint, since the Board's General Counsel has unreviewable discretion to refuse to institute an unfair labor practice complaint. See United Electrical Contractors Assn. v. Ordman, 366 F.2d 776 (C.A.2d Cir.1966), cert. denied, 385 U.S. 1026, 87 S.Ct. 753, 17 L.Ed.2d 674.[8] The existence of even a small group of cases in which the Board would be unwilling or unable to remedy a union's breach of duty would frustrate the basic purposes underlying the duty of fair representation doctrine. For these reasons, we cannot assume from the NLRB's tardy assumption of jurisdiction in these cases that Congress, when it enacted N.L. R.A. § 8(b) in 1947, intended to oust the courts of their traditional jurisdiction to curb arbitrary conduct by the individual employee's statutory representative.

B. There are also some intensely practical considerations which fore-close pre-emption of judicial cognizance of fair representation duty suits, considerations which emerge from the intricate relationship between the duty of fair representation and the enforcement of collective bargaining contracts. For the fact is that the question of whether a union has breached its duty of fair representation will in many cases be a critical issue in a suit

8. The public interest in effectuating the policies of the federal labor laws, not the wrong done the individual employee, is always the Board's principal concern in fashioning unfair labor practice remedies. See N.L.R.A. § 10(c) * * *; Phelps Dodge Corp. v. N.L. R.B., 313 U.S. 177, 61 S.Ct. 845, 85 L.Ed. 1271. Thus, the General Counsel will refuse to bring complaints on behalf of injured employees where the injury complained of is "insubstantial." See Administrative Decision of the General Counsel, Case No. K–610, Aug. 13, 1956, in CCH N.L.R.B. Decisions, 1956–1957, at Transfer Binder, ¶ 54,059.

under L.M.R.A. § 301 charging an employer with a breach of contract. To illustrate, let us assume a collective bargaining agreement that limits discharges to those for good cause and that contains no grievance, arbitration or other provisions purporting to restrict access to the courts. If an employee is discharged without cause, either the union or the employee may sue the employer under L.M.R.A. § 301. Under this section, courts have jurisdiction over suits to enforce collective bargaining agreements even though the conduct of the employer which is challenged as a breach of contract is also arguably an unfair labor practice within the jurisdiction of the NLRB. *Garmon* and like cases have no application to § 301 suits. Smith v. Evening News Assn., 371 U.S. 195, 83 S.Ct. 267, 9 L.Ed.2d 246.

The rule is the same with regard to pre-emption where the bargaining agreement contains grievance and arbitration provisions which are intended to provide the exclusive remedy for breach of contract claims. If an employee is discharged without cause in violation of such an agreement, that the employer's conduct may be an unfair labor practice does not preclude a suit by the union against the employer to compel arbitration of the employee's grievance, the adjudication of the claim by the arbitrator, or a suit to enforce the resulting arbitration award. See e.g., United Steelworkers of America v. American Mfg. Co., 363 U.S. 564, 80 S.Ct. 1343, 4 L.Ed.2d 1403.

However, if the wrongfully discharged employee himself resorts to the courts before the grievance procedures have been fully exhausted, the employer may well defend on the ground that the exclusive remedies provided by such a contract have not been exhausted. Since the employee's claim is based upon breach of the collective bargaining agreement, he is bound by terms of that agreement which govern the manner in which contractual rights may be enforced. For this reason, it is settled that the employee must at least attempt to exhaust exclusive grievance and arbitration procedures established by the bargaining agreement. Republic Steel Corp. v. Maddox, 379 U.S. 650, 85 S.Ct. 614, 13 L.Ed.2d 580. However, because these contractual remedies have been devised and are often controlled by the union and the employer, they may well prove unsatisfactory or unworkable for the individual grievant. The problem then is to determine under what circumstances the individual employee may obtain judicial review of his breach-of-contract claim despite his failure to secure relief through the contractual remedial procedures.

An obvious situation in which the employee should not be limited to the exclusive remedial procedures established by the contract occurs when the conduct of the employer amounts to a repudiation of those contractual procedures. Cf. Drake Bakeries, Inc. v. Local 50, Am. Bakery, etc., Workers, 370 U.S. 254, 260–263, 82 S.Ct. 1346, 1350–1352, 8 L.Ed.2d 474. See generally 6A Corbin, Contracts § 1443 (1962). In such a situation (and there may of course be others), the employer is estopped by his own conduct to rely on the unexhausted grievance and arbitration procedures as a defense to the employee's cause of action.

We think that another situation when the employee may seek judicial enforcement of his contractual rights arises if, as is true here, the union has sole power under the contract to invoke the higher stages of the grievance procedure, *and* if, as is alleged here, the employee-plaintiff has been prevented from exhausting his contractual remedies by the union's *wrongful* refusal to process the grievance. It is true that the employer in such a situation may have done nothing to prevent exhaustion of the exclusive contractual remedies to which he agreed in the collective bargaining agreement. But the employer has committed a wrongful discharge in breach of that agreement, a breach which could be remedied through the grievance process to the employee-plaintiff's benefit were it not for the union's breach of its statutory duty of fair representation to the employee. To leave the employee remediless in such circumstances would, in our opinion, be a great injustice. We cannot believe that Congress, in conferring upon employers and unions the power to establish exclusive grievance procedures, intended to confer upon unions such unlimited discretion to deprive injured employees of all remedies for breach of contract. Nor do we think that Congress intended to shield employers from the natural consequences of their breaches of bargaining agreements by wrongful union conduct in the enforcement of such agreements. * * *

For these reasons, we think the wrongfully discharged employee may bring an action against his employer in the face of a defense based upon the failure to exhaust contractual remedies, provided the employee can prove that the union as bargaining agent breached its duty of fair representation in its handling of the employee's grievance. We may assume for present purposes that such a breach of duty by the union is an unfair labor practice, as the NLRB and the Fifth Circuit have held. The employee's suit against the employer, however, remains a § 301 suit, and the jurisdiction of the courts is no more destroyed by the fact that the employee, as part and parcel of his § 301 action, finds it necessary to prove an unfair labor practice by the union, than it is by the fact that the suit may involve an unfair labor practice by the employer himself. The court is free to determine whether the employee is barred by the actions of his union representative, and, if not, to proceed with the case. And if, to facilitate his case, the employee joins the union as a defendant, the situation is not substantially changed. The action is still a § 301 suit, and the jurisdiction of the courts is not preempted under the *Garmon* principle. * * * And, insofar as adjudication of the union's breach of duty is concerned, the result should be no different if the employee, as Owens did here, sues the employer and the union in separate actions. There would be very little to commend a rule which would permit the Missouri courts to adjudicate the Union's conduct in an action against Swift but not in an action against the Union itself. * * *

It follows from the above that the Missouri courts had jurisdiction in this case. * * *

III.

Petitioners contend, as they did in their motion for judgment notwithstanding the jury's verdict, that Owens failed to prove that the Union breached its duty of fair representation in its handling of Owens' grievance. Petitioners also argue that the Supreme Court of Missouri, in rejecting this contention, applied a standard that is inconsistent with governing principles of federal law with respect to the Union's duty to an individual employee in its processing of grievances under the collective bargaining agreement with Swift. We agree with both contentions.

A. In holding that the evidence at trial supported the jury's verdict in favor of Owens, the Missouri Supreme Court stated:

"The essential issue submitted to the jury was whether the union * * * arbitrarily * * * refused to carry said grievance * * * through the fifth step. * * *

"We have concluded that there was sufficient substantial evidence from which the jury reasonably could have found the foregoing issue in favor of plaintiff. It is notable that no physician actually testified in the case. Both sides were content to rely upon written statements. Three physicians certified that plaintiff was able to perform his regular work. Three other physicians certified that they had taken plaintiff's blood pressure and that the readings were approximately 160 over 100. It may be inferred that such a reading does not indicate that his blood pressure was dangerously high. Moreover, plaintiff's evidence showed that he had actually done hard physical labor periodically during the four years following his discharge. We accordingly rule this point adversely to defendants." 397 S.W.2d, at 665.

Quite obviously, the question which the Missouri Supreme Court thought dispositive of the issue of liability was whether the evidence supported Owens' assertion that he had been wrongfully discharged by Swift, regardless of the Union's good faith in reaching a contrary conclusion. This was also the major concern of the plaintiff at trial: the bulk of Owens' evidence was directed at whether he was medically fit at the time of discharge and whether he had performed heavy work after that discharge.

A breach of the statutory duty of fair representation occurs only when a union's conduct toward a member of the collective bargaining unit is arbitrary, discriminatory, or in bad faith. * * * There has been considerable debate over the extent of this duty in the context of a union's enforcement of the grievance and arbitration procedures in a collective bargaining agreement. See generally Blumrosen, The Worker and Three Phases of Unionism: Administrative and Judicial Control of the Worker-Union Relationship, 61 Mich.L.Rev. 1435, 1482–1501 (1963); Comment, Federal Protection of Individual Rights under Labor Contracts, 73 Yale L.J. 1215 (1964). Some have suggested that every individual employee should have the right to have his grievance taken to arbitration.[13] Others have urged that the union be given substantial discretion (if the collective bargaining agreement so provides) to decide whether a grievance should be taken to arbitration, subject only to the duty to refrain from patently wrongful conduct such as racial discrimination or personal hostility.[14]

Though we accept the proposition that a union may not arbitrarily ignore a meritorious grievance or process it in perfunctory fashion, we do not agree that the individual employee has an absolute right to have his grievance taken to arbitration regardless of the provisions of the applicable collective bargaining agreement. * * * In providing for a grievance and

13. See Donnelly v. United Fruit Co., 40 N.J. 61, 190 A.2d 825; Report of Committee on Improvement of Administration of Union-Management Agreements, 1954, Individual Grievances, 50 Nw.U.L.Rev. 143 (1955); Murphy, The Duty of Fair Representation under Taft-Hartley, 30 Mo.L.Rev. 373, 389 (1965); Summers, Individual Rights in Collective Agreements and Arbitration, 37 N.Y.U.L.Rev. 362 (1962).

14. See Sheremet v. Chrysler Corp., 372 Mich. 626, 127 N.W.2d 313; Wyle, Labor Arbitration and the Concept of Exclusive Representation, 7 B.C.Ind. & Com.L.Rev. 783 (1966).

arbitration procedure which gives the union discretion to supervise the grievance machinery and to invoke arbitration, the employer and the union contemplate that each will endeavor in good faith to settle grievances short of arbitration. Through this settlement process, frivolous grievances are ended prior to the most costly and time-consuming step in the grievance procedures. * * * [15]

* * * For these reasons, we conclude that a union does not breach its duty of fair representation, and thereby open up a suit by the employee for breach of contract, merely because it settled the grievance short of arbitration. * * *

[T]he Supreme Court of Missouri erred in upholding the verdict in this case solely on the ground that the evidence supported Owens' claim that he had been wrongfully discharged.

B. Applying the proper standard of union liability to the facts of this case, we cannot uphold the jury's award, for we conclude that as a matter of federal law the evidence does not support a verdict that the Union breached its duty of fair representation. As we have stated, Owens could not have established a breach of that duty merely by convincing the jury that he was in fact fit for work in 1960; he must also have proved arbitrary or bad-faith conduct on the part of the Union in processing his grievance. The evidence revealed that the Union diligently supervised the grievance into the fourth step of the bargaining agreement's procedure, with the Union's business representative serving as Owens' advocate throughout these steps. When Swift refused to reinstate Owens on the basis of his medical reports indicating reduced blood pressure, the Union sent him to another doctor of his own choice, at Union expense, in an attempt to amass persuasive medical evidence of Owens' fitness for work. When this examination proved unfavorable, the Union concluded that it could not establish a wrongful discharge. It then encouraged Swift to find light work for Owens at the plant. When this effort failed, the Union determined that arbitration would be fruitless and suggested to Owens that he accept Swift's offer to send him to a heart association for rehabilitation. At this point, Owens' grievance was suspended in the fourth step in the hope that he might be rehabilitated.

* * * There was no evidence that any Union officer was personally hostile to Owens or that the Union acted at any time other than in good faith. Having concluded that * * * a breach of the duty of fair representation is not established merely by proof that the underlying grievance was meritorious, we must conclude that that duty was not breached here.

IV.

In our opinion, there is another important reason why the judgment of the Missouri Supreme Court cannot stand. Owens' suit against the Union

---

15. Under current grievance practices, an attempt is usually made to keep the number of arbitrated grievances to a minimum. An officer of the National Union testified in this case that only one of 967 grievances filed at all of Swift's plants between September 1961 and October 1963 was taken to arbitration. And the AFL–CIO's *amicus* brief reveals similar performances at General Motors Corpora- tion and United States Steel Corporation, two of the Nation's largest unionized employers: less than .05% of all written grievances filed during a recent period at General Motors required arbitration, while only 5.6% of the grievances processed beyond the first step at United States Steel were decided by an arbitrator.

was grounded on his claim that Swift had discharged him in violation of the applicable collective bargaining agreement. In his complaint, Owens alleged "that, as a direct result of said wrongful breach of said contract, by employer * * * Plaintiff was damaged in the sum of Six Thousand, Five Hundred ($6,500.00) Dollars per year, continuing until the date of trial." For the Union's role in "preventing Plaintiff from completely exhausting administrative remedies," Owens requested, and the jury awarded, compensatory damages for the above-described breach of contract plus punitive damages of $3,000. We hold that such damages are not recoverable from the Union in the circumstances of this case.

The appropriate remedy for a breach of a union's duty of fair representation must vary with the circumstances of the particular breach. In this case, the employee's complaint was that the Union wrongfully failed to afford him the arbitration remedy against his employer established by the collective bargaining agreement. But the damages sought by Owens were primarily those suffered because of the employer's alleged breach of contract. * * *

Petitioners urge that an employee be restricted in such circumstances to a decree compelling the employer and the union to arbitrate the underlying grievance. It is true that the employee's action is based on the employer's alleged breach of contract plus the union's alleged wrongful failure to afford him his contractual remedy of arbitration. For this reason, an order compelling arbitration should be viewed as one of the available remedies when a breach of the union's duty is proved. But we see no reason inflexibly to require arbitration in all cases. In some cases, for example, at least part of the employee's damages may be attributable to the union's breach of duty, and an arbitrator may have no power under the bargaining agreement to award such damages against the union. In other cases, the arbitrable issues may be substantially resolved in the course of trying the fair representation controversy. In such situations, the court should be free to decide the contractual claim and to award the employee appropriate damages or equitable relief.

A more difficult question is, what portion of the employee's damages may be charged to the union: in particular, may an award against a union include, as it did here, damages attributable solely to the employer's breach of contract? We think not. Though the union has violated a statutory duty in failing to press the grievance, it is the employer's unrelated breach of contract which triggered the controversy and which caused this portion of the employee's damages. * * * [T]he employer may be (and probably should be) joined as a defendant in the fair representation suit * * *. It could be a real hardship on the union to pay these damages, even if the union were given a right of indemnification against the employer. * * *

The governing principle, then, is to apportion liability between the employer and the union according to the damage caused by the fault of each. Thus, damages attributable solely to the employer's breach of contract should not be charged to the union, but increases if any in those damages caused by the union's refusal to process the grievance should not be charged to the employer. In this case, even if the Union had breached its duty, all or almost all of Owens' damages would still be attributable to his allegedly wrongful discharge by Swift. For these reasons, even if the Union here had properly been found liable for a breach of duty, it is clear that the damage award was improper.

Reversed.

[Justice Fortas, joined by Chief Justice Warren and Justice Harlan, concurred in the result, but on the ground that the Garmon preemption doctrine should be applied.]

MR. JUSTICE BLACK, dissenting.

The Court today opens slightly the courthouse door to an employee's incidental claim against his union for breach of its duty of fair representation, only to shut it in his face when he seeks direct judicial relief for his underlying and more valuable breach-of-contract claim against his employer.

* * *

The Court recognizes as it must, that the jury in this case found at least that Benjamin Owens was fit for work; that his grievance against Swift was meritorious, and that Swift breached the collective bargaining agreement when it wrongfully discharged him. * * * [W]hen Owens attempts to proceed with his pending breach-of-contract action against Swift, Swift will undoubtedly secure its prompt dismissal by pointing to the Court's conclusion here that the union has not breached its duty of fair representation. Thus, Owens, who now has obtained a judicial determination that he was wrongfully discharged, is left remediless, and Swift having breached its contract, is allowed to hide behind, and is shielded by the union's conduct. I simply fail to see how it should make one iota of difference, as far as the "unrelated breach of contract" by Swift is concerned, whether the union's conduct is wrongful or rightful. Neither precedent nor logic supports the Court's new announcement that it does. * * *

Henceforth, in almost every § 301 breach-of-contract suit by an employee against an employer, the employee will have the additional burden of proving that the union acted arbitrarily or in bad faith. The Court never explains what is meant by this vague phrase or how trial judges are intelligently to translate it to a jury. Must the employee prove that the union in fact acted arbitrarily, or will it be sufficient to show that the employee's grievance was so meritorious that a reasonable union would not have refused to carry it to arbitration? Must the employee join the union in his § 301 suit against the employer, or must he join the employer in his unfair representation suit against the union? However these questions are answered, today's decision, requiring the individual employee to take on both the employer and the union in every suit against the employer and to prove not only that the employer breached its contract, but that the union acted arbitrarily, converts what would otherwise be a simple breach-of-contract action into a three-ring donnybrook. It puts an intolerable burden on employees with meritorious grievances * * *.[a]

Note

1. The last sentence of Justice Black's dissent provides a portal of entry into a whole complex of important problems: "It [the Court's decision] puts an

a. For a detailed analysis of the Vaca case, see Lewis, Fair Representation in Grievance Administration: Vaca v. Sipes, 1967 Sup.Ct. Rev. 81.

intolerable burden on employees with meritorious grievances." An appropriate opening question is, how is the meritoriousness of the grievance to be ascertained? Justice Black assumes Owens' grievance to have been "meritorious" solely because the jury found in his favor. Is this justifiable? The question of meritoriousness is necessarily one of interpretation of the contract between the employer and the union. By that contract, what has the employer obligated himself to do in the event of a claimed breach on his part? If the contract expressly states that the grievance-arbitration procedures incorporated therein are the "sole and exclusive" remedy to which the employer subjects himself, on what basis can the employer be subjected to other modes of enforcement? So viewed, does not Justice Black beg the question of the meritoriousness of Owens' grievance? Indeed, was not the grievance determined to be *un*meritorious by the very procedures agreed upon in the contract for the resolution of such questions?

This is the line of thought of Justice White, writing for the majority. The line of thought encounters next this obstacle: All well and good where the union acts *fairly,* but suppose it does not. Can the employer and union reasonably be thought to have intended that the union have the authority to act *unfairly* in performing its role in the grievance-resolution process? Of course not. Thus far, no hang-ups, at least conceptually. But now let us look more closely at some very real problems of both a practical *and* conceptual nature. Suppose in Vaca these modifications: Owens, still living, joins his employer and union as defendants in a court action in which he proves the union acted unfairly in not taking his grievance to arbitration and obtains a court order compelling arbitration of the grievance. Is Owens entitled to receive notice of the hearing before the arbitrator and opportunity to appear in his own behalf, either as an observer for the purpose of "policing" the good faith of the union in presenting his cause or, beyond this, as an active participant, in one degree or another? If your answer to these questions is yes, out of some concern for procedural due process in the arbitration environment, how far would you go in "protecting" Owens: Could he participate through his own lawyer? Could he present evidence, cross-examine witnesses (including the union's), and argue the case? Could he *control* the presentation of the case on the union's side, on the theory that it is *his* grievance which is at stake?

To the extent you offer Owens such procedural protection, do you not also derogate from the union's role as collective bargaining *representative* and foist upon the employer and the union a contract other than the one produced by the free bargaining between them?

2. The foregoing questions are largely unresolved. The Hines case, which follows, lies at their core. See also Edwards, Due Process Considerations in Labor Arbitration, 25 Arb.J.(n.s.) 141 (1970); Fleming, Some Problems of Due Process and Fair Procedure in Labor Arbitration, 13 Stan.L.Rev. 235 (1961).

HINES v. ANCHOR MOTOR FREIGHT, INC.

Supreme Court of the United States, 1976.
424 U.S. 554, 96 S.Ct. 1048, 47 L.Ed.2d 231.

MR. JUSTICE WHITE delivered the opinion of the Court.

The issue here is whether a suit against an employer by employees asserting breach of a collective-bargaining contract was properly dismissed where the accompanying complaint against the union for breach of duty of fair representation has withstood the union's motion for summary judgment and remains to be tried.

I

Petitioners,[1] who were formerly employed as truck drivers by respondent Anchor Motor Freight, Inc. (Anchor), were discharged on June 5, 1967. The applicable collective-bargaining contract forbade discharges without just cause. The company charged dishonesty. The practice at Anchor was to reimburse drivers for money spent for lodging while the drivers were on the road overnight. Anchor's assertion was that petitioners had sought reimbursement for motel expenses in excess of the actual charges sustained by them. At a meeting between the company and the union, Local 377, International Brotherhood of Teamsters (the Union), which was also attended by petitioners, Anchor presented motel receipts previously submitted by petitioners which were in excess of the charges shown on the motel's registration cards; a notarized statement of the motel clerk asserting the accuracy of the registration cards; and an affidavit of the motel owner affirming that the registration cards were accurate and that inflated receipts had been furnished petitioners. The Union claimed petitioners were innocent and opposed the discharges. It was then agreed that the matter would be presented to the joint arbitration committee for the area, to which the collective-bargaining contract permitted either party to submit an unresolved grievance.[2] Pending this hearing, petitioners were reinstated. Their suggestion that the motel be investigated was answered by the Union representatives' assurances that "there was nothing to worry about" and that they need not hire their own attorney.

A hearing before the joint area committee was held on July 26, 1967. Anchor presented its case. Both the Union and petitioners were afforded an opportunity to present their case and to be heard. Petitioners denied their dishonesty, but neither they nor the Union presented any other evidence contradicting the documents presented by the company. The committee sustained the discharges. Petitioners then retained an attorney and sought rehearing based on a statement by the motel owner that he had no personal knowledge of the events, but that the discrepancy between the receipts and the registration cards could have been attributable to the motel clerk's recording on the cards less than was actually paid and retaining for himself the difference between the amount receipted and the amount recorded. The

1. Two of the original petitioners, Burtice A. Hines and Arthur D. Cartwright, are deceased. Charles A. Hines and Chyra J. Cartwright have been substituted as party petitioners. 423 U.S. 816, 96 S.Ct. 390, 46 L.Ed.2d 300 (1975).

2. The contractual grievance procedure is set out in Art. 7 of the Central Conference Area Supplement to the National Master Agreement. Grievances were to be taken up by the employee involved and if no settlement was reached, were then to be considered by the business agent of the local union and the employer representative. If the dispute remained unresolved, either party had the right to present the case for decision to the appro-

priate joint area arbitration committee. These committees are organized on a geographical area basis and hear grievances in panels made up of an equal number of representatives of the parties to the collective-bargaining agreement. Cases that deadlocked before the joint area committee could be taken to a panel of the national joint arbitration committee, composed like the area committee panels of an equal number of representatives of the parties to the agreement. If unresolved there, they would be resolved by a panel including an impartial arbitrator. The joint arbitration committee for the Detroit area is involved in this case.

committee, after hearing, unanimously denied rehearing "because there was no new evidence presented which would justify reopening this case." App. 212.

There were later indications that the motel clerk was in fact the culprit; and the present suit was filed in June 1969, against Anchor, the Union and its International. The complaint alleged that the charges of dishonesty made against petitioners by Anchor were false, that there was no just cause for discharge and that the discharges had been in breach of contract. It was also asserted that the falsity of the charges could have been discovered with a minimum of investigation, that the Union had made no effort to ascertain the truth of the charges and that the Union had violated its duty of fair representation by arbitrarily and in bad faith depriving petitioners of their employment and permitting their discharge without sufficient proof.

The Union denied the charges and relied on the decision of the joint area committee. Anchor asserted that petitioners had been properly discharged for just cause. It also defended on the ground that petitioners, diligently and in good faith represented by the Union, had unsuccessfully resorted to the grievance and arbitration machinery provided by the contract and that the adverse decision of the joint arbitration committee was binding upon the Union and petitioners under the contractual provision declaring that "[a] decision by a majority of a Panel of any of the Committees shall be final and binding on all parties, including the employee and/or employees affected." Discovery followed, including a deposition of the motel clerk revealing that he had falsified the records and that it was he who had pocketed the difference between the sums shown on the receipts and the registration cards. Motions for summary judgment filed by Anchor and the Unions were granted by the District Court on the ground that the decision of the arbitration committee was final and binding on the employees and "for failure to show facts comprising bad faith, arbitrariness or perfunctoriness on the part of the Unions." 72 Labor Cases ¶ 13,987, at 28,131 (ND Ohio 1973). Although indicating that the acts of the Union "may not meet professional standards of competency, and while it might have been advisable for the Union to further investigate the charges * * *," the District Court concluded that the facts demonstrated at most bad judgment on the part of the Union, which was insufficient to prove a breach of duty or make out a prima facie case against it. Id., at 28,132.

After reviewing the allegations and the record before it, the Court of Appeals concluded that there were sufficient facts from which bad faith or arbitrary conduct on the part of the local Union could be inferred by the trier of fact and that petitioners should have been afforded an opportunity to prove their charges.[4] To this extent the judgment of the District Court was

---

4. As summarized by the Court of Appeals, the allegations relied on were:

"They consist of the motel clerk's admission, made a year after the discharge was upheld in arbitration, that he, not plaintiffs, pocketed the money; the claim of the union's failure to investigate the motel clerk's original story implicating plaintiffs despite their requests; the account of the union officials' assurances to plaintiffs that

'they had nothing to worry about' and 'that there was no need for them to investigate;' the contention that no exculpatory evidence was presented at the hearing; and the assertion that there existed political antagonism between local union officials and plaintiffs because of a wildcat strike led by some of the plaintiffs and a dispute over the appointment of a steward, resulting in denunciation of plaintiffs as 'hillbillies' by An-

reversed. The Court of Appeals affirmed the judgment in favor of Anchor and the International. Saying that petitioners wanted to relitigate their discharges because of the recantation of the motel clerk, the Court of Appeals, quoting from its prior opinion in Balowski v. International Union, 372 F.2d 829 (CA 6 1967),[5] concluded that the finality provision of collective-bargaining contracts must be observed because there was "[n]o evidence of any misconduct on the part of the employer * * *" and wholly insufficient evidence of any conspiracy between the Union and Anchor. 506 F.2d 1157, 1158.

It is this judgment of the Court of Appeals with respect to Anchor that is now before us on our limited grant of the employees' petition for writ of certiorari.[7] We reverse that judgment.

II

Section 301 of the Labor Management Relations Act provides for suits in the district courts for violation of collective-bargaining contracts between labor organizations and employers without regard to the amount in controversy. * * * Petitioners' present suit against the employer was for wrongful discharge and is the kind of case Congress provided for in § 301.

Collective-bargaining contracts, however, generally contain procedures for the settlement of disputes through mutual discussion and arbitration. These provisions are among those which are to be enforced under § 301. * * *

* * * Since Steele v. Louisville & N. R. Co., 323 U.S. 192, 65 S.Ct. 226, 89 L.Ed. 173 (1944), with respect to the railroad industry, and * * * Syres v. Oil Workers Local 23, 350 U.S. 892, 76 S.Ct. 152, 100 L.Ed. 785 (1955), with respect to those industries reached by the National Labor Relations Act, the duty of fair representation has served as a "bulwark to prevent arbitrary union conduct against individuals stripped of traditional forms of redress by the provisions of federal labor law." Vaca v. Sipes, 386 U.S., at 182, 87 S.Ct., at 912, 17 L.Ed.2d, at 853.

gelo, the union president." 506 F.2d 1153, 1156 (CA 6 1974).

5. The quoted segment of the opinion in Balowski v. International Union, supra, at 833, was:

" '[i]t is apparent that what plaintiff is attempting to do is to relitigate his grievance in this proceeding. This he cannot do when the collective bargaining agreement provides for final and binding arbitration of all disputes, absent a showing of fraud, misrepresentation, bad faith, dishonesty of purpose, or such gross mistake or inaction as to imply bad faith on the part of the Union or the employer.' " 506 F.2d, at 1157 (citation omitted).

The rule in the Sixth Circuit, under Balowski, would appear to have been that an employee could litigate his discharge in court if he proved bad faith or gross mistake on the part of either the union or the employer.

7. Our order of April 21, 1975, was as follows:

"Petition for writ of certiorari to the United States Court of Appeals for the Sixth Circuit granted limited to Question 1, presented by the petition which reads as follows:

" '1. Whether petitioners' claim under LMRA § 301 for wrongful discharge is barred by the decision of a joint grievance committee upholding their discharge, notwithstanding that their union breached its duty of fair representation in processing their grievance so as to deprive them and the grievance committee of overwhelming evidence of their innocence of the alleged dishonesty for which they were discharged.' Mr. Justice Douglas took no part in the consideration or decision of this petition."

The affirmance of summary judgment in favor of the International is therefore not before us. Nor is the judgment of the Court of Appeals reversing the summary judgment in favor of Local 377, since the Union has not sought review of this ruling.

Claims of union breach of duty may arise during the life of a contract when individual employees claim wrongful discharge or other improper treatment at the hands of the employer. Contractual remedies, at least in their final stages controlled by union and employer, are normally provided; yet the union may refuse to utilize them or, if it does, assertedly do so discriminatorily or in bad faith. "The problem then is to determine under what circumstances the individual employee may obtain judicial review of his breach-of-contract claim despite his failure to secure relief through the contractual remedial procedures." Vaca v. Sipes, supra, at 185, 87 S.Ct., at 914, 17 L.Ed.2d, at 854. * * *

In Vaca v. Sipes, the discharged employee sued the union alleging breach of its duty of fair representation in that it had refused in bad faith to take the employee's grievance to arbitration as it could have under the contract. In the course of rejecting the claim that the alleged conduct was arguably an unfair practice within the exclusive jurisdiction of the Labor Board, we ruled that "the wrongfully discharged employee may bring an action against his employer in the face of a defense based upon the failure to exhaust contractual remedies, provided the employee can prove that the union as bargaining agent breached its duty of fair representation in its handling of the employee's grievance." 386 U.S., at 186, 87 S.Ct., at 914, 17 L.Ed.2d, at 855 (footnote omitted). This was true even though "the employer in such a situation may have done nothing to prevent exhaustion of the exclusive contractual remedies * * *," for "the employer has committed a wrongful discharge in breach of that agreement, a breach which could be remedied through the grievance process * * * were it not for the union's breach of its statutory duty of fair representation * * *." Id., at 185, 87 S.Ct., at 914, 17 L.Ed.2d, at 855. We could not "believe that Congress, in conferring upon employers and unions the power to establish exclusive grievance procedures, intended to confer upon unions such unlimited discretion to deprive injured employees of all remedies for breach of contract." Nor did we "think that Congress intended to shield employers from the natural consequences of their breaches of bargaining agreements by wrongful union conduct in the enforcement of such agreements." Id., at 186, 87 S.Ct., at 914, 17 L.Ed.2d, at 855. At the same time "we conclude[d] that a union does not breach its duty of fair representation * * * merely because it settled the grievance short of arbitration." Id., at 192, 87 S.Ct., at 918, 17 L.Ed.2d, at 859. * * * We also expressly indicated that suit against the employer and suit against the union could be joined in one action. Id., at 187, 87 S.Ct., at 915, 17 L.Ed.2d, at 856.

III

Even though under *Vaca* the employer may not insist on exhaustion of grievance procedures when the union has breached its representation duty, it is urged that when the procedures have been followed and a decision favorable to the employer announced, the employer must be protected from relitigation by the express contractual provision declaring a decision to be final and binding. We disagree. The union's breach of duty relieves the employee of an express or implied requirement that disputes be settled through contractual grievance procedures; if it seriously undermines the integrity of the arbitral process the union's breach also removes the bar of the finality provisions of the contract.

It is true that *Vaca* dealt with a refusal by the union to process a grievance. It is also true that where the union actually utilizes the grievance and arbitration procedures on behalf of the employee, the focus is no longer on the reasons for the union's failure to act but on whether, contrary to the arbitrator's decision, the employer breached the contract and whether there is substantial reason to believe that a union breach of duty contributed to the erroneous outcome of the contractual proceedings. * * *

In *Vaca* "we accept[ed] the proposition that a union may not arbitrarily ignore a meritorious grievance or process it in a perfunctory fashion," 386 U.S., at 191, 87 S.Ct., at 917, 17 L.Ed.2d, at 856; and our ruling that the union had not breached its duty of fair representation in not pressing the employee's case to the last step of the grievance process stemmed from our evaluation of the manner in which the union had handled the grievance in its earlier stages. Although "the Union might well have breached its duty had it ignored [the employee's] complaint or had it processed the grievance in a perfunctory manner," "the Union conclude[d] that arbitration would be fruitless and that the grievance should be dismissed" only after it had "processed the grievance into the fourth step, attempted to gather sufficient evidence to prove [the employee's] case, attempted to secure for [him] less vigorous work at the plant, and joined in the employer's efforts to have [him] rehabilitated." Id., at 194, 87 S.Ct., at 919, 17 L.Ed.2d, at 860.

Anchor would have it that petitioners are foreclosed from judicial relief unless some blameworthy conduct on its part disentitles it to rely on the finality rule. But it was Anchor that originated the discharges for dishonesty. If those charges were in error, Anchor has surely played its part in precipitating this dispute. Of course, both courts below held there were no facts suggesting that Anchor either knowingly or negligently relied on false evidence. As far as the record reveals it also prevailed before the joint committee after presenting its case in accordance with what were ostensibly wholly fair procedures. Nevertheless there remains the question whether the contractual protection against relitigating an arbitral decision binds employees who assert that the process has fundamentally malfunctioned by reason of the bad-faith performance of the union, their statutorily imposed collective-bargaining agent.

Under the rule announced by the Court of Appeals, unless the employer is implicated in the Union's malfeasance or has otherwise caused the arbitral process to err, petitioners would have no remedy against Anchor even though they are successful in proving the Union's bad faith, the falsity of the charges against them and the breach of contract by Anchor by discharging without cause. This rule would apparently govern even in circumstances where it is shown that a union has manufactured the evidence and knows from the start that it is false; or even if, unbeknownst to the employer, the union has corrupted the arbitrator to the detriment of disfavored union members. As is the case where there has been a failure to exhaust, however, we cannot believe that Congress intended to foreclose the employee from his § 301 remedy otherwise available against the employer if the contractual processes have been seriously flawed by the union's breach of its duty to represent employees honestly and in good faith and without invidious discrimination or arbitrary conduct.

It is urged that the reversal of the Court of Appeals will undermine not only the finality rule but the entire collective-bargaining process. Employers, it is said, will be far less willing to give up their untrammeled right to discharge without cause and to agree to private settlement procedures. But the burden on employees will remain a substantial one, far too heavy in the opinion of some.[10] To prevail against either the company or the Union, petitioners must show not only that their discharge was contrary to the contract but must also carry the burden of demonstrating breach of duty by the Union. As the District Court indicated, this involves more than demonstrating mere errors in judgment.

Petitioners are not entitled to relitigate their discharge merely because they offer newly discovered evidence that the charges against them were false and that in fact they were fired without cause. The grievance processes cannot be expected to be error-free. The finality provision has sufficient force to surmount occasional instances of mistake. But it is quite another matter to suggest that erroneous arbitration decisions must stand even though the employee's representation by the Union has been dishonest, in bad faith or discriminatory; for in that event error and injustice of the grossest sort would multiply. The contractual system would then cease to qualify as an adequate mechanism to secure individual redress for damaging failure of the employer to abide by the contract. Congress has put its blessing on private dispute settlement arrangements provided in collective agreements, but it was anticipated, we are sure, that the contractual machinery would operate within some minimum levels of integrity. In our view, enforcement of the finality provision where the arbitrator has erred is conditioned upon the Union's having satisfied its statutory duty fairly to represent the employee in connection with the arbitration proceedings. Wrongfully discharged employees would be left without jobs and without a fair opportunity to secure an adequate remedy.

Except for this case the Courts of Appeals have arrived at similar conclusions.[11] As the Court of Appeals for the Ninth Circuit put it in Margetta v. Pam Pam Corp., 501 F.2d 179, 180 (1974): "To us, it makes little difference whether the union subverts the arbitration process by refusing to proceed as in *Vaca* or follows the arbitration trail to the end, but in doing so subverts the arbitration process by failing to fairly represent the employee. In neither case does the employee receive fair representation."

10. Mr. Justice Black, for one, was of the view that where the union refused to process agreements, the employee should be allowed his suit in court without proof of the union's breach of duty. Vaca v. Sipes, 386 U.S. 171, 203, 87 S.Ct. 903, 923–924, 17 L.Ed.2d 842 (1967) (dissenting opinion).

11. Steinman v. Spector Freight System, Inc., 441 F.2d 599 (CA 2 1971); Butler v. Local Union 823, International Brotherhood of Teamsters, 514 F.2d 442 (CA 8), cert. denied, 423 U.S. 924, 96 S.Ct. 265, 46 L.Ed.2d 249 (1975); Margetta v. Pam Pam Corporation, 501 F.2d 179 (CA 9 1974); Local 13, International Longshoremen's and Warehousemen's Union v. Pacific Maritime Association, 441 F.2d 1061 (CA 9 1971), cert. denied, 404 U.S. 1016, 92 S.Ct. 677, 30 L.Ed.2d 664 (1972). See also Bieski v. Eastern Automobile Forwarding Co., 396 F.2d 32, 38 (CA 3 1968); Rothlein v. Armour & Co., 391 F.2d 574, 579–580 (CA 3 1968); Harris v. Chemical Leaman Tank Lines, Inc., 437 F.2d 167, 171 (CA 5 1971); Andrus v. Convoy Co., 480 F.2d 604, 606 (CA 9), cert. denied, 414 U.S. 989, 94 S.Ct. 286, 38 L.Ed.2d 228 (1973).

Petitioners, if they prove an erroneous discharge and the Union's breach of duty tainting the decision of the joint committee, are entitled to an appropriate remedy against the employer as well as the Union. It was error to affirm the District Court's final dismissal of petitioners' action against Anchor. To this extent the judgment of the Court of Appeals is reversed.

So ordered.

Judgment reversed.

MR. JUSTICE STEVENS took no part in the consideration or decision of this case.

MR. JUSTICE STEWART, concurring.

I agree with the Court that proof of breach of the Union's duty of fair representation will remove the bar of finality from the arbitral decision that Anchor did not wrongfully discharge the petitioners. * * * But this is not to say that proof of breach of the Union's representation duty would render Anchor potentially liable for backpay accruing between the time of the "tainted" decision by the grievance committee and a subsequent "untainted" determination that the discharges were, after all, wrongful.

If an employer relies in good faith on a favorable arbitral decision, then his failure to reinstate discharged employees cannot be anything but rightful, until there is a contrary determination. Liability for the intervening wage loss must fall not on the employer but on the Union. Such an apportionment of damages is mandated by *Vaca's* holding that "damages attributable solely to the employer's breach of contract should not be charged to the union, but increases if any in those damages caused by the union's refusal to process the grievance should not be charged to the employer." 386 U.S., at 197–198, 87 S.Ct., at 920, 17 L.Ed.2d, at 862. To hold an employer liable for back wages for the period during which he rightfully refuses to rehire discharged employees would be to charge him with a contractual violation on the basis of conduct precisely in accord with the dictates of the collective agreement.

MR. JUSTICE REHNQUIST, with whom THE CHIEF JUSTICE joins, dissenting.

Petitioners seek $1 million damages from their employer and their union on the grounds that they were wrongfully discharged from their jobs. The District Court granted summary judgment for respondents, finding that the issues had been finally decided as to respondent Anchor Motor by the arbitration committee and that petitioners had failed "to show facts comprising bad faith, arbitrariness or perfunctoriness on the part of the Unions." The Court of Appeals reversed the summary judgment as to the local Union holding that the issue of bad faith should not have been summarily decided. However, as to respondent Anchor Motor the Court of Appeals affirmed, holding that where, as here, the collective-bargaining agreement provided that arbitration would be final and binding, the decision of the arbitrator would not be upset, "absent a showing of fraud, misrepresentation, bad faith, dishonesty of purpose or such gross mistake or inaction as to imply bad faith on the part of the Union or the employer." This Court, assuming *arguendo* that the Union breached its duty of fair representation for the reasons set forth in the opinion, reversed as to Anchor Motor, holding that the *Union's* breach of its duty to its members voided an otherwise valid arbitration decision in favor of the *company*. I find this result to be anomalous and contrary to the longstanding policy of this Court favoring the finality of arbitration awards.

In Vaca v. Sipes, 386 U.S. 171, 87 S.Ct. 903, 17 L.Ed.2d 842 (1967), this Court held that, where the union has prevented the employee from taking his grievance to arbitration, as provided in the collective-bargaining agreement, he may then turn to the courts for relief. This decision bolstered the consistent policy of this Court of encouraging the parties to settle their differences according to the terms of their collective-bargaining agreement. United Steel Workers v. American Mfg. Co., 363 U.S. 564, 566, 80 S.Ct. 1343, 1345–1346, 4 L.Ed.2d 1403 (1960). By subjecting the employer to a damage suit due to the union's failure to utilize the arbitration process on behalf of the employees, the *Vaca* decision put pressure on both employers and unions to make full use of the contractual provisions for settling disputes by arbitration.

The decision in this case will have the exact opposite result. Here the Court has cast aside the policy of finality of arbitration decisions and established a new policy of encouraging challenges to arbitration decrees by the losing party on the ground that he was not properly represented.

The majority cite Margetta v. Pam Pam Corp., 501 F.2d 179, 180 (CA9 1974), for the proposition that "it makes little difference whether the union subverts the arbitration process by refusing to proceed as in Vaca or follows the arbitration trial to the end, but in doing so subverts the arbitration process by failing to fairly represent the employee." To the contrary, I believe that the existence of a final arbitration decision is the crucial difference between this case and *Vaca*. The duty of "fair representation" discussed in *Vaca* was the duty of the union to put the case to a fair and neutral arbitrator, a step which the employee could not take by himself.

Here the case *was* presented to a concededly fair and neutral arbitrator but the claim is that that arbitration decision should be vacated because the employee did not receive "fair representation" from the Union in the sense of representation by counsel at a trial. Obviously this stretches *Vaca* far beyond its original meaning and adopts the novel notion that one may vacate an otherwise valid arbitration award because his "counsel" was ineffective.

As noted, such a principle violates this Court's policy favoring the finality of arbitration awards. It also has no basis in the statutory provisions respecting arbitration. The Uniform Arbitration Act, which is in use in many States, sets forth the grounds for vacating an award. Un.Arb.Act § 12. These include awards having been procured by corruption or fraud, and arbitrators exceeding their powers or exhibiting evident partiality. The federal statute governing arbitration, 9 U.S.C.A. §§ 1–14, provides similarly narrow grounds for vacating an award. 9 U.S.C.A. § 10. Nowhere is any provision made for vacation of an award due to ineffective presentation of the case by a party's attorney or representative.

The Court's decision is particularly vexing on the facts of this case. Petitioners' had all of the information necessary to present their case at their own disposal. If they had felt that the Union had not brought this information fully to the attention of the arbitration committee or that further investigation was necessary they could have so informed the committee. There is no indication that they did so. Rather, they allowed without protest, the arbitration to proceed to a decision and when that decision was adverse they brought suit against the company and the Union.

Now the employer, which concededly acted in good faith throughout these proceedings is to be subjected to a damage suit because of the Union's alleged misconduct. In view of the fact that petitioners have an action for damages against the Union, see Czosek v. O'Mara, 397 U.S. 25, 90 S.Ct. 770, 25 L.Ed.2d 21 (1970), this additional remedy against the employer seems both undesirable and unnecessary.

For the reasons stated I would affirm the judgment of the Court of Appeals.

Note

1. How would you answer the dissent's argument that the decision in Hines undermines the finality premise upon which the whole scheme of arbitration rests?

2. What must the plaintiff employees prove on remand in order to establish breach of the duty of fair representation? If the plaintiffs had been represented by counsel of their own choosing in the original proceedings before the "joint area arbitration committee," all else remaining the same, would the decision of the Supreme Court have been different?

Should negligence on the part of the union be held to constitute a breach of the duty of fair representation? In which direction would you expect the law to be moving on this question? * * * You are right, but the movement is gingerly and circumlocutory. See, e.g., Ruzicka v. General Motors Corp., 523 F.2d 306 (6th Cir.1975) (union agent's "neglect" to file grievance within contractual time limit held "arbitrary" in the sense of "perfunctory").

3. Assuming the plaintiffs succeed on remand in proving a breach by the union of the duty of fair representation, what, if anything, must they further prove in order to establish liability on the part of the employer? If plaintiffs are successful, what relief should they get and from whom?

In Bowen v. United States Postal Service, 459 U.S. 212, 103 S.Ct. 588, 74 L.Ed.2d 402 (1983), the Court (5–4) defined more clearly the formula for apportioning hybrid 301/duty of fair representation damages between employer and union. The majority held that the liability of the employer covers the period from the time of wrongful discharge or other contract-breaching action to the time when appropriate union handling of the grievance-arbitration procedure would have provided relief for the grievant. The liability of the union covers the period from the time of the union's breach of the duty of fair representation to the time of rectification of the wrongs done to the employee through court action. In other words, liability is apportioned between the employer and the union in accordance with the damages caused by the fault of each. Justice White, joined by Justices Blackmun, Marshall and Rehnquist, dissented for the following reason:

"The Court, in effect, sustains the employer's protest to the union that 'you should be liable for all damages flowing from my wrong from and after a certain time, because you should have caught and rectified my wrong by that time.' Seymour v. Olin Corp., 666 F.2d 202, 215 (CA 5 1982). The employer's wrongful conduct clearly was the generating cause of Bowen's loss, and only the employer had the continuing ability to right the wrong and limit liability by reinstating Bowen. The employer has the sole duty to pay wages, and it should be responsible for all back wages to which Bowen is entitled." 459 U.S. at 239, 103 S.Ct. at 604, 74 L.Ed.2d at 423.

With whom do you agree?

In International Brotherhood of Electrical Workers v. Foust, 442 U.S. 42, 99 S.Ct. 2121, 60 L.Ed.2d 698 (1979), the Court concluded that punitive damages could not be awarded in a duty of fair representation case. The claim of violation of the duty was based on the union's failure to file a grievance within the contractual limitation period of 90 days, thus finalizing the discharge of the plaintiff. A jury awarded the plaintiff $40,000 actual damages and $75,000 punitive damages. As explained in the majority opinion in Bowen (459 U.S. at 227, 103 S.Ct. at 597–98, 74 L.Ed.2d at 416 n. 16): "In *Foust*, we found that a union was not liable for punitive damages. The interest in deterring future breaches by the union was outweighed by the debilitating impact that 'unpredictable and potentially substantial' awards of punitive damages would have on the union treasury and the union's exercise of discretion in deciding what claims to pursue. Id., at 50–52. An award of compensatory damages, however, normally will be limited and finite."

4. In view of the character of the "joint area arbitration committee" (see footnote 2, supra p. 754), is the product of that committee to be evaluated by quasi-legislative standards (i.e., as a product of collective bargaining) or by quasi-judicial standards? Does it make any difference?

Should, indeed, the decisions of such joint arbitration panels be accorded any deference at all? This question was addressed in Barrentine v. Arkansas-Best Freight System, Inc., 615 F.2d 1194 (8th Cir.1979), reversed on other grounds, 450 U.S. 728, 101 S.Ct. 1437, 67 L.Ed.2d 641:

"Before discussing the validity of the particular arbitration awards that were made in this case, we will take up the plaintiffs' underlying argument that it is inherently unfair and contrary to federal labor policy to submit individual employee grievances to arbitration by panels made up of representatives of management and organized labor even though an effort to achieve impartiality is made by a requirement that neither the employer nor the local union involved in the particular dispute to be submitted is to be represented on the arbitration panel.

"While the defendants strongly urge that this contention is not properly before us for consideration, we will assume *arguendo* that it is.

"A forceable argument can be made, and has been made here, that the kind of arbitration in question is subject to grave abuses, including notably, collusive secret agreements between employers and unions as a result of which the interests of individual employee grievants may be sacrificed to arrangements that management and union labor may consider to be in their own broader interests.

"This method of arbitration, which is widely used to settle individual employee grievances arising under contracts to which locals of the Teamsters Union are parties, has been criticized on account of the possibility of abuses just mentioned. See General Drivers & Helpers Union, Local No. 554 v. Young & Hay Transp. Co., 522 F.2d 562, 567 n. 5 (8th Cir.1975). See also Feller, 'A General Theory of the Collective Bargaining Agreement,' 61

Cal.L.Rev. 663, 836–38 (1973); Azoff, 'Joint Committees As An Alternative Form of Arbitration Under The NLRA,' 47 Tul.L.Rev. 325 (1973).

"However, as of this time the law seems to be established that the joint committee method of arbitration is valid, and that committee awards are final and enforceable so long as the unions involved do not breach the duty of fair representation owed to union members and so long as the awards do not radically depart from the terms of the collective bargaining agreements involved. Hines v. Anchor Motor Freight, Inc., 424 U.S. 554, 96 S.Ct. 1048, 47 L.Ed.2d 231 (1976); Humphrey v. Moore, 375 U.S. 335, 84 S.Ct. 363, 11 L.Ed.2d 370 (1964); General Drivers, Warehousemen & Helpers Local Union No. 89 v. Riss & Co., Inc., 372 U.S. 517, 83 S.Ct. 789, 9 L.Ed.2d 918 (1963).

"In view of this state of the law plaintiffs' attack on joint committee arbitration in general must be rejected." 615 F.2d at 1201.

5. In DelCostello v. International Brotherhood of Teamsters, 462 U.S. 151, 103 S.Ct. 2281, 76 L.Ed.2d 476 (1983), the Court held that the statute of limitations to be applied in hybrid 301/duty of fair representation cases is the six-month period prescribed in section 10(b) for the filing of an unfair labor practice charge. This limitation was held to be applicable to both the breach of contract action against the employer and the breach of the duty of fair representation action against the union. In so holding, the Court rejected resort to arguably relevant state statutes of limitations which are sometimes looked to when there is no express statute of limitations.

THE EROSION OF THE "EMPLOYMENT AT WILL" DOCTRINE: INDIVIDUAL RIGHTS BEYOND (OUTSIDE OF) COLLECTIVE BARGAINING

Job security is the core concern of employees and is, accordingly, the primal motivation toward unionization and collective bargaining. Most employment is "at will," i.e., not contractually protected except where there is a collective bargaining agreement. At common law, "employment at will" is, as its name connotes, terminable at any time, without cause, on the part of either the employer or the employee. As stated in the Budd Mfg. case, supra p. 241: "[A]n employer may discharge an employee for a good reason, a poor reason or no reason at all so long as the provisions of the National Labor Relations Act [or other federal or state statutes] are not violated." As a consequence, one of the first demands of a union in negotiating a collective bargaining agreement is for contractual provisions limiting an employer's right to terminate employment to instances of "just cause," and subjecting that determination to the due process of a grievance-arbitration system.

One of the most recent developments in the evolution of the law pertaining to employment relations is the emergence of challenge to the employment-at-will doctrine; this challenge seeks to provide job "tenure" for *non*unionized employees. While this development is understandable and, indeed, laudable, it holds the ironic potential of weakening the union movement through co-opting the basic job-security motivation to organize. As might be expected, the attack on the employment-at-will doctrine occurs most typically in nonunionized employment contexts; its impact, however, is by no means so restricted. The potential of this impact on traditional collective bargaining relationships is presaged in the following case.

In Garibaldi v. Lucky Food Stores, Inc., 726 F.2d 1367 (9th Cir.1984), John Garibaldi, a truck driver, had been employed for years by Lucky Food Stores, was a member of the Teamsters Union, and was covered by a collective bargaining agreement with the employer. He was discharged for refusal to deliver a load of milk which he believed to be spoiled. He had reported this belief to his employer, but was instructed nonetheless to deliver the milk. Instead, he notified the local health department, which condemned the milk and ordered that it not be delivered. He was subsequently discharged, and filed a grievance that was processed through arbitration. The arbitrator found that he had been discharged for cause.

Garibaldi thereafter filed a complaint in a California court, seeking damages for wrongful termination of his employment in violation of the public policy of the state of California as declared by a statute prohibiting the sale or delivery of adulterated milk. Lucky Food Stores removed the case to a federal district court. Garibaldi moved to remand the case to the state court. The federal court upheld the removal for the reason that the cause of action was premised upon Section 301 of the Labor Management Relations Act and thus was preempted by the federal law. Applying the federal law, the district court granted summary judgment to the employer. Garibaldi appealed to the Ninth Circuit.

Stating that the preemption issue, based on a claim for wrongful termination in violation of state public policy, was one of first impression, the Ninth Circuit confronted the question of whether the federal statute and regulatory scheme left room for state regulations. The court held that the claim for wrongful termination was not preempted and remanded the issue for decision to the state court. In so doing, the Ninth Circuit stated:

> "An action for wrongful termination exists under California law in three circumstances: when the termination would violate (1) public policy, (2) a statute, or (3) an express or implied contract term that the employee was hired to serve so long as he or she performed to the satisfaction of the employer. See Cleary v. American Airlines, 111 Cal.App.3d 443, 450, 168 Cal.Rptr. 722, 726 (1980); Patterson v. Philco Corp., 252 Cal.App.2d 63, 65, 60 Cal.Rptr. 110 (1967).[9]

> "The public policy exception was established by the California Supreme Court in Tameny v. Atlantic Richfield Co., 27 Cal.3d 167, 164 Cal.Rptr. 839, 610 P.2d 1330 (1980), where the court allowed a cause of action for wrongful discharge arising out of the plaintiff's refusal to fix retail gasoline prices in violation of federal law. The Court held that an 'employer cannot condition employment upon required participation in unlawful conduct by the employee.' 27 Cal.3d at 178, 164 Cal.Rptr. at 845, 610 P.2d at 1330. The court recognized that the 'employer's obligation to refrain from discharging an employee who refuses to commit a criminal act does not depend on any express or implied "'promises set forth in the [employment] contract'" * * *, but rather reflects a duty imposed by law upon all employers in

9. Lucky Food Stores argues that California wrongful termination law does not apply to union employees. That issue has never been addressed by the California courts. We see nothing in the cases addressing wrongful termination in violation of public policy that suggests the distinction. The argument would have considerable force in a case such as Cleary v. American Airlines, 111 Cal.App.3d 443, 168 Cal.Rptr. 722 (1980). Absent California law to support Lucky Food Stores' contention, we decline to look beyond Garibaldi's assertion of a state law claim. Removal is judged by the face of the complaint.

order to implement the fundamental public policies embodied in the state's penal statutes.' 27 Cal.3d at 176, 164 Cal.Rptr. at 844, 610 P.2d at 1330.[10] Thus, it is clear that California's interest in providing a cause of action for violation of public policy or a statute is the enforcement of the underlying statute or policy, not the regulation of the employment relationship.

"In contrast, California's interest in job security based on an express or implied contractual term of employment [in a non-unionized employment context] is quite different. In Cleary v. American Airlines, 111 Cal.App.3d 443, 168 Cal.Rptr. 722, the court held that 'the longevity of the employee's service, together with the expressed policy of the employer [of adopting specific procedures for adjudicating employee disputes], operate as a form of estoppel, precluding any discharge of such an employee by the employer without good cause.' 111 Cal.App.3d at 455, 456, 168 Cal.Rptr. at 729. The court departed from the concept that 'at will' employees could be terminated without any reason whatsoever, see Marin v. Jacuzzi, 224 Cal.App.2d 549, 553, 36 Cal.Rptr. 880 (1964), and applied in the employment context the 'covenant of good faith and fair dealing' which it had implied into insurance contracts. See Communale v. Traders & General Insurance Co., 50 Cal.2d 654, 658, 328 P.2d 198 (1958). Although the court used *Tameny* as precedent, it went beyond it to protect a different type of interest, protecting 'certain implied contract rights to *job security*, necessary to ensure social stability in our society [in the absence of a collective bargaining agreement].' 111 Cal.App.3d at 455, 168 Cal.Rptr. at 729 (emphasis added).

" * * *

"Garibaldi's 'whistle blowing' to protect the health and safety of the citizens of California is exactly the type of conduct that the California Supreme Court protected in *Tameny.* * * * In contrast, if Garibaldi had alleged that he was terminated in violation of the collective bargaining contract, or, based on Cleary v. American Airlines, in violation of an implied covenant not to terminate without cause, the result might be otherwise.[11]

"A claim grounded in state law for wrongful termination for public policy reasons poses no significant threat to the collective bargaining process; it does not alter the economic relationship between the employer and employee. The remedy is in *tort,* distinct from any contractual remedy an employee might have under the collective bargaining contract. It furthers the state's interest in protecting the general public—an interest which transcends the employment relationship. See *New York Telephone,* 440 U.S. at 533, 99 S.Ct. at 1337 [discussed supra p. 554].[12]

10. Other states have adopted doctrines similar to *Tameny.* See e.g., Trombetta v. Detroit, Toledo & Iron R.R., 81 Mich.App. 489, 496, 265 N.W.2d 385, 388 (1978) (discharge for refusal to manipulate pollution control reports—not preempted by RLA); Pierce v. Ortho Pharmaceutical Corp., 84 N.J. 58, 417 A.2d 505 (1980) (protesting testing harmful drug on humans); Nees v. Hocks, 272 Or. 210, 536 P.2d 512 (1975) (discharge for reporting for jury service).

11. As discussed in note 9, *supra,* the rationale of *Cleary* is of doubtful applicability in this case. The court relied strongly on the lack of job security possessed by *at will* employees under the former California common law. No such lack of job security exists for union employees. * * *.

12. A recent decision supports the result we reach in this case. In Machinists Automotive Trades District Lodge No. 190 v. Utility Trailer Sales, 141 Cal.App.3d 80, 190 Cal.Rptr. 98 (1st Dist.), appeal dismissed ___ U.S. ___, 104 S.Ct. 520, 78 L.Ed.2d 705 (1983), the California Court of Appeal held that an employee's statutory right of indemnity [for expenses or losses incurred in the performance of duty] by his employer under state law was not preempted by federal labor law. The court said,

the fact that a matter is a subject of collective bargaining does not preclude the state from adopting standards to protect the wel-

" * * *

"We hold that the claim for wrongful termination based on state public policy is not preempted by section 301 of the LMRA. Removal was improper. Because the district court had no jurisdiction over this case, we reverse and remand to the district court with instructions to remand to the California state court." 726 F.2d at 1373–76.

Note

1. An aspect of Garibaldi, dealt with only tangentially in the foregoing excerpt, involves the implications of the erosion of the employment-at-will doctrine for the duty of fair representation. It should be noted that John Garibaldi's claim against Lucky Food Stores was processed by the Teamster's Union through the contractual grievance procedures, including arbitration, and that the decision of the arbitrator was in favor of the employer. No charge of violation of the union's duty of fair representation was made. The recognition of the *state* wrongful-termination cause of action thus provided a kind of "end run" around the substantive and procedural requirements for successful suit against the employer, as outlined in Vaca and Hines. The court relied upon "the distinctly separate nature" of rights asserted under the collective bargaining agreement, as to which the Section 301/duty of fair representation doctrinal paraphernalia would apply, and rights asserted under state statutory and judicial policy.

Is the above circumvention sound? For an analogy, see Alexander v. Gardner-Denver Co., infra p. 928, where the Supreme Court holds an adverse arbitration award non-dispositive of an employee's claim under Title VII of the Civil Rights Act of 1964.

2. The onslaught of the "wrongful termination" cases on the "at will" doctrine is explored in Summers, Individual Protection Against Unjust Dismissal: Time For a Statute, 62 Va.L.Rev. 481 (1976); Peck, Unjust Discharges From Employment: A Necessary Change in the Law, 40 Ohio St.L.J. 1 (1979); Pierce, Mann & Roberts, Employee Termination at Will: A Principled Approach, 28 Vill.L.Rev. 1 (1983); Heinsz, The Assault on the Employment At Will Doctrine: Management Considerations, 48 Mo.L.Rev. 855 (1983); Comment, Protecting at Will Employees Against Wrongful Discharge: The Duty to Terminate Only in Good Faith, 93 Harv.L.Rev. 1816 (1980).

2. UNION SECURITY

NATIONAL LABOR RELATIONS BOARD v. GENERAL MOTORS CORP.

Supreme Court of the United States, 1963.
373 U.S. 734, 83 S.Ct. 1453, 10 L.Ed.2d 670.

MR. JUSTICE WHITE delivered the opinion of the Court.

The issue here is whether an employer commits an unfair labor practice * * * when it refuses to bargain with a certified union over the union's

---

fare of the workers * * *. Bower's statutory right to indemnity is independent of any contractual right.

190 Cal.Rptr. at 100, citing Alexander v. Gardner-Denver Co., 415 U.S. 36, 52, 94 S.Ct. 1011, 1021, 39 L.Ed.2d 147 (1974).

The Supreme Court dismissed the appeal for want of a substantial federal question. ___ U.S. ___, 104 S.Ct. 520, 78 L.Ed.2d 705. A dismissal for want of a substantial federal question is a decision on the merits. Hicks v. Miranda, 422 U.S. 332, 344, 95 S.Ct. 2281, 2289, 45 L.Ed.2d 223 (1975).

proposal for the adoption of the "agency shop." More narrowly, since the employer is not obliged to bargain over a proposal that he commit an unfair labor practice, the question is whether the agency shop is an unfair labor practice under § 8(a)(3) of the Act or else is exempted from the prohibitions of that section by the proviso thereto.[2] We have concluded that this type of arrangement does not constitute an unfair labor practice and that it is not prohibited by § 8.

Respondent's employees are represented by the United Automobile, Aerospace and Agricultural Implement Workers of America, UAW, in a single, multiplant company-wide unit. The 1958 agreement between union and company provides for maintenance of membership and the union shop.[3] These provisions were not operative, however, in such States as Indiana where state law prohibited making union membership a condition of employment.

In June 1959, the Indiana intermediate appellate court held that an agency shop arrangement would not violate the state right-to-work law. Meade Elec. Co. v. Hagberg, 129 Ind.App. 631, 159 N.E.2d 408. As defined in that opinion, the term "agency shop" applies to an arrangement under which all employees are required as a condition of employment to pay dues to the union and pay the union's initiation fee, but they need not actually become union members. The union thereafter sent respondent a letter proposing the negotiation of a contractual provision covering Indiana plants "generally similar to that set forth" in the Meade case. Continued employ-

2. "Sec. 8. (a) It shall be an unfair labor practice for an employer—

* * * * *

"(3) by discrimination in regard to hire or tenure of employment or any term or condition of employment to encourage or discourage membership in any labor organization: *Provided,* That nothing in this Act, or in any other statute of the United States, shall preclude an employer from making an agreement with a labor organization * * * to require as a condition of employment membership therein on or after the thirtieth day following the beginning of such employment or the effective date of such agreement, whichever is the later * * *."

3. "Union Security and Check-Off of Union Membership Dues

"(4) An employe who is a member of the Union at the time this Agreement becomes effective shall continue membership in the Union for the duration of this Agreement to the extent of paying an initiation fee and the membership dues uniformly required as a condition of acquiring or retaining membership in the Union.

"(4a) An employe who is not a member of the Union at the time this Agreement becomes effective shall become a member of the Union within 60 days after the thirtieth (30th)

day following the effective date of this Agreement or within 60 days after the thirtieth (30th) day following employment, whichever is later, and shall remain a member of Union, to the extent of paying an initiation fee and the membership dues uniformly required as a condition of acquiring or retaining membership in the Union, whenever employed under, and for the duration of, this Agreement.

"(4b) Anything herein to the contrary notwithstanding, an employe shall not be required to become a member of, or continue membership in, the Union, as a condition of employment, if employed in any state which prohibits, or otherwise makes unlawful, membership in a labor organization as a condition of employment.

"(4c) The Union shall accept into membership each employe covered by this Agreement who tenders to the Union the periodic dues and initiation fees uniformly required as a condition of acquiring or retaining membership in the Union.

* * * * *

"(4f) 'Member of the Union' as used in paragraphs (4) and (4a) above means any employe who is a member of the Union and is not more than sixty (60) days in arrears in the payment of membership dues."

ment in the Indiana plants would be conditioned upon the payment of sums equal to the initiation fee and regular monthly dues paid by the union members. The intent of the proposal, the National Labor Relations Board concluded, was not to require membership but to make membership available at the employees' option and on nondiscriminatory terms. Employees choosing not to join would make the required payments and, in accordance with union custom, would share in union expenditures for strike benefits, educational and retired member benefits, and union publications and promotional activities, but they would not be entitled to attend union meetings, vote upon ratification of agreements negotiated by the union, or have a voice in the internal affairs of the union. The respondent made no counterproposal, but replied to the union's letter that the proposed agreement would violate the National Labor Relations Act and that respondent must therefore "respectfully decline to comply with your request for a meeting" to bargain over the proposal.

The union thereupon filed a complaint with the National Labor Relations Board against respondent for its alleged refusal to bargain in good faith. In the Board's view of the record, "the Union was not seeking to bargain over a clause requiring nonmember employees to pay sums equal to dues and fees as a condition of employment while at the same time maintaining a closed-union policy with respect to applicants for membership," since the proposal contemplated an arrangement in which "all employees are *given the option* of becoming, or refraining from becoming members of the Union." Proceeding on this basis and putting aside the consequences of a closed-union policy upon the legality of the agency shop, the Board assessed the union's proposal as comporting fully with the congressional declaration of policy in favor of union-security contracts and therefore a mandatory subject as to which the Act obliged respondent to bargain in good faith. At the same time, it stated that it had "no doubt that an agency-shop agreement is a permissible form of union-security within the meaning of Sections 7 and 8(a)(3) of the Act." Accordingly, the Board ruled that respondent had committed an unfair labor practice by refusing to bargain in good faith with the certified bargaining representative of its employees, and it ordered respondent to bargain with the union over the proposed arrangement; no back-pay award is involved in this case. 133 N.L.R.B. 451, 456, 457.

Respondent petitioned for review in the Court of Appeals, and the Board cross-petitioned for enforcement. The Court of Appeals set the order aside on the grounds that the Act tolerates only "an agreement requiring membership in a labor organization as a condition of employment" when such agreements do not violate state right-to-work laws, and that the Act does not authorize agreements requiring payment of membership dues to a union, in lieu of membership, as a condition of employment. It held that the proposed agency shop agreement would violate §§ 7, 8(a)(1), and 8(a)(3) of the Act and that the employer was therefore not obliged to bargain over it. 303 F.2d 428 (C.A. 6th Cir.). We granted certiorari * * * and now reverse the decision of the Court of Appeals.

Section 8(3) under the Wagner Act was the predecessor to § 8(a)(3) of the present law. Like § 8(a)(3), § 8(3) forbade employers to discriminate against employees to compel them to join a union. Because it was feared that § 8(3) and § 7, if nothing were added to qualify them, might be held to outlaw union-security arrangements such as the closed shop, * * * the proviso to § 8(3) was added expressly declaring:

> "*Provided,* That nothing in this Act * * * or in any other statute of the United States, shall preclude an employer from making an agreement with a labor organization * * * to require as a condition of employment membership therein, if such labor organization is the representative of the employees as provided in section 9(a) * * *."

The prevailing administrative and judicial view under the Wagner Act was or came to be that the proviso to § 8(3) covered both the closed and union shop, as well as less onerous union-security arrangements, if they were otherwise legal. The National Labor Relations Board construed the proviso as shielding from an unfair labor practice charge less severe forms of union-security arrangements than the closed or the union shop, including an arrangement in Public Service Co. of Colorado, 89 N.L.R.B. 418, requiring nonunion members to pay to the union $2 a month "for the support of the bargaining unit." And in Algoma Plywood Co. v. Wisconsin Board, 336 U.S. 301, 307, 69 S.Ct. 584, 93 L.Ed. 691, which involved a maintenance of membership agreement, the Court, in commenting on petitioner's contention that the proviso of § 8(3) affirmatively protected arrangements within its scope, * * * said of its purpose: "The short answer is that § 8(3) merely disclaims a national policy hostile to the closed shop *or other forms of union-security agreement.*" (Emphasis added.)

When Congress enacted the Taft-Hartley Act, it added the following to the language of the original proviso to § 8(3): "on or after the thirtieth day following the beginning of such employment or the effective date of such agreement, whichever is the later * * *. *Provided further,* That no employer shall justify any discrimination against an employee for non-membership in a labor organization (A) if he has reasonable grounds for believing that such membership was not available to the employee on the same terms and conditions generally applicable to other members, or (B) if he has reasonable grounds for believing that membership was denied or terminated for reasons other than the failure of the employee to tender the periodic dues and the initiation fees uniformly required as a condition of acquiring or retaining membership." * * * These additions were intended to accomplish twin purposes. On the one hand, the most serious abuses of compulsory unionism were eliminated by abolishing the closed shop. On the other hand, Congress recognized that in the absence of a union-security provision "many employees sharing the benefits of what unions are able to accomplish by collective bargaining will refuse to pay their share of the cost." S.Rep.No. 105, 80th Cong., 1st Sess., p. 6, 1 Leg.Hist.L.M.R.A. 412. Consequently, under the new law "employers would still be permitted to enter into agreements requiring all the employees in a given bargaining unit to become members 30 days after being hired," but "expulsion from a union cannot be a ground of compulsory discharge if the worker is not delinquent in paying his initiation fee or dues." S.Rep.No. 105, p. 7, 1 Leg.Hist.L.M.R.A. 413. The amendments were intended only to "remedy the most serious abuses of compulsory union membership and yet give employers and unions who feel that such agreements promoted stability by eliminating 'free riders' the right to continue such arrangements." Ibid. As far as the federal law was concerned, all employees could be required to pay their way. The bill "abolishes the closed shop but permits voluntary agreements for requiring such forms of compulsory membership as the union shop or maintenance of membership * * *." S.Rep. No. 105, p. 3, 1 Leg.Hist.L.M.R.A. 409.

We find nothing in the legislative history of the Act indicating that Congress intended the amended proviso to § 8(a)(3) to validate only the union shop and simultaneously to abolish, in addition to the closed shop, all other union-security arrangements permissible under state law. There is much to be said for the Board's view that, if Congress desired in the Wagner Act to permit a closed or union shop and in the Taft-Hartley Act the union shop, then it also intended to preserve the status of less vigorous, less compulsory contracts which demanded less adherence to the union.

Respondent, however, relies upon the express words of the proviso which allow employment to be conditioned upon "membership": since the union's proposal here does not require actual membership but demands only initiation fees and monthly dues, it is not saved by the proviso. This position, of course, would reject administrative decisions concerning the scope of § 8(3) of the Wagner Act * * *. Moreover, the 1947 amendments not only abolished the closed shop but also made significant alterations in the meaning of "membership" for the purposes of union-security contracts. Under the second proviso to § 8(a)(3), the burdens of membership upon which employment may be conditioned are expressly limited to the payment of initiation fees and monthly dues. It is permissible to condition employment upon membership, but membership, insofar as it has significance to employment rights, may in turn be conditioned only upon payment of fees and dues. "Membership" as a condition of employment is whittled down to its financial core. * * *

We are therefore confident that the proposal made by the union here conditioned employment upon the practical equivalent of union "membership," as Congress used that term in the proviso to § 8(a)(3).[9] The proposal for requiring the payment of dues and fees imposes no burdens not imposed by a permissible union shop contract and compels the performance of only those duties of membership which are enforceable by discharge under a union shop arrangement. If an employee in a union shop unit refuses to respect any union-imposed obligations other than the duty to pay dues and fees, and membership in the union is therefore denied or terminated, the condition of "membership" for § 8(a)(3) purposes is nevertheless satisfied and the employee may not be discharged for non-membership even though he is not a formal member. Of course, if the union chooses to extend membership even though the employee will meet only the minimum financial burden, and refuses to support or "join" the union in any other affirmative way, the employee may have to become a "member" under a union shop contract, in

9. Referring to the Canadian practice, Senator Taft stated that the rule adopted by the Conference Committee "is substantially the rule now in effect in Canada" which is that "the employee must, nevertheless, pay dues, even though he does not join the union" and that if he pays the dues without joining he has the right to be employed. 93 Cong.Rec. 4887, 2 Leg.Hist.L.R.M.A. 1422.

the sense that the union may be able to place him on its rolls.[11] The agency shop arrangement proposed here removes that choice from the union and places the option of membership in the employee while still requiring the same monetary support as does the union shop. Such a difference between the union and agency shop may be of great importance in some contexts, but for present purposes it is more formal than real. To the extent that it has any significance at all it serves, rather than violates, the desire of Congress to reduce the evils of compulsory unionism while allowing financial support for the bargaining agent.

In short, the employer categorically refused to bargain with the union over a proposal for an agreement within the proviso to § 8(a)(3) and as such lawful for the purposes of this case. By the same token, § 7, and derivatively § 8(a)(1), cannot be deemed to forbid the employer to enter such agreements, since it too is expressly limited by the § 8(a)(3) proviso. We hold that the employer was not excused from his duty to bargain over the proposal on the theory that his acceding to it would necessarily involve him in an unfair labor practice. Whether a different result obtains in States which have declared such arrangements unlawful is an issue still to be resolved in Retail Clerks Ass'n v. Schermerhorn, 373 U.S. 746, 83 S.Ct. 1461, and one which is of no relevance here because Indiana law does not forbid the present contract proposal. In the context of this case, then, the employer cannot justify his refusal to bargain. He violated § 8(a)(5), and the Board properly ordered him to return to the bargaining table.

Reversed and remanded.

MR. JUSTICE GOLDBERG took no part in the consideration or decision of this case.

Note

1. Suppose the Indiana right-to-work law had been interpreted by the Indiana courts to prohibit the agency shop. Would such a prohibition be within the power of the state under Section 14(b)? In a companion case to General Motors—Retail Clerks v. Schermerhorn ("SCHERMERHORN I"), 373 U.S. 746, 83 S.Ct. 1461, 10 L.Ed.2d 678 (1963)—the Court held that the word "membership" in Section 14(b) means the same as in the proviso to Section 8(a)(3), and that, accordingly, just as the agency shop is permissible under Section 8(a)(3), it is subject to prohibition by a state under Section 14(b).

In "SCHERMERHORN II," 375 U.S. 96, 84 S.Ct. 219, 11 L.Ed.2d 179 (1963), the question was whether a state court or the NLRB was the appropriate tribunal to enforce the Florida law invalidating the agency shop (and found to be within the state's authority under Section 14(b) in Schermerhorn I). The Court declined to apply the preemption doctrine, stating: "It is argued that if there is a violation of a state union-security law authorized by § 14(b), it is a federal unfair labor practice and that the federal remedy is the exclusive one. It is urged that that course is necessary if uniformity is to be achieved. But § 14(b) gives the States power to outlaw even a union-security agreement that passes muster by

---

11. Cf. American Seating Co., 98 N.L.R.B. 800, 802, * * * approving a provision protecting those who object on conscientious grounds from being required to become "members" in the conventional sense of that term.

[Ed. note: Section 19 of the National Labor Relations Act was amended in 1980 so as to codify this right of conscientious objection. See Statutory Supplement.]

federal standards. Where Congress gives state policy that degree of overriding authority, we are reluctant to conclude that it is nonetheless enforceable by the federal agency in Washington." 375 U.S. at 103, 84 S.Ct. at 222. Florida was therefore free to enjoin the enforcement of the agency-shop provision.

But, having yielded this much, the Court proceeded to limit the area within which the state could exercise its enforcement power: "[P]icketing in order to get an employer to execute an agreement to hire all-union labor in violation of a state union-security statute lies exclusively in the federal domain * * * because state power, recognized by § 14(b), begins *only with actual negotiation and execution of the type of agreement described by § 14(b)*. Absent such an agreement, conduct arguably an unfair labor practice would be a matter for the National Labor Relations Board under Garmon." 375 U.S. at 105, 84 S.Ct. at 223.

An attentive reading of Section 14(b) will demonstrate that in Schermerhorn II the Court drew the preemption noose as tightly around that section as its language will permit, short of denying the states *all* enforcement power.

2. As is typical under agency-shop contracts, in General Motors and Schermerhorn the fees required by the union of nonmembers were precisely the same as those paid by members—the amount of the initiation fee and periodic dues— thus making the agency shop only nominally different from the union shop. (" 'Membership' as a condition of employment is whittled down to its financial core.") Suppose, instead, the "service fee" charged the nonmember were his pro-rata share of the union's cost in negotiating and administering the collective agreement. This service fee would thus be *less* than the amount paid by a member since not all union expenditures are for the negotiation and administration of the contract (e.g., recreation, insurance benefits, political action programs).[a]

Would such a "union security" arrangement suffer the same fate as in Schermerhorn? Should it? Is "membership" thus made a condition of employment? Is there any need to invoke the 8(a)(3) proviso—i.e., is 8(a)(3) itself even triggered since encouragement and discouragement of union membership are in equipoise?

3. Some twenty states have by statute or constitutional amendment prohibited the requirement of union membership as a condition of employment. (Indiana repealed its right-to-work law in 1965, leaving the number at nineteen—all in the south, southwest, plains states, and Rocky Mountains.) In Lincoln Federal Labor Union v. Northwestern Iron & Metal Co., 335 U.S. 525, 69 S.Ct. 251, 93 L.Ed. 212 (1949), the Court upheld the validity of these measures in the face of challenges under the First and Fourteenth Amendments and Article I, Section 10 (impairment of contracts) of the Constitution. The Court noted, somewhat ironically: "Claiming that the Federal Constitution itself affords protection for union members against discrimination, [appellants] nevertheless assert that the same Constitution forbids a state from providing the same protection for non-union members. Just as we have held that the due process clause erects no obstacle to block legislative protection of union members, we now hold that legislative protection can be afforded non-union workers." 335 U.S. at 537, 69 S.Ct. at 257.

a. For a discussion of such a modified service-fee approach in public employment, see Waks, Impact of the Agency Shop on Labor Relations in the Public Sector, 55 Cornell L.Rev. 547 (1970). See also Hopfl, The Agency Shop Question, 49 Cornell L.Q. 478 (1964).

4. For further discussion of union security, in the hiring hall context, see supra pp. 169–178; in the First Amendment context (use for political purposes of enforced payments to the union), see infra pp. 799–814.

3. THE UNION'S POWER TO COMPEL ITS MEMBERS TO ENGAGE IN CONCERTED ACTIVITIES

NATIONAL LABOR RELATIONS BOARD v. ALLIS-CHALMERS MFG. CO.

Supreme Court of the United States, 1967.
388 U.S. 175, 87 S.Ct. 2001, 18 L.Ed.2d 1123.

MR. JUSTICE BRENNAN delivered the opinion of the Court.

The question here is whether a union which threatened and imposed fines, and brought suit for their collection, against members who crossed the union's picket line and went to work during an authorized strike against their employer, committed the unfair labor practice under § 8(b)(1)(A) of the National Labor Relations Act of engaging in conduct "to restrain or coerce" employees in the exercise of their right guaranteed by § 7 to "refrain from" concerted activities.

Employees at the West Allis, and La Crosse, Wisconsin, plants of respondent Allis-Chalmers Manufacturing Company were represented by locals of the United Automobile Workers. Lawful economic strikes were conducted at both plants in support of new contract demands. In compliance with the UAW constitution, the strikes were called with the approval of the International Union after at least two-thirds of the members of each local voted by secret ballot to strike. Some members of each local crossed the picket lines and worked during the strikes. After the strikes were over, the locals brought proceedings against these members charging them with violation of the International constitution and bylaws. The charges were heard by local trial committees in proceedings at which the charged members were represented by counsel. No claim of unfairness in the proceedings is made. The trials resulted in each charged member being found guilty of "conduct unbecoming a Union-member" and being fined in a sum from $20 to $100. Some of the fined members did not pay the fines and one of the locals obtained a judgment in the amount of the fine against one of its members, Benjamin Natzke, in a test suit brought in the Milwaukee County Court. An appeal from the judgment is pending in the Wisconsin Supreme Court.

Allis-Chalmers filed unfair labor practice charges against the locals alleging violation of § 8(b)(1)(A). A complaint issued and after hearing a trial examiner recommended its dismissal. The National Labor Relations Board sustained the examiner on the ground that, in the circumstances of this case, the actions of the locals, even if restraint or coercion prohibited by § 8(b)(1)(A), constituted conduct excepted from the section's prohibitions by the proviso that such prohibitions "shall not impair the right of a labor organization to prescribe its own rules with respect to the acquisition or retention of membership therein." 149 N.L.R.B. 67. Upon Allis-Chalmers' petition for review to the Court of Appeals for the Seventh Circuit, a panel of that court upheld the Board's decision. Following a rehearing en banc, however, the court, three judges dissenting, withdrew the panel opinion, held that the locals' conduct violated § 8(b)(1)(A), and remanded to the Board for appropriate proceedings. 358 F.2d 656. We granted certiorari * * *. We reverse.

I.

The panel and the majority *en banc* of the Court of Appeals thought that reversal of the NLRB order would be required under a literal reading of §§ 7 and 8(b)(1)(A); under that reading union members who cross their own picket lines would be regarded as exercising their rights under § 7 to refrain from engaging in a particular concerted activity, and union discipline in the form of fines for such activity would therefore "restrain or coerce" in violation of § 8(b)(1)(A) if the section's proviso is read to sanction no form of discipline other than expulsion from the union. The panel rejected that literal reading. The majority *en banc* adopted it, stating that the panel "mistakenly took the position that such a literal reading was unwarranted in the light of the history and purposes" of the sections, 358 F.2d, at 659, and holding that "[T]he statutes in question present no ambiguities whatsoever, and therefore do not require recourse to legislative history for clarification." Id., at 660.

It is highly unrealistic to regard § 8(b)(1), and particularly its words "restrain or coerce," as precisely and unambiguously covering the union conduct involved in this case. On its face court enforcement of fines imposed on members for violation of membership obligations is no more conduct to "restrain or coerce" satisfaction of such obligations than court enforcement of penalties imposed on citizens for violation of their obligations as citizens to pay income taxes, or court awards of damages against a contracting party for nonperformance of a contractual obligation voluntarily undertaken. But even if the inherent imprecision of the words "restrain or coerce" may be overlooked, recourse to legislative history to determine the sense in which Congress used the words is not foreclosed. We have only this Term again admonished that labor legislation is peculiarly the product of legislative compromise of strongly held views, * * * and that legislative history may not be disregarded merely because it is arguable that a provision may unambiguously embrace conduct called in question. National Woodwork Mfrs. Assn. v. NLRB, 386 U.S. 612, 619–620, 87 S.Ct. 1250, 1266, 18 L.Ed.2d 357.

National labor policy has been built on the premise that by pooling their economic strength and acting through a labor organization freely chosen by the majority, the employees of an appropriate unit have the most effective means of bargaining for improvements in wages, hours, and working conditions. * * *

Integral to this federal labor policy has been the power in the chosen union to protect against erosion its status under that policy through reasonable discipline of members who violate rules and regulations governing membership. That power is particularly vital when the members engage in strikes. The economic strike against the employer is the ultimate weapon in labor's arsenal for achieving agreement upon its terms * * *. Provisions in union constitutions and bylaws for fines and expulsion of recalcitrants, including strikebreakers, are therefore commonplace and were commonplace at the time of the Taft-Hartley amendments.[9]

In addition, the judicial view current at the time § 8(b)(1)(A) was passed was that provisions defining punishable conduct and the procedures for trial and appeal constituted part of the contract between member and union and that "The courts' role is but to enforce the contract." [10] * * *

To say that Congress meant in 1947 by the § 7 amendments and § 8(b)(1)(A) to strip unions of the power to fine members for strikebreaking, however lawful the strike vote, and however fair the disciplinary procedures and penalty, is to say that Congress preceded the Landrum-Griffin amendments with an even more pervasive regulation of the internal affairs of unions. * * * More importantly, it is to say that Congress limited unions in the powers necessary to the discharge of their role as exclusive statutory bargaining agents by impairing the usefulness of labor's cherished strike weapon. It is no answer that the proviso to § 8(b)(1)(A) preserves to the union the power to expel the offending member. Where the union is strong and membership therefore valuable, to require expulsion of the member visits a far more severe penalty upon the member than a reasonable fine. Where the union is weak, and membership therefore of little value, the union faced with further depletion of its ranks may have no real choice except to condone the member's disobedience.[12] Yet it is just such weak unions for which the power to execute union decisions taken for the benefit of all employees is most critical to effective discharge of its statutory function.

Congressional meaning is of course ordinarily to be discerned in the words Congress uses. But when the literal application of the imprecise words "restrain or coerce" Congress employed in § 8(b)(1)(A) produces the extraordinary results we have mentioned we should determine whether this meaning is confirmed in the legislative history of the section.

II.

* * *

What legislative materials there are dealing with § 8(b)(1)(A) contain not a single word referring to the application of its prohibitions to traditional internal union discipline in general, or disciplinary fines in particular.

---

9. * * * It is suggested that while such provisions for fines and expulsion were a common element of union constitutions at the time of the enactment of § 8(b)(1), such background loses its cogency here because such provisions did not explicitly call for court enforcement. However, the potentiality of resort to courts for enforcement is implicit in any binding obligation. Surely it cannot be said that the absence of a "court enforceability" clause in a contract of sale implies that the parties do not foresee resort to the courts as a possible means of enforcement. It is also suggested that court enforcement of fines is "a rather recent innovation." Yet such enforcement was known as early as 1867. Master Stevedores' Assn. v. Walsh, 2 Daly 1 (NY).

10. Summers, The Law of Union Discipline: What the Courts Do in Fact, 10 Yale L.J. 175, 180 (1960).

12. "Since the union's effectiveness is based largely on the degree to which it controls the available labor, expulsions tend to weaken the union. If large numbers are expelled, they become a threat to union standards by undercutting union rates, and in case of a strike they may act as strikebreakers. * * * Therefore, expulsions must be limited to very small numbers unless the union is so strongly entrenched that it cannot be effectively challenged by the employer or another union." Summers, Disciplinary Powers of Unions, 3 Ind. & Lab.Rel.Rev. 483, 487–488 (1950).

On the contrary there are a number of assurances by its sponsors that the section was not meant to regulate the internal affairs of unions.

The provision was not contained in the Senate or House bills reported out of committee, but was introduced as an amendment on the Senate floor by Senator Ball. The amendment was adopted in the Conference Committee, without significant enlightenment from the report of that committee. The first suggestion that restraint or coercion of employees in the exercise of § 7 rights should be an unfair labor practice appears in the Statement of Supplemental Views to the Senate Report, in which a minority of the Senate Committee, including Senators Ball, Taft, and Smith, concurred. The mischief against which the Statement inveighed was restraint and coercion by unions in *organizational campaigns.* "The committee heard many instances of union coercion of employees such as that brought about by threats of reprisal against employees and their families in the course of organizing campaigns; also direct interference by mass picketing and other violence." S.Rep. No. 105, supra, at 50, I Leg.Hist. 456. Senator Ball proposed § 8(b)(1) (A) as an amendment to the Senate bill, and stated, "The purpose of the amendment is simply to provide that where unions, in their organizational campaigns, indulge in practices which, if an employer indulged in them, would be unfair labor practices, such as making threats or false promises or false statements, the unions also shall be guilty of unfair labor practices." 93 Cong.Rec. 4016, II Leg.Hist. 1018. ＊ ＊ ＊ Indeed, when Senator Holland introduced the proviso eliminating from the reach of § 8(b)(1)(A) "the right of a labor organization to prescribe its own rules with respect to the acquisition or retention of membership ＊ ＊ ＊," Senator Ball replied,

> "I merely wish to state to the Senate that the amendment offered by the Senator from Florida is perfectly agreeable to me. *It was never the intention of the sponsors of the pending amendment to interfere with the internal affairs or organization of unions."* [17] (Emphasis supplied.) ＊ ＊ ＊

＊ ＊ ＊ At the very least ＊ ＊ ＊ the proviso preserves the rights of unions to impose fines, as a lesser penalty than expulsion, and to impose fines which carry the explicit or implicit threat of expulsion for nonpayment. Therefore, under the proviso the rule in the UAW constitution governing fines is valid and the fines themselves and expulsion for nonpayment would not be an unfair labor practice. Assuming that the proviso cannot also be read to authorize court enforcement of fines, a question we need not reach,[29] the fact remains that to interpret the body of § 8(b)(1) to apply to the imposition and collection of fines would be to impute to Congress a concern with the permissible *means* of enforcement of union fines and to attribute to Congress a narrow and discrete interest in banning court enforcement of such fines. Yet there is not one word in the legislative history evidencing any such congressional concern. And, as we have pointed out, a distinction between court enforcement and expulsion would have been anomalous for several reasons. First, Congress was operating within the context of the "contract theory" of the union-member relationship which widely prevailed at that time. The efficacy of a contract is precisely its legal enforceability.

17. 93 Cong.Rec. 4272, II Leg.Hist. 1141.

29. Our conclusion that § 8(b)(1)(A) does not prohibit the locals' actions makes it un-

necessary to pass on the Board holding that the proviso protected such actions.

A lawsuit is and has been the ordinary way by which performance of private money obligations is compelled. Second, as we have noted, such a distinction would visit upon the member of a strong union a potentially more severe punishment than court enforcement of fines, while impairing the bargaining facility of the weak union by requiring it either to condone misconduct or deplete its ranks.

There may be concern that court enforcement may permit the collection of unreasonably large fines. However, even were there evidence that Congress shared this concern, this would not justify reading the Act also to bar court enforcement of reasonable fines.

The 1959 Landrum-Griffin amendments, thought to be the first comprehensive regulation by Congress of the conduct of internal union affairs, also negate the reach given § 8(b)(1)(A) by the majority *en banc* below. * * * In 1959 Congress did seek to protect union members in their relationship to the union by adopting measures to insure the provision of democratic processes in the conduct of union affairs and procedural due process to members subjected to discipline. * * * The Eighty-sixth Congress was thus plainly of the view that union self-government was not regulated in 1947. Indeed, that Congress expressly recognized that a union member may be "fined, suspended, expelled, or otherwise disciplined," and enacted only procedural requirements to be observed. 73 Stat. 523, 29 U.S.C.A. § 411(a) (5). Moreover, Congress added a proviso to the guarantee of freedom of speech and assembly disclaiming any intent "to impair the right of a labor organization to adopt and enforce reasonable rules as to the responsibility of every member toward the organization as an institution * * *." 29 U.S. C.A. § 411(a)(2). * * *

Thus this history of congressional action does not support a conclusion that the Taft-Hartley prohibitions against restraint or coercion of an employee to refrain from concerted activities included a prohibition against the imposition of fines on members who decline to honor an authorized strike and attempts to collect such fines. Rather, the contrary inference is more justified in light of the repeated refrain throughout the debates on § 8(b)(1) (A) and other sections that Congress did not propose any limitations with respect to the internal affairs of unions, aside from barring enforcement of a union's internal regulations to affect a member's employment status.

III.

The collective bargaining agreements with the locals incorporate union security clauses. Full union membership is not compelled by the clauses: an employee is required only to become and remain "a member of the Union * * * to the extent of paying his monthly dues * * *." The majority *en banc* below nevertheless regarded full membership to be "the result not of individual voluntary choice but of the insertion of [this] union security provision in the contract under which a substantial minority of the employees may have been forced into membership." 358 F.2d, at 660. But the relevant inquiry here is not what motivated a member's full membership but whether the Taft-Hartley amendments prohibited disciplinary measures against a full member who crossed his union's picket line. It is clear that the fined employees involved herein enjoyed full union membership. Each executed the pledge of allegiance to the UAW constitution and took the oath of full membership. Moreover, the record of the Milwaukee County Court case against Benjamin Natzke discloses that two disciplined employees testified that they had fully participated in the proceedings leading to the strike. They attended the meetings at which the secret strike vote and the renewed strike vote were taken. It was upon this and similar evidence that the Milwaukee County Court found that Natzke "had by his actions become a member of the union for all purposes * * *." Allis-Chalmers offered no evidence in this proceeding that any of the fined employees enjoyed other than full union membership. We will not presume the contrary. * * * Indeed, it is and has been Allis-Chalmers' position that the Taft-Hartley prohibitions apply whatever the nature of the membership. Whether those prohibitions would apply if the locals had imposed fines on members whose membership was in fact limited to the obligation of paying monthly dues is a question not before us and upon which we intimate no view.

The judgment of the Court of Appeals is reversed.

[Justice White's concurrence, which provided the "swing" vote, is omitted. He noted that: "[N]either the majority nor the dissent in this case questions the validity of the union rule against its members crossing picket lines during a properly called strike, or the propriety of expulsion to enforce the rule. * * * [T]here is no basis for thinking that Congress, having accepted expulsion as a permissible technique to enforce a rule in derogation of § 7 rights, nevertheless intended to bar enforcement by another method which may be far less coercive." 388 U.S. at 198, 87 S.Ct. at 2016, 18 L.Ed. 2d at 1137–38.]

Mr. Justice Black, whom Mr. Justice Douglas, Mr. Justice Harlan, and Mr. Justice Stewart join, dissenting. * * *

I.

In determining what the Court here holds, it is helpful to note what it does not hold. Since the union resorted to the courts to enforce its fines instead of relying on its own internal sanctions such as expulsion from membership, the Court correctly assumes that the proviso to § 8(b)(1)(A) cannot be read to authorize its holding. Neither does the Court attempt to sustain its holding by reference to § 7 which gives employees the right to refrain from engaging in concerted activities. To be sure, the Court in characterizing the union-member relationship as "contractual" and in emphasizing that its holding is limited to situations where the employee is a "full member" of the union implies that by joining a union an employee gives up or waives some of his § 7 rights. But the Court does not say that a union member is without the § 7 right to refrain from participating in such concerted activity as an economic strike called by his union. Such a holding would be clearly unwarranted even by resort to the legislative history of the 1947 addition to § 7 of "the right to refrain from any or all of such activities." According to Senator Taft, that phrase was added by the Conference Committee to "make the prohibition contained in section 8(b)(1) apply to coercive acts of unions against employees who did not wish to join *or did not care to participate in a strike or a picket line.*" 93 Cong.Rec. 6859, II Leg.Hist. 1623. (Emphasis added.)

With no reliance on the proviso to § 8(b)(1)(A) or on the meaning of § 7, the Court's holding boils down to this: a court-enforced reasonable fine for non-participation in a strike does not "restrain or coerce" an employee in the exercise of his right not to participate in the strike. In holding as it does, the Court interprets the words "restrain or coerce" in a way directly opposed to their literal meaning, for the Court admits that fines are as coercive as penalties imposed on citizens for the nonpayment of taxes. * * * The real reason for the Court's decision is its policy judgment that unions, especially weak ones, need the power to impose fines on strikebreakers and to enforce those fines in court. It is not enough, says the Court, that the unions have the power to expel those members who refuse to participate in a strike or who fail to pay fines imposed on them for such failure to participate; it is essential that weak unions have the choice between expulsion and court-enforced fines, simply because the latter are more effective in the sense of being more punitive. Though the entire mood of Congress in 1947 was to curtail the power of unions, as it had previously curtailed the power of employers, in order to equalize the power of the two, the Court is unwilling to believe that Congress intended to impair "the usefulness of labor's cherished strike weapon." I cannot agree with this conclusion or subscribe to the Court's unarticulated premise that the Court has power to add a new weapon to the union's economic arsenal whenever the Court believes that the union needs that weapon. That is a job for Congress, not this Court.

II.

* * *

In this case, each strikebreaking employee was fined from $20 to $100, and the union initiated a "test case" in state court to collect the fines. In notifying the employees of the charges against them, however, the union warned them that each day they crossed the picket line and went to work might be considered a separate offense punishable by a fine of $100. In several of the cases, the strikes lasted for many months. Thus, although the union here imposed minimal fines for the purpose of its "test case," it is not too difficult to imagine a case where the fines will be so large that the threat of their imposition will absolutely restrain employees from going to work during a strike. Although an employee might be willing to work even if it meant the loss of union membership, he would have to be well paid indeed to work at the risk that he would have to pay his union $100 a day for each day worked. Of course, as the Court suggests, he might be able to defeat the union's attempt at judicial enforcement of the fine by showing it was "unreasonable" or that he was not a "full member" of the union, but few employees would have the courage or the financial means to be willing to take that risk. * * *

[T]he Court says that disciplinary fines were commonplace at the time the Taft-Hartley Act was passed, and thus Congress could not have meant to prohibit these "traditional internal union discipline" measures without saying so. Yet there is not one word in the authorities cited by the Court that indicates that court enforcement of fines was commonplace or traditional in 1947, and, to the contrary, until recently unions rarely resorted to court enforcement of union fines. * * * Congress' unfamiliarity in 1947 with this recent innovation and consequent failure to make any distinction between union-enforced and court-enforced fines cannot support the conclusion that Congress was unconcerned with the "means" a union uses to enforce its fines. * * *

[I]f the union * * * uses threats of physical violence by its officers or other members to compel payment of its fines, I do not doubt that this too would be a violation of § 8(b)(1)(A). * * *

V.

The union here had a union security clause in its contract with Allis-Chalmers. That clause made it necessary for all employees, including the ones involved here, to pay dues and fees to the union. But § 8(a)(3) and § 8(b)(2) make it clear that "Congress intended to prevent utilization of union security agreements for any purpose other than to compel payment of union dues and fees." Radio Officers' Union etc. v. National Labor Relations Board, 347 U.S. 17, 41, 74 S.Ct. 323, 336, 98 L.Ed. 455. If the union uses the union security clause to compel employees to pay dues, characterizes such employees as members, and then uses such membership as a basis for imposing court-enforced fines upon those employees unwilling to participate in a union strike, then the union security clause is being used for a purpose other than "to compel payment of union dues and fees." It is being used to coerce employees to join in union activity in violation of § 8(b)(2). * * *

VI.

* * * A court-enforced fine is certainly coercive, certainly affects the employee's job, and certainly is not a traditional method of internal union discipline. When applied by a union to an employee who has joined it as a condition of obtaining employment in a union shop, it defeats the provisions of the Act designed to prevent union security clauses from being used for purposes other than to compel payment of dues. In such a situation it cannot be justified on any theory that the employee has contracted away or waived his § 7 rights. * * *

Note

1. Does the Court in Allis-Chalmers rely upon Section 8(b)(1)(A) or upon its proviso; i.e., did the union ever get into the 8(b)(1)(A) box or trap so as to have need for the escape hatch? Do you agree with the majority or the dissent?

A problem with the analysis in Allis-Chalmers is that not one of the opinions deals directly with the underlying question, largely one of philosophy or political science, to-wit: To what extent, if any, *should* an organization such as a labor union, be permitted, consistent with the rationale of a free society, to coerce the continued allegiance of its members other than through threat of suspension or expulsion?

2. A second question left unattended by Allis-Chalmers concerns the theory pursuant to which the union fines are to be judicially enforced. The Court stated: "Congress was operating within the context of the 'contract theory' of the union-member relationship which widely prevailed at that time. The efficacy of a contract is precisely its legal enforceability. A lawsuit is and has been the ordinary way by which performance of private money obligations is compelled." Supra pp. 777–778.

There are a number of problems obscured by this easy assertion: By what theory of the law of contracts is the *amount* of the fine to be ascertained? Are *penalties* enforceable? Are the parties to be viewed as having contracted to "arbitrate" the issue of the extent of the injury caused to the union by the breach through the internal disciplinary tribunals of the union? Is the fine to be analogized to "liquidated damages"? Is not the union-member "contract" one of adhesion (the more so in a union-shop context) and therefore to be interpreted strictly against the adherer (adheree?) rather than against the adheree (adherer?)? Some of these questions are dealt with, largely unsatisfactorily, in the state court cases cited in footnote 12 of the Boeing case, which follows. See also Comment, Court Enforcement of Union Fines, 25 Wash. & Lee L.Rev. 273 (1968).

NATIONAL LABOR RELATIONS BOARD v. BOEING CO.

Supreme Court of the United States, 1973.
412 U.S. 67, 93 S.Ct. 1952, 36 L.Ed.2d 752.

MR. JUSTICE REHNQUIST delivered the opinion of the Court.

The question presented in this case is whether the National Labor Relations Board is required by § 8(b)(1)(A) of the National Labor Relations Act to inquire into the reasonableness of a disciplinary fine imposed by a union upon a member when the Board exercises its admitted authority under that section to determine whether the fine otherwise constitutes an unfair labor practice. The Board held that the validity of union fines under the Act does not depend on their being reasonable in amount. Booster Lodge No. 405, 185 N.L.R.B. 380, 383 n. 16, 75 L.R.R.M. 1004, 1007 n. 16 (1970). On petition for judicial review of this determination, the Court of Appeals held that an unreasonably large fine is coercive and restraining within the meaning of § 8(b)(1)(A), and remanded the case to the Board with directions to consider "questions relating to the reasonableness of the fines imposed by the Union." Booster Lodge No. 405, International Association of Machinists v. NLRB, 148 U.S.App.D.C. 119, 137, 459 F.2d 1143, 1161 (1972). We granted certiorari and now reverse the judgment below.

From May 16, 1963, through September 15, 1965, Booster Lodge No. 405, International Association of Machinists & Aerospace Workers, AFL–CIO (the Union), and the Boeing Co. (the Company), were parties to a collective-bargaining agreement. Upon expiration of this agreement the Union called a lawful economic strike at the Company's Michoud plant in New Orleans and at other locations. As of October 2, 1965, the parties signed a new collective-bargaining agreement and the strikers thereafter returned to work. Both agreements contained maintenance-of-membership clauses that required Union members to retain their membership during the contract term. New employees were required to notify the Union and the Company within 40 days of accepting employment if they elected not to join the Union.

During the 18-day strike some 143 employees out of 1,900 production and maintenance employees in the bargaining unit at the Michoud plant crossed the picket lines and returned to work. All of these employees were Union members at the time the strike began, although some of them tendered their resignations either before or after crossing the picket lines.[2] In late October or early November 1965 the Union notified these employees that charges had been preferred against them for violating the International Union's constitution. The constitution provides penalties for the "improper conduct of a member," which term includes "[a]ccepting employment * * * in an establishment where a strike * * * exists." In accordance with appropriate union procedures, including notice and opportunity for a hearing, all strikebreakers were found guilty, fined $450, and barred from holding Union office for a period of five years.[3] While some of the fines were reduced and some partial payments were received by the Union, no member paid the full $450.[4] After warning members to pay their fines or face the consequences, the Union filed suits in state court against nine individual employees to collect the fines. None of these suits has been finally adjudicated.

In February 1966 the Company filed a charge with the Labor Board alleging that the attempted court enforcement of the fines violated § 8(b)(1)(A) of the National Labor Relations Act. The allegations were basically twofold: first, that the Union committed an unfair labor practice by fining employees who had resigned from the Union, an issue that we consider in the companion case, Booster Lodge No. 405, Intern. Ass'n of Machinists & Aerospace Workers, AFL–CIO v. NLRB, 412 U.S. 84, 93 S.Ct. 1961, 36 L.Ed. 2d 764; and, second, that as to the members who were otherwise validly fined, the fines were unreasonable in amount. Thereafter the Board's General Counsel issued a complaint and the case was heard by a Trial Examiner. With respect to the second issue, the Trial Examiner determined that the fines were impermissibly excessive, but the Board refused to adopt his conclusion. It relied on a case decided the same day, Machinists, Local Lodge 504 (Arrow Development Co.), 185 N.L.R.B. 365, 75 L.R.R.M. 1008 (1970), reversed sub nom. O'Reilly v. NLRB, 472 F.2d 426 (C.A.9 1972), in which it held that Congress did not intend to give the Board authority to regulate the size of union fines or to establish standards with respect to a fine's reasonableness.

Section 8(b)(1)(A) of the Act provides, in pertinent part, that it shall be an unfair labor practice for a labor organization "to restrain or coerce (A) employees in the exercise of the rights guaranteed in section 7 of this title." [5]

2. Of the 143 employees who crossed the picket lines, 24 made no attempt to resign from the Union, 61 resigned before crossing the picket lines, and 58 resigned after crossing the picket lines and reporting for work. The validity of the fines imposed against those who resigned from the Union is considered in a companion case, Booster Lodge No. 405, International Association of Machinists and Aerospace Workers, AFL–CIO v. NLRB, 412 U.S. 84, 93 S.Ct. 1961, 36 L.Ed.2d 764. See also NLRB v. Granite State Joint Board, Textile Workers Union of America, Local 1029, AFL–CIO, 409 U.S. 213, 93 S.Ct. 385, 34 L.Ed. 2d 422 (1972).

3. The Union constitution provides that members found guilty of misconduct after notice and a hearing are subject to "reprimand,

fine, suspension, or expulsion from membership or any lesser penalty or combination." The constitution sets no maximum dollar limitation on fines.

4. The base income of the employees fined ranges from $95 to $145 for a 40-hour workweek.

Fines were reduced to 50% of wages earned during the strike for 35 members who appeared for the Union trial, apologized for their actions, and pledged loyalty to the Union. Eighteen of these reduced fines have been paid in full.

5. The proviso to this section states: "That this paragraph shall not impair the right of a labor organization to prescribe its own rules with respect to the acquisition or retention of

Among the § 7 rights guaranteed to employees is the right to refrain from any of the concerted activities described in that section. We have previously held that § 8(b)(1)(A) was not intended to give the Board power to regulate internal union affairs, including the imposition of disciplinary fines, with their consequent court enforcement, against members who violate the unions' constitutions and bylaws. NLRB v. Allis-Chalmers Mfg. Co., 388 U.S. 175, 87 S.Ct. 2001, 18 L.Ed.2d 1123 (1967); Scofield v. NLRB, 394 U.S. 423, 89 S.Ct. 1154, 22 L.Ed.2d 385 (1969). In *Allis-Chalmers* we held that court enforcement of fines ranging from $20 to $100 for crossing picket lines did not "restrain or coerce" employees within the meaning of the Act. And in *Scofield* we held that the union did not violate the Act in imposing fines of $50 and $100 on members for violating a union rule relating to production ceilings.

In deciding these cases, the Court several times referred to the unions' imposition of "reasonable" fines. In particular, the *Scofield* Court concluded "that the union rule is valid and that its enforcement by *reasonable* fines does not constitute the restraint or coercion proscribed by § 8(b)(1)(A)." 394 U.S., at 436, 89 S.Ct. at 1161 (emphasis added). The Company contends, not illogically, that the Court's use of the adjective "reasonable" was intended to suggest to the Board that an unreasonable fine would amount to an unfair labor practice.

This interpretation, however, permissible as it may be is only dicta, since in both *Allis-Chalmers* and in *Scofield* the reasonableness of the fines was assumed. 388 U.S., at 192–193, 87 S.Ct., at 2013, n. 30; 394 U.S., at 430, 89 S.Ct., at 1158.[7] Being squarely presented with the issue in this case, we recede from the implications of the dicta in these earlier cases. While "unreasonable" fines may be more coercive than "reasonable" fines, all fines are coercive to a greater or lesser degree. The underlying basis for the holdings of *Allis-Chalmers* and *Scofield* was not that reasonable fines were non-coercive under the language of § 8(b)(1)(A) of the Act, but was instead that those provisions were not intended by Congress to apply to the imposition by the union of fines not affecting the employer-employee relationship and not otherwise prohibited by the Act. The reason for this determination, in turn, was that Congress had not intended by enacting this section to

membership therein." It has been the Board's position that this proviso authorizes the unions to impose disciplinary fines on union members. Minneapolis Star & Tribune Co., 109 N.L.R.B. 727, 34 L.R.R.M. 1431 (1954); Wisconsin Motor Corp., 145 N.L.R.B. 1097, 55 L.R.R.M. 1985 (1964); Allis-Chalmers Mfg. Co., 149 N.L.R.B. 67, 57 L.R.R.M. 1242 (1964). This Court, however, in holding that court enforcement of union fines was not an unfair labor practice in NLRB v. Allis-Chalmers Mfg. Co., 388 U.S. 175, 87 S.Ct. 2001, 18 L.Ed.2d 1123 (1967), relied on congressional intent only with respect to the first part of this section. The parties' principal contentions in this case do not depend on the scope of the proviso and we do not consider its interpretation necessary to our conclusion.

7. Moreover, since the Board has consistently over a long period of time interpreted the Act as not giving it authority to examine the reasonableness of disciplinary fines, infra, * * * it is not likely that the Court specifically intended, by the use of a single adjective, and without mentioning the Labor Board cases to the contrary, to overturn the Board's interpretation of the Act. Nor can it be argued that the Court was unaware of the Board's interpretation, for the *Scofield* Court stated that in *Allis-Chalmers* it

"essentially accepted the position of the National Labor Relations Board dating from Minneapolis Star & Tribune Co., 109 N.L.R.B. 727 (1954) where the Board also distinguished internal from external enforcement in holding that a union could fine a member for his failure to take part in picketing during a strike * * *." Scofield v. NLRB, 394 U.S. 423, 428, 89 S.Ct. 1154, 1157, 22 L.Ed.2d 385 (1969).

regulate the internal affairs of unions to the extent that would be required in order to base unfair labor practice charges on the levying of such fines.

The Court's examination of the legislative history of this provision in *Allis-Chalmers* led to the conclusion that:

> "What legislative materials there are dealing with § 8(b)(1)(A) contain not a single word referring to the application of its prohibitions to traditional internal union discipline in general, or disciplinary fines in particular. On the contrary there are a number of assurances by its sponsors that *the section was not meant to regulate the internal affairs of unions.*" 388 U.S., at 185–186, 87 S.Ct., at 2009 (emphasis added).[8]

In *Scofield* we decided that Congress intended to distinguish between the external and the internal enforcement of union rules, and that therefore the Board would have authority to pass on those rules affecting an individual's employment status but not on his union membership status. 394 U.S., at 428–430, 89 S.Ct., at 1157–1158.

Inquiry by the Board into the multiplicity of factors that the parties and the Court of Appeals correctly thought to have a bearing on the issue of reasonableness would necessarily lead the Board to a substantial involvement in strictly internal union affairs. While the line may not always be clear between those matters that are internal and those that are external, to the extent that the Board was required to examine into such questions as a union's motivation for imposing a fine it would be delving into internal union affairs in a manner which we have previously held Congress did not intend. Given the rationale of *Allis-Chalmers* and *Scofield,* the Board's conclusion that § 8(b)(1)(A) of the Act has nothing to say about union fines of this nature, whatever their size, is correct. Issues as to the reasonableness or unreasonableness of such fines must be decided upon the basis of the law of contracts, voluntary associations, or such other principles of law as may be applied in a forum competent to adjudicate the issue. Under our holding, state courts will be wholly free to apply state law to such issues at the suit of either the union or the member fined.

Our conclusion is also supported by the Board's longstanding administrative construction to the same effect. At least since 1954, it has been the Board's consistent position that it has "not been empowered by Congress * * * to pass judgment on the penalties a union may impose on a member so long as the penalty does not impair the member's status as an employee." Local 283, UAW, 145 N.L.R.B. 1097, 1104 (1964). See also Minneapolis Star & Tribune Co., 109 N.L.R.B. 727, 34 L.R.R.M. 1431 (1954). We have held in analogous situations that such a consistent and contemporaneous construction of a statute by the agency charged with its enforcement is entitled to great deference by the courts. Griggs v. Duke Power Co., 401 U.S. 424, 433–434, 91 S.Ct. 849, 854–855, 28 L.Ed.2d 158 (1971); Udall v. Tallman, 380 U.S. 1, 16, 85 S.Ct. 792, 801, 13 L.Ed.2d 616 (1965).[10]

---

8. As we also noted in *Allis-Chalmers,* this interpretation is supported by the Landrum-Griffin Act, where "Congress expressly recognized that a union member may be 'fined, suspended, expelled, or otherwise disciplined,' and enacted only procedural requirements to be observed. 73 Stat. 523, 29 U.S.C.A.

§ 411(a)(5)." NLRB v. Allis-Chalmers Mfg. Co., 388 U.S., at 194, 87 S.Ct., at 2014.

10. It is also noteworthy that when Congress has intended the Board to examine a fee for being excessive or unreasonable, it has specifically so stated and has provided statutory standards for the Board to follow in making

The Court of Appeals and the Company have suggested several policy reasons why the Board should not leave the determinations of reasonableness entirely to the state courts. Their basic reasons are, first, that more uniformity in the determination of what is reasonable will result if the Board suggests standards and, second, that more expertise in labor matters will be brought to bear if the issue is decided by the Board rather than solely by the courts. Even if we were to concede the relevance of policy factors in determining congressional intent, we are not persuaded that the Board is necessarily the better forum for determining the reasonableness of a fine.

As we noted in *Allis-Chalmers,* court enforcement of union fines is not a recent innovation but has been known at least since 1867. 388 U.S., at 182 n. 9, 87 S.Ct., at 2007. See also Summers, The Law of Union Discipline: What the Courts Do in Fact, 70 Yale L.J. 175 (1960). The relationship between a member and his union is generally viewed as contractual in nature, International Association of Machinists v. Gonzales, 356 U.S. 617, 618, 78 S.Ct. 923, 924, 2 L.Ed.2d 1018 (1958); Scofield v. NLRB, 394 U.S., at 426 n. 3, 89 S.Ct., at 1156; NLRB v. Granite State Joint Board, Textile Workers Union of America, Local 1029, AFL–CIO, 409 U.S. 213, 217, 93 S.Ct. 385, 387, 34 L.Ed.2d 422 (1972), and the local law of contracts or voluntary associations usually governs the enforcement of this relationship. NLRB v. Allis-Chalmers Mfg. Co., supra, 388 U.S., at 192 and 193 n. 32, 87 S.Ct., at 2012, 2013; Scofield v. NLRB, supra, 394 U.S., at 426 n. 3, 89 S.Ct., at 1156.

We alluded to state court enforcement of unusually harsh union discipline in *Allis-Chalmers* when we stated that "state courts, in reviewing the imposition of union discipline, find ways to strike down 'discipline [which] involves a severe hardship.'" 388 U.S., at 193 n. 32, 87 S.Ct., at 2013 quoting Summers, Legal Limitations on Union Discipline, 64 Harv.L.Rev. 1049, 1078 (1951). The Board assumed that in view of this statement, our reference to "reasonable" fines, when reasonableness was not in issue, in *Allis-Chalmers* and in *Scofield,* was merely adverting to the usual standard applied by state courts in deciding whether to enforce union-imposed fines. The Board reads these cases, therefore, as encouraging state courts to use a reasonableness standard, not as a directive to the Board.[11]

Our review of state court cases decided both before and after our decisions in *Allis-Chalmers* and *Scofield* reveals that state courts applying state law are quite willing to determine whether disciplinary fines are reasonable in amount.[12] Indeed, the expertise required for a determination

such a determination. See, e.g., 29 U.S.C.A. § 158(b)(5) (union initiation fees).

11. The Board's interpretation of our decisions is basically the following:

"Thus, the Court's findings that the fines in those cases were reasonable seems directed to enforcing courts, encouraging those courts to make an independent determination of the reasonableness of the fine in each case presented, in the same fashion as courts limit other union discipline which imposes a severe hardship. Such considerations are of an equitable nature rather than of the character of restraint and coercion with which the National Labor Relations Act treats." Machinists, Local Lodge 504 (Arrow Development Co.), 185 N.L.R.B. 365, 368, 75 L.R.R.M. 1008, 1010 (1970).

12. Auto Workers Local 283 v. Scofield, 50 Wis.2d 117, 183 N.W.2d 103 (1971) ($100 fine deemed reasonable); Farnum v. Kurtz, 70 L.R. R.M. 2035 (Los Angeles Mun.Ct.1968) ($592 fine deemed unreasonable and reduced to $100); McCauley v. Federation of Musicians, 26 L.R.R.M. 2304 (Pa.Ct. of Common Pleas 1950) ($300 fine deemed excessive and reduced to $100); North Jersey Newspaper Guild Local No. 173 v. Rakos, 110 N.J.Super. 77, 264 A.2d 453 (1970) ($750 fine reduced to $500, which was deemed reasonable); Walsh v.

of reasonableness may well be more evident in a judicial forum that is called upon to assess reasonableness in varying factual contexts than it is in a specialized agency. In assessing the reasonableness of disciplinary fines, for example, state courts are often able to draw on their experience in areas of the law apart from labor relations.

Nor is it clear, as contended by the Court of Appeals, that the Board's setting of standards of reasonableness will necessarily result in greater uniformity in this area even if uniformity is thought to be a desirable goal. Since state courts will have jurisdiction to determine reasonableness in the enforcement context in any event, the Board's independent determination of reasonableness in an unfair labor practice context might well yield a conflict when the two forums are called upon to review the same fine.

For all of the foregoing reasons, we conclude that the Board was warranted in determining that when the union discipline does not interfere with the employee-employer relationship or otherwise violate a policy of the National Labor Relations Act, the Congress did not authorize it "to evaluate the fairness of union discipline meted out to protect a legitimate union interest." [15] The judgment of the Court of Appeals is, therefore, reversed.

Reversed.

MR. CHIEF JUSTICE BURGER, dissenting.

It is odd, to say the least, to find a union urging on us severe limitations on NLRB authority, and telling us that state courts are the proper forum to resolve questions regarding the reasonableness of fines imposed on workers for violation of union rules. For years, there has been unrelenting union opposition to state court "intervention" into industrial disputes and union activities. We have been told countless times that the "expertise" of the Labor Board, based on its overview and intimate familiarity with labor problems, is essential in this area.

A union must, of course, have some disciplinary powers or it would disintegrate. However, the power to discipline can easily turn from a means of enforcing valid rules to an oppressive and coercive device of retribution, a weapon which, when used to extremes, may deprive a working man of his very means of sustenance. Whether a particular fine is required in a particular situation involves a weighing of the delicate balance of relations between the employers, employees, and the union involved. Such an intimate knowledge of labor relations has consistently been ascribed to the Board, often by the unions. It is the Board that deals with such matters on a daily basis. It is the Board that has the jurisdiction and experience to devise and employ national standards to govern union conduct; there are

---

Communications Workers of America, Local 2336, 259 Md. 608, 271 A.2d 148 (1970) ($500 fine deemed reasonable); Local 248, United Auto Workers v. Natzke, 36 Wis.2d 237, 153 N.W.2d 602 (1967) ($100 fine upheld); Jost v. Communications Workers of America, Local 9408, 13 Cal.App.3d Supp. 7, 91 Cal.Rptr. 722 (1970) ($299 fine upheld, the court stating that "it is the settled law in this country that such a fine becomes a debt enforceable by the courts in an amount that is not unreasonably large." Id., at 12, 91 Cal.Rptr., at 725).

15. Machinists, Local Lodge 504 (Arrow Development Co.), 185 N.L.R.B. 365, 368, 75 L.R.R.M. 1008, 1011 (1970). The Board has long held that the Act proscribes certain unacceptable methods of union coercion, such as physical violence to force an employee to join a union or to participate in a strike. In re Maritime Union, 78 N.L.R.B. 971, enforced, 175 F.2d 686 (CA2 1949), cited in Scofield v. NLRB, supra, 394 U.S., at 428 n. 4, 89 S.Ct., at 1157.

valid reasons for essential uniformity and consistency in the matters of fines. To isolate this sensitive subject and thrust it on the state courts is contrary to the entire history of the federal labor statutes and opens the door to a wide disparity of fines for the same conduct in different States.

MR. JUSTICE DOUGLAS, with whom MR. CHIEF JUSTICE BURGER and MR. JUSTICE BLACKMUN concur, dissenting.

I dissent from the holding of the Court that the Board has no jurisdiction to determine the "reasonableness" of the fines placed by the Union on its dissident members. * * *

The Union sent out a written notice saying that the unpaid fines had been referred to an attorney for collection and that the reduced fines would be restored to $450 if not paid. Suits against nine employees were filed in a state court to collect the fines plus attorneys' fees and interest; and they are unresolved.

Boeing filed a charge of an unfair labor practice against the Union under § 8(b)(1)(A) of the Act. The General Counsel issued a complaint and the Board decided that the Union had violated § 8(b)(1)(A) except for the fines on members for crossing the picket line to work and for the fines on those who resigned after returning to work during the strike, for work performed during the strike prior to their resignations. But the Board, one member dissenting, refused to pass on the reasonableness of the fines, holding it lacked the power to do so.

The unfair labor practice under § 8(b)(1)(A) is the action of a union "to restrain or coerce" an employee from the "right to refrain from" assisting a union as that right is defined in § 7. In Scofield v. NLRB, 394 U.S. 423, 89 S.Ct. 1154, 22 L.Ed.2d 385, we upheld a union rule and concluded "that its enforcement by *reasonable* fines does not constitute the restraint or coercion proscribed by § 8(b)(1)(A)." Id., at 436, 89 S.Ct., at 1161 (emphasis added). See also NLRB v. Allis-Chalmers Mfg. Co., 388 U.S. 175, 87 S.Ct. 2001, 18 L.Ed.2d 1123. The imposition of a nominal fine of $1 might suit the circumstances of a case, where a $1,000 fine would be monstrous. A nominal fine might be justified where, as here, the employees had no warning that they would or could be fined for working behind a picket line. A fine where the only sanction would be temporary suspension from the union might be "reasonable," yet unreasonable if it was court enforceable, meaning, as it does here, that attorneys' fees, costs, and interest may be added. A member who must pay the union's attorney as well as his own if he challenges the reasonableness of a fine in a state court and loses, may well be suffering an unconscionable penalty. Moreover, the fine may be imposed by a union which believed as did the present Union that the member had no "right" to resign, though NLRB v. Granite State Joint Board, Textile Workers Union of America, Local 1029, AFL–CIO, 409 U.S. 213, 93 S.Ct. 385, 34 L.Ed.2d 422, held to the contrary. The present fines seem to be swollen by that predilection of the Union. The present fines also exceed the earnings of the workers during the strike period. By what standard can that possibly be justified? As member McCulloch of the Board, dissenting, said, the excess of the fines over the wages collected during this period is in actual effect an assessment after the strike is over. If after the strike the Union caused Boeing to suspend a member without pay after the strike because he had worked during the strike, there could be no question but that the Union violated § 8(b)(1)(A). Yet, the assessment of fines greater than the wages earned during the strike has precisely that effect. Thus, in assessing an unreasonable fine the Union, in my view, goes beyond the permissible bounds of regulating its internal affairs.

It is no answer to say that the reasonableness of a fine may be tested in a state-court suit. That envisages a rich and powerful union suing a rich and powerful employee. Employees, however, are often at the bottom of the totem pole, without financial resources, and unworldly when it comes to litigation. Such a suit is likely to be no contest. The Board procedures, on the other hand, may be readily available. If an employee files a charge with any merit, the Regional Director will issue a complaint. Thereafter, the General Counsel represents the employee, and the agency bears any cost of prosecuting the claim.

But my difficulty with the Court's decision is even greater. State judges, though honest and competent have no expertise in labor-management relations. The Board does have that expertise and can evolve guidelines based on its broad experience. It is said that Congress has provided the Board with no guidelines for passing on the "reasonableness" of union-imposed fines. But the Board through case-by-case treatment has been developing an administrative common law concerning "unfair" practices of employers and unions alike. We have said on other occasions that the "experience and commonsense" which are facets of the expertise of the Board, NLRB v. Radio and Television Broadcast Engineers Union, 364 U.S. 573, 582–583, 81 S.Ct. 330, 335, 336, 5 L.Ed.2d 302, are adequate for the difficult and delicate responsibilities which Congress has entrusted to it, subject of course to judicial review. A fine discretely related to a legitimate union need and reflecting principled motivations under the law is one thing. A fine that reflects the raw power exercised by a union in its hunger for all-pervasive authority over members is quite another problem. The Labor Board, which knows the nuances of this problem better than any other tribunal, is the keeper of the conscience under the Act. It and it alone has primary responsibility to police unions, as well as employers, in protection of the rights of workers. In my view it cannot properly perform its duties under § 8(b)(1)(A) unless it determines whether the nature and amount of the fine levied by a union constitute an unfair labor practice.

Note

1. A companion case to Boeing presented the question of whether the union (same union, same employer, same strike, different strike-breaker) had violated Section 8(b)(1)(A) through court enforcement of fines against former union members for strikebreaking activities occurring after their resignation from the union. In Booster Lodge No. 405, IAM v. NLRB, 412 U.S. 84, 93 S.Ct. 1961, 36 L.Ed.2d 764 (1973), the Court upheld the Board's findings that such union conduct violated Section 8(b)(1)(A). In so ruling, the Court followed its decision to the same effect in NLRB v. Granite State Joint Board, Textile Workers, Local 1029, 409 U.S. 213, 93 S.Ct. 385, 34 L.Ed.2d 422 (1972). The Court observed:

"Here, as in *Granite State*, the Union's constitution and by-laws are silent on the subject of voluntary resignation from the Union. And here as there we leave open the question of the extent to which contractual restriction on a member's right to resign may be limited by the Act. Since there is no evidence that the employees here either knew of or had consented to any limitation on their right to resign, we need 'only to apply the law which normally is reflected in our free institutions—the right of the individual to join or to resign from associations, as he sees fit "subject of course to any financial obligations due and owing" the group with which he was associated.' Granite State, supra, at 216, 93 S.Ct. at 387." 412 U.S. at 88, 93 S.Ct. at 1964.

The Court refused to distinguish Granite State on the ground that in Booster the union's constitution expressly imposed an obligation to refrain from strikebreaking. This did not, the Court held, give rise to an "implied post-resignation commitment."

Whereas in Booster Lodge (also in Granite State) the union's constitution was silent on the subject of "voluntary resignation" from the union, in Pattern Makers' League of North America v. NLRB, ___ U.S. ___, 105 S.Ct. 3064, 87 L.Ed.2d 68 (1985), the union had amended its constitution in 1976 to provide that: "No resignation or withdrawal from [the union] shall be accepted during a strike or lockout, or at a time when a strike or lockout appears imminent." ___ U.S. at ___, 105 S.Ct. at 3066, 87 L.Ed.2d at 71. During an economic strike several employees submitted letters of resignation to the union and returned to work. Following settlement of the strike with a new collective bargaining agreement, the employees who had resigned were informed by the union that their resignations had been rejected because in violation of the foregoing constitutional provision. Each of the employees was subsequently fined approximately the equivalent of earnings during the strike. Upon the filing of an employer charge, the Board agreed that the union fines were prohibited by section 8(b)(1)(A). The Supreme Court concluded (5–4) that the Board's construction of 8(b)(1)(A) was reasonable and that this section "properly may be construed as prohibiting the fining of employees who have tendered resignations ineffective under a restriction in the union constitution. We therefore affirm the judgment of the Court of Appeals enforcing the Board's order." ___ U.S. at ___, 105 S.Ct. at 3068, 87 L.Ed.2d at 73.

The issue which sharply divided the Court may be defined as follows: whether the joining or continuing in membership of a union, the constitution of which forbids resignation during a period of economic warfare, may fairly be held to be a waiver of the section 7 right to refrain from engagement in such warfare; conversely, does the union's right, under section 8(b)(1)(A)'s proviso, to "prescribe its own rules with respect to the acquisition or retention of membership" carry with it the power not merely to expel but also to prohibit resignation during such critical period. The majority of the Court deferred to the Board's expertise. Do you agree?

2. In the Scofield case, discussed in Boeing, the Court centered on the purpose for which the union imposed its discipline in the form of court-enforced fines:

" * * * The inquiry must * * * focus on the legitimacy of the union interest vindicated by the rule and the extent to which any policy of the Act may be violated by the union-imposed production ceiling.

"[U]nion opposition to unlimited piecework pay systems is historic. Union apprehension, not without foundation, is that such systems will drive up employee productivity and in turn create pressures to lower the piece-work rate so that at the new, higher level of output employees are earning little more than they did before. The fear is that the competitive pressure generated will endanger workers' health, foment jealousies, and reduce the work force. * * *

" * * * In *Allis-Chalmers,* the union members were subject to the discipline of an internal rule which strengthened the union's hand in bargaining and in this respect benefited both the members who obeyed the rule and the non-members who did not. The same is true here, and the price of obeying the rule is not as high as in *Allis-Chalmers.* There the member could be replaced for his refusal to report to work during a strike; here he need simply limit his production and suffer whatever consequences that conduct may entail. If a member chooses not to engage in this concerted activity and is unable to prevail on the other members to change the rule, then he may leave the union and obtain whatever benefits in job advancement and extra pay may result from extra work, at the same time enjoying the protection from competition, the high piece rate, and the job security which compliance with the union rule by union members tends to promote." 394 U.S. at 431–35, 89 S.Ct. at 1158–61.

3. The Court also focused upon the purpose for which the union discipline was imposed in NLRB v. Industrial Union of Marine Workers, 391 U.S. 418, 88 S.Ct. 1717, 20 L.Ed.2d 706 (1968) (reported infra p. 858), but reached the opposite result. The Marine Workers case involved a member who filed an unfair labor practice charge against his union in violation of a provision in the union constitution requiring the exhaustion of internal union remedies before initiating any judicial or administrative proceeding against the union. For this violation he was expelled from the union, whereupon he filed a second charge against the union, alleging a violation of Section 8(b)(1)(A) by reason of the expulsion. The Board found the union guilty as charged, reasoning that the member had a Section 7 right, implied from the rights expressly declared therein, to unimpeded recourse to the NLRB for protection of the expressed rights; that the union had, by expelling him for allegedly premature pursuit of that right, "restrained or coerced" him in the exercise of that right; and that the proviso to 8(b)(1)(A) did not give so large an exemption to the union with regard to its internal affairs as to encompass the union rule here sought to be enforced. The Supreme Court agreed with the Board, stating: "§ 8(b)(1)(A) assures a union freedom of self-regulation where its legitimate internal affairs are concerned. But where a union rule penalizes a member for filing an unfair labor practice charge with the Board other considerations of public policy come into play." 391 U.S. at 424, 88 S.Ct. at 1721.

4. When *supervisors* who are also union members are disciplined or threatened with discipline by the union for their conduct during a strike, it is possible that a violation of Section 8(b)(1)(B) has occurred. The interpretation of Section 8(b)(1)(B) as applied to such a situation is dealt with in Note 3, infra p. 845.

Chapter 8

THE INDIVIDUAL AND THE UNION: "I VERSUS WE"—A STUDY IN IRONY

SCOPE NOTE

Since collective bargaining, by its very nature, entails the collectivizing of the "I" interests of the individual employees into the "we" interests of the Union, "I versus we" conflicts of several varieties are present or potential. Some of these conflicts are dealt with in other chapters. Examples are found in the materials concerning the duty of fair representation; the administration of union shops and hiring halls; discrimination because of race, religion, sex, or national origin in the union's admission policies and internal administration. Despite the germaneness of these subjects to the title of the present chapter, there will be no special attempt to cover them here, although some reference to them will be made.

The subjects to be treated in this chapter are the following: admission to union membership; basic internal organizational rights of union members; union elections; union trusteeships; union corruption; and reporting and disclosure requirements.

A. ADMISSION TO UNION MEMBERSHIP

1. RIGHT TO BE ADMITTED

Trade unions were long likened to social clubs, religious groups, and other voluntary associations. Accordingly, there was no more right to be admitted to a labor union than to the Methodists or the Moose. The first breach in this position occurred, as one would expect, in a closed shop-closed union situation. In James v. Marinship Corporation, 25 Cal.2d 721, 155 P.2d 329 (1944), plaintiff employee was a black who, along with other black employees, had been ordered by the defendant union to join, and pay initiation fee and dues to, a racially segregated affiliate of the union, or, in the alternative, to suffer discharge from his job. California courts granted injunctive relief to the plaintiff, holding that the union must either (1) admit the black employees on the same terms available to non-black employees, or (2) not seek to enforce the closed shop agreement against them. Interestingly, some three years after this decision Congress took a similar position in

Section 8(a)(3) of the Taft-Hartley amendments and did so again in the 1951 amendment to the Railway Labor Act authorizing the union shop. (Section 2, Eleventh.)

Thus, for years no union subject to the NLRA or RLA has had the legal right to cause loss or denial of work by reason of discriminatorily withheld union membership. But neither Taft-Hartley nor the 1951 amendment to the RLA reached the nonunion shop; in such a shop, no more right to union membership existed than had been the case under the Wagner Act, the RLA prior to 1951, or the common law. (For a lonely decision the other way, see Betts v. Easley, 161 Kan. 459, 169 P.2d 831 (1946), supra p. 193.) Nor did the Landrum-Griffin Act of 1959 make any change in this (despite an effort to have it do so; see supra pp. 193–194); the "Bill of Rights" declared therein was expressly limited in application to "members." It was not until the Civil Rights Act of 1964 that Congress acted to assure the right of admission to unions on a broad basis (see supra p. 194), and even then the right was extended only to those denied such membership because of "race, color, religion, sex, or national origin." An argument for a more embracing right to union membership is made in the following case.

DIRECTORS GUILD OF AMERICA, INC. v. SUPERIOR COURT OF LOS ANGELES COUNTY

Supreme Court of California, 1966.
64 Cal.2d 42, 48 Cal.Rptr. 710, 409 P.2d 934.

TOBRINER, JUSTICE. Petitioner prays for a writ of prohibition to restrain further prosecution of a pending superior court action in which plaintiff (real party in interest) sought relief by way of damages and injunction on the ground that a labor union arbitrarily excluded him from membership and discriminatorily barred him from employment which he would have otherwise obtained. Since plaintiff's action raises the issue of whether federal labor legislation preempts the state jurisdiction, we must, pursuant to United States Supreme Court decisions, decide whether or not the action essentially turns upon conduct arguably subject to the federal statute.

* * * [T]he complaint alleges that plaintiff suffered both job discrimination by the union and arbitrary exclusion from the union. In such event, as we explain, the Supreme Court holds that the issue of preemption depends on the "crux" of the cause of action: if the cause centers upon job discrimination, the state court may not proceed; if it turns upon acquisition or restoration of union membership, the state court may act. We shall show that the instant complaint speaks in the language of discrimination, alleging that the employer's refusal of employment emanated from union control of the job. Since the complaint pivots on job discrimination the federal statute preempts the state jurisdiction. * * *

The complaint sets forth that in August 1964 a motion picture production company, Stage Five Productions, determined to employ plaintiff [Joseph P. Byrne] in the capacity of second assistant director for the filming of the television series "Ozzie and Harriet." In September 1964 plaintiff applied for admission into membership in the defendant Directors Guild of America, Inc. (hereinafter called Guild), a labor organization representing directors, assistant directors, and other production personnel in the motion picture and related industries. Although plaintiff tendered the requisite initiation fee and dues and otherwise fulfilled all the formal requirements for membership prescribed in the Guild constitution and bylaws, defendants refused to admit him. Such arbitrary refusal resulted from the Guild's practice of refusing membership to any person not a relative of an existing member unless the defendant officers chose to admit him for reasons of personal friendship or favoritism.

According to plaintiff, the Guild maintains closed shop conditions in the industry both by means of oral agreements with many producers that they will employ only Guild members as well as by means of threats to the remaining producers that they will encounter labor difficulties if they do not employ Guild members. The Guild's by-laws likewise obligate the Guild members to refuse to work with an employee who is not a member of the Guild.

Plaintiff alleges that in order to coerce Stage Five not to employ him defendants notified it that if it used plaintiff as a second assistant director the Guild would call the first assistant director off the job. The Guild also wrote to the Guild members then employed by Stage Five informing them that Stage Five proposed to employ plaintiff in the stated capacity and that, since he was not a member of the Guild, the above-mentioned provision of the by-laws applied. As a result of these pressures Stage Five refused to employ plaintiff as second assistant director.

The complaint purports to set forth two causes of action. The first in substance alleges that "although Stage Five did * * * want to use plaintiff in the capacity of Second Assistant Director" it did, because of the Guild's arbitrary rejection of plaintiff from membership and because of its coercive tactics, "refuse, and has continuously refused to employ plaintiff in such capacity." The first cause further states that "as declared by the California Supreme Court in James v. Marinship Corp., 25 Cal.2d 721, 731 [155 P.2d 329, 160 A.L.R. 900] (1945), the maintenance of a closed shop industry by a union that also maintains a closed union is contrary to the public policy of the State of California." The second cause alleges that by such conduct it "tortiously interfered with and prevented plaintiff from being able to enter into such advantageous employment contract."

Subsequent to the date of filing the superior court action, plaintiff brought charges before the National Labor Relations Board alleging that defendants committed unfair labor practices under section 8 of the Act. No question arises here but that the involved employment affects interstate commerce. * * *

After a tortuous course in evolving a definition of the permissible scope of state jurisdiction in the field of labor relations, the United States Supreme Court has now held that except in cases involving the preservation of the domestic peace the state jurisdiction succumbs to the federal in matters arguably subject to the protections of section 7 or the prohibition of section 8 of the Act. * * *

Section 8(a)(3) of the Act declares in substance that it is an unfair labor practice for an employer by discrimination in regard to hire or tenure of employment or any term or condition of employment to encourage or discourage membership in any labor organization, provided that an employer may enter into an agreement, requiring membership in a union as a condition of employment, with a labor organization which is the collective bargaining agent of its employees. Section 8(b)(2) of the Act makes it an unfair labor practice for a labor organization to cause or attempt to cause an employer to discriminate against an employee to whom membership in the union has been denied on grounds other than failure to tender the periodic dues and the initiation fee uniformly required as a condition of acquiring or retaining membership.

This court has acknowledged that the federal act would foreclose the state in a case involving interstate commerce which turned upon union discrimination that prevented the complainant's employment. Thorman v. International Alliance etc. Employees (1958) 49 Cal.2d 629, 320 P.2d 494 * * *.

* * * [W]e must [now] determine whether the state is likewise preempted as to a complaint which seeks not only placement on the job but also admission to the union. Recent United States Supreme Court cases, International Ass'n of Machinists v. Gonzales (1958) 356 U.S. 617, 78 S.Ct. 923, 2 L.Ed.2d 1018; Local 100, United Ass'n of Journeymen and Apprentices v. Borden (1962) 373 U.S. 690, 83 S.Ct. 1423, 10 L.Ed.2d 638, and Local No. 207, etc., Iron Workers Union v. Perko (1963) 373 U.S. 701, 83 S.Ct. 1429, 10 L.Ed. 2d 646, indicate the proper resolution of this issue.

In *Gonzales* the United States Supreme Court held that a state court could exercise jurisdiction to entertain an action by one whom the union arbitrarily expelled; the state court could order reinstatement and award damages for lost wages. Justice Frankfurter, writing for the majority, said: " * * * the protection of union members in their rights as members from arbitrary conduct by unions and union officers has not been undertaken by federal law, and indeed the assertion of any such power has been expressly denied. * * * Thus, to preclude a state court from exerting its traditional jurisdiction to determine and enforce the rights of union membership would in many cases leave an unjustly ousted member without remedy for the restoration of his important union rights." (356 U.S. at p. 620, 78 S.Ct. at p. 925.) The Supreme Court held that Gonzales' claim did not directly turn on employment relations but upon the union's internal affairs. * * *

On the other hand, in *Borden* the court held that the questioned union activity related to job discrimination, conduct which arguably fell under the exclusive jurisdiction of the board. There the plaintiff, a member of a Louisiana local plumbers union, attempted to secure employment with a construction company in Dallas, Texas. The company did its hiring by means of referral from the local union. When the local union refused plaintiff such reference, the company in turn rejected him; plaintiff brought suit upon the ground that the union improperly discriminated against him in assignment for jobs. The Supreme Court held that the "suit involved here was focused principally, if not entirely, on the union's actions with respect to Borden's efforts to obtain employment." (373 U.S. at p. 697, 83 S.Ct. at p. 1427.) Using the language of *Gonzales* the court said: "the 'crux' of the action * * * concerned Borden's employment relations and involved conduct arguably subject to the Board's jurisdiction." (Id.) The court contrasted the situation before it with that of *Gonzales,* which "turned on the Court's conclusion that the lawsuit was focused on purely internal union matters, i.e., on relations between the individual plaintiff and the union not having to do directly with matters of employment, and that the principal relief sought was restoration of union membership rights." (Id.)

If, then, the state court is confronted with a case, such as the instant one, which apparently embraces both the union's discrimination as to employment and the union's arbitrary refusal to afford membership, we must ascertain the focus or crux of the cause of action to determine if it essentially turns upon conduct which is arguably regulated by the federal act or, instead, principally rests upon conduct for which the state affords relief.

We have concluded that plaintiff's first cause of action essentially involves discrimination as to employment. Plaintiff complains that the union's refusal to afford him membership and its concomitant coercive activities have prevented him from obtaining the second assistant directorship. The complaint is founded upon discrimination; its self-evident purpose is to obtain plaintiff's placement on the job. Plaintiff's second cause of action likewise involves such discrimination; it alleges the union's tortious interference "prevented plaintiff from being able to enter into such * * * employment contract." Thus both causes pivot upon job discrimination; yet the finding of such discrimination lies exclusively with the board. * * *

* * * Plaintiff argues that he is entitled to membership even if the union did not enforce a union shop contract or otherwise engage in discrimination against him as to employment, alleging that "an arbitrary and discriminatory membership policy is contrary to public policy *without regard to whether the defendants maintain closed shop conditions.*" (Italics added.) We have seen that the board exercises exclusive jurisdiction over a matter of union discrimination in employment; plaintiff now asks relief irrespective of such discrimination. We shall explain that a union cannot arbitrarily exclude from membership a person employed in the craft or industry whose employees are represented by the union even when the union does not have a union shop contract. But relief in such a situation can be afforded only to those who are employed in such a craft or industry. Plaintiff does not allege such employment.

If plaintiff had properly alleged that he had actually *been employed* as a second assistant director and that the union had arbitrarily refused him membership, our previous decisions, and the reasoning upon which they rest, would justify a ruling affording him union membership.

In the landmark case of James v. Marinship, supra, 25 Cal.2d 721, 155 P.2d 329, this court enjoined the enforcement of a union shop contract under which the union required Negroes to become members of an "auxiliary" local but denied them full membership in the "white" local which negotiated the contracts, handled grievances and dispatched employees to their jobs. Holding that since the union controlled a "monopoly" of jobs through its closed shop contract, it occupied a "quasi public position similar to that of a public service business and [had] * * * corresponding obligations" (p. 731, 155 P.2d p. 335), Chief Justice Gibson prophetically stated, "It is difficult to see how a union can fairly represent *all* the employees of a bargaining unit unless it is willing to admit all to membership, giving them the opportunity

to vote for union leaders and to participate in determining union policies."
(p. 735, 155 P.2d p. 337.) * * *

The philosophy of [James v. Marinship and later California] cases finds
its ultimate application in the ruling of Thorman v. International Alliance
etc. Employees, supra, 49 Cal.2d 629, 320 P.2d 494, which upheld a writ of
mandamus directing a union to admit to membership a motion picture
projectionist whom it had arbitrarily excluded. Plaintiff, a member of an
"auxiliary" union, subject to displacement from his job by senior members of
the "main" local, could not participate in the affairs of the main local or
negotiation of contracts; he could become a member of that local only by a
two-thirds vote, a requirement which the court apparently held to be
arbitrary. As one commentator points out, "It is difficult to explain such an
order except on the theory that an individual within a bargaining unit
represented by a union has a right, quite apart from his right to work, to
participate in that union's affairs. Indeed, in the case of a union operating
as statutory bargaining representative, under state or federal legislation,
that theory would seem to follow from the position of the United States
Supreme Court that such a union has a statutory, if not constitutional,
obligation to represent fairly all employees within the bargaining unit."
(Grodin, Union Government & The Law: British and American Experiences
(1961) 179.)

The decisions of this court thus recognize that membership in the union
means more than mere personal or social accommodation. Such membership affords to the employee not only the opportunity to participate in the
negotiation of the contract governing his employment but also the chance to
engage in the institutional life of the union. Although in the case which
involves interstate commerce the union must legally give fair representation
to all the appropriate employees, whether or not they are members of the
union, the union official, in the nature of political realities, will in all
likelihood more diligently represent union members, who can vote him out
of office, than employees whom he must serve only as a matter of abstract
law.

Our decisions further recognize that the union functions as the medium
for the exercise of industrial franchise. As Summers puts it, "The right to
join a union involves the right to an economic ballot." (The Right to Join a
Union (1947) 47 Colum.L.Rev. 33.) Participation in the union's affairs by the
workman compares to the participation of the citizen in the affairs of his
community. The union, as a kind of public service institution, affords to its
members the opportunity to record themselves upon all matters affecting
their relationships with the employer; it serves likewise as a vehicle for the
expression of the membership's position on political and community issues.
The shadowy right to "fair representation" by the union, accorded by the
Act, is by no means the same as the hard concrete ability to vote and to
participate in the affairs of the union.

The above grounds for condemnation of arbitrary rejection from membership apply as forcefully to the situation in which the union does not have
a union shop contract as to that in which it does. The need of the worker for
union participation is not reduced because the union does not enjoy a union

shop; the basis for membership lies in the right and desirability of representation, not in the union's economic control of the job.

Our analysis applies, however, only to union membership for those employed in the appropriate craft or industry. To hold that a union must admit *all* persons who seek membership but are not employed in the craft or industry whose employees are represented by the union would raise serious social and economic questions. Any such sweeping ruling would subject the union to an influx of unemployed persons who could distort its function from representation of those working in the relevant craft or industry to purposes alien to such objectives. It would set up for state courts a test as to the scope of the union's obligation of representation which would conflict with the National Labor Relations Board's counterpart concept of the appropriate bargaining unit.[6] It could gravely affect the basic structure of the union. Although we would hold that the union, even in the absence of the union shop, must admit to membership all qualified employed applicants, the instant complaint, lacking such allegation of employment, must fail.[7]

We conclude that the instant case does not present a matter for state court relief; that the crux of the complaint necessarily pertains to employment relations rather than to union membership. As a result, as we have said, the federal act preempts. But in so holding, we do not rule that preemption extends to the lawsuit which, in the words of *Borden*, "focused on purely internal union matters, i.e., on relations between the individual plaintiff and the union not having to do directly with matters of employment, * * *." (373 U.S. 690, 697, 83 S.Ct. 1423, 1427.) The complaint which draws into issue the right to union membership alone involves the factors which we have discussed above; as to a suit which met the foregoing requirements, relief at the state level would be appropriate.

Let a peremptory writ of prohibition issue.

TRAYNOR, C.J., and McCOMB, PETERS, PEEK, MOSK and BURKE JJ., concur.

Note

1. In the absence of legislative mandate to the contrary, and despite the reasoning in Directors Guild, the following excerpt from Oliphant v. Brotherhood of Locomotive Firemen, 262 F.2d 359, 363 (6th Cir.1958), cert. denied, 359 U.S. 935 (1959), supra p. 193, states the still prevalent view: "The Brotherhood is a private association, whose membership policies are its own affair, and this is not an appropriate case for interposition of judicial control."

6. Section 9(a) of the Act provides: "Representatives designated or selected for the purposes of collective bargaining by the majority of the *employees* in a unit appropriate for such purposes, shall be the exclusive representatives of all the *employees* in such unit * * *." Section 9(b) provides: "The Board shall decide in each case whether, in order to assure to *employees* the fullest freedom in exercising the rights guaranteed by this Act, the unit appropriate for the purposes of collective bargaining shall be the employer unit, craft unit, plant unit, or subdivision therof: * * *." (Emphasis added.) Section 2(3) provides the statutory definition of "employee."

7. Thus we do not face the issue which would be presented if the board should ultimately hold that the union *had* engaged in discriminatory conduct and ordered plaintiff's employment, which actions by the board were followed by union refusal of membership; or if, further, plaintiff were thereafter *employed* as a second assistant director, and the union had then arbitrarily refused him membership. Such a cause would necessarily be conditioned upon the arbitrary rejection of plaintiff from membership and upon the actual fact of plaintiff's employment.

The Oliphant decision is premised upon the view that the policies of a "private association," with regard to both admission and other internal matters, do not constitute "state action" and are, therefore, not subject to federal constitutional constraints. Would a contrary decision in a case where the plaintiff seeks admission to a union open a Pandora's Box, subjecting *every* internal decision of the union to constitutional scrutiny? If so, would the gain be worth the price? If not, how could the constitutional ("public policy"?—see supra p. 796) standard thus applied be rationally limited to the "admission to membership" issue? One virtue of *legislative* remedying of such problems is that Pandora's Box can be opened on a rationally limited basis.

2. The reverse side of the right-to-membership coin is presented in the materials in the next section: "All is not gold that glitters."

2. DUTY TO BELONG: "FREE RIDING" AND THE CONSTITUTION

ABOOD v. DETROIT BOARD OF EDUCATION

Supreme Court of the United States, 1977.
431 U.S. 209, 97 S.Ct. 1782, 52 L.Ed.2d 261.

MR. JUSTICE STEWART delivered the opinion of the Court.

The State of Michigan has enacted legislation authorizing a system for union representation of local governmental employees. A union and a local government employer are specifically permitted to agree to an "agency shop" arrangement, whereby every employee represented by a union—even though not a union member—must pay to the union, as a condition of employment, a service fee equal in amount to union dues. The issue before us is whether this arrangement violates the constitutional rights of government employees who object to public sector unions as such or to various union activities financed by the compulsory service fees.

I

After a secret ballot election, the Detroit Federation of Teachers (the Union) was certified in 1967 pursuant to Michigan law as the exclusive representative of teachers employed by the Detroit Board of Education (the Board). The Union and the Board thereafter concluded a collective-bargaining agreement effective from July 1, 1969, to July 1, 1971. Among the agreement's provisions was an "agency shop" clause, requiring every teacher who had not become a Union member within 60 days of hire (or within 60 days of January 26, 1970, the effective date of the clause) to pay the Union a service charge equal to the regular dues required of Union members. A teacher who failed to meet this obligation was subject to discharge. Nothing in the agreement, however, required any teacher to join the Union, espouse the cause of unionism, or participate in any other way in union affairs.

On November 7, 1969—more than two months before the agency-shop clause was to become effective—Christine Warczak and a number of other named teachers filed a class action in a state court, naming as defendants the Board, the Union, and several Union officials. Their complaint, as amended, alleged that they were unwilling or had refused to pay dues and that they opposed collective bargaining in the public sector. The amended complaint further alleged that the Union "carries on various social activities for the benefit of its members which are not available to non-members as a matter of right," and that the Union is engaged

"in a number and variety of activities and programs which are economic, political, professional, scientific and religious in nature of which Plaintiffs do not approve, and in which they will have no voice, and which are not and will not be collective bargaining activities, i.e., the negotiation and administration of contracts with Defendant Board, and that a substantial part of the sums required to be paid under said Agency Shop Clause are used and will continue to be used for the support of such activities and programs, and not solely for the purpose of defraying the cost of Defendant Federation of its activities as bargaining agent for teachers employed by Defendant Board." [3]

The complaint prayed that the agency-shop clause be declared invalid under state law and also under the United States Constitution as a deprivation of, *inter alia*, the plaintiffs' freedom of association protected by the First and Fourteenth Amendments, and for such further relief as might be deemed appropriate.

Upon the defendants' motion for summary judgment, the trial court dismissed the action for failure to state a claim upon which relief could be granted. 73 L.R.R.M. 2237 (Cir.Ct. Wayne County). The plaintiffs appealed, and while their appeal was pending the Michigan Supreme Court ruled in Smigel v. Southgate Community School Dist., 388 Mich. 531, 202 N.W.2d 305, that state law prohibited an agency shop in the public sector. Accordingly, the judgment in the *Warczak* case was vacated and remanded to the trial court for further proceedings consistent with the *Smigel* decision.

Meanwhile, D. Louis Abood and other named teachers had filed a separate action in the same state trial court. The allegations in the complaint were virtually identical to those in *Warczak*,[5] and similar relief was requested.[6] This second action was held in abeyance pending disposition of the *Warczak* appeal, and when that case was remanded the two cases were consolidated in the trial court for consideration of the defendants' renewed motion for summary judgment.

On November 5, 1973, that motion was granted. The trial court noted that following the *Smigel* decision, the Michigan Legislature had in 1973 amended its Public Employment Relations Act so as expressly to authorize an agency shop. 1973 Mich.Pub.Acts, No. 25, codified as Mich.Comp.Laws § 432.210(1)(c). This amendment was applied retroactively by the trial court to validate the agency-shop clause predating 1973 as a matter of state law, and the court ruled further that such a clause does not violate the Federal Constitution.

The plaintiffs' appeals were consolidated by the Michigan Court of Appeals, which ruled that the trial court had erred in giving retroactive application to the 1973 legislative amendment. The appellate court proceeded, however, to consider the constitutionality of the agency-shop clause, and upheld its facial validity on the authority of this Court's decision in Railway

---

3. The nature of these activities and of the objections to them were not described in any further detail.

5. The only material difference was that *Abood* was not a class action.

6. The *Abood* complaint prayed for declaratory and injunctive relief against discharge of any teacher for failure to pay the service charge, and for such other relief as might be deemed appropriate.

Employes' Department v. Hanson, 351 U.S. 225, 76 S.Ct. 714, 100 L.Ed. 1112, which upheld the constitutionality under the First Amendment of a union-shop clause, authorized by the Railway Labor Act, requiring financial support of the exclusive bargaining representative by every member of the bargaining unit. Id., at 238, 76 S.Ct., at 721. Noting, however, that Michigan law also permits union expenditures for legislative lobbying and in support of political candidates, the state appellate court identified an issue explicitly not considered in *Hanson*—the constitutionality of using compulsory service charges to further "political purposes" unrelated to collective bargaining. Although recognizing that such expenditures "could violate plaintiffs' First and Fourteenth Amendment rights," the court read this Court's more recent decisions to require that an employee who seeks to vindicate such rights must "make known to the union those causes and candidates to which he objects." Since the complaints had failed to allege that any such notification had been given, the court held that the plaintiffs were not entitled to restitution of any portion of the service charges. After the Supreme Court of Michigan denied review, the plaintiffs appealed to this Court, 28 U.S.C.A. § 1257(2), and we noted probable jurisdiction.[9]

II

A

Consideration of the question whether an agency shop provision in a collective-bargaining agreement covering governmental employees is, as such, constitutionally valid must begin with two cases in this Court that on their face go far towards resolving the issue. The cases are Railway Employes' Department v. Hanson, supra, and International Association of Machinists v. Street, 367 U.S. 740, 81 S.Ct. 1784, 6 L.Ed.2d 1141.

In the *Hanson* case a group of railroad employees brought an action in a Nebraska court to enjoin enforcement of a union-shop agreement.[10] The

9. At oral argument the suggestion was made that this case might be moot. The only agency-shop clause placed in issue by the complaints was contained in a collective-bargaining agreement that expired in 1971. That clause was unenforceable as a matter of state law after the decision in *Smigel* and the ruling of the state court of appeals in the present cases that the 1973 statute should not be given retroactive application.

But both sides acknowledged in their briefs submitted to the Michigan Court of Appeals that a successor collective-bargaining agreement effective in 1973 contained substantially the identical agency shop provision. The Court of Appeals appears to have taken judicial notice of this agreement in rendering its decision, for otherwise its ruling that the 1973 amendment was not retroactive would have disposed of the case without the need to consider any constitutional questions. Since the state appellate court considered the 1973 agreement to be part of the record in making its ruling, we proceed upon the same premise.

The fact that the 1973 agreement may have expired since the state appellate court rendered its decision does not affect the continuing vitality of this controversy for Article III purposes. Some of the plaintiffs in both *Warczak* and *Abood* either refused to pay the service charge or paid it under protest. Their contention that they cannot constitutionally be compelled to contribute the service charge, or at least some portion of it, thus survives the expiration of the collective-bargaining agreement itself.

10. Under a union-shop agreement, an employee must become a member of the union within a specified period of time after hire, and must as a member pay whatever union dues and fees are uniformly required. Under both the National Labor Relations Act and the Railway Labor Act, "[i]t is permissible to condition employment upon membership, but membership, insofar as it has significance to employment rights, may in turn be conditioned only upon payment of fees and dues." NLRB v. General Motors Corp., 373 U.S. 734, 742, 83 S.Ct. 1453, 1459, 10 L.Ed.2d 670. See 29 U.S.C.A. § 158(a)(3); 45 U.S.C.A. § 152, Eleventh. Hence, although a union shop denies an employee the option of not formally

challenged clause was authorized, and indeed shielded from any attempt by a State to prohibit it, by the Railway Labor Act, 45 U.S.C.A. § 152, Eleventh. The trial court granted the relief requested. The Nebraska Supreme Court upheld the injunction on the ground that employees who disagreed with the objectives promoted by union expenditures were deprived of the freedom of association protected by the First Amendment. This Court agreed that "justiciable questions under the First and Fifth Amendments were presented," 351 U.S., at 231, 76 S.Ct., at 718,[12] but reversed the judgment of the Nebraska Supreme Court on the merits. Acknowledging that "[m]uch might be said *pro* and *con*" about the union shop as a policy matter, the Court noted that it is Congress that is charged with identifying "[t]he ingredients of industrial peace and stabilized labor-management relations * * *." 351 U.S., at 233–234, 76 S.Ct. at 719. Congress determined that it would promote peaceful labor relations to permit a union and an employer to conclude an agreement requiring employees who obtain the benefit of union representation to share its cost, and that legislative judgment was surely an allowable one. Id., at 235, 76 S.Ct. at 719.

The record in *Hanson* contained no evidence that union dues were used to force ideological conformity or otherwise to impair the free expression of employees, and the Court noted that "[i]f 'assessments' are in fact imposed for purposes not germane to collective bargaining, a different problem would be presented." Id., at 235, 76 S.Ct., at 720. (footnote omitted). But the Court squarely held that "the requirement for financial support of the collective-bargaining agency by all who receive the benefits of its work * * * does not violate * * * the First Amendmen[t]." Id., at 238, 76 S.Ct., at 721.

The Court faced a similar question several years later in the *Street* case, which also involved a challenge to the constitutionality of a union shop authorized by the Railway Labor Act. In *Street,* however, the record contained findings that the union treasury to which all employees were required to contribute had been used "to finance the campaigns of candi-

becoming a union member, under federal law it is the "practical equivalent" of an agency shop, NLRB v. General Motors, supra, at 743, 83 S.Ct. at 1459. See also Lathrop v. Donohue, 367 U.S. 820, 828, 81 S.Ct. 1826, 1830, 6 L.Ed.2d 1191.

Hanson was concerned simply with the requirement of financial support for the union, and did not focus on the question whether the additional requirement of a union-shop arrangement that each employee formally join the union is constitutionally permissible. See NLRB v. General Motors, supra, 373 U.S. at 744, 83 S.Ct. at 1460. ("Such a difference between the union and agency shop may be of great importance in some contexts * * *."); cf. Storer v. Brown, 415 U.S. 724, 745–746, 94 S.Ct. 1274, 1286, 39 L.Ed.2d 714. As the agency shop before us does not impose that additional requirement, we have no occasion to address that question.

12. Unlike § 14(b) of the National Labor Relations Act, 29 U.S.C.A. § 164(b), the Rail-

way Labor Act pre-empts any attempt by a State to prohibit a union-shop agreement. Had it not been for that federal statute, the union-shop provision at issue in *Hanson* would have been invalidated under Nebraska law. The *Hanson* Court accordingly reasoned that government action was present: "the federal statute is the source of the power and authority by which any private rights are lost or sacrificed. * * * The enactment of the federal statute authorizing union shop agreements is the governmental action on which the Constitution operates * * *." 351 U.S., at 232, 76 S.Ct. at 718. See also ibid., n. 4 ("Once courts enforce the agreement the sanction of government is, of course, put behind them. See Shelley v. Kraemer, 334 U.S. 1, 68 S.Ct. 836, 92 L.Ed. 1161; Hurd v. Hodge, 334 U.S. 24, 68 S.Ct. 847, 92 L.Ed. 1187; Barrows v. Jackson, 346 U.S. 249, 73 S.Ct. 1031, 97 L.Ed. 1586.").

dates for federal and state offices whom [the plaintiffs] opposed, and to promote the propagation of political and economic doctrines, concepts and ideologies with which [they] disagreed." 367 U.S., at 744, 81 S.Ct., at 1787.

The Court recognized that these findings presented constitutional "questions of the utmost gravity" not decided in *Hanson,* id., at 749, 81 S.Ct., at 1789, and therefore considered whether the Act could fairly be construed to avoid these constitutional issues. Id., at 749–750, 81 S.Ct., at 1789–90.[13] The Court concluded that the Act could be so construed, since only expenditures related to the union's functions in negotiating and administering the collective bargaining agreement and adjusting grievances and disputes fell within "the reasons * * * accepted by Congress why authority to make union-shop agreements was justified," id., at 768, 81 S.Ct. at 1800. The Court ruled, therefore, that the use of compulsory union dues for political purposes violated the Act itself. Nonetheless, it found that an injunction against enforcement of the union-shop agreement as such was impermissible under *Hanson,* and remanded the case to the Supreme Court of Georgia so that a more limited remedy could be devised.

The holding in *Hanson,* as elaborated in *Street,* reflects familiar doctrines in the federal labor laws. The principle of exclusive union representation, which underlies the National Labor Relations Act as well as the Railway Labor Act, is a central element in the congressional structuring of industrial relations. * * * The designation of a single representative avoids the confusion that would result from attempting to enforce two or more agreements specifying different terms and conditions of employment. It prevents inter-union rivalries from creating dissension within the work force and eliminating the advantages to the employee of collectivization. It also frees the employer from the possibility of facing conflicting demands from different unions, and permits the employer and a single union to reach agreements and settlements that are not subject to attack from rival labor organizations. * * *

The designation of a union as exclusive representative carries with it great responsibilities. The tasks of negotiating and administering a collective-bargaining agreement and representing the interests of employees in settling disputes and processing grievances are continuing and difficult ones. They often entail expenditure of much time and money. See *Street,* supra, 367 U.S. at 760, 81 S.Ct. at 1795. The services of lawyers, expert negotiators, economists, and a research staff, as well as general administrative personnel, may be required. Moreover, in carrying out these duties, the union is obliged "fairly and equitably to represent all employees, * * * union and nonunion," within the relevant unit. Id., at 761, 81 S.Ct., at 1796. A union-shop arrangement has been thought to distribute fairly the cost of these activities among those who benefit, and it counteracts the incentive that employees might otherwise have to become "free riders"—to refuse to contribute to the union while obtaining benefits of union representation that necessarily accrue to all employees. * * *

---

13. In suggesting that *Street* "significantly undercut," and constituted a "rethinking" of, *Hanson,* the concurring opinion loses sight of the fact that the record in *Street,* unlike that in *Hanson,* potentially presented constitutional questions arising from union expenditures for ideological purposes unrelated to collective bargaining.

To compel employees financially to support their collective bargaining representative has an impact upon their First Amendment interests. An employee may very well have ideological objections to a wide variety of activities undertaken by the union in its role as exclusive representative. His moral or religious views about the desirability of abortion may not square with the union's policy in negotiating a medical benefits plan. One individual might disagree with a union policy of negotiating limits on the right to strike, believing that to be the road to serfdom for the working class, while another might have economic or political objections to unionism itself. An employee might object to the union's wage policy because it violates guidelines designed to limit inflation, or might object to the union's seeking a clause in the collective-bargaining agreement proscribing racial discrimination. The examples could be multiplied. To be required to help finance the union as a collective-bargaining agent might well be thought, therefore, to interfere in some way with an employee's freedom to associate for the advancement of ideas, or to refrain from doing so, as he sees fit. But the judgment clearly made in *Hanson* and *Street* is that such interference as exists is constitutionally justified by the legislative assessment of the important contribution of the union shop to the system of labor relations established by Congress. "The furtherance of the common cause leaves some leeway for the leadership of the group. As long as they act to promote the cause which justified bringing the group together, the individual cannot withdraw his financial support merely because he disagrees with the group's strategy. If that were allowed, we would be reversing the *Hanson* case, *sub silentio*." International Association of Machinists v. Street, supra, 367 U.S. at 778, 81 S.Ct. at 1805. (Douglas, J., concurring).

B

The National Labor Relations Act leaves regulation of the labor relations of state and local governments to the States. See 29 U.S.C.A. § 152(2). Michigan has chosen to establish for local government units a regulatory scheme which, although not identical in every respect to the NLRA or RLA, is broadly modeled after federal law. * * *

The governmental interests advanced by the agency shop provision in the Michigan statute are much the same as those promoted by similar provisions in federal labor law. The confusion and conflict that could arise if rival teachers' unions, holding quite different views as to the proper class hours, class sizes, holidays, tenure provisions, and grievance procedures, each sought to obtain the employer's agreement, are no different in kind from the evils that the exclusivity rule in the Railway Labor Act was designed to avoid. * * * The desirability of labor peace is no less important in the public sector, nor is the risk of "free riders" any smaller.

Our province is not to judge the wisdom of Michigan's decision to authorize the agency shop in public employment. Rather, it is to adjudicate the constitutionality of that decision. The same important government interests recognized in the *Hanson* and *Street* cases presumptively support the impingement upon associational freedom created by the agency shop here at issue. Thus, insofar as the service charge is used to finance expenditures by the union for the purposes of collective bargaining, contract administration, and grievance adjustment, those two decisions of this Court appear to require validation of the agency-shop agreement before us.

While recognizing the apparent precedential weight of the *Hanson* and *Street* cases, the appellants advance two reasons why those decisions should not control decision of the present case. First, the appellants note that it is *government* employment that is involved here, thus directly implicating constitutional guarantees, in contrast to the private employment that was the subject of the *Hanson* and *Street* decisions. Second, the appellants say that in the public sector collective bargaining itself is inherently "political," and that to require them to give financial support to it is to require the "ideological conformity" that the Court expressly found absent in the *Hanson* case. 351 U.S., at 238, 76 S.Ct., at 721. We find neither argument persuasive.

Because it is employment by the State that is here involved, the appellants suggest that this case is governed by a long line of decisions holding that public employment cannot be conditioned upon the surrender of First Amendment rights. But, while the actions of public employers surely constitute "state action," the union shop, as authorized by the Railway Labor Act, also was found to result from governmental action in *Hanson*.[22] The plaintiffs' claims in *Hanson* failed, not because there was no governmental action, but because there was no First Amendment violation. The appellants' reliance on the "unconstitutional conditions" doctrine is therefore misplaced.

The appellants' second argument is that in any event collective bargaining in the public sector is inherently "political" and thus requires a different result under the First and Fourteenth Amendments. This contention rests upon the important and often-noted differences in the nature of collective bargaining in the public and private sectors.[24] A public employer, unlike his private counterpart, is not guided by the profit motive and constrained by the normal operation of the market. Municipal services are typically not priced, and where they are they tend to be regarded as in some sense "essential" and therefore are often price inelastic. Although a public employer, like a private one, will wish to keep costs down, he lacks an important discipline against agreeing to increases in labor costs that in a market system would require price increases. A public sector union is correspondingly less concerned that high prices due to costly wage demands will decrease output and hence employment.

The government officials making decisions as the public "employer" are less likely to act as a cohesive unit than are managers in private industry, in

---

22. See n. 12, supra.

24. See, e.g., K. Hanslowe, The Emerging Law of Labor Relations in Public Employment (1967); H. Wellington & R. Winter, Jr., The Unions and the Cities (1971); Hildebrand, The Public Sector, in J. Dunlop and N. Chamberlain (eds.), Frontiers of Collective Bargaining 125–154 (1967); Rehmus, Constraints on Local Governments in Public Employee Bargaining, 67 Mich.L.Rev. 919 (1969); Shaw & Clark, The Practical Differences Between Public and Private Sector Collective Bargaining, 19 U.C.

L.A.L.Rev. 867 (1972); Smith, State and Local Advisory Reports on Public Employment Labor Legislation: A Comparative Analysis, 67 Mich.L.Rev. 891 (1969); Summers, Public Employee Bargaining: A Political Perspective, 83 Yale L.J. 1156 (1974); Project, Collective Bargaining and Politics in Public Employment, 19 U.C.L.A.L.Rev. 887 (1972). The general description in text of the differences between private and public sector collective bargaining is drawn from these sources.

part because different levels of public authority—department managers, budgetary officials, and legislative bodies—are involved, and in part because each official may respond to a distinctive political constituency. And the ease of negotiating a final agreement with the union may be severely limited by statutory restrictions, by the need for the approval of a higher executive authority or a legislative body, or by the commitment of budgetary decisions of critical importance to others.

Finally, decisionmaking by a public employer is above all a political process. The officials who represent the public employer are utlimately responsible to the electorate, which for this purpose can be viewed as comprising three overlapping classes of voters—taxpayers, users of particular government services, and government employees. Through exercise of their political influence as part of the electorate, the employees have the opportunity to affect the decisions of government representatives who sit on the other side of the bargaining table. Whether these representatives accede to a union's demands will depend upon a blend of political ingredients, including community sentiment about unionism generally and the involved union in particular, the degree of taxpayer resistance, and the views of voters as to the importance of the service involved and the relation between the demands and the quality of service. It is surely arguable, however, that permitting public employees to unionize and a union to bargain as their exclusive representative gives the employees more influence in the decisionmaking process than is possessed by employees similarly organized in the private sector.

The distinctive nature of public-sector bargaining has led to widespread discussion about the extent to which the law governing labor relations in the private sector provides an appropriate model. To take but one example, there has been considerable debate about the desirability of prohibiting public employee unions from striking,[25] a step that the State of Michigan itself has taken, Mich.Comp.Laws § 423.202. But although Michigan has not adopted the federal model of labor relations in every respect, it has determined that labor stability will be served by a system of exclusive representation and the permissive use of an agency shop in public employment. As already stated, there can be no principled basis for according that decision less weight in the constitutional balance than was given in *Hanson* to the congressional judgment reflected in the Railway Labor Act. The only remaining constitutional inquiry evoked by the appellants' argument, therefore, is whether a public employee has a weightier First Amendment interest than a private employee in not being compelled to contribute to the costs of exclusive union representation. We think he does not.

Public employees are not basically different from private employees; on the whole, they have the same sort of skills, the same needs, and seek the same advantages. "The uniqueness of public employment is *not in the employees* nor in the work performed; the uniqueness is in the special

---

25. See, e.g., Anderson, Strikes and Impasse Resolution in Public Employment, 67 Mich.L.Rev. 943 (1969); Burton & Krider, The Role and Consequences of Strikes by Public Employees, 79 Yale L.J. 418 (1970); Hildebrand, supra n. 24; Kheel, Strikes and Public Employment, 67 Mich.L.Rev. 931 (1969); Wellington & Winter, The Limits of Collective Bargaining in Public Employment, 78 Yale L.J. 1107 (1969); Wellington & Winter, More on Strikes by Public Employees, 79 Yale L.J. 441 (1970).

character of the employer." Summers, Public Sector Bargaining: Problems of Governmental Decisionmaking, 44 Cinn.L.Rev. 669, 670 (1976) (emphasis added). The very real differences between exclusive agent collective bargaining in the public and private sectors are not such as to work any greater infringement upon the First Amendment interests of public employees. A public employee who believes that a union representing him is urging a course that is unwise as a matter of public policy is not barred from expressing his viewpoint. Besides voting in accordance with his convictions, every public employee is largely free to express his views, in public or private, orally or in writing.   *   *   *

There can be no quarrel with the truism that because public employee unions attempt to influence governmental policymaking, their activities— and the views of members who disagree with them—may be properly termed political. But that characterization does not raise the ideas and beliefs of public employees onto a higher plane than the ideas and beliefs of private employees. It is no doubt true that a central purpose of the First Amendment "was to protect the free discussion of governmental affairs." But our cases have never suggested that expression about philosophical, social, artistic, economic, literary, or ethical matters—to take a nonexhaustive list of labels—is not entitled to full First Amendment protection. Union members in both the public and private sector may find that a variety of union activities conflict with their beliefs. Nothing in the First Amendment or our cases discussing its meaning makes the question whether the adjective "political" can properly be attached to those beliefs the critical constitutional inquiry.

The differences between public and private sector collective bargaining simply do not translate into differences in First Amendment rights. Even those commentators most acutely aware of the distinctive nature of public-sector bargaining and most seriously concerned with its policy implications agree that "[t]he union security issue in the public sector *   *   * is fundamentally the same issue *   *   * as in the private sector. *   *   * No special dimension results from the fact that a union represents public rather than private employees." H. Wellington & R. Winter, The Unions and the Cities 95–96 (1971). We conclude that the Michigan Court of Appeals was correct in viewing this Court's decisions in *Hanson* and *Street* as controlling in the present case insofar as the service charges are applied to collective bargaining, contract administration, and grievance adjustment purposes.

C

Because the Michigan Court of Appeals ruled that state law "sanctions the use of nonunion members' fees for purposes other than collective bargaining," 60 Mich.App., at 99, 230 N.W.2d, at 326, and because the complaints allege that such expenditures were made, this case presents constitutional issues not decided in *Hanson* or *Street*. Indeed, *Street* embraced an interpretation of the Railway Labor Act not without its difficulties, precisely to avoid facing the constitutional issues presented by the use of union-shop dues for political and ideological purposes unrelated to collective bargaining. Since the state court's construction of the Michigan statute is authoritative, however, we must confront those issues in this case.

Our decisions establish with unmistakable clarity that the freedom of an individual to associate for the purpose of advancing beliefs and ideas is protected by the First and Fourteenth Amendments. E.g., Elrod v. Burns, 427 U.S. 347, 355–357, 96 S.Ct. 2673, 2680–82, 49 L.Ed.2d 547 (plurality opinion); Cousins v. Wigoda, 419 U.S. 477, 487, 95 S.Ct. 541, 547, 42 L.Ed.2d 595; Kusper v. Pontikes, 414 U.S. 51, 56–57, 94 S.Ct. 303, 307, 38 L.Ed.2d 260; NAACP v. Alabama ex rel. Patterson, 357 U.S. 449, 460–461, 78 S.Ct. 1163, 1170–71, 2 L.Ed.2d 1488. Equally clear is the proposition that a government may not require an individual to relinquish rights guaranteed him by the First Amendment as a condition of public employment. E.g., Elrod v. Burns, supra, 427 U.S. at 357–360, 96 S.Ct. at 2681–2683 and cases cited; Perry v. Sindermann, 408 U.S. 593, 92 S.Ct. 2694, 33 L.Ed.2d 570; Keyishian v. Board of Regents, 385 U.S. 589, 87 S.Ct. 675, 17 L.Ed.2d 629. The appellants argue that they fall within the protection of these cases because they have been prohibited not from actively associating, but rather from refusing to associate. They specifically argue that they may constitutionally prevent the Union's spending a part of their required service fees to contribute to political candidates and to express political views unrelated to its duties as exclusive bargaining representative. We have concluded that this argument is a meritorious one.

We do not hold that a union cannot constitutionally spend funds for the expression of political views, on behalf of political candidates, or towards the advancement of other ideological causes not germane to its duties as collective bargaining representative.[32] Rather, the Constitution requires only that such expenditures be financed from charges, dues, or assessments paid by employees who do not object to advancing those ideas and who are not coerced into doing so against their will by the threat of loss of governmental employment.

There will, of course, be difficult problems in drawing lines between collective bargaining activities, for which contributions may be compelled, and ideological activities unrelated to collective bargaining, for which such compulsion is prohibited.[33] The Court held in *Street,* as a matter of statutory construction, that a similar line must be drawn under the Railway Labor Act, but in the public sector the line may be somewhat hazier. The process of establishing a written collective-bargaining agreement prescribing the terms and conditions of public employment may require not merely concord at the bargaining table, but subsequent approval by other public authorities; related budgetary and appropriations decisions might be seen as an integral part of the bargaining process. We have no occasion in this case, however, to try to define such a dividing line. The case comes to us after a judgment on the pleadings, and there is no evidentiary record of any kind. The

32. To the extent that this activity involves support of political candidates, it must, of course, be conducted consistently with any applicable (and constitutional) system of election campaign regulation. See generally Buckley v. Valeo, supra; Developments in the Law—Election Law, 88 Harv.L.Rev. 1111, 1237–1271 (1975).

33. The appellants' complaints also alleged that the Union carries on various "social ac-

tivities" which are not open to nonmembers. It is unclear to what extent such activities fall outside the Union's duties as exclusive representative or involve constitutionally protected rights of association. Without greater specificity in the description of such activities and the benefit of adversary argument, we leave those questions in the first instance to the Michigan courts.

allegations in the complaint are general ones, and the parties have neither briefed nor argued the question of what specific union activities in the present context properly fall under the definition of collective bargaining. The lack of factual concreteness and adversary presentation to aid us in approaching the difficult line-drawing questions highlight the importance of avoiding unnecessary decision of constitutional questions. All that we decide is that the general allegations in the complaint, if proven, establish a cause of action under the First and Fourteenth Amendments.

III

In determining what remedy will be appropriate if the appellants prove their allegations, the objective must be to devise a way of preventing compulsory subsidization of ideological activity by employees who object thereto without restricting the union's ability to require every employee to contribute to the cost of collective-bargaining activities.[35] This task is simplified by the guidance to be had from prior decisions. In *Street*, supra, the plaintiffs had proved at trial that expenditures were being made for political purposes of various kinds, and the Court found those expenditures illegal under the Railway Labor Act. Moreover, in that case each plaintiff had "made known to the union representing his craft or class his dissent from the use of his money for political causes which he opposes." 367 U.S., at 750, 81 S.Ct., at 1790; see id., at 771, 81 S.Ct. at 1801. The Court found that "[i]n that circumstance, the respective unions were without power to use payments thereafter tendered by them for such political causes." Ibid. Since, however, *Hanson* had established that the union-shop agreement was not unlawful as such, the Court held that to enjoin its enforcement would "[sweep] too broadly." Ibid. The Court also found that an injunction prohibiting the union from expending dues for political purposes would be inappropriate, not only because of the basic policy reflected in the Norris-La Guardia Act against enjoining labor unions, but also because those union members who do wish part of their dues to be used for political purposes have a right to associate to that end "without being silenced by the dissenters." Id., at 772–773, 81 S.Ct., at 1802.

After noting that "dissent is not to be presumed" and that only employees who have affirmatively made known to the union their opposition to political uses of their funds are entitled to relief, the Court sketched two possible remedies: first, "an injunction against expenditure for political causes opposed by each complaining employee of a sum, from those moneys

---

35. It is plainly not an adequate remedy to limit the use of the actual dollars collected from dissenting employees to collective-bargaining purposes. Such a limitation "is of bookkeeping significance only rather than a matter of real substance. It must be remembered that the service fee is admittedly the exact equal of membership initiation fees and monthly dues * * * and that * * * dues collected from members may be used for a 'variety of purposes, in addition to meeting the union's costs of collective bargaining.' Unions 'rather typically' use their membership dues 'to do those things which the members authorize the union to do in their interest and on their behalf.' If the union's total budget is divided between collective bargaining and institutional expenses and if nonmember payments, equal to those of a member, go entirely for collective bargaining costs, the nonmember will pay more of these expenses than his pro rata share. The member will pay less and to that extent a portion of his fees and dues is available to pay institutional expenses. The union's budget is balanced. By paying a larger share of collective bargaining costs the nonmember subsidizes the union's institutional activities." Retail Clerks Local 1625 v. Schermerhorn, 373 U.S. 746, 753–754, 83 S.Ct. 1461, 1465, 10 L.Ed.2d 678.

to be spent by the union for political purposes, which is so much of the moneys exacted from him as is the proportion of the union's total expenditures made for such political activities to the union's total budget," and second, restitution of a fraction of union dues paid equal to the fraction of total union expenditures that were made for political purposes opposed by the employee. 367 U.S. at 774–775, 81 S.Ct., at 1802–03.

The Court again considered the remedial question in Brotherhood of Railway & Steamship Clerks v. Allen, 373 U.S. 113, 83 S.Ct. 1158, 10 L.Ed.2d 235. In that case employees who had refused to pay union-shop dues obtained injunctive relief in state court against enforcement of the union-shop agreement. The employees had not notified the Union prior to bringing the lawsuit of their opposition to political expenditures, and at trial, their testimony was principally that they opposed such expenditures, as a general matter. Id., at 118–119, n. 5, 83 S.Ct., at 1161–62. The Court held that the employees had adequately established their cause of action by manifesting "opposition to *any* political expenditures by the union," id., at 118, 83 S.Ct. at 1162 (emphasis in original), and that the requirement in *Street* that dissent be affirmatively indicated was satisfied by the allegations in the complaint that was filed, id., at 118–119, and n. 6, 83 S.Ct., at 1161–62.[39] The Court indicated again the appropriateness of the two remedies sketched in *Street;* reversed the judgment affirming issuance of the injunction; and remanded for determination of which expenditures were properly to be characterized as political and what percentage of total union expenditures they constituted.[40]

The Court in *Allen* described a "practical decree" that could properly be entered, providing for (1) the refund of a portion of the exacted funds in the proportion that union political expenditures bear to total union expenditures, and (2) the reduction of future exactions by the same proportion. Id., at 122, 83 S.Ct., at 1163. Recognizing the difficulties posed by judicial administration of such a remedy, the Court also suggested that it would be highly desirable for unions to adopt a "voluntary plan by which dissenters would be afforded an internal union remedy." Ibid. This last suggestion is particularly relevant to the case at bar, for the Union has adopted such a plan since the commencement of this litigation.[41]

---

39. *Allen* can be viewed as a relaxation of the conditions established in *Street* governing eligibility for relief. *Street* seemed to imply that an employee would be required to identify the *particular* causes which he opposed. Any such implication was clearly disapproved in *Allen*, and, as explained today, there are strong reasons for preferring the approach of *Allen*.

40. The Court in *Allen* went on to elaborate:

"[s]ince the unions possess the facts and records from which the proportion of political to total union expenditures can reasonably be calculated, basic considerations of fairness compel that they, not the individual employees, bear the burden of proving such proportion. Absolute precision in the calculation of such proportion is not, of course, to be expected or required; we are mindful of the difficult accounting problems that may arise. And no decree would be proper which appeared likely to infringe the unions' right to expend uniform exactions under the union-shop agreement in support of activities germane to collective bargaining and, as well, to expend nondissenters' such exactions in support of political activities." 373 U.S., at 122, 83 S.Ct., at 1163.

41. Under the procedure adopted by the Union, as explained in the appellees' brief, a dissenting employee may protest at the beginning of each school year the expenditure of any part of his agency-shop fee for "activities or causes of a political nature or involving controversial issues of public importance only incidentally related to wages, hours, and conditions of employment." The employee is

Although *Street* and *Allen* were concerned with statutory rather than constitutional violations, that difference surely could not justify any lesser relief in this case. Judged by the standards of those cases, the Michigan Court of Appeals' ruling that the appellants were entitled to no relief at this juncture was unduly restrictive. For all the reasons outlined in *Street,* the court was correct in denying the broad injunctive relief requested. But in holding that as a prerequisite to any relief each appellant must indicate to the Union the *specific* expenditures to which he objects, the Court of Appeals ignored the clear holding of *Allen.* As in *Allen,* the employees here indicated in their pleadings that they opposed ideological expenditures of *any* sort that are unrelated to collective bargaining. To require greater specificity would confront an individual employee with the dilemma of relinquishing either his right to withhold his support of ideological causes to which he objects or his freedom to maintain his own beliefs without public disclosure. It would also place on each employee the considerable burden of monitoring all of the numerous and shifting expenditures made by the Union that are unrelated to its duties as exclusive bargaining representative.

The Court of Appeals thus erred in holding that the plaintiffs are entitled to no relief if they can prove the allegations contained in their complaints, and in depriving them of an opportunity to establish their right to appropriate relief, such, for example, as the kind of remedies described in *Street* and *Allen.* In view of the newly adopted union internal remedy, it may be appropriate under Michigan law, even if not strictly required by any doctrine of exhaustion of remedies, to defer further judicial proceedings pending the voluntary utilization by the parties of that internal remedy as a possible means of settling the dispute.

The judgment is vacated, and the case is remanded for further proceedings not inconsistent with this opinion.

It is so ordered.

[Justice Rehnquist concurred in the opinion and judgment of the Court in a separate opinion suggesting that the result was inconsistent with Elrod v. Burns, 427 U.S. 347, 96 S.Ct. 2673, 49 L.Ed.2d 547 (1976), in which he had dissented. In Elrod the Court had held that the First and Fourteenth Amendments were violated when noncivil service employees were terminated by the newly elected sheriff of Cook County, Illinois, in accordance with a long-standing patronage policy, for the reason that they did not obtain support from his political party.

Justice Stevens joined the Court's opinion but cautioned that he—and, in his opinion, the Court—was making no judgment on the appropriateness of any remedy since the factual basis for such a judgment was not before the Court.

Justice Powell, joined by Chief Justice Burger and by Justice Blackmun, concurred in the judgment of the Court but not in its reasoning. He disagreed with the Court's conclusion that there was no First Amendment distinction between private and public employment. He disagreed also with the conclusion that the Hanson and Street cases compelled the holding that

then entitled to a pro rata refund of his service charge in accordance with the calculation of the portion of total union expenses for the specified purposes. The calculation is made in the first instance by the Union, but is subject to review by an impartial board.

an agency-shop agreement with a government employer would necessarily be constitutionally valid with regard to each expenditure "germane to collective bargaining." In his opinion governmental *imposition* of mandatory union dues through the entering into a collective bargaining agreement which then has the force of law is fundamentally different from governmental *authorization* of such agreements in the private sector as was the case in Hanson and Street. Further, because of the political nature of all public employee bargaining, all of the expenditures of required fees may intrude upon protected speech and therefore each item of expenditure, including costs "germane to collective bargaining," must be justified by "overriding state interests." In Justice Powell's view the *state* (or other public employer), not merely the union, would have to meet that burden before the payment of any dues could be required.]

Note

1. In spite of the disagreement among the justices with regard to the constitutional implications of public sector bargaining, all of them agreed that it is unconstitutional to compel public employees to contribute to union expenditures for political purposes. There is still the question, however, of where the line is to be drawn between expenditures "germane to collective bargaining" and those which are impermissible, including, most centrally, those of a political nature.

As Justice Stewart, predicted in Abood, such line drawing has not proved an easy task. In ELLIS v. BROTHERHOOD OF RAILWAY CLERKS, 466 U.S. 435, 104 S.Ct. 1883, 80 L.Ed.2d 428 (1984), the Court confronted this problem of classification, and also the problem of remedy. There, some employees, required by a union security agreement to pay fees in amounts equivalent to union members' dues, objected (1) to the *use* of their compelled dues for certain union activities: the union's quadrennial convention, certain social functions, union publications, efforts to organize employees outside the bargaining unit, and litigation not involving the negotiation of agreements or settlement of grievances; *and* (2) to the *means* adopted by the union to refund dues which would be used for political or ideological activities—a "rebate program" under which objecting employees were required to pay a sum equal to union members' dues but were reimbursed months later for any impermissibly collected dues. The challenge to items (1) and (2) was on the grounds both of the First Amendment and of statutory interpretation (Railway Labor Act); the Court chose to deal with them on the latter ground.

The Court first determined that the rebate program was inadequate:

"By exacting and using full dues, then refunding months later the portion that it was not allowed to exact in the first place, the union effectively charges the employees for activities that are outside the scope of the statutory authorization. The cost to the employee is, of course, much less than if the money was never returned, but this is a difference of degree only. The harm would be reduced were the union to pay interest on the amount refunded, but [it] did not do so. Even then the union obtains an involuntary loan for purposes to which the employee objects.

"The only justification for this union borrowing would be administrative convenience. But there are readily available alternatives, such as advance reduction of dues and/or interest-bearing escrow accounts, that place only the slightest additional burden, if any, on the union. Given the existence of acceptable alternatives, the union cannot be allowed to commit dissenters' funds to improper uses even temporarily. A rebate scheme reduces but does not eliminate the statutory violation." 466 U.S. at 444, 104 S.Ct. at 1890, 80 L.Ed.2d at 439.

In determining the propriety of union expenditures to which the employees objected, the Court held:

"* * * [T]he test must be whether the challenged expenditures are necessarily or reasonably incurred for the purpose of performing the duties of an exclusive representative of the employees in dealing with the employer on labor-management issues. Under this standard, objecting employees may be compelled to pay their fair share of not only the direct costs of negotiating and administering a collective-bargaining contract and of settling grievances and disputes, but also the expense of activities or undertakings normally or reasonably employed to implement or effectuate the duties of the union as exclusive representative of the employees in the bargaining unit." 466 U.S. at 448, 104 S.Ct. at 1892, 80 L.Ed.2d at 442.

In assessing the particular expenditures to which the employees had objected, the Court concluded that expenses for union conventions allowed the union to "maintain [the] corporate or associational existence" necessary to perform its statutory functions; that the purchasing of refreshments for social activities, which were open to all employees, members and nonmembers, was *de minimus* and "a standard feature of union operations"; and that union publications served as a "primary means of communicating information concerning collective bargaining, contract administration, and employees' rights to employees." These expenditures were found normal and appropriate to the functioning of a union in carrying out its duties as the employees' exclusive representative.

On the other hand, the Court stated: "Using dues exacted from an objecting employee to [organize] workers outside the bargaining unit can afford only the most attenuated benefits to collective bargaining on behalf of the dues payer." Similarly, the Court found insufficient the relationship between the union's function as exclusive representative and expenditures for litigation "unless the * * * bargaining unit is directly concerned" in such litigation. 466 U.S. at 448–53, 104 S.Ct. 1892–95, 80 L.Ed.2d 442–45. Thus, such organizational and litigation expenditures could not be charged to objecting employees.

2. In CHICAGO TEACHERS UNION, LOCAL NO. 1 v. HUDSON, ___ U.S. ___, 106 S.Ct. 1066, 89 L.Ed.2d 232 (1986), a public employees union had established an internal procedure, as Justice Stewart had suggested in Abood (supra p. 810) for nonmembers to dissent from the use of agency shop fees for expenditures unrelated to the union's performance of duties as bargaining representative. The nonmember was required to object in writing, and the union would then place all of the nonmember's contribution in an escrow account. The objection would be dealt with in a three-stage procedure. First, the union's executive committee would consider the protest; second, the union's executive board would review the committee's decision; and finally, an arbitrator, chosen by the union president from a list maintained by the Illinois Board of Education and paid by the union, would determine the issue.

The union had calculated that 95% of its expenditures were germane to collective bargaining. Thus, while the union dues for member teachers were $17.35 per month, the corresponding proportionate-share payment for nonmember teachers was $16.48. Plaintiffs, nonmember teachers, challenged on First

Amendment grounds the legitimacy of the 95% figure and of the procedure established by the union for the consideration of objections thereto. The District Court rejected these challenges, 573 F.Supp. 1505 (N.D.Ill.1983), but the Seventh Circuit reversed, 743 F.2d 1187 (7th Cir.1984). The Supreme Court affirmed the Seventh Circuit's decision.

The Court focused upon the union *procedure* available for challenge of its classification of expenditures, thus mooting review of the substantive standards for such classification. So focused, the Court found the procedure for challenge constitutionally deficient because (1) it did not provide nonmembers with sufficient information as to the bases for the calculation of the 95% figure nor with the assurance of an independent auditor that, accepting those bases, the 95% figure was accurately ascertained; (2) the procedure did not "provide for a reasonably prompt decision by an impartial decisionmaker." ___ U.S. at ___, 106 S.Ct. at 1076, 89 L.Ed.2d at 247. In other words, the procedure for objection by nonmembers to the amount of the "proportionate share" did not afford them the data necessary for evaluating the germaneness of union expenditures, nor did it afford procedural wherewithal for reasonably expeditious resolution of such objection. As to the latter, the Court observed that "the procedure is * * * from start to finish * * * entirely controlled by the union, which is an interested party." ___ U.S. at ___, 106 S.Ct. at 1077, 89 L.Ed.2d at 248. The Court advised, however, that the requirement of a "reasonably prompt decision by an impartial decisionmaker" might be satisfied through arbitration "so long as the arbitrator's selection did not represent the Union's unrestricted choice." Ibid.

Summarizing, the Court concluded: "We hold today that the constitutional requirements for the Union's collection of agency fees include an adequate explanation of the basis for the fee, a reasonably prompt opportunity to challenge the amount of the fee before an impartial decisionmaker, and an escrow for the amounts reasonably in dispute while such challenges are pending." ___ U.S. at ___, 106 S.Ct. at 1078, 89 L.Ed.2d at 249.

The Court further stated, in response to the Union's suggestion that its expressed willingness to place 100% of the objecting nonmember's proportionate-share payments in escrow eliminated any valid constitutional objection to the procedure and provided in itself an adequate remedy in the case: "We reject this argument. * * * [T]he Union's 100% escrow does not cure all of the problems * * *. Two of the three flaws remain [inadequate explanation of the basis for the fee and lack of a reasonable opportunity for prompt and impartial decision]." ___ U.S. at ___, 106 S.Ct. at 1077–78, 89 L.Ed.2d at 248–249. Moreover, the Court observed, a 100% escrow was, in itself, too stringent. "Such a remedy has the serious defect of depriving the Union of access to some escrowed funds that it is unquestionably entitled to retain. If, for example, the original disclosure by the Union had included a certified public accountant's verified breakdown of expenditures, including some categories that no dissenter could reasonably challenge, there would be no reason to escrow the portion of the nonmember's fees that would be represented by those categories." Ibid.

3. Public sector bargaining, the context in Abood, is further considered in Chapter 9, Section D, infra p. 1145. The Abood case itself is further treated, infra p. 799.

B. RIGHTS OF MEMBERS

1. IMPERATIVES OF UNION DEMOCRACY: A "BILL OF RIGHTS"

SALZHANDLER v. CAPUTO

United States Court of Appeals, Second Circuit, 1963.
316 F.2d 445.

Certiorari denied 375 U.S. 946 (1963).

LUMBARD, CHIEF JUDGE. This appeal raises an important question of the rights of union members under the Labor-Management Reporting and Disclosure Act of 1959 * * *: whether a union member's allegedly libelous statements regarding the handling of union funds by union officers justify disciplinary action against the member and his exclusion from any participation in the affairs of the union for five years, including speaking and voting at meetings and even attending meetings. We hold that the LMRDA protects the union member in the exercise of his right to make such charges without reprisal by the union; that any provisions of the union constitution which make such criticism, whether libelous or not, subject to union discipline are unenforceable; and that the Act allows redress for such unlawful treatment. Accordingly we reverse the judgment rendered by Judge Wham, sitting in the United States District Court for the Southern District of New York, which dismissed the union member's complaint and we remand the case for further proceedings.

Solomon Salzhandler, a member of Local 442, Brotherhood of Painters, Decorators & Paperhangers of America, brought suit in the district court following the decision of a Trial Board of the union's New York District Council No. 9 that he had untruthfully accused Isadore Webman, the president of the local, of the crime of larceny. The Trial Board found that Salzhandler's "unsupported accusations" violated the union's constitution which prohibited "conduct unbecoming a member * * *", "acts detrimental to * * * interests of the Brotherhood", "libeling, slandering * * * fellow members [or] officers of local unions" and "acts and conduct * * * inconsistent with the duties, obligations and fealty of a member." [1]

Salzhandler's complaint alleged that his charges against Webman were an exercise of his rights as a member of the union and that the action of the Trial Board was in violation of the provisions of the LMRDA under which he was entitled to relief.

The undisputed facts developed during the trial in the district court amply support Salzhandler's claims for relief.

Salzhandler was elected financial secretary of Local 442 in 1953. He was reelected thereafter and at the times in question he was serving a three-year term which was to end June 30, 1962. His weekly compensation as an officer was $35, of which $25 was salary and $10 was for expenses. The dispute giving rise to this suit was touched off in November 1960 by Salzhandler's distribution to members of Local 442 of a leaflet which accused Webman of mishandling of union funds.

---

1. Brotherhood Constitution § 267(5), (6), (10) and (16).

Prior to the audit each July, Salzhandler obtained the checks for the auditor. In going over the union's checks in July 1960 Salzhandler noticed that two checks, one for $800 and one for $375, had been drawn to cover the expenses of Webman and one Max Schneider at two union conventions to which they were elected delegates. The $800 check, drawn on August 21, 1959 to Webman's order, was endorsed by Webman and his wife. The $375 check, drawn on March 4, 1960 to "Cash," was likewise endorsed by Webman and his wife. Schneider's endorsement did not appear on either check. Schneider had died on May 31, 1960.

On July 15, 1960 two checks, each for $6, were drawn as refunds of dues paid by Max Schneider and another deceased member. Such checks were ordinarily mailed to the widows. Webman, however, brought the two checks to Salzhandler and told him to deposit them in a special fund for the benefit of the son of Max Schneider. Salzhandler refused to do this because the checks were not endorsed. Thereafter Sol Feldman and W. Shirpin, who were trustees of the local, each endorsed one of the checks and Salzhandler made the deposit as Webman had requested.[2]

In November 1960 Salzhandler distributed to members of the local a leaflet which accused Webman of improper conduct with regard to union funds and of referring to members of the union by such names as "thieves, scabs, robbers, scabby bosses, bums, pimps, f-bums, [and] jail birds." Attached to the leaflet were photostats of the four checks. With regard to the convention checks, Salzhandler wrote:

"The last convention lasted five days, Monday August 31, to Friday, September 4, 1959. The delegates of 442 presented their credentials Monday, August 31, and on Thursday, September 3, as soon as they got the mileage fare, they disappeared. They were absent at Thursday afternoon session. The most the chairman should have gotten was a weeks pay and allowance—$250.00. The auditor's report shows he got $200 in pay and $300 in expenses—$500, or twice what was coming to him, and also $300 as expenses for the Business Agent. The check was made out to *Cash* for $800 (photostat enclosed). So was the voucher. It does not indicate that Max Schneider got any of it. The same goes for a check made out *only* to I. Webman on March 4, 1960 for another convention, where the chairman was to get $250, but got $375. It does not indicate Schneider got his share. Were the checks legal?"

The leaflet also branded Webman as a "petty robber" of the two $6 checks:

"To prove himself most unworthy of any trust, he performed the cheapest petty act ever. Two widows were refunded each $6.00 for overpayment of dues. Two checks were issued to that effect. The petty robber had two of his friends sign their names and the chairman declared these two checks as contributions to the special tax for Michael Schneider—photostats of checks enclosed."

On December 13, 1960, Webman filed charges against Salzhandler with the New York District Council No. 9 of the union, alleging that Salzhandler had violated the union constitution, § 267, by libelling and slandering him in

---

2. At the trial Webman testified that he had authorization from the widows.

implying that he, Webman, had not reimbursed Max Schneider for convention expenses, and that he had been a "petty robber" in causing the two $6 checks to be deposited in the Michael Schneider fund, rather than being paid over to the two widows. The charge went on to state that Salzhandler was guilty of "acts and conduct inconsistent with the duties, obligations and fealty of a member or officer of the Brotherhood" and that the net effect of the leaflet was untruthfully to accuse an officer of the union of the crime of larceny. For over six hours on the evening of February 23, 1961, Salzhandler was tried by a five-member Trial Board of the District Council. As the union rules permitted, Salzhandler was represented by a union member who was not a lawyer. At the trial, Webman introduced the leaflet. Salzhandler produced the photostats and was questioned by the Trial Board. Webman's witnesses testified that the convention expenditures were approved by the membership. Salzhandler produced three witnesses who testified that Webman had called members names as alleged in the leaflet.

Not until April 2, 1961 did Salzhandler receive notice of the Trial Board's decision and his removal from office and this was from a printed postal card mailed to all members:

"By a decision of the Trial Committee of District Council 9, Sol Saltzhandler [sic] is no longer Financial Secretary of Local Union 442."

Thereafter, on April 4, the District Council mailed to Salzhandler only the final paragraph of its five page "Decision" which read as follows:

"It is our decision that Brother Solomon Salzhandler be prohibited from participating in the affairs of L.U. 442, or of any other Local Union of the Brotherhood, or of District Council 9, for a period of five (5) years. He shall not be permitted during that period to attend meetings of L.U. 442, to vote on any matter, to have the floor at any meeting of any other Local Union affiliated with the District Council, or to be a candidate for any position in any local Union or in the District Council. In all other respects Brother Salzhandler's rights and obligations as a member of the Brotherhood shall be continued."

Salzhandler did not receive a copy of the full opinion of the Trial Board until after this action was commenced on June 14, 1961. Meanwhile, as the union constitution required appeal within 30 days, Salzhandler filed intraunion appeals with the Secretary-Treasurer of the Council and the General Secretary-Treasurer of the Brotherhood on April 12 and 28. At the time this action was brought, plaintiff had received no word regarding said appeals.[4]

On May 15, 1961, Salzhandler attempted to attend a meeting of the local but was prevented from doing so by Webman. The complaint alleges that Webman assaulted Salzhandler and used violence in removing him.

This action was commenced in the federal court under the Labor-Management Reporting and Disclosure Act of 1959, § 102, * * * requesting a nullification of the order of the Trial Board, reinstatement in the position as financial secretary, and damages.

Judge Wham dismissed the complaint holding that the Trial Board's conclusion that the leaflet was libelous was sufficiently supported by the

4. The parties are agreed that Salzhandler exhausted his intraunion remedies. We do not pass upon the question of whether, in a case such as this, the plaintiff must first exhaust his intraunion remedies.

evidence. He went further, however, and made an independent finding that the statements were, in fact, libelous. The court held, as a matter of law, that "The rights accorded members of labor unions under Title I of the Labor-Management Reporting and Disclosure Act of 1959 * * * do not include the right of a union member to libel or slander officers of the union." We do not agree.

The LMRDA of 1959 was designed to protect the rights of union members to discuss freely and criticize the management of their unions and the conduct of their officers. The legislative history and the extensive hearings which preceded the enactment of the statute abundantly evidence the intention of the Congress to prevent union officials from using their disciplinary powers to silence criticism and punish those who dare to question and complain. The statute is clear and explicit. Under a sub-chapter heading of "Bill of Rights of Members of Labor Organizations," §§ 101(a)(1) and (2) * * * provide:

"(1) Equal rights.—Every member of a labor organization shall have equal rights and privileges within such organization to nominate candidates, to vote in elections or referendums of the labor organization, to attend membership meetings, and to participate in the deliberations and voting upon the business of such meetings, subject to reasonable rules and regulations in such organization's constitution and bylaws.

"(2) Freedom of speech and assembly.—Every member of any labor organization shall have the right to meet and assemble freely with other members; and to express any views, arguments, or opinions; and to express at meetings of the labor organization his views, upon candidates in an election of the labor organization or upon any business properly before the meeting, subject to the organization's established and reasonable rules pertaining to the conduct of meetings: Provided, That nothing herein shall be construed to impair the right of a labor organization to adopt and enforce reasonable rules as to the responsibility of every member toward the organization as an institution and to his refraining from conduct that would interfere with its performance of its legal or contractual obligations."

Section 102 * * * safeguards the rights just enumerated by providing:

"Any person whose rights secured by the provisions of this title have been infringed by any violation of this title may bring a civil action in a district court of the United States for such relief (including injunctions) as may be appropriate. Any such action against a labor organization shall be brought in the district court of the United States for the district where the alleged violation occurred, or where the principal office of such labor organization is located."

Section 609 * * * makes doubly secure the protection of the members in the exercise of their rights by providing:

"It shall be unlawful for any labor organization, or any officer, agent, shop steward, or other representative of a labor organization, or any employee thereof to fine, suspend, expel, or otherwise discipline any of its members for exercising any right to which he is entitled under the provisions of this Act. The provisions of section 102 shall be applicable in the enforcement of this section."

Appellees argue that just as constitutionally protected speech does not include libelous utterances, Beauharnais v. Illinois, 343 U.S. 250, 266, 72 S.Ct. 725, 96 L.Ed. 919 (1952), the speech protected by the statute likewise does not include libel and slander. The analogy to the First Amendment is not convincing. In Beauharnais, the Supreme Court recognized the possibility that state action might stifle criticism under the guise of punishing libel. However, because it felt that abuses could be prevented by the exercise of judicial authority, * * * the court sustained a state criminal libel statute. But the union is not a political unit to whose disinterested tribunals an alleged defamer can look for an impartial review of his "crime." [6] It is an economic action group, the success of which depends in large measure on a unity of purpose and sense of solidarity among its members.

The Trial Board in the instant case consisted of union officials, not judges. It was a group to which the delicate problems of truth or falsehood, privilege, and "fair comment" were not familiar. Its procedure is peculiarly unsuited for drawing the fine line between criticism and defamation, yet, were we to adopt the view of the appellees, each charge of libel would be given a trial de novo in the federal court—an impractical result not likely contemplated by Congress, see 105 Cong.Rec. 6026 (daily ed. April 25, 1959) (colloquy between Senator Goldwater and Senator Clark)—and such a Trial Board would be the final arbiter of the extent of the union member's protection under § 101(a)(2).[7]

In a proviso to § 101(a)(2), there are two express exceptions to the broad rule of free expression. One relates to "the responsibility of every member toward the organization as an institution." The other deals with interference with the union's legal and contractual obligations.

While the inclusion of only two exceptions, without more, does not mean that others were intentionally excluded, we believe that the legislative history supports the conclusion that Congress intended only those exceptions which were expressed.

The expression of views by Salzhandler did not come within either exception in the proviso to § 101(a)(2). The leaflet did not interfere in any way with the union's legal or contractual obligations and the union has never claimed that it did. Nor could Salzhandler's charges against Webman be construed as a violation of the "responsibility of every member toward the organization as an institution." Quite the contrary; it would seem clearly in the interest of proper and honest management of union affairs to permit members to question the manner in which the union's officials handle the union's funds and how they treat the union's members. It is that interest which motivated the enactment of the statute and which would be immea-

---

6. Union discipline for libel has been characterized as a form of criminal sanction, Summers, The Law of Union Discipline. What Courts Do In Fact, 70 Yale L.J. 175, 178 (1960).

7. See Summers, American Legislation for Union Democracy, 25 Mod.L.Rev. 273, 287:

"The most difficult problem arises when a member is expelled for 'slandering a union officer.' Union debates are characterized by vitriol and calumny, and campaigns for of-fice are salted with overstated accusations. Defining the scope of fair comment in political contests is never easy, and in this context is nearly impossible. To allow the union to decide this issue in the first instance is to invite retaliation and repression and to frustrate one of the principal reasons for protecting this right—to enable members to oust corrupt leadership through the democratic process."

surably frustrated were we to interpret it so as to compel each dissatisfied and questioning member to draw, at the peril of union discipline, the thin and tenuous line between what is libelous and what is not. This is especially so when we consider that the Act was designed largely to curtail such vices as the mismanagement of union funds, criticism of which by union members is always likely to be viewed by union officials as defamatory.

The union argues that there is a public interest in promoting the monolithic character of unions in their dealings with employers. But the Congress weighed this factor and decided that the desirability of protecting the democratic process within the unions outweighs any possible weakening of unions in their dealings with employers which may result from the freer expression of opinions within the unions.

The democratic and free expression of opinion in any group necessarily develops disagreements and divergent opinions. Freedom of expression would be stifled if those in power could claim that any charges against them were libelous and then proceed to discipline those responsible on a finding that the charges were false. That is precisely what Webman and the Trial Board did here when they punished Salzhandler with a five-year ban of silence and stripped him of his office.

So far as union discipline is concerned Salzhandler had a right to speak his mind and spread his opinions regarding the union's officers, regardless of whether his statements were true or false. It was wholly immaterial to Salzhandler's cause of action under the LMRDA whether he spoke truthfully or not, and accordingly Judge Wham's views on whether Salzhandler's statements were true are beside the point. Here Salzhandler's charges against Webman related to the handling of union funds; they concerned the way the union was managed. The Congress has decided that it is in the public interest that unions be democratically governed and toward that end that discussion should be free and untrammeled and that reprisals within the union for the expression of views should be prohibited. It follows that although libelous statements may be made the basis of civil suit between those concerned, the union may not subject a member to any disciplinary action on a finding by its governing board that such statements are libelous. The district court erred in dismissing the complaint.

Accordingly, we reverse the judgment of the district court and direct entry of judgment for the plaintiff which, among other things, should assess damages and enjoin the defendants from carrying out any punishment imposed by the District Council Trial Board.

Note

Does the Salzhandler decision go too far in the pursuit of internal union democracy? Does it make sense that Webman can sue Salzhandler in a civil action for libel, but that he cannot press disciplinary charges within the union?

FINNEGAN v. LEU

Supreme Court of the United States, 1982.
456 U.S. 431, 102 S.Ct. 1867, 72 L.Ed.2d 239.

CHIEF JUSTICE BURGER.

The question presented in this case is whether the discharge of a union's appointed business agents by the union president, following his election over the candidate supported by the business agents, violated the Labor Management Reporting and Disclosure Act of 1959 * * *. The Court of Appeals, 652 F.2d 58 (6th Cir.) held that the Act did not protect the business agents from discharge. We granted certiorari to resolve circuit conflicts, * * * and we affirm.

I

In December 1977, respondent Harold Leu defeated Omar Brown in an election for the presidency of Local 20 of the International Brotherhood of Teamsters, Chauffeurs, Warehousemen and Helpers of America, a labor organization representing workers in a 14 county area of northwestern Ohio.[2] During the vigorously contested campaign, petitioners, then business agents of Local 20, openly supported the incumbent President, Brown. Upon assuming office in January 1978, Leu discharged petitioners and the Local's other business agents, all of whom had been appointed by Brown following his election in 1975.[3] Leu explained that he felt the agents were loyal to Brown, not to him, and therefore would be unable to follow and implement his policies and programs.

Local 20's Bylaws—which were adopted by, and may be amended by, a vote of the union membership—provide that the President shall have authority to appoint, direct, and discharge the Union's business agents. Bylaws of Teamsters, Chauffers, Warehousemen and Helpers Union Local No. 20, Art. IX, § 3 D, Joint Exhibit 1, at 15. The duties of the business agents include participation in the negotiating of collective bargaining agreements, organizing of union members, and processing of grievances. In addition, the business agents, along with the President, other elected officers, and shop stewards, sit as members of the Stewards Council, the legislative assembly of the Union. Petitioners had come up through the union ranks, and as business agents they were also members of Local 20. Discharge from their positions as business agents did not render petitioners ineligible to continue their union membership.

2. Brown challenged the election results and, following an investigation, the Secretary of Labor determined that unlawful employer contributions had affected the outcome of the election. The Secretary filed suit in the United States District Court for the Northern District of Ohio, and that court ordered a rerun election under the Secretary's supervision; the Court of Appeals for the Sixth Circuit affirmed. Marshall v. Local 20, Teamsters, 611 F.2d 645 (CA6 1979). In the second election, Leu again defeated Brown.

Brown and Leu had previously opposed each other in the 1974 election for the presidency. Although Leu defeated Brown by a slight margin, the election was set aside by the International Union because of irregularities at the polling places. Brown won the second election, which was held in 1975 under the supervision of a panel from the International Union.

3. When Brown was elected President in 1975, see n. 2, supra, the incumbent business agents resigned.

Petitioners filed suit in the United States District Court, alleging that they had been terminated from their appointed positions in violation of the Labor Management Reporting and Disclosure Act, 29 U.S.C. §§ 411(a)(1), 411(a)(2), 412, and 529. The District Court granted summary judgment for respondents Leu and Local 20, holding that the Act does not protect a union employee from discharge by the president of the union if the employee's rights as a union member are not affected. 469 F.Supp. 832. The United States Court of Appeals for the Sixth Circuit affirmed, concluding "that a union president should be able to work with those who will cooperate with his program and carry out his directives, and that these business agents, who served at the pleasure of the union president, and actively supported the president's opponent could be removed from their employment as union business agents." App. to Pet. for Cert. A3.

II

The Labor Management Reporting and Disclosure Act of 1959 was the product of congressional concern with widespread abuses of power by union leadership. The relevant provisions of the Act had a history tracing back more than two decades in the evolution of the statutes relating to labor unions. Tensions between union leaders and the rank and file members and allegations of union wrongdoing led to extended congressional inquiry. As originally introduced, the legislation focused on disclosure requirements and the regulation of union trusteeships and elections. However, various amendments were adopted, all aimed at enlarged protection for members of unions paralleling certain rights guaranteed by the Federal Constitution; not surprisingly, these amendments—ultimately enacted as Title I of the Act, * * * were introduced under the title of "Bill of Rights of Members of Labor Organizations."[4] The amendments placed emphasis on the rights of union members to freedom of expression without fear of sanctions by the union, which in many instances could mean loss of union membership and in turn loss of livelihood. Such protection was necessary to further the Act's primary objective of ensuring that unions would be democratically governed and responsive to the will of their memberships. * * *

Sections 101(a)(1) and (2) of the Act, * * * on which petitioners rely, guarantee equal voting rights, and rights of speech and assembly, to "[e]very *member* of a labor organization" (emphasis added). In addition, § 609 of the Act, * * * renders it unlawful for a union or its representatives "to fine, suspend, expel, or otherwise discipline any of its *members* for exercising any right to which he is entitled under the provisions of [the Act]." (Emphasis added). It is readily apparent, both from the language of these provisions and from the legislative history of Title I, that it was rank and file union members—not union officers or employees, as such—whom Congress sought to protect.[7]

---

4. The original "Bill of Rights" amendment was introduced on the floor of the Senate by Sen. McClellan and adopted by a vote of 47–46. 105 Cong.Rec. 5804–5827 (1959), II Legislative History of the Labor Management Reporting and Disclosure Act of 1959, 1096–1119 (1959) (hereafter Leg.Hist.). However, a compromise version of the amendment introduced by Sen. Kuchel was substituted shortly

thereafter, id., at 6020–6030, II Leg.Hist. 1229–1239, and later approved by the House of Representatives as part of the Landrum-Griffin Bill, H.R. 8400, 86th Cong., 1st Sess. (1959), I Leg.Hist. 628–633. * * *.

7. The provisions of Title I consistently refer to the rights of union "members." As originally passed by the Senate, § 101(a)(4)—

Petitioners held a dual status as both employees and members of the Union. As *members* of Local 20, petitioners undoubtedly had a protected right to campaign for Brown and support his candidacy. At issue here is whether they were thereby immunized from discharge at the pleasure of the President from their positions as appointed union *employees.*

III

Petitioners contend that discharge from a position as a union employee constitutes "discipline" within the meaning of § 609; and that termination of union employment is therefore unlawful when predicated upon an employee's exercise of rights guaranteed to members under the Act. However, we conclude that the term "discipline," as used in § 609, refers only to retaliatory actions that affect a union member's rights or status *as a member* of the union. Section 609 speaks in terms of disciplining "members"; and the three disciplinary sanctions specifically enumerated—fine, suspension, and expulsion—are all punitive actions taken against union members as members.[8] In contrast, discharge from union employment does not impinge upon the incidents of union membership, and affects union members only to the extent that they happen also to be union employees. See Sheridan v. Carpenters Local No. 626, 306 F.2d 152, 156 (CA3 1962). We discern nothing in § 609, or its legislative history, to support petitioners' claim that Congress intended to establish a system of job security or tenure for appointed union employees.

Congress used essentially the same language elsewhere in the Act with the specific intent not to protect a members' status as a union employee or officer. Section 101(a)(5) * * * states that "[n]o member of any labor organization may be fined, suspended, expelled, or otherwise disciplined" without enumerated procedural protections. The Conference Report accompanying S. 1555 as finally enacted, H.R.Rep. 1147, 86th Cong., 1st Sess. 31 (1959), I Leg.Hist. 935, explains that this "prohibition on suspension without observing certain safeguards applies only to suspension of membership in the union; *it does not refer to suspension of a member's status as an officer of the union*" (emphasis added). This too is a persuasive indication that the virtually identical language in § 609 was likewise meant to refer only to punitive actions diminishing membership rights, and not to termination of a member's status as an appointed union employee.[9]

which in its present form protects the right of "any member" to institute legal proceedings against the union * * *—applied to "any member *or officer*" of a labor organization (emphasis added). S. 1555, 86th Cong., 1st Sess. § 101(a)(4) (1959), I Leg.Hist. 520. However, the words "or officer" were deleted from the Landrum-Griffin Bill, H.R. 8400, 86th Cong., 1st Sess. § 101(a)(4) (1959), I Leg.Hist. 630–631, and the House version was retained in Conference, see H.R.Rep. 1147, 86th Cong., 1st Sess. 31 (1959), I Leg.Hist. 935. See also Sheridan v. Carpenters Local No. 626, 306 F.2d 152, 156–157 (CA3 1962).

8. Compare § 201(a)(5)(H) of the Act, * * * which requires reporting on the procedures for "discipline *or removal* of officers or

agents for breaches of their trust" (emphasis added).

9. In Grand Lodge of the International Ass'n of Machinists v. King, 355 F.2d 340, 344 (CA9), cert. denied, 379 U.S. 920, 85 S.Ct. 274, 13 L.Ed.2d 334 (1964), the court held that Congress had used the "identical words * * * with quite different meanings" in the two sections. The court found that the "legislative gloss" on the words "otherwise disciplined" in § 101(a)(5) stemmed primarily from congressional concern that "wrongdoing union officials"—and particularly those guilty of misappropriating union funds—might be permitted "to remain in control while the time-consuming 'due process' requirements of the section were met." Id., at 341–342. See 105

We hold, therefore, that removal from appointive union employment is [as with § 101(a)(5)] not within the scope of those union sanctions explicitly prohibited by § 609.

IV

* * * Section 102 states that

"[a]ny person whose rights secured by the provisions of this subchapter [Title I of the Act] have been infringed by any violation of this subchapter may bring a civil action in a district court of the United States for such relief (including injunctions) as may be appropriate."

* * *

We need not decide whether the retaliatory discharge of a union member from union office—even though not "discipline" prohibited under § 609 [and § 101(a)(5)]—might ever give rise to a cause of action under § 102. For whatever limits Title I places on a union's authority to utilize dismissal from union office as "part of a purposeful and deliberate attempt to suppress dissent within the union," cf. Schonfeld v. Penza, 477 F.2d 899, 904 (CA2 1973), it does not restrict the freedom of an elected union leader to choose a staff whose views are compatible with his own.[11] Indeed, neither, the language nor the legislative history of the Act suggests that it was intended even to address the issue of union patronage.[12] To the contrary, the Act's overriding objective was to ensure that unions would be democratically governed, and responsive to the will of the union membership as expressed in open, periodic elections. See Wirtz v. Hotel Employees, Local 6, 391 U.S. 492, 497, 88 S.Ct. 1743, 1746, 20 L.Ed.2d 763 (1968). Far from being inconsistent with this purpose, the ability of an elected union president to select his own administrators is an integral part of ensuring a union administration's responsiveness to the mandate of the union election.

Here, the presidential election was a vigorous exercise of the democratic processes Congress sought to protect. Petitioners—appointed by the defeated candidate—campaigned openly against respondent Leu, who was elected by a substantial margin. The Union's Bylaws, adopted, and subject to amendment, by a vote of the union membership, grant the President plenary

Cong.Rec. 17899 (1959) (remarks of Sen. Kennedy). However, viewing this concern as inapplicable with regard to § 609, the court concluded that "although Congress did not intend the words 'otherwise discipline' to include removal from union office in section 101(a)(5), it did intend the words to include such action in section 609." Id., at 343. See also Maciera v. Pagan, 649 F.2d 8, 14 (CA1 1981); Wood v. Dennis, 489 F.2d 849, 853–854 (CA7 1973) (en banc).

We agree that the purposes of the two sections are different, and that the distinction drawn in *King* is one Congress plausibly could have chosen to make. However, we are hard pressed to discern any such distinction from either the language or legislative history of the Act. Certainly one would expect that if Congress had intended identical language to have substantially different meanings in different sections of the same enactment it would

have manifested its intention in some concrete fashion. See Wood v. Dennis, supra, at 858 (Stevens, J., concurring).

11. We leave open the question whether a different result might obtain in a case involving nonpolicymaking and nonconfidential employees.

12. We think it virtually inconceivable that Congress would have prohibited the longstanding practice of union patronage without any discussion in the legislative history of the Act. See Wood v. Dennis, 480 F.2d 849, 858 (CA7 1973) (en banc) (Stevens, J., concurring). Had such a result been contemplated, it undoubtedly would have encountered substantial resistance. Moreover, Congress likely would have made some express accommodation to the needs of union employers to appoint and remove policymaking officials. See id.

authority to appoint, suspend, discharge, and direct the Union's business agents, who have significant responsibility for the day-to-day conduct of union affairs. Nothing in the Act evinces a congressional intent to alter the traditional pattern which would permit a union president under these circumstances to appoint agents of his choice to carry out his policies.

No doubt this poses a dilemma for some union employees; if they refuse to campaign for the incumbent they risk his displeasure, and by supporting him risk the displeasure of his successor. However, in enacting Title I of the Act, Congress simply was not concerned with perpetuating appointed union employees in office at the expense of an elected president's freedom to choose his own staff. Rather, its concerns were with promoting union democracy, and protecting the rights of union *members* from arbitrary action by the union or its officers.

We therefore conclude that petitioners have failed to establish a violation of the Act. Accordingly, the decision of the Court of Appeals is affirmed.

JUSTICE BLACKMUN, with whom JUSTICE BRENNAN joins, concurring.

I am not prepared to hold that a newly-elected president of a local union may discipline, without violating the Labor Management Reporting and Disclosure Act of 1959, * * * and as a matter of retaliation, *all* union member-employees who opposed his candidacy. As the Court notes, a union member possesses, under the Act, rights to freedom of expression and of speech and assembly, * * * and a right to support the candidate of his choice.

I must assume that what the Court holds today is that the newly-elected president may discharge the union's appointed business agents and other appointed union member-employees who will be instrumental in evolving the president's administrative policies. See Elrod v. Burns, 427 U.S. 347, 96 S.Ct. 2673, 49 L.Ed.2d 547 (1976); Branti v. Finkel, 445 U.S. 507, 100 S.Ct. 1287, 63 L.Ed.2d 574 (1980). Indeed, the Court uses the terms "staff," ante, * * * and "his own administrators," ante * * *. In addition, this particular union's bylaws expressly give the president plenary authority over the business agents. With that much, I have no difficulty.

On the understanding, but only on the understanding, that the Court by its opinion is not reaching out further to decide the same issue with respect to nonpolicy-making employees, that is, rank-and-file member-employees (a matter which, for me, presents another case for another day), I join the Court's opinion.

Note

1. Is the Finnegan v. Leu decision consistent with the pursuit of internal union democracy? If so, how far down the ladder of union staff positions should the power of "political" removal reach?

2. In United Steelworkers v. Sadlowski, 457 U.S. 102, 102 S.Ct. 2339, 72 L.Ed.2d 707 (1982), the Court held, 5 to 4, that a union constitutional provision which prohibited candidates for union office from soliciting or accepting financial support from non-members, most especially employers, did not violate Section 101(a)(2) of the LMRDA. The Court concluded that the rule was

sheltered by the proviso to Section 101(a)(2), since it served the legitimate purpose of preventing non-members from unduly influencing union affairs.

Justice White, joined by the Chief Justice and Justices Brennan and Blackmun, thought that the rule was too absolute and unbending to be deemed a reasonable restriction on the freedoms of speech and assembly guaranteed by Section 101(a)(2). The dissenters believed that the rule made the task of unseating incumbent union officers unduly onerous, given the typical one-party system in most national unions and the control accordingly wielded by the incumbents.

<h3 style="text-align:center">INTERNATIONAL BROTHERHOOD OF
BOILERMAKERS v. HARDEMAN</h3>

Supreme Court of the United States, 1971.
401 U.S. 233, 91 S.Ct. 609, 28 L.Ed.2d 10.

MR. JUSTICE BRENNAN delivered the opinion of the Court.

Section 102 of the Labor-Management Reporting and Disclosure Act (hereafter LMRDA) provides that a union member who charges that his union violated his rights under Title I of the Act may bring a civil action against the union in a district court of the United States for appropriate relief. Respondent was expelled from membership in petitioner union and brought this action under § 102 in the District Court for the Southern District of Alabama. He alleged that in expelling him the petitioner violated § 101(a)(5) of the Act * * *. A jury awarded respondent damages of $152,150. The Court of Appeals for the Fifth Circuit affirmed. 420 F.2d 485 (1969).[2] We granted certiorari limited to the questions whether the subject matter of the suit was preempted because exclusively within the competence of the National Labor Relations Board and, if not preempted, whether the courts below had applied the proper standard of review to the union proceedings * * *. We reverse.

The case arises out of events in the early part of October 1960. Respondent, George Hardeman, is a boilermaker. He was then a member of petitioner's Local Lodge 112. On October 3, he went to the union hiring hall to see Herman Wise, business manager of the Local Lodge and the official responsible for referring workmen for jobs. Hardeman had talked to a friend of his, an employer who had promised to ask for him by name for a job in the vicinity. He sought assurance from Wise that he would be referred for the job. When Wise refused to make a definite commitment, Hardeman threatened violence if no work was forthcoming in the next few days.

On October 4, Hardeman returned to the hiring hall and waited for a referral. None was forthcoming. The next day, in his words, he "went to the hall * * * and waited from the time the hall opened until we had the trouble. I tried to make up my mind what to do, whether to sue the local or Wise or beat hell out of Wise, and then I made up my mind." When Wise came out of his office to go to a local jobsite, as required by his duties as business manager, Hardeman handed him a copy of a telegram asking for

2. The affirmance was on the basis of International Brotherhood of Boilermakers v. Braswell, 388 F.2d 193 (C.A.5 1968).

Hardeman by name. As Wise was reading the telegram, Hardeman began punching him in the face.

Hardeman was tried for this conduct on charges of creating dissension and working against the interest and harmony of the Local Lodge,[3] and of threatening and using force to restrain an officer of the Local Lodge from properly discharging the duties of his office.[4] The trial committee found him "guilty as charged," and the Local Lodge sustained the finding and voted his expulsion for an indefinite period. Internal union review of this action, instituted by Hardeman, modified neither the verdict nor the penalty. Five years later, Hardeman brought this suit alleging that petitioner violated § 101(a)(5) by denying him a full and fair hearing in the union disciplinary proceedings.

I

We consider first the union's claim that the subject matter of this lawsuit is, in the first instance, within the exclusive competence of the National Labor Relations Board. The union argues that the gravamen of Hardeman's complaint—which did not seek reinstatement, but only damages for wrongful expulsion, consisting of loss of income, loss of pension and insurance rights, mental anguish and punitive damages—is discrimination against him in job referrals; that any such conduct on the part of the union is at the very least arguably an unfair labor practice under §§ 8(b)(1)(A) and 8(b)(2) of the National Labor Relations Act * * *; and that in such circumstances, "the federal courts must defer to the exclusive competence of the National Labor Relations Board if the danger of * * * interference with national policy is to be averted." San Diego Building Trades Council, Millmen's Union, Local 2020 v. Garmon, 359 U.S. 236, 245, 79 S.Ct. 773, 780, 3 L.Ed.2d 775 (1959); see Local 100 of United Ass'n of Journeymen and Apprentices v. Borden, 373 U.S. 690, 83 S.Ct. 1423, 10 L.Ed.2d 638 (1963).

We think the union's argument is misdirected. Hardeman's complaint alleged that his expulsion was unlawful under § 101(a)(5), and sought compensation for the consequences of the claimed wrongful expulsion. The critical issue presented by Hardeman's complaint was whether the union disciplinary proceedings had denied him a full and fair hearing within the meaning of § 101(a)(5)(C).[5] Unless he could establish this claim, Hardeman

---

3. Article 13, § 1, of the Subordinate Lodge Constitution then in force provided:

"Any member who endeavors to create dissension among the members; or who works against the interest and harmony of the International Brotherhood or of any District or Subordinate Lodge; who advocates or encourages a division of the funds, or the dissolution of any District or Subordinate Lodge, or the separation of any District or Subordinate Lodge from the International Brotherhood; who supports or becomes a member of any dual or subversive organization which shall be hostile to the International Brotherhood or to any of its Subordinate Lodges, or which is antagonistic to the principles and purposes of the International Brotherhood, shall, upon conviction thereof be punished by expulsion from the International Brotherhood."

4. Article 12, § 1, of the Subordinate Lodge By-Laws then in force provided that "It shall be a violation of these By-Laws for any member through the use of force or violence or the threat of the use of force or violence to restrain, coerce, or intimidate, or attempt to restrain, coerce, or intimidate any official of this International Brotherhood or Subordinate Lodge to prevent or attempt to prevent him from properly discharging the duties of his office." Violators of Article 12 are to "be punished as warranted by the offense."

5. Hardeman's complaint did not claim that the charges were insufficiently specific, or that he did not have adequate time to prepare his defense in the union proceedings.

would be out of court. We hold that this claim was not within the exclusive competence of the National Labor Relations Board. * * * Those factors suggesting that resort must be had to the administrative process are absent from the present case. The fairness of an internal union disciplinary proceeding is hardly a question beyond "the conventional experience of judges," nor can it be said to raise issues "within the special competence" of the NLRB. See N.L.R.B. v. Allis-Chalmers Mfg. Co., 388 U.S. 175, 181, 193–194, 87 S.Ct. 2001, 2007, 2013–2014, 18 L.Ed.2d 1123 (1967). As we noted in that case, the Eighty-Sixth Congress which enacted § 101(a)(5) was "plainly of the view" that the protections embodied therein were new material in the body of federal labor law. 388 U.S. at 194, 87 S.Ct. at 2014. And that same Congress explicitly referred claims under § 101(a)(5) not to the NLRB, but to the federal district courts. * * *

The union argues that Hardeman's suit should nevertheless have been dismissed because he did not seek an injunction restoring him to membership, and because he did seek damages for loss of employment said to be the consequence of his expulsion from the union. Taken together, these factors are said to shift the primary focus of the action from a review of Hardeman's expulsion to a review of alleged union discrimination against him in job referrals. Since this is a matter normally within the exclusive competence of the NLRB, see Local 100 of United Ass'n of Journeymen and Apprentices v. Borden, 373 U.S., at 695–696, 83 S.Ct., at 1426–1427, the union argues that Hardeman's suit was beyond the competence of the district court.

The argument has no merit. To begin with, the language of § 102 does not appear to make the availability of damages turn upon whether an injunction is requested as well. If anything, § 102 contemplates that damages will be the usual, and injunctions the extraordinary form of relief. Requiring that injunctive relief be sought as a precondition to damages would have little effect other than to force plaintiffs, as a matter of course, to add a few words to their complaints seeking an undesired injunction. We see no reason to import into § 102 so trivial a requirement.

Nor are our prior cases authority for such a result. We have repeatedly held, of course, that state law may not regulate conduct either protected or prohibited by the National Labor Relations Act. * * * Where it has not been clear whether particular conduct is protected, prohibited, or left to state regulation by that Act, we have likewise required courts to stay their hand * * *.

The present case, however, implicates none of the principles discussed above. There is no attempt, in this lawsuit, to apply state law to matters preempted by federal authority. * * * Nor is there an attempt to have the district court enforce the provisions of the National Labor Relations Act itself, without guidance from the NLRB. As we have said, the critical question in this action is whether Hardeman was afforded the rights guaranteed him by § 101(a)(5) of the LMRDA. If he was denied them, Congress has said that he is entitled to damages for the consequences of that denial. Since these questions are irrelevant to the legality of conduct under the National Labor Relations Act, there is no danger of conflicting interpretation of its provisions. And since the law applied is federal law explicitly made applicable to such circumstances by Congress, there is no danger that state law may come in through the back door to regulate conduct that has been removed by Congress from state control. Accordingly, this action was within the competence of the district court.

II

Two charges were brought against Hardeman in the union disciplinary proceedings. He was charged with violation of Article 13, § 1, of the Subordinate Lodge Constitution, which forbids attempting to create dissension or working against the interest and harmony of the union, and carries a penalty of expulsion. He was also charged with violation of Article 12, § 1, of the Subordinate Lodge By-Laws, which forbids the threat or use of force against any officer of the union in order to prevent him from properly discharging the duties of his office; violation may be punished "as warranted by the offense." Hardeman's conviction on both charges was upheld in internal union procedures for review.

The trial judge instructed the jury that "whether or not he [respondent] was rightfully or wrongfully discharged or expelled is a pure question of law for me to determine." He assumed, but did not decide, that the transcript of the union desciplinary hearing contained evidence adequate to support conviction of violating Article 12. He held, however, that there was no evidence at all in the transcript of the union disciplinary proceedings to support the charge of violating Article 13. This holding appears to have been based on the Fifth Circuit's decision in International Brotherhood of Boilermakers v. Braswell, 388 F.2d 193 (CA5 1968). There the Court of Appeals for the Fifth Circuit had reasoned that "penal provisions in union constitutions must be strictly construed," and that as so construed Article 13 was directed only to "threats to the union as an organization and to the effective carrying out of the union's aims," not to merely personal altercations. 388 F.2d at 199. Since the union tribunals had returned only a general verdict, and since one of the charges was thought to be supported by no evidence whatsoever, the trial judge held that Hardeman had been deprived of the full and fair hearing guaranteed by § 101(a)(5). The Court of Appeals affirmed, simply citing *Braswell.* 420 F.2d 485 (CA5 1970).

We find nothing in either the language or the legislative history of § 101(a)(5) that could justify such a substitution of judicial for union authority to interpret the union's regulations in order to determine the scope of offenses warranting discipline of union members. Section 101(a)(5) began life as a floor amendment to S. 1555, the Kennedy-Ervin Bill, in the Eighty-Sixth Congress. As proposed by Senator McClellan, and as adopted by the Senate on April 22, 1959, the amendment would have forbidden discipline of union members "except for breach of a published written rule of [the union]." 105 Cong.Rec. 6476, 6492–6493 (1959). But this language did not long survive. Two days later, a substitute amendment was offered by Senator Kuchel, who explained that further study of the McClellan amendment had raised "some rather vexing questions." Id., at 6720. The Kuchel substitute, adopted the following day, deleted the requirement that charges be based upon a previously published, written union rule; it transformed Senator McClellan's amendment, in relevant part, into the present language of § 101(a)(5). Id., at 6720, 6727. As so amended, S. 1555 passed the Senate on April 25. Id., at 6745. Identical language was adopted by the House, id., at 15884, 15891, and appears in the statute as finally enacted.

The Congress understood that Senator Kuchel's amendment was intended to make substantive changes in Senator McClellan's proposal. Senator Kennedy had specifically objected to the McClellan amendment because

"In the case of ＊ ＊ ＊ the ＊ ＊ ＊ official who bribed a judge, unless there were a specific prohibition against bribery of judicial officers written into the constitution of the union, then no union could take disciplinary action against [an] officer or member guilty of bribery. ＊ ＊ ＊

"It seems to me that we can trust union officers to run their affairs better than that." Id., at 6491.

Senator Kuchel described his substitute as merely providing "the usual reasonable constitutional basis" for union disciplinary proceedings: union members were to have "constitutionally reasonable notice and a reasonable hearing." Id., at 6720. After the Kuchel amendment passed the Senate, Senator Goldwater explained it to the House Committee on Labor and Education as follows:

"[T]he bill of rights in the Senate bill require[s] that the union member be served with written charges prior to any disciplinary proceedings but it does not require that these charges, to be valid, must be based on activity that the union had proscribed prior to the union member having engaged in such activity." Labor-Management Reform Legislation, Hearings before a Joint Subcommittee of the House Committee on Education and Labor, 86th Cong., 1st Sess. pt. 4, p. 1595 (1959).

And Senator McClellan's testimony was to the same effect. ＊ ＊ ＊

We think that this is sufficient to indicate that § 101(a)(5) was not intended to authorize courts to determine the scope of offenses for which a union may discipline its members.[11] And if a union may discipline its members for offenses not proscribed by written rules at all, it is surely a futile exercise for a court to construe the written rules in order to determine whether particular conduct falls within or without their scope.

Of course, § 101(a)(5)(A) requires that a member subject to discipline be "served with written specific charges." These charges must be, in Senator McClellan's words, "specific enough to inform the accused member of the offense that he has allegedly committed." Where, as here, the union's charges make reference to specific written provisions, § 101(a)(5)(A) obviously empowers the federal courts to examine those provisions and determine whether the union member had been misled or otherwise prejudiced in the presentation of his defense. But it gives courts no warrant to scrutinize the union regulations in order to determine whether particular conduct may be punished at all.

Respondent does not suggest, and we cannot discern, any possibility of prejudice in the present case. Although the notice of charges with which he

---

11. State law, in many circumstances, may go further [i.e., give state courts authority to determine for what offenses a union can punish]. See Summers, The Law of Union Discipline: What the Courts Do in Fact, 70 Yale L.J. 175 (1960). But Congress, which pre-served state law remedies by § 103 of the LMRDA, ＊ ＊ ＊ was well aware that even the broad language of Senator McClellan's original proposal was more limited in scope than much state law. See 105 Cong.Rec. 6481–6489 (1959).

was served does not appear as such in the record, the transcript of the union hearing indicates that the notice did not confine itself to a mere statement or citation of the written regulations that Hardeman was said to have violated: the notice appears to have contained a detailed statement of the facts relating to the fight which formed the basis for the disciplinary action, Section 101(a)(5) requires no more.

III

There remains only the question whether the evidence in the union disciplinary proceeding was sufficient to support the finding of guilt. Section 101(a)(5)(C) of the LMRDA guarantees union members a "full and fair" disciplinary hearing, and the parties and the lower federal courts are in full agreement that this guarantee requires the charging party to provide some evidence at the disciplinary hearing to support the charges made. This is the proper standard of judicial review. We have repeatedly held that conviction on charges unsupported by any evidence is a denial of due process, * * * and we feel that § 101(a)(5)(C) may fairly be said to import a similar requirement into union disciplinary proceedings. Senator Kuchel, who first introduced the provision, characterized it on the Senate floor as requiring the "usual reasonable constitutional basis" for disciplinary action, * * * and any lesser standard would make useless § 101(a)(5)(A)'s requirement of written, specific charges. A stricter standard, on the other hand, would be inconsistent with the apparent congressional intent to allow unions to govern their own affairs, and would require courts to judge the credibility of witnesses on the basis of what would be at best a cold record.[15]

Applying this standard to the present case, we think there is no question that the charges were adequately supported. Respondent was charged with having attacked Wise without warning, and with continuing to beat him for some time. Wise so testified at the disciplinary hearing, and his testimony was fully corroborated by one other witness to the altercation. Even Hardeman, although he claimed he was thereafter held and beaten, admitted having struck the first blow. On such a record there is no question but that the charges were supported by "some evidence."

Reversed.

Mr. Justice White, concurring. * * *

* * * As the Court says, Hardeman's conviction on both charges against him was upheld. Expulsion was warranted on either count. The principle of Stromberg v. California, 283 U.S. 359, 51 S.Ct. 532, 75 L.Ed. 1117 (1931) [discussed infra, dissenting opinion], has no application in this situation. * * *

Mr. Justice Douglas, dissenting.

Section 102 of the Landrum-Griffin Act * * * gives a member of a union the right of civil redress in a federal district court against his union for infringement of his rights secured by the Act at the same time § 103 * * * reserves to members any remedies they may have "under any State or Federal law or before any court or other tribunal, or under the constitution and bylaws" of their unions. Moreover, § 101(a)(5) * * * provides

---

15. Although a transcript was made of the union proceedings in the present case, we have no reason to believe that this is a universal practice.

except for nonpayment of dues, no member of a labor organization may be expelled or disciplined until there has been notice and a fair hearing.

The latter right is not exclusive for as noted the Act gives members remedies for infringement of rights under the Act or under the constitution and bylaws of the union.

In the present case respondent went to one Wise, in charge of referral of men to jobs through the union hiring hall, and during the discussion which followed there was an altercation in which respondent hit Wise. For that assault respondent was fined in a criminal court. Thereupon Wise filed charges against respondent for violations of one provision of the union's bylaws and one provision of the union's constitution.

At a hearing before a committee of the local lodge which Hardeman attended it was determined that respondent was "guilty as charged." That determination was approved by the membership of the local which voted *to suspend him from membership "indefinitely."*

Respondent appealed to the International Union, petitioner here. Acting through its president and its international executive council it denied the appeal.

Thereafter respondent sued International for consequential and punitive damages. The case was tried by a jury which returned a verdict of $152,150 and the Court of Appeals affirmed. * * *

There was evidence that there was a grudge between Wise and respondent, out of which the fist fight occurred. And there was evidence that the force or violence was an attempt to coerce Wise "to prevent him from properly discharging the duties of his office" within a rational meaning of the bylaws of the union. And the District Court so charged the jury. But, as the District Court ruled, there was no evidence that respondent endeavored "to create dissension among the members" or to work against the "interests and harmony" of the union within the meaning of Article XIII of the Constitution.

I agree that a court does not sit in review of a union as it does of an administrative agency. But by reason of § 101(a)(5) judicial oversight is much more than procedural; it provides in subsection (C) for "a full and fair hearing." Even if every conceivable procedural guarantee is provided, a hearing is not "fair" when all substantive rights are stripped away to reach a pre-ordained result. If there is to be a "fair hearing" there must, I submit, be some evidence directed to the charges to support the conclusion.

Membership in a union may be the key to livelihood itself.[7] Without membership, the member may be cast into the outer darkness, so far as employment is concerned. Just as this Court concluded Congress did not authorize exclusive bargaining agents to make invidious discriminations, Steele v. Louisville & Nashville R.Co., 323 U.S. 192, 65 S.Ct. 226, 89 L.Ed. 173, it is unthinkable to me that Congress in designing § 101(a)(5) gave unions the authority to expel members for such reasons as they chose. For courts to lend their hand to such oppressive practices is to put the judicial

---

7. Hardeman testified at trial that following the loss of his union card he was unable to   work in the boilermaker's trade beyond one job lasting five days.

imprimatur behind the union's utter disregard of due process to reach its own ends.

In International Brotherhood of Boilermakers v. Braswell, arising out of the same incident, the Court of Appeals followed that reasoning. 388 F.2d 193, 198–199. It said:

> " * * * the act charged to Braswell was a blow struck in anger, and nothing more. However reprehensible this act may be, it did not constitute a violation of the provisions in the charges. Article XIII, Section 1 of the constitution on its face is directed at threats to the union as an organization and to the effective carrying out of the union's aims. Braswell's fist was not such a threat."

As stated by a student in this area " * * * how can there be a 'full and fair hearing' when it results in a verdict which mocks the evidence?"[8] Of course the reviewing court does not give a hearing *de novo;* nor does it review the merits of the dispute. But it does sit to check intemperate use of union powers; and if it is to discharge its duties, it must conclude that there is some evidence to sustain the charge. * * *

Violation of the Article XIII of the constitution carries with it automatic expulsion. Violation of the bylaws would carry punishment "as warranted by the offense," which, I assume would justify expulsion. For respondent to use force against Wise who was in charge of referral of men to jobs through the union hiring hall may well have been an attempt "to prevent him from properly discharging the duties of his office" within the meaning of Article XII. But how an isolated fist fight could "create dissension" among union members or work against the union's interests in the other ways described in Article XIII remains a mystery.

The finding of the union was the general one "guilty as charged." Under which provision—constitution or bylaw—it suspended him indefinitely is not made clear. Perhaps it was under only one or perhaps under both provisions.

In that posture the case is in the category of Stromberg v. California, 283 U.S. 359, 51 S.Ct. 532, 75 L.Ed. 1117, where a conviction might have been valid under one charge but would have been invalid under the other; but the verdict being a general one, it was impossible to tell under which he was convicted. It is as much a denial of due process to sustain a conviction merely because a verdict of guilty *might* have been rendered on a valid ground as it is to send an accused to prison following conviction of a charge on which he was never tried. * * *

Note

1. Does the following *pre*-Landrum-Griffin case illustrate Justice Brennan's observation in footnote 11 of his opinion that state law might afford a greater latitude to courts in determining the substantive offenses for which a union member may be disciplined by his union than does federal law? In MADDEN v. ATKINS, 4 N.Y.2d 283, 174 N.Y.S.2d 633, 151 N.E.2d 73 (1958), union members were expelled for having committed the offense of "dual unionism" under

---

8. Christensen, Union Discipline Under
Federal Law, 43 N.Y.U.L.Rev. 227, 251.

circumstances where the expelled members claimed only to have been promoting a two-party system within the union. Their activities consisted of (1) the issuance of "smear sheets" during an election campaign in which they attacked incumbent officers and (2) the organization of an opposition group within the union to challenge existing policies and to promote rival candidates. The New York Court of Appeals ordered the reinstatement of the members with compensatory damages, stating:

> "If there be any public policy touching the government of labor unions, and there can be no doubt that there is, it is that traditionally democratic means of improving their union may be freely availed of by members without fear of harm or penalty. And this necessarily includes the right to criticize current union leadership and, within the union, to oppose such leadership and its policies. * * * The price of free expression and of political opposition within a union cannot be the risk of expulsion or other disciplinary action." 4 N.Y.2d at 293, 174 N.Y.S.2d at 640, 151 N.E.2d at 78.

Under Hardeman, would a federal court be authorized to second-guess union tribunals concerning what constitutes "dual unionism"? Would the Landrum-Griffin Act preclude a state court from *refusing* relief in a case such as Madden? On these questions, see Sections 101(b), 103, 603(a), and 609.

> "Congress has expressly withheld preemption of any rights or remedies which a union member may have under state law. * * *. The rights and remedies provided by the federal statute are additional to other rights of union members under state law." Posner v. Utility Workers Union, 47 Cal. App.3d 970, 974, 121 Cal.Rptr. 423, 425 (1975).

In view of the foregoing provisions of the LMRDA, is the Hardeman interpretation of Section 101(a)(5) of much significance?

2. In the absence of legislation bestowing jurisdiction, what is the common-law basis for state judicial intervention in a case like Madden? "To justify intervention, courts have adopted two established legal principles as rationales for relief. First, they have said that membership in a labor union is a property right and must be protected against any unlawful interference. Second, they have reasoned that membership in a union creates a contract. Any improper discipline is a breach of that contract for which the law will give relief." Summers, Legal Limitations on Union Discipline, 64 Harv.L.Rev. 1049, 1051 (1951).

The "property right" basis for judicial intervention found its most obvious application in cases where a union member would lose a substantial interest in some valuable property, such as fraternal insurance benefits, if his expulsion from the union were not reviewed and set aside. The doctrine "grew out of the old maxim that equity will not act except to protect property rights." Id. at 1052, n. 10. What constitutes a "property right" was given an expanding definition by some state courts, particularly in situations where justice strongly called for intervention, evolving to the point where, as stated in the quotation in the preceding paragraph, membership itself was deemed a property right.

The contract theory for judicial intervention proceeds on the premise that "a member, by joining the union, enters into a contract, the terms of which are expressed in the union constitution and bylaws. The member consents to suspension or expulsion according to the provisions of that contract, and if he is disciplined in violation of the constitution, the court will order him reinstated."

Id. at 1054. It may readily be seen that the contract approach affords the reviewing court all of the doctrinal tools of standard contract law for dealing with internal union disputes—e.g., interpretation of ambiguity, nonenforcement of illegal provisions (because "against public policy"). It is worth noting that the Landrum-Griffin Act, in one way of viewing it, simply builds on the common-law contract theory, making two basic alterations: (1) certain types of "contractual" (i.e., constitutional) provisions are statutorily incorporated in the union constitution (e.g., Section 101(b)); (2) the "contract" is expressly made enforceable as a matter of *federal* law (e.g., Section 102).

UNITED AUTO WORKERS, A MORE PERFECT UNION * * * THE UAW PUBLIC REVIEW BOARD
3–6 (1957).

On April 8, 1957, the 16th constitutional convention of the United Automobile, Aircraft and Agricultural Implement Workers of America—the UAW—took the unprecedented step of establishing a public review board of independent distinguished citizens to which members could appeal their grievances against the union * * *.

* * * The first public mention of the plan came in March 1957, in Reuther's report to the forthcoming UAW convention.

On behalf of the UAW executive board he proposed two changes in the union's trial machinery. The first was selection of local union trial boards by lot, rather than by election, to prevent the administration of justice from becoming a local political issue. The second was the public review board as an alternative—at the member's choice—to the established procedure of an appeal to the convention as the final step in a dispute between an individual or a subordinate body and the international union. * * *

In the course of the discussion [at the convention] Reuther stressed that the public review board was not merely window-dressing to counteract current anti-union propaganda.

"This is not the creation of a public board of apology," he said. "These people are going to be an essential part of our constitution and they will have broad powers and responsibilities.

"You ought to recognize that this is the real thing. There are no ifs, ands, buts or loopholes."

And in concluding the debate he added: "I think * * * you ought to recognize that this gets into an area that we are either going to have to deal with voluntarily or the government will deal with it for us."

Under the constitutional amendment adopted by the UAW convention, the public review board has broad powers * * *.

It is given the "authority and duty to make final and binding decisions" in all cases placed before it by aggrieved members or subordinate bodies of the UAW. Essentially these cases will involve individual members who feel they have been unfairly disciplined by their local unions and who have failed to obtain satisfaction upon appeal to the UAW executive board. Also included will be local unions which feel they have been unfairly disciplined by the international. * * *

* * * A member who has been disciplined by a trial committee of his own local must first appeal to a general membership meeting of the local union * * *. If still dissatisfied, he must within 30 days appeal to the international executive board, with a brief written summary of the case. Should he fail to get satisfaction from the international executive board, he may, if he chooses, take his appeal to the UAW convention, as before; but he may elect, instead, to go to the public review board. He can't go to both.

The constitution clearly denies to the public review board any jurisdiction over official collective bargaining policies of the UAW. In the same manner, it sharply limits the board's functions in cases involving grievances arising from the union contract.

Where the latter are involved, the public review board has jurisdiction only over charges, previously made to the international executive board, that the grievance was improperly handled because of fraud, discrimination or collusion with management. In other words, the public review board is in no way a super-substitute for local grievance machinery on contract matters.

However, complaints involving the processing of grievances are the only ones which might come before both the public review board and the convention. If the board decides it does not have jurisdiction, the appellant can take his complaint to the convention. But in doing so, he cannot raise any issue which the board threw out in dismissing the case.

The same safeguards are provided for proceedings before the public review board as for the previous trial procedure. To insure promptness, appeals must be filed within 30 days except when the UAW president extends the time in the interests of justice. A hearing is guaranteed on all charges, except when a complaint is "manifestly groundless or frivolous." All parties have the right to counsel. To discourage groundless charges, the public review board is empowered to impose a fine up to $500 and suspension from membership for three months or more upon an accuser who "acted in bad faith or with malicious intent and in a willful effort to divide and disrupt the union."

* * * The board is directed to make an annual report summarizing all appeals heard during the year, drawing attention to any activity it has found to be improper and commenting upon the steps taken by the union to correct it. This report must be published in full in the official publication of the UAW and released to the public press.

Members of the public review board are appointed by the president of the UAW, subject to the approval of the executive board and the convention. Their terms run to the following convention. Careful provision is made to insure the independence of the review board, even though its costs are paid by the UAW.

No one under the jurisdiction of the UAW or in any way employed by the union or its subordinate bodies is eligible for appointment. The board is instructed to make its own rules, hire its own staff and set up its own office, physically apart from any UAW office. The UAW executive board must provide for an annual operating budget for the public review board, including "reasonable compensation" for its members; the money is deposited quarterly to the review board's account, and the review board must arrange for an annual audit of its books for submission to the UAW secretary-treasurer and the convention.[b]

LOCAL 257, UAW v. ROBERT KELLOG

UAW Public Review Board, 1965.
PRB Case No. 109.

Panel Sitting: Adler, Chairman; Crane, Hanrahan, and McKelvey, Members. * * *

Appellants here challenge their convictions, affirmed on review by the International Executive Board, on charges preferred by the president of their Local Union pursuant to Article 30 of the International Constitution. The charge against each was that he " * * * did violate and conduct himself in such a manner that it was detrimental to the best interests of this Union and its members * * * (by having) crossed the picket lines of this Local while on strike and proceeded to operate the plant of our striking members." At issue is the adequacy of the Local trial procedures and the jurisdiction of the Local to try appellants for the acts allegedly committed. Representatives of appellants, the International Union and Local 257 were heard in oral argument before the Board in Detroit on December 7, 1964.

I

As of May, 1962, each of appellants was an hourly-rated supervisor in the employ of the Doehler-Jarvis Company at its plant in Grand Rapids, Michigan. Bargaining unit employees at the plant are represented by UAW Local 257. Hourly-rated supervisors constitute the first line of supervision and the positions are filled by promotion from the bargaining unit. Pursuant to the Collective Agreement, hourly-rated supervisors retain seniority in the bargaining unit and hold honorable withdrawal transfer cards from the Local during their tenure as supervisor.

In May, June and July of 1962, Local 257 struck the Grand Rapids facility as a part of a nationwide strike arising out of a dispute over the terms to be included in a new master Agreement. Prior to the commencement of the strike, representatives of the Union and the Company reached certain understandings concerning the procedures which would be followed during the course of the strike. One of these was that hourly-rated supervision would be permitted to cross the picket lines and enter the various Doehler-Jarvis plants throughout the course of the strike. Whether any agreement was also reached concerning what would be the nature of their activities, is disputed.

After the strike had been in progress for some weeks, hourly-rated supervisors at the Grand Rapids plant were instructed by their superiors to perform certain sample and close-out production work which would normally have been done by members of the bargaining unit. The work was performed as instructed.

b. The reader who seeks a fuller understanding of the unique and interesting UAW Public Review Board may find it in Oberer, Voluntary Impartial Review of Labor: Some Reflections, 58 Mich.L.Rev. 55 (1959); Brooks, Impartial Public Review of Internal Union Disputes: Experiment in Democratic Self-Discipline, 22 Ohio St.L.J. 64 (1961); Klein, UAW Public Review Board Report, 18 Rutgers L.Rev. 304 (1964); Stieber, Oberer & Harrington, Democracy and Public Review (1960).

Following the conclusion of the strike the Company found it necessary to reduce its first line supervisory staff at its Grand Rapids plant. As a result, some of the hourly-rated supervisors who crossed the picket lines and performed bargaining unit work during the course of the 1962 strike were returned to the bargaining unit. Each as he returned was charged with having committed acts detrimental to the interests of the Union by reason of his having crossed the picket lines and performed production work during the 1962 strike while holding an honorable withdrawal transfer card. That portion of the charge which pertained to the crossing of the picket line was, in every case, ultimately dropped. The trials in question occurred at various times following the conclusion of the strike. However, by stipulation of the parties the facts as developed in one of these proceedings occurring on November 7, 1963, are to apply to all appeals here pending before the Board.

II

Appellants have advanced five reasons why their convictions must be set aside: First, the Local Trial Committee was prejudiced, for one of its members stated for the record that he knew before the trial commenced the accused had committed the acts with which they were charged. Second, the verdict was contrary to the evidence in that the Local failed to offer any probative evidence to establish the charges. Third, the action of the Local taken against them was discriminatory by reason of the fact that hourly-rated supervisors at other Doehler-Jarvis plants were not similarly charged although they did the same work. Fourth, the action of the Union was contrary to a pre-strike understanding between Doehler-Jarvis and the UAW wherein it was agreed that hourly-rated supervisors would be permitted to cross the picket line and to perform limited sample and close-out production work. Finally, they maintain the Local has no jurisdiction to charge them with acts committed in a supervisory capacity.

The Union, for its part, argues that the evidence conclusively establishes that appellants operated the Plant as charged; that this conduct was clearly detrimental to the interests of the Union since it interfered with the economic pressure which the Union was at that time trying to apply to the Company; and that the Constitution expressly holds a member responsible for the acts which he commits while holding a withdrawal transfer card. The Public Review Board, it asserts, must under these circumstances affirm the convictions of appellants.

III

We are fully satisfied the Union is correct in its premise that the act of performing production work during the course of a strike is detrimental to the collective interest of its members and we so hold. The strike is simply a pressure device designed to coerce a recalcitrant employer to accepting the Union's point of view with respect to a given controversy by withholding the means of production from the employer. The success or failure of the strike as an instrument of coercion often depends in large measure upon the effectiveness of the withdrawal of the labor force in the prevention of production. If the employer, despite the absence of his normal labor force, is nevertheless able to maintain some production sufficient to satisfy at least in a minimal way his contractual obligations, he will thereby partially counter the effect of the strike and consequently diminish its effectiveness. It is clear to us therefore that appellants by assisting in the production of certain sample work and close-out runs, and thereby helping to save some of the employer's contracts, did hinder the Union in its attempt to cause the employer to yield. The critical issue, however, is not whether the Union was correct in its evaluation of the effect of appellants' acts, but whether it may properly discipline for them. We think that it may.

The relationship between member and Union is a contractual one. By joining the Union, the employee in effect contracts with the organization for it to become his exclusive collective bargaining representative. In return he agrees to become bound by the rules of the organization. Among the rules pertaining to membership in the UAW is that which is set forth in Article 17, Section 10:

> "A person who has deposited his honorable withdrawal transfer card and thus resumed membership in the Union shall thereupon be subject to charges and trial for acts or conduct detrimental to the interests of the Union or its members, committed while he was out of the Union on honorable withdrawal transfer card. The provisions of Article 30 shall be applicable in such cases."

Members of the UAW therefore must be assumed to know they are held accountable to the Union for acts or conduct detrimental to the interests of the Union committed while the member holds an honorable withdrawal transfer card from the Union.

But, appellants argue, regardless of any obligation owed the Union by virtue of the holding of an honorable withdrawal transfer card, they are not answerable to the Union for acts committed in the course of the discharge of their supervisory responsibilities. The responsibility of the supervisor, they say, is wholly to management; the Union may not intervene in this relationship. Yet, they argue, to give the Union the right to impose a penalty upon a member by reason of an act pursuant to supervisory responsibility in effect confers upon it the right to exert a measure of control over the affairs of management quite beyond the rights conferred upon it by the collective bargaining agreement. A supervisor cannot serve two masters, they declare, particularly when the interests of each will often be in direct conflict. Inevitably, in their view the situation will arise where a choice will have to be made—and there is no real choice: Should he refuse to act as directed by his superior the supervisor naturally is subject to discipline, including discharge; if discharged the Union could provide him no protection. It is entirely unreasonable, they say, for the Union to expect to exact control over those to whom it can offer no protection.

Appellants' argument, it seems to us, suffers from two intrinsic weaknesses: First, they appear to hold that upon assuming supervisory positions their relationship with the Union was completely severed. This, however, was not in fact the case. Hourly-rated supervisors under the terms of the Agreement continued to retain and accumulate seniority within the bargaining unit. First line supervisors, then, were recipients of benefits under the Agreement and as a consequence had a continuing interest in the continued well-being of the collective bargaining representative. Second, appellants assume that the fines imposed upon them by their Union were an attempt by the Union to control their activities as supervisors. We believe this view to be incorrect. The Union did not attempt to determine whether appellants properly discharged their duties as supervisors, for its inquiry was strictly limited to the question of whether appellants' activity was detrimental to the interests of the Union. Nor did it, once having made the determination that appellants' acts were harmful, attempt to affect appellants' relationship with their employer. No action was taken until after each returned to the bargaining unit and then the matter was handled as a strictly internal affair. The fines imposed thus were no more than the penalty which the Union deemed appropriate to levy upon those who had damaged the collective interest of the bargaining unit by undermining its efforts to secure a more favorable Agreement.

None of the other defenses raised by appellants impresses us as having merit. There is no evidence whatsoever to establish that there was an agreement between International Union and Doehler-Jarvis that permitted limited types of bargaining unit work which might be done during the strike. Neither does their claim that the trial committee was prejudiced against them appear to be found in fact. That the members of the trial committee may have known that appellants performed bargaining unit work would not of itself demonstrate prejudice. Knowledge may result in the prejudging of the question of guilt or innocence but appellants did not pursue this area of inquiry. On the issue of uniformity of union procedure, we need only observe that we know of no rule which requires autonomous locals to act with uniformity with respect to policy determinations of this sort.

Our dissenting colleague would overturn appellants' convictions because the charging parties failed to present probative evidence to establish the charges. We respectfully disagree. His conclusion is based on a premise which requires close examination; namely, that the same rigorous procedure which prevails in a court of law should obtain here—and hence the prosecution bears the exclusive responsibility for proving by acceptable means the charges on which the defendants are being tried. It is clearly evident that a lay tribunal cannot be held to the formal procedure which is followed in a court. The judges are not professionally trained in the law and the atmosphere in which such a tribunal meets is more in the nature of a meeting at which certain matters are considered than an official court operating in accordance with concepts and forms that have become crystallized and rooted in the life of a society as a result of centuries of struggle and development. The fact that work in the plant was actually done by the appellants was indeed established, though not by the legal methods honored in a court of law. Moreover, appellants, as the record shows, readily admitted and indeed defended the work they did.

The case must thus be seen in its context. Appellants of their own choice accepted promotion to supervisory posts, and thus passed from the jurisdiction of the Union into management, while retaining seniority rights in the Union. A strike was begun in May, 1962. Prior to the strike, the Union agreed that appellants as supervisory personnel would be permitted to cross picket lines during the strike. What is under dispute is the kind of activity they would be prohibited from performing while in the plant at the time of the strike.

These supervisors, though technically outside the Union, yet maintained a substantial relationship with it. Upon demotion they would resume their membership in the bargaining unit without suffering any loss in seniority. The choice they made in accepting the supervisory position, while conferring upon them the preferment in wages and prestige they evidently sought, likewise exposed them to a number of contingencies, which as responsible men they should have taken into account. The major one of these was the possibility of a strike by the bargaining unit and thus the possibility, if not likelihood, that during the strike management might call upon them for activity that would be detrimental to the Union. A strike in the labor-management field is analogous to a war in international affairs. Comfort and aid to one side is disloyalty to the other. The appellants by crossing the picket line entered what was, from the Union's point of view, a beleaguered city, an enemy post. While within the "enemy's" lines, were they doing aught that made the strike a less effectual instrument for bringing management to terms, than it otherwise might have been? A strike is not only an economic weapon; it is also a human situation. People are out of work. Anxiety and apprehension increase as the days pass. Workers' families are daily asking their provider when will they resume work, since some of the children need new clothing or the house requires repairs. Beyond the picket lines and within the plant were these supervisors, formerly their colleagues in the Union and at the plant. Is it not fair to expect in the light of such a tense situation, and since their present position was theirs by choice, that appellants on returning to full membership in the Union would present some evidence purporting to show that they did not render the kind of help to management which would prolong the strike and work to the detriment of their striking brethren?

To be sure, evidence should always be clearly and properly presented when charges are made. The procedures are of supreme significance and freedom weakens and dissolves in the absence of procedures that safeguard the rights of the accused. But appellants in the instant case did not come in without traces of suspicion generated by their own decision to accept supervisory status. There can be no reasonable doubt that they did work in the plant, though the fact was not arrived by the formal and painstaking procedure which is traditional in a court of law.

The entire arrangement whereby supervisory personnel retain seniority rights has its motivation, it appears, in the desire to broaden the opportunities for promotion from the Union's ranks. It is part of the Union's effort to advance the welfare of its members. Such an opportunity, however, should not become a means for hurting the Union's cause.

The decision of the International Executive Board is affirmed.

Concurring opinion by MEMBER McKELVY:

In subscribing to the above opinion I should like to emphasize that I do so only because of the state of the record in this particular case. Had the appellants rested after making their motion for a directed verdict of acquittal, I would have agreed with our dissenting colleague that the charges against the appellants had not been proved and that consequently their convictions should be set aside. But since they proceeded to present their witnesses "in the interest of getting the entire facts before this tribunal"

(Attorney Vana's statement in closing argument, Transcript of Local Trial, p. 168), I conclude that appellants in effect waived their procedural defense. I do not interpret our decision in this case as constituting any endorsement of the proposition that Local trial committees can base convictions upon assertions without adducing any proof whatsoever. It is only because I find that appellants here admitted the commission of the acts with which they were charged that I concur in the opinion.

Dissenting opinion of MEMBER HANRAHAN:

I think these convictions and the penalties imposed pursuant thereto should be set aside. While I do not necessarily disagree with our colleagues in their conclusion that the Union may properly discipline its member for acts which are committed in a supervisory capacity, I would not reach this issue for I am firmly of the opinion that the evidence presented by the charging party was insufficient to sustain a conviction.

In the course of his presentation, President Peterson, spokesman for the charging parties, did no more than reiterate the charges against the appellants. He stated that they crossed the picket line and that they produced castings. While he said he saw them cross picket lines, he admitted he did not see them operate the plant. He produced no witnesses who saw them "produce castings" nor did he apparently make any effort to do so. In short, he was content to allow common knowledge of the acts, shared by all members of the Local, establish the operative facts. At the conclusion of the presentation of Local President Peterson, counsel for appellants requested that the trial committee direct that the charges be dropped for failure to introduce any probative evidence in support of the charges. This the trial committee refused to do.

It was only following the refusal of the trial committee to direct a verdict in favor of appellants, that their counsel went ahead with the presentation of the defense on behalf of the accused. Through the testimony offered by defense witnesses it was conclusively established that all of the defendants had in fact "operated" the plant as charged. Nevertheless, neither the fact that appellants' acts were a matter of common knowledge nor the fact that testimony offered on behalf of the accused conclusively established the acts beyond all doubt alters in any way the fact that the charging party failed to produce any evidence whatsoever in support of its charges.

Since appellants timely raised the issue of the adequacy of the proof presented, we must consider the record as though it contained nothing more than President Peterson's bald, unsupported assertions that the accused had done what they were charged with doing. Viewed in this respect, the case against appellants was not established and I would so hold.

Now I recognize the difficulties with which the charging party was faced in proving these particular claims. The acts took place inside the plant when all the members of the bargaining unit were outside the plant conducting a strike. The only witnesses who could testify against the accused were either their fellow defendants or members of higher supervision. A fellow-accused might be unwilling to appear against his co-defendants for fear of implicating himself, and members of higher supervision might just be unwilling to testify in a Union proceeding. There was, of course, no way for the Union to compel either group of witnesses to testify.

Against the difficulties created by the problems of proof, however, we must balance the rights of the accused. Early in its existence the Public Review Board held that every Union member accused of wrongdoing is entitled to a full and fair trial conducted in accordance with the Union's trial procedure. This we said is "to protect to the fullest the rights of an individual member against error that might more easily occur in a less formal type of hearing * * *." Appeal of Local 469 (In re Agatha Praniewicz), PRB Case No. 13.

While the Constitution of the UAW sets forth no explicit requirements concerning the trial proceeding itself, the International Union has prepared and distributed to its Locals a booklet entitled "Guide to Local Union Trials" which sets forth suggested procedures for all stages of a trial proceeding. Concerning trial procedure the Guide provides that following the opening statements:

> "The accusing member shall then present evidence supporting his charge. Insofar as possible, such evidence should be limited to testimony of witnesses or presentation of authenticated documents. Witnesses should take an oath swearing to tell the truth. After each of the accusing member's witnesses has testified, the accused member may cross-examine. If a member of the Trial Committee feels that additional questions should be asked, he may ask them directly of a witness.

> "The Trial Committee is not bound by the rules of evidence prevailing in courts of law but may receive any evidence—oral or documentary—that the members of the Committee would consider if they were making a decision involving an extremely important personal affair. Hearsay evidence is not excluded (hearsay evidence is given when a witness testifies about what another person has told him rather than what he did, or saw himself). Trial Committee members, of course, may consider such evidence as less weighty than direct evidence, inasmuch as the person being quoted is not present to be cross-examined."

It is plain from this that while the Guide contemplates a somewhat less rigid procedure for the presentation of evidence than would be followed in a court of law, it is to be remembered the term "trial" is used in the Constitution. Unless that word is to be deleted and replaced by the more informal term "inquiry," then such proceedings should be conducted in substantial conformity with the usual adversary type procedure the term "trial" connotes, including the basic requirement for consideration of the "evidence" produced.

This is the area in which the Local 257 proceedings involving these appellants was plainly deficient. No evidence whatsoever was produced by the accuser! Even no attempt to secure witnesses was made. Had President Peterson reported to the trial committee that he had requested members of supervision to testify then he could have made an offer of proof as to what they would have related had they appeared. Or he could perhaps have found some members who knew through conversations with others that appellants had done that with which they were accused. While "evidence" of this nature would not be admissible in a court of law, under the more liberal rules which attend a local proceeding this might have been sufficient. However, having heard no evidence the trial committee was obligated to return a verdict for the accused. By failing to do so it committed reversible error.

I do not mean to imply that I would saddle the Union trial procedures in their present form with all the procedural safeguards that attend a criminal proceeding in a court of law. I stress, however, that in order to protect the substance of justice, the forms through which justice is obtained are of material importance. In that respect the "Guide to Local Trials" should be of assistance to a trial committee.

I would reverse the decision of the International Executive Board and set aside appellants' convictions.

Note

1. The transcript of the trial on November 7, 1963, before the Local Trial Committee in PRB Case No. 109 reveals the following: Peterson, the president of Local 257, was both the "prosecutor" and the sole witness for the "prosecution." The charges against the defendants were that they had acted detrimentally to the union by crossing the picket line and operating the plant. The charge of crossing the picket line was dropped by the union in the course of the proceedings, pursuant to a pre-strike agreement between the company and union permitting supervisors to enter the plant. The crucial question of fact was therefore whether the defendants had "operated the plant"—i.e., done production work ordinarily performed by those on strike. Peterson testified, under cross-examination by Vana, the attorney for the defendants, that he had not seen any of the defendants doing the production work. Moreover, he did not even testify that he had been told by anyone that the defendants had done production work.

With the case in this posture, the prosecution "rested." Vana thereupon moved that the charges against the defendants be dropped. He contended: "It is the burden of the charging party to prove that these four men did in fact * * * operate the plant. There is no testimony under oath or otherwise that they did operate the machines. * * *

"I am not trying to be technical. Please don't think that, gentlemen and madame. I am trying to say to you this: If you all believe in justice, as I am sure you do, there's not any testimony offered to you upon which you can find these four men guilty, none at all." Transcript, Trial Committee Proceedings, p. 13.

The chairman of the Local Trial Committee apparently did not understand what Vana was asking him to do; he refused to rule on the motion that the charges be dropped and requested Vana to present the testimony of the defendants' witnesses. In response, Vana stated: "All right. I want it understood * * * that the presentation of witnesses and testimony of the four gentlemen charged does not in any way prejudice their rights or waive their rights on the motion just made. We are presenting this testimony only because the Trial Committee has seen fit not to rule on our motion at this time." Transcript, p. 14.

The testimony of the defendants was to the effect that they had to obey the orders of management or be fired, that the union could not protect them if they were fired since they were not employees within the bargaining unit, and that the production work they did was helpful to the union rather than harmful because it made unnecessary the hiring of permanent replacements for the strikers by the company and prevented the loss of accounts, and therefore the loss of jobs for the strikers, once the strike had ended.

The examination of the defendants, and their cross-examination by Peterson, made clear that they had in fact done the production work as charged.

In his closing argument to the Trial Committee, Vana spoke of the burden of proof as being upon the prosecution. A member of the Committee interrupted him to state that there was no need of proof that the defendants had committed the offense charged since "we knew they did it." Vana asked: "Before we put in any testimony you as members of the Trial Committee knew they did it?" Answer: "Yes." Vana: "You state so on the record?" Answer: "Yes." Vana: "You knew before testimony was presented?" Answer: "Yes." Transcript, pp. 88–89.

2. Were the union tribunals properly found to have jurisdiction to discipline the defendants for actions "detrimental to the union" committed while the defendants were part of management, on "honorable withdrawal" from the union? Under Hardeman, would this question be open for review in a federal court?

3. A variation of the "honorable withdrawal" policy of the UAW, covering bargaining-unit employees who are promoted to supervisory positions, is found in other employment contexts. It is not uncommon, for example, in the public utilities industry for such employees to *retain* full union membership, sometimes pursuant to collective bargaining agreements mandating such division of loyalty. (You may profitably speculate as to both employer and union motivation for accepting this duality.) In FLORIDA POWER & LIGHT CO. v. IBEW, LOCAL 641, 417 U.S. 790, 94 S.Ct. 2737, 41 L.Ed.2d 477 (1974), the Court faced the question of whether union disciplinary action against such supervisors constituted a violation of the NLRA. A divided Board had found violations of Section 8(b)(1)(B) in two cases where fines ($500 in the first case, $100 to $6,000 in the second) were imposed on supervisors who were also members of the union because they performed struck work during the union's economic strike against the employer. In one of the cases the union had also expelled the offending supervisors from the union, thereby terminating their rights to pension and welfare benefits. The two cases were consolidated in the D.C. Circuit and considered en banc. In a 5-to-4 decision the circuit refused to enforce the Board's orders. The Supreme Court, also in a 5-to-4 decision, affirmed the circuit.

The majority opinion concluded that Congress, in enacting Section 8(b)(1)(B), intended to protect employers *only* where the union's conduct coerced or restrained the employer *in choosing its representatives for collective bargaining or for grievance adjustment.* With regard to the broader problem of supervisor loyalty, the majority concluded that Congress had dealt with that matter through the 1947 amendments to Section 2(3) of the NLRA which excluded individuals defined as supervisors in Section 2(11) from the coverage of the Act and through explicitly providing in Section 14(a) that, while supervisors have the right to join unions, employers cannot be compelled to consider them as employees for collective bargaining purposes. Consequently, the employer was free to require supervisors to refrain from participating in union activity if it so chose; if it did not so choose, it took the bitter of union discipline of supervisors with whatever sweet their union membership brought.

Four years later, a new facet of the supervisor loyalty problem reached the Court. In AMERICAN BROADCASTING COMPANIES v. WRITERS GUILD, 437 U.S. 411, 98 S.Ct. 2423, 57 L.Ed.2d 313 (1978), supervisory employees who were union members were threatened with union discipline for crossing picket lines for the purpose of doing *only* supervisory work, including the processing of grievances. Supervisory employees who crossed the picket lines were fined amounts varying from $100 to $50,000. The NLRB found that the union's conduct was a violation of Section 8(b)(1)(B). The court of appeals, relying on Florida Power and Light, refused enforcement of the Board's order. The Supreme Court (again 5–4) reversed, upholding the Board. The Court stated:

"We cannot agree with what appears to be the fundamental position of the Court of Appeals and the union that under § 8(b)(1)(B), as the section was construed in *FP&L,* it is never an unfair practice for a union to discipline a supervisor-member for working during a strike, regardless of the work that he may perform behind the picket line. * * * [A]n employer [can] be coerced or restrained within the meaning of § 8(b)(1)(B) not only by picketing or other direct actions aimed at him [to force him into a multi-employer bargaining unit or otherwise to dictate or control the choice of his representative for the purpose of collective bargaining or adjusting grievances in the course of administering an existing contract] but also [indirectly] by debilitating discipline imposed on his collective-bargaining or grievance-adjustment representative. Indeed, after focusing on the purposes of the section, the Court in *FP&L* delineated the boundaries of when that 'carryover' effect would violate § 8(b)(1)(B): whenever such discipline may adversely affect the supervisor's conduct in his capacity as a grievance adjustor or collective bargainer. In these situations—that is, when such impact might be felt—the employer would be deprived of the full services of his representatives and hence would be restrained and coerced in his selection of those representatives." 437 U.S. at 429, 98 S.Ct. at 2433–34, 57 L.Ed.2d at 327–28.

Based upon your reading of this Note 3, how would you describe the interpretation given Section 8(b)(1)(B) by the Court?

4. With regard to the enforcement of fines levied pursuant to union disciplinary proceedings and the role of state courts in that process, see NLRB v. Allis-Chalmers Mfg. Co., supra p. 774; NLRB v. Boeing Co., supra p. 782; and Pattern Makers' League v. NLRB, supra p. 789, Note 1.

5. Assuming that the union tribunals did have jurisdiction to discipline the defendants in PRB Case No. 109, were the defendants accorded a "full and fair" hearing within the meaning of Section 101(a)(5)? Suppose the defendants had refused to testify or present any evidence. Who should have the burden of proof? Are such defendants privileged against self-incrimination? In other words, to what extent should union disciplinary proceedings be analogized to criminal prosecutions?

The elements of a fair hearing in union disciplinary proceedings are discussed in Summers, Union Discipline: What the Courts Do in Fact, 70 Yale L.J. 175, 200 (1960).

DETROY v. AMERICAN GUILD OF VARIETY ARTISTS

United States Court of Appeals, Second Circuit, 1961.
286 F.2d 75.

Certiorari denied, 366 U.S. 929 (1961).

LUMBARD, CHIEF JUDGE. The appellant, manager and trainer of a troupe of chimpanzees with which he performs professionally under the name of the "Marquis Family" in theaters, night clubs, circuses, on television, and in motion pictures, instituted this proceeding under § 102 of the Labor-Management Reporting and Disclosure Act of 1959, * * * demanding injunctive relief and damages for an alleged violation of the procedural rights granted union members by § 101(a)(5) of the Act * * *. Upon a motion for summary judgment, the district court dismissed the complaint on the ground that under § 101(a)(4) the plaintiff could bring no court action against a labor union without first exhausting the internal remedies provided by the union, and that in this case the defendant union had established reasonable procedures by its constitution whereby claims against it by members could be heard within the four-month period permitted by the law.

The controversy between the appellant and the American Guild of Variety Artists, a labor union representing variety entertainers in the United States and Canada, arose out of a breach-of-contract claim made against the appellant by a resort hotel in Las Vegas, Nevada. After failing to settle the dispute by negotiation, the AGVA requested the parties to submit it to arbitration, which they did. A panel of three, one selected by each of the parties to the dispute and the third chosen by the two so designated, met in Los Angeles County, California, on January 12, 1960, and decided in favor of the hotel. The union then advised the appellant that if he did not abide by the award, it would place him on the "National Unfair List" appearing in its monthly periodical "AGVA News." The appellant replied that he intended to move to vacate the arbitration award in the California courts, but never began any such proceedings. When the three months provided by California law for vacating arbitration awards had elapsed, the union proceeded to publish the appellant's name in the August 1960 issue of the periodical under a heading which read as follows:

"Notice to Members.

"The rules require that you may not work for any employer, agent, booker or third party who is marked 'Unfair' by AGVA. Violation of these rules subjects you to disciplinary action.

"Notice to Agents

" * * * You are not authorized to book AGVA members in unfair establishments or book performers not in good standing in AGVA. Violation of rules subjects you to revocation of your franchise."

The appellant then began this proceeding in the Southern District of New York, claiming that the listing amounted to disciplinary action within the meaning of § 101(a)(5) of the Labor-Management Reporting and Disclosure Act of 1959, * * * and that he was, therefore, entitled to specific written charges, a reasonable time to defend, and a full and fair hearing before having his name placed on the list.

The appellant did not, however, seek to utilize the procedure made available by Article XX of the Constitution of the AGVA. This article, entitled "Claims of Members," establishes procedures whereby claims asserted against the union are heard and determined by its Board or Executive Committee. Thus, the first issue before us now is whether the proviso in § 101(a)(4), which protects the right of a union member to sue his union, "Provided, That any such member may be required to exhaust reasonable hearing procedures (but not to exceed a four-month lapse of time) within such organization, before instituting legal or administrative proceedings against such organizations or any officer thereof," required of the appellant in this case that he first have recourse to the internal procedures established by the union's constitution. The exhaustion proviso of § 101(a)(4) does not appear in § 102, which grants members who claim that their rights under § 101 have been infringed a federal forum in which to litigate their disputes with the union. It might also appear from the rejection by the House of Representatives of H.R. 8342, the bill originally reported out of the Committee on Education and Labor, which explicitly provided for exhaustion of internal remedies in § 102, that Congress did not mean to have the exhaustion doctrine apply to the rights granted by § 101, except where, as in the case of the right to sue, it was expressly provided. However, the board language of the proviso in § 101(a)(4) includes suits instituted against labor unions in any court on any claim. Absent a clear directive by Congress, the policy formulated over a course of time by courts reluctant to interfere in the internal affairs of private organizations should not be superseded. We hold, therefore, that the provision in § 101(a)(4) applies, as well, to suits brought in the federal courts for violations of the rights secured by § 101.

Judge Dimock in this case read § 101(a)(4) as imposing upon the union member an absolute duty to exhaust union remedies before applying to the federal courts. The legislative history of the section indicates, however, that Congress had no intention of establishing such a rule.[2]

---

2. For example, one of the authors of the bill passed by the House, Representative Griffin, expressed a clear opinion on the question. He said:

"The proviso which limits exhaustion of internal remedies is not intended to impose restrictions on a union member which do not otherwise exist, but rather to place a maximum on the length of time which may be required to exhaust such remedies. In other words, existing decisions which require, or do not require, exhaustion of such remedies are not to be affected except as a time limit of 4 months is superimposed. Also, by use of the phrase 'reasonable hearing procedures' in the proviso, it should be clear that no obligation is imposed to exhaust procedures where it would obviously be futile or would place an undue burden on the union member." 105 Daily Cong.Rec. App. A7915 (Sept. 4, 1959).

The statement made by Senator Kennedy, who introduced the original bill to which §§ 101–105 were added as amendments on the Senate floor, is also representative of the attitude taken by those who instituted the legislation. He said:

"Nor is it the intent or purpose of the provision to invalidate the considerable body of State and Federal court decisions of many years standing which require, or do not require, the exhaustion of internal remedies prior to court intervention depending upon the reasonableness of such requirements in terms of the facts and circumstances of a particular case. * * * The doctrine of exhaustion of reasonable internal union remedies for violation of union laws is just as firmly established as the doctrine of exhausting reasonable administrative agency provisions prior to action by

The statute provides that any member of a labor organization "may be required" to exhaust the internal union remedies, not that he "must" or "is required to" exhaust them. When read in light of the statements made on the floor of Congress by the authors of the statute, it appears clear that the proviso was incorporated in order to preserve the exhaustion doctrine as it had developed and would continue to develop in the courts, lest it otherwise appear to be Congress' intention to have the right to sue secured by § 101 abrogate the requirement of prior resort to internal procedures. In addition, the proviso dictated an outside limit beyond which the judiciary cannot extend the requirement of exhaustion—no remedy which would require proceedings exceeding four months in duration may be demanded. We therefore construe the statute to mean that a member of a labor union who attempts to institute proceedings before a court or an administrative agency may be required *by that court or agency* to exhaust internal remedies of less than four months' duration before invoking outside assistance.

Section 102, under which the appellant instituted his proceeding, provides for enforcement by federal courts of rights secured by federal law. We are not in this case, therefore, bound by the doctrine of exhaustion as developed in the New York, Nevada, or California courts with respect to suits against unions brought in the courts of those states by union members. In enforcing rights guaranteed by the new statute, whether or not similar rights would be enforced under state law by state courts, the federal courts may develop their own principles regarding the time when a union's action taken in violation of § 101 is ripe for judicial intervention. * * * The rules formulated by various state courts may suggest helpful avenues of approach, cf. Textile Workers Union of America v. Lincoln Mills, 1957, 353 U.S. 448, 457, 77 S.Ct. 912, 1 L.Ed.2d 972, but the authority granted to the federal courts by Congress to secure the rights enumerated in § 101 of the 1959 Act is accompanied by the duty to formulate federal law regarding a union member's obligation to exhaust the internal union remedies before seeking judicial vindication of those rights.

If we look to the substantial body of state law on the subject, we find that the general rule requiring exhaustion before resort to a court has been almost entirely swallowed up by exceptions phrased in broad terms. See Annotation 168 A.L.R. 1462 (1947); Summers, Legal Limitations on Union Discipline, 64 Harv.L.Rev. 1049, 1086–92 (1951). * * *

The Congressionally approved policy of first permitting unions to correct their own wrongs is rooted in the desire to stimulate labor organizations to take the initiative and independently to establish honest and democratic procedures. See Cox, The Role of Law in Preserving Union Democracy, 72 Harv.L.Rev. 609, 615 (1959). Other policies, as well, underlie the exhaustion rule. The possibility that corrective action within the union will render a member's complaint moot suggests that, in the interest of conserving judicial resources, no court step in before the union is given its opportunity. Moreover, courts may find valuable the assistance provided by prior consideration of the issues by appellate union tribunals. See Summers, The Law of Union Discipline: What the Courts Do in Fact, 70 Yale L.J. 175, 207 (1960).

courts." 105 Daily Cong.Rec. 16414 (Sept. 3, 1959).

Congress has provided a safeguard against abuse by a union of the freedom thus granted it by not requiring exhaustion of union remedies if the procedures will exceed four months in duration. But in any case, if the state of facts is such that immediate judicial relief is warranted, Congress' acceptance of the exhaustion doctrine as applied to the generality of cases should not bar an appropriate remedy in proper circumstances.

The affidavits and exhibits submitted in the district court on the motion for summary judgment establish that the only hearing given the appellant before his name was placed on the National Unfair List was that of the arbitration proceeding. The union was not a party to the arbitration, and the issue decided by the arbitrators was not whether the appellant should be disciplined by the union but whether he owed an obligation to an employer with whom he had contracted. It is undisputed that no hearing was held in which the appellant could respond to the union's intention of taking disciplinary action. Quite clearly, a hearing in which some liability between a union member and a third party is determined is not the type of hearing demanded by § 101(a)(5). At no time was the appellant given the opportunity of arguing before the union's hearing board that placing him on the Unfair List exceeded the powers granted to the union by its constitution, nor could he raise other mitigating circumstances in response to an expressed intention to place his name on such a list. The facts on their face, therefore, reveal a violation of the rights guaranteed union members by § 101(a)(5). If the question before us were whether the union's constitution authorized the listing of the appellant's name on an unfair list after a hearing with due procedural safeguards, a union tribunal might provide some insight to aid our decision. But no prior consideration by such a tribunal is necessary or helpful on the question whether the treatment of the appellant violated § 101(a)(5).

In addition, the particular form of the disciplinary action makes it difficult for the union to provide an adequate remedy. The appellant, from the date his name appeared on the list, was virtually barred from employment by those dealing regularly with the AGVA. Since he is an independent contractor whose weekly pay varies according to the terms of the contracts he signs with his employers, the precise extent of damages suffered by the appellant as a result of the listing can never be determined. Even were the union to permit him to present his case before a review board, the board could merely order his name removed from the list and, in order to provide a more satisfactory remedy, award as damages for the period during which he was barred from employment a sum which, at best, could only be an approximation. It appears unlikely that Congress intended that its expressed desire to provide minimum safeguards against arbitrary union discipline be avoided by the union's imposition of a sanction which has its most severe effect within a four-month period, if the consequences of such action cannot be precisely measured in order to assess damages. Early judicial intervention providing an adequate remedy by means of the court's power to enjoin further violations is therefore proper. * * *

Moreover, it is by no means clear that the union's own rules afforded the appellant a remedy within the organization. The section of the union's constitution which relates to disciplinary proceedings (Article XVII) authorizes fines, censure, suspension, or expulsion pursuant to a hearing and determination made by the Board or Executive Committee of the union. An appeal may be taken from such a decision to the next following annual or special convention of the union. No provision is made anywhere for any proceeding either before or after the printing of a member's name on the National Unfair List. The union maintains that Article XX of its Constitution, entitled "Claims of Members," provides a means for reviewing the correctness of this sanction. The constitution's separate provision for disciplinary proceedings in Article XVII, however, suggests that Article XX was not intended to provide an alternate procedure for review of a union's sanctions against its members, but merely to grant a forum for other monetary claims against the union. Moreover, after the arbitration award the appellant notified the Western Regional Director of the union by telegram that he intended "appealing to the National Board," and was told in a reply letter that "the decision of the arbitrators is final and * * * you cannot appeal this to the National Board of AGVA." Although this response referred not to the disciplinary measure but to the arbitrators' decision, neither that letter nor the later notification that he was being placed on the National Unfair List notified the appellant that any specific review procedure was available. Thus, an attempt to proceed under Article XX might not have proved futile, but it would have been quite uncertain. When asserting what is clearly a violation of a federal statute, a union member should not be required to first seek out remedies which are dubious. Only resort to those expressly provided in the union's constitution or those clearly called to his attention by the union officials should be demanded of him.

Taking due account of the declared policy favoring self-regulation by unions, we nonetheless hold that where the internal union remedy is uncertain and has not been specifically brought to the attention of the disciplined party, the violation of federal law clear and undisputed, and the injury to the union member immediate and difficult to compensate by means of a subsequent money award, exhaustion of union remedies ought not to be required. The absence of any of these elements might, in light of Congressional approval of the exhaustion doctrine, call for a different result. The facts of this case, however, warrant immediate judicial intervention.

Nor can we agree with the union's claim that the listing of the appellant's name did not constitute discipline within the meaning of § 101(a)(5). If a union such as the AGVA undertakes to enforce the contracts made by its members with employers, it does so because such enforcement is to the ultimate benefit of all the members, in that it promotes stability within the industry. A breach of contract or a refusal to abide by an arbitration award, therefore, is not damaging merely to the employer but to the union as well, and the union's listing of those of its members who do violate their contracts is an act of self-protection. In thus furthering its own ends the union must abide by the rules set down for it by Congress in § 101(a)(5), and any member against whom steps are taken by the union in the interest of promoting the welfare of the group is entitled to these guarantees.

In passing on the motions for summary judgment and for a temporary injunction, the district court had before it only the complaint and the affidavits of the appellant and various officers of the union. The undisputed facts of the case require that a temporary injunction issue ordering the union to remove the appellant's name from its Unfair List where it is now retained in apparent violation of § 101(a)(5).

We reverse the order of the district court dismissing the complaint and remand the case with instructions to grant the temporary injunction requested by the appellant.

Note

1. The Detroy court states that "[i]f we look to the substantial body of state law on the subject, we find that the general rule requiring exhaustion [of internal union remedies] before resort to a court has been almost entirely swallowed up by exceptions * * *." Supra p. 849. The most important exceptions are the following: (1) *The trial body lacked jurisdiction;* the proceedings were therefore void and there is nothing to appeal internally. (2) *The grounds for discipline were improper;* the proceedings were void because the offense charged was not made punishable by the union constitution or, in any event, could not be made punishable by reason of public policy. (3) *The disciplinary procedure was improper;* the proceedings were void because the provisions of the union constitution were not followed, or the specified union procedures, though followed, denied a fair trial. (4) *Exhaustion of internal appeal procedures would involve unreasonable delay;* the delay itself would preclude the doing of justice. (5) *Internal appeal would be futile;* the union tribunals to which appeal might be made are so biased as to make such appeal a waste of time. It is not uncommon to find more than one of these reasons for exception to the exhaustion requirement in the same case.

> "It is difficult to ascertain to what extent the exhaustion doctrine has really influenced results of cases and to what extent it has merely been used as make-weight in opinion-writing. First, it is always difficult to determine which of a number of different factors discussed by a court is crucial. Second, in most cases, all that is available to show what really happened in the case is the court's interpretation of the facts. It is not unnatural to expect that a court which has concluded, for example, that the plaintiff has a valid case on the merits, would state the facts so that the case appears to fit into one of the accepted formulas for avoiding the exhaustion rule."
> Vorenberg, Exhaustion of Intraunion Remedies, 2 Lab.L.J. 487, 491 (1951).

On the other hand, a court which is confronted by the "dismal swamp" of internal organizational disputation and perceives at the surface no obvious denial of justice may stay clear of the mire, at least temporarily, perhaps permanently, by invoking the exhaustion requirement.

The essence of the exhaustion doctrine is thus judicial discretion.

2. Should the "otherwise disciplined" provision of Section 101(a)(5) (also Section 609) be interpreted to include action by the union vis-à-vis the member which injures him as an *employee,* or should the provision be interpreted so as to limit its coverage to union action which injures him as a *member?* For example, does a member state a cause of action within the meaning of Section 101(a)(5) if he alleges a refusal by the union, *for the purpose of discipline,* to process his grievance against his employer? Under the reasoning of the court in Allen v. Armored Car Chauffeurs and Guards, 185 F.Supp. 492 (D.N.J.1960), the question is answered in the negative: "The disciplinary action of which this Court is

given jurisdiction * * * is not discharge from employment, but the discipline of a member by the Union as to his membership." 185 F.Supp. at 494–95. This reasoning was rejected, however, in Scovile v. Watson, 338 F.2d 678 (7th Cir. 1964), cert. denied, 380 U.S. 963 (1965), the court stating: "Although a right such as plaintiff asserts may be derivative [from the collective bargaining agreement], a refusal by the union * * * to prosecute an arbitrable grievance might be considered as a disciplinary measure relating to the employee's membership in the union." 338 F.2d at 680.

Is not the Scovile answer clearly correct? If so, is there a preemption problem? Compare NLRA Sections 8(b)(2)/8(a)(3) and 8(b)(1)(A) with Landrum-Griffin Sections 103 and 603(a). An affirmative answer to the Scovile question is given in Beaird and Player, Union Discipline of Its Membership Under Section 101(a)(5) of Landrum-Griffin: What Is "Discipline" and How Much Process Is Due?, 9 Ga.L.Rev. 383, 392 (1975). The preemption question was answered in the negative in the Hardeman case, supra p. 826, discussed in Beaird and Player, at 387–88.

MAMULA v. UNITED STEELWORKERS
Supreme Court of Pennsylvania, 1964.
414 Pa. 294, 200 A.2d 306.
Appeal dismissed and certiorari denied, 379 U.S. 17 (1964).

COHEN, JUSTICE. This is an appeal from the decree entered below dismissing appellant's amended complaint for failure to exhaust internal union remedies. Appellees are the United Steelworkers of America (International Union), Local 1211 of the United Steelworkers of America (Local Union), and various officers of Local Union.

It appears from the amended complaint that appellant formerly held the office of president in Local Union. In 1961, charges of misconduct were brought against him and after a hearing by a trial committee of Local Union, these charges were sustained and it was recommended that appellant be removed from office, fined $2,000, and be suspended from union membership until the fine was paid. When these recommendations were approved by the membership of Local Union, appellant appealed to the Executive Board of the International Union in accordance with the procedure prescribed in the International Constitution.

The Executive Board on January 20, 1962, reversed appellant's suspension from union membership and remitted the $2,000 fine, but affirmed appellant's removal from office. In addition, the Board stated that appellant should not be eligible to hold office for five years nor until he repaid $1,081.99, the amount of expense allegedly caused by his misconduct. Once this amount was tendered, however, the Board left open the possibility of decreasing the period of disqualification from office. Although the International Constitution permitted a final appeal to the International Convention of the Union which was scheduled to convene in September, 1962, appellant did not invoke this internal procedure but instead instituted the present suit complaining solely of his ineligibility to hold union office.[1] We hold that the

---

1. In prior litigation, appellant unsuccessfully attempted to challenge his removal from office and the election subsequently held in June, 1962, to fill this vacancy. See Mamula
v. United Steelworkers of America, 409 Pa. 175, 185 A.2d 595 (1962) and Mamula v. United Steelworkers of America, 304 F.2d 108 (3d Cir.1962), cert. denied, 371 U.S. 823, 83 S.Ct.

court below correctly dismissed this action for failure of appellant to exhaust his internal union remedies.

In Falsetti v. Local Union No. 2026, United Mine Workers of America, 400 Pa. 145, 161 A.2d 882, 87 A.L.R.2d 1032 (1960), we examined at length the basis and rationale for the general rule that a member of an unincorporated association must first exhaust his available internal remedies before seeking judicial relief. We concluded that such a rule not only benefits the association by promoting autonomy and internal democracy, but also aids the judicial process by settling grievances internally and, where not settled internally, by supplying our courts with the considered judgment of the association tribunals. At the same time, we sought in Falsetti to protect the rights of the grievant member by establishing certain limited exceptions to the exhaustion rule where, for example, the available remedies are illusory or resort to them would be futile or unreasonably burdensome. The experience since Falsetti has not indicated any necessity for reexamining the general principles therein set forth.

In attempting to justify his failure to appeal to the International Convention, appellant makes two contentions: (1) the general exhaustion rule is inapplicable because appeal to the Convention would have been futile and unreasonably burdensome; and (2) even if the rule is applicable, it has been modified by Section 101(a)(4) of the Landrum-Griffin Act.

With regard to the first contention, appellant's complaint alleges that the disciplinary action of Local Union was directed by the international officers who are biased against him and thus further appeal would have been "illusory, futile and vain and would only afford said international union defendant opportunity for further delaying plaintiff's rights and remedies." We held in Falsetti that the grievant member must set forth facts in his complaint to support the allegation that there exists an exception to the exhaustion rule. * * * Not only has appellant failed to do this, but the admitted facts belie his contention that the bias of the international officers made an appeal to the International Convention futile.

In the first place, we have seen that appellant's appeal to the Executive Board of the International Union resulted in a reversal of his suspension from union membership and a remittance of the $2,000 fine. This fact casts considerable doubt on appellant's assertion that the internal appellate tribunals were prejudged against him. Secondly, it appears that the international officers constituted a very small percentage of the membership at the International Convention.[2] Hence even if the international officers were biased against appellant, it does not necessarily follow that the Convention would have denied him a fair hearing. * * *

Appellant argues that the exhaustion rule is also inapplicable because it would have been unreasonably burdensome for him to appeal to the International Convention in view of the eight-month delay between the decision of the Executive Board (January, 1962) and the meeting of the Convention

42, 9 L.Ed.2d 63 (1962). Although his amended complaint is not clear on the point, appellant states in his brief that the present action is concerned solely with his ineligibility to hold union office.

2. Of the nearly 3000 delegates at the International Convention, only 33 were international officers.

(September, 1962). As we indicated in Falsetti, a grievant member need not as a general matter appeal to an International Convention which does not convene for several years. However, a two or three-step appellate procedure is not *per se* unduly burdensome, nor is it possible to set forth for all situations a time limit beyond which exhaustion of internal remedies will not be demanded. Rather, an examination must be made of the special factors in each case, especially the possible prejudice caused to the grievant member from the delay in internal appellate procedures.

Applying this test to the instant case, we find that here the eight-month time period was not unreasonably burdensome. It must be remembered that the Executive Board reinstated appellant to union membership and hence there was no loss of possible employment opportunities during this period. With regard to appellant's ineligibility to hold union office, it appears that another election did not take place until sometime in 1963, well after the meeting of the International Convention. Thus no apparent harm would have resulted to appellant from insistence on an appeal to the International Convention. Particularly is this so since the right appellant seeks to protect is his right to be a candidate for office—a right *not* protected by the "BILL OF RIGHTS OF MEMBERS OF LABOR ORGANIZATIONS", 29 U.S.C.A. §§ 411–415. We conclude, therefore, that none of the exceptions set forth in Falsetti are here applicable.

Our determination here does not mean we fail to recognize that in many instances an appeal to the International Convention is so illusory that it would be futile and unreasonably burdensome to require resort to Convention action prior to instituting suit. In fact, the whole appellate procedure of some unions is subject to the indictment of being illusory. Indeed, some new internal facility is required in some union discipline procedure—such as a public review board—which would have final jurisdiction to hear appeals from the decisions of the union. Such a board would be extremely helpful to unions, their members and the courts, and would dissipate the overtones of bias that permeates some union disciplinary action. See 73 Yale L.J. 472 (1964). Full protection of a member's individual rights of any nature is important to the concept of union democracy. Union officials should not be permitted to discipline so as to silence criticism, punish complainers and discourage reform. See Salzhandler v. Caputo, 2 Cir., 316 F.2d 445 (1963).

Appellant next contends that our exhaustion rule has been modified by Section 101(a)(4) of the Landrum-Griffin Act. That section provides as follows:

> "Protection of the right to sue.—No labor organization shall limit the right of any member thereof to institute an action in any court, or in a proceeding before any administrative agency, * * * or the right of any member of a labor organization to appear as a witness in any judicial, administrative, or legislative proceeding, or to petition any legislature or to communicate with any legislator: *Provided, That any such member may be required to exhaust reasonable hearing procedures (but not to exceed a four-month lapse of time) within such organization, before instituting legal or administrative proceedings against such organizations or any officer thereof * * *.*" (Emphasis applied).

Appellant argues that the proviso clause means that courts, both state and federal, may not compel a grievant member to invoke an internal remedy which will consume more than four months. Since the appeal to the International Convention involved an eight-month delay, appellant asserts that he was not required to exhaust this remedy. We do not agree.

We read Section 101(a)(4) as a limitation upon labor organizations and not upon the judiciary. Prior to the passage of the Landrum-Griffin Act, many unions had provisions in their constitutions stating that any member who brought suit against the union without first exhausting all available internal remedies—no matter how burdensome or time-consuming—was subject to expulsion from membership.[6] Congress' purpose in enacting Section 101(a)(4) was to invalidate such provisions,[7] thereby protecting the union member from discipline for violation thereof, where insistence on exhaustion of remedies would be either (1) unreasonable or (2) exceed a four-month time period. Congress did not intend to alter state rules relating to exhaustion of remedies which, as we have seen, are designed to aid the courts as well as the unincorporated association. Thus while appellant could not be disciplined for bringing suit before appealing to the International Convention, the failure to exhaust this internal remedy still precludes resort to our courts.

An examination of the language of Section 101(a)(4) plainly supports this interpretation. In the first place, the section states that "[n]o labor organization" shall limit the right of any member to institute suit or to take other remedial steps. There is no reference to existing judicial limitations on the ability of members of unincorporated associations to maintain action against the association. In this connection it should be remembered that the Landrum-Griffin Act was designed to promote union democracy by protecting the rights of a union member vis-à-vis his union. In fact, Title I, of which Section 101(a)(4) is a part, is labeled the "BILL OF RIGHTS OF MEMBERS OF LABOR ORGANIZATIONS" and sets forth various restrictions upon labor organizations.

Secondly, the language relied upon by appellant appears in a parenthetical clause contained in a proviso to the restrictions imposed upon labor organizations. It is highly unlikely that Congress would attempt in such a cavalier manner to alter established state court rules relating to exhaustion of internal remedies.[8]

Appellant cites two federal cases and some language contained in Falsetti in support of his interpretation of Section 101(a)(4). The federal cases[9] involved suits brought in federal court under Section 102 of the Landrum-Griffin Act to remedy alleged violations of Title I of the Act. We

---

6. See Cox, Internal Affairs of Labor Unions Under the Labor Reform Act of 1959, 58 Mich.L.Rev. 819, 839 (1960).

7. Section 101(b) of the Act states that "[a]ny provision of the constitution and by-laws of any labor organization which is inconsistent with the provisions of this section shall be of no force or effect." * * *

8. See Cox, supra note 6 at 839–41; Hickey, The Bill of Rights of Union Members, 48

Geo.L.J. 226, 254 (1959); Smith, The Labor-Management Reporting and Disclosure Act of 1959, 46 Va.L.Rev. 195 (1960).

9. Appellant cites Harris v. International Longshoremen's Association, Local No. 1291, 321 F.2d 801 (3d Cir.1963) and Detroy v. American Guild of Variety Artists, 286 F.2d 75 (2d Cir.1961).

read those decisions as merely adopting for the federal courts an exhaustion of remedies rule patterned upon the proviso clause in Section 101(a)(4). Those cases do not mean that state courts must also adopt this exhaustion rule.

* * * [W]e hold that Section 101(a)(4) does not alter the Pennsylvania exhaustion of remedies rule.

Since appellant has not shown any legal justification for his failure to exhaust internal union remedies, we conclude that the decree entered below must be affirmed.

Decree affirmed.

JONES, J., dissents.

ROBERTS, JUSTICE (dissenting).

Even a highly imaginative fiction writer would have considerable difficulty conceiving a procedure more futile, frustrating and meaningless than having an individual member appear before an International Convention, consisting of approximately 3,000 delegates, to present and argue his grievances against the leadership of the union, with the expectation of moving that body to hear, understand and decide the controversy on the merits. Such exposure to the convention arena is not a reasonable pursuit of a remedy; rather, it is a compelled involvement in a vast and undefined contest. The convention is not a tribunal conducive to the fair and impartial determination of a controversy. The customary protections, rights and rules usually associated with the hearing and decisional process are totally absent. I see no reason why the litigant here should be required to travel such a hazardous and unproductive road. In no other instance is one seeking justice required to engage in such futility. * * *

I am also unable to share the majority's interpretation of Section 101(a) (4) of the Landrum-Griffin Act and the majority's failure to apply it to this litigation. This section obviously does not alter the established substantive rule of this Commonwealth which requires exhaustion of internal union remedies. It does, however, make it unmistakably clear that "no labor organization" may delay the availability of such internal remedies for more than four months.

If appeal to the International Convention be regarded as a "remedy", as the majority holds, then clearly its availability fails to comply with the statute, since that hearing procedure was postponed more than four months.

I conclude, therefore, that appellant may not be denied relief in our courts. He has effectively exhausted all meaningful internal union remedies. Moreover, even if appeal to the International Convention be considered more than an empty gesture, as the majority holds, the Landrum-Griffin Act requires that such appeal be available within four months of the conclusion of the prior step in the appeal process.

I dissent.

BELL, C.J., joins in this opinion.

Note

The Supreme Court denied certiorari in the Mamula case with regard to the following question: Does Section 101(a)(4) of the LMRDA control or modify the exhaustion of remedies rule previously applied by state equity courts in suits by members against unions? See 58 L.R.R. (News and Background Information) 32 (1965). Fully analyzed, the question breaks down into two parts: (1) Does the proviso to Section 101(a)(4) apply to unions, courts, or both? (2) If applicable to courts, is the application confined to federal courts or does it also reach state courts?

As to question (2), do Sections 102, 103, and 603(a) shed any light? For legislative history and analysis relevant to question (2) (without, however, answering it), see Summers, Pre-emption and the Labor Reform Act—Dual Rights and Remedies, 22 Ohio St.L.J. 119 (1961).

As to question (1), are the answers given by Detroy and Mamula the same? For legislative history and analysis arguing "that Section 101(a)(4) was not intended as a limitation on the courts but only limits the unions' power to discipline members for seeking legal protection," see O'Donoghue, Protection of a Union Member's Right to Sue Under the Landrum-Griffin Act, 14 Catholic U.L. Rev. 215, 234 (1965).

Is question (1) answered by the Supreme Court in the Marine Workers case, which follows?

NATIONAL LABOR RELATIONS BOARD v. INDUSTRIAL UNION OF MARINE WORKERS

Supreme Court of the United States, 1968.
391 U.S. 418, 88 S.Ct. 1717, 20 L.Ed.2d 706.

MR. JUSTICE DOUGLAS delivered the opinion of the Court.

One Holder, a member of respondent unions, filed with the National Labor Relations Board an unfair labor practice charge, alleging that Local 22 had violated § 8(b)(1)(A) of the National Labor Relations Act * * * by causing his employer to discriminate against him because he had engaged in protected activity with respect to his employment.[2] The filing of this charge followed an accusation by Holder to Local 22 that its president had violated the constitution of the International. The local decided in favor of its president; but Holder did not pursue the intra-union appeals procedure that was available to him and filed the unfair labor practice charge instead, based on the same alleged violations by the president.

Section 5 of Article V of the constitution of the International Union, which was binding on Local 22, contained the following provision relative to grievances of union members:

2. This charge, filed with the Board February 28, 1964, was directed solely against respondent International Union and alleged that:

"On or about October 8, 196[3], the above named labor organization caused the United States Lines [employer] to discriminate against Edwin D. Holder because he engaged in concerted activities with respect to the conditions of his employment.

"By these and other acts, the above named labor organization has interfered with, restrained and coerced, and continues to interfere with, restrain and coerce the Company's employees in the exercise of rights guaranteed in Section 7 of the Act."

By letter of May 20, 1964, the Regional Director informed Holder that this charge was dismissed.

"Every member * * * considering himself * * * aggrieved by any action of this Union, the [General Executive Board], a National Officer, a Local or other subdivision of this Union shall exhaust all remedies and appeals within the Union, provided by this Constitution, before he shall resort to any court or other tribunal outside of the Union."

While Holder's charge was pending before the Board, Local 22 lodged a complaint in internal union proceedings against Holder alleging he had violated § 5 of Article V of the International's constitution by filing his charge with the Board before he had exhausted his internal remedies. After a hearing before Local 22, Holder was found guilty and expelled from both respondent unions. He then appealed to the General Executive Board of the International which affirmed the local's action on October 7, 1964.

On October 28, 1964, Holder filed a second charge with the Board, claiming his expulsion for filing the first charge was unlawful. That charge is the basis of the instant case.

A complaint issued; and the Board found that the respondent unions had violated § 8(b)(1)(A) of the Act by expelling Holder for filing a charge with the Board without first having exhausted the intra-union procedures. 159 N.L.R.B. 1065. It issued a remedial order, which the Court of Appeals refused to enforce, 3 Cir., 379 F.2d 702. The case is here on writ of certiorari * * *.

The main issue in the case is whether Holder could be expelled for filing the charge with the Board without first having exhausted "all remedies and appeals within the Union" [4] as provided in § 5 of Article V of the constitution, already quoted.

Section 8(b)(1)(A) in its proviso preserves to a union "the right of a labor organization to prescribe its own rules with respect to the acquisition or retention of membership therein."

The Court of Appeals concluded that while this proviso would not permit a union to expel a member because he filed an unfair labor practice charge against the union, it permits a rule which gives the union "a fair opportuni-

---

4. These remedies are provided for in § 3 of Article V of the constitution:

"No Union member in good standing in any Local may be suspended or expelled or otherwise disciplined or penalized without a fair and open trial, of which reasonable notice shall be given the accused member, before the Trial Board of the Local Union * * *. The accused member or members or the accusers may appeal the decision of the local Union's Executive Board [sic] to the regular meeting of the General Membership of the Local Union next following the meeting of the Executive Board at which the decision was rendered, and within thirty (30) days after the membership's decision may appeal to the General Executive Board. The General Executive Board shall, after reasonable notice to the appellant of the time and place of hearing, hold a fair and open hearing on such appeal and,

not later than 130 days after the first regular meeting of the General Executive Board following receipt of the appeal at the National Office, and in any event not later than the first day of the National Convention, shall render its decision affirming, overruling, or modifying either the findings of guilt or innocence, or the penalty imposed. Both the accused and the accuser shall have the right to file an appeal to the next National Convention by sending such appeal to the National Office of this Union by registered mail not later than thirty days after the decision by the General Executive Board."

Although Holder did not take any internal appeal from the local's original adverse decision on his charge to it against the president, he did appeal his expulsion to the General Executive Board of the International which affirmed.

ty to correct its own wrong before the injured member should have recourse to the Board." 379 F.2d at 707.

We held in NLRB v. Allis-Chalmers Mfg. Co., 388 U.S. 175, 87 S.Ct. 2001, 18 L.Ed.2d 1123, that § 8(b)(1)(A) does not prevent a union from imposing fines on members who cross a picket line created to implement an authorized strike. The strike, we said, "is the ultimate weapon in labor's arsenal for achieving agreement upon its terms" and the power to fine or expel a strikebreaker " 'is essential if the union is to be an effective bargaining agent.' " * * *

Thus § 8(b)(1)(A) assures a union freedom of self-regulation where its legitimate internal affairs are concerned. But where a union rule penalizes a member for filing an unfair labor practice charge with the Board other considerations of public policy come into play.

Section 10(b) of the Act * * * forbids issuance of a complaint based on conduct occurring more than six months prior to filing of the charge—a provision promoting promptness. A proceeding by the Board is not to adjudicate private rights but to effectuate a public policy. The Board cannot initiate its own proceedings; implementation of the Act is dependent "upon the initiative of individual persons." Nash v. Florida Industrial Comm'n, 389 U.S. 235, 238, 88 S.Ct. 362, 365, 19 L.Ed.2d 438. The policy of keeping people "completely free from coercion," ibid., against making complaints to the Board is therefore important in the functioning of the Act as an organic whole. A restriction such as we find in § 5 of Article V of the International's constitution is contrary to that policy, as it is applied here. A healthy interplay of the forces governed and protected by the Act means that there should be as great a freedom to ask the Board for relief as there is to petition any other department of government for a redress of grievances. Any coercion used to discourage, retard, or defeat that access is beyond the legitimate interests of a labor organization. That was the philosophy of the Board in the Skura case, Local 138, International Union of Operating Engineers, 148 N.L.R.B. 679; and we agree that the overriding public interest makes unimpeded access to the Board the only healthy alternative, except and unless plainly internal affairs of the union are involved.

In the present case a whole complex of public policy issues was raised by Holder's original charge. It implicated not only the union but the employer. The employer might also have been made a party and comprehensive and coordinated remedies provided. Those issues cannot be fully explored in an internal union proceeding. There cannot be any justification to make the public processes wait until the union member exhausts internal procedures plainly inadequate to deal with all phases of the complex problem concerning employer, union, and employee member. If the member becomes exhausted, instead of the remedies, the issues of public policy are never reached and an airing of the grievance never had. The Court of Appeals recognized that this might be the consequence and said that resort to an intra-union remedy would not be required if it "would impose unreasonable delay or hardship upon the complainant." 379 F.2d, at 707.

The difficulty is that a member would have to guess what a court ultimately would hold. If he guessed wrong and filed the charge with the Board without exhausting internal union procedures, he would have no recourse against the discipline of the union. That risk alone is likely to chill the exercise of a member's right to a Board remedy and induce him to forgo his grievance or pursue a futile union procedure. That is the judgment of the Board; and we think it comports with the policy of the Act. That is to say, the proviso in § 8(b)(1)(A) that unions may design their own rules respecting "the acquisition or retention of membership" is not so broad as to give the union power to penalize a member who invokes the protection of the Act for a matter that is in the public domain and beyond the internal affairs of the union.

The Court of Appeals found support for its contrary position in § 101(a) (4) of the Labor-Management Reporting and Disclosure Act of 1959 * * *. While that provision prohibits a union from limiting the right of a member "to institute an action in any court or in a proceeding before any administrative agency," it provides that a member "may be required to exhaust reasonable hearing procedures" "not to exceed a four-month lapse of time."

We conclude that "may be required" is not a grant of authority to unions more firmly to police their members but a statement of policy that the public tribunals whose aid is invoked may in their discretion stay their hands for four months, while the aggrieved person seeks relief within the union. We read it, in other words, as installing in this labor field a regime comparable to that which prevails in other areas of law before the federal courts, which often stay their hands while a litigant seeks administrative relief before the appropriate agency.[8]

The legislative history is not very illuminating. Some members of the House who spoke indicated that there was room for judicial discretion whether to remit the member to available internal union remedies. In the Senate the fear was expressed that the new section would give unions power to punish their members for filing charges with the Board prior to exhaustion of their internal remedies. In the Senate the continuance of union grievance procedures under the new section was emphasized. It was indeed expressly stated by Senator John F. Kennedy reporting from the Conference Committee: [12]

> "The 4-month limitation in the House bill also relates to restrictions imposed by unions rather than the rules of judicial administration or the action of Government agencies."

Yet it plainly appears from those speaking for the Conference Report that a member was to be permitted to complain to the Board even before the end of the four-month period. Congressman Griffin reported: [13]

8. See Myers v. Bethlehem Shipbuilding Corp., 303 U.S. 41, 58 S.Ct. 459, 82 L.Ed. 638; compare Railroad Comm'n of Texas v. Pullman Co., 312 U.S. 496, 61 S.Ct. 643, 85 L.Ed. 971. The requirement of exhaustion is a matter within the sound discretion of the courts. See, e.g., McCulloch v. Sociedad Nacional, 372 U.S. 10, 16–17, 83 S.Ct. 671, 674–675, 9 L.Ed. 2d 547. And see Leedom v. Kyne, 358 U.S. 184, 188–189, 79 S.Ct. 180, 183–184, 3 L.Ed.2d 210; Public Utilities Comm. of State of California v. United States, 355 U.S. 534, 539–540, 78 S.Ct. 446, 450, 2 L.Ed.2d 470. Exhaustion is not required when the administrative reme-

dies are inadequate. Greene v. United States, 376 U.S. 149, 84 S.Ct. 615, 11 L.Ed.2d 576; McNeese v. Board of Education, 373 U.S. 668, 83 S.Ct. 1433, 10 L.Ed.2d 622. See generally 3 K. Davis, Administrative Law Treatise § 20.07 (1958). When the complaint, as in the instant case, raises a matter that is in the public domain and beyond the internal affairs of the union, the union's internal procedures are, as previously explained, plainly inadequate.

12. 105 Cong.Rec. 17899.

13. 105 Cong.Rec. 18152.

"[T]he proviso was not intended to limit in any way the right of a union member under the Labor-Management Relations Act of 1947, as amended, to file unfair labor practice charges against a union, or the right of the NLRB to entertain such charges, even though a 4-month period may not have elapsed."

And on the Senate side, Senator Kennedy said that the proviso was not intended "to invalidate the considerable body of State and Federal court decisions of many years standing which require, *or do not require,* the exhaustion of internal remedies prior to court intervention *depending upon the reasonableness of such requirements in terms of the facts and circumstances of a particular case."* (Emphasis added.) Nor, he said, was it intended to prohibit "the National Labor Relations Board * * * from entertaining charges by a member against a labor organization even though 4 months has not elapsed." [14]

We conclude that unions were authorized to have hearing procedures for processing grievances of members, provided those procedures did not consume more than four months of time; but that a court or agency might consider whether a particular procedure was "reasonable" and entertain the complaint even though those procedures had not been "exhausted." We also conclude, for reasons stated earlier in this opinion, that where the complaint or grievance does not concern an internal union matter, but touches a part of the public domain covered by the Act, failure to resort to any intra-union grievance procedure is not ground for expulsion from a union. We hold that the Board properly entertained the complaint of Holder and that its order should be enforced.

Reversed.

MR. JUSTICE STEWART dissents. He would affirm the judgment, agreeing substantially with the opinion of the Court of Appeals for the Third Circuit. 379 F.2d 702.

MR. JUSTICE HARLAN, concurring.

I am persuaded by the legislative history, summarized in part by the Court, that the proviso to § 101(a)(4) of the Labor-Management Reporting and Disclosure Act * * * was intended simply to permit a court or agency to require a union member to exhaust internal union remedies of less than four months' duration before invoking outside assistance. See generally Detroy v. American Guild of Variety Artists, 2 Cir., 286 F.2d 75, 78. I cannot, however, agree that a union may punish a member for his invocation of his remedies before a court or agency "where the complaint or grievance * * * concern[s] an internal union matter," and thus does not touch any "part of the public domain covered by the Act * * *." * * * Assuming *arguendo* that there are member-union grievances untouched by the various federal labor statutes, this dichotomy has, it seems to me, precisely the disadvantage that the Court has found in the Third Circuit's construction of the proviso: it compels a member to gamble his union membership, and often his employment, on the accuracy of his understanding of the federal labor laws.

14. 105 Cong.Rec. 17899.

Finally, it is appropriate to emphasize that courts and agencies will frustrate an important purpose of the 1959 legislation if they do not, in fact, regularly compel union members "to exhaust reasonable hearing procedures" within the union organization. Responsible union self-government demands, among other prerequisites, a fair opportunity to function. . . . *

With these modifications, I concur in the opinion and judgment of the Court.

Note

On the basis of your reading of the Marine Workers case, how would you advise a federal district judge confronted by a Mamula-type problem—i.e., a union motion to dismiss by reason of plaintiff's failure to exhaust internal union remedies requiring *eight* months for completion?

To answer this question requires the prior answering of two other questions: (1) Whether Marine Workers speaks to the *union* exhaustion doctrine or to the *judicial* (including administrative agency) exhaustion doctrine, or both? (2) Whether that speaking is by way of holding or dictum?

2. UNION ELECTIONS

CALHOON v. HARVEY

Supreme Court of the United States, 1964.
379 U.S. 134, 85 S.Ct. 292, 13 L.Ed.2d 190.

MR. JUSTICE BLACK delivered the opinion of the Court.

This case raises important questions concerning the powers of the Secretary of Labor and federal courts to protect rights of employees guaranteed by the Labor-Management Reporting and Disclosure Act of 1959.

The respondents, three members of District No. 1, National Marine Engineers' Beneficial Association, filed a complaint in Federal District Court against the union, its president and its secretary-treasurer, alleging that certain provisions of the union's bylaws and national constitution violated the Act in that they infringed "the right of members of defendant District No. 1, NMEBA, to nominate candidates in elections of defendant, which right is guaranteed to each member of defendant, and to each plaintiff, by Section 101(a)(1) of the LMRDA. * * * " [2] It was alleged that § 102 of Title I of the Act gave the District Court jurisdiction to adjudicate the controversy. The union bylaws complained of deprived a member of the right to nominate anyone for office but himself. The national constitution in turn provided that no member could be eligible for nomination or election to a full-time elective office unless he had been a member of the national union for five years and had served 180 days or more of seatime in each of

---

* It should be noted that many union constitutions have elaborate provisions for internal appeals, and that these provisions were often added or modified as a consequence of § 101(a)(4). See Kroner, Title I of the LMRDA: Some Problems of Legal Method and Mythology, 43 N.Y.U.L.Rev. 280, 302, n. 72.

2. "Every member of a labor organization shall have equal rights and privileges within such organization to nominate candidates, to vote in elections or referendums of the labor organization, to attend membership meetings, and to participate in the deliberations and voting upon the business of such meetings, subject to reasonable rules and regulations in such organization's constitution and bylaws." 73 Stat. 522, 29 U.S.C.A. § 411(a)(1) (1958 ed., Supp. V).

two of the preceding three years on vessels covered by collective bargaining agreements with the national or its subsidiary bodies. On the basis of these allegations respondents asked that the union be enjoined from preparing for or conducting any election until it revised its system of elections so as to afford each of its members a fair opportunity to nominate any persons "meeting fair and reasonable eligibility requirements for any or all offices to be filled by such election." [4]

The union moved to dismiss the complaint on the grounds that (1) the court lacked jurisdiction over the subject matter, and (2) the complaint failed to state a claim upon which relief could be granted. The District Court dismissed for want of "jurisdiction," [5] holding that the alleged conduct of the union, even if true, failed to show a denial of the equal rights of all members of the union to vote for or nominate candidates guaranteed by § 101(a)(1) of Title I of the Act, so as to give the District Court jurisdiction of the controversy under § 102. The allegations, said the court, showed at most imposition of qualifications of eligibility for nomination and election so restrictive that they might violate § 401(e) of Title IV by denying members a reasonable opportunity to nominate and vote for candidates.[6] The District Court further held that it could not exercise jurisdiction to protect § 401(e) rights because § 402(a) of Title IV provides a remedy, declared by § 403 to be "exclusive," authorizing members to vindicate such rights by challenging elections after they have been held,[8] and then only by (1) first exhausting all remedies available with the union, (2) filing a complaint with the Secretary of Labor, who (3) may, after investigating the violation alleged in the complaint, bring suit in a United States district court to attack the validity of the election. The Court of Appeals reversed, holding that "the complaint alleged a violation of § 101(a)(1) and that federal jurisdiction existed under § 102." 324 F.2d 486, 487. Because of the importance of the questions presented and conflicting views in the courts of appeals and the district courts, we granted certiorari. * * *

I.

Jurisdiction of the District Court under § 102 of Title I depends entirely upon whether this complaint showed a violation of rights guaranteed by § 101(a)(1), for we disagree with the Court of Appeals' holding that jurisdiction under § 102 can be upheld by reliance in whole or in part on allegations which in substance charge a breach of Title IV rights. An analysis and understanding of the meaning of § 101(a)(1) and of the charges of the complaint are therefore essential to a determination of this issue. Respondents charge that the bylaws and constitutional provisions referred to above infringed their right guaranteed by § 101(a)(1) to nominate candidates. The result of their allegations here, however, is an attempt to sweep into the

---

4. The complaint also asked for damages.

5. 221 F.Supp. 545, 550.

6. "In any election required by this section which is to be held by secret ballot a reasonable opportunity shall be given for the nomination of candidates and every member in good standing shall be eligible to be a candidate and to hold office (subject to section 504 of this title and to reasonable qualifications uniform-

ly imposed) and shall have the right to vote for or otherwise support the candidate or candidates of his choice * * *." 73 Stat. 533, 29 U.S.C.A. § 481(e) (1958 ed., Supp. V).

8. Section 403 provides also that "[e]xisting rights and remedies to enforce the constitution and bylaws of a labor organization with respect to elections prior to the conduct thereof shall not be affected * * *." * * *

ambit of their right to sue in federal court if they are denied an equal opportunity to nominate candidates under § 101(a)(1), a right to sue if they are not allowed to nominate anyone they choose regardless of his eligibility and qualifications under union restrictions. But Title IV, not Title I, sets standards for eligibility and qualifications of candidates and officials and provides its own separate and different administrative and judicial procedure for challenging those standards. And the equal-rights language of § 101(a)(1) would have to be stretched far beyond its normal meaning to hold that it guarantees members not just a right to "nominate candidates," but a right to nominate anyone, without regard to valid union rules. All that § 101(a)(1) guarantees is that * * * members and classes of members shall not be discriminated against in their right to nominate and vote. And Congress carefully prescribed that even this right against discrimination is "subject to reasonable rules and regulations" by the union. The complaining union members here have not been discriminated against in any way and have been denied no privilege or right to vote or nominate which the union has granted to others. They have indeed taken full advantage of the uniform rule limiting nominations by nominating themselves for office. It is true that they were denied their request to be candidates, but that denial was not a discrimination against their right to nominate, since the same qualifications were required equally of all members. Whether the eligibility requirements set by the union's constitution and bylaws were reasonable and valid is a question separate and distinct from whether the right to nominate on an equal basis given by § 101(a)(1) was violated. The District Court therefore was without jurisdiction to grant the relief requested here unless, as the Court of Appeals held, the "*combined* effect of the eligibility requirements and the restriction to self-nomination" is to be considered in determining whether § 101(a)(1) has been violated.[12]

II.

We hold that possible violations of Title IV of the Act regarding eligibility are not relevant in determining whether or not a district court has jurisdiction under § 102 of Title I of the Act. Title IV sets up a statutory scheme governing the election of union officers, fixing the terms during which they hold office, requiring that elections be by secret ballot, regulating the handling of campaign literature, requiring a reasonable opportunity for the nomination of candidates, authorizing unions to fix "reasonable qualifications uniformly imposed" for candidates, and attempting to guarantee fair union elections in which all the members are allowed to participate. Section 402 of Title IV, as has been pointed out, sets up an exclusive method for protecting Title IV rights, by permitting an individual member to file a complaint with the Secretary of Labor challenging the validity of any election because of violations of Title IV. Upon complaint the Secretary investigates and if he finds probable cause to believe that Title IV has been violated, he may file suit in the appropriate district court. It is apparent that Congress decided to utilize the special knowledge and discretion of the Secretary of Labor in order best to serve the public interest. Cf. San Diego Building Trades Council Millmen's Union, Local 2020 v. Garmon, 359 U.S. 236, 242, 79 S.Ct. 773, 778, 3 L.Ed.2d 775, 781. In so doing Congress, with

---

12. 324 F.2d, at 489. (Emphasis supplied.)

one exception not here relevant,[13] decided not to permit individuals to block or delay union elections by filing federal-court suits for violations of Title IV. Reliance on the discretion of the Secretary is in harmony with the general congressional policy to allow unions great latitude in resolving their own internal controversies, and, where that fails, to utilize the agencies of Government most familiar with union problems to aid in bringing about a settlement through discussion before resort to the courts. Without setting out the lengthy legislative history which preceded the passage of this measure, it is sufficient to say that we are satisfied that the Act itself shows clearly by its structure and language that the disputes here, basically relating as they do to eligibility of candidates for office, fall squarely within Title IV of the Act and are to be resolved by the administrative and judicial procedures set out in that Title.

Accordingly, the judgment of the Court of Appeals is reversed and that of the District Court is affirmed. * * *

Mr. Justice Douglas would affirm the judgment of the Court of Appeals for the reasons stated in its opinion as reported in 324 F.2d 486.

Mr. Justice Stewart, whom Mr. Justice Harlan joins, concurring.

This case marks the first interpretation by this Court of the significant changes wrought by the Labor-Management Reporting and Disclosure Act of 1959 increasing federal supervision of internal union affairs. At issue are subtle questions concerning the interplay between Title I and Title IV of that Act. In part, both seem to deal with the same subject matter: Title I guarantees "equal rights and privileges * * * to nominate candidates"; Title IV provides that "a reasonable opportunity shall be given for the nomination of candidates." Where the two Titles of the legislation differ most substantially is in the remedies they provide. If a Title I right is at issue, the allegedly aggrieved union member has direct, virtually immediate recourse to a federal court to obtain an adjudication of his claim and an injunction if his complaint has merit. * * * Vindication of claims under Title IV may be much more onerous. Federal-court suits can be brought only by the Secretary of Labor, and then, only after the election has been held. An additional barrier is thus placed between the union member and the federal court. Remedies shape the significance of rights, and I think the Court too casually forecloses the direct access to a federal court which the Court of Appeals held was given these respondents by Congress.

At the time this case was brought, District 1 of the National Marine Engineers' Beneficial Association (NMEBA) had two rules of direct relevance here governing selection of candidates for election to union office. One rule, of long standing in the union, prescribed that self-nomination was the only manner by which a name could be placed before the membership for election to union office. The second rule, adopted seven months before this election was scheduled to occur, severely limited eligibility for office by requiring that prospective officers must have belonged to the national union for five years and served 180 or more days of sea duty in each of two years during

---

13. Section 401(c) of the Act permits suits prior to election in the United States District Courts by any bona fide candidate for union office to enforce the rights, guaranteed by that section, to equal treatment in the distribution of campaign literature and access to membership lists. * * *

the three-year period before the election.[1] According to the three union members who brought this action, the combination of these rules unreasonably limited their right to nominate. They alleged that, except for those members of the union who fulfilled the strict eligibility requirements, the self-nomination rule emptied of all meaning the equal right to nominate. To be sure, the "right to nominate" continued, but, they say, for the countless union members rendered ineligible for office by the new sea-duty rule, the privilege of turning in one's name for prospective candidacy was meaningless.

The Court precludes the District Court from asserting jurisdiction over this complaint by focusing on the fact that one of the imposed restrictions speaks in terms of eligibility. And since these are "possible violations of Title IV of the Act regarding eligibility" they "are not relevant in determining whether or not a district court has jurisdiction under § 102 of Title I of the Act." By this reasoning, the Court forecloses early adjudication of claims concerning participation in the election process. But there are occasions when eligibility provisions can infringe upon the right to nominate. Had the NMEBA issued a regulation that only Jesse Calhoon was eligible for office, no one could place great store on the right to self-nomination left to the rest of the membership. This Court long ago recognized the subtle ways by which election rights can be removed through discrimination at a less visible stage of the political process. The decisions in the Texas Primary Cases were founded on the belief that the equal right to vote was impaired where discrimination existed in the method of nomination. Smith v. Allwright, 321 U.S. 649, 64 S.Ct. 757, 88 L.Ed. 987; Nixon v. Herndon, 273 U.S. 536, 47 S.Ct. 446, 71 L.Ed.2d 759. * * * No less is the equal right to nominate infringed where onerous burdens drastically limit the candidates available for nomination. In scrutinizing devices designed to erode the franchise, the Court has shown impatience with arguments founded in the form of the device. * * * If Congress has told the courts to protect a union member from infringement of his equal right to nominate, the courts should do so whether such discrimination is sophisticated or simple-minded. * * *

After today, simply by framing its discriminatory rules in terms of eligibility, a union can immunize itself from pre-election attack in a federal court even though it makes deep incursions on the equal right of its members to nominate, to vote, and to participate in the union's internal affairs.

The Court justifies this conclusion by looking to the "structure and language" of the Act. The language is certainly not free from doubt. And the legislative history indicates that the structure can be misleading. What now constitutes Titles II through VI of the Act was substantially contained in the original bill presented to the Senate by Senator Kennedy. Title I, first introduced by Senator McClellan, was the product of doubt that the bill went far enough in guaranteeing internal democracy in union affairs. The concept of Title I—its stress on equal rights and judicial protection—was the subject of great controversy both in the Senate and in the House. Repeated

---

1. An additional restriction, applicable solely to the post of president, required that all candidates for that office must have served the union in some prior official capacity.

attempts were made by representatives of organized labor, among other groups, to have the strict mandate of this so-called Bill of Rights modified, or eliminated altogether. Despite these efforts to remove Title I, it endured, and indeed was amended to provide stronger remedial provisions than those contained in the original version. As originally introduced, § 102 would have required an aggrieved union member to make his complaint to the Secretary of Labor, exactly the remedy provided by Title IV. The Kuchel amendment, however, substituted the present provision permitting suit by an aggrieved member in a federal district court. * * * Senator Clark of Pennsylvania noted that the Kuchel amendment "takes the Federal bureaucracy out of this bill of rights and leaves its enforcement to union members, aided by the courts." II Leg.Hist. 1233.

Nonetheless, the Court finds a "general congressional policy" to avoid judicial resolution of internal union disputes. That policy, the Court says, was designed to limit the power of individuals to block and delay elections by seeking injunctive relief. Such an appraisal might have been accurate before the addition of Title I, but it does not explain the emphasis on prompt judicial remedies there provided. In addition to the injunctive relief authorized by § 102 and the saving provisions of § 103, § 101(a)(4) modifies the traditional requirement of exhausting internal remedies before resort to litigation.[4] Even § 403 is not conclusive on the elimination of pre-election remedies.[5] At the least, state-court actions may be brought in advance of an election to "enforce the constitution and bylaws." And as to federal courts, it is certainly arguable that recourse through the Secretary of Labor is the exclusive remedy only after the election has been held.[6] By reading Title I rights so narrowly, and by construing Title IV to foreclose absolutely pre-election litigation in the federal courts, the Court sharply reduces meaningful protection for many of the rights which Congress was so assiduous to create.[7] By so simplifying the tangled provisions of the Act, the Court renders it virtually impossible for the aggrieved union member to gain a hearing when it is most necessary—when there is still an opportunity to make the union's rules comport with the requirements of the Act.

My difference with the Court does not reach to the disposition of this particular case. Whether stated in terms of restrictions on the right to nominate or in terms of limitations on eligibility for union office, I think the

---

4. See Detroy v. American Guild of Variety Artists, 286 F.2d 75 (C.A.2d Cir.1961).

5. "Sec. 403 * * *. Existing rights and remedies to enforce the constitution and by-laws of a labor organization with respect to elections prior to the conduct thereof shall not be affected by the provisions of this title. The remedy provided by this title for challenging an election already conducted shall be exclusive."

6. See Summers, Pre-emption and the Labor Reform Act—Dual Rights and Remedies, 22 Ohio St.L.J. 119, 138–139 (1961). It would be strange indeed if only state courts were available to enforce the federal law created by the Act during the pre-election period.

7. The Court's reading of federal-court remedies available under Title I and Title IV

is particularly restrictive because of the limited powers of the district judge once the balloting has occurred. Under § 402(c), the court is confined to setting the election aside only if "the violation of section 401 may have affected the outcome." For the aggrieved union member, this protection may be totally inadequate. The function of nominating a candidate is not always to gain the office. A faction may be vitally interested in appearing on the ballot merely to show that it is part of the political structure of the union. Under the Court's view, until such a faction approaches majority status, judicial relief in the federal courts will be absent. See Summers, Judicial Regulation of Union Elections, 70 Yale L.J. 1221, 1257 (1961).

rules of a labor organization would operate illegally to curtail the members' equal right to nominate within the meaning of Title I only if those rules effectively distorted the basic democratic process. The line might be a shadowy one in some cases. But I think that in this case the respondents did not allege in their complaint nor demonstrate in their affidavits that this line was crossed. I would therefore remand the case to the District Court with directions to dismiss the complaint for failure to state a claim for relief.

Note

1. Section 402's exhaustion requirement—that a complaining member must exhaust his union remedies as a condition precedent to the right of resort to the Secretary of Labor in challenging an election already held—was given a broad interpretation in Hodgson v. Local 6799, United Steelworkers, 403 U.S. 333, 91 S.Ct. 1841, 29 L.Ed.2d 510 (1971). The complaining member, in asserting his case before the union tribunals, had protested as to several alleged violations, including the use of union facilities to prepare campaign materials for an incumbent officer who was re-elected. The member had not, however, presented to those tribunals, the claimed unreasonableness of a provision of the union constitution which required attendance at one-half or more of the regular meetings of the local union for thirty-six months immediately preceding the election as a requisite for eligibility to run for certain local offices. The Court held, 7 to 2, that the Secretary of Labor was, under these circumstances, barred from relying upon the attendance rule as a basis for challenging the election. "To accept [the Secretary's] contention that a union member, who is aware of the facts underlying an alleged violation, need not first protest this violation to his union before complaining to the Secretary would be needlessly to weaken union self-government. Plainly [the Secretary's] approach slights the interest in protecting union self-regulation and is out of harmony with the congressional purpose reflected in § 402(a)." 403 U.S. at 340, 91 S.Ct. at 1846.

2. In American Federation of Musicians v. Wittstein, 379 U.S. 171, 85 S.Ct. 300, 13 L.Ed.2d 214 (1964), a companion case to Calhoon v. Harvey, the Court held that Section 101(a)(3)(B)'s provision that the dues of an international union shall not be increased except "(i) by majority vote of the delegates voting at a regular convention" does not prohibit a weighted voting system authorized by the union's constitution, pursuant to which the delegates cast a number of votes equal to the membership of the local union from which they are elected.

3. The fact that section 403 makes a suit by the Secretary the exclusive post-election remedy for a violation of Title IV does not bar intervention by individual union members in such a suit; however, the intervenors may not assert grounds for setting aside the election other than those asserted by the Secretary. Trbovich v. United Mine Workers, 404 U.S. 528, 92 S.Ct. 630, 30 L.Ed.2d 686 (1972).

4. In Dunlop v. Bachowski, 421 U.S. 560, 95 S.Ct. 1851, 44 L.Ed.2d 377 (1975), the Court held that the Secretary's decision not to bring an action to set aside an allegedly invalid election is reviewable under the standards of section 706(2)(A) of the Administrative Procedure Act (5 U.S.C.A. § 706):

> "Two conclusions follow from * * * our [prior] decisions: (1) since the statute relies upon the special knowledge and discretion of the Secretary for the determination of both the probable violation and the probable effect, clearly the reviewing court is not authorized to substitute its judgment for

the decision of the Secretary not to bring suit; (2) therefore, to enable the reviewing court intelligently to review the Secretary's determination, the Secretary must provide the court and the complaining witness with copies of a statement of reasons supporting his determination. * * *

"Moreover, a statement of reasons serves purposes other than judicial review. Since the Secretary's role as lawyer for the complaining union member does not include the duty to indulge a client's usual prerogative to direct his lawyer to file suit, we may reasonably infer that Congress intended that the Secretary supply the member with a reasoned statement why he determined not to proceed. '[A]s a matter of law * * * the Secretary is not required to sue to set aside the election whenever the proofs before him suggest the suit *might* be successful. There remains in him a degree of discretion to select cases and it is his subjective judgment as to the probable outcome of the litigation that must control.' DeVito v. Shultz, 72 L.R.R.M. 2682, 2683 (DC 1969) (DeVito II) (emphasis added). But '[s]urely Congress must have intended that courts would intercede sufficiently to determine that the provisions of Title IV have been carried out in harmony with the implementation of other provisions of [the LMRDA].' *DeVito I,* 300 F.Supp. at 383. Finally, a 'reasons' requirement promotes thought by the Secretary and compels him to cover the relevant points and eschew irrelevancies, and as noted by the Court of Appeals in this case, the need to assure careful administrative consideration 'would be relevant even if the Secretary's decision were unreviewable.' 502 F.2d, at 88–89, n. 14.

"The necessity that the reviewing court refrain from substitution of its judgment for that of the Secretary thus helps define the permissible scope of review. Except in what must be the rare case, the court's review should be confined to examination of the 'reasons' statement, and the determination whether the statement, without more, evinces that the Secretary's decision is so irrational as to constitute the decision arbitrary and capricious. Thus, review may not extend to cognizance or trial of a complaining member's challenges to the factual bases for the Secretary's conclusion either that no violations occurred or that they did not affect the outcome of the election. The full trappings of adversary trial-type hearings would be defiant of congressional objectives not to permit individuals to block or delay resolution of post-election disputes, but rather 'to settle as quickly as practicable the cloud on the incumbents' titles to office'; and 'to protect unions from frivolous litigation and unnecessary interference with their elections.' 'If * * * the Court concludes * * * there is a rational and defensible basis [stated in the reasons statement] for [the Secretary's] determination, then that should be an end of this matter, for it is not the function of the Court to determine whether or not the case should be brought or what its outcome would be.' *DeVito II,* supra, at 2683." 421 U.S. at 571–73, 95 S.Ct. at 1860.

WIRTZ v. HOTEL, MOTEL AND CLUB EMPLOYEES UNION, LOCAL 6

Supreme Court of the United States, 1968.
391 U.S. 492, 88 S.Ct. 1743, 20 L.Ed.2d 763.

MR. JUSTICE BRENNAN delivered the opinion of the Court.

This action was brought by petitioner, the Secretary of Labor, in the District Court for the Southern District of New York for a judgment declaring void the May 1965 election of officers conducted by respondent

Local 6, and ordering a new election under the Secretary's supervision. The action is authorized by § 402(b) of the Labor-Management Reporting and Disclosure Act of 1959 * * *. The Secretary charged that a bylaw of the Local which limited eligibility for major elective offices to union members who hold or have previously held elective office was not a "reasonable qualification" within the intendment of the provision of § 401(e) of the Act * * * that "every member in good standing shall be eligible to be a candidate and to hold office (subject to * * * reasonable qualifications uniformly imposed) * * *." He charged further that enforcement of the bylaw "may have affected the outcome" of the election within the meaning of § 402(c) * * *.

The District Court, after hearing, entered a judgment which declared that the prior-office requirement was not reasonable, but also declared that it could not be found that its enforcement in violation of § 401(e) "may have affected the outcome" of the election. The court therefore refused to set aside the May 1965 election and to order a new election under the Secretary's supervision, but did grant an injunction against enforcement of the bylaw in future elections. 265 F.Supp. 510. The Court of Appeals for the Second Circuit reversed the provision of the judgment which declared the bylaw not to be reasonable and its enforcement violative of § 401(e), and set aside the injunction.[4] The court found it unnecessary in that circumstance to decide whether enforcement of the bylaw at the election may have affected the outcome. 381 F.2d 500. We granted certiorari. * * * We hold that the restriction was not reasonable and that its enforcement may have affected the outcome of the election. The Secretary is therefore entitled to an order directing a new election under his supervision.

I.

Title IV is one of the seven titles of the Labor-Management Reporting and Disclosure Act (LMRDA). Earlier this Term, we observed that "Title IV's special function in furthering the overall goals of the LMRDA is to insure 'free and democratic' elections. The legislative history shows that Congress weighed how best to legislate against revealed abuses in union elections without departing needlessly from its long-standing policy against unnecessary governmental intrusion into internal union affairs." Wirtz v. Local 153, Glass Bottle Blowers Assn., 389 U.S. 463, 470–471, 88 S.Ct. 643, 647–648, 19 L.Ed.2d 705. The Court of Appeals, however, in considering the reasonableness of the bylaw, emphasized only the congressional concern not to intervene unnecessarily in internal union affairs, stating that "[i]n deciding the issue of reasonableness we must keep in mind the fact that the Act did not purport to take away from labor unions the governance of their own internal affairs and hand that governance over either to the courts or to the Secretary of Labor. The Act strictly limits official interference in the internal affairs of unions." 381 F.2d, at 504. But this emphasis overlooks

---

4. * * * The District Court did not consider other violations alleged in the complaint because no member of Local 6 had first invoked union remedies to redress them pursuant to § 402(a). In light of our decision we need not consider the Secretary's argument that a member's protest triggers a § 402 en- forcement action in which the Secretary may challenge any violation of § 401 discovered in his investigation of the member's complaint and brought to the attention of the union. Cf. Wirtz v. Local Union No. 125, Laborers' Int'l Union, etc., 389 U.S. 477, 481–482, 88 S.Ct. 639, 641–642, 19 L.Ed.2d 716.

the fact that the congressional concern to avoid unnecessary intervention was balanced against the policy expressed in the Act to protect the public interest by assuring that union elections would be conducted in accordance with democratic principles. As we said in Wirtz v. Local 153, Glass Bottle Blowers Assn., supra, 389 U.S. at 473, 88 S.Ct. at 649, decided after the Court of Appeals decided this case, " * * * Congress, although committed to minimal intervention, was obviously equally committed to making that intervention, once warranted, effective in carrying out the basic aim of Title IV." Thus, "the freedom allowed unions to run their own elections was reserved for those elections which conform to the democratic principles written into § 401." Id., at 471, 88 S.Ct. at 648. In a companion case, Wirtz v. Local Union No. 125, Laborers' Int'l Union, etc., 389 U.S. 477, 483, 88 S.Ct. 639, 642, 19 L.Ed.2d 716, we said that the provisions of § 401 are "necessary protections of the public interest as well as of the rights and interests of union members." * * *

A pervasive theme in the congressional debates about the election provisions was that revelations of corruption, dictatorial practices and racketeering in some unions investigated by Congress indicated a need to protect the rights of rank-and-file members to participate fully in the operation of their union through processes of democratic self-government, and, through the election process, to keep the union leadership responsive to the membership. This theme is made explicit in the reports of the Labor Committees of both Houses of Congress. It is reflected in the discrete provisions of Title IV and also of Title I, the "Bill of Rights" for union members. * * * Title IV, and particularly § 401, was the vehicle by which Congress expressed its policy. That section prescribes standards to govern the conduct of union elections: International union elections must be held at least once every five years and local elections at least once every three years. Elections must be by secret ballot. Specific provisions insure equality of treatment in the mailing of campaign literature; require adequate safeguards to insure a fair election; guarantee a "reasonable opportunity" for the nomination of candidates, the right to vote, and the right of every member in good standing to be a candidate subject to "reasonable qualifications uniformly imposed," the guarantee with which we are concerned in this case. * * * Furthermore, although Congress emphatically gave unions the primary responsibility for enforcing compliance with the Act, Congress also settled enforcement authority on the Secretary of Labor to insure that serious violations would not go unremedied and the public interest go unvindicated. * * *[7]

Congress plainly did not intend that the authorization in § 401(e) of "reasonable qualifications uniformly imposed" should be given a broad reach. The contrary is implicit in the legislative history of the section and in its wording that "every member in good standing shall be eligible to be a candidate and to hold office * * *." This conclusion is buttressed by other

7. * * *

For the general background and legislative history of the Act, see generally Aaron, The Labor-Management Reporting and Disclosure Act of 1959, 73 Harv.L.Rev. 851 (1960); Cox, Internal Affairs of Labor Unions Under the Labor Reform Act of 1959, 58 Mich.L.Rev. 819 (1960); Levitan & Loewenberg, The Politics and Provisions of the Landrum-Griffin Act, in Regulating Union Government 28 (M. Estey, P. Taft, & M. Wagner eds. 1964); Rezler, Union Elections: The Background of Title IV of LMRDA, in Symposium on LMRDA 475 (R. Slovenko ed. 1961).

provisions of the Act which stress freedom of members to nominate candidates for office.[8] Unduly restrictive candidacy qualifications can result in the abuses of entrenched leadership that the LMRDA was expressly enacted to curb. * * *

It follows therefore that whether the Local 6 by law is a "reasonable qualification" within the meaning of § 401(e) must be measured in terms of its consistency with the Act's command to unions to conduct "free and democratic" union elections.

II.

Local 6 has 27,000 members, assets of $2,300,000, and assets in welfare, pension, and medical funds of some $30,000,000. The Local represents bartenders, maids, dining room employees, and kitchen employees of hotels, motels, and private clubs in New York. It is structured into six geographic districts, each with five craft departments, for hotel and motel employees, and a seventh district for private clubs. The various crafts have their own representatives in each hotel, motel, or club. An Assembly, composed in 1965 of 372 members, meets four times a year and is the basic representative body. The delegates are elected from among the craft units within each of the seven districts on the basis of one delegate for each 75 members of a craft. The Assembly in turn elects from its membership an Executive Board on the basis of one board member for each 500 members, augmented by principal officers and by nonvoting business agents, 31 of whom are elected from the seven districts and others who are appointed by the Assembly. The Executive Board meets monthly. There is also an Administrative Board made up of, in addition to general officers, seven district vice-presidents elected from the districts and elected or appointed delegates to the New York Hotel and Motel Trades Council. Finally there are four paid full-time general officers—President, Secretary-Treasurer, General Organizer, and Recording Secretary, all elected by the membership at large. Terms of office are three years. In practice the affairs of the Local are administered by the general officers and the Administrative Board.

The bylaw under challenge[9] limited eligibility for positions as a general officer, district vice-president or elected business agent to members of either the Assembly or the Executive Board or members who, "at some time in the past, have served at least one term on either the Executive Board, the Assembly, or the old Shop Delegates Council." The Shop Delegates Council was abolished in 1951 and replaced by the Assembly. These qualifications

---

8. See [Section 401(e)]: "a reasonable opportunity shall be given for the nomination of candidates * * *"; [Section 101(a)(1)]: "Every member of a labor organization shall have equal rights and privileges within such organization to nominate candidates * * *."

9. The Local has amended its bylaw to liberalize the candidacy requirements (making eligible department delegates and members of five years' good standing) and the amended bylaw was to govern an election scheduled for May 16, 1968. The District Court held the amended bylaw also unreasonable, but that ruling is not before us. 265 F.Supp., at 522–523. In any event, respondent's argument

that the amendment renders this case moot is foreclosed by Wirtz v. Local 153, Glass Bottle Blowers Assn., supra, 389 U.S. at 475–476, 88 S.Ct. at 650–651. ["We * * * hold that when the Secretary of Labor proves the existence of a § 401 violation that may have affected the outcome of a challenged election, the fact that the union has already conducted another unsupervised election does not deprive the Secretary of his right to a court order declaring the challenged election void and directing that a new election be conducted under his supervision." 389 U.S. at 475–76, 88 S.Ct. at 650.] * * *

apply, however, only to members who stand for election for office. Vacancies may not always be filled by election; the general officers may in such cases fill vacancies by appointment of members without prior office-holding experience, with the approval of the Executive Board and the Assembly.

By the terms of the bylaw, in the May 1965 election only 1,725 of the 27,000 members were eligible to run for office. Of these, 1,182, or 70%, were eligible only because of service on the Shop Delegates Council which had been abolished 14 years earlier. Thus, only 543 of the eligibles, some 2% of the membership, had at some time or other served at least a term in the Assembly, designated in the bylaws as "the highest body of the Union," since its creation in 1951.

Five elections were held between 1951 and 1965. All of them were won by the "Administration Party," whose slates were composed largely of incumbents. Until the May 1965 election there was only token opposition to those slates. Early in 1965, however, a "Membership Party" was organized. It attempted to field a slate of candidates to oppose the "Administration Party" slate for, among others, the four general offices and for 13 of the 27 vice-president and business agent posts. But enforcement of the bylaw disqualified the "Membership Party" candidates for the general office of Secretary-Treasurer and for eight of the district offices. Other "Membership Party" nominees were disqualified for lack of good standing. In result, the "Membership Party" slate was reduced to candidates for the offices of president, general organizer, and business agent in two districts. The "Administration Party" ran a full slate and elected its candidates by margins up to 7 to 1. Following the election, "Membership Party" members protested the validity of the bylaw and, after unsuccessfully exhausting internal union remedies as required by § 402(a)(1), filed the complaint with the Secretary of Labor as authorized by that section which in due course led to the Secretary's filing this action.

Plainly, given the objective of Title IV, a candidacy limitation which renders 93% of union members ineligible for office can hardly be a "reasonable qualification." The practical effect of the limitation was described by the District Court:

> "In practice it was not possible to be elected to the Assembly except with the blessing of the Administration Party conferred by selection to run for the Assembly on Row A [of a voting machine]. This was doubtless in large part because there was never a full slate of opposing candidates for the Assembly. The candidates to run on Row A for the Assembly were selected by the incumbent group of officers and were put in nomination after caucuses of invited members, attended by officers. It was only natural that candidates selected to run on Row A for the Assembly would be supporters of the administration. All candidates on Row A were pledged to support each other. Dissidents could not be elected to the Assembly. * * *
>
> "Since 1951 the only way new members could become eligible for office was to win election to the Assembly. But in this period the only candidates which won such election were those who ran on Row A, the administration ticket. The only way to run on Row A was to be selected by the administration. Thus, dissidents could not become eligible to be opposing candidates

for office and effective opposition was thus sharply curtailed." 265 F.Supp., at 516, 520.

The Local attempts to defend the restriction as a "reasonable qualification" by citing the concededly impressive record of the "Administration Party" in running the Local's affairs since 1951. There is no reason to doubt that the Local has enjoyed enlightened and aggressive leadership. But that fact does not sustain the Local's burden. Congress designed Title IV to curb the possibility of abuse by benevolent as well as malevolent entrenched leaderships.

The Local also argues that the high annual turnover in membership, the diverse interests of the various craft units and the multimillion-dollar finances of the Local justify the bylaw as a measure to limit the holding of important union offices to those members who have acquired a familiarity with the Local's problems by service in lesser offices. That argument was persuasive with the Court of Appeals, which said:

> "[I]t is not self-evident that basic minimum principles of union democracy require that every union entrust the administration of its affairs to untrained and inexperienced rank and file members. * * * It does not seem to us to be surprising that the union should hesitate to permit a cook or a waiter or a dishwasher without any training or experience in the management of union affairs to take on responsibility for the complex and difficult problems of administration of this union. * * *

> "We do not believe that it is unreasonable for a union to condition candidacy for offices of greater responsibility upon a year [sic] of the kind of experience and training that a union member will acquire in a position such as that of membership in Local 6's Assembly." 381 F.2d, at 505.

That argument is not, however, persuasive to us. It assumes that rank-and-file union members are unable to distinguish qualified from unqualified candidates for particular offices without a demonstration of a candidate's performance in other offices. But Congress' model of democratic elections was political elections in this country, and they are not based on any such assumption. Rather, in those elections the assumption is that voters will exercise common sense and judgment in casting their ballots. Local 6 made no showing that citizens assumed to make discriminating judgments in public elections cannot be relied on to make such judgments when voting as union members. Indeed the Local is not faithful to its own premise. A member need not have prior service in union office to be *appointed* to a vacancy in any office. Also, many members of the powerful Administrative Board become such by reason of their *appointments* as delegates to the New York Hotel and Motel Trades Council, another example of important officers who are not required to have had prior service. Moreover, as the District Court found, "once such an officer is appointed, he automatically becomes a member of the Assembly and immediately becomes eligible to run thereafter for any union office. This enables the incumbent group to qualify members for elective office by a procedure not available to dissidents." 265 F.Supp., at 520.

The bylaw is virtually unique in trade union practice. It has its counterpart in some other locals of this International Union but not in all; and it is not a requirement included in the International's constitution.

Among other large unions only the International Ladies Garment Workers Union has a similar restriction, but that union provides members with the alternative of a union-conducted course in union management. Of 66 unions reporting receipts over $1,000,000 for 1964, only locals of ILGWU and Local 6 reported having this requirement.

Control by incumbents through devices which operate in the manner of this bylaw is precisely what Congress legislated against in the LMRDA. * * * Accordingly, we hold that the bylaw is not a "reasonable qualification" within the meaning of § 401(e).

III.

The Secretary was not entitled to an order for a supervised election unless the enforcement of the bylaw "may have affected" the outcome of the May 1965 election, § 402(c), 29 U.S.C.A. § 482(c). The "may have affected" language appeared in the bill passed by the Senate, S. 1555. The bill passed by the House, H.R. 8342, and the Kennedy-Ervin bill introduced in the Senate, S. 505, required the more stringent showing that the violation actually "affected" the outcome. The difference was resolved in conference by the adoption of the "may have affected" language. Senator Goldwater explained,

> "The Kennedy-Ervin bill (S. 505), as introduced, authorized the court to declare an election void only if the violation of section 401 actually affected the outcome of the election rather than may have affected such outcome. The difficulty of proving such an actuality would be so great as to render the professed remedy practically worthless. Minority members in committee secured an amendment correcting this glaring defect and the amendment is contained in the conference report." 105 Cong.Rec. 19765.

The provision that the finding should be made "upon a preponderance of the evidence" was left undisturbed when the change was made. That provision is readily satisfied, however, as is the congressional purpose in changing "affected" to "may have affected" in order to avoid rendering the proposed "remedy practically worthless," by ascribing to a proved violation of § 401 the effect of establishing a prima facie case that the violation "may have affected" the outcome. This effect may of course be met by evidence which supports a finding that the violation did not affect the result. This construction is peculiarly appropriate when the violation of § 401, as here, takes the form of a substantial exclusion of candidates from the ballot. In such case we adopt the reasoning of the Court of Appeals for the Second Circuit in Wirtz v. Local Unions 410, IUOE, 366 F.2d 438, 443.

> "The proviso was intended to free unions from the disruptive effect of a voided election unless there is a meaningful relation between a violation of the Act and results of a particular election. For example, if the Secretary's investigation revealed that 20 percent of the votes in an election had been tampered with, but that all officers had won by an 8–1 margin, the proviso should prevent upsetting the election. * * * But in the cases at bar, the alleged violations caused the exclusion of willing candidates from the ballots. In such circumstances, there can be no tangible evidence available of the effect of this exclusion on the election; whether the outcome would have been different depends upon whether the suppressed candidates were potent vote-getters, whether more union members would have voted had candidates

not been suppressed, and so forth. Since any proof relating to effect on outcome must necessarily be speculative, we do not think Congress meant to place as stringent a burden on the Secretary as the district courts imposed here."

The District Court acknowledged that the issue was "governed by the teaching of Wirtz v. Local Unions 410, etc." and correctly held that under its principle "a violation by disqualification of candidates does not automatically require a finding that the outcome may have been affected." 265 F.Supp. at 520–521. We cannot make out from the court's opinion, however, whether the violation was regarded as establishing a prima facie case that the outcome was affected. But if we assume that the court accorded the violation that effect, we disagree with its conclusion that the evidence met that case. The court cited the substantial defeat of those "Membership Party" candidates who did run, the lack of evidence that any of the disqualified nominees was a proven vote-getter, the lack of a substantial grievance or issue asserted by the "Membership Party" against the incumbents and the overwhelming advantage enjoyed by the "Administration Party" of having a full slate of candidates. 265 F.Supp., at 521. We do not think that these considerations constitute proof supporting the court's conclusion. None of the factors relied on is tangible evidence against the reasonable possibility that the wholesale exclusion of members did affect the outcome. Nothing in them necessarily contradicts the logical inference that some or all of the disqualified candidates might have been elected had they been permitted to run. The defeat suffered by the few candidates allowed to run proves nothing about the performance that might have been made by those who did not. The District Court properly perceived that the bylaw necessarily inhibited the membership generally from considering making the race, but held that any inference from this was disproved by "the heavy vote in favor of the administration candidates * * *." Ibid. But since 93% of the membership was ineligible under the invalid bylaw it is impossible to know that the election would not have attracted many more candidates but for the bylaw. In short, the considerations relied on by the court are pure conjecture, not evidence. We therefore conclude that the prima facie case established by the violation was not met by evidence which supports the District Court's finding that the violation did not affect the result.

The judgment of the Court of Appeals is reversed and the case is remanded to the District Court with direction to order a new election under the Secretary's supervision.

MR. JUSTICE MARSHALL took no part in the consideration or decision of this case.

Note

Union constitutional provisions regarding eligibility for candidacy for union office frequently impose requirements designed, at least in part, to encourage involvement in union affairs and ensure the election of individuals who have some degree of familiarity with those affairs. For example, the United Steelworkers' constitution provides that eligibility for local union office is limited to individuals who have attended at least one-half of the regular meetings of the local for three years previous to the election. Unlike the rule in Hotel Employees, the Steelworkers' eligibility rule does not limit eligibility to those in the union hierarchy; an individual interested in running for office can qualify merely by attending the requisite number of meetings. Is it, therefore, a "reasonable qualification" to so limit eligibility?

In Local 3489, United Steelworkers v. Usery, 429 U.S. 305, 97 S.Ct. 611, 50 L.Ed.2d 502 (1977), the Court, resolving a conflict in the circuits, held the Steelworkers' eligibility rule to be violative of Section 401(e):

"＊ ＊ ＊ Like the bylaw in *Hotel Employees,* an attendance requirement that results in the exclusion of 96.5% of the members from candidacy for union office hardly seems to be a reasonable qualification consistent with the goal of free and democratic elections. A requirement having that result obviously severely restricts the free choice of the membership in selecting their leaders.

"Petitioners argue however that the bylaw held violative of § 401(e) in *Hotel Employees* differs significantly from the attendance rule here. Under the *Hotel Employees* bylaw no member could assure by his own efforts that he would be eligible for union office, since others controlled the criterion for eligibility. Here, on the other hand, a member can assure himself of eligibility for candidacy by attending some 18 brief meetings over a three-year period. In other words, the union would have its rule treated not as excluding a category of member from eligibility, but simply as mandating a procedure to be followed by any member who wishes to be a candidate.

"Even examined from this perspective, however, the rule has a restrictive effect on union democracy. In the absence of a permanent opposition party within the union, opposition to the incumbent leadership is likely to emerge in response to particular issues at different times, and member interest in changing union leadership is therefore likely to be at its highest only shortly before elections. Thus it is probable that to require that a member decide upon a potential candidacy at least 18 months in advance of an election when no issues exist to prompt that decision may not foster but discourage candidacies and to that extent impair the general membership's freedom to oust incumbents in favor of new leadership.

"Nor are we persuaded by the Union's argument that the Secretary has failed to show an antidemocratic effect because he has not shown that the incumbent leaders of the Union became 'entrenched' in their offices as a consequence of the operation of the attendance rule. ＊ ＊ ＊

"＊ ＊ ＊ Congress chose to guarantee union democracy by regulating not the results of a union's electoral procedure, but the procedure itself. Congress decided that if the elections are 'free and democratic,' the members themselves are able to correct abuse of power by entrenched leadership. Procedures that unduly restrict free choice among candidates are forbidden without regard to their success or failure in maintaining corrupt leadership.

"Petitioners next argue that the rule is reasonable within § 401(e) because it encourages attendance at union meetings, and assures more qualified officers by limiting election to those who have demonstrated an interest in union affairs, and are familiar with union problems. But the rule has plainly not served these goals. It has obviously done little to encourage attendance at meetings, which continue to attract only a handful of members.[8] Even as to the more limited goal of encouraging the attendance of potential dissident candidates, very few members, as we have said, are likely to see themselves as such sufficiently far in advance of the election to be spurred to attendance by the rule." 429 U.S. at 310–312, 97 S.Ct. at 615–16.

LOCAL NO. 82, FURNITURE AND PIANO MOVING DRIVERS v. CROWLEY

Supreme Court of the United States, 1984.
467 U.S. 526, 104 S.Ct. 2557, 81 L.Ed.2d 457.

JUSTICE BRENNAN delivered the opinion of the Court.

The Labor-Management Reporting and Disclosure Act of 1959 * * * was Congress' first major attempt to regulate the internal affairs of labor unions. Title I of the Act provides a statutory "Bill of Rights" for union members, including various protections for members involved in union elections, with enforcement and appropriate remedies available in district court. Title IV, in contrast, provides an elaborate post-election procedure aimed solely at protecting union democracy through free and democratic elections, with primary responsibility for enforcement lodged with the Secretary of Labor. Resolution of the question presented by this case requires that we address the conflict that exists between the separate enforcement mechanisms included in these two titles. In particular, we must determine whether suits alleging violations of Title I may properly be maintained in district court during the course of a union election.

The Court of Appeals approved a preliminary injunction issued by the District Court that enjoined an ongoing union election and ordered the staging of a new election pursuant to procedures promulgated by the court. After reviewing the complex statutory scheme created by Congress, we conclude that such judicial interference in an ongoing union election is not appropriate relief under § 102 of Title I * * *. We therefore reverse the Court of Appeals.

I

Local No. 82, Furniture and Piano Moving, Furniture Store Drivers, Helpers, Warehousemen, and Packers (Local 82) represents approximately 700 employees engaged in the furniture moving business in the Boston, Massachusetts area. The union is governed by a seven-member executive board whose officers, pursuant to § 401(b) of the LMRDA * * * must be chosen by election no less than once every three years. These elections, consistent with the executive board's discretion under the union's bylaws and constitution, have traditionally been conducted by mail referendum balloting. The dispute giving rise to the present case stems from the union election that was regularly scheduled for the last two months of 1980.

On November 9, 1980, Local 82 held a meeting to nominate candidates for positions on its executive board. The meeting generated considerable interest, in part because dissident members of the union were attempting to

---

8. Attendance at Local 3489's meetings averages 47 out of approximately 660 members. There is no indication in the record that this total represents a significant increase over attendance before the institution of the challenged rule.

turn the incumbent union officials out of office. Two aspects of the controversial meeting are especially important for present purposes. First, admission to the meeting was restricted to those members who could produce a computerized receipt showing that their dues had been paid up to date. Several union members, including respondent Jerome Crowley, were prohibited from entering the meeting because they did not have such dues receipts in their possession. Second, during the actual nominations process, there was disagreement relating to the office for which respondent John Lynch had been nominated. At the close of nominations, petitioner Bart Griffiths, the union's incumbent secretary-treasurer, declared himself the only candidate nominated for that office; at the same time, he included Lynch among the candidates selected to run for union president.

Several dissatisfied members of the union, now respondents before this Court, filed a protest with the union. On November 20, their protest was denied by Local 82.[3] Election ballots were thereafter distributed to all members of the union, who were instructed to mark and return the ballots by mail so that they would arrive in a designated post office box by 9:00 a.m. on December 13, 1980, at which time they were scheduled to be counted. Respondent Lynch's name appeared on the ballot as a candidate for president, and not for secretary-treasurer.

On December 1, 1980, after the distribution of ballots had been completed, the respondents filed this action in the United States District Court for the District of Massachusetts. They alleged, *inter alia*, that Local 82 and its officers had violated several provisions of Title I of the LMRDA, and sought a preliminary injunction. In particular, the respondents claimed that restricting admission to the nominations meeting to those members who could produce computerized dues receipts violated their "equal rights * * * to nominate candidates [and] to attend membership meetings" under § 101(a)(1) of the Act, as well as their right freely to express views at meetings of the union under § 101(a)(2) of the Act. They also alleged that the union and its officers had violated § 101(a)(1) by failing to recognize respondent Lynch as a candidate for secretary-treasurer.[6]

After preliminary papers were filed, on December 12 the District Court issued a temporary restraining order to preserve the status quo and to protect its own jurisdiction. * * * Given that the next morning (December 13) was the preestablished deadline for voting, many, if not most, of the ballots had already been returned by the union's voting members. Nonetheless, the court noted that federal court jurisdiction was available under § 102 * * * for claims alleging discriminatory application of union rules.

---

3. The respondents also filed protests with the International Brotherhood of Teamsters, Chauffeurs, Warehousemen and Helpers of America, the international union with which Local 82 is affiliated, and with Teamsters Joint Council 10, the regional body containing Local 82. No action was ever taken by the international union, and a hearing scheduled by the regional body for December 23, 1980 was cancelled after the present lawsuit was filed.

6. Several other claims under both Title I and Title IV of the LMRDA were asserted in the respondents' original complaint. These included allegations that the union failed to notify members about the nominations meeting, [and] that the union unlawfully limited candidate eligibility to members who had timely paid their dues during the preceding 24 months * * *. For a variety of reasons, however, the District Court refused to grant preliminary relief on * * * these claims, and they are not now before the Court.

Moreover, the court's order specifically required that the ballots be sealed and delivered to the court, thereby preventing the petitioners from counting the ballots until a final determination could be made on the motion for a preliminary injunction.

Several days of hearings on the preliminary injunction, and several months of negotiations concerning an appropriate court order to accompany that injunction, followed. Finally, on July 13, 1981, the District Court issued a preliminary injunction accompanied by a memorandum opinion. 521 F.Supp. 614 (Mass.1981). The court first addressed more fully the petitioners' argument that, because the challenged conduct concerned the procedures for conducting union elections, the respondents' exclusive remedy was to file a complaint with the Secretary of Labor under Title IV. The court rejected this argument, noting that, "at least with respect to actions challenging pre-election conduct, Title I of the LMRDA establishes an alternative enforcement mechanism for remedying conduct interfering with a member's right to engage in activities associated with union democracy." *Id.*, at 621 (footnote omitted). Therefore, the court concluded, it could properly invoke its jurisdiction under Title I, if only for those claims concerning dues receipts and the nomination of respondent Lynch that are now before this Court. Id., at 622–623. Because the suit concerned disputes arising out of a nominations meeting conducted in preparation for a union election, and given that the court had issued a temporary restraining order barring actual completion of the election, Title I jurisdiction could properly be asserted over this "pre-election conduct." Id., at 621, n. 12.

After concluding that the respondents had demonstrated a substantial likelihood of success on their claims,[7] the court issued its * * * injunction. The court explicitly intended to issue an order that "interfere[d] as little as possible with the nomination and election procedures" required by the union's constitution and bylaws, *id.*, at 634; moreover, the terms of the preliminary injunction were derived in large part from an ongoing process of negotiations and hearings that the court had conducted with the parties during the preceding six months. Nonetheless, the order declared the ballots cast in December 1980 to be "legally without effect," id., at 636, n. *, and provided detailed procedures to be followed by the union during a new nominations meeting and a subsequent election. Among other things, the order selected an outside group of arbitrators to conduct and supervise the election, and set forth eligibility requirements for attending the nominations meeting, being a candidate for office, and voting. The order also provided that it would remain in effect until further order of the District Court.

---

7. In particular, the court found that the dues receipt requirement for entry into the nominations meeting was "suddenly announced," was applied "in a discriminatory fashion," and was "imposed in retaliation for [the respondents'] expressed intention to nominate candidates to oppose the incumbent Local officers and with the objective of suppressing dissent within the Local." 521 F.Supp., at 627. The court also found that, despite being listed as a candidate for union president, respondent Lynch had actually been nominated for secretary-treasurer. Ibid. Finally, the court found that irreparable harm to the respondents would result if a new nominations meeting and election were not held, that the burdens imposed on the petitioners by preliminary relief were sufficiently mitigated by the full hearing accorded their arguments, and that the public interest in union democracy would be served by granting such relief. Id., at 627–628. None of these findings is being challenged before this Court. See n. 9, infra.

The petitioners appealed, and the Secretary of Labor, who until then had not participated in the proceedings, intervened on their behalf. They argued that the District Court lacked authority under Title I to enjoin the tabulation of ballots and order new nominations and elections under court supervision. The Court of Appeals rejected these arguments, however, and affirmed in all respects. 679 F.2d 978 (CA1 1982). It agreed with the District Court that Title I remedies are not foreclosed when violations of Title I occur during the course of an election. The court also held that § 403 of the Act, which explicitly provides that Title IV's remedies are exclusive for elections that are "already conducted" * * * does not apply until all the ballots have actually been tabulated.[9]

Writing in dissent, Judge Campbell was "unable to read Title I as extending so far as to allow a district court, once balloting has commenced, to invalidate an election and order a new one under its supervision and under terms and conditions extemporized by the courts and parties." 679 F.2d at 1004. He believed that "the proper accommodation between Title I and Title IV requires consideration not only of the stage which the election process has reached but [also] the nature of the relief" requested and granted. Id., at 1005.

Because of the confusion evident among the lower federal courts that have tried to reconcile the remedial provisions under Title I and Title IV of the Act,[10] we granted certiorari. 459 U.S. 1168, 103 S.Ct. 813, 74 L.Ed.2d 1012 (1983). We now reverse.[11]

II

To examine fully the relationship between the respective enforcement provisions of Title I and Title IV of the LMRDA, it is necessary first to

---

9. The Court of Appeals further concluded that "the district court committed no clear error" when finding that there existed substantial proof that the petitioners violated the provisions of Title I by imposing the dues receipt requirement and by mishandling the nomination of respondent Lynch. 679 F.2d, at 995. See n. 7, supra. The petitioners have not challenged that ruling in this Court. Our decision therefore assumes that the respondents have demonstrated a substantial likelihood of success on their two Title I claims.

10. See, e.g., Kupau v. Yamamoto, 622 F.2d 449 (CA9 1980); Driscoll v. International Union of Operating Engineers, 484 F.2d 682 (CA7 1973); Schonfeld v. Penza, 477 F.2d 899 (CA2 1973); McDonough v. Local 825, International Union of Operating Engineers, 470 F.2d 261 (CA3 1972). See also, e.g., James, Union Democracy and the LMRDA: Autocracy and Insurgency in National Union Elections, 13 Harv.C.R.–C.L.L.Rev. 247 (1978); Comment, Titles I and IV of the LMRDA: A Resolution of the Conflict of Remedies, 42 U.Chi.L.Rev. 166 (1974); Note, Pre-election Remedies Under the Landrum-Griffin Act: The "Twilight Zone" Between Election Rights Under Title IV and the Guarantees of Titles I and V, 74 Colum.L.Rev. 1105 (1974).

11. * * *

[T]he respondents claim that the entire case is moot because not only has the election ordered by the District Court taken place, but also the term to be served by the officers chosen in that election has now elapsed. We have previously held, however, that the intervention of another election does not terminate the Secretary of Labor's authority under Title IV of the LMRDA to seek invalidation of the preceding election. Wirtz v. Bottle Blowers Assn., 389 U.S. 463, 88 S.Ct. 643, 19 L.Ed.2d 705 (1968); Wirtz v. Laborers' Union, 389 U.S. 477, 88 S.Ct. 639, 19 L.Ed.2d 716 (1968). If the District Court acted beyond its authority in ordering and supervising a new election, then the ballots that were never counted in December 1980 but were sealed pursuant to the District Court's order could be tabulated, and the Secretary's remedies under Title IV would come into play. Moreover, we note that there are still pending several important collateral matters, including claims for damages, attorney's fees, and costs, that are dependent upon the propriety of the District Court's preliminary injunction. * * * We have no doubt, therefore, that the present controversy has not been mooted by intervening circumstances.

summarize the relevant statutory provisions and Congress' principal purposes in their enactment. The LMRDA was "the product of congressional concern with widespread abuses of power by union leadership." Finnegan v. Leu, 456 U.S. 431, 435, 102 S.Ct. 1867, 1870, 72 L.Ed.2d 239 (1982). Although the Act "had a history tracing back more than two decades," ibid., and was directly generated by several years of congressional hearings, see S.Rep. No. 187, 86th Cong., 1st Sess., 2 (1959), U.S.Code Cong. & Admin.News 1959, p. 2318, many specific provisions of the Act did not find their way into the statute until the proposed legislation was fully considered on the floor of the Senate, 456 U.S., at 435, n. 4, 102 S.Ct., at 1870, n. 4. It should not be surprising, therefore, that the interaction between various provisions that were finally included in the Act has generated considerable uncertainty.

A

Chief among the causes for this confusion is Title I of the Act, which provides union members with an exhaustive "Bill of Rights" enforceable in federal court.   *   *   * In particular, Title I is designed to guarantee every union member equal rights to vote and otherwise participate in union decisions, freedom from unreasonable restrictions on speech and assembly, and protection from improper discipline. See Finnegan v. Leu, supra, 456 U.S., at 435–436, 102 S.Ct., at 1870–1871; Steelworkers v. Sadlowski, 457 U.S. 102, 103, 109–110, 102 S.Ct. 2339, 2341, 2344–2345, 72 L.Ed.2d 707 (1982). Given these purposes, there can be no doubt that the protections afforded by Title I extend to union members while they participate in union elections.   *   *   *

As first introduced by Senator McClellan on the floor of the Senate, see 105 Cong.Rec. 6469–6476, 6492–6493 (1959), Title I empowered the Secretary of Labor to seek injunctions and other relief in federal district court to enforce the rights guaranteed to union members. A few days later, however, the McClellan amendment was replaced by a substitute amendment offered by Senator Kuchel. See id., at 6693–6694, 6717–6727. Among the principal changes made by this substitute was to provide for enforcement of Title I through suits by individual union members in federal district court. Id., at 6717, 6720. As so amended, the legislation was endorsed in the Senate by a vote of 77–14, id., at 6727, and was quickly accepted without substantive change by the House, see H.R. 8400, 86th Cong., 1st Sess., § 102 (1959); H.R. Conf.Rep. No. 1147, 86th Cong., 1st Sess., 31 (1959). In relevant part, therefore, § 102 of the Act now provides:

> "Any person whose rights secured by the provisions of this [title] have been infringed by any violation of this [title] may bring a civil action in a district court of the United States for such relief (including injunctions) as may be appropriate."   *   *   *

Standing by itself, this jurisdictional provision suggests that individual union members may properly maintain a Title I suit whenever rights guaranteed by that title have been violated. At the same time, however, § 102 explicitly limits the relief that may be ordered by a district court to that which is "appropriate" to any given situation. See Hall v. Cole, 412 U.S. 1, 10–11, 93 S.Ct. 1943, 1948–1949, 36 L.Ed.2d 702 (1973).

B

Nor would it be appropriate to interpret the enforcement and remedial provisions of Title I in isolation. In particular, Title IV of the LMRDA specifically regulates the conduct of elections for union officers, and therefore protects many of the same rights as does Title I. See §§ 401–403 * * *

Although Congress meant to further this basic policy with a minimum of interference in the internal affairs of unions, see Calhoon [v. Harvey, 379 U.S. 134, 140, 85 S.Ct. 292, 296, 13 L.Ed.2d 190 (1964)], § 402 of Title IV contains its own comprehensive administrative and judicial procedure for enforcing the standards established in that title of the Act * * *. See Dunlop v. Bachowski, 421 U.S. 560, 95 S.Ct. 1851, 44 L.Ed.2d 377 (1975); Trbovich v. United Mine Workers, 404 U.S. 528, 531, 92 S.Ct. 630, 632, 30 L.Ed.2d 686 (1972); *Calhoon,* supra, at 138–140, 85 S.Ct., at 295–296. "Any union member who alleges a violation [of Title IV] may initiate the enforcement procedure. He must first exhaust any internal remedies available under the constitution and bylaws of his union. Then he may file a complaint with the Secretary of Labor, who 'shall investigate' the complaint. Finally, if the Secretary finds probable cause to believe a violation has occurred, he 'shall * * * bring a civil action against the labor organization' in federal district court, to set aside the election if it has already been held, and to direct and supervise a new election." *Trbovich,* supra, at 531, 92 S.Ct., at 632 (quoting § 402 * * *). See *Calhoon,* supra, at 140, 85 S.Ct., at 296. Significantly, the court may invalidate an election already held, and order the Secretary to supervise a new election, only if the violation of Title IV "may have affected the outcome" of the previous election. § 482(c) * * *.

Congress also included in Title IV an exclusivity provision that explains the relationship between the enforcement procedures established for violations of Title IV and the remedies available for violations of potentially overlapping state and federal laws. In relevant part, § 403 of the LMRDA provides:

> "Existing rights and remedies to enforce the constitution and bylaws of a labor organization with respect to elections prior to the conduct thereof shall not be affected by the provisions of this [title]. The remedy provided by this [title] for challenging an election already conducted shall be exclusive."

Relying on this provision, and on the comprehensive nature of the enforcement scheme established by § 402, we have held that Title IV "sets up an exclusive method for protecting Title IV rights," and that Congress "decided not to permit individuals to block or delay union elections by filing federal-court suits for violations of Title IV." *Calhoon,* supra, at 140, 85 S.Ct., at 296.

III

We have not previously determined exactly how the exclusivity of Title IV's remedial scheme for enforcing rights guaranteed by that title might affect remedies available to enforce other rights, such as those protected by Title I. Nor has Congress provided any definitive answers in this area. This case requires, however, that we decide whether Title I remedies are available to aggrieved union members while a union election is being conducted.

A

It is useful to begin by noting what the plain language of the Act clearly establishes about the relationship between the remedies provided under Title I and Title IV. First, the exclusivity provision included in § 403 of Title IV plainly bars Title I relief when an individual union member challenges the validity of an election that has already been completed.[16] Second, the full panoply of Title I rights are available to individual union members "prior to the conduct" of a union election. As with the plain language of most federal labor laws, however, this simplicity is more apparent than real. Indeed, by its own terms, the provision offers no obvious solution to what remedies are available during the course of a union election, the issue presented by this case.

Even if the plain meaning of the "already conducted" language of § 403 could be read not to preclude other remedies until the actual tabulation and certification of ballots has been completed, we would hesitate to find such an interpretation determinative. First, such an approach would ignore the limitation on judicial remedies that Congress included in Title I, which allows a district court to award only "appropriate" relief. Moreover, we have previously "cautioned against a literal reading" of the LMRDA. Wirtz v. Bottle Blowers Assn., 389 U.S., at 468, 88 S.Ct., at 646. Like much federal labor legislation, the statute was "the product of conflict and compromise between strongly held and opposed views, and its proper construction frequently requires consideration of its wording against its legislative history and in light of the general objectives Congress sought to achieve." Ibid. (citing National Woodwork Mfrs. Assn. v. NLRB, 386 U.S. 612, 619, 87 S.Ct. 1250, 1254, 18 L.Ed.2d 357 (1967)). See Sadlowski, 457 U.S., at 111, 102 S.Ct., at 2345. Indeed, in many ways this admonition applies with its greatest force to the interaction between Title I and Title IV of the LMRDA, if only because of the unusual way in which the legislation was enacted.[17]

Nor does the legislative history of the LMRDA provide any definitive indication of how Congress intended § 403 to apply to Title I suits while an election is being conducted. Throughout the legislative debate on this provision, the exclusivity of Title IV was predominantly, if not only, considered in the context of a union election, such as one held at a union meeting,

---

16. This does not necessarily mean that § 403 forecloses the availability of all post-election relief under Title I. The exclusivity provision of Title IV may not bar post-election relief for Title I claims or other actions that do not directly challenge the validity of an election already conducted. See, e.g., Ross v. Electrical Workers, 513 F.2d 840 (CA9 1975) (common law tort claim); Amalgamated Clothing Workers Rank and File Committee v. Amalgamated Clothing Workers, 473 F.2d 1303 (CA3 1973) (Title I claim).

17. The remarks of a commentator who actively participated in shaping much of the LMRDA are especially pertinent:

"The legislation contains more than its share of problems for judicial interpretation because much of the bill was written on the floor of the Senate or the House of Representatives and because many sections contain calculated ambiguities or political compromises essential to secure a majority. Consequently, in resolving them the courts would be well advised to seek out the underlying rationale without placing great emphasis upon close construction of the words." Cox, Internal Affairs of Labor Unions Under the Labor Reform Act of 1959, 58 Mich.L.Rev. 819, 852 (1960). * * *

that would take place for a discrete and limited period of time.[18] Thus, Congress did not explicitly consider how the exclusivity provision might apply to an election that takes several weeks or months to complete. Moreover, the legislative history that is available on the meaning of § 403 is largely derived from congressional action that occurred prior to the time that Title I was added to the LMRDA. See, e.g., S.Rep. No. 187, supra, at 21; id., at 104 (minority views); H.R.Rep. No. 741, 86th Cong., 1st Sess., 17 (1959). The interplay between the rights and remedies provided to union members by Title I, and the exclusivity provision already included in Title IV, therefore received little, if any, attention from the Congress. Cf. H.R. Conf.Rep. No. 1147, supra, at 35 (conference report, written after both titles were included in the Act, but failing to explain what remedies are available during an election).

B

Despite this absence of conclusive evidence in the legislative history, the primary objectives that controlled congressional enactment of the LMRDA provide important guidance for our consideration of the availability of Title I remedies during a union election. In particular, throughout the congressional discussions preceding enactment of both Title I and Title IV, Congress clearly indicated its intent to consolidate challenges to union elections with the Secretary of Labor, and to have the Secretary supervise any new elections necessitated by violations of the Act. This strongly suggests that, even when Title I violations are properly alleged and proven, Congress would not have considered a court order requiring and judicially supervising a new election to be "appropriate" relief under Title I. At the same time, there is nothing in the legislative history suggesting that Congress intended to foreclose all access to federal courts under Title I during an election, especially when a statutory violation could be corrected without any major delay or disruption to an ongoing election. We therefore conclude that whether a Title I suit may properly be maintained by individual union members during the course of a union election depends upon the nature of the relief sought by the Title I claimants.

Throughout its consideration of the LMRDA, Congress clearly intended to lodge exclusive responsibility for post-election suits challenging the validity of a union election with the Secretary of Labor. The legislative history of Title IV consistently echoes this theme. For example, the election provisions contained in the committee bill as originally reported to the full Senate gave the Secretary exclusive authority to enforce Title IV and to supervise whatever new elections might be needed because of violations of its provisions. S. 1555, 86th Cong., 1st Sess., §§ 302–303 (1959). As the Report of the Senate Committee on Labor and Public Welfare explained: "[S]ince the bill provides an effective and expeditious remedy for overthrowing an improperly held election and holding a new election, the Federal remedy is made the sole remedy and private litigation would be precluded." S.Rep.

---

18. For example, speaking before Title I was added to the LMRDA, at which time state law provided the principal protection for union members before an election, Senator John F. Kennedy noted: "Prior to the day of an election an individual can sue in a State. The day after an election the Secretary of Labor assumes jurisdiction." 105 Cong.Rec. 6485 (1959).

No. 187, supra, at 21, U.S.Code Cong. & Admin.News 1959, p. 2338.[19]

* * *

[G]iven the clear congressional preference expressed in Title IV for supervision of new elections by the Secretary of Labor, we are compelled to conclude that Congress did not consider court supervision of union elections to be an "appropriate" remedy for a Title I suit filed during the course of a union election. * * *

That is not to say that a court has no jurisdiction over otherwise proper Title I claims that are filed during the course of a lengthy union election. The important congressional policies underlying enactment of Title I * * * likewise compel us to conclude that appropriate relief under Title I may be awarded by a court while an election is being conducted. Individual union members may properly allege violations of Title I that are easily remediable under that title without substantially delaying or invalidating an ongoing election. For example, union members might claim that they did not receive election ballots distributed by the union because of their opposition to the incumbent officers running for reelection. Assuming that such union members prove a statutory violation under Title I, a court might appropriately order the union to forward ballots to the claimants before completion of the election. To foreclose a court from ordering such Title I remedies during an election would not only be inefficient, but also would frustrate the purposes that Congress sought to serve by including Title I in the LMRDA. Indeed, eliminating all Title I relief in this context might preclude aggrieved union members from ever obtaining relief for statutory violations, since the more drastic remedies under Title IV are ultimately dependent upon a showing that a violation "may have affected the outcome" of the election, § 482(c), 29 U.S.C. § 482(c) * * *.

C

Our conclusion that appropriate Title I relief during the course of a union election does not include the invalidation of an ongoing election or court supervision of a new election finds further support in our prior cases interpreting the LMRDA, and in the underlying policies of the Act that have controlled those decisions. In Calhoon v. Harvey * * * for example, we were faced with a pre-election challenge to several union rules that con-

---

19. A major reason for creating federal standards to govern union elections, and for lodging primary responsibility for enforcement of those standards with the Secretary of Labor, was the inadequacy of state court remedies. Professor Archibald Cox, testifying before the Senate Subcommittee on Labor, explained in detail the inherent inability of courts to supervise elections:

"A court is also a clumsy instrument for supervising an election. The judicial process may be suitable for determining the validity of an election which has already been held; but if it is found invalid, or if no election has been held, judges have few facilities for providing an effective remedy. Merely to order an election might turn the authority to conduct the balloting over to the very same officers whose misconduct gave rise to the litigation. The court has no tellers, watchers, or similar officials. It would become mired in the details of the electoral process. To appoint a master to supervise the election would delegate the responsibility, but the master would face many of the same problems as the judge. Probably it is the consciousness of these weaknesses that has made judges so reluctant to interfere with union elections, though apparently a few court-conducted elections have been held." Labor-Management Reform Legislation: Hearings on S. 505 et al. Before the Subcommittee on Labor of the Senate Committee on Labor and Public Welfare, 86th Cong., 1st Sess., 133–134 (1959) (hereinafter Hearings).

trolled eligibility to run and nominate others for union office. The claimants in that case asked the court to enjoin the union from preparing for or conducting any election until the rules were revised. We first concluded that in substance the claims alleged violations of Title IV rather than Title I, because the latter only protects union members against the discriminatory application of union rules. Then, given that "Congress * * * decided not to permit individuals to block or delay union elections by filing federal-court suits for violations of Title IV," id., at 140 * * *, we held that the District Court could not invoke its jurisdiction under Title I to hear Title IV claims. We relied for our conclusion in part on Congress' intent "to allow unions great latitude in resolving their own internal controversies, and, where that fails, to utilize the agencies of Government most familiar with union problems to aid in bringing about a settlement through discussion before resort to the courts." 379 U.S., at 140, 85 S.Ct., at 296. * * *

In sum, whether suits alleging violations of Title I of the LMRDA may properly be maintained during the course of a union election depends upon the appropriateness of the remedy required to eliminate the claimed statutory violation. If the remedy sought is invalidation of the election already being conducted with court supervision of a new election, then union members must utilize the remedies provided by Title IV. For less intrusive remedies sought during an election, however, a district court retains authority to order appropriate relief under Title I.

IV

The procedural history of this case clearly demonstrates the undesirable consequences that follow from judicial supervision of a union election. The respondents filed suit after Local 82 had distributed election ballots to its members, but before some of the ballots had been returned or any of the ballots had been counted. Then, less than 24 hours before the election would have been completed and the ballots tabulated, the District Court issued a temporary restraining order that brought the election to a halt. This was followed by several months of negotiations between the parties and hearings before the District Court. Finally, the court issued an order declaring the interrupted election invalid, and setting forth elaborate procedures to be followed during a new election.

Several aspects of these proceedings demonstrate why they are inconsistent with the policies underlying the LMRDA. For example, the temporary restraining order and preliminary injunction issued by the court delayed the union election that was originally scheduled for December 1980 for one full year. Among other consequences, this left the incumbent union officers in power beyond the scheduled expiration of their terms. Cf. § 401(b) * * * (officers shall be elected not less than once every three years). If the procedures under Title IV had been properly followed, the December 1980 election would have been presumed valid, see § 402(a) * * * and new officers would have replaced the incumbents. Moreover, the expertise of the Secretary in supervising elections was completely ignored. Not only did the court acting alone decide that a new election was required, but its order established procedures for that election and appointed an outside arbitrator to supervise their implementation. This action by the District Court directly interfered with the Secretary's exclusive responsibilities for supervising new elections, and was inconsistent with the basic objectives of the LMRDA enforcement scheme.

V

We conclude that the District Court overstepped the bounds of "appropriate" relief under Title I of the LMRDA when it enjoined an ongoing union election and ordered that a new election be held pursuant to court-ordered procedures. Accordingly, the judgment of the Court of Appeals is reversed and the case is remanded for further proceedings consistent with this opinion.[23]

It is so ordered.

JUSTICE STEVENS, dissenting.

* * * The majority reads the statute as if Title IV had been added to the statute to limit the scope of Title I, when in reality the reverse is true. Congress wanted union members to be able to protect their own Title I rights rather than to rely on the Secretary of Labor. Because the Court's holding means that the most serious violations of Title I cannot be adequately remedied except in the discretion of the Secretary, I cannot join the Court's holding or judgment.

* * *

Note

Though the result in Calhoon and Crowley is the same (Title IV prevails over Title I), what analytical difference does the Court perceive between the cases?

3. TRUSTEESHIPS

SECRETARY OF LABOR, UNION TRUSTEESHIPS: REPORT TO THE CONGRESS UPON THE OPERATION OF TITLE III OF THE LABOR–MANAGEMENT REPORTING AND DISCLOSURE ACT

5–11 (1962).

BACKGROUND

A trusteeship is any method of supervision or control whereby a labor organization suspends the autonomy otherwise available to a subordinate body under its constitution or bylaws. The practice of imposing trusteeships by unions dates back to the 19th century, but was extremely rare until the development of strong national unions.

During hearings of the McClellan Committee it was disclosed that the power to impose trusteeship was used sometimes for the purpose of "milking" local treasuries or undemocratically controlling votes to perpetuate power. In the second and third years of the McClellan Committee hearings,

---

23. On remand, the preliminary injunction issued by the District Court should be vacated, and the ballots from the December 1980 election that were sealed and delivered to the court should be returned to the custody of the petitioners. After those ballots have been counted, and the election completed, the re- spondents will have access to the remedies available under Title IV. We note that the Solicitor General has represented to this Court that "the Secretary would himself have sought a new election for a nominations violation like the one alleged here." Brief for the Federal Respondent 11; Tr. of Oral Arg. 27.

legislation was proposed containing provisions to correct abuses through enforcement measures.

Provisions covering trusteeships were enacted as title III of the Labor-Management Reporting and Disclosure Act of 1959 * * * on September 14, 1959. This title prescribes conditions under which trusteeships may be established and continued, requires reporting and public disclosure of their stewardship by any labor organization, makes it a crime either to count the votes of delegates of the trusteed union unless democratically elected, or to transfer funds to the supervisory body, and provides redress for the union member or subordinate body either directly in court or through the Secretary of Labor.

The discussions and committee deliberations in Congress recognized that union trusteeships, although sometimes used to control subordinated organizations illegally, most often are used to provide assistance to subordinates in difficulties, to assist in maintenance and stability, and to promote rather than stifle union democracy. * * *

CHARACTERISTICS OF TRUSTEESHIPS

A total of 777 trusteeships were reported to the Department of Labor during the 2½ years following enactment of the LMRDA. By the cutoff date for this study (March 13, 1962), 590 of these were terminated, leaving 187 subordinate bodies still under trusteeship. This 187 contrasts with 487 unions under trusteeship on September 14, 1959—the effective date of the Act.

Only about one-fourth of all national unions subject to the Act have reported any trusteeship. Of the 70 organizations that have reported trusteeships, 23 had only one in effect at any time during the study period.

An analysis of the financial reports shows that the typical union under trusteeship is small, with assets of about $1,750 and annual receipts slightly in excess of $6,000. * * *

During the past 2½ years new trusteeships have continued to be imposed at a rate averaging about 10 per month and indications are that the Act has not substantially hindered national unions in the establishment of essential trusteeships.

The LMRDA states four allowable purposes for establishing trusteeships:

1. "Correcting corruption or financial malpractice." * * *

2. "Assuring the performance of collective-bargaining agreements or other duties of a bargaining representative." * * *

3. "Restoring democratic procedures." * * *

4. "Otherwise carrying out the legitimate objects of such labor organization." Included under this purpose are: *caretaker trusteeships* (accounting for about one-third of the trusteeships active during this report period), which were used when a subordinate union was relatively inactive because of the closing of a plant, a small or itinerant membership, sudden loss of leadership (e.g., by death or illness), or because it was a new local not yet able to stand on its own feet; *dissension*, a category which has shown the largest decrease in use since the LMRDA; *mismanagement*, which embraces

other than financial malpractice; and *disaffiliation,* a self-explanatory reason for establishing trusteeships. * * *

Of the 487 trusteeships reported in effect on September 14, 1959, 312 were already more than 18 months old. Of the 187 trusteeships active on March 13, 1962, 74 are more than 18 months old. The most common reason for continuing those which were still active in March 1962 was the need for a "caretaker." * * *

CONCLUSIONS

Operation of the trusteeship provisions of the Labor-Management Reporting and Disclosure Act during the first 2½ years supports the following conclusions:

1. Establishment of trusteeships has never been a widespread practice, except in a few unions. When the Act became effective, trusteeships existed in less than 1 percent of the covered unions. Now, less than half that percentage are involved.

2. The Act has been effective in correcting the malpractices disclosed by the McClellan Committee. Further, a large number of trusteeships, while not corrupt, were unnecessarily continued and have now been terminated.

3. Since enactment of the law, many national union constitutions have been amended to provide greater safeguards against unnecessary suspension of autonomy.

4. Indications are that the Act has not substantially hindered unions from establishing essential trusteeships.

5. The reporting and disclosure of the facts surrounding trusteeships, and the active cooperation of the vast majority of unions and union officers, have resulted in substantial compliance with the law with a minimum need for enforcement.

UNITED BROTHERHOOD OF CARPENTERS v. BROWN

United States Court of Appeals, Tenth Circuit, 1965.
343 F.2d 872.

HILL, CIRCUIT JUDGE.

* * * [Plaintiffs, members of Local 201,] alleged that the placing of Local 201 under trusteeship was invalid and in violation of Section 302 of the Act.

The trial court found and held that: The trusteeship was invalid and should be revoked; the members of Local 201 who were suspended by appellants [the United Brotherhood of Carpenters and Joiners of America and one J.O. Mack, Trustee] should be reinstated; all fines paid by them should be remitted by appellants; the increase in dues from $5.80 to $8.00 per month was not by secret ballot and was unlawful; the excess of $2.20 collected each month from the members from and after August 1, 1962, should be remitted and paid to the members; an accounting should be made by appellants; the members of Local 201 should be restored to their right to administer their own affairs and elect officers * * *. Judgment was entered accordingly and defendants below appealed. * * *

Appellants contend that the judgment must be reversed and the action dismissed because plaintiffs have not exhausted the administrative remedy available to them under the provisions of section 304(a) of the Act * * *.[8] The argument is that plaintiffs were required to first file a complaint with the Secretary of Labor in accordance with section 304(a) and exhaust that remedy before proceeding in court with this lawsuit. There is authority to support that argument. * * * But, there is also authority supporting the view that a local union member need not exhaust the administrative remedy provided in section 304(a) before bringing suit in the district court under that section. * * * We believe the latter view is the better rule for the reasons set forth in Judge Watkins' excellent analysis of section 304(a) in [Executive Board, Local Union No. 28, I.B.E.W. v. International Brotherhood of Electrical Workers, 184 F.Supp. 649, 655–59 (D.Md.1960)].[a] We can add nothing to that discussion and accordingly hold that appellants were not required to exhaust the administrative remedy provided in section 304(a) before instituting this action. * * *

8. That section provides as follows:

"Upon the written complaint of any member or subordinate body of a labor organization alleging that such organization has violated the provisions of this subchapter (except section [301] of this title) the Secretary shall investigate the complaint and if the Secretary finds probable cause to believe that such violation has occurred and has not been remedied he shall, without disclosing the identity of the complainant, bring a civil action in any district court of the United States having jurisdiction of the labor organization for such relief (including injunctions) as may be appropriate. Any member or subordinate body of a labor organization affected by any violation of this subchapter (except section [301] of this title) may bring a civil action in any district court of the United States having jurisdiction of the labor organization for such relief (including injunctions) as may be appropriate."

a. Judge Watkins stated (184 F.Supp. at 655–56):

"[T]his court is of the opinion that—although the Secretary of Labor may bring a suit for violations of the trusteeship provisions of [the] Act (in which event 'the jurisdiction of the district court over such trusteeship shall be exclusive * * *,' section 306)—unless and until the Secretary of Labor does so sue, 'any member * * * affected by any violation' (except of section 301) 'may bring a civil action in any district court of the United States having jurisdiction of the labor organization * * *.'

"(i) Language of the Act.

"To the court, the language is clear. Had it been intended to make the Secretary of Labor the sole enforcing medium, the most elementary draftsmanship could have made this crystal clear and unmistakable (see legislative history, infra). * * *

"(ii) Justification of Alternative Remedies.

"There is a very pragmatic justification for the provision for suits by the Secretary of Labor in trusteeship cases, or in the absence of such suit, by the members of the labor organization. Upon the written complaint of 'any member' of a labor organization alleging violations (except of section 301) 'the Secretary shall investigate the complaint and if the Secretary finds probable cause to believe that such violation has occurred and has not been remedied *he shall, without disclosing the identity of the complainant*' bring an appropriate civil action. In the alternative—no such complaint having been made to the Secretary of Labor—'any member * * * affected by any violation' (except of section 301) may bring an appropriate civil action.

"A cautious, timid, or financially poor member of a labor organization may therefore rely completely, and anonymously, upon the Secretary of Labor. A more brash, imprudent, or financially better-off member need not first invoke the aid of the Secretary of Labor.

"(iii) Legislative History.

"A review of the legislative history of the Labor Management Reporting and Disclosure Act unmistakably shows that two coordinate, alternative remedies exist for redress of violations under a trusteeship."

Appellants also contend that the judgment must be reversed and the action dismissed for the reason that the plaintiffs have failed to exhaust the internal remedies afforded by United Brotherhood's Constitution and Laws as required by section 101(a)(4) of the Act * * *. We do not agree. Section 101(a)(4) is applicable only where individual violations of the so-called Bill of Rights provisions are alleged and does not apply where, as here, the validity of a trusteeship is being challenged. As the Supreme Court said in Calhoon v. Harvey, 379 U.S. at 138, 85 S.Ct. at 295: "Jurisdiction of the District Court under § 102 of Title I depends entirely upon whether this complaint showed a violation of rights guaranteed by § 101(a)(1), * * *."

* * *

The basic issue in this case is, of course, the validity of the trusteeship imposed upon Local 201 by United Brotherhood. That issue must be determined by reference to section 302 of the Act, * * * which provides that a trusteeship may be established and administered by a labor organization over its subordinate body " * * * only in accordance with the constitution and bylaws of the organization which has assumed trusteeship * * *." The statute is mandatory in its terms and has nullified or removed whatever inherent power an international union had prior to its enactment to impose such a trusteeship. Unless the constitution and bylaws of the parent organization make provision therefor, such organization has no power to establish a trusteeship over a subordinate body. Flight Engineers International Association v. Continental Air Lines, Inc., 9 Cir., 297 F.2d 397, cert. denied, 369 U.S. 871, 82 S.Ct. 1141, 8 L.Ed.2d 276. An examination of the constitution and bylaws of United Brotherhood discloses that there is no specific provision authorizing it to impose a trusteeship on any of its subordinate local unions.

It is suggested, however, that United Brotherhood's power to impose the trusteeship in question may be derived from the general authority granted to it in sections 6B [10] and 6D [11] of its Constitution and Laws, as implemented by the provision in section 10K, which empowers the General Executive Board " * * * to take such action as is necessary and proper for the welfare * * *" of the national union. Appellant's argument is that while its constitution and laws do not specifically grant it the authority to impose trusteeships, such authority may be implied from sections 6B, 6D and 10K and that implied authority is sufficient. We do not agree. The legislative history of section 302 of the Act clearly discloses an intent on the part of Congress " * * * that there should be a 'limitation on the right of internationals to place local unions in trusteeship'" and one of those limitations was that " * * * the trusteeship must conform to the constitution and bylaws of the labor organization." 2 U.S.Code Cong. & Adm.News, 86th Cong., 1st Sess., 1959, pp. 2333–2334. Obviously, a trusteeship cannot conform to the constitution and bylaws of a labor organization where, as

---

10. "The right is reserved to the United Brotherhood through the International Body to regulate and determine all matters pertaining to the various branches and subdivisions of the trade."

11. "The right is reserved to establish jurisdiction over any Local or Auxilliary Un-

ions, District, State or Provincial Councils whose affairs are conducted in such a manner as to be detrimental to the welfare of the members and to the best interests of the International Body."

here, the constitution and bylaws make no provision for trusteeships. We think the statute not only contemplates, but requires, more than some vague general reference to the effect that the parent organization shall have power to take such action as is necessary and proper for its welfare. It requires at the very least that the organization's constitution and bylaws set forth the circumstances under which a trusteeship may be established over its local unions and the manner or procedure in which it is to be imposed. It goes without saying, of course, that the constitution and bylaws in that respect must not conflict with applicable provisions of the Act.

A second limitation upon the imposition of trusteeships is that under section 302 it must be for one of the following purposes: (1) To correct corruption or financial malpractice; (2) to assure the performance of collective bargaining agreements or other duties of a bargaining representative; or (3) to restore democratic procedures, or otherwise carry out the legitimate objects of the labor organization. Congress recognized that the use of trusteeships by an international union is a particularly effective device for the maintenance of order within the organization and that " * * * they have been widely used to prevent corruption, mismanagement of union funds, violation of collective bargaining agreements, infiltration of Communists; in short, to preserve the integrity and stability of the organization itself. * * *." But, Congress also recognized that " * * * in some instances trusteeships have been used as a means of consolidating the power of corrupt union officers, plundering and dissipating the resources of local unions, and preventing the growth of competing political elements within the organization." 2 U.S.Code Cong. & Adm.News, 86th Cong., 1st Sess., 1959, p. 2333. To preserve the legitimate use of trusteeships, Congress in enacting section 302 enumerated the purposes for which a trusteeship could be imposed in language of a broad and general nature. However, in order to prevent their misuse, Congress obviously intended those purposes to have limitations as well and therefore in determining whether a particular case meets the test, the statute must be construed in the light of the various other provisions of the Act.

The purpose of the Act as a whole is not only to stop and prevent outrageous conduct by thugs and gangsters but also to stop lesser forms of objectionable conduct by those in positions of trust and to protect democractic processes within union organizations. * * * Thus, the rights of individual members of a labor union are protected by federal statute with a view to allowing those members to conduct local matters with a minimum of outside interference. In short, local affairs are to be governed by local members under democractic processes.

With this background in mind we turn to a consideration of the purposes for which the instant trusteeship was imposed. The trial court found, and the evidence confirms, that United Brotherhood established the trusteeship over Local 201 because it would not affiliate with the District Council and would not raise its dues. The court also found, and the evidence shows, that it was not imposed because of "dissension" within the local union. The result is that the trusteeship was established for the purposes of affiliating Local 201 with the District Council and raising the dues of its membership. In determining whether these are proper purposes under section 302, we must remember that a majority of the local membership consistently voted against having anything to do with the District Council and on at least two occasions, by secret ballot, voted against the proposal to raise the monthly dues. We must also remember that the provisions of [Section 101] were designed to afford them protection in that respect. Under these circumstances, we have no hesitancy in holding that the purposes for which this trusteeship was imposed do not fall within any of the categories set forth in section 302. Beyond question, they do not come under the category of correcting corruption or financial malpractice and have nothing whatever to do with collective bargaining. It is also clear to us that the specified purposes are not within the category of restoring democratic processes or otherwise carrying out the legitimate objects of United Brotherhood. To the contrary, the imposition of the trusteeship in question could have no other effect than to stifle democratic processes by, in effect, voiding the results of the properly conducted elections on the issues involved. If we were to hold that the asserted purposes were proper, this court would be placed in the position of allowing a national union to establish a trusteeship over a local union because the members of the local union insisted upon exercising a right granted them by statute. This would in effect nullify and frustrate not only the plain purpose but the express terms of the Act.

It is true that there is a presumption as to the validity of a trusteeship for a period of eighteen months from the date of its establishment. [Section 304(c).] But, it is quite clear from the statute itself and from the legislative history that Congress intended for the presumption of validity to be available only where the trusteeship has been established " * * * in conformity with the procedural requirements of its [the labor organization's] constitution and bylaws and authorized or ratified after a fair hearing either before the executive board or before such other body as may be provided in accordance with its constitution or bylaws * * *." [Section 304(c).] Since the trusteeship in this case was not established in conformity with the constitution and bylaws, the presumption is not available to appellants.

* * *

We conclude that the trusteeship in question is invalid under the provisions of section 302 of the Act for two distinct and separate reasons. Having so concluded, it necessarily follows that the trusteeship was void from its inception and therefore the challenged actions of the Trustee during the period of the trusteeship were also unauthorized and invalid unless they can be sustained on some other legal basis. That, of course, brings us to the cross-appeal by the plaintiffs below.

The first point raised on the cross-appeal relates to the right of the plaintiffs to recover, on behalf of the members of Local 201, the sum of $28,647 paid out of the local union's funds to the District Council. It is clear from the record that the temporary officers [appointed by Trustee Mack] of Local 201 made several payments to the District Council out of local union funds upon the orders and at the directions of the Trustee, Mack. * * *

The plaintiffs contend that the trial court erred in denying recovery of the $28,647 because the payments of that sum to the District Council were made in violation of section 501 of the Act * * * and without the approval, consent or vote of the local union members. The argument is that the payments were unauthorized because they were made upon the orders of a Trustee who was invalidly appointed and, more than that, were made in violation of the trust or fiduciary obligations imposed upon labor union representatives by section 501(a). Plaintiffs point out that they obtained leave of the court below upon verified application for good cause shown in accordance with the requirements of section 501(b) and argue that they are therefore entitled to an accounting of the $28,647 under that subsection.

The court below denied recovery of the payments made to the District Council on the basis that the litigation in the state courts [b] had established that the payments under the trusteeship constituted a legal debt owing from Local 201 to the District Council and that such determination was conclusive in this case under the doctrine of res judicata, thereby precluding any such recovery. However, the court also held that there had been a raise in local dues from $5.80 per month to $8.00 per month in violation of section 101(a) (3) of the Act, * * * and therefore an accounting must be made by the defendants as to the $2.20 increase. It is apparent that these rulings are in conflict with each other. To resolve that conflict, we must first determine whether res judicata is applicable.

This court has recently held that under " * * * the doctrine of res judicata the final judgment of a court of competent jurisdiction upon the merits of a controversy is conclusive as to the parties to the litigation and their privies and it is a bar to any further litigation upon the same cause of action, either before the same or any other tribunal. * * * " Mid-Continent Casualty Company v. Everett, 10 Cir., 340 F.2d 65, 69. The state court litigation with which we are concerned here was in a court of competent jurisdiction and the judgments rendered have become final. There is admittedly privity between the parties to the state court proceedings and the parties to this action. * * *

* * * Under these circumstances, we must conclude that the doctrine of res judicata is fully applicable and the issues determined in the state court proceedings are conclusive on the parties to this action. * * *

It is suggested, however, that unless the so-called increased dues of $2.20 are ordered returned to the members of Local 201, the result will be a raise or increase in local dues without a majority vote by secret ballot after reasonable notice, in violation of section 101(a)(3). If this be so, it is directly attributable to the attempt to litigate the issues in two different forums. * * *

The second point raised on the cross-appeal is whether plaintiffs are entitled to attorney fees. The trial court denied such fees on the ground that Title I of the Act * * * makes no provision for the allowance thereof. However they may be allowed under section 501(b) which provides, in part: " * * * The trial judge may allot a reasonable part of the recovery in any action under this subsection to pay the fees of counsel prosecuting the suit at the instance of the member of the labor organization and to compensate such member for any expenses necessarily paid or incurred by him in connection with the litigation." This statute leaves the matter of the allowance of counsel fees in the sound discretion of the district court and therefore upon

b. Roush v. Hodge, 193 Kan. 473, 394 P.2d 101 (1964).

remand and the accounting the trial judge must first determine whether plaintiffs are entitled to any such fees under the provision quoted above and, if so, the amount thereof. * * *

 * * * [T]he case is remanded for further proceedings in accordance with this opinion. * * *

4. FIDUCIARY RESPONSIBILITY OF UNION OFFICERS

GILBERT v. HOISTING & PORTABLE ENGINEERS

Supreme Court of Oregon, 1963.
237 Or. 130, 384 P.2d 136.
Certiorari denied, 376 U.S. 963, 84 S.Ct. 1125, 11 L.Ed.2d 981 (1964).

O'CONNELL, JUSTICE. This is a suit in equity brought against the Hoisting & Portable Engineers Local 701 by plaintiffs as representatives of all the members of the local union. Plaintiffs pray for the appointment of a receiver, for an accounting, and for other incidental relief.

The gravamen of the complaint is that four of the officers of the local union had failed to follow "democratic processes" in the conduct of the affairs of the union in various particulars. It is charged that these officers were elected as a result of a fraudulent election in which they caused invalid ballots to be cast and that the officers, for the purpose of appropriating union property for unauthorized purposes, have refused to provide for the election of trustees and auditors as required by the bylaws of the union.

The trial court found that plaintiffs had failed to sustain their charge of fraudulent election, or that there had been a misappropriation of funds justifying the appointment of a receiver. However, the court found that defendants, in conducting the affairs of the union, had disregarded the union constitution in certain respects affecting democratic processes.[1] Although the trial judge found that there was not sufficient evidence to justify removal of the defendant officers, he considered their previous neglect in observing the democratic processes of the union a ground for setting up safeguards in

---

1. The trial judge's memorandum opinion contains the following statement:

"3. *As to Abolition of Democratic Processes.* This challenge to defendants' conduct of Local 701, its members' meetings, controls, failure to follow constitutional directives, as evidenced by absence of auditors, trustee *appointments,* inability of members to secure requested information regarding funds, elections, etc., constitute the more serious criticism of defendants' operations."

The court continued:

"4. * * *, we now address ourselves to the *'Democratic processes'* phase of charge and inquiry. As stated above, I am of the opinion defendants have in certain respects disregarded the constitution. Conduct of meetings (however, only one or two were testified to) has been criticized, and some evidence suggests unlawful means employed when observance of the by-laws would have

accomplished the same result. The Financial Secretary and Business Manager, P.R. Wages, has laid himself open to charges of 'Cronyism' and suspicion of selection of officials and committeemen who might be inclined toward Wages' policies and therefore lacking in independence. Generally, it would seem, however, these men have discharged their responsibilities adequately; the situation, however, should never have been permitted to develop when by reason of the manner and method of their selection, their actions might be 'suspect.' What judicial action is suggested in view of the fact in June, 1962, the members will participate in an election which may well resolve at least the most important issues? No serious contention is made that the up-coming election is 'rigged', no such issue appears in the pleadings, nor has it developed on the trial, other than suggestion of continuance of 'Cronyism.' Contests appear on the ballot for major offices."

the conduct of the next union election which was soon to be held. To this end the following order was entered:

"5. For the purpose of participating in supervising the election of officers and officials of the defendant Local 701 in June 1962, the certified public accountant firm of Pattullo and Gleason be and it hereby is appointed by the Court with instructions to report the conduct and results of the election to the Court.

"6. For the purpose of advising the Court as to the assets, income and expenses of the defendant Local 701 the certified public accountant firm of Pattullo and Gleason be and it hereby is appointed to check the quarterly audits of the business of said defendant and to report thereon to the Court each quarter from date hereof not to exceed one year.

"7. Jurisdiction over this suit is hereby retained by this Court so that any party may bring before the Court any matters within the issues and particularly any failure to comply with the Constitution of the International and the Bylaws of defendant Local 701 and any failure to accord to the membership their rights under the law and the said constitution and bylaws. Either party may move to terminate said jurisdiction at any time."

Assuming that there was evidence to support the charge of an abuse of democratic processes in conducting the affairs of the union relating to election of officers, the relief granted was within the power of a court of equity.[3] As we read the record, there was evidence to establish that the defendants failed to observe the union bylaws and constitution relating to the election of trustees and auditors. There also was evidence of irregularities in previous election procedures. This evidence was sufficient to support the order designed to protect the plaintiffs' right to have a fair election.

However, it is contended that even assuming such evidence was produced, plaintiffs have failed to comply with Section 501(b) of the Labor-Management Reporting and Disclosure Act of 1959, * * * requiring a union member who seeks relief against his union to first request the governing board or officers to sue or secure the appropriate relief and to obtain leave of court before bringing such proceeding.

The trial court concluded that the procedure specified in Section 501(b) was not intended to be binding upon union members bringing actions in courts of a state where there already existed procedures by which a union member could enforce the fiduciary duties of union officers. We agree with this interpretation of the act. Section 501(b) could be interpreted to mean that the procedure there specified must be followed in state court proceedings. But Section 603(a) of the Labor-Management Reporting and Disclosure Act of 1959 indicates the congressional intent to recognize the remedies available in state courts unaffected by the remedies under the federal act unless "explicitly provided to the contrary."

It is not necessary under Oregon law to obtain leave to sue under the circumstances recited in Section 501(b). Although it is necessary for a complaining union member to exhaust his remedies within the union itself

---

3. It is recognized that a court of equity may provide the necessary safeguards to assure a fair union election. See for example, Sibilia v. Western Electric Employees Ass'n, 142 N.J.Eq. 77, 59 A.2d 251 (1948); O'Neill v. United Ass'n of Journeymen Plumbers, Etc., 348 Pa. 531, 36 A.2d 325 (1944).

as a condition precedent to judicial relief, the facts in the present case indicate such procedure would have been fruitless. Plaintiffs could not expect relief through a request made to the officer of the local union whose conduct was being challenged. And, although plaintiffs brought the alleged unlawful activities of the defendant officers to the attention of the International Union of Operating Engineers, the International took no action.

We are of the opinion that the controversy was ripe for consideration by the trial court.

Defendants' attack upon the court's jurisdiction is made, not because they object to the judicial supervision of the election but because the court allowed plaintiffs' attorneys fees ($8,500) and reimbursed plaintiffs' counsel for the cost of duplicating and distributing to the union membership copies of the court's memorandum opinion ($222).

Defendants object to the allowance of attorneys' fees, first upon the ground that there is no authorization in the Oregon statutes for the allowance of attorneys' fees under the circumstances of this case, and secondly because Section 501(b) limits the allowance of attorneys' fees to cases where there is the "recovery" of money.[8] Having interpreted Section 501(b) as merely supplemental to state remedies, it follows that we would not be bound by any limitation which that section imposes upon the allowance of attorneys' fees.

Although defendants' first ground of objection presents a more serious question, we are of the opinion that the allowance of attorneys' fees was proper in this case. The authority of a court of equity to award attorneys' fees is not derived solely from the statutes. Equity may under some circumstances as a part of its inherent equitable powers award attorneys' fees. This power is frequently exercised where the plaintiff brings a representative suit on behalf of other members of an organization, as for example where a stockholder brings a derivative suit against a corporation.

Defendants contend, however, that attorneys' fees are allowed in such cases only if the prosecution of the suit results in a pecuniary benefit. Although there is authority supporting defendants' contention, more recent cases have permitted recovery where there was a non-pecuniary benefit to the corporation. We believe that these recent cases announce the sounder rule.[10] The broader rule is particularly apposite in suits brought by members of a union to correct evils in union management. The preservation of the democratic process in the functioning of unions is a matter of primary concern, not only to union members but to the public as well. Litigation which results in correcting abuses of this process frequently may not give rise to an ascertainable pecuniary benefit. But the fact that no money or property is involved does not detract from the importance of the litigation. Those members of the union who in good faith seek to preserve the internal

8. The part of Section 501(b) referred to reads as follows:

    " * * * The trial judge may allot a reasonable part of the recovery in any action under this subsection to pay the fees of counsel prosecuting the suit at the instance of the member of the labor organization * * *."

10. It has been suggested that the rule should be stated even more broadly, permitting recovery of attorneys' fees even in the absence of benefit if the public interest is served by bringing the suit. Cf., Note, 13 Stan.L.Rev. 146 (1960); 45 Minn.L.Rev. 164 (1960); Note, 48 Calif.L.Rev. 843 (1960).

democracy of their union should not have to bear the expense of a successful suit. We hold that plaintiffs were entitled to attorneys' fees. The fee allowed by the trial court was reasonable.

The trial court allowed plaintiffs $222 which was the cost of reproducing and distributing to the union membership 4800 copies of the court's order. This is not an item of disbursement within ORS 20.020. However, under proper circumstances a court of equity would have the power to order the defendants to duplicate and distribute copies of the court's opinion or to pay the cost of doing so. But we are unable to find anything in the record other than the statement of plaintiffs' counsel explaining why this cost was imposed upon defendants. Therefore it is disallowed.

The decree of the lower court, as modified by the disallowance of the sum of $222, is affirmed.

Note

1. What law did the Supreme Court of Oregon apply in determining that the conduct of the defendants was actionable—Section 501(a) or state law? (*Who* is being sued? Does it matter with regard to Section 501?) What light, if any, is cast upon the federal-or-state-law question by the following excerpt from Highway Truck Drivers v. Cohen, 182 F.Supp. 608 (E.D.Pa.1960), affirmed 284 F.2d 162 (3d Cir.1960), cert. denied, 365 U.S. 833, 81 S.Ct. 747, 5 L.Ed.2d 744 (1961)?

"Section 501 * * * attempts to define in the broadest terms possible the duty which the new federal law imposes upon a union official. Congress made no attempt to 'codify' the law in this area. It appears evident to us that they intended the federal courts to fashion a new federal labor law in this area, in much the same way that the federal courts have fashioned a new substantive law of collective bargaining contracts under § 301(a) of the Taft-Hartley Act * * *. See Textile Workers Union of America v. Lincoln Mills, 1957, 353 U.S. 448, 77 S.Ct. 923, 1 L.Ed.2d 972. In undertaking this task the federal courts will necessarily rely heavily upon the common law of the various states. Where that law is lacking or where it in any way conflicts with the policy expressed in our national labor laws, the latter will of course be our guide." 182 F.Supp. at 617.

Is the following proposition accurate: The federal law (Section 501) preempts unless the state law affords better protection to the plaintiff?

2. In fashioning a "new federal labor law in this area," how broad an interpretation should the federal courts give to the "fiduciary responsibility" imposed by Section 501(a)? Should that responsibility be confined to fiscal and property matters, or should it be held to extend to other areas, as in the Gilbert case?

This question was confronted in Guarnaccia v. Kenin, 234 F.Supp. 429 (S.D. N.Y.1964), affirmed sub nom. Gurton v. Arons, 339 F.2d 371 (2d Cir.1964):

"[P]laintiffs seek to enjoin defendants (officers of Local 802 though sued herein as individuals) from refusing to carry out the provisions of the Gurton and Rothstein resolutions. In effect, plaintiffs seek a court directive ordering the defendants, as officers of the Local, to carry out the duties imposed upon them by the two resolutions; to wit, pre-election registration of members and the conduct of the election of officers by in-person balloting.

* * *

"Jurisdiction of this Court is based on Section 501(a) & (b) of the LMRDA * * *.

" * * * [D]efendants assert that the coverage of Section 501 is limited to *financial* fiduciary duties. A plain reading of the statute would appear to support that conclusion. While the first sentence of the statute states that officers of labor organizations occupy positions of trust with respect to the organization, the second sentence of the statute clearly defines the scope of the trust and the duty imposed on the officer-trustee. The duty as set forth in the statute relates to the handling of money and property of the union. Plaintiffs place great emphasis on the duty 'to refrain from dealing with such organization[s] as an adverse party.' However, immediately subsequent to that statement and as a corollary to it, the statute provides: 'and from holding or acquiring any pecuniary or personal interest which conflicts with the interests of such organization.'

"The legislative history of the Section would appear to also be in accord with defendants' position that the Section relates solely to questions of financial dealings. Thus during the course of debate, Senators McClellan and Ervin made it quite clear that the Section would relate solely to matters of money and property. See II Leg.History 1129–31 (1959). Law Review comment, as well, in analyzing Section 501, has discussed the fiduciary obligation, solely in a financial context. See Cox, Internal Affairs of Labor Unions under the Labor Reform Act of 1959, 58 Mich.L.Rev. 819, 823–29 (1960); Dugan, Fiduciary Obligations Under the New Act, 48 Geo.L.J. 277, 294–97 (1959); Symposium, Comparative Labor Law and Law of Employment Relations; Summers, Internal Relations between Unions and Their Members: General Report, 18 Rutgers L.Rev. 236, 271–72 (1964); ibid., Aaron, United States Report, 18 Rutgers L.Rev. 279, 299–300 (1964); Note, 37 N.Y.U.L.Rev. 486, 507 (1962).

"More important, however, is the fact that plaintiffs have not cited, nor has the Court been able to find, a decision under Section 501 which involved an alleged breach of duty in respect to matters other than finances. * * *

"Plaintiffs cite the following statement in Johnson v. Nelson, 325 F.2d 646, 651 (8th Cir.1963), in support of their position:

" 'In summary, we hold that § 501 imposes fiduciary responsibility in its broadest application and is not confined in its scope to union officials only in their handling of money and property affairs.'

"However, it is important to add that the case involved a suit by union members against the treasurer of the union and the complaint alleged that the treasurer and other officers occupying a position of trust had breached their fiduciary obligation by 'their refusal to sign checks in payment of certain attorneys' fees and other expenses which had been approved by the membership.' Id. at 647. Thus the above-cited statement is at most dictum in the case. Likewise, the statement in Parks v. IBEW, 203 F.Supp. 288, 295–296 (D.Md.1962), affirmed, 314 F.2d 886 (4th Cir.), cert. denied, 372 U.S. 976, 83 S.Ct. 1111, 10 L.Ed.2d 142 (1963), that the broad statement in Section 501 emphasizes the nature of the duty as not being limited to pecuniary matters, is clearly dicta since the suit was brought under Sections 101, 302 and 609—*not* Section 501. * * *

"Accordingly, * * * the injunction petitioned for will not be granted, and the complaint is hereby dismissed." 234 F.Supp. at 441–44.

The contrary view is expressed in CLARK, THE FIDUCIARY DUTIES OF UNION OFFICIALS UNDER SECTION 501 OF THE LMRDA, 52 Minn.L.Rev. 437, 440–44 (1967):

"The question * * * is whether the broadly stated fiduciary duty imposed by the first sentence of section 501(a) is limited and qualified by the three specific obligations of the second sentence. Since these specific obligations deal almost exclusively with fiscal wrongdoing, the question may alternatively be stated as whether the fiduciary duties of union officials under the Act extend only to fiscal matters. * * *

"A majority of the courts have construed section 501(a) broadly. For instance, in Nelson v. Johnson,[24] the court held that the president and treasurer of a local union violated their fiduciary duties when they refused to abide by a resolution passed by the local membership directing the payment of the attorney's fees and costs incurred by the plaintiffs in an action under Title I of the LMRDA. While noting that section 501(a) 'speaks broadly in one breath and narrowly in the next,' the court declared that it was 'no parsimonious dole by Congress, to be in turn niggardly measured out by the Federal courts.' Accordingly, the court concluded that the fiduciary duties imposed upon union officials were 'as broad as human experience in the labor field.' In affirming the decision, the Eighth Circuit stated that section 501(a) 'imposes fiduciary responsibility in its broadest application and is not confined in its scope to union officials only in their handling of money and property affairs.'[28]

"The court in Moschetta v. Cross[29] held that the members of a union's executive board violated their fiduciary obligations under section 501(a) when they refused to hold a special convention which had been previously authorized in accordance with the union's constitution. In Parks v. IBEW,[30] the court declared that 'the broad declaration in the first sentence of section 501(a) * * * emphasizes the nature of the officers' duty, which is not limited to pecuniary matters.' In addition, the Oregon Supreme Court upheld a trial court's decision that certain union officers violated their fiduciary obligations under section 501 where 'there was evidence to support the charge of abuse of democratic processes in conducting the affairs of the union relating to election of officers. * * *'[32]"

If the broad view of Section 501(a) is adopted, does it not provide a duplicative and to some extent conflicting avenue of enforcement of rights declared in Titles I, III, and IV of the LMRDA? Should, for example, a member disciplined by his union officers in violation of Section 101(a)(5) acquire thereby a right of action under Section 501(b) (assuming the procedural requirements thereof are satisfied) and become eligible for attorney fees in case of victory, on the theory that the union and its members benefit from the purgative effect of his action? (Cf. the Gilbert case.) Speaking to this general problem, the court in Schonfeld v. Caputo, 49 CCH Lab.Cas. ¶ 19,078 (S.D.N.Y.1964), declared: "Titles I and IV of the Act are the exclusive provisions dealing with the union member's right of franchise and

24. 212 F.Supp. 233 (D.Minn.), aff'd, 325 F.2d 646 (8th Cir.1963).

28. Johnson v. Nelson, 325 F.2d 646, 651 (8th Cir.1963).

29. 48 L.R.R.M. 2669 (D.D.C.1961).

* * *

30. 203 F.Supp. 288 (D.Md.1962), rev'd on other grounds, 314 F.2d 886 (4th Cir.), cert. denied, 372 U.S. 976 (1963).

32. Gilbert v. Hoisting & Portable Eng'rs Local 700, 237 Ore. 130, 134, 384 P.2d 136, 138 (1963), cert. denied, 376 U.S. 963 (1964).

* * *

redress for its infringement. If, as hereinbefore indicated, this court lacks jurisdiction of that part of plaintiff's suit under sections 101(a)(1), 102 and 401 of the Act, it does not acquire such jurisdiction under section 501 thereof."

The dispute as to the scope of section 501(a) has not yet reached the Supreme Court. The circuits remain split along the lines delineated above. See, e.g., Head v. Brotherhood of Railway Clerks, 512 F.2d 398 (2d Cir.1975); Yanity v. Benware, 376 F.2d 197 (2d Cir.1967), certiorari denied, 389 U.S. 874, 88 S.Ct. 167, 19 L.Ed.2d 158 (1967); Pignotti v. Local No. 3 Sheet Metal Workers International Association, 477 F.2d 825 (8th Cir.1973), certiorari denied, 414 U.S. 1067, 94 S.Ct. 576, 38 L.Ed.2d 472 (1973); Lodge 1380, Brotherhood of Railway Clerks v. Dennis, 625 F.2d 819 (9th Cir.1980).

3. In the Gilbert case, the defendants objected to the allowance of attorney fees to plaintiff on the ground that Section 501(b) limits such fees to "a reasonable part of the *recovery* in any action under this subsection." (Emphasis added.) The Oregon court avoided this problem by resort to the liberal common law of Oregon. If the question were to arise in a federal court, how should it be answered? In the same liberal manner as in the Gilbert case, answers CLARK, supra Note 2 at 473–75:

"[The] legislative history [supports] the argument that there must be a fund out of which to pay counsel fees * * *. Nevertheless, the courts thus far have been unanimous in concluding that the word 'recovery' must be given an expansive interpretation so as to allow the granting of counsel fees in all cases where the union has been benefited, and not just in those cases where there has been a monetary recovery.

"In Highway Truck Drivers v. Cohen [178] the plaintiffs sought counsel fees and expenses after successfully obtaining an injunction against the use of union funds to pay the legal fees incurred by certain union officers who were charged with looting the union's treasury. The court in granting the plaintiffs' motion for counsel fees and costs said that Congress could not have intended the phrase 'a reasonable part of the recovery' to apply only to a monetary recovery. '[O]therwise,' the court noted, 'what would be the inducement to the speedy prosecution of an action? An attorney should not be penalized for seeking a timely injunction under the Act in order to prevent large unlawful expenditures by the Union.' To support its decision, the court broadly construed the term 'recovery':

"'Most important, "recovery" in the common meaning of the term means more than money. It means anything of value, as when one says he "recovered" his overcoat which was stolen. Webster's New International Dictionary, 2d. Edition, says that a "recovery" is a "Means of restoration, remedy, cure." Recovery, therefore, must include the entire remedy effectuated and thus encompasses the total benefit conferred upon the Union through the efforts of counsel.' [180]

"The court held that the obtaining of the injunction was a 'benefit in and of itself without regard to any specific monetary amount.' It failed to mention, however, any of the legislative history discussed above.

178. 220 F.Supp. 735 (E.D.Pa.1963).   180. Id. [at 737].

* * *

"The court in Bakery & Confectionery Workers v. Ratner,[182] also apparently ignoring the legislative history, held that the phrase 'a reasonable part of the recovery' was permissive in nature and meant only that '* * * where a monetary recovery has in fact been achieved, that fund may constitute a source from which the trial judge "may allot a reasonable part" for the payment of counsel fees and disbursements.' * * *

"While the result reached by the courts is desirable in terms of public policy, it is difficult to reconcile it with the legislative history and the literal wording of section 501(b). * * * Perhaps the granting of counsel fees in cases where there has been no monetary recovery can be rationalized on the ground that the legislative history did not reflect with requisite clarity a congressional plan to proscribe such payments. Certainly such a result would be in accord with the overall aims and purposes of the LMRDA."

A recent case, confirming the liberal position with regard to the recovery of attorney fees under section 501(b), is Monzillo v. Biller, 735 F.2d 1456 (D.C.Cir. 1984).

4. The showing of "good cause" is a prerequisite to suit under Section 501(b). What does "good cause" mean? As stated by CLARK, supra Note 2 at 465–69:

" 'Good cause' is not defined by the Act, but there is fairly general agreement that this provision was 'intended as a safeguard to the union against harassing and vexatious litigation brought without merit or good faith.'[130] Beyond this, however, there is no consensus as to the meaning and interpretation of the good cause provision.

"At least three interpretations as to what constitutes good cause have been suggested. First, good cause might mean nothing more than that a union member has requested the union to sue and the union has either refused or failed to do so. Such an interpretation would, however, reduce the good cause requirement to a mere redundancy. Moreover, it is a cardinal rule of statutory construction that a statute should be interpreted, if possible, to give effect to all of its provisions. Second, the phrase might mean that the court should examine the union member's complaint and then determine on its face whether it states a good cause of action. This interpretation would also render the good cause provision largely meaningless since a legally sufficient complaint could nearly always be drafted without much difficulty. The third suggested interpretation is by far the best: the court should, after a hearing if necessary, determine whether the plaintiff has made a showing of probable cause. Such an interpretation would give the good cause requirement meaning, and, in addition, would give unions some real protection against harassing and vexatious suits. The legislative history lends support to this interpretation. * * *

"In addition to these three interpretations of what constitutes good cause, several courts have added a fourth. These courts hold that the good cause requirement contemplates reference to the exhaustion of internal remedies doctrine. In Penuelas v. Moreno,[141] the court concluded 'that the exhaustion of remedies provision of Section 101(a)(4) is a prerequisite to

---

182. 335 F.2d 691 (D.C.Cir.1964).

130. Highway Truck Drivers v. Cohen, 182 F.Supp. 608, 622 n. 10, aff'd, 284 F.2d 162 (3d Cir.1960), cert. denied, 365 U.S. 833 (1961).

* * * See Aaron, The Labor-Management Reporting and Disclosure Act of 1959, 73 Harv.L.Rev. 851, 895 (1960) * * *.

141. 198 F.Supp. 441 (S.D.Cal.1961).

* * * federal jurisdiction under section 501(b) * * *.' The court noted that it was 'apparent that all policies favoring the exhaustion prerequisite to Section 101 actions apply with equal force to suits instituted pursuant to Section 501(b).'

"The holding in *Penuelas* is questionable at best, and several courts have expressly rejected it. In Holdeman v. Sheldon [144] the court reasoned:

" '[T]he fact that Congress made specific reference to exhaustion of internal remedies under § 101(a)(4), * * * and adopted a different proce-dure under § 501(b), both sections being enacted at the same time as part of a comprehensive revision of the labor law, leads to the conclusion that the concept of first exhausting internal remedies was knowingly omitted.' [145]

"In addition to section 101(a)(4), the court could have mentioned that Congress specifically provided in section 402(a) that a union member must comply with certain prescribed exhaustion of remedy requirements before filing a complaint with the Secretary of Labor alleging any violation of section 401. In any event, it is submitted that the court in *Holdeman* reached the correct result. To utilize the good cause provision in section 501(b), as the court in *Penuelas* did, and to say that the requirements of section 101(a)(4) are engrafted onto any suit brought under section 501(b) is contrary to both the language of the Act and sound statutory construction. * * *

"It has also been suggested that the requirement of demand and refusal upon the union, rather than the good cause provision, was intended as the statutory counterpart of the 'exhaustion' doctrine in this area.[150] * * *

"Finally, section 501(b) provides that application for leave of the court to sue may be made *ex parte*. * * * Some questions have been raised, however, as to the advisability of granting *ex parte* applications.[153] One court, for example, after deciding that an *ex parte* order had been improper-ly issued, made the following comment: 'After our experience with this case, we think the better practice will be to require an adversary proceeding before permitting an action under Section 501(b) to be filed.' [154] Certainly it would be far easier to detect harassing and unmeritorious suits if adversary proceedings were required. Although *ex parte* applications should be availa-ble in proper circumstances, courts should nevertheless be quite hesitant in granting them."

5. The propriety, under Section 501(a), of the use of union funds for the payment of attorney fees incurred by union officers in defending against crimi-nal and civil charges of malfeasance in office is considered in the next section.

144. 204 F.Supp. 890 (S.D.N.Y.), aff'd per curiam, 311 F.2d 2 (2d Cir.1962). * * *

145. 204 F.Supp. at 896.

150. ABA Section of Labor Relations Law, Report of Comm. on Union Administration and Procedure 123 n. 97 (1962).

153. '[C]ases which subsequently prove to have no merit are being submitted to the federal district judges, thus conveying the mis-leading impression to the membership and the public generally that there has been gross misconduct and dishonesty on the part of local union officers.' Previant, Have Titles I–VI of Landrum-Griffin Served the Stated Legisla-tive Purpose?, 14 Lab.L.J. 28, 35 (1963). * * *

154. Penuelas v. Moreno, 198 F.Supp. 441, 449 (S.D.Cal.1961). * * *

5. THE RIGHT TO BE INFORMED: REPORTING, DISCLOSURE, AND INVESTIGATION

COX, INTERNAL AFFAIRS OF LABOR UNIONS UNDER THE LABOR REFORM ACT OF 1959
58 Michigan Law Review 819, 824–27 (1960).

The LMRDA * * * requires every labor organization in an industry affecting interstate commerce to file an annual financial report disclosing its receipts and disbursements together with the sources and purposes thereof.[27] The reports are filed with the Secretary of Labor on forms prescribed by him. They are open to union members, the press and the general public. A union is required to preserve the records necessary to verify and substantiate its reports.[28] The Secretary of Labor is authorized to investigate the accuracy of reports armed with the power to subpoena.[29] Failure to file a report or filing an intentionally false report is punishable by fine or imprisonment.[30] The Secretary is also given the rather unusual power to "report to interested persons or officials concerning the facts required to be shown in any report required by this Act and concerning the reasons for failure or refusal to file such a report or any other matter which he deems to be appropriate as a result of such an investigation." [31]

This provision seeks to implement the basic theory of the statute—that the government should assure union members adequate information about the conduct of the union's financial affairs; that it should guarantee fair elections for the selection of officers; and that it should then trust the good sense of the members to remove any incompetent or dishonest officials. The Secretary's function is to furnish the members with the facts which should have been supplied by union officials. In legal usage "interested persons" means not the curious, but those who are substantially affected. Possibly the section permits an irresponsible Secretary to injure a union which displeases him by issuing hostile press releases without a hearing, but this is a power possessed by all prosecutors or investigators without express statutory authorization. The risk is a small price to pay for the safeguard. * * *

* * * The statute also requires each officer to obtain an individual bond.[33] * * *

More disturbing than the outright thievery revealed by the McClellan Committee was the evidence of the use of union office for personal profit; for one suspects that the vice of playing both sides of the street, under-cover deals, and conflicts of interest infect a good many unions whose officials believe themselves to be personally honest. * * *

Such conduct, if it occurred as reported, offends ancient moral precepts. The common law has condemned it for generations. * * *

27. Section 201.

28. Sections 205–206, 209(c).

29. Section 601.

30. Section 209.

31. Section 601(a).

33. Section 502. The interpretative bulletin issued by the Secretary of Labor rules that the bonding requirement is satisfied by a position schedule bond, i.e., one which covers any officials and union agents holding specified positions without naming the particular individuals. 29 C.F.R. § 453.18 (Supp.1960). * * *

The original Kennedy bills sought to support the underlying moral precepts by requiring every union officer annually to report to the Secretary of Labor any holdings, income or transactions which created a potential conflict between his personal interests and loyalty to the members. These sections, which reach not only cases where the official has legal title, but also beneficial ownership held through "covers," "straws" or "blinds," were carried into the LMRDA without amendment.[39] True criminals will undoubtedly ignore the duty to report but the detailed and unequivocal legislative condemnation of specific holdings and transactions should go far toward establishing a higher standard of conduct. The official whose fingers itch for a "fast buck" but who is not a criminal will be deterred by the fear of prosecution if he files no report and by fear of reprisal from the members if he does.

UNION CONSTITUTION, BYLAWS, AND PROCEDURES

In addition to the reporting requirements outlined in the foregoing article, Section 201(a) of Title II (the "Reporting" Title) requires that every labor organization "adopt a constitution and bylaws and * * * file a copy thereof with the Secretary," together with a report containing certain specified information, such as the names of the officers, the initiation fee and dues, membership requirements, and the procedures for calling meetings and disciplining members. Section 101(b) of Title I explicitly (and, one may conclude, unnecessarily) states: "Any provision of the constitution and bylaws of any labor organization which is inconsistent with the provisions of this section [or any other, presumably] shall be of no force and effect."

INTERNATIONAL BROTHERHOOD OF TEAMSTERS v. WIRTZ

United States Court of Appeals, District of Columbia Circuit, 1965.
346 F.2d 827.

BURGER, CIRCUIT JUDGE. The District Court on application of the Secretary of Labor ordered enforcement of a subpoena duces tecum issued by the Secretary directing International Brotherhood of Teamsters, Chauffeurs, Warehousemen and Helpers of America, the "Teamsters Union" in ordinary parlance, to produce records containing information as to financial matters required to be reported under §§ 201(a) and 201(b) of the Labor-Management Reporting and Disclosure Act of 1959 * * *. On this appeal the Teamsters Union challenges the power of the Secretary under Section 601 of the Act * * * to subpoena records of a labor organization for the purpose of investigating, evaluating and publicizing the existence of alleged violations of Section 501(a) of the Act, * * * which imposes certain fiduciary duties upon officers, agents and other representatives of labor organizations, on the ground that the Secretary has no remedial or enforcement powers as to Section 501(a) violations.

Certain background facts are important. On May 11, 1964 the Secretary issued a press release stating that the Department of Labor had begun an investigation into the possible use of union funds by Appellant to pay legal fees incurred by James Hoffa, its president. The release also disclosed

---

39. Section 202.

that sixteen members of a Teamsters Union local had complained that Hoffa had used union funds for private purposes in violation of Section 501. Additionally, the Secretary's announcement stated that the complaining local union members requested prompt investigation of the complaint and publication of the results of the inquiry.

The stated purpose of the challenged subpoena, issued three days later on May 14, was to implement an investigation to determine whether any person had violated or was about to violate any provision of the Labor-Management Reporting and Disclosure Act of 1959 (except Title I and amendments made by the Act to other statutes).[1]

Shortly after the Secretary's announcement of his investigation, six members of the same Teamsters Union local referred to in the press release brought suit on behalf of the union and its members against various union officers, including James Hoffa, charging that union treasury funds had been wrongfully diverted by the union to pay legal expenses of Hoffa and other union officials in defense of various criminal prosecutions and demanding an accounting for and restitution of the diverted funds to the union. The action was brought under Section 501(b) of the Labor-Management Reporting and Disclosure Act and the complaint alleged that the claimed diversion of funds violated Section 501(a) of the Act.

On the return date fixed in the subpoena, Appellant refused to deliver any records pending action on its request that the Secretary withdraw the subpoena. Its request was based primarily on contentions (a) that the Secretary has no enforcement role or power to remedy violations of Section 501(a) and hence his investigatory powers under Section 601 do not extend to inquiry into violations of Section 501(a); (b) that a civil action had been brought by members of Teamsters Local 107 who allegedly were among those whose complaints to the Secretary led to issuance of the subpoena and that the Secretary is without power so to assist private litigants for whom all discovery procedures of the Federal Rules of Civil Procedure are available; (c) that even if the Secretary has such powers he may not use them when union members have not exhausted their rights to examine union records on demand; (d) that the subpoena is oppressive, burdensome and duplicitous.

The Solicitor of Labor on behalf of the Secretary then advised Appellant that the scope of the demand would be reduced to cover only the period from January 1, 1962 to a current date; the original subpoena was withdrawn and an amended subpoena issued. On June 1, 1964 in a hearing on the return of the new subpoena, Appellant, while still challenging the Secretary's powers, offered to comply with the demands if the Secretary would give assurances not to make any public disclosure of findings as to the expenditures of

---

1. Thus, it will be seen that the scope of the subpoena is commensurate with the Secretary's power under the Act. Section 601 of the Act provides as follows:

"(a) The Secretary shall have power when he believes it necessary in order to determine whether any person has violated or is about to violate any provision of this Act (except title I or amendments made by this Act to other statutes) to make an investigation and in connection therewith he may enter such places and inspect such records and accounts and question such persons as he may deem necessary to enable him to determine the facts relative thereto. The Secretary may report to interested persons or officials concerning the facts required to be shown in any report required by this Act and concerning the reasons for failure or refusal to file such a report or any other matter which he deems to be appropriate as a result of such an investigation. * * *"

Teamsters Union funds to pay litigation expenses of criminal proceedings against Hoffa. The Secretary declined to give any such assurances and proceeded in the District Court for enforcement of the subpoena. The District Court ordered enforcement and granted a stay pending resolution of this appeal.

The contentions on appeal are essentially those urged unsuccessfully on the Secretary, i.e., chiefly that the Secretary lacks power under the Labor-Management Reporting and Disclosure Act to investigate and publicize findings as to violations of Section 501(a) of the Act.

The powers of the Secretary under the Labor-Management Reporting and Disclosure Act are broad and, as with visitorial powers in other contexts, they are to be construed in such a way as to give effect to the purposes of the Act. That the Secretary's public announcement cites Section 501(a) as the basis of complaints by union members cannot in any sense limit the scope of his investigation.[2] An inquiry prompted by reports of violations in one area of the statutory coverage might reveal violations in other areas. Nor can the pendency of class actions brought by union members and aimed at the related objective of accounting and restitution operate to circumscribe the Secretary's powers.

It would be an anomaly if private persons, for whatever motives, could determine what the Secretary could or could not do with information which he secures in the exercise of his overseeing functions under the Act. The Secretary has the power under Section 601 to investigate and report to "interested persons or officials" concerning facts required to be reported under the Act, reasons for failure to report and "any other matter which he deems to be appropriate * * *." See note 1 supra. A basic purpose of the Act was to aid union members in securing information as to the financial affairs of their unions and the employment of union assets. The power to report to "interested persons" in addition to "officials" such as the Attorney General includes the power to inform the public at large and union members. To give the Act a lesser scope would be to lose sight of the fiduciary nature which Congress has attributed to the offices of union leadership.[3]

Congress afforded a broad range of remedies, civil and criminal, and authorized investigations as a means of aiding union members in pursuit of their remedies; there is nothing in the language of the statute, its history or the announced legislative purpose which should lead us to accept the Union's narrow reading of this remedial legislation.

2. Indeed neither the press release nor the subpoena itself purports to limit the Secretary's concern to violations of Section 501.

3. The union's position that the proposed investigation seeks information limited to Section 501(a) violations is without merit as without record support even if we assume the correctness of the legal conclusions the union would draw from such a state of facts. The Secretary's press release simply indicated what prompted his action, not the scope of his search. The subpoena itself is drawn as broadly as the Act will permit. Use of union funds to pay private bills of officers might violate both Sections 209 and 501(c). These provisions are *enforceable* by the Attorney General, but the Secretary is expressly given the enforcement-related role of supplying that official with pertinent evidence disclosed by investigations. 73 Stat. 540, 29 U.S.C.A. § 527. Moreover, the search could afford a basis for civil actions by the Secretary under Section 210. Thus the record will not support the assertion that the subpoena has nothing to do with the Secretary's enforcement duties: Appellant's legal argument lacks a factual underpinning.

It is not without significance that Congress considered and rejected a limitation on the Secretary's powers in the form of a requirement that the Secretary first find probable cause to believe that violations had occurred before issuing a subpoena. See Int'l Bhd. of Teamsters, Chauffeurs, Warehousemen and Helpers of America v. Goldberg, 112 U.S.App.D.C. 391, 303 F.2d 402 (1962), approving Goldberg v. Truck Drivers Local Union No. 299, 293 F.2d 897 (6th Cir.), cert. denied 368 U.S. 938, 82 S.Ct. 379, 7 L.Ed.2d 337 (1961). While Appellant does not here argue for such a requirement, we note Congress' rejection of a probable cause limitation as probative of its intent to confer broad investigative powers on the Secretary.

The public disclosure functions of Section 601 have a certain similarity of purpose with the disclosure concepts of the Securities and Exchange Act; to a degree each has as its purpose ventilation of facts in which the public at large as well as a particular segment—here union members—have a genuine interest. A labor union is not a private enterprise. Congress seems to have thought that reporting and disclosure would serve a prophylactic function, deterring some of the corrupt practices and acts of untrustworthiness on the part of union officers which Congress had found prevalent, and would enable union members to govern their organizations more intelligently.

The objectives of the Act read as a whole do not warrant our reading into Section 601 the implied exception Appellant seeks to add to the exceptions therein expressed by Congress. The plain, unambiguous language of the statute renders resort to legislative history unnecessary as an aid to interpretation, but the language of one of the reports illuminates the legislative objectives:

> "This provision in insures [sic] that union members will have all the vital information necessary for them to take effective action in regulating affairs of their trade union, *either through voluntary compliance of the labor organization with the reporting requirements* of the act *or as a result of investigation and reports by the Secretary of Labor.* The committee is confident that union members armed with adequate information and having the benefit of secret elections * * * would rid themselves of untrustworthy or corrupt officers. In addition, the exposure to public scrutiny of all vital information concerning the operation of trade unions will help deter repetition of the financial abuses disclosed by the McClellan committee.[4]"

Appellant's next contention is that the Secretary may not use his investigatory power to furnish information to those local members who requested it, since certain of the latter allegedly have instituted an action under Section 501(b), as an incident of the prosecution of which the normal discovery devices afforded by the Federal Rules of Civil Procedure are available to them. This contention, like that discussed above, suffers first from the fact that the record does not demonstrate the Secretary's sole or primary purpose to have been to come to the aid of any individual union members. And even if such a purpose can be assumed, there has been no showing that any of the six suing members was among the sixteen who called on the Secretary for aid. Assuming, *arguendo*, that these facts were

---

4. S.Rep. No. 187, 86th Cong., 1st Sess. 9 (1959), U.S.Code Congressional and Administrative News 1959, p. 2325. (Emphasis added.) Moreover, the Senate Report indicates that one purpose of reporting and publicity is to facilitate legal actions by union members. Id. at 16.

shown, we find Appellant's argument untenable. The institution of action by union members does not deprive the Secretary of his broad powers to deal with facts involved in such litigation.

Appellant's final contention that the union members failed to exhaust available remedies by first requesting the desired information from the Union before petitioning the Secretary must fail for a variety of reasons. As just noted, the Secretary's powers are independent of the action or inaction of union members. Nothing in the Act expressly requires members to ask the Union for information as a condition to receiving information secured by the Secretary under the statute; moreover, there is little reason to assume that the Union will give to its "hostile" members the very information which it refuses to give the Secretary of Labor unless the Secretary agrees not to reveal it to the public or "interested persons." Certainly one purpose served by granting the Secretary independent powers is to make sure that relevant information can be secured in the public interest if members are too complacent or too cowed to ask the union for it.

Even if we assume that an action by members under Section 201(c) requires a prior demand on the union, that cannot affect the Secretary's broad powers under the Act. We read the Act as authorizing action on a broad front to accomplish the objective of enforcing recognition of the essentially fiduciary relationship between union officials on the one hand and members on the other, with all the duties and obligations which follow. * * * See generally Note, The Fiduciary Duty of Union Officers Under the LMRDA, 37 N.Y.U.L.Rev. 486 (1962). * * *

Affirmed.

Note

1. The action (referred to in the Wirtz case) by the six members of the Teamsters Union against James Hoffa and other officers of the union for restitution of union funds allegedly wrongfully diverted to pay legal expenses of Hoffa and the others (International Brotherhood of Teamsters v. Hoffa, 242 F.Supp. 246 (D.C.1965)) had its predecessor in Highway Truck Drivers and Helpers Local 107 v. Cohen, 182 F.Supp. 608 (E.D.Pa.1960), aff'd, 284 F.2d 162 (3d Cir.1960), cert. denied, 365 U.S. 833 (1961). In that case the plaintiffs, rank-and-file members of Local 107 of the Teamsters, sued to enjoin their local officers from using union funds to defray certain legal expenses. The question presented was stated by the district court to be: "Does the expenditure of union funds to pay for legal fees in the defense of both criminal and civil actions brought against the various defendant officers for an alleged conspiracy to cheat and defraud their union of large sums of money constitute a breach of that fiduciary duty imposed upon them by Section 501(a) * * *, notwithstanding the purported authorization of such expenditures by a resolution of the union membership passed at a regular union meeting?" 182 F.Supp. at 616. The court answered the question in the affirmative, finding the expenditures to be ultra vires and therefore not protected by the resolution of the union membership. The court explained: "To allow a union officer to use the power and wealth of the very union which he is accused of pilfering, to defend himself against such charges, is totally inconsistent with Congress' effort to eliminate the undesirable element which has been uncovered in the labor-management field. To allow even a majority of members in that union to authorize such action, when, if the charges

made against these defendants are true, it is these very members whom the officers have deceived, would be equally inconsistent with the Act. If some of those members have not been deceived by the defendants, but because of the immediate gains in their income and working conditions which Local 107 has won for them, they are content to accept as officers anyone who produces immediate results, regardless of what other wrongs those officers may commit in so doing, this Court would still not feel constrained to bow to their will in the light of its duty both to those members of Local 107 who place honesty above material gain as well as to the millions of others in the labor movement whose cause would be seriously injured by such an attitude." 182 F.Supp. at 620–21.

In 1961, the International Brotherhood of Teamsters, as a counter to the Cohen decision, amended its constitution so as to authorize the payment by the union, or locals thereof, of legal fees incurred by union officers in defending themselves against charges of the sort involved in the Cohen case. The purpose of the amendment was to circumvent the ultra vires pitfall previously encountered by the Cohens and Hoffas of the union. This effort, too, aborted. In subsequent litigation it was held that "the action of the International [in amending the constitution] was just as inconsistent with Section 501 of the * * * Act as was the local's ill conceived resolution." Highway Truck Drivers and Helpers Local 107 v. Cohen, 334 F.2d 378, 381 (3d Cir.1964).

In International Brotherhood of Teamsters v. Hoffa, supra, the court, while acknowledging the right of the International Brotherhood to defend against the effort to invalidate the 1961 amendment to its constitution, held that it must be represented in such cause by counsel independent of the individual defendants. The court stated:

"As a matter of general common law in this jurisdiction [District of Columbia], the 'funds of a union are not available to defend officers charged with wrongdoing which, if the charges were true, would be seriously detrimental to the union and its membership,' and the same broad principle flows from the Act. Simultaneous representation of the organization and an individual defendant charged with unauthorized disbursement of its funds would not only to that extent provide assistance of a forbidden type but would produce other detrimental consequences as well. * * *

"* * * Where, as here, union officials are charged with breach of fiduciary duty, the organization is entitled to an evaluation and representation of its institutional interests by independent counsel, unencumbered by potentially conflicting obligations to any defendant officer." 242 F.Supp. at 255–56.

Is it a violation of Section 501 for union officers to pay legal fees incurred by a union officer where such payment is made only in the case of the exoneration of the defendant officer and after the fact of exoneration? This question was left open in the Cohen litigation. (See 182 F.Supp. at 622, 284 F.2d at 164, 215 F.Supp. at 941.) It was answered in the negative in Morrissey v. Segal, 526 F.2d 121, 128 (2d Cir.1975), the court stating: 'The beneficient aims of § 501 should not be frustrated by construing its terms with such uncompromising rigor that competent individuals are discouraged from assuming a fiduciary role in union affairs."

2. Should the authority of the Secretary of Labor to investigate a past union election under Section 601 be held conditional upon the prior satisfaction of Section 402(a) (requiring the filing of a complaint with the Secretary by a union member who has first exhausted, or sought for three months to exhaust,

the internal union remedies)? Consistently with the resolution of the Section 601-versus-Section 501 conflict in the Teamsters v. Wirtz case, the Section 601–Section 402 competition was resolved in favor of broad investigatorial powers on the part of the Secretary in Local 57, International Union of Operating Engineers v. Wirtz, 346 F.2d 552 (1st Cir.1965); satisfaction of the Section 402(a) conditions was held to be unnecessary. Does this mean that the Secretary could bring a suit, based upon a Section 601 investigation, without more, to set aside an election? Consider the impact of Section 403.

3. The investigatory powers under the LMRDA are not confined to the Secretary of Labor. "Self-help" on the part of union members is encouraged by Section 201(c), which requires unions to make available to "all" of their members "information required to be contained in" their Section 201 reports to the Secretary. This duty is enforceable in a suit by any member in a state or federal court upon a showing of "just cause"; such a showing entitles the member "to examine any books, records, and accounts necessary to verify" his union's 201 report. Costs and attorney fees may be allowed by the court in such an action. As to the meaning of "just cause," the courts have taken a liberal view from the standpoint of the plaintiff member. E.g., Mallick v. International Brotherhood of Electrical Workers, 749 F.2d 771 (D.C.Cir.1984); Fruit & Vegetable Packers Local 760 v. Morley, 378 F.2d 738 (9th Cir.1967); Rekant v. Rabinowitz, 194 F.Supp. 194 (E.D.Pa.1961).

Personal involvement and responsibility on the part of union members in policing their own rights is also encouraged by Section 104, requiring unions to make copies of collective bargaining agreements available to the members.

4. The reporting and disclosure provisions of Title II apply not only to unions and their officials, but also to employers with regard to certain payments and expenditures affecting the right of their employees to organize and to bargain collectively. Section 203(a) requires an employer who has made a payment or expenditure of the sort described in subsections (1), (2), (3), and (5) thereof to file with the Secretary of Labor a report setting forth the details of the transaction. Reports are also required of any "labor relations consultant" who enters an agreement with an employer (Section 203(a)(4)) to "persuade employees to exercise or not to exercise, or * * * as to the manner of exercising, the right to organize and bargain collectively * * *, or undertakes to supply such employer with information concerning the activities of employees or a labor organization in connection with a labor dispute involving such employer * * *." The details of such agreements between employers and labor relations consultants are required to be reported by both the employer (Section 203(a)(4)) and the labor relations consultant (Section 203(b)). Section 203(c) excludes from this reporting requirement what might be described as the normal, lawful services rendered to an employer by an attorney or other labor relations specialist in connection with the employer's rights and responsibilities under applicable labor laws.

Simply stated, the purpose of the reporting obligations placed upon employers and labor relations consultants by the ample verbiage of Section 203 is to provide a balancing "open window" on the employer side; anti-Section 7 "shenanigans" may thus be more difficult to conceal and, accordingly, less widely practiced. See Beaird, Reporting Requirements for Employers and Labor Relations Consultants in the Labor-Management Reporting and Disclosure Act of 1959, 53 Geo.L.J. 267 (1965); Bethel, Profiting from Unfair Labor Practices: A Proposal to Regulate Management Representatives, 79 Nw.U.L.Rev. 506 (1984).

6. THE RIGHT NOT TO BE LED BY CERTAIN LEADERS OF THEIR CHOICE: OF COMMUNISTS AND FELONS

UNITED STATES v. BROWN

Supreme Court of the United States, 1965.
381 U.S. 437, 85 S.Ct. 1707, 14 L.Ed.2d 484.

Mr. Chief Justice Warren delivered the opinion of the Court.

In this case we review for the first time a conviction under § 504 of the Labor-Management Reporting and Disclosure Act of 1959, which makes it a crime for a member of the Communist Party to serve as an officer or (except in clerical or custodial positions) as an employee of a labor union.[1] Section 504, the purpose of which is to protect the national economy by minimizing the danger of political strikes, was enacted to replace § 9(h) of the National Labor Relations Act, as amended by the Taft-Hartley Act, which conditioned a union's access to the National Labor Relations Board upon the filing of affidavits by all of the union's officers attesting that they were not members of or affiliated with the Communist Party.

Respondent has been a working longshoreman on the San Francisco docks, and an open and avowed Communist, for more than a quarter of a century. He was elected to the Executive Board of Local 10 of the International Longshoremen's and Warehousemen's Union for consecutive one-year terms in 1959, 1960, and 1961. On May 24, 1961, respondent was charged in a one-count indictment returned in the Northern District of California with "knowingly and wilfully serv[ing] as a member of an executive board of a labor organization * * * while a member of the Communist Party, in wilful violation of Title 29, United States Code, Section 504." It was neither charged nor proven that respondent at any time advocated or suggested illegal activity by the union, or proposed a political strike.[4] The jury found respondent guilty, and he was sentenced to six months' imprisonment. The Court of Appeals for the Ninth Circuit, sitting *en banc*, reversed and remanded with instructions to set aside the conviction and dismiss the indictment, holding that § 504 violates the First and Fifth Amendments to the Constitution. 334 F.2d 488. We granted certiorari * * *.

Respondent urges—in addition to the grounds relied on by the court below—that the statute under which he was convicted is a bill of attainder, and therefore violates Art. I, § 9, of the Constitution. We agree that § 504 is void as a bill of attainder and affirm the decision of the Court of Appeals

---

1. * * * § 504 * * * provides, in pertinent part:

"(a) No person who is or has been a member of the Communist Party * * * shall serve—

"(1) as an officer, director, trustee, member of any executive board or similar governing body, business agent, manager, organizer, or other employee (other than as an employee performing exclusively clerical or custodial duties) of any labor organization,

* * *

* * * * *

"during or for five years after the termination of his membership in the Communist Party * * *.

"(b) Any person who willfully violates this section shall be fined not more than $10,000 or imprisoned for not more than one year, or both."

4. Evidence that the executive board had never called a strike was, upon the motion of the Government, stricken from the record, and a defense offer to prove that the union had not been involved in a strike since 1948 was rejected by the court.

on that basis. We therefore find it unnecessary to consider the First and Fifth Amendment arguments.

I.

The provisions outlawing bills of attainder were adopted by the Constitutional Convention unanimously, and without debate.

"No Bill of Attainder or ex post facto Law shall be passed [by the Congress]." Art. I, § 9, cl. 3.

"No State shall * * * pass any Bill of Attainder, ex post facto Law, or Law impairing the Obligation of Contracts * * *." Art. I, § 10.

A logical starting place for an inquiry into the meaning of the prohibition is its historical background. The bill of attainder, a parliamentary act sentencing to death one or more specific persons, was a device often resorted to in sixteenth, seventeenth and eighteenth century England for dealing with persons who had attempted, or threatened to attempt, to overthrow the government. In addition to the death sentence, attainder generally carried with it a "corruption of blood," which meant that the attainted party's heirs could not inherit his property. The "bill of pains and penalties" was identical to the bill of attainder, except that it prescribed a penalty short of death, e.g., banishment, deprivation of the right to vote, or exclusion of the designated party's sons from Parliament. Most bills of attainder and bills of pains and penalties named the parties to whom they were to apply; a few, however, simply described them. While some left the designated parties a way of escaping the penalty, others did not. The use of bills of attainder and bills of pains and penalties was not limited to England. During the American Revolution, the legislatures of all thirteen States passed statutes directed against the Tories; among these statutes were a large number of bills of attainder and bills of pains and penalties. While history thus provides some guidelines, the wide variation in form, purpose and effect of ante-Constitution bills of attainder indicates that the proper scope of the Bill of Attainder Clause, and its relevance to contemporary problems, must ultimately be sought by attempting to discern the reasons for its inclusion in the Constitution, and the evils it was designed to eliminate. The best available evidence, the writings of the architects of our constitutional system, indicates that the Bill of Attainder Clause was intended not as a narrow, technical (and therefore soon to be outmoded) prohibition, but rather as an implementation of the separation of powers, a general safeguard against legislative exercise of the judicial function, or more simply—trial by legislature.

The Constitution divides the National Government into three branches—Legislative, Executive and Judicial. This "separation of powers" was obviously not instituted with the idea that it would promote governmental efficiency. It was, on the contrary, looked to as a bulwark against tyranny. For if governmental power is fractionalized, if a given policy can be implemented only by a combination of legislative enactment, judicial application, and executive implementation, no man or group of men will be able to impose its unchecked will. * * *

The authors of the Federalist Papers took the position that although under some systems of government (most notably the one from which the United States had just broken), the Executive Department is the branch most likely to forget the bounds of its authority, "in a representative republic * * * where the legislative power is exercised by an assembly * * * which is sufficiently numerous to feel all the passions which actuate a multitude; yet not so numerous as to be incapable of pursuing the objects of its passions * * *," barriers had to be erected to ensure that the legislature would not overstep the bounds of *its* authority and perform the functions of the other departments.[17] The Bill of Attainder Clause was regarded as such a barrier. Alexander Hamilton wrote:

> "Nothing is more common than for a free people, in times of heat and violence, to gratify momentary passions, by letting into the government principles and precedents which afterwards prove fatal to themselves. Of this kind is the doctrine of disqualification, disfranchisement, and banishment by acts of the legislature. * * *" [18]

Thus the Bill of Attainder Clause not only was intended as one implementation of the general principle of fractionalized power, but also reflected the Framers' belief that the Legislative Branch is not so well suited as politically independent judges and juries to the task of ruling upon the blameworthiness of, and levying appropriate punishment upon, specific persons. * * * By banning bills of attainder, the Framers of the Constitution sought to guard against such dangers by limiting legislatures to the task of rulemaking. "It is the peculiar province of the legislature to prescribe general rules for the government of society; the application of those rules to individuals in society would seem to be the duty of other departments." Fletcher v. Peck, 6 Cranch 87, 136, 3 L.Ed. 162.

II.

It is in this spirit that the Bill of Attainder Clause was consistently interpreted by this Court—until the decision in American Communications Ass'n v. Douds, 339 U.S. 382, 70 S.Ct. 674, 94 L.Ed. 925, which we shall consider hereafter. * * *

[This] approach * * * was followed in the twin post-Civil War cases of Cummings v. State of Missouri, 4 Wall. 277, 18 L.Ed. 356, and Ex parte Garland, 4 Wall. 333, 18 L.Ed. 366. Cummings involved the constitutionality of amendments to the Missouri Constitution of 1865 which provided that no one could engage in a number of specified professions (Cummings was a priest) unless he first swore that he had taken no part in the rebellion against the Union. At issue in Garland was a federal statute which required attorneys to take a similar oath before they could practice in federal courts. This Court struck down both provisions as bills of attainder on the ground that they were legislative acts inflicting punishment on a specific group: clergymen and lawyers who had taken part in the rebellion and therefore could not truthfully take the oath. * * *

The next extended discussion of the Bill of Attainder Clause came in 1946, in United States v. Lovett, 328 U.S. 303, 66 S.Ct. 1073, 90 L.Ed. 1252, where the Court invalidated § 304 of the Urgent Deficiency Appropriation Act, 1943, 57 Stat. 431, 450, which prohibited payment of further salary to three named federal employees, as a bill of attainder.

17. The Federalist, No. 48, pp. 383–384 (Hamilton ed. 1880) (Madison).

18. III (John C.) Hamilton, History of the Republic of the United States, p. 34 (1859), quoting Alexander Hamilton. * * *

"[L]egislative acts, no matter what their form, that apply either to named individuals or to easily ascertainable members of a group in such a way as to inflict punishment on them without a judicial trial are bills of attainder prohibited by the Constitution. * * * This permanent proscription from any opportunity to serve the Government is punishment, and of a most severe type. * * * No one would think that Congress could have passed a valid law, stating that after investigation it had found Lovett, Dodd, and Watson 'guilty' of the crime of engaging in 'subversive activities,' defined that term for the first time, and sentenced them to perpetual exclusion from any government employment. Section 304, while it does not use that language, accomplishes that result." Id., at 315–316, 66 S.Ct., at 1079.[23]

III.

Under the line of cases just outlined, § 504 of the Labor-Management Reporting and Disclosure Act plainly constitutes a bill of attainder. Congress undoubtedly possesses power under the Commerce Clause to enact legislation designed to keep from positions affecting interstate commerce persons who may use such positions to bring about political strikes. In § 504, however, Congress has exceeded the authority granted it by the Constitution. The statute does not set forth a generally applicable rule decreeing that any person who commits certain acts or possesses certain characteristics (acts and characteristics which, in Congress' view, make them likely to initiate political strikes) shall not hold union office, and leave to courts and juries the job of deciding what persons have committed the specified acts or possess the specified characteristics. Instead, it designates in no uncertain terms the persons who possess the feared characteristics and therefore cannot hold union office without incurring criminal liability— members of the Communist Party.[24] * * *

The Solicitor General points out that in Board of Governors of Federal Reserve System v. Agnew, 329 U.S. 441, 67 S.Ct. 411, 91 L.Ed. 408, this Court applied § 32 of the Banking Act of 1933, which provides:

"No officer, director, or employee of any corporation or unincorporated association, no partner or employee of any partnership, and no individual, primarily engaged in the issue, flotation, underwriting, public sale, or distribution, at wholesale or retail, or through syndicate participation, of stocks, bonds, or other similar securities, shall serve the same time as an officer, director, or employee of any member bank except in limited classes of cases in which the Board of Governors of the Federal Reserve System may allow such service by general regulations when in the judgment of the said

---

23. Although it may be that underinclusiveness is a characteristic of most bills of attainder, we doubt that it is a necessary feature. We think it clear from the Lovett opinion that § 304 would have been voided even if it could have been demonstrated that no one other than Lovett, Watson and Dodd possessed the characteristics which Congress was trying to reach. The vice of attainder is that the legislature has decided for itself that certain persons possess certain characteristics and are therefore deserving of sanction, not that it has failed to sanction others similarly situated.

24. We of course take no position on whether or not members of the Communist Party are in fact likely to incite political strikes. The point we make is rather that the Constitution forbids Congress from making such determinations.

Board it would not unduly influence the investment policies of such member bank or the advice it gives its customers regarding investments." [27]

He suggests that for purposes of the Bill of Attainder Clause, such conflict-of-interest laws are not meaningfully distinguishable from the statute before us. We find this argument without merit. First, we note that § 504, unlike § 32 of the Banking Act, inflicts its deprivation upon the members of a political group thought to present a threat to the national security. As we noted above, such groups were the targets of the overwhelming majority of English and early American bills of attainder. Second, § 32 incorporates no judgment censuring or condemning any man or group of men. In enacting it, Congress relied upon its general knowledge of human psychology, and concluded that the concurrent holding of the two designated positions would present a temptation to *any* man—not just certain men or members of a certain political party. Thus insofar as § 32 incorporates a condemnation, it condemns all men. Third, we cannot accept the suggestion that § 32 constitutes an exercise in specification rather than rule-making. It seems to us clear that § 32 establishes an objective standard of conduct. Congress determined that a person who both (a) held a position in a bank which could be used to influence the investment policies of the bank or its customers, and (b) was in a position to benefit financially from investment in the securities handled by a particular underwriting house, might well be tempted to "use his influence in the bank to involve it or its customers in securities which his underwriting house has in its portfolio or has committed itself to take." 329 U.S., at 447, 67 S.Ct., at 414. In designating bank officers, directors and employees as those persons in position (a), and officers, directors, partners and employees of underwriting houses as those persons in position (b), Congress merely expressed the characteristics it was trying to reach in an alternative, shorthand way.

* * *

It is argued, however, that in § 504 Congress did no more than it did in enacting § 32: it promulgated a general rule to the effect that persons possessing characteristics which make them likely to incite political strikes should not hold union office, and simply inserted in place of a list of those characteristics an alternative, shorthand criterion—membership in the Communist Party. Again, we cannot agree. The designation of Communists as those persons likely to cause political strikes is not the substitution of a semantically equivalent phrase; on the contrary, it rests, as the Court in Douds explicitly recognized, 339 U.S., at 389, 70 S.Ct., at 679, upon an empirical investigation by Congress of the acts, characteristics and propensities of Communist Party members. In a number of decisions, this Court has pointed out the fallacy of the suggestion that membership in the Communist Party, or any other political organization, can be regarded as an alternative, but equivalent, expression for a list of undesirable characteristics. For, as the Court noted in Schneiderman v. United States, 320 U.S. 118, 136, 63 S.Ct. 1333, 1342, 87 L.Ed. 1796, "under our traditions beliefs are personal and not a matter of mere association, and * * * men in adhering to a political party or other organization notoriously do not subscribe unqualified-

---

27. 48 Stat. 194, as amended, 49 Stat. 709, 12 U.S.C.A. § 78 (1964 ed.).

ly to all of its platforms or asserted principles." Just last Term, in Aptheker v. Secretary of State, 378 U.S. 500, 84 S.Ct. 1659, 12 L.Ed.2d 992, we held § 6 of the Subversive Activities Control Act to violate the Constitution because it "too broadly and indiscriminately" restricted constitutionally protected freedoms. One of the factors which compelled us to reach this conclusion was that § 6 inflicted its deprivation upon all members of Communist organizations without regard to whether there existed any demonstrable relationship between the characteristics of the person involved and the evil Congress sought to eliminate. Id., at 509–511, 84 S.Ct., at 1665–1666. These cases are relevant to the question before us. Even assuming that Congress had reason to conclude that some Communists would use union positions to bring about political strikes, "it cannot automatically be inferred that all members shar[e] their evil purposes or participat[e] in their illegal conduct." Schware v. Board of Bar Examiners of State of New Mexico, 353 U.S. 232, 246, 77 S.Ct. 752, 760, 1 L.Ed.2d 796. In utilizing the term "members of the Communist Party" to designate those persons who are likely to incite political strikes, it plainly is not the case that Congress has merely substituted a convenient shorthand term for a list of the characteristics it was trying to reach.[31]

IV.

The Solicitor General argues that § 504 is not a bill of attainder because the prohibition it imposes does not constitute "punishment." In support of this conclusion, he urges that the statute was enacted for preventive rather than retributive reasons—that its aim is not to punish Communists for what they have done in the past, but rather to keep them from positions where they will in the future be able to bring about undesirable events. He relies on American Communications Ass'n v. Douds, 339 U.S. 382, 70 S.Ct. 674, 94 L.Ed. 925, which upheld § 9(h) of the National Labor Relations Act, the predecessor of the statute presently before us. In Douds the Court distinguished Cummings, Garland and Lovett on the ground that in those cases

> "the individuals involved were in fact being punished for *past* actions; whereas in this case they are subject to possible loss of position only because there is substantial ground for the congressional judgment that their beliefs and loyalties will be transformed into *future* conduct." Id., at 413, 70 S.Ct. at 691.

This case is not necessarily controlled by Douds. For to prove its assertion that § 9(h) was preventive rather than retributive in purpose, the Court in Douds focused on the fact that members of the Communist Party could escape from the class of persons specified by Congress simply by resigning from the Party:

> "Here the intention is to forestall future dangerous acts; there is no one who may not by a voluntary alteration of the loyalties which impel him to action, become eligible to sign the affidavit. We cannot conclude that this section is a bill of attainder." Id., at 414, 70 S.Ct. at 692.

---

31. We rely on the "overbroadness" cases only to buttress our conclusion that § 504 cannot be rationalized on the ground that membership in the Communist Party is merely an equivalent, shorthand way of expressing those characteristics which render likely the incitement of political strikes. We of course do not hold that overbroadness is a necessary characteristic of a bill of attainder.

Section 504, unlike § 9(h), disqualifies from the holding of union office not only present members of the Communist Party, but also anyone who has within the past five years been a member of the Party. However, even if we make the assumption that the five-year provision was inserted not out of desire to visit retribution but purely out of a belief that failure to include it would lead to *pro forma* resignations from the Party which would not decrease the threat of political strikes, it still clearly appears that § 504 inflicts "punishment" within the meaning of the Bill of Attainder Clause. It would be archaic to limit the definition of "punishment" to "retribution." Punishment serves several purposes; retributive, rehabilitative, deterrent— and preventive. One of the reasons society imprisons those convicted of crimes is to keep them from inflicting future harm, but that does not make imprisonment any the less punishment.

Historical considerations by no means compel restriction of the bill of attainder ban to instances of retribution. A number of English bills of attainder were enacted for preventive purposes—that is, the legislature made a judgment, undoubtedly based largely on past acts and associations (as § 504 is) that a given person or group was likely to cause trouble (usually, overthrow the government) and therefore inflicted deprivations upon that person or group in order to keep it from bringing about the feared event.[34] It is also clear that many of the early American bills attainting the Tories were passed in order to impede their effectively resisting the Revolution. * * *

The Solicitor General urges us to distinguish Lovett on the ground that the statute struck down there "singled out three identified individuals." It is of course true that § 504 does not contain the words "Archie Brown," and that it inflicts its deprivation upon more than three people. However, the decisions of this Court, as well as the historical background of the Bill of Attainder Clause, make it crystal clear that these are distinctions without a difference. It was not uncommon for English acts of attainder to inflict their deprivations upon relatively large groups of people, sometimes by description rather than name. Moreover, the statutes voided in Cummings and Garland were of this nature. We cannot agree that the fact that § 504 inflicts its deprivation upon the membership of the Communist Party rather than upon a list of named individuals takes it out of the category of bills of attainder.

We do not hold today that Congress cannot weed dangerous persons out of the labor movement, any more than the Court held in Lovett that subversives must be permitted to hold sensitive government positions. Rather, we make again the point made in Lovett: that Congress must accomplish such results by rules of general applicability. * * *

The judgment of the Court of Appeals is affirmed.

---

34. * * * Professor Chafee has pointed out that even the death penalty was often inflicted largely for preventive purposes: "There was no good middle ground between beheading and doing nothing. If the ousted adviser were left at liberty, he could readily turn his resentment into coercion or rebellion and make a magnificent comeback to the utter ruin of those who had driven him from his high place. Therefore, the usual object of Parliamentary proceedings against an important minister was to put him to death." Chafee, Three Human Rights in the Constitution of 1787, pp. 103–104 (1956). * * *

Mr. Justice White, with whom Mr. Justice Clark, Mr. Justice Harlan, and Mr. Justice Stewart join, dissenting.

* * * When an enactment is challenged as an attainder, the central inquiry must be whether the disability imposed by the act is "punishment" (i.e., is directed at an individual or a group of individuals) or is "regulation" (i.e., is directed at controlling future conduct). Flemming v. Nestor, 363 U.S. 603, at 613–614, 80 S.Ct. 1367, at 1374–1375, 4 L.Ed.2d 1435; accord, Trop v. Dulles, 356 U.S. 86, 95–96, 78 S.Ct. 590, 595–596, 2 L.Ed.2d 630 (Warren, C.J., announcing judgment). Whether a punitive purpose would be inferred has depended in past cases on a number of circumstances, including the nature of the disability, whether it was traditionally regarded as punishment, whether it is rationally connected to a permissible legislative objective, as well as the specificity of the legislature's designation of the persons to be affected. * * *

In this case, however, the Court discards this meticulous multifold analysis that has been deemed necessary in the past. * * *

* * * [T]he Court implies that legislation is sufficiently general if it specifies a characteristic that makes it *likely* that individuals falling within the group designated will engage in conduct Congress may prohibit. But the Court then goes on to reject the argument that Communist Party membership is in itself a characteristic raising such a likelihood. The Court declares that "[e]ven assuming that Congress had reason to conclude that *some* Communists would use union positions to bring about political strikes, ' * * * it cannot automatically be inferred that *all* members shar[e] their evil purposes or participat[e] in their illegal conduct.'" (Emphasis added.) This sudden shift in analysis—from likelihood to certainty—must mean that the Bill of Attainder Clause proscribes legislative action with respect to any group smaller than the total class possessing the characteristic upon which legislative power is premised whenever the legislation is based only on a finding about the average characteristics of the subgroup. The legislature may focus on a particular group or class only when the group designation is a "shorthand phrase" for the feared characteristic—i.e., when it is common knowledge that all, not just some, members of the group possess the feared characteristic and thus such legislative designation would require no legislative fact-finding about individuals.[1]

In the Court's view, therefore, § 504 is too narrow in specifying the particular class; but it is also too broad in treating all members of the class alike. On both counts—underinclusiveness and overinclusiveness—§ 504 is invalid as a bill of attainder because Congress has engaged in forbidden fact-finding about individuals and groups and has thus strayed into the area reserved to the judiciary by the Constitution.

I.

It is not difficult to find some of the cases and statutes which the necessary implications of the Court's approach will overrule or invalidate.

---

1. An overbroadness challenge could also be made under the First Amendment on the ground that in § 504 Congress has too broadly and indiscriminately visited disabilities on a class defined in terms of associational ties. See Aptheker v. Secretary of State, 378 U.S. 500, 84 S.Ct. 1659, 12 L.Ed.2d 992. But the Court expressly disavows decision of First Amendment claims, and I likewise put such questions aside.

American Communications Ass'n v. Douds, 339 U.S. 382, 70 S.Ct. 674, 94 L.Ed. 925, which upheld the predecessor statute to § 504 is obviously overruled. In that case the Court accepted the congressional findings about the Communist Party and about the propensity of Party members "to subordinate legitimate trade union objectives to obstructive strikes when dictated by Party leaders, often in support of the policies of a foreign government." 339 U.S., at 388, 70 S.Ct., at 678. Moreover, Congress was permitted to infer from a person's "political affiliations and beliefs" that such a person would be likely to instigate political strikes. 339 U.S., at 391–392, 70 S.Ct., at 680. Like § 504, the statute there under consideration did not cover all persons who might be likely to call political strikes. Nevertheless, legislative findings that *some* Communists would engage in illegal activities were sufficient to sustain the exercise of legislative power. The Bill of Attainder Clause now forbids Congress to do precisely what was validated in Douds.

Similarly invalidated are statutes denying positions of public importance to groups of persons identified by their business affiliations, commonly known as conflict-of-interest statutes. In the Douds case the Court found in such statutes support for its conclusion that Congress could rationally draw inferences about probable conduct on the basis of political affiliations and beliefs, which it considered comparable to business affiliations. The majority in the case now before us likewise recognizes the pertinency of such statutes and, in its discussion of Board of Governors of Federal Reserve System v. Agnew, 329 U.S. 441, 67 S.Ct. 411, 91 L.Ed. 408, strenuously—and unsuccessfully—attempts to distinguish them.

The statute involved in Agnew, § 32 of the Banking Act of 1933, 48 Stat. 194, as amended, 12 U.S.C.A. § 78 (1964 ed.), forbade any partner or employee of a firm primarily engaged in underwriting securities from being a director of a national bank. The Court expressly recognized that the statute was directed to the *"probability or likelihood"* that a bank director who was also a partner or employee of an underwriting firm *"may use his influence in the bank to involve it or its customers in securities which his underwriting house has in its portfolio or has committed itself to take."* 329 U.S., at 447, 67 S.Ct., at 414. (Emphasis added.) And, as we noted in Douds, 339 U.S., at 392, 70 S.Ct., at 681, "[t]here was no showing, nor was one required, that all employees of underwriting firms would engage in such conduct." See also Agnew, 329 U.S., at 449, 67 S.Ct., at 415.

In terms of the Court's analysis of the Bill of Attainder Clause, no meaningful distinction may be drawn between § 32 of the Banking Act and § 504. Both sections disqualify a specifically described group, officers and employees of underwriting firms in the one case and members of the Communist Party in the other. Both sections may be said to be underinclusive: others besides underwriters may have business interests conflicting with the duties of a bank director and others than Communists may call political strikes. Equally, both sections may be deemed overinclusive: neither section finds that all members of the group affected would violate their obligations to the office from which they are disqualified; some members would and perhaps others would not. Both sections are based on a probability or likelihood that this would occur. Both sections leave to the courts the task of determining whether particular persons are members of the designated groups and occupy the specified positions.

In attempting to distinguish the two sections, the Court states that in enacting § 32 of the Banking Act Congress made no judgment or condemnation of any specific group of persons. Instead, the Court reasons, "Congress relied upon its general knowledge of human psychology, and concluded that the concurrent holding of the two designated positions would present a temptation to *any* man—not just certain men or members of a certain political party." But § 32 disqualifies only partners and employees of underwriting firms, not other businessmen with conflicting interests. And § 504 applies to *any* man who occupies the two positions of labor union leader and member of the Communist Party. If based upon "its general knowledge of human psychology" Congress may make findings about a group including members and employees of underwriting firms which disqualify such persons from a certain office, why may not Congress on a similar basis make such a finding about members of the Communist Party? "Because of their business connections, carrying as they do certain loyalties, interests and disciplines," § 32 disqualifies members and employees of underwriting firms as posing "a continuing threat of participation in the harmful activities * * *." Douds, 339 U.S., at 392, 70 S.Ct., at 681. The same might be said about § 504, as was said about its predecessor: "Political affiliations of the kind here involved, no less than business affiliations, provide rational ground for the legislative judgment that those persons proscribed by § 9(h) would be subject to 'tempting opportunities' to commit acts deemed harmful to the national economy. * * *" Id., at 392, 70 S.Ct., at 681.

* * * If the Court would save the conflict-of-interest statutes, which apparently it would, it is difficult to understand why § 504 is stricken down as a bill of attainder.

Other legislative enactments relevant here are those statutes disqualifying felons from occupying certain positions. The leading case is Hawker v. People of State of New York, 170 U.S. 189, 18 S.Ct. 573, 42 L.Ed. 1002, which upheld a provision prohibiting convicted felons from practicing medicine against a claim that, as applied to one convicted before its enactment, it was an *ex post facto* law. The Court noted that a legislature may establish qualifications for the practice of medicine, and character may be such a qualification. Conviction of a felony, the Court reasoned, may be evidence of character:

> "* * * When the legislature declares that whoever has violated the criminal laws of the state shall be deemed lacking in good moral character, it is not laying down an arbitrary or fanciful rule, one having no relation to the subject-matter, but is only appealing to a well-recognized fact of human experience. * * *

> "It is no answer to say that this test of character is not in all cases absolutely certain, and that sometimes it works harshly. Doubtless, one who has violated the criminal law may thereafter reform, and become in fact possessed of a good moral character. But the legislature has power in cases of this kind to make a rule of universal application, and no inquiry is permissible back of the rule to ascertain whether the fact of which the rule

is made the absolute test does or does not exist." 170 U.S., at 196–197, 18 S.Ct., at 576. * * *

Like § 504, the legislation challenged in Hawker was both overinclusive and underinclusive. Felons were not the only persons who might possess character defects making them unsuitable practitioners of medicine; and, as the Court expressly noted, not all felons would lack good moral character. Nevertheless, the legislature was permitted to disqualify all members of the class, rather than being required to delegate to the courts the responsibility of determining the character of each individual based on all relevant facts, including the prior conviction. The legislative findings that sustained the legislation attacked in Hawker were simply that a substantial number of felons would be likely to abuse the practice of medicine because of their bad character. It is just such findings respecting the average propensities of a given class of persons to engage in particular conduct that the Court will not now permit under the Bill of Attainder Clause. Though the Court makes no attempt to distinguish the Hawker-type laws it apparently would save them, see Trop v. Dulles, 356 U.S. 86, 96–97, 78 S.Ct. 590, 595–596, 2 L.Ed.2d 630 (Warren, C.J., announcing judgment), and with them the provision of the statute now before the Court which disqualifies felons from holding union office.[3] * * *

* * * Section 504 is said to impose punishment on specific individuals because it has disqualified all Communist Party members without providing for a judicial determination as to each member that he will call a political strike. A likelihood of doing so based on membership is not enough. By the same token, a statute disqualifying Communists (or authorizing the Executive Branch to do so) from holding sensitive positions in the Government would be automatically infirm, as would a requirement that employees of the Central Intelligence Agency or the National Security Agency disclaim membership in the Communist Party, unless in each case it is proved by evidence other than membership in the Communist Party, the nature of which has already been adjudicated, that the individual would commit acts of disloyalty or subordinate his official undertakings to the interests of the Party.

But how does one prove that a person would be disloyal? The Communist Party's illegal purpose and its domination by a foreign power have already been adjudicated, both administratively and judicially. [Communist Party of United States v. Subversive Activities Control Board, 367 U.S. 1, 81 S.Ct. 1357, 6 L.Ed.2d 625 (1961).] If this does not in itself provide a sufficient probability with respect to the individual who persists in remaining a member of the Party, or if a probability is in any event insufficient, what evidence with regard to the individual will be sufficient to disqualify him? If he must be apprehended in the act of calling one political strike or in one act of disloyalty before steps can be taken to exclude him from office, there is little or nothing left of the preventive or prophylactic function of § 504 or of the statutes such as the Court had before it in Hawker and Agnew. * * *

---

3. For a partial listing of similar statutes, see De Veau v. Braisted, 363 U.S. 144, 159, 80 S.Ct. 1146, 1154, 4 L.Ed.2d 1109 (Frankfurter, J., announcing judgment). De Veau v. Braisted itself sustained against a bill of attainder challenge, without dissent on this issue, a state statute disqualifying felons from holding office in waterfront labor unions.

III.

The basic flaw in the Court's reasoning * * * is its too narrow view of the legislative process. The Court is concerned to separate the legislative and judicial functions by ensuring that the legislature does not infringe the judicial function of applying general rules to specific circumstances. Congress is held to have violated the Bill of Attainder Clause here because, on the one hand, § 504 does not encompass the whole class of persons having characteristics that would make them likely to call political strikes and, on the other hand, § 504 does single out a particular group, members of the Communist Party, not all of whom possess such characteristics. Because of this combination of underinclusiveness and overinclusiveness the Court concludes that Communist Party members were singled out for punishment, thus rejecting the Government's contention that § 504 has solely a regulatory aim.

The Court's conclusion that a statute which is both underinclusive and overinclusive must be deemed to have been adopted with a punitive purpose assumes that legislatures normally deal with broad categories and attack all of an evil at a time. Or if partial measures are undertaken, a legislature singles out a particular group for regulation only because the group label is a "shorthand phrase" for traits that are characteristic of the broader evil. But this Court has long recognized in equal protection cases that a legislature may prefer to deal with only part of an evil. * * * And it is equally true that a group may be singled out for regulation without any punitive purpose even when not all members of the group would be likely to engage in the feared conduct. * * * That is, the focus of legislative attention may be the substantially greater likelihood that some members of the group would engage in the feared conduct compared to the likelihood that members of other groups would do so. This is true because legislators seldom deal with abstractions but with concrete situations and the regulation of specific abuses. Thus many regulatory measures are enacted after investigation into particular incidents or the practices of particular groups and after findings by the legislature that the practices disclosed are inimical to the public interest and should be prevented in the future. Not surprisingly, the resulting legislation may reflect in its specificity the specificity of the preceding legislative inquiry. * * * But the fact that it does should not be taken, in itself, to be conclusive that the legislature's purpose is punitive. Admittedly the degree of specificity is a relevant factor—as when individuals are singled out by name—but because in many instances specificity of the degree here held impermissible may be wholly consistent with a regulatory, rather than a punitive purpose, the Court's *per se* approach cuts too broadly and invalidates legitimate legislative activity.

      * * *

Note

1. Does the Court's reasoning in the Brown case draw into the bill of attainder trap the felony portion of Section 504, along with the Communist portion?

In De Veau v. Braisted, 363 U.S. 144, 80 S.Ct. 1146, 4 L.Ed.2d 1109 (1960), the Court upheld the validity of Section 8 of the New York Waterfront Commission Act of 1953, which made it a crime for any person to collect dues on behalf of any labor organization "if any officer or agent of such organization has been convicted * * * of a felony * * *." The Court stated that the provision in question "is neither a bill of attainder nor an *ex post facto* law. * * * The question in each case * * * is whether the legislative aim was to punish that individual for past activity, or whether the restriction of the individual comes about as a relevant incident to a regulation of the present situation, such as the proper qualifications for a profession. See Hawker v. People of State of New York, 170 U.S. 189, 18 S.Ct. 573, 42 L.Ed. 1002. No doubt is justified regarding the legislative purpose of § 8." 363 U.S. at 160, 80 S.Ct. at 1155.

Does this reasoning apply to Section 504?

2. The court of appeals had reversed Brown's conviction on the grounds of the First and Fifth Amendments: conviction on the basis of mere membership constituted both (1) a denial of freedom of association under the First Amendment and (2) a deprivation of liberty without due process because of inadequacy of proof of guilt (impermissible imputation of guilt by reason of association) under the Fifth Amendment. There was not a "sufficiently close relationship between the regulation and the achievement of the Congressional objective [avoidance of political strikes]." 334 F.2d at 495. In short, Section 504 was a case of legislative over-kill; Congress had shot with a blunderbuss instead of a rifle, thereby hitting "innocent" Party members as well as those who harbored the intent to foment political strikes.

The Supreme Court eschewed the First-Fifth Amendment ground for decision, relying instead upon what it considered to be a simpler and sounder doctrinal vehicle for analysis. Wisely? Which analytical apparatus—that of the First Amendment (and its alter ego, under the facts, the Fifth Amendment) or that of the bill of attainder—best facilitates the isolation, weighing, and balancing of the competing societal values involved in the Brown case?

Chapter 9

THE CONFLICT BETWEEN FREE COLLECTIVE BARGAINING AND OTHER PUBLIC INTERESTS

INTRODUCTORY NOTE

The first three sections of this chapter deal with areas of conflict between the national labor policy of free collective bargaining and the national public interest in (Section A) the elimination of discrimination in employment because of race, color, religion, sex, or national origin; (Section B) the maintenance of a competitive economy through enforcement of the antitrust laws; and (Section C) protection against national emergency disputes. The fourth section, D, deals with the conflict in public interests engendered by the importation of the concepts of free collective bargaining, as developed in the private sector, into the public sector.

Sections A and D—employment discrimination and public employment collective bargaining—are now subjects of law school courses unto themselves. Accordingly, the treatment here will be frugal and spinal-cord in character—to relate these latter-day developments to the main course of the national labor policy.

Similarly, the antitrust laws dealt with in Section B constitute a separate law school course and are treated herein only insofar as they are relevant to, indeed conflict with, the National Labor Relations Act.

Section C, dealing with national emergency disputes, is historically a lean subject and is here accorded lean treatment.

A. EMPLOYMENT DISCRIMINATION

The law of employment discrimination is large and growing. Title VII of the Civil Rights Act of 1964, as amended by the Equal Employment Opportunity Act of 1972,[a] is the major, but not the only, component. The Supreme Court has held that the Civil Rights Act of 1866, 42 U.S.C.A. § 1981, also affords a federal remedy against discrimination in private employment on the basis of race. Johnson v. Railway Express Agency, Inc., 421 U.S. 454, 95 S.Ct. 1716, 44 L.Ed.2d 295 (1975). The requirement of

a. The statute, as amended, is set forth in the Statutory Supplement.

927

affirmative action as an element of federal contract compliance (discussed in United Steelworkers v. Weber, 443 U.S. 193, 99 S.Ct. 2721, 61 L.Ed.2d 480 (1979), infra p. 968) is a third formidable factor in the legal mix.

A result of this multi-pronged approach to implementing the national policy against employment discrimination is the existence of overlapping and competing fora, procedures, and remedies. This problem is considerably exacerbated where a collective bargaining relationship exists. Where the union is involved in the discriminatory practice, or is its originator, the matter may become the subject of judicial proceedings based on the duty of fair representation (Vaca v. Sipes, supra p. 742) and of NLRB proceedings based on the theory that the violation of the duty of fair representation is an unfair labor practice (Local 12, supra p. 737). Where the Union is supportive of the employee or group of employees claiming discrimination, the grievance-arbitration machinery of the collective bargaining agreement may be invoked.

Detailed exploration of the many legal approaches to employment discrimination problems is beyond the scope of this subchapter, as is a detailed analysis of Title VII. It is our limited purpose to focus on two specific areas of conflict between the labor law and the law governing employment discrimination.

First, the Gardner-Denver case (which follows) and the Robbins & Myers case (infra p. 938) deal with the problem of reconciling the pro-arbitration policy reflected in the "Steelworkers Trilogy" (supra p. 632) and in the Collyer-Spielberg deferral doctrine (supra p. 725) with the mandate to the federal courts under Title VII to afford a forum to the victims of discrimination. Second, the remaining three principal cases in the section focus on a conflict between a primary goal of collective bargaining—job security based on seniority—and a primary goal of the civil rights acts—remedying the effects of generations of employment discrimination; as we shall see, Congress passed a hot potato to the federal courts, and the courts are still juggling it.

ALEXANDER v. GARDNER–DENVER CO.

Supreme Court of the United States, 1974.
415 U.S. 36, 94 S.Ct. 1011, 39 L.Ed.2d 147.

MR. JUSTICE POWELL delivered the opinion of the Court.

This case concerns the proper relationship between federal courts and the grievance-arbitration machinery of collective-bargaining agreements in the resolution and enforcement of an individual's rights to equal employment opportunities under Title VII of the Civil Rights Act of 1964 * * *. Specifically, we must decide under what circumstances, if any, an employee's statutory right to a trial *de novo* under Title VII may be foreclosed by prior submission of his claim to final arbitration under the nondiscrimination clause of a collective-bargaining agreement.

I

In May 1966, petitioner Harrell Alexander, Sr., a black, was hired by respondent Gardner-Denver Company (the "company") to perform maintenance work at the company's plant in Denver, Colorado. In June 1968, petitioner was awarded a trainee position as a drill operator. He remained at that job until his discharge from employment on September 29, 1969. The company informed petitioner that he was being discharged for producing too many defective or unusable parts that had to be scrapped.

On October 1, 1969, petitioner filed a grievance under the collective-bargaining agreement in force between the company and petitioner's union, Local No. 3029 of the United Steelworkers of America (the "union"). The grievance stated: "I feel I have been unjustly discharged and ask that I be reinstated with full seniority and pay." No explicit claim of racial discrimination was made.

Under Art. 4 of the collective-bargaining agreement, the company retained "the right to hire, suspend or discharge [employees] for proper cause." Art. 5, § 2 provided, however, that "there shall be no discrimination against any employee on account of race, color, religion, sex, national origin, or ancestry," and Art. 23, § 6(a) stated that "[n]o employee will be discharged, suspended or given a written warning notice except for just cause." The agreement also contained a broad arbitration clause covering "differences aris[ing] between the Company and the Union as to the meaning and application of the provisions of this Agreement" and "any trouble aris[ing] in the plant." Disputes were to be submitted to a multi-step grievance procedure, the first four steps of which involved negotiations between the company and the union. If the dispute remained unresolved, it was to be remitted to compulsory arbitration. The company and the union were to select and pay the arbitrator, and his decision was to be "final and binding upon the Company, the Union, and any employee or employees involved." The agreement further provided that "[t]he arbitrator shall not amend, take away, add to, or change any of the provisions of this Agreement, and the arbitrator's decision must be based solely on an interpretation of the provisions of this Agreement." The parties also agreed that there "shall be no suspension of work" over disputes covered by the grievance-arbitration clause.

The union processed petitioner's grievance through the above machinery. In the final prearbitration step, petitioner raised, apparently for the first time, the claim that his discharge resulted from racial discrimination. The company rejected all of petitioner's claims, and the grievance proceeded to arbitration. Prior to the arbitration hearing, however, petitioner filed a charge of racial discrimination with the Colorado Civil Rights Commission, which referred the complaint to the Equal Employment Opportunity Commission on November 5, 1969.

At the arbitration hearing on November 20, 1969, petitioner testified that his discharge was the result of racial discrimination and informed the arbitrator that he had filed a charge with the Colorado Commission because he "could not rely on the union." The union introduced a letter in which petitioner stated that he was "knowledgeable that in the same plant others have scrapped an equal amount and sometimes in excess, but by all logical reasoning I * * * have been the target of preferential discriminatory treatment." The union representative also testified that the company's usual practice was to transfer unsatisfactory trainee drill operators back to their former positions.

On December 30, 1969, the arbitrator ruled that petitioner had been "discharged for just cause." He made no reference to petitioner's claim of racial discrimination. The arbitrator stated that the union had failed to produce evidence of a practice of transferring rather than discharging trainee drill operators who accumulated excessive scrap, but he suggested that the company and the union confer on whether such an arrangement was feasible in the present case.

On July 25, 1970, the Equal Employment Opportunity Commission determined that there was not reasonable cause to believe that a violation of Title VII of the Civil Rights Act of 1964 * * * had occurred. The Commission later notified petitioner of his right to institute a civil action in federal court within 30 days. Petitioner then filed the present action in the United States District Court for the District of Colorado, alleging that his discharge resulted from a racially discriminatory employment practice in violation of § 703(a)(1) of the Act. * * *

The District Court granted respondent's motion for summary judgment and dismissed the action. 346 F.Supp. 1012 (1971). The court found that the claim of racial discrimination had been submitted to the arbitrator and resolved adversely to petitioner.[4] It then held that petitioner, having voluntarily elected to pursue his grievance to final arbitration under the nondiscrimination clause of the collective-bargaining agreement, was bound by the arbitral decision and thereby precluded from suing his employer under Title VII. The Court of Appeals for the Tenth Circuit affirmed *per curiam* on the basis of the District Court's opinion. 466 F.2d 1209 (1972).

We granted petitioner's application for certiorari. * * * We reverse.

II

Congress enacted Title VII of the Civil Rights Act of 1964 * * * to assure equality of employment opportunities by eliminating those practices and devices that discriminate on the basis of race, color, religion, sex, or national origin. McDonnell Douglas Corp. v. Green, 411 U.S. 792, 800, 93 S.Ct. 1817, 1823, 36 L.Ed.2d 668 (1973); Griggs v. Duke Power Co., 401 U.S. 424, 429–430, 91 S.Ct. 849, 852–853, 28 L.Ed.2d 158 (1971). Cooperation and voluntary compliance were selected as the preferred means for achieving this goal. To this end, Congress created the Equal Employment Opportunity Commission and established a procedure whereby existing State and local equal employment opportunity agencies, as well as the Commission, would have an opportunity to settle disputes through conference, conciliation, and persuasion before the aggrieved party was permitted to file a lawsuit. In the Equal Employment Opportunity Act of 1972, Pub.L. 92–261, 86 Stat. 103, Congress amended Title VII to provide the Commission with further authority to investigate individual charges of discrimination, to promote voluntary compliance with the requirements of Title VII, and to institute civil actions against employers or unions named in a discrimination charge.

---

4. In reaching this conclusion, the District Court relied on petitioner's deposition acknowledging that he had raised the racial discrimination claim during the arbitration hearing. 346 F.Supp. 1012, 1014.

Even in its amended form, however, Title VII does not provide the Commission with direct powers of enforcement. The Commission cannot adjudicate claims or impose administrative sanctions. Rather, final responsibility for enforcement of Title VII is vested with federal courts. The Act authorizes courts to issue injunctive relief and to order such affirmative action as may be appropriate to remedy the effects of unlawful employment practices. 42 U.S.C.A. §§ 2000e–5(f) and (g) [§§ 706(f) and (g)]. Courts retain these broad remedial powers despite a Commission finding of no reasonable cause to believe that the Act has been violated. McDonnell Douglas Corp. v. Green, supra, 411 U.S., at 798–799, 93 S.Ct., at 1822–1823. Taken together, these provisions make plain that federal courts have been assigned plenary powers to secure compliance with Title VII.

In addition to reposing ultimate authority in federal courts, Congress gave private individuals a significant role in the enforcement process of Title VII. Individual grievants usually initiate the Commission's investigatory and conciliatory procedures. And although the 1972 amendment to Title VII empowers the Commission to bring its own actions, the private right of action remains an essential means of obtaining judicial enforcement of Title VII. 42 U.S.C.A. § 2000e–5(f)(1) [§ 706(f)(1)]. In such cases, the private litigant not only redresses his own injury but also vindicates the important congressional policy against discriminatory employment practices. Hutchings v. United States Industries, Inc., 428 F.2d 303, 310 (CA5 1970); Bowe v. Colgate-Palmolive Co., 416 F.2d 711, 715 (CA7 1969); Jenkins v. United Gas Corp., 400 F.2d 28, 33 (CA5 1968). See also Newman v. Piggie Park Enterprises, Inc., 390 U.S. 400, 402, 88 S.Ct. 964, 966, 19 L.Ed.2d 1263 (1968).

Pursuant to this statutory scheme, petitioner initiated the present action for judicial consideration of his rights under Title VII. The District Court and the Court of Appeals held, however, that petitioner was bound by the prior arbitral decision and had no right to sue under Title VII. Both courts evidently thought that this result was dictated by notions of election of remedies and waiver and by the federal policy favoring arbitration of labor disputes, as enunciated by this Court in Textile Workers Union v. Lincoln Mills, 353 U.S. 448, 77 S.Ct. 912, 923, 1 L.Ed.2d 972 (1957), and the *Steelworkers Trilogy.* ＊　＊　＊ We disagree.

III

Title VII does not speak expressly to the relationship between federal courts and the grievance-arbitration machinery of collective-bargaining agreements. It does, however, vest federal courts with plenary powers to enforce the statutory requirements; and it specifies with precision the jurisdictional prerequisites that an individual must satisfy before he is entitled to institute a lawsuit. In the present case, these prerequisites were met when petitioner (1) filed timely a charge of employment discrimination with the Commission, and (2) received and acted upon the Commission's statutory notice of the right to sue. 42 U.S.C.A. §§ 2000e–5(b), (e), and (f) [§§ 706(b), (e), and (f)]. See McDonnell Douglas Corp. v. Green, supra, 411 U.S., at 798, 93 S.Ct. at 1822. There is no suggestion in the statutory scheme that a prior arbitral decision either forecloses an individual's right to sue or divests federal courts of jurisdiction.

In addition, legislative enactments in this area have long evinced a general intent to accord parallel or overlapping remedies against discrimination.[7] In the Civil Rights Act of 1964 * * * Congress indicated that it considered the policy against discrimination to be of the "highest priority." Newman v. Piggie Park Enterprises, Inc., supra, 390 U.S., at 402, 88 S.Ct. at 966. Consistent with this view, Title VII provides for consideration of employment-discrimination claims in several forums. See 42 U.S.C.A. § 2000e–5(b) [§ 706(b)] (EEOC); 42 U.S.C.A. § 2000e–5(c) [§ 706(c)] (State and local agencies); 42 U.S.C.A. § 2000e–5(f) [§ 706(f)] (federal courts). And, in general, submission of a claim to one forum does not preclude a later submission to another.[8] Moreover, the legislative history of Title VII manifests a congressional intent to allow an individual to pursue independently his rights under both Title VII and other applicable state and federal statutes.[9] The clear inference is that Title VII was designed to supplement, rather than supplant, existing laws and institutions relating to employment discrimination. In sum, Title VII's purpose and procedures strongly suggest that an individual does not forfeit his private cause of action if he first pursues his grievance to final arbitration under the nondiscrimination clause of a collective-bargaining agreement.

In reaching the opposite conclusion, the District Court relied in part on the doctrine of election of remedies. That doctrine, which refers to situations where an individual pursues remedies that are legally or factually inconsistent, has no application in the present context. In submitting his grievance to arbitration, an employee seeks to vindicate his contractual right under a collective-bargaining agreement. By contrast, in filing a lawsuit under Title VII, an employee asserts independent statutory rights accorded by Congress. The distinctly separate nature of these contractual and statutory rights is not vitiated merely because both were violated as a result of the same factual occurrence. And certainly no inconsistency results from permitting both rights to be enforced in their respectively appropriate forums. The resulting scheme is somewhat analogous to the procedure

7. See, e.g. 42 U.S.C.A. § 1981 (Civil Rights Act of 1866); 42 U.S.C.A. § 1983 (Civil Rights Act of 1871).

8. For example, Commission action is not barred by "findings and orders" of state or local agencies. See 42 U.S.C.A. § 2000e–5(b) [§ 706(b)]. Similarly, an individual's cause of action is not barred by a Commission finding of no reasonable cause to believe that the Act has been violated. See 42 U.S.C.A. § 2000e–5(f) [§ 706(f)]; McDonnell Douglas Corp. v. Green, supra.

9. For example, Senator Joseph Clark, one of the sponsors of the bill, introduced an interpretive memorandum which stated: "Nothing in Title VII or anywhere else in this bill affects the rights and obligations under the NLRA or the Railway Labor Act * * *. Title VII is not intended to and does not deny to any individual, rights and remedies which he may pursue under other federal and state statutes. If a given action should violate both Title VII and the National Labor Relations Act, the National Labor Relations Board

would not be deprived of jurisdiction." 110 Cong.Rec. 7207 (1964). Moreover, the Senate defeated an amendment which would have made Title VII the exclusive federal remedy for most unlawful employment practices. 110 Cong.Rec. 13650–13652 (1964). And a similar amendment was rejected in connection with the Equal Employment Opportunity Act of 1972. See H.R. 9247, 92d Cong., 1st Sess. (1971). See also 2 U.S.Code Cong. & Admin. News, 92d Cong., 2d Sess. (1972), pp. 2137, 2179, 2181–2182. The report of the Senate Committee responsible for the 1972 Act explained that the "provisions regarding the individual's right to sue under Title VII, nor any of the provisions of this bill, are meant to affect existing rights granted under other laws." S.Rep. No. 415, at 24, 92d Cong., 1st Sess. (1971). For a detailed discussion of the legislative history of the 1972 Act, see Sape and Hart, Title VII Reconsidered: The Equal Opportunity Act of 1972, 40 Geo.Wash.L.Rev. 824 (1972).

under the National Labor Relations Act, as amended, where disputed transactions may implicate both contractual and statutory rights. Where the statutory right underlying a particular claim may not be abridged by contractual agreement, the Court has recognized that consideration of the claim by the arbitrator as a contractual dispute under the collective-bargaining agreement does not preclude subsequent consideration of the claim by the National Labor Relations Board as an unfair labor practice charge or as a petition for clarification of the union's representation certificate under the Act. Carey v. Westinghouse Electric Corp., 375 U.S. 261, 84 S.Ct. 401, 11 L.Ed.2d 320 (1964). Cf. Smith v. Evening News Assn., 371 U.S. 195, 83 S.Ct. 267, 9 L.Ed.2d 246 (1962). There, as here, the relationship between the forums is complementary since consideration of the claim by both forums may promote the policies underlying each. Thus, the rationale behind the election of remedies doctrine cannot support the decision below.[14]

We are also unable to accept the proposition that petitioner waived his cause of action under Title VII. To begin, we think it clear that there can be no prospective waiver of an employee's rights under Title VII. It is true, of course, that a union may waive certain statutory rights related to collective activity, such as the right to strike. Mastro Plastics Corp. v. NLRB, 350 U.S. 270, 76 S.Ct. 349, 100 L.Ed. 309 (1956); Boys Markets, Inc. v. Retail Clerks Union, 398 U.S. 235, 90 S.Ct. 1583, 26 L.Ed.2d 199 (1970). These rights are conferred on employees collectively to foster the processes of bargaining and properly may be exercised or relinquished by the union as collective-bargaining agent to obtain economic benefits for unit members. Title VII, on the other hand, stands on plainly different ground; it concerns not majoritarian processes, but an individual's right to equal employment opportunities. Title VII's strictures are absolute and represent a congressional command that each employee be free from discriminatory practices. Of necessity, the rights conferred can form no part of the collective-bargaining process since waiver of these rights would defeat the paramount congressional purpose behind Title VII. In these circumstances, an employee's rights under Title VII are not susceptible to prospective waiver. See Wilko v. Swan, 346 U.S. 427, 74 S.Ct. 182, 98 L.Ed. 168 (1953).

The actual submission of petitioner's grievance to arbitration in the present case does not alter the situation. Although presumably an employee may waive his cause of action under Title VII as part of a voluntary settlement,[15] mere resort to the arbitral forum to enforce contractual rights constitutes no such waiver. Since an employee's rights under Title VII may

---

14. Nor can it be maintained that election of remedies is required by the possibility of unjust enrichment through duplicative recoveries. Where, as here, the employer has prevailed at arbitration, there of course can be no duplicative recovery. But even in cases where the employee has first prevailed, judicial relief can be structured to avoid such windfall gains. * * * Furthermore, if the relief obtained by the employee at arbitration were fully equivalent to that obtainable under Title VII, there would be no further relief for the court to grant and hence no need for the employee to institute suit.

15. In this case petitioner and respondent did not enter into a voluntary settlement expressly conditioned on a waiver of petitioner's cause of action under Title VII. In determining the effectiveness of any such waiver, a court would have to determine at the outset that the employee's consent to the settlement was voluntary and knowing. In no event can the submission to arbitration of a claim under the nondiscrimination clause of a collective-bargaining agreement constitute a binding waiver with respect to an employee's rights under Title VII.

not be waived prospectively, existing contractual rights and remedies against discrimination must result from other concessions already made by the union as part of the economic bargain struck with the employer. It is settled law that no additional concession may be exacted from any employee as the price for enforcing those rights. J.I. Case Co. v. National Labor Relations Board, 321 U.S. 332, 338–339, 64 S.Ct. 576, 580–581, 88 L.Ed. 762 (1944).

Moreover, a contractual right to submit a claim to arbitration is not displaced simply because Congress also has provided a statutory right against discrimination. Both rights have legally independent origins and are equally available to the aggrieved employee. This point becomes apparent through consideration of the role of the arbitrator in the system of industrial self-government.[16] As the proctor of the bargain, the arbitrator's task is to effectuate the intent of the parties. His source of authority is the collective-bargaining agreement, and he must interpret and apply that agreement in accordance with the "industrial common law of the shop" and the various needs and desires of the parties. The arbitrator, however, has no general authority to invoke public laws that conflict with the bargain between the parties * * *. Thus the arbitrator has authority to resolve only questions of contractual rights, and this authority remains regardless of whether certain contractual rights are similar to, or duplicative of, the substantive rights secured by Title VII.

IV

The District Court and the Court of Appeals reasoned that to permit an employee to have his claim considered in both the arbitral and judicial forums would be unfair since this would mean that the employer, but not the employee, was bound by the arbitral award. In the District Court's words, it could not "accept a philosophy which gives the employee two strings to his bow when the employer has only one." 346 F.Supp., at 1019. This argument mistakes the effect of Title VII. Under the *Steelworker's Trilogy,* an arbitral decision is final and binding on the employer and employee, and judicial review is limited as to both. But in instituting an action under Title VII, the employee is not seeking review of the arbitrator's decision. Rather, he is asserting a statutory right independent of the arbitration process. An employer does not have "two strings to his bow" with respect to an arbitral decision for the simple reason that Title VII does not provide employers with a cause of action against employees. An employer cannot be the victim of discriminatory employment practices. * * *

The District Court and the Court of Appeals also thought that to permit a later resort to the judicial forum would undermine substantially the

---

16. See Meltzer, Labor Arbitration and Overlapping and Conflicting Remedies for Employment Discrimination, 39 U.Chi.L.Rev. 30, 32–35 (1971); Meltzer, Ruminations About Ideology, Law, and Arbitration, 34 U.Chi.L. Rev. 545 (1967). As the late Dean Shulman stated:

"A proper conception of the arbitrator's function is basic. He is not a public tribunal imposed upon the parties by superior authority which the parties are obliged to accept. He has no general charter to administer justice for a community which transcends the parties. He is rather part of a system of industrial self-government created by and confined to the parties. He serves their pleasure only, to administer the rule of law established by their collective agreement." Shulman, Reason, Contracts and Law in Labor Relations, 68 Harv.L.Rev. 999, 1016 (1955).

employer's incentive to arbitrate and would "sound the death knell for arbitration clauses in labor contracts." 346 F.Supp., at 1019. Again, we disagree. The primary incentive for an employer to enter into an arbitration agreement is the union's reciprocal promise not to strike. As the Court stated in Boys Markets, Inc. v. Retail Clerk's Union, 398 U.S. 235, 248, 90 S.Ct. 1583, 1591, 26 L.Ed.2d 199 (1970), "a no strike obligation, express or implied, is the *quid pro quo* for an undertaking by an employer to submit grievance disputes to the process of arbitration." It is not unreasonable to assume that most employers will regard the benefits derived from a no-strike pledge as outweighing whatever costs may result from according employees an arbitral remedy against discrimination in addition to their judicial remedy under Title VII. Indeed, the severe consequences of a strike may make an arbitration clause almost essential from both the employees' and the employer's perspective. Moreover, the grievance-arbitration machinery of the collective-bargaining agreement remains a relatively inexpensive and expeditious means for resolving a wide range of disputes, including claims of discriminatory employment practices. Where the collective-bargaining agreement contains a nondiscrimination clause similar to Title VII, and where arbitral procedures are fair and regular, arbitration may well produce a settlement satisfactory to both employer and employee. An employer thus has an incentive to make available the conciliatory and therapeutic processes of arbitration which may satisfy an employee's perceived need to resort to the judicial forum, thus saving the employer the expense and aggravation associated with a lawsuit. For similar reasons, the employee also has a strong incentive to arbitrate grievances, and arbitration may often eliminate those misunderstandings or discriminatory practices that might otherwise precipitate resort to the judicial forum.

V

Respondent contends that even if a preclusion rule is not adopted, federal courts should defer to arbitral decisions on discrimination claims where: (i) the claim was before the arbitrator; (ii) the collective-bargaining agreement prohibited the form of discrimination charged in the suit under Title VII; and (iii) the arbitrator has authority to rule on the claim and to fashion a remedy.[17] Under respondent's proposed rule, a court would grant summary judgment and dismiss the employee's action if the above conditions were met. The rule's obvious consequence in the present case would be to deprive the petitioner of his statutory right to attempt to establish his claim in a federal court.

At the outset, it is apparent that a deferral rule would be subject to many of the objections applicable to a preclusion rule. The purpose and procedures of Title VII indicate that Congress intended federal courts to exercise final responsibility for enforcement of Title VII; deferral to arbitral decisions would be inconsistent with that goal. Furthermore, we have long recognized that "the choice of forums inevitably affects the scope of the substantive right to be vindicated." U.S. Bulk Carriers v. Arguelles, 400 U.S. 351, 358, 359–360, 91 S.Ct. 409, 413, 414, 27 L.Ed.2d 456 (1971) (Harlan,

---

17. Respondent's proposed rule is analogous to the NLRB's policy of deferring to arbitral decisions on statutory issues in certain cases. See Spielberg Manufacturing Co., 112 N.L.R.B. 1080, 1082 (1955).

J., concurring). Respondent's deferral rule is necessarily premised on the assumption that arbitral processes are commensurate with judicial processes and that Congress impliedly intended federal courts to defer to arbitral decisions on Title VII issues. We deem this supposition unlikely.

Arbitral procedures, while well suited to the resolution of contractual disputes, make arbitration a comparatively inappropriate forum for the final resolution of rights created by Title VII. This conclusion rests first on the special role of the arbitrator, whose task is to effectuate the intent of the parties rather than the requirements of enacted legislation. Where the collective-bargaining agreement conflicts with Title VII, the arbitration must follow the agreement. To be sure, the tension between contractual and statutory objectives may be mitigated where a collective-bargaining agreement contains provisions facially similar to those of Title VII. But other facts may still render arbitral processes comparatively inferior to judicial processes in the protection of Title VII rights. Among these is the fact that the specialized competence of arbitrators pertains primarily to the law of the shop, not the law of the land. United Steelworkers of America v. Warrior & Gulf Navigation Co., 363 U.S. 574, at 581–583, 80 S.Ct. 1347, at 1352–1353, 4 L.Ed.2d 1409.[18] Parties usually choose an arbitrator because they trust his knowledge and judgment concerning the demands and norms of industrial relations. On the other hand, the resolution of statutory or constitutional issues is a primary responsibility of courts, and judicial construction has proven especially necessary with respect to Title VII, whose broad language frequently can be given meaning only by reference to public law concepts.

Moreover, the fact-finding process in arbitration usually is not equivalent to judicial fact-finding. The record of the arbitration proceedings is not as complete; the usual rules of evidence do not apply; and rights and procedures common to civil trials such as discovery, compulsory process, cross-examination, and testimony under oath, are often severely limited or unavailable. * * * And as this Court has recognized, "[a]rbitrators have no obligation to the court to give their reasons for an award." United Steelworkers of America v. Enterprise Wheel & Car Corp., 363 U.S. 593, at 598, 80 S.Ct. 1358, at 1361, 4 L.Ed.2d 1424. Indeed, it is the informality of arbitral procedure that enables it to function as an efficient, inexpensive, and expeditious means for dispute resolution. This same characteristic, however, makes arbitration a less appropriate forum for final resolution of Title VII issues than the federal courts.[19]

---

18. See also Gould, Labor Arbitration of Grievances Involving Racial Discrimination, 118 U.Pa.L.Rev. 40, 47–48 (1969); Platt, The Relationship between Arbitration and Title VII of the Civil Rights Act of 1964, 3 Ga.L. Rev. 398 (1969). Significantly, a substantial proportion of labor arbitrators are not lawyers. See Note, The NLRB and Deference to Arbitration, 77 Yale L.J. 1191, 1194, n. 28 (1968). This is not to suggest, of course, that arbitrators do not possess a high degree of competence with respect to the vital role in implementing the federal policy favoring arbitration of labor disputes.

19. A further concern is the union's exclusive control over the manner and extent to which an individual grievance is presented. See Vaca v. Sipes, 386 U.S. 171, 87 S.Ct. 903, 17 L.Ed.2d 842 (1967); Republic Steel Co. v. Maddox, 379 U.S. 650, 85 S.Ct. 614, 13 L.Ed.2d 580 (1965). In arbitration, as in the collective-bargaining process, the interests of the individual employee may be subordinated to the collective interests of all employees in the bargaining unit. See J.I. Case Co. v. National Labor Relations Board, 321 U.S. 332, 64 S.Ct. 576, 88 L.Ed. 762 (1944). Moreover, harmony of interest between the union and the individual employee cannot always be presumed, especially where a claim of racial discrimination is made. See, e.g., Steele v. Louisville & N.R. Co., 323 U.S. 192, 65 S.Ct. 226, 89 L.Ed. 173

It is evident that respondents' proposed rule would not allay these concerns. Nor are we convinced that the solution lies in applying a more demanding deferral standard, such as that adopted by the Fifth Circuit in Rios v. Reynolds Metals Co., 467 F.2d 54 (1972).[20] As respondent points out, a standard that adequately insured effectuation of Title VII rights in the arbitral forum would tend to make arbitration a procedurally complex, expensive, and time-consuming process. And judicial enforcement of such a standard would almost require courts to make *de novo* determinations of the employees' claims. It is uncertain whether any minimal savings in judicial time and expense would justify the risk to vindication of Title VII rights.

A deferral rule also might adversely affect the arbitration system as well as the enforcement scheme of Title VII. Fearing that the arbitral forum cannot adequately protect their rights under Title VII, some employees may elect to bypass arbitration and institute a lawsuit. The possibility of voluntary compliance or settlement of Title VII claims would thus be reduced, and the result could well be more litigation, not less.

We think, therefore, that the federal policy favoring arbitration of labor disputes and the federal policy against discriminatory employment practices can best be accommodated by permitting an employee to pursue fully both his remedy under the grievance-arbitration clause of a collective-bargaining agreement and his cause of action under Title VII. The federal court should consider the employee's claim *de novo*. The arbitral decision may be admitted as evidence and accorded such weight as the court deems appropriate.[21]

The judgment of the Court of Appeals is reversed.

(1944) * * *. And a breach of the union's duty of fair representation may prove difficult to establish. See Vaca v. Sipes, supra; Humphrey v. Moore, 375 U.S. 335, 342, 348–351, 84 S.Ct. 363, 367, 371–373, 11 L.Ed.2d 370. In this respect, it is noteworthy that Congress thought it necessary to afford the protections of Title VII against unions as well as employers. * * *

20. In *Rios*, the court set forth the following deferral standard: "First, there may be no deference to the decision of the arbitrator unless the contractual right coincides with rights under Title VII. Second, it must be plain that the arbitrator's decision is in no way violative of the private rights guaranteed by Title VII, nor of the public policy which inheres in Title VII. In addition, before deferring, the district court must be satisfied that (1) the factual issues before it are identical to those decided by the arbitrator; (2) the arbitrator had power under the collective agreement to decide the ultimate issue of discrimination; (3) the evidence presented at the arbitral hearing dealt adequately with all factual issues; (4) the arbitrator actually decided the factual issues presented to the court; (5) the arbitration proceeding was fair and regular and free of procedural infirmities. The burden of proof in establishing these conditions of limitation will be upon the respondent

as distinguished from the claimant." 467 F.2d, at 58. For a discussion of the problems posed by application of the *Rios* standard, see Note, Judicial Deference to Arbitrators' Decisions in Title VII Cases, 26 Stan.L.Rev. 421 (1974).

21. We adopt no standards as to the weight to be accorded an arbitral decision, since this must be determined in the court's discretion with regard to the facts and circumstances of each case. Relevant factors include the existence of provisions in the collective-bargaining agreement that conform substantially with Title VII, the degree of procedural fairness in the arbitral forum, adequacy of the record with respect to the issue of discrimination, and the special competence of particular arbitrators. Where an arbitral determination gives full consideration to an employee's Title VII rights, a court may properly accord it great weight. This is especially true where the issue is solely one of fact, specifically addressed by the parties and decided by the arbitrator on the basis of an adequate record. But courts should ever be mindful that Congress, in enacting Title VII, thought it necessary to provide a judicial forum for the ultimate resolution of discriminatory employment claims. It is the duty of courts to assure the full availability of this forum.

Note

1. Mr. Alexander won the battle but lost the war. In Alexander v. Gardner-Denver Co., 519 F.2d 503 (10th Cir.1975), cert. denied, 423 U.S. 1058, 96 S.Ct. 793, 46 L.Ed.2d 648 (1976), the court of appeals, on remand, affirmed the trial court's decision granting judgment for the employer. The only mention made of the arbitration award is in the factual recitation: "The arbitrator did not consider whether racial discrimination was involved in the discharge." 519 F.2d at 505.

2. Are you in agreement with the proposition advanced in the last sentence of footnote 15 of Gardner-Denver: "In no event can the submission to arbitration of a claim under the nondiscrimination clause of a collective-bargaining agreement constitute a binding waiver with respect to an employee's rights under Title VII." Why should not an employee's "voluntary and knowing" waiver of the right to sue his employer under Title VII be viewed as the quid pro quo for the employer's willingness to arbitrate the particular grievance? If the right to a jury trial in a criminal case may be so waived, why is not waiver of the Title VII right a fortiori? Is the employer bound by the arbitration provision to arbitrate grievances as to which no finality of award attaches?

ELECTRICAL WORKERS, LOCAL 790 v. ROBBINS & MYERS, INC.

Supreme Court of the United States, 1976.
429 U.S. 229, 97 S.Ct. 441, 50 L.Ed.2d 427.

MR. JUSTICE REHNQUIST delivered the opinion of the Court.

Petitioners seek review of a decision of the Court of Appeals for the Sixth Circuit holding that a claim brought by petitioner Dortha Guy under Title VII was barred by her failure to file a charge with the Equal Employment Opportunity Commission (EEOC) within the statutory limitations period. They present three contentions: the existence and utilization of grievance procedures postpones the date on which an allegedly discriminatory firing took place; the existence and utilization of grievance procedures tolls the running of the limitations period which would otherwise begin on the date of the firing; and the 1972 amendments to Title VII, Equal Employment Opportunity Act of 1972, extending the limitations period from 90 to 180 days, apply to the charge in this case.

I

Respondent terminated the employment of petitioner Guy on October 25, 1971, and assigned as its reason for doing so her failure to comply with procedures contained in the collective-bargaining agreement pertaining to leaves of absence. Two days later petitioner caused a grievance alleging the "unfair action" of the Company in firing her to be filed on her behalf in accordance with the provisions of the collective-bargaining agreement then in force between petitioner Local 790 of the International Union of Electrical, Radio and Machine Workers (Local 790) and respondent. That agreement's dispute resolution procedure, which is to be commenced within "five (5) working days of the commission of the act originating the grievance," consists of three grievance steps followed by one arbitration step. Guy's grievance was processed through the third step of the grievance procedure where it was denied on November 18, 1971, with the finding that her termination had been in accordance with the provisions of the collective-bargaining agreement.

On February 10, 1972, a date 84 days after the denial of her grievance at the third stage, but 108 days after the date of her discharge, Guy, who is black, filed a charge of racial discrimination with the EEOC directed against both Robbins & Myers and Local 790. The EEOC in due course issued its determination and "right to sue" letter finding that there was "no reason to believe that race was a factor in the decision to discharge" Guy. Her suit in the United States District Court for the Western District of Tennessee under 42 U.S.C.A. § 2000e–5 was met by a motion to dismiss on the ground, *inter alia*, that it was barred because of her failure to file a charge with the EEOC within 90 days of her discharge, § 706(d), 42 U.S.C.A. § 2000e–5(d).[1] The District Court dismissed her action,[2] and the Court of Appeals affirmed that judgment by a divided vote, 6 Cir., 525 F.2d 124. That court felt that it would be "utterly inconsistent" with our opinions in Johnson v. Railway Express Agency, 421 U.S. 454, 95 S.Ct. 1716, 44 L.Ed.2d 295 (1975) and in Alexander v. Gardner-Denver Co., 415 U.S. 36, 94 S.Ct. 1011, 39 L.Ed.2d 147 (1974) to hold that the pursuit of a contractual grievance procedure operates to toll a Title VII remedy "which the employee has a right to resort to concurrently." 525 F.2d at 126. Then, noting the question of the applicability of the 1972 amendments to Title VII raised by the EEOC as *amicus curiae* (also noting without more that "[s]ince this issue was not raised in the District Court by any party to the case, we are not required to consider it") the Court of Appeals stated

"Plaintiff Guy's claim was barred on January 24, 1972. She did not file her charge with EEOC until February 10, 1972. The amendments to Title VII, increasing the time within which to file her charge to 180 days, did not become effective until March 24, 1972. 42 U.S.C.A. § 2000e–5(e). The subsequent increase of time to file the charge enacted by Congress could not revive plaintiff's claim which had been previously barred and extinguished." 525 F.2d, at 128.

The dissenting judge disagreed on this point, believing that the case should be remanded for consideration of the effect of the 1972 amendments.

We granted certiorari to resolve an apparent circuit conflict on two of these issues: tolling during the pendency of a collective-bargaining-contract's grievance mechanism, and the applicability of the 1972 amendments to charges filed more than 90 days from the date of the alleged discriminatory act but less than 180 days before the time the amendments became effective.

---

1. At the time of her discharge, and at the time the charge was filed with the EEOC, § 706(d) stated, in pertinent part: "A charge under subsection (a) [of this section] shall be filed within ninety days after the alleged unlawful employment practice occurred * * *." Section 706(d) was renumbered as § 706(e), 42 U.S.C.A. § 2000e–5(e), as a result of the 1972 amendments to the Act. Whenev-

er § 706(d) is cited in this opinion, it refers to the pre-1972 version of what is now § 706(e).

2. Guy also alleged a cause of action under 42 U.S.C.A. § 1981. By order dated May 30, 1974, the District Court dismissed this cause of action because of a failure to meet the applicable Tennessee statute of limitations. No appeal was taken from this decision.

II

Before reaching either of those questions, however, petitioners Guy and Local 790 assert that the complaint with the EEOC was timely filed, not because of any tolling concept, but simply because the date "the alleged unlawful employment practice occurred" is the date of the conclusion of the collective-bargaining agreement's grievance-arbitration procedures. Until that time, we are told, the October 25th discharge of Guy (although itself an "occurrence" allowing immediate resort to the EEOC) was "tentative" and "non-final," and remained so until she terminated the grievance and arbitration process, at which time the "final" occurrence transpired.[4] As a consequence, according to petitioners, the unfavorable termination of the grievance procedures, making the discharge "final," constituted an "occurrence" enabling Guy to start the 90-day period running from that date.

While the parties could conceivably have agreed to a contract under which management's ultimate adoption of a supervisor's recommendation would be deemed the relevant statutory "occurrence," this was not such a contract. For all that appears Guy was fired as of October 25, 1971, and all parties so understood. She stopped work and ceased receiving pay and benefits as of that date. Unless the grievance procedures resulted in her reinstatement, she would not be entitled to be paid for the period during which the grievance procedures were being implemented. The grievance lodged on October 27, 1971, protests the "unfair action of *Co.* for discharge" (emphasis added), while the Complaint filed in the District Court alleges Guy's disagreement, after learning of her discharge, "with the *Company's* determination that she had 'voluntarily quit,'" (emphasis added). Throughout the proceedings both in the District Court and in the Court of Appeals, both sides appeared to have assumed, as did the courts, that the date of discharge was October 25, 1971. There being no indication that either party viewed the October 25th discharge as anything other than "final," there is certainly no reason for us to now torture this mutual understanding by accepting the bare assertions to the contrary raised by petitioners for the first time before this Court.

III

We think that petitioners' arguments for tolling the statutory period for filing a claim with the EEOC during the pendency of grievance or arbitration procedures under the collective-bargaining contract are virtually foreclosed by our decisions in Alexander v. Gardner-Denver Co., and in Johnson v. Railway Express Agency. In *Alexander* we held that an arbitrator's decision pursuant to provisions in a collective-bargaining contract was not binding on an individual seeking to pursue his Title VII remedies in court. We reasoned that the contractual rights under a collective-bargaining agreement and the statutory right provided by Congress under Title VII "have legally independent origins and are equally available to the aggrieved

---

4. This assertion, which is also adopted by the EEOC as *amicus curiae*, is premised on the proposition that "[u]se of the grievance resolution process is not an 'appeal' of a 'final' decision, but is a method of obtaining the judgment of higher management on whether the employee should be retained," EEOC Brief *Amicus Curiae*, at 21; Brief for Petitioner Local 790, at 17–18.

employee," 415 U.S., at 52, 94 S.Ct. at 1022, and for that reason we concluded that:

> "in instituting an action under Title VII, the employee is not seeking review of the arbitrator's decision. Rather, he is asserting a statutory right independent of the arbitration process." 415 U.S., at 54, 94 S.Ct. at 1022.

One Term later, we reaffirmed the independence of Title VII remedies from other pre-existing remedies available to an aggrieved employee. In Johnson v. Railway Express Agency, we held that the timely filing of a charge with the EEOC pursuant to § 706 of Title VII did not toll the running of the statute of limitations applicable to an action, based on the same facts, brought under 42 U.S.C.A. § 1981. In reaffirming the independence of Title VII remedies from other remedies, we noted that such independence might occasionally be a two-edged sword,[9] but "in the face of congressional emphasis upon the existence and independence of the two remedies," we were disinclined "to infer any positive preference for one over the other, without a more definite expression in the legislation Congress has enacted," 421 U.S., at 461, 95 S.Ct. at 1720.

Petitioners insist that notwithstanding these decisions, equitable tolling principles should be applied to this case, and that the application of such principles would toll the 90-day period pending completion of the grievance procedures. This is so, they say, because in this case the "policy of repose, designed to protect defendants," Burnett v. New York Central R. Co., 380 U.S. 424, 428, 85 S.Ct. 1050, 1055, 13 L.Ed.2d 941 (1965), is "outweighed [because] the interests of justice require vindication of the plaintiff's rights," ibid.

But this is quite a different case from *Burnett,* supra. There the plaintiff in an FELA action *had* asserted his FELA claim in the state courts, which had concurrent jurisdiction with the federal courts, but he had the misfortune of filing his complaint in an Ohio state court where venue did not lie under Ohio law. This Court held that such a filing was sufficient to toll the statutory limitations period, even though the state court action was dismissed for improper venue and a new complaint ultimately filed in the United States District Court. The Court said:

> "Petitioner here did not sleep on his rights but brought an action within the statutory period in the state court of competent jurisdiction. Service of process was made upon the respondent notifying him that petitioner was asserting his cause of action." 380 U.S., at 429, 85 S.Ct. at 1055.

Here petitioner Guy in the grievance proceedings was not asserting the same statutory claim in a different forum, nor giving notice to respondent of that statutory claim, but was asserting an independent claim based on a *contract* right, Alexander v. Gardner-Denver Co., supra, 415 U.S. at 53–54,

9. "Conciliation and persuasion through the administrative process [e.g., Title VII], to be sure, often constitute a desirable approach to settlement of disputes based on sensitive and emotional charges of invidious employment discrimination. We recognize, too, that the filing of a lawsuit might tend to deter efforts at conciliation, that lack of success in the legal action could weaken the Commission's efforts to induce voluntary compliance, and that a suit is privately oriented and narrow, rather than broad, in application, as successful conciliation tends to be. But these are the natural effects of the choice Congress has made available to the claimant by its conferring upon him independent administrative and judicial remedies. The choice is a valuable one," Johnson v. Railway Express Agency, supra, 421 U.S. at 461, 95 S.Ct. at 1720.

56–58, 94 S.Ct. at 1022. *Burnett* cannot aid this petitioner, see Johnson v. Railway Express Agency, supra, 421 U.S. at 467–468, and n. 14, 95 S.Ct. at 1724.

Petitioners advance as a corollary argument for tolling the premise that substantial policy considerations, based on the central role of arbitration in labor-management relations, see United Steelworkers v. American Mfg. Co., 363 U.S. 564, 80 S.Ct. 1343, 4 L.Ed.2d 1403 (1960), Textile Workers Union v. Lincoln Mills, 353 U.S. 448, 77 S.Ct. 912, 1 L.Ed.2d 972 (1957), also dictate a finding that the Title VII limitations period is tolled in this situation. Similar arguments by the employer in Alexander v. Gardner-Denver Co., supra, urging the superiority and pre-eminence of the arbitration process were rejected by us in that case, and we find the reasoning of that case controlling in rejecting this claim made by petitioners.

Petitioners also advance a related argument that the danger of possible conflict between the concurrent pursuit of both collective bargaining and Title VII remedies should result in tolling the limitations period for the latter while the former proceeds to conclusion. Similar arguments to these, albeit relating to § 1981 and not to private labor agreements, were, however, raised and rejected in *Johnson,* supra. We think the language we used in that case is sufficient to dispose of this claim:

> "it is conceivable, and perhaps almost to be expected, that failure to toll will have the effect of pressing a civil rights complainant who values his § 1981 claim into court before the EEOC has completed its administrative proceeding. One answer to this, although perhaps not a highly satisfactory one, is that the plaintiff in his § 1981 suit may ask the court to stay proceedings until the administrative efforts at conciliation and voluntary compliance have been completed. But the fundamental answer to petitioner's argument lies in the fact—presumably a happy one for the civil rights claimant—that Congress clearly has retained § 1981 as a remedy against private employment discrimination separate from and independent of the more elaborate and time consuming procedures of Title VII." 421 U.S., at 465–466, 95 S.Ct. at 1722.

Petitioners contend at some length that tolling would impose almost no costs, as the delays occasioned by the grievance-arbitration process would be "slight," [12] noting that the maximum delay in invoking the three-stage grievance procedure (although not including the arbitration step) under the collective-bargaining agreement in force in this case would be 35 days. But the principal answer to this contention is that Congress has already spoken with respect to what it considers acceptable delay when it established a 90-day limitations period, and gave no indication that it considered a "slight" delay followed by 90 days equally acceptable. In defining Title VII's jurisdictional prerequisites "with precision," Alexander v. Gardner-Denver Co., supra, 415 U.S. at 47, 94 S.Ct. at 1019, Congress did not leave to courts the decision as to which delays might or might not be "slight."

Congress did provide in § 706(d) one exception for this 90-day limitations period, when it provided that the limitations period should run for a

---

12. Petitioners contend that the vast majority of collective-bargaining agreements have stringent time restrictions on the resolution of disputes through the grievance stages, see, e.g., Brief of Petitioner Local 790, at 38–39; see also EEOC Brief *Amicus Curiae,* at 23 n. 13.

maximum additional 120 days when there existed "a State or local law prohibiting the unlawful employment practice alleged and establishing or authorizing a State or local authority to grant or seek relief from such practice or to institute criminal proceedings with respect thereto upon receiving notice thereof," § 706(b). Where Congress has spoken with respect to a claim much more closely related to the Title VII claim than is the contractual claim pursued under the grievance procedure, and then firmly limited the maximum possible extension of the limitations period applicable thereto, we think that all of petitioners' arguments taken together simply do not carry sufficient weight to overcome the negative implication from the language used by Congress, cf. Johnson v. Railway Express Agency, supra, 421 U.S. at 461, 95 S.Ct. at 1720.[14]

IV

Guy filed her charge with the EEOC on February 10, 1972, 108 days after her October 25, 1971 discharge. On March 24, 1972, the Equal Employment Opportunity Act of 1972 extended to 180 days the time within which to file a claim with the EEOC, § 706(e). Petitioners contend that this expanded limitations period should apply to Guy's charge as the occurrence she was complaining of took place within 180 days of the enactment of the 1972 amendments. We agree.

Section 14 of the Equal Employment Opportunity Act of 1972 states:

> "The amendments made by this Act to section 706 of the Civil Rights Act of 1964 shall be applicable with respect to charges pending with the Commission on the date of enactment of this Act and to all charges filed thereafter."

Robbins & Myers asserts that § 14, which was added by amendment to the bill on the floor of the House by Senator Jacob Javits, 118 Cong.Rec. 4816, was designed for the sole purpose of having the new enforcement powers given to the EEOC apply to pending charges, see letter from David L. Norman, Assistant Attorney General, Civil Rights Division of the Department of Justice to Senator Peter H. Dominick, quoted in Equal Employment Opportunity Commission v. Christiansburg Garment Co., 376 F.Supp. 1067, 1074 (W.D.Va.1974). However, the explicit statutory language used applies to *all* amendments made by the Act to § 706, not simply to the new enforcement provisions. As Senator Javits did not limit his remarks on the floor so as to indicate that § 14's retroactivity was designed to apply only to the new enforcement provisions,[15] the legislative history does not make this one of those unusual cases in which a court may infer, contrary to the language actually used, that Congress intended to so limit the scope of § 14, cf. also S.Rep. No. 91–1137, 91st Cong., 2d Sess., 31 (1970).

---

14. Adherence to the limitations period assures prompt notification to the employer of a charge of an alleged violation of Title VII, see § 706(b). The grievance process assures no such comparable notice. In the instant case, the grievance alleged only an "unfair action." Even if racial discrimination is explicitly discussed, however, the grievance procedure properly involves only *contractual* questions, and would but fortuitously implicate the Title VII standards ＊ ＊ ＊.

15. Indeed, the comment of Senator Javits implied precisely the opposite:

> "MR. JAVITS. Mr. President, this amendment would make whatever we do enact into law applicable to pending cases. The Department of Justice has requested it in a letter to the minority leader; that is my reason for offering it." 118 Cong.Rec. 4816 (1972).

Robbins & Myers also contends that the amendment is not applicable to the charge filed by Guy with the EEOC, since, being untimely when filed, her charge could not have been "pending with the Commission on the date of enactment of this Act." This reading of "pending"—confining it to charges still before the Commission *and* timely when filed—is not the only possible meaning of the word, is largely rebutted by the legislative history,[16] and renders the language of § 14 virtually meaningless insofar as the enlarged limitations period is concerned. Since Congress also applied the enlarged limitations period to charges, whether or not untimely on March 24th, "filed thereafter," we should not presume Congress created this odd hiatus in retroactivity suggested by Robbins & Myers unless congressional intent to do so was conveyed by language more precise than "pending," cf. Love v. Pullman Co., 404 U.S. 522, 92 S.Ct. 616, 30 L.Ed.2d 679 (1972). "Pending" is simply not a term of art that unambiguously carries with it a meaning precisely suited for this situation; equally as logical, for example, would be an interpretation that read "pending" to mean "filed and not yet rejected," cf. Committee Legis.Hist., at 1851. We hold that Congress intended the 180-day period to be applicable to charges such as that filed by Guy, where the charge was filed with the EEOC prior to March 24, 1972, and alleged a discriminatory occurrence within 180 days of the enactment of the Act.

Robbins & Myers contends, finally, that Congress was without constitutional power to revive, by enactment, an action which, when filed, is already barred by the running of a limitations period. This contention rests on an unwarrantedly broad reading of our opinion in William Danzer Co. v. Gulf & Ship Island R. Co., 268 U.S. 633, 45 S.Ct. 612, 69 L.Ed. 1126 (1925). *Danzer* was given a narrow reading in the later case of Chase Securities Corp. v. Donaldson, 325 U.S. 304, 311–312, 65 S.Ct. 1137, 1141, 89 L.Ed. 1628 (1945). The latter case states the applicable constitutional test in this language:

> "The Fourteenth Amendment does not make an act of state legislation void merely because it has some retrospective operation. What it does forbid is taking of life, liberty or property without due process of law. * * * Assuming that statutes of limitation, like other types of legislation, could be so manipulated that their retroactive effects would offend the Constitution, certainly it cannot be said that lifting the bar of a statute of limitation so as to restore a remedy lost through mere lapse of time is *per se* an offense against the Fourteenth Amendment." 325 U.S., at 315–316, 65 S.Ct. at 1143.

Applying that test to this case, we think that Congress might constitutionally provide for retroactive application of the extended limitations period which it enacted.

We thus resolve against petitioners their first two contentions, but resolve the third in their favor. The judgment of the Court of Appeals for the Sixth Circuit is therefore reversed, and the case remanded for further proceedings not inconsistent with this opinion.

Reversed and remanded.

MR. JUSTICE BRENNAN, MR. JUSTICE STEWART, MR. JUSTICE MARSHALL, and MR. JUSTICE STEVENS agree that the expanded 180-day limitations period

---

16. Section 14 was stated to be designed to cover "charges filed with the Commission pri- or to the effective date of the Act," Committee Legis.Hist., at 1851; see, also id., at 1777.

enacted by 86 Stat. 103 applied to Guy's charge and would reverse the Court of Appeals on that ground without addressing the questions discussed in Parts II and III of the Court's opinion.

Note

1. In Johnson v. Railway Express Agency, discussed in Robbins & Myers, the Court held that the statute of limitations applicable to Section 1981 cases would ordinarily be one provided by state law. In Occidental Life Insurance Co. v. EEOC, 432 U.S. 355, 97 S.Ct. 2447, 53 L.Ed.2d 402, (1977), the Court held that Title VII itself imposes *no* time limitation on the EEOC's right to bring an enforcement action and furthermore that it would be inappropriate to apply a state statute of limitations "[i]n view of the federal policy requiring employment discrimination claims to be investigated by the EEOC and, whenever possible, administratively resolved before suit is brought in a federal court * * *." 432 U.S. at 368, 97 S.Ct. at 2456. The consequence of this holding is that *no* statute of limitations applies to the EEOC's suits.

2. In these statute of limitations cases the Court has attempted to achieve a balance between the policies favoring (1) dispute settlement in the collective bargaining-arbitration context, (2) conciliation of disputes by the EEOC and similar state agencies, and (3) preservation of alternative remedies for victims of discrimination. The Court has declared the following principles:

a. Title VII, the Civil Rights Act of 1866, and a collective bargaining agreement create separate rights, and resort to one avenue of redress does not constitute a waiver of the other avenues.

b. Since the rights are separate, a statute of limitations applicable to one avenue of redress is not tolled by the pursuit of another.

c. Since there is no express statute of limitations in Section 1981, it is appropriate to apply a state statute even though the consequent starting of Section 1981 cases may interfere with the conciliation process. However, a state statute cannot be applied to limit suits by the EEOC itself since this would unduly impinge on the EEOC's conciliation responsibilities.

Is it possible to distill from these principles a ranking of priorities as among dispute settlement in the collective bargaining context, conciliation, and preservation of alternate remedies? Suppose a union and an employer negotiating a collective bargaining agreement ask you whether it might be advisable for them to exclude from the grievance-arbitration process all grievances based upon allegations which, if proved, would be the basis for Title VII or Section 1981 relief. How would you respond? Is the union's duty of fair representation implicated here?

3. In Johnson v. Railway Express Agency, quoted in relevant part in Robbins & Myers, supra p. 942, Justice Blackmun responded to the concern that the filing of a Section 1981 case might impair the conciliation efforts of the EEOC by stating: "One answer to this, although perhaps not a highly satisfactory one, is that the plaintiff in his § 1981 suit may ask the court to stay the proceedings until the administrative efforts at conciliation and compromise have been completed." Why "not a highly satisfactory" answer? Is it possible that the Supreme Court decisions rejecting tolling reflect an underlying uneasiness with the alternate remedy approach? While these decisions do not restrict the number of available remedies, they do place time constraints on those alternatives.

FRANKS v. BOWMAN TRANSPORTATION CO.

Supreme Court of the United States, 1976.
424 U.S. 747, 96 S.Ct. 1251, 47 L.Ed.2d 444.

MR. JUSTICE BRENNAN delivered the opinion of the Court.

This case presents the question whether identifiable applicants who were denied employment because of race after the effective date and in violation of Title VII of the Civil Rights Act of 1964 may be awarded seniority status retroactive to the dates of their employment applications.[1]

Petitioner Franks brought this class action in the United States District Court for the Northern District of Georgia against his former employer, respondent Bowman Transportation Company, and his unions, the International Union of District 50, Allied and Technical Workers of the United States and Canada and its local, No. 13600, alleging various racially discriminatory employment practices in violation of Title VII. Petitioner Lee intervened on behalf of himself and others similarly situated alleging racially discriminatory hiring and discharge policies limited to Bowman's employment of over-the-road (OTR) truck drivers. Following trial, the District Court found Bowman had engaged in a pattern of racial discrimination in various company policies, including the hiring, transfer, and discharge of employees, and found further that the discriminatory practices were perpetrated [perpetuated?] in Bowman's collective-bargaining agreement with the unions. The District Court certified the action as a proper class action under Fed.Rule Civ.Proc. 23(b)(2), and of import to the issues before this Court, found that petitioner Lee represented all black applicants who sought to be hired or to transfer to OTR driving positions prior to January 1, 1972. In its final order and decree, the District Court subdivided the class represented by petitioner Lee into a class of black non-employee applicants for OTR positions prior to January 1, 1972 (class 3), and a class of black employees who applied to transfer to OTR positions prior to the same date (class 4).

In its final judgment entered July 14, 1972, the District Court permanently enjoined the respondents from perpetuating the discriminatory practices found to exist, and, in regard to the black applicants for OTR positions, ordered Bowman to notify the members of both subclasses within 30 days of their right to priority consideration for such jobs. The District Court declined, however, to grant to the unnamed members of classes 3 and 4 any other specific relief sought, which included an award of backpay and seniority status retroactive to the date of individual application for an OTR position.

On petitioners' appeal to the Court of Appeals for the Fifth Circuit, raising for the most part claimed inadequacy of the relief ordered respecting unnamed members of the various subclasses involved, the Court of Appeals affirmed in part, reversed in part, and vacated in part. 495 F.2d 398. The Court of Appeals held that the District Court had exercised its discretion under an erroneous view of law insofar as it failed to award backpay to the unnamed class members of both classes 3 and 4, and vacated the judgment in that respect. The judgment was reversed insofar as it failed to award any

---

1. Petitioners also alleged an alternative claim for relief for violations of 42 U.S.C.A. § 1981. In view of our decision we have no occasion to address that claim.

seniority remedy to the members of class 4 who after the judgment of the District Court sought and obtained priority consideration for transfer to OTR positions. As respects unnamed members of class 3—nonemployee black applicants who applied for and were denied OTR prior to January 1, 1972— the Court of Appeals affirmed the District Court's denial of any form of seniority relief. Only this last aspect of the Court of Appeals' judgment is before us for review under our grant of the petition for certiorari. 420 U.S. 989, 95 S.Ct. 1421, 43 L.Ed.2d 669 (1975). * * *

II

In affirming the District Court's denial of seniority relief to the class 3 group of discriminatees, the Court of Appeals held that the relief was barred by § 703(h) of Title VII. We disagree. Section 703(h) provides in pertinent part that:

> "Notwithstanding any other provision of this title, it shall not be an unlawful employment practice for an employer to apply different standards of compensation, or different terms, conditions, or privileges of employment pursuant to a bona fide seniority or merit system * * * provided that such differences are not the result of an intention to discriminate because of race, color, religion, sex, or national origin * * *."

The Court of Appeals reasoned that a discriminatory refusal to hire "does not affect the bona fides of the seniority system. Thus, the differences in the benefits and conditions of employment which a seniority system accords to older and newer employees is protected as 'not an unlawful employment practice' [by § 703(h)]." 495 F.2d, at 417. Significantly, neither Bowman nor the unions undertake to defend the Court of Appeals judgment on that ground. It is clearly erroneous.

The black applicants for OTR positions composing class 3 are limited to those whose applications were put in evidence at the trial.[10] The underlying legal wrong affecting them is not the alleged operation of a racially discriminatory seniority system but of a racially discriminatory hiring system. Petitioners do not ask modification or elimination of the existing seniority system, but only an award of the seniority status they would have individually enjoyed under the present system but for the illegal discriminatory refusal to hire. It is this context that must shape our determination as to the meaning and effect of § 703(h).

On its face, § 703(h) appears to be only a definitional provision; as with the other provisions of § 703, subsection (h) delineates which employment practices are illegal and thereby prohibited and which are not.[11] Section

10. By its terms, the judgment of the District Court runs to all black applicants for OTR positions prior to January 1, 1972, and is not qualified by a limitation that the discriminatory refusal to hire must have taken place after the effective date of the Act. However, only post-Act victims of racial discrimination are members of class 3. Title VII's prohibition on racial discrimination in hiring became effective on July 2, 1965, one year after the date of its enactment. Pub.L. 88–352, § 716(a)–(b); 78 Stat. 253. Petitioners sought relief in this case for identifiable applicants for OTR positions "whose applications were put in evidence at the trial." App., at 20a. There are 206 unhired black applicants prior to January 1, 1972, whose written applications are summarized in the record and none of the applications relates to years prior to 1970. App., at 52a, Table VA.

11. See Last Hired, First Fired Seniority, Layoffs, and Title VII: Questions of Liability and Remedy, 11 Colum.J.L. & Soc.Prob. 343, 376, 378 (1975).

703(h) certainly does not expressly purport to qualify or proscribe relief otherwise appropriate under the remedial provisions of Title VII, § 706(g), in circumstances where an illegal discriminatory act or practice is found. Further, the legislative history of § 703(h) plainly negates its reading as limiting or qualifying the relief authorized under § 706(g). The initial bill reported by the House Judicial Committee as H.R. 7152 and passed by the full House on February 10, 1964, did not contain § 703(h). Neither the House bill nor the majority Judiciary Committee Report even mentioned the problem of seniority. That subject thereafter surfaced during the debate of the bill in the Senate. This debate prompted Senators Clark and Case to respond to criticism that Title VII would destroy existing seniority systems by placing an Interpretive Memorandum in the Congressional Record. The Memorandum stated that "Title VII would have no effect on established seniority rights. Its effect is prospective and not retrospective." 110 Cong. Rec. 7213 (1964).[15] Senator Clark also placed in the Congressional Record a Justice Department statement concerning Title VII which stated that "it has been asserted that Title VII would undermine vested rights of seniority. This is not correct. Title VII would have no effect on seniority rights existing at the time it takes effect." 110 Cong.Rec. 7207 (1964).[16] Several

---

15. The full text of the Memorandum pertaining to seniority states:

"Title VII would have no effect on established seniority rights. Its effect is prospective and not retrospective. Thus, for example, if a business has been discriminating in the past and as a result has an all-white working force, when the title comes into effect the employer's obligation would be simply to fill future vacancies on a nondiscriminatory basis. He would not be obliged—or indeed, permitted—to fire whites in order to hire Negroes, or to prefer Negroes for future vacancies, or, once Negroes are hired, to give them special seniority rights at the expense of the white workers hired earlier. (However, where waiting lists for employment or training are, prior to the effective date of the title, maintained on a discriminatory basis, the use of such lists after the title takes effect may be held an unlawful subterfuge to accomplish discrimination.)" 110 Cong.Rec. 7213 (1964).

16. The full text of the Statement introduced by Senator Clark pertinent to seniority states:

"First, it has been asserted that title VII would undermine vested rights of seniority. This is not correct. Title VII would have no effect on seniority rights existing at the time it takes effect. If, for example, a collective bargaining contract provides that in the event of layoffs, those who were hired last must be laid off first, such a provision would not be affected in the least by title VII. This would be true even in the case where owing to discrimination prior to the effective date of the title, white workers had more seniority than Negroes. Title VII is directed at discrimination based on race,

color, religion, sex, or national origin. It is perfectly clear that when a worker is laid off or denied a chance for promotion because under established seniority rules he is "low man on the totem pole" he is not being discriminated against because of his race. Of course, if the seniority rule itself is discriminatory, it would be unlawful under title VII. If a rule were to state that all Negroes must be laid off before any white man, such a rule could not serve as the basis for a discharge subsequent to the effective date of the title. I do not know how anyone could quarrel with such a result. But, in the ordinary case, assuming that seniority rights were built up over a period of time during which Negroes were not hired, these rights would not be set aside by the taking effect of title VII. Employers and labor organizations would simply be under a duty not to discriminate against Negroes because of their race. Any differences in treatment based on established seniority rights would not be based on race and would not be forbidden by the title." 110 Cong.Rec. 7207 (1964).

Senator Clark also introduced into the Congressional Record a set of answers to a series of questions propounded by Senator Dirksen. Two of these questions and answers are pertinent to the issue of seniority:

"Question. Would the same situation prevail in respect to promotions, when that management function is governed by a labor contract calling for promotions on the basis of seniority? What of dismissals? Normally, labor contracts call for 'last hired, first fired.' If the last hired are Negroes, is the employer discriminating if his

weeks thereafter, following several informal conferences among the Senate leadership, the House leadership, the Attorney General and others, see Vaas, Title VII: Legislative History, 7 B.C.Ind. & Com.L.Rev. 431, 445 (1966), a compromise substitute bill prepared by Senators Mansfield and Dirksen, Senate majority and minority leaders respectively, containing § 703(h) was introduced on the Senate floor. Although the Mansfield-Dirksen substitute bill, and hence § 703(h), was not the subject of a committee report, see generally Vaas, supra, Senator Humphrey, one of the informal conferees, later stated during debate on the substitute that § 703(h) was not designed to alter the meaning of Title VII generally but rather "merely clarifies its present intent and effect." 110 Cong.Rec. 12,723 (1964) (remarks of Sen. Humphrey). Accordingly, whatever the exact meaning and scope of § 703(h) in light of its unusual legislative history and the absence of the usual legislative materials, see Vaas, supra, at 457–458, it is apparent that the thrust of the section is directed toward defining what is and what is not an illegal discriminatory practice in instances in which the post-Act operation of a seniority system is challenged as perpetuating the effects of discrimination occurring prior to the effective date of the Act. There is no indication in the legislative materials that § 703(h) was intended to modify or restrict relief otherwise appropriate once an illegal discriminatory practice occurring after the effective date of the Act is proved—as in the instant case, a discriminatory refusal to hire. This accords with the apparently unanimous view of commentators, see Cooper and Sobol, Seniority and Testing Under Fair Employment Laws: A General Approach to Objective Criteria of Hiring and Promotion, 82 Harv.L.Rev. 1598, 1632 (1969); Stacy, Title VII Seniority Remedies in a Time of Economic Downturn, 28 Vand.L.Rev. 487, 506 (1975).[18] We therefore hold that the Court of Appeals erred in concluding that, as a matter of law, § 703(h) barred the award of seniority relief to the unnamed class 3 members.

III

There remains the question whether an award of seniority relief is appropriate under the remedial provision of Title VII, specifically, § 706(g).[19]

contract requires they be first fired and the remaining employees are white?

"Answer. Seniority rights are in no way affected by the bill. If under a 'last hired, first fired' agreement a Negro happens to be the 'last hired,' he can still be 'first fired' as long as it is done because of his status as 'last hired' and not because of his race.

"Question. If an employer is directed to abolish his employment list because of discrimination what happens to seniority?

"Answer. The bill is not retroactive, and it will not require an employer to change existing seniority lists." 110 Cong.Rec. 7217 (1964).

18. Cf. Gould, Employment Security, Seniority and Race: The Role of Title VII of the Civil Rights Act of 1964, 13 How.L.J. 1, 8–9 and n. 32 (1967); see also Jurinko v. Edwin L. Wiegand Company, 477 F.2d 1038 (C.A.3), vacated and remanded on other grounds 414

U.S. 970, 94 S.Ct. 293, 38 L.Ed.2d 214 (1973), wherein the court awarded back seniority in a case of discriminatory hiring after the effective date of Title VII without any discussion of the impact of § 703(h) on the propriety of such a remedy.

19. Section 706(g) of Title VII provides:

"If the court finds that the respondent has intentionally engaged in or is intentionally engaging in an unlawful employment practice charged in the complaint, the court may enjoin the respondent from engaging in such unlawful employment practice, and order such affirmative action as may be appropriate, which may include, but is not limited to, reinstatement or hiring of employees, with or without back pay (payable by the employer, employment agency, or labor organization, as the case may be, responsible for the unlawful employment practice), or any other equitable relief as

We begin by repeating the observation of earlier decisions that in enacting Title VII of the Civil Rights Act of 1964, Congress intended to prohibit all practices in whatever form which create inequality in employment opportunity due to discrimination on the basis of race, religion, sex, or national origin, Alexander v. Gardner-Denver Co., 415 U.S. 36, 44, 94 S.Ct. 1011, 1017, 39 L.Ed.2d 147, 155 (1974); McDonnell Douglas Corp. v. Green, 411 U.S. 792, 800, 93 S.Ct. 1817, 1823, 36 L.Ed.2d 668, 676 (1973); Griggs v. Duke Power Co., 401 U.S. 424, 429–430, 91 S.Ct. 849, 852–853, 28 L.Ed.2d 158, 163–164 (1971), and ordained that its policy of outlawing such discrimination should have the "highest priority," Alexander, supra, 415 U.S., at 47, 94 S.Ct. at 1019, 39 L.Ed.2d at 158; Newman v. Piggie Park Enterprises, Inc., 390 U.S. 400, 402, 88 S.Ct. 964, 966, 19 L.Ed.2d 1263, 1265 (1968). Last Term's Albermarle Paper Company v. Moody, 422 U.S. 405, 95 S.Ct. 2362, 45 L.Ed.2d 280 (1975), consistently with the congressional plan, held that one of the central purposes of Title VII is "to make persons whole for injuries suffered on account of unlawful employment discrimination." Id., at 418, 95 S.Ct., at 2372, 45 L.Ed.2d, at 297. To effectuate this "make-whole" objective, Congress in § 706(g) vested broad equitable discretion in the federal courts to "order such affirmative action as may be appropriate, which may include, but is not limited to, reinstatement or hiring of employees, with or without backpay * * *, or any other equitable relief as the court deems appropriate." Ibid. The legislative history supporting the 1972 Amendments of § 706(g) of Title VII affirms the breadth of this discretion. "The provisions of [Section 706(g)] are intended to give the courts wide discretion exercising their equitable powers to fashion the most complete relief possible. * * * [T]he Act is intended to make the victims of unlawful employment discrimination whole and * * * the attainment of this objective * * * requires that persons aggrieved by the consequences and effects of the unlawful employment practice be, so far as possible, restored to a position where they would have been were it not for the unlawful discrimination." Section by Section Analysis of H.R. 1746, accompanying The Equal Employment Opportunity Act of 1972—Conference Report, 118 Cong.Rec. 7166, 7168 (1972). This is emphatic confirmation that federal courts are empowered to fashion such relief as the particular circumstances of a case may require to effect restitution, making whole insofar as possible the victims of racial discrimination in hiring. * * *

Seniority standing in employment with respondent Bowman, computed from the departmental date of hire, determines the order of layoff and recall of employees. Further, job assignments for OTR drivers are posted for competitive bidding and seniority is used to determine the highest bidder. As OTR drivers are paid on a per-mile basis, earnings are therefore to some extent a function of seniority. Additionally, seniority computed from the

the court deems appropriate. Back pay liability shall not accrue from a date more than two years prior to the filing of a charge with the Commission. Interim earnings or amounts earnable with reasonable diligence by the person or persons discriminated against shall operate to reduce the back pay otherwise allowable. No order of the court shall require the admission or reinstatement of an individual as a member of a union, or the hiring, reinstatement, or promotion of an individual as an employee, or the payment to him of any back pay, if such individual was refused admission, suspended, or expelled, or was refused employment or advancement or was suspended or discharged for any reason other than discrimination on account of race, color, religion, sex, or national origin or in violation of section 2000e–3(a) of this title."

company date-of-hire determines the length of an employee's vacation and pension benefits. Obviously merely to require Bowman to hire the class 3 victim of discrimination falls far short of a "make whole" remedy. A concomitant award of the seniority credit he presumptively would have earned but for the wrongful treatment would also seem necessary in the absence of justification for denying that relief. Without an award of seniority dating from the time at which he was discriminatorily refused employment, an individual who applies for and obtains employment as an OTR driver pursuant to the District Court's order will never obtain his rightful place in the hierarchy or seniority according to which these various employment benefits are distributed. He will perpetually remain subordinate to persons who, but for the illegal discrimination, would have been in respect to entitlement to these benefits his inferiors.

The Court of Appeals apparently followed this reasoning in holding that the District Court erred in not granting seniority relief to class 4 Bowman employees who were discriminatorily refused transfer to OTR positions. Yet the class 3 discriminatees in the absence of a comparable seniority award would also remain subordinated in the seniority system to the class 4 discriminatees. The distinction plainly finds no support anywhere in Title VII or its legislative history. Settled law dealing with the related "twin" areas of discriminatory hiring and discharges violative of National Labor Relations Act provides a persuasive analogy. "[I]t would indeed be surprising if Congress gave a remedy for the one which it denied for the other." Phelps Dodge Corp. v. NLRB, 313 U.S. 177, 187, 61 S.Ct. 845, 849, 85 L.Ed. 1271, 1279 (1941). For courts to differentiate without justification between the classes of discriminatees "would be a differentiation not only without substance but in defiance of that against which the prohibition of discrimination is directed." Id., at 188, 61 S.Ct., at 850, 85 L.Ed., at 1280.

Similarly, decisions construing the remedial section of the National Labor Relations Act, § 10(c), the model for § 706(g), Albermarle Paper, 422 U.S., at 419, 95 S.Ct., at 2372, 45 L.Ed.2d., at 297—make clear that remedies constituting authorized "affirmative action" include an award of seniority status, for the thrust of "affirmative action" redressing the wrong incurred by an unfair labor practice is to make "the employees whole, and thus restor[e] the economic status quo that would have obtained but for the company's wrongful [act]." NLRB v. J.H. Rutter-Rex Manufacturing Company, 396 U.S. 258, 263, 90 S.Ct. 417, 420, 24 L.Ed.2d 405, 411 (1969). The task of the NLRB in applying § 10(c) is "to take measures designed to recreate the conditions and relationships that would have been had there been no unfair labor practice." Local 60, United Brotherhood of Carpenters and Joiners of America, AFL–CIO v. NLRB, 365 U.S. 651, 657, 81 S.Ct. 875, 879, 6 L.Ed.2d 1, 5 (1961) (Harlan, J., concurring). And the NLRB has often required that the hiring of employees who had been discriminatorily refused employment be accompanied by an award of seniority equivalent to that which they would have enjoyed but for the illegal conduct. See, e.g., In re Phelps Dodge Corp., 19 N.L.R.B. 547, 600 & n. 39, 603–604 (1940), modified on other grounds, 313 U.S. 177, 61 S.Ct. 845, 85 L.Ed. 1271 (1941) (ordering persons discriminatorily refused employment hired "without prejudice to their other rights and privileges"); In re Nevada Consolidated Copper Corp., 26 N.L.R.B. 1182, 1235 (1940), enforced, 316 U.S. 105, 62 S.Ct. 960, 86 L.Ed.

1305 (1942) (ordering persons discriminatorily refused employment hired with "any seniority or other rights and privileges which they would have acquired, had the respondent not unlawfully discriminated against them"). Plainly the "affirmative action" injunction of § 706(g) has no lesser reach in the district courts. "Where racial discrimination is concerned, 'the [district] court has not merely the power but the duty to render a decree which will so far as possible eliminate the discriminatory effects of the past as well as bar like discrimination in the future.'" Albemarle Paper, supra, 422 U.S., at 418, 95 S.Ct., at 2372, 45 L.Ed.2d at 297.

IV

We are not to be understood as holding that an award of seniority status is requisite in all circumstances. The fashioning of appropriate remedies invokes the sound equitable discretion of the district courts. Respondent Bowman attempts to justify the District Court's denial of seniority relief for petitioners as an exercise of equitable discretion, but the record is its own refutation of the argument.

Albemarle Paper, supra, at 416, 95 S.Ct., at 2371, 45 L.Ed.2d, at 296, made clear that discretion imports not the Court's "inclination, but * * * its judgment; and its judgment is to be guided by sound legal principles." Discretion is vested not for purposes of "limit[ing] appellate review of trial courts, or * * * invit[ing] inconsistency and caprice," but rather to allow the most complete achievement of the objectives of Title VII that is attainable under the facts and circumstances of the specific case. Id., at 421, 95 S.Ct., at 2373, 45 L.Ed.2d, at 298. Accordingly, the District Court's denial of any form of seniority remedy must be reviewed in terms of its effect on the attainment of the Act's objectives under the circumstances presented by this record. No less than with the denial of the remedy of backpay, the denial of seniority relief to victims of illegal racial discrimination in hiring is permissible "only for reasons which, if applied generally, would not frustrate the central statutory purposes of eradicating discrimination throughout the economy and making persons whole for injuries suffered through past discrimination." Ibid.

The District Court stated two reasons for its denial of seniority relief for the unnamed class members. The first was that those individuals had not filed administrative charges under the provisions of Title VII with the Equal Employment Opportunity Commission and therefore class relief of this sort was not appropriate. We rejected this justification for denial of class-based relief in the context of backpay awards in *Albemarle Paper,* and for the same reasons reject it here. This justification for denying class-based relief in Title VII suits has been unanimously rejected by the courts of appeals, and Congress ratified that construction by the 1972 Amendments. Albemarle Paper, supra, at 414 n. 8, 95 S.Ct., at 2370, 45 L.Ed.2d., at 294.

The second reason stated by the District Court was that such claims "presuppose a vacancy, qualification, and performance by every member. There is no evidence on which to base these multiple conclusions." The Court of Appeals rejected this reason insofar as it was the basis of the District Court's denial of backpay, and of its denial of retroactive seniority relief to the unnamed members of class 4. We hold that it is also an improper reason for denying seniority relief to the unnamed members of class 3.

We read the District Court's reference to the lack of evidence regarding a "vacancy, qualification and performance" for every individual member of the class as an expression of concern that some of the unnamed class members (unhired black applicants whose employment applications were summarized in the record) may not in fact have been actual victims of racial discrimination. That factor will become material however only when those persons reapply for OTR positions pursuant to the hiring relief ordered by the District Court. Generalizations concerning such individually applicable evidence cannot serve as a justification for the denial of relief to the entire class. Rather, at such time as individual class members seek positions as OTR drivers, positions for which they are presumptively entitled to priority hiring consideration under the District Court's order,[31] evidence that particular individuals were not in fact victims of racial discrimination will be material. But petitioners here have carried their burden of demonstrating the existence of a discriminatory hiring pattern and practice by the respondents and, therefore, the burden will be upon respondents to prove that individuals who reapply were not in fact victims of previous hiring discrimination. Cf. McDonnell Douglas Corp. v. Green, 411 U.S., at 802, 93 S.Ct., at 1824, 36 L.Ed.2d, at 677, Baxter v. Savannah Sugar Refining Corp., 495 F.2d 437, 443–444 (C.A.5), cert. denied, 419 U.S. 1033, 95 S.Ct. 515, 42 L.Ed.2d 308 (1974). Only if this burden is met may retroactive seniority—if otherwise determined to be an appropriate form of relief under the circumstances of the particular case—be denied individual class members.

Respondent Bowman raises an alternative theory of justification. Bowman argues that an award of retroactive seniority to the class of discriminatees will conflict with the economic interests of other Bowman employees. Accordingly, it is argued, the District Court acted within its discretion in denying this form of relief as an attempt to accommodate the competing interests of the various groups of employees.[33]

We reject this argument for two reasons. First, the District Court made no mention of such considerations in its order denying the seniority relief. As we noted in Albemarle Paper, supra, 422 U.S., at 421 n. 14, 95 S.Ct., at 2373, 45 L.Ed.2d, at 299, if the District Court declines due to the peculiar circumstances of the particular case to award relief generally appropriate under Title VII, "[i]t is necessary * * * that * * * it carefully articulate its reasons" for so doing. Second and more fundamentally, it is apparent that denial of seniority relief to identifiable victims of racial discrimination on the sole ground that such relief diminishes the expectations of other, arguably innocent, employees would if applied generally frustrate the cen-

---

31. The District Court order is silent whether applicants to OTR positions who were previously discriminatorily refused employment must be presently qualified for those positions in order to be eligible for priority hiring under that order. The Court of Appeals however, made it plain that they must be. 495 F.2d, at 417. We agree.

33. Even by its terms, this argument could apply only to the award of retroactive seniority for purposes of "competitive status" benefits. It has no application to a retroactive award for purposes of "benefit" seniority—extent of vacation leave and pension benefits. Indeed, the decision concerning the propriety of this latter type of seniority relief is analogous, if not identical, to the decision concerning an award of backpay to an individual discriminatee hired pursuant to an order redressing previous employment discrimination.

tral "make-whole" objective of Title VII. These conflicting interests of other employees will of course always be present in instances where some scarce employment benefit is distributed among employees on the basis of their status in the seniority hierarchy. But, as we have said, there is nothing in the language of Title VII, or in its legislative history, to show that Congress intended generally to bar this form of relief to victims of illegal discrimination, and the experience under its remedial model in the National Labor Relations Act points to the contrary.[34] Accordingly, we find untenable the conclusion that this form of relief may be denied merely because the interests of other employees may thereby be affected. "If relief under Title VII can be denied merely because the majority group of employees, who have not suffered discrimination, will be unhappy about it, there will be little hope of correcting the wrongs to which the Act is directed." United States v. Bethlehem Steel Corp., 446 F.2d 652, 663 (C.A.2 1971). * * *[38]

Certainly there is no argument that the award of retroactive seniority to the victims of hiring discrimination in any way deprives other employees of indefeasibly vested rights conferred by the employment contract. This Court has long held that employee expectations arising from a seniority system agreement may be modified by statutes furthering a strong public policy interest. Tilton v. Missouri Pacific Railroad Co., 376 U.S. 169, 84 S.Ct. 595, 11 L.Ed.2d 590 (1964) (construing §§ 9(c)(1) and 9(c)(2) of the Universal Military Training and Service Act of 1948, 50 U.S.C.A.App. §§ 459(c)(1)–(2), which provided that a re-employed returning veteran should enjoy the seniority status he would have acquired but for his absence in military service); Fishgold v. Sullivan Drydock & Repair Corp., 328 U.S. 275, 66 S.Ct. 1105, 90 L.Ed. 1230 (1946) (construing the comparable provision of the Selective Training and Service Act of 1940). The Court has also held that a collective-bargaining agreement may go further, enhancing the seniority status of certain employees for purposes of furthering public policy interests beyond what is required by statute, even though this will to some extent be detrimental to the expectations acquired by other employees under the previous seniority agreement. Ford Motor Company v. Huffman, 345 U.S., 330, 73 S.Ct. 681, 97 L.Ed. 1048 (1953). And the ability of the union and employer voluntarily to modify the seniority system to the end of ameliorating the effects of past racial discrimination, a national policy objective of the "highest priority," is certainly no less than in other areas of public policy

34. * * *

The dissent has cited no case, and our research discloses none, wherein the Board has ordered hiring relief and yet withheld the remedy of retroactive seniority status.

* * *

38. In arguing that an award of the seniority relief established as presumptively necessary does nothing to place the burden of the past discrimination on the wrongdoer in most cases—the employer—the dissent of necessity addresses issues not presently before the Court. Further remedial action by the district courts, having the effect of shifting to the employer the burden of the past discrimination in respect to competitive status benefits, raises such issues as the possibility of an in-

junctive "hold harmless" remedy respecting all affected employees in a layoff situation, Brief of Amicus Curiae for Local 862, United Automobile Workers, the possibility of an award of monetary damages (sometimes designated "front pay") in favor of each employee and discriminatee otherwise bearing some of the burden of the past discrimination, ibid.; Brief for the United States and the Equal Employment Opportunity Commission as Amici Curiae, and the propriety of such further remedial action in instances wherein the union has been adjudged a participant in the illegal conduct. Such issues are not presented by the record before us, and we intimate no view regarding them.

interests. Pellicer v. Brotherhood of Railway and Steamship Clerks, 217 F.2d 205 (C.A.5 1954), cert. denied, 349 U.S. 912, 75 S.Ct. 601, 99 L.Ed. 1246 (1955). See also Cooper and Sobol, 82 Harv.L.Rev. at 1605.

V

In holding that class-based seniority relief for identifiable victims of illegal hiring discrimination is a form of relief generally appropriate under § 706(g), we do not in any way modify our previously expressed view that the statutory scheme of Title VII "implicitly recognizes that there may be cases calling for one remedy but not another, and—owing to the structure of the federal judiciary—these choices are of course left in the first instance to the district courts." Albemarle Paper, supra, 422 U.S. at 416, 95 S.Ct., at 2370, 45 L.Ed.2d at 295. Circumstances peculiar to the individual case may of course justify the modification or withholding of seniority relief for reasons that would not if applied generally undermine the purposes of Title VII.[41]

* * *

Accordingly, the judgment of the Court of Appeals affirming the District Court's denial of seniority relief to class 3 is reversed, and the case remanded to the District Court for further proceedings consistent with this opinion.

It is so ordered.

Reversed and remanded.

MR. JUSTICE STEVENS took no part in the consideration or decision of this case.

MR. CHIEF JUSTICE BURGER, concurring in part and dissenting in part.

I concur in the judgment in part and generally with MR. JUSTICE POWELL, but I would stress that although retroactive benefit-type seniority relief may sometimes be appropriate and equitable, competitive-type seniority relief at the expense of wholly innocent employees can rarely, if ever, be equitable if that term retains traditional meaning. More equitable would be a monetary award to the person suffering the discrimination. An award such as "front pay" could replace the need for competitive-type seniority relief. See, ante, n. 38. (Majority opinion.) Such monetary relief would serve the dual purpose of deterring the wrongdoing employer or union—or both—as well as protecting the rights of innocent employees. In every respect an innocent employee is comparable to a "holder-in-due-course" of negotiable paper or a bona fide purchaser of property without notice of any defect in the seller's title. In this setting I cannot join in judicial approval of "robbing Peter to pay Paul."

I would stress that the Court today does not foreclose claims of employees who might be injured by this holding from petitioning the District Court for equitable relief on their own behalf.

41. Accordingly, to no "significant extent" do we "[strip] the district courts of [their] equitable powers." Rather our holding is that in exercising their equitable powers, district courts should take as their starting point the presumption in favor of rightful place seniority relief, and proceed with further legal analysis from that point; and that such relief may not be denied on the abstract basis of adverse impact upon interests of other employees but rather only on the basis of unusual adverse impact arising from facts and circumstances that would not be generally found in Title VII cases. To hold otherwise would be to shield "inconsisten[t] and capri[cious]" denial of such relief from "thorough appellate review." Albemarle Paper, 422 U.S., at 416, 421, 95 S.Ct., at 2371, 2373, 45 L.Ed.2d, at 296, 299.

[Justice Powell, joined by Justice Rehnquist, agreed with the majority that § 703(h) was not a bar to the award of retroactive seniority. However, he asserted that the court erred in recognizing no meaningful distinction between "benefit" type seniority and "competitive" type seniority. In the latter type, he said, there should be no presumption favoring the retroactive granting of seniority. The District Court should not be precluded from considering the impact of such a remedy upon innocent employees, particularly since the employer who has discriminated is not directly affected by such an award. Further, §§ 703(h) and 703(j), while not limitations on § 706(g), indicate a congressional concern for seniority rights and an opposition to preferential treatment which argue against restricting the discretion of the district court.]

Note

The dissenting Justices stressed that an award of "competitive" seniority penalizes other employees without punishing the employer who has discriminated. Should this be a relevant consideration in determining remedy? If so, should it make a difference whether the discriminatory act was participated in or initiated by the union? See footnote 38, supra p. 954.

INTERNATIONAL BROTHERHOOD OF TEAMSTERS v. UNITED STATES

Supreme Court of the United States, 1977.
431 U.S. 324, 97 S.Ct. 1843, 52 L.Ed.2d 396.

MR. JUSTICE STEWART delivered the opinion of the Court.

This litigation brings here several important questions under Title VII of the Civil Rights Act of 1964, as amended. The issues grow out of alleged unlawful employment practices engaged in by an employer and a union. The employer is a common carrier of motor freight with nationwide operations, and the union represents a large group of its employees. The District Court and the Court of Appeals held that the employer had violated Title VII by engaging in a pattern and practice of employment discrimination against Negroes and Spanish-surnamed Americans, and that the union had violated the Act by agreeing with the employer to create and maintain a seniority system that perpetuated the effects of past racial and ethnic discrimination. In addition to the basic questions presented by these two rulings other subsidiary issues must be resolved if violations of Title VII occurred—issues concerning the nature of the relief to which aggrieved individuals may be entitled.

I

The United States brought an action in a Tennessee federal court against the petitioner T.I.M.E.–D.C., Inc. (the company) pursuant to § 707(a) of the Civil Rights Act of 1964.[1] The complaint charged that the company

1. At the time of suit the statute provided as follows:

"(a) Whenever the Attorney General has reasonable cause to believe that any person or group of persons is engaged in a pattern or practice of resistance to the full enjoy-

ment of any of the rights secured by this subchapter, and that the pattern or practice is of such a nature and is intended to deny the full exercise of the rights herein described, the Attorney General may bring a civil action in the appropriate district court

had followed discriminatory hiring, assignment, and promotion policies against Negroes at its terminal in Nashville, Tenn. The Government brought a second action against the company almost three years later in a federal district court in Texas, charging a pattern and practice of employment discrimination against Negroes and Spanish-surnamed persons throughout the company's transportation system. The petitioner International Brotherhood of Teamsters (the union) was joined as a defendant in that suit. The two actions were consolidated for trial in the Northern District of Texas.

The central claim in both lawsuits was that the company had engaged in a pattern or practice of discriminating against minorities in hiring so-called line drivers. Those Negroes and Spanish-surnamed persons who had been hired, the Government alleged, were given lower paying less desirable jobs as servicemen or local city drivers, and were thereafter discriminated against with respect to promotions and transfers.[3] In this connection the complaint also challenged the seniority system established by the collective-bargaining agreements between the employer and the union. The Government sought a general injunctive remedy and specific "make whole" relief for all individual discriminatees, which would allow them an opportunity to transfer to line-driver jobs with full company seniority for all purposes.

The cases went to trial[4] and the District Court found that the Government had shown "by a preponderance of the evidence that T.I.M.E.–D.C. and

of the United States by filing with it a complaint (1) signed by him (or in his absence the Acting Attorney General), (2) setting forth facts pertaining to such pattern or practice, and (3) requesting such relief, including an application for a permanent or temporary injunction, restraining order or other order against the person or persons responsible for such pattern or practice, as he deems necessary to insure the full enjoyment of the rights herein described."

Section 707 was amended by § 5 of the Equal Employment Opportunity Act of 1972, 86 Stat. 107, 42 U.S.C.A. § 2000e–6(c) (Supp. V), to give the Equal Employment Opportunity Commission, rather than the Attorney General, the authority to bring "pattern or practice" suits under that section against private-sector employers. In 1974, an order was entered in this action substituting the EEOC for the United States but retaining the United States as a party for purposes of jurisdiction, appealability, and related matters. See 42 U.S.C.A. § 2000e–6(d) (Supp. V).

3. *Line drivers*, also known as over-the-road drivers, engage in long-distance hauling between company terminals. They compose a separate bargaining unit at T.I.M.E.–D.C. Other distinct bargaining units include *servicemen*, who service trucks, unhook tractors and trailers and perform similar tasks; and *city operations*, composed of dockmen, hostlers, and city drivers who pick up and deliver freight within the immediate area of a particular terminal. All of these employees were

represented by the petitioner International Brotherhood of Teamsters.

4. Following the receipt of evidence, but before decision, the Government and the company consented to the entry of a Decree in Partial Resolution of Suit. The consent decree did not constitute an adjudication on the merits. The company agreed, however, to undertake a minority recruiting program; to accept applications from all Negroes and Spanish-surnamed Americans who inquired about employment, whether or not vacancies existed, and to keep such applications on file and notify applicants of job openings; to keep specific employment and recruiting records open to inspection by the Government and to submit quarterly reports to the District Court; and to adhere to certain uniform employment qualifications respecting hiring and promotion to line driver and other jobs.

The decree further provided that future job vacancies at any T.I.M.E.–D.C. terminal would be filled first "[b]y those persons who may be found by the Court, if any, to be individual or class discriminatees suffering the present effects of past discrimination because of race or national origin prohibited by Title VII of the Civil Rights Act of 1964." Any remaining vacancies could be filled by "any other persons," but the company obligated itself to hire one Negro or Spanish-surnamed person for every white person hired at any terminal until the percentage of minority workers at that terminal equaled the percentage of minority group members in the population of the met-its predecessor companies were engaged in a plan and practice of discrimination in violation of Title VII * * *." [5] The court further found that the seniority system contained in the collective-bargaining contracts between the company and the union violated Title VII because it "operate[d] to impede the free transfer of minority groups into and within the company." Both the company and the union were enjoined from committing further violations of Title VII.

With respect to individual relief the court accepted the Government's basic contention that the "affected class" of discriminatees included all Negro and Spanish-surnamed incumbent employees who had been hired to fill city operations or serviceman jobs at every terminal that had a line-driver operation. All of these employees, whether hired before or after the effective date of Title VII, thereby became entitled to preference over all other applicants with respect to consideration for future vacancies in line-driver jobs. Finding that members of the affected class had been injured in different degrees the court created three subclasses. Thirty persons who had produced "the most convincing evidence of discrimination and harm" were found to have suffered "severe injury." The court ordered that they be offered the opportunity to fill line-driver jobs with competitive seniority dating back to July 2, 1965, the effective date of Title VII.[8] A second subclass included four persons who were "very possibly the objects of discrimination" and who "were likely harmed," but as to whom there had been no specific evidence of discrimination and injury. The court decreed that these persons were entitled to fill vacancies in line-driving jobs with competitive seniority as of January 14, 1971, the date on which the Government had filed its systemwide lawsuit. Finally, there were over 300 remaining members of the affected class as to whom there was "no evidence to show that these individuals were either harmed or not harmed individually." The court ordered that they be considered for line-driver jobs ahead of any applicants from the general public but behind the two other subclasses. Those in the third subclass received no retroactive seniority; their competitive seniority as line drivers would begin with the date they were hired as line drivers. The court further decreed that the right of any class member to fill a line-driver vacancy was subject to the prior recall rights of laid-off line drivers, which under the collective-bargaining agreements then in effect extended for three years.

ropolitan area surrounding the terminal. Finally, the company agreed to pay $89,500 in full settlement of any backpay obligations. Of this sum, individual payments not exceeding $1,500 were to be paid to "alleged individual and class discriminatees" identified by the Government.

The Decree in Partial Resolution of Suit narrowed the scope of the litigation, but the District Court still had to determine whether unlawful discrimination had occurred. If so, the Court had to identify the actual discriminatees entitled to fill future job vacancies under the decree. The validity of the collective-bargaining contract's seniority system also remained for decision, as did the question whether any discriminatees should be awarded additional equitable relief such as retroactive seniority.

5. The District Court's Memorandum Decision in United States v. T.I.M.E. D.C., Inc., Civ. No. 5–868 (Oct. 19, 1972), is not officially reported. It is unofficially reported at 6 FEP Cases 690 and 6 EPD ¶ 8979.

8. If an employee in this class had joined the company after July 2, 1965, then the date of his initial employment rather than the effective date of Title VII was to determine his competitive seniority.

The Court of Appeals for the Fifth Circuit agreed with the basic conclusions of the District Court: that the company had engaged in a pattern or practice of employment discrimination and that the seniority system in the collective-bargaining agreements violated Title VII as applied to victims of prior discrimination. United States v. T.I.M.E.–D.C., Inc., 517 F.2d 299. The appellate court held, however, that the relief ordered by the District Court was inadequate. Rejecting the District Court's attempt to trisect the affected class, the Court of Appeals held that all Negro and Spanish-surnamed incumbent employees were entitled to bid for future line-driver jobs on the basis of their company seniority, and that once a class member had filled a job, he could use his full company seniority—even if it predated the effective date of Title VII—for all purposes, including bidding and layoff. This award of retroactive seniority was to be limited only by a "qualification date" formula, under which seniority could not be awarded for periods prior to the date when (1) a line-driving position was vacant, *and* (2) the class member met (or would have met, given the opportunity) the qualifications for employment as a line driver.[12] Finally, the Court of Appeals modified that part of the District Court's decree that had subjected the rights of class members to fill future vacancies to the recall rights of laid-off employees. Holding that the three-year priority in favor of laid-off workers "would unduly impede the eradication of past discrimination," id., at 322, the Court of Appeals ordered that class members be allowed to compete for vacancies with laid-off employees on the basis of the class members' retroactive seniority. * * *

The Court of Appeals remanded the case to the District Court to hold the evidentiary hearings necessary to apply these remedial principles. We granted both the company's and the union's petitions for certiorari to consider the significant questions presented under the Civil Rights Act of 1964.

II

In this Court the company and the union contend that their conduct did not violate Title VII in any respect, asserting first that the evidence introduced at trial was insufficient to show that the company engaged in a "pattern or practice" of employment discrimination. The union further contends that the seniority system contained in the collective-bargaining agreements in no way violated Title VII. If these contentions are correct, it is unnecessary, of course, to reach any of the issues concerning remedies that so occupied the attention of the Court of Appeals.

A

Consideration of the question whether the company engaged in a pattern or practice of discriminatory hiring practices involves controlling legal principles that are relatively clear. The Government's theory of discrimination was simply that the company, in violation of § 703(a) of Title VII, regularly and purposefully treated Negroes and Spanish-surnamed Ameri-

---

12. For example, if a class member began his tenure with the company on January 1, 1966, at which time he was qualified as a line driver and a line-driving vacancy existed, his competitive seniority upon becoming a line driver would date back to January 1, 1966. If he became qualified or if a vacancy opened up only at a later date, then that later date would be used.

cans less favorably than white persons. The disparity in treatment allegedly involved the refusal to recruit, hire, transfer, or promote minority group members on an equal basis with white people, particularly with respect to line-driving positions. The ultimate factual issues are thus simply whether there was a pattern or practice of such disparate treatment and, if so, whether the differences were "racially premised." McDonnell Douglas Corp. v. Green, 411 U.S. 792, 805 n. 18, 93 S.Ct. 1817, 1825, 36 L.Ed.2d 668.

As the plaintiff, the Government bore the initial burden of making out a prima facie case of discrimination. Albemarle Paper Co. v. Moody, 422 U.S. 405, 425, 95 S.Ct. 2362, 2375, 45 L.Ed.2d 280; McDonnell Douglas Corp. v. Green, supra, 411 U.S., at 802, 93 S.Ct., at 1824. And, because it alleged a systemwide pattern or practice of resistance to the full enjoyment of Title VII rights, the Government ultimately had to prove more than the mere occurrence of isolated or "accidental" or sporadic discriminatory acts. It had to establish by a preponderance of the evidence that racial discrimination was the company's standard operating procedure—the regular rather than the unusual practice.

We agree with the District Court and the Court of Appeals that the Government carried its burden of proof. As of March 31, 1971, shortly after the Government filed its complaint alleging systemwide discrimination, the company had 6,472 employees. Of these, 314 (5%) were Negroes and 257 (4%) were Spanish-surnamed Americans. Of the 1,828 line drivers, however, there were only 8 (0.4%) Negroes and 5 (0.3%) Spanish-surnamed persons, and all of the Negroes had been hired after the litigation had commenced. With one exception—a man who worked as a line driver at the Chicago terminal from 1950 to 1959—the company and its predecessors *did not employ a Negro on a regular basis as a line driver until 1969.* And, as the Government showed, even in 1971 there were terminals in areas of substantial Negro population where all of the company's line drivers were white. A great majority of the Negroes (83%) and Spanish-surnamed Americans (78%) who did work for the company held the lower-paying city operations and serviceman jobs, whereas only 39% of the non-minority employees held jobs in those categories.

The Government bolstered its statistical evidence with the testimony of individuals who recounted over 40 specific instances of discrimination. Upon the basis of this testimony the District Court found that "[n]umerous qualified black and Spanish-surnamed American applicants who sought line-driving jobs at the company over the years had their requests ignored, were given false or misleading information about requirements, opportunities, and application procedures, or were not considered and hired on the same basis that whites were considered and hired." Minority employees who wanted to transfer to line-driver jobs met with similar difficulties.

The company's principal response to this evidence is that statistics can never in and of themselves prove the existence of a pattern or practice of discrimination, or even establish a prima facie case shifting to the employer the burden of rebutting the inference raised by the figures. But, as even our brief summary of the evidence shows, this was not a case in which the Government relied on "statistics alone." The individuals who testified about their personal experiences with the company brought the cold numbers convincingly to life.

In any event, our cases make it unmistakably clear that "[s]tatistical analyses have served and will continue to serve an important role" in cases in which the existence of discrimination is a disputed issue. Mayor of Philadelphia v. Educational Equality League, 415 U.S. 605, 620, 94 S.Ct. 1323, 1333, 39 L.Ed.2d 630. See also McDonnell Douglas Corp. v. Green, supra, 411 U.S., at 805, 93 S.Ct., at 1825. Cf. Washington v. Davis, 426 U.S. 229, 241–242, 96 S.Ct. 2040, 2048–2049, 48 L.Ed.2d 597. We have repeatedly approved the use of statistical proof, where it reached proportions comparable to those in this case, to establish a prima facie case of racial discrimination in jury selection cases, see, e.g., Turner v. Fouche, 396 U.S. 346, 90 S.Ct. 532, 24 L.Ed.2d 567; Hernandez v. Texas, 347 U.S. 475, 74 S.Ct. 667, 98 L.Ed. 866; Norris v. Alabama, 294 U.S. 587, 55 S.Ct. 579, 79 L.Ed. 1074. Statistics are equally competent in proving employment discrimination. We caution only that statistics are not irrefutable; they come in infinite variety and, like any other kind of evidence, they may be rebutted. In short, their usefulness depends on all of the surrounding facts and circumstances. See, e.g., Hester v. Southern R. Co., 497 F.2d 1374, 1379–1381 (CA5).

In addition to its general protest against the use of statistics in Title VII cases, the company claims that in this case the statistics revealing racial imbalance are misleading because they fail to take into account the company's particular business situation as of the effective date of Title VII. The company concedes that its line drivers were virtually all white in July 1965, but it claims that thereafter business conditions were such that its work force dropped. Its argument is that low personnel turnover, rather than post-Act discrimination, accounts for more recent statistical disparities. It points to substantial minority hiring in later years, especially after 1971, as showing that any pre-Act patterns of discrimination were broken.

The argument would be a forceful one if this were an employer who, at the time of suit, had done virtually no new hiring since the effective date of Title VII. But it is not. Although the company's total number of employees apparently dropped somewhat during the late 1960's, the record shows that many line drivers continued to be hired throughout this period, and that almost all of them were white.   *   *   *

The District Court and the Court of Appeals, on the basis of substantial evidence, held that the Government had proved a prima facie case of systematic and purposeful employment discrimination, continuing well beyond the effective date of Title VII. The company's attempts to rebut that conclusion were held to be inadequate. For the reasons we have summarized, there is no warrant for this Court to disturb the findings of the District Court and the Court of Appeals on this basic issue.   *   *   *

B

The District Court and the Court of Appeals also found that the seniority system contained in the collective-bargaining agreements between the company and the union operated to violate Title VII of the Act.

For purposes of calculating benefits, such as vacations, pensions, and other fringe benefits, an employee's seniority under this system runs from the date he joins the company, and takes into account his total service in all jobs and bargaining units. For competitive purposes, however, such as determining the order in which employees may bid for particular jobs, are laid off, or are recalled from layoff, it is bargaining-unit seniority that controls. Thus, a line driver's seniority, for purposes of bidding for particular runs and protection against layoff, takes into account only the length of time he has been a line driver at a particular terminal. The practical effect is that a city driver or serviceman who transfers to a line-driver job must forfeit all the competitive seniority he has accumulated in his previous bargaining unit and start at the bottom of the line-drivers' "board."

The vice of this arrangement, as found by the District Court and the Court of Appeals, was that it "locked" minority workers into inferior jobs and perpetuated prior discrimination by discouraging transfers to jobs as line drivers. While the disincentive applied to all workers, including whites, it was Negroes and Spanish-surnamed persons who, those courts found, suffered the most because many of them had been denied the equal opportunity to become line drivers when they were initially hired, whereas whites either had not sought or were refused line-driver positions for reasons unrelated to their race or national origin.

The linchpin of the theory embraced by the District Court and the Court of Appeals was that a discriminatee who must forfeit his competitive seniority in order finally to obtain a line-driver job will never be able to "catch up" to the seniority level of his contemporary who was not subject to discrimination.[27] Accordingly, this continued, built-in disadvantage to the prior discriminatee who transfers to a line-driver job was held to constitute a continuing violation of Title VII, for which both the employer and the union who jointly created and maintain the seniority system were liable.

The union, while acknowledging that the seniority system may in some sense perpetuate the effects of prior discrimination, asserts that the system is immunized from a finding of illegality by reason of § 703(h) of Title VII, which provides in part:

> "Notwithstanding any other provision of this subchapter, it shall not be an unlawful employment practice for an employer to apply different standards of compensation, or different terms, conditions, or privileges of employment pursuant to a bona fide seniority * * * system, * * * provided that such differences are not the result of an intention to discriminate because of race * * * or national origin * * *."

It argues that the seniority system in this case is "bona fide" within the meaning of § 703(h) when judged in light of its history, intent, application, and all of the circumstances under which it was created and is maintained. More specifically, the union claims that the central purpose of § 703(h) is to ensure that mere perpetuation of *pre-Act* discrimination is not unlawful

---

27. An example would be a Negro who was qualified to be a line driver in 1958 but who, because of his race, was assigned instead a job as a city driver, and is allowed to become a line driver only in 1971. Because he loses his competitive seniority when he transfers jobs, he is forever junior to white line drivers hired between 1958 and 1970. The whites, rather than the Negro, will henceforth enjoy the preferable runs and the greater protection against layoff. Although the original discrimination occurred in 1958—before the effective date of Title VII—the seniority system operates to carry the effects of the earlier discrimination into the present.

under Title VII. And, whether or not § 703(h) immunizes the perpetuation of *post-Act* discrimination, the union claims that the seniority system in this case has no such effect. Its position in this Court, as has been its position throughout this litigation, is that the seniority system presents no hurdle to post-Act discriminatees who seek retroactive seniority to the date they would have become line drivers but for the company's discrimination. Indeed, the union asserts that under its collective-bargaining agreements the union will itself take up the cause of the post-Act victim and attempt, through grievance procedures, to gain for him full "make whole" relief, including appropriate seniority.

The Government responds that a seniority system that perpetuates the effects of prior discrimination—pre- or post-Act—can never be "bona fide" under § 703(h); at a minimum Title VII prohibits those applications of a seniority system that perpetuate the effects on incumbent employees of prior discriminatory job assignments.

The issues thus joined are open ones in this Court.[28] We considered § 703(h) in Franks v. Bowman Transportation Co., 424 U.S. 747, 96 S.Ct. 1251, 47 L.Ed.2d 444, but there decided only that § 703(h) does not bar the award of retroactive seniority to job applicants who seek relief from an employer's post-Act hiring discrimination. We stated that "the thrust of [§ 703(h)] is directed toward defining what is and what is not an illegal discriminatory practice in instances in which the post-Act operation of a seniority system is challenged as perpetuating the effects of discrimination occurring prior to the effective date of the Act." 424 U.S., at 761, 96 S.Ct., at 1263. Beyond noting the general purpose of the statute, however, we did not undertake the task of statutory construction required in this case.

(1)

Because the company discriminated both before and after the enactment of Title VII, the seniority system is said to have operated to perpetuate the effects of both pre- and post-Act discrimination. Post-Act discriminatees, however, may obtain full "make whole" relief, including retroactive seniority under Franks v. Bowman, supra, without attacking the legality of the seniority system as applied to them. *Franks* made clear and the union acknowledges that retroactive seniority may be awarded as relief from an employer's discriminatory hiring and assignment policies even if the seniority system agreement itself makes no provision for such relief. 424 U.S., at 778–779, 96 S.Ct., at 1271. Here the Government has proved that the

---

28. Concededly, the view that § 703(h) does not immunize seniority systems that perpetuate the effects of prior discrimination has much support. It was apparently first adopted in Quarles v. Philip Morris, Inc., 279 F.Supp. 505 (ED Va.). The court there held that "a departmental seniority system *that has its genesis in racial discrimination* is not a *bona fide* seniority system." Id., at 517 (first emphasis added). The *Quarles* view has since enjoyed wholesale adoption in the Courts of Appeals. See, e.g., Local 189, United Paperworkers v. United States, 416 F.2d 980, 987–988 (CA5); United States v. Sheet Metal Workers Local 36, 416 F.2d 123, 133–134, n. 20

(CA8); United States v. Bethlehem Steel Corp., 446 F.2d 652, 658–659 (CA2); United States v. Chesapeake & Ohio R. Co., 471 F.2d 582, 587–588 (CA4). Insofar as the result in *Quarles* and in the cases that followed it depended upon findings that the seniority systems were themselves "racially discriminatory" or had their "genesis in racial discrimination," 279 F.Supp., at 517, the decisions can be viewed as resting upon the proposition that a seniority system that perpetuates the effects of pre-Act discrimination cannot be bona fide if an intent to discriminate entered into its very adoption.

company engaged in a post-Act pattern of discriminatory hiring, assignment, transfer and promotion policies. Any Negro or Spanish-surnamed American injured by those policies may receive all appropriate relief as a direct remedy for this discrimination.[30]

(2)

What remains for review is the judgment that the seniority system unlawfully perpetuated the effects of *pre-Act* discrimination. We must decide, in short, whether § 703(h) validates otherwise bona fide seniority systems that afford no constructive seniority to victims discriminated against prior to the effective date of Title VII, and it is to that issue that we now turn.

The primary purpose of Title VII was "to assure equality of employment opportunities and to eliminate those discriminatory practices and devices which have fostered racially stratified job environments to the disadvantage of minority citizens." McDonnell Douglas Corp. v. Green, supra, 411 U.S., at 800, 93 S.Ct., at 1823. * * * To achieve this purpose, Congress "proscribe[d] not only overt discrimination but also practices that are fair in form, but discriminatory in operation." *Griggs,* 401 U.S., at 431, 91 S.Ct., at 853. * * *

One kind of practice "fair in form, but discriminatory in operation" is that which perpetuates the effects of prior discrimination. As the Court held in *Griggs:* "Under the Act, practices, procedures, or tests neutral on their face, and even neutral in terms of intent, cannot be maintained if they operate to 'freeze' the status quo of prior discriminatory employment practices." 401 U.S., at 430, 91 S.Ct., at 853.

Were it not for § 703(h), the seniority system in this case would seem to fall under the *Griggs* rationale. The heart of the system is its allocation of the choicest jobs, the greatest protection against layoffs, and other advantages to those employees who have been line drivers for the longest time. Where, because of the employer's prior intentional discrimination, the line drivers with the longest tenure are without exception white, the advantages of the seniority system flow disproportionately to them and away from Negro and Spanish-surnamed employees who might by now have enjoyed those advantages had not the employer discriminated before the passage of the Act. This disproportionate distribution of advantages does in a very real sense "operate to 'freeze' the status quo of prior discriminatory employment practices." Ibid. But both the literal terms of § 703(h) and the legislative history of Title VII demonstrate that Congress considered this very effect of many seniority systems [and] extended a measure of immunity to them.

---

30. The legality of the seniority system insofar as it perpetuates post-Act discrimination nonetheless remains at issue in this case, in light of the injunction entered against the union. * * * Our decision today in United Air Lines v. Evans [431 U.S. 553, 97 S.Ct. 1885, 52 L.Ed.2d 571,] is largely dispositive of this issue. *Evans* holds that the operation of a seniority system is not unlawful under Title VII even though it perpetuates post-Act discrimination that has not been the subject of a timely charge by the discriminatee. Here, of course, the Government has sued to remedy the post-Act discrimination directly, and there is no claim that any relief would be time-barred. But this is simply an additional reason not to hold the seniority system unlawful, since such a holding would in no way enlarge the relief to be awarded. See Franks v. Bowman, 424 U.S. at 778–779, 96 S.Ct. at 1271. Section 703(h) on its face immunizes all bona fide seniority systems, and does not distinguish between the perpetuation of pre- and post-Act discrimination.

Throughout the initial consideration of H.R. 7152, later enacted as the Civil Rights Act of 1964, critics of the bill charged that it would destroy existing seniority rights. The consistent response of Title VII's congressional proponents and of the Justice Department was that seniority rights would not be affected, even where the employer had discriminated prior to the Act. An interpretative memorandum placed in the Congressional Record by Senators Clark and Case stated:

"Title VII would have no effect on established seniority rights. Its effect is prospective and not retrospective. Thus, for example, *if a business has been discriminating in the past and as a result has an all-white working force, when the title comes into effect the employer's obligation would be simply to fill future vacancies on a non-discriminatory basis.* He would not be obliged—or indeed, permitted—to fire whites in order to hire Negroes or to prefer Negroes for future vacancies, or, once Negroes are hired to give them special seniority rights at the expense of the white workers hired earlier." 110 Cong.Rec. 7213 (1964) (emphasis added).[35]

A Justice Department statement concerning Title VII placed in the Congressional Record by Senator Clark, voiced the same conclusion:

"Title VII would have no effect on seniority rights existing at the time it takes effect. If, for example, a collective bargaining contract provides that in the event of layoffs, those who were hired last must be laid off first, such a provision would not be affected in the least by title VII. *This would be true even in the case where owing to discrimination prior to the effective date of the title, white workers had more seniority than Negroes.*" Id., at 7207 (emphasis added).[36]

While these statements were made before § 703(h) was added to Title VII, they are authoritative indicators of that section's purpose. Section 703(h) was enacted as part of the Mansfield-Dirksen compromise substitute bill that cleared the way for the passage of Title VII. The drafters of the compromise bill stated that one of its principal goals was to resolve the ambiguities in the House-passed version of H.R. 7152. See, e.g., id., at 11935–11937 (remarks of Sen. Dirksen); id. at 12707 (remarks of Sen. Humphrey). As the debates indicate, one of those ambiguities concerned Title VII's impact on existing collectively bargained seniority rights. It is apparent that § 703(h) was drafted with an eye toward meeting the earlier criticism on this issue with an explicit provision embodying the understanding and assurances of the Act's proponents: namely, that Title VII would not outlaw such differences in treatment among employees as flowed from a bona fide seniority system that allowed for full exercise of seniority accumulated before the effective date of the Act. * * *.

In sum, the unmistakable purpose of § 703(h) was to make clear that the routine application of a bona fide seniority system would not be unlawful under Title VII. As the legislative history shows, this was the intended result even where the employer's pre-Act discrimination resulted in whites having greater existing seniority rights than Negroes. Although a seniority system inevitably tends to perpetuate the effects of pre-Act discrimination in

---

35. Senators Clark and Case were the "bipartisan captains" responsible for Title VII during the Senate debate. * * *

36. The full text of the statement is set out in Franks v. Bowman [supra p. 948, n. 16].

such cases, the congressional judgment was that Title VII should not outlaw the use of existing seniority lists and thereby destroy or water down the vested seniority rights of employees simply because their employer had engaged in discrimination prior to the passage of the Act.

To be sure, § 703(h) does not immunize all seniority systems. It refers only to "bona fide" systems, and a proviso requires that any differences in treatment not be "the result of an intention to discriminate because of race * * * or national origin * * *." But our reading of the legislative history compels us to reject the Government's broad argument that no seniority system that tends to perpetuate pre-Act discrimination can be "bona fide." To accept the argument would require us to hold that a seniority system becomes illegal simply because it allows the full exercise of the pre-Act seniority rights of employees of a company that discriminated before Title VII was enacted. It would place an affirmative obligation on the parties to the seniority agreement to subordinate those rights in favor of the claims of pre-Act discriminatees without seniority. The consequence would be a perversion of the congressional purpose. We cannot accept the invitation to disembowel § 703(h) by reading the words "bona fide" as the Government would have us do.[38] Accordingly, we hold that an otherwise neutral, legitimate seniority system does not become unlawful under Title VII simply because it may perpetuate pre-Act discrimination. Congress did not intend to make it illegal for employees with vested seniority rights to continue to exercise those rights, even at the expense of pre-Act discriminatees.

* * *

(3)

The seniority system in this case is entirely bona fide. It applies equally to all races and ethnic groups. To the extent that it "locks" employees into non-line-driver jobs, it does so for all. The city drivers and servicemen who are discouraged from transferring to line-driver jobs are not all Negroes or Spanish-surnamed Americans; to the contrary, the overwhelming majority are white. The placing of line drivers in a separate bargaining unit from other employees is rational in accord with the industry practice, and consistent with NLRB precedents.[42] It is conceded that the seniority system did not have its genesis in racial discrimination, and that it was negotiated and has been maintained free from any illegal purpose. In these circumstances,

---

38. For the same reason, we reject the contention that the proviso in § 703(h), which bars differences in treatment resulting from "an intention to discriminate," applies to any application of a seniority system that may perpetuate past discrimination. In this regard the language of the Justice Department memorandum introduced at the legislative hearings is especially pertinent: "It is perfectly clear that when a worker is laid off or denied a chance for promotion because he is 'low man on the totem pole' he is not being discriminated against because of his race * * *. Any differences in treatment based on established seniority rights would not be based on race and would not be forbidden by the title." 110 Cong.Rec. 7207 (1964).

42. See Georgia Highway Express, 150 N.L.R.B. 1649, 1651: "The Board has long held that local drivers and over-the-road drivers constitute separate appropriate units where they are shown to be clearly defined, homogeneous, and functionally distinct groups with separate interests which can effectively be represented separately for bargaining purposes. * * * In view of the different duties and functions, separate supervision, and different bases of payment, it is clear that the over-the-road drivers have divergent interests from those of the employees in the [city operations] unit * * * and should not be included in that unit."

the single fact that the system extends no retroactive seniority to pre-Act discriminatees does not make it unlawful.

Because the seniority system was protected by § 703(h), the union's conduct in agreeing to and maintaining the system did not violate Title VII. On remand, the District Court's injunction against the union must be vacated.

III

Our conclusion that the seniority system does not violate Title VII will necessarily affect the remedy granted to individual employees on remand of this litigation to the District Court. Those employees who suffered only pre-Act discrimination are not entitled to relief, and no person may be given retroactive seniority to a date earlier than the effective date of the Act.

*   *   *

MR. JUSTICE MARSHALL, with whom MR. JUSTICE BRENNAN joins, concurring in part and dissenting in part.

*   *   *

As the Court quite properly acknowledges, the seniority provision at issue here clearly would violate Title VII absent § 703(h), which exempts at least some seniority systems from the reach of the Act. *   *   *

As the Court also concedes, with a touch of understatement, "the view that § 703(h) does not immunize seniority systems that perpetuate the effects of prior discrimination has much support." Ante, n. 28. Without a single dissent, six courts of appeals have so held in over 30 cases, and two other courts of appeals have indicated their agreement, also without dissent. In an unbroken line of cases, the EEOC has reached the same conclusion. And the overwhelming weight of scholarly opinion is in accord. *   *   *.

Note

The Court states: "It is conceded that the seniority system did not have its genesis in racial discrimination, and that it was negotiated and maintained free from any illegal purpose [i.e., the intention to discriminate because of race, color, religion, sex, or national origin]." (Supra p. 966.) Since minority employees hired prior to 1965 were assigned to less desirable jobs because of their race and since the seniority system then effectively locked them into those jobs, what kind of seniority system *would* have "its genesis in racial discrimination"? Is a seniority system which has the lock-in effect described above "negotiated and maintained free from any illegal purpose" when it is *retained* in collective bargaining agreements negotiated *after* the Act?

If your answer to the last question is yes, because otherwise a pre-Act seniority system legitimated by the Teamsters decision would expire with the post-Act expiration of the pertinent collective bargaining agreement, how would you react to a post-Act *initiation* of a seniority provision which locked in a pre-Act discriminatory *hiring* practice? In American Tobacco Co. v. Patterson, 456 U.S. 63, 102 S.Ct. 1534, 71 L.Ed.2d 748 (1982), the Court held, 5–4, the latter to be exempted under § 703(h) because "[s]ection 703(h) makes no distinction between seniority systems adopted before its effective date and those adopted after its effective date." 456 U.S. at 76, 102 S.Ct. at 1541, 71 L.Ed.2d at 760.

"[O]n its face [section 703(h)] immunized *all* bona fide seniority systems, and does not distinguish between the perpetuation of pre- and post-Act discriminatory impact. *Teamsters,* * * * 431 U.S. at 348, n. 30, 97 S.Ct. at 1861, n. 30 (emphasis added)." 456 U.S. at 75–76, 102 S.Ct. at 1541, 71 L.Ed.2d at 759–60.

UNITED STEELWORKERS v. WEBER

Supreme Court of the United States, 1979.
443 U.S. 193, 99 S.Ct. 2721, 61 L.Ed.2d 480.

MR. JUSTICE BRENNAN delivered the opinion of the Court.

Challenged here is the legality of an affirmative action plan—collectively bargained by an employer and a union—that reserves for black employees 50% of the openings in an in-plant craft training program until the percentage of black craft workers in the plant is commensurate with the percentage of blacks in the local labor force. The question for decision is whether Congress, in Title VII of the Civil Rights Act of 1964 as amended, * * * left employers and unions in the private sector free to take such race-conscious steps to eliminate manifest racial imbalances in traditionally segregated job categories. We hold that Title VII does not prohibit such race-conscious affirmative action plans.

I

In 1974 petitioner United Steelworkers of America (USWA) and petitioner Kaiser Aluminum & Chemical Corporation (Kaiser) entered into a master collective-bargaining agreement covering terms and conditions of employment at 15 Kaiser plants. The agreement contained, *inter alia,* an affirmative action plan designed to eliminate conspicuous racial imbalances in Kaiser's then almost exclusively white craft work forces. Black craft hiring goals were set for each Kaiser plant equal to the percentage of blacks in the respective local labor forces. To enable plants to meet these goals, on-the-job training programs were established to teach unskilled production workers—black and white—the skills necessary to become craft workers. The plan reserved for black employees 50% of the openings in these newly created in-plant training programs. This case arose from the operation of the plan at Kaiser's plant in Gramercy, La. Until 1974 Kaiser hired as craft workers for that plant only persons who had had prior craft experience. Because blacks had long been excluded from craft unions,[1] few were able to present such credentials. As a consequence, prior to 1974 only 1.83% (five out of

---

1. Judicial findings of exclusion from crafts on racial grounds are so numerous as to make such exclusion a proper subject for judicial notice. See, e.g., United States v. International Union of Elevator Constructors, 538 F.2d 1012 (CA3 1976); Associated General Contractors of Massachusetts v. Altshuler, 490 F.2d 9 (CA1 1973); Southern Illinois Builders Association v. Ogilve, 471 F.2d 680 (CA7 1972); Contractors Association of Eastern Pennsylvania v. Secretary of Labor, 442 F.2d 159 (CA3 1971); Local 53 of International Association of Heat & Frost, etc. v. Vogler, 407 F.2d 1047 (CA5 1969); Buckner v. Goodyear, 339 F.Supp. 1108 (NDAla.1972), aff'd without opinion, 476 F.2d 1287 (CA5 1973). See also United States Commission on Civil Rights, The Challenge Ahead: Equal Opportunity in Referral Unions 58–94 (1976), (summarizing judicial findings of discrimination by craft unions); G. Myrdal, An American Dilemma (1944) 1079–1124; R. Marshall and V. Briggs, The Negro and Apprenticeship (1967); S. Spero and A. Harris, The Black Worker (1931); United States Commission on Civil Rights, Employment 97 (1961), State Advisory Committee, United States Commission on Civil Rights, 50 States Report 209 (1961); Marshall, "The Negro in Southern Unions," in The Negro and the American Labor Movement (ed. Jacobson, Anchor 1968) p. 145; App., 63, 104.

273) of the skilled craft workers at the Gramercy plant were black, even though the work force in the Gramercy area was approximately 39% black.

Pursuant to the national agreement Kaiser altered its craft hiring practice in the Gramercy plant. Rather than hiring already trained outsiders, Kaiser established a training program to train its production workers to fill craft openings. Selection of craft trainees was made on the basis of seniority, with the proviso that at least 50% of the new trainees were to be black until the percentage of black skilled craft workers in the Gramercy plant approximated the percentage of blacks in the local labor force. See 415 F.Supp. 761, 764.

During 1974, the first year of the operation of the Kaiser-USWA affirmative action plan, 13 craft trainees were selected from Gramercy's production work force. Of these, 7 were black and 6 white. The most junior black selected into the program had less seniority than several white production workers whose bids for admission were rejected. Thereafter one of those white production workers, respondent Brian Weber, instituted this class action in the United States District Court for the Eastern District of Louisiana.

The complaint alleged that the filling of craft trainee positions at the Gramercy plant pursuant to the affirmative action program had resulted in junior black employees receiving training in preference to more senior white employees, thus discriminating against respondent and other similarly situated white employees in violation of §§ 703(a)[2] and (d)[3] of Title VII. The District Court held that the plan violated Title VII, entered a judgment in favor of the plaintiff class, and granted a permanent injunction prohibiting Kaiser and the USWA "from denying plaintiffs, Brian F. Weber and all other members of the class, access to on-the-job training programs on the basis of race." 415 F.Supp. 761 (1976). A divided panel of the Court of Appeals for the Fifth Circuit affirmed, holding that all employment preferences based upon race, including those preferences incidental to bona fide affirmative action plans, violated Title VII's prohibition against racial discrimination in employment. 563 F.2d 216 (1978). We granted certiorari. * * * We reverse.

II

We emphasize at the outset the narrowness of our inquiry. Since the Kaiser-USWA plan does not involve state action, this case does not present

2. Section 703(a), * * * provides:

"(a) It shall be an unlawful employment practice for an employer—

"(1) to fail or refuse to hire or to discharge any individual, or otherwise to discriminate against any individual with respect to his compensation, terms, conditions, or privileges of employment, because of such individual's race, color, religion, sex, or national origin; or

"(2) to limit, segregate, or classify his employees or applicants for employment in any way which would deprive or tend to deprive any individual of employment opportunities or otherwise adversely af-

fect his status as an employee, because of such individual's race, color, religion, sex, or national origin."

3. Section 703(d), * * * provides:

"It shall be an unlawful employment practice for any employer, labor organization, or joint labor-management committee controlling apprenticeship or other training or retraining, including on-the-job training programs to discriminate against any individual because of his race, color, religion, sex, or national origin in admission to, or employment in, any program established to provide apprenticeship or other training."

an alleged violation of the Equal Protection Clause of the Constitution. Further, since the Kaiser-USWA plan was adopted voluntarily, we are not concerned with what Title VII requires or with what a court might order to remedy a past proven violation of the Act. The only question before us is the narrow statutory issue of whether Title VII *forbids* private employers and unions from voluntarily agreeing upon bona fide affirmative action plans that accord racial preferences in the manner and for the purpose provided in the Kaiser-USWA plan. That question was expressly left open in McDonald v. Santa Fe Trail Trans. Co., 427 U.S. 273, 281 n. 8, 96 S.Ct. 2574, 2579, 49 L.Ed.2d 493 (1976), which held, in a case not involving affirmative action, that Title VII protects whites as well as blacks from certain forms of racial discrimination.

Respondent argues that Congress intended in Title VII to prohibit all race-conscious affirmative action plans. Respondent's argument rests upon a literal interpretation of §§ 703(a) and (d) of the Act. Those sections make it unlawful to "discriminate * * * because of * * * race" in hiring and in the selection of apprentices for training programs. Since, the argument runs, McDonald v. Santa Fe Trail Trans. Co., supra, settled that Title VII forbids discrimination against whites as well as blacks, and since the Kaiser-USWA affirmative action plan operates to discriminate against white employees solely because they are white, it follows that the Kaiser-USWA plan violates Title VII.

Respondent's argument is not without force. But it overlooks the significance of the fact that the Kaiser-USWA plan is an affirmative action plan voluntarily adopted by private parties to eliminate traditional patterns of racial segregation. In this context respondent's reliance upon a literal construction of § 703(a) and (d) and upon *McDonald* is misplaced. See McDonald v. Santa Fe Trail Trans Co., supra, at 281, n. 8, 96 S.Ct., at 2579. It is a "familiar rule that a thing may be within the letter of the statute and yet not within the statute, because not within its spirit nor within the intention of its makers." Holy Trinity Church v. United States, 143 U.S. 457, 459, 12 S.Ct. 511, 512, 36 L.Ed. 226 (1892). The prohibition against racial discrimination in §§ 703(a) and (d) of Title VII must therefore be read against the background of the legislative history of Title VII and the historical context from which the Act arose. * * * Examination of those sources makes clear that an interpretation of the sections that forbade all race-conscious affirmative action would "bring about an end completely at variance with the purpose of the statute" and must be rejected. United States v. Public Utilities Comm'n, 345 U.S. 295, 315, 73 S.Ct. 706, 718, 97 L.Ed. 1020 (1953). * * *

Congress' primary concern in enacting the prohibition against racial discrimination in Title VII of the Civil Rights Act of 1964 was with "the plight of the Negro in our economy." 110 Cong.Rec. 6548 (remarks of Sen. Humphrey). Before 1964, blacks were largely relegated to "unskilled and semi-skilled jobs." Id., at 6548 (remarks of Sen. Humphrey); id., at 7204 (remarks of Sen. Clark); id., at 7279–7280 (remarks of Sen. Kennedy). Because of automation the number of such jobs was rapidly decreasing. See 110 Cong.Rec., at 6548 (remarks of Sen. Humphrey); id., at 7204 (remarks of Sen. Clark). As a consequence "the relative position of the Negro worker

[was] steadily worsening. In 1947 the non-white unemployment rate was only 64 percent higher than the white rate; in 1962 it was 124 percent higher." Id., at 6547 (remarks of Sen. Humphrey). See also id., at 7204 (remarks of Sen. Clark). Congress considered this a serious social problem. As Senator Clark told the Senate:

> "The rate of Negro unemployment has gone up consistently as compared with white unemployment for the past 15 years. This is a social malaise and a social situation which we should not tolerate. That is one of the principal reasons why this bill should pass." Id., at 7220.

Congress feared that the goals of the Civil Rights Act—the integration of blacks into the mainstream of American society—could not be achieved unless this trend were reversed. And Congress recognized that that would not be possible unless blacks were able to secure jobs "which have a future." Id., at 7204 (remarks of Sen. Clark). See also id., at 7279–7280 (remarks of Sen. Kennedy). As Senator Humphrey explained to the Senate.

> "What good does it do a Negro to be able to eat in a fine restaurant if he cannot afford to pay the bill? What good does it do him to be accepted in a hotel that is too expensive for his modest income? How can a Negro child be motivated to take full advantage of integrated educational facilities if he has no hope of getting a job where he can use that education?" Id., at 6547.
>
>   *   *   *
>
> "Without a job, one cannot afford public convenience and accommodations. Income from employment may be necessary to further a man's education, or that of his children. If his children have no hope of getting a good job, what will motivate them to take advantage of educational opportunities." Id., at 6552.

These remarks echoed President Kennedy's original message to Congress upon the introduction of the Civil Rights Act in 1963.

> "There is little value in a Negro's obtaining the right to be admitted to hotels and restaurants if he has no cash in his pocket and no job." Id., at 11159.

Accordingly, it was clear to Congress that "the crux of the problem [was] to open employment opportunities for Negroes in occupations which have been traditionally closed to them," id., at 6548 (remarks of Sen. Humphrey), and it was to this problem that Title VII's prohibition against racial discrimination in employment was primarily addressed.

It plainly appears from the House Report accompanying the Civil Rights Act that Congress did not intend wholly to prohibit private and voluntary affirmative action efforts as one method of solving this problem. The Report provides:

> "No bill can or should lay claim to eliminating all of the causes and consequences of racial and other types of discrimination against minorities. There is reason to believe, however, that national leadership provided by the enactment of Federal legislation dealing with the most troublesome problems *will create an atmosphere conducive to voluntary or local resolution of other forms of discrimination.*" H.R.Rep. No. 914, 88th Cong., 1st Sess. (1963), at 18, U.S.Code Cong. & Admin.News 1964, pp. 2355, 2393. (Emphasis supplied.)

Given this legislative history, we cannot agree with respondent that Congress intended to prohibit the private sector from taking effective steps to accomplish the goal that Congress designed Title VII to achieve. The very statutory words intended as a spur or catalyst to cause "employers and unions to self-examine and to self-evaluate their employment practices and to endeavor to eliminate, so far as possible, the last vestiges of an unfortunate and ignominious page in this country's history." Albemarle v. Moody, 422 U.S. 405, 418, 95 S.Ct. 2362, 2372, 45 L.Ed.2d 245 (1975), cannot be interpreted as an absolute prohibition against all private, voluntary, race-conscious affirmative action efforts to hasten the elimination of such vestiges.[4] It would be ironic indeed if a law triggered by a Nation's concern over centuries of racial injustice and intended to improve the lot of those who had "been excluded from the American dream for so long," 110 Cong. Rec., at 6552 (remarks of Sen. Humphrey), constituted the first legislative prohibition of all voluntary, private, race-conscious efforts to abolish traditional patterns of racial segregation and hierarchy.

Our conclusion is further reinforced by examination of the language and legislative history of § 703(j) of Title VII.[5] Opponents of Title VII raised two related arguments against the bill. First, they argued that the Act would be interpreted to *require* employers with racially imbalanced work forces to grant preferential treatment to racial minorities in order to integrate. Second, they argued that employers with racially imbalanced work forces would grant preferential treatment to racial minorities, even if not required to do so by the Act. See 110 Cong.Rec. 8618–8619 (remarks of Sen. Sparkman). Had Congress meant to prohibit all race-conscious affirmative action, as respondent urges, it easily could have answered both objections by providing that Title VII would not require or *permit* racially preferential integration efforts. But Congress did not choose such a course. Rather Congress added § 703(j) which addresses only the first objection. The section provides that nothing contained in Title VII "shall be interpreted to *require* any employer * * * to grant preferential treatment * * * to any group because of the race * * * of such * * * group on account of" a de facto

---

4. The problem that Congress addressed in 1964 remains with us. In 1962 the nonwhite unemployment rate was 124% higher than the white rate. See 110 Cong.Rec. 6547 (remarks of Sen. Humphrey). In 1978 the black unemployment rate was 129% higher. See Monthly Labor Review, U.S. Department of Labor Bureau of Labor Statistics 78 (Mar. 1979).

5. Section 703(j) of Title VII * * * provides:

"Nothing contained in this subchapter shall be interpreted to require any employer, employment agency, labor organization, or joint labor-management committee subject to this subchapter to grant preferential treatment to any individual or to any group because of the race, color, religion, sex, national origin of such individual or group on account of an imbalance which may exist with respect to the total number or percentage of persons of any race, color, religion,

sex, or national origin employed by any employer, referred or classified for employment by any employment agency or labor organization, admitted to membership or classified by any labor organization, or admitted to, or employed in, any apprenticeship or other training program, in comparison with the total number or percentage of persons of such race, color, religion, sex, or national origin in any community, State, section, or other area, or in the available work force in any community, State, section, or other area."

Section 703(j) speaks to substantive liability under Title VII, but it does not preclude courts from considering racial imbalance as evidence of a Title VII violation. See Teamsters v. United States, 431 U.S. 324, 339–340, n. 20, 97 S.Ct. 1843, 1856, 52 L.Ed.2d 396 (1977). Remedies for substantive violations are governed by § 706(g) * * *.

racial imbalance in the employer's work force. The section does *not* state that "nothing in Title VII shall be interpreted to *permit*" voluntary affirmative efforts to correct racial imbalances. The natural inference is that Congress chose not to forbid all voluntary race-conscious affirmative action.

The reasons for this choice are evident from the legislative record. Title VII could not have been enacted into law without substantial support from legislators in both Houses who traditionally resisted federal regulation of private business. Those legislators demanded as a price for their support that "management prerogatives and union freedoms * * * be left undisturbed to the greatest extent possible." H.R.Rep. No. 914, 88th Cong., 1st Sess., Pt. 2 (1963), at 29, U.S.Code Cong. & Admin.News 1964, p. 2391. Section 703(j) was proposed by Senator Dirksen to allay any fears that the Act might be interpreted in such a way as to upset this compromise. The section was designed to prevent § 703 of Title VII from being interpreted in such a way as to lead to undue "Federal Government interference with private businesses because of some Federal employee's ideas about racial balance or imbalance." 110 Cong.Rec., at 14314 (remarks of Sen. Miller).[6] * * * Clearly, a prohibition against all voluntary, race-conscious, affirmative action efforts would disserve these ends. Such a prohibition would augment the powers of the Federal Government and diminish traditional management prerogatives while at the same time impeding attainment of the ultimate statutory goals. In view of this legislative history and in view of Congress' desire to avoid undue federal regulation of private businesses, use of the word "require" rather than the phrase "require or permit" in § 703(j) fortifies the conclusion that Congress did not intend to limit traditional business freedom to such a degree as to prohibit all voluntary, race-conscious affirmative action.

We therefore hold that Title VII's prohibition in §§ 703(a) and (d) against racial discrimination does not condemn all private, voluntary, race-conscious affirmative action plans.

III

We need not today define in detail the line of demarcation between permissible and impermissible affirmative action plans. It suffices to hold that the challenged Kaiser-USWA affirmative action plan falls on the permissible side of the line. The purposes of the plan mirror those of the statute. Both were designed to break down old patterns of racial segregation and heirarchy. Both were structured to "open employment opportunities for

6. Title VI of the Civil Rights Act of 1964, considered in University of California Regents v. Bakke, 438 U.S. 265, 98 S.Ct. 2733, 57 L.Ed. 2d 750 (1978), contains no provision comparable to § 703(j). This is because Title VI was an exercise of federal power over a matter in which the Federal Government was already directly involved: the prohibitions against race-based conduct contained in Title VI governed "program[s] or activit[ies] receiving Federal financial assistance." 42 U.S.C. § 2000d. Congress was legislating to assure federal funds would not be used in an improper manner. Title VII, by contrast, was enacted pursuant to the Commerce power to regulate purely private decisionmaking and was not intended to incorporate and particularize the commands of the Fifth and Fourteenth Amendments. Title VII and Title VI, therefore, cannot be read *in pari materia*. See 110 Cong.Rec. 8315 (1964) (remarks of Sen. Cooper). See also id., at 11615 (remarks of Sen. Cooper).

Negroes in occupations which have been traditionally closed to them." 110 Cong.Rec. 6548 (remarks of Sen. Humphrey).[8]

At the same time the plan does not unnecessarily trammel the interests of the white employees. The plan does not require the discharge of white workers and their replacement with new black hires. Cf. McDonald v. Santa Fe Trail Trans. Co., supra. Nor does the plan create an absolute bar to the advancement of white employees; half of those trained in the program will be white. Moreover, the plan is a temporary measure; it is not intended to maintain racial balance, but simply to eliminate a manifest racial imbalance. Preferential selection of craft trainees at the Gramercy plant will end as soon as the percentage of black skilled craft workers in the Gramercy plant approximates the percentage of blacks in the local labor force.

* * *

We conclude, therefore, that the adoption of the Kaiser-USWA plan for the Gramercy plant falls within the area of discretion left by Title VII to the private sector voluntarily to adopt affirmative action plans designed to eliminate conspicuous racial imbalance in traditionally segregated job categories.[9] Accordingly, the judgment of the Courts of Appeals for the Fifth Circuit is reversed.

MR. JUSTICE POWELL and MR. JUSTICE STEVENS took no part in the consideration or decision of this case.

MR. JUSTICE REHNQUIST, with whom THE CHIEF JUSTICE joins, dissenting.

In a very real sense, the Court's opinion is ahead of its time: it could more appropriately have been handed down five years from now, in 1984, a year coinciding with the title of a book from which the Court's opinion borrows, perhaps subconsciously, at least one idea. Orwell describes in his book a governmental official of Oceania, one of the three great world powers, denouncing the current enemy, Eurasia, to an assembled crowd:

> "It was almost impossible to listen to him without being first convinced and then maddened. * * * The speech had been proceeding for perhaps twenty minutes when a messenger hurried onto the platform and a scrap of paper was slipped into the speaker's hand. He unrolled and read it without pausing in his speech. Nothing altered in his voice or manner, or in the content of what he was saying, but suddenly the names were different. Without words said, a wave of understanding rippled through the crowd. Oceania was at war with Eastasia! * * * The banners and posters with which the square was decorated were all wrong! * * *
>
> "[T]he speaker had switched from one line to the other actually in mid-sentence, not only without a pause, but without even breaking the syntax."
> G. Orwell, Nineteen Eighty-Four, 182–183 (1949).

Today's decision represents an equally dramatic and equally unremarked switch in this Court's interpretation of Title VII.

---

8. See n. 1, supra. This is not to suggest that the freedom of an employer to undertake race-conscious affirmative action efforts depends on whether or not his effort is motivated by fear of liability under Title VII.

9. Our disposition makes unnecessary consideration of petitioners' argument that their plan was justified because they feared that black employees would bring suit under Title VII if they did not adopt an affirmative action plan. Nor need we consider petitioners' contention that their affirmative action plan represented an attempt to comply with Executive Order 11246 [see dissent, footnote 2 infra p. 976].

The operative sections of Title VII prohibit racial discrimination in employment *simpliciter*. Taken in its normal meaning and as understood by all Members of Congress who spoke to the issue during the legislative debates, see infra, ＊ ＊ ＊ this language prohibits a covered employer from considering race when making an employment decision, whether the race be black or white. Several years ago, however, a United States District Court held that "the dismissal of white employees charged with misappropriating company property while not dismissing a similarly charged Negro employee does not raise a claim upon which Title VII relief may be granted." McDonald v. Santa Fe Trail Transp. Co., 427 U.S. 273, 278, 96 S.Ct. 2574, 2578, 49 L.Ed.2d 493 (1976). This Court unanimously reversed, concluding from the "uncontradicted legislative history" that "[T]itle VII prohibits racial discrimination against the white petitioners in this case upon the same standards as would be applicable were they Negroes ＊ ＊ ＊." 427 U.S., at 280, 96 S.Ct., at 2579.

We have never wavered in our understanding that Title VII "prohibits *all* racial discrimination in employment, without exception for any particular employees." Id., at 283, 96 S.Ct., at 2580 (emphasis in original). In Griggs v. Duke Power Co., 401 U.S. 424, 431, 91 S.Ct. 849, 853, 28 L.Ed.2d 158 (1971), our first occasion to interpret Title VII, a unanimous court observed that "[d]iscriminatory preference, for any group, minority or majority, is precisely and only what Congress has proscribed." And in our most recent discussion of the issue, we uttered words seemingly dispositive of this case: "It is clear beyond cavil that the obligation imposed by Title VII is to provide an equal opportunity for *each* applicant regardless of race, without regard to whether members of the applicant's race are already proportionately represented in the work force." Furnco Construction Corp. v. Waters, 438 U.S. 567, 579, 98 S.Ct. 2943, 2951, 57 L.Ed.2d 957 (1978) (emphasis in original).[1]

Today, however, the Court behaves much like the Orwellian speaker earlier described as if it had been handed a note indicating that Title VII would lead to a result unacceptable to the Court if interpreted here as it was in our prior decisions. Accordingly, without even a break in syntax, the Court rejects "a literal construction of § 703(a)" in favor of newly discovered "legislative history," which leads it to a conclusion directly contrary to that compelled by the "uncontradicted legislative history" unearthed in *McDonald* and our other prior decisions. Now we are told that the legislative history of Title VII shows that employers are free to discriminate on the basis of race: an employer may, in the Court's words, "trammel the interests of white employees" in favor of black employees in order to eliminate "racial imbalance." Ante ＊ ＊ ＊. Our earlier interpretations of Title VII, like the banners and posters decorating the square in Oceania, were all wrong.

As if this were not enough to make a reasonable observer question this Court's adherence to the oft-stated principle that our duty is to construe rather than rewrite legislation, ＊ ＊ ＊ the Court also seizes upon § 703(j) of Title VII as an independent, or at least partially independent, basis for its holding. Totally ignoring the wording of that section, which is obviously

1. Our statements in *Griggs* and *Furnco Construction* patently inconsistent with to-   day's holding, are not even mentioned, much less distinguished, by the Court.

addressed to those charged with the responsibility of interpreting the law rather than those who are subject to its proscriptions, and totally ignoring the months of legislative debates preceding the section's introduction and passage, which demonstrate clearly that it was enacted to prevent precisely what occurred in this case, the Court infers from § 703(j) that "Congress chose not to forbid all voluntary race-conscious affirmative action."   *   *   *

Thus, by a *tour de force* reminiscent not of jurists such as Hale, Holmes, and Hughes, but of escape artists such as Houdini, the Court eludes clear statutory language, "uncontradicted" legislative history and uniform precedent in concluding that employers are, after all, permitted to consider race in making employment decisions.   It may be that one or more of the principal sponsors of Title VII would have preferred to see a provision allowing preferential treatment of minorities written into the bill.   Such a provision, however, would have to have been expressly or impliedly excepted from Title VII's explicit prohibition on all racial discrimination in employment.   There is no such exception in the Act.   And a reading of the legislative debates concerning Title VII, in which proponents and opponents alike uniformly denounced discrimination in favor of, as well as discrimination against, Negroes, demonstrates clearly that any legislator harboring an unspoken desire for such a provision could not possibly have succeeded in enacting it into law.

I

Kaiser opened its Gramercy, La., plant in 1958.   Because the Gramercy facility had no apprenticeship or in-plant craft training program, Kaiser hired as craft workers only persons with prior craft experience.   Despite Kaiser's efforts to locate and hire trained black craftsmen, few were available in the Gramercy area, and as a consequence, Kaiser's craft positions were manned almost exclusively by whites.   In February 1974, under pressure from the Office of Federal Contract Compliance to increase minority representation in craft positions at its various plants,[2] and hoping to deter the filing of employment discrimination claims by minorities, Kaiser entered into a collective-bargaining agreement with the United Steelworkers of

---

2. The Office of Federal Contract Compliance (OFCC), subsequently renamed the Office of Federal Contract Compliance Programs (OFCCP), is an arm of the Department of Labor responsible for ensuring compliance by government contractors with the equal employment opportunity responsibilities established by Executive Order 11246, 30 Fed.Reg. 12319 (1965), as amended by Executive Order 11375, 32 Fed.Reg. 14303 (1967), and by Executive Order 12086, 43 Fed.Reg. 46501 (1978).

Executive Order 11246 requires all applicants for federal contracts to refrain from employment discrimination and to "take affirmative action to ensure that applicants are employed, and that employees are treated during employment, without regard to their race, color, religion, sex or national origin." § 202(j), 3 CFR § 169 (1974), reprinted following 42 U.S.C. § 200e (1970).   The Executive Order empowers the Secretary of Labor to issue rules and regulations necessary and ap-

propriate to achieve its purpose.   He, in turn, has delegated most enforcement duties to the OFCC.   See 41 CFR § 60-20.1 et seq.; 41 CFR § 60-2.24.

The affirmative action program mandated by 41 CFR § 60-2 (Revised order No. 4) for nonconstruction contractors requires a "utilization" study to determine minority representation in the work force.   Goals for hiring and promotion must be set to overcome any "underutilization" found to exist.

The OFCC employs the "power of the purse" to coerce acceptance of its affirmative action plans.   Indeed, in this case, "the district court found that the 1974 collective bargaining agreement reflected less of a desire on Kaiser's part to train black craft workers than a self-interest in satisfying the OFCC in order to retain lucrative government contracts."   563 F.2d 216, 226 (CA5 1977).

America (Steelworkers) which created a new on-the-job craft training program at 15 Kaiser facilities, including the Gramercy plant. The agreement required that no less than one minority applicant be admitted to the training program for every nonminority applicant until the percentage of blacks in craft positions equaled the percentage of blacks in the local work force. Eligibility for the craft training programs was to be determined on the basis of plant seniority, with black and white applicants to be selected on the basis of their relative seniority within their racial group.

Brian Weber is white. He was hired at Kaiser's Gramercy plant in 1969. In April 1974 Kaiser announced that it was offering a total of nine positions in three on-the-job training programs for skilled craft jobs. Weber applied for all three programs, but was not selected. The successful candidates—five black and four white applicants—were chosen in accordance with the 50% minority admission quota mandated under the 1974 collective-bargaining agreement. Two of the successful black applicants had less seniority than Weber. Weber brought the instant class action in the United States District Court for the Eastern District of Louisiana, alleging that use of the 50% minority admission quota to fill vacancies in Kaiser's craft training programs violated Title VII's prohibition on racial discrimination in employment. The District Court and the Court of Appeals for the Fifth Circuit agreed, enjoining further use of race as a criterion in admitting applicants to the craft training programs.[6]

6. In upholding the District Court's injunction, the Court of Appeals affirmed the District Court's finding that Kaiser had not been guilty of any past discriminatory hiring or promotion at its Gramercy plant. The court thus concluded that this finding removed the instant case from this Court's line of "remedy" decisions authorizing fictional seniority in order to place proven victims of discrimination in as good a position as they would have enjoyed absent the discriminatory hiring practices. See Franks v. Bowman Transp. Co., 424 U.S. 747, 96 S.Ct. 1251, 47 L.Ed.2d 444 (1976). "In the absence of prior discrimination," the Court of Appeals observed, "a racial quota loses its character as an equitable *remedy* and must be banned as an unlawful racial *preference* prohibited by Title VII, §§ 703(a) and (d). Title VII outlaws preferences for any group, minority or majority, if based on race or other impermissible classifications, but it does not outlaw preferences favoring victims of discrimination." 563 F.2d, at 224 (emphasis in original). Nor was the Court of Appeals moved by the claim that Kaiser's discriminatory admission quota is justified to correct a lack of training of Negroes due to past societal discrimination: "Whatever other effects societal discrimination may have, it has had—by the specific finding of the court below—*no effect* on the seniority of any party here." Id.,

at 226 (emphasis in original). Finally, the Court of Appeals rejected the argument that Kaiser's admission quota does not violate Title VII because it is sanctioned, indeed compelled, by Executive Order 11246 and regulations issued by the OFCC mandating affirmative action by all government contractors. See n. 2, supra. Citing Youngstown Sheet & Tube Co. v. Sawyer, 343 U.S. 579, 72 S.Ct. 863, 96 L.Ed. 1153 (1952), the court concluded that "[i]f Executive Order 11246 mandates a racial quota for admission to on-the-job training by Kaiser, *in the absence of any prior hiring or promotion discrimination,* the Executive Order must fall before the direct congressional prohibition [of § 703(d)]." Id., at 227 (emphasis in original).

Judge Wisdom, in dissent, argued that "[i]f an affirmative action plan, adopted in a collective bargaining agreement, is a reasonable remedy for an *arguable* violation of Title VII, it should be upheld." Id., at 230. The United States, in its brief before this Court, and Mr. Justice Blackmun [, concurring,] largely adopt Judge Wisdom's theory, which apparently rests on the conclusion that an employer is free to correct *arguable* discrimination against his black employees by adopting measures that he *knows* will discriminate against his white employees.

II

Were Congress to act today specifically to prohibit the type of racial discrimination suffered by Weber, it would be hard pressed to draft language better tailored to the task than that found in § 703(d) of Title VII:

> "It shall be an unlawful employment practice for any employer, labor organization, or joint labor-management committee controlling apprenticeship or other training or retraining, including on-the-job training programs to discriminate against any individual because of his race, color, religion, sex, or national origin in admission to, or employment in, any program established to provide apprenticeship or other training." * * *

Equally suited to the task would be § 703(a)(2), which makes it unlawful for an employer to classify his employees "in any way which would deprive or tend to deprive any individual of employment opportunities or otherwise adversely affect his status as an employee, because of such individual's race, color, religion, sex, or national origin." * * *

Entirely consistent with these two express prohibitions is the language of § 703(j) of Title VII, which provides that the Act is not to be interpreted "to require any employer * * * to grant preferential treatment to any individual or to any group because of the race * * * of such individual or group" to correct a racial imbalance in the employer's work force. * * * Seizing on the word "require," the Court infers that Congress must have intended to "permit" this type of racial discrimination. Not only is this reading of § 703(j) outlandish in the light of the flat prohibitions of §§ 703(a) and (d), but, as explained in Part III, it is totally belied by the Act's legislative history.

Quite simply, Kaiser's racially discriminatory admission quota is flatly prohibited by the plain language of Title VII. This normally dispositive fact, however, gives the Court only momentary pause. An "interpretation" of the statute upholding Weber's claim would, according to the Court, " 'bring about an end completely at variance with the purpose of the statute.' " Ante, * * * quoting United States v. Public Utilities Comm'n, 345 U.S. 295, 315, 73 S.Ct. 706, 718, 97 L.Ed. 1020 (1953). To support this conclusion, the Court calls upon the "spirit" of the Act, which it divines from passages in Title VII's legislative history indicating that enactment of the statute was prompted by Congress' desire "to open employment opportunities for Negroes in occupations which [had] been traditionally closed to them." Ante, * * * quoting 110 Cong.Rec. 6548 (1964) (remarks of Sen. Humphrey).[10] But the legislative history invoked by the Court to avoid the plain language of §§ 703(a) and (d) simply misses the point. To be sure, the reality of

---

10. In holding that Title VII cannot be interpreted to prohibit use of Kaiser's racially discriminatory admission quota, the Court reasons that it would be "ironic" if a law inspired by the history of racial discrimination in employment against blacks forbade employers from voluntarily discriminating against whites in favor of blacks. I see no irony in a law that prohibits *all* voluntary racial discrimination, even discrimination directed at whites in favor of blacks. The evil inherent in discrimination against Negroes is that it is based on an immutable characteristic, utterly irrelevant to employment decisions. The characteristic becomes no less immutable and irrelevant, and discrimination based thereon becomes no less evil, simply because the person excluded is a member of one race rather than another. Far from ironic, I find a prohibition on all preferential treatment based on race as elementary and fundamental as the principle that "two wrongs do not make a right."

employment discrimination against Negroes provided the primary impetus for passage of Title VII. But this fact by no means supports the proposition that Congress intended to leave employers free to discriminate against white persons. In most cases, "[l]egislative history * * * is more vague than the statute we are called upon to interpret." United States v. Public Utilities Comm'n, 345 U.S. 295, 321, 73 S.Ct. 706, 720, 97 L.Ed. 1020 (1954) (Jackson, J., concurring). Here, however, the legislative history of Title VII is as clear as the language of §§ 703(a) and (d), and it irrefutably demonstrates that Congress meant precisely what it said in §§ 703(a) and (d)—that *no* racial discrimination in employment is permissible under Title VII, not even preferential treatment of minorities to correct racial imbalance.

III

In undertaking to review the legislative history of Title VII, I am mindful that the topic hardly makes for light reading, but I am also fearful that nothing short of a thorough examination of the congressional debates will fully expose the magnitude of the Court's misinterpretation of Congress' intent.

A

Introduced on the floor of the House of Representatives on June 20, 1963, the bill—H.R. 7152—that ultimately became the Civil Rights Act of 1964 contained no compulsory provisions directed at private discrimination in employment. The bill was promptly referred to the Committee on the Judiciary, where it was amended to include Title VII. With two exceptions, the bill reported by the House Judiciary Committee contained §§ 703(a) and (d) as they were ultimately enacted. Amendments subsequently adopted on the House floor added § 703's prohibition against sex discrimination and § 703(d)'s coverage of "on the job training."

After noting that "[t]he purpose of [Title VII] is to eliminate * * * discrimination in employment based on race, color, religion, or national origin," the Judiciary Committee's report simply paraphrased the provisions of Title VII without elaboration. H.R.Rep. No. 914, 88th Cong., 1st Sess., 26 (1963) (hereinafter H.R.Rep.), U.S.Code Cong. & Admin.News 1964, p. 2401. In a separate Minority Report, however, opponents of the measure on the Committee advanced a line of attack which was reiterated throughout the debates in both the House and Senate and which ultimately led to passage of § 703(j). Noting that the word "discrimination" was nowhere defined in H.R. 7152, the Minority Report charged that the absence from Title VII of any reference to "racial imbalance" was a "public relations" ruse and that "the administration intends to rely upon its own construction of 'discrimination' as including the lack of racial balance * * *." H.R.Rep., at 67–68, U.S.Code Cong. & Admin.News 1964, p. 2436. To demonstrate how the bill would operate in practice, the Minority Report posited a number of hypothetical employment situations, concluding in each example that the employer "*may be forced to hire according to race,* to 'racially balance' those who work for him *in every job classification* or be in violation of Federal law." Id., at 69, U.S.Code Cong. & Admin.News 1964, p. 2438 (emphasis in original).

When H.R. 7152 reached the House floor, the opening speech in support
of its passage was delivered by Representative Celler, Chairman of the House
Judiciary Committee and the Congressman responsible for introducing the
legislation. A portion of that speech responded to criticism "seriously
misrepresent[ing] what the bill would do and grossly distort[ing] its effects":

> "[T]he charge has been made that the Equal Employment Opportunity
> Commission to be established by title VII of the bill would have the power to
> prevent a business from employing and promoting the people it wished, and
> that a 'Federal inspector' could then order the hiring and promotion only of
> employees of certain races or religious groups. This description of the bill is
> entirely wrong.
>
> * * *
>
> "Even [a] court could not order that any preference be given to any
> particular race, religion or other group, but would be limited to ordering an
> end of discrimination. The statement that a Federal inspector could order
> the employment and promotion only of members of a specific racial or
> religious group is therefore patently erroneous.
>
> * * *
>
> " * * * The Bill would do no more than prevent * * * employers
> from discriminating against *or in favor* of workers because of their race,
> religion, or national origin.
>
> "It is likewise not true that the Equal Employment Opportunity Com-
> mission would have power to rectify existing 'racial or religious imbalance'
> in employment by requiring the hiring of certain people without regard to
> their qualifications simply because they are of a given race or religion.
> Only actual discrimination could be stopped." 110 Cong.Rec. 1518 (1964)
> (emphasis added).

Representative Celler's construction of Title VII was repeated by several
other supporters during the House debate.

Thus, the battle lines were drawn early in the legislative struggle over
Title VII, with opponents of the measure charging that agencies of the
federal government such as the Equal Employment Opportunity Commission
(EEOC), by interpreting the word "discrimination" to mean the existence of
"racial imbalance," would "require" employers to grant preferential treatment to minorities, and supporters responding that the EEOC would be
granted no such power and that, indeed, Title VII prohibits discrimination
"in favor of workers because of their race." Supporters of H.R. 7152 in the
House ultimately prevailed by a vote of 290 to 130, and the measure was
sent to the Senate to begin what became the longest debate in that body's
history.

B

The Senate debate was broken into three phases: the debate on sending
the bill to Committee, the general debate on the bill prior to invocation of
cloture, and the debate following cloture.

1

When debate on the motion to refer the bill to Committee opened,
opponents of Title VII in the Senate immediately echoed the fears expressed

by their counterparts in the House, as is demonstrated by the following colloquy between Senators Hill and Ervin:

"Mr. ERVIN. I invite attention to * * * Section [703(a)] * * *

"I ask the Senator from Alabama if the Commission could not tell an employer that he had too few employees, that he had limited his employment, and enter an order, under [Section 703(a)], requiring him to hire more persons, not because the employer thought he needed more persons, but because the Commission wanted to compel him to employ persons of a particular race.

"Mr. HILL. The Senator is correct. That power is written into the bill. The employer could be forced to hire additional persons * * *." 110 Cong. Rec. 4764 (1964).

Senator Humphrey, perhaps the primary moving force behind H.R. 7152 in the Senate, was the first to state the proponents' understanding of Title VII. Responding to a political advertisement charging that federal agencies were at liberty to interpret the word "discrimination" in Title VII to require racial balance, Senator Humphrey stated: "[T]he meaning of racial or religious discrimination is perfectly clear. * * * [I]t means a distinction and treatment given to different individuals because of their different race, religion, or national origin." Id., at 5423. Stressing that Title VII "does not limit the employer's freedom to hire, fire, promote, or demote for any reasons—or no reasons—so long as his action is not based on race," Senator Humphrey further stated that "nothing in the bill would permit any official or court to require any employer or labor union to give preferential treatment to any minority group." Ibid.[17]

After 17 days of debate the Senate voted to take up the bill directly, without referring it to a committee. Id., at 6455. Consequently, there is no Committee Report in the Senate.

2

Formal debate on the merits of H.R. 7152 began on March 30, 1964. Supporters of the bill in the Senate had made elaborate preparations for this second round. Senator Humphrey, the Majority Whip, and Senator Kuchel, the Minority Whip, were selected as the bipartisan floor managers on the entire civil rights bill. Responsibility for explaining and defending each important title of the bill was placed on bipartisan "captains." Senators Clark and Case were selected as the bipartisan captains responsible for Title VII. Vaas, Title VII: Legislative History, 7 B.C.Indus. & Com.L.Rev. 431, 444–445 (1966) (hereinafter Title VII: Legislative History).

17. Earlier in the debate, Senator Humphrey had introduced a newspaper article quoting the answers of a Justice Department "expert" to the "ten most common objections to Title VII." Insofar as is pertinent here, the article stated:

"Objection: The law would empower Federal 'inspectors' to require employers to hire by race. White people would be fired to make room for Negroes. Seniority rights would be destroyed * * *.

"Reply: The bill requires no such thing. The five-member Equal Employment Opportunity Commission that would be created would have no powers to order anything * * *.

" * * * The bill would not authorize anyone to order hiring or firing to achieve racial or religious balance. An employer will remain wholly free to hire on the basis of his needs and of the job candidate's qualifications. What is prohibited is the refusal to hire someone because of his race or religion. Similarly, the law will have no effect on union seniority rights." 110 Cong.Rec. 5094 (1964).

In the opening speech of the formal Senate debate on the bill, Senator Humphrey addressed the main concern of Title VII's opponents, advising that not only does Title VII not require use of racial quotas, *it does not permit* their use. "The truth," stated the floor leader of the bill, "is that this title forbids discriminating against anyone on account of race. This is the simple and complete truth about title VII." 110 Cong.Rec. 6549 (1964). Senator Humphrey continued:

"Contrary to the allegations of some opponents of this title, there is nothing in it that will give any power to the Commission or to any courts to require hiring, firing, or promotion of employees in order to meet a racial 'quota' or to achieve a certain racial balance.

"That bugaboo has been brought up a dozen times; but it is nonexistent. In fact, *the very opposite is true. Title VII prohibits discrimination.* In effect, it says that race, religion, and national origin are not to be used as the basis for hiring and firing. Title VII is designed to encourage hiring on the basis of ability and qualifications, not race or religion." Ibid. (emphasis added).

At the close of his speech, Senator Humphrey returned briefly to the subject of employment quotas: "It is claimed that the bill would require racial quotas for all hiring, when in fact it provides that race shall not be a basis for making personnel decisions." Id., at 6553.

Senator Kuchel delivered the second major speech in support of H.R. 7152. In addressing the concerns of the opposition, he observed that "[n]othing could be further from the truth" than the charge that "Federal inspectors" would be empowered under Title VII to dictate racial balance and preferential advancement of minorities. Id., at 6563. Senator Kuchel emphasized that seniority rights would in no way be affected by Title VII: "Employers and labor organizations could not discriminate *in favor of or against* a person because of his race, his religion, or his national origin. In such matters * * * the bill now before us * * * is color-blind." Id., at 6564 (emphasis added).

A few days later the Senate's attention focused exclusively on Title VII, as Senators Clark and Case rose to discuss the title of H.R. 7152 on which they shared floor "captain" responsibilities. In an interpretative memorandum submitted jointly to the Senate, Senators Clark and Case took pains to refute the opposition's charge that Title VII would result in preferential treatment of minorities. Their words were clear and unequivocal:

"There is no requirement in title VII that an employer maintain a racial balance in his work force. On the contrary, any deliberate attempt to maintain a racial balance, whatever such a balance may be, would involve a violation of title VII because maintaining such a balance would require an employer to hire or to refuse to hire on the basis of race. It must be emphasized that discrimination is prohibited as to any individual." Id., at 7213.

Of particular relevance to the instant case were their observations regarding seniority rights. As if directing their comments at Brian Weber, the Senators said:

"Title VII would have no effect on established seniority rights. Its effect is prospective and not retrospective. Thus, for example, if a business has been discriminating in the past and as a result has an all-white working force, when the title comes into effect the employer's obligation would be simply to fill future vacancies on a nondiscriminatory basis. He would not be obliged—*or indeed permitted*—to fire whites in order to hire Negroes, *or to prefer Negroes for future vacancies, or, once Negroes are hired, to give them special seniority rights at the expense of the white workers hired earlier."* Ibid. (emphasis added).

Thus with virtual clairvoyance the Senate's leading supporters of Title VII anticipated precisely the circumstances of this case and advised their colleagues that the type of minority preference employed by Kaiser would violate Title VII's ban on racial discrimination. To further accentuate the point, Senator Clark introduced another memorandum dealing with common criticisms of the bill, including the charge that racial quotas would be imposed under Title VII. The answer was simple and to the point: "Quotas are themselves discriminatory." Id., at 7218.

Despite these clear statements from the bill's leading and most knowledgeable proponents, the fears of the opponents were not put to rest. Senator Robertson reiterated the view that "discrimination" could be interpreted by a federal "bureaucrat" to require hiring quotas. Id., at 7418–7420. Senators Smathers and Sparkman, while conceding that Title VII does not in so many words require the use of hiring quotas, repeated the opposition's view that employers would be coerced to grant preferential hiring treatment to minorities by agencies of the Federal Government. Senator Williams was quick to respond:

> "Those opposed to H.R. 7152 should realize that to hire a Negro solely because he is a Negro is racial discrimination, just as much as a 'white only' employment policy. Both forms of discrimination are prohibited by title VII of this bill. The language of that title simply states that race is not a qualification for employment. * * * Some people charge that H.R. 7152 favors the Negro, at the expense of the white majority. But how can the language of equality favor one race or one religion over another? Equality can have only one meaning, and that meaning is self-evident to reasonable men. Those who say that equality means favoritism do violence to common sense." Id., at 8921.

Senator Williams concluded his remarks by noting that Title VII's only purpose is "the elimination of racial and religious discrimination in employment." Ibid. On May 25, Senator Humphrey again took the floor to defend the bill against "the well-financed drive by certain opponents to confuse and mislead the American people." Id., at 11846. Turning once again to the issue of preferential treatment, Senator Humphrey remained faithful to the view that he had repeatedly expressed:

> "The title does not provide that any preferential treatment in employment shall be given to Negroes or to any other persons or groups. It does not provide that any quota systems may be established to maintain racial balance in employment. In fact, *the title would prohibit preferential treatment for any particular group,* and any person, whether or not a member of any minority group would be permitted to file a complaint of discriminatory employment practices." Id., at 11848 (emphasis added).

While the debate in the Senate raged, a bipartisan coalition under the leadership of Senators Dirksen, Mansfield, Humphrey, and Kuchel was working with House leaders and representatives of the Johnson Administration on a number of amendments to H.R. 7152 designed to enhance its prospects of passage. The so-called "Dirksen-Mansfield" amendment was introduced on May 26 by Senator Dirksen as a substitute for the entire House-passed bill. The substitute bill, which ultimately became law, left unchanged the basic prohibitory language of §§ 703(a) and (d), as well as the remedial provisions in § 706(g). It added, however, several provisions defining and clarifying the scope of Title VII's substantive prohibitions. One of those clarifying amendments, § 703(j), was specifically directed at the opposition's concerns regarding racial balancing and preferential treatment of minorities, providing in pertinent part: "Nothing contained in [Title VII] shall be interpreted to require any employer * * * to grant preferential treatment to any individual or to any group because of the race * * * of such individual or group on account of" a racial imbalance in the employer's work force. * * *

The Court draws from the language of § 703(j) primary support for its conclusion that Title VII's blanket prohibition on racial discrimination in employment does not prohibit preferential treatment of blacks to correct racial imbalance. Alleging that opponents of Title VII had argued (1) that the act would be interpreted to require employers with racially imbalanced work forces to grant preferential treatment to minorities and (2) that "employers with racially imbalanced work forces would grant preferential treatment to racial minorities even if not required to do so by the Act," ante, * * * the Court concludes that § 703(j) is responsive only to the opponents' first objection and that Congress therefore must have intended to permit voluntary, private discrimination against whites in order to correct racial imbalance.

Contrary to the Court's analysis, the language of § 703(j) is precisely tailored to the objection voiced time and again by Title VII's opponents. Not once during the 83 days of debate in the Senate did a speaker, proponent or opponent, suggest that the bill would allow employers *voluntarily* to prefer racial minorities over white persons.[23] In light of Title VII's flat prohibition

23. The Court cites the remarks of Senator Sparkman in support of its suggestion that opponents had argued that employers would take it upon themselves to balance their work forces by granting preferential treatment to racial minorities. In fact, Senator Sparkman's comments accurately reflected the opposition's "party line." He argued that while the language of Title VII does not expressly require imposition of racial quotas (no one, of course, had ever argued to the contrary), the law would be applied by federal agencies in such a way that "some kind of quota system will be used." 110 Cong.Rec. 8619 (1964). Senator Sparkman's view is reflected in the following exchange with Senator Stennis:

"Mr. SPARKMAN. At any rate, when the Government agent came to interview an employer who had 100 persons in his employ, the first question would be, 'How many Negroes are you employing?' Suppose the population of that area was 20

percent Negro. Immediately the agent would say, 'You should have at least 20 Negroes in your employ, and they should be distributed among your supervisory personnel and in all the other categories'; and the agent would *insist* that that be done immediately.

"Mr. STENNIS. * * *

"The Senator from Alabama has made very clear his point about employment on the quota basis. Would not the same basis be applied to promotions?

"Mr. SPARKMAN. Certainly it would. As I have said, when the Federal agents came to check on the situation in a small business which had 100 employees, and when the agents said to the employer, 'You must hire 20 Negroes, and some of them must be employed in supervisory capacities,' and so forth, and so on, the agent would also say, 'And you must promote the Negroes,

on discrimination "against any individual * * * because of such individual's race," § 703(a), * * * such a contention would have been, in any event, too preposterous to warrant response. Indeed, speakers on both sides of the issue, as the legislative history makes clear, recognized that Title VII would tolerate no *voluntary* racial preference, whether in favor of blacks or whites. The complaint consistently voiced by the opponents was that Title VII, particularly the word "discrimination," would be *interpreted* by federal agencies such as the Equal Employment Opportunity Commission to *require* the correction of racial imbalance through the granting of preferential treatment to minorities. Verbal assurances that Title VII would not require—indeed, would not permit—preferential treatment of blacks having failed, supporters of H.R. 7152 responded by proposing an amendment carefully worded to meet, and put to rest, the opposition's charge. Indeed, unlike §§ 703(a) and (d), which are by their terms directed at entities—e.g., employers, labor unions—whose actions are restricted by Title VII's prohibitions, the language of § 703(j) is specifically directed at entities—federal agencies and courts—charged with the responsibility of interpreting Title VII's provisions.

In light of the background and purpose of § 703(j), the irony of invoking the section to justify the result in this case is obvious. The Court's frequent references to the "voluntary" nature of Kaiser's racially discriminatory admission quota bear no relationship to the facts of this case. Kaiser and the Steelworkers acted under pressure from an agency of the Federal Government, the Office of Federal Contract Compliance, which found that minorities were being "underutilized" at Kaiser's plants. See n. 2, supra. That is, Kaiser's work force was racially imbalanced. Bowing to that pressure, Kaiser instituted an admissions quota preferring blacks over whites, thus confirming that the fears of Title VII's opponents were well founded. Today § 703(j), adopted to allay those fears, is invoked by the Court to uphold imposition of a racial quota under the very circumstances that the section was intended to prevent.[25]

too, in order to distribute them evenly among the various ranks of your employees.'" Id., at 8618 (emphasis added).

Later in his remarks, Senator Sparkman stated: "Certainly the suggestion will be made to a small business that may have a small government contract * * * that if it does not carry out the suggestion that has been made to the company by an inspector, its Government contract will not be renewed." Ibid. Except for the size of the business, Senator Sparkman has seen his prophecy fulfilled in this case.

25. In support of its reading of § 703(j), the Court argues that "a prohibition against all voluntary, race-conscious, affirmative action efforts would disserve" the important policy, expressed in the House Report on H.R. 7152, that Title VII leave "management prerogatives and union freedoms * * * undisturbed to the greatest extent possible." H.R.Rep., Part II, at 29, quoted ante * * * The Court thus concludes that "Congress did not intend to limit traditional business freedom to such a

degree as to prohibit all voluntary, race-conscious affirmative action." * * *

The sentences in the House Report immediately following the statement quoted by the Court, however, belie the Court's conclusion: "Internal affairs of employers and labor organizations must not be interfered with *except to the limited extent that correction is required in discrimination practices.* Its primary task is to make certain that the channels of employment are open to persons *regardless of their race* and that jobs in companies or membership in unions are strictly filled on the basis of qualification." H.R.Rep., Part II, at 29 (emphasis added).

Thus, the House Report invoked by the Court is perfectly consistent with the countless observations elsewhere in Title VII's voluminous legislative history that employers are free to make employment decisions without governmental interference, so long as those decisions are made *without regard to race.* The whole purpose of Title VII was to deprive employers of their "traditional business free-

Section 703(j) apparently calmed the fears of most of the opponents; after its introduction complaints concerning racial balance and preferential treatment died down considerably. Proponents of the bill, however, continued to reassure the opposition that its concerns were unfounded. In a lengthy defense of the entire civil rights bill, Senator Muskie emphasized that the opposition's "torrent of words * * * cannot obscure this basic, simple truth: Every American citizen has the right to equal treatment—not favored treatment, not complete individual equality—just equal treatment." 110 Cong.Rec. 12614 (1964). With particular reference to Title VII, Senator Muskie noted that the measure "seeks to afford to all Americans equal opportunity in employment without discrimination. Not equal pay, not 'racial balance.' Only equal opportunity." Id., at 12617.

* * *

On June 9, Senator Ervin offered an amendment that would entirely delete Title VII from the bill. In answer to Senator Ervin's contention that Title VII "would make the members of a particular race special favorites of the laws," id., at 13079, Senator Clark retorted:

> "The bill does not make anyone higher than anyone else. It establishes no quotas. It leaves an employer free to select whomever he wishes to employ. * * *" Id., at 13080.

The Ervin amendment was defeated * * *.

3

On June 10 the Senate, for the second time in its history, imposed cloture on its members. The limited debate that followed centered on proposed amendments to the Dirksen-Mansfield substitute. Of some 24 proposed amendments, only 5 were adopted.

As the civil rights bill approached its final vote, several supporters rose to urge its passage. Senator Muskie adverted briefly to the issue of preferential treatment: "It has been said that the bill discriminates in favor of the Negro at the expense of the rest of us. It seeks to do nothing more than to lift the Negro from the status of inequality to one of *equality* of treatment." 110 Cong.Rec. 14328 (1964) (emphasis added). Senator Moss in a speech delivered on the day that the civil rights bill was finally passed, had this to say about quotas:

> "The bill does not accord to any citizen advantage or preference—it does not fix quotas of employment or school population—it does not force personal association. What it does is to prohibit public officials and those who invite the public generally to patronize their businesses or to apply for employment, to utilize the offensive, humiliating, and cruel practice of discrimination on the basis of race. In short, the bill does not accord special consideration; it establishes *equality*." Id., at 14484 (emphasis added).

Later that day, June 19, the issue was put to a vote, and the Dirksen-Mansfield substitute bill was passed.

dom" to discriminate on the basis of race. In this case, the "channels of employment" at Kaiser were hardly "open" to Brian Weber.

C

The Act's return engagement in the House was brief. The House Committee on Rules reported the Senate version without amendments on June 30, 1964. By a vote of 289 to 126, the House adopted House Resolution 789, thus agreeing to the Senate's amendments of H.R. 7152. Later that same day, July 2, the President signed the bill and the Civil Rights Act of 1964 became law.

IV

Reading the language of Title VII, as the Court purports to do, "against the background of [its] legislative history * * * and the historical context from which the Act arose," * * * one is led inescapably to the conclusion that Congress fully understood what it was saying and meant precisely what it said. Opponents of the civil rights bill did not argue that employers would be permitted under Title VII voluntarily to grant preferential treatment to minorities to correct racial imbalance. The plain language of the statute too clearly prohibited such racial discrimination to admit of any doubt. They argued, tirelessly, that Title VII would be interpreted by federal agencies and their agents to require unwilling employers to racially balance their work forces by granting preferential treatment to minorities. Supporters of H.R. 7152 responded, equally tirelessly, that the Act would not be so interpreted because not only does it not require preferential treatment of minorities, it does not *permit* preferential treatment of any race for any reason. It cannot be doubted that the proponents of Title VII understood the meaning of their words, for "[s]eldom has similar legislation been debated with greater consciousness for the need for 'legislative history' or with greater care in the making thereof, to guide the courts in interpreting and applying the law." Title VII: Legislative History, at 444.

To put an end to the dispute, supporters of the civil rights bill drafted and introduced § 703(j). Specifically addressed to the opposition's charge, § 703(j) simply enjoins federal agencies and courts from interpreting Title VII to require an employer to prefer certain racial groups to correct imbalances in his work force. The section says nothing about voluntary preferential treatment of minorities because such racial discrimination is plainly proscribed by §§ 703(a) and (d). Indeed, had Congress intended to except voluntary, race-conscious preferential treatment from the blanket prohibition on racial discrimination in §§ 703(a) and (d), it surely could have drafted language better suited to the task than § 703(j). It knew how. Section 703(i) provides:

> "Nothing contained in [title VII] shall apply to any business or enterprise on or near an Indian reservation with respect to any publicly announced employment practice of such business or enterprise under which a preferential treatment is given to any individual because he is an Indian living on or near a reservation." * * *

V

Our task in this case, like any other case involving the construction of a statute, is to give effect to the intent of Congress. To divine that intent, we traditionally look first to the words of the statute and, if they are unclear, then to the statute's legislative history. Finding the desired result hopelessly foreclosed by these conventional sources, the Court turns to a third source—the "spirit" of the Act. But close examination of what the Court proffers as the spirit of the Act reveals it as the spirit animating the present majority, not the Eighty-eighth Congress. For if the spirit of the Act eludes the cold words of the statute itself, it rings out with unmistakable clarity in the words of the elected representatives who made the Act law. It is *equality*. Senator Dirksen, I think, captured that spirit in a speech delivered on the floor of the Senate just moments before the bill was passed:

"[T]oday we come to grips finally with a bill that advances the enjoyment of living; but, more than that, it advances the equality of opportunity.

"I do not emphasize the word 'equality' standing by itself. It means equality of opportunity in the field of education. It means equality of opportunity in the field of employment. It means equality of opportunity in the field of participation in the affairs of government * * *.

"That is it.

"Equality of opportunity, if we are going to talk about conscience, is the mass conscience of mankind that speaks in every generation, and it will continue to speak long after we are dead and gone." 110 Cong.Rec. 14510 (1964).

There is perhaps no device more destructive to the notion of equality than the *numerus clausus* —the quota. Whether described as "benign discrimination" or "affirmative action," the racial quota is nonetheless a creator of castes, a two-edged sword that must demean one in order to prefer another. In passing Title VII Congress outlawed *all* racial discrimination, recognizing that no discrimination based on race is benign, that no action disadvantaging a person because of his color is affirmative. With today's holding, the Court introduces into Title VII a tolerance for the very evil that the law was intended to eradicate, without offering even a clue as to what the limits on that tolerance may be. We are told simply that Kaiser's racially discriminatory admission quota "falls on the permissible side of the line." * * * By going not merely *beyond,* but directly *against* Title VII's language and legislative history, the Court has sown the wind. Later courts will face the impossible task of reaping the whirlwind.

[The concurring opinion of JUSTICE BLACKMUN and the dissenting opinion of THE CHIEF JUSTICE are omitted.]

Note

1. The duty of fair representation was not expressly dealt with in Weber, but is it not a proper concern for a union negotiating a voluntary affirmative action program with an employer? Conversely, would a refusal by a union to seek such a program run afoul of that duty? By what standards should the union's performance in these regards be measured?

2. The pendulum swung wide in Weber for affirmative action, but it swung back in FIREFIGHTERS LOCAL UNION NO. 1784 v. STOTTS, 467 U.S. 561, 104 S.Ct. 2576, 81 L.Ed.2d 483 (1984). There the Court reversed a Fifth Circuit affirmance of a district court's order enjoining the City of Memphis from following its seniority system in determining which firefighters should be laid off as a result of a budgetary shortfall. The injunction was issued in support of an affirmative action program which was the product of a consent decree climaxing

a previous class action suit by black firefighters against the City, complaining of a "pattern or practice of making hiring and promotion decisions on the basis of race in violation of Title VII." In accordance with the consent decree, the City agreed to promote 13 named individuals and also prescribed "the long-term goal of increasing the proportion of minority representation in each job classification in the Fire Department to approximately the proportion of blacks in the [local] labor force." The City did not, however, "by agreeing to the decree admit 'any violations of law, rule or regulation with respect to the allegations' in the complaint." A year after the consent decree was approved and entered, and as a result of a budget deficit, the City announced a reduction of nonessential personnel throughout the City government, the layoffs to be based on the "last hired, first fired" rule incorporated in a "memorandum of understanding between the City and the Union." In response to this action, the district court issued an injunction which supported the affirmative action program contained in the consent decree and precluded the honoring of the seniority provision. As a consequence, some non-minority employees with more seniority than minority employees were laid off or demoted in rank. The City and the Firefighters Union (the Union had not previously been a party to the court proceedings, but had been permitted to intervene with regard to the application for injunctive relief) filed separate petitions for certiorari, both of which were granted and the cases consolidated.

A plurality of the Court (Justice White wrote for himself and three others; Justices O'Connor and Stevens wrote concurring opinions; Justice Blackmun, joined by Justices Brennan and Marshall, dissented) stated:

> "The issue at the heart of this case is whether the District Court exceeded its powers in entering an injunction requiring white employees to be laid off, when the otherwise applicable seniority system would have called for the layoff of black employees with less seniority. We are convinced that the Court of Appeals erred in resolving this issue and in affirming the District Court.
>
> "   *   *   *
>
> "   *   *   * The District Court held that the City could not follow its seniority system in making its proposed layoffs because its proposal was discriminatory in effect and hence not a bona fide plan. Section 703(h), however, permits the routine application of a seniority system absent proof of an intention to discriminate. Teamsters v. United States, 431 U.S. 324, 352, 97 S.Ct. 1843, 1963, 52 L.Ed.2d 396 (1977). Here, the District Court itself found that the layoff proposal was not adopted with the purpose or intent to discriminate on the basis of race. Nor had the City in agreeing to the decree admitted in any way that it had engaged in intentional discrimination. The Court of Appeals was therefore correct in disagreeing with the District Court's holding that the layoff plan was not a bona fide application of the seniority system, and it would appear that the City could not be faulted for following the seniority plan expressed in its agreement with the Union. The Court of Appeals nevertheless held that the injunction was proper even though it conflicted with the seniority system. This was error.
>
> "   *   *   *
>
> "   *   *   * The court concluded that *   *   * the District Court *   *   * 'had the authority to override the Firefighter's Union security provisions to effectuate the purpose of the 1980 [Consent] Decree.' 679 F.2d at 566.

"The difficulty with this approach is that it overstates the authority of the trial court to disregard a seniority system in fashioning a remedy after a plaintiff has successfully proved that an employer has followed a pattern or practice having a discriminatory effect on black applicants or employees. If individual members of a plaintiff class demonstrate that they have been actual victims of the discriminatory practice, they may be awarded competitive seniority and given their rightful place on the seniority roster. This much is clear from Franks v. Bowman Tranportation Co., 424 U.S. 747, 96 S.Ct. 1251, 47 L.Ed.2d 444 (1976), and Teamsters v. United States, 431 U.S. 324, 97 S.Ct. 1843, 52 L.Ed.2d 396 (1977). *Teamsters*, however, also made clear that mere membership in the disadvantaged class is insufficient to warrant a seniority award; each individual must prove that the discriminatory practice had an impact on him. 431 U.S., at 367–371, 97 S.Ct., at 1860–1872. Even when an individual shows that the discriminatory practice has had an impact on him, he is not automatically entitled to have a non-minority employee laid off to make room for him. He may have to wait until a vacancy occurs,[11] and if there are non-minority employees on layoff, the Court must balance the equities in determining who is entitled to the job. *Teamsters*, supra, 431 U.S., at 371–376, 97 S.Ct., at 1872–1875. See also Ford Motor Co. v. EEOC, 458 U.S. 219, 236–240, 103 S.Ct. 3057, 3068–3070, 73 L.Ed.2d 721 (1982). Here, there was no finding that any of the blacks protected from layoff had been a victim of discrimination and no award of competitive seniority to any of them. Nor had the parties in formulating the consent decree purported to identify any specific employee entitled to particular relief other than those listed in the exhibits attached to the decree. It therefore seems to us that, in light of *Teamsters*, the Court of Appeals imposed on the parties as an adjunct of settlement something that could not have been ordered had the case gone to trial and the plaintiffs proved that a pattern or practice of discrimination existed.

"Our ruling in *Teamsters* that a court can award competitive seniority only when the beneficiary of the award has actually been a victim of illegal discrimination is consistent with the policy behind § 706(g) of Title VII, which affects the remedies available in Title VII litigation. That policy, which is to provide make-whole relief only to those who have been actual victims of illegal discrimination, was repeatedly expressed by the sponsors of the Act during the congressional debates. * * *" 467 U.S. at 572–80, 104 S.Ct. at 2585–89, 81 L.Ed.2d at 495–500.

The dissent's position on the pivotal Section 706(g) issue is distilled in the following:

"In determining the nature of 'appropriate' relief under § 706(g), courts have distinguished between individual relief and race-conscious class relief. Although overlooked by the Court, this distinction is highly relevant here. In a Title VII class-action suit of the type brought by respondents, an individual plaintiff is entitled to an award of individual relief only if he can establish that he was the victim of discrimination. That requirement grows out of the general equitable principles of 'make whole' relief; an individual who has suffered no injury is not entitled to an individual award. See

---

11. Lower courts have uniformly held that relief for actual victims does not extend to bumping employees previously occupying jobs. See e.g., Patterson v. American Tobacco Co., 535, F.2d 257, 267 (CA4), cert. denied, 429 U.S. 920, 97 S.Ct. 314, 50 L.Ed.2d 286 (1976); Local 189, United States Papermakers and Paperworkers v. United States, 416 F.2d 980, 988 (CA5 1969), cert. denied, 397 U.S. 919, 90 S.Ct. 926, 25 L.Ed.2d 100 (1970).

Teamsters v. United States, 431 U.S. 324, 347–348, 364–371, 97 S.Ct. 1843, 1860–1861, 1869–1872, 52 L.Ed.2d 396 (1977). If victimization is shown, however, an individual is entitled to whatever retroactive seniority, backpay, and promotions are consistent with the statute's goal of making the victim whole. Franks v. Bowman Transportation Co., 424 U.S. 747, 762, 770, 96 S.Ct. 1251, 1263–1266, 47 L.Ed.2d 444 (1976).

"In Title VII class-action suits, the Courts of Appeals are unanimously of the view that race-conscious affirmative relief can also be 'appropriate' under § 706(g).[10] * * * The purpose of such relief is not to make whole any particular individual, but rather to remedy the present class-wide effects of past discrimination or to prevent similar discrimination in the future. Because the discrimination sought to be alleviated by race-conscious relief is the classwide effects of past discrimination, rather than discrimination against identified members of the class, such relief is provided to the class as a whole rather than to its individual members. The relief may take many forms, but in class actions it frequently involves percentages—such as those contained in the 1980 consent decree between the city and respondents—that require race to be taken into account when an employer hires or promotes employees. The distinguishing feature of race-conscious relief is that no individual member of the disadvantaged class has a claim to it, and individual beneficiaries of the relief need not show that they were themselves victims of the discrimination for which the relief was granted.

"In the instant case * * * the District Court order required the city to conduct its layoffs in a race-conscious manner; specifically, the injunction prohibited the city from conducting layoffs that would 'decrease the percentage of black[s]' in certain job categories. The city remained free to lay off any individual black so long as the percentage of black representation was maintained.

"Because these cases arise out of a consent decree, and a trial on the merits has never taken place, it is of course impossible for the Court to know the extent and nature of any past discrimination by the city. * * *" 104 U.S. at 612–614, 104 S.Ct. at 2605–06, 81 L.Ed.2d at 520–21.

The watershed potential of Stotts is demonstrated by the Supreme Court's having granted certiorari in three courts of appeals' cases which present the question of the validity of affirmative action hiring, promotion, and layoff programs in the context of collective bargaining agreements containing seniority provisions. Wygant v. Jackson Board of Education, 746 F.2d 1152 (6th Cir. 1984), cert. granted ___ U.S. ___, 105 S.Ct. 2015, 85 L.Ed.2d 298 (1985); Vanguards of Cleveland v. Cleveland, 753 F.2d 479 (6th Cir. 1985), cert. granted sub nom. Local No. 93, International Association of Firefighters v. Cleveland, ___

---

10. See e.g., Boston Chapter, NAACP, Inc. v. Beecher, 504 F.2d 1017, 1027–1028 (CA1 1974), cert. denied, 421 U.S. 910, 95 S.Ct. 1561, 43 L.Ed.2d 775 (1975); Rios v. Enterprise Ass'n Steamfitters Local 638, 501 F.2d 622, 629 (CA2 1974); E.E.O.C. v. American Tel. & Tel. Co., 556 F.2d 167, 174–177 (CA3 1977), cert. denied, 438 U.S. 915, 98 S.Ct. 3145, 57 L.Ed.2d 1161 (1978); Chisholm v. United States Postal Service, 665 F.2d 482, 499 (CA4 1981); United States v. City of Alexandria, 614 F.2d 1358, 1363–1366 (CA5 1980); United States v. I.B.E.W. Local No. 38, 428 F.2d 144 (CA6), cert. denied, 400 U.S. 943, 91 S.Ct. 245, 27 L.Ed.2d 248 (1970); United States v. City of Chicago, 663 F.2d 1354 (CA7 1981) (en banc); Firefighters Institute v. City of St. Louis, 616 F.2d 350, 364 (CA8 1980), cert. denied, 452 U.S. 938, 101 S.Ct. 3079, 69 L.Ed.2d 951 (1981); United States v. Ironworkers Local 86, 443 F.2d 544, 553–554 (CA9), cert. denied, 404 U.S. 984, 92 S.Ct. 447, 30 L.Ed.2d 367 (1971); United States v. Lee Way Motor Freight, Inc., 625 F.2d 918, 944 (CA10 1979); Thompson v. Sawyer, 219 U.S.App.D.C. 393, 430, 678 F.2d 257, 294 (1982).

U.S. __, 106 S.Ct. 59, 88 L.Ed.2d 48 (1985); EEOC v. Local 638, 753 F.2d 1172 (2d Cir. 1985), cert. granted sub nom. Local 28, Sheet Metal Workers' International Association v. EEOC, __ U.S. __, 106 S.Ct. 58, 88 L.Ed.2d 47 (1985). In the first, the issue of a racial preference arises out of an *express* provision in a collective bargaining agreement prescribing priority for minority personnel in the event of layoffs "during economically required reduction in staff"; in the second, the issue arises out of a consent decree requiring affirmative action in promotion of employees; in the third, the "race conscious" "quota" remedy approved by the court of appeals was the product of a court order.

What future-ordaining answers to these questions does *your* "crystal ball" foretell? [P.S.: The Supreme Court's decisions in these three cases were announced while this book was in the process of publication. The following characterization of them is accordingly interstitial and abbreviated.

In Wygant v. Jackson Board of Education, __ U.S. __, 106 S.Ct. 1842, 90 L.Ed.2d 260 (1986), a badly split Court held that a school board violated the Equal Protection Clause (no Title VII claim was raised before the Court) when it considered race in laying off non-minority teachers with more seniority than some minority teachers it had retained, even though the school board acted under the terms of a collective bargaining agreement. Justice Powell, joined by Chief Justice Burger and Justice Rehnquist, delivered the opinion of the Court. Justice O'Connor and Justice White wrote separate concurring opinions. Justice Marshall, joined by Justices Brennan and Blackmun, and Justice Stevens wrote dissenting opinions. Justice Powell and Justice O'Connor agreed that the school board's goal of alleviating the effects of societal discrimination by providing minority role models for minority students could not justify the discriminatory layoffs. Justice Powell noted that there had never been a judicial finding that the school board engaged in racial discrimination and that requiring non-minority teachers with greater seniority to lose their jobs was too intrusive a burden on them. Justice White held simply to the position that laying off white employees who would otherwise be retained in order to keep black employees on the job violated the Equal Protection Clause.

Justice Marshall dissented on the ground that the layoff policy was embodied in a collective bargaining agreement and was necessary to achieve the remedial purpose of an integrated workforce. Justice Stevens in his dissent asserted that the goal of the affirmative action plan to maintain a racially balanced faculty was a sound educational purpose, which outweighed any harm to the laid-off white teachers.

In Local No. 93, International Association of Firefighters v. Cleveland, __ U.S. __, 106 S.Ct. 3063, __ L.Ed.2d __ (1986), the Supreme Court, by a 6–3 vote, upheld a federal district court's entry of a consent decree between the city and minority firefighters, over the objection of the union which represented all city firefighters, that provided for an affirmative action program in promoting firefighters. The majority opinion, written by Justice Brennan, held that, Section 706(g) which states that "[n]o order of the court shall require the * * * promotion of an individual * * * if such individual * * * was refused * * * advancement * * * for any reason other than discrimination on account of race * * *," was inapplicable to a consent decree even though the decree might benefit individuals who were not the actual victims of the city's prior discriminatory promotion practices. The intent of Title VII, as the Court had held in Steelworkers v. Weber, and of Section 706(g) in particular, was both to foster voluntary compliance with the statutory purpose of eradicating discrimination and to avoid undue governmental interference with private agreements of parties to accomplish such end. Since the consent decree was such a voluntary agreement, it did not conflict with Section 706(g), and the district court was not barred from entering the consent decree merely because the decree provided broader relief than a court could have awarded after a trial. The majority distinguished Firefighters v. Stotts on the ground that the entering of the injunctive order by the district court to modify the consent decree involved there would have conflicted with the provisions of Title VII.

Justice White dissented on the ground that the Weber case was inapplicable since there had been no determination that the city had engaged in past discrimination in regard to promotions, which finding he considered the "necessary predicate" to any racial preference in either a voluntary agreement or a judicial order. Justice Rehnquist, in an opinion joined by Chief Justice Burger, dissented on the basis that the language and legislative history of Section 706(g), as decided in Firefighters v. Stotts, precluded any order allowing a preference to individuals who had not been the actual victims of discriminatory practices. According to Justice Rehnquist, the entering of a consent decree by a district court was as much an "order of the court" under Section 706(g) as was the modification of the consent decree in Stotts.

Finally, in Local 28, Sheet Metal Workers v. Equal Employment Opportunity Commission, ___ U.S. ___, 106 S.Ct. 3019, ___ L.Ed.2d ___ (1986), the Court, again in a split decision, held that a district court under Section 706(g) and the equal protection guarantees embodied in the Fifth Amendment could order an affirmative action remedy to nonvictims of discrimination in appropriate circumstances. A federal district court found that the defendant union had engaged in long-term and egregious discrimination against minorities in denial of membership and ordered a 29.23% nonwhite membership goal. Justice Brennan authored an opinion, in which three other members agreed, that the affirmative action remedy in this case was proper; Justice Powell concurred in part; Justices White, O'Connor, Rehnquist, and Chief Justice Burger dissented on this issue.

Justice Brennan's plurality opinion looked to the broad language of Section 706(g) granting to district courts the authority to award "appropriate" equitable relief. He noted that the legislative history regarding Section 706(g) did not indicate that Congress intended to limit affirmative relief only to the identified victims of past discrimination. The fears that were expressed concerning quotas were directed only to the contention that Title VII should not require an employer or a union to adopt quotas or preferences simply because of racial imbalance in a workforce or membership. Congress addressed these qualms by the enactment of Section 703(j), which limited the requirement of preferences in determining liability; but Congress placed no similar limits on the remedial powers of a district court under Section 706(g). Justice Brennan distinguished Firefighters v. Stotts as a case where there had been no proof of discrimination against any individual in the operation of a seniority system in a layoff situation, and so no affirmative action relief could be awarded. In the present case there was a proven pattern of racial discrimination in denial of membership against the class of plaintiffs as a whole. In such an instance the court had the authority to order race-conscious affirmative action for beneficiaries who need not show that they were victims of discrimination, in order to dismantle the prior patterns of employment discrimination and to prevent discrimination in the future. The plurality also held that there was no constitutional bar to the court order of affirmative action relief since the remedy was narrowly tailored to further the government's interest in remedying past discrimination and would not disadvantage any existing union members.

Justice Powell, providing the fifth vote, concurred in the judgment in an opinion in which he noted that under the circumstances of the case, where the union had engaged in particularly egregious conduct, the affirmative action remedy to persons other than actual victims of discrimination violated neither Title VII nor the Constitution.

Justice White, in his dissent, noted that, although Title VII does not bar relief for nonvictims in all circumstances, the affirmative action remedy in this case was an impermissible strict racial quota. Justice O'Connor also opposed the implementation of the remedy as an improper quota and accused the plurality opinion of overturning the decision of the Court in Stotts to the effect that Sections 703(j) and 706(g) did not permit such a remedy to nonvictims. Similarly, Justice Rehnquist, in an opinion joined by Chief Justice Burger, determined that Section 706(g), as interpreted in Stotts, would not allow a court to order racial preferences except to minority individuals who have been the actual victims of discrimination.

While the number of opinions and the complexity of the issues make it extremely difficult to say with clarity where the "law" is, after the foregoing decisions, is the following characterization accurate? In a layoff situation, as in Stotts and Wygant, the displacement of nonminority with minority employees with less seniority is too intrusive a burden on the (innocent) nonminority employees; in the hiring or admission to membership situation, as in Local 28, Sheet Metal Workers, the racial preference does not deprive nonminorities of existing employment or membership rights; the promotion situation, as encountered in Local No. 93, International Association of Firefighters, lies somewhere in between?]

B. COLLECTIVE BARGAINING AND THE ANTITRUST LAWS

INTRODUCTORY NOTE

The reader has already had substantial exposure to the application of the antitrust laws to labor relations. The story of the beginning of such application, its burgeoning, and ultimate near-demise has been told in Loewe v. Lawlor, supra p. 55, Duplex Printing Press Co. v. Deering, supra p. 62, Coronado Coal Co. v. United Mine Workers, supra p. 75, U.S. v. Hutcheson, supra p. 92, Apex Hosiery Co. v. Leader, supra p. 97, and Allen Bradley v. Local 3, IBEW, supra p. 156. The last of these cases, Allen Bradley, provided, as relatively recent litigation demonstrates, the line of analysis for a second cycle of labor-antitrust cases. An understanding of this seminal case, reported below, will be expedited by a rereading of the brief textual statement of its facts, holding, and reasoning, supra p. 156.

ALLEN BRADLEY v. LOCAL 3, IBEW

Supreme Court of the United States, 1945.
325 U.S. 797, 65 S.Ct. 1533, 89 L.Ed. 1939.

MR. JUSTICE BLACK delivered the opinion of the Court.

The question presented is whether it is a violation of the Sherman Anti-Trust Act for labor unions and their members, prompted by a desire to get and hold jobs for themselves at good wages and under high working standards, to combine with employers and with manufacturers of goods to restrain competition in, and to monopolize the marketing of, such goods.

Upon the complaint of petitioners and after a lengthy hearing the District Court held that such a combination did violate the Sherman Act, entered a declaratory judgment to that effect, and entered an injunction restraining respondents from engaging in a wide range of specified activities. 41 F.Supp. 727, 51 F.Supp. 36. The Circuit Court of Appeals reversed the decision and dismissed the cause, holding that combinations of unions and business men which restrained trade and tended to monopoly were not in violation of the Act where the bona fide purpose of the unions was to raise wages, provide better working conditions, and bring about better conditions of employment for their members. 2 Cir., 145 F.2d 215. The Ninth Circuit Court of Appeals having reached a contrary conclusion in a similar case, Lumber Products Ass'n v. United States, 144 F.2d 546, we granted certiorari in both cases. * * *

Petitioners are manufacturers of electrical equipment. Their places of manufacture are outside of New York City, and most of them are outside of New York State as well. They have brought this action because of their desire to sell their products in New York City, a market area that has been closed to them through the activities of respondents and others.

Respondents are a labor union, its officials and its members. The union, Local No. 3 of the International Brotherhood of Electrical Workers, has jurisdiction only over the metropolitan area of New York City. It is therefore impossible for the union to enter into a collective bargaining agreement with petitioners. Some of petitioners do have collective bargaining agreements with other unions, and in some cases even with other locals of the I.B.E.W.

Some of the members of respondent union work for manufacturers who produce electrical equipment similar to that made by petitioners; other members of respondent union are employed by contractors and work on the installation of electrical equipment, rather than in its production.

The union's consistent aim for many years has been to expand its membership, to obtain shorter hours and increased wages, and to enlarge employment opportunities for its members. To achieve this latter goal—that is, to make more work for its own members—the union realized that local manufacturers, employers of the local members, must have the widest possible outlets for their product. The union therefore waged aggressive campaigns to obtain closed shop agreements with all local electrical equipment manufacturers and contractors. Using conventional labor union methods, such as strikes and boycotts, it gradually obtained more and more closed shop agreements in the New York City area. Under these agreements, contractors were obligated to purchase equipment from none but local manufacturers who also had closed shop agreements with Local No. 3; manufacturers obligated themselves to confine their New York City sales to contractors employing the Local's members. In the course of time, this type of individual employer-employee agreement expanded into industry-wide understandings, looking not merely to terms and conditions of employment but also to price and market control. Agencies were set up composed of representatives of all three groups to boycott recalcitrant local contractors and manufacturers and to bar from the area equipment manufactured outside its boundaries. The combination among the three groups, union, contractors, and manufacturers, became highly successful from the standpoint of all of them. The business of New York City manufacturers had a phenomenal growth, thereby multiplying the jobs available for the Local's members. Wages went up, hours were shortened, and the New York electrical equipment prices soared, to the decided financial profit of local contractors and manufacturers. The success is illustrated by the fact that some New York manufacturers sold their goods in the protected city market at one price and sold identical goods outside of New York at a far lower price. All of this took place, as the Circuit Court of Appeals declared [145 F.2d 218], "through the stifling of competition", and because the three groups, in combination as "co-partners", achieved "a complete monopoly which they used to boycott the equipment manufactured by the plaintiffs." Interstate sale of various types of electrical equipment has, by this powerful combination, been wholly suppressed.

Quite obviously, this combination of business men has violated both Sections (1) and (2) of the Sherman Act,[2] unless its conduct is immunized by the participation of the union. For it intended to and did restrain trade in and monopolize the supply of electrical equipment in the New York City area to the exclusion of equipment manufactured in and shipped from other states, and did also control its price and discriminate between its would-be customers. Apex Hosiery Co. v. Leader, 310 U.S. 469, 512, 513, 60 S.Ct. 982, 1002, 1003, 84 L.Ed. 1311, 128 A.L.R. 1044. Our problem in this case is therefore a very narrow one—do labor unions violate the Sherman Act when, in order to further their own interests as wage earners, they aid and abet business men to do the precise things which that Act prohibits?

* * *

2. Sections 1 and 2 provide in part as follows:

"Sec. 1. Every contract, combination in the form of trust or otherwise, or conspiracy, in restraint of trade or commerce among the several States, or with foreign nations, is hereby declared to be illegal * * *.

"Sec. 2. Every person who shall monopolize, or attempt to monopolize, or combine or conspire with any other person or persons, to monopolize any part of the trade or commerce among the several States, or with foreign nations, shall be deemed guilty of a misdemeanor, * * *".

[The Court reviewed the history of antitrust and labor legislation and their interrelationship.]

The result of all this is that we have two declared congressional policies which it is our responsibility to try to reconcile. The one seeks to preserve a competitive business economy; the other to preserve the rights of labor to organize to better its conditions through the agency of collective bargaining. We must determine here how far Congress intended activities under one of these policies to neutralize the results envisioned by the other.

Aside from the fact that the labor union here acted in combination with the contractors and manufacturers, the means it adopted to contribute to the combination's purpose fall squarely within the "specified acts" declared by Section 20 [of the Clayton Act] not to be violations of federal law. For the union's contribution to the trade boycott was accomplished through threats that unless their employers bought their goods from local manufacturers the union laborers would terminate the "relation of employment" with them and cease to perform "work or labor" for them; and through their "recommending, advising, or persuading others by peaceful and lawful means" not to "patronize" sellers of the boycotted electrical equipment. Consequently, under our holdings in [United States v. Hutcheson, 312 U.S. 219, 61 S.Ct. 463, 85 L.Ed. 788 (1941), supra p. 92] and other cases which followed it, had there been no union-contractor-manufacturer combination the union's actions here, coming as they did within the exemptions of the Clayton and Norris-LaGuardia Acts, would not have been violations of the Sherman Act. We pass to the question of whether unions can with impunity aid and abet business men who are violating the Act.

*   *   * [W]e think Congress never intended that unions could, consistently with the Sherman Act, aid non-labor groups to create business monopolies and to control the marketing of goods and services.

Section 6 of the Clayton Act declares that the Sherman Act must not be so construed as to forbid the "existence and operation of labor, agricultural, or horticultural organizations, instituted for the purposes of mutual help *   *   *." But "the purposes of mutual help" can hardly be thought to cover activities for the purpose of "employer-help" in controlling markets and prices. And in an analogous situation where an agricultural association joined with other groups to control the agricultural market, we said:

"The right of these agricultural producers thus to unite in preparing for market and in marketing their products, and to make the contracts which are necessary for that collaboration, cannot be deemed to authorize any combination or conspiracy *with other persons* in restraint of trade that these producers may see fit to devise." United States v. Borden Co., 308 U.S. 188, 204, 205, 60 S.Ct. 182, 191, 84 L.Ed. 181. (Italics supplied.)

We have been pointed to no language in any act of Congress or in its reports or debates, nor have we found any, which indicates that it was ever suggested, considered, or legislatively determined that labor unions should be granted an immunity such as is sought in the present case. It has been argued that this immunity can be inferred from a union's right to make bargaining agreements with its employer. Since union members can without violating the Sherman Act strike to enforce a union boycott of goods, it is said they may settle the strike by getting their employers to agree to refuse to buy the goods. Employers and the union did here make bargaining agreements in which the employers agreed not to buy goods manufactured by companies which did not employ the members of Local No. 3. We may assume that such an agreement standing alone would not have violated the Sherman Act. But it did not stand alone. It was but one element in a far larger program in which contractors and manufacturers united with one another to monopolize all the business in New York City, to bar all other business men from that area, and to charge the public prices above a competitive level. It is true that victory of the union in its disputes, even had the union acted alone, might have added to the cost of goods, or might have resulted in individual refusals of all of their employers to buy electrical equipment not made by Local No. 3. So far as the union might have achieved this result acting alone, it would have been the natural consequence of labor union activities exempted by the Clayton Act from the coverage of the Sherman Act. Apex Hosiery Co. v. Leader, supra, 310 U.S. 503, 60 S.Ct. 997, 84 L.Ed. 1311, 128 A.L.R. 1044. But when the unions participated with a combination of business men who had complete power to eliminate all competition among themselves and to prevent all competition from others, a situation was created not included within the exemptions of the Clayton and Norris-LaGuardia Acts.

It must be remembered that the exemptions granted the unions were special exemptions to a general legislative plan. The primary objective of all the Anti-trust legislation has been to preserve business competition and to proscribe business monopoly. It would be a surprising thing if Congress, in order to prevent a misapplication of that legislation to labor unions, had bestowed upon such unions complete and unreviewable authority to aid business groups to frustrate its primary objective. For if business groups, by combining with labor unions, can fix prices and divide up markets, it was little more than a futile gesture for Congress to prohibit price fixing by business groups themselves. Seldom, if ever, has it been claimed before, that by permitting labor unions to carry on their own activities, Congress intended completely to abdicate its constitutional power to regulate interstate commerce and to empower interested business groups to shift our society from a competitive to a monopolistic economy. Finding no purpose of Congress to immunize labor unions who aid and abet manufacturers and traders in violating the Sherman Act, we hold that the district court correctly concluded that the respondents had violated the Act.

Our holding means that the same labor union activities may or may not be in violation of the Sherman Act, dependent upon whether the union acts alone or in combination with business groups. This, it is argued, brings about a wholly undesirable result—one which leaves labor unions free to engage in conduct which restrains trade. But the desirability of such an exemption of labor unions is a question for the determination of Congress. * * * It is true that many labor union activities do substantially interrupt the course of trade and that these activities, lifted out of the prohibitions of the Sherman Act, include substantially all, if not all, of the normal peaceful activities of labor unions. It is also true that the Sherman Act "draws no distinction between the restraints effected by violence and those achieved by peaceful * * * means * * *," Apex Hosiery Co. v. Leader, supra, 310 U.S. 513, 60 S.Ct. 1002, 84 L.Ed. 1311, 128 A.L.R. 1044, and that a union's exemption from the Sherman Act is not to be determined by a judicial "judgment regarding the wisdom or unwisdom, the rightness or wrongness, the selfishness or unselfishness of the end of which the particular union activities are the means." United States v. Hutcheson, supra, 312 U.S. 232, 61 S.Ct. 466, 85 L.Ed. 788. Thus, these congressionally permitted union activities may restrain trade in and of themselves. There is no denying the fact that many of them do so, both directly and indirectly. Congress evidently concluded, however, that the chief objective of Anti-trust legislation, preservation of business competition, could be accomplished by applying the legislation primarily only to those business groups which are directly interested in destroying competition. The difficulty of drawing legislation primarily aimed at trusts and monopolies so that it could also be applied to labor organizations without impairing the collective bargaining and related rights of those organizations has been emphasized both by congressional and judicial attempts to draw lines between permissible and prohibited union activities. There is, however, one line which we can draw with assurance that we follow the congressional purpose. We know that Congress feared the concentrated power of business organizations to dominate markets and prices. It intended to outlaw business monopolies. A business monopoly is no less such because a union participates, and such participation is a violation of the Act. * * *

Respondents objected to the form of the injunction and specifically requested that it be amended so as to enjoin only those prohibited activities in which the union engaged in combination "with any person, firm or corporation which is a non-labor group * * *." Without such a limitation, the injunction as issued runs directly counter to the Clayton and the Norris-LaGuardia Acts. The district court's refusal so to limit it was error.

The judgment of the Circuit Court of Appeals ordering the action dismissed is accordingly reversed and the cause is remanded to the district court for modification and clarification of the judgment and injunction, consistent with this opinion.

MR. JUSTICE MURPHY, dissenting.

My disagreement with the Court rests not so much with the legal principles announced as with the application of those principles to the facts of the case.

If the union in this instance had acted alone in its self-interest, resulting in a restraint of interstate trade, the Sherman Act concededly would be inapplicable. But if the union had aided and abetted manufacturers or traders in violating the Act, the union's statutory immunity would disappear. I cannot agree, however, that the circumstances of this case demand the invocation of the latter rule.

The union here has not in any true sense "aided" or "abetted" a primary violation of the Act by the employers. In the words of the union, it has been "the dynamic force which has driven the employer-group to enter into agreements" whereby trade has been affected. The fact that the union has expressed its self-interest with the aid of others rather than solely by its own activities should not be decisive of statutory liability. What is legal if done alone should not become illegal if done with the assistance of others and with the same purpose in mind. Otherwise a premium of unlawfulness is placed on collective bargaining.

Had the employers embarked upon a course of unreasonable trade restraints and had they sought to immunize themselves from the Sherman Act by using the union as a shield for their nefarious practices, we would have quite a different case. The union then could not be said to be acting in its self-interest in combining with the employers to carry out trade restraints primarily for the employers' interests, even though incidental benefits might accrue to the union. Under such conditions the union fairly could be said to be aiding and abetting a violation of the Act and its immunity would be lost. The facts of this case, however, do not allow such conclusions to be drawn.

I would therefore affirm the judgment of the court below.

MR. JUSTICE ROBERTS.

While I should reverse the judgment, I am unable to concur in the court's opinion. I think it conveys an incorrect impression of the genesis and character of the conspiracy charged in the complaint, and misapplies recent decisions of the court. * * *

The course of decision in this court has now created a situation in which, by concerted action, unions may set up a wall around a municipality of millions of inhabitants against importation of any goods if the union is careful to make separate contracts with each employer, and if union and employers are able to convince the court that, while all employers have such agreements, each acted independently in making them,—this notwithstanding the avowed purpose to exclude goods not made in that city by the members of the union; notwithstanding the fact that the purpose and inevitable result is the stifling of competition in interstate trade and the creation of a monopoly.

The only answer I find in the opinion of the court is that Congress has so provided. I think it has not provided any such thing and that the figmentary difference between employers negotiating jointly with the only union with which they can deal,—which imposes like conditions on all employers—and each employer dealing separately with the same union is unrealistic and unworkable. And the language of § 20 of the Clayton Act makes no such distinction. * * *

Note

Assuming the antitrust law to be the same as at the time of the Allen Bradley decision, could Local 3 lawfully achieve *at present* the same goals it pursued in Allen Bradley by dealing and contracting *separately* with each manufacturer and contractor? See Sections 8(b)(4) and 8(e) of the NLRA.

UNITED MINE WORKERS v. PENNINGTON

Supreme Court of the United States, 1965.
381 U.S. 657, 85 S.Ct. 1585, 14 L.Ed.2d 626.

MR. JUSTICE WHITE delivered the opinion of the Court.

This action began as a suit by the trustees of the United Mine Workers of America Welfare and Retirement Fund against the respondents, individually and as owners of Phillips Brothers Coal Company, a partnership, seeking to recover some $55,000 in royalty payments alleged to be due and payable under the trust provisions of the National Bituminous Coal Wage Agreement of 1950, as amended, September 29, 1952, executed by Phillips and United Mine Workers of America on or about October 1, 1953, and re-executed with amendments on or about September 8, 1955, and October 22, 1956. Phillips filed an answer and a cross claim against UMW, alleging in both that the trustees, the UMW and certain large coal operators had conspired to restrain and to monopolize interstate commerce in violation of §§ 1 and 2 of the Sherman Antitrust Act, as amended * * *. Actual damages in the amount of $100,000 were claimed for the period beginning February 14, 1954, and ending December 31, 1958.

The allegations of the cross claim were essentially as follows: Prior to the 1950 Wage Agreement between the operators and the union, severe controversy had existed in the industry, particularly over wages, the welfare fund and the union's efforts to control the working time of its members. Since 1950, however, relative peace has existed in the industry, all as the result of the 1950 Wage Agreement and its amendments and the additional understandings entered into between UMW and the large operators. Allegedly the parties considered overproduction to be the critical problem of the coal industry. The agreed solution was to be the elimination of the smaller companies, the larger companies thereby controlling the market. More specifically, the union abandoned its efforts to control the working time of the miners, agreed not to oppose the rapid mechanization of the mines which would substantially reduce mine employment, agreed to help finance such mechanization and agreed to impose the terms of the 1950 agreement on all operators without regard to their ability to pay. The benefit to the union was to be increased wages as productivity increased with mechanization, these increases to be demanded of the smaller companies whether mechanized or not. Royalty payments into the welfare fund were to be increased also, and the union was to have effective control over the fund's use. The union and large companies agreed upon other steps to exclude the marketing, production, and sale of nonunion coal. Thus the companies agreed not to lease coal lands to non-union operators, and in 1958 agreed not to sell or buy coal from such companies. The companies and the union jointly and successfully approached the Secretary of Labor to obtain establishment under the Walsh-Healey Act, as amended, * * * of a minimum wage for employees of contractors selling coal to the TVA, such minimum wage being much higher than in other industries and making it difficult for small companies to compete in the TVA term contract market. At a later time, at a meeting attended by both union and company representatives, the TVA was urged to curtail its spot market purchases, a substantial portion of which were exempt from the Walsh-Healey order. Thereafter four of the larger companies waged a destructive and collusive price-cutting campaign in the TVA spot market for coal, two of the companies, West Kentucky Coal Co. and its subsidiary Nashville Coal Co., being those in which the union had large investments and over which it was in position to exercise control.

The complaint survived motions to dismiss and after a five-week trial before a jury, a verdict was returned in favor of Phillips and against the trustees and the union, the damages against the union being fixed in the amount of $90,000, to be trebled under 15 U.S.C.A. § 15 (1958 ed.). The trial court set aside the verdict against the trustees but overruled the union's motion for judgment notwithstanding the verdict or in the alternative for a new trial. The Court of Appeals affirmed. 325 F.2d 804. It ruled that the union was not exempt from liability under the Sherman Act on the facts of this case, considered the instructions adequate and found the evidence generally sufficient to support the verdict. We granted certiorari. * * * We reverse and remand the case for proceedings consistent with this opinion.

I.

We first consider UMW's contention that the trial court erred in denying its motion for a directed verdict and for judgment notwithstanding the verdict, since a determination in UMW's favor on this issue would finally resolve the controversy. The question presented by this phase of the case is whether in the circumstances of this case the union is exempt from liability under the antitrust laws. We think the answer is clearly in the negative and that the union's motions were correctly denied.

The antitrust laws do not bar the existence and operation of labor unions as such. Moreover § 20 of the Clayton Act * * * and § 4 of the Norris-LaGuardia Act * * * permit a union, acting alone, to engage in the conduct therein specified without violating the Sherman Act. United States v. Hutcheson, 312 U.S. 219, 61 S.Ct. 463, 95 L.Ed. 788 * * *.

But neither § 20 nor § 4 expressly deals with arrangements or agreements between unions and employers. Neither section tells us whether any or all such arrangements or agreements are barred or permitted by the antitrust laws. Thus Hutcheson itself stated:

> "So long as a union acts in its self-interest *and does not combine with non-labor groups,* the licit and the illicit under § 20 are not to be distinguished by any judgment regarding the wisdom or unwisdom, the rightness or wrongness, the selfishness or unselfishness of the end of which the particular union activities are the means." 312 U.S. at 232, 61 S.Ct. at 466. (Emphasis added.)

And in Allen Bradley Co. v. Local Union No. 3, IBEW, 325 U.S. 797, 65 S.Ct. 1533, 89 L.Ed. 1939, this Court made explicit what had been merely a qualifying expression in Hutcheson and held that "when the unions participated with a combination of business men who had complete power to eliminate all competition among themselves and to prevent all competition from others, a situation was created not included within the exemptions of the Clayton and Norris-LaGuardia Acts." Id., 325 U.S. at 809, 65 S.Ct. at 1540. * * * Subsequent cases have applied the Allen Bradley doctrine to such combinations without regard to whether they found expression in a collective bargaining agreement, United Brotherhood of Carpenters v. United States [330 U.S. 395, 67 S.Ct. 775, 91 L.Ed. 973]; see Local 24 of International Brotherhood of Teamsters, etc. v. Oliver, 358 U.S. 283, 296, 79 S.Ct. 297, 304, 3 L.Ed.2d 312, and even though the mechanism for effectuating the purpose of the combination was an agreement on wages, see Adams Dairy Co. v. St. Louis Dairy Co., 260 F.2d 46 (C.A.8th Cir.1958), or on hours of work, Philadelphia Record Co. v. Manufacturing Photo-Engravers Assn., 155 F.2d 799 (C.A.3d Cir.1946).

If the UMW in this case, in order to protect its wage scale by maintaining employer income, had presented a set of prices at which the mine operators would be required to sell their coal, the union and the employers who happened to agree could not successfully defend this contract provision if it were challenged under the antitrust laws by the United States or by some party injured by the arrangement. Cf. Allen Bradley Co. v. Local Union No. 3, IBEW, 325 U.S. 797, 65 S.Ct. 1533, 89 L.Ed. 1939. * * * In such a case, the restraint on the product market is direct and immediate, is of the type characteristically deemed unreasonable under the Sherman Act and the union gets from the promise nothing more concrete than a hope for better wages to come.

Likewise, if as is alleged in this case, the union became a party to a collusive bidding arrangement designed to drive Phillips and others from the TVA spot market, we think any claim to exemption from antitrust liability would be frivolous at best. For this reason alone the motions of the unions were properly denied.

A major part of Phillips' case, however, was that the union entered into a conspiracy with the large operators to impose the agreed-upon wage and royalty scales upon the smaller, nonunion operators, regardless of their ability to pay and regardless of whether or not the union represented the employees of these companies, all for the purpose of eliminating them from the industry, limiting production and pre-empting the market for the large, unionized operators. The UMW urges that since such an agreement concerned wage standards, it is exempt from the antitrust laws.

It is true that wages lie at the very heart of those subjects about which employers and unions must bargain and the law contemplates agreements on wages not only between individual employers and a union but agreements between the union and employers in a multi-employer bargaining unit. National Labor Relations Board v. Truck Drivers Union [Buffalo Linen], 353 U.S. 87, 94–96, 77 S.Ct. 643, 646–647, 1 L.Ed.2d 676. The union benefit from the wage scale agreed upon is direct and concrete and the effect on the product market, though clearly present, results from the elimination of competition based on wages among the employers in the bargaining unit, which is not the kind of restraint Congress intended the Sherman Act to proscribe. Apex Hosiery Co. v. Leader, 310 U.S. 469, 503–504, 60 S.Ct. 982, 997, 84 L.Ed. 1311 * * *. We think it beyond question that a union may conclude a wage agreement with the multi-employer bargaining unit without violating the antitrust laws and that it may as a matter of its own policy, and not by agreement with all or part of the employers of that unit, seek the same wages from other employers.

This is not to say that an agreement resulting from union-employer negotiations is automatically exempt from Sherman Act scrutiny simply because the negotiations involve a compulsory subject of bargaining, regardless of the subject or the form and content of the agreement. Unquestionably the Board's demarcation of the bounds of the duty to bargain has great relevance to any consideration of the sweep of labor's antitrust immunity, for we are concerned here with harmonizing the Sherman Act with the national policy expressed in the National Labor Relations Act of promoting "the peaceful settlement of industrial disputes by subjecting labor-management controversies to the mediatory influence of negotiation." Fibreboard Paper Prods. Corp. v. National Labor Relations Board, 379 U.S. 203, 211, 85 S.Ct. 398, 403, 13 L.Ed.2d 233. But there are limits to what a union or an employer may offer or extract in the name of wages, and because they must bargain does not mean that the agreement reached may disregard other laws. Local 24 of Intern. Broth. of Teamsters, etc. v. Oliver, 358 U.S. 283, 296, 79 S.Ct. 297, 304, 3 L.Ed.2d 312 * * *.

We have said that a union may make wage agreements with a multi-employer bargaining unit and may in pursuance of its own union interests seek to obtain the same terms from other employers. No case under the antitrust laws could be made out on evidence limited to such union behavior.[2] But we think a union forfeits its exemption from the antitrust laws when it is clearly shown that it has agreed with one set of employers to impose a certain wage scale on other bargaining units. One group of employers may not conspire to eliminate competitors from the industry and the union is liable with the employers if it becomes a party to the conspiracy. This is true even though the union's part in the scheme is an undertaking to secure the same wages, hours, or other conditions of employment from the remaining employers in the industry.

We do not find anything in the national labor policy that conflicts with this conclusion. This Court has recognized that a legitimate aim of any national labor organization is to obtain uniformity of labor standards and that a consequence of such union activity may be to eliminate competition based on differences in such standards. Apex Hosiery Co. v. Leader, 310 U.S. 469, 503, 60 S.Ct. 982, 997, 84 L.Ed. 1311. But there is nothing in the labor policy indicating that the union and the employers in one bargaining unit are free to bargain about the wages, hours and working conditions of other bargaining units or to attempt to settle these matters for the entire industry. On the contrary, the duty to bargain unit by unit leads to a quite different conclusion. The union's obligation to its members would seem best served if the union retained the ability to respond to each bargaining situation as the individual circumstances might warrant, without being straitjacketed by some prior agreement with the favored employers.

So far as the employer is concerned it has long been the Board's view that an employer may not condition the signing of a collective bargaining agreement on the union's organization of a majority of the industry. American Range Lines, Inc., 13 N.L.R.B. 139, 147 (1939); Samuel Youlin, 22 N.L.R.B. 879, 885 (1940); Newton Chevrolet, Inc., 37 N.L.R.B. 334, 341 (1941); see National Labor Relations Board v. George P. Pilling & Son Co., 119 F.2d 32, 38 (C.A.3d Cir.1941). In such cases the obvious interest of the employer is to ensure that acceptance of the union's wage demands will not adversely affect his competitive position. In American Range Lines, Inc., supra, the Board rejected that employer interest as a justification for the demand. "[A]n

---

2. Unilaterally, and without agreement with any employer group to do so, a union may adopt a uniform wage policy and seek vigorously to implement it even though it may suspect that some employers cannot effectively compete if they are required to pay the wage scale demanded by the union. The union need not gear its wage demands to wages which the weakest units in the industry can afford to pay. Such union conduct is not alone sufficient evidence to maintain a union-employer conspiracy charge under the Sherman Act. There must be additional direct or indirect evidence of the conspiracy. There was, of course, other evidence in this case, but we indicate no opinion as to its sufficiency.

employer cannot lawfully deny his employees the right to bargain collectively through their designated representative in an appropriate unit because he envisions competitive disadvantages accruing from such bargaining." 13 N.L.R.B., at 147. Such an employer condition, if upheld, would clearly reduce the extent of collective bargaining. Thus, in Newton Chevrolet, Inc., supra, where it was held a refusal to bargain for the employer to insist on a provision that the agreed contract terms would not become effective until five competitors had signed substantially similar contracts, the Board stated that "[t]here is nothing in the Act to justify the imposition of a duty upon an exclusive bargaining representative to secure an agreement from a majority of an employer's competitors as a condition precedent to the negotiation of an agreement with the employer. To permit individual employers to refuse to bargain collectively until some or all of their competitors had done so clearly would lead to frustration of the fundamental purpose of the Act to encourage the practice of collective bargaining." 37 N.L.R.B., at 341. Permitting insistence on an agreement by the union to attempt to impose a similar contract on other employers would likewise seem to impose a restraining influence on the extent of collective bargaining, for the union could avoid an impasse only by surrendering its freedom to act in its own interest vis-à-vis other employers, something it will be unwilling to do in many instances. Once again, the employer's interest is a competitive interest rather than an interest in regulating its own labor relations, and the effect on the union of such an agreement would be to limit the free exercise of the employees' right to engage in concerted activities according to their own views of their self-interest. In sum, we cannot conclude that the national labor policy provides any support for such agreements.

On the other hand, the policy of the antitrust laws is clearly set against employer-union agreements seeking to prescribe labor standards outside the bargaining unit. One could hardly contend, for example, that one group of employers could lawfully demand that the union impose on other employers wages that were significantly higher than those paid by the requesting employers, or a system of computing wages that, because of differences in methods of production, would be more costly to one set of employers than to another. The anticompetitive potential of such a combination is obvious, but is little more severe than what is alleged to have been the purpose and effect of the conspiracy in this case to establish wages at a level that marginal producers could not pay so that they would be driven from the industry. And if the conspiracy presently under attack were declared exempt it would hardly be possible to deny exemption to such avowedly discriminatory schemes.

From the viewpoint of antitrust policy, moreover, all such agreements between a group of employers and a union that the union will seek specified labor standards outside the bargaining unit suffer from a more basic defect, without regard to predatory intention or effect in the particular case. For the salient characteristic of such agreements is that the union surrenders its freedom of action with respect to its bargaining policy. Prior to the agreement the union might seek uniform standards in its own self-interest but would be required to assess in each case the probable costs and gains of a strike or other collective action to that end and thus might conclude that the objective of uniform standards should temporarily give way. After the agreement the union's interest would be bound in each case to that of the favored employer group. It is just such restraints upon the freedom of economic units to act according to their own choice and discretion that run counter to antitrust policy.   *   *   *

Thus the relevant labor and antitrust policies compel us to conclude that the alleged agreement between UMW and the large operators to secure uniform labor standards throughout the industry, if proved, was not exempt from the antitrust laws.

II.

The UMW next contends that the trial court erroneously denied its motion for a new trial based on claimed errors in the admission of evidence.

In Eastern R.R. Presidents Conf. v. Noerr Motor Freight Inc., 365 U.S. 127, 81 S.Ct. 523, 5 L.Ed.2d 464, the Court rejected an attempt to base a Sherman Act conspiracy on evidence consisting entirely of activities of competitors seeking to influence public officials. The Sherman Act, it was held, was not intended to bar concerted action of this kind even though the resulting official action damaged other competitors at whom the campaign was aimed. Furthermore, the legality of the conduct "was not at all affected by any anticompetitive purpose it may have had," id., at 140, 81 S.Ct. at 531—even though the "sole purpose in seeking to influence the passage and enforcement of laws was to destroy the truckers as competitors for the long-distance freight business," id., at 138, 81 S.Ct. at 530. Nothing could be clearer from the Court's opinion than that anticompetitive purpose did not illegalize the conduct there involved.

We agree with the UMW that both the Court of Appeals and the trial court failed to take proper account of the Noerr case. In approving the instructions of the trial court with regard to the approaches of the union and the operators to the Secretary of Labor and to the TVA officials, the Court of Appeals considered Noerr as applying only to conduct "unaccompanied by a purpose or intent to further a conspiracy to violate a statute. It is the illegal purpose or intent inherent in the conduct which vitiates the conduct which would otherwise be legal." 325 F.2d, at 817. Noerr shields from the Sherman Act a concerted effort to influence public officials regardless of intent or purpose. The Court of Appeals, however, would hold the conduct illegal depending upon proof of an illegal purpose.

The instructions of the trial court to the jury exhibit a similar infirmity. The jury was instructed that the approach to the Secretary of Labor was legal unless part of a conspiracy to drive small operators out of business and that the approach to the TVA was not a violation of the antitrust laws "unless the parties so urged the TVA to modify its policies in buying coal for the purpose of driving the small operators out of business." If, therefore, the jury determined the requisite anticompetitive purpose to be present, it was free to find an illegal conspiracy based solely on the Walsh-Healey and TVA episodes, or in any event to attribute illegality to these acts as part of a general plan to eliminate Phillips and other operators similarly situated. Neither finding, however, is permitted by Noerr for the reasons stated in that case. Joint efforts to influence public officials do not violate the antitrust laws even though intended to eliminate competition. Such conduct is not illegal, either standing alone or as part of a broader scheme itself violative of the Sherman Act. The jury should have been so instructed and, given the obviously telling nature of this evidence, we cannot hold this lapse to be mere harmless error.

There is another reason for remanding this case for further proceedings in the lower courts. It is clear under Noerr that Phillips could not collect any damages under the Sherman Act for any injury which it suffered from the action of the Secretary of Labor. The conduct of the union and the operators did not violate the Act, the action taken to set a minimum wage for government purchases of coal was the act of a public official who is not claimed to be a co-conspirator, and the jury should have been instructed, as UMW requested, to exclude any damages which Phillips may have suffered as a result of the Secretary's Walsh-Healey determinations.   *   *   *

The judgment is reversed and the case remanded for further proceedings consistent with this opinion.   *   *   *

MR. JUSTICE DOUGLAS, with whom MR. JUSTICE BLACK and MR. JUSTICE CLARK agree, concurring.

As we read the opinion of the Court, it reaffirms the principles of Allen Bradley Co. v. Local Union No. 3, IBEW, 325 U.S. 797, 65 S.Ct. 1533, 89 L.Ed. 1939, and tells the trial judge:

First. On the new trial the jury should be instructed that if there were an industry-wide collective bargaining agreement whereby employers and the union agreed on a wage scale that exceeded the financial ability of some operators to pay and that if it was made for the purpose of forcing some employers out of business, the union as well as the employers who participated in the arrangement with the union should be found to have violated the antitrust laws.

Second. An industry-wide agreement containing those features is prima facie evidence of a violation.

  *   *   * If the allegations in this case are to be believed, organized labor joined hands with organized business to drive marginal operators out of existence. According to those allegations the union used its control over West Kentucky Coal Co. and Nashville Coal Co. to dump coal at such low prices that respondents, who were small operators, had to abandon their business. According to those allegations there was a boycott by the union and the major companies against small companies who needed major companies' coal land on which to operate. According to those allegations, high wage and welfare terms of employment were imposed on the small, marginal companies by the union and the major companies with the knowledge and intent that the small ones would be driven out of business.

The only architect of our economic system is Congress. We are right in adhering to its philosophy of the free enterprise system as expressed in the antitrust laws and as enforced by Allen Bradley Co. v. Union until the Congress delegates to big business and big labor the power to remold our economy in the manner charged here.

[For the opinion of JUSTICE GOLDBERG, dissenting from the Court's opinion but concurring in the reversal, see infra p. 1018.]

LOCAL 189, AMALGAMATED MEAT CUTTERS v. JEWEL TEA CO.

Supreme Court of the United States, 1965.
381 U.S. 676, 85 S.Ct. 1596, 14 L.Ed.2d 640.

Mr. Justice White announced the judgment of the Court and delivered an opinion, in which The Chief Justice and Mr. Justice Brennan join.

Like No. 48, United Mine Workers of America v. Pennington, * * * decided today, this case presents questions regarding the application of §§ 1 and 2 of the Sherman Antitrust Act * * * to activities of labor unions. In particular, it concerns the lawfulness of the following restriction on the operating hours of food store meat departments contained in a collective bargaining agreement executed after joint multi-employer, multi-union negotiations:

"Market operating hours shall be 9:00 a.m. to 6:00 p.m. Monday through Saturday, inclusive. No customer shall be served who comes into the market before or after the hours set forth above."

This litigation arose out of the 1957 contract negotiations between the representatives of 9,000 Chicago retailers of fresh meat and the seven union petitioners, who are local affiliates of the Amalgamated Meat Cutters and Butcher Workmen of North America, AFL–CIO, representing virtually all butchers in the Chicago area. During the 1957 bargaining sessions the employer group presented several requests for union consent to a relaxation of the existing contract restriction on marketing hours for fresh meat, which forbade the sale of meat before 9 a.m. and after 6 p.m. in both service and self-service markets.[1] The unions rejected all such suggestions, and their own proposal retaining the marketing-hours restriction was ultimately accepted at the final bargaining session by all but two of the employers, National Tea Co. and Jewel Tea Co. (hereinafter "Jewel"). Associated Food Retailers of Greater Chicago, a trade association having about 1,000 individual and independent merchants as members and representing some 300 meat dealers in the negotiations, was among those who accepted. Jewel, however, asked the union negotiators to present to their membership, on behalf of it and National Tea, a counter offer that included provision for Friday night operations. At the same time Jewel voiced its belief, as it had midway through the negotiations, that any marketing-hours restriction was illegal. On the recommendation of the union negotiators, the Jewel offer was rejected by the union membership, and a strike was authorized. Under the duress of the strike vote, Jewel decided to sign the contract previously approved by the rest of the industry.

In July 1958 Jewel brought suit against the unions, certain of their officers, Associated, and Charles H. Bremann, Secretary-Treasurer of Associ-

---

1. The practice in the Chicago area is for the employers and the butchers to execute separate, but similar, collective bargaining agreements for self-service and service markets. A self-service market is "one in which fresh beef, veal, lamb, mutton or pork are available for sale on a prepackage self-service basis." Semi-self-service markets, those in which fresh meat is made available on a prepackaged basis but there is also a service counter offering custom cutting for those who prefer it, are governed by the self-service contract. Service markets are those in which no fresh meat is made available on a self-service basis.

ated, seeking invalidation under §§ 1 and 2 of the Sherman Act of the contract provision that prohibited night meat market operations. The gist of the complaint was that the defendants and others had conspired together to prevent the retail sale of fresh meat before 9 a.m. and after 6 p.m. As evidence of the conspiracy Jewel relied in part on the events during the 1957 contract negotiations—the acceptance by Associated of the market-hours restriction and the unions' imposition of the restriction on Jewel through a strike threat. Jewel also alleged that it was a part of the conspiracy that the unions would neither permit their members to work at times other than the hours specified nor allow any grocery firm to sell meat, with or without employment of their members, outside those hours; that the members of Associated, which had joined only one of the 1957 employer proposals for extended marketing hours, had agreed among themselves to insist on the inclusion of the marketing-hours limitation in all collective bargaining agreements between the unions and any food store operator; that Associated, its members and officers had agreed with the other defendants that no firm was to be permitted to operate self-service meat markets between 6 p.m. and 9 p.m.; and that the unions, their officers and members had acted as the enforcing agent of the conspiracy.

The complaint stated that in recent years the prepackaged, self-service system of marketing meat had come into vogue, that 174 of Jewel's 196 stores were equipped to vend meat in this manner, and that a butcher need not be on duty in a self-service market at the time meat purchases were actually made. The prohibition of night meat marketing, it was alleged, unlawfully impeded Jewel in the use of its property and adversely affected the general public in that many persons find it inconvenient to shop during the day. An injunction, treble damages and attorneys' fees were demanded.

The trial judge held the allegations of the complaint sufficient to withstand a motion to dismiss made on the grounds, *inter alia,* that (a) the alleged restraint was within the exclusive regulatory scope of the National Labor Relations Act and was therefore outside the jurisdiction of the Court and (b) the controversy was within the labor exemption to the antitrust laws. That ruling was sustained on appeal. Jewel Tea Co. v. Local Unions Nos. 189, etc., Amalgamated Meat Cutters, AFL–CIO, 274 F.2d 217 (C.A.7th Cir. 1960), cert. denied, 362 U.S. 936, 80 S.Ct. 757, 4 L.Ed.2d 747. After trial, however, the District Judge ruled the "record was devoid of any evidence to support a finding of conspiracy" between Associated and the unions to force the restrictive provision on Jewel. 215 F.Supp. 839, 845. Testing the unions' action standing alone, the trial court found that even in self-service markets removal of the limitation on marketing hours either would inaugurate longer hours and night work for the butchers or would result in butchers' work being done by others unskilled in the trade. Thus, the court concluded, the unions had imposed the marketing-hours limitation to serve their own interests respecting conditions of employment, and such action was clearly within the labor exemption of the Sherman Act established by Hunt v. Crumboch, 325 U.S. 821, 65 S.Ct. 1545, 89 L.Ed. 1954; United States v. Hutcheson, 312 U.S. 219, 61 S.Ct. 463, 85 L.Ed. 788 * * *. Alternatively, the District Court ruled that even if this was not the case, the arrangement did not amount to an unreasonable restraint of trade in violation of the Sherman Act.

The Court of Appeals reversed the dismissal of the complaint as to both the unions and Associated. Without disturbing the District Court's finding that, apart from the contractual provision itself, there was no evidence of conspiracy, the Court of Appeals concluded that a conspiracy in restraint of trade had been shown. The court noted that "[t]he rest of the Industry agreed with the Defendant Local Unions to continue the ban on night operations," while plaintiff resisted, and concluded that Associated and the unions "entered into a combination or agreement, which constituted a conspiracy, as charged in the complaint. * * * [w]hether it be called an agreement, a contract or a conspiracy, is immaterial." 331 F.2d 547, 551.

Similarly, the Court of Appeals did not find it necessary to review the lower court's finding that night marketing would affect either the butchers' working hours or their jurisdiction, for the court held that an employer-union contract respecting working hours would be unlawful. "One of the proprietary functions is the determination of what days a week and what hours of the day the business will be open to supply its customers. * * * As long as all rights of employees are recognized and duly observed by the employer, including the number of hours per day that any one shall be required to work, any agreement by a labor union, acting in concert with business competitors of the employer, designed to interfere with his operation of a retail business * * * is a violation of the Sherman Act. * * * [T]he furnishing of a place and advantageous hours of employment for the butchers to supply meat to customers are the prerogatives of the employer." 331 F.2d 547, 549.

We granted certiorari on the unions' petition * * * [3] and now reverse the Court of Appeals.

I.

We must first consider the union's attack on the appropriateness of the District Court's exercise of jurisdiction, which is encompassed in their contention that this controversy is within the exclusive primary jurisdiction of the National Labor Relations Board. On this point, which is distinct from the unions' argument that the operating-hours restriction is subject to regulation only by the Board and is thus wholly exempt from the antitrust laws, the unions' thesis is that the pivotal issue is whether the operating-hours restriction is a "term or condition of employment" and that the District Court should have held the case on its docket pending a Board proceeding to resolve that issue, which is said to be peculiarly within the competence of the Board.

3. The grant of certiorari was limited to the following questions:

"1. Based on the District Court's undisturbed finding that the limitation 'was imposed after arm's length bargaining, * * * and was fashioned exclusively by the unions to serve their own interests—how long and what hours, members shall work, what work they shall do, and what pay they shall receive,' whether the limitation upon mar-

ket operating hours and the controversy concerning it are within the labor exemption of the Sherman Antitrust Act.

"2. Whether a claimed violation of the Sherman Antitrust Act which falls within the regulatory scope of the National Labor Relations Act is within the exclusive primary jurisdiction of the National Labor Relations Board."

"The doctrine of primary jurisdiction * * * applies where a claim is originally cognizable in the courts, and comes into play whenever enforcement of the claim requires the resolution of issues which, under a regulatory scheme, have been placed within the special competence of an administrative body; in such a case the judicial process is suspended pending referral of such issues to the administrative body for its views." United States v. Western Pac. R. Co., 352 U.S. 59, 63–64, 77 S.Ct. 161, 165, 1 L.Ed.2d 126. The doctrine is based on the principle "that in cases raising issues of fact not within the conventional experience of judges or cases requiring the exercise of administrative discretion, agencies created by Congress for regulating the subject matter should not be passed over," Far East Conference v. United States, 342 U.S. 570, 574, 72 S.Ct. 492, 494, 96 L.Ed. 576, and "requires judicial abstention in cases where protection of the integrity of a regulatory scheme dictates preliminary resort to the agency which administers the scheme," United States v. Philadelphia Nat. Bank, 374 U.S. 321, 353, 83 S.Ct. 1715, 1736, 10 L.Ed.2d 915.

Whether a proposed bargaining subject is a term or condition of employment is an issue that the Board frequently determines in considering charges that an employer or union has violated the duty to bargain in good faith concerning "wages, hours, and other terms and conditions of employment," the mandatory subjects of bargaining described in § 8(d) of the National Labor Relations Act * * *. Such an issue may be raised by an unfair labor practice charge of violation of § 8(a)(5) or § 8(b)(3) through, for example, a refusal to bargain on a mandatory subject of bargaining, see National Labor Relations Board v. Katz, 369 U.S. 736, 82 S.Ct. 1107, 8 L.Ed. 2d 230, or insistence on a nonmandatory subject, see National Labor Relations Board v. Wooster Division of Borg-Warner Corp., 356 U.S. 342, 78 S.Ct. 718, 2 L.Ed.2d 823. Thus, the unions contend, Jewel could have filed an unfair labor practice charge with the Board on the ground that the unions had insisted on a nonmandatory subject—the marketing-hours restriction. Obviously, classification of bargaining subjects as "terms or conditions of employment" is a matter concerning which the Board has special expertise. Nevertheless, for the reasons stated below we cannot conclude that this is a proper case for application of the doctrine of primary jurisdiction.

To begin with, courts are themselves not without experience in classifying bargaining subjects as terms or conditions of employment. Just such a determination must be frequently made when a court's jurisdiction to issue an injunction affecting a labor dispute is challenged under the Norris-LaGuardia Act, which defines "labor dispute" as including "any controversy concerning terms or conditions of employment." Norris-LaGuardia Act, § 13(c). * * *

Finally, we must reject the unions' primary-jurisdiction contention because of the absence of an available procedure for obtaining a Board determination. The Board does not classify bargaining subjects in the abstract but only in connection with unfair labor practice charges of refusal to bargain. The typical antitrust suit, however, is brought by a stranger to the bargaining relationship, and the complaint is not that the parties have refused to bargain but, quite the contrary, that they have agreed. Jewel's conspiracy allegation in the present case was just such a complaint. Agreement is of course not a refusal to bargain, and in such cases the Board affords no mechanism for obtaining a classification of the subject matter of the agreement. Moreover, even in the few instances when the antitrust action could be framed as a refusal to bargain charge, there is no guarantee of Board action. It is the function of the Board's General Counsel rather than the Board or a private litigant to determine whether an unfair labor practice complaint will ultimately issue. National Labor Relations Act, § 3(d) * * *. And the six-month limitation period of § 10(b) of the Act * * * would preclude many litigants from even filing a charge with the General Counsel. Indeed, Jewel's complaint in this very case was filed more than six months after it signed the 1957 collective bargaining agreement. * * *

II.

Here, as in United Mine Workers of America v. Pennington, * * * the claim is made that the agreement under attack is exempt from the antitrust laws. We agree, but not on the broad grounds urged by the union.

It is well at the outset to emphasize that this case comes to us stripped of any claim of a union-employer conspiracy against Jewel. The trial court found no evidence to sustain Jewel's conspiracy claim and this finding was not disturbed by the Court of Appeals. We therefore have a situation where the unions, having obtained a marketing-hours agreement from one group of employers, have successfully sought the same terms from a single employer, Jewel, not as a result of a bargain between the unions and some employers directed against other employers, but pursuant to what the unions deemed to be in their own labor union interests.

Jewel does not allege that it has been injured by the elimination of competition among the other employers within the unit with respect to marketing hours; Jewel complains only of the unions' action in forcing it to accept the same restriction, the unions acting not at the behest of any employer group but in pursuit of their own policies. It might be argued that absent any union-employer conspiracy against Jewel and absent any agreement between Jewel and any other employer, the union-Jewel contract cannot be a violation of the Sherman Act. But the issue before us is not the broad substantive one of a violation of the antitrust laws—was there a conspiracy or combination which unreasonably restrained trade or an attempt to monopolize and was Jewel damaged in its business?—but whether the agreement is immune from attack by reason of the labor exemption from the antitrust laws. See note 3, supra. The fact that the parties to the agreement are but a single employer and the unions representing its employees does not compel immunity for the agreement. We must consider the subject matter of the agreement in the light of the national labor policy. * * *

We pointed out in Pennington that exemption for union-employer agreements is very much a matter of accommodating the coverage of the Sherman Act to the policy of the labor laws. Employers and unions are required to bargain about wages, hours and working conditions, and this fact weighs heavily in favor of antitrust exemption for agreements on these subjects. But neither party need bargain about other matters and either party commits an unfair labor practice if it conditions its bargaining upon discussions of a nonmandatory subject. National Labor Relations Board v. Division of Wooster Borg-Warner Corp., 356 U.S. 342, 78 S.Ct. 718. Jewel, for example, need not have bargained about or agreed to a schedule of prices at which its meat would be sold and the unions could not legally have insisted that it do so. But if the unions had made such a demand, Jewel had agreed and the United States or an injured party had challenged the agreement under the antitrust laws, we seriously doubt that either the unions or Jewel could claim immunity by reason of the labor exemption whatever substantive questions of violation there might be.

Thus the issue in this case is whether the marketing-hours restriction, like wages, and unlike prices, is so intimately related to wages, hours and working conditions that the unions' successful attempt to obtain that provision through bona fide, arm's-length bargaining in pursuit of their own labor union policies, and not at the behest of or in combination with nonlabor groups, falls within the protection of the national labor policy and is therefore exempt from the Sherman Act.[5] We think that it is.

The Court of Appeals would classify the marketing-hours restriction with the product-pricing provision and place both within the reach of the Sherman Act. In its view, labor has a legitimate interest in the number of hours it must work but no interest in whether the hours fall in the daytime, in the nighttime or on Sundays. "[T]he furnishing of a place and advantageous hours of employment for the butchers to supply meat to customers are the prerogatives of the employer." 331 F.2d 547, 549. That reasoning would invalidate with respect to both service and self-service markets the 1957 provision that "eight hours shall constitute the basic work day, Monday through Saturday; *work to begin at 9:00 a.m. and stop at 6:00 p.m.* * * *" as well as the marketing-hours restriction.

Contrary to the Court of Appeals, we think that the particular hours of the day and the particular days of the week during which employees shall be required to work are subjects well within the realm of "wages, hours, and other terms and conditions of employment" about which employers and unions must bargain. National Labor Relations Act, § 8(d); see Timken Roller Bearing Co., 70 N.L.R.B. 500, 504, 515–516, 521 (1946), rev'd on other grounds, 161 F.2d 949 (C.A. 6th Cir.1947) (employer's unilateral imposition of Sunday work was refusal to bargain); Massey Gin & Machine Works, Inc., 78 N.L.R.B. 189, 195, 199 (1948) (change in starting and quitting time); Camp & McInnes, Inc., 100 N.L.R.B. 524, 532 (1952) (reduction of lunch hour and

5. The crucial determinant is not the form of the agreement—e.g., prices or wages—but its relative impact on the product market and the interests of union members. Thus in Local 24 of Intern. Broth. of Teamsters Union v. Oliver, 358 U.S. 283, 79 S.Ct. 297, we held that federal labor policy precluded application of state antitrust laws to an employer-union agreement that when leased trucks were driven by their owners, such owner-drivers should receive, in addition to the union wage, not less than a prescribed minimum rental. Though in form a scheme fixing prices for the supply of leased vehicles, the agreement was designed "to protect the negotiated wage scale against the possible undermining through diminution of the owner's wages for driving which might result from a rental which did not cover his operating costs." Id., at 293–294, 79 S.Ct. at 303. As the agreement did not embody a " 'remote and indirect approach to the subject of wages' * * * but a direct frontal attack upon a problem thought to threaten the maintenance of the basic wage structure established by the collective bargaining contract," id., at 294, 79 S.Ct. at 304, the paramount federal policy of encouraging collective bargaining proscribed application of the state law. * * *

advancement of quitting time). And, although the effect on competition is apparent and real, perhaps more so than in the case of the wage agreement, the concern of union members is immediate and direct. Weighing the respective interests involved, we think the national labor policy expressed in the National Labor Relations Act places beyond the reach of the Sherman Act union-employer agreements on when, as well as how long, employees must work. An agreement on these subjects between the union and the employers in a bargaining unit is not illegal under the Sherman Act, nor is the union's unilateral demand for the same contract of other employers in the industry.

Disposing of the case, as it did, on the broad grounds we have indicated, the Court of Appeals did not deal separately with the marketing-hours provision, as distinguished from hours of work, in connection with either service or self-service markets. The dispute here pertains principally to self-service markets.

The unions argue that since night operations would be impossible without night employment of butchers, or an impairment of the butchers' jurisdiction, or a substantial effect on the butchers' workload, the marketing-hours restriction is either little different in effect from the valid working-hours provision that work shall stop at 6 p.m. or is necessary to protect other concerns of the union members. If the unions' factual premises are true, we think the unions could impose a restriction on night operations without violation of the Sherman Act; for then operating hours, like working hours, would constitute a subject of immediate and legitimate concern to union members.

Jewel alleges on the other hand that the night operation of self-service markets requires no butcher to be in attendance and does not infringe any other legitimate union concern. Customers serve themselves; and if owners want to forgo furnishing the services of a butcher to give advice or to make special cuts, this is not the unions' concern since their desire to avoid night work is fully satisfied and no other legitimate interest is being infringed. In short, the connection between working hours and operating hours in the case of the self-service market is said to be so attenuated as to bring the provision within the prohibition of the Sherman Act.

If it were true that self-service markets could actually operate without butchers, at least for a few hours after 6 p.m., that no encroachment on butchers' work would result and that the workload of butchers during normal working hours would not be substantially increased, Jewel's position would have considerable merit. For then the obvious restraint on the product market—the exclusion of self-service stores from the evening market for meat—would stand alone, unmitigated and unjustified by the vital interests of the union butchers which are relied upon in this case. In such event the limitation imposed by the unions might well be reduced to nothing but an effort by the unions to protect one group of employers from competition by another, which is conduct that is not exempt from the Sherman Act. Whether there would be a violation of §§ 1 and 2 would then depend on whether the elements of a conspiracy in restraint of trade or an attempt to monopolize had been proved.[6]

Thus the dispute between Jewel and the unions essentially concerns a narrow factual question: Are night operations without butchers, and without infringement of butchers' interests, feasible? The District Court resolved this factual dispute in favor of the unions. It found that "in stores where meat is sold at night it is impractical to operate without either butchers or other employees. Someone must arrange, replenish and clean the counters and supply customer services." Operating without butchers would mean that "their work would be done by others unskilled in the trade," and "would involve an increase in workload in preparing for the night work and cleaning the next morning." 215 F.Supp., at 846. Those findings were not disturbed by the Court of Appeals, which, as previously noted, proceeded on a broader ground. Our function is limited to reviewing the record to satisfy ourselves that the trial judge's findings are not clearly erroneous. Fed.Rules Civ.Proc. 52(a).

The trial court had before it evidence concerning the history of the unions' opposition to night work, the development of the provisions respecting night work and night operations, the course of collective bargaining negotiations in 1957, 1959, and 1961[7] with regard to those provisions, and the characteristics of meat marketing insofar as they bore on the feasibility of night operations without butchers.

The unions' opposition to night work has a long history. Prior to 1919 the operating hours of meat markets in Chicago were 7 a.m. to 7 p.m., Monday through Friday; 7 a.m. to 10 p.m. on Saturday, and 7 a.m. to 1 p.m. on Sunday. Butchers worked the full 81-hour, seven-day week. The Chicago butchers' strike of 1919 was much concerned with shortening working hours, and the resulting contract, signed in 1920, set the working day at 8 a.m. to 6 p.m., Monday through Friday, and 8 a.m. to 9 p.m. on Saturday. Various alterations in the hours were made in 1937, 1941, 1945, 1946, and again in 1947, when the present working hours (9 a.m. to 6 p.m., Monday through Saturday) were established. In a mail ballot conducted by the unions in October 1962, Jewel's meat cutters voted 759 to 28 against night work.

Concomitant with the unions' concern with the working hours of butchers was their interest in the hours during which customers might be served. The 1920 agreement provided that "no customers will be served who come into the market after 6 P.M. and 9 P.M. on Saturdays and on days preceding holidays * * *." That provision was continued until 1947, when it was superseded by the formulation presently in effect and here claimed to be unlawful:

---

6. One issue, for example, would be whether the restraint was unreasonable. Judicial pronouncements regarding the reasonableness of restraints on hours of business are relatively few. Some cases appear to have viewed such restraints as tantamount to limits on hours of work and thus reasonable, even though contained in agreements among competitors. * * *

7. In 1959, and again in 1961, new collective bargaining agreements containing the challenged provision were executed. In each instance Jewel reserved its position with respect to this litigation.

"Market operating hours shall be 9:00 a.m. to 6:00 p.m. Monday through Saturday, inclusive. No customer shall be served who comes into the market before or after the hours set forth above."

In 1947, Jewel had just started investigating the self-service method of meat vending. It introduced that method in the Chicago area in 1948 and in the territory of these unions in 1953.

During the 1957 negotiations numerous proposals for relaxation of the operating-hours restriction were presented by the employer group. Each of these proposals, including that submitted separately by Jewel for consideration at the unions' ratification meetings, combined a provision for night operations with a provision for a more flexible workday that would permit night employment of butchers. Such juxtaposition of the two provisions could, of course, only serve to reinforce the unions' fears that night operations meant night work. Jewel did allege in its complaint, filed in July 1958, that night operations were possible without butchers, but even in the 1959 bargaining sessions Jewel failed to put forth any plan for night operations that did not also include night work. Finally, toward the end of the 1961 negotiations, Jewel did make such a suggestion, but, as the trial judge remarked, the "unions questioned the seriousness of that proposal under the circumstances." 215 F.Supp., at 843.

The unions' evidence with regard to the practicability of night operations without butchers was accurately summarized by the trial judge as follows:

"[I]n most of plaintiff's stores outside Chicago, where night operations exist, meat cutters are on duty whenever a meat department is open after 6 P.M. * * *. Even in self-service departments, ostensibly operated without employees on duty after 6 P.M., there was evidence that requisite customer services in connection with meat sales were performed by grocery clerks. In the same vein, defendants adduced evidence that in the sale of delicatessen items, which could be made after 6 P.M. from self-service cases under the contract, 'practically' always during the time the market was open the manager, or other employees, would be rearranging and restocking the cases. There was also evidence that even if it were practical to operate a self-service meat market after 6 P.M. without employees, the night operations would add to the workload in getting the meats prepared for night sales and in putting the counters in order the next day." 215 F.Supp., at 844.

Jewel challenges the unions' evidence on each of these points—arguing, for example, that its preference to have butchers on duty at night, where possible under the union contract, is not probative of the feasibility of not having butchers on duty and that the evidence that grocery clerks performed customer services within the butchers' jurisdiction was based on a single instance resulting from "entrapment" by union agents. But Jewel's argument—when considered against the historical background of union concern with working hours and operating hours and the virtually uniform recognition by employers of the intimate relationship between the two subjects, as manifested by bargaining proposals in 1957, 1959, and 1961—falls far short of a showing that the trial judge's ultimate findings were clearly erroneous.

Judgment reversed and case remanded to the United States District Court for the Northern District of Illinois for further proceedings in conformity with the judgment of this Court.

MR. JUSTICE DOUGLAS, with whom MR. JUSTICE BLACK and MR. JUSTICE CLARK concur, dissenting.

If we followed Allen Bradley Co. v. Local Union No. 3, * * * we would hold with the Court of Appeals that this multi-employer agreement with the union not to sell meat between 6 p.m. and 9 a.m. was not immunized from the antitrust laws and that respondent's evidence made out a prima facie case that it was in fact a violation of the Sherman Act.

If, in the present case, the employers alone agreed not to sell meat from 6 p.m. to 9 a.m., they would be guilty of an anti-competitive practice, barred by the antitrust laws. Absent an agreement or conspiracy, a proprietor can keep his establishment open for such hours as he chooses. Cf. Textile Workers v. Darlington Mfg. Co., 380 U.S. 263, 85 S.Ct. 994. My Brother WHITE recognizes, as he must, that the agreement in this case has an "effect on competition [that] is apparent and real" and that it is an "obvious restraint on the product market." That Jewel has been coerced by the unions into respecting this agreement means that Jewel cannot use convenience of shopping hours as a means of competition. * * *

At the conclusion of respondent's case, the District Court dismissed Associated and Bromann from the action, which was tried without a jury, on the ground that there was no evidence of a conspiracy between Associated and the unions. But in the circumstances of this case the collective bargaining agreement itself, of which the District Court said there was clear proof, was evidence of a conspiracy among the employers with the unions to impose the marketing-hours restriction on Jewel via a strike threat by the unions. This tended to take from the merchants who agreed among themselves their freedom to work their own hours and to subject all who, like Jewel, wanted to sell meat after 6 p.m. to the coercion of threatened strikes, all of which if done in concert only by businessmen would violate the antitrust laws. * * *

In saying that there was no conspiracy, the District Court failed to give any weight to the collective bargaining agreement itself as evidence of a conspiracy and to the context in which it was written. This Court makes the same mistake. We said in Allen Bradley Co. v. Local Union No. 3, supra, 325 U.S. at 808, 65 S.Ct. at 1539, "* * * we think Congress never intended that unions could, consistently with the Sherman Act, aid nonlabor groups to create business monopolies and to control the marketing of goods and services." Here the contract of the unions with a large number of employers shows it was planned and designed not merely to control but entirely to prohibit "the marketing of goods and services" from 6 p.m. until 9 a.m. the next day. Some merchants relied chiefly on price competition to draw trade; others employed courtesy, quick service, and keeping their doors open long hours to meet the convenience of customers. The unions here induced a large group of merchants to use their collective strength to hurt others who wanted the competitive advantage of selling meat after 6 p.m. Unless Allen Bradley is either overruled or greatly impaired, the unions can no more aid a group of businessmen to force their competitors to follow uniform store marketing hours than to force them to sell at fixed prices. Both practices take away the freedom of traders to carry on their business in their own competitive fashion.

My Brother WHITE'S conclusion that the concern of the union members over *marketing* hours is "immediate and direct" depends upon there being a necessary connection between marketing hours and working hours. That connection is found in the District Court's finding that "in stores where meat is sold at night it is impractical to operate without either butchers or other employees." 215 F.Supp. 839, 846. It is, however, undisputed that on some nights Jewel does so operate in some of its stores in Indiana, and even in Chicago it sometimes operates without butchers at night in the sale of fresh poultry and sausage, which are exempt from the union ban.

It is said that even if night self-service could be carried on without butchers, still the union interest in store hours would be immediate and direct because competitors would have to stay open too or be put at a disadvantage—and some of these competitors would be non-self-service stores that would have to employ union butchers at night. But Allen Bradley forecloses such an expansive view of the labor exemption to the antitrust laws.

MR. JUSTICE GOLDBERG, with whom MR. JUSTICE HARLAN and MR. JUSTICE STEWART join, dissenting from the opinion but concurring in the reversal in No. 48 [Pennington] and concurring in the judgment of the Court in No. 240 [Jewel Tea].

Stripped of all the pejorative adjectives and reduced to their essential facts, both Pennington and Jewel Tea represent refusals by judges to give full effect to congressional action designed to prohibit judicial intervention via the antitrust route in legitimate collective bargaining. The history of these cases furnishes fresh evidence of the observation that in this area, necessarily involving a determination of "what public policy in regard to the industrial struggle demands," Duplex Printing Press Co. v. Deering, 254 U.S. 443, 479, 485, 41 S.Ct. 172, 183, 65 L.Ed. 349 (dissenting opinion of Mr. Justice Brandeis), "courts have neither the aptitude nor the criteria for reaching sound decisions." Cox, Labor and the Antitrust Laws—A Preliminary Analysis, 104 U.Pa.L.Rev. 252, 269–270 (1955); see Winter, Collective Bargaining and Competition: The Application of Antitrust Standards to Union Activities, 73 Yale L.J. 14 (1963).

I.

Pennington presents a case of a union negotiating with the employers in the industry for wages, fringe benefits, and working conditions. Despite allegations of conspiracy, which connotes clandestine activities, it is no secret that the United Mine Workers acting to further what it considers to be the best interest of its members, espouses a philosophy of achieving uniform high wages, fringe benefits, and good working conditions. As the *quid pro quo* for this, the Union is willing to accept the burdens and consequences of automation. Further, it acts upon the view that the existence of marginal operators who cannot afford these high wages, fringe benefits, and good working conditions does not serve the best interests of the working miner but, on the contrary, depresses wage standards and perpetuates undesirable conditions. This has been the articulated policy of the Union since 1933. See Baratz, The Union and the Coal Industry 62–74 (1955). The Mine Workers has openly stated its preference, if need be, for a reduced working force in the industry, with those employed working at high wages rather than for greater total employment at lesser wage rates. Ibid. * * * Consistent with this view, the Union welcomes automation, insisting only that the workers participate in its benefits.[1]

Jewel Tea presents another and different aspect of collective bargaining philosophy. The Chicago Local of the Amalgamated Meat Cutters bargains for its members with small, independent service butchers as well as large automated self-service chains. It seeks from both a uniform policy that no fresh meat be sold after 6 p.m. This union policy, as my Brother WHITE recognizes, * * * has a long history dating back to 1919 and has grown out of the Union's struggle to reduce the long, arduous hours worked by butchers, which in 1919 were 81 hours per week. It took a long strike to achieve the first limitation on hours in 1920, and it has required hard extensive collective bargaining since then to maintain the policy and further reduce the number of hours worked. While it is claimed by Jewel Tea, a large operator of automated self-service markets, that it can operate beyond the set hours without increasing the work of butchers or having others do butchers' work—a claim rejected by the trial court and the majority of this Court—it is conceded, on this record, that the small, independent service operators cannot do so. Therefore to the extent that the Union's uniform policy limiting hours of selling fresh meat has the effect of aiding one group of employers at the expense of another, here the union policy, unlike that in Pennington, aids the small employers at the expense of the large.

Although evidencing these converse economic effects, both Pennington and Jewel Tea * * * involve conventional collective bargaining on wages, hours, and working conditions—mandatory subjects of bargaining under the National Labor Relations Act * * *. Yet the Mine Workers' activity in Pennington was held subject to an antitrust action by two lower courts. This decision was based upon a jury determination that the Union's economic philosophy is undesirable, and it resulted in an award against the Union of treble damages of $270,000 and $55,000 extra for respondent's attorneys' fees. In Jewel Tea, the Union has also been subjected to an antitrust suit in which a court of appeals, with its own notions as to what butchers are legitimately interested in, would subject the Union to a treble damage judgment in an as yet undetermined amount.

Regretfully these cases, both in the lower courts and in expressions in the various opinions filed today in this Court, * * * constitute a throwback to past days when courts allowed antitrust actions against unions and employers engaged in conventional collective bargaining, because "a judge considered" the union or employer conduct in question to be "socially or economically" objectionable. Duplex Printing Press Co. v. Deering, supra, 254 U.S. at 485, 41 S.Ct. at 183 (dissenting opinion of Mr. Justice Brandeis).

1. For these policies, John L. Lewis, the long-time head of the Mine Workers, has been variously condemned and praised. * * *

It is necessary to recall that history to place the cases before us in proper perspective.

II.

[JUSTICE GOLDBERG reviewed the antitrust legislation and the earlier cases.]

To round out this history it should be noted that, while rejecting attempts to restrict or eliminate the labor exemption from the antitrust laws, Congress, in the 1947 Taft-Hartley Act * * * and the 1959 Landrum-Griffin Act, * * * has taken steps to proscribe union activities which, in its legislative judgment, it considers to be detrimental to the public good. Consistent, however, with its policy of not turning the lawfulness of union conduct on subjective judgments of purpose or effect, a policy expressed in §§ 6 and 20 of the Clayton Act and in the Norris-LaGuardia Act, Congress did this by making unlawful certain specific union activities under the National Labor Relations Act. Congress, for example, has curbed the secondary boycott in § 8(b)(4)(B) of the National Labor Relations Act * * *. The jurisdictional strike is regulated by § 8(b)(4)(D) in conjunction with § 10(k) of the Act.[10] Union opposition to automation has been regulated to the limited extent Congress wished to do so by § 8(b)(6) of the Act. Strikes and pressure by minority unions for organization or recognition are controlled by §§ 8(b)(4)(C) and 8(b)(7) of the Act. Union restrictions on contracting out and subcontracting of work are delineated by § 8(e) of the Act.[13] For the issue presently before us, it is most significant that in enacting this last prohibition, Congress in the exercise of its legislative judgment, specifically excepted the unusual situations existing in the garment and building industries. Such exceptions for particular industries which may be proper subjects of legislative discretion, would, of course, be most difficult for courts to make in employing a broad proscription like the Sherman Act.

III.

In my view, this history shows a consistent congressional purpose to limit severely judicial intervention in collective bargaining under cover of the wide umbrella of the antitrust laws, and, rather, to deal with what Congress deemed to be specific abuses on the part of labor unions by specific proscriptions in the labor statutes. I believe that the Court should respect this history of congressional purpose * * *. [T]he Court should hold that, in order to effectuate congressional intent, collective bargaining activity concerning mandatory subjects of bargaining under the Labor Act is not subject to the antitrust laws. This rule flows directly from the Hutcheson holding that a union acting as a union, in the interests of its members, and not acting to fix prices or allocate markets in aid of an employer conspiracy to accomplish these objects, with only indirect union benefits, is not subject to challenge under the antitrust laws. To hold that mandatory collective

10. As an antitrust issue, see United States v. Hutcheson, supra.

13. In Pennington the collective bargaining agreement restricted subleasing, which is a mining form of subcontracting. Indeed, the Pennington case bristles with potential unfair labor practices. * * * A "protective wage clause" in the national wage agreement provided that signatory companies would not buy coal mined under terms and conditions less favorable than those in the national wage agreement. The Labor Board has held that this type of clause violates § 8(e) of the NLRA * * *.

bargaining is completely protected would effectuate the congressional policies of encouraging free collective bargaining, subject only to specific restrictions contained in the labor laws, and of limiting judicial intervention in labor matters via the antitrust route * * *.

* * * [The] national scheme [of free collective bargaining] would be virtually destroyed by the imposition of Sherman Act criminal and civil penalties upon employers and unions engaged in such collective bargaining. To tell the parties that they must bargain about a point but may be subject to antitrust penalties if they reach an agreement is to stultify the congressional scheme.

Moreover, mandatory subjects of bargaining are issues as to which union strikes may not be enjoined by either federal or state courts. To say that the union can strike over such issues but that both it and the employer are subject to possible antitrust penalties for making collective bargaining agreements concerning them is to assert that Congress intended to permit the parties to collective bargaining to wage industrial warfare but to prohibit them from peacefully settling their disputes. * * *

Congress has also recognized that some labor organizations seek, as in Pennington, through industry-wide bargaining, to eliminate differences in labor standards among employers. This was common knowledge in 1935 when the Wagner Act was enacted. The aims and practices of unions engaging in industry-wide bargaining were well known in 1947 at the time of the Taft-Hartley revision. Then and on subsequent occasions Congress refused to enact bills to restrict or prohibit industry-wide bargaining. * * * Nor can it be seriously argued that multi-employer bargaining, as in Jewel Tea, introduces an illegal element or is otherwise opposed to the national labor policy. Indeed, this Court to implement congressional policy sanctioning multi-employer bargaining, permitted employers to resort, under certain circumstances, to lockouts to protect the integrity of the multi-employer bargaining unit. See National Labor Relations Board v. Truck Drivers Local Union No. 449, etc. [Buffalo Linen], 353 U.S. 87, 77 S.Ct. 643, 1 L.Ed.2d 676; National Labor Relations Board v. Brown, 380 U.S. 278, 85 S.Ct. 980.[20] The wisdom of permitting industry-wide and multi-employer bargaining is for Congress to decide * * *.

IV.

The Court in Pennington today ignores this history of the discredited judicial attempt to apply the antitrust laws to legitimate collective bargaining activity, and it flouts the clearly expressed congressional intent that, since "[t]he labor of a human being is not a commodity or article of

20. Today, between 80% and 100% of the workers under union agreement are covered by multi-employer contracts in such important industries as men's and women's clothing, coal mining, building construction, hotel, longshoring, maritime, trucking and warehousing. Between 60% and 80% of unionized workers are under multi-employer pacts in baking, book and job printing, canning and preserving, textile dyeing and finishing, glass and glassware, malt liquor, pottery and retail trades. See Reynolds, Labor Economics and Labor Relations 170 (3d ed. 1959). Furthermore, in some other major industries relatively uniform terms of employment are obtained through the negotiation of a contract with one leading employer and the subsequent acceptance of that contract's key provisions, with only minor modifications by the other employers in the industry. See Chamberlain, Collective Bargaining 259–263 (1951).

commerce," [21] the antitrust laws do not proscribe, and the national labor policy affirmatively promotes, the "elimination of price competition based on differences in labor standards," Apex Hosiery Co. v. Leader, supra, 310 U.S., at 503, 60 S.Ct., at 997. While purporting to recognize the indisputable fact that the elimination of employer competition based on substandard labor conditions is a proper labor union objective endorsed by our national labor policy and that, therefore, "a union may make wage agreements with a multi-employer bargaining unit and may in pursuance of its own union interests seek to obtain the same terms from other employers," Pennington, 381 U.S., at 665, 85 S.Ct., at 1591, the Court holds that "a union forfeits its exemption from the antitrust laws when it is clearly shown that it has agreed with one set of employers to impose a certain wage scale on other bargaining units." Ibid.

This rule * * * will severely restrict free collective bargaining. Since collective bargaining inevitably involves and requires discussion of the impact of the wage agreement reached with a particular employer or group of employers upon competing employers, the effect of the Court's decision will be to bar a basic element of collective bargaining from the conference room. If a union and employer are prevented from discussing and agreeing upon issues which are, in the great majority of cases, at the central core of bargaining, unilateral force will inevitably be substituted for rational discussion and agreement. Plainly and simply, the Court would subject both unions and employers to antitrust sanctions, criminal as well as civil, if in collective bargaining they concluded a wage agreement and, as part of the agreement, the union has undertaken to use its best efforts to have this wage accepted by other employers in the industry. Indeed, the decision today even goes beyond this. Under settled antitrust principles which are accepted by the Court as appropriate and applicable, which were the basis for jury instructions in Pennington, and which will govern it upon remand, there need not be direct evidence of an express agreement. Rather the existence of such an agreement, express or implied, may be inferred from the conduct of the parties. See, e.g., Interstate Circuit, Inc. v. United States, 306 U.S. 208, 59 S.Ct. 467, 83 L.Ed. 610; American Tobacco Co. v. United States, 328 U.S. 781, 66 S.Ct. 1125, 90 L.Ed. 1575; United States v. Paramount Pictures, Inc., 334 U.S. 131, 68 S.Ct. 915, 92 L.Ed. 1260; Theatre Enterprises, Inc. v. Paramount Film Distributing Corp., 346 U.S. 537, 74 S.Ct. 257, 98 L.Ed. 273. * * * As the facts of Pennington illustrate, the jury is therefore at liberty to infer such an agreement from "clear" evidence that a union's philosophy that high wages and mechanization are desirable has been accepted by a group of employers and that the union has attempted to achieve like acceptance from other employers. For, as I have pointed out, stripped of all adjectives, this is what Pennington presents. Yet the Court today holds "the alleged agreement between UMW and the large operators to secure uniform labor standards throughout the industry, if proved, was not exempt from the antitrust laws." * * *

The rational thing for an employer to do, when faced with union demands he thinks he cannot meet, is to explain why, in economic terms, he believes that he cannot agree to the union requests. Indeed, the Labor Act's

---

21. Section 6 of the Clayton Act.

compulsion to bargain in good faith requires that he meaningfully address himself to the union's requests. See National Labor Relations Board v. Truitt Mfg. Co., 351 U.S. 149, 76 S.Ct. 753, 100 L.Ed. 1027. A recurring and most understandable reason given by employers for their resistance to union demands is that competitive factors prevent them from accepting the union's proposed terms. Under the Court's holding today, however, such a statement by an employer may start both the employer and union on the road to antitrust sanctions, criminal and civil. For a jury may well interpret such discussion and subsequent union action as showing an implicit or secret agreement to impose uniform standards on other employers. Nor does the Court's requirement that there be "direct or indirect evidence of the conspiracy" * * *—whatever those undefined terms in the opinion may mean— provide any substantial safeguard for uninhibited collective bargaining discussions. * * *

Furthermore, in order to determine whether, under the Court's standard, a union is acting unilaterally or pursuant to an agreement with employers, judges and juries will inevitably be drawn to try to determine the purpose and motive of union and employer collective bargaining activities. The history I have set out, however, makes clear that Congress intended to foreclose judges and juries from roaming at large in the area of collective bargaining, under cover of the antitrust laws, by inquiry into the purpose and motive of the employer and union bargaining on mandatory subjects. Such roaming at large, experience shows, leads to a substitution of judicial for congressional judgment as to how collective bargaining should operate. * * *

In Pennington, central to the alleged conspiracy is the claim that hourly wage rates and fringe benefits were set at a level designed to eliminate the competition of the smaller nonunion companies by making the labor cost too high for them to pay. Indeed, the trial judge charged that there was no violation of the Sherman Act in the establishing of wages and welfare payments through the national contract, "provided" the mine workers and the major coal producers had not agreed to fix "high" rates "in order to drive the small coal operators out of business." Under such an instruction, if the jury found the wage scale too "high" it could impute to the union the unlawful purpose of putting the nonunion operators out of business. It is clear that the effect of the instruction, therefore, was to invite 12 jurymen to become arbiters of the economic desirability of the wage scale in the Nation's coal industry. The Court would sustain the judgment based on this charge and thereby put its stamp of approval on this role for courts and juries.

The Court's approval of judges and juries determining the permissible wage scale for working men in an industry is confirmed by the Court's express statement "there are limits to what a union or an employer may offer or extract in the name of wages," Pennington, 381 U.S., at 665, 85 S.Ct., at 1591. To allow a jury to infer an illegal "conspiracy" from the agreed-upon wage scale means that the jury must determine at what level the wages could be fixed without impelling the parties into the ambit of the antitrust laws. Is this not another way of saying that, via the antitrust route, a judge or jury may determine, according to its own notions of what is economically sound, the amount of wages that a union can properly ask for or that an employer can pay? It is clear, as experience shows, that judges and juries neither have the aptitude nor possess the criteria for making this kind of judgment. In Pennington, absent the alleged conspiracy, would the wage rate and fringe benefits have been lower? Should they have been lower? If Pennington were an action for injunctive relief, what would be the appropriate remedy to reach the labor cost which is at the heart of the alleged antitrust violation? A judicial determination of the wage rate? A judicial nullification of the existing rate with a direction to negotiate a lower one? I cannot believe that Congress has sanctioned judicial wage control under the umbrella of the Sherman Act, for, absent a national emergency, Congress has never legislated wage control in our free-enterprise economy.

* * *

* * * Only rarely will there be direct evidence of an express agreement between a union and an employer to impose a particular wage scale on other employers. In most cases, as was true of Pennington, the trial court will instruct the jury that such an illegal agreement may be inferred from the conduct—"indirect evidence"—of the union and employers. To allow a court or a jury to infer an illegal agreement from collective bargaining conduct inevitably requires courts and juries to analyze the terms of collective bargaining agreements and the purposes and motives of unions and employers in agreeing upon them. Moreover, the evidence most often available to sustain antitrust liability under the Court's theory would show, as it did in Pennington, simply that the motives of the union and employer coincide—the union seeking high wages and protection from low-wage, nonunion competition, and the employer who pays high wages seeking protection from competitors who pay lower wages. When there is this coincidence of motive, does the illegality of the "conspiracy" turn on whether the Union pursued its goal of a uniform wage policy through strikes and not negotiation? As I read the Court's opinion this is precisely what the result turns on and thus unions are forced, in order to show that they have not illegally "agreed" with employers, to pursue their aims through strikes and not negotiations. Yet, it is clear that such a result was precisely what the National Labor Relations Act was designed to prevent. The only alternative to resolution of collective bargaining issues by force available to the parties under the Court's holding is the encouragement of fraud and deceit. An employer will be forced to take a public stand against a union's wage demands, even if he is willing to accept them, lest a too ready acceptance be used by a jury to infer an agreement between the union and employer that the same wages will be sought from other employers. Yet I have always thought that in collective bargaining, even more than in other areas of contractual agreement, the objective is open covenants openly arrived at.

* * *

[L]abor contracts establishing more or less standardized wages, hours, and other terms and conditions of employment in a given industry or market area are often secured either through bargaining with multi-employer associations or through bargaining with market leaders that sets a "pattern" for agreements on labor standards with other employers. These are two similar systems used to achieve the identical result of fostering labor peace through the negotiation of uniform labor standards in an industry. Yet the Court makes antitrust liability for both unions and employers turn on which of these two systems is used. It states that uniform wage agreements may be made with multi-employer units but an agreement cannot be made to affect employers outside the formal bargaining unit. I do not believe that the Court understands the effect of its ruling in terms of the practical realities of the automobile, steel, rubber, shipbuilding, and numerous other industries which follow the policy of pattern collective bargaining. See Chamberlain, Collective Bargaining 259–263 (1951); note 20, supra. I also do not understand why antitrust liability should turn on the form of unit determination rather than the substance of the collective bargaining impact on the industry.

Finally, it seems clear that the essential error at the core of the Court's reasoning is that it ignores the express command of Congress that "[t]he labor of a human being is not a commodity or article of commerce," and therefore that the antitrust laws do not prohibit the "elimination of price competition based on differences in labor standards." Apex Hosiery Co. v. Leader, supra, 310 U.S. at 503, 60 S.Ct. at 997. This is made clear by a simple question that the Court does not face. Where there is an "agreement" to seek uniform wages in an industry, in what item is competition restrained? The answer to this question can only be that competition is restrained in employee wage standards. That is, the union has agreed to restrain the free competitive market for labor by refusing to provide labor to other employers below the uniform rate. Under such an analysis, it would seem to follow that the existence of a union itself constitutes a restraint of trade, for the object of a union is to band together the individual workers in an effort, by common action, to obtain better wages and working conditions—i.e., to obtain a higher price for their labor. The very purpose and effect of a labor union is to limit the power of an employer to use competition among workingmen to drive down wage rates and enforce substandard conditions of employment. If competition between workingmen to see who will work for the lowest wage is the ideal, all labor unions should be eliminated. * * *

V.

The judicial expressions in Jewel Tea represent another example of the reluctance of judges to give full effect to congressional purpose in this area and the substitution by judges of their views for those of Congress as to how free collective bargaining should operate. In this case the Court of Appeals would have held the Union subject to the Sherman Act's criminal and civil penalties because in the court's social and economic judgment, the determination of the hours at which meat is to be sold is a "proprietary" matter within the exclusive control of management and thus the Union had no legitimate interest in bargaining over it. My Brother DOUGLAS * * * would affirm this judgment apparently because the agreement was reached through a multi-employer bargaining unit. But, as I have demonstrated above, there is nothing even remotely illegal about such bargaining. * * *

* * * [M]y Brother WHITE indicates that he would sustain a judgment here, even absent evidence of union abetment of an independent conspiracy of employers, if the trial court had found "that self-service markets could actually operate without butchers, at least for a few hours after 6 p.m., that no encroachment on butchers' work would result and that

the workload of butchers during normal working hours would not be substantially increased * * *." * * * Such a view seems to me to be unsupportable. It represents a narrow, confining view of what labor unions have a legitimate interest in preserving and thus bargaining about. Even if the self-service markets could operate after 6 p.m., without their butchers and without increasing the work of their butchers at other times, the result of such operation can reasonably be expected to be either that the small, independent service markets would have to remain open in order to compete, thus requiring their union butchers to work at night, or that the small, independent service markets would not be able to operate at night and thus would be put at a competitive disadvantage.[26] Since it is clear that the large, automated self-service markets employ fewer butchers per volume of sales than service markets do, the Union certainly has a legitimate interest in keeping service markets competitive so as to preserve jobs. Job security of this kind has been recognized to be a legitimate subject of union interest. See Order of Railroad Telegraphers v. Chicago & N.W.R. Co., 362 U.S. 330, 80 S.Ct. 761, 4 L.Ed.2d 774; Local 24 of the Intern. Broth. of Teamsters, etc. v. Oliver, 358 U.S. 283, 79 S.Ct. 297, 3 L.Ed.2d 312. * * * The direct interest of the union in not working undesirable hours by curtailing all business at those hours is, of course, a far cry from the indirect "interest" in Allen Bradley in fixing prices and allocating markets solely to increase the profits of favored employers.

Indeed, if the Union in Jewel Tea were attempting to aid the small service butcher shops and thus save total employment against automation, perhaps at a necessarily reduced wage scale, the case would present the exact opposite union philosophy from that of the Mine Workers in Pennington. Putting the opinion of the Court in Pennington together with the opinions of my Brothers DOUGLAS and WHITE in Jewel Tea, it would seem that unions are damned if their collective bargaining philosophy involves acceptance of automation (Pennington) and are equally damned if their collective bargaining philosophy involves resistance to automation (Jewel Tea). Again, the wisdom of a union adopting either philosophy is not for judicial determination. * * *

VI.

Moreover, while these cases involve suits against unions, we should not overlook the fact that if unions are held liable under the antitrust laws for collective bargaining activities concerning mandatory subjects, then the employer parties to this mandatory collective bargaining would also be subject to antitrust penalties, criminal and civil. * * * The unfairness to employers of this situation is aptly illustrated by the record facts of Pennington. From 1930 until the formation of the Bituminous Coal Operators' Association and the negotiation of a uniform wage agreement between the Association and the union in 1950, bargaining in the coal industry was highlighted by bitter and protracted negotiations. * * *

* * * Since this change in 1950, collective bargaining has been, to a marked degree, stabilized in the industry. There have been no governmen-

---

26. It is clear that the small service butcher shops cannot operate at night without butchers on duty. There is no doubt that the Union could bargain with them as to the hours its members worked.

tal seizures or nation-wide strikes. Collective bargaining problems have not ended as a matter of course in Labor Board or court proceedings, or in governmental seizure or other intervention. While the negotiations have not always been easy and many difficult issues have arisen, the procedure for solving them has gone from the earlier jungle-type economic warfare to the reasoned and rational process of the conference table. * * * To apply the antitrust laws at this late date to such activities would endanger the stability which now characterizes collective bargaining in the coal industry and other basic industries with similar collective bargaining histories.
* * *

VII.

My view that Congress intended that collective bargaining activity on mandatory subjects of bargaining under the Labor Act not be subject to the antitrust laws does not mean that I believe that Congress intended that activity involving all non-mandatory subjects of bargaining be similarly exempt. The direct and overriding interest of unions in such subjects as wages, hours, and other working conditions, which Congress has recognized in making them subjects of mandatory bargaining, is clearly lacking where the subject of the agreement is price-fixing and market allocation. Moreover, such activities are at the core of the type of anticompetitive commercial restraint at which the antitrust laws are directed.

Nor does my view mean that where a union operates as a businessman, exercising a proprietary or ownership function, it is beyond the reach of the antitrust laws merely because it is a union. On the contrary, the labor exemption is inapplicable where the union acts not as a union but as an entrepreneur. * * *

Note

1. In their respective opinions in Pennington and Jewel Tea, Justices White, Douglas, and Goldberg articulate three differing points of view with regard to the drawing of the line between that which is lawful by reason of the National Labor Relations Act and that which is unlawful by reason of the antitrust laws; they disagree, in other words, on the proper accommodation of national labor and antitrust policy. How would each of them decide the three following variations of the Jewel Tea case, and why?

Case 1: The collective bargaining agreement contains no provision concerning when the markets may or may not be open for business but on this subject says merely: "No butcher shall be required or permitted to work before 9 A.M. or after 6 P.M., Monday through Saturday inclusive."

Case 2: The finding of the trial court, adequately supported by the evidence, is: "In self-service markets it is practicable to sell meat at night without either butchers or other additional employees and without any substantial effect upon the workload of butchers employed at the self-service markets."

Case 3: The finding of the trial court, adequately supported by the evidence, is: "The unions and employers in the bargaining unit agreed that the unions would use their 'best efforts' to impose the 9 A.M. to 6 P.M. marketing-hour restriction upon Jewel Tea and all other Chicago retailers of fresh meat."

2. With whom do you agree concerning the accommodation of the labor and antitrust laws—Justice White, Douglas, or Goldberg?

3. On remand of the Pennington case, the district court found the evidence insufficient to convict the United Mine Workers of a violation of the Sherman Act. Lewis v. Pennington, 257 F.Supp. 815 (E.D.Tenn.1966), affirmed, 400 F.2d 806 (6th Cir.1968). In affirming, the court of appeals stated:

> "While the jury by its verdict in the first trial of this case had found a conspiracy between the UMW and large mine operators to put smaller mine operators out of business by a preponderance of the evidence, [Trial] Judge Taylor found such a conspiracy not to have been shown by 'clear proof' at the second trial. Judge Taylor properly concluded that a degree of proof less than the 'beyond a reasonable doubt' requirement in criminal cases but greater than the 'preponderance of the evidence' standard of civil actions is necessary. 257 F.Supp. at 829. The District Court's determination that judged by this standard evidence of sufficient probity had not been offered is supported by a review of the record and is not clearly erroneous. Rule 52 F.R.Civ.P." 400 F.2d at 814.

The Sixth Circuit proved to be wrong on the "clear proof" point. In Ramsey v. United Mine Workers, 401 U.S. 302, 91 S.Ct. 658, 28 L.Ed.2d 64 (1971), a case much similar to Pennington, the Court held, 5 to 4, that the ordinary "preponderance of evidence" standard is applicable in civil antitrust actions against labor unions except with regard to proving the authority of alleged agents of the union to perform on behalf of the union the acts complained of, as to which the "clear proof" standard of Section 6 of the Norris-LaGuardia Act applies. The Court further declared: "[W]e * * * adhere to the decision in *Pennington:* * * * [T]he relevant labor and antitrust policies compel us to conclude that the alleged agreement between UMW and the large operators to secure uniform labor standards throughout the industry, if proved, was not exempt from the antitrust laws.' 381 U.S., at 669, 85 S.Ct., at 1593. Where a union, by agreement with one set of employers, insists on maintaining in other bargaining units specified wage standards ruinous to the business of those employers, it is liable under the antitrust laws for the damages caused by its agreed upon conduct." 401 U.S. at 313, 91 S.Ct. at 665.

H.A. ARTISTS & ASSOCIATES, INC. v. ACTORS' EQUITY ASSOCIATION

Supreme Court of the United States, 1981.
451 U.S. 704, 101 S.Ct. 2102, 68 L.Ed.2d 558.

Justice Stewart delivered the opinion of the Court.

The respondent, Actors' Equity Association (Equity), is a union representing the vast majority of stage actors and actresses in the United States. It enters into collective-bargaining agreements with theatrical producers that specify minimum wages and other terms and conditions of employment for those whom it represents. The petitioners are independent theatrical agents who place actors and actresses in jobs with producers. The Court of Appeals for the Second Circuit held that the respondents' system of regulation of theatrical agents is immune from antitrust liability by reason of the statutory labor exemption from the antitrust laws, H.A. Artists & Associates,

Inc. v. Actors' Equity Assn., 622 F.2d 647.[2] We granted certiorari to consider the availability of that exemption in the circumstances presented by this case. * * *

I

A

Equity is a national union that has represented stage actors and actresses since early in this century. Currently representing approximately 23,000 actors and actresses, it has collective-bargaining agreements with virtually all major theatrical producers in New York City, on and off-Broadway, and with most other theatrical producers throughout the United States. The terms negotiated with producers are the minimum conditions of employment (called "scale"); an actor or actress is free to negotiate wages or terms more favorable than the collectively bargained minima.

Theatrical agents are independent contractors who negotiate contracts and solicit employment for their clients. The agents do not participate in the negotiation of collective-bargaining agreements between Equity and the theatrical producers. If an agent succeeds in obtaining employment for a client, he receives a commission based on a percentage of the client's earnings. Agents who operate in New York City must be licensed as employment agencies and are regulated by the New York City Department of Consumer Affairs pursuant to New York law, which provides that the maximum commission a theatrical agent may charge his client is 10% of the client's compensation.

In 1928, concerned with the high unemployment rates in the legitimate theater and the vulnerability of actors and actresses to abuses by theatrical agents,[3] including the extraction of high commissions that tended to undermine collectively bargained rates of compensation, Equity unilaterally established a licensing system for the regulation of agents. The regulations permitted Equity members to deal only with those agents who obtained Equity licenses and thereby agreed to meet the conditions of representation prescribed by Equity. Those members who dealt with nonlicensed agents were subject to union discipline.

The system established by the Equity regulations was immediately challenged.[4] In Edelstein v. Gillmore, 35 F.2d 723, the Court of Appeals for the Second Circuit concluded that the regulations were a lawful effort to improve the employment conditions of Equity members. In an opinion written by Judge Swan and joined by Judge Augustus N. Hand, the court said:

> "The evils of unregulated employment agencies (using this term broadly to include also the personal representative) are set forth in the defendants' affidavits and are corroborated by common knowledge. * * * Hence the

2. The basic sources of organized labor's exemption from federal antitrust laws are §§ 6 and 20 of the Clayton Act, 38 Stat. 731 and 738, 15 U.S.C. § 17 and 29 U.S.C. § 52, and the Norris-LaGuardia Act, 47 Stat. 70, 71, and 73, 29 U.S.C. §§ 104, 105, and 113.

3. Such vulnerability was, and still remains, particularly acute for actors and ac-

tresses without established professional reputations, who have always comprised the overwhelming majority of Equity's members.

4. The challenge was grounded on allegations of common law tortious interference with business relationships.

requirement that, as a condition to writing new business with Equity's members, old contracts with its members must be made to conform to the new standards, does not seem to us to justify an inference that the primary purpose of the requirement is infliction of injury upon plaintiff, and other personal representatives in a similar situation, rather than a protection of the supposed interests of Equity's members. *The terms they insist upon are calculated to secure from personal representatives better and more impartial services, at uniform and cheaper rates, and to improve conditions of employment of actors by theater managers.* Undoubtedly the defendants intend to compel the plaintiff to give up rights under existing contracts which do not conform to the new standards set up by Equity, but, as already indicated *their motive in so doing is to benefit themselves and their fellow actors in the economic struggle.* The financial loss to plaintiff is incidental to this purpose." 35 F.2d, at 726 (emphasis added).

The essential elements of Equity's regulation of theatrical agents have remained unchanged since 1928. A member of Equity is prohibited, on pain of union discipline, from using an agent who has not, through the mechanism of obtaining an Equity license (called a "franchise") agreed to comply with the regulations. The most important of the regulations requires that a licensed agent must renounce any right to take a commission on an employment contract under which an actor or actress receives scale wages.[8] To the extent a contract includes provisions under which an actor or actress will sometimes receive scale pay—for rehearsals or "chorus" employment, for example—and sometimes more, the regulations deny the agent any commission on the scale portions of the contract. Licensed agents are also precluded from taking commissions on out-of-town expense money paid to their clients. Moreover, commissions are limited on wages within 10% of scale pay,[9] and an agent must allow his client to terminate a representation contract if the agent is not successful in procuring employment within a specified period.[10] Finally, agents are required to pay franchise fees to Equity. The fee is $200 for the initial franchise, $60 a year thereafter for each agent, and $40 for any subagent working in the office of another. These fees are deposited by Equity in its general treasury and are not segregated from other union funds.

8. The minimum, or "scale" wage varies. In August 1977, for example, the minimum weekly salary was $335 for Broadway performances, and $175 for performances off-Broadway. Scale wages are set by a collective-bargaining agreement between Equity and the producers, to which the agents are not parties. When an agent represents an actor or actress whose professional reputation is not sufficient to demand a salary higher than scale, the agent hopes to develop a relationship that will become continually more remunerative as the performer's professional reputation grows, and with it the power to demand an ever higher salary. No agent is required to represent an actor or actress whom he does not wish to represent.

9. It is Equity's view that commissions in the industry are not necessarily related to

efforts by the agents, and that an agent often functions as little more than an "order taker," who is able to collect a percentage of a client's wages for the duration of a show for doing little more than answering a producer's telephone call. Indeed, an agent may collect a commission on the salary of an actor or actress he represents even if the client obtains the job without the agent.

10. Equity argues that this restriction is necessary because there is an incentive for agents to represent as many actors and actresses as possible—and not necessarily to serve them all well—because an agent receives a commission whenever his client is employed at a salary higher than scale, regardless of the extent of his involvement in obtaining employment for the client.

In 1977, after a dispute between Equity and Theatrical Artists Representatives Associates (TARA)—a trade association representing theatrical agents—a group of agents, including the petitioners, resigned from TARA because of TARA's decision to abide by Equity's regulations. These agents also informed Equity that they would not accept Equity's regulations, or apply for franchises. The petitioners instituted this lawsuit in May 1978, contending that Equity's regulations of theatrical agents violated §§ 1 and 2 of the Sherman Act, 15 U.S.C. §§ 1, 2.

B

The District Court found, after a bench trial, that Equity's creation and maintenance of the agency franchise system were fully protected by the statutory labor exemptions from the antitrust laws, and accordingly dismissed the petitioners' complaint. H.A. Artists & Associates, Inc. v. Actors' Equity Assn., 478 F.Supp. 496 (SDNY). Among its factual conclusions, the trial court found that in the theatrical industry, agents play a critical role in securing employment for actors and actresses:

> "As a matter of general industry practice, producers seek actors and actresses for their productions through agents. Testimony in this case convincingly established that an actor without an agent does not have the same access to producers or the same opportunity to be seriously considered for a part as does an actor who has an agent. * * *" Id., at 497 * * *.

The court also found "no evidence to suggest the existence of any conspiracy between Actors' Equity and TARA or between Actors' Equity and Producers," and concluded that "[t]he Actors Equity franchising system was employed by Actors' Equity for the purpose of protecting the wages and working conditions of its members." Id., at 499.

The Court of Appeals unanimously affirmed the judgment of the District Court. It determined that the threshold issue was, under United States v. Hutcheson, 312 U.S. 219, 232, 61 S.Ct. 463, 466, 85 L.Ed. 788, whether Equity's franchising system involved any combination between Equity and any "non-labor groups" or persons who are not "parties to a labor dispute." 622 F.2d 647, 648–649. If it did, the court reasoned, the protection of the statutory labor exemption would not apply.

First, the Court of Appeals held that the District Court had not been clearly erroneous in finding no agreement, explicit or tacit, between Equity and the producers to establish or police the franchising system. Ibid. Next, the court turned to the relationship between the union and those agents who had agreed to become franchised, in order to determine whether those agreements would divest Equity's system of agency regulation of the statutory exemption. Relying on American Federation of Musicians v. Carroll, 391 U.S. 99, 88 S.Ct. 1562, 20 L.Ed.2d 460, the court concluded that the agents were themselves a "labor group," because of their substantial "economic interrelationship" with Equity, under which "the union could not eliminate wage competition among its members without regulation of the fees of the agents." 622 F.2d, at 650, 651. Accordingly, since the elimination of wage competition is plainly within the area of a union's legitimate self-interest, the court concluded that the exemption was applicable.[11]

After deciding that the central feature of Equity's franchising system—the union's exaction of an agreement by agents not to charge commissions on certain types of work—was immune from antitrust challenge, the Court of Appeals turned to the petitioners' challenge of the franchise fees exacted from agents. Equity had argued that the fees were necessary to meet its expenses in administering the franchise system, but no evidence was presented at trial to show that the costs justified the fees actually levied. The Court of Appeals suggested that if the exactions exceeded the true costs, they could not legally be collected, as such exactions would be unconnected with any of the goals of national labor policy that justify the labor antitrust exemption. Despite the lack of any cost evidence at trial, however, the appellate court reasoned that the fees were sufficiently low that a remand to the District Court on this point "would not serve any useful purpose." 622 F.2d, at 651.

II

A

Labor unions are lawful combinations that serve the collective interests of workers, but they also possess the power to control the character of competition in an industry. Accordingly, there is an inherent tension between national antitrust policy, which seeks to maximize competition, and national labor policy, which encourages co-operation among workers to improve the conditions of employment. * * *

Section 6 of the Clayton Act, 15 U.S.C. § 17, declares that human labor "is not a commodity or article of commerce," and immunizes from antitrust liability labor organizations and their members "lawfully carrying out" their "legitimate objectives." Section 20 of the Act prohibits injunctions against specified employee activities, such as strikes and boycotts, that are undertaken in the employees' self-interest and that occur in the course of disputes "concerning terms or conditions of employment," and states that none of the specified acts can be "held to be [a] violation * * * of any law of the United States." 29 U.S.C. § 52. This protection is re-emphasized and expanded in the Norris-LaGuardia Act, which prohibits federal court injunctions against single or organized employees engaged in enumerated activities,[14] and specifically forbids such injunctions notwithstanding the claim of an unlawful combination or conspiracy. While the Norris-LaGuardia Act's bar of federal court labor injunctions is not explictly phrased as an exemption from the antitrust laws, it has been interpreted broadly as a statement

---

11. The Court of Appeals recognized that even if there had been an agreement between Equity and a "non-labor group," the agreement might still have been protected from the antitrust laws under the "non-statutory" exemption. 622 F.2d, at 649, n. 1. See Connell Construction Co. v. Plumbers Local 100, 421 U.S. 616, 622, 95 S.Ct. 1830, 1835, 44 L.Ed.2d 418. See n. 19, infra.

14. As is true under the Clayton Act, the specified activities are protected only in the context of a labor dispute. The Norris-La-Guardia Act defines a labor dispute to include "any controversy concerning terms or conditions of employment, or concerning the association or representation of persons in negotiating, fixing, maintaining, changing, or seeking to arrange terms or conditions of employment, regardless of whether or not the disputants stand in the proximate relation of employer and employee. 29 U.S.C. § 113."

of congressional policy that the courts must not use the antitrust laws as a vehicle to interfere in labor disputes.

In United States v. Hutcheson, 312 U.S. 219, 61 S.Ct. 463, 85 L.Ed. 788, the Court held that labor unions acting in their self-interest and not in combination with nonlabor groups enjoy a statutory exemption from Sherman Act liability. After describing the congressional responses to judicial interference in union activity, id., at 229–230, 61 S.Ct., at 464–465, the Court declared that

> "[s]o long as a union acts in its self-interest and does not combine with non-labor groups, the licit and the illicit under § 20 [of the Clayton Act] are not to be distinguished by any judgment regarding the wisdom or unwisdom, the rightness or wrongness, the selfishness or unselfishness of the end of which the particular union activities are the means," Id., at 232, 61 S.Ct., at 466 (footnote omitted).

The Court explained that this exemption derives not only from the Clayton Act, but also from the Norris-LaGuardia Act, particularly its definition of a "labor dispute," see n. 14, supra, in which Congress "reasserted the original purpose of the Clayton Act by infusing into it the immunized trade union activities as redefined by the later Act." 312 U.S., at 236, 61 S.Ct., at 468. Thus under *Hutcheson,* no federal injunction may issue over a "labor dispute," and "§ 20 [of the Clayton Act] removes all such allowable conduct from the taint of being a 'violation of any law of the United States,' including the Sherman Act." Ibid.[16]

The statutory exemption does not apply when a union combines with a "non-labor group." *Hutcheson,* 312 U.S., at 232, 61 S.Ct., at 466. * * * Congress "intended to outlaw business monopolies. A business monopoly is no less such because a union participates, and such participation is a violation of the Act." [Allen Bradley v. Electrical Workers, 325 U.S.], at 811, 65 S.Ct., at 1540.[19]

16. See also Apex Hosiery Co. v. Leader, 310 U.S. 469, 60 S.Ct. 982, 84 L.Ed. 1311. There, in the Term preceding that in which the *Hutcheson* case was decided, the Court reasoned that the Sherman Act prohibits only restraints on "commercial competition," id., at 497, 499, 510–511, 60 S.Ct., at 994, 995, 1001— or those market restraints designed to monopolize supply, control prices, or allocate product distribution—and that unions are not liable where they merely further their own goals in the labor market.

19. Even where there are union agreements with nonlabor groups that may have the effect of sheltering the nonlabor groups from competition in product markets, the Court has recognized a "nonstatutory" exemption to shield such agreements if they are intimately related to the union's vital concerns of wages, hours and working conditions. See, e.g., Meat Cutters v. Jewel Tea, 381 U.S. 676, 85 S.Ct. 1596, 14 L.Ed.2d 640. This nonstatutory exemption was described as follows in Connell Construction Co. v. Plumbers & Steamfitters, 421 U.S. 616, 622, 95 S.Ct. 1830, 1835, 44 L.Ed.2d 418:

"The Court has recognized * * * that a proper accommodation between the congressional policy favoring collective bargaining under the NLRA and the congressional policy favoring free competition in business markets requires that some union-employer agreements be accorded a limited nonstatutory exemption from antitrust sanctions.

* * *

"The nonstatutory exemption has its source in the strong labor policy favoring the association of employees to eliminate competition over wages and working conditions. Union success in organizing workers and standardizing wages ultimately will affect price competition among employers, but the goals of federal labor law never could be achieved if this effect on business competition were held a violation of the antitrust laws. The Court therefore has acknowledged that labor policy requires tolerance for the lessening of business competition based on differences in wages and working conditions." (Citation omitted.)

Neither the District Court nor the Court of Appeals in this case decided whether the non-

B

The Court of Appeals properly recognized that the threshold issue was to determine whether or not Equity's franchising of agents involved any combination between Equity and any "non-labor groups," or persons who are not "parties to a labor dispute." 622 F.2d, at 649 (quoting *Hutcheson,* 312 U.S., at 232, 61 S.Ct., at 466). And the court's conclusion that the trial court had not been clearly erroneous in its finding that there was no combination between Equity and the theatrical producers [21] to create or maintain the franchise system is amply supported by the record.

The more difficult problem is whether the combination between Equity and the agents who agreed to become franchised was a combination with a "nonlabor group." The answer to this question is best understood in light of Musicians v. Carroll, 391 U.S. 99, 88 S.Ct. 1562, 20 L.Ed.2d 460. There, four orchestra leaders, members of the American Federation of Musicians, brought an action based on the Sherman Act challenging the union's unilateral system of regulating "club dates," or one-time musical engagements. These regulations, *inter alia,* enforced a closed shop; required orchestra leaders to engage a minimum number of "sidemen," or instrumentalists; prescribed minimum prices for local engagements; [22] prescribed higher minimum prices for traveling orchestras; and permitted leaders to deal only with booking agents licensed by the union.

Without disturbing the finding of the Court of Appeals that the orchestra leaders were employers and independent contractors, the Court concluded that they were nonetheless a "labor group" and parties to a "labor dispute" within the meaning of the Norris-LaGuardia Act, and thus that their involvement in the union regulatory scheme was not an unlawful combination between "labor" and "non-labor" groups. The Court agreed with the trial court that the applicable test was whether there was "job or wage competition or some other economic interrelationship affecting legitimate union interests between the union members and the independent contractors." 391 U.S., at 106, 88 S.Ct., at 1567.

The Court also upheld the restrictions on booking agents, who were *not* involved in job or wage competition with union members. Accordingly, these restrictions had to meet the "other economic interrelationship" branch of the disjunctive test quoted above. And the test was met because those restrictions were "at least as intimately bound up with the subject of wages ' * * * as the price floors.' " Id., at 113, 88 S.Ct., at 1570. The Court noted that the booking agent restriction had been adopted, in part, because

---

statutory exemption would independently shield the respondent from the petitioner's antitrust claims. See n. 11, supra.

21. As the employers of Equity's members, producers are plainly a "non-labor group." Employers almost always will be a "non-labor group," although an exception has been recognized, for example, when the employer himself is in job competition with his employees. See American Federation of Musicians v. Carroll, 391 U.S. 99, 88 S.Ct. 1562, 20 L.Ed.2d 460 (orchestra leaders who both lead an orchestra and play an instrument).

22. These consisted of a minimum scale for sidemen, a "leader's fee," which was twice the sidemen's scale in orchestras of at least four, and an additional 8% for social security, unemployment insurance, and other expenses. In addition, if a leader did not appear but designated a subleader, and four or more musicians performed, the leader was required to pay from his leader's fee 1.5 times the sidemen's scale to the subleader.

agents had "charged exorbitant fees, and booked engagements for musicians at wages * * * below union scale." [23]

C

The restrictions challenged by the petitioners in this case are very similar to the agent restrictions upheld in the *Carroll* case. The essential features of the regulatory scheme are identical: members are permitted to deal only with agents who have agreed (1) to honor their fiduciary obligations by avoiding conflicts of interest, (2) not to charge excessive commissions and (3) not to book members for jobs paying less than the union minimum. And as in *Carroll*, Equity's regulation of agents developed in response to abuses by employment agents who occupy a critical role in the relevant labor market. The agent stands directly between union members and jobs, and is in a powerful position to evade the union's negotiated wage structure.

The peculiar structure of the legitimate theater industry, where work is intermittent, where it is customary if not essential for union members to secure employment through agents, and where agents' fees are calculated as a percentage of a member's wage, makes it impossible for the union to defend even the integrity of the minimum wages it has negotiated without regulation of agency fees.[27] The regulations are "brought within the labor exemption * * * [because they are] necessary to assure that scale wages will be paid. * * *" *Carroll*, 391 U.S., at 112, 88 S.Ct., at 1570. They "embody a direct frontal attack upon a problem thought to threaten the maintenance of the basic wage structure." Teamsters Union v. Oliver, 358 U.S. 283, at 294, 79 S.Ct. 297, at 303, 3 L.Ed.2d 312. Agents must, therefore, be considered a "labor group," and their controversy with Equity is plainly a "labor dispute" as defined in the Norris-LaGuardia Act: "representation of persons in negotiating, fixing, maintaining, changing, or seeking to arrange terms or conditions of employment, regardless of whether or not the disputants stand in the proximate relation of employer and employee." 29 U.S.C. § 113.

Agents perform a function—the representation of union members in the sale of their labor—that in most nonentertainment industries is performed exclusively by unions. In effect, Equity's franchise system operates as a substitute for maintaining a hiring hall as the representative of its members seeking employment.

Finally, Equity's regulations are clearly designed to promote the union's legitimate self-interest. *Hutcheson*, 312 U.S., at 232, 61 S.Ct., at 466. In a case such as this, where there is no direct wage or job competition between the union and the group it regulates, the *Carroll* formulation to determine the presence of a nonlabor group—whether there is "some * * * economic

23. The court did not explicitly determine whether the second prong of the *Hutcheson* test for the statutory exemption had been met, i.e., whether the union had acted in its "self-interest." But given its various findings that the challenged restrictions were designed to cope with job competition and to protect wage scales and working conditions, 391 U.S., at 108, 109, 110, 113, 88 S.Ct., at 1568, 1569, 1570, it clearly did so sub silentio.

27. The Court of Appeals found that "the union *cannot* eliminate wage competition among its members without regulation of the fees of the agents." 622 F.2d 647, 651 (emphasis added). Wage competition is prevented not only by the rule precluding commissions on scale jobs. Actors and actresses could also compete over the percentage of their wages they were willing to cede to an agent, subject only to the restrictions imposed by state law.

interrelationship affecting legitimate union interests * * *," 391 U.S., at 106, 88 S.Ct., at 1667—necessarily resolves this issue.

D

The question remains whether the fees that Equity levies upon the agents who apply for franchises are a permissible component of the exempt regulatory system. We have concluded that Equity's justification for these fees is inadequate. Conceding that *Carroll* did not sanction union extraction of franchise fees from agents, Equity suggests, only in the most general terms, that the fees are somehow related to the basic purposes of its regulations: elimination of wage competition, upholding of the union wage scale, and promotion of fair access to jobs. But even assuming that the fees no more than cover the costs of administering the regulatory system, this is simply another way of saying that without the fees, the union's regulatory efforts would not be subsidized—and that the dues of Equity's members would perhaps have to be increased to offset the loss of a general revenue source. If Equity did not impose these franchise fees upon the agents, there is no reason to believe that any of its legitimate interests would be affected.[31]

III

For the reasons stated, the judgment of the Court of Appeals is affirmed in part and reversed in part, and the case is remanded for proceedings consistent with this opinion.

It is so ordered.

JUSTICE BRENNAN, with whom THE CHIEF JUSTICE and JUSTICE MARSHALL join, concurring in part and dissenting in part.

I join all but Part II–D of the Court's opinion. That part holds that respondents' exaction of a franchise fee is not a "permissible component of the exempt regulatory system." Rather, I agree with the Court of Appeals that the approximately $12,000 collected annually in fees is not "incommensurate with Equity's expenses in maintaining a full-time employee to administer the system," 622 F.2d 647, 651 (CA2 1980), and thus is not "unconnected with any of the goals of national labor policy which justify the antitrust exemption for labor," ibid.

The Court justifies its conclusion by suggesting that, since the union could increase its dues to offset the revenue lost from invalidation of the fee system, "there is no reason to believe that any of [the union's] legitimate interests would be affected," if the fee system were found to violate the antitrust laws. The union could of course raise its dues, but the issue here is whether the conceded antitrust immunity of the franchising system includes the franchise fee.

---

31. The respondents offer union hiring hall fees as an analogy in support of Equity's collection of franchise fees. In that context, the respondents argue, without citation, a union may impose reasonable fees upon employers to meet the costs of maintaining a union-run hiring hall. But even if the respondents' statement of labor law is correct, the analogy would not be persuasive. Assuming that hiring hall fees are so imposed, the fees are borne by parties who directly benefit from the employment services of the hiring halls and are collected by the parties that provide them. That is not true in the present case.

The view expressed in the separate opinion filed today as to who are the beneficiaries of the franchising system will undoubtedly surprise the agents who brought this lawsuit.

I find somewhat incongruous the Court's conclusion that an incident of the overall system constitutes impermissible regulation, but that agents in general may be significantly regulated because they are not a "non-labor group." This incongruity is highlighted by the similarity between union hiring halls and the franchising system, a similarity which the Court itself acknowledges: "Equity's franchise system operates as a substitute for maintaining a hiring hall as the representative of its members seeking employment." The Court disregards this similarity in concluding that the franchising system does not "directly benefit" the agents who are required to pay the fees. Ante, at n. 31. It reaches this conclusion by incorrectly assuming that the only parties who directly benefit from the hiring hall and the franchising system are employers and employees and producers and actors, as the case may be. But surely the agents also benefit from the franchising system, which provides an orderly and protective mechanism for pairing actors who seek jobs with producers who seek actors. The system is thus the means by which the agents ultimately receive their commissions; it is as much the source of their livelihood as it is that of the actors.

Because the fee is an incident of a legitimate scheme of regulation and because it is commensurate in amount with the purpose for which it is sought, I would also affirm this holding of the Court of Appeals.

Note

In many parts of the country most barbers belong to the Barbers Union. The union sets minimum prices for haircuts and other services rendered by barbers. Barber shops are owned by working barbers, most of whom belong to the union. If an owner-barber is successful enough, he will hire other barbers to work in his shop. An employee-barber gets a percenctage (e. g., 75%) of the fees collected for the services he renders to customers. Would this arrangement constitute a violation of a state "Little Sherman" Act? Does the following case cast light on this question?

In Riviello v. Journeymen Barbers, 88 Cal.App.2d 499, 199 P.2d 400 (1948), three employer-barbers, operating as a partnership and employing employee-barbers, all of whom were members of the Journeymen Barbers Union, sought to enjoin that union from carrying out a threatened strike and supportive picketing. The purpose of the strike was to compel plaintiffs to enter a new collective bargaining agreement containing, inter alia, a clause requiring the plaintiffs to become members of the union. With respect to the issue thus posed, the court stated:

> "While § 921 of the Labor Code prohibits employees from attempting to compel an employer to join or refrain from joining an employer organization, that is not the problem here under discussion. Here the agreement does not attempt to compel the employer to join an employer organization, but it attempts to compel such employer, who works at the trade in competition with union members, to join an employee organization. That is clearly a proper labor objective, and is for the 'mutual aid or protection' of employees as provided in § 923 of the Labor Code, the section declaring the state policy on such questions. The effort to organize all barbers who work in the trade is clearly a legitimate interest of the barbers' union. It is evident that an employer-worker is in competition with all other barbers who are not employers. Without being subject to union sanctions for

violating the wages, hours and conditions of employment imposed on union members, the employer-worker could gain a great advantage to the detriment of the union members." 88 Cal.App.2d at 504, 199 P.2d at 403.

(The injunction was nonetheless granted against the union for the reason that the membership it sought to impose upon the employer-barbers was a "non-active" variety, shorn of the right to vote, hold office, or participate in any of the union affairs, rather than full union membership.)

CONNELL CONSTRUCTION CO. v. PLUMBERS AND STEAMFITTERS LOCAL UNION NO. 100.

Supreme Court of the United States, 1975.
421 U.S. 616, 95 S.Ct. 1830, 44 L.Ed.2d 418.

Mr. Justice Powell delivered the opinion of the Court.

The building trades union in this case supported its efforts to organize mechanical subcontractors by picketing certain general contractors, including petitioner. The union's sole objective was to compel the general contractors to agree that in letting subcontracts for mechanical work they would deal only with firms that were parties to the union's current collective-bargaining agreement. The union disclaimed any interest in representing the general contractors' employees. In this case the picketing succeeded, and petitioner seeks to annul the resulting agreement as an illegal restraint on competition under federal and state law. The union claims immunity from federal antitrust statutes and argues that federal labor regulation preempts state law.

I

Local 100 is the bargaining representative for workers in the plumbing and mechanical trades in Dallas. When this litigation began, it was party to a multiemployer bargaining agreement with the Mechanical Contractors Association of Dallas, a group of about 75 mechanical contractors. That contract contained a "most favored nation" clause, by which the union agreed that if it granted a more favorable contract to any other employer it would extend the same terms to all members of the Association.

Connell Construction Co. is a general building contractor in Dallas. It obtains jobs by competitive bidding and subcontracts all plumbing and mechanical work. Connell has followed a policy of awarding these subcontracts on the basis of competitive bids, and it has done business with both union and nonunion subcontractors. Connell's employees are represented by various building trade unions. Local 100 has never sought to represent them or to bargain with Connell on their behalf.

In November 1970, Local 100 asked Connell to agree that it would subcontract mechanical work only to firms that had a current contract with the union. It demanded that Connell sign the following agreement:

"WHEREAS, the contractor and the union are engaged in the construction industry, and

"WHEREAS, the contractor and the union desire to make an agreement applying in the event of subcontracting in accordance with Section 8(e) of the Labor Management Relations Act;

"WHEREAS, it is understood that by this agreement the contractor does not grant, nor does the union seek, recognition as the collective bargaining representative of any employees of the signatory contractor; and

"WHEREAS, it is further understood that the subcontracting limitation provided herein applies only to mechanical work which the contractor does not perform with his own employees but uniformly subcontracts to other firms;

"THEREFORE, the contractor and the union mutually agree with respect to work falling within the scope of this agreement that is to be done at the site of construction, alteration, painting or repair of any building, structure, or other works, that [if] the contractor should contract or subcontract any of the aforesaid work falling within the normal trade jurisdiction of the union, said contractor shall contract or subcontract such work only to firms that are parties to an executed, current collective bargaining agreement with Local Union 100 of the United Association of Journeymen and Apprentices of the Plumbing and Pipefitting Industry."

When Connell refused to sign this agreement, Local 100 stationed a single picket at one of Connell's major construction sites. About 150 workers walked off the job, and construction halted. Connell filed suit in state court to enjoin the picketing as a violation of Texas antitrust laws. Local 100 removed the case to federal court. Connell then signed the subcontracting agreement under protest. It amended its complaint to claim that the agreement violated §§ 1 and 2 of the Sherman Act, * * * and was therefore invalid. Connell sought a declaration to this effect and an injunction against any further efforts to force it to sign such an agreement.

By the time the case went to trial, Local 100 had submitted identical agreements to a number of other general contractors in Dallas. Five others had signed, and the union was waging a selective picketing compaign against those who resisted.

The District Court held that the subcontracting agreement was exempt from federal antitrust laws because it was authorized by the construction industry proviso to § 8(e) of the National Labor Relations Act * * *. The court also held that federal labor legislation pre-empted the State's antitrust laws. 78 L.R.R.M. 3012 (ND Tex.1971). The Court of Appeals for the Fifth Circuit affirmed, 483 F.2d 1154 (1973), with one judge dissenting. It held that Local 100's goal of organizing nonunion subcontractors was a legitimate union interest and that its efforts toward that goal were therefore exempt from federal antitrust laws. On the second issue, it held that state law was pre-empted under San Diego Building Trades Council v. Garmon, 359 U.S. 236, 79 S.Ct. 773, 3 L.Ed.2d 775 (1959). We granted certiorari on Connell's petition. * * * We reverse on the question of federal antitrust immunity and affirm the ruling on state law pre-emption.

II

The basic sources of organized labor's exemption from federal antitrust laws are §§ 6 and 20 of the Clayton Act, * * * and the Norris-LaGuardia Act * * *. These statutes declare that labor unions are not combinations or conspiracies in restraint of trade, and exempt specific union activities, including secondary picketing and boycotts, from the operation of the antitrust laws. See United States v. Hutcheson, 312 U.S. 219, 61 S.Ct. 463, 85 L.Ed. 788 (1941). They do not exempt concerted action or agreements between unions and nonlabor parties. Mine Workers v. Pennington, 381 U.S. 657, 662, 85 S.Ct. 1585, 1589, 14 L.Ed.2d 626 (1965). The Court has recognized, however, that a proper accommodation between the congressional policy favoring collective bargaining under the NLRA and the congressional policy favoring free competition in business markets requires that some union-employer agreements be accorded a limited nonstatutory exemption from antitrust sanctions. Meat Cutters v. Jewel Tea Co., 381 U.S. 676, 85 S.Ct. 1596, 14 L.Ed.2d 640 (1965).

The nonstatutory exemption has its source in the strong labor policy favoring the association of employees to eliminate competition over wages and working conditions. Union success in organizing workers and standardizing wages ultimately will affect price competition among employers, but the goals of federal labor law never could be achieved if this effect on business competition were held a violation of the antitrust laws. The Court therefore has acknowledged that labor policy requires tolerance for the lessening of business competition based on differences in wages and working conditions. See Mine Workers v. Pennington, supra, 381 U.S. at 666, 85 S.Ct. at 1591; *Jewel Tea*, supra, 381 U.S. at 692–693, 85 S.Ct. at 1603–1604 (opinion of White, J.). Labor policy clearly does not require, however, that a union have freedom to impose direct restraints on competition among those who employ its members. Thus, while the statutory exemption allows unions to accomplish some restraints by acting unilaterally, e.g., Federation of Musicians v. Carroll, 391 U.S. 99, 88 S.Ct. 1562, 20 L.Ed.2d 460 (1968), the nonstatutory exemption offers no similar protection when a union and a nonlabor party agree to restrain competition in a business market. See Allen Bradley Co. v. Electrical Workers, 325 U.S. 797, 806–811, 65 S.Ct. 1533, 1538–1541, 89 L.Ed. 1939 (1945); Cox, Labor and the Antitrust Laws—A Preliminary Analysis, 104 U.Pa.L.Rev. 252 (1955); Meltzer, Labor Unions, Collective Bargaining, and the Antitrust Laws, 32 U.Chi.L.Rev. 659 (1965).

In this case Local 100 used direct restraints on the business market to support its organizing campaign. The agreements with Connell and other general contractors indiscriminately excluded nonunion subcontractors from a portion of the market, even if their competitive advantages were not derived from substandard wages and working conditions but rather from more efficient operating methods. Curtailment of competition based on efficiency is neither a goal of federal labor policy nor a necessary effect of the elimination of competition among workers. Moreover, competition based on efficiency is a positive value that the antitrust laws strive to protect.

The multiemployer bargaining agreement between Local 100 and the Association, though not challenged in this suit, is relevant in determining the effect that the agreement between Local 100 and Connell would have on the business market. The "most favored nation" clause in the multiemployer agreement promised to eliminate competition between members of the Association and any other subcontractors that Local 100 might organize. By giving members of the Association a contractual right to insist on terms as favorable as those given any competitor, it guaranteed that the union would make no agreement that would give an unaffiliated contractor a competitive advantage over members of the Association.[1] Subcontractors in the Association thus stood to benefit from any extension of Local 100's organization, but the method Local 100 chose also had the effect of sheltering them from outside competition in that portion of the market covered by subcontracting agreements between general contractors and Local 100. In that portion of the market, the restriction on subcontracting would eliminate competition on all subjects covered by the multiemployer agreement, even on subjects unrelated to wages, hours, and working conditions.

Success in exacting agreements from general contractors would also give Local 100 power to control access to the market for mechanical subcontracting work. The agreements with general contractors did not simply prohibit subcontracting to any nonunion firm; they prohibited subcontracting to any firm that did not have a contract with Local 100. The union thus had complete control over subcontract work offered by general contractors that had signed these agreements. Such control could result in significant adverse effects on the market and on consumers—effects unrelated to the union's legitimate goals of organizing workers and standardizing working conditions. For example, if the union thought the interests of its members would be served by having fewer subcontractors competing for the available work, it could refuse to sign collective-bargaining agreements with marginal firms. Cf. Mine Workers v. Pennington, supra. Or, since Local 100 has a well-defined geographical jurisdiction, it could exclude "traveling" subcontractors by refusing to deal with them. Local 100 thus might be able to create a geographical enclave for local contractors, similar to the closed market in *Allen Bradley,* supra.

This record contains no evidence that the union's goal was anything other than organizing as many subcontractors as possible.[2] This goal was legal, even though a successful organizing campaign ultimately would reduce the competition that unionized employers face from nonunion firms. But the methods the union chose are not immune from antitrust sanctions simply because the goal is legal. Here Local 100, by agreement with several contractors, made nonunion subcontractors ineligible to compete for a portion of the available work. This kind of direct restraint on the business market has substantial anticompetitive effects, both actual and potential,

---

1. The primary effect of the agreement seems to have been to inhibit the union from offering any other employer a more favorable contract. When asked at trial whether another subcontractor could get an agreement on any different terms, Local 100's business agent answered:

"No. The agreement says that no one will be given a more favorable agreement. I couldn't, if I desired, as an agent, sign an agreement other than the ones in existence between the local contractors and the Local 100.

*　　*　　*　　*　　*

"Q. I see. So that's—in other words, once you sign that contract with the Mechanical Contractors' Association, that sets the only type of agreement which your Union can enter into with any other mechanical contractors; is that correct, sir?

"A. That is true." Tr. 45–46.

2. There was no evidence that Local 100's organizing campaign was connected with any agreement with members of the multiemployer bargaining unit, and the only evidence of agreement among those subcontractors was the "most favored nation" clause in the collective-bargaining agreement. In fact, Connell has not argued the case on a theory of conspiracy between the union and unionized subcontractors. It has simply relied on the multiemployer agreement as a factor enhancing the restraint of trade implicit in the subcontracting agreement it signed.

that would not follow naturally from the elimination of competition over wages and working conditions. It contravenes antitrust policies to a degree not justified by congressional labor policy, and therefore cannot claim a nonstatutory exemption from the antitrust laws.

There can be no argument in this case, whatever its force in other contexts, that a restraint of this magnitude might be entitled to an antitrust exemption if it were included in a lawful collective-bargaining agreement. Cf. Mine Workers v. Pennington, 381 U.S., at 664–665, 85 S.Ct., at 1590, 1591; *Jewel Tea,* 381 U.S., at 689–690, 85 S.Ct., at 1601–1602 (opinion of White, J.); id., at 709–713, 732–733, 85 S.Ct. 1614, 1616, 1626–1627 (opinion of Goldberg, J.). In this case, Local 100 had no interest in representing Connell's employees. The federal policy favoring collective bargaining therefore can offer no shelter for the union's coercive action against Connell or its campaign to exclude nonunion firms from the subcontracting market.

III

Local 100 nonetheless contends that the kind of agreement it obtained from Connell is explicitly allowed by the construction-industry proviso to § 8(e) and that antitrust policy therefore must defer to the NLRA. The majority in the Court of Appeals declined to decide this issue, holding that it was subject to the "exclusive jurisdiction" of the NLRB. 483 F.2d, at 1174. This Court has held, however, that the federal courts may decide labor law questions that emerge as collateral issues in suits brought under independent federal remedies, including the antitrust laws.[3] We conclude that § 8(e) does not allow this type of agreement.

Local 100's argument is straightforward: the first proviso to § 8(e) allows "an agreement between a labor organization and an employer in the construction industry relating to the contracting or subcontracting of work to be done at the site of the construction, alteration, painting, or repair of a building, structure or other work."[4] Local 100 is a labor organization, Connell is an employer in the construction industry, and the agreement

---

3. Meat Cutters v. Jewel Tea Co., 381 U.S. 676, 684–688, 85 S.Ct. 1596, 1599–1601, 14 L.Ed.2d 640 (1965) (opinion of White, J.); id., at 710 n. 18, 85 S.Ct., at 1614 (opinion of Goldberg, J.); cf. Vaca v. Sipes, 386 U.S. 171, 176–188, 87 S.Ct. 903, 909–916, 17 L.Ed.2d 842 (1967); Smith v. Evening News Assn., 371 U.S. 195, 83 S.Ct. 267, 9 L.Ed.2d 246 (1962).

4. Section 8(e) provides:

"It shall be an unfair labor practice for any labor organization and any employer to enter into any contract or agreement, express or implied, whereby such employer ceases or refrains or agrees to cease or refrain from handling, using, selling, transporting or otherwise dealing in any of the products of any other employer, or to cease doing business with any other person, and any contract or agreement entered into heretofore or hereafter containing such an agreement shall be to such extent unenforceable and void: *Provided,* That nothing in this subsection shall apply to an agreement between a labor organization and an employer in the construction industry relating to the contracting or subcontracting of work to be done at the site of the construction, alteration, painting, or repair of a building, structure, or other work: *Provided further,* That for the purposes of this subsection and subsection (b) [(4)(B)] of this section the terms 'any employer', 'any person engaged in commerce or an industry affecting commerce', and 'any person' when used in relation to the terms 'any other producer, processor, or manufacturer', 'any other employer', or 'any other person' shall not include persons in the relation of a jobber, manufacturer, contractor, or subcontractor working on the goods or premises of the jobber or manufacturer or performing parts of an integrated process of production in the apparel and clothing industry: *Provided further,* That nothing in this subchapter shall prohibit the enforcement of any agreement which is within the foregoing exception." 29 U.S.C. § 158(e).

covers only work "to be done at the site of construction, alteration, painting or repair of any building, structure, or other works." Therefore, Local 100 says, the agreement comes within the proviso. Connell responds by arguing that despite the unqualified language of the proviso, Congress intended only to allow subcontracting agreements within the context of a collective-bargaining relationship; that is, Congress did not intend to permit a union to approach a "stranger" contractor and obtain a binding agreement not to deal with nonunion subcontractors. On its face, the proviso suggests no such limitation. This Court has held, however, that § 8(e) must be interpreted in light of the statutory setting and the circumstances surrounding its enactment:

> "It is a 'familiar rule, that a thing may be within the letter of the statute and yet not within the statute, because not within its spirit nor within the intention of its makers.' Holy Trinity Church v. United States, 143 U.S. 457, 459, 12 S.Ct. 511, 512, 36 L.Ed. 226." National Woodwork Mfrs. Assn. v. NLRB, 386 U.S. 612, 619, 87 S.Ct. 1250, 1255, 18 L.Ed.2d 357 (1967).

Section 8(e) was part of a legislative program designed to plug technical loopholes in § 8(b)(4)'s general prohibition of secondary activities. In § 8(e) Congress broadly proscribed using contractual agreements to achieve the economic coercion prohibited by § 8(b)(4). See *National Woodwork Mfrs. Assn.,* supra, 386 U.S. at 634, 87 S.Ct. at 1262. The provisos exempting the construction and garment industries were added by the Conference Committee in an apparent compromise between the House bill which prohibited all "hot cargo" agreements, and the Senate bill, which prohibited them only in the trucking industry.[5] Although the garment-industry proviso was supported by detailed explanations in both Houses,[6] the construction-industry proviso was explained only by bare references to "the pattern of collective bargaining" in the industry.[7] It seems, however, to have been adopted as a partial substitute for an attempt to overrule this Court's decision in NLRB v. Denver Building & Construction Trades Council, 341 U.S. 675, 71 S.Ct. 943, 95 L.Ed. 1284 (1951).[8] Discussion of "special problems" in the construction

5. See H.R.Conf.Rep. No. 1147, 86th Cong., 1st Sess., 39–40 (1959), U.S.Code Cong. & Admin.News, p. 2318.

6. 105 Cong.Rec. 17327 (1959) (remarks by Sen. Kennedy); id., at 17381 (remarks by Sens. Javits and Goldwater); id., at 15539 (memorandum by Reps. Thompson and Udall); id., at 16590 (memorandum by Sen. Kennedy and Rep. Thompson). These debates are reproduced in 2 NLRB, Legislative History of the Labor-Management Reporting and Disclosure Act of 1959, pp. 1377, 1385, 1576, 1708 (1959) (hereinafter Leg.Hist. of LMRDA).

7. 105 Cong.Rec. 17899 (1959) (remarks by Sen. Kennedy); id., at 18134 (remarks by Rep. Thompson); 2 Leg.Hist. of LMRDA 1432, 1721.

8. President Eisenhower's message to Congress recommending labor reform legislation urged amendment of the secondary-boycott provisions to permit secondary activity "under certain circumstances, against secondary employers engaged in work at a *common con-* *struction site* with the primary employer." S.Doc. No. 10, 86th Cong., 1st Sess., 3 (1959) (emphasis added). Various bills introduced in both Houses included such provisions, see 2 Leg.Hist. of LMRDA 1912–1915, but neither the bill that passed the Senate nor the one that passed the House contained a *Denver Building Trades* provision. The Conference Committee proposed to include such an amendment to § 8(b)(4)(B) in the Conference agreement, along with a closely linked construction-industry exemption from § 8(e). 105 Cong.Rec. 17333 (1959) (proposed Senate resolution), 2 Leg.Hist. of LMRDA 1383. But a parliamentary obstacle killed the § 8(b)(4)(B) amendment, and only the § 8(e) proviso survived. See 105 Cong.Rec. 17728–17729, 17901–17903, 2 Leg.Hist. of LMRDA 1397–1398, 1434–1436. References to the proviso suggest that the Committee may have intended the § 8(e) proviso simply to preserve the status quo under Carpenters v. NLRB (Sand Door). 357 U.S. 93, 78 S.Ct. 1011, 2 L.Ed.2d 1186 (1958), pending action on the *Denver* industry, applicable to both the § 8(e) proviso and the attempt to overrule *Denver Building Trades,* focused on the problems of picketing a single nonunion subcontractor on a multiemployer building project, and the close relationship between contractors and subcontractors at the jobsite.[9] Congress limited the construction-industry proviso to that single situation, allowing subcontracting agreements only in relation to work done on a jobsite. In contrast to the latitude it provided in the garment-industry proviso, Congress did not afford construction unions an exemption from § 8(b)(4)(B) or otherwise indicate that they were free to use subcontracting agreements as a broad organizational weapon. In keeping with these limitations, the Court has interpreted the construction-industry proviso as

> "a measure designed to allow agreements pertaining to certain secondary activities on the construction site because of the close community of interests there, but to ban secondary-objective agreements concerning nonjobsite work, in which respect the construction industry is no different from any other." *National Woodwork Mfrs. Assn.,* 386 U.S., at 638–639, 87 S.Ct., at 1265 (footnote omitted).

Other courts have suggested that it serves an even narrower function:

> "[T]he purpose of the section 8(e) proviso was to alleviate the frictions that may arise when union men work continuously alongside nonunion men on the same construction site." Drivers Local 695 v. NLRB, 124 U.S.App.D.C. 93, 99, 361 F.2d 547, 553 (1966).

See also *Denver Building Trades,* 341 U.S., at 692–693, 71 S.Ct., at 953, (Douglas, J., dissenting); Essex County & Vicinity District Council of Carpenters v. NLRB, 332 F.2d 636, 640 (CA 3 1964).

Local 100 does not suggest that its subcontracting agreement is related to any of these policies. It does not claim to be protecting Connell's employees from having to work alongside nonunion men. The agreement apparently was not designed to protect Local 100's members in that regard, since it was not limited to jobsites on which they were working. Moreover, the subcontracting restriction applied only to the work Local 100's members would perform themselves and allowed free subcontracting of all other work, thus leaving open a possibility that they would be employed alongside nonunion subcontractors. Nor was Local 100 trying to organize a nonunion subcontractor on the building project it picketed. The union admits that it sought the agreement solely as a way of pressuring mechanical subcontractors in the Dallas area to recognize it as the representative of their employees.

If we agreed with Local 100 that the construction-industry proviso authorizes subcontracting agreements with "stranger" contractors, not limited to any particular jobsite, our ruling would give construction unions an

---

Building Trades problem in the following session. See H.R.Rep. No. 1147, *supra,* n. 5, at 39–40; 105 Cong.Rec. 17900 (1959) (report of Sen. Kennedy on Conference agreement); 2 Leg.Hist. of LMRDA 1433. Although Senator Kennedy introduced a bill to amend § 8(b)(4), S. 2643, 86th Cong., 1st Sess. (1959), it was never reported out of committee.

9. See 105 Cong.Rec. 17881 (1959) (remarks by Sen. Morse); id., at 15541 (memorandum by Reps. Thompson and Udall); id., at 15551–15552 (memorandum by Sen. Elliott); id., at 15852 (remarks by Rep. Goodell); see also id., at 20004–20005 (post-legislative remarks by Rep. Kearns); 2 Leg.Hist. of LMRDA 1425, 1577, 1588, 1684, and 1861.

almost unlimited organizational weapon.[10] The unions would be free to enlist any general contractor to bring economic pressure on nonunion subcontractors, as long as the agreement recited that it only covered work to be performed on some jobsite somewhere. The proviso's jobsite restriction then would serve only to prohibit agreements relating to subcontractors that deliver their work complete to the jobsite.

It is highly improbable that Congress intended such a result. One of the major aims of the 1959 Act was to limit "top-down" organizing campaigns, in which unions used economic weapons to force recognition from an employer regardless of the wishes of his employees.[11] Congress accomplished this goal by enacting § 8(b)(7), which restricts primary recognitional picketing, and by further tightening § 8(b)(4)(B), which prohibits the use of most secondary tactics in organizational campaigns. Construction unions are fully covered by these sections. The only special consideration given them in organizational campaigns is § 8(f), which allows "pre-hire" agreements in the construction industry, but only under careful safeguards preserving workers' rights to decline union representation. The legislative history accompanying § 8(f) also suggests that Congress may not have intended that strikes or picketing could be used to extract prehire agreements from unwilling employers.[12]

These careful limits on the economic pressure unions may use in aid of their organizational campaigns would be undermined seriously if the proviso to § 8(e) were construed to allow unions to seek subcontracting agreements, at large, from any general contractor vulnerable to picketing. Absent a clear indication that Congress intended to leave such a glaring loophole in its restrictions on "top-down" organizing, we are unwilling to read the construction-industry proviso as broadly as Local 100 suggests.[13] Instead, we

---

10. Local 100 contends, unsoundly we think, that the NLRB has decided this issue in its favor. It cites Los Angeles Building & Construction Trades Council (B & J Investment Co.), 214 N.L.R.B. No. 86, 87 L.R.R.M. 1424 (1974), and a memorandum from the General Counsel explaining his decision not to file unfair labor practice charges in a similar case, Plumbers Local 100 (Hagler Construction Co.), No. 16–CC–447 (May 1, 1974). In B & J Investment the Board approved, without comment, an administrative law judge's conclusion that the § 8(e) proviso authorized a subcontracting agreement between the Council and a general contractor who used none of his own employees in the particular construction project. The agreement in question may have been a prehire contract under § 8(f), and it is not clear that the contractor argued that it was invalid for lack of a collective-bargaining relationship. The General Counsel's memorandum in *Hagler Construction* is plainly addressed to a different argument—that a subcontracting clause should be allowed only if there is a *pre-existing* collective-bargaining relationship with the general contractor or if the general contractor has employees who perform the kind of work covered by the agreement.

11. 105 Cong.Rec. 6428–6429 (1959) (remarks of Sen. Goldwater); id., at 6648–6649 (remarks of Sen. McClellan); id., at 6664–6665 (remarks of Sen. Goldwater); id., at 14348 (memorandum of Rep. Griffin); 2 Leg.Hist. of LMRDA 1079, 1175–1176, 1191–1192, 1523.

12. H.R.Rep. No. 1147, supra, n. 5, at 42; 105 Cong.Rec. 10104 (1959) (memorandum of Sen. Goldwater); id., at 18128 (remarks by Rep. Barden); 2 Leg.Hist. of LMRDA 1289, 1715. The NLRB has taken this view. Operating Engineers Local 542, 142 N.L.R.B. 1132 (1963), enforced, 331 F.2d 99 (CA 3), cert. denied, 379 U.S. 889, 85 S.Ct. 161, 13 L.Ed.2d 93 (1964).

13. As noted above, supra, at 1837–1839, the garment-industry proviso reflects different considerations. The text of the proviso and the treatment in congressional debates and reports suggest that Congress intended to authorize garment workers' unions to continue using subcontracting agreements as an organizational weapon. See Danielson v. Joint Board, 494 F.2d 1230 (CA 2 1974) (Friendly, J.).

think its authorization extends only to agreements in the context of collective-bargaining relationships and in light of congressional references to the *Denver Building Trades* problem, possibly to common-situs relationships on particular jobsites as well.[14]

Finally, Local 100 contends that even if the subcontracting agreement is not sanctioned by the construction-industry proviso and therefore is illegal under § 8(e), it cannot be the basis for antitrust liability because the remedies in the NLRA are exclusive. This argument is grounded in the legislative history of the 1947 Taft-Hartley amendments. Congress rejected attempts to regulate secondary activities by repealing the antitrust exemptions in the Clayton and Norris-LaGuardia Acts, and created special remedies under the labor law instead.[15] It made secondary activities unfair labor practices under § 8(b)(4), and drafted special provisions for preliminary injunctions at the suit of the NLRB and for recovery of actual damages in the district courts. § 10(*l*) of the NLRA, 49 Stat. 453, as added, 61 Stat. 149, as amended, 29 U.S.C. § 160l, and § 303 of the Labor Management Relations Act, 61 Stat. 158, as amended, 29 U.S.C. § 187. But whatever significance this legislative choice has for antitrust suits based on those secondary activities prohibited by § 8(b)(4), it has no relevance to the question whether Congress meant to preclude antitrust suits based on the "hot cargo" agreements that it outlawed in 1959. There is no legislative history in the 1959 Congress suggesting that labor-law remedies for § 8(e) violations were intended to be exclusive, or that Congress thought allowing antitrust remedies in cases like the present one would be inconsistent with the remedial scheme of the NLRA.[16]

We therefore hold that this agreement, which is outside the context of a collective-bargaining relationship and not restricted to a particular jobsite, but which nonetheless obligates Connell to subcontract work only to firms that have a contract with Local 100, may be the basis of a federal antitrust

14. Connell also has argued that the subcontracting agreement was subject to antitrust sanctions because the construction-industry proviso authorizes only voluntary agreements. The foundation of this argument is a contention that § 8(b)(4)(B) forbids picketing to secure an otherwise lawful "hot cargo" agreement in the construction industry. Because we hold that the agreement in this case is outside the § 8(e) proviso, it is unnecessary to consider this alternative contention.

15. See H.R.Conf.Rep. No. 510, 80th Cong., 1st Sess. (House Managers' statement), 65–67 (1947); 93 Cong.Rec. 4757, 4770, 4834–4874 (1947) (debates over Sen. Ball's proposal for antitrust sanctions and Sen. Taft's compromise proposal for actual damages, which became § 303 of the NLRA).

16. The dissenting opinion of Mr. Justice Stewart argues that § 303 provides the exclusive remedy for violations of § 8(e), thereby precluding recourse to antitrust remedies. For that proposition the dissenting opinion relies upon "considerable evidence in the legislative materials." Post, at 1848. In our view, these materials are unpersuasive. In the first place, Congress did not amend § 303 expressly to provide a remedy for violations of § 8(e). See Labor-Management Reporting and Disclosure Act of 1959, §§ 704(d), (e), 73 Stat. 544–545. The House in 1959 did reject proposals by Representatives Hiestand, Alger, and Hoffman to repeal labor's antitrust immunity. Post, at 1848–1851. Those proposals, however, were much broader than the issue in this case. The Hiestand-Alger proposal would have repealed antitrust immunity for any action in concert by two or more labor organizations. The Hoffman proposal apparently intended to repeal labor's antitrust immunity entirely. That the Congress rejected these extravagant proposals hardly furnishes proof that it intended to extend labor's antitrust immunity to include agreements with nonlabor parties, or that it thought antitrust liability under the existing statutes would be inconsistent with the NLRA. The bill introduced by Senator McClellan two years later provides even less support for that proposition. Like most bills introduced in Congress, it never reached a vote.

suit because it has a potential for restraining competition in the business market in ways that would not follow naturally from elimination of competition over wages and working conditions.

IV

Although we hold that the union's agreement with Connell is subject to the federal antitrust laws, it does not follow that state antitrust law may apply as well. The Court has held repeatedly that federal law pre-empts state remedies that interfere with federal labor policy or with specific provisions of the NLRA. E.g., Motor Coach Employees v. Lockridge, 403 U.S. 274, 91 S.Ct. 1909, 29 L.Ed.2d 473 (1971); Teamsters v. Morton, 377 U.S. 252, 84 S.Ct. 1253, 12 L.Ed.2d 280 (1964); Teamsters v. Oliver, 358 U.S. 283, 79 S.Ct. 297, 3 L.Ed.2d 312 (1959).[17] The use of state antitrust law to regulate union activities in aid of organization must also be pre-empted because it creates a substantial risk of conflict with policies central to federal labor law.

* * *

V

Neither the District Court nor the Court of Appeals decided whether the agreement between Local 100 and Connell, if subject to the antitrust laws, would constitute an agreement that restrains trade within the meaning of the Sherman Act. The issue was not briefed and argued fully in this Court. Accordingly, we remand for consideration whether the agreement violated the Sherman Act.[19]

Reversed in part, affirmed in part, and remanded.

MR. JUSTICE DOUGLAS, dissenting.

While I join the opinion of MR. JUSTICE STEWART, I write to emphasize what is, for me, the determinative feature of the case. Throughout this litigation, Connell has maintained only that Local 100 coerced it into signing the subcontracting agreement. With the complaint so drawn, I have no difficulty in concluding that the union's conduct is regulated solely by the labor laws. The question of antitrust immunity would be far different,

17. In most cases a decision that state law is pre-empted leaves the parties with recourse only to the federal labor law, as enforced by the NLRB. See Motor Coach Employees v. Lockridge, 403 U.S. 274, 91 S.Ct. 1909, 29 L.Ed.2d 473 (1971); San Diego Building Trades Council v. Garmon, 359 U.S. 236, 79 S.Ct. 773, 3 L.Ed.2d 775 (1959). But in cases like this one, where there is an independent federal remedy that is consistent with the NLRA, the parties may have a choice of federal remedies. Cf. Vaca v. Sipes, 386 U.S. 171, 176–188, 87 S.Ct. 903, 909–915, 17 L.Ed.2d 842 (1967); Smith v. Evening News Assn., 371 U.S. 195, 83 S.Ct. 267, 9 L.Ed.2d 246 (1962).

19. In addition to seeking a declaratory judgment that the agreement with Local 100 violated the antitrust laws, Connell sought a permanent injunction against further picketing to coerce execution of the contract in litigation. Connell obtained a temporary restraining order against the picketing on Janu-

ary 21, 1971, and thereafter executed the contract—under protest—with Local 100 on March 28, 1971. So far as the record in this case reveals, there has been no further picketing at Connell's construction sites. Accordingly, there is no occasion for us to consider whether the Norris-LaGuardia Act forbids such an injunction where the specific agreement sought by the union is illegal, or to determine whether, within the meaning of the Norris-LaGuardia Act, there was a "labor dispute" between these parties. If the Norris-LaGuardia Act were applicable to this picketing, injunctive relief would not be available under the antitrust laws. See United States v. Hutcheson, 312 U.S. 219, 61 S.Ct. 463, 85 L.Ed. 788 (1941). If the agreement in question is held on remand to be invalid under federal antitrust laws, we cannot anticipate that Local 100 will resume picketing to obtain or enforce an illegal agreement.

however, if it were alleged that Local 100 had conspired with mechanical subcontractors to force nonunion subcontractors from the market by entering into exclusionary agreements with general contractors like Connell. An arrangement of that character was condemned in Allen Bradley Co. v. Electrical Workers, 325 U.S. 797, 65 S.Ct. 1533, 89 L.Ed. 1939 (1945) * * *.

MR. JUSTICE STEWART, with whom MR. JUSTICE DOUGLAS, MR. JUSTICE BRENNAN, and MR. JUSTICE MARSHALL join, dissenting.

As part of its effort to organize mechanical contractors in the Dallas area, the respondent Local Union No. 100 engaged in peaceful picketing to induce the petitioner Connell Construction Co., a general contractor in the building and construction industry, to agree to subcontract plumbing and mechanical work at the construction site only to firms that had signed a collective-bargaining agreement with Local 100. None of Connell's own employees were members of Local 100, and the subcontracting agreement contained the union's express disavowal of any intent to organize or represent them. The picketing at Connell's construction site was therefore secondary activity, subject to detailed and comprehensive regulation pursuant to § 8(b)(4) of the National Labor Relations Act * * * and § 303 of the Labor Management Relations Act * * *. Similarly, the subcontracting agreement under which Connell agreed to cease doing business with nonunion mechanical contractors is governed by the provisions of § 8(e) of the National Labor Relations Act, 29 U.S.C. § 158(e). The relevant legislative history unmistakably demonstrates that in regulating secondary activity and "hot cargo" agreements in 1947 and 1959, Congress selected with great care the sanctions to be imposed if proscribed union activity should occur. In so doing, Congress rejected efforts to give private parties injured by union activity such as that engaged in by Local 100 the right to seek relief under federal antitrust laws. Accordingly, I would affirm the judgment before us.

I

For a period of 15 years, from passage of the Norris-LaGuardia Act * * * in 1932 [1] until enactment of the Labor Management Relations Act (the Taft-Hartley Act) * * * in 1947, union economic pressure directed against a neutral, secondary employer was not subject to sanctions under either federal labor law or antitrust law, at least in the absence of proof that the union was coercing the secondary employer in furtherance of a conspiracy with a nonlabor group. See United States v. Hutcheson, 312 U.S. 219, 61 S.Ct. 463, 85 L.Ed. 788; Allen Bradley Co. v. Electrical Workers, 325 U.S. 797, 65 S.Ct. 1533, 89 L.Ed. 1939. * * *

Congressional concern over labor abuses of the broad immunity granted by the Norris-LaGuardia Act was one of the considerations that resulted in passage of the Taft-Hartley Act in 1947, which, among other things, prohibited specified union secondary activity. * * * [H]owever, Congress deliber-

1. Before 1932 this Court had held that secondary strikes and boycotts were not exempt from the coverage of the antitrust laws. E.g., Duplex Printing Press Co. v. Deering, 254 U.S. 443, 41 S.Ct. 172, 65 L.Ed. 349; Bedford Cut Stone Co. v. Journeymen Stone Cutters' Assn., 274 U.S. 37, 47 S.Ct. 522, 71 L.Ed. 916. *Duplex* and its progeny were overruled by

Congress with passage of the Norris-LaGuardia Act, 47 Stat. 70. See Milk Wagon Drivers' Union v. Lake Valley Farm Products, Inc., 311 U.S. 91, 100–103, 61 S.Ct. 122, 126–128, 85 L.Ed. 63; United States v. Hutcheson, 312 U.S. 219, 229–231, 235–237, 61 S.Ct. 463, 464–466, 467–469, 85 L.Ed. 788.

ately chose not to subject unions engaging in prohibited secondary activity to the sanctions of the antitrust laws.

* * * [B]oth Houses of Congress agreed to regulate union secondary activity by making specified activity an unfair labor practice under § 8(b)(4) of the National Labor Relations Act, authorizing the Board to seek injunctions against such activity, 29 U.S.C. § 160(*l*), and providing for recovery of actual damages in a suit by a private party under Senator Taft's compromise proposal, which became § 303 of the Labor Management Relations Act, 29 U.S.C. § 187. Congress in 1947 did not prohibit all secondary activity by labor unions, see Carpenters v. NLRB, 357 U.S. 93, 78 S.Ct. 1011, 2 L.Ed.2d 1186; and those practices which it did outlaw were to be remedied only by seeking relief from the Board or by pursuing the newly created, exclusive federal damages remedy provided by § 303. Teamsters v. Morton, supra.

II

Contrary to the assertion in the Court's opinion * * *, the deliberate congressional decision to make § 303 the exclusive private remedy for unlawful secondary activity is clearly relevant to the question of Local 100's antitrust liability in the case before us. The Court is correct, of course, in noting that § 8(e)'s prohibition of "hot cargo" agreements was not added to the Act until 1959, and that § 303 was not then amended to cover § 8(e) violations standing alone. But as part of the 1959 amendments designed to close "technical loopholes" perceived in the Taft-Hartley Act, Congress amended § 8(b)(4) to make it an unfair labor practice for a labor organization to threaten or coerce a neutral employer, either directly or through his employees, where an object of the secondary pressure is to force the employer to enter into an agreement prohibited by § 8(e). At the same time, Congress expanded the scope of the § 303 damages remedy to allow recovery of the actual damages sustained as a result of a union's engaging in secondary activity to force an employer to sign an agreement in violation of § 8(e). In short, Congress has provided an employer like Connell with a fully effective private damages remedy for the allegedly unlawful union conduct involved in this case.

The essence of Connell's complaint is that it was coerced by Local 100's picketing into "conspiring" with the union by signing an agreement that limited its ability to subcontract mechanical work on a competitive basis. If, as the Court today holds, the subcontracting agreement is not within the construction-industry proviso to § 8(e), then Local 100's picketing to induce Connell to sign the agreement constituted a § 8(b)(4) unfair labor practice, and was therefore also unlawful under § 303(a) * * *. Accordingly, Connell has the right to sue Local 100 for damages sustained as a result of Local 100's unlawful secondary activity pursuant to § 303(b) * * *. Although "limited to actual, compensatory damages," Teamsters v. Morton, 377 U.S., at 260, 84 S.Ct. at 1258, Connell would be entitled under § 303 to recover all damages to its business that resulted from the union's coercive conduct, including any provable damage caused by Connell's inability to subcontract mechanical work to nonunion firms. Similarly, any nonunion mechanical contractor who believes his business has been harmed by Local 100's having coerced Connell into signing the subcontracting agreement is entitled to sue the union for compensatory damages; for § 303 broadly grants its damages action to "[w]hoever shall be injured in his business or property" by reason of a labor organization's engaging in a § 8(b)(4) unfair labor practice.[9]

[Discussion by the dissent of the legislative history referred to in note 16 of the majority opinion is omitted.]

[T]he legislative history of the 1947 and 1959 amendments and additions to national labor law clearly demonstrates that Congress did not intend to restore antitrust sanctions for secondary boycott activity such as that engaged in by Local 100 in this case, but rather intended to subject such activity only to regulation under the National Labor Relations Act and § 303 of the Labor Management Relations Act. The judicial imposition of "independent federal remedies" not intended by Congress, no less than the application of state law to union conduct that is either protected or prohibited by federal labor law,[13] threatens "to upset the balance of power between labor and management expressed in our national labor policy." Teamsters v. Morton, 377 U.S., at 260, 84 S.Ct., at 1258. See Carpenters v. NLRB, 357 U.S., at 98–100, 78 S.Ct., at 1015, 1017; National Woodwork Mfrs. Assn. v. NLRB, 386 U.S., at 619–620, 87 S.Ct., at 1254–1255. Accordingly, the judgment before us should be affirmed.

Note

1. In Kaiser Steel Corp. v. Mullins, 455 U.S. 72, 102 S.Ct. 851, 70 L.Ed.2d 833 (1982), the Court, 6–3, reiterated its Connell holding that enforcement of Section 8(e) and its prohibition of "hot cargo" provisions is not preempted by the federal labor laws. There, the United Mine Workers, in a collective bargaining agreement with a multi-employer association of coal producers, had elicited a promise by the producers to contribute to employee health and retirement funds on the basis of each ton of coal they produced *and also* each ton of coal they purchased from producers who were *not under contract* with the union. Kaiser

---

9. If Connell and Local 100 had entered into a purely voluntary "hot cargo" agreement in violation of § 8(e), an injured nonunion mechanical subcontractor would have no § 303 remedy because the union would not have engaged in any § 8(b)(4) unfair labor practice. The subcontractor, however, would still be able to seek the full range of Board remedies available for a § 8(e) unfair labor practice. Moreover, if Connell had truly agreed to limit its subcontracting without any coercion whatsoever on the part of Local 100, the affected subcontractor might well have a valid antitrust claim on the ground that Local 100 and Connell were engaged in the type of conspiracy aimed at third parties with which this Court dealt in Allen Bradley Co. v. Electrical Workers, 325 U.S. 797, 65 S.Ct. 1533, 89 L.Ed. 1939. At the very least, an antitrust suit by an injured subcontractor under circumstances in which Congress had failed to provide any form of private remedy for damage resulting from an illegal "hot cargo" agreement would present a very different question from the one before us—a question which it is not now necessary to answer. Cf.

Meat Cutters v. Jewel Tea Co., 381 U.S. 676, 708 n. 9, 85 S.Ct. 1607, 1613, 14 L.Ed.2d 640 (opinion of Goldberg, J.)

On the other hand, the signatory of a purely voluntary agreement that violates § 8(e) is fully protected from any damage that might result from the illegal "hot cargo" agreement by his ability simply to ignore the contract provision that violates § 8(e). If the union should attempt to enforce the illicit "hot cargo" clause through any form of coercion, the employer may then bring a § 303 damages suit or may file an unfair labor practice charge with the Board. See 29 U.S.C. § 158(b)(4)(B). Since § 8(e) provides that any prohibited agreement is "unenforcible and void," any union effort to invoke legal processes to compel the neutral employer to comply with his purely voluntary agreement would obviously be unavailing.

13. I fully agree with the Court's conclusion, * * * that federal labor law preempts the state law that Connell sought to apply to Local 100's secondary activity in this case.

failed to make contributions as required by the "purchased-coal" clause, thus prompting the trustees of the union welfare funds to sue the company in a federal district court for enforcement of this provision under Section 301 of the Labor Management Relations Act. Kaiser admitted its failure to comply with the purchased-coal clause, but contended that the clause was unenforceable as violative of Sections 1 and 2 of the Sherman Act and Section 8(e). The Court held, *inter alia,* that Kaiser's defense, based upon the illegality of the provision sought to be enforced, was cognizable by the district court.

The Court stated: "We * * * do not agree that the question of the legality of the purchased-coal clause under § 8(e) * * * was within the exclusive jurisdiction of the National Labor Relations Board and that the District Court was therefore without authority to adjudicate Kaiser's defense in this respect. * * * In *Connell,* we decided the § 8(e) issue in the first instance. It was necessary to do so to determine whether the agreement was immune from the antitrust laws. Here a court must decide whether the purchased-coal clause violates § 8(e) in order to determine whether to enforce the clause. * * * While only the Board may provide affirmative remedies for unfair labor practices, a court may not enforce a contract provision which violates § 8(e)." 455 U.S. at 83–86, 102 S.Ct. at 859–861, 70 L.Ed.2d at 843–845.

2. For a thorough discussion of Connell and its relationship to the Pennington and Jewel Tea cases, see St. Antoine, Connell: Antitrust Law at the Expense of Labor Law, 62 Va.L.Rev. 603 (1976). Further post-Connell fallout in the federal courts is thoughtfully analyzed in Handler & Zifchak, Collective Bargaining and the Antitrust Laws: The Emasculation of the Labor Exemption, 1981 Colum.L.Rev. 459.

C. EMERGENCY DISPUTES

Whether or not a labor dispute

Is of an emergency nature

Depends on the size and the time and the trade

But mostly on one's nomenclature.

For what is the meaning of "national health"?

Is it periled by localized cancers?

Are national "safety" and "welfare" the same?

Does the following case hold the answers?

—Anon.

UNITED STEELWORKERS v. UNITED STATES
Supreme Court of the United States, 1959.
361 U.S. 39, 80 S.Ct. 1, 177, 4 L.Ed.2d 12, 169.

PER CURIAM. The Attorney General sought and obtained in the District Court for the Western District of Pennsylvania an injunction against the continuation of an industry-wide strike of workers in the basic steel industry pursuant to § 208 of the Labor Management Relations Act, 1947 * * *. We granted certiorari * * * to review the judgment of the Court of Appeals for the Third Circuit, 271 F.2d 676, affirming the District Court, 178 F.Supp. 297. In pertinent part, § 208 provides that if the District Court—

"finds that   *   *   * [a] threatened or actual strike or lockout—

"(i) affects an entire industry or a substantial part thereof engaged in trade, commerce, transportation, transmission, or communication among the several States or with foreign nations, or engaged in the production of goods for commerce; and

"(ii) if permitted to occur or to continue, will imperil the national health or safety, it shall have jurisdiction to enjoin any such strike or lockout, or the continuing thereof, and to make such other orders as may be appropriate."

The arguments of the parties here and in the lower courts have addressed themselves in considerable part to the propriety of the District Court's exercising its equitable jurisdiction to enjoin the strike in question once the findings set forth above had been made. These arguments have ranged widely into broad issues of national labor policy, the availability of other remedies to the Executive, the effect of a labor injunction on the collective bargaining process, consideration of the conduct of the parties to the labor dispute in their negotiations, and conjecture as to the course of those negotiations in the future. We do not believe that Congress in passing the statute intended that the issuance of injunctions should depend upon judicial inquiries of this nature. Congress was not concerned with the merits of the parties' positions or the conduct of their negotiations. Its basic purpose seems to have been to see that vital production should be resumed or continued for a time while further efforts were made to settle the dispute. To carry out its purposes, Congress carefully surrounded the injunction proceedings with detailed procedural devices and limitations. The public report of a board of inquiry, the exercise of political and executive responsibility personally by the President in directing the commencement of injunction proceedings, the statutory provisions looking toward an adjustment of the dispute during the injunction's pendency, and the limited duration of the injunction, represent a congressional determination of policy factors involved in the difficult problem of national emergency strikes. This congressional determination of the policy factors is of course binding on the courts.

The statute imposes upon the courts the duty of finding, upon the evidence adduced, whether a strike or lockout meets the statutory conditions of breadth of involvement and peril to the national health or safety. We have accordingly reviewed the concurrent findings of the two lower courts. Petitioner here contests the findings that the continuation of the strike would imperil the national health and safety. The parties dispute the meaning of the statutory term "national health"; the Government insists that the term comprehends the country's general well-being, its economic health; petitioner urges that simply the physical health of the citizenry is meant. We need not resolve this question, for we think the judgment below is amply supported on the ground that the strike imperils the national safety.* Here we rely upon the evidence of the strike's effect on specific

---

* The evidence in this regard is reflected in the District Court's findings of fact Nos. 15(a), (b), (c), and (d), as follows:

"(a) Certain items of steel required in top priority military missile programs of the United States are not made by any mill now operating, nor available from any inventory or from imports. Any further delay in resumption of steel production would result in an irretrievable loss of time in the supply of weapons systems essential to the national defense projects; we need not pass on the Government's contention that "national safety" in this context should be given a broader construction and application.

The petitioner suggests that a selective reopening of some of the steel mills would suffice to fulfill specific defense needs. The statute was designed to provide a public remedy in times of emergency; we cannot construe it to require that the United States either formulate a reorganization of the affected industry to satisfy its defense needs without the complete reopening of closed facilities, or demonstrate in court the unfeasibility of such a reorganization. There is no room in the statute for this requirement which the petitioner seeks to impose on the Government.

We are of opinion that the provision in question as applied here is not violative of the constitutional limitation prohibiting courts from exercising powers of a legislative or executive nature, powers not capable of being conferred upon a court exercising solely "the judicial power of the United States." * * * Petitioner contends that the statute is constitutionally invalid because it does not set up any standard of lawful or unlawful conduct on the part of labor or management. But the statute does recognize certain rights in the public to have unimpeded for a time production in industries vital to the national health or safety. It makes the United States the guardian of these rights in litigation. * * * The availability of relief, in the common judicial form of an injunction, depends on findings of fact, to be judicially made. Of the matters decided judicially, there is no review by other agencies of the Government. * * * We conclude that the statute entrusts the courts only with the determination of a "case or controversy," on which the judicial power can operate, not containing any element capable of only legislative or executive determination. We do not find that the termination of the injunction after a specified time, or the machinery established in an attempt to obtain a peaceful settlement of the underlying dispute during the injunction's pendency, detracts from this conclusion.

The result is that the judgment of the Court of Appeals for the Third Circuit, affirming that of the District Court, is affirmed. Our mandate shall issue forthwith.

defense plans of the United States and its allies.

"(b) The planned program of space activities under the direction of the National Aeronautics and Space Administration has been delayed by the strike and will be further delayed if it is continued. Specifically, project MERCURY, the nation's manned satellite program, which has the highest national priority, has been delayed by reason of delay in construction of buildings essential to its operation. This program is important to the security of the nation. Other planned space programs will be delayed or threatened with delay by a continuation of the strike.

"(c) Nuclear Submarines and the naval shipbuilding program other than subma-

rines, including new construction, modernization, and conversion, have been affected by reason of the inability to secure boilers, compressors, and other component parts requiring steel. Products of the steel industry are indispensable to the manufacture of such items and delay in their production will irreparably injure national defense and imperil the national safety.

"(d) Exported steel products are vital to the support of United States bases overseas and for the use of NATO allies and similar collective security groups. The steel strike, if permitted to continue, will seriously impair these programs, thus imperiling the national safety."

MR. JUSTICE FRANKFURTER and MR. JUSTICE HARLAN: In joining the Court's opinion we note our intention to file in due course an amplification of our views upon the issues involved which could not be prepared within the time limitations imposed by the necessity of a prompt adjudication in this case. * * *

MR. JUSTICE DOUGLAS, dissenting.*

Great cases, like this one, are so charged with importance and feeling that, as Mr. Justice Holmes once remarked (Northern Securities Co. v. United States, 193 U.S. 197, 400–401, 24 S.Ct. 436, 468, 48 L.Ed. 679, dissenting opinion), they are apt to generate bad law. We need, therefore, to stick closely to the letter of the law we enforce in order to keep this controversy from being shaped by the intense interest which the public rightfully has in it. The statute, which Congress had authority to pass, speaks in narrow and guarded terms. Section 206 of the Labor Management Relations Act 1947 * * * gives the President power to invoke the aid of a board of inquiry whenever he is of the opinion that a strike or lock out will imperil "the national health or safety." The President, in appointing the board of inquiry in this case, stated:

> "The strike has closed 85 percent of the nation's steel mills, shutting off practically all new supplies of steel. Over 500,000 steel workers and about 200,000 workers in related industries, together with their families, have been deprived of their usual means of support. Present steel supplies are low and the resumption of full-scale production will require some weeks. If production is not quickly resumed, severe effects upon the economy will endanger the economic health of the nation."

It is plain that the President construed the word "health" to include the material well-being or public welfare of the Nation. When the Attorney General moved under § 208 for an injunction in the District Court based on the opinion of the President and the conclusions of the board of inquiry, the union challenged the conclusion that "the national health or safety" was imperiled, as those words are used in the Act. The District Court found otherwise, stating five ways in which the strike would, if permitted to continue, imperil "the national health and safety": [The first four—(a), (b), (c), and (d)—are set forth in the footnote to the Court's opinion.]

> "(e) A continuation of the strike will have the ultimate effect of adversely affecting millions of small business enterprises, almost all of which are directly or indirectly dependent upon steel products and most of which lack the resources to stock large inventories. In addition, it will have the effect of idling millions of workers and a large proportion of the facilities in industries dependent upon steel for their continued operation. Manufacturing industries directly dependent on steel mill products account for the employment of approximately 6,000,000 workers and normal annual wages and salaries totalling approximately $34,000,000,000. The products of these industries are valued at over $125,000,000,000. The national health will be imperiled if the strike is permitted to continue."

* [Reporter's Note: This dissenting opinion was filed November 7, 1959, and was revised later in the light of the concurring opinion [filed December 7, 1959]. It is reported here as revised.]

Here again it is obvious that "national health" was construed to include the economic well-being or general welfare of the country. The Court of Appeals, in sustaining the injunction, was apparently of the same view. This seems to me to be an assumption that is unwarranted. I think that Congress, when it used the words "national health," was safeguarding the heating of homes, the delivery of milk, the protection of hospitals, and the like. The coal industry, closely identified with physical health of people, was the industry paramount in the debates on this measure. * * * There were those in the Senate who wanted to go so far as to outlaw strikes "in utilities and key Nation-wide industries" in order to protect the "public welfare." 93 Cong.Rec. A1035. Reference was, indeed, made to strikes in industries "like coal or steel" among those to be barred in "the public interest." Ibid. But the Senate did not go that far. The Senate bill reached only situations where there was peril to the "national health or safety." The House bill went further and included cases where there was peril to "the public health, safety, or interest." The Senate view prevailed, its version being adopted by the Conference. Some light is thrown on the wide difference between those two standards—if words are to be taken in their usual sense—by the following colloquy on the floor of the House: [4]

"Mr. KENNEDY. I believe that this country should certainly be in a position to combat a strike that affects the health and safety of the people. Therefore, I feel that the President must have the power to step in and stop those strikes. I am not in the position of opposing everything in this bill, but there are certain things in the bill that are wrong. I do not see how the President is going to have the power to stop strikes that will affect the health and safety of the people under the procedure listed in section 203. I think he must have that power.

"I agree with you that any bill providing for an injunction should carefully consider the position of the striking union and make sure that their rights are protected. I think that in those cases Federal seizure until the dispute is settled would perhaps equalize the burden in the fairest possible manner.

"Mr. OWENS. Will not the gentleman admit that we have a third word in there? It is 'interest.' Could we not better use the word 'welfare' instead of 'interest,' because the word 'welfare' occurs in the Constitution? It is just as broad as the word 'interest' and more practical.

"Mr. KENNEDY. The proposal embraces two separate things, health and safety. Because the remedy is drastic these two, in my opinion, are sufficient. I believe we should apply this remedy when the strike affects health or safety, but not the welfare and interest, which may mean anything. I would not interfere in an automobile strike because while perhaps that affects national interest, it does not affect health and safety.

"Mr. OWENS. Does not the gentleman agree that 'welfare' is the stronger and in line with the President's idea?

"Mr. KENNEDY. No. Both 'welfare' and 'interest' are too indefinite. They could cover anything. I would not have the law apply except in cases where the strike affected health and safety."

4. 93 Cong.Rec. 3513.

To read "welfare" into "health" gives that word such a vast reach that we should do it only under the most compelling necessity. We must be mindful of the history behind this legislation. In re Debs, 158 U.S. 564, 584, 15 S.Ct. 900, 906, 39 L.Ed. 1092, stands as ominous precedent for the easy use of the injunction in labor disputes. Freewheeling Attorneys General used compelling public demands to obtain the help of courts in stilling the protests of labor. The revulsion against that practice was deep, and it led ultimately to the enactment of the Norris-LaGuardia Act ＊ ＊ ＊.

We deal, of course, with a later Congress and an Act that by § 208(b) sets aside *pro tanto* the earlier Act. What Congress has created Congress can refashion. But we should hesitate to conclude that Congress meant to restore the use of the injunction in labor disputes whenever that broad and all-inclusive concept of the public welfare is impaired. The words used— "national health or safety"—are much narrower. ＊ ＊ ＊

It is a fact of which we can take judicial notice that steel production in its broadest reach may have a great impact on "national health." Machinery for processing food is needed; hospitals require surgical instruments; refrigeration is dependent on steel; and so on. Whether there are such shortages that imperil the "national health" is not shown by this record. But unless these particularized findings are made no case can be made out for founding the injunction on impending peril to the "national health."

Nor can this broad injunction be sustained when it is rested solely on "national safety." The heart of the District Court's finding on this phase of the case is in its statement, "Certain items of steel required in top priority military missile programs of the United States are not made by any mill now operating, nor available from any inventory or from imports." Its other findings, already quoted, are also generalized. One cannot find in the record the type or quantity of the steel needed for defense, the name of the plants at which those products are produced, or the number or the names of the plants that will have to be reopened to fill the military need. We do know that for one and a half years ending in mid-1959 the shipments of steel for defense purposes accounted for less than 1% of all the shipments from all the steel mills. If 1,000 men, or 5,000 men, or 10,000 men can produce the critical amount the defense departments need, what authority is there to send 500,000 men back to work?

There can be no doubt that the steel strike affects a "substantial" portion of the industry. Hence the first requirement of § 208(a) of the Act is satisfied. But we do know that only a fraction of the production of the struck industry goes to defense needs. We do not know, however, what fraction of the industry is necessary to produce that portion. Without that knowledge the District Court is incapable of fashioning a decree that will safeguard the national "safety," and still protect the rights of labor. Will a selective reopening of a few mills be adequate to meet defense needs? Which mills are these? Would it be practical to reopen them solely for defense purposes or would they have to be reopened for all civilian purposes as well? This seems to me to be the type of inquiry that is necessary before a decree can be entered that will safeguard the rights of all the parties. Section 208(a) gives the District Court "jurisdiction to enjoin" the strike. There is no command that it *shall* enjoin 100% of the strikers when only 1%

or 5% or 10% of them are engaged in acts that imperil the national "safety." We are dealing here with equity practice which has several hundred years of history behind it. We cannot lightly assume that Congress intended to make the federal judiciary a rubber stamp for the President. His findings are entitled to great weight, and I along with my Brethren accept them insofar as national "safety" is concerned. But it is the court, not the President, that is entrusted by Article III of the Constitution to shape and fashion the decree. If a federal court is to do it, it must act in its traditional manner, not as a military commander ordering people to work willy-nilly, nor as the President's Administrative Assistant. If the federal court is to be merely an automaton stamping the papers an Attorney General presents, the judicial function rises to no higher level than an IBM machine. Those who grew up with equity and know its great history should never tolerate that mechanical conception.

An appeal to the equity jurisdiction of the Federal District Court is an appeal to its sound discretion. One historic feature of equity is the molding of decrees to fit the requirements of particular cases. * * * We should hesitate long before we conclude that Congress intended an injunction to issue against 500,000 workers when the inactivity of only 5,000 or 10,000 of the total imperils the national "safety." That would be too sharp a break with traditional equity practice for us to accept, unless the statutory mandate were clear and unambiguous. * * *

* * * If more men are sent back to work than are necessary to fill the defense needs of the country, other objectives are being served than those specified in the statute. What are these other objectives? What right do courts have in serving them? * * * I cannot believe that Congress intended the federal courts to issue injunctions that bludgeon all workers merely because the labor of a few of them is needed in the interest of "national safety."

Labor goes back to work under the present injunction on terms dictated by the industry, not on terms that have been found to be fair to labor and to industry. The steel industry exploits a tremendous advantage:

> "Our steel mills can produce in nine months all the metal the country can use in a year. That means a three-month strike costs the companies nothing in annual sales, and Uncle Sam picks up the tab for half of their out-of-pocket strike losses in the form of eventual tax adjustments.

> "The industry's final insurance against any acute financial pinch is the certainty that the President will have to step in with a national emergency injunction under the Taft-Hartley Act whenever steel stockpiles shrink to the danger level. This takes much of the bite out of the union's assault on the pocketbooks of the steel producers." [10]

This is a matter which equity should take into consideration. For a chancellor sits to do equity. * * *

Though unlikely, it is possible that, had the District Court given the problem the consideration that it deserves, it could have found that the only way to remove the peril to national safety caused by the strike was to issue

10. Raskin, To Prove Karl Marx Was Wrong, N.Y. Times Magazine, Oct. 25, 1959, pp. 12, 84.

the broad, blanket injunction. It may be that it would be found impractical to send only part of the steelworkers back to work. The record in this case, however, is devoid of evidence to sustain that position.[12] Furthermore, there is no indication that the District Court ever even considered such a possibility. I am unwilling to take judicial notice that it requires 100% of the workers to produce the steel needed for national defense when 99% of the output is devoted to purposes entirely unconnected with defense projects.

The trier of fact under our federal judicial system is the District Court—not this Court nor the Court of Appeals. No finding was made by the District Court on the feasibility of a limited reopening of the steel mills and it is not, as the concurring opinion suggests, the province of the Court of Appeals to resolve conflicts in the evidence that was before the District Court.

I would reverse this decree and remand the cause to the District Court for particularized findings as to how the steel strike imperils the "national health" and what plants need to be reopened to produce the small quantity of steel now needed for the national "safety." There would also be open for inquiry and findings any questions pertaining to "national health" in the narrow sense in which the Act uses those words.

Separate opinion of MR. JUSTICE FRANKFURTER and MR. JUSTICE HARLAN, concurring * * *.

* * * The strike which was the concern of the action arose out of a labor dispute between petitioner, the collective bargaining agent of the workers, and the steel companies, and was nationwide in scope. The strike began on July 15, 1959, fifteen days after the contracts between the steel companies and petitioner expired. On October 9, 1959, the President created the Board of Inquiry provided by §§ 206 and 207 of the Act * * * to inquire into the issues involved in the dispute. The President deemed the strike to affect a "substantial part of * * * an industry," and concluded that, if allowed to continue, it would imperil the national "health and safety." On October 19 the Board submitted its report, which concluded: "[T]he parties have failed to reach an agreement and we see no prospects for an early cessation of the strike. The Board cannot point to any single issue of any consequence whatsoever upon which the parties are in agreement." The President filed the report with the Federal Mediation and Conciliation Service and made its contents public, in accordance with § 206, and ordered the Attorney General to commence this action, reiterating his former pronouncements that the continuance of the strike constituted a threat to the national health and safety.

Pursuant to stipulations of the parties, the District Court heard the case on affidavits. On October 21 it granted the injunction. Its order was stayed by the Court of Appeals for the Third Circuit, pending that court's final determination of petitioner's appeal. On October 27 it affirmed the decision of the District Court (one judge dissenting) and granted an additional stay to enable petitioner to seek relief here. On October 28 this Court denied the

---

12. Such an opinion was stated in an affidavit by the Chairman of the Council of Economic Advisers; but that is conclusional only. There has been no sifting of the facts to determine whether defense needs can be satisfied by practical means short of sending all men back to work.

motion of the United States to modify the stay. On October 30 we granted certiorari, set the argument down for November 2, and extended the stay pending final disposition. In a *per curiam* opinion on November 7, this Court affirmed the decision of the Court of Appeals, Mr. Justice Douglas dissenting. * * *

The injunction was challenged on three grounds: (1) the lower courts were not entitled to find that the national emergency, upon which the District Court's jurisdiction is dependent under § 208, existed; (2) even if the emergency existed, the District Court failed to exercise the discretion, claimed to be open to it under § 208, whether or not to grant the relief sought by the United States; (3) even if the injunction was otherwise unassailable it should have been denied because § 208 seeks to charge the District Courts with a duty outside the scope of "judicial power" exercisable under Art. III, § 2, of the Constitution. * * *

In its finding of fact No. 15, the District Court described four instances of serious impediment to national defense programs as a result of existing and prospective procurement problems due to the strike. The programs affected included the missile, nuclear submarine and naval shipbuilding, and space programs. Each of these findings had, as the Court of Appeals found, ample support in the affidavits submitted by the United States. * * *

In view of such demonstrated unavailability of defense materials it is irrelevant that, as petitioner contended and the United States conceded, somewhat in excess of 15% of the steel industry remained unaffected by the stoppage, and that only about 1% of the gross steel product is ordinarily allocated to defense production.

     * * *

Moreover, under § 208 the trier of these facts was called upon to make a judgment already twice made by the President of the United States: once when he convened the Board of Inquiry; and once when he directed the Attorney General to commence this action. His reasoned judgment was presumably based upon the facts we have summarized, and it is not for us to set aside findings consistent with them. The President's judgment is not controlling; § 208 makes it the court's duty to "find" the requisite jurisdictional fact for itself. But in the discharge of its duty a District Court would disregard reason not to give due weight to determinations previously made by the President, who is, after all, the ultimate constitutional executive repository for assuring the safety of the Nation, and upon whose judgment the invocation of the emergency provisions depends.

The petitioner next asserted that the findings made were insufficient as a matter of law to support the District Court's jurisdiction under § 208. Conceding that peril to the national defense is peril to the national safety, it asserted that the peril to the national safety which is made an element of the court's jurisdiction by part (ii) of § 208(a) must result from the substantial character of the effect upon an industry required by part (i), and that if it does not so result a District Court is without power to enjoin the stoppage or any part of it. Alternately, it urged that the jurisdiction which is conferred by the section is limited to relief against such part of the total stoppage as is found to be the cause in fact of the peril. Petitioner claimed that as a matter of fact the procurement embarrassments found by the

PUBLIC INTERESTS

courts below were the result not of the entire steel stoppage or even of a substantial part of it, but only of the closing of a "handful" of the hundreds of plants affected; and that therefore the entire industry-wide strike should not have been enjoined under either construction of § 208 which it asserted.

In the first place, the requisite fact was found against petitioner's contention. The Court of Appeals found that "[t]he steel industry is too vast and too complicated to be segmented" so as to alleviate the existing and foreseeable peril to the national defense by the mere reopening of a few plants. It expressly relied upon the affidavit of Dr. Raymond J. Saulnier, Chairman of the Council of Economic Advisers of the Federal Government, which was before both the lower courts. Dr. Saulnier stated that:

> "Steel is produced through closely interrelated processes that often cannot be separated technically or economically to allow production of items 'needed' * * * while omitting items 'not needed.' * * * '[I]n order to satisfy defense requirements alone from the standpoint of size, grade, and product, it would be necessary to reactivate 25 to 30 hot rolling mills, together with supporting blast furnaces, and Bessemer, electric, open hearth, and vacuum-melting furnaces. Additional facilities for pickling, coating, heat treating, cold finishing, shearing, cutting, testing, and the like would also be required. To reopen these plants for the production of steel products to meet only defense requirements would be totally impracticable. The problems of scheduling the limited tonnages involved, plus the cost and technical difficulty of start-ups and shut-downs would appear to be insurmountable.'"

* * *

Nor was it a refutation of the finding of the Court of Appeals to suggest, as petitioner did here, that "needed" facilities might be opened for all purposes. The problem is self-evidently one of programming months in advance every specialized commodity needed for defense purposes, a project which itself would require months of effort and the delays such effort would entail. Other obvious difficulties are not less formidable. Upon what basis would the plants to be reopened be chosen, assuming the number of plants needed could be determined? According to what standard would the production of particular complexes of plants be regulated? What of problems of cost and overhead, and the cost of and time required for intra-company planning to determine the practicality of partially restricting the operation of giant complexes such as those of the major producers?

No doubt a District Court is normally charged with the duty of independently shaping the details of a decree when sitting in equity in controversies that involve simple and relatively few factors; factors, that is, far less in number, less complicated and less interrelated than in the case before us. But a court is not qualified to devise schemes for the conduct of an industry so as to assure the securing of necessary defense materials. It is not competent to sit in judgment on the existing distribution of factors in the conduct of an integrated industry to ascertain whether it can be segmented with a view to its reorganization for the supply exclusively, or even primarily, of government-needed materials. Nor is it able to readjust or adequately to reweigh the forces of economic competition within the industry or to appraise the relevance of such forces in carrying out a defense program for the Government. Against all such assumptions of competence, the finding of the Court of Appeals was amply supported by the record.

* * *

The legislative history confirms what the provisions themselves amply reveal, that this portion of the Taft-Hartley Act contains a dual purpose, on the one hand to alleviate, at least temporarily, a threat to the national health or safety; and on the other to promote settlement of the underlying dispute of industry-wide effect. The former purpose is to be accomplished by the injunction, and by whatever additional remedies the President may seek and the Congress grant in pursuance of the command of § 210 of the Act that the matter be returned to Congress by the President with full report in the event of a failure of settlement within the injunction period. The latter purpose is to be accomplished by the command of § 209 that the parties to the dispute "make every effort to adjust and settle their differences"; by the secret ballot of employees provided by § 209 with reference to the last offer of the companies; and finally by further action by the President and Congress pursuant to § 210. To hold, as petitioner alternatively urged, that a District Court may enjoin only that part of the total stoppage which is shown to be the cause in fact of the peril, would at best serve only the purpose of alleviating the peril, while stultifying the provisions designed to effect settlement of the underlying dispute.

[T]he evidentiary burdens upon the Government which would have resulted from the adoption of either of the constructions urged by petitioner would tend to cripple the designed effectiveness of the Act. It is extremely doubtful whether in strikes of national proportion information would be available to the United States within a reasonable time to enable it to show that particular critical orders were placed with particular facilities no longer available; or whether the United States could, within such time, effect a theoretical reorganization of its procurement program so as to demonstrate to a court that it cannot successfully be conducted without the reopening of particular facilities.

[Section] 208 is not to be construed narrowly, as if it were merely an exception to the policies which led to the restrictions on the use of injunctions in labor disputes embodied in the Norris-LaGuardia Act * * *. Totally different policies led to the enactment of the national emergency provisions of the 1947 Act. The legislative history of these provisions is replete with evidence of the concern of both the proponents and the opponents of the bill to deal effectively with large-scale work stoppages which endanger the public health or safety. To stop or prevent public injury, both management and labor were brought within the scope of the injunctive power, and both were subjected to the command to "make every effort to adjust and settle their differences * * *." § 209. * * *

Because the District Court's finding of peril to the national safety resulting from impediments to the programs for national defense was itself sufficient to satisfy the requirement of § 208(a)(ii), it is not necessary to determine whether perils to defense exhaust the scope of "safety" as used in this statute, or to consider its findings with regard to peril to the national health.

Having decided that the strike was one which created a national emergency within the terms of the statute, the next question is whether, upon that finding, alone, the "eighty-day" injunction for which the Government prayed should have issued, or whether the District Court was to exercise the conventional discretionary function of equity in balancing conveniences as a preliminary to issuing an injunction. The petitioner argued that under the Act a District Court has "discretion" whether to issue an "eighty-day" injunction, even though a national emergency be found. It argued that the district judge in this case did not consider that he had such "discretion." Alternatively, it argued that if the district judge did exercise "discretion" he abused it, for the broad injunctive relief he granted was not justifiable in this case. * * * We do not think it necessary to embark upon the speculative consideration whether the district judge in fact made a discretionary determination, and, if he did, whether that determination was justifiable. We conclude that under the national emergency provisions of the Labor Management Relations Act it is not for judges to exercise conventional "discretion" to withhold an "eighty-day" injunction upon a balancing of conveniences.

* * *

In the national emergency provisions of the Labor Management Relations Act, Congress has with particularity described the duration of the injunction to be granted and the nature of specific collateral administrative procedures which are to be set in motion upon its issuance. We think the conclusion compelling that Congress has thereby manifested that a District Court is not to indulge its own judgment regarding the wisdom of the relief Congress has designed. * * * The statute embodies a legislative determination that the particular relief described is appropriate to the emergency, when one is found to exist. Moreover, it is a primary purpose of the Act to stop the national emergency at least for eighty days, which would be defeated if a court were left with discretion to withhold an injunction and thereby permit continuation of an emergency it has found to exist. The hope is that within the period of the injunction voluntary settlement of the labor dispute will be reached, and to that end the statute compels bargaining between the parties during that time. If no voluntary settlement is concluded within the period of the injunction, the President is to report to Congress so that that body may further draw upon its constitutional legislative powers. How else can these specific directions be viewed but that the procedures provided are, in the view of Congress, the way to meet the emergencies which come within the statute? It is not for a court to negative the direction of Congress because of its own confident prophecy that the "eighty-day" injunction and the administrative procedures which follow upon it will not induce voluntary settlement of the dispute, or are too drastic a way of dealing with it. * * *

We come finally to the petitioner's contention that the grant to the District Courts by § 208(a) of the Labor Management Relations Act of jurisdiction to enjoin strikes such as this one is not a grant of "judicial Power" within the meaning of Art. III, § 2, of the Constitution, and was therefore beyond the power of Congress to confer on the District Courts. What proceedings are "Cases" and "Controversies" and thus within the "judicial Power" is to be determined, at the least, by what proceedings were recognized at the time of the Constitution to be traditionally within the power of courts in the English and American judicial systems. ✱ ✱ ✱

Beginning at least as early as the sixteenth century the English courts have issued injunctions to abate public nuisances. The judicial power to enjoin public nuisance at the instance of the Government has been a commonplace of jurisdiction in American judicial history. ✱ ✱ ✱

The jurisdiction given the District Courts by § 208(a) of the Labor Management Relations Act to enjoin strikes creating a national emergency is a jurisdiction of a kind that has been traditionally exercised over public nuisances. The criterion for judicial action—peril to health or safety—is much like those upon which courts ordinarily have acted. Injunctive relief is traditionally given by equity upon a showing of such peril, and the court, as was traditional, acts at the request of the Executive. There can therefore be no doubt that, being thus akin to jurisdiction long historically exercised, the function to be performed by the District Courts under § 208(a) is within the "judicial Power" as contemplated by Art. III, § 2, and is one which Congress may thus confer upon the courts. It surely does not touch the criteria for determining what is "judicial Power" that the injunction to be issued is not a permanent one, and may last no longer than eighty days. Given the power in Congress to vest in the federal courts the function to enjoin absolutely, it does not change the character of the power granted or undermine the professional competence of a court for its exercise that Congress has directed the relief to be tempered.

These controlling constitutional considerations were sought to be diverted by the petitioner through abstract discussion about the necessity for Congress to define legal rights and duties. The power of Congress to deal with the public interest does not derive from, nor is it limited by, rights and duties as between parties. Congress may impose duties and enforce obligations to the Nation as a whole, as it has so obviously done in the Labor Management Relations Act. Such congressional power is not to be subordinated to a sterile juristic dialectic.

DIVISION 1287, AMALGAMATED ASSOCIATION OF STREET, ELECTRIC RAILWAY AND MOTOR COACH EMPLOYEES v. MISSOURI

Supreme Court of the United States, 1963.
374 U.S. 74, 83 S.Ct. 1657, 10 L.Ed.2d 763.

Opinion of the Court by MR. JUSTICE STEWART, announced by MR. JUSTICE WHITE.

The appellant union is the certified representative of a majority of the employees of Kansas City Transit, Inc., a Missouri corporation which operates a public transit business in Kansas and Missouri. A collective bargaining agreement between the appellant and the company was due to expire on October 31, 1961, and in August of that year, after appropriate notices, the parties commenced the negotiation of an amended agreement. An impasse in these negotiations was reached, and in early November the appellant's members voted to strike. The strike was called on November 13.

The same day the Governor of Missouri acting under the authority of a state law known as the King-Thompson Act,[1] issued a proclamation that the public interest, health and welfare were jeopardized by the threatened interruption of the company's operations, and by an executive order purported to take possession "of the plants, equipment, and all facilities of the Kansas City Transit, Inc., located in the State of Missouri, for the use and operation by the State of Missouri in the public interest." A second executive order provided in part that "All rules and regulations ＊ ＊ ＊ governing the internal management and organization of the company, and its duties and responsibilities, shall remain in force and effect throughout the term of operation by the State of Missouri."

Pursuant to a provision of the Act which makes unlawful any strike or concerted refusal to work as a means of enforcing demands against the utility or the State after possession has been taken by the State, the State petitioned the Circuit Court of Jackson County for an injunction on November 15, 1961.[2] A temporary restraining order was issued on that day, and the strike and picketing were discontinued that evening. After a two-day trial, the order was continued in effect, and the Circuit Court later entered a permanent injunction barring the continuation of the strike "against the State of Missouri."

On appeal to the Supreme Court of Missouri, the appellants argued that the King-Thompson Act is in conflict with and is pre-empted by federal labor legislation, and that it abridges rights guaranteed by the First, Thirteenth, and Fourteenth Amendments. Reaffirming its earlier decisions in cases arising under the Act, the Supreme Court of Missouri rejected these arguments and affirmed the issuance of the injunction. 361 S.W.2d 33. We noted probable jurisdiction. ＊ ＊ ＊

The King-Thompson Act defines certain public utilities as "life essentials of the people" and declares it to be the policy of the State that "the possibility of labor strife in utilities operating under governmental franchise or permit or under governmental ownership and control is a threat to the welfare and health of the people." The Act imposes requirements in connection with the duration and renewal of collective bargaining agreements, and creates a State Board of Mediation and public hearing panels whose services are to be invoked whenever the parties cannot themselves agree upon the terms to be included in a new agreement. And where, as here, the recommendations of these agencies are not accepted, and the continued operation of the utility is threatened as a result, the Governor is empowered to "take immediate possession of" the utility "for the use and operation by the state of Missouri in the public interest."

1. The King-Thompson Act is Chapter 295 of the Revised Statutes of Missouri, 1959. The section of the statute authorizing seizure is Mo.Rev.Stat., 1959, § 295.180, V.A.M.S.

2. Missouri Rev.Stat., 1959, § 295.200, par. 1, provides:

"It shall be unlawful for any person, employee, or representative as defined in this chapter to call, incite, support or participate in any strike or concerted refusal to work for any utility or for the state after any plant, equipment or facility has been taken over by the state under this chapter, as means of enforcing any demands against the utility or against the state."

Section 295.200, par. 6, provides:

"The courts of this state shall have power to enforce by injunction or other legal or equitable remedies any provision of this chapter or any rule or regulation prescribed by the governor hereunder."

In Amalgamated Ass'n of Street, Electric Ry. & Motor Coach Employees of America, Division 998 v. Wisconsin Employment Relations Board, 340 U.S. 383, 71 S.Ct. 359, 95 L.Ed. 364, this Court held that the Wisconsin Public Utility Anti-Strike Law, which made it a misdemeanor for public utility employees to engage in a strike which would cause an interruption of an essential public utility service, conflicted with the National Labor Relations Act and was therefore invalid under the Supremacy Clause of the Constitution. The Supreme Court of Missouri in the present case rejected the appellants' argument that the Wisconsin Board decision was determinative of the unconstitutionality of the Missouri statute here in issue. The court held that the provisions of the King-Thompson Act dealing with the mediation board and public hearing panels were severable from the remainder of the statute, and refused to pass on any but those provisions which authorize the seizure and the issuance of injunctions against strikes taking place after seizure has been imposed. These provisions, the court ruled, do not—as in the Wisconsin Board case—provide a comprehensive labor code conflicting with federal legislation, but rather represent "strictly emergency legislation" designed solely to authorize use of the State's police power to protect the public from threatened breakdowns in vital community services. Emphasizing that the company was not a party to the injunction suit, the court concluded that, although the State did not actively participate in the management of the utility's operations, the Governor's executive order had been sufficient to convert the strike into one against the State, and that an injunction barring such a strike is therefore not barred by the provisions of federal labor legislation. 361 S.W.2d, at 44, 46, 48–52.

We disagree. None of the distinctions drawn by the Missouri court between the King-Thompson Act and the legislation involved in Wisconsin Board seem to us to be apposite. First, whatever the status of the title to the properties of Kansas City Transit, Inc., acquired by the State as a result of the Governor's executive order, the record shows that the State's involvement fell far short of creating a state-owned and operated utility whose labor relations are by definition excluded from the coverage of the National Labor Relations Act. The employees of the company did not become employees of Missouri. Missouri did not pay their wages, and did not direct or supervise their duties. No property of the company was actually conveyed, transferred, or otherwise turned over to the State. Missouri did not participate in any way in the actual management of the company, and there was no change of any kind in the conduct of the company's business. As summed up by the Chairman of the State Mediation Board: "So far as I know the company is operating now just as it was two weeks ago before the strike."

Secondly, the Wisconsin Board case decisively rejected the proposition that a state enactment affecting a public utility operating in interstate commerce could be saved from a challenge based upon a demonstrated conflict with the standards embodied in federal law simply by designating it as "emergency legislation." There the Court said that where "the state seeks to deny entirely a federally guaranteed right which Congress itself restricted only to a limited extent in case of national emergencies, however serious, it is manifest that the state legislation is in conflict with federal law." 340 U.S., at 394, 71 S.Ct. at 365.

The short of the matter is that Missouri, through the fiction of "seizure" by the State, has made a peaceful strike against a public utility unlawful, in direct conflict with federal legislation which guarantees the right to strike against a public utility, as against any employer engaged in interstate commerce.[9] In forbidding a strike against an employer covered by the National Labor Relations Act, Missouri has forbidden the exercise of rights explicitly protected by § 7 of that Act. Collective bargaining, with the right to strike at its core, is the essence of the federal scheme. As in Wisconsin Board, a state law which denies that right cannot stand under the Supremacy Clause of the Constitution.

It is hardly necessary to add that nothing we have said even remotely affects the right of a State to own or operate a public utility or any other business, nor the right or duty of the chief executive or legislature of a State to deal with emergency conditions of public danger, violence, or disaster under appropriate provisions of the State's organic or statutory law.

Reversed.

Note

1. Is the Missouri case consistent with other pre-emption cases previously encountered, supra pp. 330–373.

2. The most famous case of government seizure is YOUNGSTOWN SHEET AND TUBE CO. v. SAWYER, 343 U.S. 579, 72 S.Ct. 863, 96 L.Ed. 1153 (1952). In order to head off an imminent strike in the steel industry during the Korean War, President Truman issued an executive order directing the Secretary of Commerce to seize and operate most of the steel mills. The Secretary, in turn, ordered the presidents of the seized companies to serve as operating managers for the United States in accordance with regulations and directions of the Secretary. The companies obeyed the Secretary's orders under protest, at the same time bringing suit against him in the federal district court, charging that the seizure was not authorized by any act of Congress nor by the Constitution and asking that the orders of the President and the Secretary be declared invalid and their enforcement enjoined. The Court held, 6 to 3, that, where Congress has enacted legislation for dealing with national emergency disputes, as in Sections 206–210 of the Taft-Hartley Act, the President does not have the inherent power, either as President or as Commander in Chief of the Armed Forces, to take action contrary to that authorized by Congress; in issuing the seizure order, the President had usurped a legislative function. (President Truman's hostility to the Taft-Hartley Act, including its emergency provisions, had been earlier dramatized by his veto of the Bill, which was then passed, over his veto, by a two-thirds majority of both Houses.) What reasons might President Truman have had for preferring seizure to the Taft-Hartley procedures?

3. The Railway Labor Act, like the Taft-Hartley Act, contains provisions for the resolution of "emergency disputes." Such disputes were once quite common in the railroad industry (see, e.g., Brotherhood of Locomotive Firemen and Enginemen v. Chicago, Burlington & Quincy Railroad, 225 F.Supp. 11

9. In enacting the Taft-Hartley Act, Congress expressly rejected the suggestion that public utilities be treated differently from other employers. As explained by Senator Taft, "If we begin with public utilities, it will be said that coal and steel are just as important as public utilities. I do not know where we could draw the line. So far as the bill is concerned, we have proceeded on the theory that there is a right to strike and that labor peace must be based on free collective bargaining." 93 Cong.Rec. 3835.

(D.D.C.1964), affirmed 331 F.2d 1020 (D.C.Cir.1964), cert. denied 377 U.S. 918, 84 S.Ct. 1181, 12 L.Ed.2d 187 (1964)), but, as with American industry generally, have been of diminished importance in recent years. The procedures for dealing with such disputes (see RLA Section 10, Statutory Supplement) are briefly discussed supra p. 101.

4. Compulsory arbitration is the most straightforward of the variety of techniques advanced for the resolution of bargaining impasses without resort to the strike, a concern not only in emergency disputes but also in public-sector labor relations (dealt with in Section D infra). This very strength, if so it be, is also the weakness of compulsory arbitration, for it is feared that parties potentially subject to compulsory arbitration will cease to engage in a sincere effort to resolve their differences through negotiation. Instead, they will be motivated to conduct their "bargaining" in such a fashion as to leave them in the best position possible once the arbitral stage is reached. This means that concessions which might otherwise be made during negotiations will be withheld for fear that the other side will not make responsive concessions, thus prejudicing the conceding side when the arbitration tribunal seeks to compromise the positions (as typically it does). If the union, for example, has demanded a 15% increase in wages, and the employer has responded with a 5% offer, any lowering of its demand by the union would be at the risk of the employer's standing pat; the union would then go into arbitration with, say, a 10% figure, instead of 15%, to play off against the employer's 5%. To circumvent this undesired side-effect of compulsory arbitration, the suggestion has been made that the arbitration tribunal be confined in its award to a choice of one or the other side's final offer—a "winner take all" scheme. See, e.g., Stern, Final-Offer Arbitration (1975); Stevens, Is Compulsory Arbitration Compatible with Bargaining? 5 Indus. Relations, No. 2, 38, 45–47 (February 1966); Fleischli, Some Problems with the Administration of Compulsory Final Offer Arbitration Procedures, 56 Chi.-Kent L.Rev. 559 (1980); Rehmus, Varieties of Final Offer Arbitration, 37 Arb.J. 4 (1982); Grebey, Another Look at Baseball's Salary Arbitration, 38 Arb.J. 24 (1983); Miller, Arbitration of Baseball Salaries: Impartial Adjudication in Place of Management Fiat, 38 Arb.J. 31 (1983); Dworkin, Salary Arbitration in Baseball: An Impartial Assessment After Ten Years, 41 Arb.J. 63 (1986).

In short, the argument against compulsory arbitration as a method for the resolution of emergency labor disputes is that it destroys genuine collective bargaining. Is this loss worth the gain?

CONCLUDING COMMENT ON EMERGENCY DISPUTES

The emergency dispute provisions of the Taft-Hartley Act have drawn fire. The strongest criticism has been directed at their rigidity and predictability. What they come down to in every case is an injunction against the continuation of the strike, the injunction to be in effect for a period of up to eighty days. As noted by A.H. Raskin in the article quoted by Justice Douglas, dissenting in the Steelworkers case, supra p. 1057, the employer can in many situations incorporate the anticipated strike-ending injunction as a part of its bargaining strategy.

Criticism of a lesser degree has been leveled at the ballot required by Section 209(b) on the employer's final offer and at the preclusion under Sections 206 and 209(b) of recommendations for settlement of the dispute by the board of inquiry appointed by the President. The effect of the last-offer ballot has been to solidify the union position; the employer's last offer is typically rejected. The forbidding of recommendations for settlement by the presidential boards of inquiry is said to deny to the public an essential ingredient for the rallying of informed opinion as a pressure toward settlement.

Those advocating reform of emergency-dispute provisions most commonly espouse what has been variously styled a "choice of procedures," "arsenal of weapons," "bag of tricks" approach. See, e.g., Wirtz, The "Choice of Procedures" Approach to National Emergency Disputes, in Emergency Disputes and National Policy 149 (Bernstein, Enarson, and Fleming, eds. 1955). Under this scheme the President (or some other officer or agency) would choose from among several courses of action the one deemed most appropriate in the particular case. The options would include the cooling-off injunction, government seizure, fact finding with recommendations, compulsory arbitration. The premise of the choice-of-procedures approach is that the parties will be unable to predict what course of action will be taken to deal with their dispute, and will accordingly feel a pressure to resolve the dispute themselves through intensified bargaining rather than run the risk of uncertainty.

A novel and somewhat intriguing option argued by some to belong in the "bag of tricks" is the so-called "non-stoppage" or "statutory" strike. See Goble, The Nonstoppage Strike, 2 Lab.L.J. 105 (1951); Goble, An Alternative to the Strike, 6 id. 83 (1955). See also Marshall and Marshall, Nonstoppage Strikes and National Labor Policy—A Critique, 7 id. 299 (1956). The potential variations on this theme are manifold, but the core of the idea is the following: During such a "strike" a specified percentage of the employer's profits, of management salaries, and of workers' wages would be impounded by some government agency and held for a period of time—say, ninety days. If agreement were reached by the parties to the dispute within the ninety-day period, the impounded sums would be paid over, in toto, to those from whom they had been withheld. If, on the other hand, agreement were not reached within the ninety-day period, the impounded funds would be deemed forfeited, and a second ninety-day period would begin with the same rules obtaining. An obvious permutation would be to scale the forfeiture *within* each ninety-day period. A major problem with the "non-stoppage strike" is that it would require enabling legislation. No such legislation is currently in existence. Do you find this surprising?

The materials in this section have been concerned with the public interest in private employment labor disputes which create public emergencies. In such situations, techniques for settlement other than the usual weapons of economic warfare have been sought. A much similar concern characterizes *public* employment labor disputes, the subject matter of the succeeding section.

D. COLLECTIVE BARGAINING IN PUBLIC EMPLOYMENT

Collective bargaining in public employment has both similarities to and differences from collective bargaining in private employment. Insofar as the two are similar, collective bargaining in public employment presents no special problems for the student of labor relations and of the law pertaining thereto. The differences are what merit special attention. The materials which follow have been selected in accordance with this criterion. They present the major differences in the public sector context. It should be the student's effort to perceive these differences and to reflect upon their implications for a system of collective bargaining. A brief review of the DeLury case, supra p. 196, and of the note which follows it, will afford a running start.

UNITED FEDERATION OF POSTAL CLERKS v. BLOUNT

United States District Court, District of Columbia, 1971.
325 F.Supp. 879.

Affirmed without opinion, 404 U.S. 802 (1971).

Before WRIGHT and MACKINNON, CIRCUIT JUDGES, and PRATT, DISTRICT JUDGE.

PER CURIAM. This action was brought by the United Federation of Postal Clerks (hereafter sometimes referred to as "Clerks"), an unincorporated public employee labor organization which consists primarily of employees of the Post Office Department, and which is the exclusive bargaining representative of approximately 305,000 members of the clerk craft employed by defendant. Defendant Blount is the Postmaster General of the United States. The Clerks seek declaratory and injunctive relief invalidating portions of 5 U.S.C.A. § 7311, 18 U.S.C.A. § 1918, an affidavit required by 5 U.S.C.A. § 3333 to implement the above statutes, and Executive Order 11491, C.F.R., Chap. II, p. 191. The Government, in response, filed a motion to dismiss or in the alternative for summary judgment, and plaintiff filed its opposition thereto and cross motion for summary judgment. A three-judge court was convened pursuant to 28 U.S.C.A. § 2282 and § 2284 to consider this issue.

The Statutes Involved

5 U.S.C.A. § 7311(3) prohibits an individual from accepting or holding a position in the federal government or in the District of Columbia if he "(3) participates in a strike * * * against the Government of the United States or the government of the District of Columbia * * *."

Paragraph C of the appointment affidavit required by 5 U.S.C.A. § 3333, which all federal employees are required to execute under oath, states (POD Form 61).[1]

---

1. Punishments for false statements under oath are provided by the general perjury statute, 18 U.S.C.A. § 1621 (1964). Conviction requires proof that the individual wilfully swore falsely and that such wilfulness existed at the time the oath was taken. See United States v. Hvass, 355 U.S. 570, 574, 78 S.Ct. 501, 2 L.Ed.2d 496 (1958); United States v.

"I am not participating in any strike against the Government of the United States or any agency thereof, and I will not so participate while an employee of the Government of the United States or any agency thereof."

18 U.S.C.A. § 1918, in making a violation of 5 U.S.C.A. § 7311 a crime, provides:

"Whoever violates the provision of section 7311 of title 5 that an individual may not accept or hold a position in the Government of the United States or the government of the District of Columbia if he * * *

"(3) participates in a strike, or asserts the right to strike, against the Government of the United States or the District of Columbia * * *

"shall be fined not more than $1,000 or imprisoned not more than one year and a day, or both."

Section 2(e)(2) of Executive Order 11491 exempts from the definition of a labor organization any group which:

"asserts the right to strike against the Government of the United States or any agency thereof, or to assist or participate in such a strike, or imposes a duty or obligation to conduct, assist or participate in such a strike * * *."

Section 19(b)(4) of the same Executive Order makes it an unfair labor practice for a labor organization to:

"call or engage in a strike, work stoppage, or slowdown; picket an agency in a labor-management dispute; or condone any such activity by failing to take affirmative action to prevent or stop it; * * *."

Plaintiff's Contentions

Plaintiff contends that the right to strike is a fundamental right protected by the Constitution, and that the absolute prohibition of such activity by 5 U.S.C.A. § 7311(3) and the other provisions set out above thus constitutes an infringement of the employees' First Amendment rights of association and free speech and operates to deny them equal protection of the law. Plaintiff also argues that the language to "strike" and "participates in a strike" is vague and overbroad and therefore violative of both the First Amendment and the due process clause of the Fifth Amendment. For the purposes of this opinion, we will direct our attention to the attack on the constitutionality of 5 U.S.C.A. § 7311(3), the key provision being challenged. To the extent that the present wording of 18 U.S.C.A. § 1918(3) and Executive Order 11491 does not reflect the actions of two statutory courts in Stewart v. Washington, 301 F.Supp. 610 (D.C.D.C.1969) and N.A.L.C. v. Blount, 305 F.Supp. 546 (D.C. D.C.1969), said wording, insofar as it inhibits the *assertion* of the right to strike, is overbroad because it attempts to reach activities protected by the First Amendment and is therefore invalid. With this *caveat*, our treatment of the issue raised by plaintiffs with respect to the constitutionality of 5 U.S. C.A. § 7311(3) will also apply to 18 U.S.C.A. § 1918, the penal provision, and to Form 61, the affidavit required by 5 U.S.C.A. § 3333. For the reasons set

Debrow, 346 U.S. 374, 376, 74 S.Ct. 113, 98 L.Ed. 92 (1953); Application of 18 U.S.C.A. § 1621 to the oath here under consideration gives rise to no problems of constitutional dimension. See generally Screws v. United States, 325 U.S. 91, 65 S.Ct. 1031, 89 L.Ed. 1495 (1945).

forth below, we deny plaintiff's request for declaratory and injunctive relief and grant defendant's motion to dismiss.

I. PUBLIC EMPLOYEES HAVE NO CONSTITUTIONAL RIGHT TO STRIKE

At common law no employee, whether public or private, had a constitutional right to strike in concert with his fellow workers. Indeed, such collective action on the part of employees was often held to be a conspiracy. When the right of private employees to strike finally received full protection, it was by statute, Section 7 of the National Labor Relations Act, which "took this conspiracy weapon away from the employer in employment relations which affect interstate commerce" and guaranteed to employees in the private sector the right to engage in concerted activities for the purpose of collective bargaining. See discussion in International Union, U.A.W.A., A.F. of L. Local 232 v. Wisconsin Employment Relations Board, 336 U.S. 245, 257–259, 69 S.Ct. 516, 93 L.Ed. 651 (1948). It seems clear that public employees stand on no stronger footing in this regard than private employees and that in the absence of a statute, they too do not possess the right to strike. The Supreme Court has spoken approvingly of such a restriction, see Amell v. United States, 384 U.S. 158, 161, 86 S.Ct. 1384, 16 L.Ed.2d 445 (1965), and at least one federal district court has invoked the provisions of a predecessor statute, 5 U.S.C.A. § 118p–r, to enjoin a strike by government employees. Tennessee Valley Authority v. Local Union No. 110 of Sheet Metal Workers, 233 F.Supp. 997 (D.C.W.D.Ky.1962). Likewise, scores of state cases have held that state employees do not have a right to engage in concerted work stoppages, in the absence of legislative authorization. * * * It is fair to conclude that, irrespective of the reasons given, there is a unanimity of opinion on the part of courts and legislatures that government employees do not have the right to strike. See Moberly, The Strike and Its Alternative in Public Employment, University of Wisconsin Law Review (1966) pp. 549–550, 554.

Congress has consistently treated public employees as being in a different category than private employees. The National Labor Relations Act of 1935 and the Labor Management Relations Act of 1947 (Taft-Hartley), both defined "employer" as not including any governmental or political subdivisions, and thereby indirectly withheld the protections of § 7 from governmental employees. Congress originally enacted the no-strike provision separately from other restrictions on employee activity, i.e., such as those struck down in Stewart v. Washington and N.A.L.C. v. Blount, supra, by attaching riders to appropriations bills which prohibited strikes by government employees. See for example the Third Urgent Deficiency Appropriation Act of 1946,[4] which provided that no part of the appropriation could be used to pay the salary of anyone who engaged in a strike against the Government. Section 305 of the Taft-Hartley Act made it unlawful for a federal employee to participate in a strike, providing immediate discharge and forfeiture of civil service status for infractions. Section 305 was repealed in 1955 by Public Law 330,[6] and re-enacted in 5 U.S.C.A. § 118p–r, the predecessor to the present statute.

4. 60 Stat. 268 (1946).   6. 69 Stat. 624 (1955).

Given the fact that there is no constitutional right to strike, it is not irrational or arbitrary for the Government to condition employment on a promise not to withhold labor collectively, and to prohibit strikes by those in public employment, whether because of the prerogatives of the sovereign, some sense of higher obligation associated with public service, to assure the continuing functioning of the Government without interruption, to protect public health and safety or for other reasons. Although plaintiff argues that the provisions in question are unconstitutionally broad in covering all Government employees regardless of the type or importance of the work they do, we hold that it makes no difference whether the jobs performed by certain public employees are regarded as "essential" or "non-essential," or whether similar jobs are performed by workers in private industry who do have the right to strike protected by statute. Nor is it relevant that some positions in private industry are arguably more affected with a public interest than are some positions in the Government service. While the Fifth Amendment contains no Equal Protection Clause similar to the one found in the Fourteenth Amendment, concepts of Equal Protection do inhere in Fifth Amendment Principles of Due Process. Bolling v. Sharpe, 347 U.S. 497, 74 S.Ct. 693, 98 L.Ed. 884 (1954). The Equal Protection Clause, however, does not forbid all discrimination. Where fundamental rights are not involved, a particular classification does not violate the Equal Protection Clause if it is not "arbitrary" or "irrational," i.e., "if any state of facts reasonably may be conceived to justify it." McGowan v. Maryland, 366 U.S. 420, 426, 81 S.Ct. 1101, 1105, 6 L.Ed.2d 393 (1961). Compare Kramer v. Union Free School District, 395 U.S. 621, 627–628, 89 S.Ct. 1886, 23 L.Ed.2d 583 (1969). Since the right to strike cannot be considered a "fundamental" right, it is the test enunciated in *McGowan* which must be employed in this case. Thus, there is latitude for distinctions rooted in reason and practice, especially where the difficulty of drafting a no-strike statute which distinguishes among types and classes of employees is obvious.

Furthermore, it should be pointed out that the fact that public employees may not strike does not interfere with their rights which are fundamental and constitutionally protected. The right to organize collectively and to select representatives for the purposes of engaging in collective bargaining is such a fundamental right. Thomas v. Collins, 323 U.S. 516, 65 S.Ct. 315, 89 L.Ed. 430 (1945); N.L.R.B. v. Jones & Laughlin, 301 U.S. 1, 33, 57 S.Ct. 615, 81 L.Ed. 893 (1937); Hague v. C.I.O., 307 U.S. 496, 59 S.Ct. 954, 83 L.Ed. 1423 (1939). But, as the Supreme Court noted in International Union, etc., Local 232 v. Wisconsin Employment Relations Board, supra, "The right to strike, because of its more serious impact upon the public interest, is more vulnerable to regulation than the right to organize and select representatives for lawful purposes of collective bargaining which this Court has characterized as a 'fundamental right' and which, as the Court has pointed out, was recognized as such in its decisions long before it was given protection by the National Labor Relations Act." 336 U.S. at 259, 69 S.Ct. at 524.

Executive Order 11491 recognizes the right of federal employees to join labor organizations for the purpose of dealing with grievances, but that Order clearly and expressly defines strikes, work stoppages and slow-downs as unfair labor practices. As discussed above, that Order is the culmination of a long-standing policy. There certainly is no compelling reason to imply the existence of the right to strike from the right to associate and bargain collectively. In the private sphere, the strike is used to equalize bargaining power, but this has universally been held not to be appropriate when its object and purpose can only be to influence the essentially political decisions of Government in the allocation of its resources. Congress has an obligation to ensure that the machinery of the Federal Government continues to function at all times without interference. Prohibition of strikes by its employees is a reasonable implementation of that obligation.

II. THE PROVISIONS ARE NEITHER UNCONSTITUTIONALLY VAGUE NOR OVERBROAD.

Plaintiff contends that the word "strike" and the phrase "participates in a strike" used in the statute are so vague that "men of common intelligence must necessarily guess at [their] meaning and differ as to [their] application," Connally v. General Construction Co., 269 U.S. 385, 391, 46 S.Ct. 126, 127, 70 L.Ed. 322 (1926), and are therefore violative of the due process clause of the Fifth Amendment. Plaintiff also contends that the provisions are overly broad. While there is no sharp distinction between vagueness and overbreadth, an overly broad statute reaches not only conduct which the Government may properly prohibit but also conduct which is beyond the reach of governmental regulation. A vague statute is merely imprecise in indicating which of several types of conduct which could be restricted has in fact been prohibited.

These concepts of "striking" and "participating in a strike" occupy central positions in our labor statutes and accompanying caselaw, and have been construed and interpreted many times by numerous state and federal courts. "Strike" is defined in § 501(2) of the Taft-Hartley Act to include "any strike or other concerted stoppage of work by employees * * * and any concerted slowdown or other concerted interruption of operations by employees." On its face this is a straightforward definition. It is difficult to understand how a word used and defined so often could be sufficiently ambiguous as to be constitutionally suspect. "Strike" is a term of such common usage and acceptance that "men of common intelligence" need not guess at its meaning. Connally v. General Construction Co., supra, at 391, 46 S.Ct. at 127.

Plaintiff complains that the precise parameters of "participation" are so unclear that employees may fail to exercise other, protected First Amendment rights for fear of overstepping the line, and that in any event, "participates" is too broad to withstand judicial scrutiny. Plaintiff urges that Congress is required to more specifically define exactly what activities are to be caught up in the net of illegality.

The Government, however, represented at oral argument that it interprets "participate" to mean "striking," the essence of which is an actual refusal in concert with others to provide services to one's employer. We adopt this construction of the phrase, which will exclude the First Amendment problems raised by the plaintiff in that it removes from the strict reach of these statutes and other provisions such conduct as speech, union membership, fund-raising, organization, distribution of literature and informational picketing, even though those activities may take place in concert during a strike by others. We stress that it is only an actual refusal by particular employees to provide services that is forbidden by 5 U.S.C.A. § 7311(3) and penalized by 18 U.S.C.A. § 1918. However, these statutes, as all criminal statutes, must be read in conjunction with 18 U.S.C.A. §§ 2 (aiding and abetting) and 371 (conspiracy). We express no views as to the extent of their application to cases that might arise thereunder as it is practically impossible to fashion a meaningful declaratory judgment in such a broad area.

This case does not involve a situation where we are concerned with a prior construction by a state supreme court, but rather one in which we are faced with the interpretation to be given a federal statute in the first instance by a federal court. Under such circumstances federal courts have broad latitude, the language of the statute permitting, to construe a statute in such terms as will save it from the infirmities of vagueness and over-breadth. Kent v. Dulles, 357 U.S. 116, 78 S.Ct. 1113, 2 L.Ed.2d 1204 (1958). This principle of interpretation is equally true of cases which involve rights under the First Amendment. United States v. C.I.O., 335 U.S. 106, 120–122, 68 S.Ct. 1349, 92 L.Ed. 1849 (1948); Chaplinsky v. New Hampshire, 315 U.S. 568, 573–574, 62 S.Ct. 766, 86 L.Ed. 1031 (1942); see also Williams v. District of Columbia, 136 U.S.App.D.C. 56, 419 F.2d 638 (en banc, 1969). Such construction of the word "strike" and the phrase "participates in a strike" achieves the objective of Congress and, in defining the type of conduct which is beyond the reach of the statute, saves it from the risk of vagueness and overbreadth.

Accordingly, we hold that the provisions of the statute, the appointment affidavit and the Executive Order, as construed above, do not violate any constitutional rights of those employees who are members of plaintiff's union. The Government's motion to dismiss the complaint is granted. Order to be presented.

J. SKELLY WRIGHT, CIRCUIT JUDGE (concurring):

I concur in Part II of the majority's opinion and in the result. My following comments are addressed to the main issue raised in Part I of the opinion—the validity of the flat ban on federal employees' strikes under the Fifth Amendment of the Constitution. This question is, in my view, a very difficult one, and I cannot concur fully in the majority's handling of it.

It is by no means clear to me that the right to strike is not fundamental. The right to strike seems intimately related to the right to form labor organizations, a right which the majority recognizes as fundamental and which, more importantly, is generally thought to be constitutionally protected under the First Amendment—even for public employees. See Melton v. City of Atlanta, 324 F.Supp. 315 (N.D.Ga.1971); Atkins v. City of Charlotte, 296 F.Supp. 1068 (W.D.N.C.1969). If the inherent purpose of a labor organization is to bring the workers' interests to bear on management, the right to strike is, historically and practically, an important means of effectuating that purpose. A union that never strikes, or which can make no credible threat to strike, may wither away in ineffectiveness. That fact is not irrelevant to the constitutional calculations. Indeed, in several decisions, the Supreme Court has held that the First Amendment right of association is at least concerned with essential organizational activities which give the particular association life and promote its fundamental purposes. See

Williams v. Rhodes, 393 U.S. 23, 89 S.Ct. 5, 21 L.Ed.2d 24 (1968); United Mine Workers, etc. v. Illinois State Bar Assn., 389 U.S. 217, 88 S.Ct. 353, 19 L.Ed.2d 426 (1967). I do not suggest that the right to strike is co-equal with the right to form labor organizations. Nor do I equate striking with the organizational activities protected in *Williams* (access to the ballot) or *United Mine Workers* (group legal representation). But I do believe that the right to strike is, at least, within constitutional concern and should not be discriminatorily abridged without substantial or "compelling" justification.

Hence the real question here, as I see it, is to determine whether there is such justification for denying federal employees a right which is granted to other employees of private business. Plaintiff's arguments that not all federal services are "essential" and that some privately provided services are no less "essential" casts doubt on the validity of the flat ban on federal employees' strikes. In our mixed economic system of governmental and private enterprise, the line separating governmental from private functions may depend more on the accidents of history than on substantial differences in kind.

Nevertheless, I feel that I must concur in the result reached by the majority in Part I of its opinion. As the majority indicates, the asserted right of public employees to strike has often been litigated and, so far as I know, never recognized as a matter of law. The present state of the relevant jurisprudence offers almost no support for the proposition that the government lacks a "compelling" interest in prohibiting such strikes. No doubt, the line between "essential" and "non-essential" functions is very, very difficult to draw. For that reason, it may well be best to accept the demarcations resulting from the development of our political economy. If the right of public employees to strike—with all its political and social ramifications—is to be recognized and protected by the judiciary, it should be done by the Supreme Court which has the power to reject established jurisprudence and the authority to enforce such a sweeping rule.

Note

In 1971, Executive Order 11491 was amended by Executive Order 11616, which, along with other changes, eliminated the requirement that labor organizations refrain from *asserting* the right to strike. The Executive Orders have been superseded by Title VII (Federal Service Labor-Management Relations) of the Civil Service Reform Act of 1978, 5 U.S.C.A. §§ 7101–7135, set forth in the Statutory Supplement. This enactment is briefly described infra, p. 1146.

COUNTY SANITATION DISTRICT NO. 2 OF LOS ANGELES COUNTY v. LOS ANGELES COUNTY EMPLOYEES ASSOCIATION, LOCAL 660

Supreme Court of California, 1985.
38 Cal.3d 564, 214 Cal.Rptr. 424, 699 P.2d 835.

BROUSSARD, JUSTICE.

Defendants appeal from a judgment awarding plaintiff sanitation district damages and prejudgment interest in connection with defendant union's involvement in a labor strike against plaintiff. The case squarely presents issues of great import to public sector labor-management relations, namely whether all strikes by public employees are illegal and, if so, whether the striking union is liable in tort for compensatory damages. After careful review of a long line of case law and policy arguments, we conclude that the common law prohibition against all public employee strikes is no longer supportable. Therefore, the judgment for the plaintiff finding the strike to be unlawful and awarding damages, interest and costs must be reversed.

I. STATEMENT OF THE CASE.

Defendant union (Local 660 or the union) is a labor organization affiliated with the Service Employees International Union, AFL–CIO, and has been the certified bargaining representative of the blue collar employees of the Los Angeles Sanitation District since 1973. Plaintiff is one of 27 sanitation districts within Los Angeles County and is charged with providing, operating and maintaining sewage transport and treatment facilities and landfill disposal sites throughout the county. The District employs some 500 workers who are directly or indirectly responsible for the operation and maintenance of its facilities and who are members of, or represented by, Local 660. Since 1973, the District and Local 660 have bargained concerning wages, hours and working conditions pursuant to the Meyers-Milias-Brown Act (MMBA). (Gov.Code, §§ 3500–3511.) Each year these negotiations have resulted in a binding labor contract or memorandum of understanding (MOU). * * *

On July 5, 1976, approximately 75 percent of the District's employees went out on strike after negotiations between the District and the union for a new wage and benefit agreement reached an impasse and failed to produce a new MOU. The District promptly filed a complaint for injunctive relief and damages and was granted a temporary restraining order. The strike continued for approximately 11 days, during which time the District was able to maintain its facilities and operations through the efforts of management personnel and certain union members who chose not to strike. On July 16, the employees voted to accept a tentative agreement on a new MOU, the terms of which were identical to the District's offer prior to the strike.

The District then proceeded with the instant action for tort damages. The trial court found the strike to be unlawful and in violation of the public policy of the State of California and thus awarded the District $246,904 in compensatory damages, prejudgment interest in the amount of $87,615.22 and costs of $874.65.

II. THE TRADITIONAL PROHIBITION AGAINST PUBLIC EMPLOYEE STRIKES.

Common law decisions in other jurisdictions at one time held that no employee, whether public or private, had a right to strike in concert with fellow workers. In fact, such collective action was generally viewed as a conspiracy and held subject to both civil and criminal sanctions.[5] Over the

---

5. See Commonwealth v. Pullis (Mayor's Ct.Phil. 91806) reported in 3 Commons, Documentary History of American Industrial Society (1910) p. 59; Walker v. Cronin (1871) 107 Mass. 555; Vegelahn v. Guntner (1896) 167 Mass. 92, 44 N.E. 1077; Loewe v. Lawlor (1908) 208 U.S. 274, 28 S.Ct. 301, 52 L.Ed. 488.

course of the 20th century, however, courts and legislatures gradually acted to change these laws as they applied to private sector employees; today, the right to strike is generally accepted as indispensable to the system of collective bargaining and negotiation, which characterizes labor-management relations in the private sector.[6]

By contrast, American law continues to regard public sector strikes in a substantially different manner. A strike by employees of the United States government may still be treated as a crime,[7] and strikes by state and local employees have been explicitly allowed by courts or statute in only 10 states.[8]

Contrary to the assertions of the plaintiff as well as various holdings of the Court of Appeal,[9] this court has repeatedly stated that the legality of strikes by public employees in California has remained an open question. In Los Angeles Met. Transit Authority v. Brotherhood of Railroad Trainmen (1960) 54 Cal.2d 684, 687–688, 8 Cal.Rptr. 1, 355 P.2d 905, this court stated in dictum that "[i]n the absence of legislative authorization public employees in general do not have the right to strike . . ." but proceeded to hold that a statute affording public transit workers the right " 'to engage in other concerted activities for the purpose of collectively bargaining or other mutual aid or protection' " granted these employees a right to strike. However, in our very next opinion on the issue, In re Berry (1968) 68 Cal.2d 137, 65 Cal.Rptr. 273, 436 P.2d 273, we invalidated an injunction against striking public employees as unconstitutionally overbroad, and expressly

---

6. Congress gradually, through a series of legislative enactments, not only granted private sector employees a right to strike and to engage in other concerted activities, but also deprived employers of their traditional remedies of injunction and damage suits. (See 38 Stat. 730 (1914) [Clayton Antitrust Act], codified as amended at 15 U.S.C. §§ 15, 17, 26 (1970), 29 U.S.C. § 52 (1970); 47 Stat. 70 (1930) [Norris-La Guardia Act], codified at 29 U.S.C. §§ 101–115 (1970); 44 Stat., pt. II 577 (1926) [Railway Labor Act], codified as amended at 45 U.S.C. §§ 151–88 (1970); 49 Stat. 449 (1935) [Wagner Act], codified as amended at 29 U.S.C. §§ 141–197 (1970).)

7. Employees of the federal government are statutorily prohibited from striking under 5 United States Code section 7311 (1976), which prohibits an individual from holding a federal position if he "participates in a strike, or asserts the right to strike against the Government of the United States. ✳ ✳ ✳" In United Federation of Postal Clerks v. Blount (D.D.C.1971) 325 F.Supp. 879, affd., 404 U.S. 802, 92 S.Ct. 80, 30 L.Ed.2d 38 (1971), the court upheld the constitutionality of the strike prohibitions, yet declared unconstitutional the "wording insofar as it inhibits the *assertion* of the right to strike. ✳ ✳ ✳" (Id. at p. 881 [emphasis in original].) In 1947, Congress originally denied federal employees the right to strike in section 305 of the Labor Management Relations Act (Taft-Hartley Act), chap-

ter 120, 61 Statutes at Large 136 (1947). This act was repealed and ultimately replaced by section 7311.

8. Those 10 states are Alaska, Hawaii, Idaho, Illinois, Minnesota, Montana, Oregon, Pennsylvania, Vermont, and Wisconsin. (See further discussion below.) Interestingly, the United States is virtually alone among Western industrial nations in upholding a general prohibition of public employee strikes. Most European countries have permitted them, with certain limitations, for quite some time as has Canada. See, e.g., Anderson, Strikes and Impasse Resolution in Public Employment (1969) 67 Mich.L.Rev. 943, 961–964.

9. See, e.g., Stationary Engineers v. San Juan Water Dist. (1979) 90 Cal.App.3d 796, 801, 153 Cal.Rptr. 666; Pasadena Unified Sch. Dist. v. Pasadena Federation of Teachers (1977) 72 Cal.App.3d 100, 140 Cal.Rptr. 41; Service Employees' International Union, Local No. 22 v. Roseville Community Hosp. (1972) 24 Cal.App.3d 400, 408, 101 Cal.Rptr. 69; Trustees of Cal. State Colleges v. Local 1352, S.F. State etc. Teachers (1970) 13 Cal. App.3d 863, 867, 92 Cal.Rptr. 134; City of San Diego v. American Federation of State etc. Employees (1970) 8 Cal.App.3d 308, 310, 87 Cal.Rptr. 258; Almond v. County of Sacramento (1969) 276 Cal.App.2d 32, 35, 80 Cal. Rptr. 518.

reserved opinion on "the question whether strikes by public employees can be lawfully enjoined." (Id., p. 151, 65 Cal.Rptr. 273, 436 P.2d 273.)

In our next opportunity to examine public employee strikes, City and County of San Francisco v. Cooper (1975) 13 Cal.3d 898, 120 Cal.Rptr. 707, 534 P.2d 403, which involved a suit challenging the validity of a strike settlement agreement enacted by the city, we held only that such settlement agreements are valid. After noting the Court of Appeal holdings that public employee strikes are illegal and the employees' counterargument that such strikes are impliedly authorized by statute, our unanimous opinion declared that we had no occasion to resolve that controversy in that action. (Id., p. 912, 120 Cal.Rptr. 707, 534 P.2d 403.)

In a similar vein, this court has carefully and explicitly reserved judgment on the issue of the legality of public employee strikes on at least three other occasions in recent years.[10] Indeed, our reluctance to address the issue head-on has elicited critical commentary from both dissenting and concurring opinions, which have urged us to resolve the question once and for all.[11] While we had ample reason for deciding the aforementioned cases without determining the broader question of the right of public employees to strike, the instant case presents us with the proper circumstances for direct consideration of this fundamental issue.

Before commencing our discussion, however, we must note that the Legislature has also chosen to reserve judgment on the general legality of strikes in the public sector. As Justice Grodin observed in his concurring opinion in El Rancho Unified School Dist. v. National Education Assn., supra, 33 Cal.3d 946, 964, 192 Cal.Rptr. 123, 663 P.2d 893, "the Legislature itself has steadfastly refrained from providing clearcut guidance." With the exception of firefighters (Lab.Code, § 1962), no statutory prohibition against strikes by public employees in this state exists. The MMBA, the statute under which the present controversy arose, does not directly address the question of strikes.

The MMBA sets forth the rights of municipal and county employees in California.[13] (Gov.Code, §§ 3500–3511.) The MMBA protects the right of

10. San Diego Teachers Assn. v. Superior Court (1979) 24 Cal.3d 1, 154 Cal.Rptr. 893, 593 P.2d 838; El Rancho Unified School Dist. v. National Education Assn. (1983) 33 Cal.3d 946, 192 Cal.Rptr. 123, 663 P.2d 893; and International Brotherhood of Electrical Workers, Local Union 1245 v. City of Gridley (1983) 34 Cal.3d 191, 193 Cal.Rptr. 518, 666 P.2d 960.

11. See, e.g., dissenting opinion of Richardson, J., in San Diego Teachers Assn. v. Superior Court, supra, 24 Cal.3d 1, 154 Cal.Rptr. 893, 593 P.2d 838 and concurring opinion of Richardson, J., in El Rancho Unified School Dist. v. National Education Assn., supra, 33 Cal.3d at page 962, 192 Cal.Rptr. 123, 663 P.2d 893, where he stated that "[t]his court should no longer continue its hesitant, tentative ritual dance around the perimeter of this central legal principle. * * *"

13. The MMBA revised its predecessor, the Brown Act, in 1968. The MMBA amend-

ments, however, apply only to local government employees because the MMBA deleted reference to the "State of California" and explicitly defined "public employee" as one employed by any political subdivision of the state. (See Gov.Code, § 3501.) Presently, state employees are governed by the State Employer-Employee Relations Act (Gov.Code, §§ 3512–3524).

Additional groups of employees were excepted from coverage under the Brown Act by previous legislation. These employees are consequently not covered by the MMBA. (See Pub.Util.Code, §§ 25051–25052, added by Stats.1955, ch. 1036, § 2 at pp. 1960–1961 [governing bargaining between employees of the Alameda-Contra Costa Transit District and their employers]; Pub.Util.Code, Appen. 1, § 3.6(b)–(g) [governing bargaining in the Los Angeles Metropolitan Transit Authority]; Ed.

such employees "to form, join, and participate in the activities of employee organizations * * * for the purpose of representation on all matters of employer-employee relations." It also requires public employers to "meet and confer" in good faith with employee representatives on all issues within the scope of representation. As explained in its preamble, one of the MMBA's main purposes is to improve communications between public employees and their employers by providing a reasonable method for resolving disputes. A further stated purpose is to promote improved personnel relations by "providing a uniform basis for recognizing the right of public employees to join organizations of their own choice." [14]

On its face, the MMBA neither denies nor grants local employees the right to strike. This omission is noteworthy since the Legislature has not hesitated to expressly prohibit strikes for certain classes of public employees. For example, the above-noted prohibition against strikes by firefighters was enacted nine years before the passage of the MMBA and remains in effect today. Moreover, the MMBA includes firefighters within its provisions. Thus, the absence of any such limitation on other public employees covered by the MMBA at the very least implies a lack of legislative intent to use the MMBA to enact a general strike prohibition.

* * *

In sum, the MMBA establishes a system of rights and protections for public employees which closely mirrors those enjoyed by workers in the private sector. The Legislature, however, intentionally avoided the inclusion of any provision which could be construed as either a blanket grant or prohibition of a right to strike, thus leaving the issue shrouded in ambiguity. In the absence of clear legislative directive on this crucial matter, it becomes the task of the judiciary to determine whether, under the law, strikes by public employees should be viewed as a prohibited tort.

III. THE COMMON LAW PROHIBITION AGAINST PUBLIC EMPLOYEE STRIKES.

As noted above, the Court of Appeal and various lower courts in this and other jurisdictions have repeatedly stated that, absent a specific statutory grant, all strikes by public employees are per se illegal. A variety of policy rationales and legal justifications have traditionally been advanced in support of this common law "rule," and numerous articles and scholarly treatises have been devoted to debating their respective merits.[18] The

Code, §§ 13080–13089 [governing educational employees].)

For a detailed discussion of the scope and purposes of the MMBA, see Grodin, Public Employees Bargaining in California: The Meyers-Milias-Brown Act in the Courts (1972) 23 Hastings L.J. 719; Note, Collective Bargaining Under the Meyers-Milias-Brown Act— Should Local Employees Have the Right to Strike (1984) 35 Hastings L.J. 523.

14. However, the MMBA contains no clear mechanism for resolving disputes. It merely provides that if the parties fail to reach an agreement, they may agree to appoint a mediator or use other impasse resolution procedures agreed upon by the parties. Additional-

ly, the MMBA does not authorize the establishment of an administrative agency to resolve controversies arising under its provisions. In contrast, statutes governing other public employees in California authorize the Public Employee Relations Board (PERB) to resolve disputes and enforce the provisions of the legislation. (See Gov.Code, § 3541.3 (setting the powers and duties of the PERB under the Educational Employment Relations Act (EERA)); and Gov.Code, § 3513, subd. (g) [making the powers and duties of the PERB under the EERA applicable to the State Employees Relations Act].)

18. Among the more notable works to appear recently on the subject of labor relations

various justifications for the common law prohibition can be summarized into four basic arguments. First—the traditional justification—that a strike by public employees is tantamount to a denial of governmental authority/ sovereignty. Second, the terms of public employment are not subject to bilateral collective bargaining, as in the private sector, because they are set by the legislative body through unilateral lawmaking. Third, since legislative bodies are responsible for public employment decision making, granting public employees the right to strike would afford them excessive bargaining leverage, resulting in a distortion of the political process and an improper delegation of legislative authority. Finally, public employees provide essential public services which, if interrupted by strikes, would threaten the public welfare.

Our determination of the legality of strikes by public employees necessarily involves an analysis of the reasoning and current viability of each of these arguments. The first of these justifications, the sovereignty argument, asserts that government is the embodiment of the people, and hence those entrusted to carry out its function may not impede it. This argument was particularly popular in the first half of the 20th century, when it received support from several American Presidents.[20]

The sovereignty concept, however, has often been criticized in recent years as a vague and outdated theory based on the assumption that "the King can do no wrong." As Judge Harry T. Edwards has cogently observed, "the application of the strict sovereignty notion—that governmental power

in the public sector are: Hanslowe & Acierno, The Law and Theory of Strikes By Government Employees (1982) 67 Cornell L.Rev. 1055; Comment, Public Employees (1982) 67 Cornell L.Rev. 1055; Comment, Public Employee Legislation: An Emerging Paradox, Impact, and Opportunity (1976) 13 San Diego L.Rev. 931; Comment, California Assembly Advisory Council's Recommendations on Impasse Resolution Procedures and Public Employee Strikes (1974) 11 San Diego L.Rev. 473; Comment, The Collective Bargaining Process at the Municipal Level Lingers in Its Chrysalis Stage (1974) 14 Santa Clara Law. 397; Grodin, Public Employee Bargaining in California: The Meyers-Milias-Brown Act in the Courts (1972) 23 Hastings L.J. 719; Shaw & Clark, The Practical Differences Between Public and Private Sector Collective Bargaining (1972) 19 UCLA L.Rev. 867; Lev, Strikes by Government Employees: Problems and Solutions (1971) 57 A.B.A.J. 771; Witt, The Public Sector Strike: Dilemma of the Seventies (1971) 8 Cal.Western L.Rev. 102; Bernstein, Alternatives to the Strike in Public Labor Relations (1971) 85 Harv.L.Rev. 459; Burton & Krider, The Role and Consequences of Strikes by Public Employees (1970) 79 Yale L.J. 418; Wellington & Winter, More on Strikes by Public Employees (1970) 79 Yale L.J. 441; Kheel, Strikes and Public Employment (1969) 67 Mich.L.Rev. 931; Anderson, Strikes and Impasse Resolution in Public Employment (1969) 67 Mich.L.Rev. 943; Wellington & Winter, The Limits of Collective Bar-

gaining in Public Employment (1969) 78 Yale L.J. 1107; Thorne, The Government Employee and Organized Labor (1962) 2 Santa Clara Law. 147; Note, Labor Relations in the Public Service (1961) 75 Harv.L.Rev. 391; Annot., Labor Law: Right of Public Employees to Strike or Engage in Work Stoppage (1971) 37 A.L.R.3d 1147.

20. Commenting on the Boston police strike, Calvin Coolidge asserted that "[t]here is no right to strike against public safety by anybody, anywhere, at any time" (quoted in Norwalk Teachers Ass'n v. Board of Education (1951) 138 Conn. 269, 273, 83 A.2d 482, 484). Woodrow Wilson, commenting on the same strike, stated that the strike is "'an intolerable crime against civilization'" (quoted in id., at p. 273, 83 A.2d at p. 484).

In another famous pronouncement of the sovereignty argument, President Franklin Roosevelt stated: "'[M]ilitant tactics have no place in the functions of any organization of Government employees. * * * [A] strike of public employees manifests nothing less than an intent on their part to prevent or obstruct the operations of Government until their demands are satisfied. Such action, looking toward the paralysis of Government by those who have sworn to support it, is unthinkable and intolerable.'" (Id., at pp. 273–274, 83 A.2d at p. 484 [quoting a letter from President Roosevelt to the president of the National Federation of Federal Employees (Aug. 16, 1937)].)

can never be opposed by employee organizations—is clearly a vestige from another era, an era of unexpanded government. * * * With the rapid growth of the government, both in sheer size as well as in terms of assuming services not traditionally associated with the 'sovereign,' government employees understandably no longer feel constrained by a notion that The King can do no wrong. The distraught cries by public unions of disparate treatment merely reflect the fact that, for all intents and purposes, public employees occupy essentially the same position vis a vis the employer as their private counterparts." Edwards, The Developing Labor Relations Law in the Public Sector (1972) 10 Duq.L.Rev. 357, 359–360.

In recent years, courts have rejected the very same concept of sovereignty as a justification for governmental immunity from tort liability. In California, the death knell came in Muskopf v. Corning Hospital Dist. (1961) 55 Cal.2d 211, 11 Cal.Rptr. 89, 359 P.2d 457, where this court stated that, "[t]he rule of governmental immunity for tort is an anachronism, without rational basis, and has existed only by the force of inertia." (55 Cal.2d at p. 216, 11 Cal.Rptr. 89, 359 P.2d 457.) As noted by this court in *Muskopf,* perpetuation of the doctrine of sovereign immunity in tort law led to many inequities, and its application effected many incongruous results. Similarly, the use of this archaic concept to justify a per se prohibition against public employee strikes is inconsistent with modern social reality and should be hereafter laid to rest.

The second basic argument underlying the common law prohibition of public employee strikes holds that since the terms of public employment are fixed by the Legislature, public employers are virtually powerless to respond to strike pressure, or alternatively that allowing such strikes would result in "government by contract" instead of "government by law." (See City of L.A. v. Los Angeles etc. Council (1949) 94 Cal.App.2d 36, 46, 210 P.2d 305.) This justification may have had some merit before the California Legislature gave extensive bargaining rights to public employees. However, at present, most terms and conditions of public employment are arrived at through collective bargaining under such statutes as the MMBA.

We have already seen that the MMBA establishes a variety of rights and protections for public employees—including the right to join and participate in union activities and to meet and confer with employer representatives for the purpose of resolving disputed labor-management issues. The importance of mandating these rights, particularly the meet and confer requirement, cannot be ignored. The overall framework of the MMBA represents a nearly exact parallel to the private sector system of collective bargaining—a system which sets forth the guidelines for labor-management relations in the private sphere and which protects the right of private employees to strike. By enacting these significant and parallel protections for public employees through the MMBA, the Legislature effectively removed many of the underpinnings of the common law per se ban against public employee strikes. While the MMBA does not directly address the issue of such strikes, its implications regarding the traditional common law prohibition are significant.

This argument was eloquently explained by Justice Grodin in his concurring opinion in El Rancho Unified Sch. Dist. v. National Education Assn., supra, 33 Cal.3d at page 963, 192 Cal.Rptr. 123, 663 P.2d 893, where he pointed out that "[t]he premise underlying the court's opinion in *City of L.A.* [94 Cal.App.2d 36, 210 P.2d 305]—that it is necessarily contrary to public policy to establish terms and conditions of employment for public employees through the bilateral process of collective bargaining rather than through unilateral lawmaking—has since been rejected by the Legislature. The heart of the statute under consideration in this case [the Educational Employment Relations Act], for example, contemplates that matters relating to wages, hours, and certain other terms and conditions of employment for teachers will be the subject of negotiation and agreement between a public school employer and organizations representing its employees. (Gov.Code, §§ 3543.2, 3543.3, 3543.7.) Thus, the original policy foundation for the 'rule' that public employee strikes are illegal in this state has been substantially undermined, if not obliterated."

The remaining two arguments have not served in this state as grounds for asserting a ban on public employee strikes but have been advanced by commentators and by courts of other states. With the traditional reasons for prohibiting such strikes debunked, these additional reasons do not convince us of the necessity of a judicial ukase prohibiting all such strikes.

The first of these arguments draws upon the different roles of market forces in the private and public spheres. This rationale suggests that because government services are essential and demand is generally inelastic, public employees would wield excessive bargaining power if allowed to strike. Proponents of this argument assume that economic constraints are not present to any meaningful degree in the public sector. Consequently, in the absence of such constraints, public employers will be forced to make abnormally large concessions to workers, which in turn will distort our political process by forcing either higher taxes or a redistribution of resources between government services.[22]

There are, however, several fundamental problems with this "distortion of the political process" argument. For one, as will be discussed more fully below, a key assumption underlying the argument—that all government services are essential—is factually unsupportable. Modern governments engage in an enormous number and variety of functions, which clearly vary as to their degree of essentiality. As such, the absence of an unavoidable nexus between most public services and essentiality necessarily undercuts the notion that public officials will be forced to settle strikes quickly and at any cost. The recent case of the air-traffic controllers' strike [23] is yet another example that governments have the ability to hold firm against a strike for a considerable period, even in the face of substantial inconve-

22. See e.g., United Federation of Postal Clerks v. Blount, supra, 325 F.Supp. 879, 884. ("In the private sphere, the strike is used to equalize bargaining power, but this has universally been held not to be appropriate when its object and purpose can only be to influence the essentially political decisions of Government in the allocation of its resources.")

For an even more extensive elaboration of this "distortion of the political process" argument, see Wellington & Winter, The Limits of Collective Bargaining in Public Employment, supra, 78 Yale L.J. 1107.

23. In August 1981, the Professional Air Traffic Controllers Organization (PATCO)

nience. As this court concluded in Los Angeles Met. Transit Authority v. Brotherhood of Railroad Trainmen, supra, "Permitting employees to strike does *not* delegate to them authority to fix their own wages to the exclusion of the employer's discretion. In collective bargaining negotiations, whether or not the employees strike, the employer is free to reject demands if he determines that they are unacceptable." (54 Cal.2d at p. 693, 8 Cal.Rptr. 1, 355 P.2d 905, italics added.)

Other factors also serve to temper the potential bargaining power of striking public employees and thus enable public officials to resist excessive demands: First, wages lost due to strikes are as important to public employees as they are to private employees. Second, the public's concern over increasing tax rates will serve to prevent the decision-making process from being dominated by political instead of economic considerations. A third and related economic constraint arises in such areas as water, sewage and, in some instances, sanitation services, where explicit prices are charged. Even if representatives of groups other than employees and the employer do not formally enter the bargaining process, both union and local government representatives are aware of the economic implications of bargaining which leads to higher prices which are clearly visible to the public. A fourth economic constraint on public employees exists in those services where subcontracting to the private sector is a realistic alternative. For example, Warren, Michigan resolved a bargaining impasse with an American Federation of State, County and Municipal Employees (AFSCME) local by subcontracting its entire sanitation service; Santa Monica, California, ended a strike of city employees by threatening to subcontract its sanitation operations; in fact, San Francisco has chosen to subcontract its entire sanitation system to *private* firms. If this subcontract option is preserved, wages in the public sector clearly need not exceed the rate at which subcontracting becomes a realistic alternative.

The proponents of a flat ban on public employee strikes not only ignore such factors as the availability of subcontracting, but also fail to adequately consider public sentiment towards most strikes and assume that the public will push blindly for an early resolution at any cost. In fact, public sentiment toward a strike often limits the pressure felt by political leaders, thereby reducing the strike's effectiveness. A Pennsylvania Governor's Commission Report stressed just such public sentiment as an important reason to *grant* a limited right to strike: "[T]he limitations on the right to strike which we propose * * * will appeal to the general public as so much fairer than a general ban on strikes that the public will be less likely to tolerate strikes beyond these boundaries. Strikes can only be effective so long as they have public support. *In short, we look upon the limited and*

launched a nationwide strike against the federal government. President Ronald Reagan ordered the discharge of 11,000 striking controllers who had not returned to work within a two-day grace period. Up to the time of this writing, the Administration has rejected all suggestions for a general amnesty, its position being that the strikers, by violating the federal government's prohibition on strikes and their own "no-strike" oath, have forfeited their jobs with the Federal Aviation Administration forever. Federal courts upheld the government's position in PATCO v. Federal Labor Relations Authority (D.C.Cir.1982) 685 F.2d 547. For a more detailed analysis of the strike, see Meltzer & Sunstein, Public Employee Strikes, Executive Discretion, and the Air Traffic Controllers (1983) 50 U.Chi.L.Rev. 731.

carefully defined right to strike as a safety valve that will in fact prevent strikes." [25] (Italics in original.)

In sum, there is little, if any empirical evidence which demonstrates that governments generally capitulate to unreasonable demands by public employers in order to resolve strikes. The result of the strike in the instant case clearly suggests the opposite. During the 11-day strike, negotiations resumed, and the parties subsequently reached an agreement on a new MOU, the terms of which were *precisely the same* as the District's last offer prior to the commencement of the strike. Such results certainly do not illustrate a situation where public employees wielded excessive bargaining power and thereby caused a distortion of our political process.

The fourth and final justification for the common law prohibition is that interruption of government services is unacceptable because they are essential. As noted above, in our contemporary industrial society the presumption of essentiality of most government services is questionable at best. In addition, we tolerate strikes by private employees in many of the same areas in which government is engaged, such as transportation, health, education, and utilities; in many employment fields, public and private activity largely overlap.

* * *

We of course recognize that there are certain "essential" public services, the disruption of which would seriously threaten the public health or safety. In fact, defendant union itself concedes that the law should still act to render illegal any strikes in truly essential services which would constitute a genuine threat to the public welfare. Therefore, to the extent that the "excessive bargaining power" and "interruption of essential services" arguments still have merit, specific health and safety limitations on the right to strike should suffice to answer the concerns underlying those arguments.

In addition to the various legal arguments advanced to persuade the courts to impose a judicial ban on public employee strikes—arguments which, as we have seen, are decidedly unpersuasive in the context of modern jurisprudence and experience—there is the broader concern that permitting public employees to strike may be, on balance, harmful to labor-management relations in the public sector. This is essentially a political argument, best addressed to the Legislature. We review the matter only to point out that the issue is not so clear cut as to justify judicial intervention, since the Legislature could reasonably conclude that recognizing public employees' right to strike may actually enhance labor-management relations.

At least 10 states have granted most of their public employees a right to strike,[26] and the policy rationale behind this statutory recognition further

25. Governor's Commission to Revise the Public Employee Law of Pennsylvania, Report and Recommendations, reprinted in 251 Govt. Empl.Rel.Rep. (BNA) E–1, E–3 (1968). This report is discussed in detail in Hanslowe & Acierno, The Law and Theory of Strikes by Government Employees, supra, 67 Cornell L.Rev. 1055.

26. See footnote 8, ante, for a list of the 10 states. Typically these statutes permit public sector strikes, unless such strikes endanger the public health, safety, or welfare. The statutes generally prohibit strikes by police and fire-protection employees, employees in correctional facilities, and those in health-care institutions. In some instances, statutes provide binding arbitration to resolve certain disputes for which strikes are proscribed. Thus, the public sector strike has begun to achieve some degree of legitimacy, despite the strong opposition of critics.

undercuts several of the basic premises relied upon by strike-ban advocates. As the aforementioned Pennsylvania Governor's Commission Report concluded: "The collective bargaining process will be strengthened if this qualified right to strike is recognized. It will be some curb on the possible intransigence of an employer; and the limitations on the right to strike will serve notice on the employee that there are limits to the hardships that he can impose." (251 Govt.Empl.Rel.Rep., supra, at p. E–3.)

It is unrealistic to assume that disputes among public employees and their employers will not occur; in fact, strikes by public employees are relatively frequent events in California. For example, 46 strikes occurred during 1981–1983, which actually marks a significant decline when compared to the number during the 5 previous years.[27] Although the circumstances behind each individual strike may vary somewhat, commentators repeatedly note that much of the reason for their occurrence lies in the fact that without the right to strike, or at least a credible strike threat, public employees have little negotiating strength. This, in turn, produces frustrations which exacerbate labor-management conflicts and often provoke "illegal" strikes.

The noted labor mediator, Theodore W. Kheel, aptly described this process when analyzing New York's Taylor Law (which makes all public employee strikes illegal) and its resultant effect on labor relations in that state: "It would be unfair to place upon the legal machinery sole responsibility for these interruptions of critical services on which the welfare of New York depends. But the fact remains that the machinery—including the prohibition on strikes with attendant penalties and the fact-finding boards with their power to make recommendations—did not work to settle these disputes or stop the strikes, slowdowns, or threats. In fact it is probable that the Taylor Law exacerbated these conflicts. For one thing, it made subversive a form of conduct society endorsed for private workers. It encouraged unions to threaten to strike to achieve the bargaining position participants in collective bargaining must possess. It made the march to jail a martyr's procession and a badge of honor for union leaders. * * * In simple point of fact, it did not and is not likely to work as a mechanism for resolving conflicts in public employment relations through joint determination, whether called collective bargaining or collective negotiations." (Kheel, Strikes and Public Employment, supra, 67 Mich.L.Rev. 931, 936.)[28]

---

27. Public employee strikes in California, 1970–1983: *

1970	1971	1972	1973	1974	1975	1976
20	14	18	15	45	44	23

1977	1978	1979	1980	1981	1982	1983
59	29	87	55	20	6	20

* Source: An Analysis of 1981–1983 Strikes in California's Public Sector (1984) (Mar. 1984 Inst. of Ind. Rel., U.C. Berkeley) 60 Cal.Pub. Empl.Rel. 7, 9. Public employees include all workers in public agencies in California, excluding federal service and public utilities.

28. Indeed the per se prohibition is notoriously ineffective. See Comment, California Assembly Advisory Council's Recommendations on Impasse Resolution Procedures and Public Employee Strikes, supra, 11 San Diego L.Rev. 473, 480. The council's study found that the "present laws do not deter strikes, and furthermore, that once an illegal strike is instituted the law has very little effect in compelling the strikers to return to work. Part of the reason for this is that many public employers hesitate to request an injunction because they believe that the employees would continue to strike, thereby forcing the employer to either initiate contempt proceedings and subject his employees to quasi-criminal penalties, or stand idly and ineffectually by as the illegal strike continues. Either of these alternatives, if pursued, would have a deleterious effect on future employee-management relations once the strike is settled."

It is universally recognized that in the private sector, the bilateral determination of wages and working conditions through a collective bargaining process, in which both sides possess relatively equal strength, facilitates understanding and more harmonious relations between employers and their employees. In the absence of some means of equalizing the parties' respective bargaining positions, such as a credible strike threat, both sides are less likely to bargain in good faith; this in turn leads to unsatisfactory and acrimonious labor relations and ironically to more and longer strikes. Equally as important, the possibility of a strike often provides the best impetus for parties to reach an agreement at the bargaining table, because *both* parties lose if a strike actually comes to pass. Thus by providing a clear incentive for resolving disputes, a credible strike threat may serve to avert, rather than to encourage, work stoppages.

Theodore Kheel has explained this argument very well: "[W]e should acknowledge the failure of unilateral determination, and turn instead to true collective bargaining, even though this must include the possibility of a strike. We would then clearly understand that we must seek to improve the bargaining process and the skill of the negotiators to prevent strikes. * * * With skillful and responsible negotiators, no machinery, no outsiders, and no fixed rules are needed to settle disputes. For too long our attention has been directed to the mechanics and penalties rather than to the participants in the process. It is now time to change that, to seek to prevent strikes by encouraging collective bargaining to the fullest extent possible." [30]

A final policy consideration in our analysis addresses a more philosophical issue—the perception that the right to strike, in the public sector as well as in the private sector, represents a basic civil liberty.[31] The widespread acceptance of that perception leads logically to the conclusion that the right to strike, as an important symbol of a free society, should not be denied

---

* * *

See also Cebulski, An Analysis of 22 Illegal Strikes and California Law (1973) 18 Cal.Pub. Empl.Rel. 2, 9 (chart showing that strikes in which public sector employers imposed legal sanctions lasted *twice as long* as strikes in which the employers did not attempt to impose sanctions).

30. Kheel, op. cit. supra, 67 Mich.L.Rev. at pages 940–941.

31. Another interesting and related policy argument in support of granting a right to strike to public employees rests on a recognition of the changing shape and values of the American economic system itself. In essence, it focuses on the fact that our market economy has evolved from its classical model into an increasingly mixed and pluralistic form. In this process of increased government intervention, the line between public and private enterprise has become increasingly blurred. At the same time, a concomitant blurring has occurred between traditional political and economic activity, and it is this latter overlap which renders a flat ban on all public sector strikes so difficult to defend.

The argument then analogizes the deviation of the American system from classical economic models and the corresponding reevaluation of public strike prohibitions to the Solidarity-inspired developments in Poland prior to the latest military crackdown. Ironically, the traditional common law argument that public sector bargaining and striking is antidemocratic and inimical to our political process, closely mirrors the Polish government's view that unions and strikes are antisocial—indeed revisionist and reactionary—conduct in a system operated purportedly for the benefit of all. Deviations from classical models and beliefs thus confront both ideological viewpoints. The argument for a right to strike for public employees in a capitalist system clearly gains strength as society evolves away from the classical ideal of a pure market economy where the public and private sectors are clearly separated. Similarly, the case for a right to strike in a socialist system grows stronger as that society deviates from the classical ideals of the socialist model. For a more detailed analysis of this theory, see Hanslowe & Acierno, supra, 67 Cornell L.Rev. at pages 1072–1073.

unless such a strike would substantially injure paramount interests of the larger community.

Plaintiff's argument that only the Legislature can reject the common law doctrine prohibiting public employee strikes flies squarely in the face of both logic and past precedent. Legislative silence is not the equivalent of positive legislation and does not preclude judicial reevaluation of common law doctrine. If the courts have created a bad rule or an outmoded one, the courts can change it.

This court has long recognized the need to redefine, modify or even abolish a common law rule "when reason or equity demand it" or when its underlying principles are no longer justifiable in light of modern society. (See Rodriquez v. Bethlehem Steel Corp. (1974) 12 Cal.3d 382, 394, 115 Cal. Rptr. 765, 525 P.2d 669; Muskopf v. Corning Hospital Dist. (1961) 55 Cal.2d 211, 216, 11 Cal.Rptr. 89, 359 P.2d 457; Green v. Superior Court (1974) 10 Cal.3d 616, 629, 111 Cal.Rptr. 704, 517 P.2d 1168; Li v. Yellow Cab Co. (1975) 13 Cal.3d 804, 808, 119 Cal.Rptr. 858, 532 P.2d 1228.)

This court's history provides numerous examples of this principle. In Li v. Yellow Cab Co., supra, 13 Cal.3d at page 812, 119 Cal.Rptr. 858, 532 P.2d 1228, when this court first adopted a rule of comparative negligence, we expressly rejected the contention that any change in the law of contributory negligence was exclusively a matter for the Legislature, and overturned more than a century of precedent. In Rodriguez v. Bethlehem Steel Corp., supra, we directly repudiated the assertion that recognition of a spousal action for loss of consortium required legislative action (see 12 Cal.3d pp. 393–395, 115 Cal.Rptr. 765, 525 P.2d 669) and reversed numerous prior decisions in endorsing that cause of action. Furthermore, "[w]hen the law governing a subject has been shaped and guided by judicial decision, legislative inaction does not necessarily constitute a tacit endorsement of the precise stage in the evolution of the law extant at the time when the Legislature did nothing; it may signify that the Legislature is willing to entrust the further evolution of legal doctrine to judicial development." (People v. Drew (1978) 22 Cal.3d 333, 347, fn. 11, 149 Cal.Rptr. 275, 583 P.2d 1318.)

For the reasons stated above, we conclude that the common law prohibition against public sector strikes should not be recognized in this state. Consequently, strikes by public sector employees in this state as such are neither illegal nor tortious under California common law. We must immediately caution, however, that the right of public employees to strike is by no means unlimited. Prudence and concern for the general public welfare require certain restrictions.

The Legislature has already prohibited strikes by firefighters under any circumstance. It may conclude that other categories of public employees perform such essential services that a strike would invariably result in imminent danger to public health and safety, and must therefore be prohibited.[32]

32. See, e.g., Minnesota Statutes Annotated section 179.63(11) (1981) (firefighters, peace officers, guards at correctional facilities), Oregon Revised Statutes section 243.736 (1979) (firefighters, police officers and guards at correctional or mental health institutions); Pennsylvania Statutes Annotated title 43, section 1101.1001 (guards at correctional or mental health institutions and employees necessary to the functioning of the courts). For a further discussion of these provisions, see Hanslowe & Acierno, The Law and Theory of

While the Legislature may enact such specific restrictions, the courts must proceed on a case-by-case basis. Certain existing statutory standards may properly guide them in this task. As noted above, a number of states have granted public employees a limited right to strike, and such legislation typically prohibits strikes by a limited number of employees involved in clearly essential services. In addition, several statutes provide for injunctive relief against other types of striking public employees when the state clearly demonstrates that the continuation of such strikes will constitute an imminent threat or "clear and present danger" to public health and safety.[33] Such an approach guarantees that essential public services will not be disrupted so as to genuinely threaten public health and safety, while also preserving the basic rights of public employees.

After consideration of the various alternatives before us, we believe the following standard may properly guide courts in the resolution of future disputes in this area: strikes by public employees are not unlawful at common law unless or until it is clearly demonstrated that such a strike creates a substantial and imminent threat to the health or safety of the public. This standard allows exceptions in certain essential areas of public employment (e.g., the prohibition against firefighters and law enforcement personnel) and also requires the courts to determine on a case-by-case basis whether the public interest overrides the basic right to strike.

Although we recognize that this balancing process may impose an additional burden on the judiciary, it is neither a novel nor unmanageable task.[34] Indeed, an examination of the strike in the instant case affords a

Strike by Government Employees, supra, 67 Cornell L.Rev. 1055, 1079–1083.

See also Burton & Kinder, supra, 79 Yale L.J. at page 437 (advocating a presumption of illegality in strikes involving truly essential services, thereby relieving the state of the burden to demonstrate the elements necessary for an injunction).

33. See, e.g., Alaska Statutes section 23.40.200(c) (strikes by most public employees may not be enjoined unless it can be shown that it has begun to threaten the health, safety and welfare of the public); Oregon Revised Statutes section 243.762(3)(a) (injunctive relief available when strike creates a clear and present danger or threat to the health, safety or welfare of the public); Pennsylvania Statutes Annotated title 43, section 1101.1003 (injunctive relief available when strike creates a clear and present danger or threats to the health, safety or welfare of the public); Wisconsin Statutes Annotated section 111.70(7m)(b) (injunctive relief available if strike poses an imminent threat to the public health or safety). See also School District for City of Holland v. Holland Educ. Ass'n (1968) 380 Mich. 314, 157 N.W.2d 206, 210 (Mich.Supreme Ct., in teachers strike cases, declaring state's policy is not "to issue injunctions in labor disputes absent a showing of violence, irreparable injury, or breach of the peace"); Timberlane Reg. Sch. Dist. v. Timberlane Reg. Ed. Ass'n (1974) 114 N.H. 245, 317 A.2d 555,

559 (N.H. Supreme Ct. refused to rule on the legality of teachers' strikes but stated that in determining whether to issue a strike injunction, a court should consider "whether the public health, safety and welfare will be substantially harmed if the strike is allowed to continue."). The Federal Labor Management Relations Act of 1947 [29 U.S.C. §§ 141–187], follows a similar approach with respect to private sector strikes. It empowers the President to direct the Attorney General to enjoin a threatened or actual strike if it affects an industry involved in interstate commerce and if permitted to occur or continue would imperil the national health or safety. (29 U.S.C. §§ 176–180.)

34. Legislation in several states already requires the courts to make this precise determination. (See e.g., the relevant statutory provisions in Alaska, Ore., Pa. and Wis.) For just one example, under the Pennsylvania Public Employee Relations Act, public employees are not prohibited from striking after they have submitted to mediation and fact finding, unless or until such a strike creates a clear and present danger or threat to the health, safety and welfare of the public. (Pa.Stat.Ann., tit. 43, § 1101.1003.) In such cases, the employer may petition for equitable relief, including injunctions, and is entitled to relief if the court finds that the strike creates the danger or threat. (Id.) The Pennsylvania courts have applied this standard to several classes of pub-

good example of how this new standard should be applied. The 11-day strike did not involve public employees, such as firefighters or law enforcement personnel, whose absence from their duties would clearly endanger the public health and safety. Moreover, there was no showing by the District that the health and safety of the public was at any time imminently threatened. That is not to say that had the strike continued indefinitely, or had the availability of replacement personnel been insufficient to maintain a reasonable sanitation system, there could not have been at some point a clear showing of a substantial threat to the public health and welfare.[35] However, such was not the case here, and the legality of the strike would have been upheld under our newly adopted standard.[36]

Defendant union has also urged this court to find that a per se prohibition of all public employee strikes violates the California Constitution's guarantees of freedom of association, free speech, and equal protection. They do not contend that such a constitutional infringement is present when a court exercises its equitable authority to enjoin a strike based on a showing that the strike represents a substantial and imminent danger to the public health or safety. Instead, the union argues that in the absence of such a showing, per se prohibition is constitutionally unsupportable.

The right to form and be represented by unions is a fundamental right of American workers that has been extended to public employees through constitutional adjudication [37] as well as by statute; in this case, it is specifically mandated by the provisions of the MMBA itself. * * *.

lic employees. (See, e.g., Bethel Park Sch. v. Bethel Park Fed. of Tchrs. Local 1607, Am. Fed'n of Teachers (1980) 54 Pa.Commw. 49, 52, 420 A.2d 18 (teacher's strike constituted a clear and present danger to the public's health, safety and welfare and school district entitled to back-to-work order in view of potential losses of state subsidies, instructional days vocational job, higher education opportunities, counseling, social and health services, extracurricular enrichment programs and employees' work opportunities and wages); Bristol Township Education Ass'n v. School District (1974) 14 Pa. Commw. 463, 468–470, 322 A.2d 767 (school district entitled to injunction against teacher's strike under similar circumstances); Highland Sewer and Water Auth. v. Local Union 459; I.B.E.W. (1973) 67 Pa.D. & C.2d 564, 565–567 (sewer and water authority not entitled to injunction forcing striking employees back to work since there was no clear and present danger in view of the fact that the services provided by the authority could still be performed during the strike, apparently by supervisors, with relatively little inconvenience).

35. Had such a showing been made, the trial court would then have had the authority to issue an injunction and declare the strike illegal. In cases involving sanitation strikes, it is often the length of the strike which will ultimately require issuance of an injunction. (See, e.g., Highland Sewer and Water Auth. v. Local Union 459, I.B.E.W., supra, 67 Pa.D. & C.2d 564, 565–567.) In addition, if particular

jobs performed by striking sanitation or other public employees require unique skills and training, it is conceivable that a public agency might be unable to find adequate replacements. In the instant matter, however, replacement personnel adequately maintained needed sanitation services without any significant threat of harm to the public. Further, the District's allegations of vandalism by the strikers * * *, while perhaps citing individual illegal acts, were by no means enough to render the entire strike illegal or even a substantial public threat.

36. The trial court in this matter had no reason to make a finding regarding the threat to public health and safety posed by the strike. The court merely relied on prior Court of Appeal opinions, which had held that public employee strikes were per se illegal in the absence of a specific statutory grant. In the future, trial courts will clearly be required to make such a finding. In these cases, the scope of appellate review will ordinarily be limited to determining whether reasonable grounds existed for the trial court's decision.

37. In upholding the National Labor Relations Act against constitutional attack, the United States Supreme Court recognized that the right of employees to organize for the purpose of collective bargaining is fundamental. (Labor Board v. Jones & Laughlin (1937) 301 U.S. 1, 33, 57 S.Ct. 615, 622, 81 L.Ed. 893.)

* * *

* * * As yet, however, the right to strike has not been accorded full constitutional protection, the prevailing view being that "[t]he right to strike, because of its more serious impact upon the public interest, is more vulnerable to regulation than the right to organize and select representatives for lawful purposes of collective bargaining which this Court has characterized as a 'fundamental right. * * *'" (Auto Workers v. Wis. Board (1949) 336 U.S. 245, 259, 69 S.Ct. 516, 524, 93 L.Ed. 651.)

Further, the federal ban on public employee strikes has been specifically upheld as constitutionally permissible. (See United Federation of Postal Clerks v. Blount, supra, 325 F.Supp. 879, 884; affd. (1971) 404 U.S. 802, 92 S.Ct. 80, 30 L.Ed.2d 38.) In the absence of any explicit constitutional protection of the right to strike, the *Blount* court reasoned that the law prohibiting only public employees from striking need only have a rational basis to avoid offending constitutional guarantees. The court then easily found that the common law policy justifications (discussed in detail above) did indeed provide a rational basis for the per se prohibition. (See, United Federation of Postal Clerks v. Blount, supra, at p. 883.)

Thoughtful judges and commentators, however, have questioned the wisdom of upholding a per se prohibition of public employee strikes. They have persuasively argued that because the right to strike is so inextricably intertwined with the recognized fundamental right to organize and collectively bargain, some degree of constitutional protection should be extended to the act of striking in both the public and private sectors.

* * *

We are not persuaded that the personal freedoms guaranteed by the United States and California Constitutions confer an *absolute right* to strike,[38] but the arguments above may merit consideration at some future date. If the right to strike is afforded some constitutional protection as derivative of the fundamental right of freedom of association, then this right cannot be abridged absent a substantial or compelling justification.

* * *

Since we have already concluded that the traditional per se prohibition against public employee strikes can no longer be upheld on common law grounds, we do not find it necessary to reach the issue in constitutional terms. Although we are not inclined to hold that the right to strike rises to the magnitude of a fundamental right, it does appear that associational rights are implicated to a substantial degree. As such, the close connection between striking and other constitutionally protected activity adds further weight to our rejection of the traditional common law rationales underlying the per se prohibition. (Cf. Environmental Planning & Information Council v. Superior Court (1984) 36 Cal.3d 188, 195, 203 Cal.Rptr. 127, 680 P.2d 1086.)

We conclude that it is not unlawful for public employees to engage in a concerted work stoppage for the purpose of improving their wages or conditions of employment, unless it has been determined that the work

---

38. As stated in the United States Supreme Court in Dorchy v. Kansas: "Neither the common law nor the Fourteenth Amendment confers the absolute right to strike." (Dorchy v. Kansas (1926) 272 U.S. 306, 311, 47 S.Ct. 86, 87, 71 L.Ed. 248.) Similarly, we do not find that the comparable personal freedoms guaranteed by the California Constitution confer an absolute right to strike. (See, e.g., In re Porterfield (1946) 28 Cal.2d 91, 114, 168 P.2d 706.)

stoppage poses an imminent threat to public health or safety. Since the trial court's judgment for damage in this case was predicated upon an erroneous determination that defendants' strike was unlawful, the judgment for damages cannot be sustained.

The judgment is reversed.

MOSK and GRODIN, JJ., concur.

KAUS, JUSTICE, [joined by REYNOSO, JUSTICE,] concurring.

I concur in the judgment insofar as it holds that a peaceful strike by public employees does not give rise to a tort action for damages against the union. I am aware of nothing in the Meyers-Milias-Brown Act which suggests that the Legislature intended that common law tort remedies should be applied in this context, and without such legislative endorsement I believe it is improper to import tort remedies that were devised for different situations into this sensitive labor relations arena. * * *.

* * * I believe it is equally unwise to venture an opinion on potential constitutional challenges to future legislative action in this field. In my view, we should—if anything—be encouraging the Legislature to attempt to deal with the difficult public policy questions in this area, not frightening it away with premature warnings of possible constitutional minefields.

BIRD, CHIEF JUSTICE, concurring.

I write separately because I believe it is only fair to give the Legislature some guidance in an area filled with constitutional problems. * * *

* * * [T]oday's holding is compelled not only by common law principles but also by the California Constitution.

LUCAS, JUSTICE, dissenting.

* * * In my view, public employees in this state neither have the right to strike, nor should they have that right. * * *

Note

While the Los Angeles County Sanitation case may indicate a trend in the direction of more permissive dealing with public employee strikes, it is still the fact that in most American jurisdictions such strikes are illegal. Moreover, there are some strikes in public employment which cannot be tolerated, however liberal the approach in the particular jurisdiction. This brings into focus the major problem confronting any effort at strike prohibition—enforcement. "Basically, there are four types of sanctions that may be brought to bear: (1) The injunctive power of the courts. This has the virtue of flexibility, inherent in the discretionary power of the court. If the court's injunction is violated, it may impose penalties, including imprisonment of individuals and fines upon individuals and/or organizations, for contempt of its order. [A court may also impose a judgment for damages on a tort theory as done by the trial court in the Los Angeles County Sanitation case.]

(2) The imposition of penalties by the employer for misconduct, including reprimand, fine, loss of benefits, demotion, suspension, and dismissal. (3) The denial or revocation of recognition of the employee organization [and/or revoca-

tion of dues "check off" privileges].   (4) The imposition of criminal penalties
* * *." ᵃ

Unfortunately, strike penalties, however fierce they may sound in statutory recital, are not self-executing.   Experience teaches that a cohesive and militant union, whose members provide an important public service for which there is no ready substitute, is hard to control by the most carefully constructed statutory scheme.   The strength of the union is frequently manifested in the amnesty provisions it is able to compel in strike settlements.

Given these pressures and this experience, which sanctions would you want available and seek to utilize if you were a public employer?

IN THE MATTER OF THE IMPASSE BETWEEN THE BOARD OF EDUCATION OF THE CITY OF BUFFALO AND THE BUFFALO TEACHERS FEDERATION

Report and Recommendations of Fact-Finding Panel, 1969.
2 P.E.R.B. 6417.

INTRODUCTION

The existing contract between the Board of Education of the City of Buffalo (hereinafter referred to as the Board) and the Buffalo Teachers Federation (hereinafter referred to as the BTF) [a local affiliate, despite its name, of the National Education Association (NEA) rather than of the American Federation of Teachers (AFT)], expiring on June 30, 1970, contains a provision permitting the reopening of the contract "by November 1, 1968 concerning any matters of mutual concern."   In accordance with this provision, the contract was reopened, and the parties exchanged proposals for its revision.

On January 9, 1969, the New York State Public Employment Relations Board, after consultation with the parties, determined that an impasse existed in the negotiations and appointed the three undersigned as members of a mediation panel, pursuant to Civil Service Law, Article 14 (Taylor Law), Section 209,ᵇ to seek to resolve the impasse.   As a consequence of extensive

a. Doherty and Oberer, Teachers, School Boards, and Collective Bargaining: A Changing of the Guard 106 (1967).

b. § 209 [as amended in 1969]. Resolution of disputes in the course of collective negotiations.

1. For purposes of this section, an impasse may be deemed to exist if the parties fail to achieve agreement at least sixty days prior to the budget submission date of the public employer.

2. Public employers are hereby empowered to enter into written agreements with recognized or certified employee organizations setting forth procedures to be invoked in the event of disputes which reach an impasse in the course of collective negotiations.   Such agreements may include the undertaking by each party to submit unresolved issues to impartial arbitration.   In the absence or upon the failure of such procedures, public employ-

ers and employee organizations may request the board to render assistance as provided in this section, or the board may render such assistance on its own motion, as provided in subdivision three of this section.

3. On request of either party or upon its own motion, as provided in subdivision two of this section, and in the event the board determines that an impasse exists in collective negotiations between such employee organization and a public employer as to the conditions of employment of public employees, the board shall render assistance as follows:

(a) to assist the parties to effect a voluntary resolution of the dispute, the board shall appoint a mediator or mediators representative of the public from a list of qualified persons maintained by the board;

(b) if the impasse continues, the board shall appoint a fact-finding board of not more than three members, each representa-

further negotiations, an agreement was reached in mid-January, 1969, between the negotiating teams of the Board and the BTF, which agreement was shortly thereafter ratified by both the Board and the membership of the BTF. A copy of this "Memorandum of Agreement" is attached hereto as Appendix A. [Appendix A has been deleted.]

The Board presented its budget request for 1969–70 to the Mayor of the City of Buffalo by February 1, 1969, as it is required by law to do. This budget request was in the amount of $68,011,439, an increase of $8,268,439 over the Board's 1968–69 budget of $59,743,000. Of the over eight million increase, some three million represented the cost of previously mandated increases, some two million represented the cost of new or expanded programs, and the remaining three million represented the improvement in teachers' salaries and fringe benefits resulting from the Memorandum of Agreement of January, 1969.

The Mayor, in turn, required by law to present his budgetary recommendations for all city departments and for the Board of Education to the City Council by May 1, 1969, recommended an increase in the Board's budget for 1969–70 of only $16,760 over the amount appropriated for the Board in 1968–69. The effect of this recommendation, as viewed by the Board, was to deny the wherewithal to the Board for fulfilling its tentative agreement of January 1969 with the BTF.

In this posture of affairs, the New York State Public Employment Relations Board, on May 9, 1969, again after consulting the parties and pursuant to Section 209 of the Taylor Law, reconstituted the original three-member mediation panel as a fact-finding panel. Responding to this charge, the undersigned, now serving as fact finders, conducted hearings in Buffalo

tive of the public, from a list of qualified persons maintained by the board, which fact-finding board shall have, in addition to the powers delegated to it by the board, the power to make public recommendations for the resolution of the dispute;

(c) if the dispute is not resolved at least twenty days prior to the budget submission date, the fact-finding board, acting by a majority of its members, (i) shall immediately transmit its findings of fact and recommendations for resolution of the dispute to the chief executive officer of the government involved and to the employee organization involved, (ii) may thereafter assist the parties to effect a voluntary resolution of the dispute, and (iii) shall within five days of such transmission make public such findings and recommendations;

(d) in the event that the findings of fact and recommendations are made public by a fact-finding board established pursuant to procedures agreed upon by the parties under subdivision two of this section, and the impasse continues, the public employment relations board shall have the power to take whatever steps it deems appropriate to resolve the dispute, including (i) the making of recommendations after giving due consideration to the findings of fact and recommen-

dations of such fact-finding board, but no further fact-finding board shall be appointed, and (ii) upon the request of the parties assistance in providing for voluntary arbitration;

(e) in the event that either the public employer or the employee organization does not accept in whole or part the recommendations of the fact-finding board, (i) the chief executive officer of the government involved, shall within ten days after receipt of the findings of fact and recommendations of the fact-finding board, submit to the legislative body of the government involved a copy of the findings of fact and recommendations of the fact-finding board, together with his recommendations for settling the dispute; (ii) the employee organization may submit to such legislative body its recommendations for settling the dispute; (iii) the legislative body or a duly authorized committee thereof shall forthwith conduct a hearing at which the parties shall be required to explain their positions with respect to the report of the fact-finding board; and (iv) thereafter, the legislative body shall take such action as it deems to be in the public interest, including the interest of the public employees involved.

on May 14 and 26, 1969, and in the process received evidence and heard argument from representatives of the Board and the BTF, and from the Director of the Budget and the Corporation Counsel as representatives of the City administration.

PRELIMINARY QUESTIONS CONFRONTING THE FACT FINDERS

The Buffalo Board of Education is fiscally dependent upon the Buffalo City Council, which interacts with the Mayor in appropriating funds for the operation and maintenance of public education in Buffalo. (In this regard, the Buffalo School District is in the same position as the other five of the so-called "Big Six" school districts in the State of New York—New York City, Yonkers, Albany, Syracuse, and Rochester.) The City Council, in the ordinary course of things, presents its budgetary determinations by June 1.

An initial problem confronting the fact finders in these proceedings was to ascertain just who the parties to the dispute were. Was it the board and the BTF who were at impasse, despite the fact of their agreement of January, 1969? Or was it the Mayor and City Council, on the one hand, and the BTF, on the other, who were at impasse? Or, indeed, was it the Mayor and the City Council, on the one side, and the BTF *and* Board, on the other?

These preliminary questions were resolved, as a practical matter, by hearing from representatives of all three of the interest groups which had yet acted in the matter: the Board, the BTF, and the City administration. As a matter of law, however, the disputants are quite clearly the BTF and the Board. (See Sections 201.7 [c] and .12,[d] and 209, among others, of the Taylor Law.)

The Board took the position that the agreement which it entered with the BTF in January, 1969, was contingent upon sufficient funds being appropriated by the City Council to permit the Board, without cutting back other services, to meet the obligations of the agreement. The BTF, in forthright and commendable fashion, conceded the contingency of the agreement in this regard.

All of which leaves the impasse in this posture before the fact finders: (1) the statutory parties to the existing impasse are the Board and the BTF; (2) those parties are indeed at impasse since both agree that the Memorandum of Agreement of January, 1969 (Appendix A) is not binding; (3) the impasse as to which findings of fact and recommendations are to be made by the fact finders concerns the "terms and conditions of employment" (see Sections 204 [e] and 209 of the Taylor Law), qualified by the concession of the

---

c. § 201.7. The term "government" or "public employer" means (a) the state of New York, (b) a county, city, town, village or any other political subdivision or civil division of the state, (c) a school district or any governmental entity operating a public school, college or university, (d) a public improvement or special district, (e) a public authority, commission, or public benefit corporation, or (f) any other public corporation, agency or instrumentality or unit of government which exercises governmental powers under the laws of the state.

d. § 201.12. The term "legislative body of the government" in the case of school districts, means the board of education, board of trustees or sole trustee, as the case may be. [For the relevance of this provision, see § 209.3(e), supra footnote b.]

e. § 204.2. Where an employee organization has been certified or recognized pursuant to the provisions of this article, the appropriate public employer shall be, and hereby is, required to negotiate collectively with such employee organization in the determination of, and administration of grievances arising

parties that only "economic" provisions of the January agreement are in dispute.

THE CONTROLLING ISSUE

In the circumstances described, the fact finders have concluded that the controlling issue presented is the effect to be given to the Memorandum of Agreement of January, 1969, between the Board and the BTF (Appendix A).

RECOMMENDATIONS AND SUPPORTIVE FINDINGS

The fact finders hereby recommend that the impasse between the Board and the BTF as to the terms and conditions of employment of the subject employees for the year 1969–70 be resolved in accordance with the agreement between the parties of January, 1969. The reasons for this recommendation include the following:

1. The January agreement was conceded by the representatives of the Board and BTF in the proceedings before the fact finders to be a "fair and reasonable" disposition of the matters at issue between them. Not one person appearing before the fact finders so much as suggested the contrary.

2. The January agreement was the product of hard bargaining on both sides, conducted in good faith, with substantial concessions from original positions having been made by each. The fact finders, in their then role of mediators, were present during the final, crucial negotiating sessions, out of which agreement came, and observed, among other things, the exemplary protection of the public and taxpayers' interest by the Board negotiators. The Board negotiators pressed the "inability to pay" arguments with great tenacity and skill and succeeded in achieving agreement by the BTF representatives at levels considerably below those which the BTF representatives had previously determined they could not drop.

3. The January agreement is, objectively viewed, as fair and reasonable as all participants in the proceedings before the fact finders conceded it to be. It is in line with settlements reached or expected to be reached for 1969–70 in school districts properly to be looked to for purposes of comparison. It is by no means in the vanguard of such settlements. Indeed, Appendix B [omitted herefrom] demonstrates, for example, the low standing of the Buffalo School District in 1968–69 vis-à-vis other Erie County school districts in several important respects; the improvement contained in the January agreement would by no means vault Buffalo to leadership in the listed categories even as measured against the *1968–69* salary schedules of other districts in the county; as measured against the *1969-70* salary schedules yet to be finalized in those districts, the improvement contained in the January agreement can hardly do better than leave Buffalo in the also-ran category it presently occupies. All of this is in the face of the fact that urban teaching is generally regarded as more difficult than suburban and that urban districts, to remain competitive in the recruitment and retention of competent teachers, should lead rather than follow suburban districts.

4. The "poverty" justification of the Board representatives for refusing to adhere to the January agreement, i.e., that the Board is imprisoned in the

under, the terms and conditions of employment of the public employees as provided in this article, and to negotiate and enter into written agreements with such employee organizations in determining such terms and conditions of employment.

confines of a drastically bobbed Mayoral budgetary recommendation (anticipated to be followed by the City Council) and therefore cannot properly
adhere to that agreement, is not persuasive. No contention was made before
the fact finders that the Board budget, even as cut back by the Mayor, would
not be adequate to compensate the teachers in accordance with the January
agreement. The Board's contention, on the contrary, was that too great a
reduction in educational programs and services would be required to honor
the January agreement with the teachers in the face of the Mayor's drastic
reduction in the Board's budget. This position of the Board necessarily
raises the question of whether the cost of providing adequate public educational services in Buffalo should be subsidized by the school teachers of
Buffalo through working for salaries below the fair and reasonable level.
Since the Board representatives conceded the provisions of the January
agreement to be fair and reasonable, the inference fairly to be drawn from a
refusal to abide by that agreement is that the school teachers should work
for less than they might fairly and reasonably claim in order that educational services not otherwise available might be provided to the public. The fact
finders are as unwilling to take the position that the services of public school
teachers should be available to the government without fair compensation as
they would be to take the position that property should be subject to
appropriation (condemnation) by the government without fair compensation.

In this regard, it is not irrelevant to point out that the Buffalo School
District spent, according to the unchallenged evidence of the BTF, less in
1968–69 per public school pupil ($792) than any other of the Big Six cities
(range: $808 to $1,200), and less even than the average school district in the
State of New York ($925).

5. From the standpoint of building effective relationships in collective
negotiations, the present situation in public education in Buffalo is most
lamentable and, if not quickly corrected, augurs serious breakdown. A brief
review of the history of the current negotiations will suffice to establish this
concern. Negotiations began last fall and after twelve negotiating sessions,
some of considerable length, culminated in a hard bargain in mid-January of
this year. The hardness of the bargain finally struck is intimately known to
this fact-finding panel since, as previously noted, it was then functioning in a
mediation role. The bargain reached by the negotiating teams was quickly
ratified by the Board and by the members of the BTF. For almost three
months thereafter, both the Board and the BTF and its constituents, particularly the latter, had reason to believe they had a deal. While the Board
members, closer to the politics of the Buffalo situation, being appointees of
the Mayor themselves, may have had reason to hedge their reliance upon
the firmness of the bargain, and while the officers of the BTF may have had
occasion for sober second concern as to whether the deal would "keep," the
members of the BTF, the school teachers of Buffalo, had necessarily less
awareness of the situation in City Hall. Expectations seeded in January had
taken root by May. To tear these expectations out, root and all, at this late
date can hardly have other than deleterious consequences for future employment relations in the Buffalo School District. Such a course of action hardly
seems consistent with the "statement of policy" in Section 200 of the Taylor
Law, that "the legislature of the state of New York declares that it is the
public policy of the state and the purpose of this act to promote harmonious

and cooperative relationships between government and its employees
* * *."

Perhaps the lesson for the future is that the City should take a more active role in collective negotiations with the Buffalo school teachers at the point where the effective negotiations take place, i.e., in the period before the Board's budget request is finalized and presented to the Mayor. An alternative would be for effective bargaining with the Buffalo teachers to take place at a later date and with City representatives playing a more active role. In any event, it is clear from the standpoint of anyone experienced in collective negotiations that requiring the employees of the Buffalo Board of Education to go through the ordeal of bargaining with Board representatives, of surrendering bargaining goals in the process of probing for the best deal that hard bargaining on both sides can produce, and then of seeing that bottom-dollar deal go up in smoke three months later can only produce labor relations problems of a traumatic order. Frustration, disillusionment, loss of confidence are the products of such a course, and they portend ill for employer-employee relations.

The fact finders therefore recommend adherence to the agreement, conceded by all involved to be fair and reasonable and now independently found to be so by the fact finders themselves, reached between the Board and the BTF last January and memorialized in Appendix A.

DATED: May 28, 1969

> Irving R. Markowitz
>
> Julian S. Peasant, Jr.
>
> Walter E. Oberer
> Chairman

Note

1. The impasse-resolving procedures which the Taylor Law substitutes for the right to strike—i.e., mediation and fact finding with nonbinding recommendations (see Section 209, supra p. 1092 footnote b)—are, in one variation or another, the techniques typically relied upon in public employment bargaining statutes. What are the distinctive contributions of each of these techniques? Since mediators sometimes, in the process of mediation, make recommendations for settlement, and fact finders sometimes, in the process of fact finding, mediate, what reasons are there for differentiating the two functions and prescribing them separately, with mediation first? What are the implications of having the same personnel perform both functions in the same impasse situation, as in the Buffalo case (where, incidentally, the school board and the teacher organization consented to the arrangement)?

For a study of the effectiveness of fact finding in several of the states where it has been adopted, see McKelvey, Fact Finding in Public Employment Disputes: Promise or Illusion?, 22 Indus. & Lab.Rel.Rev. 528 (1969). This article provides basis for answering the title question either way. The author offers the following "Trends and Conclusions":

"1. There will be an increasing emphasis on the need for high quality mediation skills in the public sector whether exercised by mediators or nominal fact finders.

"2. Contractual impasse procedures will become more prevalent and may well replace statutory procedures.

"3. Voluntary arbitration of impasses will gain acceptability and may well have a spill-over impact on the private sector.[48]

"4. Increasingly, state laws will be enacted or revised to permit a limited right to strike or to mandate compulsory arbitration in the public sector. The legalization of strikes may paradoxically reduce their incidence.[49]

"5. Since all proposals for legalizing strikes in public employment contemplate the prior exhaustion of mediation and fact finding, there may develop an automatic resort to fact finding. In this event, fact finding may become, as it has under the Railway Labor Act, an addictive habit, the first and not the final step in collective negotiations.

"It is this last prospect which gives this writer most cause for alarm. As indicated above, under some circumstances, especially for unsophisticated and inexperienced public bargainers, fact finding has performed both an educational and a dispute-resolving function well beyond what the precepts of orthodox teaching would lead one to expect. In this sense it has shown promise. It has been useful, if not entirely successful. In another and more profound sense, however, it may prove ultimately to be not only an illusion, but what is worse, an exercise in futility." Id. at 543.

For a later study of fact finding, somewhat more optimistic than the foregoing, see Yaffe and Goldblatt, Factfinding in Public Employment Disputes in New York State: More Promise than Illusion (1971).

2. In the Buffalo case the main contention of the employer was that the city was unable to pay the salaries sought by the teachers, however fair and reasonable these might be, because of having almost exhausted its statutory and constitutional taxing powers. Such an inability-to-pay argument on the part of public employers is the one most commonly encountered. How much weight should fact finders give to this plaint? In considering this question, what significance, if any, would you accord to the fact (if it be a fact—a fair assumption when the first edition of this casebook was published; perhaps not so now) that after an illegal strike of some duration, sufficient money usually materializes for a settlement to be reached—whether from newly bestowed

---

48. Orthodox theory which holds that binding arbitration will destroy collective bargaining is partially refuted by Canadian experience. Under the Public Service Staff Relations Act which has governed federal employment labor relations in Canada for the last 2 years, the bargaining agents must choose in advance whether to refer contract disputes to binding arbitration or to conciliation with the ultimate right to strike. Only 8 units, including the postal workers, have chosen the strike option. Some 20 units representing the preponderance of federal employees have chosen binding arbitration. None of these groups has resorted to arbitration, however, and only 2 or 3 have gone to conciliation

boards. The president of the largest of these organizations, the Public Service Alliance, has stated that the parties still prefer to reach their own agreements because of the risks involved in living with an arbitration decision "that would be much worse than anything we might bargain." Toronto Globe and Mail, Oct. 25, 1968.

49. The proposition that it may "be easier to control a legal strike than an illegal one" is developed by Boyd Hight, "Teachers, Bargaining, and Strikes: Perspectives from the Swedish Experience," in UCLA Law Review, Vol. 15, p. 840.

taxing authority, the largesse of higher government (county, state, or federal), the "discovery" of money "hidden" in some reserve account, or the reallocation of previously available funds?

3. What are the implications of collective bargaining in public employment for decision-making as to the allocation of public resources and the priority of public services? The earlier state statutes authorizing collective bargaining in the public sector adopted essentially the same language as that of the National Labor Relations Act in defining the scope of negotiations. For example, under the Taylor Law involved in the Buffalo case, the scope of negotiations is defined as "the terms and conditions of employment." (See supra p. 1094, footnote e). The potential for expansive impact of collective bargaining upon public policy under such a criterion is apparent. Taking public education as an illustration: "Almost no policy decision of a school board is without its effect upon the working conditions of teachers. As a consequence, there is room under the 'conditions of employment' formula for teacher representatives to assert bargaining rights over such diverse matters as promotions, discipline procedures, transfers, class size, televised instruction, additions to the staff, extension of the school day or year, curriculum content, text books, allocation of money in the school budget."[f]

As a consequence of concerns generated by the expansive tendencies of collective bargaining and by the implications of this for public policy, more recently-enacted statutes reflect efforts to narrow the scope of bargaining. Those of Hawaii (Hawaii Rev.Stat. ch. 89, § 89–9(d)), Pennsylvania (Pa.Stat.Ann. tit. 43, § 1101.702), and Delaware (Del.Code Ann. tit. 14, §§ 4002, 4005), for example, exclude from the subjects for negotiation certain "management rights," such as direction of the work force, determination of standards for performance, and decisions as to the functions and programs of the public employer.

What is your view of the wisdom and viability of these efforts to restrict the scope of negotiability in public employment? Pertinently, both the Hawaii and the Pennsylvania statutes impose a second variety of "negotiating" duty upon public employers, in addition to the duty to bargain or negotiate in good faith as to the narrowly-defined terms and conditions of employment—to wit, the duty to "meet and discuss," or to "consult with" concerning, policy decisions affecting employment conditions but not the subject of the duty to bargain or negotiate. The Hawaii statute, for example, declares: "The employer shall make every reasonable effort to consult with the exclusive representatives prior to effecting changes in any major policy affecting employee relations." Hawaii Rev.Stat. ch. 89, § 89–9(c). What is the precise content of this secondary duty to "consult with" or "meet and discuss" as compared to the content of the duty to bargain or negotiate in good faith? The Pennsylvania statute attempts a definition: "'Meet and discuss' means the obligation of a public employer upon request to meet at reasonable times and discuss recommendations submitted by representatives of public employes: Provided, That any decisions or determinations on matters so discussed shall remain with the public employer and be deemed final on any issue or issues raised." Pa.Stat.Ann. tit. 43, § 1101.301(17).

Would consultation or discussion in "bad faith" satisfy the secondary duty so defined?

f. Doherty and Oberer, Teachers, School Boards and Collective Bargaining: A Changing of the Guard 91–92 (1967).

Why have efforts not been made in the private sector to confine *by statute* the scope of "terms and conditions of employment"?

4. As evidenced in the Buffalo case, one of the major differences between private and public sector bargaining is the existence in the latter of budgetary deadlines established by law. The existence of these deadlines presents problems at both the selection-of-representative stage and the negotiation stage. A few moments' reflection should reveal these problems. * * * Did it?

5. One of the most troublesome differences between private and public employment with regard to collective bargaining is the difficulty of identifying the "employer" in the public sector. This problem was at the core of the Buffalo dispute. The case which follows presents a variant of the same problem, equally mischievous and amusing.

CIVIL SERVICE COMMISSION FOR THE COUNTY OF WAYNE v. WAYNE COUNTY BOARD OF SUPERVISORS, WAYNE COUNTY LABOR RELATIONS BOARD, AND WAYNE COUNTY BOARD OF ROAD COMMISSIONERS

Court of Appeals of Michigan, Division 1, 1970.
22 Mich.App. 287, 177 N.W.2d 449.
Reversed in part, 384 Mich. 363, 184 N.W.2d 201 (1971).

FITZGERALD, PRESIDING JUDGE.

This Court is faced with two cases which have been consolidated for purposes of this appeal, the same statement of facts being applicable in both instances. The original actions dealt with and arose out of the amendment to the statute known as the "Hutchinson Act." It is concerned with the right of county employees to organize and bargain collectively with their respective governmental employers over rates of pay, wages, conditions of employment and hours of work.

The initial dispute arose on March 22, 1966, when the Wayne County Board of Supervisors adopted a resolution which established a three-member labor relations board for the express purpose of complying with the requirements of P.A. 1965, No. 379, M.C.L.A. § 423.209 [Stat.Ann. 1968 Rev. § 17.455(9)], amending P.A. 1947, No. 336, and establishing collective bargaining for public employees. The act provides that:

> "It shall be lawful for public employees to organize together or to form, join or assist in labor organizations, to engage in lawful concerted activities for the purpose of collective negotiation or bargaining or other mutual aid and protection, or to negotiate or bargain collectively with their public employers through representatives of their own free choice."

In § 15 of the act, collective bargaining is made an employer duty, the act specifically providing that:

> "A public employer shall bargain collectively with the representative of its employees as defined in section 11 and is authorized to make and enter into collective bargaining agreements with such representatives."

The Labor Relations Board, which consisted of representatives of the Board of Supervisors, Wayne County Civil Service Commission and the Wayne County Road Commission, began collective bargaining sessions.

This, in effect, displaced the Civil Service Commission in bargaining for rates of pay and terms and conditions of employment.

In April, 1967, the Wayne County Civil Service Commission filed an action against the Wayne County Board of Supervisors, the Wayne County Road Commission and the Wayne County Labor Relations Board, seeking a declaratory judgment for determination of the collective bargaining rights of the respective parties. The case came on to be heard by a three-judge panel of the Wayne county circuit court.

On March 26, 1968, the court entered a declaratory judgment, with one judge dissenting, which determined that the county of Wayne was the employer under P.A. 1965, No. 379, M.C.L.A. § 423.209 [Stat.Ann.1968 Rev. § 17.455(9)], and that the Wayne County Board of Supervisors was empowered to act for the employer in establishing rates of pay and other terms and conditions of employment through the labor relations board. All parts of P.A.1941, No. 370 (M.C.L.A. § 38.401 et seq. [Stat.Ann.1961 Rev. § 5.1191(1) et seq.]), which were inconsistent were declared repealed by implication or suspended.[1] * * *

We are primarily concerned with the issue of whether the trial court erred in its determination that the county of Wayne was the employer under P.A.1965, No. 379, and that the Wayne County Board of Supervisors was empowered to act for the employer in establishing rates of pay and other terms and conditions of employment through the Labor Relations Board. More succinctly stated, we are asked to determine who actually is the employer of employees of Wayne county for the purpose of collective bargaining and negotiation. We note that this problem exists because the legislature in drafting P.A. 1965, No. 379, failed to specifically define the term "employer" for purposes of collective bargaining under the act.

It is the contention of the plaintiff Civil Service Commission that the county of Wayne is the employer and that the Civil Service Commission is the exclusive body to represent the county of Wayne and all bodies within the county in matters dealing with terms and conditions of employment, salaries and wages of all employees of this governmental unit in the classified service. On the other hand, defendant Board of Wayne County Road Commissioners avers that it is the employer of its own employees.

The Board of Wayne County Supervisors takes a slightly different tack and maintains that the county of Wayne is composed of joint employers and the Board of Supervisors is the branch of government within the county upon whom the duties and responsibilities arising under P.A. 1965, No. 379, are imposed.

We note that this whole action comes to us as a by-product of the passage of P.A.1965, No. 379, supra. After a careful examination of the pertinent provisions of this act, nowhere within it is the term "public employer" defined. This oversight is the crux of the problem with which we are faced. Nowhere within the statutory confines of "P.E.R.A." [Public Employment Relations Act] can be found any standards to aid in this determination.

---

1. P.A.1941, No. 370 (M.C.L.A. § 38.401 [Stat.Ann.1961 Rev. § 5.119(1)]), established   a Civil Service System for the county of Wayne.

In reviewing the dissenting opinion entered in this cause, we find the general characteristics of identification of an employer are: 1) that they select and engage the employee; 2) that they pay the wages; 3) that they have the power of dismissal; 4) that they have the power and control over the employee's conduct (35 Am.Jur., Master & Servant, § 3, p. 445). A most significant requisite of one who is an employer is his right to exercise control over the method by which the employee carries out his work. Hence, before we can reach a proper conclusion to this controversy it is necessary to determine what authority and power each of the parties to this litigation have with regard to the employment relationship.

The powers of the Wayne County Civil Service Commission are set forth in P.A.1941, No. 370 (M.C.L.A. § 38.409 [Stat.Ann.1961 Rev. § 5.1191[9]). Thus, the Civil Service Commission has authority to:

> "Provide by regulation for the hours and conditions of service, for the length and period of vacations, and for the regulation of sick leaves in the county service, and for such other matters pertaining to the carrying out of the provisions of this act * * *."

Its powers are more specifically delineated in M.C.L.A. § 38.412 (Stat. Ann.1969 Cum.Supp. § 5.1191[12]) which states:

> "(a) It shall classify all the offices and positions of employment with reference to the examinations herein provided for, excepting as herein otherwise provided;

> "(b) Shall from time to time make, in accordance with the provisions hereof, rules adapted to carry out the purposes of this act and not inconsistent with its provisions for the examination and selection of persons to fill the offices and positions in the classified service, which are required to be filled by appointment, and for the selection of persons to be employed in the service of the county;

> "(c) Shall supervise the administration of the civil service rules, hold examinations thereunder from time to time, giving notice thereof, prepare and keep an eligible list of persons passing such examinations and certify the names of persons thereon to the appointing officers of the several departments;

> "(d) Shall, by itself or otherwise, investigate the enforcement of the provisions of this act, of its own rules and of the action of appointees in the classified service. In the course of such investigation, the commission or its authorized representative, shall have the power to administer oaths, and the commission shall have power by its subpoena, to secure both the attendance and testimony of witnesses and the production of books and papers relevant to such investigation;

> "(e) Shall provide, through the purchasing department of the county, all needed supplies for the use of the commission.

> "(f) The classification shall be subdivided into groups and shall be based upon, and graded according to the duties and responsibilities of such positions, and shall be so arranged as to permit the filling of the higher grades through promotion. All salaries shall be uniform for like service in each grade of the classified service as the same shall be classified and standardized by the commission. *Such classification and standardization of salaries shall not be final until approved by the board of supervisors and such*

salaries shall not be paid except in accordance with such classification and standardization;

"(g) Shall have such other powers and perform such other duties as may be necessary to carry out the provisions hereof."

As can readily be seen from an examination of the aforementioned powers and duties, the Civil Service Commission is clothed with some of the characteristics of an employer. However, while the plaintiff must classify positions and submit uniform pay plans for standardizing salaries, it does not have exclusive control over classification and standardization of salaries, for this must be approved by the Board of Supervisors.

The Wayne County Board of Supervisors has a duty to represent the county and to have "care and management of the property and business of the county in all cases where no other provisions shall be made." M.C.L.A. § 46.11 [Stat.Ann.1969 Cum.Supp. § 5.331]. The Board of Supervisors must also approve all decisions made by the County Civil Service Commission. Hence, it is clear that the responsibility for final approval of all contract salary provisions lies with the supervisors.

It appears from the foregoing that the Board of Supervisors does not hold all of the identifying characteristics of an employer and must function in conjunction with the Civil Service Commission and the particular appointing authority.

The Wayne County Road Commission is also a creature of statute, with specific duties and functions. (M.C.L.A. § 224.9 [Stat.Ann.1958 Rev. § 9.109]). * * *

The parties have stipulated: the Road Commission has the power to hire, fire, demote, promote, discipline and pay its employees performing road work, subject to P.A.1941, No. 370 as amended, since its adoption in 1942. * * *

In view of the above analysis of the obligations and powers of the parties to the present litigation, it is apparent that there exists no single agency in Wayne county which has the exclusive right or responsibility to represent the county in all matters pertinent to the process of collective bargaining.

In its majority opinion, the trial court ruled that provisions of P.A.1941, No. 370, which were inconsistent with P.A.1965, No. 379, were repealed by implication. We disagree with this position, as both statutes are capable of being reconciled. P.A.1965, No. 379, has changed the field of public employment only to the extent that the employees may now join a union and bargain collectively with employers. Since Act No. 379 does not specifically define the word "employer," bargaining must be carried out within the framework of the law already in existence. From an examination of both statutes, it seems fair to say that P.A.1965, No. 379 did not undertake to change the character of the employer or transfer any duties, but gave the representative of the employees the right to deal with the particular employer as he found him. Therefore, the statutory enactments dividing up the prerequisites and functions among several county agencies will have to be recognized.

While this is not the simplest solution to the difficult problem with which we are faced, and though it may even tend to confuse and complicate the area of collective bargaining within Wayne County, it is the only plausible solution under the confines of the present statutory law. Our holding is most adequately explained by the dissenting opinion which states in part:

> "The courts are without authority to bring their concept of judicial order out of what the litigants feel is legislative chaos, unless, of course, the statute is unconstitutional. Nor is it the prerogative of the courts to simplify the procedure by ignoring statutes, no matter how numerous or difficult."

We therefore reverse the decision of the lower court and adopt in full the answer in the dissenting opinion to the questions posed in the prayer of the original complaint, which is as follows:

> "1. Plaintiff performs some of the functions of the public employer, but certainly not all; that plaintiff's contention that the Civil Service Commission is the only body empowered to negotiate with public employee unions on matters set out in Section 11 of Act 379 is unsupported by law; that the 'public employer' is the County of Wayne and that Plaintiff, the Board of Supervisors, the County Road Commission and other agencies of the County are empowered by law to, and therefore must, perform those functions delegated to them in dealing with public employees and their conditions of employment; * * *

> "III. The Board of Supervisors—in carrying out its statutory function (MSA 5.331) of having the 'care and management of the property and business of the county in all cases *where no other provisions shall be made*' (Emphasis supplied) has the right and responsibility to carry out the requirements of Act 379 as to determining adequate bargaining units and the recognition of exclusive agents of employees and may utilize a vehicle such as the Labor Relations Board to investigate and recommend appropriate action to the Board of Supervisors.

> "IV. There is no single body or individual in county government who has the right or responsibility, exclusively, to represent the County in matters dealing with the establishment of salaries, wages, terms and conditions of employment of employees in the classified service.

> "V. Act 379 has not terminated or modified the power and authority of the Civil Service Commission under Act 370, except that as the repository of some of the powers of the employer, they as well as others holding such powers, have the duty to bargain in good faith, etc.

> "VI. Neither the Board of Supervisors nor the Wayne County Road Commission has the authority to delegate to the Labor Relations Board the duties and responsibilities of the Civil Service Commission under Act 370."

Reversed. No costs, a public question.

LEVIN, JUDGE (concurring).

I am in almost complete agreement with my colleagues. It has not been demonstrated that the objectives and language of Act 379 (public employee collective bargaining) cannot be reconciled with the objectives and language of Act 370 (merit system of civil service).

This case comes to us upon appeal from a declaratory judgment; the relevant facts have not been fully developed.

Although the record is incomplete, it is apparent that the road commission has the authority to hire,[3] promote and dismiss road commission employees and to control the method by which they perform their work; and, as stated in the opinion of the court, these are generally regarded as critical indicia of an employer-employee relationship. Undoubtedly, there are other major units of county government like the road commission which exercise employer functions.

The board of supervisors is willing to undertake the employer's negotiating responsibility as to all county employees. The road commission is willing to assume that responsibility as to road commission employees. Although the position of the board of supervisors has fluctuated during the course of this litigation, the board at one time in this litigation recognized that the true employer of road commission employees is the road commission.

The principal issues to be negotiated in labor-management collective bargaining are usually economic, and even so-called non-economic issues are generally tinged with an economic cost to the employer and an economic value to the employee. The civil service commission simply does not have the power to authorize the disbursement of county or road commission funds, nor does it have the responsibility of running the units of county government where civil service employees work. Understandably, those who have those powers and responsibilities think that it is their duty to undertake the public employer's collective bargaining responsibility. The employing unit is bound to be more conversant than the civil service commission with the day-to-day problems that must be resolved to maintain a productive employment relationship. Meaningful collective bargaining cannot occur unless there is a unity of responsibility and authority at the employer end of the bargaining table.[6]

True, the Wayne county civil service commission has the power under Act 370 to "provide by regulation for the hours and conditions of service, for the length and period of vacations, and for the regulation of sick leaves," and to "classify and standardize" positions and salaries in the county civil service. The superimposition of such regulations does not, however, eliminate the employer-employee relationship existent between the employing unit and its employees, nor does it change the essence of that relationship. The employing unit remains the employer, albeit an employer with an obligation to conform to the lawful regulations of the civil service commission regarding matters within its "regulatory" control.

The provisions of Act 370 (merit system of civil service) are to be construed in the light of its declared purpose:

> "The purpose of this act is to guarantee to all citizens a fair and equal opportunity for public service; to establish conditions of service which will attract officers and employees of character and capacity, and to increase the

---

3. While the civil service commission classifies positions and holds competitive examinations and keeps lists of eligible persons, it does not actually hire employees. This is done by the operating unit or department of county government.

6. Under § 13 of Act 379 (M.C.L.A. § 423.213 [Stat.Ann.1968 Rev. § 17.455(13)]) the State Labor Mediation Board determines the unit of employees appropriate for the purposes of collective bargaining.

efficiency of the county governmental departments, commissions, boards and agencies, by the improvement of methods of personnel administration."

The civil service commission's regulatory power concerning hours, conditions of service, vacations and sick leaves and its power to classify and standardize positions and salaries, which are required to be "uniform for like service in each grade," enables the commission to harmonize disparities between like positions. A civil service career is, thereby, made more attractive and more competitive with private employment opportunities.

The power of the civil service commission to classify and standardize positions and salaries does not, however, confer upon the commission the authority to fix or limit salaries;[11] nor does the power to "provide by regulation" as to hours and conditions of service, vacations, and sick leaves give the commission authority to require hours and conditions of service and vacation and sick leave benefits less liberal than those which a major unit of county government having the hiring, supervisory, disciplinary and budgetary responsibility is willing to provide.

If a contract that has or shall be negotiated is deemed by the civil service commission to conflict with the merit system objectives of Act 370 and the exercise by the civil service commission of its powers,[12] then a far clearer issue will be posed for judicial consideration than the somewhat

---

11. In Bischoff v. County of Wayne (1948), 320 Mich. 376, 392, 393, 31 N.W.2d 798, the plaintiff, Bischoff, was chief deputy circuit court clerk of Wayne county and executive secretary of the Wayne county road commission. The principal issue was whether he should be classified executive II or clerk IV. There was an additional issue arising from the road commission's recommendation that it pay Bischoff $1,200 a year for his part-time services. This was $200 more than the amount ($1,000) which the civil service commission thought proper; the civil service commission's determination was sustained by the Supreme Court. The language of the Court, which described the commission's action as "fixing plaintiff's classification or his compensation," was entirely appropriate on the facts there presented of a single part-time employee. This opinion of the Court need not be read as recognizing in the civil service commission the power to prevent general increases in compensation or benefits which a major unit of county government, like the road commission, is willing to provide.

12. In one of its briefs the civil service commission recognizes that its rules and regulations and its Official Salary Plan could be conformed to collective bargaining agreements that may be negotiated. While this was said in support of the civil service commission's claim that it can negotiate as the employer of all county civil service employees, no reason appears why the rules and regulations and Official Salary Plan could not be conformed to collective bargaining agreements negotiated by the board of supervisors or the road commission or other units of county government

provided the provisions of such agreements are consistent with the objectives of a merit system of civil service.

That the commission recognizes an obligation to accommodate its practices to the requirements of meaningful collective bargaining appears from the following statement in one of its briefs:

"The requirement of uniform salaries does not specify that they shall be uniform throughout the County service. Certainly, this would be desirable, and has been practiced by the Commission in order to be fair to all employees no matter in which department employed. But, there is no restriction that such uniformity cannot be maintained *within* the appropriate bargaining units. It is clearly *within* the power of the Commission to maintain such uniformity to the extent that it is possible *between* bargaining units, and the fact that it is so obligated by law, will strongly tend to keep some uniformity for all County employees." (Emphasis by the civil service commission.)

Similarly, the grievance procedure set out in § 16 of P.A.1941, No. 370 (M.C.L.A. § 38.416 [Stat.Ann.1961 Rev. § 5.1191(16)]), under which a civil service employee may appeal to the civil service commission an order of removal, suspension or reduction, is not necessarily in conflict with—it may appear to be merely supplementary of—any negotiated grievance procedure.

Constructively approached by all parties, the task of reconciling and implementing the objectives of both acts may very well be achieved.

nebulous question we are being asked to resolve in this declaratory judgment action.

To the extent that the Wayne county labor relations board constitutes a vehicle through which all concerned units, departments and agencies of county government may meet with employee representatives, it may be a useful *ad hoc* device to implement and reconcile the purposes and objectives of the two acts. In this connection, it should be borne in mind that Wayne is the only county with countywide civil service; no doubt the legislature intended that civil service employees of this most populous county should enjoy the same right to meaningful collective bargaining as do other public employees.

I am in agreement with my colleagues that, to the extent it may have been sought by the creation of the Wayne county labor relations board to supersede the functions of the civil service commission or the road commission or the board of supervisors, it would violate the statutes which confer upon them their respective powers and responsibilities.

[P.S.: The Michigan Supreme Court, in reversing the court of appeals, held that the 1965 bargaining statute impliedly repealed the 1941 civil service statute to the extent of any repugnance between them. As applied to the present case, this meant that the Wayne County Road Commission was, for the purposes of the bargaining statute, the "employer" and the *sole* "employer" of its employees; "the plaintiff Civil Service Commission has no lawful part in the administration, directly or indirectly, of the act of 1965."]

Note

1. In the Wayne County case the court of appeals characterizes the problem as one of legislative "oversight" in failing to define the term "public employer." Is this persuasive? Or, on the contrary, is the problem one which inheres in the very structure of government? Under the Taylor Law of the State of New York, the term "public employer" is defined in some detail (see supra p. 1094, footnote c), and yet that definition did nothing to alter the echelonning and fragmentation of managerial authority which was at the root of the problem in the Buffalo fact-finding case. In that case, authority pertinent to collective bargaining was held by each of the following entities: the school board; the mayor; the city council; the taxpayers of the City of Buffalo; the governor (who proposes the state budget, including a substantial amount of state aid for local school districts); the state legislature (which passes upon that budget); the taxpayers of the state; various agencies of the federal government, including Congress because of the increasing amount of federal aid for local education; the federal taxpayers.

If it may fairly be said in public employment, as in private, that the "employer" is the one against whom the employees strike, then a strong case can be made that the "employer" is the body of taxpayers; the function of the strike in public employment, adequately analyzed, is to "educate" the pertinent taxpayers to an enhanced evaluation of the public service involved, thereby insulating elective office holders from political retribution at the polls because of increased tax burdens necessitated by improved employee benefits.

2. The conflict between the new public employment bargaining statutes and the preexisting civil service laws is the product of a head-on collision between the bilateralism of collective bargaining and the paternalism of civil service systems. Can these two systems coexist?

3. There is a close relationship between (1) the question of who the public employer is, (2) the scope of negotiations, and (3) the determination of the appropriate bargaining unit. This proposition, not always perceived, was implicit in the Wayne County case and is explicit in the case which follows.

IN THE MATTER OF STATE OF NEW YORK
(STATE UNIVERSITY OF NEW YORK),
EMPLOYER, ET AL.

Decision and Order of Director of Representation, New York State Public Employment Relations Board, 1969.
2 P.E.R.B. 4183.
Affirmed, 2 P.E.R.B. 3492 (N.Y. PERB 1969).

On November 15, 1967, the State of New York, herein referred to as the employer,[1] defined three negotiating units for its employees, one of which was for professional employees at the State University of New York exclusive of those determined to be management. No employee organization, however, was recognized to represent the employees within this unit for purposes of collective negotiations, since the employer felt that there was no clear indication which organization, if any, was the choice of its professional employees.

On May 1 and May 21, 1968, various locals of the State University Federation of Teachers, herein collectively referred to as the federation, filed, in accordance with the Rules of Procedure, herein referred to as the Rules, of the New York State Public Employment Relations Board, herein referred to as the Board, timely petitions to be individually certified as the exclusive negotiating representative of certain professional employees at five campuses of the State University of New York, herein referred to as SUNY.[2] An extensive consolidated hearing was held before Howard A. Rubenstein, a trial examiner of the Board, between July 16, 1968 and March 7, 1969, with

1. For purposes of this proceeding, the employer has been designated as "State of New York (State University of New York)."

2. The federation's petitions claimed the following units:

(a) Case No. C–0253—"teaching faculty defined as teaching 6 hrs. or more; and professional librarians; teachers in campus school" at the State University College at Buffalo, excluding administrators.

(b) Case No. C–0260—"instructional staff" at the Cortland campus excluding the president, vice president, deans, assistant deans, directors, assistant directors, principals, and assistant principals.

(c) Case No. C–0262—"instructional staff" at New Paltz, excluding the president, vice president, and deans.

(d) Case No. C–0263—"[f]ull and part-time faculty members whose major regular as-

signment is instruction, including those with released time for research, and department and division chairmen without other administrative titles" at Brockport, excluding the president, vice president, deans, associate deans and others whose primary function is not instruction.

(e) Case No. C–0264—"instructional staff including librarians and technical assistants" at Delhi Agriculture and Technical College, excluding the president, vice president, deans, associate deans, divisional chairmen and others not holding academic rank.

During the course of the hearing, the federation modified its unit position as set forth in these petitions and is now seeking a uniting structure to be described below.

all parties present and represented by counsel, including the Civil Service Employees Association, Inc., herein referred to as CSEA, the Faculty Senate, herein referred to as the senate,[4] and the Council of Affiliated Chapters of the American Association of University Professors in the State University of New York, herein referred to as AAUP.

STATUS OF THE FACULTY SENATE

The senate's status as an "employee organization" as that term is defined in § 201(6) of the Public Employees' Fair Employment Act [Taylor Law], herein referred to as the Act[6] is being challenged by the federation, which argues that the senate is not primarily concerned with working to improve the terms and conditions of employment of SUNY's employees.[7] The federation further argues that the senate is employer-dominated because it is financially dependent upon SUNY, its constitution is incorporated into the "policies" of SUNY's board of trustees, and it admits management personnel to membership.

Any discussion of the senate's status as an employee organization must first place this issue in its proper context. A university is an historically unique employer in that faculty members, although they are technically "rank-and-file" employees, share authority for managing the university with managerial personnel. At SUNY, the vehicle for faculty participation in management has been the senate, a representative body,[8] which has functioned as a structural component of SUNY since the early 1950's. * * * The chancellor of SUNY and two of his designated representatives are constitutionally ordained members of the senate, with one representative entitled under the senate's constitution to sit on its executive committee.

The senate charges no dues and relies upon SUNY for funding. Thus, each year, the senate presents its budget request to SUNY which, after review, is incorporated into SUNY's budget request and made part of the executive budget which is submitted to the State Legislature for adoption. Once the Legislature has approved the executive budget and appropriated funds for the senate, the senate is free to spend such funds in any way it chooses.

The record makes it clear that the senate, in its role as faculty governor, has represented the faculty position with regard to economic goals as well as a number of matters of educational concern, such as admissions policies, faculty hiring, promotion and tenure procedures, curriculum, and class size. It is equally clear that many of these matters would constitute, to some degree, negotiable terms and conditions of faculty employment. Moreover,

---

4. On January 20, 1969, during the course of the hearing, the senate filed, in accordance with the Rules, a timely petition for certification (Case No. C–0351) as the exclusive negotiating representative of "all members of the professional staff of the State University of New York" excluding all persons holding management positions.

6. Section 201(6) reads, in relevant part, as follows:

"The term 'employee organization' means an organization of any kind having as its

primary purpose the improvement of terms and conditions of employment of public employees. * * *"

7. It has been stipulated, and I find, that the federation, CSEA, and AAUP are employee organizations within the meaning of the Act.

8. The professional staff at each campus elects one to four senators, depending upon the number of full-time faculty members with academic rank at each campus.

the "purpose" clause of the senate's constitution was revised in late 1968 to specifically mandate the senate to work to improve the terms and conditions of employment of all members of the professional staff. Clearly then, there is no basis in fact for finding that the senate's "primary purpose" is other than the improvement of terms and conditions of employment. Therefore, I find that the senate satisfies the statutory definition of an "employee organization."

However, as noted above, the federation claims that the senate is employer-dominated, and thus should be disqualified from further participation in this proceeding. Despite the outward indicia of employer control, the record, at least to some extent, supports a conclusion that the senate has operated in fact as an independent organization inasmuch as it has adopted positions which were opposed by management personnel. Further, as I have previously noted, prior to the passage of the Act there was no need for an organization " * * * to delineate, for purposes of collective negotiations, between 'rank-and-file' employees and 'management'." [10] This principle applies with equal force and validity to the senate's history of financial dependence on SUNY. Moreover, regarding its financial arrangements, the senate has placed on the record assurances that it will in the future adhere to whatever standards of financing this Board may establish for employee organizations. As a beginning, it has pledged to finance its election campaign at SUNY and its negotiating activities, should it be certified herein, through voluntary contributions and educational foundation grants. With regard to management participation in senate affairs, the senate also testified that, as has been its practice since the passage of the Act, it will continue to exclude the chancellor and his two representatives from the deliberations of its economic status committee concerning proposals made in negotiations. Further, the senate intends to exclude all senators not included in a negotiating unit which it may represent from involvement in senate consideration of matters relevant to its status as a negotiating representative.

In any event, on March 10, 1969, the Act was amended in a manner most relevant to this issue. The Board, effective September 1, 1969, will have the authority to process "improper practice" charges brought against public employers and employee organizations. Thus, § 201-a of the amended Act provides that it shall be an improper practice for a public employer or its agents deliberately " * * * to dominate or interfere with the formation or administration of any employee organization" for the purpose of depriving public employees of their protected rights under the Act. Accordingly, by its action, the Legislature has indicated its intent that questions of employer domination be treated in this new context, rather than during the course of a representation proceeding. Without, of course, deciding whether the present relationship between the senate and SUNY would fall within a proscribed improper practice, it is clear to me that the issue of employer domination should not be resolved herein.[12]

---

10. In the Matter of New York State Thruway, 1 PERB 4062, 4063 (1968), aff'd, 1 PERB 3214 (1968).

12. This approach is consistent with the private sector cases relied upon by the federation in its brief, which were all litigated as alleged unfair labor practices under § 8(a)(2) of the National Labor Relations Act, as amended.

Accordingly, * * * I find that [the senate] is an employee organization within the meaning and intent of § 201(6) of the Act. * * *

UNIT CONTENTIONS

I now move to the unit contentions of the parties. The federation concedes in its brief that the individual campus units it initially sought are inappropriate. It has, therefore, modified its position so as to seek a "dual-unit" type of structure. It argues that subjects of negotiations are divisible into local and state-wide issues. With regard to issues it believes are local, it contends that negotiating agents elected separately at each campus should separately negotiate these matters with the appropriate local campus administrator. A council of local campus winners would additionally be created [14] to represent unit employees on a state-wide level and would negotiate state-wide issues with the central administration of SUNY. The federation now seeks to include in these units members of the academic staff and specified nonacademic professional employees performing teaching and research functions, and also certain nonacademic professionals engaged in related aspects of instruction or research. It would exclude from its units all other professional employees.

The employer, CSEA, AAUP, and the senate argue that any form of negotiations on a campus-by-campus basis are unfeasible and only a single state-wide unit is appropriate. AAUP, however, would limit this unit to those employees in the basic teaching and research unit, thereby excluding administrative personnel, while the others take the position that the negotiating unit should include all professional employees of the employer, excluding only management and "students." [17] * * *

The employer, in addition to arguing the merits of its unit position, claims that its unit determination of November 15, 1967 was an expert educational judgment to which this Board must defer, as have the courts in reviewing other SUNY determinations, unless SUNY is found to have been arbitrary or capricious. The employer, in making this contention, misconstrues the Act and the function of this Board in resolving representation disputes, and erroneously relies upon the recent decision of the appellate division in In the Matter of Civil Service Employees Association, Inc. v. Helsby, 32 A.D.2d 131, 134 (1969) (per curiam), aff'd, 303 N.Y.S.2d 690 (July 1, 1969). In that decision, the court stated:

> "While the public employer, in the course of extending recognition to employee organizations, may initially designate bargaining units * * * [citation omitted], the statute (§ 207, subd. 1) expressly authorizes the Board to establish appropriate employer-employee negotiating units, applying those standards prescribed by the Legislature. Such determination must be made by providing a resolution of a particular dispute as to representation status on petitions filed with it pursuant to section 205, but we do not

---

14. The federation does not indicate whether the formation of the council would be by Board fiat or on a voluntary basis.

17. The parties stipulated to exclude " * * * any person who has as a primary objective study at one of the State University campuses under the supervision of a faculty [sic] for the established purpose of obtaining a graduate or undergraduate degree and who performs instructional, research or other services at a campus of the University. * * * " This stipulation is not intended to apply to any individual holding academic rank.

construe the Board's function as being limited to a review of the employer's designation. * * * "

Thus, and inasmuch as the Act makes no provision for the special handling of representation disputes involving SUNY, it is clear that this Board has the power and indeed the obligation, to resolve the instant dispute by applying the statutory criteria.[g] The rest of this decision shall be devoted to that task.

THE GEOGRAPHIC SCOPE OF THE UNIT

A. Facts: SUNY was created in 1948 as a corporation within the State Education Department, pursuant to Education Law § 352. At the present time, SUNY consists of four university centers, eleven four-year colleges, two medical centers, the College of Forestry at Syracuse, the Maritime College at Fort Schuyler, four contract colleges at Cornell and the College of Ceramics at Alfred University, six two-year agricultural and technical colleges; and thirty-one community colleges.[18] * * *

The instant proceeding involves only employees in the professional service at SUNY, which includes the academic staff and all other professionals. The employer states in its brief that "[t]here were approximately 11,371 persons in the professional service as of 1968, comprising 7,817 faculty and 3,554 other professionals."

SUNY is structured like a pyramid. At its apex sits the board of trustees, with statutory authority to exercise all corporate powers. The trustees are appointed by the Governor and are responsible, inter-alia, for "the over-all central administration, supervision and coordination" of all constituent institutions, the appointment of all staff members, the promulgation of rules and regulations for SUNY's governance, the management of SUNY's endowment funds, and the drafting of SUNY's annual budget. At four year intervals, they must also submit for the approval of the regents of the university of the State of New York and the Governor, a master plan for the projected long-range development of SUNY.

None of the constituent institutions of SUNY, with the exception of the College of Forestry, has an independent Board of Trustees. Each campus does have an affiliated council of gubernatorial appointees, but these function almost exclusively as advisory and review bodies, not as policy making groups, and they are subject to the supervision and control of the board of trustees.

The board of trustees, in its official "Policies," has designated the chancellor as SUNY's chief executive officer and delegated to him the day-to-day responsibility for the conduct of its affairs. The trustees have delegated

---

g. § 207.1: (a) [T]he definition of the unit shall correspond to a community of interest among the employees to be included in the unit;

(b) the officials of government at the level of the unit shall have the power to agree, or to make effective recommendations to other administrative authority or the legislative body with respect to, the terms and conditions of employment upon which the employees desire to negotiate; and

(c) the unit shall be compatible with the joint responsibilities of the public employer and public employees to serve the public.

18. The parties stipulated that the professional staff at the Cornell contract colleges and the community colleges should not be included in any negotiating unit or units deemed herein to be appropriate.

authority, subject to the limitations to be discussed infra, for the administration of the individual colleges to the chief administrative officer of each college (usually the president), and have made him responsible in this respect to both the chancellor of SUNY and the trustees.

General educational, fiscal, and personnel policies are determined by the trustees and the chancellor. The key to SUNY's purposefully integrated structure is the quadrennial master plan. This document is required by statute to contain proposals for new curricula, new facilities, and new student admissions policies in light of projected enrollment figures. It is developed by the office of the vice chancellor for long range planning from campus development plans submitted by the individual campuses. There is considerable dialogue between the vice chancellor's office and the campuses on the content of the campus plans and on the draft of the master plan, including consultation with such groups as the senate, student government presidents, and campus presidents. But, since the plan is intended to deal with the balanced educational requirements of the entire state, final responsibility for its content lies with central administration as the only authority able to resolve factional and regional conflicts. Thus, the vice chancellor, and then the chancellor, have the power to accept or reject any part of a campus plan and to include in the final plan proposals of their own design. So important is the concept of a unified plan for the higher educational development of the State, that no new project may be funded or initiated which has not been programmed in the master plan or one of the annual revisions; in addition, no campus may deviate from the master plan's blueprint without prior approval from central administration.

Budgetary procedures are similarly centralized, a reflection of the fact that the annual budget is, in one sense, the fiscal medium for implementing the recommendations of the master plan. Accordingly, the vice chancellor for finance and management reviews, modifies, and coordinates the individual campus budgets with an eye to maintaining the balance among the various campuses envisioned in the master plan. Then, the trustees prepare a comprehensive budget for inclusion in the executive budget which is submitted to the legislature by the Governor. Each campus is listed as a line item in the executive budget. Once the executive budget has been passed by the legislature, the authority of an individual campus to modify its monetary allocation is limited. A transfer of funds from one program to another requires the prior approval of the chancellor, while the approval of both the chancellor and the budget director is required before funds allocated in the budget to a given campus may be diverted to another campus. The campus president may transfer funds from one department to another within a given program, i.e., instructional, research, public service, etc., if they are to be used for the same general purpose as originally budgeted. Each campus president is further limited in that he may not increase by more than one percent the number of full time equivalent positions which his campus has been authorized in the budget, regardless of any excess funds he may possess.

The trustees' official "Policies" sets forth the applicable rules for the entire professional staff with regard to appointment, promotion, and termination, as well as vacations, sick leave, maternity leave, and sabbatical leave. Campus presidents may determine the recipients of sabbatical leaves and make all appointments (initial and promotional) to the professional staff which do not confer tenure [23] and which involve annual salaries of $15,000 or less. Even this limited power of appointment is reviewed by central administration. The chancellor makes all other academic appointments with the exceptions of distinguished professor, distinguished service professor, and university professor, which may be filled only by act of the trustees. The trustees also appoint non-academic members of the professional staff whose salaries exceed $15,000.

Other benefits uniformly conferred upon the entire professional staff either by statute or by trustees' determination are health insurance, retirement plans, disability benefits, tax-deferred annuities, reimbursement for moving expenses, workmen's compensation, and free tuition. Any professional transferring from one SUNY institution to another retains all his accrued benefits and credits, including service time.

With regard to salaries, maximums for the professional staff are uniform at all campuses (except for the medical centers) and are set by central administration subject to the approval of the director of the budget. Individual salaries, particularly of academic staff members, are subject to negotiation at the campus level within the ceiling limits and will reflect the impact of market forces. Merit increases and general salary increases are governed by standards and guidelines set by central administration.[26]

A number of other matters which are of possible concern to various members of the professional staff are also centrally coordinated and regulated. * * *

B. Conclusion: The initial uniting issue presented for determination is whether the state-wide unit defined by the employer should be geographically fragmented in accordance with the federation's "dual-unit" position. The federation bases its plan upon the proposition that potential negotiating issues may easily be divided into "state-wide" and "local" categories. Subjects such as salaries, retirement plans, most fringe benefits, and general personnel policies are conceded by the federation to be negotiable only on a state-wide level since only the board of trustees has the power to determine or to make effective recommendations with regard to them. However, the federation argues that individual campus presidents have effective authority to negotiate concerning other issues, such as policy and procedure with regard to merit salary increases, appointments and reappointments, teacher load, secretarial services, length of the college year, vacation periods, evening assignments, and research staff facilities. Each of [the three] statutory standards [h] will be dealt with below in resolving the issue at hand.

The record makes it abundantly clear that all professional employees of SUNY across the state have a substantial community of interest in that almost all fundamental terms and conditions of employment are uniform at all campuses or locally determined in accordance with uniformly applicable standards or guidelines. This significant fact has not been contravened by

---

23. The parties have stipulated that no distinction shall be made between faculty members on the basis of tenure for purposes of the unit determination herein.

26. The recipients of merit salary increases are determined, however, at the campus level.

h. See footnote g, supra, p. 1112.

the federation. Although, as the federation points out, there is some degree of local autonomy as set forth above, surely the concomitant differences among the campuses do not establish such conflicts of interest between their respective professionals as to warrant geographic fragmentation. It would appear that this broad-based community of interest mandates that negotiations, to be effective, should be conducted on a state-wide basis.

The power to set general personnel and education policies, fringe benefits, and salary scales, and to determine other economic and non-economic terms and conditions of employment resides in the chancellor or the board of trustees subject, of course, to legislative approval where necessary. Any power the campus presidents have is effectively circumscribed by the existence of the master plan and the comprehensive budget for the entire university, both of which are under the control and implementation of the board of trustees. Centralized control of the planning and budget processes also means that almost all allegedly "local" issues will have serious state-wide ramifications, either of an economic or policy nature. For these reasons, it is only during the course of state-wide negotiations with the board of trustees, if at all, that "local" issues could be properly defined and the scope of authority of campus presidents to negotiate on them could be insured. Any attempt to frame local issues independently would be putting the cart before the horse. Until such state-wide negotiations are conducted with a certified employee organization, it is clearly impossible for any sort of meaningful negotiations to take place at the campus level. Thus, the conclusion is inescapable that the establishment of negotiating units on a campus level would run counter to the statutory requirement that a negotiating unit be established at a level where officials of the employer have the power to make determinations or effective recommendations concerning terms and conditions of employment. This defect goes to the heart of the federation's case and is not cured by the proposed creation of a council of campus negotiating representatives to handle negotiations at the state level, since this coalition is premised on a unit structure which cannot be justified under the Act.

[The] third statutory factor relates to the administrative inconvenience which unwarranted fragmentation would cause, and thus mandates consideration of the desire of the employer. The employer's strong desire for state-wide negotiations and its conviction that the underlying concept of SUNY as a "community of scholars" bound together by a uniform administrative pattern would be destroyed by adoption of the federation's position, are not rebutted by any evidence in the record. To the contrary, the record is replete with evidence that the structured pyramid that is SUNY would crumble if its components were removed, and the conclusion is manifest that the federation's proposed "dual-unit" negotiating format is incompatible with the structure of SUNY. * * *

In addition, there are many other procedural and substantive difficulties with the "dual-unit" concept. For example, it apparently contemplates a purely voluntary and therefore hypothetical merger of the organizations that establish majority status at each of the campuses. Further, it would seem to require this Board to determine prematurely the type and nature of negotiable items. Finally, it would impose a system upon SUNY's professionals that would result in an unforeseen "council" negotiating on their behalf with regard to arbitrarily determined issues. A much more logical way of insuring that the faculty on each campus will be democratically represented by an organization that is eventually certified, would be for that organization to establish locals at each campus.

Accordingly, I find that only a statewide unit or units will satisfy all three uniting criteria of the Act.[35] The federation's proposal to the contrary must be rejected.

COMPOSITION OF THE STATE-WIDE UNIT

* * * The second uniting issue presented for resolution is the proper allocation of positions in the professional service, which have been divided by the "Policies" of the board of trustees into academic and nonacademic categories. The parties have stipulated to the appropriateness of a basic teaching and research unit which includes the academic staff and nonacademic professionals with teaching and research functions. The remaining nonacademic professionals, whose placement by the employer within the same unit as the academic staff is in dispute, may be loosely referred to as administrative personnel * * *.

* * * The answer to the question of whether administrative professionals should be included in the same negotiating unit as academic professionals is not free from doubt. However, I must be guided by a recent statement of the Board which indicates a disinclination to fragment employees having a basic community of interest: [44]

"[T]his statutory standard [CSL § 207(1)(c)] requires the designation of as small a number of units as possible consistent with the overriding requirement that the employees be permitted to form organizations of their own choosing to represent them in a meaningful and effective manner."

Thus, the issue to be determined is whether the differences between the two groups in terms and conditions of employment, as set forth above, are sufficiently important or significant so as to constitute conflicts of interest that would prevent meaningful and effective negotiations and warrant fragmentation. For the reasons set forth below, I find that they are not.
* * *

* * * [T]he basic community of interest between academic and nonacademic professionals as evidenced by their common fringe benefits, related salaries, common mission, and substantial amount of interchange, is not overshadowed by any demonstrable conflicts and would seem to mandate a conclusion that the two groups be included in the same unit for purposes of

---

35. The case of In the Matter of State Colleges of New Jersey, P.E.R.C. # 1 (April 9, 1969), relied upon by the federation, is inapposite. First, as the federation concedes, the case is factually distinguishable. Thus, the New Jersey Public Employment Relations Commission, in reaching its conclusion that separate negotiating units at each college were more appropriate than a single statewide unit, relied principally upon the legislative design in the New Jersey Education Law granting considerable autonomy to each campus. The statute accomplishes this by vesting in the board of trustees of each campus the power to manage and administer its own affairs. The situation with SUNY is, needless to say, precisely contrary to that existing in New Jersey. Second, this case merely adopts the approach that the federation itself has now rejected, i.e., campus units for all purposes; it does not even consider a "dual-unit" approach.

44. In the Matter of State of New York, [IPERB 3226] at 3231 (1968).

collective negotiations. * * * Fragmentation of the unit designated by the employer is not warranted by the record and might well cause the employer unnecessary difficulties in continuing to achieve its goal of providing quality higher education. For example, fragmentation would result in a seemingly inevitable curtailment of the present interchange and co-operation among all professional personnel. * * *

Accordingly, I find that the most appropriate unit in this matter is one that includes both academic and nonacademic professional employees. * * *

* * * IT IS ORDERED that an election by secret ballot shall be held under the supervision of the undersigned among the employees of the employer in the unit determined above to be appropriate, who are employed by the employer on the first payroll date of the 1969–1970 academic year. * * *

Paul E. Klein

Director of Representation

Dated: August 12, 1969
        Albany, New York

Note

1. An amusing sidelight on the "who is the employer?" theme appears in PERB's characterization of the employer in the very title of the SUNY case: "State of New York (State University of New York)." Who is the "employer" for collective negotiation purposes—the "State of New York" or the parenthetical "State University of New York"? Who, to get downright practical, calls the signals for management's side of the table—the governor or the chancellor and board of trustees? This question was one of great interest and concern to SUNY when the relationship between the Office of Employee Relations (N.Y.Exec.Law art. 24) and the SUNY administration was in the process of definition. The OER is headed by a Director of Employee Relations who is appointed by, and holds office at the pleasure of, the governor. (N.Y.Exec.Law § 652). The job of the director is to conduct collective negotiations on behalf of the state as the governor's agent. "Notwithstanding any inconsistent provision of law, any state officer, department, board, commission or agency shall, upon written request from the director, take such * * * action as is necessary to implement * * * the provisions of any binding agreement between the state and [any employee organization pursuant to the Taylor Law]. Such action may include * * * the adoption, repeal or amendment of rules, regulations or other procedures." N.Y. Exec.Law § 654(a). As may readily be seen, substantial changes in the way the University is run, and by whom are highly potential. These are entirely unintended, indeed even unforeseen, byproducts of the introduction of collective negotiations.

When the situation of SUNY is multiplied by the many other governmental agencies covered by the Taylor Law and similar enactments, the catalytic character of such laws may be more fully appreciated. Because so much of this change is both unintended and unforeseen, the ultimate impact of the emerging system of collective bargaining in public employment upon the structure and philosophy of American government can, at present, only be guessed at.

2. The ballots in the SUNY representation election (conducted by mail) were counted on December 29, 1970. They showed the following:

Votes

Potential	15,746
Cast	9,893
Challenged	– 469
Total counted	9,424

Results

State University Federation of Teachers	3,287
Senate Professional Association (formed by Faculty Senate)	2,974
American Association of University Professors	1,912
Civil Service Employees Association	705
No representation	546
Total	9,424

The ballots in the run-off election were counted on January 26, 1971, and showed:

Votes

Potential	15,746
Cast	10,804
Void	– 140
Challenged	– 378
Total counted	10,286

Results

Senate Professional Association	5,491
State University Federation of Teachers	4,795
Total	10,286

3. Is not some kind of "dual unit" system, as espoused by the State University Federation of Teachers, a necessity in public employment situations like the one involved in the SUNY case if the employees are to have the right of collective negotiations with regard to *all* of their "terms and conditions of employment"?

4. A significant difference between unit determination by the NLRB and that done under public employment relations acts is that the NLRB's criteria are satisfied if a proposed unit is *an* appropriate unit, whereas there is a tendency in the public sector to accept only *the* most appropriate unit, usually as comprehensive in size as is consistent with the avoidance of dangerous conflicts of interest within the unit. See Crowley, The Resolution of Representation Status Disputes Under the Taylor Law, 37 Ford.L.Rev. 517, 518–20 (1969), discussed and quoted supra p. 218, text and footnote d.

5. We have seen that the scope of collective bargaining in the public sector is closely connected to problems of unit determination. Another distinguishing feature of public sector bargaining is its interrelationship with the various bodies of law governing public enterprises. These bodies of law, already encountered in the preceding materials, include legislation concerning fiscal and budgetary

matters, civil service laws and regulations, and the like. Their relationship to the scope of bargaining is explored in the materials which follow.

DETERMINING THE SCOPE OF NEGOTIATIONS UNDER PUBLIC EMPLOYMENT RELATIONS STATUTES

24 Industrial and Labor Relations Review 432 (1971)

[The Public Employees' Fair Employment Act of the State of New York (N.Y.Civil Service Law, art. 14; N.Y. Judiciary Law § 751), enacted in 1967 and popularly known as the Taylor Law, was amended in 1969 so as to make it an "improper practice," inter alia, for public employers to refuse to negotiate with duly authorized employee representatives concerning terms and conditions of employment (Section 209–a, effective September 1, 1969). The Public Employment Relations Board (PERB) is charged under the amendments with enforcement of the duty to negotiate (Section 205.5(d)). In determining the scope of the matters over which a public employer must negotiate, PERB encounters problems peculiar to public employment. Other tribunals and agencies of the state have long been in the business of deciding questions now seemingly within the bailiwick of PERB. If, for example, the state comptroller, in the exercise of a supervisory power over proper subjects for public expenditure, rules that a public employer within the state cannot lawfully spend public funds for a purpose otherwise falling within the Taylor Law ambit of negotiability (that is, "terms and conditions of employment"), what effect should PERB give to the ruling? Among PERB's other competitors for jurisdiction to define the scope of negotiability are the courts, attorney general, Civil Service Commission, State Education Department, and local legislative bodies.

A separate but related question concerning the scope of negotiations under the Taylor Law, also peculiar to public employment, grows out of the fact that management at the level of the negotiating unit may not have authority over a subject otherwise clearly within "terms and conditions of employment," the authority residing instead in a higher echelon of public management. Should orders to negotiate be issued with regard to such subjects? A further question is that of the role of fact finders and mediators in the determination of the scope of negotiability. A final question, cutting across all of the rest, concerns the impact of the Taylor Law on the pre-Taylor scope of employer power to confer employee benefits within the meaning of "terms and conditions of employment." Is the scope of the unilateral power exercised by a particular public employer under preexisting law the same as the scope of negotiability under the Taylor Law, or is the latter greater?

Concerned with the foregoing and related problems, PERB commissioned Kurt L. Hanslowe and Walter E. Oberer, experienced third parties in public employment disputes and professors of law and industrial and labor relations at Cornell University, to analyze the problems and advise as to the course of action PERB should follow. These two consultants, although compensated by PERB for the time invested in this project, exercised judgments solely oriented to sound resolution of the problems. Their memorandum to PERB culminating their analysis is, with their permission and that of PERB, reproduced below. The problems and suggested dispositions, although examined in the frame of reference of the State of New York, are relevant to other jurisdictions having a public employment relations scheme entailing the duty to negotiate and enforcement of that duty by an administering agency.—EDITOR]

MEMORANDUM

To: Jerome Lefkowitz

         Deputy Chairman

         Public Employment Relations Board

From: Kurt L. Hanslowe and Walter E. Oberer

Subject: PERB AND THE SCOPE OF NEGOTIATIONS UNDER THE TAYLOR LAW

Dated: June 1, 1970

1. *General Problem*

The general problem examined herein is the relationship of the Taylor Law and of PERB to other laws of the State of New York and to the agencies which administer them, with regard to the determination of the scope of negotiations under the Taylor Law—i.e., the subjects as to which there is a duty to negotiate.

A question within the foregoing question is: What impact, if any, does the Taylor Law have on the pre-existing authority of public employers to determine "terms and conditions of employment" of their employees? In other words, is the scope of negotiations under the Taylor Law coterminous with or greater than the scope of the unilateral power held by the particular public employer under pre-existing law, as declared by the Constitution, Legislature, courts, State Comptroller, Attorney General, etc.?

2. *A Hypothetical Case: PERB vs. the Comptroller as to Local Government Conditions of Employment*

Employee Organization, duly certified representative of certain professional employees, presents to School Board, the public employer, a list of negotiating demands which includes the following item: "Payment of accrued sick leave to the estate of a deceased employee."

School Board refuses to discuss the above item on the ground that inclusion of such a provision in the collective agreement would be illegal, citing 23 Op.State Compt. 649 (1967, # 67–735) and Article VIII, § 1 of the State Constitution, prohibiting government entities, including school districts, from giving gifts.

Employee Organization files a charge with PERB under Section 209–a.–1(d), alleging that the above-described action of the School Board constitutes a refusal to negotiate concerning "terms and conditions of employment."

What should PERB do?

Under the 1969 amendments it is clearly PERB's responsibility to determine whether or not the alleged improper practice occurred. Section 205.5, as amended, provides:

In addition to its powers and functions provided in other sections of this article, the board shall have the following powers and functions:

"* * * (d) To establish procedures for the prevention of improper employer and employee organization practices as provided in section two hundred nine-a of this article. * * * The board shall exercise exclusive nondelegable jurisdiction of the powers granted to it by this paragraph. * * *"

PERB must, therefore, determine whether the unused sick leave demand falls within the scope of "terms and conditions of employment," within the meaning of the Taylor Law.

Concerning the relationship of the above-cited opinion of the State Comptroller to this determination, PERB has three courses of action available: PERB might accept the opinion of the Comptroller as conclusive of the matter and dismiss the charge; PERB might ignore the opinion of the Comptroller as irrelevant; PERB might take into account the opinion of the Comptroller, giving it, however, only such weight as, in the judgment of PERB, its persuasive force merits.

The third course of action is patently the proper one. The decision as to the scope of negotiability is PERB's in the first instance. The first two options—abandonment of decision to the Comptroller and ignoring the opinion of the Comptroller—have little to commend them. As to the first, the Comptroller has no mandate under the law to resolve such questions; his opinions with respect to such local government expenditures are admitted by himself to be "informal and advisory" only. * * * As to the second, the Comptroller has, by arrogation or otherwise, been in the business of advising local governments as to their powers under a broad body of law for a substantial period of time; in the process he has accumulated considerable experience concerning the legal framework within which local governments of the State of New York operate. For PERB to ignore completely this source of potential guidance would seem unwise.

The burden of demarcating those subjects which are within the scope of the statutory criterion "terms and conditions of employment" is initially PERB's, not merely because PERB has been designated by the State Legislature to make such determinations in the first instance, but because the vitality of the administrative process lies in the development and application of expertise in specially difficult areas of government regulation. The definition of the scope of negotiations under the Taylor Law is such an area.

One way of validating the foregoing position is to consider the matter of judicial review. However the decision as to the scope of negotiability under the Taylor Law is made in the first instance, it is subject to review in the courts. Such review is dependent upon the quality of the record made below and the sophistication of the trial tribunal with regard to the questions before it. Employment relations, as several decades of experience in the private sector demonstrate, is a complex and delicate area in which the adequacy of judicial review is particularly dependent upon the quality of the proceedings, record, and judgment below.

It is instructive to note, in the foregoing regard, that Comptroller opinions are typically rendered on the basis of a mere exchange of letters, without the sharpening of issues through pleadings, the presentation of evidence, confrontation and cross examination of witnesses, oral or written argument. Proceedings before PERB, on the contrary, under sections 209–a and 205.5(d), entail all of these aids to administrative adjudication and judicial review.

Turning now to the merits of the hypothetical case posed, namely, whether the issue of "payment of accrued sick leave to the estate of a deceased employee" is within the statutory mandate of "terms and conditions of employment," the problems presented to PERB are the following: (1) whether the demand concerning the treatment of accrued sick leave is a term or condition of employment, and (2) whether Article VIII, § 1 of the State Constitution and/or some other state constitutional or legislative provision takes the matter out of the scope of negotiability. The answer to the first question would seem quite clearly to be yes. The real question for the purposes of this memorandum is the second. As to this, PERB must determine, within the limiting context of all relevant constitutional and statutory provisions (i.e., all relevant "law"), whether, as a matter of sound employment relations in the public sector, including such a subject within the scope of negotiability makes sense.

Stated more clearly perhaps, in cases such as the hypothetical one posed PERB has two questions potentially before it: (1) whether the particular subject should be deemed, as a matter of sound public employment relations, to be within "terms and conditions of employment," (2) whether, even if it should be so deemed, the particular subject has been withheld or withdrawn from negotiability by the operation of some competing provision of law. Where the answer to the second question is unclear by reason of ambiguity in the competing law, the question of negotiability should be decided by PERB on the basis of sound public employment relations.

Whatever the determination of PERB, that determination is of course reviewable in the courts pursuant to Section 210.4 of the Taylor Law.

3. *Another Hypothetical Case: PERB vs. the Comptroller as to State Government Conditions of Employment*

Fuller understanding of the Comptroller's role vis-à-vis PERB requires the posing of a second hypothetical case. Let us assume that the demand with regard to unused sick leave were to be made by an organization of employees of the State of New York, rather than by an organization of local employees. Let us further assume that the State Comptroller has previously ruled that such an expenditure of state funds would be illegal. Accordingly, the state employer refuses to negotiate with the organization of state employees concerning the demand. The employees file a charge of refusal to negotiate against the state employer.

Is the problem regarding PERB's response to the Comptroller's ruling any different here from the preceding case? The answer is both yes and no. No, because PERB must again make the initial determination as to whether the subject of the demand falls within the statutory definition "terms and conditions of employment." Yes, because in making this determination PERB may be required to pay more respect to the prior determination of the Comptroller that the expenditure involved would not be a lawful one. This greater respect is the product of the difference in the role of the Comptroller under state law with regard to (1) *local* finance and (2) *state* finance.

As to the Comptroller's role with regard to *local* finance, we find no express or clearly implied power granted to the Comptroller by either the Constitution or the Legislature to pass on the *substantive* propriety of public expenditures. (At least there is no such *general* power. The myriad of statutes touching the Comptroller in one respect or another may contain some such grant in specific and narrow instances.) The assumption of authority by the Comptroller in cases presenting questions of substantive propriety is an interesting and instructive example of an institution expanding to fill the need of municipalities and other local governments for "authoritative" legal advice (a need more typically filled, one would guess, by Attorneys General).

As to the Comptroller's role with regard to *state* finance, the picture is quite different. There, the Comptroller exercises authority derived from the State Constitution itself. Article 5, § 1 provides that: "The comptroller shall be required: (1) To audit all vouchers before payment. * * * The payment of any money of the state, or of any money under its control * * * except upon audit by the comptroller, shall be void. * * *" More specifically, Article 2, § 8, subdivision 8 of the State Finance Law specifies as one of the duties of the Comptroller that he shall: "Draw warrants on the treasury for the payment of the moneys directed by law to be paid out of the treasury, but no such warrant shall be drawn unless authorized by law, and every such warrant shall refer to the law under which it is drawn."

What the foregoing demonstrates is the primary role played by the Comptroller with regard to the expenditure of *state* funds. That role is to determine in the first instance the lawfulness of any proposed expenditure. This is not a final power, however. The action of the Comptroller in refusing any expenditure is subject to judicial review. (N.Y.Civil Practice Law and Rules §§ 7801, 7802, 7803, 7804, 7806; see Quayle v. State, 192 N.Y. 47, 54, 84 N.E. 583, 585 (1908) ("If the comptroller exceeded his power in allowing as payment less than the contract prices, the claimant's remedy was by direct proceeding against him to review that audit."); Nicholoulias v. Regent Restaurant, 175 Misc. 526, 25 N.Y.S.2d 181 (Sup.Ct., Albany Co., 1940); Guardian Life Insurance Company of America v. Bohlinger, 308 N.Y. 174, 183, 124 N.E.2d 110, 114 (1954) ("* * * the courts have the power and the duty to make certain that the administrative official has not acted in excess of the grant of authority given him by statute or in disregard of the standard prescribed by the legislature.")

One of the questions presented in judicial review of a determination of the Comptroller is whether it "was affected by an error of law." (CPLR § 7803.3.) Any determination of the Comptroller which poses a problem for PERB with regard to scope of negotiations is almost certain to be the product of interpretation (or misinterpretation) of relevant (or irrelevant) provisions of law (or unlaw). Accordingly, such a determination should be overturned by a court for "error of law" where, in the court's judgment, the Comptroller has misapplied or misinterpreted the law.

Returning to our hypothetical situation concerning the unused sick leave, PERB's relationship to the Comptroller is akin to that of a court called upon to review one of his determinations. What the Comptroller has hypothetically done in the unused sick leave case, in one way of putting it, is to interpret "terms and conditions of employment" in such a fashion as to exclude that subject from the scope of negotiations. The question before PERB on the improper practice charge of refusal to negotiate is the same. For PERB to take the position that the Comptroller's decision is final and unreviewable by PERB would be to make the Comptroller the controller of this vital aspect of employment relations (viz., scope of negotiations), rather than PERB, the tribunal expressly created and empowered to perform this function. Such a course might also be said to constitute an illegal delegation of PERB's duty and power to determine the alleged improper employer practice in the first instance. (See § 205.5(d).) Important questions of employment relations would be decided by a "tribunal" inexpert in that area and without the due process protections of a full hearing. Again, judicial review of any decision made with regard to the scope of negotiations would be considerably enhanced where the decision under review was made by an expert body on the basis of a full record.

All of which leads to the conclusion that PERB's relationship to the Comptroller is not significantly different in the state employment area from what it is in the local employment area. In each area PERB makes its own determination of negotiability, giving such weight to prior determinations of the Comptroller as it deems appropriate in the particular case. One should be alerted, however, to the following qualification. An argument might be made in a particular case that the Comptroller has *discretionary* power with respect to particular expenditures, and that, as a consequence, his decision against such a proposed expenditure is reversible only upon a showing of abuse of discretion, i.e., of arbitrariness or unreasonableness. (See, e.g., the discussion of the Comptroller's role re the State Employees' Retirement System in Part 5 infra.) To sustain such an argument, one would have to point to rather clear statutory language in the particular case—language which would support the proposition that the Legislature has delegated to the Comptroller a discretion ordinarily exercised by the Legislature itself, namely, the setting of the standards by which state funds are to be expended. We find no reason to conclude that such is the case with regard to the *general* grants of power to the Comptroller, either constitutional or statutory. And even where the Comptroller may fairly be said to possess a discretionary power over a subject otherwise within the Taylor Law's "terms and conditions of employment," there still is room for *some* judicial review, and therefore, for some review by PERB. Indeed, PERB may be validly claimed to have the *same* degree of discretionary power with regard to defining the scope of negotiations under the Taylor Law, thus presenting a court called upon to review PERB's determination (assuming it is inconsistent with the Comptroller's) with competing exercises of discretion by the two agencies. The question of primary or priority of discretion as between the Comptroller and PERB would thus be "up for grabs." There is no reason to assume, a priori, that PERB would lose in this contest for ultimate judicial acceptance. (See Part 7 herein for further relevant discussion.)

4. *The Relationship of PERB to Other Competing Agencies*

What has been said of the Comptroller is dispositive of PERB's relationship with other potentially competing agencies of state government. Whatever the competing agency, the question of negotiability is to be answered by PERB in the first instance. In the process of answering the question, PERB should take into account all pertinent constitutional and statutory provisions; its consideration should not be confined to the Taylor Law alone. Neither the Taylor Law nor PERB exits in a void. (Cf., e.g., Southern Steamship Co. v. NLRB, 316 U.S. 31, 47 (1942) (" * * * the Board has not been commissioned to effectuate the policies of the Labor Relations Act so singlemindedly that it may wholly ignore other and equally important Congressional objectives. Frequently the entire scope of Congressional purpose calls for careful accommodation of one statutory scheme to another, and it is not too much to demand of an administrative body that it undertake this accommodation without excessive emphasis upon its immediate task."); American News Co., 55 NLRB 1302 (1944).)

In addition to taking into account other constitutional and statutory provisions, PERB should consider the decisions of tribunals competent to interpret those constitutional and statutory provisions. The weight which PERB gives to any aspect of the foregoing array of law (constitutional, statutory, decisional) should depend on PERB's own interpretation of such of that law as it deems relevant. PERB's interpretation would, of course, be oriented to sound public employment relations as perceived through its own expertise. While PERB cannot and should not ignore clear mandates from the Constitution, the Legislature, or the Court of Appeals [New York's highest court], it should deem itself free in the absence of such mandates to exercise its own best judgment, understanding of course that its decisions are themselves subject to judicial review. It would be obviously wasteful for PERB to determine questions of negotiability in the context of the Taylor Law alone, leaving to the reviewing courts in the first instance the questions of the relevance and force of competing law. Such an approach would deny to the reviewing courts the benefit of PERB's developing expertise with respect to the implications of such competing law for sound public employment relations (which is to say, sound public policy in a public employment context) in the State of New York. * * *

5. *The Relationship of Scope of Negotiations to the Unit Problem*

A somewhat different variety of scope of negotiations question confronts PERB in the following type of situation: where the subject sought to be negotiated is quite clearly within the statutory scope, "terms and conditions of employment," but is not within the authority of management at the unit level. An example of this type of subject is annuities and pensions under the State Employees' Retirement System. (Retirement and Social Security Law, Article 2.) This system applies not only to state employees but also to the employees of "participating" municipalities and other local government entities. The State Comptroller is declared by § 11 of the Retirement and Social Security Law to be the "administrative head" of the Retirement System, with the express power, among others, to adopt and amend "rules and regulations for the administration and transaction of the business of the retirement system. * * *"

Without delving more deeply into the Retirement and Social Security Law, it may be seen that two sets of potential questions for PERB as to scope of negotiations are presented thereunder. The first set of questions has to do with negotiations in *state* employment; the second set has to do with negotiations in *local* employment.

As to the *state* negotiations, a tug-of-war seems possible between the Office of Employee Relations, on the one hand, and the State Comptroller, on the other. With whom, it may be asked, do state employees have the right to negotiate concerning those aspects of the pension program which the Legislature has expressly placed in the discretionary control of the Comptroller. Those aspects may be said to be (1) not negotiable except with the Comptroller himself (is the Comptroller a "public employer" with regard to employees not employed in the Department of Audit and Control?), (2) negotiable only if the Comptroller *chooses* to negotiate concerning the exercise of his discretionary authority, (3) negotiable only to the extent that the state employer (Office of Employee Relations?) and the employee organization involved may agree upon joint recommendations to be made to the Comptroller and/or to the Legislature.

A possible legislative resolution of the foregoing type of problem may be foreshadowed by a very recent amendment to § 8 of the State Finance Law. The duties of the Comptroller with regard to a related matter have been modified as follows in subdivision 16 thereof:

> "Notwithstanding any inconsistent provision of law, no change shall be made in the rate or eligibility standards for state employees' travel, meals, lodging, and other expenses for which the state makes payment (either in advance or by reimbursement), without the approval of the director of employee relations."

As to negotiations over pensions involving *local* governments participating in the State Retirement System, the only practical effect of such would be to produce joint proposals to be presented in the form of requests to the Comptroller and/or the State Legislature. This is an instance of a larger question which will confront PERB in several different contexts. The question is whether PERB should require a particular public employer to negotiate with regard to a subject as to which the employer has no control *except* the power to make recommendations. This question is dealt with in the ensuing section.

6. *Subjects of Negotiation: Mandatory, Permissible, Illegal?*

The subjects of bargaining in the private sector have been trichotomized into mandatory, permissible, and illegal. Mandatory subjects are those which fall within the meaning of "wages, hours, and other terms and conditions of employment" (National Labor Relations Act, Section 8(d)); as to these, the proposing party may bargain to impasse, and the other party has a duty to bargain in response. Permissible subjects are those not within "wages, hours, and other terms and conditions of employment," but not illegal; as to these, the proponent may propose, but not insist upon, and the other party need not, but may, bargain; if agreement is reached on a permissible subject, that agreement is an enforceable part of the contract. Illegal subjects are those which, even if agreed upon, are unenforceable; of course there is no duty to bargain over such a subject. (See generally, sections 8(a)(5), 8(b)(3), 9(a), and 8(d) of the National Labor Relations Act, and NLRB v. Wooster Division of Borg-Warner Corporation, 356 U.S. 342 (1958).)

The situation in public employment is sufficiently different as to impugn the relevance of the trichotomy. The *terminology* may, however, be helpful for purposes of analysis. Assuming a subject to be clearly within "terms and conditions of employment" and at the same time not within the authority of management at the level of the unit, should PERB enforce a duty to negotiate at that level? To put it otherwise, should such a subject be treated as mandatory, permissible, or illegal—i.e., should negotiation be required, permitted, prohibited?

The real choice would seem to lie between the mandatory and permissible approaches; little purpose would be served in *prohibiting* negotiations on such a subject. Even where public management at the level of the unit is without authority to control subject X, it would ordinarily have authority to agree with the employee organization involved to make a joint recommendation to the appropriate higher echelon of authority as to the desired disposition of subject X. Accordingly, subjects found to be within the statutory language "terms and conditions of employment" but not within the authority of management at the unit level might, nonetheless, be treated as mandatory subjects and negotiations over them therefore required. A difficulty with this approach is that it might tend to clutter up negotiations with a laundry list of demands for joint importuning of distant and perhaps intractable holders of pertinent powers. On the other hand, a good deal of negotiations in the public sector concerning the most central of subjects is conducted by "public employers" who lack authority to resolve finally those issues. Examples of this are (1) a dependent school board negotiating teacher salaries and (2) the State Office of Employee Relations negotiating state employee salaries; in the case of the first, the pertinent authority resides in the city council; in the second, it resides in the State Legislature.

Perhaps guidance toward a middle course between the mandatory and permissible approaches is offered by Section 207.1(b) of the Taylor Law when it speaks of "*effective* recommendations." Subjects which the particular employer does not control but as to which he has the power to make *effective* recommendations might be treated as mandatory subjects. On the other hand, subjects as to which the employer could make only *ineffective* recommendations might be treated as permissible subjects only.

7. *The Impact of the Taylor Law on the Pre-Existing Authority of Public Employers*

The array of positions with regard to the effect of the enactment of the Taylor Law on the pre-existing authority of public employers to confer benefits on their employees ranges from the response of the Comptroller at the right extreme, "nil," to a hypothetical position at the left extreme to the effect that the Taylor Law impliedly repeals all prior inconsistent legislation and judicial and administrative rulings.   *   *   *

The Comptroller's position, "a fundamental premise which underlies every Opinion of the State Comptroller, concerning situations involving Article 14, of the Civil Service Law (known as the Taylor Law)" (see Comptroller's Memorandum of Law in the *Town of Huntington case,* page 4), was stated in 23 Op. State Compt. 316, 318–19 (1967, # 67–378):

> "The new statutory provisions [the Taylor Law] do not in any way enlarge the legal benefits which public employers may confer on their employees nor has there been any expansion of the authority of such public employers in regard to these benefits. Therefore, it will be necessary for us to consider in order each of the employee demands herein to determine whether, irrespective of collective bargaining, this school district may legally comply with the same."

We disagree with the position thus taken by the Comptroller (and also with the position at the opposite extreme of the spectrum). At least two pertinent changes, both, in our judgment, rather basic, have been produced by the Taylor Law. The effect of these two changes is potentially to expand the scope of negotiations beyond the scope of pre-Taylor *exercise* of employer power. The first change is that a new public agency, PERB, has been created and empowered by the Legislature to deal with and decide issues of public employment relations in the State of New York—issues previously presided over (to the extent they were presided over at all) by other agencies. To the extent that those other agencies lacked authority or occasion to render final decisions on questions of employer power presently falling within the purview of PERB, such questions are still open. This means that the only questions of employer power definitively answered at the time of this writing are those questions which have heretofore been unambiguously resolved by the Constitution of the State of New York, the State Legislature, or the Court of Appeals. Opinions of the State Comptroller, and even decisions of lower state courts never challenged in the ultimate through appellate review to the Court of Appeals, establish no controlling precedents.

A second basic change in the public policy of the State of New York occasioned by the enactment of the Taylor Law is the introduction into public employment relations of the whole new concept of resolving employer-employee disagreements through the institution of collective negotiations. We concede that matters unambiguously resolved by the State Constitution, by statutory enactment, or by Court of Appeals interpretation of either of the foregoing are not affected by the passage of the Taylor Law. Where ambiguity exists, however, or where the source of the competing "law" is of a lower order than Constitution, Legislature, Court of Appeals—i.e., in the gray area of public employer authority over "terms and conditions of employment"—strong reason exists for concluding that the legislative intent was to have such gray-area problems resolved through the process of collective negotiations. Indeed, the Taylor Law declares it to be the public policy of the State of New York to resolve disputes between public employees and public employers by that process. (Section 200.)   ∗   ∗   ∗

Summary of Conclusions

The Taylor Law, as amended, places upon PERB the duty to determine in the first instance, subject to judicial review, the scope of negotiability, when that issue is presented in refusal to negotiate cases. In such a case PERB has two questions actually or potentially before it: (1) whether the subject of the dispute, viewed solely in the context of the Taylor Law, is within the statutory definition "terms and conditions of employment"; (2) whether some competing law precludes such inclusion. Considerable guidance as to the first question exists in the thirty-five years of experience with the scope of bargaining under a similar definition in the private sector. The second question is, on the contrary, almost unique to public employment; the purpose of this memorandum is to seek to chart a sensible course through these strange waters.

In discharging its function of determining negotiability in the first instance, PERB should take into account not merely the Taylor Law, but other relevant statutory and constitutional provisions, including the interpretation and application of these provisions by other tribunals, judicial and administrative. Subjects claimed to be non-negotiable by reason of the dictates of such other laws or enforcement agencies should be dealt with by PERB in two categories. Category 1 consists of constitutional and statutory provisions and Court of Appeals decisions which *unambiguously* remove a subject from the scope of "terms and conditions of employment" under the Taylor Law. As to these pre-empted subjects, PERB should issue no order to negotiate, however much it might have done so absent the competing law. Category 2 consists of (a) constitutional and statutory provisions and Court of Appeals decisions of *questionable* relevance to the matter before PERB, and (b) enactments, decisions, and opinions emanating from sources of law lower than Constitutional Convention, State Legislature, Court of Appeals—i.e., courts inferior to the Court of Appeals, executive officers, administrative agencies other than PERB, local legislatures. As to subjects falling in Category 2, PERB should make its own fresh analysis of the issue of preemption and decide it on the basis of the soundest public employment policy permitted by the competing law, having in mind, of course, that its decision will be subject to judicial review.

A related problem, unique to public employment, is that management at the level of the negotiating unit may not have authority over a subject otherwise clearly within "terms and conditions of employment," authority over that subject residing in a higher echelon of public management. Should such a subject, as to which management at the unit level has at most a power to make recommendations, be deemed a "mandatory" subject of negotiations, failure to negotiate in good faith producing an order to negotiate by PERB, or should it be deemed merely a "permissible" subject of negotiations, as to which the non-proposing party may, but need not, negotiate? Our suggestion to PERB is that it consider the dividing of such subjects into two categories: those as to which management at the unit level has the capacity to make "*effective* recommendations" to the appropriate echelon of higher authority, and those as to which it lacks such capacity. Orders to negotiate would be issued by PERB with regard to the first, but not the second. * * *

A question cutting across all of the problems pertaining to negotiability concerns the impact of the Taylor Law upon the pre-existing scope of employer power to confer employee benefits within the ambit of "terms and conditions of employment." Is the scope of negotiations under the Taylor Law coterminous with or greater than the scope of unilateral power held by the particular public employer under pre-existing law? Our conclusion is that the scope of negotiations under the Taylor Law may well be broader than the scope of previously unilaterally *exercised* employer authority. The Taylor Law works two basic changes which, in our judgment, provide the wherewithal for the conclusion expressed. First, it creates and empowers a new agency, PERB, for resolving gray-area questions, never previously *authoritatively* resolved, as to the pertinent scope of employer authority. Second, the Taylor Law introduces a whole new concept for the resolution of problems of public employer-employee relationships, including problems in the gray area of employer authority—i.e., the concept of *bilateral* determination of conflicts over "terms and conditions of employment." Without espousing the extreme position that the Taylor Law constitutes an implied repeal of all prior inconsistent legislation, our conclusion is that the two basic changes noted render the pre-Taylor scope of exercised employer power an inadequate guide to the post-Taylor scope of negotiations. * * *

BOARD OF EDUCATION OF UNION FREE SCHOOL DISTRICT NO. 3 v. ASSOCIATED TEACHERS OF HUNTINGTON, INC.

Court of Appeals of New York, 1972.
30 N.Y.2d 122, 331 N.Y.S.2d 17, 282 N.E.2d 109.

FULD, CHIEF JUDGE.

We are called upon to decide (1) whether a school board has the authority to enter into a collective bargaining agreement granting economic benefits to schoolteachers, absent specific statutory authorization to do so and (2) whether such a board lacks the power to enter into a collective bargaining agreement containing a clause which provides for the arbitration of disputes concerning disciplinary action taken against tenure teachers.

The facts are undisputed. The plaintiff (hereafter called the "Board"), as a public employer under the Taylor Law (Civil Service Law, art. 14), recognized the defendant (hereafter referred to as the "Association") as the employee organization representing the school district teachers. The parties—following recommendations by a fact-finding panel appointed by the New York State Public Employment Relations Board—entered into a collective bargaining agreement for the 1969–70 school year. Included in this agreement are five provisions which gave rise to this litigation. Four of them relate to the payment of economic benefits in the form of either salary increases or reimbursement for certain expenses incurred, and the fifth provides for arbitration in cases in which tenure teachers have been disciplined.

The first two challenged provisions deal with the reimbursement of teachers for job related personal property damage (the damage reimbursement provision).[1] The next provides partial reimbursement to teachers for

1. These clauses—contained in article VIII—read as follows:

"E. The Board will provide protection of teachers by reimbursement for cost of re-

placing or repairing dentures, eyeglasses, etc., not covered by Workmen's Compensation, destroyed or lost as the result of an

graduate courses taken with the approval of the school administration (the tuition reimbursement provision).[2] The fourth questioned clause (art. XXI) provides for a salary increment for teachers during their last year of service before retirement (the retirement award provision) and reads as follows:

> "Each teacher who hereafter indicates his intention to retire one year prior to such retirement under the New York State Teachers Retirement System or whose retirement is mandatory under such system shall receive at the start of the last school year of service a salary increase for that year equal to $^5/_{10}$ of 1% (0.5%) of his current salary multiplied by the number of years of service in this school district, such salary increase not to exceed $1500."

The remaining disputed provision (art. XVIII, § C) relates to the arbitration of disputes regarding disciplinary action taken against tenure teachers (the grievance provision):

> "No tenure teacher shall be disciplined, reprimanded, reduced in rank or compensation, suspended, demoted, transferred, terminated or otherwise deprived of any professional advantage without just cause. * * * Any such action, including adverse evaluation of teacher performance or a violation of professional ethics asserted by the Board or any agent thereof, shall be subject to the grievance procedure set forth in this Agreement."

The Board, questioning its own power to agree and bind itself to the provisions set out above, raised the issue of their legality in September, 1969, during the negotiations leading up to the execution of the collective bargaining agreement, and shortly thereafter it brought this action for a judgment (1) declaring those provisions illegal and of no effect and (2) staying arbitration proceedings which had been commenced by the Association under the grievance provision. The court at Special Term, 310 N.Y.S.2d 929, held that the provisions relating to tuition reimbursement and to the grievance procedure were illegal but sustained the validity of the remaining provisions. On appeal, the Appellate Division agreed with Special Term in all respects except one; it concluded that the tuition reimbursement provision was also valid (36 A.D.2d 753, 319 N.Y.S.2d 469). Two of the justices dissenting in part, believed that the retirement award provision was illegal.

In our view, all of the challenged provisions are valid.

The basic question posed by this appeal is whether there is any fundamental conflict between the provisions of the Taylor Law and the provisions of any other statute dealing with the powers and duties of school boards. Under the Taylor Law, a public employer, in order "to promote harmonious and cooperative relationships between government and its employees"

injury sustained in the course of his or her employment.

"F. The Board will provide reimbursement for repair or value, whichever is less, of clothing and personal effects damaged or destroyed during the course of and incident to employment, provided loss is not caused by negligence of the claimant. Personal effects do not include automobiles and/or other vehicles."

2. The provision (art. XI, § A) reads in this way:

"Any member of the professional staff shall, upon presentation of his transcript and a bursar's receipt, be reimbursed in a lump sum in an amount equal to 50% of the cost per credit hour of such work up to a maximum of ten hours per year; provided the courses are of a content related to the curriculum or course of study taught by the teacher and are approved in advance by the Principal and Superintendent. The benefits provided above may be extended to other courses with the approval of the Superintendent."

(§ 200), is empowered to recognize an employee organization for the purpose of collective bargaining negotiations (§ 204, subd. 1). When such an organization is recognized, the public employer "is, required to negotiate collectively with such employee organization in the determination of, and administration of grievances arising under, *the terms and conditions of employment of the public employees as provided in this article,* and to negotiate and enter into written agreements with such employee organizations in determining such terms and conditions of employment" (§ 204, subd. 2; italics supplied).

In other words, the validity of a provision found in a collective agreement negotiated by a public employer turns upon whether it constitutes a term or condition of employment. If it does, then, the public employer must negotiate as to such term or condition and, upon reaching an understanding, must incorporate it into the collective agreement unless some statutory provision circumscribes its power to do so.

It is manifest that each of the provisions here challenged constitutes a term or condition of employment. It is certainly not uncommon for collective agreements in the public sector, as well as in the private sector, to contain "damage reimbursement" provisions similar to the one before us. If, during the course of performing his duties, an employee has his clothing, eyeglasses or other personal effects damaged or destroyed, it is certainly reasonable to reimburse him for the cost of repairing or replacing them.

The tuition reimbursement provision, as well, clearly relates to a term and condition of employment. School boards throughout the State pay teachers a salary differential for completing a specified number of credit hours above the baccalaureate degree. Since graduate work tends to increase teacher skills and is beneficial to the school district, there is no reason why the Board should not encourage such work by absorbing one half of the tuition expense.

The so-called retirement award provision also involves a term and condition of employment.[3] Employers, both in the public and private sectors, have traditionally paid higher salaries based upon length of service and training. In addition to the fact that the payment was to be for services actually rendered during their last year of employment, the benefit provided for served the legitimate purpose of inducing experienced teachers to remain in the employ of the school district.[4] It is not, therefore, a constitutionally prohibited "gift" of public moneys (N.Y. Const. art. VII, § 8, subd. 1; art. VIII, § 1), since the retiring teachers who benefit from this provision have furnished a "corresponding benefit or consideration to the State". (Matter of Teachers Assn. [Bd. of Educ.], 34 A.D.2d 351, 353, 312 N.Y.S.2d 252, 254.) Nor may the provision be regarded as creating a retirement plan since the additional compensation was made payable only upon completion of the required services during the year prior to retirement. If this were to be deemed a retirement benefit, then, it would be equally logical to argue that

3. The final year salary increment is comparable to the salary increment which was— pursuant to section 3102 (subd. 3) of the Education Law (repealed L.1971, ch. 123)—formerly granted by the Board unilaterally after a teacher had been employed for 30 years.

4. In addition, it tends to assure that those teachers who plan to retire give the Board sufficient advance notice so that it may acquire adequate replacements.

increases in compensation in the years immediately prior to retirement were part and parcel of the retirement plan.

This brings us to the grievance provision. It assures teachers with tenure that no disciplinary action will be taken against them without just cause and that any dispute as to the existence of such cause may be submitted to arbitration. It is a provision commonly found in collective bargaining agreements in the private and public sectors and carries out Federal and State policy favoring arbitration as a means of resolving labor disputes. (See Steelworkers v. Warrior & Gulf Co., 363 U.S. 574, 583–585; Matter of Associated Teachers [Bd. of Educ.], 60 Misc.2d 443, 447, 303 N.Y.S. 2d 469, 473; Klaus, The Evolution of a Collective Bargaining Relationship in Public Education, 67 Mich.L.Rev. 1033, 1040–1041; Krislov & Peters, Arbitration of Grievances in Educational Units, 23 Lab.L.J. 25.)

In sum, each of the provisions under attack relates to a term or condition of employment and, accordingly, the Board was, in light of the Taylor Law, required to negotiate—unless its contentions, to which we turn, compel a different conclusion.

Although the Board raises specific objections that are peculiar to each of the challenged items, its basic premise is the same—that, absent a statutory provision *expressly* authorizing a school board to provide for a particular term or condition of employment, it is legally prohibited from doing so. Proceeding from that premise, the Board would have us hold that school boards possess only those powers granted by a single provision, section 1709, of the Education Law. Quite apart from the fact that that section contains a broad grant of powers,[5] the Board's premise is fallacious. Under the Taylor Law, the obligation to bargain as to all terms and conditions of employment is a broad and unqualified one, and there is no reason why the mandatory provision of that act should be limited, in any way, except in cases where some other applicable statutory provision explicitly and definitively prohibits the public employer from making an agreement as to a particular term or condition of employment.

Were it otherwise, a school board would have a hard time bargaining effectively with its teachers concerning terms of employment, since it would frequently be difficult, if not impossible, to find an express grant of power with respect to any particular subject. To adhere to the restrictive view advanced by the Board "would", the Appellate Division recently wrote in Matter of Teachers Assn. (Bd. of Educ.) (34 A.D.2d, supra, at p. 356, 312 N.Y.S.2d 252, 257), "virtually destroy the bargaining powers which public policy has installed in the field of public employment and throttle the ability of a Board of Education to meet the changing needs of employer-employee relations within its district."

Public employers must, therefore, be presumed to possess the broad powers needed to negotiate with employees as to all terms and conditions of employment. The presumption may, of course, be rebutted by showing statutory provisions which expressly prohibit collective bargaining as to a particular term or condition but, "[i]n the absence of an express legislative

5. Subdivision 33 of section 1709 recites that the Board shall have "all the powers reasonably necessary to exercise powers granted expressly or by implication and to discharge duties imposed expressly or by implication by this chapter or other statutes."

restriction against bargaining for that term of an employment contract between a public employer and its employees, the authority to provide for such [term] resides in the [school board] under the broad powers and duties delegated by the statutes." (Matter of Teachers Assn. [Bd. of Educ.], 34 A.D.2d 351, 355, 312 N.Y.S.2d 252, 256, supra; see, also, Rayburn v. Board of Educ., 71 LRRM 2177, 2178 [Mich.Cir.Ct.].) It is hardly necessary to say that, if the Board asserts a lack of power to agree to any particular term or condition of employment, it has the burden of demonstrating the existence of a specific statutory provision which circumscribes the exercise of such power. It has failed to meet this burden in the present case.

The Board cites no legislation which expressly or even impliedly prevented it from including the tuition and damage reinbursement provisions. Nor does section 113 (subd. a) of the Retirement and Social Security Law—to which the Board points—prohibit inclusion of the retirement award provision; that provision merely provided for the payment of a salary increment based upon length of service.[6] We also find without substance the Board's claim that the grievance provision violates section 3020–a of the Education Law, generally known as the Tenure Law. That statute provides that, prior to any disciplinary action being taken against a teacher, the latter must be afforded a hearing before an impartial panel, which then submits recommendations to the school board (Education Law, § 3020–a, subds. 2, 3, 4). The Board is not bound by these recommendations and may disregard them in making its decision. Since a decision by the Board itself to impose discipline is a prerequisite to arbitration, the grievance provision in no way supplants this aspect of the Tenure Law. In addition, section 3020–a (subd. 5) declares that any employee "feeling himself aggrieved" may either appeal to the Commissioner of Education or commence an article 78 proceeding. The procedure thus set up is not mandatory, its implementation resting entirely in the teacher's discretion. Thus, the Legislature has given a tenure teacher a choice of two methods of statutory appeal if he desires to challenge an adverse decision of the school board. But it does not follow from this that the Board is inhibited from agreeing that the teacher may choose arbitration as a third method of reviewing its determination.

It is of more than passing significance that the Taylor Law explicitly vests employee organizations with the right to represent public employees not only in connection with negotiations as to the terms and conditions of employment but also as to *"the administration of grievances arising thereunder"* (Civil Service Law, § 203; italics supplied). Indeed, it is the declared policy of this State to encourage "public employers and * * * employee

---

6. It should be noted that section 431 of the Retirement and Social Security Law, enacted last year (L.1971, ch. 503), provides in subdivision 3 that, in a retirement or pension plan to which the State or a municipality thereof contributes, the salary base for the computation of retirement benefits shall not include "any additional compensation paid in anticipation of retirement" earned or received "on or after April first, nineteen hundred seventy-two". Quite apart from the fact that the collective agreement in this case antedated enactment of section 431, it is obvious that the statute, whatever impact it might have on the payment of retirement benefits, does not invalidate a salary increment payable, pursuant to the "retirement award provision", for services rendered during the final year of employment. (See Kranker v. Levitt, 30 N.Y.2d 574, 330 N.Y.S.2d 791, 281 N.E.2d 840.) And we have no need or occasion to consider the impact of any other statute (e.g., Education Law, § 501, subd. 11) upon a retirement award provision such as is contained in article XXI.

organizations to agree upon procedures for resolving disputes" (§ 200, subd. [c]). And arbitration is, of course, part and parcel of the administration of grievances. (See Steelworkers v. Warrior & Gulf Co., 363 U.S. 574, 578, 80 S.Ct. 1347, 4 L.Ed.2d 1409, supra; McGuire v. Humble Oil & Refining Co., 355 F.2d 352, 358; see, also, Krislov & Peters, Arbitration of Grievances in Educational Units, 23 Lab.L.J. 25, 29.) There is, therefore, no reason to infer that the Legislature intended that the provisions of the Tenure Law should, by implication, deprive employee organizations of a right to represent employees in the administration of disciplinary grievances.

Nor can we agree that a board of education is better qualified than an arbitrator to decide whether a teacher in its employ should be dismissed for incompetency or misconduct. It may not be gainsaid that arbitrators, selected because of their impartiality and their intimate knowledge of school board matters are fully qualified to decide issues such as those under consideration. Moreover, if the school board's contentions were sustained, it would be the Supreme Court, not the board of education, which would pass upon the correctness of the determination in an article 78 proceeding. In any event, though, we cannot subscribe to the view that the legality of an arbitration provision turns on the relative competency of arbitrator and judge.

We would but add that there is no basis for the fear expressed that to permit the grievance to go to arbitration will enable the employee to appeal—pursuant to section 3020–a, subdivision 5, of the Education Law—to the arbitrator after he has lost before the commissioner or the court or, conversely, to the Commissioner of Education or the Supreme Court after he has submitted to arbitration and lost before the arbitrator.[8] Once the controversy is heard and a decision arrived at either by the arbitrator or by the commissioner or by the judge, that is the end of the matter. As already indicated, the collective bargaining agreement does no more than give the employee a possible third means of reviewing a Board determination.

The order appealed from should be modified, without costs, by reversing so much thereof as holds illegal the provision permitting arbitration with respect to the disciplining of tenure teachers and, except as so modified, affirmed.

BREITEL, JUDGE (dissenting in part):

I quite agree with all but one feature of the majority determination, that dealing with the retirement award. While that feature may seem a small part of the collective bargaining agreement negotiated and executed, it has, as a precedent, marked significance in the relations between public employers and employees and critical impact on public retirement systems. Moreover, the retirement feature is one that falls in an area where government has been especially concerned because of accumulating economic burdens on retirement systems and the public fisc out of which some or all retirement reserves come. Indeed, the condition has become so critical that the Legislature in recent sessions has, as is publicly known, invoked a "freeze" on the general increase of retirement benefits.

8. We assume, of course, that the arbitration proceeding is fair and regular and free from any procedural infirmities that might invalidate the award. (Cf., e.g., Spielberg Manufacturing Company, 112 N.L.R.B. 1080.)

As did two dissenting Justices at the Appellate Division, I conclude that the collective bargaining provision granting to retiring teachers a salary increase for their terminal year is invalid. Unlike the dissenting Justices, however, I do not find that the provision violates constitutional limitations on making gifts (N.Y. Const., art. VII, § 8, subd. 1); but do find in agreement with the dissenters that it is invalid because it violates applicable statute law.

Article XXI of the collective agreement reads:

"Retirement Award

"Each teacher who hereafter indicates his intention to retire one year prior to such retirement under the New York State Teachers Retirement System or whose retirement is mandatory under such system shall receive at the start of the last school year of service a salary increase for that year equal to $5/10$ of 1% (0.5%) of his current salary multiplied by the number of years of service in this school district, such salary increase not to exceed $1500."

Preliminarily, the provision is entitled as a "retirement award", and, therefore, the parties so regarded it. Moreover, it reads as a retirement formula would with a fraction determined by years of service as a numerator and the current salary as a base.

Section 113 of the Retirement and Social Security Law forbids any municipality from creating any retirement system for its officers or employees (subd. a). Section 526 of the Education Law provided since the merger of school retirement systems into the State system in 1923 for the abolition and discontinuance of local school retirement systems.

The "retirement award" provided by the collective agreement violates both statutes. Nor may the provision be regarded simply as a salary increase payable out of funds available to the school district. Its pivotal effect, by increasing final average salary in determining retirement allowances, is to increase the allowances payable by the State teachers' retirement system out of its reserves contributed by employers and employees (see, e.g., Education Law, §§ 510, 511, 511–a).

There may be a further consequential effect. Because the agreement, if valid, affects retirement system benefits it may be prospectively binding under the constitutional provision prohibiting the diminishment or impairment of retirement benefits (art. V, § 7; Kranker v. Levitt, 30 N.Y.2d 574). All this under a locally-negotiated agreement and, of course, subject to arbitration in the event of disputes.

If there were any doubt, and there should be none, that the provision, or its like, has direct bearing on retirement systems, and that "increases" in benefits of precisely this kind have been a matter of deep current concern, the recent enactment of chapter 503 of the Laws of 1971 resolves the doubt. Chapter 503 enacts, among others, a new section 431 to the Retirement and Social Security Law, which reads:

"In any retirement or pension plan to which the state or municipality thereof contributes, the salary base for the computation of retirement benefits shall in no event include any of the following earned or received, on or after April first, nineteen hundred seventy-two:

* 　 * 　 * 　 * 　 * 　 * 　 * 　 * 　 *

"2. any form of termination pay,

"3. any additional compensation paid in anticipation of retirement, or

"4. that portion of compensation earned during any twelve months included in such salary base period which exceeds that of the preceding twelve months by more than twenty per centum."

It is difficult to avoid the conclusion that everyone, including the Legislature, and even the parties to the collective agreement, regard a final year's salary in anticipation of retirement, as a retirement benefit under a retirement system. That tinkering locally or administratively with such benefits may invoke constitutional limitations on impairment, see Kranker v. Levitt (supra).

To further point the analysis, the State Comptroller in opinions rendered in 1967 and 1968 held invalid, because beyond the statutory power of local boards of education, salary increases for final years in anticipation of retirement (opn. No. 67–355, June 5, 1967, 23 Op.St.Comp., 1967, p. 291; opn. No. 68–232, March 26, 1968, 24 Op.St.Comp., 1968, p. 244).

Obviously, the Taylor Law (Civil Service Law, art. 14) was not intended, and should not have the effect, of overriding the statutes discussed, simply because it authorizes collective bargaining between public employers and employees over the terms and conditions of employment (Civil Service Law, § 204). Otherwise, the whole body of statute and decisional law affecting public employment, penal and civil, would be subject to repeal or revision in public collective agreements so long as there is any effect on "the terms and conditions of employment".

Nor do the strictures apply to any increases in compensation which happen to occur in the final years of employment. The strictures do apply to increases in anticipation of and conditioned on retirement. Which also suggests that the provision is hardly an inducement to continued employment. On the contrary, it is an inducement to retire. To say that the purpose is to induce "experienced teachers to remain in the employ of the school district" is to state the contrary of the provision's effect. Of course, it is irrelevant whether the retirement award promotes or deters earlier retirement, so long as there is no power by local agreement to vary the retirement system's balanced incentives for encouraging continued employment and at certain points to encourage retirement.

Accordingly, I dissent in part and vote to modify except as to the provision for a retirement award which should be held invalid for the reasons indicated.

BURKE, BERGAN and GIBSON, JJ., concur with FULD, C.J.

BREITEL, J., dissents in part and votes to further modify in a separate opinion in which SCILEPPI and JASEN, JJ., concur.

Ordered accordingly.

Note

1. To what extent does the court's majority in the Huntington case adopt the approach taken in the Hanslowe-Oberer memorandum reported supra p.

1119? Is the latter approach sound? Reconsider Note 3, supra p. 1099, following the Buffalo fact-finding report. Should not the court in Huntington have reserved decision and deferred to PERB's primary administrative jurisdiction over scope-of-bargaining questions? Why was not the plaintiff Board of Education in Huntington in any event estopped from asserting the illegality of contract provisions to which it had agreed?

2. "Exclusivity" of status as bargaining representative has become almost as common-place in public employment as it is in the private sector. Does exclusivity raise problems which are peculiar to public employment due to the fact that governmental employers, unlike private employers, are inherently engaged in "state action" and are therefore subject to constitutional restraints? The next case speaks to an aspect of this question.

MINNESOTA STATE BOARD FOR COMMUNITY COLLEGES v. KNIGHT

Supreme Court of the United States, 1984.
465 U.S. 271, 104 S.Ct. 1058, 79 L.Ed.2d 299.

JUSTICE O'CONNOR delivered the opinion of the Court.

The State of Minnesota authorizes its public employees to bargain collectively over terms and conditions of employment. It also requires public employers to engage in official exchanges of views with their professional employees on policy questions relating to employment but outside the scope of mandatory bargaining. If professional employees forming an appropriate bargaining unit have selected an exclusive representative for mandatory bargaining, their employer may exchange views on nonmandatory subjects only with the exclusive representative. The question presented in this case is whether this restriction on participation in the nonmandatory-subject exchange process violates the constitutional rights of professional employees within the bargaining unit who are not members of the exclusive representative and who may disagree with its views. We hold that it does not.

I

A

In 1971, the Minnesota legislature adopted the Public Employment Labor Relations Act (PELRA), Minn.Stat. §§ 179.61 et seq. (1982), to establish "orderly and constructive relationships between all public employers and their employees. * * *" Id., § 179.61. The public employers covered by the law are, broadly speaking, the state and its political subdivisions, agencies, and instrumentalities. Id., § 179.63. In its amended form, as in its original form, PELRA provides for the division of public employees into appropriate bargaining units and establishes a procedure, based on majority support within a unit, for the designation of an exclusive bargaining agent for that unit. Id., §§ 179.67, 179.71, 179.741. The statute requires public employers to "meet and negotiate" with exclusive representatives concerning the "terms and conditions of employment," which the statute defines to mean "the hours of employment, the compensation therefor * * *, and the employer's personnel policies affecting the working conditions of the employees." Id., §§ 179.63, 179.67, 179.71. The employer's and employees' representatives must seek an agreement in good faith. Id., § 179.63, subd. 16.

PELRA also grants professional employees, such as college faculty, the right to "meet and confer" with their employers on matters related to employment that are outside the scope of mandatory negotiations. Id., §§ 179.63, 179.65. This provision rests on the recognition "that professional employees possess knowledge, expertise, and dedication which is helpful and necessary to the operation and quality of public services and which may assist public employers in developing their policies." Id., § 179.73. The statute declares it to be the state's policy to "encourage close cooperation between public employers and professional employees" by providing for "meet and confer" sessions on all employment-related questions not subject to mandatory bargaining. Ibid. There is no statutory provision concerning the "meet and confer" process, however, that requires good faith efforts to reach agreement. See Minneapolis Federation of Teachers Local 59 v. Minneapolis Special School Dist. No. 1, Minn., 258 N.W.2d 802, 804, n. 2 (1977).

PELRA requires professional employees to select a representative to "meet and confer" with their public employer. Minn.Stat. § 179.73. If professional employees in an appropriate bargaining unit have an exclusive representative to "meet and negotiate" with their employer, that representative serves as the "meet and confer" representative as well. Indeed, the employer may neither "meet and negotiate" nor "meet and confer" with any members of that bargaining unit except through their exclusive representative. Id., § 179.66, subd. 7. This restriction, however, does not prevent professional employees from submitting advice or recommendations to their employer as part of their work assignment. Ibid. Moreover, nothing in PELRA restricts the right of any public employee to speak on any "matter related to the conditions or compensation of public employment or their betterment" as long as doing so "is not designed to and does not interfere with the full, faithful and proper performance of the duties of employment or circumvent the rights of the exclusive representative if there be one." Id., § 179.65, subd. 1.

B

Appellant Minnesota State Board for Community Colleges (State Board) operates the Minnesota community college system. At the time of trial, the system comprised eighteen institutions located throughout the state. Each community college is administered by a president, who reports, through the chancellor of the system, to the State Board.

Prior to 1971, Minnesota's community colleges were governed in a variety of ways. On some campuses, faculty had a strong voice in administrative policymaking, expressed through organizations such as faculty senates. On other campuses, the administration consulted very little with the faculty. Irrespective of the level of faculty involvement in governance, however, the administrations of the colleges retained final authority to make policy.

Following enactment of PELRA, appellant Minnesota Community College Faculty Association (MCCFA)[1] was designated the exclusive representative of the faculty of the state's community colleges, which had been deemed a single bargaining unit.[2] MCCFA has "met and negotiated" and "met and conferred" with the State Board since 1971. The result has been the negotiation of successive collective bargaining agreements in the intervening years and, in order to implement the "meet and confer" provision, a restructuring of governance practices in the community college system.

On the state level, MCCFA and the Board established "meet and confer" committees to discuss questions of policy applicable to the entire system. On the campus level, the MCCFA chapters and the college administrations created local "meet and confer" committees—also referred to as "exchange of views" committees—to discuss questions of policy applicable only to the campus. The committees on both levels have discussed such topics as the selection and evaluation of administrators, academic accreditation, student affairs, curriculum, and fiscal planning—all policy matters within the control of the college administrations and the State Board. * * *.

The State Board considers the views expressed by the state-wide faculty "meet and confer" committees to be the faculty's official collective position. It recognizes, however, that not every instructor agrees with the official faculty view on every policy question. Not every instructor in the bargaining unit is a member of MCCFA, and MCCFA has selected only its own members to represent it on "meet and confer" committees. Accordingly, all faculty have been free to communicate to the State Board and to local administrations their views on questions within the coverage of the statutory "meet and confer" provision. * * * They have frequently done so.[3] With the possible exception of a brief period of adjustment to the new governance structure, during which some administrators were reluctant to communicate informally with faculty, individual faculty members have not been impeded by either MCCFA or college administrators in the communication of their views on policy questions. Nor has PELRA ever been construed to impede such communication.[4]

1. MCCFA is affiliated with the Minnesota Education Association (MEA) and the National Education Association (NEA), also appellants in this case.

2. Since 1980, the "community college instructional unit" has been defined by statute. Minn.Stat. § 179.741.

3. [W]hile the meet and confer process gives weight to an official collective faculty position as formulated by the faculty's exclusive representative, all instructors have ample opportunity to express their views to their employer on subjects within the purview of the "meet and confer" process.

4. The repeated suggestions in Justice Stevens' dissent that the state employer and state employees have been prohibited or deterred by the statute from talking with each other on policy questions, misunderstand the statute

and are flatly contradicted by the District Court's findings. All that the statute prohibits is the formal exchange of views called a "meet and confer" session. It in no way impairs the ability of individual employees or groups of employees to express their views to their employer outside that formal context, and there has been no suggestion in this case that, after an initial period of adjustment to PELRA, any such communication of views has ever been restrained because it was challenged as constituting a formal "meet and confer" session. * * *

Indeed, the District Court made the following findings of fact: "All faculty have the right to informally communicate their individual views to administrators and [the State Board] and MCCFA have never attempted to deny or abridge such rights." * * *

C

Appellees are twenty Minnesota community college faculty instructors who are not members of MCCFA. In December 1974, they filed suit in the United States District Court for the District of Minnesota, challenging the constitutionality of MCCFA's exclusive representation of community college faculty in both the "meet and negotiate" and "meet and confer" processes. A three-judge District Court was convened to hear the case. * * *

The court rejected appellees' attack on the constitutionality of exclusive representation in bargaining over terms and conditions of employment, relying chiefly on Abood v. Board of Education, 431 U.S. 209, 97 S.Ct. 1782, 52 L.Ed.2d 261 (1977). The court agreed with appellees, however, that PELRA, as applied in the community college system, infringes First and Fourteenth Amendment speech and associational rights of faculty who do not wish to join MCCFA. By granting MCCFA the right to select the faculty representatives for the "meet and confer" committees and by permitting MCCFA to select only its own members, the court held, PELRA unconstitutionally deprives non-MCCFA instructors of "a fair opportunity to participate in the selection of governance representatives." * * * The court granted declaratory relief in accordance with its holdings and enjoined MCCFA from selecting "meet and confer" representatives without providing all faculty the fair opportunity that its selection practice had unconstitutionally denied.

Appellees, the State Board, and MCCFA all filed appeals with this Court, invoking jurisdiction under 28 U.S.C. § 1253. The Court summarily affirmed the judgment insofar as the District Court held the "meet and negotiate" provisions of PELRA to be valid. * * * 460 U.S. 1048, 103 S.Ct. 1493, 75 L.Ed.2d 927 (1983). The Court thus rejected appellees' argument, based on A.L.A. Schechter Poultry Corp. v. United States, 295 U.S. 495, 55 S.Ct. 837, 79 L.Ed. 1570 (1935), and on Carter v. Carter Coal Co., 298 U.S. 238, 56 S.Ct. 855, 80 L.Ed. 1160 (1936), that PELRA unconstitutionally delegated legislative authority to private parties. The Court's summary affirmance also rejected the constitutional attack on PELRA's restriction to the exclusive representative of participation in the "meet and negotiate" process.

On March 28, 1983, the Court noted probable jurisdiction in the appeals by the Board and MCCFA. 460 U.S. 1050, 103 S.Ct. 1496, 75 L.Ed.2d 928. * * * We now reverse the District Court's holding that the "meet and confer" provisions of PELRA deprive appellees of their constitutional rights.

II

A

Appellees do not and could not claim that they have been unconstitutionally denied access to a public forum. A "meet and confer" session is obviously not a public forum. It is a fundamental principle of First Amendment doctrine, articulated most recently in Perry Education Assn. v. Perry Local Educators' Assn., 460 U.S. 37, 45–46, 103 S.Ct. 948, 954, 74 L.Ed.2d 794 (1983), that for government property to be a public forum, it must by long tradition or by government designation be open to the public at large for assembly and speech. Minnesota college administration meetings convened to obtain faculty advice on policy questions have neither by long tradition nor by government designation been open for general public participation. The District Court did not find * * * and appellees do not contend otherwise.

The rights at issue in this case are accordingly wholly unlike those at stake in City of Madison Joint School District v. Wisconsin Public Employment Relations Comm'n, 429 U.S. 167, 97 S.Ct. 421, 50 L.Ed.2d 376 (1976). The Court in that case upheld a claim of access to a public forum, applying standard public-forum First Amendment analysis. * * * The school board meetings at issue there were "opened [as] a forum for direct citizen involvement," 429 U.S., at 175, 97 S.Ct., at 426, and "public participation [was] permitted," id., at 169, 97 S.Ct., at 423. The First Amendment was violated when the meetings were suddenly closed to one segment of the public even though they otherwise remained open for participation by the public at large. This case, by contrast, involves no selective closure of a generally open forum, and hence any reliance on the City of Madison case would be misplaced.

* * *

"Meet and confer" sessions are occasions for public employers, acting solely as instrumentalities of the state, to receive policy advice from their professional employees. Minnesota has simply restricted the class of persons to whom it will listen in its making of policy. Thus, appellees' principal claim is that they have a right to force officers of the state acting in an official policymaking capacity to listen to them in a particular formal setting. * * *

This conclusion is erroneous. Appellees have no constitutional right to force the government to listen to their views. They have no such right as members of the public, as government employees, or as instructors in an institution of higher education.

* * *

Policymaking organs in our system of government have never operated under a constitutional constraint requiring them to afford every interested member of the public an opportunity to present testimony before any policy is adopted. Legislatures throughout the nation, including Congress, frequently enact bills on which no hearings have been held or on which testimony has been received from only a select group. Executive agencies likewise make policy decisions of widespread application without permitting unrestricted public testimony. Public officials at all levels of government daily make policy decisions based only on the advice they decide they need and choose to hear. To recognize a constitutional right to participate directly in government policymaking would work a revolution in existing government practices.

Not least among the reasons for refusing to recognize such a right is the impossibility of its judicial definition and enforcement. Both federalism and separation-of-powers concerns would be implicated in the massive intrusion into state and federal policymaking that recognition of the claimed right would entail. * * *

However wise or practicable various levels of public participation in various kinds of policy decisions may be, this Court has never held, and nothing in the Constitution suggests it should hold, that government must provide for such participation. ＊ ＊ ＊ It is inherent in a republican form of government that direct public participation in government policymaking is limited. See The Federalist No. 10 (Madison). Disagreement with public policy and disapproval of officials' responsiveness ＊ ＊ ＊ is to be registered principally at the polls.

Appellees thus have no constitutional right as members of the public to a government audience for their policy views. As public employees, of course, they have a special interest in public policies relating to their employment. Minnesota's statutory scheme for public-employment labor relations recognizes as much. Appellees' status as public employees, however, gives them no special constitutional right to a voice in the making of policy by their government employer.

＊ ＊ ＊

B

Although there is no constitutional right to participate in academic governance, the First Amendment guarantees the right both to speak and to associate. Appellees' speech and associational rights, however, have not been infringed by Minnesota's restriction of participation in "meet and confer" sessions to the faculty's exclusive representative. The state has in no way restrained appellees' freedom to speak on any education-related issue or their freedom to associate or not to associate with whom they please, including the exclusive representative. Nor has the state attempted to suppress any ideas.

It is doubtless true that the unique status of the exclusive representative in the "meet and confer" process amplifies its voice in the policymaking process. But that amplification [does not impair] individual instructors' constitutional freedom to speak ＊ ＊ ＊. Moreover, the exclusive representative's unique role in "meet and negotiate" sessions amplifies its voice as much as its unique role in "meet and confer" sessions, yet the Court summarily affirmed the District Court's approval of that role in this case. Amplification of the sort claimed is inherent in government's freedom to choose its advisers. A person's right to speak is not infringed when government simply ignores that person while listening to others.

Nor is appellees' right to speak infringed by the ability of MCCFA to "retaliate" for protected speech, as the District Court put it, by refusing to appoint them to the "meet and confer" committees. The state of Minnesota seeks to obtain MCCFA's views on policy questions, and MCCFA has simply chosen representatives who share its views on the issues to be discussed with the state. MCCFA's ability to "retaliate" by not selecting those who dissent from its views no more unconstitutionally inhibits appellees' speech than voters' power to reject a candidate for office inhibits the candidate's speech.

＊ ＊ ＊

Similarly, appellees' associational freedom has not been impaired. Appellees are free to form whatever advocacy groups they like. They are not required to become members of MCCFA, and they do not challenge the monetary contribution they are required to make to support MCCFA's representation activities.[11] Appellees may well feel some pressure to join the exclusive representative in order to give them the opportunity to serve on the "meet and confer" committees or to give them a voice in the representative's adoption of positions on particular issues. That pressure, however, is no different from the pressure they may feel to join MCCFA because of its unique status in the "meet and negotiate" process, a status the Court has summarily approved. Moreover, the pressure is no different from the pressure to join a majority party that persons in the minority always feel. Such pressure is inherent in our system of government; it does not create an unconstitutional inhibition on associational freedom.

C

Unable to demonstrate an infringement of any First Amendment right, appellees contend that their exclusion from "meet and confer" sessions denies them equal protection of the laws in violation of the Fourteenth Amendment. This final argument is meritless. The interest of appellees that is affected—the interest in a government audience for their policy views—finds no special protection in the Constitution. There being no other reason to invoke heightened scrutiny, the challenged state action "need only rationally further a legitimate state purpose" to be valid under the Equal Protection Clause. Perry Education Assn. v. Perry Local Educators' Assn., supra, 460 U.S., at 54, 103 S.Ct., at 960. PELRA certainly meets that standard. The state has a legitimate interest in ensuring that its public employers hear one, and only one, voice presenting the majority view of its professional employees on employment-related policy questions, whatever other advice they may receive on those questions. Permitting selection of the "meet and confer" representatives to be made by the exclusive representative, which has its unique status by virtue of majority support within the bargaining unit, is a rational means of serving that interest.

If it is rational for the state to give the exclusive representative a unique role in the "meet and negotiate" process, as the summary affirmance in appellees' appeal in this case presupposes, it is rational for the state to do the same in the "meet and confer" process. The goal of reaching agreement makes it imperative for an employer to have before it only one collective view of its employees when "negotiating." See Abood v. Detroit Board of Education, supra, 431 U.S., at 224, 97 S.Ct., at 1793. Similarly, the goal of basing policy decisions on consideration of the majority view of its employees makes it reasonable for an employer to give only the exclusive representative a particular formal setting in which to offer advice on policy. Appellees' equal protection challenge accordingly fails.

III

The District Court erred in holding that appellees had been unconstitutionally denied an opportunity to participate in their public employer's

---

11. Under PELRA, public employees are not required to join the organization that acts as their exclusive representative. Minn.Stat. § 179.65, subd. 2. Nonmembers may, however, be required to pay a fair-share fee to the exclusive representative to cover costs related to negotiating on behalf of the entire bargaining unit. Minn.Stat. § 179.65, subd. 2. This requirement is not at issue in this lawsuit, although it is subject to certain constitutional constraints. See Abood v. Detroit Board of Education, 431 U.S. 209, 217–237, 97 S.Ct. 1782, 1790–1800, 52 L.Ed.2d 261 (1977) (mandatory contributions valid if for bargaining, administration, and grievance activities of exclusive representative but not if for other, ideological activities).

making of policy. Whatever the wisdom of Minnesota's statutory scheme for professional employee consultation on employment-related policy, in academic or other settings, the scheme violates no provision of the Constitution. The judgment of the District Court is therefore

Reversed.

[The concurring opinion of Justice Marshall is omitted.]

[The dissenting opinions of Justices Stevens and Brennan (the former joined by Justice Powell) are omitted. The essence of their disagreement with the majority lies in their perception of the greatly enlarged scope of the duty to "meet and confer" as compared to the relatively narrow confines of the duty to "meet and negotiate." Whereas the latter is defined under the Minnesota statute to concern the "terms and conditions of employment," which the statute limits to "the hours of employment, the compensation therefor * * *, and the employer's personnel policies affecting the working conditions of the employees," the former covers, potentially, an amorphous range of policies with implicit political dimensions. Accordingly, the effort to formalize the resolution of this broad range of issues within the channels of "exclusivity" raised constitutional concerns not encountered in the more traditional and confined scope of collective bargaining. The majority's resolution of these constitutional concerns is epitomized in footnote 4 of its opinion, distinguishing between "formal" and "informal" means of communication on subjects within the purview of the "meet and confer" process. The dissents, on the other hand, viewed the very formalizing of discussions of these broad issues as stultifying the opportunity for *non*members of the MCCFA to participate "effectively" in this decisional process.]

Note

Statutory powers of exclusive representation are, it will be recalled, accompanied by the duty of fair representation. Incorporation of this duty, has, in turn, produced demands from public employee organizations for the requirement that all represented employees bear a proportionate share of this representation. The form of union security widely advocated for the public sector is the agency shop or its variant, involved in the preceding case (supra p. 1144 footnote 11), the so-called "fair share" agreement pursuant to which nonmember employees are compelled to pay a service or representation fee reflecting that portion of union dues devoted to such collective bargaining activities as contract negotiation and grievance processing. In Abood v. Detroit Bd. of Educ., 431 U.S. 209, 97 S.Ct. 1782, 52 L.Ed.2d 261 (1977), supra p. 799, the Court addressed the constitutional problems posed by such compulsory payments as a condition of public employment. The majority of the Court, giving great weight to the importance of the exclusivity concept in public as well as private collective bargaining, concluded that so long as the payments were to be used for purposes "germane to collective bargaining," they could be required without offending the constitution.

Does the "germane to collective bargaining" test cover the exclusive bargaining representative's expenditures in "meet and confer" functions? *Should* it? (This question was not raised in the Knight case [perhaps because the dissenting teachers had "larger fish to fry"?]; see footnote 11 and accompanying text supra p. 1144.)

LABOR–MANAGEMENT RELATIONS IN THE
FEDERAL SERVICE

While President Kennedy's Executive Order 10988 of January 17, 1962 (27 Fed.Reg. 551), signaled the real advent of collective bargaining in public employment relations across the country, the version extant in the federal service is less like that in the private sector than are most of the state schemes. The main reason for this is the narrow range of issues subject to bilateral determination in federal employment. At the core of collective bargaining is the question of the compensation to be paid for services rendered; this question was not open to negotiations under Executive Order 10988 or Executive Order 11491 (34 Fed.Reg. 17605 (1969)), issued by President Nixon as a replacement for 10988, effective January 1, 1970. It continues not to be a subject for bilateral determination under Title VII of the Civil Service Reform Act of 1978, 5 U.S.C.A. §§ 7101–7135, which has superseded the Executive Orders. The scope of bargaining under both Executive Orders was "personnel policies and practices and matters affecting working conditions" (E.O. 11491, Section 11(a)); this continues to be the scope under Section 7103(a)(14) of the Civil Service Reform Act. Even these non-dollars-and-cents subjects are tightly circumscribed by broad management-rights reservations. (See Section 7106 of the Act.) In state and local public employment negotiations, by way of contrast, money is the name of the game.

A major premise of the Civil Service Reform Act of 1978 is continued denial of the right to strike, striking against the federal government remaining a felony. See United Federation of Postal Clerks v. Blount, supra p. 1069. While bilateral determination of issues is circumscribed as noted above, in other major respects the pattern of rights and procedures under the statute is similar to other systems for the collective resolution of employment issues, entailing: declaration of the right to organize; provision of standards and procedures for achieving recognition; proscription of the usual unfair labor practices; authorization of grievance procedures, including arbitration; administration by a Federal Labor Relations Authority and a General Counsel.

The Federal Labor Relations Authority is composed of three presidential appointees (subject to Senate approval) holding staggered five-year terms. The powers of the Authority are modeled after those of the NLRB. It may conduct representation elections, confer exclusive representation status, find unfair labor practices, and, for the first time in federal sector labor relations, seek enforcement of its orders in the Courts of Appeals. In contrast, decisions of the predecessor Federal Labor Relations Council, under the Executive Orders, were self-enforcing within the Executive Branch. The Act continues the Federal Services Impasses Panel, as conceived under the Executive Orders. As its name implies, the Panel is charged with the resolution of "negotiation impasses," by recommending procedures for resolution or by taking appropriate action itself.

The provisions of Title VII of the Civil Service Reform Act are set forth in full in the Statutory Supplement. The scope and structure of the Act are dealt with in the following case.

BUREAU OF ALCOHOL, TOBACCO AND FIREARMS v. FEDERAL LABOR RELATIONS AUTHORITY

Supreme Court of the United States, 1983.
464 U.S. 89, 104 S.Ct. 439, 78 L.Ed.2d 195.

JUSTICE BRENNAN delivered the opinion of the Court.

Title VII of the Civil Service Reform Act of 1978 ("Act"), Pub.L. No. 95–454, 92 Stat. 1111, 5 U.S.C. § 7131(a), requires federal agencies to grant "official time" to employees representing their union in collective bargaining with the agencies. The grant of official time allows the employee negotiators to be paid as if they were at work, whenever they bargain during hours they would otherwise be on duty. The Federal Labor Relations Authority ("FLRA" or "Authority") concluded that the grant of official time also entitles employee union representatives to a per diem allowance and reimbursement for travel expenses incurred in connection with collective bargaining. 2 F.L.R.A. 265 (1979). In this case, the Court of Appeals for the Ninth Circuit enforced an FLRA order requiring an agency to pay a union negotiator travel expenses and a per diem, finding the Authority's interpretation of the statute "reasonably defensible." 672 F.2d 732 (1982). Three other Courts of Appeals have rejected the FLRA's construction of the Act.[1] We granted certiorari to resolve this conflict, * * * and now reverse.

I

A

Title VII of the Civil Service Reform Act, part of a comprehensive revision of the laws governing the rights and obligations of civil servants, contains the first statutory scheme governing labor relations between federal agencies and their employees. Prior to enactment of Title VII, labor-management relations in the federal sector were governed by a program established in a 1962 Executive Order.[2] The Executive Order regime, under which federal employees had limited rights to engage in concerted activity, was most recently administered by the Federal Labor Relations Council, a body composed of three Executive Branch management officials whose decisions were not subject to judicial review.[3]

The new Act, declaring that "labor organizations and collective bargaining in the civil service are in the public interest," 5 U.S.C. § 7101(a), significantly strengthened the position of public employee unions while carefully preserving the ability of federal managers to maintain "an effective and efficient Government," § 7101(b).[4] Title VII expressly protects the

1. Florida National Guard v. FLRA, 699 F.2d 1082 (CA11 1983), cert. pending, No. 82–1970; United States Department of Agriculture v. FLRA, 691 F.2d 1242 (CA8 1982), cert. pending, No. 82–979; Division of Military & Naval Affairs v. FLRA, 683 F.2d 45 (CA2 1982), cert. pending, No. 82–1021.

2. Exec.Order No. 10988, 3 CFR 521 (1959–1963 Comp.). The Executive Order program was revised and continued by Exec.Order No. 11491, 3 CFR 861 (1966–1970 Comp.), as amended by Exec.Orders Nos. 11616, 11636, and 11838, 3 CFR 605, 634 (1971–1975 Comp.) and 3 CFR 957 (1971–1975 Comp.).

3. The Council was established by Executive Order 11491 in 1970.

4. Certain federal employees, including members of the military and the Foreign Service, and certain federal agencies, including the Federal Bureau of Investigation and the Central Intelligence Agency, are excluded

rights of federal employees "to form, join, or assist any labor organization, or to refrain from any such activity," § 7102, and imposes on federal agencies and labor organizations a duty to bargain collectively in good faith, §§ 7116(a)(5) and (b)(5). The Act excludes certain management prerogatives from the scope of negotiations, although an agency must bargain over the procedures by which these management rights are exercised. See § 7106. In general, unions and federal agencies must negotiate over terms and conditions of employment, unless a bargaining proposal is inconsistent with existing federal law, rule, or regulation. See §§ 7103(a), 7114, 7116, and 7117(a). Strikes and certain other forms of concerted activities by federal employees are illegal and constitute unfair labor practices under the Act, § 7116(b)(7)(A).

The Act replaced the management-controlled Federal Labor Relations Council with the FLRA, a three-member independent and bipartisan body within the Executive Branch with responsibility for supervising the collective-bargaining process and administering other aspects of federal labor relations established by Title VII. § 7104. The Authority, the role of which in the public sector is analogous to that of the National Labor Relations Board in the private sector, see H.R.Rep. No. 95-1403, p. 41 (1978), adjudicates negotiability disputes, unfair labor practice complaints, bargaining unit issues, arbitration exceptions, and conflicts over the conduct of representational elections. See § 7105(a)(2)(A)–(I). In addition to its adjudicatory functions, the Authority may engage in formal rulemaking, § 7134, and is specifically required to "provide leadership in establishing policies and guidance relating to matters" arising under the Act, § 7105(a)(1). The FLRA may seek enforcement of its adjudicatory orders in the United States Courts of Appeals, § 7123(b), and persons, including federal agencies, aggrieved by any final FLRA decision may also seek judicial review in those courts, § 7123(a).

B

Petitioner, the Bureau of Alcohol, Tobacco and Firearms ("BATF" or "Bureau"), an agency within the Department of the Treasury, maintained a regional office in Lodi, California. Respondent, the National Treasury Employees Union ("NTEU" or "Union") was the exclusive representative of BATF employees stationed in the Lodi office. In November 1978, the Bureau notified NTEU that it intended to move the Lodi office to Sacramento and to establish a reduced duty post at a new location in Lodi. The Union informed BATF that it wished to negotiate aspects of the move's impact on employees in the bargaining unit. As its agent for these negotiations, the Union designated Donald Pruett, a BATF employee and NTEU steward who lived in Madera, California and was stationed in Fresno. Bureau officials agreed to meet with Pruett at the new offices and discuss the planned move. Pruett asked that his participation in the discussions be classified as "official time" so that he could receive his regular salary while attending the meetings. The Bureau denied the request and directed Pruett to take either annual leave or leave without pay for the day of the meeting.

from the coverage of Title VII. 5 U.S.C. § 7102(a)(2) and (3).

On February 23, 1979, Bureau officials met with Pruett at the proposed new Sacramento offices and inspected the physical amenities, including the restrooms, dining facilities, and parking areas. Pruett and the BATF officials then drove to Lodi where they conducted a similar inspection of the new reduced duty post. Finally, the group repaired to the existing Lodi office where they discussed the planned move. After Pruett expressed his general satisfaction with the new facilities, he negotiated with the agency officials about such matters as parking arrangements, employee assignments, and the possibility of excusing employee tardiness for the first week of operations in the Sacramento office. Once the parties reached an agreement on the move, Pruett drove back to his home in Madera.

Pruett had spent 11 and one half hours travelling to and attending the meetings, and had driven more than 300 miles in his own car. When he renewed his request to have his participation at the meetings classified as official time, the Bureau informed him that it did not reimburse employees for expenses incurred in negotiations and that it granted official time only for quarterly collective-bargaining sessions and not for mid-term discussions like those involved here. In June 1979, the Union filed an unfair labor practice charge with the FLRA, claiming that BATF had improperly compelled Pruett to take annual leave for the February 23 sessions.

While the charge was pending, the FLRA issued an "Interpretation and Guidance" of general applicability which required federal agencies to pay salaries, travel expenses, and per diem allowances to union representatives engaged in collective bargaining with the agencies.[5] 2 F.L.R.A. 265 (1979). The Interpretation relied on § 7131(a) of the Act, which provides that "[a]ny employee representing an exclusive representative in the negotiation of a collective bargaining agreement * * * shall be authorized official time for such purposes. * * *" The Authority concluded that an employee's entitlement to official time under this provision extends to "all negotiations between an exclusive representative and an agency, regardless of whether such negotiations pertain to the negotiation or renegotiation of a basic collective bargaining agreement." 2 F.L.R.A., at 268. The Authority further determined that § 7131(a) requires agencies to pay a per diem allowance and travel expenses to employees representing their union in such negotiations. Id., at 270.

Based on the NTEU's pending charge against the Bureau, the General Counsel of the Authority issued a complaint and notice of hearing, alleging that the BATF had committed an unfair labor practice by refusing to grant Pruett official time for the February 23 meetings.[6] During the course of a

---

5. Although the Authority invited interested persons to express their views prior to adoption of the Interpretation, see Notice Relating to Official Time, 44 Fed.Reg. 42,788 (July 20, 1979), the decision apparently was issued not under the FLRA's statutory power to promulgate regulations, § 7134, but rather under § 7105(a)(1), which requires the Authority to provide leadership in establishing policies and guidance relating to federal labor-management relations. See Brief for Respondent FLRA at 11 n. 10.

6. Section 7118 of the Act provides in part:

"(a)(1) If any agency or labor organization is charged with having engaged in or engaging in an unfair labor practice, the General Counsel shall investigate the charge and may issue and cause to be served upon the agency or labor organization a complaint. * * *"

The complaint issued by the General Counsel in this case relied on § 7116 of the Act, which provides in part:

"(a) For the purposes of this chapter, it shall be an unfair labor practice for an agency—

subsequent hearing on the charge before an Administrative Law Judge, the complaint was amended to add a claim that, in addition to paying Pruett's salary for the day of the meetings, the BATF should have paid his travel expenses and a per diem allowance. Following the hearing, the ALJ determined that negotiations had in fact taken place between Pruett and BATF officials at the February 23 meetings. Bound to follow the recent FLRA Interpretation and Guidance, the ALJ concluded that the Bureau had committed an unfair labor practice by failing to comply with § 7131. Accordingly, he ordered the Bureau to pay Pruett his regular salary for the day in question, as well as his travel costs and a per diem allowance. The ALJ also required the BATF to post a notice stating that the agency would do the same for all employee union representatives in future negotiations. The Bureau filed exceptions to the decision with the Authority, which, in September 1980, affirmed the decision of the ALJ, adopting his findings, conclusions, and recommended relief. 4 F.L.R.A. No. 40 (1980).

The Bureau sought review in the United States Court of Appeals for the Ninth Circuit, and the Union intervened as a party in that appeal. The Bureau challenged both the FLRA's conclusion that § 7131(a) applies to mid-term negotiations and its determination that the section requires payment of travel expenses and a per diem allowance. After deciding that the Authority's construction of its enabling Act was entitled to deference if it was "reasoned and supportable," 672 F.2d at 735–736, the Court of Appeals enforced the Authority's order on both issues. Id., at 737, 738. On certiorari to this Court, petitioner does not seek review of the holding with respect to mid-term negotiations. Only that aspect of the Court of Appeals' decision regarding travel expenses and per diem allowances is at issue here.

II

The FLRA order enforced by the Court of Appeals in this case was, as noted, premised on the Authority's earlier construction of § 7131(a) in its Interpretation and Guidance. Although we have not previously had occasion to consider an interpretation of the Civil Service Reform Act by the FLRA, we have often described the appropriate standard of judicial review in similar contexts.[7] Like the National Labor Relations Board, see, e.g., NLRB v. Erie Resistor Corp., 373 U.S. 221, 236, 83 S.Ct. 1139, 1149, 10 L.Ed.2d 308 (1963), the FLRA was intended to develop specialized expertise in its field of labor relations and to use that expertise to give content to the principles and goals set forth in the Act. See § 7105; H.R.Rep. No. 95–1403, p. 41 (1978). Consequently, the Authority is entitled to considerable deference when it exercises its "special function of applying the general provisions of the Act to

"(1) to interfere with, restrain, or coerce any employee in the exercise by the employee of any right under this chapter;

*   *   *   *   *

"(8) to otherwise fail or refuse to comply with any provision of this chapter."

7. The decisions of the FLRA are subject to judicial review in accordance with the Administrative Procedure Act (APA), 5 U.S.C. § 706. See 5 U.S.C. § 7123(c). The APA requires a reviewing court to "decide all relevant ques-

tions of law, interpret constitutional and statutory provisions, and determine the meaning or applicability of the terms of an agency action." § 706. The court must set aside agency actions and conclusions found to be "arbitrary, capricious, an abuse of discretion, or otherwise not in accordance with law" or "in excess of statutory jurisdiction, authority, or limitations, or short of statutory right." § 706(2)(A) and (C).

the complexities" of federal labor relations. Cf., NLRB v. Erie Resistor Corp., supra, at 236, 83 S.Ct., at 1149. * * *

On the other hand, the "deference owed to an expert tribunal cannot be allowed to slip into a judicial inertia which results in the unauthorized assumption by an agency of major policy decisions properly made by Congress." American Ship Building Co. v. NLRB, 380 U.S. 300, 318, 85 S.Ct. 955, 967, 13 L.Ed.2d 85 (1965). Accordingly, while reviewing courts should uphold reasonable and defensible constructions of an agency's enabling Act, * * * they must not "rubber-stamp * * * administrative decisions that they deem inconsistent with a statutory mandate or that frustrate the congressional policy underlying a statute." NLRB v. Brown, 380 U.S. 278, 291–292, 85 S.Ct. 980, 988–989, 13 L.Ed.2d 839 (1965). * * * Guided by these principles, we turn to a consideration of the FLRA's construction of § 7131(a).

III

Section 7131(a) of the Civil Service Reform Act provides in full:

"Any employee representing an exclusive representative in the negotiation of a collective bargaining agreement under this chapter shall be authorized official time for such purposes, including attendance at impasse proceeding, during the time the employee otherwise would be in a duty status. The number of employees for whom official time is authorized under this subsection shall not exceed the number of individuals designated as representing the agency for such purposes."

According to the House Committee that reported the bill containing § 7131, Congress used the term "official time" to mean "paid time." See H.R.Rep. No. 95–1403, p. 58 (1978). In light of this clear expression of congressional intent, the parties agree that employee union negotiators are entitled to their usual pay during collective-bargaining sessions that occur when the employee "otherwise would be in a duty status." Both the Authority, 2 F.L. R.A., at 269, and the Court of Appeals, 672 F.2d, at 737, recognized that there is no corresponding expression, either in the statute or the extensive legislative history, of a congressional intent to pay employee negotiators travel expenses and per diem allowances as well.

Despite this congressional silence, respondents advance several reasons why the FLRA's determination that such payments are required is consistent with the policies underlying the Act. Each of these arguments proceeds from the assumption that, by providing employee negotiators with official time for bargaining, Congress rejected the model of federal labor relations that had shaped prior administrative practice. In its place, according to respondents, Congress substituted a new vision of collective bargaining under which employee negotiators, like management representatives, are considered "on the job" while bargaining and are therefore entitled to all customary forms of compensation, including travel expenses and per diem allowances. In order to evaluate this claim, it is necessary briefly to review the rights of employee negotiators to compensation prior to adoption of the Act.

A

Under the 1962 Executive Order establishing the first federal labor relations program, the decision whether to pay union representatives for the time spent in collective bargaining was left within the discretion of their employing agency, apparently on the ground that, without some control by management, the length of such sessions could impose too great a burden on government business. See Report of the President's Task Force on Employee-Management Relations in the Federal Service, reprinted in Legislative History of the Federal Service Labor-Management Relations Statute, Title VII of the Civil Service Reform Act of 1978, at 1177, 1203 (Comm.Print 1979) (hereinafter "Legis.Hist."). Under this early scheme, employee negotiators were not entitled to per diem allowances and travel expenses, on the view that they were engaged, not in official business of the government, but rather in activities "primarily in the interest of the employee organization." 44 Comp.Gen. 617, 618 (1965).

Executive Order No. 11491, which became effective in 1970, cut back on the previous Order by providing that employees engaged in negotiations with their agencies could not receive official time, even at the agencies' discretion. See 3 CFR 861–862, 873–874 (1966–1970 Comp.). Again, the prohibition was based on the view that employee representatives work for their union, not for the government, when negotiating an agreement with their employers. See Legis.Hist. at 1167. In 1971, however, at the recommendation of the Federal Labor Relations Council, an amending Executive Order allowed unions to negotiate with agencies to obtain official time for employee representatives, up to a maximum of either 40 hours, or 50% of the total time spent in bargaining. Exec.Order No. 11616, 3 CFR 605 (1971–1975 Comp.). The Council made clear that this limited authorization, which was intended "to maintain a reasonable policy with respect to union self-support and an incentive to economical and businesslike bargaining practices," Legis. Hist. at 1169, did not permit "overtime, premium pay, or travel expenditures." Id., at 1264.

The Senate version of the bill that became the Civil Service Reform Act would have retained the last Executive Order's restrictions on the authorization of official time. S.Rep. No. 95–969, p. 112 (1978), U.S.Code Cong. & Admin.News 1978, 2723. Congress instead adopted the section in its present form, concluding, in the words of one congressman, that union negotiators "should be allowed official time to carry out their statutory representational activities just as management uses official time to carry out its responsibilities." 124 Cong.Rec. 29,188 (1978) (remarks of Rep. Clay). See H.R.Conf. Rep. No. 95–1717, p. 111 (1978), U.S.Code Cong. & Admin.News 1978, 2723.

B

Respondents suggest that, by rejecting earlier limitations on official time, Congress repudiated the view that employee negotiators work only for their union and not for the government. Under the new vision of federal labor relations postulated by respondents, civil servants on both sides of the bargaining table are engaged in official business of the government and must be compensated equally. Because federal employees representing the views of management receive travel expenses and per diem allowances, federal employees representing the views of labor are entitled to such payments as well. In support of this view, respondents rely on the Act's declaration that public sector collective bargaining is "in the public interest" and "contributes to the effective conduct of public business," § 7101(a), as well as on a number of specific provisions in the Act intended to equalize the position of management and labor. For instance, the Act requires agencies to deduct union dues from employees' paychecks and to transfer the funds to the union at no cost, § 7115(a);[12] in addition, agencies must furnish a variety of data useful to unions in the collective-bargaining process, § 7114(b)(4). Respondents also contend that Congress employed the term "official time" in § 7131 specifically to indicate that employee negotiators are engaged in government business and therefore entitled to all of their usual forms of compensation.

Although Congress certainly could have adopted the model of collective bargaining advanced by respondents, we find no indications in the Act or its legislative history that it intended to do so. The Act's declaration that collective bargaining contributes to efficient government and therefore serves the public interest does not reflect a dramatic departure from the principles of the Executive Order regime under which employee negotiators had not been regarded as working for the government. To the contrary, the declaration constitutes a strong congressional endorsement of the policy on which the federal labor relations program had been based since its creation in 1962. * * * See * * * 124 Cong.Rec. 29182 (1978) (remarks of Rep. Udall) ("What we really do is to codify the 1962 action of President Kennedy in setting up a basic framework of collective bargaining for Federal employees").[13]

Nor do the specific provisions of the Act aimed at equalizing the positions of management and labor suggest that Congress intended employee representatives to be treated as though they were "on the job" for all purposes. Indeed, the Act's provision of a number of specific subsidies for union activities supports precisely the opposite conclusion. As noted above, Congress expressly considered and ultimately rejected the approach to paid time that had prevailed under the Executive Order regime. * * * In contrast, there is no reference in the statute or the legislative history to travel expenses and per diem allowances * * *. There is, of course, nothing inconsistent in paying the salaries, but not the expenses, of union negotiators. Congress might well have concluded that, although union representatives should not be penalized by a loss in salary while engaged in collective bargaining, they need not be further subsidized with travel and per diem allowances. The provisions of the Act intended to facilitate the

12. Under the Executive Order regime, unions had to negotiate for dues deductions and were generally charged a fee for the service. See Information Announcement, 1 F.L.R.C. 676, 677 (1973).

13. We do not read Representative Udall's remark to suggest that the Authority is bound by administrative decisions made under the Executive Order regime. The Act explicitly encourages the Board to establish policies and provide guidance in the federal labor relations field, § 7105(a)(1), and there are undoubtedly areas in which the FLRA, like the National Labor Relations Authority, enjoys considerable freedom to apply its expertise to new problems, provided it remains faithful to the fundamental policy choices made by Congress. * * * See * * * § 7135(b) (decisions under Executive Order regime remain in effect unless revised by President or superseded by Act or regulations or decisions thereunder).

collection of union dues, see § 7115, certainly suggest that Congress contemplated that unions would ordinarily pay their own expenses.

Respondents also find their understanding of the role of union representatives supported by Congress's use of the phrase "official time" in § 7131(a). For respondents, the use of this term indicates an intent to treat employee negotiators "as doing the government's work for all the usual purposes," and therefore entitled to "all attributes of employment," including travel expenses and a per diem allowance. Brief for NTEU at 24–28. They suggest that, if Congress intended to maintain only the employees' salaries, it would have granted them "leave without loss of pay," a term it has used in other statutes. See, e.g., 5 U.S.C. § 6321 (absence of veterans to attend funeral services), § 6322(a) (jury or witness duty), and § 6323 (military reserve duty). * * *

The difficulty with respondents' argument is that * * * the right to a salary conferred by § 7131(a) obtains only when "the employee would *otherwise* be in a duty status." (Emphasis supplied). This qualifying language strongly suggests that union negotiators engaged in collective bargaining are not considered *in* a duty status and thereby entitled to all of their normal forms of compensation. Nor does the phrase "official time," borrowed from prior administrative practice, [support the respondents' contention]. As noted above, employees on "official time" under the Executive Order regime were not generally entitled to travel expenses and a per diem allowance. * * * Moreover, as respondents' own examples demonstrate, Congress does not rely on the mere use of the word "official" when it intends to allow travel expenses and per diems. * * * Congress generally provides explicit authorization for such payments. * * * In the Civil Service Reform Act itself, for instance, Congress expressly provided that members of the Federal Service Impasses Panel are entitled to travel expenses and a per diem allowance, in addition to a salary. See §§ 5703, 7119(c)(4).

Perhaps recognizing that authority for travel expenses and per diem allowances cannot be found within the four corners of § 7131(a), respondents alternatively contend that the Authority's decision is supported by the Travel Expense Act, 5 U.S.C. § 5702, which provides that a federal employee "travelling on official business away from his designated post of duty * * * is entitled to * * * a per diem allowance." The Travel Expense Act is administered by the Comptroller General who has concluded that agencies may authorize per diem allowances for travel that is "sufficiently in the interest of the United States so as to be regarded as official business." 44 Comp.Gen. 188, 189 (1964). Under the Executive Order regime, the Comptroller General authorized per diem payments to employee negotiators pursuant to this statute upon a certification that the employees' travel served the convenience of the employing agency. * * *

Based on its view that employee negotiators are "on the job," the Authority determined that union representatives engaged in collective bargaining are on "official business" and therefore entitled to a per diem allowance under the Travel Expense Act. 2 F.L.R.A., at 269. In support of this reasoning, the Authority notes that § 5702 has been construed broadly to authorize reimbursement in connection with a variety of "quasi-official" activities, such as employees' attendance at their own personnel hearings and at privately-sponsored conferences. See, e.g., Comptroller General of the United States, Travel in the Management and Operation of Federal Programs 1, App. I at 5 (Rpt. No. FPCD–77–11, Mar. 17, 1977); 31 Comp.Gen. 346 (1952). In each of these instances, however, the travel in question was presumably for the convenience of the agency and therefore clearly constituted "official business" of the government. As we have explained, neither Congress's declaration that collective bargaining is in the public interest nor its use of the term of art "official time" warrants the conclusion that employee negotiators are on "official business" of the government.[17]

IV

In passing the Civil Service Reform Act, Congress unquestionably intended to strengthen the position of federal unions and to make the collective-bargaining process a more effective instrument of the public interest than it had been under the Executive Order regime. * * * There is no evidence, however, that the Act departed from the basic assumption underlying collective bargaining in both the public and the private sector that the parties "proceed from contrary and to an extent antagonistic viewpoints and concepts of self-interest." NLRB v. Insurance Agents, 361 U.S. 477, 488, 80 S.Ct. 419, 426, 4 L.Ed.2d 454 (1960) * * *. Nor did the Act confer on the FLRA an unconstrained authority to equalize the economic positions of union and management. See American Ship Building v. NLRB, supra, 380 U.S., at 316–318, 85 S.Ct., at 966–967. We conclude, therefore, that the FLRA's interpretation of § 7131(a) constitutes an "unauthorized assumption by [the] agency of [a] major policy decision properly made by Congress." Id., at 318, 85 S.Ct., at 967.

The judgment of the Court of Appeals is

Reversed.

Note

1. As previously noted, the strike continues to be illegal in federal service. For reasons not entirely clear, the federal ban has been more effective than the state bans. The first major breach was the postal strike of 1970. That strike resulted in the passage on August 12, 1970, of the Postal Reorganization Act, 39 U.S.C.A. § 101, creating the "United States Postal Service" as an "independent establishment of the executive branch," directed by a "Board of Governors," and setting forth a special body of law for the regulation of labor relations in the Postal Service (the federal agency, incidentally, which has been the longest and most fully organized). The new plan removed the Postal Service from the ambit

---

17. Our conclusion that federal agencies may not be required under § 7131(a) to pay the travel expenses and per diem allowances of union negotiators does not, of course, preclude an agency from making such payments upon a determination that they serve the convenience of the agency or are otherwise in the primary interest of the government, as was the practice prior to passage of the Act. * * *. Furthermore, unions may presumably negotiate for such payments in collective bargaining as they do in the private sector.

See Midstate Tel. Corp. v. NLRB, 706 F.2d 401, 405 (CA2 1983); Axelson, Inc. v. NLRB, 599 F.2d 91, 93–95 (CA5 1979). Indeed, we are informed that many agencies presently pay the travel expenses of employee representatives pursuant to collective-bargaining agreements. Letter from Ruth E. Peters, Counsel for Respondent FLRA, Nov. 9, 1983. See also J.P. Stevens & Co., 239 NLRB 738, 739 (1978) (employer required to pay travel expenses as remedy for failing to bargain in good faith).

of the Executive Orders and subjected it instead, with major modifications, to the provisions of the National Labor Relations Act. (Id., Section 1209(a).)

The most important modification is the continued denial of the right to strike and the substitution, as a means for achieving finality in bargaining impasses, of compulsory arbitration before a tripartite board. (Section 1207(c) and (d).) Another interesting and significant modification is the express adoption of a "comparability" formula in determining compensation of postal workers: "It shall be the policy of the Postal Service to maintain compensation and benefits for all officers and employees on a standard of comparability to the compensation and benefits paid for comparable levels of work in the private sector of the economy." (Section 1003(a).) This applies the "prevailing rate" concept, long utilized with regard to so-called "wage board" employees, to postal workers. "Wage board" or "prevailing rate" employees are blue-collar workers, skilled and unskilled, such as painters, plumbers, janitors, who are employed by federal agencies, such as shipyards and the Tennessee Valley Authority, and who are paid the prevailing rate, as determined by a "wage board," of painters, plumbers, janitors in private employment in the particular geographical area. There are approximately 800,000 of these wage-board employees in over fifty different, executive departments and agencies.[i] They have their counterparts at the state and local level. The determinations of these wage boards constitute what might, with fair accuracy, be termed a form of compulsory arbitration—in effect, incidentally, for over a hundred years.

2. This concluding Section of the casebook (Collective Bargaining in Public Employment) began with United Federation of Postal Clerks v. Blount, supra p. 1069, which upholds the prohibition of strikes in federal employment against constitutional challenge. It perorates in this concluding note with recognition of the relative effectiveness of the federal ban as opposed to that of most of the states. As the first major breach of the federal ban was the postal strike of 1970, so the last and most dramatic was that launched by the Professional Air Traffic Controllers Organization in August of 1981. The debacle suffered by PATCO in that abortive strike is briefly observed in footnote 23 of the Los Angeles County Sanitation case, supra pp. 1082–1083. In the Los Angeles case, ironically, the strike in public employment is held to be lawful under the common law of California. This juxtaposing of the antipodal views on the role and propriety of the strike in public employment frames what has proved to be the most enduring question for government labor relations. We leave where we came in: The strike or not the strike? ("The Lady or the Tiger?" Which is which?)

i. Hearings on the Coordinated Federal Wage System Before the Subcommittee on Manpower and Civil Service of the House Committee on Post Office and Civil Service, 90th Cong., 2d Sess., at 3 (1968); Donoian, A New Approach to Setting the Pay of Federal Blue-Collar Workers, 92 Monthly Lab. Rev. 30 (April 1969).

Index

References are to Pages

†